CORPORATE GOVERNANCE AT THE CROSSROADS

A Book of Readings

The McGraw-Hill/IRWIN Series in Finance, Insurance and Real Estate

Stephen A. Ross
Franco Modigliani Professor of Finance and Economics
Sloan School of Management
Massachusetts Institute of Technology
Consulting Editor

FINANCIAL MANAGEMENT

Benninga and Sarig
Corporate Finance:
A Valuation Approach

Block and Hirt
Foundations of Financial Management
Eleventh Edition

Brealey and Myers
Principles of Corporate Finance
Seventh Edition

Brealey, Myers and Marcus
Fundamentals of Corporate Finance
Fourth Edition

Brooks
FinGame Online 4.0

Bruner
Case Studies in Finance:
Managing for Corporate Value Creation
Fourth Edition

Chew
The New Corporate Finance:
Where Theory Meets Practice
Third Edition

Chew and Gillan
Corporate Governance at the Crossroads:
A Book of Readings
First Edition

DeMello
Cases in Finance

Grinblatt and Titman
Financial Markets and Corporate Strategy
Second Edition

Helfert
Techniques of Financial Analysis:
A Guide to Value Creation
Eleventh Edition

Higgins
Analysis for Financial Management

Seventh Edition

Kester, Ruback and Tufano
Case Problems in Finance
Twelfth Edition

Ross, Westerfield and Jaffe
Corporate Finance
Seventh Edition

Ross, Westerfield and Jordan
Essentials of Corporate Finance
Fourth Edition

Ross, Westerfield and Jordan
Fundamentals of Corporate Finance
Sixth Edition

Smith
The Modern Theory of Corporate Finance
Second Edition

White
Financial Analysis with an Electronic Calculator
Fifth Edition

INVESTMENTS

Bodie, Kane and Marcus
Essentials of Investments
Fifth Edition

Bodie, Kane and Marcus
Investments
Sixth Edition

Cohen, Zinbarg and Zeikel
Investment Analysis and Portfolio Management
Fifth Edition

Corrado and Jordan
Fundamentals of Investments:
Valuation and Management
Third Edition

Farrell
Portfolio Management:
Theory and Applications
Second Edition

Hirt and Block
Fundamentals of Investment Management
Seventh Edition

FINANCIAL INSTITUTIONS AND MARKETS

Cornett and Saunders
Fundamentals of Financial Institutions Management

Rose and Hudgins
Commercial Bank Management
Sixth Edition

Rose
Money and Capital Markets:
Financial Institutions and Instruments in a Global Marketplace
Eighth Edition

Santomero and Babbel
Financial Markets, Instruments, and Institutions
Second Edition

Saunders and Cornett
Financial Institutions Management:
A Risk Management Approach
Fourth Edition

Saunders and Cornett
Financial Markets and Institutions:
A Modern Perspective
Second Edition

INTERNATIONAL FINANCE

Beim and Calomiris
Emerging Financial Markets

Eun and Resnick
International Financial Management
Third Edition

Levich
International Financial Markets:
Prices and Policies
Second Edition

REAL ESTATE

Brueggeman and Fisher
Real Estate Finance and Investments
Twelfth Edition

Corgel, Ling and Smith
Real Estate Perspectives:
An Introduction to Real Estate
Fourth Edition

Ling and Archer
Real Estate Principles:
A Value Approach
First Edition

FINANCIAL PLANNING AND INSURANCE

Allen, Melone, Rosenbloom and Mahoney
Pension Planning:
Pension, Profit-Sharing, and Other Deferred Compensation Plans
Ninth Edition

Crawford
Life and Health Insurance Law
Eighth Edition (LOMA)

Harrington and Niehaus
Risk Management and Insurance
Second Edition

Hirsch
Casualty Claim Practice
Sixth Edition

Kapoor, Dlabay and Hughes
Personal Finance
Seventh Edition

Williams, Smith and Young
Risk Management and Insurance
Eighth Edition

CORPORATE GOVERNANCE AT THE CROSSROADS

A Book of Readings

EDITED BY

Donald H. Chew, Jr. and
Stuart L. Gillan

McGraw-Hill Irwin

Boston   Burr Ridge, IL   Dubuque, IA   Madison, WI   New York   San Francisco   St. Louis
Bangkok   Bogotá   Caracas   Kuala Lumpur   Lisbon   London   Madrid   Mexico City
Milan   Montreal   New Delhi   Santiago   Seoul   Singapore   Sydney   Taipei   Toronto

McGraw-Hill Irwin

CORPORATE GOVERNANCE AT THE CROSSROADS: A BOOK OF READINGS
Published by McGraw-Hill/Irwin, a business unit of The McGraw-Hill Companies, Inc.,
1221 Avenue of the Americas, New York, NY, 10020. Copyright © 2005 by The McGraw-Hill
Companies, Inc. All rights reserved. No part of this publication may be reproduced or
distributed in any form or by any means, or stored in a database or retrieval system, without
the prior written consent of The McGraw-Hill Companies, Inc., including, but not limited to,
in any network or other electronic storage or transmission, or broadcast for distance learning.
Some ancillaries, including electronic and print components, may not be available to
customers outside the United States.

This book is printed on acid-free paper.

1 2 3 4 5 6 7 8 9 0 DOC/DOC 0 9 8 7 6 5 4

ISBN   0-07-295708-5

Vice president and editor-in-chief: *Robin J. Zwettler*
Publisher: *Stephen M. Patterson*
Sponsoring editor: *Michele Janicek*
Editorial coordinator: *Barbara Hari*
Executive marketing manager: *Rhonda Seelinger*
Project manager: *Laura Griffin*
Senior production supervisor: *Sesha Bolisetty*
Designer: *Mary E. Kazak*
Senior digital content specialist: *Brian Nacik*
Cover design: *Asylum Studios*
Cover photo: *© Photodisc*
Compositor: *Concepts Unlimited®*
Printer: *R. R. Donnelley*

Library of Congress Cataloging-in-Publication Data

Corporate governance at the crossroads : a book of readings / [compiled by] Donald H.
  Chew, Jr., Stuart L. Gillan.
    p. cm. – (The McGraw-Hill/Irwin Series in finance, insurance, and real estate)
  ISBN 0-07-295708-5 (alk.paper)
  1. Corporate governance. I. Gillan, Stuart L. II. Series.
HD2741.C77497 2005
658.4–dc22

                                                                    2003066489

www.mhhe.com

To our wives, Susan Emerson and Laura Gillan

TABLE OF CONTENTS

FOREWORD

by Charles M. Elson
Edgar S. Woolard, Jr., Chair
John L. Weinberg Center for
Corporate Governance
Lerner College of Business & Economics
University of Delaware

For many years, interest in corporate governance was limited to a self-contained camp of enthusiasts. It included legal and financial academics, shareholder activists, and a small core of institutional investors. That has all changed dramatically in the past year or so. The collapse of the famed Enron Corporation has proven not only to have been a seminal business event, as rarely does a company as large and respected as Enron fail, but along with several coincident corporate scandals, has proven a watershed moment in U.S. corporate governance. A significant change in approach to corporate board composition, conduct and responsibility has occurred at the legal and regulatory levels, largely in response to a perceived failure by the Enron Board to have prevented management conduct that led to the company's downfall. At last, the belief, long held by the small coterie of governance activists, that effective corporate governance leads to greater management accountability and enhanced corporate performance, has become widely and popularly accepted. That is why this collection of essays on corporate governance assembled by Chew and Gillan is so relevant and important. The readings presented within provide the reader with a challenging and comprehensive overview of the myriad of issues, both theoretical and practical, arising out of the current debate on creating effective corporate governance. It will prove most useful to those seeking a thorough introduction to the subject for both academic and applied purposes.

INTRODUCTION

Writing in *The Wealth of Nations* in 1776, Adam Smith was skeptical about the future of the publicly traded corporation, or what back then was called the "joint stock company." Given the role of self-interest in human affairs, the proposition that a faceless and uncoordinated group of outside investors could be brought to entrust their savings to professional corporate managers—people whose interests were almost sure to diverge from their own—was doubtful at best. Faced with the challenge of controlling this divergence of interests, Smith argued that joint stock companies would end up being well suited only to "turnkey operations"—enterprises like banks, canal operators, and water suppliers—that did not require managerial genius or initiative, but mainly just the ability to administer a pre-established and well-understood set of rules.

But Smith turned out to be wrong. During the past two centuries, publicly traded corporations with dispersed ownership have come to dominate business activity in the U.S. and U.K. And in Continental Europe and Asia, where private and closely held corporations have long been the rule, listed companies are beginning to account for an expanding share of GDP.

What Smith failed to foresee was the development of effective corporate governance systems. Critical to this development were innovations in regulation and law, including the enactment of limited liability for shareholders, that offered protection to minority stockholders. But in addition to such legal and regulatory changes, the emergence of effective corporate governance systems has required the evolution of corporate procedures and financial institutions that work together to assure investors that professional managers will make efficient use of their capital.

In the U.S., and indeed all national economies, corporate governance mechanisms can be seen as falling into two main categories, either internal or external. Internal governance mechanisms include the board of directors, subcommittees of the board (including audit, compensation, and nominating committees), compensation programs designed to align the interests of managers and shareholders, and other corporate control systems. External governance mechanisms include accounting rules and regulatory reporting requirements, external auditors, investment bankers (who help companies raise capital), securities analysts (who issue buy-sell recommendations), credit analysts (who issue credit ratings), local laws (based on where the company is incorporated), and the shareholders themselves (through their willingness to buy and sell shares). Other forces with potential for disciplining corporate managers are product markets (in the sense that consumer dissatisfaction will soon show up in declining profits and stock prices) and the market for executive labor (since a high-level manager's reputation for building shareholder value is likely to be a key determinant of his or her next job). If all of these different mechanisms fail to get managers to work to increase shareholder value, the "market for corporate control"—in its most extreme forms, hostile takeovers and LBOs—is available as a last resort.

As Bengt Holmstrom and Steve Kaplan begin by observing in their assessment of *"The State of the U.S. Corporate Governance System"* (which appears early in this book), the U.S. economy and stock markets have outperformed those of other nations for at least the past two decades. And while Kaplan and Holmstrom are careful to avoid asserting a cause-and-effect relationship, most business laypersons would be willing to attribute at least part of this success to the U.S. corporate governance system. But with the recent and well-publicized failures of companies like Enron and WorldCom, U.S. corporate governance practices are once again under attack by our mass media and politicians. This time, however, the charge is a little different.

In the past, the criticism has been directed mainly at the *external* corporate governance—at U.S. capital markets and their relentless pressuring of U.S. companies to increase profits. In the 1980s, for example, the popular story was that the threat of takeover by corporate "raiders" was forcing managers to lay off productive employees and cut back on promising investment to meet near-term earnings targets. And in a claim that has been proven wrong by time (and by an impressive body of research documenting the shareholder gains of the '80s), such cutbacks were in turn said to be weakening the competitive position of American companies relative to their Japanese and European counterparts.

In the current attack on U.S. corporate governance, although public accountants and securities analysts have certainly come in for their share of the blame, the main focus has shifted to *internal* corporate governance. In particular, U.S. boards and managers are now being subjected to unprecedented scrutiny. The principal charge appears to be this: Many executives of U.S. companies, having received large awards of stock options, cashed out their holdings when their stock prices proved to be unsustainably high. Making matters worse, in a number of cases like Enron and WorldCom, the stock price run-ups were fueled in part by accounting manipulation or outright falsification of reported earnings. Whether achieved by accident or design, the resulting transfers of wealth from "long-term" shareholders to top management have aroused increased skepticism about U.S. financial reporting and executive pay practices—so much so that the U.S. corporate governance system is now said to be suffering a crisis of confidence.

But are things as bad as they seem? The article by Holmstrom and Kaplan offers a number of reasons to be optimistic about the future. After pointing to the superior performance of the U.S. economy and stock market, Holmstrom and Kaplan go on to argue that the most important changes in U.S. corporate governance during the 1980s and 1990s—especially the increased ownership of U.S. companies by institutional shareholders and the dramatic increase in equity-based executive pay— have been positive developments on the whole, serving mainly to strengthen the accountability of

U.S. managers to their shareholders and to reinforce the bond of common interest between them. The growth of institutional share ownership that accelerated in the '80s helped corporate raiders launch the highly productive restructuring of U.S. companies that took place during that decade. And after the shutdown of the leveraged restructuring movement at the end of the '80s, an explosion of equity-based pay motivated U.S. managers to initiate their own value-increasing restructurings—particularly M&A and divestitures—throughout the '90s.

But if equity incentives played an important role in the corporate value creation of the '90s, they have also been implicated in the recent scandals, where fraudulent behavior has been linked to significant holdings of stock or options. As Holmstrom and Kaplan see it, however, the problem here is not the use of stock or options per se, but rather a serious flaw in the design of equity pay plans. The extraordinary growth of executive stock option grants by U.S. public companies that began in the early '90s was premised in large part on the accomplishments (also well documented by academic research) of the LBO movement in the '80s. But while achieving their goal of getting significant equity ownership into the hands of top management, the corporate boards of U.S. public companies failed to recognize a critical feature of the equity typically provided the key managers of LBO firms—namely, its "illiquidity," resulting from the lack of a public market and extensive restrictions on selling. Without such restrictions, and in the midst of the bull market of the late '90s, the top managers of U.S. public companies found themselves not only with the opportunity to unload stock during price run-ups, but also under considerable pressure to sustain or propel such run-ups by putting the best face on quarterly accounting results.

For Holmstrom and Kaplan, then, any reform of internal U.S. corporate governance practices should begin with the attempt to make executive pay in public companies more like that of private LBOs. And this message is repeated in a number of articles scattered throughout this book, including Brian Hall's "*Six Challenges in Designing Equity-Based Pay.*" Besides recommending the use of longer vesting periods and other restrictions on executive stock and option holdings, Hall argues that the current, clearly unrealistic accounting treatment of options (discussed in another article in this book by the late Merton Miller and compensation consultant Bud Crystal) has obscured some important advantages of restricted stock over options, including its tendency to be valued more highly by executives and employees (per dollar of cost to shareholders); its ability to provide reasonably strong ownership incentives and retention power even if the stock price falls sharply; and the greater "transparency" of its value to stockholders, employees, and the press.

Another recurrent theme of the articles in this book is the failure of U.S. accounting rules to reflect economic reality and the problems caused by top executives' pursuit of continuous increases in reported EPS. For example, in "*How to Fix Accounting—Measure and Report Economic Profit*," Bennett Stewart argues that corporate efforts to "manage" earnings, besides misleading investors, often involve the sacrifice of long-term value through shortsighted cutbacks in R&D and other forms of corporate investment that must be immediately expensed under U.S. GAAP. Stewart proposes to remedy this problem with a complete overhaul of GAAP that aims to measure and report *economic* profit. Stated in brief, Stewart's concept of economic profit begins with a definition of accounting income known as "residual income" and then proposes a series of additional adjustments to GAAP that are designed to produce a reliable measure of a company's sustainable annual *cash*-generating capacity.

But in "*Accounting Doesn't Need Much Fixing (Just Reinterpreting)*," Emory University's distinguished accounting scholar George Benston responds to Stewart's proposal with a classic defense of traditional accounting practices and standards. Like the recent efforts of the FASB to achieve greater balance-sheet realism through "fair value accounting," Stewart's call to make economic profit the centerpiece of GAAP is said to stem from the mistaken premise that audited financial statements are intended *primarily* to guide equity investors in setting stock prices. But if he rejects Stewart's proposal, Benston nevertheless agrees with Stewart's claim that GAAP accounting is of limited use for investors in valuing companies and that the single-minded pursuit of higher GAAP earnings by corporate managers can lead to value-reducing investment and operating decisions. Accordingly, he endorses many of Stewart's proposed modifications of GAAP both for *internal* purposes, such as performance evaluation and incentive compensation, and for *voluntary supplemental* reporting to the investment community.

In sum, the U.S. corporate governance system now appears to be at a critical point in its evolution-ary course, with major accomplishments behind it and challenges ahead. And to the extent the U.S. system serves as a model for other national governance systems (which are also discussed in this book), the concerns about U.S. corporate governance have become a global preoccupation.

This book consists of 40 articles on several important aspects of U.S. and international corporate governance, with special focus on the U.S. system and the challenge of designing effective management incentives. All but one of the articles in this book were previously published in the *Journal of Applied Corporate Finance*, which has been devoting roughly one issue per year to the subject of corporate governance for at least the past decade. In many if not most cases, the relevance of such articles appears to have only increased with the passage of time.

Chapter 1 consists of articles that provide general perspectives on corporate governance and incentives. Section 1.1 focuses on the objective of the publicly traded corporation, different types of corporate governance mechanisms, and the role of law and politics in shaping our current governance structures. Section 1.2 provides an economic perspective on incentives, ethics, and the influence of organizational structure on employee behavior. In this fashion, we begin by giving the reader a broad context and a framework for considering both governance structures and the incentives of participants in corporate governance systems.

Chapter 2 contains three sections that each address an important aspect of internal corporate governance. The articles in section 2.1 examine the role of the corporate board of directors, which we view as the linchpin of corporate governance. As the shareholders' representatives, corporate boards are charged with hiring, firing, and compensating the senior management team. Yet many contend that boards have failed in their duties and function mainly as puppets of management. Nevertheless, the articles do furnish some evidence that some boards have become more independent and effective, and that boards can make a difference for shareholders.

Section 2.2 addresses what is perhaps the second most important element of internal corporate governance—incentives and compensation. Effective compensation plans reward, retain, and motivate employees while aligning employee interests with those of shareholders. However, concerns about the level of compensation and a breakdown in the link between pay and performance have again focused the spotlight on corporate pay practices. The articles in this section address the compensation controversy and discuss issues pertaining to different types of compensation plans, option-based compensation, and the debate surrounding the expensing of stock options.

Section 2.3 recognizes that internal governance mechanisms do not arise in a vacuum, and that other aspects of organizational architecture may affect board and compensation structures. Specifically, the articles in this section focus on the role of the CEO, the business environment, the structure of the organization (be it centralized or decentralized decision-making), and the firm's financing polices and how these factors interact to influence other elements of a firm's governance structure.

Chapter 3 shifts the focus to external corporate governance. Section 3.1 focuses on corporate ownership and control, with emphasis on the role of institutional investors in the U.S. and on differences in ownership structure between the U.S., France, Germany, and the U.K. The readings in Section 3.2 examine the market for corporate control, and how the legal environment and financial markets may influence external governance mechanisms. The articles in the book's final section discuss corporate

accounting and reporting issues and propose ways of addressing them.

During the last half of the 1990s—a period when stock prices appeared to become almost completely detached from "fundamentals"—investors appear to have been lulled into a false sense of well-being. Indeed, there is an important sense in which the current dissatisfaction with U.S. governance can be traced directly to its past accomplishments. It was arguably *excessive* investor confidence in the U.S. system (aided by the widespread misconception that accounting earnings reflect economic reality) that helped U.S. stock prices reach such extraordinary levels. For it was those high levels that, while enabling many insiders to cash out their holdings, also made possible (some would argue inevitable) the plunge in prices that has put corporate governance on the front pages of our newspapers.

As a consequence, all aspects of the U.S. corporate governance system are now being reexamined. And while the possibility of "overregulation" always remains a concern, the combination of new laws and regulations with the prospect of more effective board monitoring and better designed incentives is likely to end up, in Holmstrom and Kaplan's words, making "a good system a better one." That is our hope and our expectation.

—*Don Chew and Stuart Gillan*

CHAPTER 1
CORPORATE GOVERNANCE PERSPECTIVES

1

CHAPTER 1: SECTION 1.1
An Overview of Corporate Governance

Chapter 1 provides a broad perspective on corporate governance by focusing on internal and external governance mechanisms, and the role of politics and law in shaping governance systems.

In our lead article, ***Value Maximization, Stakeholder Theory, and the Corporate Objective Function***, Michael Jensen attempts to dispel a major source of confusion in the current corporate governance debate—the continuing disagreement about the fundamental purpose of the corporation. As Jensen begins by noting, there are two main views of the corporate "objective function" that are contending for the minds and hearts of social scientists and policy makers not just in the United States, but in all nations with industrialized economies. The first is what Jensen refers to as "the value maximization proposition," which is rooted in 200 years of economic theory and research. Starting with Adam Smith's *Wealth of Nations*, economists have argued that social wealth and welfare are likely to be greatest when corporations seek to maximize the stream of profits that can be divided among their investors. And, as transformed by financial economists like Jensen, this goal has become "maximization of the long-run market value of the firm"—a value that is determined mainly, though not entirely, by a company's stock price.

The main rival to value maximization is called "stakeholder theory." Stakeholder theory, in brief, says that corporations should attempt to maximize not the value of their shares (or financial claims), but rather the total value that is distributed among all corporate "stakeholders," including employees, customers, suppliers, local communities, and tax collectors. What is perhaps most remarkable about the theory, at least to an economist like Jensen, is its extraordinary popularity. The language and concepts of stakeholder theory have been adopted by many professional organizations, politicians, and special interest groups—and the theory itself has even received formal endorsement by the current British government. And as Jensen goes on to note, stakeholder theory has also received implicit support from many U.S. corporate managers, as reflected in the widespread use of the Balanced Scorecard—a multi-dimensional performance measurement system that Jensen describes as the "managerial equivalent" of stakeholder theory.

One of the major aims of Jensen's paper is to explain the appeal of stakeholder theory (and, by extension, the Balanced Scorecard). Of course, it's not difficult to see how stakeholder theory increases the demand for the services of "outside" stakeholders, such as legislators, regulators, and other representatives of the "public" interest. Politicians in particular have always looked for ways to divert corporate wealth to their voters (even though an increasing number of them are now shareholders). And it's also not hard to see why some corporate executives—particularly those who don't own much stock in their own companies—have proven receptive to the theory. As Jensen points out, corporate CEOs who are forced to be accountable to many corporate constituencies end up being accountable to none. But there is more than the inevitable workings of self-interest in this story. Drawing on the writings of Friedrich von Hayek, Jensen shows how stakeholder theory draws much of its emotional power by conjuring up images of "tribe and family"—images that, when applied to the publicly traded corporation, are not only anachronistic, but a source of managerial confusion that ends up contributing to corporate failure.

And this, in essence, is Jensen's verdict on stakeholder theory: Those nations and companies who embrace its principles will find themselves handicapped in the global race for competitive advantage. In Jensen's words, "*Without the clarity of mission provided by a single-valued objective function, companies embracing stakeholder theory will experience managerial confusion, conflict, inefficiency, and perhaps even competitive failure. And the same fate is likely to be visited on those companies that use the so-called "Balanced Scorecard" approach—the managerial equivalent of stakeholder theory—as a performance measurement system.*"

But if stakeholder theory and the Balanced Scorecard are likely to reduce efficiency and value by obscuring the overriding corporate goal, does that mean they have no useful insights for corporate managers? And can top management of a large corporation succeed just by holding up value maximization as the goal and ignoring stakeholders? The answer Jensen provides to both questions is an "emphatic no":

In order to maximize value, corporate managers must not only satisfy, but enlist the support of, all corporate stakeholders—customers, employees, managers, suppliers, local communities. Top management plays a critical role in this function through its leadership and effectiveness in creating, projecting, and sustaining the company's strategic vision.

With this new twist on the economist's concept of value maximization, Jensen goes on to propose a "somewhat new" version that he calls "*enlightened* value maximization." As Jensen describes it, "*Enlightened value maximization uses much of the structure of stakeholder theory but accepts maximization of the long-run value of the firm as the criterion for making the requisite tradeoffs among its stakeholders.*" He also ends with a strongly qualified endorsement of the Balanced Scorecard: although likely to be disastrous as the basis of a performance measurement system with its dozen or so measures (it is more a "dashboard" or "instrument panel" than a scorecard), it can nevertheless play a valuable role in helping managers and employees understand the different drivers of value in their business.

Our second article, also by Jensen, provides a good illustration of the difficult choices that even enlightened value maximizers must sometimes make. Written in the early '90s, *The Modern Industrial Revolution, Exit, and the Failure of Internal Control Systems* argues that one of the most critical functions of the U.S. economy and governance system—and, indeed, the economies of all industrialized nations—is to squeeze out excess capital and capacity. In making this argument, Jensen draws striking parallels between the 19th-century Industrial Revolution and worldwide economic developments during the 1970s and 1980s. In both periods, technological advances led to sharp increases in productivity, dramatic price reductions, and massive obsolescence and overcapacity. And much as the great mergers and acquisitions wave of the 1890s reduced capacity (by consolidating some 1,800 firms into roughly 150), the leveraged takeovers, LBOs, and other leveraged recapitalizations of the 1980s provided "healthy adjustments" to overcapacity that was building in many sectors of the U.S. economy: for example, oil and gas, tires, tobacco, commodity chemicals, food processing, paper and forest products, financial services, publishing, and broadcasting.

Jensen, however, interprets the shareholder gains from corporate restructuring transactions during the 1980s (which he estimates at $750 billion) as evidence of the failure of U.S. internal corporate control systems—that is, the failure of managements as supervised by boards of directors to deal *voluntarily* with the problem of excess capacity. Moreover, with the shutdown of the takeover market, intensifying global competition, worldwide protectionism, and other causes of potential overcapacity around this time, Jensen views reform of the U.S. corporate governance system as an urgent matter. Notable among his proposals is that large public companies should seek to replicate certain governance features of venture capital and LBO firms like Kleiner Perkins and KKR—specifically, significant equity ownership by managers and directors, greater participation by outside "active" investors, and smaller and better informed boards.

In our third article, **Is American Corporate Governance Fatally Flawed?**, Nobel-Prize-winning economist the late Merton Miller provides an answer to both Jensen's pessimism about U.S. corporate control systems and to proponents (who were once legion) of the Japanese corporate governance system, with their criticism of U.S. managers' "short-sighted" focus on stock prices. In a classic defense of the "shareholder-value principle," Miller argues that U.S. managers' concern about stock prices, far from representing a flaw, is "one of the primary strengths" of the U.S. economy. "Myopia," as he points out, "is not the only disease of vision afflicting business managers. They may suffer from astigmatism or even from excessive far-sightedness or hyperopia." During the last 20 years, as Miller goes on to argue, some American firms facing strong stockholder pressures to pay out funds invested too little. But many Japanese firms, facing no such pressures, clearly overinvested during the same period, creating problems that continue to plague the Japanese economy to this day.

Moreover, Miller contends that two sets of market forces constantly pressure corporate management to employ assets in an efficient manner—the market for corporate control, as discussed by Jensen, and the product markets. In Miller's words:

The ultimate discipline for the managers of one firm in the U.S. will always be the managers of other firms, including foreign firms, competing with them head to head for customer business. As long as we continue to have plenty of that kind of competition in the U.S., I, for one, can't become terribly concerned about the supposedly fatal flaws in our governance system.

We switch gears in the next two articles, with law and economics scholars Mark Roe and Frank Easterbrook offering contrasting perspectives on the origins of the U.S. governance system. In *The Political Roots of American Corporate Finance*, Roe argues that politics, in the form of laws and regulations affecting equity ownership by banks and institutions, have had a profound influence on ownership and governance structure of large U.S. corporations. The fact that large U.S. companies tend to have dispersed shareholders, a board of directors that defers to the CEO, and a powerful, centralized management is usually seen as a natural economic outcome of technological requirements for large-scale enterprises and substantial amounts of outside capital. However, Roe argues that current U.S. corporate structures are the result not only of such economic factors, but of political forces that restricted the size and activities of U.S. commercial banks and other financial intermediaries. Populist fears of concentrated economic power, interest group maneuvering, and a federalist American political structure all had a role in pressuring Congress to fragment U.S. financial institutions and limit their ability to own stock and participate in corporate governance.

Had U.S. politics been different, Roe suggests, the present ownership structure of some American public companies might have been different. Truly national U.S. financial institutions might have been able to participate as substantial owners in the wave of end-of-the-century mergers and then used their large blocks of stock to sit on the boards of the merged enterprises (much as Warren Buffett, venture capitalists, and LBO firms like KKR do today). Such a concentrated ownership and governance structure might have helped to address monitoring, information, and coordination problems that continue to reduce the value of some U.S. companies.

The emergence of U.S. shareholder activism in the last 10 or 15 years is also said to cast doubt on the standard explanation of American corporate ownership structure. The activism of U.S. financial institutions—primarily pension funds and mutual funds—can be interpreted as the delayed outbreak of an impulse to participate in corporate ownership and governance that was historically suppressed by American politics.

In *International Corporate Differences: Markets or Law*, Frank Easterbrook offers a very different view of how our current governance system came to be. Easterbrook argues that differences in international corporate ownership and governance systems primarily reflect differences in the efficiency of capital markets, not differences in corporate law. Law is mainly a result or output of this process, not an input. In countries where financial markets are more efficient, there is both less law and greater investor protection. Unlike nations in Asia and most of Europe, the United States and the U.K. have large and efficient capital markets, with no restrictions on cross-border capital flows. It is thus not surprising that when American and English banks, mutual funds, and insurers are allowed by law to increase the concentration of their holdings, they don't do so. With efficient markets, there is no money to be made by holding undiversified blocks in public corporations. If public markets were inefficient, entrepreneurs would arrange for large blocks of stock (or take companies private), just as they grant powers of control to venture capitalists.

Easterbrook contends that the effect of law on corporate governance and ownership is far less pronounced in America than in Europe and Japan. Restrictions on U.S. banks aside, corporate law in the United States is "enabling" —that is, it lets people do largely what they want in organizing, managing, and financing the firm. Corporate law in Europe and Japan is much more "directory." And there is a straightforward explanation for this difference: When capital markets are efficient, the valuation process works better, which in turn provides investors with stronger assurances of fairness. When markets are less efficient, some substitute must be found — law, perhaps, or the valuation procedures of banks. Thus, banks play larger corporate governance roles in nations with less extensive capital markets—and corporate law, as the European Union's company directives show, is more restrictive. In Easterbrook's words, *"European corporate law is today about as meddlesome and directory as U.S. law in the late 19th century, before U.S. capital markets became efficient."*

The section concludes with Bengt Holmstrom and Steven Kaplan's assessment of *The State of U.S. Corporate Governance*. The recent wave of corporate failures at Enron, WorldCom, and other prominent American companies and the resulting public outcry have served as catalysts for legislative and regulatory changes that include the Sarbanes-Oxley

Act of 2002 and new governance guidelines from the NYSE and NASDAQ. But is the U.S. corporate governance system really as bad as critics suggest? And will the recent legislative and regulatory changes lead to a more effective system?

The authors begin by noting that the broad evidence is not consistent with a failed U.S. governance system. During the past two decades, the U.S. economy and stock market have performed well both on an absolute basis and relative to other countries, even in the wake of the corporate scandals in 2001. Moreover, the most notable changes in U.S. corporate governance in the 1980s and 1990s—including the institutionalization of U.S. shareholders and the dramatic increase in equity-based pay—have served mainly (though not always) to strengthen the accountability of U.S. managers to their shareholders. The authors' message, then, is that while parts of the U.S. corporate governance system gave way under the exceptional strain created by the bull market of the 1990s, the overall system—which includes oversight by the public and government and the corrective market forces that Miller had so much faith in—has reacted quickly and decisively to address its weaknesses. The net effect of the recent legislative and regulatory changes has been to make a good governance system an even better one. But, as the authors caution, perhaps the greatest risk now facing the U.S. financial market system (of which corporate governance is a critical part) is that of overregulation.

VALUE MAXIMIZATION, STAKEHOLDER THEORY, AND THE CORPORATE OBJECTIVE FUNCTION

by Michael C. Jensen,
The Monitor Group and
*Harvard Business School**

I n most industrialized nations today, economists, management scholars, policy makers, corporate executives, and special interest groups are engaged in a high-stakes debate over corporate governance. In some scholarly and business circles, the discussion focuses mainly on questions of policies and procedures designed to improve oversight of corporate managers by boards of directors. But at the heart of the current global corporate governance debate is a remarkable division of opinion about the fundamental purpose of the corporation. Much of the discord can be traced to the complexity of the issues and to the strength of the conflicting interests that are likely to be affected by the outcome. But also fueling the controversy are political, social, evolutionary, and emotional forces that we don't usually think of as operating in the domain of business and economics. These forces serve to reinforce a model of corporate behavior that draws on concepts of "family" and "tribe." And as I argue in this paper, this model is an anachronism—a holdover from an earlier period of human development that nevertheless continues to cause much confusion among corporate managers about what it is that they and their organizations are supposed to do.

At the level of the individual organization, the most basic issue of governance is the following. Every organization has to ask and answer the question: What are we trying to accomplish? Or, to put the same question in more concrete terms: How do we keep score? When all is said and done, how do we measure better versus worse?

At the economy-wide or social level, the issue is this: If we could dictate the criterion or objective function to be maximized by firms (and thus the performance criterion by which corporate executives choose among alternative policy options), what would it be? Or, to put the issue even more simply: How do we want the firms in our economy to measure their own performance? How do we want them to determine what is better versus worse?

Most economists would answer simply that managers must have a criterion for evaluating performance and deciding between alternative courses of action, and that the criterion should be maximization of the long-term market value of the firm. (And "firm value," by the way, means not just the value of the equity, but the sum of the values of *all* financial claims on the firm—debt, warrants, and preferred stock, as well as equity.) This Value Maximization proposition has its roots in 200 years of research in economics and finance.

The main contender to value maximization as the corporate objective is called "stakeholder theory." Stakeholder theory says that managers should make decisions that take account of the interests of *all* the stakeholders in a firm. Stakeholders include all

*© 2001 Michael C. Jensen. An earlier version of this paper appears in *Breaking the Code of Change,* Michael Beer and Nithan Norhia, eds, Harvard Business School Press, 2000. This research has been supported by the The Monitor Group and Harvard Business School Division of Research. I am indebted to Nancy Nichols, Pat Meredith, Don Chew, and Janice Willett for many valuable suggestions.

individuals or groups who can substantially affect, or be affected by, the welfare of the firm—a category that includes not only the financial claimholders, but also employees, customers, communities, and government officials.[1] In contrast to the grounding of value maximization in economics, stakeholder theory has its roots in sociology, organizational behavior, the politics of special interests, and, as I will discuss below, managerial self-interest. The theory is now popular and has received the formal endorsement of many professional organizations, special interest groups, and governmental bodies, including the current British government.[2]

But, as I argue in this paper, stakeholder theory should not be viewed as a legitimate contender to value maximization because it fails to provide a *complete* specification of the corporate purpose or objective function. To put the matter more concretely, whereas value maximization provides corporate managers with a single objective, stakeholder theory directs corporate managers to serve "many masters." And, to paraphrase the old adage, when there are many masters, all end up being shortchanged. Without the clarity of mission provided by a single-valued objective function, companies embracing stakeholder theory will experience managerial confusion, conflict, inefficiency, and perhaps even competitive failure. And the same fate is likely to be visited on those companies that use the so-called "Balanced Scorecard" approach—the managerial equivalent of stakeholder theory—as a performance measurement system.

But if stakeholder theory and the Balanced Scorecard can destroy value by obscuring the overriding corporate goal, does that mean they have no legitimate corporate uses? And can corporate managers succeed by simply holding up value maximization as the goal and ignoring their stakeholders? The answer to both is an emphatic no. In order to maximize value, corporate managers must not only satisfy, but enlist the support of, all corporate stakeholders—customers, employees, managers, suppliers, local communities. Top management plays a critical role in this function through its leadership and effectiveness in creating, projecting, and sustaining the company's strategic vision. And even if the Balanced Scorecard is likely to be counterproductive as a performance evaluation and reward system, the *process* of creating the scorecard can add significant value by helping managers understand both the company's strategy and the drivers of value in their businesses.

With this in mind, I clarify what I believe is the proper relation between value maximization and stakeholder theory by proposing a (somewhat) new corporate objective function. I call it *enlightened* value maximization, and it is identical to what I call *enlightened* stakeholder theory. Enlightened value maximization uses much of the structure of stakeholder theory but accepts maximization of the long-run value of the firm as the criterion for making the requisite tradeoffs among its stakeholders. Enlightened stakeholder theory, while focusing attention on meeting the demands of all important corporate constituencies, specifies long-term value maximization as the firm's objective. In so doing, it solves the problems arising from the multiple objectives that accompany traditional stakeholder theory by giving managers a clear way to think about and make the tradeoffs among corporate stakeholders.

The answers to the questions of how managers should define better vs. worse, and how managers in fact do define it, have important implications for social welfare. Indeed, the answers provide the business equivalent of the medical profession's Hippocratic Oath. It is an indication of the infancy of the science of management that so many in the world's business schools, as well as in professional business organizations, seem to understand so little of the fundamental issues in contention.

With this introduction of the issues, let me now move to a detailed examination of value maximization and stakeholder theory.

---

1. Under some interpretations, stakeholders also include the environment, terrorists, blackmailers, and thieves. Edward Freeman, for example, writes: "The...definition of 'stakeholder' [is] any group or individual who can affect or is affected by the achievement of an organization's purpose....For instance, some corporations must count 'terrorist groups' as stakeholders." (Edward R. Freeman, *Strategic Management: A Stakeholder Approach*, Pittman Books Limited, 1984, p. 53.)

2. See, for example, *Principles of Stakeholder Management: The Clarkson Principles*. The Clarkson Centre for Business Ethics, Joseph L. Rotman School of Management, Univ. of Toronto, Canada. For a critical analysis of stakeholder theory, I especially recommend the following articles by Elaine Sternberg:

"Stakeholder Theory Exposed," *The Corporate Governance Quarterly* 2, no. 1 (1996); "The Stakeholder Concept: A Mistaken Doctrine," London: Foundation for Business Responsibilities, Issue Paper No.4 (November, 1999) (also available from the Social Science Research Network at: http://papers.ssrn.com/paper=263144). See also Sternberg's recent book, *Just Business: Business Ethics in Action*: Oxford University Press, 2000, which surveys the acceptance of stakeholder theory by the Business Roundtable and the *Financial Times*, and its recognition by law in 38 American states. On the latter issue, see also James L. Hanks, "From the Hustings: The Role of States with Takeover Control Laws." *Mergers & Acquisitions* 29, no. 2 (1994), September-October.

Telling a manager to maximize current profits, market share, future growth in profits, and anything else one pleases will leave that manager with no way to make a reasoned decision. In effect, it leaves the manager with *no* objective.

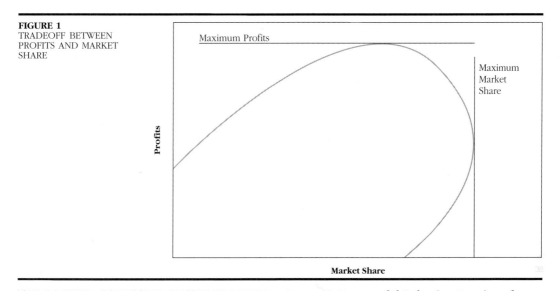

FIGURE 1
TRADEOFF BETWEEN PROFITS AND MARKET SHARE

Maximum Profits

Maximum Market Share

Profits

Market Share

THE LOGICAL STRUCTURE OF THE PROBLEM

In discussing whether firms should maximize value or not, we must separate two distinct issues:
1. Should the firm have a single-valued objective?
2. And, if so, should that objective be value maximization or something else (for example, maintaining employment or improving the environment)?

The debate over whether corporations should maximize value or act in the interests of their stakeholders is generally couched in terms of the second issue, and is often mistakenly framed as stockholders *versus* stakeholders. The real conflict here, though this is rarely stated or even recognized, is over the first issue—that is, whether the firm should have a single-valued objective function or scorecard. The failure to frame the problem in this way has contributed greatly to widespread misunderstanding and contentiousness.

What is commonly known as stakeholder theory, while not totally without content, is fundamentally flawed because it violates the proposition that a single-valued objective is a prerequisite for purposeful or rational behavior by any organization. In particular a firm that adopts stakeholder theory will be handicapped in the competition for survival because, as a basis for action, stakeholder theory politicizes the corporation and leaves its managers empowered to exercise their own preferences in spending the firm's resources.

Issue #1: Purposeful Behavior Requires the Existence of a Single-Valued Objective Function.

Consider a firm that wishes to increase both its current-year profits and its market share. Assume, as shown in Figure 1, that over some range of values of market share, profits increase. But, at some point, increases in market share come only at the expense of reduced current-year profits—say, because increased expenditures on R&D and advertising, or price reductions to increase market share, reduce this year's profit. Therefore, it is not logically possible to speak of maximizing both market share and profits.

In this situation, it is impossible for a manager to decide on the level of R&D, advertising, or price reductions because he or she is faced with the need to make tradeoffs between the two "goods"—profits and market share—but has no way to do so. While the manager knows that the firm should be at the point of maximum profits or maximum market share (or somewhere between them), there is no purposeful way to decide where to be in the area in which the firm can obtain more of one good only by giving up some of the other.

Multiple Objectives Is No Objective

It is logically impossible to maximize in more than one dimension at the same time unless the dimensions are what are known as "monotonic transformations" of one another. Thus, telling a manager to maximize current profits, market share, future growth in profits, and anything else one pleases will leave that manager with no way to make a reasoned decision. In effect, it leaves the manager with *no* objective. The result will be confusion and a lack of purpose that will handicap the firm in its competition for survival.[3]

A company can resolve this ambiguity by specifying the tradeoffs among the various dimensions, and doing so amounts to specifying an overall objective such as $V = f(x, y, \ldots)$ that explicitly incorporates the effects of decisions on *all* the performance criteria—all the goods or bads (denoted by $(x, y, \ldots)$) that can affect the firm (such as cash flow, risk, and so on). At this point, the logic above does not specify what V is. It could be anything the board of directors chooses, such as employment, sales, or growth in output. But, as I argue below, social welfare and survival will severely constrain the boards' choices.

Nothing in the analysis so far has said that the objective function f must be well behaved and easy to maximize. If the function is non-monotonic, or even chaotic, it makes it more difficult for managers to find the overall maximum. (For example, as I discuss later, the relationship between the value of the firm and a company's current earnings and investors' expectations about its future earnings and investment expenditures will often be difficult to formulate with much precision.) But even in these situations, the meaning of "better" or "worse" is defined, and managers and their monitors have a "principled"—that is, an objective and theoretically consistent—basis for choosing and auditing decisions. Their choices are not just a matter of their own personal preferences among various goods and bads.

Given managers' uncertainty about the exact specification of the objective function f, it is perhaps better to call the objective function "value seeking" rather than value maximization. This way one avoids the confusion that arises when some argue that

maximizing is difficult or impossible if the world is structured in sufficiently complicated ways.[4] It is not necessary that we be able to maximize, only that we can tell when we are getting better—that is moving in the right direction.

Issue #2: Total Firm Value Maximization Makes Society Better Off.

Given that a firm must have a single objective that tells us what is better and what is worse, we then must face the issue of what that definition of better is. Even though the single objective will always be a complicated function of many different goods or bads, the short answer to the question is that 200 years' worth of work in economics and finance indicate that social welfare is maximized when all firms in an economy attempt to maximize their own total firm value. The intuition behind this criterion is simple: that value is created—and when I say "value" I mean "social" value—whenever a firm produces an output, or set of outputs, that is valued by its customers at more than the value of the inputs it consumes (as valued by their suppliers) in the production of the outputs. Firm value is simply the long-term market value of this expected stream of benefits.

To be sure, there are circumstances when the value-maximizing criterion does not maximize social welfare—notably, when there are monopolies or "externalities." Monopolies tend to charge prices that are too high, resulting in less than the socially optimal levels of production. By "externalities," economists mean situations in which decision-makers do not bear the full cost or benefit consequences of their choices or actions. Examples are cases of air or water pollution in which a firm adds pollution to the environment without having to purchase the right to do so from the parties giving up the clean air or water. There can be no externalities as long as alienable property rights in all physical assets are defined and assigned to some private individual or firm. Thus, the solution to these problems lies not in

3. For a case study of a small non-profit firm that almost destroyed itself while trying to maximize over a dozen dimensions at the same time, see Michael Jensen, Karen H. Wruck, and Brian Barry, "Fighton, Inc. (A) and (B)," Harvard Business School Case #9-391-056, March 20, 1991; and Karen Wruck, Michael Jensen, and Brian Barry, "Fighton, Inc., (A) and (B) Teaching Note," Case #5-491-111, Harvard Business School, 1991. For an interesting empirical paper that formally tests the proposition that multiple objectives handicap firms, see Kees Cools and Mirjam van Praag (2000), "The Value Relevance of a Single-Valued Corporate Target: An Empirical Analysis." Available from the Social Science Research Network eLibrary

at: http://papers.ssrn.com/paper=244788. In their test using 80 Dutch firms in the 1993-1997 period, the authors conclude: "Our findings show the importance of setting *one* single target for value creation." (emphasis in original)

4. I'd like to thank David Rose for suggesting this simple and more descriptive term for value maximizing. See David C. Rose, "Teams, Firms, and the Evolution of Profit Seeking Behavior," May, 1999, Dept. of Economics, University of Missouri-St. Louis, St. Louis, MO, Unpublished Manuscript, available from the Social Science Research Network eLibrary at: http://papers.ssrn.com/paper=224438.

> **200 years' worth of work in economics and finance indicate that social welfare is maximized when all firms in an economy attempt to maximize their own total firm value. The intuition behind this criterion is simple: that value is created whenever a firm produces an output that is valued by its customers at more than the value of the inputs it consumes.**

telling firms to maximize something other than profits, but in defining and then assigning to some private entity the alienable decision rights necessary to eliminate the externalities.[5] In any case, resolving externality and monopoly problems, as I will discuss later, is the legitimate domain of the government in its rule-setting function.[6]

Maximizing the total market value of the firm—that is, the sum of the market values of the equity, debt and any other contingent claims outstanding on the firm—is the objective function that will guide managers in making the optimal tradeoffs among multiple constituencies (or stakeholders). It tells the firm to spend an additional dollar of resources to satisfy the desires of each constituency as long as that constituency values the result at more than a dollar. In this case, the payoff to the firm from that investment of resources is at least a dollar (in terms of market value). Although there are many single-valued objective functions that could guide a firm's managers in their decisions, value maximization is an important one because it leads under most conditions to the maximization of social welfare. But let's look more closely at this.

VALUE MAXIMIZING AND SOCIAL WELFARE

Much of the discussion in policy circles about the proper corporate objective casts the issue in terms of the conflict among various constituencies, or "stakeholders," in the corporation. The question then becomes whether shareholders should be held in higher regard than other constituencies, such as employees, customers, creditors, and so on. But it is both unproductive and incorrect to frame the issue in this manner. The real issue is what corporate behavior will get the most out of society's limited resources—or equivalently, what behavior will result in the least social waste—not whether one group is or should be more privileged than another.

Profit Maximization: A Simplified Case

To see how value maximization leads to a socially efficient solution, let's first consider an objective function, profit maximization, in a world in which all production runs are infinite and cash flow streams are level and perpetual. This scenario with level and perpetual streams allows us to ignore the complexity introduced by the tradeoffs between current and future-year profits (or, more accurately, cash flows). Consider now the social welfare effects of a firm's decision to take resources out of the economy in the form of labor hours, capital, or materials purchased voluntarily from their owners in single-price markets. The firm uses these inputs to produce outputs of goods or services that are then sold to consumers through voluntary transactions in single-price markets.

In this simple situation, a company that takes inputs out of the economy and puts its output of goods and services back into the economy increases aggregate welfare if the prices at which it sells the goods more than cover the costs it incurs in purchasing the inputs (including, of course, the cost of the capital the firm is using). Clearly the firm should expand its output as long as an additional dollar of resources taken out of the economy is valued by the consumers of the incremental product at more than a dollar. Note that it is precisely because profit is the amount by which revenues exceed costs—by which the value of output exceeds the value of inputs—that profit maximization[7] leads to an efficient social outcome.[8]

Because the transactions are voluntary, we know that the owners of the inputs value them at a level less than or equal to the price the firm pays—otherwise they wouldn't sell them. Therefore, as long as there are no negative externalities in the input factor markets,[9] the opportunity cost to society of those inputs is no higher than the total cost to the firm of acquiring them. I say "no higher" because

---

5. See Ronald H. Coase, "The Problem of Social Cost," *Journal of Law and Economics* 3, no. October 1960: pp. 1-44; and Michael C. Jensen and William H. Meckling, "Specific and General Knowledge, and Organization Structure," in ed. Lars Werin and Hans Wijkander, *Contract Economics*: (Oxford: Basil Blackwell, 1992), pp. 251-274. Available from the Social Science Research Network eLibrary at: http://papers.ssrn.com/paper=6658.

6. In the case of a monopoly, profit maximization leads to a loss of social product because the firm expands production only to the point where an additional dollar's worth of inputs generates incremental revenues equal to a dollar, not where consumers value the incremental product at a dollar. In this case the firm produces less of a commodity than that which would result in maximum social welfare.

In addition, we should recognize that when a complete set of claims for all goods for each possible time and state of the world do not exist, the social maximum will be constrained; but this is just another recognition of the fact that we must take into account the costs of creating additional claims and markets in time/state delineated claims. See Kenneth J. Arrow, "The Role of Securities in the Optimal Allocation of Risk Bearing." *Review of Economic Studies* 31, no. 86 (1964): pp. 91-96; and Gerard Debreu, *Theory of Value* (New York: John Wiley & Sons, 1959).

7. Again, provided there are no externalities.

8. I am indebted to my colleague George Baker for this simple way of expressing the social optimality of profit maximization.

9. An example would be a case where the supplier of an input was imposing negative externalities on others by polluting water or air.

some suppliers of inputs to the firm are able to earn "rents" by obtaining prices higher than the value of the goods to them. But such rents do not represent social costs, only transfers of wealth to those suppliers. Likewise, as long as there are no externalities in the output markets, the value to society of the goods and services produced by the firm is at least as great as the price the firm receives for the sale of those goods and services. If this were not true, the individuals purchasing them would not do so. Again, as in the case of producer surplus on inputs, the benefit to society is higher to the extent that consumer surplus exists (that is, to the extent that some consumers are able to purchase the output at prices lower than the value to them).

In sum, when the a company acquires an additional unit of any input(s) to produce an additional unit of any output, it increases social welfare by at least the amount of its profit—the difference between the value of the output and the cost of the input(s) required in producing it.[10] And thus the signals to the management are clear: Continue to expand purchases of inputs and sell the resulting outputs as long as an additional dollar of inputs generates sales of at least a dollar.

Value and Tradeoffs through Time

In a world in which cash flows, profits, and costs are not uniform over time, managers must deal with the tradeoffs of these items through time. A common case is when a company's capital investment comes in lumps that have to be funded up front, while production and revenue occurs in the future. Knowing whether society will be benefited or harmed requires knowing whether the future output will be valuable enough to offset the cost of having people give up their labor, capital, and material inputs in the present. Interest rates help us make this decision by telling us the cost of giving up a unit of a good today for receipt at some time in the future. So long as people take advantage of the opportunity to borrow or lend at a given interest rate, that rate determines the value of moving a marginal dollar of resources (inputs or consumption goods) forward or backward

in time.[11] In this world, individuals are as well off as possible if they maximize their wealth as measured by the discounted present value of all future claims.

In addition to interest rates, managers also need to take into account the risk of their investments and the premium the market charges for bearing such risk. But, when we add uncertainty and risk into the equation, nothing of major importance is changed in this proposition as long as there are capital markets in which the individual can buy and sell risk at a given price. In this case, it is the risk-adjusted interest rate that is used in calculating the market value of risky claims. The corporate objective function that maximizes social welfare thus becomes "maximize current total firm market value." It tells firms to expand output and investment to the point where the present market value of the firm is at a maximum.[12]

STAKEHOLDER THEORY

To the extent that stakeholder theory says that firms should pay attention to all their constituencies, the theory is unassailable. Taken this far stakeholder theory is completely consistent with value maximization or value-seeking behavior, which implies that managers must pay attention to all constituencies that can affect the value of the firm.

But there is more to the stakeholder story than this. Any theory of corporate decision-making must tell the decision-makers—in this case, managers and boards of directors—how to choose among multiple constituencies with competing and, in some cases, conflicting interests. Customers want low prices, high quality, and full service. Employees want high wages, high-quality working conditions, and fringe benefits, including vacations, medical benefits, and pensions. Suppliers of capital want low risk and high returns. Communities want high charitable contributions, social expenditures by companies to benefit the community at large, increased local investment, and stable employment. And so it goes with every conceivable constituency. Obviously any decision criterion—and the objective function is at the core of any decision criterion—must specify how to make the tradeoffs between these demands.

---

10. Equality holds only in the special case where consumer and producer surpluses are zero, and there are no externalities or monopoly.

11. For those unfamiliar with finance and present values, the value one year from now of a dollar today saved for use one year from now is thus $1 x (1+r)$, where r is the interest rate. Alternatively, the value today of a dollar of resources to be received one year from now is its present value of $1/(1+r)$.

12. Without going into the details here, the same criterion applies to all organizations whether they are public corporations or not. Obviously, even if the financial claims are not explicitly valued by the market, social welfare will be increased as long as managers of partnerships or non-profits increase output so long as the imputed market value of claims on the firm continue to increase.

> **Value maximization provides the following answer to the tradeoff question: Spend an additional dollar on any constituency provided the long-term value added to the firm from such expenditure is a dollar or more. Stakeholder theory, by contrast, contains no conceptual specification of how to make the tradeoffs among stakeholders.**

The Specification of Tradeoffs and the Incompleteness of Stakeholder Theory

Value maximization (or value seeking) provides the following answer to the tradeoff question: Spend an additional dollar on any constituency provided the long-term value added to the firm from such expenditure is a dollar or more. Stakeholder theory, by contrast,[13] contains no conceptual specification of how to make the tradeoffs among stakeholders. And as I argue below, it is this failure to provide a criterion for making such tradeoffs, or even to acknowledge the need for them, that makes stakeholder theory a prescription for destroying firm value and reducing social welfare. This failure also helps explains the theory's remarkable popularity.

Implications for Managers and Directors

Because stakeholder theory leaves boards of directors and executives in firms with no principled criterion for decision-making, companies that try to follow the dictates of stakeholder theory will eventually fail if they are competing with firms that are aiming to maximize value. If this is true, why do so many managers and directors of corporations embrace stakeholder theory?

One answer lies in their personal short-run interests. By failing to provide a definition of better, stakeholder theory effectively leaves managers and directors unaccountable for their stewardship of the firm's resources. Without criteria for performance, managers cannot be evaluated in any principled way. Therefore, stakeholder theory plays into the hands of managers by allowing them to pursue their own interests at the expense of the firm's financial claimants and society at large. It allows managers and directors to devote the firm's resources to their own favorite causes—the environment, art, cities, medical research—without being held accountable for the effect of such expenditures on firm value. (And this can be true even though managers may not consciously recognize that adopting stakeholder theory leaves them unaccountable—especially, for example when such managers have a strong personal interest in social issues.) By expanding the power of managers in this unproductive way, stakeholder theory increases agency costs in the economic system. And since it expands the power of managers, it is not surprising that stakeholder theory receives substantial support from them.

In this sense, then, stakeholder theory can be seen as gutting the foundations of the firm's internal control systems. By "internal control systems," I mean mainly the corporate performance measurement and evaluation systems that, when properly designed, provide strong incentives for value-increasing behavior. There is simply no principled way within the stakeholder construct (which fails to specify what better is) that anyone could say that a manager has done a good or bad job. Stakeholder theory supplants or weakens the power of such control systems by giving managers more power to do whatever they want, subject only to constraints that are imposed by forces *outside* the firm—by the financial markets, the market for corporate control (e.g., the market for hostile takeovers), and, when all else fails, the product markets.

Thus, having observed the efforts of stakeholder theory advocates to weaken internal control systems, it is not surprising to see the theory being used to argue for government restrictions, such as state anti-takeover provisions, on financial markets and the market for corporate control. These markets are driven by value maximization and will limit the damage that can be done by managers who adopt stakeholder theory. And, as illustrated by the 1990s campaigns against globalization and free trade, the stakeholder argument is also being used to restrict product-market competition as well.

But there is something deeper than self-interest—something rooted in the evolution of the human psyche—that is driving our attraction to stakeholder theory.

FAMILIES VERSUS MARKETS: THE ROOTS OF STAKEHOLDER THEORY

Stakeholder theory taps into the deep emotional commitment of most individuals to the family and tribe. For tens of thousands of years, those of our ancestors who had little respect for or loyalty to the family, band, or tribe were much less likely to survive than those who did. In the last few hundred years, we have experienced the emergence of a market exchange system of prices and the private property rights on which they are based. This system of voluntary and decentralized coordination of human action has brought huge increases in human welfare and freedom of action.

---

13. At least as advocated by Freeman (1984), Clarkson Principles (1999) and others.

As Friedrich von Hayek points out, we are generally unaware of the functioning of these market systems because no single mind invented or designed them—and because they work in very complicated and subtle ways. In Hayek's words:

We are led—for example, by the pricing system in market exchange—to do things by circumstances of which we are largely unaware and which produce results that we do not intend. In our economic activities we do not know the needs which we satisfy nor the sources of the things which we get. Almost all of us serve people whom we do not know, and even of whose existence we are ignorant; and we in turn constantly live on the services of other people of whom we know nothing. All this is possible because we stand in a great framework of institutions and traditions—economic, legal, moral—into which we fit ourselves by obeying certain rules of conduct that we never made, and which we have never understood in the sense in which we understand how the things that we manufacture function.[14]

Moreover, these systems operate in ways that limit the options of the small group or family, and these constraints are neither well understood nor instinctively welcomed by individuals. Many people are drawn to stakeholder theory through their evolutionary attachment to the small group and the family. As Hayek puts it:

Constraints on the practices of the small group, it must be emphasized and repeated, are hated. *For, as we shall see, the individual following them, even though he depends on them for life, does not and usually cannot understand how they function or how they benefit him. He knows so many objects that seem desirable but for which he is not permitted to grasp, and he cannot see how other beneficial features of his environment depend on the discipline to which he is forced to submit—a discipline forbidding*

him to reach out for these same appealing objects. Disliking these constraints so much, we hardly can be said to have selected them; rather, these constraints selected us: they enabled us to survive.[15]

Thus we have a system in which human beings must simultaneously exist in two orders, what Hayek calls the "micro-cosmos" and the "macro-cosmos":

Moreover, the structures of the extended order are made up not only of individuals but also of many, often overlapping, suborders within which old instinctual responses, such as solidarity and altruism, continue to retain some importance by assisting voluntary collaboration, even though they are incapable, by themselves, of creating a basis for the more extended order. Part of our present difficulty is that we must constantly adjust our lives, our thoughts and our emotions, in order to live simultaneously within different kinds of orders according to different rules. If we were to apply the unmodified, uncurbed rules of the micro-cosmos (i.e. of the small band or troop, or of, say, our families) to the macro-cosmos (our wider civilization), as our instincts and sentimental yearnings often make us wish to do, we would destroy it. Yet if we were always to apply the rules of the extended order to our more intimate groupings, we would crush them. So we must learn to live in two sorts of worlds at once. To apply the name 'society' to both, or even to either, is hardly of any use, and can be most misleading.[16]

Stakeholder theory taps into this confusion and antagonism towards markets and relaxes constraints on the small group in ways that are damaging to society as a whole and (in the long run) to the small group itself. Such deeply rooted and generally unrecognized conflict between allegiances to family and tribe and what is good for society as whole has had a major impact on our evolution. And in this case, the conflict does not end up serving our long-run collective interests.[17]

14. F. A. Hayek, *The Fatal Conceit.* Edited by W. W. Bartley. The Collected Works of F. A. Hayek. Chicago: University of Chicago Press, 1988, p.14.

15. Ibid., pp. 13, 14; emphasis in original.

16. Ibid., p. 18; emphasis in original.

17. It is useful here to briefly summarize the positive arguments (those refutable by empirical data) and normative arguments (those propositions that say what should be rather than what is in the world) I have made thus far. I have argued positively that firms that follow stakeholder theory as it is generally advocated will do less well in the competition for survival than those who follow a well-defined single-valued objective such as value creation. I have also argued positively that if firms follow value creation, social welfare will be greater and normatively that this is desirable. I have also argued positively that the self-interests of managers and directors will lead them to prefer stakeholder theory because it increases their power and means they cannot be held accountable for their actions. I have also argued positively that the self-interest of special interest groups who wish to acquire legitimacy in corporate governance circles to enhance their influence over the allocation of corporate resources will advocate the use of stakeholder theory by managers and directors. This leads to the positive prediction that society will be poorer if they are successful, and to the normative conclusion that this is undesirable. For a discussion of the role of normative, positive (or instrumental), and descriptive theory in the literature on stakeholder theory, see Thomas Donaldson and Lee E. Preston, "The Stakeholder Theory of the Corporation: Concepts, Evidence, and Implications." *Academy of Management Review* 20, no. 1 (1995): pp. 65-91.

Stakeholder theory taps into this confusion and antagonism towards markets and relaxes constraints on the small group in ways that are damaging to society as a whole and (in the long run) to the small group itself.

ENLIGHTENED VALUE MAXIMIZATION AND ENLIGHTENED STAKEHOLDER THEORY

For those intent on improving management, organizational governance, and performance, there is a way out of the conflict between value maximizing and stakeholder theory. It lies in the melding together of what I call "enlightened value maximization" and "enlightened stakeholder theory."

Enlightened Value Maximization

Enlightened value maximization recognizes that communication with and motivation of an organization's managers, employees, and partners is extremely difficult. What this means in practice is that if we simply tell all participants in an organization that its sole purpose is to maximize value, we will not get maximum value for the organization. Value maximization is not a vision or a strategy or even a purpose; it is the scorecard for the organization. We must give people enough structure to understand what maximizing value means so that they can be guided by it and therefore have a chance to actually achieve it. They must be turned on by the vision or the strategy in the sense that it taps into some human desire or passion of their own—for example, a desire to build the world's best automobile or to create a film or play that will move people for centuries. All this can be not only consistent with value seeking, but a major contributor to it.

And this brings us up against the limits of value maximization *per se.* Value seeking tells an organization and its participants how their success in achieving a vision or in implementing a strategy will be assessed. But value maximizing or value seeking says nothing about how to create a superior vision or strategy. Nor does it tell employees or managers how to find or establish initiatives or ventures that create value. It only tells them how we will measure success in their activity.

Defining what it means to score a goal in football or soccer, for example, tells the players nothing about how to win the game; it just tells them how the score will be kept. That is the role of value maximization in organizational life. It doesn't tell us how to have a great defense or offense, or what kind of plays to create, or how much to train and practice, or whom to hire, and so on. All of these critical functions are part of the competitive and organizational strategy of any team or organization. Adopting value creation as the scorekeeping measure does

nothing to relieve us of the responsibility to do all these things and more in order to survive and dominate our sector of the competitive landscape.

This means, for example, that we must give employees and managers a structure that will help them resist the temptation to maximize short-term financial performance (as typically measured by accounting profits or, even worse, earnings per share). Short-term profit maximization at the expense of long-term value creation is a sure way to destroy value. This is where enlightened stakeholder theory can play an important role. We can learn from stakeholder theorists how to lead managers and participants in an organization to think more generally and creatively about how the organization's policies treat all important constituencies of the firm. This includes not just the stockholders and financial markets, but employees, customers, suppliers, and the community in which the organization exists.

Indeed, it is a basic principle of enlightened value maximization that *we cannot maximize the long-term market value of an organization if we ignore or mistreat any important constituency.* We cannot create value without good relations with customers, employees, financial backers, suppliers, regulators, and communities. But having said that, we can now use the value criterion for choosing among those competing interests. I say "competing" interests because no constituency can be given full satisfaction if the firm is to flourish and survive. Moreover, we can be sure—again, apart from the possibility of externalities and monopoly power—that using this value criterion will result in making society as well off as it can be.

As stated earlier, resolving externality and monopoly problems is the legitimate domain of the government in its rule-setting function. Those who care about resolving monopoly and externality issues will not succeed if they look to corporations to resolve these issues voluntarily. Companies that try to do so either will be eliminated by competitors who choose not to be so civic minded, or will survive only by consuming their economic rents in this manner.

Enlightened Stakeholder Theory

Enlightened stakeholder theory is easy to explain. It can make use of most of what stakeholder theorists offer in the way of processes and audits to measure and evaluate the firm's management of its relations with all important constituencies. Enlightened stakeholder theory adds the simple specification that the objective function—the overriding goal—of the firm is to maximize total long-term firm market value. In short, the change in the total long-term market value of the firm is the scorecard by which success is measured.

I say "long-term" market value to recognize the possibility that financial markets, although forward looking, may not understand the full implications of a company's policies until they begin to show up in cash flows over time. In such cases, management must communicate to investors the policies' anticipated effect on value, and then wait for the market to catch up and recognize the real value of its decisions as reflected in increases in market share, customer and employee loyalty, and, finally, cash flows. Value creation does not mean responding to the day-to-day fluctuations in a firm's value. The market is inevitably ignorant of many managerial actions and opportunities, at least in the short run. In those situations where the financial markets clearly do not have this private competitive information, directors and managers must resist the pressures of those markets while making every effort to communicate their expectations to investors.

In this way, enlightened stakeholder theorists can see that although stockholders are not some special constituency that ranks above all others, long-term stock value is an important determinant (along with the value of debt and other instruments) of total long-term firm value. They would recognize that value creation gives management a way to assess the tradeoffs that must be made among competing constituencies, and that it allows for principled decision making independent of the personal preferences of managers and directors. Also important, managers and directors become accountable for the assets under their control because the value scorecard provides an objective yardstick against which their performance can be evaluated.

Measurability and Imperfect Knowledge

It is important to recognize that none of the above arguments depends on value being easily observable. Nor do they depend on perfect knowledge of the effects on value of decisions regarding any of a firm's constituencies. The world may be complex and difficult to understand. It may leave us in deep uncertainty about the effects of any decisions we may make. It may be governed by complex dynamic systems that are difficult to optimize in the usual sense. But that does not remove the necessity of making choices on a day-to-day basis. And to do this in a purposeful way we must have a scorecard.

The absence of a scorecard makes it easier for people to engage in value-claiming activities that satisfy one or more group of stakeholders at the expense of value creation. We can take random actions, and we can devise decision rules that depend on superstitions. But none of these is likely to serve us well in the competition for survival.

We must not confuse optimization with value creation or value seeking. To create value we need not know exactly what maximum value is and precisely how it can be achieved. What we must do, however, is to set up our organizations so that managers and employees are clearly motivated to seek value—to institute those changes and strategies that are most likely to cause value to rise. To navigate in such a world in anything close to a purposeful way, we must have a notion of "better," and value seeking is such a notion. I know of no other scorecard that will score the game as well as this one. Under most circumstances and conditions, it tells us when we are getting better, and when we are getting worse. It is not perfect, but that is the nature of the world.

THE BALANCED SCORECARD

The Balanced Scorecard is the managerial equivalent of stakeholder theory. Like stakeholder theory, the notion of a "balanced" scorecard appeals to many, but it suffers from many of the same flaws. When we use multiple measures on the balanced scorecard to evaluate the performance of people or business units, we put managers in the same impossible position as managers trying to manage under stakeholder theory. We are asking them to maximize in more than one dimension at a time with no idea of the tradeoffs between the measures. As a result, purposeful decisions cannot be made.

The balanced scorecard arose from the belief of its originators, Robert Kaplan and David Norton, that purely financial measures of performance are not sufficient to yield effective management decisions.[18]

---

18. See Robert S. Kaplan and David P. Norton, "The Balanced Scorecard—Measures That Drive Performance," *Harvard Business Review*, no. January-February 1992: pp. 71-79; and Robert Kaplan and David P. Norton, *The Balanced Scorecard*. Boston, MA: Harvard Business School Press, 1996.

The Balanced Scorecard is best described not as a scorecard, but as a dashboard or instrument panel. It can tell managers many interesting things about their business, but it does not give a score for the organization's performance, or even for the performance of its business units. It does not allow us to distinguish winners from losers.

I agree with this conclusion though, as I suggest below, they have inadvertently confused this with the unstated, but implicit conclusion that there should never be a *single* measure of performance. Moreover, especially *at lower levels of an organization*, a single pure financial measure of performance is unlikely to properly measure a person's or even a business unit's contribution to a company. In the words of Kaplan and Norton:

The Balanced Scorecard complements financial measures of past performance with measures of the drivers of future performance. The objectives and measures of the scorecard are derived from an organization's vision and strategy. The objectives and measures view organizational performance from four perspectives: financial, customer, internal business process, and learning and growth. . . .

The Balanced Scorecard expands the set of business unit objectives beyond summary financial measures. Corporate executives can now measure how their business units create value for current and future customers and how they must enhance internal capabilities and the investment in people, systems, and procedures necessary to improve future performance. The Balanced Scorecard captures the critical value-creation activities created by skilled, motivated organizational participants. While retaining, via the financial perspective, an interest in short-term performance, the Balanced Scorecard clearly reveals the value drivers for superior long-term financial and competitive performance.[19]

As Kaplan and Norton go on to say,

The measures are balanced *between the outcome measures—the results of past efforts—and the measures that drive future performance. And the scorecard is* balanced *between objective easily quantified outcome measures and subjective, somewhat judgmental performance drivers of the outcome measures. . . .*

A good balanced scorecard should have an appropriate mix of outcomes (lagging indicators) and performance drivers (leading indicators) that have been customized to the business unit's strategy."[20]

The aim of Kaplan and Norton, then, is to capture both past performance and expected future performance in scorecards with multiple measures—in fact, as many as two dozen of them—that are intimately related to the organization's strategy.[21] And this is where my misgivings about the Balanced Scorecard lie. For an organization's strategy to be implemented effectively, each person in the organization must clearly understand what he or she has to do, how their performance measures will be constructed, and how their rewards and punishments are related to those measures.

But, as we saw earlier in the case of multiple constituencies (or the multiple goals represented in Figure 1), decision makers cannot make rational choices without some overall single dimensional objective to be maximized. Given a dozen or two dozen measures and no sense of the tradeoffs between them, the typical manager will be unable to behave purposefully, and the result will be confusion.

Kaplan and Norton generally do not deal with the critical issue of how to weight the multiple dimensions represented by the two-dozen measures on their scorecards. And this is where problems with the Balanced Scorecard are sure to arise: without specifying what the tradeoffs are among these two dozen or so different measures, there is no "balance" in their scorecard. Adding to the potential for confusion, Kaplan and Norton also offer almost no guidance on the critical issue of how to tie the performance measurement system to managerial incentives and rewards. Here is their concluding statement on this important matter:

Several approaches may be attractive to pursue. In the short term, tying incentive compensation of all senior managers to a balanced set of business unit scorecard measures will foster commitment to overall organizational goals, rather than suboptimization within functional departments... Whether such linkages should be explicit... or applied judgmentally... will likely vary from company to company. More knowledge about the benefits and costs of explicit linkages will undoubtedly continue to be accumulated in the years ahead.[22]

What the Balanced Scorecard fails to provide, then, is a clear linkage (and a rationale for that

19. Kaplan and Norton (1996), p. 8.
20. Ibid., p. 10 and p. 150, emphasis in original.
21. Ibid., p. 162.
22. Ibid., p. 222.

linkage) between the performance measures and the corporate system of rewards and punishments. Indeed, the Balanced Scorecard does not provide a scorecard in the traditional sense of the word. And, to make my point, let me push the sports analogy a little further. A scorecard in any sport yields a single number that determines the winner among all contestants. In most sports the person or team with the highest score wins. Very simply, a scorecard yields a score, not multiple measures of different dimensions like yards rushing and passing. These latter drivers of performance affect who wins and who loses, but they do not themselves distinguish the winner.

To reiterate, the Balanced Scorecard does not yield a score that would allow us to distinguish winners from losers. For this reason, the system is best described not as a scorecard, but as a dashboard or instrument panel. It can tell managers many interesting things about their business, but it does not give a score for the organization's performance, or even for the performance of its business units. As a senior manager of a large financial institution that spent considerable time implementing a balanced scorecard system explained to me: "We never figured out how to use the scorecard to measure performance. We used it to transfer information, a lot of information, from the divisions to the senior management team. At the end of the day, however, your performance depended on your ability to meet your targets for contribution to bottom-line profits."

Thus, because of the lack of a way for managers to think through the difficult task of determining an unambiguous performance measure in the Balanced Scorecard system, the result in this case was a fallback to a single and inadequate financial measure of performance (in this case, accounting profits)— the very approach that Kaplan and Norton properly wish to change. The lack of a single one-dimensional measure by which an organization or department or person will score their performance means these units or people cannot make purposeful decisions. They cannot do so because if they do not understand the tradeoffs between the multiple measures, they cannot know whether they are becoming better off (except in those rare cases when all measures are increasing in some decision).

In sum, the appropriate measure for the organization is value creation, the change in the market value of all claims on the firm. And for those organizations that wish a "flow" measure of value

creation on a quarterly or yearly basis, I recommend Economic Value Added (EVA). But I hasten to add that, as the performance measures are cascaded down through the organization, neither value creation nor the year-to-year measure, EVA, is likely to be the proper performance measure at all levels. To illustrate this point, let's now look briefly at performance measurement for business units.

Measuring Divisional Performance

The proper measure for any person or business unit in a multi-divisional company will be determined mainly by two factors: the company's strategy and the actions that the person or division being evaluated can take to contribute to the success of the strategy. There are two general ways in principle that this score or objective can be determined: a centralized way and a decentralized way.

To see this let us begin by distinguishing clearly between the measure of performance (single dimensional) for a unit or person, and the drivers that the unit or person can use to affect the performance measure. In the decentralized solution, the organization determines the appropriate performance measure for the unit, and it is the person or unit's responsibility to figure out what the performance drivers are, how they influence performance, and how to manage them. The distinction here is the difference between an outcome (the performance measure) and the inputs or decision variables (the management of the performance drivers). And managers at higher levels in the hierarchy may be able to help the person or unit to understand what the drivers are and how to manage them. But this help can only go so far because the specific knowledge regarding the drivers will generally lie not in headquarters, but in the operating units. Therefore, in the end it is the accountable party, not headquarters, who will generally have the relevant specific knowledge and therefore must determine the drivers, their changing relation to results, and how to manage them, not headquarters.

At the opposite extreme is the completely centralized solution, in which headquarters will determine the performance measure by giving the functional form to the unit that lists the drivers and describes the weight that each driver receives in the determination of the performance measure. The performance for a period is then determined by calculating the weighted average of the measures of

> **As a performance measurement system, the Balanced Scorecard will lead to confusion, conflict, inefficiency, and lack of focus. This is bound to happen as operating managers guess at what the tradeoffs might be between each of the dimensions of performance.**

the drivers for the period.[23] This solution effectively transfers the job of learning how to create value at all levels in the organization to the top managers, and leaves the operating managers only the job of managing the performance drivers that have been dictated to them by top management. The problem with this approach, however, is that is likely to work only in a fairly narrow range of circumstances— those cases where the specific knowledge necessary to understand the details of the relation between changes in each driver and changes in the performance measure lies higher in the hierarchy. Although this category may include a number of very small firms, it will rule out most larger, multidivisional companies, especially in today's rapidly changing business environment.

CLOSING THOUGHTS ON THE BALANCED SCORECARD AND VALUE MAXIMIZATION

In summary, the Kaplan-Norton Balanced Scorecard is a tool to help managers understand what creates value in their business. As such, it is a useful analytical tool, and I join with Kaplan and Norton in urging managers to do the hard work necessary to understand what creates value in their organization and how to manage those value drivers. As they put it,

> *…[A] properly constructed Balanced Scorecard should tell the story of the business unit's strategy. It should identify and make explicit the sequence of hypotheses about the cause-and-effect relationships between outcome measures and the performance drivers of those outcomes. Every measure selected for a Balanced Scorecard should be an element in a chain of cause-and-effect relationships that communicates the meaning of the business unit's strategy to the organization.[24]*

But managers are almost inevitably led to try to use the multiple measures of the Balanced Scorecard as a performance measurement system. And as a performance measurement system, the Balanced Scorecard will lead to confusion, conflict, inefficiency, and lack of focus. This is bound to happen

as operating managers guess at what the tradeoffs might be between each of the dimensions of performance. And this uncertainty will generally lead to conflicts with managers at headquarters, who are likely to have different assessments of the tradeoffs. Such conflicts, besides causing disappointments and confusion about operating decisions, could also lead to attempts by operating managers to game the system—by, say, performing well on financial measures while sacrificing nonfinancial ones. Moreover, there is no logical or principled resolution of the resulting conflicts unless all the parties come to agreement about what they are trying to accomplish; and this means specifying how the score is calculated—in effect, figuring out how the balance in the Balanced Scorecard is actually attained.

As we saw earlier, even if it were possible to come up with a truly "optimizing" system where all the weights and the tradeoffs among the multiple measures and drivers were specified—a highly doubtful proposition—reaching agreement between headquarters and line management over the proper weighting of the measures and their linkage to the corporate reward system would be an enormously difficult, if not an impossible, undertaking. In addition, it would surely be impossible to keep the system continuously updated so as to reflect all the changes in a dynamic local and worldwide competitive landscape.

A 1996 survey of Balanced Scorecard implementations by Towers Perrin gives a fairly clear indication of the problems that are likely to arise with it.[25] Perhaps most troubling, 70% of the companies using a scorecard also reported using it for compensation—and an additional 17% were considering doing so. And, not surprisingly, 40% of the respondents said they believed that the large number of measures weakened the effectiveness of the measurement system. What's more, in their empirical test of the effects of the balanced scorecard implementation in a global financial services firm, a 1997 study by Christopher Ittner, David Larcker, and Marshall Meyer concluded that the first issue their study raises for future research is "defining precisely what 'balance' is and the mechanisms through which 'balance' promotes performance."[26] As I have argued in

---

23. And of course I do not mean to imply that the functional relationship between the value drivers and the performance measure will always be a simple weighted average. Indeed, in general it will be more complicated than this.
24. Ibid., p. 31.

25. Towers Perrin, "Inside 'the balanced scorecard'," *Compuscan Report*, January 1996: pp. 1-5.
26. Ittner, Cristopher, David F. Larcker, and Marshal W. Meyer, "Performance, Compensation, and the Balanced Scorecard," Unpublished, Wharton School, U. of Pennsylvania, November 1, 1997.

this paper, this question cannot be answered because "balance" is a term used by Balanced Scorecard advocates as a substitute for thorough analysis of one of the more difficult parts of the performance measurement system—the necessity to evaluate and make tradeoffs. They and others have been seduced by this hurrah word (who can argue for "unbalanced"?) into avoiding careful thought on the issues.

In fact, the sooner we get rid of the word "balance" in these discussions, the better we will be able to sort out the solutions. Balance cannot ever substitute for having to deal with the difficult issues associated with specifying the tradeoffs among multiple goods and bads that determine the overall score for an organization's success. We must do this to stand a chance of creating an organizational scoreboard that actually gives a score—which is something every good scoreboard must do.

Closing Thoughts on Stakeholder Theory

Stakeholder theory plays into the hands of special interests that wish to use the resources of corporations for their own ends. With the widespread failure of centrally planned socialist and communist economies, those who wish to use non-market forces to reallocate wealth now see great opportunity in the playing field that stakeholder theory opens to them. Stakeholder theory gives them the appearance of legitimate political access to the sources of decision-making power in organizations, and it deprives those organizations of a principled basis for rejecting those claims. The result is to undermine the foundations of value-seeking behavior that have enabled markets and capitalism to generate wealth and high standards of living worldwide.

If widely adopted, stakeholder theory will reduce social welfare even as its advocates claim to increase it—much as happened in the failed communist and socialist experiments of the last century. And, as I pointed out earlier, stakeholder theorists will often have the active support of managers who wish to throw off the constraints on their power provided by the value-seeking criterion and its enforcement by capital markets, the market for corporate control, and product markets. For example, stakeholder arguments played an important role in persuading the U.S. courts and legislatures to limit hostile takeovers through legalization of poison pills and state control shareholder acts. And we will continue to see more political action limiting the power of these markets to constrain managers. In sum, special interest groups will continue to use the arguments of stakeholder theory to legitimize their positions, and it is in our collective interest to expose the logical fallacy of these arguments.

THE MODERN INDUSTRIAL REVOLUTION, EXIT, AND THE FAILURE OF INTERNAL CONTROL SYSTEMS

by Michael C. Jensen,
Harvard Business School*

F undamental technological, political, regulatory, and economic forces are radically changing the worldwide competitive environment. We have not seen such a metamorphosis of the economic landscape since the industrial revolution of the 19th century. The scope and pace of the changes over the past two decades qualify this period as a modern industrial revolution, and I predict it will take decades more for these forces to be worked out fully in the worldwide economy.

Although the current and 19th-century transformations of the U.S. economy are separated by almost 100 years, there are striking parallels between them—most notably, rapid technological and organizational change leading to declining production costs and increasing average (but decreasing marginal) productivity of labor. During both periods, moreover, these developments resulted in widespread excess capacity, reduced rates of growth in labor income, and, ultimately, downsizing and exit.

The capital markets played a major role in eliminating excess capacity both in the late 19th century and in the 1980s. The merger boom of the 1890s brought about a massive consolidation of independent firms and closure of marginal facilities. In the 1980s the capital markets helped eliminate excess capacity through leveraged acquisitions, stock buybacks, hostile takeovers, leveraged buyouts, and divisional sales.

And much as the takeover specialists of the 1980s were disparaged by managers, policymakers, and the press, their 19th-century counterparts were vilified as "robber barons." In both cases, the popular reaction against "financiers" was followed by public policy changes that restricted the capital markets. The turn of the century saw the passage of antitrust laws that restricted business combinations; the late 1980s gave rise to re-regulation of the credit markets, antitakeover legislation, and court decisions that all but shut down the market for corporate control.

*This is a shortened version of a paper by the same title that was originally published in the *Journal of Finance* (July 1993), which was based in turn on my Presidential Address to the American Finance Association in January 1993. It is reprinted here by permission of the American Finance Association. I wish to express my appreciation for the research assistance of Chris Allen, Brian Barry, Susan Brumfield, Karin Monsler, and particularly Donna Feinberg, the support of the Division of Research of the Harvard Business School, and the comments of and discussions with George Baker, Carliss Baldwin, Joe Bower, Alfred Chandler, Harry and Linda DeAngelo, Ben Esty, Takashi Hikino, Steve Kaplan, Nancy Koehn, Claudio Loderer, George Lodge, John Long, Kevin Murphy, Malcolm Salter, Rene Stulz, Richard Tedlow, and, especially, Robert Hall, Richard Hackman, and Karen Wruck.

Although the vast increases in productivity associated with the 19th-century industrial revolution increased aggregate welfare, the resulting obsolescence of human and physical capital caused great hardship, misunderstanding, and bitterness. As noted in 1873 by Henry Ward Beecher, a well-known commentator and influential clergyman of the time,

The present period will always be memorable in the dark days of commerce in America. We have had commercial darkness at other times. There have been these depressions, but none so obstinate and none so universal... Great Britain has felt it; France has felt it; all Austria and her neighborhood has experienced it. It is cosmopolitan. It is distinguished by its obstinacy from former like periods of commercial depression. Remedies have no effect. Party confidence, all stimulating persuasion, have not lifted the pall, and practical men have waited, feeling that if they could tide over a year they could get along; but they could not tide over the year. If only one or two years could elapse they could save themselves. The years have lapsed, and they were worse off than they were before. What is the matter? What has happened? Why, from the very height of prosperity without any visible warning, without even a cloud the size of a man's hand visible on the horizon, has the cloud gathered, as it were, from the center first, spreading all over the sky?[1]

Almost 20 years later, on July 4, 1892, the Populist Party platform adopted at the party's first convention in Omaha reflected continuing unrest while pointing to financiers as the cause of the current problems:

We meet in the midst of a nation brought to the verge of moral, political, and material ruin... The fruits of the toil of millions are boldly stolen to build up colossal fortunes for the few, unprecedented in the history of mankind; and the possessors of these in turn despise the republic and endanger liberty. From the same prolific womb of government injustice are bred two great classes of tramps and millionaires.[2]

Technological and other developments that began in the mid-20th century have culminated in the past two decades in a similar situation: rapidly improving productivity, the creation of overcapacity, and, consequently, the requirement for exit. Although efficient exit has profound import for productivity and social wealth, research on the topic[3] has been relatively sparse since the 1942 publication of Joseph Schumpeter's famous description of capitalism as a process of "creative destruction." In Schumpeter's words,

Every piece of business strategy...must be seen in its role in the perennial gale of creative destruction... The usual theorist's paper and the usual government commission's report practically never try to see that behavior... as an attempt by those firms to keep on their feet, on ground that is slipping away from under them. In other words, the problem that is usually being visualized is how capitalism administers existing structures, whereas the relevant problem is how it creates and destroys them.[4]

Current technological and political changes are bringing the question of efficient exit to the forefront, and the adjustments necessary to cope with such changes will receive renewed attention from managers, policymakers, and researchers in the coming decade.

In this paper, I begin by reviewing the industrial revolution of the 19th century to shed light on current economic trends. Drawing parallels with the 1800s, I discuss in some detail worldwide changes driving the demand for exit in today's economy. I also describe the barriers to efficient exit in the U.S. economy, and the role of the market for corporate control—takeovers, LBOs, and other leveraged restructurings—in surmounting those barriers during the 1980s.

1. Walter W. Price, *We Have Recovered Before!* (Harper & Brothers: New York, 1933), p. 6.
2. Donald L., McMurray, *Coxey's Army: A Study of the Industrial Army Movement of 1894* (Little, Brown: Boston, 1929), p. 7.
3. For a rare study of exit in the finance literature, see the analysis of the retrenchment of the U.S. steel industry in Harry DeAngelo and Linda DeAngelo, "Union Negotiations and Corporate Policy: A Study of Labor Concessions in the Domestic Steel Industry during the 1980s," *Journal of Financial Economics* 30 (1991), 3-43. See also Pankaj Ghemawat and Barry Nalebuff, "Exit," *Rand Journal of Economics* 16 (Summer, 1985), 184-194. For a detailed comparison of U.S. and Japanese retrenchment in the 1970s and early 1980s, see Douglas Anderson, "Managing Retreat: Disinvestment Policy," in Thomas K. McCraw, ed., *America Versus Japan* (Harvard Business School Press: Boston, 1986), 337-372. Joseph L. Bower analyzes the private and political responses to decline in the petrochemical industry in *When Markets Quake* (Harvard Business School Press: Boston, 1986). Kathryn Harrigan presents detailed firm and industry studies in two of her books: *Managing Maturing Businesses: Restructuring Declining Industries and Revitalizing Troubled Operations* (Lexington Books, 1988) and *Strategies for Declining Businesses* (Lexington Books, 1980).
4. Joseph A., Schumpeter, *Capitalism, Socialism, and Democracy* (Harper Torchbook Edition: New York, 1976), p. 83.

With the shutdown of the capital markets in the 1990s, the challenge of accomplishing efficient exit has been transferred to corporate internal control systems. With few exceptions, however, U.S. managements and boards have failed to bring about timely exit and downsizing without external pressure. Although product market competition will eventually eliminate overcapacity, this solution generates huge unnecessary costs. (The costs of this solution have now become especially apparent in Japan, where a virtual breakdown of the internal control systems, coupled with a complete absence of capital market influence, has resulted in enormous overcapacity—a problem that Japanese companies are only beginning to address.)

At the close of the paper, I offer suggestions for reforming U.S. internal corporate control mechanisms. In particular, I hold up several features of venture capital and LBO firms such as Kleiner Perkins and KKR for emulation by large, public companies—notably (1) smaller, more active, and better informed boards; and (2) significant equity ownership by board members as well as managers. I also urge boards and managers to encourage larger holdings and greater participation by people I call "active" investors.

THE SECOND INDUSTRIAL REVOLUTION[5]

The Industrial Revolution was distinguished by a shift to capital-intensive production, rapid growth in productivity and living standards, the formation of large corporate hierarchies, overcapacity, and, eventually, closure of facilities. Originating in Britain in the late 18th century, the First Industrial Revolution witnessed the application of new energy sources to methods of production. The mid-19th century saw another wave of massive change with the birth of modern transportation and communication facilities, including the railroad, telegraph, steamship, and cable systems. Coupled with the invention of high-speed consumer packaging technology, these innovations gave rise to the mass production and distribution systems of the

late 19th and early 20th centuries—the Second Industrial Revolution.

The dramatic changes that occurred from the middle to the end of the century clearly warrant the term "revolution." Inventions such as the McCormick reaper in the 1830s, the sewing machine in 1844, and high-volume canning and packaging devices in the 1880s exemplified a worldwide surge in productivity that "substituted machine tools for human craftsmen, interchangeable parts for hand-tooled components, and the energy of coal for that of wood, water, and animals."[6] New technology in the paper industry allowed wood pulp to replace rags as the primary input material. Continuous rod rolling transformed the wire industry: within a decade, wire nails replaced cut nails as the main source of supply. Worsted textiles resulting from advances in combing technology changed the woolen textile industry. Between 1869 and 1899, the capital invested per American manufacturer grew from about $700 to $2,000; and, in the period 1889-1919, the annual growth of total factor productivity was almost six times higher than that which had occurred for most of the 19th century.[7]

As productivity climbed steadily, production costs and prices fell dramatically. The 1882 formation of the Standard Oil Trust, which concentrated nearly 25% of the world's kerosene production into three refineries, reduced the average cost of a gallon of kerosene by 70% between 1882 and 1885. In tobacco, the invention of the Bonsack machine in the early 1880s reduced the labor costs of cigarette production by 98%. The Bessemer process reduced the cost of steel rails by 88% from the early 1870s to the late 1890s, and the electrolytic refining process invented in the 1880s reduced the price of aluminum by 96% between 1888 and 1895. In chemicals, the mass production of synthetic dyes, alkalis, nitrates, fibers, plastics, and film occurred rapidly after 1880. Production costs of synthetic blue dye, for example, fell by 95% from the 1870s to 1886.[8]

Such sharp declines in production costs and prices led to widespread excess capacity—a problem that was exacerbated by the fall in demand that

---

5. This section draws extensively on excellent discussions of the period by Alfred Chandler, Thomas McCraw, and Naomi Lamoreux. See the following works by Chandler: "The Emergence of Managerial Capitalism," Harvard Business School #9-384-081, revised by Thomas J. McCraw, July 1, 1992; *Scale and Scope, The Dynamics of Industrial Capitalism* (Harvard University Press, 1990); and *The Visible Hand: The Managerial Revolution in American Business* (Harvard University Press, 1977). See also Naomi R. Lamoreaux, *The Great Merger Movement in American Business, 1895-1904* (Cambridge University Press: Cambridge, England,

1985); and Thomas K. McCraw, "Antitrust: The Perceptions and Reality in Coping with Big Business," Harvard Business School #N9-391-292 (1992), and "Rethinking the Trust Question," in T. McCraw, ed., *Regulation in Perspective* (Harvard University Press, 1981).

6. McCraw (1981), p. 3.

7. McCraw (1981), p. 3.

8. For most of the examples of cost reduction cited in this paragraph, see Chandler (1992), pp. 4-6.

accompanied the recession and panic of 1893. Although attempts were made to eliminate excess capacity through pools, associations, and cartels, the problem was not substantially resolved until the capital markets facilitated exit by means of the 1890s' wave of mergers and acquisitions. Capacity was reduced through consolidation and the closing of marginal facilities in the merged entities. From 1895 to 1904, over 1,800 firms were bought or combined by merger into 157 firms.[9]

THE MODERN INDUSTRIAL REVOLUTION

The major restructuring of the American business community that began in the 1970s and continues in the 1990s is being driven by a variety of factors, including changes in physical and management technology, global competition, new regulation and taxes, and the conversion of formerly closed, centrally planned socialist and communist economies to capitalism, along with open participation in international trade. These changes are significant in scope and effect; indeed, they are bringing about the Third Industrial Revolution. To appreciate the challenge facing current control systems in light of this change, we must understand more about these general forces sweeping the world economy, and why they are generating excess capacity and thus the requirement for exit.

What has generally been referred to as the "decade of the '80s" in the United States actually began in the early 1970s, with the 10-fold increase in energy prices from 1973 to 1979, and the emergence of the modern market for corporate control and high-yield, non-investment-grade ("junk") bonds in the mid-1970s. These events were associated with the beginnings of the Third Industrial Revolution which—if I were to pick a particular date—would be the time of the oil price increases beginning in 1973.

The Decade of the '80s: Capital Markets Provide an Early Response to the Modern Industrial Revolution

The macroeconomic data for the 1980s show major productivity gains. In fact, 1981 was a watershed year. Total factor productivity growth in the manufacturing sector more than doubled after 1981, from 1.4% per year in the period 1950-1981 (including a period of zero growth from 1973-1980) to 3.3% in the period 1981-1990.[10] Over the same period, nominal unit labor costs stopped their 17-year rise, and real unit labor costs declined by 25%. These lower labor costs came not from reduced wages or employment, but from increased productivity: nominal and real hourly compensation increased by a total of 4.2% and 0.3% per year, respectively, over the 1981-1989 period.[11] Manufacturing employment reached a low in 1983, but by 1989 had experienced a small cumulative increase of 5.5%.[12] Meanwhile, the annual growth in labor productivity increased from 2.3% between 1950-1981 to 3.8% between 1981-1990, while a 30-year decline in capital productivity was reversed when the annual change in the productivity of capital increased from –1.0% between 1950-1981 to 2.0% between 1981-1990.[13]

---

9. Lamoreux (1985), p. i.

10. Measured by multifactor productivity, as reported in Table 3 of U.S. Department of Labor, Bureau of Labor Statistics, 1990, *Multifactor Productivity Measures*, Report #USDL 91-412. Manufacturing labor productivity also grew at an annual rate of 3.8% in 1981-1990, as compared to 2.3% in the period 1950-1981 (U. S. Department of Labor, 1990, Table 3). By contrast, productivity growth in the overall (or "non-farm") business sector actually fell from 1.9% in the 1950-1981 period to 1.1% in the 1981-1990 period (U. S. Department of Labor, 1990, Table 2). The reason for the fall apparently lies in the relatively large growth in the service sector relative to the manufacturing sector and the low measured productivity growth in services. But there is considerable controversy over the adequacy of the measurement of productivity in the service sector. For example, the U.S. Department of Labor has no productivity measures for services employing nearly 70% of service workers, including, among others, health care, real estate, and securities brokerage. In addition, many believe that service sector productivity growth measures are downward biased. Service sector price measurements, for example, take no account of the improved productivity and lower prices of discount outlet clubs such as Sam's Club. As another example, the Commerce Department measures the output of financial services as the value of labor used to produce it. Because labor productivity is defined as the value of total output divided by total labor inputs, it is impossible for measured productivity to grow. Between 1973 and 1987, however, total equity shares traded daily grew from 5.7 million to 63.8 million, while employment only doubled, thus implying considerably more productivity growth than the zero growth reflected in the statistics.

11. Nominal and real hourly compensation, *Economic Report of the President*, Table B42 (1993).

12. U.S. Department of Labor, Bureau of Labor Statistics, 1991, *International Comparisons of Manufacturing Productivity and Unit Labor Cost Trends*, Report #USDL 92-752.

13. U.S. Department of Labor (1990). Trends in U.S. productivity have been controversial issues in academic and policy circles in the last decade. One reason, I believe, is that it takes time for these complicated changes to show up in the aggregate statistics. For example, in their recent book Baumol, Blackman, and Wolff changed their formerly pessimistic position. In their words: "This book is perhaps most easily summed up as a compendium of evidence demonstrating the error of our previous ways... The main change that was forced upon our views by careful examination of the long-run data was abandonment of our earlier gloomy assessment of American productivity performance. It has been replaced by the guarded optimism that pervades this book. This does *not* mean that we believe retention of American leadership will be automatic or easy. Yet the statistical evidence did drive us to conclude that the many writers who have suggested that the demise of America's traditional position has already occurred or was close at hand were, like the author of Mark Twain's obituary, a bit premature... It should, incidentally, be acknowledged that a number of distinguished economists have also been driven to a similar evaluation..." William Baumol, Sue Anne Beattey Blackman, and Edward Wolff, *Productivity and American Leadership* (MIT Press, Boston, 1989), pp. ix-x.

What has generally been referred to as the "decade of the 80s" in the United States actually began in the early 1970s, with the 10-fold increase in energy prices from 1973 to 1979, and the emergence of the modern market for corporate control and high-yield, non-investment-grade ("junk") bonds in the mid-1970s.

Reflecting these increases in the productivity of U.S. industry, the real value of public corporations' equity more than doubled during the 1980s from $1.4 to $3 trillion.[14] In addition, real median income increased at the rate of 1.8% per year between 1982 and 1989, reversing the 1.0% per year decline that occurred from 1973 to 1982.[15] Contrary to generally held beliefs, real R&D expenditures set record levels every year from 1975 to 1990, growing at an average annual rate of 5.8%.[16] In one of the media's few accurate portrayals of this period, a 1990 issue of *The Economist* noted that from 1980 to 1985, "American industry went on an R&D spending spree, with few big successes to show for it."[17]

Regardless of the gains in productivity, efficiency, and welfare, the 1980s are generally portrayed by politicians, the media, and others as a "decade of greed and excess." The media attack focused with special intensity on M&A transactions, 35,000 of which occurred from 1976 to 1990, with a total value of $2.6 trillion (in 1992 dollars). Contrary to common belief, only 364 of these offers were contested, and of those only 172 resulted in successful hostile takeovers.[18]

The popular verdict on takeovers was pronounced by prominent takeover defense lawyer Martin Lipton, when he said,

The takeover activity in the U.S. has imposed short-term profit maximization strategies on American Business at the expense of research, development, and capital investment. This is minimizing our ability to compete in world markets and still maintain a growing standard of living at home.[19]

But the evidence provided by financial economists, which I summarize briefly below, is starkly inconsistent with this view.

The most careful academic research strongly suggests that takeovers—along with leveraged restructurings prompted (in many, if not most cases) by the threat of takeover—have produced large gains for shareholders and for the economy as a whole. Based on this research,[20] my estimates indicate that over the 14-year period from 1976 to 1990, the $1.8 trillion volume of corporate control transactions—that is, mergers, tender offers, divestitures, and LBOs—generated over $750 billion in market value "premiums"[21] for selling investors. Given a reasonably efficient market, such premiums (the amounts buyers are willing to pay sellers over current market values) represent, in effect, the minimum increases in value forecast by the buyers. This $750 billion estimate of total shareholder gains thus neither includes the gains (or the losses)[22] to the buyers in such transactions, nor does it account for the value of efficiency improvements by companies pressured by control market activity into reforming without a visible control transaction.

Important sources of the expected gains from takeovers and leveraged restructurings include synergies from combining the assets of two or more organizations in the same or related industries (especially those with excess capacity) and the replacement of inefficient managers or governance systems.[23] Another possible source of the premiums, however, are transfers of wealth from other corporate stakeholders such as employees, bondholders, and the IRS. To the extent the value gains are merely wealth transfers, they do not represent efficiency improvements. But little evidence has been found to date to support substantial wealth transfers from any group,[24] and thus most of the reported gains appear to represent increases in efficiency.

Part of the attack on M&A and LBO transactions has been directed at the high-yield (or "junk") bond

---

14. As measured by the Wilshire 5,000 index of all publicly held equities.

15. Bureau of the Census, Housing and Household Economic Statistics Division (1991).

16. *Business Week* Annual R&D Scoreboard, 1991.

17. "Out of the Ivory Tower," *The Economist*, February 3, 1990.

18. *Mergerstat Review*, 1991, Merrill Lynch, Schaumburg, Illinois.

19. Martin Lipton, "Corporate Governance: Major Issues for the 1990's," Address to the Third Annual Corporate Finance Forum at the J. Ira Harris Center for the Study of Corporate Finance, University of Michigan School of Business, April 6, 1989, p. 2.

20. For a list of such studies, see the Appendix at the end of this article.

21. Measured in 1992 dollars. On average, selling-firm shareholders in all M&A transactions in the period 1976-1990 were paid premiums over market value of 41%. Annual premiums reported by *Mergerstat Review* (1991, Fig. 5) were weighted by value of transactions in the year for this estimate.

In arriving at my estimate of $750 billion of shareholder gains, I also assumed that all transactions without publicly disclosed prices had a value equal to 20% of

the value of the average publicly disclosed transaction in the same year, and that they had average premiums equal to those for publicly disclosed transactions.

22. In cases where buyers overpay, such overpayment does not represent an efficiency gain, but rather only a wealth transfer from the buying firm's claimants to those of the selling firm. My method of calculating *total* shareholder gains thus assumes that the losses to buyers are large enough to offset all gains (including those of the "raiders" whose allegedly massive "paper profits" became a favorite target of the media).

23. A 1992 study by Healy, Palepu, and Ruback estimates the total gains to buying- and selling-firm shareholders in the 50 largest mergers in the period 1979-1984 at 9.1% of the total equity value of both companies. Because buyers in such cases were typically much larger than sellers, such gains are roughly consistent with 41% acquisition premiums. They also find a strong positive cross-sectional relation between the value change and the operating cash flow changes resulting from the merger. See Paul Healy, Krishna Palepu, and Richard Ruback, "Does Corporate Performance Improve After Mergers?," *Journal of Financial Economics* 31, vol. 2 (1992), 135-175.

market. Besides helping to provide capital for corporate newcomers to compete with existing firms in the product markets, junk bonds also eliminated mere size as an effective takeover deterrent. This opened America's largest companies to monitoring and discipline from the capital markets. The following statement by Richard Munro, while Chairman and CEO of Time Inc., is representative of top management's hostile response to junk bonds and takeovers:

Notwithstanding television ads to the contrary, junk bonds are designed as the currency of 'casino economics'... they've been used not to create new plants or jobs or products but to do the opposite: to dismantle existing companies so the players can make their profit... This isn't the Seventh Cavalry coming to the rescue. It's a scalping party.[25]

As critics of leveraged restructuring have suggested, the high leverage incurred in the 1980s did contribute to a sharp increase in the bankruptcy rate of large firms in the early 1990s. Not widely recognized, however, is the major role played by other, external factors in these bankruptcies. First, the recession that helped put many highly leveraged firms into financial distress can be attributed at least in part to new regulatory restrictions on credit markets such as FIRREA—restrictions that were implemented in late 1989 and 1990 to offset the trend toward higher leverage.[26] And when companies did get into financial trouble, revisions in bankruptcy procedures and the tax code made it much more difficult to reorganize outside the courts, thereby *encouraging* many firms to file Chapter 11 and increasing the "costs of financial distress."[27]

But, even with such interference by public policy and the courts with the normal process of private adjustment to financial distress, the general economic consequences of financial distress in the high-yield markets have been greatly exaggerated. While precise numbers are difficult to come by, I estimate that the total bankruptcy losses to junk bond and bank HLT loans from inception of the market in the mid-1970s through 1990 amounted to less than $50 billion. (In comparison, IBM alone lost $51 billion—almost 65% of the total market value of its equity—from its 1991 high to its 1992 close.[28]) Perhaps the most telling evidence that losses have been exaggerated, however, is the current condition of the high-yield market, which is now financing record levels of new issues.

Of course, mistakes were made in the takeover activity of the 1980s. Indeed, given the far-reaching nature of the restructuring, it would have been surprising if there were none. But the popular negative assessment of leveraged restructuring is dramatically inconsistent with both the empirical evidence and the near-universal view of finance scholars who have studied the phenomenon. In fact, takeover activities were addressing an important set of problems in corporate America, and doing it before the companies faced serious trouble in the product markets. They were providing, in effect, an early warning system that motivated healthy adjustments to the excess capacity that was building in many sectors of the worldwide economy.

Causes of Excess Capacity

Excess capacity can arise in at least four ways, the most obvious of which occurs when market demand falls below the level required to yield returns that will support the currently installed production capacity. This *demand-reduction* scenario is most familiarly associated with recession episodes in the business cycle.

24. A 1989 study by Laura Stiglin, Steven Kaplan, and myself demonstrates that, contrary to popular assertions, LBO transactions resulted in increased tax revenues to the U. S. Treasury—increases that average about 60% per annum on a permanent basis under the 1986 IRS code. (Michael C. Jensen, Steven Kaplan, Laura Stiglin, "Effects of LBOs on Tax Revenues of the U.S. Treasury," *Tax Notes*, Vol. 42, No. 6 (February 6, 1989), pp. 727-733.)

The data presented by a study of pension fund reversions reveal that only about 1% of the premiums paid in all takeovers can be explained by reversions of pension plans in the target firms (although the authors of the study do not present this calculation themselves). (Jeffrey Pontiff, Andrei Shleifer, and Michael S. Weisbach, "Reversions of Excess Pension Assets after Takeovers," *Rand Journal of Economics*, Vol. 21, No. 4 (Winter 1990), pp. 600-613.)

Joshua Rosett, in analyzing over 5,000 union contracts in over 1,000 listed companies in the period 1973 to 1987, shows that less than 2% of the takeover premiums can be explained by reductions in union wages in the first six years after the change in control. Pushing the estimation period out to 18 years after the change

in control increases the percentage to only 5.4% of the premium. For hostile takeovers only, union wages *increase* by 3% and 6% for the two time intervals. (Joshua G. Rosett, "Do Union Wealth Concessions Explain Takeover Premiums? The Evidence on Contract Wages," *Journal of Financial Economics*, Vol. 27, No. 1 (September 1990), pp. 263-282.)

25. J. Richard Munro, "Takeovers: The Myths Behind the Mystique," May 15, 1989, published in *Vital Speeches*, p. 472.

26. See the collection of articles on the "credit crunch" in Vol. 4 No. 1 (Spring 1991) of the *Journal of Applied Corporate Finance*.

27. I make this case in "Corporate Control and the Politics of Finance," *Journal of Applied Corporate Finance* (Summer, 1991), 13-33. See also Karen Wruck, "Financial Distress, Reorganization, and Organizational Efficiency," *Journal of Financial Economics* 27 (1990), 420-444.

28. Its high of $139.50 occurred on 2/19/91 and it closed at $50.38 at the end of 1992.

> **Takeover activities were addressing an important set of problems in corporate America, and doing it before the companies faced serious trouble in the product markets. They were providing, in effect, an early warning system that motivated healthy adjustments to the excess capacity that was building in many sectors of the worldwide economy.**

Excess capacity can also arise from two types of technological change. The first type, *capacity-expanding* technological change, increases the output of a given capital stock and organization. An example of the capacity-expanding type of change is the Reduced Instruction Set CPU (RISC) processor innovation in the computer workstation market. RISC processors have brought about a ten-fold increase in power, but can be produced by adapting the current production technology. With no increase in the quantity demanded, this change implies that production capacity must fall by 90%. Of course, such price declines increase the quantity demanded in these situations, thereby reducing the extent of the capacity adjustment that would otherwise be required. Nevertheless, the new workstation technology has dramatically increased the effective output of existing production facilities, thereby generating excess capacity.

The second type is *obsolescence-creating* change—change that makes obsolete the current capital stock and organization. For example, Wal-Mart and the wholesale clubs that are revolutionizing retailing are dominating old-line department stores, thereby eliminating the need for much current retail capacity. When Wal-Mart enters a new market, total retail capacity expands, and some of the existing high-cost retail operations must go out of business. More intensive use of information and other technologies, direct dealing with manufacturers, and the replacement of high-cost, restrictive work-rule union labor are several sources of the competitive advantage of these new organizations.

Finally, excess capacity also results when many competitors simultaneously rush to implement new, highly productive technologies without considering whether the aggregate effects of all such investment will be greater capacity than can be supported by demand in the final product market. The winchester disk drive industry provides an example. Between 1977 and 1984, venture capitalists invested over $400 million in 43 different manufacturers of winchester disk drives; initial public offerings of common stock infused additional capital in excess of $800 million. In mid-1983, the capital markets assigned a value of $5.4 billion to twelve publicly-traded, venture-capital-backed hard disk drive manufacturers. Yet, by the end of 1984, overcapacity had caused the value assigned to those companies to plummet to $1.4 billion. My Harvard colleagues William Sahlman and Howard Stevenson have attributed this overcapacity to an "investment mania" based on implicit assumptions about long-run growth and profitability "*for each individual company* [that,]...had they been stated explicitly, would not have been acceptable to the rational investor."[29]

Such "overshooting" has by no means been confined to the winchester disk drive industry.[30] Indeed, the 1980s saw boom-and-bust cycles in the venture capital market generally, and also in commercial real estate and LBO markets. As Sahlman and Stevenson have also suggested, something more than "investment mania" and excessive "animal spirits" was at work here. Stated as simply as possible, my own analysis traces such overshooting to a gross misalignment of incentives between the "dealmakers" who promoted the transactions and the lenders, limited partners, and other investors who funded them.[31] During the mid to late '80s, venture capitalists, LBO promoters, and real estate developers were all effectively being rewarded simply for doing deals rather than for putting together successful deals. Reforming the "contracts" between dealmaker and investor—most directly, by reducing front-end-loaded fees and requiring the dealmakers to put up significant equity—would go far toward solving the problem of too many deals. (As I argue later, public corporations in mature industries face an analogous, though potentially far more costly (in terms of shareholder value destroyed and social resources wasted), distortion of investment priorities and incentives when their managers and directors do not have significant stock ownership.)

Current Forces Leading to Excess Capacity and Exit

The ten-fold increase in crude oil prices between 1973-1979 had ubiquitous effects, forcing contraction in oil, chemicals, steel, aluminum, and

---

29. See William A. Sahlman and Howard H. Stevenson, "Capital Market Myopia," *Journal of Business Venturing* 1 (1985), p. 7.

30. Or to the 1980s. There is evidence of such behavior in the 19th century, and in other periods of U.S. history.

31. Stated more precisely, my argument attributes overshooting to "incentive, information, and contracting" problems. For more on this, see Jensen (1991), cited in note 27, pp. 26-27. For some supporting evidence, see Steven N. Kaplan and Jeremy Stein, 1993, "The Evolution of Buyout Pricing and Financial Structure in the 1980s, *Quarterly Journal of Economics* 108, no. 2, 313-358. For a shorter, less technical version of the same article, see Vol. 6 No. 1 (Spring 1993) of the *Journal of Applied Corporate Finance.*

international shipping, among other industries. In addition, the sharp crude oil price increases that motivated major changes to economize on energy had other, longer-lasting consequences. The general corporate re-evaluation of organizational processes stimulated by the oil shock led to dramatic increases in efficiency above and beyond the original energy-saving projects. (In fact, I view the oil shock as the initial impetus for the corporate "process re-engineering" movement that still continues to accelerate throughout the world.)

Since the oil price increases of the 1970s, we have again seen systematic overcapacity problems in many industries similar to those of the 19th century. While the reasons for this overcapacity appear to differ somewhat among industries, there are a few common underlying causes.

Macro Policies. Major deregulation of the American economy (including trucking, rail, airlines, telecommunications, banking, and financial services industries) under President Carter contributed to the requirement for exit in these industries, as did important changes in the U.S. tax laws that reduced tax advantages to real estate development, construction, and other activities. The end of the Cold War has had obvious consequences for the defense industry and its suppliers. In addition, I suspect that two generations of managerial focus on growth as a recipe for success has caused many firms to overshoot their optimal capacity, thus setting the stage for cutbacks. In the decade from 1979 to 1989, *Fortune* 100 firms lost 1.5 million employees, or 14% of their workforce.[32]

Technology. Massive changes in technology are clearly part of the cause of the current industrial revolution and its associated excess capacity. Both within and across industries, technological developments have had far-reaching impact. To give some examples, the widespread acceptance of radial tires (which last three to five times longer than the older bias ply technology and provide better gas mileage) caused excess capacity in the tire industry; the personal computer revolution forced contraction of the market for mainframes; the advent of aluminum and plastic alternatives reduced demand for steel and glass containers; and fiberoptic, satellite, digital (ISDN), and new compression technolo-gies dramatically increased capacity in telecommunication. Wireless personal communication such as cellular phones and their replacements promise further to extend this dramatic change.

The changes in computer technology, including miniaturization, have not only revamped the computer industry, but also redefined the capabilities of countless other industries. Some estimates indicate the price of computing capacity fell by a factor of 1,000 over the last decade. This means that computer production lines now produce boxes with 1,000 times the capacity for a given price. Consequently, computers are becoming commonplace—in cars, toasters, cameras, stereos, ovens, and so on. Nevertheless, the increase in quantity demanded has not been sufficient to avoid overcapacity, and we are therefore witnessing a dramatic shutdown of production lines in the industry—a force that has wracked IBM as a high-cost producer. A change of similar magnitude in auto production technology would have reduced the price of a $20,000 auto in 1980 to under $20 today. Such increases in capacity and productivity in a basic technology have unavoidably massive implications for the organization of work and society.

Fiberoptic and other telecommunications technologies such as compression algorithms are bringing about similarly vast increases in worldwide capacity and functionality. A Bell Laboratories study of excess capacity indicates, for example, that, given three years and an additional expenditure of $3.1 billion, three of AT&T's new competitors (MCI, Sprint, and National Telecommunications Network) would be able to absorb the entire long-distance switched service that was supplied by AT&T in 1990.[33]

Organizational Innovation. Overcapacity can be caused not only by changes in physical technology, but also by changes in organizational practices and management technology. The vast improvements in telecommunications, including computer networks, electronic mail, teleconferencing, and facsimile transmission are changing the workplace in major ways that affect the manner in which people work and interact. It is far less valuable for people to be in the same geographical location to work together effectively, and this is encouraging smaller,

---

32. Source: Compustat.
33. Federal Communications Commission, *Competition in the Interstate Interexchange Marketplace*, FCC 91-251 (Sept. 16, 1991), p. 1140.

> **During the mid to late '80s, venture capitalists, LBO promoters, and real estate developers were all effectively being rewarded simply for doing deals... Reforming the "contracts" between dealmaker and investor—most directly, by requiring the dealmakers to put up significant equity—would go far toward solving the problem of too many deals.**

more efficient, entrepreneurial organizing units that cooperate through technology.[34] This in turn leads to even more fundamental changes. Through competition, "virtual organizations"—networked or transitory organizations in which people come together temporarily to complete a task, then separate to pursue their individual specialties—are changing the structure of the standard large bureaucratic organization and contributing to its shrinkage. Virtual organizations tap talented specialists, avoid many of the regulatory costs imposed on permanent structures, and bypass the inefficient work rules and high wages imposed by unions. In so doing, they increase efficiency and thereby further contribute to excess capacity.

In addition, Japanese management techniques such as total quality management, just-in-time production, and flexible manufacturing have significantly increased the efficiency of organizations where they have been successfully implemented throughout the world. Some experts argue that such new management techniques can reduce defects and spoilage by an order of magnitude. These changes in managing and organizing principles have contributed significantly to the productivity of the world's capital stock and economized on the use of labor and raw materials, thus also contributing to excess capacity.

Globalization of Trade. Over the last several decades, the entry of Japan and other Pacific Rim countries such as Hong Kong, Taiwan, Singapore, Thailand, Korea, Malaysia, and China into worldwide product markets has contributed to the required adjustments in Western economies. And, competition from new entrants to the world product markets promises only to intensify.

With the globalization of markets, excess capacity tends to occur worldwide. The Japanese economy, for example, is currently suffering from enormous overcapacity caused in large part by what I view as the "breakdown" of its corporate control system.[35] As a consequence, Japan now faces a massive and long-overdue restructuring—one that includes the prospect of unprecedented (for Japanese companies) layoffs, a pronounced shift of corporate focus from market share to profitability, and even the adoption of pay-for-performance executive compensation contracts (something heretofore believed to be profoundly "un-Japanese").

Yet even if the requirement for exit were isolated in just Japan and the U.S., the interdependency of today's world economy would ensure that such overcapacity would have global implications. For example, the rise of efficient high-quality producers of steel and autos in Japan and Korea has contributed to excess capacity in those industries worldwide. Between 1973 and 1990, total capacity in the U.S. steel industry fell by 38% from 157 to 97 million tons, and total employment fell over 50% from 509,000 to 252,000 (and had fallen further to 160,000 by 1993). From 1985 to 1989 multifactor productivity in the industry increased at an annual rate of 5.3%, as compared to 1.3% for the period 1958 to 1989.[36]

Revolution in Political Economy. The rapid pace of development of capitalism, the opening of closed economies, and the dismantling of central control in communist and socialist states is occurring in various degrees in Eastern Europe, China, India, Indonesia, other Asian economies, and Africa. In Asia and Africa alone, this development will place a potential labor force of almost a billion people—

---

34. The *Journal of Financial Economics*, which I have been editing with several others since 1973, is an example. The *JFE* is now edited by seven faculty members with offices at three universities in different states, and the main editorial administrative office is located in yet another state. The publisher, North Holland, is located in Amsterdam, the printing is done in India, and mailing and billing is executed in Switzerland. This "networked organization" would have been extremely inefficient two decades ago without fax machines, high-speed modems, electronic mail, and overnight delivery services.

35. A collapse I predicted in print as early as 1989. (See Michael C. Jensen, "Eclipse of the Public Corporation," *Harvard Business Review*, Vol. 89, No. 5 (September-October, 1989), pp. 61-74.)

In a 1991 article published in this journal, I wrote the following: "As our system has begun to look more like the Japanese, the Japanese economy is undergoing changes that are reducing the role of large active investors and thus making their system resemble ours. With the progressive development of U.S.-like capital markets, Japanese managers have been able to loosen the controls once exercised by the banks. So successful have they been in bypassing banks that the top third of Japanese companies are no longer net bank borrowers. As a result of their past success in product market competition, Japanese companies are now 'flooded'

with free cash flow. Their competitive position today reminds me of the position of American companies in the late 1960s. And, like their U.S. counterparts in the 60s, Japanese companies today appear to be in the process of creating conglomerates.

"My prediction is that, unless unmonitored Japanese managers prove to be much more capable than American executives of managing large, sprawling organizations, the Japanese economy is likely to produce large numbers of those conglomerates that U.S. capital markets have spent the last 10 years trying to pull apart. And if I am right, then Japan is likely to experience its own leveraged restructuring movement." ("Corporate Control and the Politics of Finance," *Journal of Applied Corporate Finance*, Vol. 4 No. 2, p. 24, fn. 47.)

For some interesting observations attesting to the severity of the Japanese overinvestment or "free cash flow" problem, see Carl Kester, "The Hidden Costs of Japanese Success," *Journal of Applied Corporate Finance* (Volume 3 Number 4, Winter 1990).

36. See James D. Burnham, *Changes and Challenges: The Transformation of the U.S. Steel Industry*, Policy Study No. 115 (Center for the Study of American Business, Washington University: St. Louis, 1993), Table 1 and p. 15.

whose current average income is less than $2 per day—on world markets. The opening of Mexico and other Latin American countries and the transition of some socialist Eastern European economies to open capitalist systems could add almost 200 million more laborers with average incomes of less than $10 per day to the world market.

To put these numbers into perspective, the average daily U.S. income per worker is slightly over $90, and the total labor force numbers about 117 million, and the European Economic Community average wage is about $80 per day with a total labor force of about 130 million. The labor forces that have affected world trade extensively in the last several decades (those in Hong Kong, Japan, Korea, Malaysia, Singapore, and Taiwan) total about 90 million.

While the changes associated with bringing a potential 1.2 billion low-cost laborers onto world markets will significantly increase average living standards throughout the world, they will also bring massive obsolescence of capital (manifested in the form of excess capacity) in Western economies as the adjustments sweep through the system. Such adjustments will include a major redirection of Western labor and capital away from low-skilled, labor-intensive industries and toward activities where they have a comparative advantage. While the opposition to such adjustments will be strong, the forces driving them will prove irresistible in this day of rapid and inexpensive communication, transportation, miniaturization, and migration.

One can also confidently forecast that the transition to open capitalist economies will generate great conflict over international trade as special interests in individual countries try to insulate themselves from competition and the required exit. And the U.S., despite its long-professed commitment to "free trade," will prove no exception. Just as U.S. managers and employees demanded protection from the capital markets in the 1980s, some are now demanding protection from international competition in the product markets, generally under the guise of protecting jobs. The dispute over NAFTA is but one general example of conflicts that are also occurring in the steel, automobile, computer chip, computer screen, and textile industries.

It would not even surprise me to see a return to demands for protection from *domestic* competition. This is currently happening in the deregulated airline industry, an industry faced with significant excess capacity.

We should not underestimate the strains this continuing change will place on worldwide social and political systems. In both the first and second industrial revolutions, the demands for protection from competition and for redistribution of income became intense. It is conceivable that Western nations could face the modern equivalent of the English Luddites, who destroyed industrial machinery (primarily knitting frames) in the period 1811-1816, and were eventually subdued by the militia. In the U.S. during the early 1890s, large groups of unemployed men (along with some vagrants and criminals), banded together in a cross-country march on Congress. The aim of "Coxey's industrial army," as the group became known, was to demand relief from "the evils of murderous competition; the supplanting of manual labor by machinery; the excessive Mongolian and pauper immigration; the curse of alien landlordism."[37]

Although Coxey's army disbanded peacefully after arriving in Washington and submitting a petition to Congress, some democratic systems may not survive the strain of adjustment, and may revert under pressure to a more totalitarian system. We need look no farther than current developments in Mexico or Russia to see such threats to democracy in effect.

The bottom line, then, is that with worldwide excess capacity and thus greater requirement for exit, the strains put on the internal control mechanisms of Western corporations are likely to worsen for decades to come. The experience of the U.S. in the 1980s demonstrated that the capital markets can play an important role in forcing managers to address this problem. In the absence of capital market pressures, competition in product markets will eventually bring about exit. But when left to the product markets, the adjustment process is greatly protracted and ends up generating enormous additional costs. This is the clear lesson held out by the most recent restructuring of the U.S. auto industry— and it's one that many sectors of the Japanese economy are now experiencing firsthand.

---

37. McMurray (1929), pp. 253-262, cited in note 2.

> **When left to the product markets, the adjustment process [to excess capacity] is greatly protracted and ends up generating enormous additional costs. This is the clear lesson held out by the most recent restructuring of the U.S. auto industry— and it's one that many sectors of the Japanese economy are now experiencing firsthand.**

THE DIFFICULTY OF EXIT

The Asymmetry between Growth and Decline

Exit problems appear to be particularly severe in companies that for long periods enjoyed rapid growth, commanding market positions, and high cash flow and profits. In these situations, the culture of the organization and the mindset of managers seem to make it extremely difficult for adjustment to take place until long after the problems have become severe and, in some cases, even unsolvable. In a fundamental sense, there is an "asymmetry" between the growth stage and the contraction stage in the corporate life cycle. Financial economists have spent little time thinking about how to manage the contracting stage efficiently or, more important, how to manage the growth stage to avoid sowing the seeds of decline.

In industry after industry with excess capacity, managers fail to recognize that they themselves must downsize; instead they leave the exit to others while they continue to invest. When all managers behave this way, exit is significantly delayed at substantial cost of real resources to society. The tire industry is an example. Widespread consumer acceptance of radial tires meant that worldwide tire capacity had to shrink by two thirds (because radials last 3 to 5 times longer than bias ply tires). Nonetheless, the response by the managers of individual companies was often equivalent to: "This business is going through some rough times. We must invest so that we will have a chair when the music stops."

The Case of Gencorp. William Reynolds, Chairman and CEO of GenCorp, the maker of General Tires, illustrates this reaction in his 1988 testimony before the U.S. House Committee on Energy and Commerce:

The tire business was the largest piece of GenCorp, both in terms of annual revenues and its asset base. Yet General Tire was not GenCorp's strongest performer. Its relatively poor earnings performance was due in part to conditions affecting all of the tire industry... In 1985 worldwide tire manufacturing capacity substantially exceeded demand. At the same time, due to a series of technological improvements in *the design of tires and the materials used to make them, the product life of tires had lengthened significantly... The economic pressure on our tire business was substantial. Because our unit volume was far below others in the industry, we had less competitive flexibility... We made several moves to improve our competitive position: We increased our investment in research and development. We increased our involvement in the high performance and light truck tire categories, two market segments which offered faster growth opportunities. We developed new tire products for those segments and invested heavily in an aggressive marketing program designed to enhance our presence in both markets. We made the difficult decision to reduce our overall manufacturing capacity by closing one of our older, less modern plants... I believe that the General Tire example illustrates that we were taking a rational, long-term approach to improving GenCorp's overall performance and shareholder value...*

Like so many U.S. CEOs, Reynolds then goes on to blame the capital markets for bringing about what he fails to recognize is a solution to the industry's problem of excess capacity:

As a result of the takeover attempt... [and] to meet the principal and interest payments on our vastly increased corporate debt, GenCorp had to quickly sell off valuable assets and abruptly lay off approximately 550 important employees.[38]

Without questioning the genuineness of Reynolds' concerns about his company and employees, it nevertheless now seems clear that GenCorp's increased investment was neither going to maximize the value of the firm nor to be a socially optimal response in a declining industry with excess capacity. In 1987, GenCorp ended up selling its General Tire subsidiary to Continental AG of Hannover, thus furthering the process of consolidation necessary to reduce overcapacity.

Information Problems

Information problems hinder exit because the high-cost capacity in the industry must be eliminated

---

38. A. William Reynolds, in testimony before the Subcommittee on Oversight and Investigations, U.S. House Committee on Energy and Commerce, February 8, 1988.

if resources are to be used efficiently. Firms often do not have good information about their own costs, much less the costs of their competitors. Thus, it is sometimes unclear to managers that they are the high-cost firm that should exit the industry.[39]

But even when managers do acknowledge the requirement for exit, it is often difficult for them to accept and initiate the shutdown. For the managers who must implement these decisions, shutting plants or liquidating the firm causes personal pain, creates uncertainty, and interrupts or sidetracks careers. Rather than confronting this pain, managers generally resist such actions as long as they have the cash flow to subsidize the losing operations. Indeed, firms with large positive cash flow will often invest in even more money-losing capacity—situations that illustrate vividly what I call the "agency costs of free cash flow."[40]

Contracting Problems

Explicit and implicit contracts in the organization can become major obstacles to efficient exit. Unionization, restrictive work rules, and lucrative employee compensation and benefits are other ways in which the agency costs of free cash flow can manifest themselves in a growing, cash-rich organization. Formerly dominant firms became unionized in their heyday (or effectively unionized in organizations like IBM and Kodak) when managers spent some of the organization's free cash flow to buy labor peace. Faced with technical innovation and worldwide competition—often from new, more flexible, and non-union organizations—these dominant firms have not adjusted quickly enough to maintain their market dominance. Part of the problem is managerial and organizational defensiveness that inhibits learning and prevents managers from changing their model of the business.

Implicit contracts with unions, other employees, suppliers, and communities add to formal union

barriers to change by reinforcing organizational defensiveness and delaying change long beyond the optimal time—often even beyond the survival point for the organization. While casual breach of implicit contracts will destroy trust in an organization and seriously reduce efficiency, all organizations must retain the flexibility to modify contracts that are no longer optimal.[41] In the current environment, it takes nothing less than a major shock to bring about necessary change.

THE ROLE OF THE MARKET FOR CORPORATE CONTROL

The Four Control Forces Operating on the Corporation

There are four basic control forces bearing on the corporation that act to bring about a convergence of managers' decisions with those that are optimal from society's standpoint. They are (1) the capital markets, (2) the legal, political, and regulatory system, (3) the product and factor markets, and (4) the internal control system headed by the board of directors.

The capital markets were relatively constrained by law and regulatory practice from about 1940 until their resurrection through hostile tender offers in the 1970s. Prior to the 1970s, capital market discipline took place primarily through the proxy process.

The legal/political/regulatory system is far too blunt an instrument to handle the problems of wasteful managerial behavior effectively. (Nevertheless, the break-up and deregulation of AT&T is one of the court system's outstanding successes; I estimate that it has helped create over $125 billion of increased value between AT&T and the Baby Bells.[42])

While the product and factor markets are slow to act as a control force, their discipline is inevitable; firms that do not supply the product that customers desire at a competitive price will not survive.

---

39. Total quality management programs strongly encourage managers to benchmark their firm's operations against the most successful worldwide competitors, and good cost systems and competitive benchmarking are becoming more common in well-managed firms.

40. Briefly stated, the "agency costs of free cash flow" means the loss in value caused by the tendency of managements of large public companies in slow-growth industries to reinvest corporate cash flow in projects with expected returns below the cost of capital. See Michael Jensen, "The Agency Costs of Free Cash Flow: Corporate Finance and Takeovers," *American Economic Review* 76, no. 2 (May,1986), 323-329.

41. Much press coverage and official policy seems to be based on the notion that *all* implicit contracts should be immutable and rigidly enforced. But while I

agree that the security of property rights and the enforceability of contracts are essential to the growth of real output and efficiency, it is also clear that, given unexpected and unforeseeable events, *not all* contracts, whether explicit or implicit, can (or even should) be fulfilled. (For example, bankruptcy is essentially a state-supervised system for breaking (or, more politely, rewriting) explicit contracts that have become unenforceable. All developed economies devise such a system.) Implicit contracts, besides avoiding the costs incurred in the writing process, provide the opportunity to revise the obligation if circumstances change; presumably, this is a major reason for their existence.

42. For this calculation, see the original version of this article in the *Journal of Finance* (Jensen (1993)).

> **In industry after industry with excess capacity, managers fail to recognize that they themselves must downsize; instead they leave the exit to others while they continue to invest. When all managers behave this way, exit is significantly delayed at substantial cost of real resources to society.**

Unfortunately, by the time product and factor market disciplines take effect, large amounts of investor capital and other social resources have been wasted, and it can often be too late to save much of the enterprise.

Which brings us to the role of corporate internal control systems and the need to reform them. As stated earlier, there is a large and growing body of studies documenting the shareholder gains from corporate restructurings of the '80s.[43] The size and consistency of such gains provide strong support for the proposition that the internal control systems of publicly held corporations have generally failed to cause managers to maximize efficiency and value in slow-growth or declining industries.

Perhaps more persuasive than the formal statistical evidence, however, is the scarcity of large, public firms that have voluntarily restructured or engaged in a major strategic redirection without either a challenge from the capital markets or a crisis in product markets. By contrast, partnerships and private or closely held firms such as investment banking, law, and consulting firms have generally responded far more quickly to changing market conditions.

Capital Markets and the Market for Corporate Control

Until they were shut down in 1989, the capital markets were providing one mechanism for accomplishing change before losses in the product markets generated a crisis. While the corporate control activity of the 1980s has been widely criticized as counterproductive to American industry, few have recognized that many of these transactions were necessary to accomplish exit over the objections of current managers and other corporate constituencies such as employees and communities.

For example, the solution to excess capacity in the tire industry came about through the market for corporate control. Every major U.S. tire firm was either taken over or restructured in the 1980s.[44] In

total, 37 tire plants were shut down in the period 1977-1987, and total employment in the industry fell by over 40%.

Capital market and corporate control transactions such as the repurchase of stock (or the purchase of another company) for cash or debt accomplished exit of resources in a very direct way. When Chevron acquired Gulf for $13.2 billion in cash and debt in 1984, the net assets devoted to the oil industry fell by $13.2 billion as soon as the checks were mailed out. In the 1980s the oil industry had to shrink to accommodate the reduction in the quantity of oil demanded and the reduced rate of growth of demand. This meant paying out to shareholders its huge cash inflows, reducing exploration and development expenditures to bring reserves in line with reduced demands, and closing refining and distribution facilities. Leveraged acquisitions and equity repurchases helped accomplish this end for virtually all major U.S. oil firms.

Exit also resulted when KKR acquired RJR-Nabisco for $25 billion in cash and debt in its 1986 leveraged buyout. The tobacco industry must shrink, given the change in smoking habits in response to consumer awareness of cancer threats, and the payout of RJR's cash accomplished this to some extent. RJR's LBO debt also prevented the company from continuing to squander its cash flows on wasteful projects it had planned to undertake prior to the buyout. Thus, the buyout laid the groundwork for the efficient reduction of capacity and resources by one of the major firms in the industry. The recent sharp declines in the stock prices of RJR and Philip Morris are signs that there is much more downsizing to come.

The era of the control market came to an end, however, in late 1989 and 1990. Intense controversy and opposition from corporate managers—assisted by charges of fraud, the increase in default and bankruptcy rates, and insider trading prosecutions—led to the shutdown of the control market through court decisions, state antitakeover amendments, and regulatory restrictions on the availability of

---

43. For a partial list of such studies, see the Appendix at the end of this article.
44. In May 1985, Uniroyal approved an LBO proposal to block hostile advances by Carl Icahn. About the same time, BF Goodrich began diversifying out of the tire business. In January 1986, Goodrich and Uniroyal independently spun off their tire divisions and together, in a 50-50 joint venture, formed the Uniroyal-Goodrich Tire Company. By December 1987, Goodrich had sold its interest in the venture to Clayton and Dubilier; Uniroyal followed soon after. Similarly, General Tire moved away from tires: the company, renamed GenCorp in 1984, sold its tire division to Continental in 1987. Other takeovers in the industry during this period

include the sale of Firestone to Bridgestone and Pirelli's purchase of the Armstrong Tire Company. By 1991, Goodyear was the only remaining major American tire manufacturer. Yet it too faced challenges in the control market: in 1986, following three years of unprofitable diversifying investments, Goodyear initiated a major leveraged stock repurchase and restructuring to defend itself from a hostile takeover from Sir James Goldsmith. Uniroyal/Goodrich was purchased by Michelin in 1990. See Richard Tedlow, "Hitting the Skids: Tires and Time Horizons," Unpublished manuscript, Harvard Business School, 1991.

financing.[45] In 1991, the total value of transactions fell to $96 billion from $340 billion in 1988.[46] Leveraged buyouts and management buyouts fell to slightly over $1 billion in 1991 from $80 billion in 1988.[47]

The demise of the control market as an effective influence on American corporations has not ended the restructuring. But it has allowed many organizations to postpone addressing major problems until forced to do so by financial difficulties generated by the product markets. Unfortunately, the delay means that some of these organizations will not survive—or will survive as mere shadows of their former selves.

THE FAILURE OF CORPORATE INTERNAL CONTROL SYSTEMS

With the shutdown of the capital markets as an effective mechanism for motivating change, exit, and renewal, we are left to depend on the internal control system to act to preserve organizational assets, both human and otherwise. Throughout corporate America, the problems that motivated much of the control activity of the 1980s are now reflected in lackluster performance, financial distress, and pressures for restructuring. General Motors, Kodak, IBM, Xerox, Westinghouse, ITT, and many others have faced or are now facing severe challenges in the product markets. We therefore must understand why these internal control systems have failed and learn how to make them work.

By nature, organizations abhor control systems. Ineffective governance is a major part of the problem with internal control mechanisms; they seldom respond in the absence of a crisis. The recent GM board "revolt," which resulted in the firing of CEO Robert Stempel, exemplifies the failure, not the success, of GM's governance system. Though clearly one of the world's high-cost producers in a market with substantial excess capacity, GM avoided making major changes in its strategy for over a decade. The revolt came too late; the board acted to remove the CEO only in 1992, after the company had reported losses of $6.5 billion in 1990 and 1991.

Unfortunately, GM is not an isolated example. IBM is another testimony to the failure of internal control systems. The company failed to adjust to the substitution away from its mainframe business following the revolution in the workstation and personal computer market—ironically enough, a revolution that it helped launch with the invention of the RISC technology in 1974. Like GM, IBM is a high-cost producer in a market with substantial excess capacity. It too began to change its strategy significantly and removed its CEO only after reporting huge losses—$2.8 billion in 1991 and further losses in 1992—while losing almost 65% of its equity value.

Eastman Kodak, another major U.S. company formerly dominant in its market, also failed to adjust to competition and has performed poorly. Largely as a result of a disastrous diversification program designed to offset the maturing of its core film business, its $37 share price in 1992 was roughly unchanged from 1981. After several reorganizations attempting relatively modest changes in its incentives and strategy, the board finally replaced the CEO in October 1993.

General Electric is a notable exception to my proposition about the failure of corporate internal control systems. Under CEO Jack Welch since 1981, GE has accomplished a major strategic re-direction, eliminating 104,000 of its 402,000 person workforce (through layoffs or sales of divisions) in the period 1980-1990 without a threat from capital or product markets. But there is little evidence to indicate this is due to the influence of GE's governance system; it appears attributable almost entirely to the vision and leadership of Jack Welch.

General Dynamics provides another exceptional case. The appointment of William Anders as CEO in September 1991 resulted in a rapid adjustment to excess capacity in the defense industry—again, with no apparent threat from any outside force. The company generated $3.4 billion of increased value on a $1 billion company in just over two years. One of the key elements in this success story, however, was a major change in the company's management compensation system[48] that tied bonuses directly to increases in stock value (a subject I return to later).

My colleague Gordon Donaldson's account of General Mills' strategic redirection is yet another

45. For a more detailed account, see my article in this journal, "Corporate Control and the Politics of Finance," Summer 1991.
46. In 1992 dollars, calculated from *Mergerstat Review*, 1991, p. 100f.
47. In 1992 dollars, *Mergerstat Review*, 1991, Figs. 29 and 38.

48. See Kevin J. Murphy and Jay Dial, "Compensation and Strategy at General Dynamics (A) and (B)," Harvard Business School #N9-493-032 and N9-493-033, 1992.

Capital market and corporate control transactions such as the repurchase of stock (or the purchase of another company) for cash or debt accomplished exit of resources in a very direct way. When Chevron acquired Gulf for $13.2 billion in cash and debt in 1984, the net assets devoted to the oil industry fell by $13.2 billion as soon as the checks were mailed out.

case of a largely voluntary restructuring.[49] But the fact that it took more than ten years to accomplish raises serious questions about the social costs of continuing the waste caused by ineffective control. It appears that internal control systems have two faults: they react too late, and they take too long to effect major change. Changes motivated by the capital market are generally accomplished quickly—typically, within one to three years. No one has yet demonstrated social benefits from relying on internally motivated change that would offset the costs of the decade-long delay in the restructuring of General Mills.

In summary, it appears that the infrequency with which large corporate organizations restructure or redirect themselves solely on the basis of the internal control mechanisms—that is, in the absence of intervention by capital markets or a crisis in the product markets—is strong testimony to the inadequacy of these control mechanisms.

[At this point, the original Journal of Finance *paper contains a section, omitted here because of space constraints, called "Direct Evidence of the Failure of Internal Control Systems." It presents estimates of the productivity of corporate capital expenditure and R&D spending programs of 432 firms that suggest "major inefficiencies in a substantial number of firms."]*

REVIVING INTERNAL CORPORATE CONTROL SYSTEMS

Remaking the Board as an Effective Control Mechanism

The problems with corporate internal control systems start with the board of directors. The board, at the apex of the internal control system, has the final responsibility for the functioning of the firm. Most important, it sets the rules of the game for the CEO. The job of the board is to hire, fire, and compensate the CEO, and to provide high-level counsel. Few boards in the past decades have done

this job well in the absence of external crises. This is particularly unfortunate, given that the very purpose of the internal control mechanism is to provide an early warning system to put the organization back on track before difficulties reach a crisis stage.

The reasons for the failure of the board are not completely understood, but we are making progress toward understanding these complex issues. The available evidence does suggest that CEOs are removed after poor performance;[50] but this effect, while statistically significant, seems too late and too small to meet the obligations of the board. I believe bad systems or rules, not bad people, are at the root of the general failings of boards of directors.

Board Culture. Board culture is an important component of board failure. The great emphasis on politeness and courtesy at the expense of truth and frankness in boardrooms is both a symptom and cause of failure in the control system. CEOs have the same insecurities and defense mechanisms as other human beings; few will accept, much less seek, the monitoring and criticism of an active and attentive board.

The following example illustrates the general problem. John Hanley, retired Monsanto CEO, accepted an invitation from a CEO

… to join his board—subject, Hanley wrote, to meeting with the company's general counsel and outside accountants as a kind of directorial due diligence. Says Hanley: "At the first board dinner the CEO got up and said, 'I think Jack was a little bit confused whether we wanted him to be a director or the chief executive officer.' I should have known right there that he wasn't going to pay a goddamn bit of attention to anything I said." So it turned out, and after a year Hanley quit the board in disgust.[51]

The result is a continuing cycle of ineffectiveness. By rewarding consent and discouraging conflicts, CEOs have the power to control the board, which in turn ultimately reduces the CEO's and the company's performance. This downward spiral makes corporate difficulties likely to culminate in a crisis

---

49. See Gordon Donaldson, "Voluntary Restructuring: The Case of General Mills," *Journal of Financial Economics* 27, no. 1 (1990), 117-141. For a shorter, less technical version of the same article, see Vol. 4 No. 3 (Fall 1991) of the *Journal of Applied Corporate Finance*.

50. CEO turnover approximately doubles from 3% to 6% after two years of poor performance (stock returns less than 50% below equivalent-risk market returns, Weisbach (1988)), or increases from 8.3% to 13.9% from the highest to

the lowest performing decile of firms, Warner, Watts, and Wruck (1988). See Michael Weisbach, "Outside Directors and CEO Turnovers," *Journal of Financial Economics* 20 (January-March, 1988), 431-460. and Jerold Warner, Ross Watts, and Karen Wruck, "Stock Prices and Top Management Changes," *Journal of Financial Economics* 20 (1989), 461-492.

51. Myron Magnet, "Directors, Wake Up!," *Fortune* (June 15, 1992), p. 86.

requiring drastic steps, as opposed to a series of small problems met by a continuously self-correcting mechanism.

Information Problems. Serious information problems limit the effectiveness of board members in the typical large corporation. For example, the CEO almost always determines the agenda and the information given to the board. This limitation on information severely restricts the ability of even highly talented board members to contribute effectively to the monitoring and evaluation of the CEO and the company's strategy.

Moreover, board members should have the financial expertise necessary to provide useful input into the corporate planning process—especially, in forming the corporate objective and determining the factors which affect corporate value. Yet such financial expertise is generally lacking on today's boards. And it is not only the inability of most board members to evaluate a company's current business and financial strategy that is troubling. In many cases, boards (and managements) fail to understand that their basic mission is to maximize the (long-run) market value of the enterprise.

Legal Liability. The incentives facing modern boards are generally not consistent with shareholder interests. Boards are motivated to serve shareholders primarily by substantial legal liabilities through class action suits initiated by shareholders, the plaintiff's bar, and others—lawsuits that are often triggered by unexpected declines in stock price. These legal incentives are more often consistent with minimizing downside risk than maximizing value. Boards are also concerned about threats of adverse publicity from the media or from the political or regulatory authorities. Again, while these incentives often provide motivation for board members to reduce potential liabilities, they do not necessarily provide strong incentives to take actions that create efficiency and value for the company.

Lack of Management and Board-Member Equity Holdings. Much of corporate America's governance problem arises from the fact that neither managers nor board members typically own sub-stantial fractions of their firm's equity. While the average CEO of the 1,000 largest firms (measured by market value of equity) owned 2.7% of his or her firm's equity in 1991, the median holding was only 0.2%—and 75% of CEOs owned less than 1.2%.[52] Encouraging outside board members to hold substantial equity interests would provide better incentives.

Of course, achieving significant direct stock ownership in large firms would require huge dollar outlays by managers or board members. To get around this problem, Bennett Stewart has proposed an interesting approach called the "leveraged equity purchase plan" (LEPP) that amounts to the sale of slightly (say, 10%) in-the-money stock options.[53] By requiring significant out-of-pocket contributions by managers and directors, and by having the exercise price of the options rise every year at the firm's cost of capital, Stewart's plan helps overcome the "free-option" aspect (or lack of downside risk) that limits the effectiveness of standard corporate option plans. It also removes the problem with standard options that allows management to reap gains on their options while shareholders are losing.[54]

Boards should have an implicit understanding or explicit requirement that new members must invest in the stock of the company. While the initial investment could vary, it should seldom be less than $100,000 from the new board member's personal funds; this investment would force new board members to recognize from the outset that their decisions affect their own wealth as well as that of remote shareholders. Over the long term, the investment can be made much larger by options or other stock-based compensation. The recent trend to pay some board-member fees in stock or options is a move in the right direction. Discouraging board members from selling this equity is also important so that holdings will accumulate to a significant size over time.

Oversized Boards. Keeping boards small can help improve their performance. When boards exceed seven or eight people, they are less likely to function effectively and are easier for the CEO to

---

52. See Kevin Murphy, *Executive Compensation in Corporate America, 1992*, United Shareholders Association, Washington, DC, 1992. For similar estimates based on earlier data, see also Michael Jensen and Kevin Murphy, "Performance Pay and Top-Management Incentives," *Journal of Political Economy* 98, no. 2 (1990), 225-264; and Michael Jensen and Kevin Murphy, "CEO Incentives—It's Not How Much You Pay, But How," *Harvard Business Review* 68, no. 3 (May-June, 1990).

53. See G. Bennett Stewart III, "Remaking the Public Corporation From Within," *Harvard Business Review* 68, no. 4 (July-August, 1990), 126-137.

54. This happens when the stock price rises but shareholder returns (including both dividends and capital gains) are less than the opportunity cost of capital.

> **Much of corporate America's governance problem arises from the fact that neither managers nor board members typically own substantial fractions of their firm's equity. While the average CEO of the 1,000 largest firms owned 2.7% of his or her firm's equity in 1991, the median holding was only 0.2%—and 75% owned less than 1.2%.**

control.[55] Since the possibility for animosity and retribution from the CEO is too great, it is almost impossible for direct reports to the CEO to participate openly and critically in effective evaluation and monitoring of the CEO. Therefore, the only inside board member should be the CEO; insiders other than the CEO can be regularly invited to attend board meetings in an unofficial capacity. Indeed, board members should be given regular opportunities to meet with and observe executives below the CEO—both to expand their knowledge of the company and CEO succession candidates, and to increase other top-level executives' exposure to the thinking of the board and the board process.

The CEO as Chairman of the Board. It is common in U.S. corporations for the CEO also to hold the position of Chairman of the Board. The function of the Chairman is to run board meetings and oversee the process of hiring, firing, evaluating, and compensating the CEO. Clearly, the CEO cannot perform this function apart from his or her personal interest. Without the direction of an independent leader, it is much more difficult for the board to perform its critical function. Therefore, for the board to be effective, it is important to separate the CEO and Chairman positions.[56] The independent Chairman should, at a minimum, be given the rights to initiate board appointments, board committee assignments, and (jointly with the CEO) the setting of the board's agenda. All these recommendations, of course, should be made conditional on the ratification of the board.

An effective board will often experience tension among its members as well as with the CEO. But I hasten to add that I am not advocating continuous war in the boardroom. In fact, in well-functioning organizations the board will generally be relatively inactive and will exhibit little conflict. It becomes important primarily when the rest of the internal control system is failing, and this should be a relatively rare event. The challenge is to create a system that will not fall into complacency during periods of prosperity and good management, and therefore be unable to rise early to the challenge of correcting a failing management system. This is a difficult task because there are strong tendencies for boards to develop a culture and social norms that reflect optimal behavior under prosperity, and these norms make it extremely difficult for the board to respond early to failure in its top management team.

Attempts to Model the Process on Political Democracy. There have been a number of proposals to model the board process after a democratic political model in which various constituencies are represented. Such a process, however, is likely to make the internal control system even less accountable to shareholders than it is now. To see why, we need look no farther than the inefficiency of representative political democracies (whether at the local, state or federal level) and their attempts to manage quasi-business organizations such as the Post Office, schools, or power-generation entities such as the TVA.

Nevertheless, there would likely be significant benefits to opening up the corporate governance process to the firm's largest shareholders. Proxy regulations by the SEC severely restrict communications between management and shareholders, and among shareholders themselves. Until recently, for example, it was illegal for any shareholder to discuss company matters with more than ten other shareholders without previously filing with and receiving the approval of the SEC. The November 1992 relaxation of this restriction now allows an investor to communicate with an unlimited number of other stockholders provided the investor owns less than 5% of the shares, has no special interest in the issue being discussed, and is not seeking proxy authority. But these remaining restrictions still have the obvious drawback of limiting effective institutional action by those investors most likely to pursue it.

As I discuss below, when equity holdings become concentrated in institutional hands, it is easier to resolve some of the free-rider problems that limit the ability of thousands of individual shareholders to engage in effective collective action. In principle, such institutions can therefore begin to exercise corporate control rights more effectively.

---

55. In their excellent analysis of boards, Martin Lipton and Jay Lorsch also criticize the functioning of traditionally configured boards, recommend limiting membership to 7 or 8 people, and encourage equity ownership by board members. (See Lipton and Lorsch, "A Modest Proposal for Improved Corporate Governance," *The Business Lawyer* 48, no. 1 (November, 1992), 59-77. Research supports the proposition that, as groups increase in size, they become less effective because the coordination and process problems overwhelm the advantages gained from having more people to draw on. See, for example, I. D. Steiner, *Group Process and Productivity* (Academic Press: New York, 1972) and Richard Hackman, ed., *Groups That Work* (Jossey-Bass: San Francisco, 1990).

56. Lipton and Lorsch (1992) stop short of recommending appointment of an independent chairman, recommending instead the appointment of a "lead director" whose function would be to coordinate board activities.

Legal and regulatory restrictions, however, have prevented financial institutions from playing a major corporate monitoring role. Therefore, if institutions are to aid in effective governance, we must continue to dismantle the rules and regulations that have prevented them and other large investors from accomplishing this coordination.

Resurrecting Active Investors

A major set of problems with internal control systems are associated with the curbing of what I call "active investors."[57] Active investors are individuals or institutions that hold large debt and/or equity positions in a company and actively participate in its strategic direction. Active investors are important to a well-functioning governance system because they have the financial interest and independence to view firm management and policies in an unbiased way. They have the incentives to buck the system to correct problems early rather than late when the problems are obvious but difficult to correct. Financial institutions such as banks, pension funds, insurance companies, mutual funds, and money managers are natural active investors, but they have been shut out of boardrooms and firm strategy by the legal structure, by custom, and by their own practices.

Active investors are important to a well-functioning governance system, and there is much we can do to dismantle the web of legal, tax, and regulatory apparatus that severely limits the scope of active investors in this country.[58] But even without such regulatory changes, CEOs and boards can take actions to encourage investors to hold large positions in their debt and equity and to play an active role in the strategic direction of the firm and in monitoring the CEO.

Wise CEOs can recruit large block investors to serve on the board, even selling new equity or debt to them to encourage their commitment to the firm. Lazard Frères Corporate Partners Fund is an example of an institution set up specifically to perform this function, making new funds available to the firm and taking a board seat to advise and monitor management performance. Warren Buffet's activity through Berkshire Hathaway provides another example of a well-known active investor. He played an important role in helping Salomon Brothers through its recent legal and organizational difficulties following the government bond bidding scandal.

Learning from LBOs and Venture Capital Firms

Organizational Experimentation in the 1980s. The evidence from LBOs, leveraged restructurings, takeovers, and venture capital firms has demonstrated dramatically that leverage, payout policy, and ownership structure (that is, who owns the firm's securities) affect organizational efficiency, cash flow, and hence value.[59] Such organizational changes show that these effects are especially important in low-growth or declining firms where the agency costs of free cash flow are large.

Evidence from LBOs. LBOs provide a good source of estimates of the value increases resulting from changing leverage, payout policies, and the control and governance system. After the transaction, the company has a different financial policy and control system, but essentially the same managers and the same assets. Leverage increases from about 18% of value to 90%, there are large payouts to prior shareholders, and equity becomes concentrated in the hands of managers and the board (who own about 20% and 60%, on average, respectively). At the same time, boards shrink to about seven or eight people, the sensitivity of managerial pay to performance rises, and the companies' equity usually becomes private (although debt is often publicly traded).

Studies of LBOs indicate that premiums to selling-firm shareholders are roughly 40% to 50% of the pre-buyout market value, cash flows increase by 96% from the year before the buyout to three years after the buyout, and value increases by 235% (96% adjusted for general market movements) from two months prior to the buyout offer to the time of

---

57. See my article in this journal, "LBOs, Active Investors, and the Privatization of Bankruptcy," *Journal of Applied Corporate Finance* (Spring 1989).

58. For discussions of such legal, tax, and regulatory barriers to active investors (and proposals for reducing them), see Mark Roe, "A Political Theory of American Corporate Finance," *Columbia Law Review* 91 (1991) 10-67; Mark Roe, "Political and Legal Restraints on Ownership and Control of Public Companies," *Journal of Financial Economics* 27, No. 1 (September, 1990); Bernard Black,

"Shareholder Passivity Reexamined," *Michigan Law Review* 89 (December, 1990), 520-608; and John Pound, "Proxy Voting and the SEC: Investor Protection versus Market Efficiency," *Journal of Financial Economics* 29, no. 2, 241-285.

59. See the Appendix at the end of this article for a listing of broad-based statistical studies of these transactions, as well as detailed clinical and case studies that document the effects of the changes on incentives and organizational effectiveness.

Wise CEOs can recruit large block investors to serve on the board. Active investors are important to a well-functioning governance system because they have the financial interest and independence to view firm management and policies in an unbiased way. They have the incentives to buck the system to correct problems early rather than late when the problems are obvious but difficult to correct.

going-public, sale, or recapitalization (about three years later, on average).[60] Large value increases have also been documented in voluntary recapitalizations—those in which the company stays public but buys back a significant fraction of its equity or pays out a significant dividend.[61]

A Proven Model of Governance Structure. LBO associations and venture capital funds provide a blueprint for managers and boards who wish to revamp their top-level control systems to make them more efficient. LBO firms like KKR and venture capital funds such as Kleiner Perkins are among the pre-eminent examples of active investors in recent U.S. history, and they serve as models that can be emulated in part or in total by most public corporations. The two have similar governance structures, and have been successful in resolving the governance problems of both slow-growth or declining firms (LBO associations) and high-growth entrepreneurial firms (venture capital funds).

Both LBO associations and venture capital funds tend to be organized as limited partnerships. In effect, the institutions that contribute the funds to these organizations are delegating the task of being active investors to the general partners of the organizations. Both governance systems are characterized by the following:

- limited partnership agreements at the top level that prohibit headquarters from cross-subsidizing one division with the cash from another;
- high equity ownership by managers and board members;
- board members (mostly the LBO association partners or the venture capitalists) who in their funds directly represent a large fraction of the equity owners of each subsidiary company;
- small boards (in the operating companies) typically consisting of no more than eight people;
- CEOs who are typically the only insider on the board; and
- CEOs who are seldom the chairman of the board.

LBO associations and venture funds also solve many of the information problems facing typical boards of directors. First, as a result of the due diligence process at the time the deal is done, both the managers and the LBO and venture partners have extensive and detailed knowledge of virtually all aspects of the business. In addition, these boards have frequent contact with management, often weekly or even daily during times of difficult challenges. This contact and information flow is facilitated by the fact that LBO associations and venture funds both have their own staffs. They also often perform the corporate finance function for the operating companies, providing the major interface with the capital markets and investment banking communities. Finally, the close relationship between the LBO partners or venture fund partners and the operating companies encourages the board to contribute its expertise during times of crisis. It is not unusual for a partner to join the management team, even as CEO, to help an organization through such emergencies.

CONCLUSION

Beginning with the oil price shock of the 1970s, technological, political, regulatory, and economic forces have been transforming the worldwide economy in a fashion comparable to the changes experienced during the 19th-century Industrial Revolution. As in the 19th century, technological advances in many industries have led to sharply declining costs, increased average (but declining marginal) productivity of labor, reduced growth rates of labor income, excess capacity, and the requirement for downsizing and exit.

Events of the last two decades indicate that corporate internal control systems have failed to deal effectively with these changes, especially excess capacity and the requirement for exit. The corporate control transactions of the 1980s—mergers and acquisitions, LBOs, and other leveraged recapitalizations—represented a capital market solution to this problem of widespread overcapacity. But because of the regulatory shutdown of the corporate control markets beginning in 1989, finding a solution to the problem now rests once more with the internal control systems, with corporate boards, and, to a lesser degree, with the large institutional shareholders who bear the consequences of corporate losses in value. Making corporate internal control systems work is the major challenge facing us in the 1990s.

---

60. For a review of research on LBOs, their governance changes, and their productivity effects, see Krishna Palepu, "Consequences of Leveraged Buyouts," *Journal of Financial Economics* 27, no. 1 (1990), 247-262.

61. See David and Diane Denis, "Managerial Discretion, Organizational Structure, and Corporate Performance: A Study of Leveraged Recapitalizations," *Journal of Accounting and Economics* (January 1993); and Karen Wruck and Krishna Palepu, "Consequences of Leveraged Shareholder Payouts: Defensive versus Voluntary Recapitalizations," Working paper, Harvard Business School, 1992.

APPENDIX:
Studies Documenting the Shareholder Wealth Effects of Capital Market Transactions

■ **Baker, George and Karen Wruck**, 1989, "Organizational Changes and Value Creation in Leveraged Buyouts: The Case of O.M. Scott and Sons Company," *Journal of Financial Economics* 25, no. 2, 163-190. For a shorter, less technical version of the same article, see Vol. 4 No. 1 (Spring 1991) of the *Journal of Applied Corporate Finance*.

■ **Brickley, James A., Gregg A. Jarrell, and Jeffrey M. Netter**, 1988, "The Market for Corporate Control: The Empirical Evidence Since 1980," *Journal of Economic Perspectives* 2, no. 1, 49-68, Winter.

■ **Dann, Larry Y. and Harry DeAngelo**, 1988, "Corporate Financial Policy and Corporate Control: A Study of Defensive Adjustments in Asset and Ownership Structure, *Journal of Financial Economics* 20, 87-127.

■ **DeAngelo, Harry, Linda DeAngelo, and Edward Rice**, 1984, "Going Private: Minority Freezeouts and Stockholder Wealth," *Journal of Law and Economics* 27, 367-401.

■ **David and Diane Denis**, 1993, "Managerial Discretion, Organizational Structure, and Corporate Performance: A Study of Leveraged Recapitalizations," *Journal of Accounting and Economics* (January). For a shorter, less technical version of the same article, see Vol. 6 No. 1 (Spring 1993) of the *Journal of Applied Corporate Finance*.

■ **Denis, David J.**, 1994, "Organizational Form and the Consequences of Highly Leveraged Transactions: Kroger's Recapitalization and Safeway's LBO," *Journal of Financial Economics*, forthcoming.

■ **Donaldson, Gordon**, 1990, "Voluntary Restructuring: The Case of General Mills," *Journal of Financial Economics* 27, no. 1, 117-141. For a shorter, less technical version of the same article, see Vol. 4 No. 3 (Fall 1991) of the *Journal of Applied Corporate Finance*.

■ **Healy, Paul M., Krishna G. Palepu, and Richard S. Ruback**, 1992, "Does Corporate Performance Improve After Mergers?," *Journal of Financial Economics* 31, vol. 2, 135-175.

■ **Holderness, Clifford G. and Dennis P. Sheehan**, 1991, "Monitoring An Owner: The Case of Turner Broadcasting," *Journal of Financial Economics* 30, no. 2, 325-346.

■ **Jensen, Michael C. and Brian Barry**, 1992, "Gordon Cain and the Sterling Group (A) and (B)," Harvard Business School, #9-942-021 and #9-942-022, 10/15.

■ **Jensen, Michael C., Willy Burkhardt, and Brian K. Barry**, 1992, "Wisconsin Central Ltd. Railroad and Berkshire Partners (A): Leverage Buyouts and Financial Distress," Harvard Business School #9-190-062, 11/13.

■ **Jensen, Michael C., Jay Dial, and Brian K. Barry**, 1992, "Wisconsin Central Ltd. Railroad and Berkshire Partners (B): LBO Associations and Corporate Governance," Harvard Business School #9-190-070, 11/13.

■ **Jensen, Michael C.**, 1986, "The Agency Costs of Free Cash Flow: Corporate Finance and Takeovers," *American Economic Review* 76, no. 2, 323-329, May.

■ **Jensen, Michael C.**, 1986, "The Takeover Controversy: Analysis and Evidence," *The Midland Corporate Finance Journal*, 4, no. 2, 6-32, Summer.

■ **Kaplan, Steven N.**, 1993, "Campeau's Acquisition of Federated: Post-bankruptcy Results," *Journal of Financial Economics* 35, 123-136.

■ **Kaplan, Steven N.**, 1989, "The Effects of Management Buyouts on Operating Performance and Value," *Journal of Financial Economics* 24, 581-618.

■ **Kaplan, Steven N.**, 1989, "Campeau's Acquisition of Federated: Value Added or Destroyed," *Journal of Financial Economics* 25, 191-212.

■ **Kaplan, Steven**, 1989, "Management Buyouts: Evidence on Taxes as a Source of Value," *Journal of Finance* 44, 611-632.

■ **Kaplan, Steven N. and Jeremy Stein**, 1993, "The Evolution of Buyout Pricing and Financial Structure in the 1980s," *Quarterly Journal of Economics* 108, no. 2, 313-358. For a shorter, less technical version of the same article, see Vol. 6 No. 1 (Spring 1993) of the *Journal of Applied Corporate Finance*.

■ **Kaplan, Steven N. and Jeremy Stein**, 1990, "How Risky is the Debt in Highly Leveraged Transactions?," *Journal of Financial Economics* 27, no. 1, 215-245.

■ **Lang, Larry H.P., Annette Poulsen, and Rene M. Stulz**, 1994, "Asset Sales, Leverage, and the Agency Costs of Managerial Discretion," *Journal of Financial Economics*, forthcoming.

■ **Lichtenberg, Frank R.**, 1992, *Corporate Takeovers and Productivity*, (MIT Press: Cambridge, MA). For a shorter, less technical summary of the findings, see Vol. 2 No. 2 (Summer 1989) of the *Journal of Applied Corporate Finance*.

■ **Lichtenberg, Frank R. and Donald Siegel**, 1990, "The Effects of Leveraged Buyouts on Productivity and Related Aspects of Firm Behavior," *Journal of Financial Economics* 27, volume 1, 165-194, September.

■ **Mann, Steven V. and Neil W. Sicherman**, 1991, "The Agency Costs of Free Cash Flow: Acquisition Activity, and Equity Issues," *Journal of Business* 64, no. 2, 213-227.

■ **Murphy, Kevin J. and Jay Dial**, 1992, "Compensation and Strategy at General Dynamics (A) and (B)," Harvard Business School #N9-493-032 and N9-493-033, Boston, MA, 11/19.

■ **Palepu, Krishna G.**, 1990, "Consequences of Leveraged Buyouts," *Journal of Financial Economics* 27, no. 1, 247-262.

■ **Rosett, Joshua G.**, 1990, "Do Union Wealth Concessions Explain Takeover Premiums? The Evidence on Contract Wages," *Journal of Financial Economics* 27, no. 1, 263-282.

■ **Smith, Abbie J.**, 1990, "Corporate Ownership Structure and Performance: The Case of Management Buyouts," *Journal of Financial Economics* 27, 143-164.

■ **Tedlow, Richard**, 1991, "Hitting the Skids: Tires and Time Horizons," Unpublished manuscript, Harvard Business School, Cambridge, MA.

■ **Tiemann, Jonathan**, 1990, "The Economics of Exit and Restructuring: The Pabst Brewing Company," Unpublished manuscript, Harvard Business School.

■ **Wruck, Karen H.**, 1991, "What Really Went Wrong at Revco?," *Journal of Applied Corporate Finance* 4, 79-92, Summer.

■ **Wruck, Karen H.**, 1990, "Financial Distress, Reorganization, and Organizational Efficiency," *Journal of Financial Economics* 27, 420-444.

■ **Wruck, Karen H.**, 1994, "Financial Policy, Internal Control, and Performance: Sealed Air Corporation's Leveraged Special Dividend," *Journal of Financial Economics*, forthcoming.

■ **Wruck, Karen H. and Krishna Palepu**, 1992, "Consequences of Leveraged Shareholder Payouts: Defensive versus Voluntary Recapitalizations," Working paper, Harvard Business School, August.

■ **Wruck, Karen H. and Steve-Anna Stephens**, 1992, "Leveraged Buyouts and Restructuring. The Case of Safeway, Inc.," Harvard Business School Case #192-095.

■ **Wruck, Karen H. and Steve-Anna Stephens**, 1992, "Leveraged Buyouts and Restructuring: The Case of Safeway, Inc.: Media Response," Harvard Business School Case #192-094.

IS AMERICAN CORPORATE GOVERNANCE FATALLY FLAWED?

by Merton H. Miller,
University of Chicago*

Are the investment horizons of U.S. firms too short? Yes, was the conclusion of *Capital Choices*, a report published in August 1992 by 25 academic scholars under the leadership of Professor Michael Porter of the Harvard Business School. The Porter Report was widely acclaimed not only by the U.S. financial press, but by many Japanese observers. Mr. Katsuro Umino, for one, Vice President of the Osaka-based Kotsu Trading Company, was quoted in the Chicago *Tribune* of August 24, 1992 as saying:

It's interesting to see that somebody in America is finally waking up to the real culprit behind the decline of American corporate competitiveness. I think many of us in Japan have known for a long time that America's capital allocation system is inherently flawed.

The flaw seen by Messrs. Porter and Umino and ever so many others is the overemphasis on stock prices and shareholder returns in the American system of corporate governance. By contrast, a survey of 1,000 Japanese and 1,000 American firms by Japan's Economic Planning Agency, reported in the same Chicago *Tribune* story, finds that on a scale of 0 to 3—3 being most important—Japanese firms give "Higher Stock Price" a rating of only 0.02. "Increasing Market Share" gets a reported rating of 1.43 in Japan, almost twice its rating in the United States.

Surveys must never be taken too literally, of course. Japanese managers surely cannot believe that increasing market share is the overriding corporate goal. Achieving a 100 percent market share for your product is too easy: just give it away! Profitability must also and always be considered. And, indeed, the Japanese firms surveyed did give a rating of 1.24 to Return on Investment—far less than the 2.43 rating given by the American firms, but still much much more than the virtually zero weight given to Higher Stock Prices.

For all its technical limitations, however, the survey does, I believe, accurately reflect differences in managerial behavior in the two countries. American managers *are* more concerned with current movements in their own stock prices than are Japanese managers. And rightly so. The emphasis American managers place on shareholder returns is not a flaw in the U.S. corporate governance system, but one of its primary strengths.

Some of my academic colleagues believe, in fact, that American big-business management has been putting put too *little* weight on stockholder returns, leading to massive waste of both shareholder and national wealth. Their argument has not, in my view, been convincingly established. The billion-dollar losses of companies like IBM and General Motors in recent years, offered by such critics as evidence for their case, testify less to failures in the U.S. governance system than to the vigorously competitive environment in which U.S. firms must operate.

*My thanks for helpful comments from my colleagues Steven Kaplan and Anil Kashyap and from Donald Chew.

MAXIMIZING SHAREHOLDER VALUE AS THE PRIMARY OBJECTIVE OF THE BUSINESS CORPORATION

Let me begin my defense of U.S. corporate governance by emphasizing that managerial concern with shareholder value is merely one specific application of the more general proposition that in American society the individual is king. Not the nation, not the government, not the producers, not the merchants, but the individual—and especially the individual consumer—is sovereign. Certainly that has not been the accepted view of ultimate economic sovereignty here in Japan, though the first signs of change are beginning to appear.

The connection between consumer sovereignty and corporate governance lies not just in the benefits customers derive from the firm's own output. The customers are not the only consumers the firm serves. The shareholders, the investors, the owners—however one chooses to call them—are also consumers and their consumption, actual and potential, is what drives the shareholder-value principle.

To see how and why, consider the directors of a firm debating how much of the firm's current profits, say $10 million, to pay out as dividends to the shareholders. If the $10 million is paid as dividends, the shareholders clearly have an additional $10 million in cash to spend. Suppose, however, that the $10 million is not paid out, but used instead for investment in the firm—buying machinery, expanding the factory, setting up a new branch, or what have you. The stockholders now do not get the cash, but they need not be disadvantaged thereby. That will depend on how the stock market values the proposed new investment projects.

If the market believes the firm's managers have invested wisely, the value of the shares may rise by $10 million or even more. Stockholders seeking to convert this potential consumption into actual consumption need only sell the shares and spend the proceeds. But if the market feels that the managers have spent the money foolishly, the stock value will rise by less than the forgone dividend of $10 million—perhaps by only $5 million, or possibly not at all. Those new investments may have expanded the firm's market share; they may have vastly improved the firm's image and the prestige of its managers. But they have not increased shareholder wealth and potential consumption. They have reduced it.

Current Market Values and Future Earnings

Using the stock market's response to measure the true worth of the proposed new investments may strike many here in Japan as precisely the kind of short-termism that has led so many American firms astray. Let it be clearly understood, therefore, that, in a U.S.-style stock market, focusing on current *stock* prices is not short-termism. Focusing on current *earnings* might be myopic, but not so for stock prices, which reflect not just today's earnings, but the earnings the market expects in all future years as well.

Just how much weight expected future earnings carry in determining current stock prices always surprises those not accustomed to working with present-value formulas and, especially, with growth formulas. Growth formulas, however, whether of dividends or earnings, rarely strike my Japanese friends or my Japanese students as very compelling. Many Japanese firms, after all, pay only nominal dividends, and the formulas don't make sufficiently clear what investors are really buying when they buy a stock.

Let me therefore shift the focus from a firm's rate of sales or earnings growth to where it ought to be—namely, to the competitive conditions facing the firm over meaningful horizons. And let me, for reasons that will become clear later, measure the strength of those competitive conditions by the currently fashionable market value-to-book value ratio (also known as the "market-to-book" or "price-to-book" ratio). The book-value term in the ratio, based as it is on original cost, approximates what management actually spent for the assets the market is valuing. A market-to-book ratio of 1.0 (abstracting from any concerns about pure price inflation) is thus a natural benchmark, signifying a firm with no competitive advantage or disadvantage. The firm is expected to earn only normal profits in the economists' sense of that term, that is, profits just large enough to give the stockholders the average, risk-adjusted return for equities generally.

To sell for more than an unremarkable market-to-book ratio of 1.0—that is, to have a positive "franchise value," as some put it—a firm must have long-term competitive advantages allowing it to earn a higher than normal rate of return on its productive assets. And that's not as easy to do as it may seem. Above-normal profits always carry with them the seeds of their own decay. They attract competitors, both from within a country and from abroad, driving profits and share prices relentlessly back toward the competitive norm. Investors buying into a firm are thus making judgments not only about whether the firm and its managers have produced a competitive advantage over their rivals, but also about how far into the future that competitive advantage can be expected to last.

Some specific numbers may help to fix ideas.[1] Consider a U.S. firm with a market-to-book ratio of 3.0—and there still are many such. And suppose, further, that it will be plowing back its entire cash flow into investments expected to earn *twice* the normal competitive rate of return. By paying three times book value for the shares, investors are in effect anticipating that the firm will expand and stay that far ahead of its competitors *for the next 20 years*!

That's *really* forward-looking—much too forward looking, some would say, in this highly uncertain world. And perhaps that's why so many Japanese managers are instinctively skeptical about using the stock market to guide or evaluate managerial decision-making. They don't really trust the prices in the Japanese stock market where, at the height of the stock market boom of 1989, market-to-book ratios were not just 3.0 but, even after adjusting for real estate and for other corporate shares in cross-holdings, ran routinely to 5.0 or even 10.0. Such ratios implied that investors saw opportunities for these companies to earn above-normal, competitor-proof returns for centuries to come!

Prices and market-to-book ratios have fallen substantially since then, but are still hard to take seriously because they are not completely free-market prices. The values are not only distorted by the pervasive cross-holdings of nontraded shares, but the prices of the thinly-traded minority of shares in the floating supply often reflect the heroic scale of market intervention by the Ministry of Finance (MOF). Japanese managers can be pardoned for wondering whether the stock market may be just a *Bunraku* theater, with the bureaucrats from MOF backstage manipulating the puppets.

MOF's notorious market support activities also interact in other ways with the issue of corporate governance in Japan. Many academic observers in the U.S. (myself, in particular)[2] have attributed MOF's famous P.K.O. (Price Keeping Operations, and a Japanese pun on the country's participation in the U.N.'s Peace Keeping Operations in Cambodia) to its role as cartel manager for the Japanese brokerage industry. Another motivation traces, however, to the Japanese banking industry. Japanese banks, unlike those in the U.S., can hold equity positions in the companies to which they are also lending—a dual role that, in turn, has often been cited as the real key to Japanese managerial success. The bank connection is said to reduce corporate agency costs, provide better monitoring of corporate decisions, and, above all, allow management to undertake profitable but risky long-run ventures while confident of having the continued financial support needed to carry projects through to completion.

But any gains to the Japanese economy on the governance front have come at a substantial cost on other fronts. Corporate equities can be great assets for banks when the stock market is booming as it was in Japan in the 1980s. The price appreciation then provides the banks with substantial regulatory capital to support their lending activities. But when the stock market collapses, as it did in Japan after 1989, the disappearance of those hidden equity reserves can threaten the solvency of the banks and the integrity of the country's payment system.

The prospect becomes even more frightening when we remember that shareholdings in Japan run in both directions. Not only do banks hold the firm's shares but the firms—again, presumably with a view to better governance—also hold the *banks'* shares. The result is a classic, unstable, positive-feedback asset pyramid. No wonder MOF must keep supporting stock prices and always seems to be running around, like the proverbial Dutch boy on the dikes, plugging holes and leaks in its regulations.

Stock Prices and Information

To say that the stock market in the U.S. is much closer to the free-market ideal than the Japanese

---

1. The calculations to follow are adapted from the finite growth model presented in Merton H. Miller and Franco Modigliani, "Dividend Policy, Growth and the Valuation of Shares," *Journal of Business*, Vol. 24, No. 4 (October 1961), pp. 411-433. I have taken the value of *rho* (the risk-adjusted cost of capital) as 10 percent (what else?) and the value of *k* (the investment-to-earnings ratio) as 1.0. A firm with a market-to-book ratio of 1.0 corresponds to a "no growth-premium firm" with average internal rate of return (*rho-star*) just equal to the cost of capital.

2. For an account of how MOF systematically uses its regulatory powers to sustain the Japanese brokerage industry cartel and to support the level of stock prices, see my articles, "The Economics and Politics of Index Arbitrage in the U.S. and Japan," *Pacific-Basin Finance Journal*, Vol. 1, No. 1 (May 1993), pp. 3-11; and "Japanese-American Trade Relations in the Financial Services Industry," Working Paper, Graduate School of Business, University of Chicago (September 1993).

stock market is not to suggest that valuations in the U.S. are always correct. But at least those investors with bearish opinions about particular stocks or the market as a whole can express their pessimism by selling, even selling short, without encountering the kind of anti-selling rules and taboos for which MOF has become notorious. Those pessimists may well be wrong, of course. And so in their turn may be those who are optimistically anticipating a rise in future earnings and prices.

No serious student of stock markets has ever suggested that stock prices always "correctly" measure the true "fundamentals," whatever those words might mean. The most claimed is that the prices are not systematically distorted, like those in Japan where MOF's heavy thumb often tilts the scales against selling. Nor are the prices in the U.S. just some artificial numbers driven by whims and fads, as some academics have argued (and quite unsuccessfully so, in my opinion). The evidence overwhelmingly supports the view that prices reflect in an unbiased way all the information about a company that is available to the investing public.

The word "available" is worth stressing, however. Stockholders and potential outside investors can't be expected to value management's proposed investment projects properly if they don't have the information on which management has based those plans. And management may well hesitate to disclose that information for fear of alerting competitors. This inevitable "asymmetry" in information, to use the fashionable academic jargon, is what many see as the real flaw in the shareholder-value principle. Projects with positive net present values, possibly even with substantial net present values, may not be undertaken because outside investors cannot value the projects properly and will condemn management for wasting the stockholders' money. That, essentially, is the Porter position. As one way to deal with it, the Porter study recommends that U.S. governance rules be changed to permit firms to disclose proprietary, competitively-sensitive information *selectively* to that subset of the stockholders willing to commit to long-term investing in the company.

Can investment be discouraged by inability to disclose selectively? Possibly. Has it happened? And on what scale? That is much harder to say. The main evidence cited for its pervasiveness in the U.S. is the supposedly superior earnings and growth performance of bank-disciplined Japanese manufacturing firms relative to their impatient American stock-holder-disciplined counterparts. Note that I stress Japanese *manufacturing* firms. No one has ever suggested that Japanese market-share-oriented firms were superior in the service industries, notably retailing, or in commercial banking.

And I should say that manufacturing *was* the main evidence for Japanese governance superiority cited before the current recession hit Japan. That recession, painful as has been and still is its impact on the Japanese economy, has at least served to remind us that myopia is not the only disease of vision afflicting business managers. They may suffer from astigmatism (distorted vision) or even from hyperopia or excessive far-sightedness. Looking back over the last 20 years, one may well find cases in which American firms facing strong stockholder pressures to pay out funds invested too little in some kinds of capital-intensive technology. But many Japanese firms, facing no such pressures, have clearly *over*invested during that same period in highly capital-intensive plants that will never come close to recovering their initial investment, let alone earning a positive rate of return. And I won't even mention the trillions of yen poured into land and office buildings both at home and abroad.

No form of corporate governance, needless to say, whether Japanese or American, can guarantee 20-20 vision by management. Mistakes, both of omission and of commission, will always be made. My claim is only that those American managers who *do* focus on maximizing the market value of the firm have a better set of correcting lenses for properly judging the trade-off between current investment and future benefits than those who focus on maximizing growth, market share, or some other, trendy, presumed strategic advantage.

MANAGEMENT OBJECTIVES AND STOCKHOLDER INTERESTS

Glasses help you see better, of course, only if you wear them. And the complaint of at least one wing of American academic opinion, especially in the field of finance, is precisely that U.S. managers don't always wear their stockholder-corrected lenses to work. Because ownership of American corporations is so widely dispersed among a multitude of passive individual and institutional investors, U.S. managers, so the argument runs, are left free to pursue objectives that may, but need not, conform to those of the stockholders.

Japanese stock prices, even at current levels, are still hard to take seriously because they are not completely free-market prices. Japanese managers can be pardoned for wondering whether the stock market may be just a Bunraku theater, with the bureaucrats from MOF backstage manipulating the puppets.

Shareholders, however, are not powerless. Although neither able nor willing to perform day-by-day monitoring of management operating decisions, shareholders do have the right to elect the company's Board of Directors. And the Board, in turn, by its power to unseat management, and even more by its power to design the program for executive compensation, has command over important levers for aligning management's objectives with those of the shareholders.

Compensation Packages and Management Incentives

The Board of Directors has a tool-box full of levers but not, alas, any simple or fool-proof set of instructions for using them. In fact, academic "agency cost" theory suggests that *no* all-purpose optimal scheme—no "first-best" as opposed to, say, second-best or even lower-best solution—really exists for aligning interests when success depends on luck as well as skill.

To see why, ask yourself how the directors could make the managers accept the stockholders' attitudes toward risk. Suppose, to be specific, that the directors try what may seem the obvious performance-based compensation strategy of giving the managers shares in the company. Will that make managers act like the shareholders would? More so, probably, than if the directors just offered a flat—and presumably high—salary supplemented with generous retirement benefits. Managers so compensated are more likely to be working for the bondholders than for the stockholders. Salaried managers clearly have little incentive to consider projects with serious downside risk.

Giving managers stock at least lets them participate in the gains from their successful moves, but still does not solve the problem of excessive managerial timidity—excessive, that is, relative to the interests of the outside stockholders. Those stockholders are, or at least in principle ought to be, well diversified. They can thus afford risking their entire investment in the company even for only 50:50 odds because their stockholding is only a small part of their total wealth. That, after all, is a key social benefit of the corporate form with fractional and easily transfer-able ownership interests: more efficient sharing of the business risks. But the managers are typically *not* diversified. A major fraction of their personal wealth and their human capital is tied to the corporation. Caution, not boldness, inevitably becomes their watchword.

The executive stock option was invented in the U.S. in the 1950s precisely to offset the play-it-safe tendencies of underdiversified corporate managers (though tax considerations and accounting conventions have since blurred the original incentive-driven motivation for options).[3] Stock options, suitably structured, work by magnifying the upside potential for the manager relative to the down. A bet paying $1,000 if a coin comes up heads and losing $1,000 if tails would hardly be tempting to the typical risk-averse manager. But tossing a fair coin might well seem attractive if heads brought $5,000 and tails cost only $500.

Options and their many variations—including option-equivalents like highly leveraged corporate capital structures—not only can reduce management's natural risk-aversion, but may overdo it and tempt managers into excessively risky ventures. If these long-odds strategies do happen to pay off, the managers profit enormously. If not, the bulk of the losses are borne by the shareholders, and probably the bondholders and other prior claimants as well. Many observers feel that a payoff asymmetry of precisely this kind for undercapitalized owner-managers was the root cause of the U.S. Savings and Loan disaster.

The inability to align management interests and risk attitudes more closely with those of the stockholders shows up most conspicuously, some academic critics would argue, in the matter of corporate diversification. Corporate diversification does reduce risk for the managers. But because stockholders can diversify directly, they have little to gain—except perhaps for some tax benefits, large in some cases, from internal rather than carryforward of losses—when a General Motors, say, uses funds that might otherwise have been paid as dividends to buy up Ross Perot's firm, Electronic Data Services (EDS). In fairness, however, let it be noted that the stockholders, by the same token, would have little to lose by such acquisitions unless the acquiring firm

---

3. See Merton Miller and Myron Scholes, "Executive Compensation, Taxes and Incentives," in *Financial Economics: Essays in Honor of Paul Cootner,* William Sharpe and Catheryn Cootner (Eds.), Prentice-Hall, Englewood Cliffs, NJ, 1982.

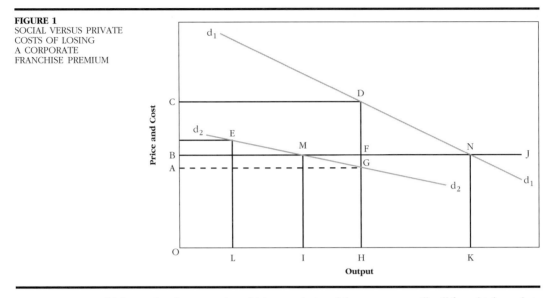

FIGURE 1
SOCIAL VERSUS PRIVATE
COSTS OF LOSING
A CORPORATE
FRANCHISE PREMIUM

were to pay too high a price for control—which certainly has been known to happen.

Stockholders could also lose if diversification predictably and consistently means sacrificing the efficiencies from specialization. Some evidence suggests that it does—although hardly enough, in my view, to justify claims by some academic critics of corporate diversification that loss of corporate focus and related failures of governance by GM or IBM or Sears in recent years have destroyed *hundreds of billions* of dollars of their stockholders' and, by extension, of the nation's wealth.

For those firms, certainly, aggregate stock market values have declined substantially. But to treat such declines as a national disaster like some gigantic earthquake is to overlook the distinction between social costs and private costs. Consider, for example, the story told in Figure 1, which pictures an IBM-type firm about to be hit unexpectedly with an anti-trust suit (and let it be clearly understood that this is an illustration, and not necessarily a recommendation). The company's initial demand curve is $d_1 d_1$, and its long-run marginal cost is BJ (assumed, for simplicity, to be constant and hence equal to its average cost). Because the firm had "market power," it set its product price at OC (i.e., above average and marginal cost), earning thereby the above-normal profits indicated by the rectangle BCDF. Those above-competitive profits will be capitalized by the stock

market and the company will sell for a high market-to-book value premium.

Now let the government win its anti-trust suit against the company and immediately force the company's price and output to their competitive levels (OB for price and OK for quantity). The abnormal profits will vanish, the stock price will fall, and the market-to-book value premium will disappear. Yet no net loss in *national* wealth or welfare has occurred in this instance. Wealth and economic welfare have simply been transferred from the company's shareholders to its customers; producer surplus has been transformed into consumers' surplus. In fact, in the case pictured, society is better off on balance, not worse off. Because output increases to the competitive level, consumers gain additional consumers' surplus in the form of the ("Harberger") triangle DFN.

The social and private consequences are easily distinguished in this anti-trust scenario. But what if the decline in stock-market value is a self-inflicted wound? IBM, after all, did *not* lose its anti-trust case. Its market value was eroded by the entry of new firms with new technologies.

That kind of value erosion, however, surely cannot be the national disaster to which the governance critics are pointing. Why, after all, should society's consumers care whether the new products were introduced by IBM or by Intel or Apple; by

Myopia is not the only disease of vision afflicting business managers. They may suffer from astigmatism or even from excessive far-sightedness. Looking back over the last 20 years, one will find cases in which American firms facing strong stockholder pressures to pay out funds invested too little. But many Japanese firms, facing no such pressures, have clearly over*invested during that same period.*

Wal-Mart or by Sears; or, for that matter, by General Motors or by Toyota? The complaint of the critics may be rather that the managements of those firms have failed to downsize and restructure fast enough even *after* the new competition had penetrated the market. Entrenched managements, unchecked by the hand-picked sycophants on their Boards, kept pouring money into the old, money-losing lines of the firm's business rather than letting their stock-holders redeploy the funds to better advantage elsewhere.

But continuing to make positive investments in a declining industry—"throwing good money after bad," as the cliché would have it—cannot automatically be taken as evidence of economic inefficiency, and certainly not of bad management. Nothing in economic logic or commonsense suggests the best exit path is always the quickest one. A firm withdraws its capital by making its *net* investment negative, that is, by holding its rate of gross investment below the rate of depreciation. The marginal rate of return on that gross investment may well be high even though the average rate of return on the past capital sunk in the division or the firm as a whole is low or even negative. When the direct costs of exit (such as severance payments) are high, and when the firm is at least covering its variable costs (unlike many in Russia, so we are told), investing to reduce a loss can often be a highly positive net-present-value project indeed.

Suppose, however, for the sake of argument that some entrenched managers *were* too slow in downsizing. The losses reported by their firms still cannot be equated dollar for dollar with the social costs of bad governance. To see why, turn again to Figure 1, which can also be used to show the new condition of our original firm—that is, after the entry of the new competition attracted by its earlier high profits. The firm's demand curve is now the much more elastic demand curve d_1d_2, and its new long-run equilibrium level of output will be OL, smaller than its earlier equilibrium output level OH.

Should the firm seek to maintain its earlier market share of OH, however, net losses of ABFG will be incurred, exactly as the critics insist. But only the triangle MFG represents the social cost of the failure to downsize. The rest, given by the area ABMG is, again, merely a transfer to consumer surplus. How much of the reported loss goes one way and how much goes the other cannot be settled, of course, merely from a schematic diagram. That

requires specific empirical research of a kind not yet found in the recent academic literature so critical of U.S. corporate governance.

That the losses suffered in recent years by firms like IBM or Sears or General Motors may not be social losses will be of little comfort, of course, to those stockholders who have seen so much of their retirement nest eggs in those companies vanish. One can hardly blame them for wishing that the directors had somehow prodded management to abandon their formerly successful strategies *before* the success of the newer competitive strategies had been so decisively confirmed. Fortunately, however, shareholders whose personal stake is too small to justify costly monitoring of management have another and well-tested way to protect their savings from management's mistakes of omission or commission: diversify! A properly diversified shareholder would have the satisfaction of knowing that his or her loss on IBM shares or Sears or General Motors was not even a *private* loss since it was offset in the portfolio by gains on Microsoft, Intel, Apple, WalMart and other new-entrant firms, foreign and domestic, that did pioneer in the new technologies.

CONCLUSION

Summing up, then, we have seen two quite different views of what is wrong with American corporate management. One view, widely accepted in Japan and by the Michael Porter wing of academic opinion, is that American managers pay too much attention to current shareholder returns. The other view, widely held among U.S. academic finance specialists, is that American managers pay too little attention to shareholder returns.

Which view is right? Both. And neither. Both sides can point to specific cases or examples seeming to support their positions. But both are wrong in claiming any permanent or systematic bias for U.S. firms in the aggregate toward myopia or hyperopia, toward underinvestment or overinvestment relative either to the shareholders' or to society's best interests. There is no inherent bias because market forces are constantly at work to remove control over corporate assets from managers who lack the competence or the vision to deploy them efficiently.

We saw those forces most dramatically perhaps in the takeover battles, leveraged buyouts, and corporate restructurings of the 1980s and, more recently, in many well-publicized board-led insur-

> There is no permanent or systematic bias for U.S. firms in the aggregate toward myopia or hyperopia, toward underinvestment or overinvestment, because market forces are constantly at work to remove control over corporate assets from managers who lack the competence or the vision to deploy them efficiently.

gencies. But, for all their drama, those events (which often seem little more than struggles over how the corporate franchise premium is to be shared between the executives and the shareholders) represent only one part—and by no means the most important part—of the process of allocating society's productive capital among firms. The ultimate disci-pline for the managers of one firm in the U.S. will always be the managers of other firms, including foreign firms, competing with them head to head for customer business. As long as we continue to have plenty of *that* kind of competition in the U.S., I, for one, can't become terribly concerned about the supposedly fatal flaws in our governance system.

THE POLITICAL ROOTS OF AMERICAN CORPORATE FINANCE

by Mark J. Roe,
Columbia University Law School*

I n 1990, two of General Motor's largest institutional shareholders, unhappy with the company's declining market share and profits during the 1980s, sought to talk to GM's leaders about a successor to the retiring CEO. GM's senior managers rebuffed the shareholders. They could do that because the two large stockholders each owned less than 1% of the company's stock.

How such a corporate ownership structure—many shareholders with small percentage holdings and, until recently, little voice in governance—came to be the dominant form of large business enterprise in the United States is usually understood as a purely economic story, one of business adaptation to economies of scale and investor diversification. The reigning explanation of U.S. corporate ownership structure continues to be the one provided over 60 years ago by Adolf Berle and Gardiner Means in their classic, *The Modern Corporation and Private Property*. According to Berle and Means, economies of scale made possible by new technologies required U.S. companies at the turn of the century to become so large that their enormous capital needs could be satisfied only by selling stock to many outside investors—investors who, by and large, wanted diversified portfolios. Ownership was thus dispersed, and this dispersion shifted decision-making power over the firm from shareholders (or, more precisely, shareholder-managers) to professional managers. This had benefits: it facilitated the exit of company founders and their heirs, professionalized U.S. management, and set the stage for large mergers. But, as Berle and Means warned, the separation of ownership from control also had offsetting costs stemming from weakened managerial incentives and accountability.

What Berle and Means failed to foresee were the many corporate governance mechanisms that were devised by both corporate insiders and outside investors to reduce such "agency costs"—things like proxy fights, hostile takeovers, incentive compensation plans, and, more recently, active outside directors prodded by institutional investors. The continued domination of the large public corporation in the U.S. suggests that such governance mechanisms, coming on top of intense competition in American product markets, worked to minimize the problems from the separation of ownership from control. For if the U.S. system had failed to "adapt" in a way that solved this governance problem, the current U.S. ownership structure would have been supplanted by a more efficient alternative. Survival implies efficiency—or at least greater efficiency than available alternatives.

In 1994, I published *Strong Managers Weak Owners: The Political Roots of American Corporate Finance*, in which I argued that this explanation, although correct as far as it goes, is incomplete. Economics alone cannot fully account for the evolution of the U.S. corporation into its present form. Politics, in the form of laws and regulations affecting commercial banks and other financial institutions, played a key role in fragmenting stock ownership beyond what was required to have big firms and well-diversified investors. From the middle of the 19th century onward, both state and federal laws restricted the growth and activities of the largest American financial institutions. U.S. commercial banks were prevented from branching nationally, and thus they lacked both the size and the information networks to fund big pieces of the capital required by the large American firms emerging at the end of the 19th century. Banks' products and portfolios were also restricted—most important, banks were barred from the securities business and from owning stock. U.S. insurance companies were barred from buying stock for most of this century. Mutual funds, thanks

*The political argument in this essay is adapted from *Strong Managers, Weak Owners: The Political Roots of American Corporate Finance* (Princeton University Press: 1994); the evolutionary argument is adapted from "Chaos and Evolution in Law and Economics," 109 *Harvard Law Review* 641 (1996).

to rules established in the 1930s and 1940s, cannot easily devote their portfolios solely to big blocks; and they face legal problems if they go into the boardroom. And, finally, pension funds cannot take very big blocks without structural and legal problems; the big private pensions are under managerial control (not the other way around) and ERISA rules make it more comfortable for pension managers to avoid big blocks than to take them.

The rules that restricted the size and scope of U.S. financial institutions were neither random nor economically inevitable. While the public interest goals of protecting financial institutions explain some rules, they do not explain all of them. Two major forces lay behind many of the restrictions: American populism, with its profound distrust of large private accumulations of power, and interest group politics. There were businesses and individuals—mostly local bankers—who gained from the early fragmentation of U.S. financial institutions. These winners in the political process had a large voice in Congress, in part because their private goals happened to line up well with popular sentiment.

The environment in which the large American firm evolved was conditioned by more than engineers' requirements for huge economies of scale and investors' demand for diversification. It was also a political environment that precluded very large-scale finance and raised the costs to financial institutions of participating in the governance of large firms. A richer story of evolution toward efficiency must account for political influences that shunted the large firm's evolution down some paths and not others.

The Limits of Economics in Explaining Corporate Ownership

Corporate finance and corporate governance are primarily economic matters. The financing goal is typically to secure funding for the corporation at the lowest possible cost; the governance goal is to maximize the value of the firm to its owners. Given these economic priorities, politics and law are rarely viewed as fundamental influences on the organization of finance and corporate governance. But the structure at the top of a nation's companies—the place where the board of directors, shareholders, and senior managers interact—is the outcome not just of economic evolution toward efficiency, but of political developments such as laws and regulations that limited the range of adaptive possibilities.

Of particular importance are historical events that influenced, and occasionally dictated, the ways in which financial intermediaries—particularly banks and insurance companies—channelled savings from households to firms. America's historical aversion to private concentrations of economic power sharply limited the size and activities of its financial institutions. Such restrictions in turn influenced how stock (and debt) has been owned in the U.S., in large part by making it costly—if not illegal—for such institutions to own large blocks of a single company's stock or play an active role in corporate governance.

To put the same thought a little differently, U.S. law and politics historically denied firms and investors the use of certain corporate governance tools, and so the American governance system evolved in ways that enabled them to make the best use possible of the other available tools. Corporate managers and investors used the tools at their disposal. Had more tools been available, some companies may well have chosen a different mix to make themselves as efficient as possible.

That politics affected the *forms* of corporate ownership seems likely. But did these political forces on U.S. corporate ownership structure also affect corporate *efficiency and security values*? Even if U.S. corporations and their investors successfully "adapted," it seems plausible that American laws reduced corporate efficiency and increased the cost of capital for some firms in some periods of U.S. history. Adaptation, after all, has costs. And, although the evidence is uncertain, it also seems plausible that denying use of a potentially effective governance tool could have continuing costs for some American firms.

In the next part of this article, I summarize the considerable evidence that U.S. politics, laws, and regulations influenced the forms of ownership and top-level governance of the American corporation. Evidence of large increases in costs of capital is harder to come by, and less persuasive. Nevertheless, in the second half of the article, I discuss three potential problems—(1) monitoring (or "agency") costs, (2) information costs, and (3) costs of coordinating long-term investments involving different parties—that could each raise the cost of capital for companies with fragmented ownership. By foreclosing the possibility of concentrated ownership, American politics denied U.S. companies one of the governance tools that could have helped to control these problems.

Like modern-day venture capitalists and merchant bankers, Morgan and other influential investment bankers sat on corporate boards and participated in strategic decision-making.

I close by offering some policy prescriptions. There is enough basis for arguing that concentrated ownership could at times be helpful that those restrictive rules lacking a policy justification ought to be pulled back. The reason to do so is not to favor one governance tool over another, but to encourage *both* ownership structures. Competition among alternative governance systems *within the U.S. economy* has the potential to increase the efficiency of American firms.

POLITICAL ROOTS

Political influences shaped American financial institutions and, in the process, American corporate finance and ownership patterns. Begin by looking at the large U.S. corporation as it emerged at the end of the 19th century. Coming near the close of the Second Industrial Revolution, this period saw remarkable advances in technology. One major consequence of the new technologies was enormous economies of scale, which meant that the cheapest production accrued to the firms with the largest operations. Among industrialized nations at the time, only America had a continent-wide economy with low internal trade barriers; and thus it alone provided a sufficiently large market for those enterprises that could achieve large-scale efficiencies.

But achieving the tremendous output necessary to realize the new scale economies required huge capital inputs to build the manufacturing facilities and the distribution system. Where could that capital come from? Much of it came from internal growth and retained earnings, some of it came from investors. Individuals, even when assembled into small groups, lacked sufficient capital to fund such undertakings. As Alfred Chandler described the railroads, the first of the modern business enterprises,

Ownership and management soon separated. The capital required to build a railroad was far more than that required to purchase a plantation, a textile mill, or even a fleet of ships. Therefore, a single entrepreneur, family, or small group of associates was rarely able to own a railroad. Nor could the many stockholders or their representatives manage it. The administrative tasks were too numerous, too varied, and too complex. They required special skills

and training which could only be commanded by a full-time salaried manager. Only in the raising and allocating of capital, in the setting of financial policies, and in the selection of top managers did the owners or their representatives have a real say in railroad management.[1]

Even John Rockefeller, the richest man in America, ended up owning only a fraction of Standard Oil. New technologies allowed for vertical integration of several steps in production and distribution; transactions that once occurred across markets—making raw materials in one firm, manufacturing them into a final product in another, and distributing them in yet another—were brought inside a single firm, with managers visibly coordinating the steps of production. Managers had to avoid shortages at each stage of production and ensure a smooth flow from raw material to final sale. *Management* thus became an even more critical determinant of the success or failure of large enterprises.

Eventually these new large-scale enterprises had to draw capital from many different shareholders whose holdings tended to be small in relation to the size of the enterprise. Although the early growth was financed by the founders' own capital and by retained earnings, a growing firm's capital requirements tended to outstrip its ability to finance itself from its own earnings. Commercial banks would often lend capital to fund part of this growth, but banks could not play a full range of roles because of their size (national banks were limited to a single location) and limited powers (they could not own stock). In the U.S. at the turn of the century, there were no financial institutions of sufficient size and geographical diversity to provide the bulk of needed capital directly to America's new large enterprises.

For the large family-owned businesses that made up most of American industry at this time, founders (or their heirs) wanting to cash out thus had only two basic choices: (1) they could sell their stock into the securities market; or (2) they could merge with another firm, in which case the securities market would finance the merger. (Indeed, the primary role of the securities market at the turn of the century was not to raise new capital, but to finance the massive mergers at the end of the 19th century and to allow founders to cash out.[2])

---

1. Alfred Chandler, *The Visible Hand—The Managerial Revolution in American Business*, p. 87 (1977).

2. Ibid., p. 373.

The dispersion of ownership that eventually resulted from such equity financing determined that professional, salaried managers (with perhaps modest stock holdings) would assume control of the day-to-day operations. Although descendants sometimes took over running the firm from the founders, that role tended to fall to hired managers. Then, over time, concentrated stock ownership dissipated into fragmented holdings as the heirs sold off the inheritance and the managers occasionally raised new capital in public markets.

The resulting combination of a large-scale enterprise, a professional (non-owner) management, and fragmented, diversified stockholders shifted control of public corporations from shareholders to managers. In contrast to business enterprises in Europe and elsewhere, dispersed shareholders and concentrated management became the distinguishing characteristics of the large American firm.

What Might Have Been? (Or the "Venture Capital" Model of Corporate Governance)

The separation of ownership and control proved functional and, in many cases, a major source of value in its own right.[3] Good managers replaced often less motivated or sometimes incompetent heirs. Specialization of risk-bearing and management meant that good managers didn't need to have their own source of capital to get to run large enterprises.

But separation via public stock markets was not the only plausible path. Some founders might have preferred that banks, insurers, or other financial institutions had instead become part owners of their businesses. Then the power of professional managers could have been balanced by financiers with large stakes and a continuing interest in the firm—much as happens in the small firms financed by U.S. venture capitalists.

Financiers like J.P. Morgan, it's true, were able to play a major role in corporate governance at the turn of the century even without holding big blocks of stock, particularly when the client firms needed outside capital. Like modern-day venture capital and merchant bankers, Morgan and other influential investment bankers sat on corporate boards and participated in strategic decision-making. But this role proved to be short-lived, at least partly because political reprisals against the "money-trusts" in the early 20th century induced Morgan and other bankers to keep a low corporate governance profile.[4]

Had national financing beyond the securities markets been available, a different pattern might have emerged. Larger financial institutions with nationwide scope may well have been able to finance more rapid expansion than that allowed by securities issuance or internally generated funds. Truly national financial institutions may also have been able to participate *as substantial owners* in the wave of end-of-the-century mergers and cash-outs. In that case, the institutions could have used their large blocks of stock to sit on the boards of the merged enterprises (much as venture capitalists and LBO firms like KKR do today) and so shared power with senior management. As I explain later, such a concentrated ownership and governance structure could have been one tool in the bundle to help control monitoring, information, and coordination problems that may well reduce the value of many U.S. companies today.

But, as things turned out, this "venture capital" model was not widely adopted for large firm governance in the U.S. Shareholders, it's true, get to elect the board of directors, and the board appoints the CEO. But the actual flow of power, as everyone recognized, ran in reverse: The CEO recommended nominees to the board. Board members were typically either insider-employees or other CEOs with little reason to invest time and energy in second-guessing the incumbent CEO. The CEO's recommendation for the board went out to the shareholders, whose small shareholdings gave them little incentive—or means—to find alternatives; they checked off the proxy card and returned it to the incumbents. In this fashion, the CEO dominated the election and the firm. And, although the balance of power may have shifted with the recent increase in shareholder and board-level activism, as recently as the 1980s many directors continued to "feel they are serving at the pleasure of the CEO-Chairman."[5]

3. William Lazonick, "Controlling the Market for Corporate Control: The Historical Significance of Managerial Capitalism," 1 *Industrial and Corporate Change* 445, 447, 462-63 (1992).

4. A notable focus for such political reprisals was the Pujo investigation early in the 20th century. Alfred D. Chandler, *The Visible Hand—The Managerial Revolution in American Business* 491-92 (1977).

5. Jay Lorsch and Elizabeth MacIver, *Pawns or Potentates: The Reality of America's Corporate Boards* (1989).

> When the Japanese banking system faced a rash of failures in 1927, the Japanese
> business authorities reacted by merging many banks into larger ones. Such mergers
> were one of the major steps in the evolution of Japanese banks into the main banks
> at the center of the Japanese *keiretsu* after World War II.

WHY U.S. BANKS WERE NOT READY FOR THE EXPANSION

When the large American corporation was emerging around the turn of the century, the dominant financial institutions—commercial banks and insurance companies—were in no shape to hold large blocks of stock. Industrial companies had learned how to operate nationally, but banks and insurers operated locally and could not own stock. When industries needed capital for expansion or to fund consolidations during the end-of-the-century merger wave, they could not go directly to a handful of commercial banks, much less to a single bank, that could provide all of the needed equity and debt from their own sources. National banks were national in name only, able to operate only from a *single* physical location.

When attempting to identify the origins of such restrictions on banking, most people think of the New Deal legislation of the 1930s—particularly, the Glass-Steagall Act, which separated commercial banks from investment banks. But the most serious restrictions on both banks and insurers *came well before* the New Deal. For banks, they were in place at the end of the 19th century; for insurance companies, they came shortly after the turn of the century. The New Deal was important in confirming the financial and ownership structures that already prevailed—and in confirming them during a period of flux when those structures could have been changed, but were not.

Restrictions on Branching

As two Federal Reserve economists put it, "*For much of its history, the United States has had a banking system like no other in the industrialized world. Since the early 1800s, the U.S. banking system has been highly fragmented, consisting of numerous small banks without extensive branch systems.*"[6] States chartered their own banks, and Congress, influenced by local interests, refused to charter national banks that could operate more extensively than the politically powerful local banks.

Every few decades, the lack of diversification resulting from such geographic restrictions either caused or aggravated a U.S. banking "crisis." This emboldened some political leaders to propose nationwide branching in order to strengthen the banking system. But, as happened when President Cleveland endorsed proposals to allow "national" banks to branch in 1895, the proposals were repeatedly blocked in Congress by well-organized unit bankers (bankers that operated from a single physical location). Indeed, the well-organized unit bankers not only stymied truly national branching for national banks, but induced Congress to reduce the capital requirement for rural national banks. The result was the establishment of many new banks, thus sowing the seeds for future bank crises and further strengthening the anti-branching banker constituency. Having more weak, local banks meant there were more players willing to invest in political action to block creation of national financial institutions.

Different political structures could have yielded different outcomes. Historically undemocratic Japan did not have the same open political structure that made American populism such a potent force. Japanese interest group configurations also differed from those in the U.S., and the national political structure was less responsive to local banking interests than the American structure. And, so, when the Japanese banking system faced a rash of failures in 1927, the Japanese authorities reacted by merging many banks into larger ones.

Such mergers were one of the major steps in the evolution of Japanese banks into the main banks that were at the center of the Japanese *keiretsu* after World War II. So, while American regulation was keeping banks small and local, Japanese regulation was making them much bigger. For better or worse, the Japanese banks had the financial strength to be able to take equity positions in most large firms after World War II. Large stock purchases of industrial firms by groups of four or five Japanese banks and insurers then produced the Japanese *keiretsu*, the networks of cross-ownership and influence among both industrial and financial firms that have dominated the Japanese economy since the 1950s.

Contrast Japanese policymakers' decision to concentrate finance during its 1927 banking crisis

---

6. Robert T. Clair and Paula K. Tucker, "Interstate Banking and the Federal Reserve: A Historical Perspective," *Federal Reserve Bank of Dallas, Economic Review*, Nov. 1989, at 1.

with the outcome of the American banking crisis that took place soon after. Instead of encouraging bank mergers and allowing nationwide branching, U.S. legislators responded to the Depression-era bank crisis by enacting deposit insurance (which was intended to *protect* small banks from larger competitors) and separating commercial from investment banking (to prevent concentration of power among the larger banking operations).

What explains the American result? The answer has much to do with differences in politics. Most members of the U.S. Congress, given the strength of their ties to their local districts, had an interest in keeping banks small and local.[7] Small-town American bankers were influential people; and, by exploiting the public sentiment against concentrated financial power, this interest group was consistently effective in Congress. And, so, Congress predictably chose to prop up the small banks with deposit insurance and other regulations designed to protect their ability to compete with larger banks at roughly the same time that an authoritarian Japan was concentrating its banking system.

Product Restrictions

Although geographic restrictions on U.S. banks were crucial, product restrictions also played an important role—and they too were in place well before the turn of the century. The National Bank Acts of 1863 and 1864 gave national banks only limited powers.[8] Control of an industrial company was not even contemplated and, hence, out of the question. And, in 1892, when the controversy over whether national banks could own stocks got the attention of the Supreme Court, the ruling came down that the power to own stock was not listed in the Act, and so it was not granted.[9]

Were Other Paths Possible?

We have already provided glimpses of alternative ownership structures in the form of the Japanese keiretsu and U.S. venture capital practices. But another way to see what might have been is to look at early American financial arrangements. Two of these are worth examining in some detail: (1) the close connections between banks and industry in New England in the early 19th century (before banking restrictions became as important); and (2) the structure and history of the Second Bank of the United States.

Economic historians have shown that, in the first part of the 19th century, New England entrepreneurs bound their operating firms to the local banks. Yet these banks did not grow into national financial institutions, and the ties between the entrepreneurs and their local banks eventually withered. The primary reason these relationships failed to grow appears to be that, as economic opportunities shifted from New England to the national economy, the New England banks could not get good information about distant firms, and the bankers were able to participate in the national economy only as passive buyers of short-term commercial paper. As economic historian Naomi Lamoreaux put it, *"[F]irms could issue their IOUs through note brokers, who would market them to banks and financial intermediaries across the country... [and] banks lost their ability to assess a customer's total indebtedness."*[10]

Since evaluating the creditworthiness of companies is usually a banker's strength, one wonders why the New England bankers ceded the profits to these note brokers. The most likely answer to this puzzle is that the bankers probably did not cede the profits voluntarily. Rather, because banks in regions with a capital surplus could not branch into capital-importing areas, the money could not move inside a single organization. But investment bankers could market notes and commercial paper throughout the country. Thus, entrepreneurs affiliated with banks could pursue economic opportunities to go national while their bankers, because of branching restrictions, could not. The commercial paper market—short-term IOUs from a debtor—was the way financiers and industrialists found to "contract around" the geographic restrictions on banks.

7. Federal Reserve Committee on Branch, Group, and Chain Banking, Branch Banking in the United States 174 (1937); Eugene N. White, "The Political Economy of Banking Regulation, 1864-1933," 42 *Journal of Economic History* 33, 35 (1982); Eugene N. White, "The Regulation and Reform of the American Banking System, 1900-1929," *Journal of Economic History*, at 65, 161 (1983).

8. National Bank Act of 1864, ch. 106, 13 Stat. 99 (1864) (codified as amended at 12 U.S.C. § 38 (1988)).

9. California Bank v. Kennedy, 167 U.S. 362 (1892); National Bank Act of Feb. 25, 1863, ch. 58, § 11, 12 Stat. 665; 12 U.S.C. § 24 (Seventh) (1988). State member banks of the Federal Reserve System were later similarly restricted. 12 U.S.C. § 335 (1988).

10. Naomi R. Lamoreaux, "Information Problems and Banks' Specialization in Short-Term Commercial Lending: New England in the Nineteenth Century," in *Inside the Business Enterprise: Historical Perspectives on the Use of Information* 161, 180 (Peter Temin ed., 1991).

The three largest American insurers showed promise of developing into institutions that would rival the German universal banks or the main banks in Japan. At the very least, they seemed ready to become much like the large modern British insurers, which hold considerable stock and play a more important governance role than their passive American counterparts.

The Fate of America's First National Financial Institution

Ironically, one of the first American national business institutions was a bank, the Second Bank of the United States. Described by Alfred Chandler as the "first prototype of modern business enterprise in American commerce," its organizational structure allowed it to coordinate complex financial transactions through its many branches to enable capital to move across the nation to support the flow of trade.[11] But, as is well-known, Andrew Jackson killed this first national financial intermediary with his famous veto message refusing to re-charter the Bank.

The Second Bank had a double importance for the history of U.S. banking. It was not only a precursor of the modern-day central bank necessary for a strong banking industry, it was also a semi-private institution with an interstate branching network. Had it survived, its national branch network could have been a model for future private banking charters. The Second Bank, or more private but truly national banks, might have played a central financial role in the construction and merger of large national firms at the end of the 19th century.

Jackson's veto of the renewal of the Second Bank's charter can be attributed to both of the two key forces that would determine the future structure of U.S. financial institutions: interest group infighting and American populism. State banks felt threatened by the Second Bank, which competed with them and had some power to control them. This opposition was an early reflection of the local bank power thats American federalism fostered and that tended to keep America's financial institutions small.[12]

Jackson's refusal to renew the Bank's charter also tapped the rich vein of populism in American politics. The veto message attacked the Bank as an elitist institution owned "by foreigners... and a few hundred of our own citizens, chiefly of the richest class." The Bank had the potential to be run by a small group of people. "It is easy to conceive that great evils to our country and its institutions might flow from such a concentration of power in the hands of a few men irresponsible to the people..."[13] Jackson's forceful rhetoric helped imprint on the national psyche frightening images of an elitist concentration of private economic power. For decades following the veto, the message itself was assigned reading for schoolchildren.

Not until the 1990s were American laws changed to permit nationwide banks, at a time when banks were of diminishing importance in the economy.

HOW U.S. INSURERS LOST THEIR POWERS

Banks, though, were not the only powerful financial institution in the U.S at the turn of the century. In an era that preceded the rise of pension funds and mutual funds, life insurers were a central depositary for middle-class savings. Were they similarly affected by politics?

The early history of the life insurers suggests they were not. At the beginning of the 20th century, several of the largest American financial institutions were insurance companies, not banks. Although banks were confined to a single state, insurers were not. The largest New York insurers were twice as large as the largest banks and were moving into related financial activities. Some insurers were underwriting securities; some were buying bank stock and controlling large banks; and some were assembling securities portfolios with the potential for exercising control. Some insurance companies had already put as much as 12% of their assets into stock. Indeed, the three largest American insurers at the time—Equitable, Mutual, and New York Life—were growing so rapidly that they showed promise of developing into institutions that would rival the powerful German universal banks or the main banks in Japan. At the very least, they seemed ready to become much like the large modern British insurers, which hold considerable stock and play a more important governance role than their passive American counterparts.

But then politics intervened. In 1905, the insurance industry was rocked by scandal, revealing nepotism, insider financial chicanery, and bribery of legislatures. The New York legislature responded with a political inquiry, which came to be called the "Armstrong investigation" after the state legislator who chaired the committee. In 1906, new insurance

---

11. Chandler, cited in footnote 1, pp. 30-31, 42-43. Temin evaluates it as an inter-regional financier and a crypto-central bank. Peter Temin, *The Jacksonian Economy* 28-58 (1969).

12. Bray Hammond, "Jackson, Biddle, and the Bank of the United States," 7 *Journal of Economic History* 1 (1947).

13. Edward L. Symons, Jr. and James J. White, *Banking Law—Teaching Materials,* 13-16 (3d ed. 1991).

laws barred insurers from owning stock, controlling banks, or underwriting securities. For the next 50 years, insurers were banned from owning any stock at all—and serious deregulation of this ban on stock ownership by insurance companies did not begin until the 1980s.

In short, American politics limited the insurance industry to its core business of writing insurance and investing in debt. Today, although insurance companies have stock holdings that amount to about 5% of the total market (which puts them a distant third behind mutual funds' share of about 10% and pension funds' 30%), they play a negligible role in corporate governance.[14]

MODERN TIMES: MUTUAL FUNDS AND PENSION FUNDS

Mutual funds and pension funds, although long overshadowed by commercial banks and insurers, now account for the bulk of institutionally owned stock in the U.S., and their share of financial assets under management is expected to continue rising. Although the potential role of such funds in corporate governance has also been somewhat limited by legal and regulatory factors, political influences on laws and regulations that govern mutual funds and pension funds are less direct and clearcut than those that constrained the historical structure of American banking and insurance. But such laws and regulations do raise the costs of such funds becoming involved in corporate governance—and it's too early to say whether the funds will come to play a bigger governance role.

For example, mutual funds face portfolio limits that stop them from deploying much of their assets in big block positions with boardroom influence.[15] And it is generally not worthwhile for funds with a small stake to attempt to play a big (which often means "expensive") public role in governance. The few

public exceptions seem to arise when a mutual fund, or a complex of funds, finds itself with a sizeable block. For example, when Kodak was in crisis and Fidelity found that its group of funds owned about 7% of the company, Fidelity became involved.

As for pension funds, although the laws governing such funds do not explicitly bar big blocks and boardroom activity, such activities are deterred by the reality that funds that deviate from prevailing practice expose themselves to greater business risks and the threat of litigation.[16] Similarly, "little" mistakes with small ownership positions can be hidden and don't usually lead to a lawsuit against the pension funds' managers. But a misstep with a large block (even if embedded in a diversified portfolio) is more readily targeted for a lawsuit. Private pension funds are also typically under the control of the sponsor company's managements, and most senior managers have usually not supported strong corporate governance activity. The *public* pension funds, by contrast, have been more active. For example, CalPERS and others have prodded boards to set up governance and review procedures.

Although the new institutional activism is about a decade old, it is still too early to say where it will all end up. Current arrangements could be the long-term, continuing result—that is, occasional institutional activism, usually following bad firm performance, but with few big blocks of stock and little continuing inside-the-boardroom role. On the other hand, the current moderate levels of activism could be an evolutionary step *toward* new roles such as acquiring industry and governance expertise, and even putting institutional representatives in the boardroom (thus moving along a path once cut off).[17] But if this happens in a way that threatens corporate managers, one wonders whether the hostile takeover tensions of the 1980s will reemerge, and managers will once again call on state legislatures for protection.[18]

---

14. Warren Buffett's insurers are property and casualty companies, not life insurers; property and casualty insurers overall have a much smaller asset base than the life insurers have. Buffett's authority to use even the property and casualty insurers for big blocks of stock required changes in the governing law, changes made in the 1980s.

15. To be sure, mutual funds' positions rarely even come near these limits, but this could be the result of such limits in combination with other constraints that have prevented mutual funds from taking large blocks in the past.

16. And, because the historical structures and rules for banks and insurers have not looked kindly on governance activity, the pension law's imitation rules favor the diversified, fragmented structures. See Mark Roe, "Mutual Funds in the Boardroom," *Journal of Applied Corporate Finance*, Vol. 5, No. 4 (Winter 1993); Roe, *Strong Managers, Weak Owners*, ch 8 (mutual funds), ch 9 (pension funds).

17. See Ronald Gilson and Reinier Kraakman, "Reinventing the Outside Director: An Agenda for Institutional Investors," 43 *Stanford Law Review* 863 (1991). The in-the-boardroom models haven't been adopted, and the first data results doesn't suggest that from-the-distance governance role has yet to become profitable. John Wagster and Andrew K. Prevost, "Wealth Effects of the CalPERS' 'Hit List' to SEC Changes in the Proxy Rules," 1996 working paper; Stuart L. Gillan and Laura T. Starks, "Relationship Investing and Shareholder Activism by Institutional Investors," *Journal of Finance* (1995).

18. Roe, *Strong Managers*, ch. 10 (takeover politics), and chs 16 and 21 (speculating on possible political influences today and in the future).

> Monitoring and corporate governance should matter least in highly competitive markets with little fixed, long-term capital and lots of growth opportunities. But when markets are concentrated, or the firms' fixed investments are large and its growth opportunities few, managers will be somewhat free from competitive and capital market pressures.

MODERN TIMES: SECURITIES LAW LIMITS ON SHAREHOLDERS' JOINT ACTION

With historical regulation of the banks and insurers barring big equity blocks, and with mutual funds and pension funds too new or too constrained for all but a few to be capable of taking big blocks in big industrial firms, *joint action* by a number of large shareholders may be today's most realistic corporate governance alternative to concentrated ownership for large U.S. firms. Given the institutionalization of stock ownership in the past couple of decades, ten or twenty owners of 1% of a firm could band together to involve themselves in corporate governance.

Obvious business reasons tend to frustrate this kind of coordination: some of the players don't want to work with a competitor (if you identify a problem, sell fast rather than alert competitors with whom you'd work to fix it), the institutions are only rarely going to be able to contribute functionally, and so on. But on top of this, securities rules discouraged joint shareholder action by, for example, classifying informal meetings (and even telephone calls) among a handful of investors as proxy solicitations requiring public filings with the SEC. Such laws saw to it that financial players who wanted to be active but keep a low profile could not do both; they instead needed their lawyers every step of the way and had to "go public" to be active. If the ownership stake was small, the profitable action was usually to do nothing.[19]

Then, in the early 1990s, the SEC relaxed its view that made many informal communications among investors come under rules requiring proxy filings. That change increased the activity of some investors with sizeable (though far from control) blocks in working with other investors to bring about change. As one example, Michael Price's recent actions in prodding Chase to merge with Chemical, taken largely through a mutual fund, were said to have been impossible before the SEC assured institutional investors that some forms of coordination would not be viewed as proxy solicitations.[20]

POTENTIAL COSTS: COULD OWNERSHIP STRUCTURE AFFECT PERFORMANCE?

It is hard to deny that American politics contributed historically to smaller and weaker banks and insurers than would otherwise have developed. And it's quite possible that larger and stronger institutions would have taken bigger ownership stakes, such as those that are common in venture capital financing and in large firms in Japan and Germany. Big blockholding has costs in reducing diversification, and bigger institutions of course can hold bigger blocks at lower cost. But even if the form of corporate ownership was affected, long-term performance might not have been. Substitute tools accomplish at least part of what alternative ownership might do—and some of the substitute tools may well work better for some firms than ownership by a financial institution.

This brings us to the question posed at the beginning of this article: If the fragmented ownership of U.S. corporations was not economically inevitable, were the governance substitutes for concentrated ownership devised by U.S. firms and capital markets as efficient as the governance alternative that was foreclosed? To put the same another way, did the American adaptations demanded by U.S. law and politics end up imposing major costs on shareholders and the economy?

Although such costs are difficult to quantify, they can be divided into two major categories: (1) the costs of the original adaptation; and (2) the continuing costs of a less than optimal governance system.

First of all, even if the adaptations proved to be *perfect* substitutes, adaptation still cost something: new structures had to be built, experiments were tried and some failed, people who might have devoted themselves to another economic activity found themselves most profitably engaged in building these adaptive structures. As one example of such costs, some recent evidence indicates that at the time of one politically motivated restructuring—the Pujo investigation, which prompted Morgan and other investment bankers to leave the many boardrooms—the stock prices of Morgan's client firms declined.[21] While the reasons for the decline could have been several, one plausible interpretation is

---

19. Roe, "Political Roots"; Bernard S. Black, "Next Steps in Proxy Reform," 18 *Journal of Corporation Law* (1992).

20. Andrew E. Serwer, "Mr. Price is on the Line," *Fortune*, Dec. 9, 1996, at 70 (Price takes bigger blocks through mutual funds when he can use proxy law rollback to coordinate with other owners to engineer changes at Chase.)

21. Miguel Cantillo, "The Rise and Fall of Bank Control in the United States: 1890-1920 (University of California at Berkeley Working Paper No. 254, Oct. 1995).

that the governance structure would be weakened, at least for a time. Adaptation, even if effective, usually isn't costless; the stockholders at the time adaptations take place pay a price.

The harder question is whether there are continuing costs from America's historical aversion to concentrated financial institutions with significant power in the boardroom. Given the many governance substitutes, it's hard to see how these costs can be very great—unless the main substitutes have problems or are themselves subject to political constraints. But if the substitute tools are less effective for some firms in some situations, then such companies may bear ongoing governance costs—say, reacting a little too slowly to a shift in demand in some cases, or failing to ramp up a new profitable project as fast as possible.

Three kinds of cost could affect companies even today: monitoring costs, information costs, and industrial organization costs. Each has the potential to raise a company's cost of capital and reduce its productivity.[22] The next three sections spell them out.

Monitoring Costs

Monitoring costs are well-known and hardly need explanation. As suggested earlier, the separation of ownership from control could weaken managerial incentives and accountability. Directors representing institutions with large blocks of stock would presumably have the means, and their institutions the incentive, for more effective monitoring of managers.

When Monitoring is Likely to Be Important. Monitoring and corporate governance should matter least in highly competitive markets with little fixed, long-term capital and lots of growth opportunities. Managers who destroy value in such cases, or fail to increase it fast enough, will be unable to raise capital for growth and eventually be replaced. But when markets are concentrated, or the firms' fixed investments are large and its growth opportunities few, managers will be somewhat free from competitive and capital market pressures. In that setting, managers who fail to use their capital efficiently need not face the consequences of error immediately; whether because oligopoly provides "slack," or the firm has lots of long-lived capital in place, the firm can slowly waste away until one of the governance mechanisms kicks in to make managers do their job better (or replaces them).

Take the case of GM in the early 1990s. After almost a decade of shrinking market share and substandard stock-price performance, the company's competitive problems culminated in 1991 with a loss of $7 billion from North American operations. At this late stage, pressures from institutional shareholders finally combined with competitive failure to force GM's board to replace two senior management groups. If better internal governance mechanisms had been in place—ones that could have kicked in earlier—much of the loss in GM's competition position and shareholder value might have been avoided.

As this example is meant to suggest, pressures for better governance can be seen as reinforcing the effects of competition in product markets. Good governance encourages a quicker response to competitive forces, bad governance slows the response. Because many companies have long-term, fixed capital, and some U.S. and global markets are still oligopolistic, governance reform can play an important monitoring role.

A Qualification. One obvious qualification needs to be made at this point: Because the institutional representatives would themselves be agents for others owning the stock, they would not be perfect monitors. Moreover, the blockholder itself, or the individuals managing the positions, could face conflicting incentives. For example, a commercial lender who is also a blockholder might overlook the poor shareholder returns of its borrowers while collecting fees and charging higher interest rates.

Thus, concentrated ownership by institutional is not a panacea, and some ownership forms could introduce their own monitoring costs.[23] But the question is not whether changes in ownership structure would be costless (although public policy concerns must of course be considered when deciding to allow such changes). The question is whether block ownership and boardroom representation would reduce the overall agency costs faced by the corporation and its investors.

22. See Roe, *Strong Managers*, chs. 17, 18, and 19.
23. See Roe, at pp. 260-262; Jonathan Macey and Geoffrey Miller, "Corporate Governance and Commercial Banking: A Comparative Examination of Germany, Japan, and the United States, *Stanford Law Review* Vol. 48 No.1 (Nov. 1995), pp. 73-112.

The ability to communicate the prospective value of a high-quality middle management team, or the import of technical data generated inside the firm, may well be greatly improved by regular, private interaction between large stable stockholders and managers. In this sense, concentrated ownership may be able to lower the cost of capital by reducing information costs.

Information Costs

When information about a company's strategy or prospects is complex or "soft" (i.e., difficult to quantify), management often finds it hard to communicate it to outsiders. Stockholders with small holdings—and the equity analysts who write research reports for them—may not have the incentives to spend much time trying to understand complex, technological information; so they might choose to ignore it and just look at the bottom line. And managers with good, but *proprietary* information would not want to reveal such information to the stock market because it could benefit their competitors. In either event, the stock market never gets the information; and, to the extent the market discounts share values for greater uncertainty (i.e., assumes the worst), information costs end up raising the firm's cost of capital.

But such soft, complex, or proprietary information may be more readily conveyed to those who sit regularly in the boardroom. The ability to communicate the prospective value of a high-quality and cohesive middle management team, or the import of technical data generated inside the firm, may well be greatly improved by regular, private interaction between large stable stockholders and managers. In this sense, concentrated ownership may be able to lower the cost of capital by reducing information costs.

Another potentially important source of information costs are distortions of management's incentives that could occur when managers are unable to communicate effectively with the market. If managers increase the long-run value of the firm in ways that investors cannot see right away, the managers may not get the "credit" right away (say, in the form of bonuses or payoffs from short-term stock options) their performance merits. Managers may then pass up profitable investments with long-term payoffs while blaming the "short termism" of the stock market. And both managers and markets will be behaving "rationally"—managers because they believe their superior performance will not be rewarded during their tenure, and investors because they lack both the information necessary to evaluate the profitability of such investments and the influence to bring about necessary changes if managers are wrong. Managers may even try to insulate themselves from the stock market (as many did during the hostile takeovers of the 1980s) by erecting anti-takeover defenses.

In theory, then, concentrated ownership structures can improve the flow of information from inside the firm to large shareholders, thus helping to deter the short-term propensities often seen in managerial behavior and sometimes in the stock market. Large holdings give the owner the scale economies needed to justify investing in the capability to acquire and process complex information. Big blockholders can afford to hire an engineering or marketing consultant that a small stockholder wouldn't think of hiring. Finally, size and boardroom presence give large stockholders a strong incentive to protect proprietary information (because to behave otherwise would reduce the value of their own large stock positions).

Coordination Costs in Joint Long-term Investments

Multiple complex investments need coordination: An auto company builds an assembly line and needs a supplier to build a big facility to make the chassis or the transmissions or the engines. What stops one of them from extorting the other later on, after the other has built specific machinery that can't be used for anything else? What stops the one who is stuck from finding their supply prices driven down to their variable costs, so that it can't recover its original investment in the factory and machines?

This problem of coordinating joint long-term investments recurs in organizing industry, and *can be especially costly* when highly specific contracts cannot be written to govern the investments. The specific contracts can't be written many times because business will change in ways the two parties can't anticipate or because pricing formulas can't be made before the business gets going.

One solution to this "contracting and coordination" problem is, of course, complete vertical integration: The customer—the assembly-line firm—buys up the supplier firms, or builds itself all of the necessary machinery, parts, and distribution systems. Although this "solves" the coordination and hold-up problems, it creates other problems, which can be more costly. Combining customers and their suppliers within a single firm tends to reduce managerial accountability for each and blunts incentives for efficiency.

A promising alternative lies in the multiple cross-holdings of stock by customers and suppliers, especially when a half-dozen suppliers and customers must simultaneously make such commitments. A customer that partly owns, say, 5% of the stock of a supplier has less incentive to exploit the supplier than one who doesn't. A customer that is a 5% stockholder and sits on a supplier's board gets information with which to monitor management not just as a buyer of the supplier's products, but also as a board member and stockholder. If the customer tried to take advantage of the supplier after the supplier has committed itself, a "*keiretsu*-like" coalition of shareholders could intervene to stop the opportunism.[24]

A third-party financier could cement these partial relationships, acting as an "escrow" agent that owns some of the equity of both the suppliers and the customers. Financial institutions big enough to hold, say, 5-10% of the stock of each of the suppliers and customers in a network could play this role. Although there's evidence of this in Japan,[25] one could also imagine a role for such arrangements in the U.S. Using such financing, for example, the bust-ups of the 1980s could have taken a somewhat different course. In the U.S. the choice has tended to be an "either/or" one, with possibilities lying only at the ends of the spectrum of independence versus integration. But, with third-party financing, some related companies might have been broken off from large vertical organizations, but networks of coordination could have been retained when it was important to do so. Under such arrangements, the financing institutions would broker deals when disputes between customers and suppliers came up, and smooth relationships during normal times.[26]

THE CASE FOR COMPETING GOVERNANCE SYSTEMS

Today, each nation tends to have its own semi-proprietary governance system, in which the largest public companies have relatively homogeneous ownership structures. In Japan, main banks both lend to and own 5% of the stock of large firms, with other banks also taking 5% blocks as well. In Germany, a handful of banks and insurers have many large blocks of stock, some owned directly,

some built from custodial holdings for individual investors. Thus, whereas most large U.S. companies have fragmented ownership structures, most large Japanese firms and many European firms have large-block shareholders. There is little diversity within national economies.

One major advantage of the U.S. financial system is its flexibility. When large organizational structures become inefficient in the U.S., entrepreneurs set up new firms that compete with old firms—and, through the securities markets, small competitors can often quickly raise the financing they need to be viable. And, by competing with the large organizations, small firms either end up improving the large firms, or replacing them. American-style hostile takeovers, though much reduced since the 1980s, also help bring about such changes. The U.S. system also seems to excel at big-leap improvements, because whole new structures (MCI is a good example) can be quickly built by American entrepreneurs using venture capital financing and a vibrant securities market.

By contrast, in centralized financial systems like those of Japan and Germany, the central players seem less willing to finance new ventures, either because they fail to see the advantages of the innovation or because the new ventures would compete with their own large corporate clients. On the other hand, foreign bank-centered systems may be able to make stronger commitments to established firms that help enable those companies to make steady improvements in known technologies. To the extent they are successful in reducing the information and monitoring costs faced by outside investors, bank-dominated systems may enable such companies to carry out their investment plans during difficult periods.

But, for purposes of public policy, where does this comparison leave us? The recognition that the U.S. securities markets has greater flexibility, but less ability to make long-term commitments, than bank-centered economies like Japan and German might seem to fail to yield any clear policy recommendations. It would be a mistake to list the advantages and disadvantages of all the different systems, weigh them, and then pronounce one the winner. It would

24. Ronald J. Gilson & Mark J. Roe, "Understanding the Japanese Keiretsu: Overlaps Between Corporate Governance and Industrial Organization," 102 *Yale Law Journal* 871 (1993).

25. David Flath, "The Keiretsu Puzzle," 10 *Journal of the Japanese and International Economies* 101-121 (1996).

26. To be sure here, cross-ownership is not without its own costs in creating conflicts of interest—a supplier may ignore bad management if it gets a better price. Industrial companies are not set up for stock ownership and are taxed unfavorably on their stock returns.

A national economy with competing forms of governance should, all else equal, eventually outperform an economy dominated by a single form. Such a mixed system could enable its firms to make more rapid and productive responses to changes in their markets and technologies.

also be a mistake to decide that if there is no clear winner—or even if the securities markets were the winner—we ought then to preserve *all* aspects of the current American system.[27]

Such arguments are flawed because they exclude an important middle ground: the possibility of encouraging *competition* among organizational forms in the same national economy. Competition between the two forms should bring out the best of both. Indeed, a national economy with competing forms of governance should, all else equal, eventually outperform an economy dominated by a single form. A mixed system could enable its firms to make more rapid and productive responses to changes in their markets and technologies.

Here's the basic idea: Begin by imagining that the ownership structure of the firms in two industries, A and B, are evenly divided between American-style fragmented ownership and Japanese-German concentrated ownership. Industry A is a high-tech, high-growth industry with lots of investment opportunities and large requirements for new capital. By contrast, Industry B is a low-tech, slow-growth industry with few investment requirements and excess capital.

High Growth, Shortage of Capital. Assume that in Industry A the value of a certain technology becomes apparent to inside managers, but the payoff from such investment is not the kind that can be communicated effectively to scattered outside stockholders. In that case, the managers of the 50% of the firms in that industry with fragmented ownership choose not to invest because because they expect to be penalized in the short-run (with smaller salary increases or reductions in the value of their stock options). At the same time, the managers of the other half of Industry A's firms can talk privately to their large-block stockholders, who are able to understand the needed change. In these circumstances, the firms with concentrated ownership get a competitive advantage by reacting faster. Eventually, however, product market competition brings even the slower-moving, diffusely owned firms into line, as they react with a lag.

And here's the benefit of competing governance systems: If none of the firms in the industry had large blockholders, managers of all companies

might be more reluctant to make the investment because of their fear that the stock market would punish them until the supporting information was diffused throughout the economy.

Low Growth, Excess Capital. Now let's turn to Industry B, with limited growth opportunities and heavy fixed capital. In this case, it is likely to be those companies with concentrated ownership that respond most slowly. The insiders—a group that includes the managers and the big blockholders—may be reluctant to acknowledge that downsizing outmoded facilities is necessary because demand isn't going to come back to the industry. In this scenario, companies with dispersed ownership sometimes may act first. After the stock price is driven down, either insiders are forced to reform from within, or outsiders launch a hostile takeover and oust the incumbents. And then, once this information gets pounded into the industry in the form of higher stock prices for the downsized firms, then the big blockholders might help to speed change in their own firms.

As these two examples are intended to suggest, competition among different governance forms can speed change and adaptation. Product market competition, to be sure, will eventually bring about necessary change if all else fails. But even the increasingly global character of product market competition is no guarantor that the needed changes will be the quickest and most productive possible. Better governance can speed along needed change.

One might mistakenly imagine that global competition is enough to bring about change and that governance is therefore irrelevant. But this isn't true; a nation can insulate its firms from competitive forces. It must pay a price in lower living standards, but that doesn't mean that insulation can't be bought.

Imagine a nation that resists building a modern governance system and perpetuates some state ownership of enterprises, entrenches old managerial elites in the private businesses, or keeps outmoded labor arrangements. Let's assume further that such entrenchment leads to substandard management in the majority of that nation's firms. Must this governance system collapse under the threat of heightened international competition? Is it unstable?

27. Nor is it correct to "measure" how much politics shaped the institutions of governance and pronounce as the winner the nation that had the "least" political influence. That is, in France, Germany, and Japan, politics probably had more impact on the structure of the corporation and the institutions that own them than it had in the U.S. In Germany, securities markets were stifled, mandatory co-determination was added, and a rigid corporate law was kept in place. Therefore, one might (mistakenly) reject the idea that politics influenced the form and possibly the costs of organizing the large American firm.

The answer is "no" to both; it need not collapse and it could be stable. While global competition pressures that country's firms to improve, it doesn't *require* that they change. What counts is whether the firms produce competitive products that can be sold. The firm can continue to compete with an outmoded governance structure if it "saves" somewhere else with an offsetting advantage. It can save somewhere else by paying its employees (or some other immobile input) less. This result, while reducing that nation's standard of living relative to others', does not necessarily lead to economic instability. Stability depends as much on a nation's politics as it does on global competition.

CONCLUSION

America's fragmented ownership, a shift in power to professional managers, and the suppression of large owners did not threaten the widely held American corporation as an organizational form because the U.S. firm and its investors adapted. Even if the structure had some weaknesses, its weaknesses were outweighed by its strengths. While the separation of ownership from control reduced managerial accountability and incentives, and made the communication of strategic information more difficult, dispersed ownership facilitated economies of scale and the substitution of professionalized management for the often less capable heirs of the founders.

Competition often makes companies efficient regardless of their governance structure. Competition in product markets—and in managerial labor and capital markets as well—helped to align the interests of shareholders and managers, because the firm must get out a competitive product to survive in the long run. In the 1930s, 1940s and 1950s, America was the world's only continent-wide open market, which meant that nowhere else in the world could several firms in an industry reach economies of scale *and* have workable competition *and* political stability. Markets abroad were closed, other nations were too small, transportation and communication costs were too high, and political upheaval was common.

But, besides the stimulus provided by competition, the large U.S. public firm also prevailed primarily because of its (and its investors') ability to strengthen managerial accountability and incentives. Through both internal and external adaptations, the public corporation succeeded in balancing the problems of managerial control with the demand

for outside capital and diffusion of risk. Internally, the firm controlled managerial agency problems with outside directors, with a managerial headquarters staff responsible for overseeing the operating divisions, and with the use of managerial incentive compensation. Externally, hostile takeovers, proxy contests, and the threat of both further disciplined managers. A remaining question, however, is whether another tool in the governance toolbox—more concentrated ownership—would have helped some firms to adapt more quickly or with fewer costs.

Today, stock is moving from individuals to institutions. This trend toward greater institutional ownership and voice is critically important, and we can interpret it in two ways. Seen through the sweep of 100 years of American financial history, it can be viewed as yet one more adaptation to political constraints on U.S. financial institutions. But it can also be understood as the long-delayed break-out of more concentrated ownership and shareholder voice after previous institutional alternatives—concentrated ownership by banks and insurers—were suppressed.

That a dispersed ownership system may have costs does not, of course, mean that we should force firms to have more concentrated ownership structures—or that we should "subsidize" big blocks, or "tax" fragmented holders who trade vigorously. But we should also resist the temptation to add up the costs and benefits of each national governance system, pronounce one the winner, and then use law to move a system to the preferred governance model. Even if securities markets are better overall than concentrated ownership, concentrated ownership might be better for enough firms now and then that allowing such ownership structures could encourage better overall corporate performance in the future. There are enough tantalizing possibilities that we should permit outcomes that have been discouraged by laws and regulation. In America, that would mean loosening restrictions such as some of the current residual portfolio rules and securities law hindrances.

No corporate governance silver bullet will cure whatever governance ills occasionally afflict some American firms. Since a casual look at the concentrated governance systems in Germany and Japan shows lots of governance failures, one should be skeptical of any claim that concentrated ownership is superior and thus should be adopted by most companies. Institutional strength has obvious defects. It creates severe conflicts of interest, particularly if the institution sells something—a product, debt, or financial services—to the firm in which it owns stock. Such relationships could deteriorate into mutual managerial self-protection and, in so doing, discourage entrepreneurial initiative and leadership. And increased institutional power could lead to political pressure for more government intervention, which has tended not to work well in the U.S., and may yet prove to work poorly abroad. These imponderables are so large that any policy conclusion must be tentative, keeping in mind that where there are expected benefits there are likely to be some costs, too.

At the same time, one should not collect the stories of foreign failures at Metallgesellschaft, Daimler-Benz and others, and then unequivocally endorse American-style corporate governance (with its own failures, such as ADM and the decade-long delay before GM seriously addressed its problems). Rather one should recognize that each system has strengths and weaknesses. Because America is big and capable of absorbing multiple governance sys-

tems, the U.S. has a greater potential than other nations of facilitating both organizational forms (and their hybrids), and allowing them both to compete.

So, my policy prescription is simple: since no governance form seems obviously superior for all firms at all times, we ought to allow competition among governance systems. Vestigial rules that serve little public purpose but hinder the emergence of competing governance structures should be revised. In most nations where the evidence is available, politics has favored some forms of organization and ownership over others. In Germany, bank influence has been favored, stock markets suppressed. In Japan, regulation blocked the growth of public capital markets and channeled post-war financing through banks. America, as we have seen, has not been immune to these political influences, which have favored liquid public markets and small-town bankers at the expense of concentrated finance. In suppressing alternatives to the diffusely held public corporation, American law and political history have suppressed competition among ownership forms.

INTERNATIONAL CORPORATE DIFFERENCES: MARKETS OR LAW?

by Frank H. Easterbrook*

Strong Managers, Weak Owners: The Political Roots of American Corporate Finance *is a constructive response to the fallacy that whatever is, is best. Many of us whose scholarly interests center around corporate law and finance have verged on if not committed this fallacy, though usually unintentionally. Many economic studies show that what is, is *not* best. Statutes are among the worst offenders; many are designed to transfer wealth, and they reduce it in the process. Institutions of corporate law and governance can be flawed for the same reason. Still, we must understand that American corporate structure has evolved through long competitive pressure to maximize welfare, *given the constraints*. This caveat avoids the fallacy Roe's book identifies.[1] The constraints include politics. If some external force really means that American mutual funds can't own more than a few percent of the shares of any large corporation, that handicap may lead to a reduction in efficiency; but such a reduction does not imply that investors, managers, and corporations have fallen short of optimality. Organizations, like species, adapt to their surroundings.

One wonders only briefly whether businesses can't control their surroundings, instead of the other way 'round. More than one thoughtful person has believed that business leaders could have defeated efficiency-reducing bills by applying the tools of political suasion, but that they were content instead to negotiate the terms of surrender. Yet this occurs because, as Michael Jensen has pointed out more than once, the "corporation" is as diffuse and disorganized as voters at large. Corporations are numerous, have different agendas, are at each others' throats in product and financial markets alike, and can't organize well because they can't overcome their free riding problem—a very serious one, given the liquidity of capital markets.[2] Laws imposing handicaps on some businesses create market opportunities for others, who support them even as consumers and investors lose ground. So it may be inevitable that well-organized segments of the financial-services industry will combine with ill-informed public sentiment to secure and defend laws such as the National Bank Act and the Glass-Steagall Act—laws that increase their own profits while injuring the investors in the short run, and depressing the rate of growth (by reducing return on investment) and hence injuring society as a whole in the long run.

---

*This essay is an extended version of oral remarks on Mark J. Roe, *Strong Managers, Weak Owners: The Political Roots of American Corporate Finance* (Princeton University Press, 1994), delivered at a conference at the Law & Economics Center of George Mason University School of Law on May 4, 1996, and is copyrighted 1996 by Frank H. Easterbrook.

1. See generally Frank H. Easterbrook & Daniel R. Fischel, *The Economic Structure of Corporate Law* 22-39 (Cambridge: Harvard University Press 1991).

2. See Frank H. Easterbrook, "The Demand for Judicial Review," 88 *Northwestern L. Rev.* 372 (1993), which addresses the question why corporations file suits (and pay taxes) that in the aggregate make them worse off. The answer is the same as the reason why corporations increase output and reduce prices, even though that prevents them from making monopoly profits: competition.

> **Political reactions *never* stop competition, unless the market is so concentrated as to be monopolized—which finance is not. It is less concentrated in the United States than elsewhere, and we should therefore expect more risk-taking, and more novel forms of organization.**

Corporations usually must take law as given and adapt. It doesn't take chaos theory to show that the evolutionary path will diverge in different nations,[3] as it has in nature (a trip to Australia will make that point). Nor does it take great wisdom to see that increasing connections among finance systems worldwide will create pressure to extirpate these differences. Paring the maladapted laws from the statute books is a slow process, but it is inevitable. Nations that do not adapt will lag behind in competition. Change is going on now, but the need to assemble political coalitions makes for halting, two-step-forward-and-one-step-back movement.

POLITICS VS. ECONOMICS

The most interesting question is whether the existing (or historical) legal differences among economic systems matter very much. Roe believes that they do, but this is unproven. American politics may be uniquely populist, as Roe contends—though one wonders why it should be—but there are lots of ways for small firms to play with the big boys. The Second Bank of Burlap can raise money locally and participate in a syndicated loan to IBM. Huge ownership blocks can then coexist with low levels of concentration in the banking business.[4] J.P. Morgan didn't own the House of Morgan; other people's money predominated. And I have a lot of difficulty with the idea that modern money managers tremble in fear of Ferdinand Pecora, whose hearings recessed 62 years ago, or that insurance companies disdain the corporate control market because, as a result of repealed legislation, they lack the expertise to play. Expertise can be hired.

Consider how little the legal system matters to what seem to be important aspects of corporate organization and control. When United States law is changed to allow mutual funds and insurance companies to hold larger positions, they don't take advantage of that opportunity (Roe develops the details of this non-event nicely). Warren Buffett of Berkshire Hathaway is an outlier. (Other insurers and mutual funds, such as Oppenheimer, that have elected to use the options recently allowed in the United States have declined to take seats on their portfolio firms' boards.) In the United Kingdom, the law has long allowed banks to hold large blocks of shares, but English firms *do not* do this—although their counterparts on the other side of the Channel (and the Pacific) do.

These differences require an explanation more powerful than reluctance or political fear or missing expertise. Political reactions *never* stop competition, unless the market is so concentrated as to be monopolized—which finance is not. It is less concentrated in the United States than elsewhere, and we should therefore expect more risk-taking, and more novel forms of organization, rather than fewer (as Roe believes). If Firm A's financing innovations bring the glare of klieg lights and hearings down on the industry's head, what of it? In the interim, Firm A makes a lot of money; afterward it makes the normal rate of return. One paper after another by students of industrial organization shows how firms innovate and boost their output even though they know that in the long run prices will fall, and profits vanish. The industry would be better off if each firm refused to build that new plant, but each reasons that if it does not build, someone else will, and take the profits.

Just so in financial markets. If Insurer X or Investment Bank Y refuses to acquire blocks of stock, and if that step is profitable, someone else will do so. Tender offers make this point nicely. Until the mid-1960s, one could have said of the market for corporate control what Roe says about mutual funds and banks and insurers: managers just don't muscle in on friendly firms, and "reputable" investment banks didn't like the hostile tender offer. But firms

3. Roe extends on this point nicely in "Chaos and Evolution in Law and Economics," 109 *Harv. L. Rev.* 641 (1996). See also Theodor Baums, Richard M. Buxbaum & Klaus J. Hopt, eds., *Institutional Investors and Corporate Governance* (Berlin: de Gruyter 1994) (chapters discuss the law and economics of arrangements in many nations); Mats Isaksson & Rolf Skog, *Aspects of Corporate Governance* (Stockholm: Juristförlaget 1993) (similar project); Gary Gorton & Frank Schmid, "Universal Banking and the Performance of German Firms," (Wharton School, University of Pennsylvania, Working Paper January 1996); Andre Shleifer & Robert W. Vishny, "A Survey of Corporate Governance," (paper presented at the Nobel Symposium on Law and Finance, Stockholm, August 1995); William J. Carney, "The Political Economy of Competition for Corporate Charters," (Emory University Working Paper May 1995); Takeo Hoshi, Anil Kashyap & David Sharfstein, "The Role of Banks in Reducing the Costs of Financial Distress in Japan," 27 *J. Fin. Econ.*

67 (1990); David G. Litt, Jonathan R. Macey, Geoffrey P. Miller & Edward L. Rubin, "Politics, Bureaucracies, and Financial Markets: Bank Entry into Commercial Paper Underwriting in the United States and Japan," 139 *U. Pa. L. Rev.* 369 (1990); Stephen D. Prowse, "Institutional Investment Patterns and Corporate Financial Behavior in the United States and Japan," 27 *J. Fin. Econ.* 43 (1990); J. Mark Ramseyer, "Legal Rules in Repeated Deals: Banking in the Shadow of Defection in Japan," 20 *J. Leg. Stud.* 91 (1991).

4. If it even makes sense to compute concentration among banks by country—as if the levels of concentration among Pennsylvania banks mattered! Concentration of ownership from the firms' side is more important, and ownership of the American corporation is considerably more concentrated than most people suppose. See, for example, Harold Demsetz & Kenneth Lehn, "The Structure of Corporate Ownership: Causes and Consequences," 93 *J. Pol. Econ.* 1155 (1985).

at the fringes of respectability began to assemble financing, and before long all the white-shoe firms had to follow suit. Throughout the 1970s and 1980s there was an explosion of tender offers, leveraged buyouts, spinoffs, splitups, and related restructuring devices. As many predicted, this brought retaliation in the legislature. Did that risk cause anyone to back off? Not at all; someone else (Michael Milken, in particular) would have taken even more of the business. So legislation happened, and clever people have found ways around *that*—with the result that corporate control transactions are on an upswing, and in 1996 set a record despite the tighter laws and antitrust scrutiny.[5]

These developments readily could have been replicated in miniature, by taking 10% blocks rather than by taking 51% or 80% or 100% blocks. But they were not. We need an economic rather than a political or sociological explanation for why this is so rare. Financial intermediaries and investors cannot be at once dynamic and risk-taking (as the takeover wars show) yet passive and risk-averse (as Roe tells us American financial intermediaries are). Unfortunately, Roberta Romano and Mark Ramseyer, who have had a lot to say about this question,[6] are not with us today. So I offer an explanation of my own—not quite the same as theirs, but with some elements in common.

NOT POPULISM, BUT THE POLITICS OF SELF-INTEREST

Let us put populism aside as an explanatory variable. Populist talk is cheap, but the wishes of the unwashed rarely explain laws or economic institutions even for a few years; for popular sentiment to dominate an entire century is out of the question. Milk producers win higher prices in the political arena even though they are few in number and opposed to the most popular cause of all—good nutrition for children. Why should things be different in financial markets? More to the point, why is there so little resistance to the laws and rules that fracture holdings in the United States? And why is England's structure of holdings so similar to that of the United States, even though its laws are like those of Japan and Germany?

If not populism, then what? There are real interest groups, with money at stake. Securities dealers want to keep other financial intermediaries from poaching; local banks want to restrict competition from securities dealers; and so on. This has the makings of a good coalition to suppress money-center banks and other financial institutions.

None of this is inconsistent with anything in Professor Roe's book. The big question is why there is so little fighting back. Roe attributes this to the ghost of Ferdinand Pecora, but I would rather attribute it to the nature of the stakes. Money-center institutions don't fight back for two reasons: first, they are not an effective interest group for the same reason corporations as a whole are not an effective group—they can't solve their free riding problem given the ease of exit in financial markets; second, it is these very markets that make fighting back not worthwhile. Securities markets in the United States are as close as one gets to Adam Smith's atomistic competition. Information is plentiful, transactions costs low.

With efficient markets, there is no money to be made by holding undiversified blocks in public corporations.[7] Competition bids down the price of securities so that the excess risk created by the lack of diversification is not compensated. Even when the holder has inside information, the likelihood that the information will come out before the investor can capitalize by selling is high. Concentrated earnings therefore create uncompensated risk. Why should the money-center financial intermediaries expend political capital to win the right to reduce their earnings?

Public markets meanwhile put managers under the same kind of pressure that concentrated holdings would do. And because entrepreneurs can't raise as

5. According to the *Wall Street Journal*, the U.S. merger and acquisition business in 1996 was $659 billion, an all-time top (Section 3, page R8 (Jan. 2, 1997)).

6. See Roberta Romano, *The Genius of American Corporate Law* 118-47 (Washington, D.C.: American Enterprise Institute 1993); Romano, "A Cautionary Note on Drawing Lessons from Comparative Corporate Law," 102 *Yale L.J.* 2021 (1993); J. Mark Ramseyer, "Columbian Cartel Launches Bid for Japanese Firms," 102 *Yale L.J.* 2005 (1993).

7. The qualifier "in public corporations" is important. There may be substantial gains from taking a corporation private by a leveraged buyout or similar transaction. Many of these gains come not from the greater concentration of holdings *per se*, but from the radical alteration in the incentives (including compensation) that managers face. Once the firm is closely held, however, large blocks are essential to facilitate monitoring, for the market institutions serving this function are gone. For discussions of the sources of gain in going-private transactions, see Michael C. Jensen,"Active Investors, LBOs, and the Privatization of Bankruptcy," 2 *J. Applied Corp. Fin.*, 35 (1989); Frank H. Easterbrook, "High-Yield Debt as an Incentive Device," 11 *Int'l Rev. L. & Econ.* 183 (1991). Once these changes have accomplished their goal of reforming corporate operations, many of these firms return to public ownership so that investors may avoid the risk of holding these undiversified blocks.

*Because assembling capital in large markets cuts down risk through diversification,
the cost is lower. We should therefore expect nations with more efficient capital
markets to have less concentration of ownership, and this is exactly what occurs.
Law appears to have little independent force.*

much capital with inefficient governance devices as with good ones—for the entrepreneurs themselves bear the cost of inefficiency in a lower price realized for stock—they choose whichever device has the lowest total costs. If public markets were inefficient, entrepreneurs would arrange for large blocks of stock, just as they grant powers of control to venture capitalists. Managers' incentives are in the long run aligned with investors' incentives.

No surprise, therefore, that even when banks, mutual funds, and insurers are allowed by law to increase the concentration of their holdings, they don't do so—not in the United States, and not in the United Kingdom, whose financial markets also are quite large and efficient. Capital is freely imported and exported, so financial markets in both countries are *world* markets. The United States and the United Kingdom have this in common even when the United Kingdom is experiencing one of its occasional bouts of socialism; and I think the two nations' similar financial structure is explained by this commonality in the markets rather than by legal differences. Put otherwise, the law of corporate finance is endogenous rather than exogenous; that is to say, current corporate law should be viewed more as the consequence of other forces than as the primary cause of corporate structure.

DEVELOPMENTS ABROAD

While efficient markets in the United States and United Kingdom allowed these developments, much of Europe and Asia was under corporative, fascist, or even feudal organization. Public markets were rare and inefficient. After World War II, revitalization took time, and many of the investments had to be large, producing concentrated holdings (much like the United States at the end of the 19th century) that take time to dissipate. Often markets were confined by law to a single country; and the market in Illinois (or France) is much less liquid than the market in the United States (or the European Union). The United States and England have large, efficient, internal markets and welcome capital from outside. This is not universally true; often politics works the other way (in Japan, banks got the upper hand and squelched trading markets); and as the size of the public market decreases, or outside capital is disfavored by the government, the debt-equity ratio and concentration of ownership must be higher to compensate. To be fair, I must acknowledge that Roe

discusses this possibility at page 185, for a single paragraph. But I think he dismisses it too quickly, without subjecting it to analysis or an empirical test (on which more below).

Let me put this in a different way. There are many substitute means of controlling the agency costs that arise from professional management and the separation of ownership from control. Concentrated holdings are one; forcing managers to return often to capital markets is another.

■ Greater concentration of ownership means that the firm has curtailed or forgone the ability to raise money in capital markets from diversified investors, a major loss. The large blockholder is taking undiversified risk, which requires compensation; and to deal with the risk the blockholder will monitor more closely, which also must be paid for. Other investors have to pay for these risk-bearing and monitoring services. Less concentration means that risk can be diversified away, liquidity increased, and the cost of capital lowered. As long as the agency costs of management do not rise by more than the savings from diversification, there is a social gain. There is on average less concentration in the United States than in the European Union, and costs of capital in United States are lower, which implies that there is a net gain. And there is a related point: a *really* large firm can't have concentrated total investment because no one has enough wealth, even if one person is willing to bear the risk. Concentration comes through financial intermediation, and the intermediary has the same problems the firm itself did.

■ Greater concentration *among equity investors* is not necessarily the same as greater concentration among all investors. One way to have votes concentrated, while reducing the total stake of the largest investor (and thus the undiversified risk-bearing that needs to be compensated), is to increase the debt-equity ratio. Take an extreme case: a firm with 99% debt and 1% equity can be controlled by a person holding 51% of the equity, or only 1/2% of the firm's capital. Some holding companies with pyramidal structures achieved such ratios but such companies generally have not survived in competition. Why? The "concentrated" equity owner can control management, but it is in his own interest to exploit debt investors *ex post* by increasing volatility. Debt investors know this and charge more for capital. Debt-heavy holding company structures lose out in competition with rivals that hire capital more cheaply. So too with nonvoting shares, which are functionally equivalent to debt (or preferred stock) with respect to their effect on control (that is, they leave control to someone else) but without the mandatory payout that for debt offsets the separation of control from the residual claim.

I suggested a decade ago[8] that the principal role of dividends is to force firms into capital markets. If companies pay money out, they have to raise it too. The need to raise money, rather than any formal "governance" device, is the principal constraint on managers—since they must pay the current price for money, reflecting the market's evaluation of their willingness and ability to pay investors. If the cost of money rises, the firm fails in its product markets; to avert this, managers repay investors and make credible promises of future controls.

Michael Jensen has made the same point about public debt[9]—and of course debt ordinarily entails a mandatory distribution, while dividends are optional (though there is a price to be paid for reducing or omitting them). One should say the same thing about bank debt. I suspect that, in the long run, most "governance" devices are insignificant compared to the discipline of capital markets. Unless they are planning to liquidate, firms need to raise money—if only from trade creditors, whose financing is often vital. To raise new money they must repay old money; otherwise promises are not believed. And *if* they can raise money at competitive prices in public markets, they don't need concentrated holdings, which create uncompensated risk.

One occasional response to an argument of this kind is that mature firms do not return to capital markets. This is not so. It confuses equity markets with capital markets. Mature firms raise capital all the time—from banks, from bondholders (debt is issued in series to require periodic payments and therefore periodic rollovers of debt), and in commercial paper markets. The institution of "commercial paper," essentially confined to mature firms, shows how managers find it in their interest to be in capital markets continually. Raising new money and repaying existing investors *at the same time* is puzzling until you see this function. Commercial paper has a short maturity (nine months or less), so firms that issue it are always under the scrutiny of capital markets, and small changes in risk bring perceptible

changes in interest rates. Even a few basis points are costly, and they catch other investors' eyes.

When managers raise new money, firms must pay the rate of return appropriate to their *current* strategies and risk. In a nation with large and efficient capital markets, this valuation is done on the fly, for new securities and existing ones. Efficiency means accurate valuation on average—and "accurate" compared not with an ideal but with alternatives such as discounted cash flow analysis, done by large blockholders who can't rely on trading markets. Cash flow analysis has high error rates indeed. Because assembling capital in large markets cuts down risk through diversification, the cost is lower. We should therefore expect nations with more efficient capital markets to have less concentration of ownership, and this is exactly what occurs. Law appears to have little independent force. The less efficient is the valuation process in charging managers with the true, current cost of capital, the more substitution toward banks or other block holdings. As the European Union becomes increasingly integrated, concentration among investors will fall.

This leads to a suggestion for an empirical test: examine the relation between ownership concentration and cost of capital. Average return on public investment (which is to say, the cost of capital) should fall as concentration of holdings falls. But I think that Mark Roe would predict the opposite: that when concentration is low, agency costs of management rise, and capital can be attracted only by higher returns to public investors.

ENABLING VS. REAL RULES OF LAW

So like Roe I think that history and culture matter; but I do think that these are aligned with, rather than opposed to, the economics of agency cost control. Indeed, I think that the influence of law on corporate governance and structure is far less in the United States than in Europe and Japan. Perhaps the courts play a larger role in the United States, in the course of enforcing contracts and fiduciary duties, but law plays less.

Corporate law in the United States is "enabling"—which is to say that it lets people do largely what they want in organizing, managing, and financing the firm. Europe and Japan are much more

---

8. Frank H. Easterbrook, "Two Agency-Cost Explanations of Dividends," *Am. Econ. Rev.* 74, 650-59 (1984).

9. Michael Jensen, "Agency Costs of Free Cash Flow, Corporate Finance and Takeovers," *Am. Econ. Rev.* 76, 323-29 (1986).

When markets are less efficient, some substitute must be found. Thus we have greater bank roles in nations with less extensive capital markets—and, as the European Union's company directives show, we have more law, too. European corporate law is today about as meddlesome and directory as U.S. law in the late 19th century, before U.S. capital markets became efficient.

directory. There are rules, which people must follow even if everyone would prefer to do things differently. Even the features of United States law that look prescriptive—for example, the regulation of securities—have little to do with corporate governance. Firms must make disclosures when issuing stock, but the shares can carry most any *substantive* rights people can dream up, and they sell for whatever price investors are willing to pay. Even the vaunted "fiduciary duty" of managers is just a matter of enforcing agreements. If the manager writes himself a bonus check, that's fine; if he takes the same amount without authorization, that's theft; the difference is approval by authorized corporate actors, not any decision of the state. Fiduciary duty means keeping one's promises. Courts in the United States sometimes try to interpolate terms into incomplete contracts, but they do this to achieve what parties would have bargained for had they thought about the question.[10] Courts almost never fail to enforce terms actually bargained for. When they try to do more, they generally fail.[11]

By contrast to the enabling structure of United States corporate governance, the European Union and its constituent member states use real rules of law. If in the United States you want to create a firm in which one person contributes capital and the other labor, and they get equal amounts of stock, that's fine. If in the European Union you want to do this, you can't; the Second Directive forbids the issuance of stock in exchange for a promise to perform services. If investors in the United States want to authorize their firm to sell new stock to outsiders without first offering it to insiders, that's fine. In the European Union, they can't do so; preemptive rights are mandatory.[12] Now preemptive rights help guard against dilution, so investors could benefit from them—though, given the differences among firms, *universal* preemptive rights are surely a bad idea. My point here, though, is not to debate the wisdom of preemptive rights, but rather to note that in Europe they are achieved by law, and in the

United States they are achieved, if at all, by contract. In the United States equity investors have no right to dividends; a firm can go from cradle to grave without issuing them, and investors cannot force dissolution to get at undistributed profits. In the European Union, according to the Fourth Directive, firms must announce anticipated dividends and adhere to these schedules, and compulsory dissolution is available.

Devices such as these in the European Union affect markets, too. Because firms cannot create and offer the full menu of devices, some risk-return combinations will be missing from the trading markets. As a consequence, the markets will be less efficient—and the lack of efficiency makes them less liquid (and still less efficient) by inducing substitution toward large blocks.

Firms make many promises in the United States, and courts enforce them, while law in the European Union is more bureaucratic. This explains my paradoxical statement that the United States relies more on courts but less on law. Good thing, too! For judges are just bureaucrats with general portfolios. Bureaucrats have poor information and worse incentives—they have their own agendas and do not share in the firm's profits and losses. Just so with judges. Even the Chancery Court of Delaware, our greatest corporate tribunal, mixes corporate mergers with divorces and child-custody cases. Few judges are chosen for business expertise, and none are fired for poor decisions. Professor Jensen thinks that managers' profit share of 0.3% in the United States is too low to align incentives properly;[13] judges' share is 0.0%. Interest-alignment devices thought essential to make corporations work, when applied to judges, are called bribes.

On the other hand, judges can enforce contracts. For then the investors and managers themselves lay down the rules. Judges serve as neutral umpires, enforcing the contracts without regard to who gains and loses in a particular case. The contents of the contracts, however, come from competition in financial markets, rather than from law.

10. See Frank H. Easterbrook & Daniel R. Fischel, "Contract and Fiduciary Duty," *J.L. & Econ.* 36, 425-46 (1993); see also John H. Langbein, "The Contractarian Basis of the Law of Trusts," 105 *Yale L.J.* 625, 657-69 (1995).

11. Litigation designed to improve the managers' fidelity often depresses stock prices; courts' inability to separate good from bad management, coupled with the risk aversion of managers, leads to settlements that do not respect the probable merit of the claim. See Janet Cooper Alexander, "Do the Merits Matter? A Study of Settlements in Securities Class Actions," 43 *Stan. L. Rev.* 497 (1991). See also Reinier Kraakman, Hyun Park & Steven Shavell, "When are Shareholder Suits in Shareholder Interests?," 82 *Geo. L.J.* 1733 (1994); Janet Cooper Alexander, "The Value of Bad News in Securities Class Actions," 41 *UCLA L. Rev.* 1421 (1994); Roberta

Romano, "The Shareholder Suit: Litigation Without Foundation?," 7 *J.L. Econ. & Org.* 55 (1991); Mark L. Cross, Wallace N. Davidson & John H. Thornton, "The Impact of Directors' and Officers' Liability Suits on Firm Value," 56 *J. Risk & Insurance* 128 (1989); Daniel R. Fischel & Michael Bradley, "The Role of Liability Rules and the Derivative Suit in Corporate Law: A Theoretical and Empirical Analysis," 71 *Cornell L. Rev.* 261 (1986). But see Joel Seligman, "The Merits Do Matter," 108 *Harv. L. Rev.* 438 (1994).

12. William J. Carney, "The Political Economy of Competition for Corporate Charters," supra note 3, canvasses many of these details.

13. Michael Jensen, "Performance Pay and Top Management Incentives," 98 *J. Pol. Econ.* 225 (1990).

Markets are costly and imperfect, but they beat the political process every time. And the more efficient financial markets are, the better competition among entrepreneurs works. This is a point Jensen and Meckling made a generation ago.[14] Entrepreneurs make promises to investors. If these promises are not optimal from investors' perspective, then investors pay less and the entrepreneurs themselves bear the costs of suboptimality. Of course, this mechanism depends on investors being able to evaluate the promises made to them. When capital markets are efficient, the valuation process works better; when markets are less efficient, some substitute must be found—law, perhaps, or the valuation procedures of banks. Thus we have greater bank roles in nations with less extensive capital markets—and, as the European Union's company directives show, we have more law, too. European corporate law is today about as meddlesome and directory as United States law was in the late 19th century, before U.S. capital markets became efficient.

What would *really* be nice is for Europe and Japan to abolish their meddlesome restrictions on corporations and financial markets, while the United States abolishes its meddlesome restrictions on banks and other financial intermediaries, and everyone abolishes meddlesome restrictions on trans-border investments. Then we might see where competition takes us. On this subject, Mark Roe and I agree wholeheartedly, but we both know it won't happen—too many interest groups.

One may ask how corporate law came to be enabling rather than directory in the United States. The answer lies in competition among jurisdictions—still another form of investor protection. States that tried inefficient regulation would drive capital and corporate structures out of their jurisdictions. Ease of movement within the large United States market made this possible. So states lost the ability to do substantial injury. Could they do good? Well, they could be more hospitable to competition, and the structure of federalism in the United States made this possible. Courts restricted states' ability to discriminate against corporations that had their headquarters in other states. Firms could move their charters without moving their operations—quite unlike the "real seat" doctrine in Europe, which was created by France in the 19th century to block competition from England! And it happened that Delaware was small enough to make a binding *commitment* to have an efficient law. It gathers about 20% of the state budget from corporate charter fees, a bond of good faith toward corporations that lack votes in the legislature. No surprise when the head of the committee that drafted the most recent version of the Delaware Code became Chief Justice of Delaware.

To sum up: international differences in corporate governance are attributable more to differences in markets than to differences in law. Law is an output of this process, not an input. When financial markets are more efficient and interjurisdictional competition blooms, there will be less law and more investor protection at the same time.

---

14. Michael Jensen & William Meckling, "Theory of the Firm: Managerial Behavior, Agency Costs and Ownership Structure," *J. Fin. Econ.* 3, 305-60 (1976).

THE STATE OF U.S. CORPORATE GOVERNANCE: WHAT'S RIGHT AND WHAT'S WRONG?

by Bengt Holmstrom,
Massachusetts Institute of Technology,
and
Steven N. Kaplan,
University of Chicago*

T o a casual observer, the United States corporate governance system must seem to be in terrible shape. The business press has focused relentlessly on the corporate board and governance failures at Enron, WorldCom, Tyco, Adelphia, Global Crossing, and others. Top executive compensation is also routinely criticized as excessive by the press, academics, and even top Federal Reserve officials.[1] These failures and concerns in turn have served as catalysts for legislative change—in the form of the Sarbanes-Oxley Act of 2002—and regulatory change, including new governance guidelines from the NYSE and NASDAQ.

The turmoil and the responses to it suggest two important questions that we attempt to answer in this article. First, has the U.S. corporate governance system performed that poorly—is it really that bad? Second, will the proposed changes lead to a more effective system?

In addressing the first question, we begin by examining two broad measures of economic performance for evidence of failure of the U.S. system. Despite the alleged flaws in its governance system, the U.S. economy has performed very well, both on an absolute basis and particularly relative to other countries. U.S. productivity gains in the past decade have been exceptional, and the U.S. stock market has consistently outperformed other world indices over the last two decades, including the period since the scandals broke. In other words, the broad evidence is not consistent with a failed U.S. system. If anything, it suggests a system that is well above average.

Next, we discuss how important aspects of the U.S. corporate governance system have evolved over the last two decades and the implications of those changes. Again, contrary to the popular impression, the major changes in U.S. corporate governance in the past 20 years— notably, the dramatic increase in equity-based pay and the institutionalization of U.S. shareholders—appear to have been positive overall. As we discuss below, such changes played a central role in the highly productive restructuring of U.S. corporations that took place during the 1980s and 1990s. But the changes did have an unfortunate side effect. Besides spurring productivity improvements, the rise of equity-based pay—particularly the explosion of stock options—and the run-up in stock prices in the late '90s created incentives for the shortsighted and at times illegal managerial behavior that has attracted so much criticism. Our view, however, is that the costs associated with such incentives and behavior have been far outweighed by the benefits.

Having addressed where the U.S. system is today and how it got there, we finally consider the probable near-term effects of the legislative, regulatory, and market responses to the perceived governance "problem." We conclude that the current changes are likely to make a good U.S. system a better one, although not without imposing some unnecessary costs. In fact, the greatest risk now facing the U.S. corporate governance system is the possibility of overregulation.

---

*Warren Batts, Don Chew, Art Kelly, Rick Melcher, Andrew Nussbaum, and Per Stromberg provided helpful comments. Address correspondence to Steven Kaplan, Graduate School of Business, The University of Chicago, 1101 East 58th Street, Chicago, IL 60637 or e-mail at steven.kaplan@gsb.uchicago.edu. Part of this article draws on our earlier article, "Corporate Governance and Takeovers in the U.S.: Making Sense of the '80s and '90s," *Journal of Economic Perspectives* (Spring 2001), pp. 121-144.

1. For example, see Marco Becht, Patrick Bolton, and Ailsa Roell, "Corporate Governance and Control," in *Handbook of Economics and Finance*, G. Constantinides, M. Harris, and R. Stulz, eds. (North Holland, 2002), "CEOs Are Overpaid, Says Fed Banker," *The Washington Post*, September 11, 2002, and "After 10 Years, Corporate Oversight Is Still Dismal," by Claudia Deutsch, *The New York Times*, January 26, 2003.

TABLE 1		U.S.		Europe	Pacific
STOCK MARKET PERFORMANCE*	From 1982 (January)	1,222%		1,145%	276%
	From 1987	436%		266%	3%
	From 1992	164%		113%	−27%
	From 1997	28%		13%	−39%
	From 2001	−32%		−34%	−32%

	U.S.	Great Britain	France	Germany	Japan
From 1982	1,222%	1,223%	1,567%	595%	90%
From 1987	436%	290%	236%	93%	−37%
From 1992	164%	121%	147%	84%	−42%
From 1997	28%	11%	47%	5%	−39%
From 2001	−32%	−32%	−45%	−53%	−34%

*Stock returns reported by Ibbotson Associates for total return on Morgan Stanley Capital International (MSCI) Indices for the United States, Europe, Pacific, Great Britain, France, Germany, and Japan from January 1 of the given year through the end of December 2002.

HOW BAD IS U.S. CORPORATE GOVERNANCE?

Given the volume and intensity of criticism of U.S. corporate governance, one would think that the U.S. stock market must have performed quite badly, particularly since the scandals broke in 2001. But the data summarized in Table 1 indicate otherwise. Table 1 reports the total returns (measured in dollars) to the Morgan Stanley Capital International indices for the aggregate U.S., European, and Pacific stock markets over five different time periods through the end of 2002. Although the U.S. stock market has had negative returns over the last several years, it has performed well relative to other stock markets, both recently and over the longer term. In fact, the U.S. market has generated returns at least as high as those of the European and Pacific markets during each of the five time periods considered—since 2001, since 1997, since 1992, since 1987, and since 1982. The returns to the U.S. stock market also compare favorably to the returns to the stock markets of the larger individual countries (including France, Germany, Great Britain, and Japan) that make up the indices.

Because many factors affect stock returns, it would be inappropriate to claim that superior U.S. corporate governance explains the differences in returns. We can conclude, however, that whatever the shortcomings of the U.S. system, they have not been sufficiently great to prevent the stock returns of U.S. companies from outperforming those of the rest of the world.

It is worth pointing out two additional implications of the stock performance results. First, the returns to U.S. stocks have been at least as large as the returns to European and Pacific stocks since 2001, the period in which the U.S. corporate governance scandals first emerged. One possible explanation is that the effects of the governance scandals on U.S. stock values have not been particularly large relative to other factors that have weighed on most national economies. Another possibility is that while there may be some problems with the U.S. corporate governance system, the problems confronting the governance systems of other nations are even worse. But in our view, the most plausible explanation is that while parts of the U.S. system failed under the exceptional strain of the 1990s' boom market, the damage was limited because the overall system reacted quickly to address the problems.

The second important point to keep in mind about stock returns is that they reflect publicly available information about executive compensation. Returns, therefore, are measured *net* of executive compensation payments. The fact that the shareholders of U.S. companies earned higher returns *even after* payments to management does not support the claim that the U.S. executive pay system is designed inefficiently; if anything, shareholders appear better off with the U.S. system of executive pay than with the systems that prevail in other countries. As we discuss later, however, the higher U.S. returns do not rule out the possibility that some

TABLE 2		U.S.	Great Britain	France	Germany	Japan
CHANGES IN REAL GDP PER CAPITA*	From 1982 (beginning) to 2000	54%	58%	37%	44%	55%
	From 1987 to 2000	38%	36%	28%	29%	36%
	From 1992 to 2000	29%	24%	12%	12%	8%
	From 1997 to 2000	14%	11%	11%	8%	3%

*Changes in real GDP per capita for the U.S., Great Britain, France, Germany, and Japan. Calculated using the Penn World Tables.

top U.S. executives are paid more than is necessary for incentive purposes and that our incentive pay system can be improved.

Overall country productivity provides another broad measure of performance. Again, one might expect a less effective corporate governance system to lead to lower productivity growth. Table 2 presents calculations of the percentage change in GDP per capita for developed countries since 1982. The results do not suggest the presence of an ineffective U.S. governance system. From the beginning of 1992 to the end of 2000,[2] growth in GDP per capita was greater in the U.S. than in France, Germany, Great Britain, or Japan. And given the strong U.S. productivity numbers through the recent downturn, this gap has probably widened since then.

Again, these results do not necessarily demonstrate that the U.S. corporate governance system is the principal cause of the larger productivity improvements. Many other forces operate at the same time. The results do suggest, however, that any deficiencies in the U.S. corporate governance system have not prevented the U.S. economy from outperforming its global competitors.

CHANGES IN U.S. CORPORATE GOVERNANCE OVER THE LAST 20 YEARS

Corporate governance in the U.S. has changed dramatically since 1980.[3] As a number of business and finance scholars have pointed out, the corporate governance structures in place before the 1980s gave the managers of large public U.S. corporations little reason to make shareholder interests their primary focus. Before 1980, corporate managements tended to think of themselves as representing not the shareholders, but rather "the corporation." In this view, the goal of the firm was not to maximize shareholder wealth, but to ensure the growth (or at least the stability) of the enterprise by "balancing" the claims of all important corporate "stakeholders"—employees, suppliers, and local communities, as well as shareholders.[4]

The external governance mechanisms available to dissatisfied shareholders were seldom used. Raiders and hostile takeovers were relatively uncommon. Proxy fights were rare and didn't have much chance of succeeding. And corporate boards tended to be cozy with and dominated by management, making board oversight weak.

Internal incentives from management ownership of stock and options were also modest. For example, in 1980 only 20% of the compensation of U.S. CEOs was tied to stock market performance.[5] Long-term performance plans were widely used, but they were typically based on accounting measures like sales growth and earnings per share that tied managerial incentives less directly, and sometimes not at all, to shareholder value.

Partly in response to the neglect of shareholders, the 1980s ushered in a large wave of takeover and restructuring activity. This activity was distinguished by its use of hostility and aggressive leverage. The 1980s saw the emergence of the corporate raider and hostile takeovers. Raiders like Carl Icahn and T. Boone Pickens became household names. Nearly half of all major U.S. corporations received a takeover offer in the 1980s—and many companies that were not taken over responded to hostile

2. This is the most recent period for which data are available.
3. This section summarizes some of the arguments in Bengt Holmstrom and Steven Kaplan, "Corporate Governance and Takeovers in the U.S.: Making Sense of the '80s and '90s," *Journal of Economic Perspectives* (Spring 2001), pp. 121-144, and Steven Kaplan, "The Evolution of U.S. Corporate Governance: We Are All Henry Kravis Now," *Journal of Private Equity*, pp. 7-14 (1997).

4. See Gordon Donaldson and Jay Lorsch, *Decision Making at the Top* (Basic Books, New York, 1983), and Michael Jensen, "The Modern Industrial Revolution," *Journal of Finance*, pp. 831-880 (1993).
5. See Brian Hall and Jeffrey Liebman, "Are CEOs Really Paid like Bureaucrats?," *Quarterly Journal of Economics*, Vol. 112 (1998), pp. 653-691.

pressure with internal restructurings that made themselves less attractive targets.[6]

The use of debt financing by U.S. companies was so extensive that, from 1984 to 1990, more than $500 billion of equity was retired (net of new equity issuances), as many firms repurchased their own shares, borrowed to finance takeovers, or were taken private in leveraged buyouts (LBOs). As a result, corporate leverage ratios increased substantially. Leveraged buyouts were extreme in this respect, with debt levels typically exceeding 80% of total capital.

In the 1990s, the pattern of corporate governance activity changed again. After a steep but brief drop in merger activity around 1990, takeovers rebounded to the levels of the 1980s. Hostility and leverage, however, declined substantially. At the same time, other corporate governance mechanisms began to play a larger role, particularly executive stock options and the greater involvement of boards of directors and shareholders.

The preponderance of the evidence is consistent with an overall explanation as follows: In the early 1980s, the wedge between actual and potential corporate performance became increasingly apparent. In some cases, changes in markets, technology, or regulation led to a large amount of excess capacity—for example, in the oil and tire industries. In others, it became apparent that diversification strategies carried out in the late '60s and '70s were underperforming.[7] The top managers of such companies, however, were slow to respond to opportunities to increase value. As mentioned above, limited ownership of stock and options gave managers little monetary incentive to make major changes that might weaken their "partnership" with other corporate stakeholders. But perhaps equally important, some corporate leaders persisted in their conviction that growth and stability were the "right" corporate goals and they simply refused to believe what the capital markets were telling them. This appears to have been true, for example, of the U.S. oil industry in the early 1980s, when oil companies traded below the value of their oil holdings because of industry-wide overinvestment in exploration.

At the same time that many U.S. companies were failing to maximize value, the U.S. capital markets were becoming more powerful because of increased stock ownership by large institutions. It was the potential for improved corporate performance, combined with the increased ownership of institutional investors, that gave birth to the takeovers, junk bonds, and LBOs of the 1980s. In some cases, the capital markets reversed ill-advised diversification through "bust-up" transactions (such as KKR's acquisition of Beatrice Foods in 1986). In other cases, the financial markets effectively forced managers to eliminate excess capacity (as in Chevron's leveraged acquisition of Gulf Oil in 1984). More generally, the capital markets disciplined managers who had ignored shareholders for the benefit of themselves and other stakeholders. As we discuss below, the incentive and governance features of LBOs are particularly representative of the discipline that the capital markets imposed.

The initial response of U.S. executives was to fight takeovers with legal maneuvers and to attempt to enlist political and popular support against corporate raiders. Over time, these efforts met with some legislative, regulatory, and judicial success. As a result, hostile takeovers became far more costly in the 1990s than in the previous decade.

But the accomplishments of the 1980s were by no means forgotten. By the 1990s, U.S. managers, boards, and institutional shareholders had seen what LBOs and other market-driven restructurings could do. With the implicit assent of institutional investors, boards substantially increased the use of stock option plans that allowed managers to share in the value created by restructuring their own companies. Shareholder value thus became an ally rather than a threat.

This general embrace of shareholder value helps to explain why restructurings continued at a high rate in the 1990s, but for the most part on amicable terms. There was also less of a need for high leverage because deals could now be paid for with stock without raising investors' concerns that managers would pursue their own objectives at the expense of shareholders.

The merger wave of the 1990s also appears to have had a somewhat different purpose than the wave of the 1980s, representing a different stage in the overall restructuring process. The deals of the

---

6. See Mark Mitchell and Harold Mulherin, "The Impact of Industry Shocks on Takeover and Restructuring Activity," *Journal of Financial Economics*, pp. 193-229 (1996).

7. See Jensen (1993), cited earlier, and Andrei Shleifer and Robert Vishny, "The Takeover Wave of the 1980s," *Science*, Vol. 249 (1990), pp. 745-749.

> **Whatever the shortcomings of the U.S. system of governance, they have not been sufficiently great to prevent the stock returns of U.S. companies from outperforming those of the rest of the world.**

1980s were more of a bust-up wave whose main effect was to force corporate assets out of the hands of managers who could not or would not use them efficiently. The transactions of the 1990s, by contrast, had more of a "build-up" effect in which assets were reconfigured to take advantage of growth opportunities in new technologies and markets. This logic also fits with the increased use of equity rather than debt in funding the deals of the 1990s.

The move toward shareholder value and increased capital market influence has also been apparent in the way corporations have reorganized themselves. For example, there has been a broad trend toward decentralization. Large companies have been working hard to become more nimble and to find ways to offer employees higher-powered incentives. At the same time, external capital markets have taken on a larger role in capital reallocation, as evidenced by the large volume of mergers and divestitures throughout the '90s. During the same period, the amounts of funds raised and invested by U.S. venture capitalists—who help perform the key economic function of transferring funds from mature to new high-growth industries—also increased by an order of magnitude over the 1990s.[8]

In sum, while corporate managers still reallocate vast amounts of resources in the economy through internal capital and labor markets, the boundary between markets and managers appears to have shifted. As managers have ceded authority to the markets, the scope and independence of their decision-making have narrowed.

We now focus more specifically on changes in three key elements of the U.S. (and indeed any) corporate governance system: executive compensation, shareholders, and boards of directors.

Changes in Executive Compensation

The total pay of top U.S. executives, particularly option-based compensation, has increased substantially over the last two decades. For example, a study published in the late '90s reported that during the 15-year period from 1980 to 1994, the average compensation of CEOs of large U.S. companies tripled in real terms. The study also concluded that the average annual CEO option grant (valued at issuance) increased roughly sevenfold and, as a result, equity-based compensation in 1994 made up almost 50% of total CEO compensation (up from less than 20% in 1980).[9] Moreover, as reported in a more recent study, this trend continued from 1994 to 2001, with CEO pay more than doubling and option-based compensation increasing at an even faster rate.[10]

Overall, then, CEO compensation appears to have increased by a factor of six over the last two decades, with a disproportionate increase in equity-based compensation. The effect of the increase in equity-based compensation has been to increase CEO pay-to-performance sensitivities by a factor of more than ten times from 1980 to 1999.[11]

These increases in executive compensation, particularly options, have generated enormous controversy. The recent scandals and stock market declines have led some observers to argue that such increases represent unmerited transfers of shareholder wealth to top executives with limited if any beneficial incentive effects. For example, one recent survey of corporate governance concludes: "It is widely recognized...that these options are at best an inefficient financial incentive and at worst create new incentive or conflict-of-interest problems of their own."[12]

There are several reasons to be skeptical of these conclusions. First, as we have already pointed out, the performance of the U.S. stock market and the strong growth in U.S. productivity provide no support for such arguments.

Second, the primary effect of the large shift to equity-based compensation has been to align the interests of CEOs and their management teams with shareholders' interests to a much greater extent than in the past. Large stock option grants fundamentally changed the mind-set of CEOs and made them much more receptive to value-increasing transactions. The tenfold increase in pay-for-performance sensitivities

---

8. See Raghu Rajan and Julie Wulf, "The Flattening Firm," Working paper, University of Chicago (2002), and Paul Gompers and Josh Lerner, "The Venture Capital Revolution," *Journal of Economic Perspectives*, pp. 145-168 (2001).

9. Hall and Liebman (1998), cited earlier.

10. See Brian Hall and Kevin Murphy, "Stock Options for Undiversified Executives," *Journal of Accounting and Economics*, pp. 3-42 (2002) and Brian Hall, "Six Challenges in Designing Equity-Based Pay," in this issue of the *JACF*.

11. The levels of executive compensation and managerial equity ownership appear to be high not only relative to 1980, but also relative to earlier periods. One study compares equity ownership by officers and directors in 1935 and 1995 and finds that equity ownership was substantially greater in 1995 than in 1935; see Cliff Holderness, Randall Kroszner, and Dennis Sheehan, "Were the Good Old Days That Good? Changes in Managerial Stock Ownership Since the Great Depression," *Journal of Finance*, pp. 435-470 (1999).

12. See Becht, Bolton, and Roell (2002), cited earlier. See also Lucian Bebchuk, Jesse Fried, and David Walker, "Managerial Power and Rent Extraction in the Design of Executive Compensation," *University of Chicago Law Review*, pp. 751-846 (2002).

implies that a one dollar increase in a company's stock price was ten times more valuable to a CEO at the end of the 1990s than at the beginning of the 1980s. As we noted earlier, this shift played a significant role in the continued restructuring of corporations in the 1990s.[13] It also helps explain the 1997 decision of the Business Roundtable—a group of 200 CEOs of the largest American companies—to change its position on business objectives (after years of opposition and ambivalence to shareholder value) to read "the paramount duty of management and the board is to the shareholder and not to...other stakeholders."

A third reason to be skeptical of the criticism of U.S. top executive pay practices is that both buyout investors and venture capital investors have made, and continue to make, substantial use of equity-based and option compensation in the firms they invest in. A 1989 study by one of the authors reported that the CEOs of companies taken private in LBOs increased their ownership stake by more than a factor of four, from an average of 1.4% before the LBO to 6.4% after. The study also found that management teams as a whole typically obtained 10% to 20% of the post-buyout equity.[14] More recent research and anecdotal evidence suggest that such levels of managerial equity ownership are still typical in today's buyout transactions.[15]

This feature of LBOs is particularly notable. LBO sponsor firms such as KKR, Texas Pacific Group, and Thomas Lee typically buy majority control of the companies they invest in through the partnerships that the sponsors manage. The individual partners of the LBO sponsors have strong incentives to make profitable investments since the sponsors typically receive 20% of the profits of a particular buyout partnership, and the sponsors' ability to raise other funds is strongly related to the performance of their existing investments.[16] And the fact that such sponsors also insist on providing the managers of their companies with high-powered incentives suggests that incentives have been a critical ingredient in the success of LBOs.

Two other aspects of compensation contracts designed by LBO sponsors for the top executives of their portfolio companies are worth mentioning. First, the equity and options held by those top executives are typically illiquid—usually by necessity because most of the companies are private—unless and until the company has clearly succeeded through an IPO or a sale to another company. This means that top management cannot trade in and out of the stock (nor can it easily hedge its positions). Second, neither LBO sponsors nor venture capitalists typically index the executive compensation contracts they employ to industry performance or market performance. If non-indexed options and equity grants were so inefficient, as critics of executive compensation have argued, we would expect to see more indexing of private equity contracts.

Unfortunately, while the greater use of stock-based compensation has likely been a positive development overall, critics of the U.S. governance system are correct in pointing out that higher-powered incentives have not come without costs.[17] First, as executive stock and option ownership has increased, so has the incentive to manage and manipulate accounting numbers in order to inflate stock market values and sell shares at those inflated values.[18] This arguably was important in the cases of Global Crossing and WorldCom, among others.

Second, and related to the first, much of the compensation of top U.S. executives is fairly liquid—and, as we argue below, considerably more liquid than shareholders would like it to be. Unlike LBO sponsors, boards do not put strong restrictions on the ability of top executives to unwind their equity-based compensation by exercising options, selling shares, or using derivatives to hedge their positions. And finding a workable solution to the problem of optimal liquidity for top executive compensation is an important challenge faced by today's boards.

13. For additional evidence consistent with this conclusion, see John Core and David Larcker, "Performance Consequences of Mandatory Increases in Executive Stock Ownership," *Journal of Financial Economics* (2002), who find that option grants or increases in equity ownership are related to improvements in stock and accounting performance.

14. See Steven Kaplan, "The Effects of Management Buyouts on Operations and Value," *Journal of Financial Economics*, pp. 217-254 (1989).

15. P. Rogers, T. Holland, and D. Haas, "Value Acceleration: Lessons from Private-Equity Masters," *Harvard Business Review* (June 2002).

16. See Steven Kaplan and Antoinette Schoar, "Private Equity Returns: Persistence and Capital Flows," Working paper, University of Chicago (December 2002).

17. Other critiques are offered in Lucien Bebchuk, Jesse Fried, and David Walker, "Managerial Power and Rent Extraction in the Design of Executive Compensation," *University of Chicago Law Review*, Vol. 69 (2002), pp. 751-846; Becht, Bolton, and Roell (2002) cited earlier; Brian Hall, "Equity-Pay Design for Executives," Working paper, Harvard Business School (2002); and Tod Perry and Marc Zenner, "CEO Compensation in the 1990s: Shareholder Alignment or Shareholder Expropriation?," *Wake Forest Law Review* (2001).

18. See Jeremy Stein, "Efficient Capital Markets, Inefficient Firms: A Model of Myopic Corporate Behavior," *Quarterly Journal of Economics*, Vol. 104 (1989), pp. 655-669 for a model explaining this behavior. See also Joseph Fuller and Michael Jensen, "Just Say No to Wall Street," *Journal of Applied Corporate Finance*, Vol. 14, No. 4 (2002).

> The corporate governance structures in place before the 1980s gave the managers of large public U.S. corporations little reason to make shareholder interests their primary focus... Since the mid-1980s, the American style of corporate governance has reinvented itself and the rest of the world seems to be following the U.S. lead.

Third, most options are issued at the money because accounting rules do not require the cost of such options to be expensed. It is plausible that because the cost of the options does not appear as an expense, some boards of directors underestimate the cost of an option grant. It is undeniable that the size of some of the option grants has been far greater than what is necessary to retain and motivate the CEOs. In 2001, for example, the ten most highly rewarded CEOs in the S&P 500 were granted option packages with an estimated average value (at time of grant) of $170 million per person. Even if some of these grants represent multiyear awards, the amounts are still staggering. It is particularly disconcerting that among the executives receiving the largest grants in the past three years, several already owned large amounts of stock, including Larry Ellison of Oracle, Tom Siebel of Siebel Systems, and Steve Jobs of Apple. It is hard to argue that these people need stronger shareholder incentives. An obvious explanation is that they have been able to use their positions of power to command excessive awards.

Even so, it would be a mistake to condemn the entire system based on a few cases. That such cases are far from representative can be seen from the pronounced skew in the distribution of CEO incomes. In 2001, for example, the same year the top ten U.S. CEOs received average option grants of $170 million, the median value of total compensation for CEOs of S&P 500 companies was about $7 million. Thus, U.S. executive pay may not be quite the runaway train that has been portrayed in the press.[19]

Changes in Shareholders

As mentioned above, the composition of U.S. shareholders also has changed significantly over the past two decades. Large institutional investors own an increasingly large share of the overall stock market. For example, from 1980 to 1996, large institutional investors nearly doubled their share of ownership of U.S. corporations from less than 30% to more than 50%. (Conversely, individual owner-ship declined from 70% in 1970 to 60% in 1980 and to 48% in 1994.[20])

There are at least two reasons public company shareholders are likely to monitor management more effectively today than in the 1980s. First, the large increase in the shareholdings of institutional investors means that professional investors—who have strong incentives to generate greater stock returns and are presumably more sophisticated—own an increasingly large fraction of U.S. corporations.

Second, in 1992 the SEC substantially reduced the costs to shareholders of challenging management teams. Under the old rules, a shareholder had to file a detailed proxy statement with the SEC before talking to more than ten other shareholders. Under the new rules, shareholders can essentially communicate at any time and in any way as long as they send a copy of the substance of the communication to the SEC afterward. The rule change has lowered the cost of coordinating shareholder actions and blocking management proposals. (Not surprisingly, the Business Roundtable and other management organizations were extremely hostile to this rule change when it was proposed.)

Consistent with these two changes, shareholder activism has increased in the U.S. since the late 1980s. The evidence on the impact of such activism, however, is mixed. For example, a 1998 summary of the results of 20 empirical studies of the effects of formal shareholder proposals and private negotiations with managements reported evidence of small or no effects on shareholder value.[21] When interpreting such evidence, however, it is important to keep in mind the difficulty of measuring the extent and effects of shareholder activity, in part because so much of this activity takes place behind the scenes and is not reported. And the fact that a recent study reported that stock returns over the period 1980-1996 were higher for companies with greater institutional ownership suggests that our large institutions may indeed be playing a valuable monitoring role—one that translates into higher stock prices.[22]

---

19. A part of the problem is that the press has traditionally reported the value of exercised options instead of the value of options at the time they have been granted. This is changing, too.

20. See Paul Gompers and Andrew Metrick, "Institutional Investors and Equity Prices, " *Quarterly Journal of Economics* (2001), and James Poterba and Andrew Samwick, "Stock Ownership Patterns, Stock Market Fluctuations, and Consumption," Brookings Papers on Economic Activity, pp. 295-357 (1995).

21. Jonathan Karpoff, "The Impact of Shareholder Activism on Target Companies: A Survey of Empirical Findings," Working paper, University of Washington (1998).

22. Paul Gompers and Andrew Metrick, "Institutional Investors and Equity Prices," *Quarterly Journal of Economics*, Vol. 116 (2001), pp. 229-260.

Changes in Boards of Directors

In an influential study of U.S. corporate boards in the second half of the 1980s, Jay Lorsch and Elizabeth MacIver pointed out a number of deficiencies and offered several recommendations. Chief among them were the following: (1) board selection by a nominating committee rather than the CEO; (2) more equity compensation for directors; and (3) more director control of board meetings through appointment of a lead director or outside chairman, annual CEO reviews, and regular sessions with outside directors only ("executive sessions").[23]

Since the publication of that study in 1989, the boards of U.S. companies have made progress in implementing all three of these recommendations. U.S. companies have significantly expanded the use of nominating committees and lead directors. Executive sessions are increasingly common (although, as suggested below, not as common as directors would like). Boards of U.S. companies now include a larger percentage of independent and outside directors, and have become somewhat smaller over time (smaller boards are thought to be more effective in disciplining CEOs and tend to be associated with higher valuations).[24] Also encouraging, directors today receive a significantly larger amount of their total compensation in the form of stock or options. For example, one study reported that stock-based directors' compensation increased from 25% in 1992 to 39% in 1995, and that trend has since continued.[25]

The CEO turnover process—one of the most widely used measures of the effectiveness of a governance system—suggests that the CEO labor market has become broader and, arguably, more efficient. One recent study of CEO turnover for large companies from 1971 to 1994 found a marked increase in both forced CEO departures and the hiring of new CEOs from outside the company. Within the study, the incidence of forced turnovers and outside succession was highest from 1989 to

1994,[26] a trend that also appears to have continued. The same study reported that CEO turnover was more sensitive to poor performance—as measured by reductions in operating income—during the 1989-1994 period than in earlier years.[27, 28]

On the negative side, however, anti-takeover measures such as poison pills and staggered boards have increased substantially in the past two decades. And recent research finds that during the 1990s, companies with a high level of anti-shareholder provisions experienced substantially lower returns than firms with a low level of such provisions.[29]

Despite the improvements noted above, the recent events at companies like Enron, Tyco, and WorldCom suggest that the boards of U.S. companies continue to exhibit less than the optimal amount of independence and oversight. The Senate report on Enron's board is particularly critical in this respect. When a company is not doing well, everyone pays close attention—lenders and investors as well as board members. But when a company appears to be doing well, as was the case with both Enron and Tyco, investors and the board are likely to be less critical.

A recent survey of more than 2,000 directors by Korn Ferry in early 2002 (and thus before the passage of Sarbanes-Oxley and the issuance of the new NYSE and NASDAQ regulations) is very interesting in this regard. The directors who responded to the survey consistently favored more monitoring than was the practice on the boards on which they served. For example, although 71% of the directors said they believed boards should hold executive sessions without the CEO, only 45% said their boards actually did so. And whereas almost 60% felt their boards should have a lead director, only 37% reported that their boards had one.

Our bottom line on boards, then, is that the structure and operating procedures of U.S. corporate boards have improved since the 1980s, but they are still far from perfect.

23. Jay Lorsch and Elizabeth MacIver, *Pawns or Potentates* (Harvard Business School Press, 1989).

24. See David Yermack, "Higher Market Valuation of Companies with a Small Board of Directors," *Journal of Financial Economics*, Vol. 40 (1996), pp. 185-202.

25. For a summary of these changes, see Ben Hermalin and Michael Weisbach, "Boards of Directors as an Endogenously Determined Institution: A Survey of the Economic Literature," *Economic Policy Review* (2003).

26. See M. Huson, Robert Parrino, and Laura Starks, "Internal Monitoring Mechanisms and CEO Turnover: A Long-Term Perspective," *Journal of Finance*, pp. 2265-2297 (2001).

27. On the other hand, research shows that CEO turnover is less sensitive to industry-adjusted stock performance from 1990 to 1995 than in earlier years; see

Kevin J. Murphy, "Executive Compensation," in O. Ashenfelter and D. Card (eds.), *Handbook of Labor Economics* (North Holland, 1999), pp. 2485-2525.

28. Rakesh Khurana in *Searching for a Corporate Savior: The Irrational Quest for Charismatic CEOs* (Princeton University Press, 2002) has argued that the CEO labor market is flawed because it is overly focused on outsider, charismatic CEOs. The operating performance evidence in Rakesh Khurana and Nitin Nohria, "The Effects of CEO Turnover in Large Industrial Corporations: A Study of the *Fortune* 200 from 1978-1993," Harvard Business School (1997), however, is not consistent with such a conclusion.

29. Paul Gompers, Joy Ishi, and Andrew Metrick, "Corporate Governance and Equity Prices," Working Paper 8449, NBER, 2001.

> While the greater use of stock-based compensation has been a positive development
> overall, critics of the U.S. governance system are correct in pointing out that
> higher-powered incentives have not come without costs.

International Developments

Indirect evidence of the effectiveness of the U.S. governance system is provided by changes in corporate governance in other countries. In recent years, as the forces of deregulation, globalization, and information technology have continued to sweep across the world economy, other countries have begun to move toward the U.S. model. Traditionally, European and Japanese firms have reallocated capital from sunset industries to sunrise industries mainly through internal diversification. External market interventions of the sort seen in the U.S. were almost unheard of. In the late 1990s, however, Europe experienced a sudden rise in hostile takeovers. In 1999 alone, 34 listed companies in Continental Europe received hostile bids, representing a total value of $406 billion (as compared to 52 bids for just $69 billion over the entire period 1990-1998).[30] These transactions included Vodafone's bid for Mannesmann, TotalFina's bid for Elf Aquitaine, and Olivetti's bid for Telecom Italia.

Shareholder activism has also been on the rise, with strong support from American institutional investors. For example, Telecom Italia's attempt to split off its wireless unit (at an unacceptable price) was blocked when TIAA-CREF put pressure on the Italian government. In France, shareholder activists managed to defeat a poison-pill proposal by Rhone-Poulenc. European universal banks also have begun to pay more attention to the value of their financial stakes than to their positions of power. These actions appear to have been very much influenced by the U.S. model of market intervention and by the fact that more than $1 trillion of U.S. funds has been invested in Western Europe in the 1980s and 1990s.

Another way in which companies can make use of the market to reallocate capital more effectively is to repurchase their own shares. In the last several years, Japan, France, Germany, and several other countries have relaxed prohibitions or restrictions on share repurchases, and companies in those countries have responded by buying back increasing numbers of shares. Finally, the use of stock options for executives and boards is increasing around the world. Japan recently eliminated a substantial tax

penalty on executive stock options, and a 2002 study based on Towers Perrin's yearly surveys reported that the rate of adoption of stock options in Europe has matched that of the U.S. in the 1990s.[31]

In sum, the conventional wisdom on corporate governance has changed dramatically since the 1970s and early 1980s, when the U.S. market-based system was subjected to heavy criticism and the bank-centered systems of Japan and Germany were held up as models.[32] Since the mid-1980s, the American style of corporate governance has reinvented itself and the rest of the world seems to be following the U.S. lead.

RECENT REGULATORY CHANGES

The Sarbanes-Oxley Act (SOX), which was enacted in the summer of 2002, mandated a number of changes in corporate governance for publicly traded companies. The NYSE and NASDAQ also mandated corporate governance changes for firms listed on their respective exchanges. In this section, we discuss the likely effect of these changes on U.S. corporate governance.

Sarbanes-Oxley

SOX mandated changes that will affect executive compensation, shareholder monitoring, and, particularly, board monitoring.

One provision requires the CEO and CFO to disgorge any profits from bonuses and stock sales during the 12-month period that follows a financial report that is subsequently restated because of "misconduct." (We assume this provision also covers any hedging transactions the CEO or CFO undertakes.) Until "misconduct" is clearly defined, this provision increases the risk to a CEO or CFO of selling a large amount of stock or options in any one year while still in office. Some CEOs and CFOs will choose to wait until they are no longer in those positions before selling equity or exercising options. To the extent CEOs and CFOs behave this way, their equity holdings become less liquid and they will care less about short-term stock price movements. This would be a positive

---

30. Rick Escherich and Paul Gibbs, *Global Mergers and Acquisitions Review*, JP Morgan (April 2002).
31. Brian Hall, "Incentive Strategy II: Executive Compensation and Ownership Structure," Harvard Business School, Teaching Note N9-902-134 (2002).

32. See, for example, Michael Porter, "Capital Disadvantage: America's Failing Capital Investment System," *Harvard Business Review*, September-October (1992), pp. 65-83.

change. In addition, the rule will act as a deterrent to negligent or deliberate misreporting.[33]

Shareholder-related provisions include changes in restrictions on insider trading regulation and enhanced financial disclosure. Executives will now have to report sales or purchases of company stock within two days rather than the current ten days, which will have the effect of making executive shares somewhat less liquid. SOX also requires more detailed disclosure of off-balance-sheet financings and special purpose entities, which should make it more difficult for companies to manipulate their financial statements in a way that boosts the current stock price.

SOX also includes a number of provisions meant to improve board monitoring. These focus largely on increasing the power, responsibility, and independence of the audit committee. SOX requires that the audit committee hire the outside auditor and that the committee consist entirely of directors with no other financial relationship with the company.

Finally, SOX increases management's and the board's responsibility for financial reporting and the criminal penalties for misreporting. The increased responsibility and penalties have clearly increased the amount of time that executives of all companies must spend on accounting matters. For companies that are already well governed, that extra time is unnecessary and therefore costly. At least initially, some of the extra time meeting SOX's requirements will be time that could have been devoted to discussing strategy or managing the business. SOX has also caused companies to increase their use of outside accountants and lawyers. But part of the resulting increase in costs is likely to be recouped in the form of valuable new information not previously available to some CEOs, CFOs, and boards. Furthermore, the additional time and costs should decline as companies become more efficient at complying with SOX.

So, what has the new legislation really accomplished? The provisions of SOX deal both directly and indirectly with some of the deficiencies of U.S. corporate governance. But many U.S. companies would have instituted some of these changes anyway. The law already punished fraudulent reporting, including the misreporting uncovered in Enron,

Tyco, and WorldCom. Furthermore, the Enron scandal brought the costs of such misreporting into sharp focus before the passage of SOX. No CEO wants to be the CEO of the next Enron. And no board member wants to be on the board of the next Enron.

There are two potentially significant dangers associated with SOX. First, the ambiguity in some of the provisions, particularly those that overlap with and even contradict aspects of state corporate law, will almost certainly invite aggressive litigation. The fear of such litigation will lead CEOs and CFOs to direct corporate resources to protect themselves against potential lawsuits. Fear of litigation is also making it harder to attract qualified board members—certainly an unintended consequence of all the effort to improve board effectiveness. The second, broader concern is that SOX represents a shift to more rigid Federal regulation and legislation of corporate governance, as distinguished from the more flexible corporate governance that has evolved from state law, particularly Delaware law.[34]

At this point, SOX has probably helped to restore confidence in the U.S. corporate governance system. Apart from that, the Act's expected overall effect is as yet unclear. Our guess is that the effects will be positive for companies with poor governance practices and negative for companies with good governance practices. Because some of the additional costs of complying with SOX are fixed rather than variable, the effects will be more negative for smaller companies than for larger ones. At the margin, this may lead some public companies to go private and deter some private companies from going public. And because of companies' initial uncertainty about how to comply with the Act, we expect the effects of SOX to be somewhat negative in the short term, with compliance costs declining over time.

NYSE and NASDAQ Corporate Governance Proposals

In 2002, both the New York Stock Exchange and NASDAQ submitted proposals designed to strengthen the corporate governance of their listed firms. Both exchanges will require the following:

(1) shareholder approval of most equity compensation plans;

---

33. This provision could lead to a modest substitution of cash compensation for equity-based compensation. However, this would have to be accomplished entirely through salary increases because cash bonuses are also subject to the same disgorgement provisions.

34. We thank Andrew Nussbaum for suggesting this possibility.

At this point, the Sarbanes-Oxley Act has probably helped to restore confidence in the U.S. corporate governance system. Apart from that, the Act's expected overall effect is as yet unclear.

(2) a majority of independent directors with no material relationships with the company;

(3) a larger role for independent directors in the compensation and nominating committees; and

(4) regular meetings of only nonmanagement directors.

Compared to SOX, these proposals address U.S. corporate governance deficiencies both more directly and with lower costs. The three provisions relating to board monitoring are particularly noteworthy in that they directly address some of the concerns mentioned by Lorsch and MacIver in 1989 and by outside directors in the recent Korn Ferry survey.

The closest historical parallel to these proposals is the Code of Best Practices (based upon the recommendations of the Cadbury Committee) that was adopted by the London Stock Exchange (LSE) in 1992. The Code included recommendations that boards have at least three outside directors and a nonexecutive chairperson. Although the Code is voluntary, the LSE requires companies to state whether they are in compliance.

There is evidence that the Code can make a difference. A recent study of all LSE companies reported that both CEO turnover and the sensitivity of CEO turnover to performance increased following the adoption of the Code—and that such increases were concentrated among those firms that had adopted the recommendations. Furthermore, the changes in turnover appear to have been driven by the increase in the fraction of outsiders on the board rather than the separation of the chairperson and CEO.[35]

Overall, then, the NYSE and NASDAQ changes should prove to be unambiguously positive.

The Conference Board Recommendations

In response to the recent scandals, the Conference Board—an association of prominent U.S. companies—put together a Commission on Public Trust and Private Enterprise with the aim of advising companies on best practices in corporate governance. The first report by the Commission, released in September 2002, provides a set of principles to guide boards in designing top executive compensation. The report begins by noting the exceptional

circumstances that led to the abuse of stock options—the equivalent of a "Perfect Storm"—and then makes the following recommendations:

(1) compensation committees should be independent and should avoid benchmarking;

(2) performance-based compensation should correspond to the corporation's long-term goals—"cost of capital, return on equity, economic value added, market share, environment goals, etc."—and should avoid windfalls related to stock market volatility;

(3) equity-based compensation should be "reasonable and cost effective";

(4) key executives and directors should "acquire and hold" a meaningful amount of company stock; and

(5) compensation disclosure should be transparent and accounting-neutral—that is, stock options should be expensed.[36]

Overall, we have a mixed reaction to these recommendations. Several are clearly beneficial. In particular, greater transparency and appropriate expensing of options will make the costs of options more clear not only to shareholders but also to boards. It also will "level the playing field" for options versus other forms of equity-based compensation.

Requiring key executives to hold a meaningful amount of company stock will reduce the temptation to manipulate earnings and stock prices in the short term by making executive stock holdings less liquid. Typically, stock options vest in one to four years, which is short given that most options are exercised and sold fairly soon after vesting. Economic logic suggests that boards should encourage longer-term holdings and a build-up of sizable executive stakes.

The Commission also endorses indexation of some kind to eliminate windfall gains. Indexation has been recommended by economists for a long time, yet practitioners have not adopted it. It is true that there has been an important accounting disadvantage to indexation in that indexed options must be expensed. But the fact that indexed options are rarely used by LBO investors and venture capitalists also suggests that there are hidden costs to indexation or that the benefits are low.

While it may be useful to experiment with some forms of indexation, we think it would probably be

35. J. Dahya, J. McConnell, and Nickolaos Travlos, "The Cadbury Committee, Corporate Performance, and Top Management Turnover," *Journal of Finance*, Vol. 57 (2002), pp. 461-483.

36. Andy Grove, Chairman of Intel, disagreed with the majority in not recommending expensing of stock options, while Paul Volcker, former Chairman of the Board of Governors of the Federal Reserve System, argued that fixed-price stock options should not be used at all. Both filed dissenting opinions.

just as effective and more transparent to index implicitly by granting stock-based incentives more frequently and in smaller amounts. Mega-grants covering several years at a fixed price have proved too unstable; the options may go underwater and then need to be bailed out (to maintain incentives), making it hard initially to determine the true expected cost of the incentive plans. In general, the incentives from stock options are more fragile than those provided by restricted stock, a problem that more frequent, smaller awards would help alleviate.[37]

We are also skeptical of the recommendation to use performance-based compensation tied to a long list of potential long-term goals, including cost of capital, return on equity, market share, revenue growth, and compliance and environmental protection goals. Such performance plans would appear to take us back to the 1970s, an era that few incentive experts remember fondly. If the problem is windfall gains, then indexed stock options or, more simply, frequent (quarterly) issues of stock options are much preferred. If the problem is manipulation of the market, it should be evident that accounting measures of the kind endorsed by the Conference Board are very problematic. It was in large part because of their vulnerability to manipulation that standard performance plans were replaced by stock-based incentives in the 1980s. This is not to say that accounting-based incentives should never be used, just that they should not form the core of a CEO's incentive plan.

We are also somewhat skeptical of the recommendation that the compensation committee "act independently of management...and avoid benchmarking that keeps continually raising the compensation levels for executives." First, dictating terms without consulting with the executives about their preferences goes against efficient contracting principles; contracting is a two-sided affair. Second, the intent seems to be to give individual compensation committees the responsibility for the overall level of executive compensation. But it is hard to see how pay levels can be set in a fair and efficient way without benchmarking. Prices, including wages, are ultimately set by supply and demand, and benchmarking is nothing more than looking at market prices. The main

problem with executive pay levels is not the overall level, but the extreme skew in the awards, as we noted earlier. To deal with this problem, we need more effective benchmarking, not less of it.

Despite good intentions, then, we see potentially serious flaws in the recommendations of the Conference Board. It is also important to keep in mind that good incentive designs are sensitive to economic circumstances and to the desired performance. One size does not fit all. And because each situation requires its own compensation plan, the need to customize that plan will often conflict with the goals of benchmarking and transparency.

WHAT WILL THE FUTURE BRING?

Working together with normal market forces, the Sarbanes-Oxley Act, the new NYSE and NASDAQ regulations, and the guidelines offered by groups like the Conference Board will significantly influence U.S. corporate governance.

Board behavior will be most strongly affected by these measures. External pressure will lead most boards to monitor top management more aggressively. Yet the relationship between boards and directors need not become more adversarial. The new regulatory requirements provide cover for a more independent and inquisitive board. Actions that in the past might have been construed as hostile will now be interpreted as following best practice. The mandated changes may in fact help reduce the tension inherent in the dual role boards play as monitors of management, on the one hand, and as advisors and sounding boards, on the other.

In addition to the changes in oversight and monitoring, boards also are likely to change their approaches to executive compensation (even though SOX and the exchanges did not address executive compensation directly). In particular, boards will increasingly restrict top executives' exercising options, selling stock, and hedging their positions. As noted earlier, some of the incentives for the executives at Global Crossing, Tyco, and WorldCom to manage earnings came from their ability to sell shares when their stock prices were overvalued. Restrictions on such selling reduce the incentive to

---

37. See Brian Hall and Thomas Knox, "Managing Option Fragility," Harvard NOM Research Paper 02-19, Harvard Business School (2002). It is interesting that fairness arguments often lead people to advocate options with exercise prices set well above current market price (for instance, Michael Jensen argues that the exercise price should rise with the cost of capital). Given the problems of fragility, this takes us in exactly the wrong direction. Restricted stock (an option with a zero exercise price) is more appealing, because its incentive effect is robust to variations in the stock price.

manage short-term earnings. While such restrictions have costs, particularly in the form of lack of diversification, the benefits in terms of improved incentives arguably outweigh them. Private equity firms routinely impose such restrictions on the managements of their portfolio companies. Furthermore, CEOs typically are wealthy enough that the benefits of diversification may not be so great.

Many corporate boards will decide to expense options and equity compensation even if they are not required to do so. We suspect that boards will discover that investors and the stock market have neutral or even positive reactions to such expensing (in contrast to the predictions of many executives). Sophisticated investors already know the extent of option issuance from its disclosure in footnotes. Expensing will provide the additional signal to these investors that the board and the company are serious about compensation and corporate governance.[38]

Boards of directors and compensation committees also will begin to change their behavior in issuing options and equity-based compensation. This will be particularly true of boards that decide to expense options. Expensing the options will make their costs more clear and will reduce the size of option grants, particularly large, one-shot grants. Moreover, some companies that do expense equity compensation will choose to issue restricted stock rather than options. Restricted stock grants have the advantages of being easier to value, providing incentives that do not vary with stock price movements, and thus being less vulnerable to repricing.[39]

CONCLUDING REMARKS

Despite its alleged flaws, the U.S. corporate governance system has performed very well, both on an absolute basis and relative to other countries. It is important to recognize that there is no perfect system and that we should try to avoid the pendulum-like movement so typical of politically inspired system redesigns. The current problems arose in an exceptional period that is not likely to happen again soon. After all, it was almost 70 years ago that the corporate governance system last attracted such intervention.

The fact that the American public and political system became outraged and involved in corporate governance does not mean the system was broken. The U.S. public and the political system are part of the broader system of corporate governance. At the same time, an effort to regulate the system so that such outrage will never again occur would be overly costly and counterproductive. It would lead to inflexibility and fear of experimentation. In today's uncertain climate, we probably need more organizational experimentation than ever. The New Economy is moving forward and, in order to exploit the potential efficiencies inherent in the new information technologies, new business models and new organizational structures are likely to be desirable and valuable. Enron was an experiment that failed. We should take advantage of its lessons not by withdrawing into a shell, but rather by improving control structures and corporate governance so that other promising experiments can be undertaken.

---

38. The argument that options cannot be expensed because no one knows their true value is wrong. On that basis, one could argue that we should not depreciate assets because it is impossible to measure the assets' true rate of depreciation. Nevertheless, it remains to be seen how fluctuations in the value of stock options will influence the information content of reported earnings. The never-ending debate over the best way to handle depreciation suggests that expensing options is going to be discussed for years to come.

39. See Hall (2002), cited earlier, for a detailed discussion.

CHAPTER 1: SECTION 1.2
Ethics and Incentives

With the recent wave of corporate scandals has come an increased focus on managerial incentives and ethics. Indeed, the Sarbanes Oxley Act of 2002 mandates that corporations disclose whether they have adopted a code of ethics for their senior financial officers and the contents of that code. Moreover, any change in, or waiver of, an issuer's code of ethics requires immediate public disclosure—a provision that appears to stem from the case of Enron, where the Board waived the firm's code of conduct on at least two occasions to allow CFO Andrew Fastow to engage in transactions with Enron in his capacity as head of external entities.

Despite the increased attention to corporate ethics, however, there is a good deal of confusion about what constitutes ethical behavior by corporations. There is general agreement, of course, that corporate managers and employees should abide by the law, and that they should be honest and forthright in their dealings with customers and fellow employees. This chapter explores the relationships among corporate ethics, incentives, and organizational structure. The predominant view in the papers—most of which are written by financial economists—is that the people who work for corporations are neither better nor worse than others. Moreover, widespread ethical problems in organizations tend to come not so much from "bad people" as from flawed organizational structures that fail to provide sufficient accountability and proper incentives.

In this section's lead article, ***The Nature of Man***, Michael Jensen and William Meckling, the founding fathers of agency theory, provide a foundation for the other articles by developing a model of human behavior they call the Resourceful, Evaluative, Maximizing Model (REMM for short). The authors define REMM in part by showing how it addresses the failings of four other models commonly used in the social sciences: the Economic Model, which views people as single-minded money-maximizers; the Sociological Model, which views behavior as largely a process of acculturation (even to the point of turning people into social victims); the Psychological Model based on Maslow's well-known hierarchy of needs; and the Political Model, which views people as perfect agents for their organizations, whether they operate in the public or the private sector.

James Brickley, Clifford Smith, and Jerold Zimmerman also adopt an economic perspective in ***Corporate Governance, Ethics, and Organizational Architecture***. The authors argue that effective corporate leadership involves more than developing a good strategic plan and setting high ethical standards. It also means developing an organizational design that encourages managers and employees to carry the firm's business plan and maintain its ethical standards. In this article, the authors use the term *organizational architecture* to refer to three key elements of a company's design: (1) the assignment of decision-making authority—who gets to make what decisions; (2) performance evaluation—the key measures of performance for evaluating business units and individual employees; and (3) compensation structure—how employees are rewarded for meeting performance goals. In well-designed companies, each of these elements is mutually reinforcing and supportive of the company's overall business strategy. Decision-making authority is assigned to managers and employees who have the knowledge and experience needed to make the best investment and operating decisions. And to ensure that those decision makers have the incentive as well as the knowledge to make the best decisions, the corporate systems used to evaluate and reward their performance are based on measures that are linked as directly as possible to the corporate goal of creating value.

Moreover, a flawed organizational design can lead to far worse than missed opportunities to create value. As the authors note, the recent corporate scandals involved not just improper behavior by senior executives, but corporate structures that, far from safeguarding against such behavior, in some ways encouraged it.

In ***Incentives, Rationality, and Society***, Michael Brennan offers a dissenting view from that provided by financial economists like Jensen and Brickley et al. Brennan objects, first of all, to the tendency of economists to identify rationality with self interest. He also objects to the "cynicism" of agency theory and its call for the widespread use of financial incentives in compensating corporate executives. Brennan argues that agency theory "assumes both too much and too little about human nature." It assumes too much when it asserts that people are capable of identifying and pursuing their own best interests without regulation or guidance from others. It assumes too little when it implies that incentive compensation contracts are necessary to motivate people to perform well on behalf of the organizations they represent. In support of his argument, Brennan notes that the lion's share of corporate executive incentive bonuses are awarded on a subjective, or discretionary, rather than a purely objective or contractual basis.

In *Self-interest, Altruism, Incentives, and Agency* Michael Jensen responds to Brennan by arguing that the pursuit of self-interest "in no way rules out or devalues altruistic behavior." But, as Jensen goes on to insist, the fact that people often devote time and resources to others by no means makes them perfect agents for the organizations that employ them. Costly conflicts of interest abound in business and political organizations; and, for this reason, the management of agency costs is an important social undertaking. Reflecting on his years of teaching agency theory, Jensen remarks:

I find that students and business people are excited by the central proposition of agency theory. And the proposition that excites them is not that people are self-interested, or that conflicts abound. The central proposition of agency theory is that rational self-interested people involved in cooperative endeavors always have incentives to reduce or control conflicts of interest so as to reduce the losses resulting from them.

The concluding article in this chapter is an edited transcript of a *Roundtable on Integrity in Financial Reporting* held at Baylor University in November of 2002. At the center of the U.S. corporate governance controversy are questions about the integrity of the U.S. financial reporting system: Can investors trust the numbers now being reported in corporate financial statements? And, if not, what steps are being taken to bring about the return of investor trust and confidence? The academics and practitioners who took part in this discussion began by expressing their reluctance to describe the current situation as a "crisis." The consensus was that the recent governance failures are not the reflection of a general decline in corporate moral standards, but rather the work of a handful of opportunists who found ways to exploit some weaknesses in the present system. Part of the discussion focused on the expected benefits (and costs) of the heightened regulatory scrutiny provided by the Sarbanes-Oxley Act and the newly formed Public Company Accounting Oversight Board. But most of the panelists placed greater emphasis on the role of self-regulation in resolving problems such as the conflicts of interest within auditing and brokerage firms that played a major role in scandals like Enron and WorldCom. And rather than relying on more vigorous SEC oversight of financial statements, a number of panelists argued that top priority should be given to comprehensive reform of U.S. accounting standards, which are said to be a major source of confusion for both managers and investors. This last argument becomes a main focus of the articles in the final section of this book.

THE NATURE OF MAN*

*by Michael C. Jensen,
Harvard University, and
William H. Meckling,
University of Rochester*

U nderstanding human behavior is fundamental to understanding how organizations function, whether they be profit-
making firms in the private sector, non-
profit enterprises, or government agencies intended to serve the "public interest." Much policy
disagreement among managers, scientists, policy
makers, and citizens derives from substantial, though
usually implicit, differences in the way we think
about human nature—about the strengths, frailties,
intelligence, ignorance, honesty, selfishness, gener-
osity, and altruism of individuals.

The usefulness of any model of human nature
depends on its ability to explain a wide range of
social phenomena; the test of such a model is the
degree to which it is consistent with observed human
behavior. A model that explains behavior only in one
small geographical area, or only for a short period in
history, or only for people engaged in certain pursuits
is not very useful. For this reason we must use a
limited number of general traits to characterize
human behavior. Greater detail limits the explanatory ability of a model because individual people
differ so greatly. We want a set of characteristics that
captures the essence of human nature, but no more.

While this may sound abstract and complex, it
is neither. Each of us has in mind and uses models
of human nature every day. We all understand, for
example, that people are willing to make trade-offs
among things that they want. Our spouses, partners,
children, friends, business associates, or perfect
strangers can be induced to make substitutions of all
kinds. We offer to go out to dinner Saturday night
instead of the concert tonight. We offer to substitute
a bicycle for a stereo as a birthday gift. We allow an
employee to go home early today if the time is made
up next week.

If our model specified that individuals were
never willing to substitute some amount of a good
for some amounts of other goods, it would quickly
run aground on inconsistent evidence. It could not
explain much of the human behavior we observe.
While it may sound silly to characterize individuals
as unwilling to make substitutions, that view of
human behavior is not far from models that are
widely accepted and used by many social scientists
(for example, Maslow's hierarchy of human needs
and sociologists' models portraying individuals as
cultural role players or social victims).

We investigate five alternative models of human behavior that are used frequently enough
(though usually implicitly) in the social science
literature and in public discussion to merit attention.
For convenience we label the models as follows:
1. **The Resourceful, Evaluative, Maximizing Model
(or REMM)**
2. **The Economic (or Money-Maximizing) Model**
3. **The Sociological (or Social Victim) Model**
4. **The Psychological (or Hierarchy of Needs) Model**
5. **The Political (or Perfect Agent) Model**

---

*We use the word "man" here in its use as a non-gender-specific reference to
human beings. We have attempted to make the language less gender-specific
because the models being discussed describe the behavior of both sexes. We have
been unable to find a genderless term for use in the title which has the same desired
impact.

The first draft of this paper was written in the early 1970s. Since then it has
been used annually in our course on Coordination and Control at both Rochester
and Harvard. We are indebted to our students for much help in honing these ideas
over the years. An earlier version of some of the ideas in this paper appeared in

William H. Meckling, "Values and the Choice of the Model of the Individual in the
Social Sciences," *Schweizerische Zeitschrift fur Volkswirtshaft und Statistik Revue
Suisse d'Economie Politique et de Statistique* (December 1976).

This research has been supported by the Managerial Economics Research
Center, University of Rochester, and the Division of Research, Harvard Business
School. We are grateful for the advice and comments of many people, including
Chris Argyris, George Baker, Fischer Black, Donald Chew, Perry Fagan, Donna
Feinberg, Amy Hart, Karin Monsler, Kevin Murphy, Natalie Jensen, Steve-Anna
Stephens, Richard Tedlow, Robin Tish, Karen Wruck, and Abraham Zaleznik.

These alternative models are pure types characterized in terms of only the barest essentials. We are sensitive to the dangers of creating straw men and concede that our characterization of these models fails to represent the complexity of the views of scientists in each of these fields. In particular, these models do not describe what all individual economists, sociologists, or psychologists use as their models of human behavior. Nevertheless, we believe that enough use is made of such admittedly reductive models throughout the social sciences, and by people in general, to warrant our treatment of them in these pages.

RESOURCEFUL, EVALUATIVE, MAXIMIZING MODEL: REMM

The first model is REMM: the Resourceful, Evaluative, Maximizing Model. While the term is new, the concept is not. REMM is the product of over 200 years of research and debate in economics, the other social sciences, and philosophy. As a result, REMM is now defined in very precise terms, but we offer here only a bare-bones summary of the concept. Many specifics can be added to enrich its descriptive content without sacrificing the basic foundation provided here.

Postulate I. Every individual cares; he or she is an evaluator.

(a) The individual cares about almost everything: knowledge, independence, the plight of others, the environment, honor, interpersonal relationships, status, peer approval, group norms, culture, wealth, rules of conduct, the weather, music, art, and so on.

(b) REMM is always willing to make trade-offs and substitutions. Each individual is always willing to give up some sufficiently small amount of any particular good (oranges, water, air, housing, honesty, or safety) for some sufficiently large quantity of other goods. Furthermore, valuation is relative in the sense that the value of a unit of any particular good decreases as the individual enjoys more of it relative to other goods.

(c) Individual preferences are transitive—that is, if A is preferred to B, and B is preferred to C, then A is preferred to C.

Postulate II. Each individual's wants are unlimited.

(a) If we designate those things that REMM values positively as "goods," then he or she prefers more goods to less. Goods can be anything from art objects to ethical norms.

(b) REMM cannot be satiated. He or she always wants more of some things, be they material goods such as art, sculpture, castles, and pyramids; or intangible goods such as solitude, companionship, honesty, respect, love, fame, and immortality.

Postulate III. Each individual is a maximizer.

He or she acts so as to enjoy the highest level of value possible. Individuals are always constrained in satisfying their wants. Wealth, time, and the laws of nature are all important constraints that affect the opportunities available to any individual. Individuals are also constrained by the limits of their own knowledge about various goods and opportunities; and their choices of goods or courses of action will reflect the costs of acquiring the knowledge or information necessary to evaluate those choices.[1]

The notion of an opportunity set provides the limit on the level of value attainable by any individual. The opportunity set is usually regarded as something that is given and external to the individual. Economists tend to represent it as a wealth or income constraint and a set of prices at which the individual can buy goods. But the notion of an individual's opportunity set can be generalized to include the set of activities he or she can perform during a 24-hour day—or in a lifetime.

Postulate IV. The individual is resourceful.

Individuals are creative. They are able to conceive of changes in their environment, foresee the consequences thereof, and respond by creating new opportunities.

Although an individual's opportunity set is limited at any instant in time by his or her knowledge and the state of the world, that limitation is not immutable. Human beings are not only capable of learning about new opportunities, they also engage in resourceful, creative activities that expand their opportunities in various ways.

The kind of highly mechanical behavior posited by economists—that is, assigning probabilities and

---

1. When one takes into account information costs, much behavior that appears to be suboptimal "satisficing" can be explained as attempts to maximize subject to such costs. Unfortunately, "satisficing" (a much misused term originated by Herbert A. Simon in "A Behavioral Model of Rational Choice," *Quarterly Journal of Economics*, Vol. 69 (1955)) does not suggest this interpretation.

expected values to various actions and choosing the action with the highest expected value—is formally consistent with the evaluating, maximizing model defined in Postulates I through III. But such behavior falls short of the human capabilities posited by REMM; it says nothing about the individual's ingenuity and creativity.

REMMs AT WORK

One way of capturing the notion of resourcefulness is to think about the effects of newly imposed constraints on human behavior. These constraints might be new operating policies in a corporation or new laws imposed by governments. No matter how much experience we have with the response of people to changes in their environment, we tend to overestimate the impact of a new law or policy intended to constrain human behavior. Moreover, the constraint or law will almost always generate behavior which was never imagined by its sponsors. Why? Because of the sponsors' failure to recognize the creativity of REMMs.

REMMs' response to a new constraint is to begin searching for substitutes for what is now constrained, a search that is not restricted to existing alternatives. REMMs will invent alternatives that did not previously exist.

An excellent illustration of how humans function as REMMs is the popular response to the 1974 federal imposition of a 55-mile-per-hour speed limit in all states under penalty of loss of federal transportation and highway moneys. The primary reason offered for this law was the conservation of gasoline and diesel fuel (for simplicity, we ignore the benefits associated with the smaller number of accidents that occur at slower speeds).[2]

The major cost associated with slower driving is lost time. At a maximum speed of 55 mph instead of 70 mph, trips take longer. Those who argue that lost time is not important must recognize that an hour of time consumed is just as irreplaceable as— and generally more valuable than—the gallon of gasoline consumed. On these grounds, the law created inefficiencies, and the behavior of drivers is consistent with that conclusion.[3]

Let's calculate the dollar benefits of fuel saved by the 55 mph speed limit and the value of these savings per additional hour of driving time. These dollar savings can then be compared to the value of the driver's time. Suppose driving at 55 mph instead of 70 saves 10% on gasoline consumption, so that, for example, if gasoline mileage is 14 mpg at 70 mph, it will be 15.4 mpg at 55 mph. To travel 70 miles at 55 mph will take 1.273 hours instead of one hour at 70 mph. The gasoline consumed is 4.545 gallons at 55 mph instead of 5 gallons at 70 mph. This means that for every additional hour of travel time required by the slower speed, a driver saves 1.665 gallons of gasoline = (5.0 − 4.545) divided by (1.273 − 1.0).

At a price of $1.20 per gallon for gasoline, the driver saves $2.00 per hour of additional travel time— a sum significantly less than the minimum wage. If there are two occupants in the car, they each save $1.00 per hour; and the rate sinks to 66¢ per hour per person if there are three occupants. Therefore, the law requires that drivers and their passengers spend time in an activity that earns them about $2.00 per hour or less, depending on the particular car, the driver's habits, and the number of passengers.

Judging from the widespread difficulties state authorities have had in enforcing the law, drivers understand the value of their time quite well. People responded in REMM-like fashion to this newly imposed constraint in a number of ways. One was to reduce their automobile, bus, and truck travel, and, in some cases, to shift to travel by other means such as airplanes and trains. Another response was to defy the law by driving at speeds exceeding the 55 mph maximum. Violating the speed limit, of course, exposes offenders to potential costs in the form of fines, higher insurance rates, and possible loss of driver's licenses. This, in turn, provides incentives for REMMs to search out ways to reduce such costs.

The result has been an entire new industry, and the rapid growth of an already existing one. Citizen's Band radios (CBs), which had been used primarily by truckers, suddenly became widely used by passenger car drivers and almost all truckers. There were about 800,000 FCC CB radio licenses outstanding throughout the period 1966-1973. By

---

2. The original temporary law was made permanent in 1975 with safety being cited as a primary reason.

3. Moreover, in 1987 the law was changed to allow states the option of raising the speed limit to 65 mph on interstate highways outside highly populated areas, and later extended to certain non-interstate highways.

the end of 1977, there were 12.25 million licensed CBs in use.[4] These two-way radios with relatively short ranges (less than 15 miles) allowed drivers to inform each other about the location of police cars, radar traps, unmarked cars, and so on. They significantly reduced the likelihood of arrest for speeding. REMMs by the millions were willing to pay from $50 to $300 for radios in order to save time and avoid speeding tickets.

CB radios have been largely replaced by radar detectors that warn drivers of the presence of police radar. These devices have become so common that police have taken countermeasures, such as investing in more expensive and sophisticated radar units that are less susceptible to detection. Manufacturers of radar detectors retaliated by manufacturing increasingly sophisticated units.

The message is clear: people who drive value their time at more than $2 per hour. When the 55 mph maximum speed limit was imposed, few would have predicted the ensuing chain of events. One seemingly modest constraint on REMMs has created a new electronic industry designed to avoid the constraint. And such behavior shows itself again and again in a variety of contexts—for example, in

- taxpayers' continuous search for, and discovery of, "loopholes" in income tax laws;
- the development of so-called clubs with private liquor stock in areas where serving liquor at public bars is prohibited;
- the ability of General Dynamics' CEO George Anders and his management team, when put under a lucrative incentive compensation plan tied to shareholder value, to quadruple the market value of the company even as the defense industry was facing sharp cutbacks; and
- the growth in the number of hotel courtesy cars and gypsy cabs in cities where taxi-cab licensing results in monopoly fares.

These examples are typical of behavior consistent with the REMM model, but not, as we shall see, with other models that prevail in the social sciences. The failure of the other models is important because the individual stands in relation to organizations as the atom is to mass. From small groups to entire societies, organizations are composed of individuals. If we are to have a science of such organizations, it will have to be founded on building blocks that capture as simply as possible the most important traits of humans. Although clearly not a complete description of human behavior, REMM is the model of human behavior that best meets this criterion.[5]

REMM MEANS THERE ARE NO "NEEDS"

REMM implies that there is no such thing as a need, a proposition that arouses considerable resistance. The fallacy of the notion of needs follows from the proposition that the individual is always willing to make trade-offs. That proposition means individuals are always willing to substitute—that is, *they are always willing to give up a sufficiently small amount of any good for a sufficiently large amount of other goods.*[6] Failure to take account of substitution is one of the most frequent mistakes in the analysis of human behavior.

George Bernard Shaw, the famous playwright and social thinker, reportedly once claimed that while on an ocean voyage he met a celebrated actress on deck and asked her whether she would be willing to sleep with him for a million dollars. She was agreeable. He followed with a counterproposal: "What about ten dollars?" "What do you think I am?," she responded indignantly. He replied, "We've already established that—now we're just haggling over price."

Like it or not, individuals are willing to sacrifice a little of almost anything we care to name, even reputation or morality, for a sufficiently large quantity of other desired things, and these things do not have to be money or even material goods. Moreover, the fact that all individuals make trade-offs (or substitute in virtually every dimension imaginable) means that there are no such things as human "needs" in the sense that word is often used. There are only human wants, desires, or, in the economist's language, demands. If something is more costly, less will be wanted, desired, demanded than if it were cheaper.

---

4. Obtained in private communication with the Federal Communications Commission.

5. REMM is not meant to describe the behavior of any particular individual. To do so requires more complete specification of the preferences, values, emotions, and talents of each person. Moreover, individuals respond very differently to factors such as stress, tension, and fear, and, in so doing, often violate the predictions of the REMM model. For purposes of organizational and public policy, many of these violations of REMM "cancel out" in the aggregate across large groups of people and over time—but by no means all. For a discussion of a Pain Avoidance Model (PAM) that complements REMM by accommodating systematically non-rational behavior, see Michael C. Jensen, "Economics, Organizations, and Non-Rational Behavior," forthcoming *Economic Inquiry* (1995).

6. The word need has meaning only when used in the conditional sense. For example: An individual needs X cubic liters of air per hour in order to live. This statement, or others like it, do not imply, however, that individuals are willing to pay an infinite price for that air.

> No matter how much experience we have with the response of people to changes in
> their environment, we tend to overestimate the impact of a new law or policy
> intended to constrain human behavior. It will almost always generate behavior
> which was never imagined by its sponsors.

Using the word need as an imperative is semantic trickery. The media and press are filled with talk about housing needs, education needs, food needs, energy needs, and so on. Politicians and others who use that language understand that the word need carries emotional impact. It implies a requirement at any cost; if the need is not met, some unspecified disaster will take place. Such assertions have a far different impact if restated to reflect the facts. The proposition that "people want more housing if they can get it cheaply enough" does not ring out from the podium or over the airwaves with the same emotional appeal as "people *need* more housing."

If individuals are required to specify what they mean by need, the emotional specter of the unexamined catastrophe that lies behind the need simply becomes another cost. Needs would be exposed for what they are—desires or wants—and discussion would focus on alternatives, substitutes, and costs in a productive manner.

ECONOMISTS, POLITICIANS, AND BUREAUCRATS AS REMMs

National Planning and Needs

While economists generally profess fidelity to REMM, their loyalty is neither universal nor constant. Their economic models of human behavior often fall short of REMM—such as, for example, when they characterize the individual as a pure money-income maximizer. Moreover, in matters of public policy, there is a systematic relationship between the policies espoused and the degree of infidelity to REMM. One of the better-known members of the economics profession and a recipient of the Nobel Prize, Professor Wassily Leontieff, was featured as a proponent of "national economic planning" in a *New York Times* advertisement that said:

No reliable mechanism in the modern economy relates needs to available manpower, plant and material... The most striking fact about the way we organize our economic life is that we leave so much to chance. We give little thought to the direction in which we would like to go. (March 16, 1975)

Notice that the emotional content and force of the statement is considerably strengthened by the authors' use of the word "needs" rather than "desires" or "wants."

But let's examine this statement more closely. If by "needs" the authors mean *individual* preferences, wants, or desires, the first sentence is simply false. There *is* a mechanism that relates such needs or wants to "manpower, plant, and materials" and it is central to the study of economics: namely, the price system. What the authors are saying is that no one organization or group of individuals *directs* (not plans) production in such a way that what is actually produced is what the advertisement's authors would define as needs. When they go on to say, "We give little thought to the direction we would like to go," the antecedent of we is meant to be "we the general public." But, of course, we as individuals (and REMMs) give a great deal of thought to where we want to study and work, how much we will save, where we will invest our savings, what we will buy, what we will produce, and so on.

Professor Leontieff's reputation rests largely on his work on input-output models. It is not surprising that he is a planning buff, for input-output models generally ignore most of the adjustment processes (that is, price changes and substitutions) that serve to balance supply and demand in a market economy. His input-output models specify fixed relations between inputs like labor, materials, and capital—and outputs like tons of steel. More or less steel can be produced only by adding or subtracting inputs in fixed proportions. There are no resourceful, evaluative maximizers in Leontieff's models. Like ants in an ant colony, his individuals possess productive capacities but very limited adaptability. In a society of such dolts, planning (or, more accurately, directing) appears unavoidable. In the words of another Nobel Prize winner, Professor Friedrich von Hayek, the real planning issue is not *whether* individuals should plan their affairs, but rather *who* should plan their affairs.[7]

The implication of input-output models, then, is that people are incapable of planning and thus require the direction and leadership of "planners." This import has not escaped the notice of bureaucrats, politicians, and managers, who themselves

---

7. See Friedrich von Hayek, "The Use of Knowledge in Society," *American Economic Review,* Vol. 35, No. 4 (September, 1945); and "'Planning' Our Way to Serfdom," *Reason* (March, 1977).

behave as REMMs when they recognize the value of models and theories that imply an increased demand for their services. By their very framing of the issue, Leontieff and politicians assume the answer to Hayek's question: planning does not exist unless the government does it.

For example, politicians are likely to see the value of an energy industry input-output model which, given projections of future energy "needs" (no prices and no substitutions here), tells how many nuclear energy plants must be built, how many strip mines should be opened, and how many new coal cars must be produced in order to become independent of foreign oil sources. The model suggests that, without extensive government intervention, the country cannot achieve energy independence. Such intervention, of course, implies an increase in politicians' power.

It is worth noting that the "we" in the Leontieff-endorsed planning statement is a common but generally unrecognized debating trick. It is standard practice in the political arena to label one's own preferences as the "people's preferences" or as the "public's preferences," and to label the policies one supports as "in the public interest." But organizations or groups of individuals cannot have preferences; only individuals can have preferences. One could supply content to terms like the people's preferences or the public interest by making them synonymous with other concepts—for example, with what a majority would support or what every voter would approve in a referendum. But the typical user would then find the terms far less persuasive, therefore less attractive, and, in the case of a complete consensus, never relevant.

Self-Interest and the Demand for Disequilibrium

Bureaucrats and politicians, like many economists, are also predisposed to embrace the concept of market "failure" or "disequilibrium" with the same enthusiasiasm they have shown for input-output models, and for the same reasons. If something is in disequilibrium, government action is required to bring about equilibrium.

Generally, economists tend to identify equilibrium with stable prices and quantities: a market is in equilibrium when there are no forces causing changes in the price or the quantity exchanged. Yet it is reasonable to argue that all markets are always in equilibrium, and all forces must always be in balance at all times—just as there is an equilibrium rate of heat transfer when heat is applied to one end of a steel bar. This is simply another way of saying that sophisticated, rational individuals always adapt to their opportunity set, where the opportunity set is defined to take account of the cost of adapting. That is, all voluntary exchanges will take place that will make both parties better off (taking all costs into account).

The view that markets are always in equilibrium does not depend on the stability of prices; prices and quantities can change dramatically. Their rate of change, however, is controlled by individual behavior—a balance is struck between the cost of change and the benefits. For example, if the dollar price of a good is prevented by law from changing, the opposing forces are balanced by the introduction of other costs such as queues and waiting time, or by the introduction of other goods as a consideration in the exchange.[8]

Although it is a tautology, the view that markets are always in equilibrium has important advantages. It focuses attention on interesting adjustment phenomena, on information and search costs and how they affect behavior, and on qualitative characteristics of the exchanges that arise to balance the opposing forces. If markets are always in equilibrium, the task of the scientist is to explain how the equilibrium is brought about.

In contrast, the word disequilibrium has strong emotional content. It denotes something unnatural, unsightly, and undesirable that requires "corrective action." A market—whether for labor, energy, sugar, health care, or derivative securities—described as being "in disequilibrium" is generally regarded as bad, and we are immediately led to think of the desirability of some form of government intervention (e.g., price controls, embargoes, subsidies, or output restrictions) to eliminate the assumed problem.

One popular pursuit of bureaucrats—making projections of supply and demand—is the outgrowth of their preoccupation with disequilibrium. Such projections usually consist of estimates of numbers of physicists, doctors, mining engineers,

---

8. For example, it is common practice in rent controlled areas for new tenants to make higher-than-market-price payments to old tenants and/or landlords for furniture or minor improvements they have no use for to get the right to rent the apartment for a below-market rate.

The implication of input-output models is that people are incapable of planning and thus require the direction and leadership of "planners." This import has not escaped the notice of bureaucrats and politicians, who themselves behave as REMMs when they recognize the value of models and theories that imply an increased demand for their services.

barrels of oil, or tons of steel "required and/or available" at some future date, again without reference to prices. Not surprisingly, the projections invariably imply a disequilibrium (a shortage or surplus) that requires government action.

But if these supply and demand projections are interpreted as forecasts of the quantities *and* prices that will prevail in a future economy in equilibrium, they lose all interest for policy makers. None of the usual policy implications follow—no subsidies, taxes, or constraints on individual behavior are called for, nor can any governmental enterprise be justified. Yet the practice of making projections goes on because politicians and bureaucrats, as REMMs, find them useful tools for expanding the role of government and the market for their services.

THE ECONOMIC MODEL
OF HUMAN BEHAVIOR

The economic model is a reductive version of REMM. This individual is an evaluator and maximizer who has only one want: money income. He or she is a short-run *money maximizer* who does not care for others, art, morality, love, respect, or honesty. In its simplest form, the economic model characterizes people as unwilling to trade current money income for future money income, no matter what rate of return they could earn.

The economic model is, of course, not very interesting as a model of human behavior. People do not behave this way. In most cases, use of this model reflects economists' desire for simplicity in modeling; the exclusive pursuit of wealth or money income is easier to model than the complexity of the actual preferences of individuals. As a consequence, however, noneconomists often use this model as a foil to discredit economics, that is, to argue that economics is of limited use because economists focus only on a single characteristic of behavior—and one of the least attractive at that, the selfish desire for money.

THE SOCIOLOGICAL MODEL
OF HUMAN BEHAVIOR

In the sociological model, individuals are viewed as the product of their cultural environment. Humans are not evaluators any more than ants, bees, or termites are evaluators. They are conventional and conformist, and their behavior is determined by the taboos, customs, mores, and traditions of the society in which they were born and raised. In this model, individuals are also often viewed as *social victims*, a concept that has gained widespread acceptance in many quarters.

By contrast, REMM is an evaluator. The REMM model recognizes that customs and mores serve as important constraints on human behavior, and that individuals who violate them incur costs in many forms. But REMMs compare the consequences of alternative courses of action, including those that involve the flouting of social norms, and consciously choose actions that lead to their preferred outcome. Moreover, if the costs or benefits of alternative courses of action change, REMMs change their behavior. In the sociological model individuals do not.

To be sure, social practices, customs, and mores play an important role in determining the attitudes and actions of individuals at any point in time. They represent a major force for teaching, learning, disciplining, and rewarding members of a group, organization, or society. But if the group or organization is to prosper—and, indeed, if the society itself is to survive—these cultural practices or values must adapt to approximate optimal behavior given the costs and benefits implied by the opportunity set faced by individuals in the society.

Changes in knowledge, technology, or the environment change the opportunity set. Therefore, a scientist who uses REMM to model behavior would predict that changes in knowledge, technology, and the environment that alter the costs or benefits of actions of large numbers of people will result in changes over time in social customs and mores. In contrast, the sociological model leaves social scientists with no explanation of changes in social customs, mores, taboos, and traditions.

For example, social scientists who use the sociological model would look to changes in morals and social attitudes to explain the increase in sexuality and the simultaneous decline in birth rates over the past several decades. By contrast, a social scientist using REMM to explain the same phenomena would place greater emphasis on advances in birth control techniques. Why? One major cost of sexual intercourse is the cost associated with bearing and rearing a child. By making it possible for those who do not want children to avoid conception more effectively, better birth control techniques substantially reduce the cost of sexual intercourse.

In addition, extramarital sex and cohabitation of unmarried couples are more acceptable now than prior to the introduction of effective birth control techniques. In this sense, the culture has adapted to the changes in optimal behavior implied by changes in the costs of sexual activity. At the same time, however, one can also predict that increases in the costs of sexual activity through the appearance of new untreatable sexually transmitted diseases will cause a resurgence of puritan ethics and a renewed emphasis on the family. This is consistent with the changes occurring as a result of the AIDS epidemic.

But the cultural changes required by the new birth control technology go well beyond the family and changes in sexual mores. By allowing women more control over the timing of childbirth, the new technology increases their labor market choices substantially. The lag in cultural and institutional practices in reflecting this newly optimal behavior is both inefficient and a major catalyst for the feminist movement. But the changes required to adjust to optimal behavior under the new cost conditions are unavoidable. Inefficient practices such as discrimination against women in hiring provide profit opportunities for those REMMs with the vision to perceive and act upon the gap between current and optimal practices.[9]

There is a crucial distinction, then, between the REMM model's recognition that cultural factors are *reflected* in human behavior and the sociological model's assertion that cultural factors *determine* human behavior. If behavior is completely determined by acculturation, as the sociological model suggests, then choice, purpose, and conscious adaptation are meaningless. Indeed, if humans are endowed with little originality, have no ability to evaluate, and simply imitate what they see and do what they are told, it is not clear how *any* social change could take place.

The REMM model, in contrast, explains the evolution of customs and mores as the reflection in habits, unquestioned beliefs, and religion of behavior patterns that reflect optimal responses to the costs and benefits of various actions. When the underlying costs and benefits of various actions change, individuals are faced with a conflict between new, optimal forms of behavior and culturally accepted but inefficient forms. In this situation there

will be social conflict. And if the new behavior patterns are indeed optimal, the population will—through experience, education and death—gradually accommodate the new behavior in the culture.

For example, consider the clash of economic reality with cultural values that lies behind the fairly recent decision by IBM's top management to abandon its longstanding (and socially revered) policy of lifetime employment. Beginning with the post-war prosperity of the 1950s and lasting well into the restructuring wave of the 1980s, the concept of lifetime employment by large U.S. corporations became a social expectation—an "implicit contract"—and top executives who resorted to layoffs just to maintain profitability (that is, unless threatened by bankruptcy or extinction) were harshly criticized by the media if not ostracized by their communities.

Although vigorous social criticism of layoffs persisted throughout the restructurings of the '80s, corporate America has been forced by increasing global competition to recognize that lifetime employment ends up debilitating rather than strengthening companies. Because the expectation of long-term job security became so engrained in the culture, it has been much more difficult for companies to adjust their practices. In the meantime, Japanese and European companies—traditionally far more committed to lifetime employment than their U.S. counterparts—are also being forced to rethink the policy while confronting their own problems of chronic industrial overcapacity and the resulting inefficiencies [10]

Because of its ability to explain such remarkable shifts in cultural values, REMM also provides the foundation for thinking about how to change corporate culture. The shared beliefs, attitudes, customs, and values of people within an organization can be a critical determinant of success or failure. And although an organization's culture constitutes a barrier to valuable innovation at any given moment, culture can be molded through conscious, coordinated effort over time. The values and attitudes of people within an organization will respond over time to view positively those actions which are rewarded in the organization and negatively those

---

9. In particular, employment or wage discrimination against women implies profit opportunities for new firms that can therefore hire superior women at market rates. Such profits can be shared with the employees through profit sharing or partnership structures.

10. For an account of the role of corporate restructuring in addressing both the U.S. and worldwide problem of industrial overcapacity, see Michael C. Jensen, "The Modern Industrial Revolution, Exit, and the Failure of Internal Control Systems," *Journal of Finance*, Vol. 48 No. 3 (July, 1993), pp. 831-880.

Social practices, customs, and mores represent a major force for teaching, learning, disciplining, and rewarding members of a group, organization, or society. But if the group or organization is to prosper—and, indeed, if the society itself is to survive—these cultural practices or values must adapt so as to approximate optimal behavior given the costs and benefits implied by the opportunity set.

actions which are punished. It will also respond to selection policies designed to bring into the company people with values and attitudes consistent with the desired culture.

The sociological model, then, has serious shortcomings as the basis for a body of theory about social behavior. With its near-exclusive focus on cultural continuity, it cannot account for the enormous diversity of human behavior at any given time. Nor can it explain dramatic changes in behavior such as those brought about by improved birth control and other technological advances. The model also ignores the process of conscious deliberation by individuals and organizations when contemplating different courses of action.

Given its limitations, why is the sociological model so popular?

The popularity of the sociological model can be traced to the relationship between models of human behavior and policy positions, as well as the human tendency to deny personal causal responsibility. If people's behavior is largely determined by factors beyond their control, they are victims and therefore cannot be held responsible for their actions or the states of their lives.

The appeal of such a theory to those who find themselves in trouble or wanting in any way is obvious; and the extent to which this theory is played out everyday in the media, courtrooms, families, and organizations is discussed at length by Charles Sykes in *A Nation of Victims* (St. Martin's Press, 1992). Several all-too-common examples from the book (p. 3): an employee fired for repeatedly late arrival sues his employer, arguing that he is a victim of "chronic lateness syndrome"; an FBI agent is reinstated after being fired for embezzling funds to repay his gambling debts because the court rules that gambling with the money of others is a "handicap" and hence protected under federal law.

Under the social victim model, if an individual steals, it is only because society has made him or her a thief, not because he or she has chosen that activity. And the solution is not to punish the individual for such actions because no thief chooses to be a thief. In this model, raising the costs of thievery can have no effect on the amount of thievery. The solution is to educate and rehabilitate.

Although education and rehabilitation programs can help to change people, they alone are unlikely to reduce criminal behavior significantly. As these programs become more widespread, and as they are accompanied by a reduction in the penalties and other "costs" of criminal behavior, we should not be surprised to find that REMMs more frequently choose to be criminals.

For the same reason, it is not surprising from the viewpoint of REMM that Singapore has no drug problem. Arrivals to the country must sign a statement recognizing that they have been informed that possession or sale of drugs is punishable by death. And the population is well aware of these policies; as illustrated by the recent caning of an American for vandalism, punishment for infractions of Singapore law is carried out swiftly and publicly.

Educating people about the effects of their choices does, of course, affect behavior; and it takes time for cultural attitudes to change. A complete programmatic attack on crime would include the use of both formal punishments and rewards as well as education and consensus building among the population. Properly carried out, such education and consensus building can tap social rejection and approval as additional (and decentralized) sources of punishments and rewards to reinforce sanctions against criminal or other undesirable behavior.

As another illustration of the workings of the sociological model, consider the current debate over the causes of homelessness. The very use of the term "homeless" suggests no choice on the part of street people (who are therefore victims of the system); it also carries little or none of the social disapprobation of "vagrant," a now unfashionable label. This change in language and attitudes reduces the decentralized sources of social or cultural punishment for being a street person—again, something the REMM model predicts would result in an increase in this socially undesirable behavior. New York City now spends in excess of a half billion dollars a year on subsidies for the homeless, and the problem shows no signs of going away, even with the improvement in the economy. (And the "de-institutionalizing" of the mentally ill, a common explanation, by no means accounts for the vast increase in the numbers of street people.)

The sociological model suggests that if an individual's income and wealth are small, it is entirely due to cultural factors, environmental adversity, or bad luck—not to conscious effort, the choice of leisure over work, the choice of a particular type of work, or the failure to invest in learning. Therefore, "justice" requires that we confiscate the wealth of the more fortunate to recompense the unfortunate.

Of course, the higher the recompense, the more attractive it is to be poor, and REMMs will respond by taking more leisure, by choosing occupations in which employment is more unstable, and by investing less in learning. The REMM model predicts that if we make the payoff high enough, we can attract an arbitrarily large number of people to become poor or unemployed—or at least to meet the established criteria for those programs. This describes important aspects of our welfare and unemployment systems.

Politicians, bureaucrats, and special interest groups understand that public policy choices are affected by the concept that individuals are responsible for their own fates. Strong popular support for the principle that individuals ought to be rewarded or punished in accordance with their own behavior means that measures that aim to redistribute wealth, or rehabilitate criminals rather than punish them, would encounter strong opposition. But resourceful politicians and others who want to put such measures into effect can neutralize public opposition by persuading people that everything we do is forced on us by our cultural environment—we are social victims, and thus neither our behavior nor our status is a product of deliberate choice. By undermining the link between choice and consequences, they can overcome the resistance that stems from beliefs that individuals are responsible for their own behavior.

In addition, individuals constantly face a conflict when attempting to help others who are experiencing difficulty, especially those related through family or other ties. The conflict is between the desire to ease or eliminate the difficulties of others through gifts or charity, and the reluctance to distort the incentives of people to take charge of their own lives—say, by investing in education and making other efforts to improve their condition. All parents face such trade-offs when deciding how much help to give their children, and the choices are not easy. The short-term pain associated with denying help to a loved one is very difficult to bear. But casual observation together with evidence of the futility of various social programs seem to indicate that people systematically underestimate the counterproductive long-run effects on individuals of actions that we take to shield them from the consequences of their own choices.[11]

The Sociological Model and Marxism

A discussion of the sociological model would be incomplete without touching upon the use of that concept by Marxists, socialists, and other groups around the world. Marxist politicians understand that the sociological model is the foundation for the centralization of power. Marxism has received wide support in Europe. It has also had substantial support among the Catholic clergy and American academics. Recent evidence on the widespread failure of Russian, Eastern European, and other economies dominated by Marxist thought has revealed the shortcomings of this view and diminished, but not eliminated, support for it. Ironically, as many formerly socialist Eastern European and Asian countries are moving toward capitalism, the U.S. is moving toward more socialistic regulatory and political policies.

Socialism is supported by a philosophy that idolizes the state. The urge to subordinate the individual to the organization has ancient roots going back at least to Plato. In portraying his ideal state, Plato says:

...[T]here is common property of wives, of children, and of all chattels. And everything possible has been done to eradicate from our life everywhere and in every way all that is private and individual. So far as it can be done, even those things which nature herself has made private and individual have somehow become the common property of all. Our very eyes and ears and hands seem to see, to hear, and to act, as if they belonged not to individuals but to the community. All men are molded to be unanimous to the utmost degree in bestowing praise and blame, and they even rejoice and grieve about the same things, and at the same time.... Nor should the mind of anybody be habituated to letting him do anything at all on his own initiative, neither out of zeal, nor even playfully... But in war and in the midst of peace—to his leader he shall direct his eye, and follow him faithfully. And even in the smallest matters he should stand under leadership. For example, he should get up, or move, or wash, or take his means... only if he has been told to do so... In a word, he should teach his soul, by long habit, never to dream of acting independently, and to become utterly incapable of it.[12]

---

11. The "tough love" movement and twelve-step programs such as AA for treating substance dependence are designed to provide help while insisting that individuals maintain their personal responsibility for their fate.

12. Plato, *Laus*, 739c, ff and 942a, f, as cited by Karl Popper in *The Open Society and Its Enemies* (2nd ed.) (Princeton, New Jersey: Princeton University Press, 1950), p. 102.

Politicians, bureaucrats, and special interest groups understand that public policy choices are affected by the concept that individuals are responsible for their own fates.

Plato's ideal state is an example of the most extreme anti-individualist position, one which makes the organization itself the ultimate end. The state is treated as a living organism; it is the overriding value. Individual purpose is not only unimportant, it is an evil that must be stamped out.

Plato's views are not very different from those of most Marxists. The role of the individual poses a dilemma for Marxists. Avowed Marxist states around the world such as the former USSR, China, and Cuba display an attitude with respect to individual citizens that is close to Plato's utopia. Party doctrine denounces individualistic motivation and invokes the common good. In intellectual discourse, Marxist theorists press for an organizational or social class approach to the study of society. In Marxist theory, the worker and the capitalist play out their roles regardless of the costs and benefits of their actions. Capitalists are what they are and do what they do because they are capitalists, and so too for workers. In the Marxist model, individuals do not evaluate, choose, or maximize; they behave according to the sociological model.

The sociological model is devoid of prescriptive content, yet it is commonly used for normative purposes. If humans are not evaluators (they only play the roles given to them by the culture), it is meaningless to talk about making people better off. While Marxists reject the Western economic tradition of considering the individual as the basic unit of analysis, they also express great concern for the plight of the less fortunate, and make much of concepts such as class conflict and exploitation.

Thus, these concerns for the welfare of people (primarily the workers or underclass) exhibit an obvious and fatal inconsistency. To repeat, unless we attribute preferences to the individual, language that describes differences in an individual's well-being makes no sense. Notions like equality and justice are popular among those who employ the sociological model of humanity, but such ethical norms are not internally meaningful because they imply that individuals care about their condition— that is, that they are evaluators, they experience envy, and they choose.

Furthermore, if the state is all that matters, as Marxist doctrine maintains, concern for the plight of the individual is irrelevant at best and can be inimical to the general good. Concepts such as exploitation and conflict can be used in a group context to refer to more than one individual, but such language has meaning only in terms of individuals. Organizations cannot be exploited any more than machines or rocks can be exploited. Only individuals can be exploited, can suffer, can make war; only individuals can be objects of compassion. Organizations are purely conceptual artifacts, even when they are assigned the legal status of individuals. In the end, we can do things *to* and *for* individuals only.

THE PSYCHOLOGICAL MODEL OF HUMAN BEHAVIOR

The psychological model is a step up the evolutionary ladder from the sociological model. Like REMM, humans in this model are resourceful, they care, they have wants and drives. But the individual's wants are viewed essentially as absolutes that are largely independent of one another. Therefore, substitutions or trade-offs are not part of individual human behavior. In effect, the individual is said to have "needs" in the sense of that word which we have already rejected.

Perhaps the best-known formulation of what we call the psychological model was provided by A. H. Maslow. "Human needs," wrote Maslow in 1943, "arrange themselves in hierarchies of prepotency. That is to say, the appearance of one need usually rests on the prior satisfaction of another more prepotent need."[13] Maslow's needs, in order of their "prepotency" from high to low, are physiological (food, water), safety, love, and self-actualization.

In contrast to REMM, in Maslow's *hierarchy of needs* model the individual is unwilling to give up any food for any amount of safety until his or her food needs are satisfied. Only after the food needs are completely satisfied will he or she be concerned about safety. What Maslow and his followers have done is to confuse two entirely different issues: how an individual allocates resources among alternative goods at a given level of wealth, and how that allocation pattern varies as an individual's wealth rises.

Maslow himself, in the latter part of his famous article, qualifies his early statements that deny substitution. He argues that he did not mean that literally

---

13. A.H. Maslow, "A Theory of Human Motivation," *Psychological Review*, Vol. 50, (January, 1943), p. 370.

100% of a person's food need had to be satisfied in order for him or her to begin to satisfy the safety needs, and so on.[14] Although most of Maslow's followers have ignored his qualifications, these latter statements show him moving toward the notion of substitution and the income elasticity of demand, a relationship known to economists for many years and incorporated in REMM.[15]

Moreover, ample evidence of human behavior contradicts Maslow's hierarchy of needs model. We see astronauts, skiers, and car racers accepting less safety in return for wealth, fame, and just plain thrills. Poets, artists, and gurus go without material comforts to devote their time to contemplation and art, and, to us, these pursuits sound closer to self-actualization than physiological goods.

The psychological model, like the sociological model, is not satisfactory for describing the behavior of individuals in the study of social phenomena. Yet there is some content in Maslow's model. His ordering of wants probably corresponds to how most people would allocate a $1,000 increment of wealth on expenditures at increasing levels of wealth. Wealthier people tend to spend less of their additional wealth on goods satisfying physiological wants, and more on each of the categories of goods higher in Maslow's hierarchy.[16] Nevertheless, inconsistent with Maslow's model, individuals at any level of wealth are willing to sacrifice some amounts of any good for sufficiently large amounts of all other goods.

Thus, while Maslow's ordering of categories of human wants tends to describe how expenditures increase with increased wealth, it is neither a hierarchy nor does it describe needs. It is difficult to infer much else about social behavior from the hierarchy of needs model that is not trivial or false. The psychological model predicts that if the cost of any good rises, the individual will reduce outlays on whatever is the highest-ranking good he or she currently buys, a behavioral reaction clearly contradicted by actual consumer behavior. When the price of one good rises relative to other goods, consumers react by reducing purchases of the good whose price has risen, not the purchases of goods that are highest on Maslow's list.

Once substitution is ruled out, the individual's attempt to maximize by reconciling wants with means is largely ignored, and attention focuses instead on the study of individual wants (or classes of wants). Examples from the field of organizational behavior (OB) are numerous. One general problem (an extremely important one) is how to get employees to be more productive. The general answer is to reward them by satisfying their needs.

The OB literature does not generally recognize that the employer's problem is one of designing an overall employment package that takes into account the potential for trade-offs. Instead, each good that the employer can provide the employee is considered in isolation. Job enrichment and the quality of the working environment are examples. More of each is always taken to be better than less, and not only is the optimality criterion seldom applied to determine the correct level of job enrichment or quality of the environment, optimality itself is rarely discussed.

The prevalence of Maslow's model in the behavioral science field is, we believe, a major reason for the failure of the field to develop a unified body of theory. Theory erected on the basis of individuals who are driven by wants, but who cannot or will not make substitutions, will necessarily consist of a series of independent propositions relating particular drives to actions and will never be able to capture the complexity of human behavior.

THE POLITICAL MODEL OF HUMAN BEHAVIOR

While resourceful and, in a certain sense, evaluators and maximizers, individuals under the political model are assumed to evaluate and maximize in terms of other individuals' preferences rather than their own. Unlike REMM, the individual is a *perfect agent*

---

14. "So far, our theoretical discussion may have given the impression that these five sets of needs are somehow in a step-wise, all-or-none relationship to each other... This... might give the false impression that a need must be satisfied 100 per cent before the next need emerges. In actual fact, most members of our society who are normal, are partially satisfied in all their basic needs and partially unsatisfied in all their basic needs at the same time. A more realistic description of the hierarchy would be in terms of decreasing percentages of satisfaction as we go up the hierarchy of prepotency...

As for the concept of emergence of a new need after satisfaction of the prepotent need, this emergence is not a sudden, salutatory phenomenon but rather a gradual emergence by slow degrees from nothingness." Maslow (1943, p. 388-9).

15. The income elasticity of demand describes how an individual's consumption of a good changes with a given change in income. It is the percentage change in the quantity of a good demanded by an individual divided by the percentage change in the individual's income (holding all prices and quantities of other goods constant).

16. Economists call such goods "necessities" and "luxury" goods. They are defined by their income- or wealth-elasticity of demand.

While Marxists reject the Western economic tradition of considering the individual as the basic unit of analysis, they also express great concern for the plight of the less fortunate. But, unless we attribute preferences to the individual, language that describes differences in an individual's well-being makes no sense.

seeking to maximize "the public good" rather than his or her own welfare.

It is important to distinguish between altruism (that is, a willingness to sacrifice some of one's own goods, time, or welfare for the benefit of others) and the political model. Altruists do not behave according to the political model. Since they have their own preferences, they cannot be perfect agents. A perfect agent is a person that will maximize with respect to the preferences of the principal while, if necessary, denying his or her own. Perfect agents would be equally satisfied working to save the whales, feed the poor, make computers, or care for the musical interests of the rich through the local symphony orchestra at the bidding of their employers. Altruist that she is, Mother Teresa's devotion to caring for the poor of Calcutta does not make her a perfect agent. It is highly doubtful that she would agree to (or effectively) represent the interests of someone who wished to save the whales or make computers. Like all REMMs, she has her own preferences and will exercise her choice over whom or what cause she devotes her time to helping.

The logic in which the political model figures so prominently is simple, though it will not withstand careful scrutiny. Whenever individuals acting on their own behalf will not bring about the "desired" outcome, government must take a hand. If consumers might be misled by deceptive advertising, have government regulate advertising. If sellers might market products that are harmful to consumers, have government regulate consumer product safety. If consumers might not understand the terms of lending contracts, have government regulate the language that can be used in such contracts.

The fatal flaw in the above propositions is their assumption that when politicians intervene, they act to accomplish the desired result—that is, they act in the public interest. Those who argue for such government intervention simply assume that politicians can and will behave in accord with the desires of the electorate.

This political or perfect agent model lies at the heart of virtually all campaigns that purport to solve

problems by creating a governmental agency or appointing a political body. Worried about too many dangerous drugs or injuries in coal mines? Establish an FDA to regulate drug testing and grant approval for the marketing of new drugs. To reduce injuries in coal mines, pass a mine safety law with the Department of Mines to administer it. Unfortunately, the results of such programs do not lend support to the political model. After the 1962 amendments regulating the efficacy of new drugs, the number of new drugs approved in the U.S. fell by half.[17] Moreover, between 1966 and 1970, more than 2,000 small nonunion coal mines closed down with no measurable reduction of injury or death rates in coal mines.[18]

These results occur—and are indeed predictable—because the people who enact and administer the laws are REMMs. The bureaucrats in the FDA, for instance, face high costs if they err and allow a drug that has injurious side effects (such as Thalidomide) to be marketed. On the other hand, the people who suffer and die because FDA procedures have kept a new drug bottled up in the testing laboratories for several years (or perhaps never let it on the market) usually don't even know that they have been harmed. Patients now able to get efficacious drug treatments in Europe that are not available in the U.S. are becoming aware of the consequences of FDA regulations, but their number is small. Political action by AIDS patients and their advocates has persuaded the FDA to relax restrictions limiting access to promising AIDS treatments before they have satisfied all normal FDA regulations for public use.

The mine safety law that closed down many nonunion mines was passed after active lobbying by both the United Mine Workers Union and the Bituminous Coal Operators Association (which represents the mining firms unionized by the United Mine Workers). Both of these groups faced competition from small mines that were generally staffed by nonunion labor. The costs imposed on these mines by the law were so onerous that many of them were driven out of business.

Allegiance to the political model has been a major deterrent to the development of a body of

---

17. See Sam Peltzman, *Regulation of Pharmaceutical Innovation* (American Enterprise Institute, 1974), pp. 15-16. See also William M. Wardell, Mohammed Hassar, Sadanand N. Anavekar, and Louis Lasagna, "The Rate of Development in New Drugs in the United States, 1963 through 1975," *Clinical Pharmacology and Therapeutics*, Vol. 24, No. 2 (August 1978). For a review of the literature on the effectiveness of the FDA drug regulation procedures, see Ronald W. Hansen, "The Relationship Between Regulation and R&D in the Pharmaceutical Industry: A

Review of Literature and Public Policy Proposals," *The Effectiveness of Medicines in Containing Health Care Costs: Impact of Innovation, Regulation and Quality* (National Pharmaceutical Council, 1982).

18. See David R. Henderson, "Coal Mine Safety Legislation: Safety or Monopoly?," Graduate School of Management, University of Rochester (November 1977).

theory that could explain with reasonable accuracy how the political system operates. Social scientists, especially political scientists, have been aware of the anxiety politicians exhibit to be reelected, and they have usually tacitly assumed that this induces them to behave in accord with the wishes of the majority. But this model of the legislative process is incapable of explaining what actually occurs.

We know that legislators consistently vote for measures that cannot possibly be in the interest of a majority of their constituents.[19] Except Wisconsin (and even there it is doubtful), there surely is no state in the Union where a majority benefits from government sponsorship of a cartel among milk producers. Other examples are tariffs on TV sets, oil import quotas, "voluntary" quotas on foreign automobiles, and punitive tariffs on flat-panel computer screens, to name just a few.

Elected officials who are REMMs sense that they have the opportunity to become entrepreneurs. They have access at relatively low cost to mass advertising via television, radio, newspapers, and magazines. Resourceful politicians also ally themselves with organized groups that get media attention and encourage the organization of new groups. Indeed, now that the general nature of the process and the payoff to such organizations have been perceived, popular fronts have proliferated, each vying for publicity, even to the point of using violence to demonstrate their sincerity.

Individually and collectively, legislators have an interest in enlarging the role of the state and, as REMMs, they engage in continuous marketing of programs to achieve that end. If crises do not exist, they create them, or at least the illusion of crises. Then, they rescue their constituents from disaster with legislation that sacrifices the general welfare to benefit special interests.

The Current Health Care Debate. For example, in recent years members of the Clinton Administration and associated special interest groups have campaigned to create the public impression of a health care crisis and mobilize support for legislation to "reform" the U.S. health care system. The proposed changes would result in massive new regulations and centralization of the system. In so doing, it would transfer substantial control over an additional 14% of the U.S. gross national product to the government, with obvious implications for the power base of the bureaucracy.

Almost as clear, unfortunately, is the import of these changes for the efficiency and quality of U.S. health care. The proposed changes would result in a centralization and cartelization of the health industry in the hands of government and newly proposed private bodies. This is exactly the wrong way to go with this industry. Because the specific knowledge of each case lies in the hands of the doctor and the patient, decision-making in the health care industry, to be effective, must be decentralized and thus kept in the hands of doctor and patient. The proposed centralized process for deciding on patient treatment and care will inevitably result in large declines in the quality of health care. Even ignoring the effects of the centralization, the Administration's original plan to take $150 billion of annual costs (and therefore real resources) out of the system while adding as many as 37 million people to it would reduce the quality and timeliness of future care; it would also create shortages and lead to rationing.

There is a U.S. health care *cost* problem, to be sure; but it does not stem from too little regulation and too few subsidies. Rather, it comes from our third-party insurance system that effectively removes responsibility for the costs from the most important decision-maker—that is, the patient. The key to solving this problem is to impose the financial consequences of their medical decisions on patients through greater use of co-pay insurance with larger deductibles that place first-dollar costs on patients while protecting them against catastrophic illness.

The Political Model in the Private Sector

The political (or perfect agent) model is also widely used by managers of private organizations in managing their employees. Corporate managers often wish to believe that people are perfect agents with no preferences of their own. If there is a problem in part of the organization with a manager who is making the wrong decisions, the problems must come from having a "bad" person in the job. The solution is then to fire the manager and replace him or her with a new person. Tell that person (who is assumed to be a perfect agent) what you want done, and then wait for it to happen.

---

19. See James M. Buchanan and Gordon Tullock, *The Calculus of Consent* (Ann Arbor, Michigan: University of Michigan Press (1965).

> **Legislators have an interest in enlarging the role of the state and, as REMMs, they engage in continuous marketing of programs to achieve that end. If crises do not exist they create them, or at least the illusion of crises.**

In contrast, managers using the REMM model would predict that if the manager has the proper talent and training, it is the organizational structure and incentives that are at the root of the problem. The solution would then be not to fire the manager, but to reform the organizational policies.

Problems in organizations often arise because managers are rewarded for doing things that harm the organization—for example, empire building or maximizing market share at the expense of shareholder value. In compensating managers according to negotiated budgets, many companies effectively induce line managers to negotiate budget targets that are well below the level that would maximize the value of the organization. The managers do this, of course, to ensure they can easily meet the target.

In a related problem, large public corporations also regularly retain and tend to waste large amounts of free cash flow—that is, cash flow in excess of that required to fund all profitable projects of the firm. Spending the cash on acquisitions or other unprofitable projects (undertaken with the aid of unrealistically high forecasts of future profitability) gives management a bigger company to run, thereby increasing their power and prestige in the community. Because managerial pay tends to be positively related to the size of the company, these actions generally increase their compensation as well. In addition, keeping the cash in the firm gives them a cushion for spending during tough times, whether it is economic or not. Retaining the excess cash also makes it easier to avoid closing plants, laying off employees, cutting charitable contributions, and making the other hard choices associated with freeing up underutilized resources. Yet it is important for managers to make these difficult choices so that the resources can be put to higher-valued uses in the rest of society.[20]

IN CLOSING

We argue that the explanatory power of REMM, the resourceful, evaluative, maximizing model of human behavior, dominates that of all the other models summarized here. To be sure, each of the other models captures an important aspect of behavior, while failing in other respects. REMM incorporates the best of each of these models.

From the economic model, REMM takes the assumption that people are resourceful, self-interested maximizers, but rejects the notion that they are interested only in money income or wealth.

From the psychological model, REMM takes the assumption that the income elasticity of demand for various goods has certain regularities the world over. Nevertheless, in taking on this modified notion of a hierarchy of needs, it does not violate the principle of substitution by assuming people have "needs."

From the sociological model, REMM takes the assumption that "society" imposes costs on people for violating social norms, which in turn affect behavior; but it also assumes that individuals will depart from such norms if the benefits are sufficiently great. Indeed, this is how social change takes place.

From the political model, REMM takes the assumption that people have the capacity for altruism. They care about others and take their interests into account while maximizing their own welfare. REMM rejects, however, the notion that people are perfect agents.

In using REMM, detail must be added (as we have done implicitly in the examples above) to tailor the model to serve as a decision guide in specific circumstances. We must specify more about people's tastes and preferences that are relevant to the issue at hand—for example, by making explicit assumptions that people have a positive rate of discount for future as opposed to present goods and that they value leisure as well as intangibles such as honor, companionship, and self-realization. Finally, combining these assumptions with knowledge of the opportunity set from which people are choosing in any situation (that is, the rates at which people can trade off or substitute among various goods) leads to a powerfully predictive model.

REMM is the basic building block that has led to the development of a more or less unified body of theory in the social sciences. For example, some economists, like recent Nobel laureate Gary Becker, have applied REMM in fields previously reserved to sociologists such as discrimination, crime, marriage,

20. See the following articles by Michael C. Jensen, "The Agency Costs of Free Cash Flow: Corporate Finance and Takeovers," *American Economic Review*, Vol. 76, No. 2 (May 1986); "Takeovers: Their Causes and Consequences," *Journal of Economic Perspectives*, Vol. 2, No. 1 (Winter 1988), pp. 21-48; "Eclipse of the Public Corporation," *Harvard Business Review*, Vol. 89, No. 5 (September-October 1989), pp. 61-74.; and Larry Lang, Annette Poulsen, Rene Stulz, "Asset Sales, Firm Performance, and the Agency Costs of Managerial Discretion," *Journal of Financial Economics* (1994) and the references therein.

> **Problems in organizations often arise because top managers are rewarded for doing things that harm the organization—for example, empire building or maximizing market share at the expense of shareholder value.**

and the family.[21] Political scientists in company with economists have also employed utility-maximizing models of political behavior to explain voter behavior and the behavior of regulators and bureaucrats.[22] Still others are using REMM to explain organizational problems inside firms.[23]

For all its diversity, this growing body of research has one common message: Whether they are politicians, managers, academics, professionals, philanthropists, or factory workers, individuals are resourceful, evaluative maximizers. They respond creatively to the opportunities the environment presents to them, and they work to loosen constraints that prevent them from doing what they wish to do. They care about not only money, but almost everything—respect, honor, power, love, and the welfare of others. The challenge for our society, and for all organizations in it, is to establish rules of the game and educational procedures that tap and direct the creative energy of REMMs in ways that increase the effective use of our scarce resources.

REMMs are everywhere.

21. See Gary Becker, "A Theory of Marriage: Part 1," *Journal of Political Economy*, Vol. 82 (July/August, 1973); and "Crime and Punishment: An Economic Approach," *Journal of Political Economy*, Vol. 76 (March/April, 1968)

22. For discussions of political choice, see Anthony Downs, *An Economic Theory of Democracy* (New York: Harper & Row, 1957); and James M. Buchanan and Gordon Tullock, *The Calculus of Consent* (Ann Arbor, Michigan: University of Michigan Press, 1965). For an analysis of bureaucracies, see William A. Niskanen, Jr., *Bureaucracy and Representative Government* (Aldine-Atherton, Inc., 1971).

23. For discussions of organizational problems, see Armen Alchian and Harold Demsetz, "Production, Information Costs, and Economic Organization," *American Economic Review*, Vol. LXII, No. 5 (1972), pp. 77-79; Kenneth J. Arrow, "Control in Large Organizations," *Essays in the Theory of Risk-Bearing* (Markham Publishing Co., 1971); Michael C. Jensen and William H. Meckling, "Theory of the Firm: Managerial Behavior, Agency Costs and Ownership Structure," *Journal of Financial Economics*, Vol. 4, No. 4 (October 1976); Michael C. Jensen and William H. Meckling, "Specific and General Knowledge and Organizational Structure," in *Contract Economics*, Lars Werm and Hans Wijkander, eds. (Blackwell, Oxford 1992; Oliver E. Williamson, *Corporate Control and Business Behavior* (Prentice-Hall, 1970); and Paul Milgrom and John Roberts, *Economics, Organization, and Management* (Prentice-Hall: 1992).

CORPORATE GOVERNANCE, ETHICS, AND ORGANIZATIONAL ARCHITECTURE

*by James A. Brickley,
Clifford W. Smith, Jr., and
Jerold L. Zimmerman,
University of Rochester**

T he recent highly publicized incidents of corporate wrongdoing have opened the floodgates of criticism and recrimination. Blame has been laid at the feet of everything from corporate greed to lax accounting oversight to Wall Street's insistence on ever-rising earnings to a general deterioration in ethics and standards. Corporate governance in general, and the pursuit of shareholder value in particular, have increasingly come under fire for what is perceived to be an excessively narrow focus on the stock price and its surrogate, accounting earnings, as the ultimate measure of corporate performance.[1]

But the practical implementation of any concept of corporate governance, whether aimed at value maximization or some other corporate objective, rests on the organizational underpinnings of the firm. In our view, the recent corporate scandals stem not so much from a general failure of corporate governance as from flaws in an important facet of corporate governance—the organizational design of the firm. We use the term *organizational architecture* to refer to three key elements of organizational design:

- The assignment of decision-making authority— who gets to make what decisions?
- Performance evaluation—how is the performance of business units and employees measured?
- Compensation structure—how are employees rewarded (or penalized) for meeting (or failing to meet) performance goals?

Successful companies assign decision-making authority in ways that effectively link that authority with the knowledge and experience needed to make good decisions. This linkage is bolstered by performance measurement systems that accurately and consistently gauge shareholder value creation, and is then reinforced by compensation systems that provide decision makers with the appropriate incentives to make value-increasing decisions. The three organizational elements are fundamentally interdependent. Indeed, they are like the three legs of a stool—they must be designed jointly to ensure that the stool is balanced and functional. A weakness in any one leg can undermine a company's organizational architecture and cause the corporate governance system to fail. And because inadequate corporate governance can torpedo even the most brilliant business strategy, managers must structure internal systems that enable a company to achieve its value potential.

Enron is a case in point. This "sleepy, regulated natural gas company" of the 1980s transformed itself in the 1990s by embracing a New Economy corporate culture with a flatter management structure, a dramatically reduced reliance on hard assets, and an entrepreneurial, risk-taking environment open to creative and unconventional products and practices. In August 2000, Enron's market cap reached a peak of nearly $70 billion, and the company was everybody's favorite success story. But then the

*This article is drawn from our book *Designing Organizations to Create Value: From Strategy to Structure* (New York: McGraw-Hill, 2002). We acknowledge a great debt to Michael Jensen and the late William Meckling, whose pioneering research in organization theory kindled much of our own research. We thank Don Chew and Janice Willett for editorial assistance.

1. While "corporate governance" is not precisely defined here, this term generally refers to the roles of shareholders, managers, directors, and others as laid out by both the underlying legal system (through, for example, state incorporation laws and SEC regulations) and firm-specific mechanisms such as corporate charters, corporate bylaws, and internal operating policies.

wheels came off, ending in a bankruptcy filing, a near-total evaporation of market cap, and the draining of $1 billion of assets from employee retirement accounts.

What went wrong? According to *BusinessWeek*,

Enron didn't just fail because of improper accounting or alleged corruption at the top...The unrelenting emphasis on earnings growth and individual initiative, coupled with a shocking absence of the usual corporate checks and balances, tipped the culture from one that rewarded aggressive strategy to one that increasingly relied on unethical cornercutting. In the end, too much leeway was given to young, inexperienced managers without the necessary controls to minimize failures. This was a company that simply placed a lot of bad bets on businesses that weren't so promising to begin with.[2]

In other words, Enron's problems were rooted in a fundamentally flawed organizational design. And each of the three architectural elements was at fault. First, in the course of flattening its management structure, Enron ended up delegating too much decision-making authority deeper into the company without retaining the appropriate degree of control at higher levels. Second, performance was evaluated largely on the basis of near-term earnings growth, which can distort managerial decision-making. Third, the company offered enormous compensation to its top performers, also on the basis of near-term earnings growth, which encouraged excessive risk-taking as well as business decisions geared toward propping up earnings.[3]

Remarkably enough, Enron's own internal risk manual pointed to the core of the problem when it acknowledged that "the rules and principles of accounting...do not always create measures consistent with underlying economics." Still, as the manual went on to say, Enron's "risk management strategies are therefore directed at accounting rather than economic performance" because "corporate management's performance is generally measured by accounting income, not underlying economics."[4] Although the internal risk management group was charged with reviewing business deals, the perfor-

mance appraisals of the employees in that group were based in part on the recommendations of the very people generating the deals. And the legal staff was decentralized throughout the organization, where they were more vulnerable to pressures to meet their individual business units' performance targets. As the Enron story suggests, there is clear potential for trouble—and even breaches in ethical behavior—when performance measurement and compensation systems are designed around accounting earnings, and a flatter, more decentralized management structure permits freewheeling decision-making.

The critical question, however, is whether managers can reasonably be expected to identify these and other potential problems before they materialize, and to structure a productive, well-balanced, value-oriented organization. We believe that the answer to this question is a resounding *yes*. As described in this article, our approach to organizational architecture provides an integrated framework that can be applied on a consistent basis. Of course, no two companies are likely to adopt precisely the same structure—and that's not surprising since the optimal organizational architecture will generally differ from company to company. Depending on its specific circumstances, top management should decentralize certain decisions and centralize others, tailoring the performance measurement system accordingly to detect whether employees are making value-adding decisions, and structuring its compensation system to reward them appropriately. And when a company adopts an incentive compensation plan, it is important that employees have the decision authority to respond to the new incentives and that their performance be measured accurately.

As the celebrated architect Louis H. Sullivan, designer of the first skyscraper and founder of the American school of architecture, once observed, "Form ever follows function." Applying this same principle to organizational architecture, we see that significant changes in the business environment and hence in a company's strategy will typically call for changes in decision authority, performance measurement, and compensation. Well-designed companies focus on—and ensure consistency among—all three design elements.

---

2. "At Enron, 'The Environment Was Ripe for Abuse,'" *BusinessWeek*, February 25, 2002.

3. Any system in which managers participate in annual profits but not in losses can encourage excessive risk-taking. This perverse incentive is most pronounced when a small bet fails and the employee tries to make it up by doubling the bet.

If this second bet also fails, the employee can have a strong incentive to double up again and "go for broke."

4. These statements by Enron were presented in testimony by Professor Frank Partnoy, University of San Diego School of Law, in hearings before the U.S. Senate Committee on Government Affairs, January 24, 2002.

As the Enron story suggests, there is clear potential for trouble—even breaches in ethical behavior—when performance measurement and compensation systems are designed around accounting earnings, and a flatter, more decentralized management structure permits freewheeling decision-making.

THE CORPORATE GOAL: SHAREHOLDER VALUE

Since the restructurings of the 1980s, maximizing shareholder value has become the premier business mantra. Managers constantly profess their fundamental allegiance to shareholder value, typically measured by the stock price. When a company is rumored to be a possible takeover target, management's first response is to make clear to employees, communities, the media, and stock analysts that their top priority is to increase shareholder returns through value creation.

And there is good reason for this development. With increased competition from both foreign and domestic producers, as well as changes in technology that have altered production processes and product demand, companies have had to refocus their attention on shareholder value to survive.[5] A senior manager of a German beer company, reflecting on the current business environment in Germany, noted that "it used to be about beer, beer, beer—now it's about shareholders."[6] Even the Keidanren, an association of over 1,000 major Japanese companies, recently concluded that it is "necessary for Japanese companies to place more importance on shareholder value" and recommended the increased use of stock options to compensate managers as well as the addition of outside directors to Japanese boards.[7]

But what does it mean to maximize shareholder value? Shareholders invest in a company's stock because they expect to earn returns comparable to those available on other similar investments. Ultimately, shareholder returns are determined by the payouts they receive, whether in the form of dividends, stock repurchases, or realized capital gains. But the underlying source of such payouts, of course, is the cash generated by the business—the operating cash flow that is left after all other bills have been paid, including taxes and debt interest. Therefore, as finance theory says, managers increase shareholder value when they increase the present value of the company's net cash flows.[8] A firm's stock price is a useful barometer of performance because it reflects not just the value the company has created

(or destroyed) historically but also the value of its expected future cash flow.

Of course, future cash flows are not known for certain and must be forecast by investors, who look to earnings statements for information that is useful in developing these forecasts. There is obviously a strong correspondence in many companies between reported earnings and cash flows, and in fact managers who work to maximize reported earnings over time will also generally be working to maximize cash flows and share value. Nonetheless, accounting earnings are relevant only to the extent they provide information about a company's ongoing ability to generate cash flow. Window-dressing will at best be disregarded by astute investors and may even be seen as a signal that management is trying to conceal poor operating performance. What's more, manipulating the timing or reporting of sales or expenses to artificially boost accounting earnings will actually decrease share value if it reduces the cash that can ultimately be paid out to shareholders.

Boards of directors have a legal responsibility to make decisions on behalf of shareholders and to adopt performance measures and compensation plans that provide managers with cost-effective incentives to maximize current and future cash flows, or the company's economic "bottom line." And as we discuss next, managers should concentrate on developing and executing a solid long-term business strategy, rather than slavishly focusing on accounting earnings.

STRATEGY AND ARCHITECTURE

Managers must continually seek new ways to create and capture value if their companies are to remain successful. Competitors who work to develop new and better products or production processes will eventually overwhelm any company that fails to innovate. In rapidly changing industries, new ways to create and capture value are likely to be critical. But even a long-time producer of a standard commodity will lose out to the competition if it fails to minimize production and distribution costs and to enhance customer benefits.

---

5. As we will discuss later, allocating corporate resources among multiple constituencies, such as employees and local communities, does not conflict with maximizing shareholder value.

6. *The Wall Street Journal*, June 21, 2001, p. A1.

7. See http://www.keidanren.or.jp/.

8. To be precise, the current value of a firm's shares is determined by the expected cash flows that ultimately will be paid out to shareholders, discounted at a rate that reflects the returns that investors could earn on alternative investments with similar risk, liquidity, and tax consequences.

The central message of the "core competency" literature is that managers need to identify what their firms are good at and devise ways to leverage those competencies to create and capture value. For example, Sony's skills in electronics might be leveraged in any number of ways, from office equipment to toys. At the same time, managers should avoid investing in businesses with little potential for creating or capturing value—witness the general lack of success of the unrelated diversifications of the 1970s. Similarly, Enron's demise is attributable in large part to the mistaken belief that its "business model" and its considerable skills in the energy business would translate into areas like water, wind, or bandwidth projects.

It is also critical to consider competitors' responses when making major strategic decisions. Sound strategy formulation often requires "putting yourself behind your rival's desk." Kodak decided to invest heavily in producing writable CD-ROMs, which had been quite a profitable business for the company, but management failed to anticipate the threat of potential competition and ultimately lost money in that business. According to then-CEO George Fisher, "I think we screwed up. We should have known that prices would fall as manufacturers worldwide ramped up production."[9]

But perhaps most important in any evaluation of strategy is the relationship between strategy and organizational architecture. If a key aspect of an industry's operating environment changes, managers in most companies in that industry will react by reappraising and modifying their strategies—too often without considering whether the existing organizational architecture will remain effective. Before the rise in foreign competition, large American companies such as ITT, IBM, and General Motors enjoyed substantial market power and faced little external pressure to focus on rapid product development, high-quality production, or competitive pricing. Their organizations were extremely bureaucratic, with centralized decision-making and limited incentive compensation. Competition has forced these companies to rethink their basic strategies and to increase their emphasis on quality, customer service, cost control, and competitive pricing. In the process, decision authority has been pushed lower within the organization—to employees with more detailed knowledge about customer preferences. This change has been accompanied by the introduction of performance measures tied to quality and customer service as well as an increased reliance on incentive compensation.

Not only changes in the competitive environment but changes in technology can precipitate changes in strategy and architecture, too. Purchasing decisions at many retailers used to be relatively centralized, with buyers in New York City selecting a company's clothing lines for the year. But the introduction of satellite communications and closed-circuit television allowed central buyers to display goods to regional store managers, who could then stock their stores based on their knowledge of local fashions and tastes. With the new strategic emphasis on local competition, purchasing decisions became more decentralized. More generally, changes in technology, including email and intranets, have facilitated communication between senior management and lower-level employees, thus reducing the need for mid-level managers and allowing many companies to flatten their management structures.

And strategy can in turn be influenced by organizational architecture. A company might decide to enter a new market in part because its decision and control systems are especially well suited for the new undertaking. Before the 1980s, Atlanta was widely acknowledged to be the banking center of the South. Yet at the beginning of the 21st century, Charlotte, North Carolina claims that title. Unlike Georgia, North Carolina had always permitted statewide branching, so when restrictions on interstate banking eased in the 1980s, the North Carolina banks—especially NCNB (now Bank of America) and Wachovia—exploited their experience in establishing and managing statewide systems to forge regional and then national banks. Their organizational architectures were better suited to the new regulatory environment.

THE FIRST LEG: DECISION-MAKING AUTHORITY

The principal challenge in organizational design is to ensure that decision makers have both the relevant information to make good decisions and the incentives to use their information productively.

---

9. *The Democrat and Chronicle* (Rochester, NY), Nov. 2, 1997.

Boards of directors have a legal responsibility to make decisions on behalf of shareholders and to adopt performance measures and compensation plans that provide managers with cost-effective incentives to maximize current and future cash flows, or the company's economic "bottom line."

The decision-making process generally comprises four steps:[10]
- Initiation: Formulating and then choosing among potential decisions
- Ratification: Approval of the selected decision with possible modifications
- Implementation: Executing the selected decision
- Monitoring: Evaluating the outcome and rewarding the decision makers appropriately

Initiation and implementation can be grouped into a category called decision management, while ratification and monitoring constitute decision control. A company's annual budgeting process encompasses all four steps and illustrates how decision authority is assigned within the company. Once managers are given a budget for their operations, they have decision authority over these resources (decision management). The performance of these managers is then judged relative to budget (decision control).

As a general principle of corporate governance, decision management and decision control should be separated unless decision makers have a significant ownership stake in corporate cash flows. The most prominent example of this separation is the presence at the top of the corporation of a board of directors with fiduciary responsibility for ratifying and monitoring important decisions initiated by the CEO.[11] If the board of directors does a poor job, it can be replaced through a proxy fight or a corporate takeover. In the U.S. corporate governance system, it is takeover specialists, financial analysts, and large blockholders (such as public pension funds) who perform the role of "monitoring the monitor."

The principle of separating decision management and control also explains the use of hierarchies within organizations, permitting decisions by certain employees to be monitored and ratified by other employees who are above them in the hierarchy. The same employee might have both decision control and decision management functions, but not for the same decision. For example, division managers might have approval authority over certain initiatives of lower-level employees while at the same time requiring authorization for the division's capital expenditure plan. In some

cases, managers might pre-authorize decisions within a particular range—what is known as boundary setting—while retaining monitoring authority. In smaller organizations, decision management and decision control are often combined. In these cases, the decision maker also tends to be an owner, which "internalizes" most incentive problems—although recent events at Martha Stewart Living Omnimedia, Inc. suggest that value destruction can occur even when principal decision makers have significant ownership stakes.

A key issue in designing a company's organizational architecture is how far down within the organization to delegate decision authority. When operating managers have specialized knowledge about markets and processes, decentralization strengthens the link between decision-making and relevant knowledge within the company, and encourages the conversion of employee expertise into shareholder value. Decentralization will tend to add even more value as a company enters more diverse markets because senior managers are less likely to have all the information necessary to make good decisions across the various businesses.

A principal drawback of decentralization, however, is that incentive conflicts increase as decision authority is pushed down into the organization to lower-level employees who may not see maximizing shareholder value as their primary goal. For example, managers may continue to operate unprofitable divisions rather than laying off colleagues and friends; and managers who are nearing retirement are less inclined to worry about cash flows that extend beyond their tenure. Fortunately, as we discuss next, the other two legs of the organizational architecture stool can help to control these incentive conflicts.

THE SECOND LEG: PERFORMANCE EVALUATION

There are at least two reasons to evaluate employee or business unit performance. The first is to provide feedback on whether the company is making the best use of its resources and to guide new resource allocation. For example, additional employee training in particular areas might be

---

10. See E. Fama and M. Jensen, "Separation of Ownership and Control," *Journal of Law and Economics*, Vol. 26 (1983), pp. 301-326.

11. Of course, the fact that the CEO has a significant ownership stake does not preclude the existence of a board of directors; yet when the CEO is essentially the sole owner, the firm will tend to operate without a board.

indicated. Employee reviews are also useful to managers who want to assign people to jobs that will make the best use of their skills. Business unit performance should be monitored for ways to increase productivity. Second, performance evaluation provides an indication of an employee's or business unit's contribution to shareholder value, which in turn is useful in determining rewards and penalties for compensation purposes.

But it's important to keep in mind that these two purposes create different incentives. If performance were evaluated strictly for feedback purposes, employees would have little reason to distort their evaluations to make themselves look better. But when compensation is based on measured performance, employees and managers are more likely to try to find ways to inflate their own or their business unit's evaluations. Senior management's challenge is to recognize these dysfunctional incentives and to craft reasonably accurate performance measures that are consistent with the strategic objectives of the firm—measures that help to motivate value-adding effort and decision-making.

Evaluating Individual Employees

We argued earlier that shareholder value is measured by the present value of all cash flows expected to accrue to the shareholders and that the firm's stock price is a reliable barometer of such value. Ideally, then, we would assess an employee's performance by his or her individual contribution to the change in stock price after each day's work. But this of course is impossible. Shareholder value is determined by the collective actions of employees throughout the company. Even in relatively small companies, the impact of an individual employee's efforts simply cannot be detected with any precision. And shareholder value is also subject to random factors from outside the company, such as conditions in the general economy—tax rates, the Federal Reserve rate, the level of unemployment, oil price levels, and so on—that are well beyond any individual employee's control. Even when it appears that an employee's contribution to value would be neatly reflected in the stock price, as when a scientist in the research lab discovers a new wonder drug and the stock price goes up $10, that employee also contributes to shareholder value in other ways that are not so readily measured, such as by guiding the work of fellow employees.

We therefore look to other measures as proxies for an employee's actual contribution to value. These measures typically try to capture the employee's productivity or output, as determined by the employee's skill level and training and by the amount of effort he or she exerts. Different measures will correspond to varying degrees with the employee's actual productivity. If output and quality are easily measured, piecework corresponds quite closely to performance, assuming that output is not affected by factors such as random machine failures and the quality and timely availability of parts and supplies. Other measures, such as the number of hours worked, will correspond somewhat less closely; for example, employees may be at their desks, but whether productive energy is being expended is another matter. Of course, evaluations based only on the quantifiable aspects of a job can cause the employee to emphasize those aspects to the detriment of other, less quantifiable aspects such as training fellow employees. Subjective performance appraisals can help to capture other dimensions of the employee's output that are of value to the company. While no performance measure is perfect, they all provide some basis for assessing an employee's contribution to value.

In choosing among performance measures, managers must keep several things in mind. First, the costs incurred in evaluating an employee's performance must not exceed the gains from doing so. The gains generally stem from the incentive effect of tying compensation to performance—but there are certainly administrative costs associated with using more precise measures, as well as costs related to employees trying to "game" the system. Second, because an employee's productivity is subject to random factors beyond the employee's control (weather, delivery schedules, raw material quality, and so on), greater reliance on incentive pay will introduce greater variability in the employee's compensation. In these cases, it will make sense to design a (perhaps costlier) measurement system that will gauge employee performance more precisely so as to reduce the compensation impact of random factors.

Thus, the degree of incentive pay and the accuracy with which performance is measured are interdependent. Because these two legs of the stool are complements, *greater reliance on incentive compensation should be accompanied by an increase in the precision with which performance is measured.*

If a key aspect of an industry's operating environment changes, managers in most companies in that industry will react by reappraising and modifying their strategies—too often without considering whether the existing organizational architecture will remain effective.

Evaluating Operating Units: ROA versus Residual Income

Business unit performance evaluation serves the same two basic purposes: feedback on how the company is doing—which units are creating value and which are destroying value—and input to the reward system. What ultimately matters is a business unit's contribution to shareholder value, as determined principally by the present value of its net operating cash flows. But there are different measures of value creation.

The most commonly used measure of performance is return on assets, or ROA. ROA is the accounting net income generated by the business unit divided by the total assets employed in that unit. It has intuitive appeal because it can be compared to competitors' rates of return to provide a benchmark for a business unit's performance.[12] However, ROA does not accurately measure the business unit's *economic* rate of return. For one thing, ROA is calculated on the basis of reported accounting numbers, with all their attendant problems (see, for instance, the article, *"How to Fix Accounting— Measure and Report Economic Profit"* by Bennett Stewart starting on page 472 of this book). Accounting income (the numerator) is not always an accurate measure of economic profit, which represents the change in value over the period, and accounting assets (the denominator) do not necessarily reflect the current value of the division's investment base.

Perhaps the biggest problem with ROA, however, is that a division manager will be inclined to reject value-creating projects whose ROAs would lower the division's overall ROA. For example, suppose the division has a current ROA of 20%, a 15% cost of capital, and the opportunity to take on a new investment project of similar risk with a 17% ROA. Accepting the project lowers the division's overall ROA, even though it increases shareholder value— and if the division manager is evaluated on the basis of maintaining or increasing division ROA, the manager will reject the project.

To overcome this problem, some companies use *residual income* (or a variant such as economic profit or EVA) to evaluate performance. Residual income is calculated by subtracting the dollar cost of capital employed in the business unit from the operating profits of the business unit. In our previous example, the new project will increase residual income (and shareholder value) because the project return is greater than the division's cost of capital, even though overall division ROA will fall slightly.

Nonetheless, both ROA and residual income have several common drawbacks, and any weaknesses must be addressed before these or any other performance metrics can be used as inputs to other systems, particularly the compensation system. First, management must estimate each division's cost of capital—or even a project-specific cost of capital— to control for risk differences (so that managers don't have incentives to plunge their divisions into risky projects to boost measured performance). These risk adjustments may cause division managers to lobby central management to reevaluate their risk and lower their required capital costs, thereby improving their reported performance. What's more, both ROA and residual income measure performance over a single year only. As a result, they can be increased by cutting maintenance or R&D, but at the expense of future cash flows and hence shareholder value. Or a division manager might take on projects that increase ROA or residual income immediately, even if they are uneconomic in the long run.[13] And neither ROA nor residual income reflects the interdependencies among divisions—one division might raise the quality of its products and thereby enhance the perceived quality of the company's brand name, but its divisional ROA or residual income will not capture the additional value created elsewhere in the company as a result.

More fundamentally, both metrics rely on accounting measures of operating profits and assets. The internal accounting system plays an important role in organizational architecture, as we discuss in more detail in the box insert. But all accounting (and other) performance measures are prone to manipulation. And because accounting numbers measure performance over only a single period, they reinforce the "horizon" problem wherein managers emphasize short-term performance at the expense of future cash flows. Therefore, any accounting-based performance measurement system requires careful oversight by senior managers to control behavior by operating managers that is not consistent with

---

12. For companies with debt financing, it is important to add back interest expense net of taxes to accounting income before comparing ROA with external rates of return.

13. Of course, many companies have long-run performance plans such as Stern Stewart's bonus banks.

The Accounting System and Performance Measurement

Many people think of the accounting system in terms of the company's external financial reports—to shareholders, taxing authorities, regulators, and lenders. But these external financial reports (both quarterly and annual) aggregate an enormous amount of internal accounting data. Managers use internal accounting data on expenses, product costs, inventories, customer account balances, and so on for both decision management and decision control.

Decision management (initiation and implementation) typically requires estimates of future costs and revenues, and accounting numbers provide a starting point in developing these estimates. Similarly, managers develop forecasts of costs and revenues for the next year in preparing their operating budgets. This process encourages managers to be forward-looking, to coordinate their operations with other managers who are directly affected by their decisions, and to share specialized knowledge of their markets and production technologies. Accounting-based budgets thus provide the framework for knowledge sharing and coordination.

Accounting budgets also serve to "hard-wire" the process of converting employee expertise into shareholder value. For example, suppose a production employee discovers a faster way to set up the machines in the production process. This discovery is translated into a plant production policy—a new set-up algorithm—and becomes part of the company's formula for value creation. Next year's budget will be adjusted to incorporate fewer labor hours for machine set-ups. If the set-up efficiencies do not materialize as anticipated, the accounting system will report this in the form of unfavorable variances.

Decision control (ratification and monitoring) relies to an even greater extent on accounting systems. In fact, accounting systems evolved primarily for this purpose. They protect against fraud, embezzlement, and theft of company assets. They also provide a scorecard for a business unit's past performance by measuring its costs, profits, or residual income. Monitoring is by definition a historical function and is well served by the accounting system. But because accounting systems are primarily designed for decision control—to prevent malfeasance and to measure past performance—they are based on historical costs and revenues and in this sense are *backward-looking*. As a result, they are often found wanting when it comes to providing managers with the information they need for decision management.

In response to these deficiencies, operating managers develop their own, often nonfinancial, information systems to provide more of the data that they need for decision management. At the same time, of course, they rely on the output of the accounting system to monitor the managers who report to them. One survey confirmed that managers rely on nonfinancial data (labor counts, units of output, units in inventory, units scrapped) to run their day-to-day operations. But when asked about their "most useful report in general," managers cited the monthly income or expense statements that are typically used to judge their own performance.[14]

---

14. S. McKinnon and W. Bruns, *The Information Mosaic* (Boston: Harvard Business School, 1992).

---

maximizing shareholder value. (The governance failure at Enron stemmed in part from senior management's failures with regard to oversight.)

Most companies employ a single accounting system for multiple purposes, making adjustments as necessary to bring the numbers more into line with economic reality. Shareholder reports, taxes, internal decision management and control, regulatory compliance, debt agreements, and management compensation plans all use accounting-based numbers. Moreover, compa-nies tend to use the same accounting procedures for all of these different purposes, which helps to control incentives to distort the numbers for any single purpose. And although managers have considerable discretion, particularly for internal purposes, the underlying accounting procedures are regulated—managers must choose among methods permitted by generally accepted accounting principles (GAAP). External, independent auditors can then attest to the accuracy and consistency of these accounting reports.

Appropriately designed incentive compensation strengthens the link between the company's organizational architecture and its business strategy. In fact, if a company has settled on a strategic course—and has assigned decision authority and established performance measurement systems that will be consistent with its strategic objectives—incentive compensation should fall readily into place.

But no accounting system works perfectly; no system eliminates all opportunities for managers to increase their well-being at the expense of the shareholders. The key question is whether the system outperforms the next best alternative after all the costs and benefits are factored in. It is thus important to avoid the "Nirvana fallacy," whereby a system is discarded or revamped if it allows *any* managerial opportunism, no matter how minor, in favor of an unachievable "perfect" system. By virtue of the simple fact that they have survived, most accounting systems would appear to be useful. Yet all accounting systems are vulnerable, partly because of "play" in the accounting rules—although it is prohibitively expensive to eliminate all managerial discretion—and sometimes because of lapses in ethics, which we discuss later. And particular attention must be paid to the use of accounting numbers for compensation purposes, a topic to which we now turn.

THE THIRD LEG: COMPENSATION AND INCENTIVE PAY

The term *incentive pay* conjures up images of piece rates, commissions, and cash bonus plans, with the employee paid on the basis of some quantifiable measure of output. More recently, the emphasis has been on stock and stock option awards, although stock ownership is unlikely to provide very powerful incentives to rank-and-file employees in large organizations. Whatever its form, the fundamental purpose of incentive pay is to increase shareholder value by motivating value-adding effort. Rewards do not have to be monetary, but can consist of anything that the employees value—corner offices, parking places, dining room privileges, and the like.

The important question is how to create incentives in a cost-effective way—to design a compensation plan whose benefits outweigh any potential disadvantages. If an employee's contribution to shareholder value could be measured precisely, it would be relatively easy to design a compensation program that would motivate the appropriate level of effort. Some of the inefficiencies that result from incentive conflicts can thus be reduced by improvements in performance measurement. This is where adjustments to accounting earnings can be important in motivating value-adding behavior. And although the standard indicator of an employee's effort is

typically the employee's direct output, there are many ways to determine whether the employee has worked hard.

In determining the year-end bonus for a salesperson on commission, for example, the sales manager should look at overall sales in addition to individual results. If a particular salesperson's performance in a given year was poor, but average sales in the company also declined substantially, it is likely that the salesperson's results were simply affected by general market conditions. If other salespeople had great results, however, the salesperson may have slacked off. Similarly, corporate earnings targets can be set with respect to the growth of other companies in the same industry. Appropriate use of relative performance information increases the precision with which an employee's or business unit's contribution to value can be measured and, when included in the compensation contract, increases the effectiveness of the incentive mechanism.

But just as employees can be penalized for factors beyond their control, they can also be *rewarded* for results in which they played no direct part. Strong market conditions can amplify the results of mediocre effort and make "normal" effort appear spectacular. For example, many executives profited enormously from stock and stock options that increased in value simply as a result of the general bull market of the 1990s. In response, some companies have experimented with industry stock indexes as benchmarks for their stock's performance, with any increase in the firm's own stock netted against the change in value of the industry index. Unfortunately, these plans can be administratively unmanageable and difficult to communicate to plan participants. Current accounting rules—which require companies to expense indexed options but not standard options—also reduce the perceived desirability of indexed options for most companies.

Perhaps most important, appropriately designed incentive compensation strengthens the link between the company's organizational architecture and its business strategy. Once the firm has identified certain strategic objectives, those objectives should be factored into the design of the incentive plan—just as they should play a role in the assignment of decision authority and the development of performance measures. If quality is an overriding objective, then incentive compensation might be based on measures such as customer satisfaction (based on surveys), the percentage of product returns, the percentage of warranty claims, and the like. If cost control is a priority, the incentive plan might incorporate measures of cost reduction. In fact, if a company has settled on a strategic course—and has assigned decision authority and established performance measurement systems that will be consistent with its strategic objectives—incentive compensation should fall readily into place. Employees will already know what is expected of them, and the incentive plan will serve to reinforce their understanding and motivate them to work toward achieving the company's goals. Yet there is the danger, as in Enron's case, that incentive compensation works *too* well—that it fosters unethical behavior. In the next section, we discuss how corporate ethics can be addressed through organizational architecture as well.

ORGANIZATIONAL ARCHITECTURE AND ETHICS

People generally have a pretty good idea of what is meant by "ethical" behavior. Most of us feel an emotional allegiance to the Golden Rule that urges us to treat others as we would have them treat us, and we value such qualities as honesty, integrity, fairness, and commitment to the task at hand. But some behaviors or activities are not so clear-cut—witness the debates over affirmative action, animal testing, genetically engineered crops, stem cell research, and sweatshops, to name but a few. In these cases, there is simply no universally accepted code of ethics by which one can readily assess right and wrong. What's more, behavior that might have been acceptable ten or twenty years ago may not be acceptable today because of changes brought about by movements as disparate as civil rights and women's rights, on the one hand, and corporate restructuring and stakeholder theory, on the other. As a result, ethics and corporate responsibility have increasingly come under scrutiny.

U.S. corporations have responded by issuing formal codes of conduct, appointing ethics officers, and instituting training programs in ethics. A corporate code of ethics helps to eliminate uncertainty about ethical standards and how to live up to them; it informs employees that certain activities can damage the reputation of the company and will be severely penalized. At a minimum, a code of ethics will typically proscribe actions such as giving or taking extravagant gifts, bribing government offi-

cials, misrepresenting data, and discriminatory hiring practices. And although many of these acts are also illegal, legality alone is not always sufficient to frame policy. Using child labor in a textile mill may be legal in Pakistan, for example, but American or European customers might object because the practice is illegal in the United States and Europe. Business norms help to codify ethics, and yet these norms can vary in different countries. (A useful approach might be to draft a press release explaining a particular business practice and then consider the potential reaction not only internally but when it appears in *The Wall Street Journal*.)

Of course, a more cynical view is that a corporate code of ethics serves merely to help the company defend itself against charges of illegal behavior. When an individual is found guilty of wrongdoing, his or her employer is also subject to federal penalties, but these penalties can be reduced as much as 50% simply by demonstrating that the employer has a compliance program in place that meets the U.S. Sentencing Commission's standards. (A compliance program minimally consists of a code of ethics and a training program.)

In any case, adopting a code of ethics is not sufficient to guarantee ethical behavior. Intangible aspects of corporate culture such as codes of ethics and internal communications must be reinforced by more tangible structures if a company is to become both a value-based and a *values*-based organization. That is, the formal organizational systems that assign decision authority and measure and reward performance must all be internally consistent and designed to encourage value-adding, ethical behavior. In fact, the critical question is whether the incentives established by the current organizational architecture of the company truly encourage ethical behavior. Strategy, business ethics, and organizational architecture are linked, and it is important to structure the company so that employees work to implement the corporate vision with regard to both strategy and ethics. In other words, all three legs of the stool—decision authority, performance measurement systems, and compensation systems—must be designed to promote the corporate mission.

One source of confusion is the concept of "corporate social responsibility," which is sometimes used interchangeably with corporate ethics. In 1969, Ralph Nader and several other lawyers launched their Project on Corporate Responsibility with the following statement:

> Intangible aspects of corporate culture such as codes of ethics and internal
> communications must be reinforced by more tangible structures if a company is to
> become both a value-based and a *values*-based organization.

Today we announce an effort to develop a new kind of citizenship around an old kind of private government—the large corporation. It is an effort which rises from the shared concern of many citizens over the role of the corporation in American society and the uses of its complex powers. It is an effort which is dedicated toward developing a new constituency for the corporation that will harness these powers for the fulfillment of a broader spectrum of democratic values.[15]

As this statement suggests, the goal of some advocates of corporate social responsibility is nothing less than to change the purpose of the corporation. In Nader's view, the corporation is to be transformed from a means of maximizing investor wealth to a vehicle for using private wealth to redress social ills. The corporate social responsibility movement seeks to make business managers responsible for upholding "a broader spectrum of democratic values." Corporate support for such values could take the form of philanthropic activities, the provision of subsidized goods and services to certain segments of the community, or the expenditure of corporate resources on public projects such as education, environmental improvement, and neighborhood reclamation projects. Stakeholder theory, popular today, embodies many of these principles.

In contrast, most economists and managers are inclined to endorse Milton Friedman's prescription that the social mission of the corporation is "to make as much money for its owners as possible while conforming to the basic rules of society."[16] In this view—embodied in value-based management—it is more efficient for the corporation to focus on creating wealth and to let shareholders, employees, and customers undertake their own charitable efforts. By maximizing shareholder value, corporations effectively enlarge the pool of individual (noncorporate) resources available for all stakeholders.

But the contrast between the two views is not as pronounced as it might appear. Corporations that wish to maximize shareholder value generally find it in their interest to devote corporate resources to constituencies such as employees, customers, suppliers, and local communities. For example, a company with a large plant in an inner city might decide that investing corporate resources and personnel to improve area schools would lead to better-trained job applicants, more productive employees, and thus lower-cost products. Giving money to the local university might benefit the company by improving its research and development, increasing its access to top graduates, or enhancing cultural and educational opportunities for its employees. Improving the environment might make it easier to attract and retain employees as well as lowering the company's legal exposure to environmental damage claims. Creating shareholder value involves allocating corporate resources to all constituencies that affect the process of shareholder value creation, but only to the point at which the benefits from such expenditures do not exceed their additional costs. If the corporation maximizes the size of the pie, each constituency—including shareholders, bondholders, managers, employees, customers, suppliers, charities, and local communities—receives a larger slice.

In short, ethical behavior can help to create shareholder value. And to the extent that the corporate ethics problem involves the issue of incentives, it can be resolved within the context of our organizational architecture framework. In many of the recent corporate scandals, ethical breaches arose from a lack of balance among the three legs of the stool. People may be honest in general, but the promptings of conscience and the desire to maintain a good reputation are neither universal nor constant, and they can certainly be influenced by the firm's decision authority, performance measurement, and reward systems.

For example, consider the transfer pricing problem faced by a corporation with multiple divisions that buy from and sell to one another. The efforts of division managers to increase their respective divisions' profits may come at the expense of the other divisions' profits and possibly also at the expense of firmwide profits. Top management might hope that instituting a code of ethics will encourage division managers to adopt a less provincial attitude and look beyond their own self-interest. But as long as the division managers are *paid* on the basis of the profits of their own divisions, they are unlikely to drastically alter their behavior. The firm's organizational architecture will have to be redesigned to change the division managers' incentives, perhaps by tying compensation to the overall value of the company as well as to divisional performance.

---

15. T. Donaldson and P. Werhane, Eds., *Ethical Issues in Business: A Philosophical Approach*, 6th ed. (Englewood Cliffs, NJ: Prentice-Hall, 1979), p. 90.

16. *New York Times Magazine*, Sept. 13, 1970.

If the compensation plan sometimes rewards unethical behavior, then unethical behavior is what the company will get, as we saw with Enron. Corporations develop ethics programs in an effort to persuade employees to put the interests of the organization or its customers ahead of their own. Executive leadership can be equally important in this effort. But internal consistency in the organizational architecture of the firm is crucial.

CONCLUSION

Effective leadership involves a great deal more than just developing an appropriate strategic or ethical vision for the company—it is also critical to motivate people to implement that vision. And while leadership is clearly important in the internal marketing of a strategic or ethical vision, it plays an even bigger role in recognizing which organizational architecture will best help fulfill that vision and then making the necessary alterations to the current design. Of course, part of good leadership is knowing when and how to work within the existing structure. Not all managers are empowered to make changes in the allocation of decision authority or in the performance measurement or compensation systems. And because too-frequent changes can discourage employees from making long-range decisions and developing effective relationships with colleagues, it is sometimes preferable to exercise leadership within the existing organizational architecture.

In fact, before undertaking any architectural changes, managers should understand how their company arrived at its existing structure and, more generally, develop a broader perspective on why specific structures work well in particular settings. Outside consultants may argue that a company's long-standing organizational practices are inefficient and propose replacing them with popular management techniques such as reengineering, total quality management (TQM), worker empowerment, the Balanced Scorecard, and so on. But most management fads address only one or at most two elements of organizational architecture. For example, reengineering focuses almost exclusively on decision authority. Total quality management ignores the reward system. Activity-based costing (ABC) changes only the performance evaluation systems. Management should resist jettisoning its current architecture without careful analysis—particularly if the business environment has been relatively stable. Uncritical experimentation with the organizational innovation *du jour* can leave the company's architecture out of balance. The focus should be on ensuring that the three elements of organizational design are synchronized with the company's strategy.

The framework outlined in this article accepts people's self-interest as given and rests on the principle that incentives work when the performance evaluation and reward systems are properly designed. Achieving the right balance among decision authority, performance evaluation, and compensation will ultimately drive shareholder value as well as ethical behavior. Whatever an organization's objectives, our approach to organization provides a solid foundation for creating value. Companies that are successful, particularly over the long run, seem to excel at creating and maintaining effective networks of employees and maximizing their potential. A key factor that these companies have in common is an effective organizational architecture—a customized design that promotes and tracks the business strategy and rewards employees for making value-maximizing decisions. And when one digs for the reasons behind spectacular corporate failures such as Enron's, a seriously flawed organizational architecture is underneath the debris.

INCENTIVES, RATIONALITY, AND SOCIETY

by Michael J. Brennan,
*University of California at Los Angeles**

S elf-image is a major determinant of behaviour. If I think of myself as a criminal, I shall behave in a criminal fashion. If I think of myself as a coward, I shall behave in a cowardly fashion. If I think of myself as an honest person, I shall behave in an honest way. If I think of myself as a rational person, must I always behave in a self-interested manner? A surprising number of economists apparently think so—though, fortunately for the rest of us, most non-economists disagree.

I would like to take the opportunity this evening to talk to you about incentives and rationality, and even a little about society as well. I am not an expert on these matters, but I think that it may be useful to try to place in a little more perspective the economic model that we in the field of corporate finance rely on in discussing such issues as managerial incentives and executive compensation. For our model of man has profound social implications, and the professional economist's model, while extremely useful in some contexts, may be misleading in others.

The well-known biologist, Stephen J. Gould, is an opponent of what he calls "cardboard Darwinism," the thesis that all biological phenomena can be explained by adaptation to the environment. He writes, "Adaptation is a powerful force, but its sway is not exclusive—and we both caricature the process and ignore a central theme in current revisions of Darwinian theory when we equate evolutionary reconstructions with our ability to tell a story about optimal behaviour in the absence of definite evidence."[1]

When I read this, I was reminded of what we might call cardboard economics—the claim that all social phenomena can be explained in terms of the working out of the implications of individual self-interest. The game that many of us (myself included) play is to take some apparently inexplicable phenomenon, like dividend payments,[2] and show that it is consistent with rational self-interested (or, in the case of corporations, value-maximizing) behaviour. As you are aware, the signalling model has proven an especially fertile source of rationalisations of phenomena that did not seem to be consistent with rational self-interested behaviour.[3]

But this game has its limits. To paraphrase Gould, "Self-interest is a powerful force, but its sway is not exclusive." I shall argue that the tendency to identify self-interest with rationality is mistaken—and that it represents a serious oversimplification of, for example, Adam Smith's view of human nature. It was, after all, Smith's *Wealth of Nations*, published in 1776, that first set modern-day economists down this road with its famous statement that "it is not from the benevolence of the butcher, the brewer, or the baker that we expect our dinner, but from their regard to their own interest." What most economists fail to remember, however, is that Smith was Professor not of Economics (there was no such thing in those days), but of Moral Philosophy at the University of Glasgow. And that Smith did not take this position lightly is evident from his other great work, *The Theory of Moral Sentiments*, in which he says that "to restrain our selfish, and to indulge our benevolent affections, constitutes the perfection of human nature."[4]

*Based on a talk given at the University of Maryland on April 2, 1993.

1. *An Urchin in the Storm* (W.W. Norton, New York, 1987).
2. Financial economists find it difficult to account for the payment of dividends by corporations, since cash can be returned to investors just as well by share repurchases which have the advantage, in most jurisdictions, that they are taxed more lightly.
3. In signalling models, individuals with superior but unobservable characteristics incur signalling costs to distinguish themselves from their less well endowed

brethren. An example from the natural world is offered by the tail feathers of the peacock which, while dysfunctional for the male bird, serve to signal its health and breeding potential to females. In the world of finance, companies may pay higher dividends or take on more financial leverage than might otherwise be optimal in order to convince outside investors of the value of their prospects.
4. Adam Smith, *The Theory of Moral Sentiments* (Liberty Press, Indianapolis, 1991), D. Reisman, 1982, *Tawney, Galbraith and Adam Smith* (New York, St. Martin's Press, 1982), p. 25.

With this as background, I shall take up the issue of executive compensation and ask whether an adequate theory of executive compensation can be based simply on the hypothesis of rational self-interest. Here I shall argue that an exclusive emphasis on self-interest and incentives fails to provide a satisfactory basis for either a descriptive theory of executive compensation (that is, one that attempts to explain why companies pay executives as they do) or a normative theory (as opposed to what they should be doing instead). Finally, I shall argue briefly that a mistaken effort to identify self-interest with rationality will, if successful, have a profoundly negative effect on our society.

First, however, I will take issue with the identification of self-interest with rationality that many professional economists are accustomed to make.

RATIONALITY AND SELF INTEREST

I have used the term "rational self-interested" behaviour. Are these adjectives synonymous? In the formal analysis of pure economic theory, rationality is assumed to embody no more than consistency in choice.[5] And even that definition seems to leave out a lot of human experience. For example, the economist[6] has no room for statements of regret, such as, for example, "I wish I had done more for my parents while they were alive, saved more for my retirement, learned Japanese etc."

In practical analysis—for example, in trying to understand executive compensation—economists are inclined to identify rationality with self-interest. At least one writer has suggested that 20th-century economics is modelled on 18th-century physics, and that self-interest is the gravity of economics. And George Stigler has even gone so far as to claim that self-interest rather than ethical considerations explain not only economic phenomena, but marital, child-bearing, criminal, and other social behaviour.[7]

Although economists certainly have no special insight into human nature, I do not doubt the usefulness of the hypothesis of self-interest for a wide range of technical economic problems. It is obviously most appropriate in the perfectly competitive setting of neoclassical theory—those situations where the individual can have no influence on the welfare of others since he is by definition a price-taker.[8] It may be less appropriate in other circumstances, such as when the individual is placed in a position of responsibility for others (and I shall say more about this later).

It can be argued that the narrow concept of rational self-interest that underlies the agency approach to discussions of compensation assumes both too much and too little about human nature. Two military examples may help here. The first suggests that it may be too much to expect people always to behave according to their rational self-interest.

In an article entitled "Incentives, Routines, and Self-Command," Steven Postrel and Richard Rumelt offer the following account of a situation in the Korean War when the Chinese army intervened after the American invasion of North Korea:

During the next 40 days, U.S. forces retreated south, suffering terrible losses. During this period, many units of the U.S. 8th Army were declared "combat ineffective", having ceased to function with any cohesion. By contrast the 1st Marine Division's retreat from the Chosin Reservoir was marked by continued cohesion and the maintenance of combat effectiveness despite heavy casualties inflicted both by China's 9th Army Group, and by the bitterly cold winter.

One of the main sources of this difference in performance between the 8th Army and the Marines was the difference in enforcement of basic routines and field discipline. A noted military historian described Baker Company of the 8th Army's 2nd Infantry Division, just before it became the first unit to experience the Chinese onslaught, in this way: "For all its heaviness of spirit, Baker was remarkably light on foot on that morning. In fact, it was much too

5. As Amartya Sen has pointed out, under this definition obsessions are regarded as rational as long as they are consistently pursued—that is, so long as there are no intervening periods of lucidity! A.K. Sen, *On Ethics and Economics* (Blackwell, Oxford, 1987).

6. In making this statement, I knowingly exclude George Akerlof, who presents an economist's model of a man subject to the normal human frailty. See G.A. Akerlof, "Procrastination and Obedience," *American Economic Review*, 81 (2) 1991: 1-19.

7. G. Stigler, "Economics or Ethics?," in S. McMurrin (Ed.), *Tanner Lectures on Human Values*, Vol II, Cambridge University Press (1981).

8. However, some economists have shown in experiments that people prefer a more equal (fair) outcome that gives them less money to a less equal outcome that gives them more, even when the two players do not know each other and do not deal face to face. See D. Kahneman, J.L. Knetsch, and R. Thaler, "Fairness and the Assumptions of Economics," *Journal of Business*, 59 (1986):Supp. 285-300. Another study by the same authors presents evidence that, even in market settings individuals may be influenced by considerations of fairness. See D. Kahneman, J.L. Knetsch and R. Thaler, "Fairness as a Constraint on Profit-Seeking; Entitlements in the Market," *American Economic Review*, 76 (1986).

light...All but twelve men had thrown away their steel helmets. The grenade load averaged less than one per man. About one half of the company had dispensed with trenching tools and so on."

This loose discipline cost the company dear in the ensuing retreat. By contrast, in the 1st Marine Division discipline never broke. Battalion commanders checked that troops had dug foxholes before turning in...company commanders watched each man perform the painful but necessary task of changing his sweat soaked socks each evening, despite the howling cold wind, to prevent frostbite...By maintaining such drudgery the marines maintained their fighting effectiveness.[9]

Postrel and Rumelt remark that the individual soldiers surely had an interest in their own unit's ability to resist attack, and certainly in their own protection against gunfire and cold. Why should it be necessary for the organization to enforce basic rituals that are clearly in each soldier's best interest to perform? They argue that an important function of organization is to give aid and strength to people in their struggles for self control. We might add that this story also illustrates the importance of good leadership.

Postrel and Rumelt claim that incentive design must therefore have two components: first, *rational preference alignment*, which, like the traditional economic theory of agency, is concerned with the assignment of payoffs across observable states to make the agent's long-term, reflective choices consistent with the principal's goals. Second, *impulse control*, which requires positioning the payments in time and context to maximize their behaviour modifying effects. Agency theory, they claim, by ignoring the significance of the timing and context of rewards, effectively ignores the problem of impulse control and the importance of developing good habits.

They illustrate their argument with quotations from an interview with the founder of ABC Supply, a rapidly growing wholesaler of roofing products:

When managers don't work out, it's usually because of character problems. Of the ones that get

fired, I'd say that 80% just plain don't care about anybody else. For example, they would not love their customers; they wanted to screw their customers. When employees see that, it destroys the character of the business.

ABC Supply aims to change the behaviour of the managers of the new stores that it acquires by training and teaching good habits through regular feedback. Incentives are the last part of ABC's behaviour modification process, and by themselves are insufficient to induce good practices.

Postrel and Rumelt's account of an incident in the Korean War suggests that people are not always capable of doing what is clearly in their self-interest.[10] Now let me use Plato's recommendation for military organisation in the *Symposium* to argue that men are also capable of rising above their narrowly defined self-interest:

Imagine a man in love being found out doing something humiliating, or letting someone else do something degrading to him, because he was too cowardly to stop it. It would embarrass him more to be found out by the boy he loved than by his father or friends, or anyone...so if there was some way of arranging that a state or an army could be made up entirely of pairs of lovers, it is impossible to imagine a finer population. They would avoid all dishonour, and compete with one another for glory...

Plato's early contribution to the debate about gays in the military suggests that higher-level concerns about honour and reputation may be as important in understanding certain kinds of behaviour as narrower and more traditional economic models of man. Incidentally, Plato's basic point that men fight out of loyalty to their fellow platoon members, and that for this reason it is important to retain social cohesion within the group, is well understood in the military today,[11] though it may have different implications for recruiting than those envisioned by him.

Adam Smith, whom James Q. Wilson describes as "the pre-eminent moral philosopher of his time,"[12]

---

9. S. Postrel and R. Rumelt, "Incentives, Routines, and Self-Command," *Industrial and Corporate Change*, 1: 1992, 397-425.

10. Note that the inability of individuals to control their own impulses provides a rationale for such phenomena as anti-drug laws and mandatory retirement systems. Economists who take their model of rational self-interested behaviour seriously are often opposed to both of these, whereas non-economists tend to favour them.

11. The same principle is employed by the British army which has for many years organised its regiments on a county basis, so that soldiers would fight alongside their neighbours.

12. J.Q. Wilson, *The Moral Sense*, The Free Press, New York, 1993, p. 30.

also recognizes that man seeks not just his self-interest but also virtue. Consider these words from *Wealth of Nations*:

> *Man naturally desires, not only to be loved, but to be lovely; or to be that thing which is the natural and proper object of love. He naturally dreads, not only to be hated but to be hateful; or to be that thing which is the natural and proper object of hatred. He desires, not only praise, but praiseworthiness; or to be that thing which, though it should be praised by nobody, is however the natural and proper object of praise. He dreads, not only blame, but blameworthiness; or to be that thing which, though it should be blamed by nobody, is the natural and proper object of blame.*[13]

Noting that we desire "both to be respectable, and to be respected" and we dread "both to be contemptible and to be contemned," Smith castigates those "splenetic philosophers" who attribute praiseworthy action to the love of praise, and remarks that "they are the most frivolous and superficial of mankind only who can be much delighted with that praise which they themselves know to be altogether unmerited." Rather than identifying rationality with self-interest, Smith claims that "it is the great precept of nature to love ourselves only as we love our neighbour, or what comes to the same thing, as our neighbour is capable of loving us."

In sum, although Smith evidently believed that self-interest could be used to explain many economic phenomena, he was far from claiming that it explains all, or that it was in any way synonymous with rationality.

INCENTIVES AND EXECUTIVE COMPENSATION

The narrowly self-interested model of economic man is commonly viewed as an object of scorn among non-economists. The economic man lacks both virtue and (most) vice. While he is never resentful at being treated unfairly, he is never angry at the unfair treatment of others. While he is never discouraged by failure, he will never perform without incentives. While unerring in his pursuit of (suitably discounted) long-term gain, he has no honour or self-esteem, and feels no shame or pride in accomplishment.[14]

It is perhaps not surprising, then, to find that such an emasculated model of man provides a poor basis for designing incentive schemes—even for low-level employees who, after all, have been known to strike in protest at the unfair dismissal of a fellow worker. According to a recent article in the *Economist*, "Having fallen in love with performance related pay in the 1980's, many managers are turning against it, complaining that it is expensive..., clumsy and *demotivating* (the winners are encouraged only briefly, while the losers fall into permanent sulk)."[15]

If "economically rational" incentive schemes work poorly with relatively low-level employees, I would be inclined to hazard they are likely to work even less well with more senior employees, since such higher-level concerns as self-actualization, honour, reputation, and job-satisfaction are likely to assume greater importance as one moves up the corporate hierarchy towards the CEO. First, for most people economic incentives are likely to decline in their effectiveness as wealth increases—remember the backward bending supply curve of labour. There is little point in earning an extra $5 million per year unless one takes the time to spend it—and spending money on such expensive luxuries as race-horses, yachts, and multiple residences takes time and effort which detract from that available for the primary task. Secondly, as one moves up the ladder, the greater is one's responsibility to others and the more is one's behaviour likely to be influenced by that responsibility.[16] I do not mean to say that there is no

13. Adam Smith, *The Wealth of Nations*, Everyman, London (1976), pp. 113-114.

14. In surveying the failure of simple agency theory to make accurate predictions about compensation schemes, George Baker, Michael Jensen, and Kevin Murphy, "it may be that psychologists, behaviourists, human resource consultants, and personnel executives understand something about human behaviour and motivation that is not yet captured in our economic models." G. Baker, M.C. Jensen, and K. Murphy, "Compensation and Incentives: Practice vs. Theory," *Journal of Finance*, 43 (1988):593-616.

15. "Gifts, on the other hand," as the passage continues, "seem to allow a show of appreciation for one person's outstanding work without annoying everyone else. For example, at Avon Products managers are instructed to send hand-written thank you notes to their Avon Ladies, while Levi Strauss gives everyone a small number of 'You are Great' coupons which they can hand out to anyone doing a particularly good job, and each division regularly holds formal events where employees, spouses, and friends gather to hand out 'personal hero'" awards to top performers." *Economist*, April 23, 1994, p. 91.

16. As Adam Smith writes in *Wealth of Nations*, "When the happiness or misery of others depends in any respect upon our conduct, we dare not, as self-love might suggest to us, prefer the interest of one to that of many...The man within immediately calls to us...that, by doing so, we render ourselves the proper object of the contempt and indignation of our brethren. Neither is this sentiment confined to men of extraordinary magnanimity and virtue." (1976, p. 137)

> If "economically rational" incentive schemes work poorly with relatively low-level
> employees, I would be inclined to hazard they are likely to work even less well with
> more senior employees, since such higher-level concerns as self-actualization,
> honour, reputation, and job-satisfaction are likely to assume greater importance as
> one moves up the corporate hierarchy towards the CEO.

place for economic incentives—only that they are less likely to be paramount.

A clear statement of the opposing view, the view that I would characterize as cardboard economics, is provided by Stephen O'Byrne, head of Stern Stewart's executive compensation consulting practice. "The average CEO's total compensation program," says O'Byrne, "needs a lot more performance incentive to *fully* align the CEO's interests with those of the shareholders."[17] This contains more than an echo of the standard agency model popularized in this context by Michael Jensen and William Meckling.[18] O'Byrne is referring to the finding of the much-cited study by Jensen and Kevin Murphy which purported to show that, on average, the total wealth of a CEO changes on average by only $3.25 for every $1000 change in shareholder wealth (and this includes the effect of CEO stockholdings as well as stock options and other incentive schemes). On the basis of this finding, Jensen and Murphy conclude that "the small observed pay-performance sensitivity seems inconsistent with the implications of formal principal-agent models."[19]

Why might the predictions of the simple agency model fail to explain the structure of executive compensation? Why are performance incentives not greater than they are?

One possibility is that there are political constraints on the feasible reward structures.[20] The welfare consequences of such restrictions do not seem to be readily analyzable in a purely economic model, for economic man has neither envy nor notions of fairness, and *schadenfreude* is foreign to his nature. Perhaps the restrictions should be interpreted as a political response to the disfranchisement of the shareholder. However, I am struck by the fact that the simple agency model fails in other contexts as well.

Thus, the need for monetary incentives to be tied directly to actions is apparently confined to business executives and a few others. I do not know whether the Swiss mercenaries received bonuses for

victories, but the Western mercenaries in the Gulf did not, and it is not customary to pay generals by results. However, generals do sometimes receive *ex gratia* payments from grateful countries. For example, the Duke of Wellington received a grant of 200,000 pounds from a grateful parliament after the defeat of Napoleon at the Battle of Waterloo. Similarly, Blenheim Palace outside Oxford, where Winston Churchill was born, stands as a gift from the nation to the Duke of Marlborough, following his victory over the French at the battle of Blenheim. I also believe that General Montgomery received a grant at the end of World War II.

Would it not have been efficient to have written these rewards into the generals' contracts *ex ante*? Was it incentive-compatible to grant the awards after the fact when they could have no possible incentive effects? Was there some reputational consideration that I have overlooked here?

Has your doctor ever told you that if you survive heart surgery the fee will be higher than if you die under the knife? You should be pleased when he does offer you such a contract, for it is not only incentive-compatible, but also a signal about your prospects, since the doctor would not offer such a contract unless he was optimistic about your survival.

Have you considered offering your new dean a contract that bases his remuneration on your position in the *Business Week* ratings—that is a tournament that, I am told, has certain efficiency prospects.[21] And if you are not interested in the *BW* ratings, then why not give the dean a percentage of the money that he raises?

I use these rather light-hearted examples to show that much is accomplished without the direct incentives we think we need for business executives. What is it about business executives that makes them require large financial incentives to perform their tasks, if indeed they do?

Adam Smith gives one answer. He suggests that men are influenced by the environment of their profession or calling, and that industry and trade

---

17. S. O' Byrne, "What Pay for Performance Really Looks Like: the Case of Michael Eisner," *Journal of Applied Corporate Finance*, 5 (1992), 135-136.

18. M.C. Jensen, and W.H. Meckling, Theory of The Firm: Managerial Behaviour, Agency Costs and Ownership Structure, *Journal of Financial Economics*, 3 (1976), pp. 305-360.

19. M. Jensen and K. Murphy, "Performance, Pay and Top Management Incentives," *Journal of Political Economy* (April, 1990).

20. Subsequent restrictions on the tax-deductibility of executive compensation by firms suggest that this may be a real consideration. However, Baker, Jensen and Murphy (1988) find such an explanation unsatisfactory.

21. By rewarding individuals on the basis of their performance relative to their peers rather than their absolute performance, it is possible to abstract from random factors that affect the performance of all members of the comparison group. Interestingly enough, the chairman of Salomon Brothers is now rewarded on the basis of the performance of the firm relative to that of its competitors (*Financial Times*, May 5, 1994).

naturally form in an individual habits of "order, economy and attention," but also, unfortunately, such vices as "mean rapacity" and "avarice and ambition." Whatever the truth of this in the 18th century, it hardly seems a fair portrait of the modern businessman. Of course, some individuals are drawn to a business career precisely because they are especially motivated by money; but this is very different from claiming that most businessmen are motivated only by money.

I would like to throw out for consideration the suggestion that the origin of executive bonuses may lie not so much in incentives as in notions of equity and fairness. As if to confirm this argument, Graef Crystal reports, "The vast majority of companies prefer a discretionary approach to establishing executive bonus levels. Within broad limits therefore, the company's board decides, after the year is over, just how much in the way of a bonus it wishes to give to its CEO."[22]

I would also suggest that such bonuses are not too far removed from the *ex-post* rewards made to generals. Somewhat like the Duke of Wellington, Hamish Maxwell was given a reward of $24 million on retirement as CEO of Philip Morris, and Roberto Goizueta of Coca-Cola was granted $80 million in stock as reward for the performance of the company over the past ten years. If we accept Crystal's characterization of executive bonuses, then much of the compensation for CEOs can be regarded as a reward for past performance rather than an incentive for future performance.

Such rewards can be understood as rewards not only for effort, but also for risk-taking. A CEO will often be placing his reputation and human capital at risk in making difficult decisions. Thus, even if there were no need to pay him a bonus in order to motivate him, it might well be appropriate to reward him well if the outcome is successful to make up for the costs he would have borne (loss of employment, reputation) if the outcome was unsuccessful.[23]

Of course, we do observe the granting of executive stock options that tie executives' wealth directly to company performance. While the use of executive stock options is usually explained in terms of agency theory (and tax planning), it is also consistent with the hypothesis that individuals like to have a sense of control over their investment returns, and to participate in the fruits of their labours. While portfolio theory would suggest that an executive would prefer, all things equal, to have a flat and thus riskless wage, and to be able to invest his wealth in a diversified portfolio of common stocks, the evidence of defined contribution pension plans is that workers tend to invest a disproportionate share of their wealth in their own company stock. There is no reason to believe that executives behave any differently. It would be interesting in this regard to examine the timing of executives' exercise of stock options and sale of shares to determine whether it is affected by more than the standard considerations of portfolio diversification and tax minimisation.

Why might CEO compensation be largely on an ex-post discretionary basis? Clearly, one reason is the difficulty of writing sufficiently explicit contracts. This difficulty is perhaps particularly acute for a person in a position of responsibility, by which I mean an individual whose actions affect the welfare of others in complex ways. The standard models of agency with which I am familiar necessarily omit much of the richness of the CEO decision-making— in these models more effort leads to more output. There is no question of the output being a joint product of the efforts of the group, whose morale may be adversely affected either by excessive pay for the leader, or by a payment scheme that directly rewards the leader for gains wrung from the group— as for example in the form of wage concessions or the cancellation of post-retirement health benefits. To the extent that the leader benefits directly from the sacrifices of other members of the group, it becomes harder to ask for such sacrifices, and his effectiveness as a leader is impaired.[24]

Secondly, the standard agency model presumes a one-to-one relation between effort and expected output. It is by no means clear that a CEO will become more effective simply by working harder.

Thirdly, the prerequisite consumption model of Jensen and Meckling that is often invoked in favour of a large managerial share of profits rests on the

---

22. G. Crystal, *In Search of Excess: The Overcompensation of American Executives* (New York: Norton, 1991).

23. Among the causes of inequality in wages among different employments, Adam Smith notes "the small or great trust in those who exercise them" and "the probability or improbability of success in them." *The Theory of Moral Sentiments* (Liberty Press, Indianapolis, 1991), pp. 89-90.

24. Such concerns were expressed in 1993 as news of the compensation package for Lou Gerstner as the new CEO of IBM appeared almost simultaneously with news of further layoffs at IBM.

> **The standard models of agency with which I am familiar necessarily omit much of the richness of the CEO decision-making. There is no question of the output being a joint product of the efforts of the group, whose morale may be adversely affected either by excessive pay for the leader, or by a payment scheme that directly rewards the leader for gains wrung from the group.**

assumption that the manager will steal what he does not own, so that it is probably more efficient to give it to him at the outset rather than put him to the trouble of stealing it. I would argue that if your manager needs such incentives to stop him from stealing, then you probably need a new manager.

Fourthly, CEO's have responsibilities to others besides the shareholders. Firms have implicit contracts with workers and suppliers and induce those parties to make significant commitments to the firm. A CEO whose pecuniary interest in short-term profitability is too great may be unable to resist the temptation to abrogate its implicit contracts, with adverse consequences for the ability of the firm to deal in a trustworthy fashion with these parties. Similar considerations apply to suppliers of debt finance, whose interests are often at odds with those of stockholders.[25] Thus, recognition of the complex inter-relationships between the various parties to a firm's activities, which are supported not only by formal contracts, but by implicit understandings and informal agreements, suggests that a CEO must act as a referee over these competing claims rather than simply as the agent of the stockholders. Indeed, to further the long-run interests of the stockholders, he must be willing to eschew short-term advantage, which may be difficult if his pecuniary reward for acting solely in the stockholders' interest is too great.[26]

Finally, a significant weakness of contractual incentives is that the need to base them on precise quantitative goals may create incentives that are not aligned with the true goals of the organisation. The recent example of a bond trader at Kidder Peabody who was able to manufacture large but economically fictitious "profits" on which his bonus was based points to the difficulty of designing such contracts even in relatively simple situations.

Where I think that the incentive model may have some power is in formalizing and clarifying the

goals of the organization—explicit criteria for reward make clear what kind of performance is sought, even when the incentive payments are modest.[27] A good horseman uses the bridle lightly to guide his mount; a bad horseman uses it roughly and, in so doing, ruins the horse's mouth and coarsens the beast. Similarly, incentives, if used wisely, will be used moderately to indicate the goals of the organization and to provide encouragement. If they are used aggressively to induce an agent to do things which are otherwise against his will, they will coarsen the agent and encourage him to do nothing without the appropriate incentive payments.

Evidence that the simple agency model may not be descriptive of the decisions of those in positions of responsibility for others is provided by a recent study by Robert Gibbons and Kevin Murphy of corporate investment in plant and equipment, advertising, and R&D around the time of CEO retirements.[28] Gibbons and Murphy argue that existing compensation arrangements give CEOs an incentive to reduce these expenditures as they near retirement—at least, this is the clear prediction of the simple agency model. What the study finds, however, is that "R&D, advertising expenditures, and capital expenditures increase rather than decrease as the CEO nears retirement."[29]

In summary, agency theory represents a promising start to thinking about executive compensation, along with other considerations such as taxes. However, the simple model of rational self-interest that underlies it is likely to be too simple in many contexts to yield reliable predictions or, more importantly, reliable prescriptions. On the one hand, we are often incapable of pursuing our own self-interest without support from the environment—witness the soldiers in the Korean War and plentiful other examples. On the other hand, we are also capable of rising above our own narrow self-interest, and we are more likely to do so the greater is our

---

25. Bondholders are most concerned with the safety of their investment, while stockholders may have an interest in pursuing relatively high risk strategies that will transfer wealth from the bondholders to them. And the concern of bondholders with managerial incentives is apparent from the finding of one recent study that bond prices tend to fall when executive stock option plans are adopted. See R.A. Defusco, R.R. Johnson and T.S. Zorn, 1990, The Effect of Executive Stock Option Plans on Stockholders and Bondholders, *Journal of Finance*, 45:617-627.

26. Agency theorists would argue that any divergence between the long-term and short-term interests of stockholders may be overcome by writing appropriate contracts, for example with rewards based on the stock price, which in theory reflects the long-run interests of stockholders. However, lack of knowledge by market participants about the inner workings of the firm will make this problematic. In other words, in setting the stock price, the market will tend to reflect the influence of managerial decisions on the long-run prospects of the firm only imperfectly.

27. Michael Jensen, as Editor of the *Journal of Financial Economics*, found that a very modest financial reward was sufficient to induce reviewers to return manuscripts in a timely fashion.

28. R. Gibbons and K.J. Murphy, "Does Executive Compensation Affect Investment?," *Journal of Applied Corporate Finance*, 5 (1992), pp. 99-109.

29. Another study, it is true, claims to find a decline in the rate of growth of these expenditures around CEO retirements as the size of the CEO's shareholding relative to his cash compensation falls. (See P.M. Deechow and R.G. Sloan, "Executive Incentives and the Horizon Problem," *Journal of Accounting and Economics*, 14 (1991):51-89.) This seems like nice support for the simple agency theory, for with a larger shareholding the CEO should have less incentive to act for short-term advantage. However, their measure of CEO shareholding is constructed so that it is likely to be lower for firms whose growth has declined—such firms will of course show lower growth in R&D regardless of agency considerations.

responsibility for the welfare of others. There is nothing irrational in that, and readers of popular sociobiology will recognize the same phenomenon in the animal world.

SELF-INTEREST, ECONOMICS, AND SOCIETY

There is a misconception, perhaps particularly common among economists, that self-interest is not only individually rational but socially rational as well, in the sense that it leads to the maximisation of some appropriately defined social welfare function. The popular argument for this position is, of course, the famous quotation of Adam Smith about the self-interest of the "butcher, the brewer, or the baker" that I cited earlier. However, appeal to authority can be a two-edged sword, and the economics textbooks that cite this passage rarely cite another from the *Wealth of Nations* that has a decidedly normative tone:

a man ought to regard himself, not as something separated and detached, but as a citizen of the world, a member of the vast commonwealth of nations...and to the interest of this great community, he ought at all times to be willing that his own little interest be sacrificed.[30]

This second quotation gives one a somewhat different view of the ideal society than the supposedly Smithian view encapsulated in the Second Theorem of Welfare Economics, that hymn of praise to the beneficial effects of self-interest, that emollient of the troubled conscience. Indeed Smith, in emphasizing the beneficial effects of self-interest, was doing so in the particular historical context of a system of state regulated monopolies. There is no evidence to suggest that he would have supported Reaganite or Thacherite policies, or have been opposed to policies of income redistribution.

It is perhaps surprising to find that this kinder and gentler side of Smith is echoed a hundred years later in the writings of Richard Ely, the founder of the American Economic Association, in whose name an annual lecture on economics is still given. Ely writes, "The fundamental organizing principle of social organisation is the biblical commandment 'thou shalt love thy neighbour as thyself'...This commandment extends even to all our daily acts, in our buying, selling and getting gain." Richard Ely was opposed by William Sumner, the other leading American economist of the day, a Yale professor who favoured social Darwinism and opposed all government effort to relieve the poor. "The fact that a man is here," wrote Sumner in a characteristic statement, "is no demand on other people that they shall keep him alive and sustain him." Contrast this with Smith, who criticized the harshness of the English Poor Laws.

Interestingly enough, Sumner, the social Darwinist, was an episcopal clergyman until he was appointed to his Chair at Yale (and I assume that the above quotation comes from his professorial rather than his clerical days). I must add that the days of influence with the AEA of the kinder and gentler Ely were rather short-lived, and that it was the views of the social Darwinist and former clergyman William Sumner that had the most influence in the end.

As American economists, we are heirs of Smith and of Ely as well as of Sumner. In trying to understand the nature of human motivation, as we must, if we are to have a theory of executive compensation, let alone a theory of society, we should be neither too optimistic nor too cynical about human nature. The simple theory of agency is too cynical for my taste, and I hope for yours also.

In reality, a purely individualistic society would be miserable to live in, for many of our activities do not lend themselves to quantitative measurement and reward. This is particularly true of the caring professions, of the law, and of much of the teaching profession where informational asymmetries, to use modern economists' jargon, put the patient, client, or student at a substantial disadvantage. It is for this reason that professions adopt codes of professional conduct and doctors swear to uphold the Hippocratic Oath. Indeed, in most transactions with others we rely on trust, and are only infrequently disappointed.[31] Most tellingly, when we are cheated, we react with anger and moral disapprobation—we do not simply recognize that we are dealing with an economically rational agent who has found it expedient to cheat us.

---

30. Ibid., p. 140.
31. As Wilson (1993, p. 13) remarks, "Most of us do not break the law most of the time, not simply because we worry about even a small chance of getting caught, but also because our conscience forbids us doing what is wrong. By the same token, most of us honour most promises, play games by the rules, respect the rights and claims of others, and *work at our jobs even when the boss isn't looking.*"

In reality, a purely individualistic society would be miserable to live in, for many of our activities do not lend themselves to quantitative measurement and reward.

However, I do have a sneaking concern. It is that if we go on hammering into our students the mistaken notion that rationality is identical with self-interest, we shall gradually make our agency models come true,[32] but at the cost of producing a society that will not function. For, as I have argued, and contrary to popular economists' misconception, unbridled self-interest leads not to utopia, but to the Hobbesian jungle where, as in parts of our cities, life is nasty, brutish and short.

---

32. One recent study reports evidence that training in economics reduces the likelihood that students will co-operate with others, and suggests that "With an eye toward both the social good and the well-being of their own students, economists may wish to stress a broader view of human motivation in their training." See R.H. Frank, T. Gilovich, D.T. Regan, "Does Studying Economics Inhibit Co-operation?," *Journal of Economic Perspectives*, 7 (1993), pp. 159-171. Wilson (1993, p. 9) attributes worldwide rising crime rates to a "profound cultural shift in the strength of either cultural constraints or internal conscience or both," and remarks that "much of modern philosophy abandoned morality without even a hint."

SELF-INTEREST, ALTRUISM, INCENTIVES, AND AGENCY THEORY

by Michael C. Jensen,
Harvard University*

In his article in this book entitled "Incentives, Rationality, and Society," Michael Brennan attacks the use of incentives for corporate executive compensation and, by implication, for society at large. Professor Brennan argues that the tendency of economists to equate rationality with the pursuit of self-interest is wrong both in a positive sense (that is, people don't behave that way) and in a normative sense (because if they did behave that way, the world would be a much less desirable place). Brennan is correct that people do not always behave rationally, but this provides no support for his opposition to incentives, or for his opposition to self-interest.

Professor Brennan's arguments, although popular in many quarters, are both logically flawed and empirically incorrect. Underlying his argument is a strong aversion to incentives, an opposition that reveals itself in several places to be primarily, if not wholly, an antagonism to the use of monetary incentives. (He cites approvingly the incentives provided by awards banquets and small prizes.) He also is not fond of the agency model; indeed, he concludes (p. 123) that "if we go on hammering into our students the mistaken notion that rationality is identical with self-interest we shall make our agency models come true, but at the cost of producing a society that will not function."

These views are based on misconceptions held by many people and, for this reason alone, are worthy of discussion. I set out by explaining what Bill Meckling and I intended to accomplish with our original paper on agency theory, and then go on to discuss the roles of self-interest, incentives, and altruism in our model. The paper ends with an introduction to what I view as a new line of approach for agency theory—systematically non-rational behavior.

AGENCY THEORY

In the early 1970s, William Meckling and I wrote an article entitled "Theory of the Firm: Managerial Behavior, Agency Costs and Ownership Structure." The purpose of that article, published in the *Journal of Financial Economics* in 1976, was to pry open the "black box" in economics and finance called the firm. In so doing, we reexamined the standard economists' assumption that public companies systematically attempt to maximize firm value.

A large part of our article was devoted to demonstrating the potential for costly conflicts of interest between corporate managers and shareholders—particularly over the optimal size of the firm—and the means by which such conflicts are (or could be) managed so as to preserve value. In the absence of significant stock holdings by managers, we argued that one potentially effective method for controlling such conflicts was incentive compensation contracts tied to performance.

Professor Brennan, in criticizing the widespread corporate use of incentives and the "cynicism" of agency theory, appeals repeatedly to the kinder, gentler side of Adam Smith as authority for moderating what he (Brennan, not Smith) sees as the "harshness" and inhumanity of free-market economics. I find this repeated appeal to Smith ironic, not because I disagree with any of Smith's sentiments, but because Smith himself properly deserves to be regarded as the father of agency theory. Although he didn't use the language of agency costs, he clearly understood the problems arising from inevitable conflicts of interest between the professional managers and owners of a business. Indeed, our agency paper begins with the following words from *Wealth of Nations*:

*This research has been supported by the Division of Research, Harvard Business School. I am also indebted to many for comments and discussions over the years that have helped me understand these issues. Although they bear no responsibility for the views expressed herein, I am grateful to Chris Argyris, George Baker, Donald Chew, Perry Fagan, Donna Feinberg, Gerald Fischbach, Jack Gabarro, Richard Hackman, Steven Hyman, William Meckling, Steve-Anna Stephens, Richard Thaler, Karen Wruck, Abraham Zaleznik, the participants in the Mind, Brain, Behavior initiative at Harvard University, and my former colleagues at the University of Rochester.

The directors of such [joint stock] companies... being the managers rather of other people's money than their own...cannot be expected...[to] watch over it with the same anxious vigilance with which the partners in a private copartnery frequently watch over their own... Negligence and profusion, therefore, must always prevail, more or less, in the management of the affairs of such a company. (*The Wealth of Nations*, 1776 (Modern Library, p. 700))

In fact, Smith believed so strongly in the power of self-interest and the conflicts it generates that he was pessimistic about the ability of the joint stock company to survive in any but the simplest of activities. As he goes on to say:

Without a monopoly... a joint stock company, it would appear from experience, cannot long carry on any branch of foreign trade. To buy in one market, in order to sell, with profit, in another, when there are many competitors in both; to watch over, not only the occasional variations in the demand, but the much greater and more frequent variations in the competition...is a species of warfare...which can scarce ever be conducted successfully, without such an unremitting exertion of vigilance and attention, as cannot long be expected from the directors of a joint stock company. (Smith, 1776, pp. 712-713)

Observing the failure of dozens of stock companies in his day, Smith concluded that the only activities a joint stock company (the forerunner of the modern public corporation) could carry on successfully without a state-granted monopoly were those that were easily monitored—in his words, those in "which all the operations are capable of being reduced to what is called a routine, or to such a uniformity of method as admits of little or no variation" (p. 713). In Smith's view, this limited the probable future success of joint stock companies to banking, fire and marine insurance, canals, and municipal water supply. Thus, Smith's principal error as the first agency theorist was his failure to anticipate the evolution of the corporate governance mechanisms—including incentive compensation contracts—that have helped enable the corporation to survive and indeed dominate most economic activities throughout the world.

Agency theory says that because people pursue their own best interests, conflicts of interests inevitably arise over at least some issues when they engage in cooperative endeavors. Such activities include not only the commerce conducted by partnerships and corporations, but also the interaction among members of families and other social organizations.

Bill Meckling and I argued that because conflicts of interest cause problems and therefore losses to the parties involved, the parties themselves have strong incentives to find ways to reduce the "agency costs" (as we called them) of such cooperation. This *conservation of value principle* is the basic force that motivates both principals and their agents (and partners) to work together to minimize the sum of the costs of writing and enforcing contracts (implicit as well as explicit), the costs of monitoring and bonding activities, and the residual losses incurred because it will not pay to enforce all contracts perfectly. The theory provides a structure within which to understand and model a broad array of human organizational arrangements, including incentive compensation, auditing, and bonding arrangements of all kinds.

To the extent we can judge from the subsequent theoretical and empirical work stemming from our agency concepts, the academic finance and economics profession has found the approach a productive one. The agency cost literature is large and continues to grow. (And, toward the end of this paper I describe what I believe will come to be recognized as a second important source of agency costs—namely, *internal* conflicts of interest, or self-control problems, that manifest themselves in the universal human tendency to take actions that are not consistent with one's self-interest.)

THE MEANING AND ROLE OF INCENTIVES IN THE LOGIC OF CHOICE

Professor Brennan's objection to the use of incentives appears to be premised on the assumption that there are no major conflicts between the interests of corporate managers and the corporate goal of maximizing firm value. But, when he complains that economic man "will never perform without incentives" (p. 34), he appears to be envisioning a world in which people have no incentives of any kind; at times he seems to suggest that action in the absence of incentives is the natural and, therefore, desirable state of affairs. Many managers, policy makers, and religious leaders share this view.

It is inconceivable that purposeful action on the part of human beings can be viewed as anything other than a response to incentives. The issue of incentives goes to the heart of what it means to optimize, or achieve the greatest possible good— indeed, it goes to the very core of what it means to choose. Rational individuals always choose the option that makes them best off as they see it. It is the difference in well-being expected from taking one action instead of another that provides incentives and results in choice.

Much of the resistance to the use of incentives appears to be based, then, on the notion of a natural state of affairs in which there are no incentives and thus no conflicts of interest. In a world without incentives, all alternative courses of action or choices must promise the same degree of utility as viewed by the individual. Such a world is virtually inconceivable. It does not exist in the state of nature: not all land is equally fertile, nor are all paths equally level or unobstructed. Incentives exist (like it or not) in all cases in which people have real choice.

Managers in every organization, even one with no pay-for-performance, face complicated incentives, including incentives to weaken the organization (by making it too large or too diversified) as well as to strengthen it. Thus, the issue for any organization is not whether to introduce incentives to motivate its employees. There are always incentives; the issue is simply which incentives do we want to encourage and which do we want to suppress.

Managerial decisions designed to strengthen organizations often meet with opposition (and even retribution) from colleagues, employees, communities, policy makers, regulators, and others with conflicting interests—thereby providing managers with incentives to compromise their decisions. To increase the chances that managers will take the best actions possible, we must ensure that the incentives (that is, the trade-offs) they face encourage them to move in the correct direction.

The main advantage of money in this mosaic of organizational incentives is that general purchasing power is valued by almost everyone (because it is a claim on all resources), and it can be varied easily with performance. In contrast, it often is difficult to vary nonmonetary forms of reward—praise, prizes, sometimes even promotions—in ways that relate to organizational, group, or individual performance.

I hasten to add that, for a variety of reasons, monetary incentives are not the best way to motivate every action. Because monetary incentives are so potent, and because it is sometimes difficult to specify the proper performance measure, monetary incentives are often dominated by other approaches. But, in the end, where money incentives are required, they are required precisely because people are motivated by things other than money.

SELF-INTEREST, ALTRUISM, AND PERFECT AGENTS

Professor Brennan, like many social scientists outside the field of economics, also criticizes the economist's model of human behavior. By identifying rationality with self-interest, he suggests, such a model not only fails to capture the full range of human feeling and action, it also works to the detriment of society by encouraging narcissism and discouraging concern for others.

But the model of self-interested behavior that Brennan has in mind here is not ours. (Nor is it the one used by most economists in practice—that is, apart from their most perfunctory kinds of model-building.) People do care about failure and success; they do have emotions and care about honor and self-esteem; and they feel shame and pride.

In our paper "The Nature of Man" in this issue, Bill Meckling and I discuss at length the minimal characterization capable of capturing the complexity of human beings. We describe people as Resourceful, Evaluative Maximizers—REMMs, for short—and argue that these three characteristics are effective in explaining much (though not all) human behavior. As we show in the paper, the model is especially powerful in predicting the aggregate behavior underlying general economic and social change.

Moreover, although Professor Brennan's definition of self-interest excludes the possibility of altruism, our REMM model explicitly acknowledges the willingness of people to sacrifice their own time or resources for the betterment of others. The satisfaction people get from helping others is another "good" to be sought in their efforts to maximize their own utility. In seeking to achieve the greatest possible good for themselves, people choose from an "opportunity set" that includes love, honor, and the welfare of others as well as money and material objects. In short, there is nothing in REMM or agency theory that excludes or in any way devalues altruistic behavior.

We agree with Brennan, then, that people are much more than money maximizers. But he takes this argument one step farther than we are willing

Because it is sometimes difficult to specify the proper performance measure, monetary incentives are often dominated by other approaches. But, in the end, where money incentives are required, they are required precisely because people are motivated by things other than money.

to go when he suggests that people "are more likely to rise above [their] own narrow self-interest...the greater is [their] responsibility for the welfare of others" (p. 121). If by this he means that people in positions of authority are more likely to have genuinely altruistic motives, then I might at least entertain the premise (although the behavior of politicians generally, and of national leaders of countries like Romania, Yugoslavia, and the old USSR, should give us pause). But Brennan's statement comes very close to the assertion that, because some people devote more of their time and energies to others, they are also "perfect agents." By perfect agents, I mean people who make decisions with no concern for their own preferences, but only for those of their principals.

As we point out in "The Nature of Man," there is compelling evidence—in family life and social organizations as well as the worlds of business and politics—that people are not perfect agents. How else can we explain the widespread failure of internal control systems at large corporations like IBM, Gulf Oil, and GM, which systematically wasted billions of dollars of resources until curbed by the market for corporate control and shareholder activism?[1] And if government officials are perfect agents, how can we explain the massive deficits combined with ineffective social programs that characterize most governments around the world? Or consider the recent scandals—and evidence of chronic mismanagement—that seem to be proliferating at non-profit organizations like Blue Cross and United Way.

The fact that further evidence of scandal, waste, and inefficiency in the U.S. public and non-profit sectors now seems to furnish daily headlines for our newspapers lends force to Adam Smith's endorsement of the social value of profit-making activities. As Smith showed us over 200 years ago, the pursuit of one's enlightened self-interest, far from reducing the public welfare, leads to general prosperity provided governments set the proper rules of the game. And, as I suggest in the next section of this paper, greater attention to self-interest or rational behavior would make the world a better, not worse, place to live.

NON-RATIONAL BEHAVIOR

Brennan cites several examples from an article by Steven Postrel and Richard Rumelt[2] in which soldiers and managers behave in ways that are clearly inconsistent with their own near-term self-interest. The soldiers fail to take obvious steps (such as keeping their helmets and arms, changing wet clothing, and digging fox holes) to maintain their own protection and fighting capability, while the managers routinely mistreat customers. Such self-damaging behavior is not unusual, and economists viewing the world through their lens of rationality generally fail to see that such behavior is common to virtually everyone.

Moreover, the fact people do not always act in their own self-interest provides no support for Brennan's call for less use of incentives. In fact, Postrel and Rumelt correctly see the import of their stories as calling for even more precise use of incentives to address self-control problems—for example, by paying attention to the timing and context of rewards and punishments to help individuals resist self-destructive impulses.

REMM provides great predictive power and a solid basis for policy decisions in business as well as personal and public life; but it is not complete. It fails to acknowledge the essentially dualistic nature of human behavior—the fact that the same people exhibit non-rational as well as rational behavior. While this may appear to be a contradiction, such internal division or inconsistency is not an aberration but an integral part of normality itself. The soldier example illustrates behavior that contradicts REMM, but the contradiction goes far beyond the extreme conditions of war. Clinical psychological records as well as daily observations of family, organizational, and social action abound with examples of non-rational behavior.

By non-rational I do not mean "random" or "unexplainable"; I mean behavior that systematically harms the individual. Although inconsistent with REMM, I believe that such non-rational behavior can be modeled and then integrated with REMM. By so doing, we can significantly increase the predictive power of our analytical apparatus.

---

1. For an account of the role of corporate restructuring in addressing both the U.S. and a worldwide problem of chronic overcapacity, see Michael C. Jensen, "The Modern Industrial Revolution, Exit, and the Failure of Internal Control Systems," *Journal of Finance* (1993); for a shorter, less technical version, see the article by the same title in the *Journal of Applied Corporate Finance*, Volume 6 Number 4 (Winter 1994).

2. S. Postrel and R. Rumelt, "Incentives, Routines, and Self Command," *Industrial and Corporate Change*, V. 1, 1992, pp. 397-425.

In a paper entitled "Economics, Organizations, and Non-Rational Behavior" that will be published in *Economic Inquiry* next year, I formulate a Pain Avoidance Model (PAM) that is intended to complement REMM.[3] PAM describes non-rational human behavior that arises under conditions of fear. While attempting (generally subconsciously) to avoid the pain associated with acknowledging their mistakes, people often end up incurring far more pain, and making themselves worse off, than if they had simply recognized and responded to their errors.

Unfortunately, this non-rational behavior is not random, but systematic and indeed virtually universal. Recent brain research suggests that such counterproductive defensive responses derive from the biological and chemical structure of the brain, and are connected to the brain's "fight or flight" response.[4]

What is surprising about this defensive behavior is the seeming triviality of the events or challenges that arouse fear, and the extent to which this fear is registered, and the defensive response takes place, below the level of conscious awareness. That is, the mechanisms of the brain commonly blind people so that they are unaware of their own fear and defensiveness. Such defensive behavior often occurs, for example, when we are faced with evidence or theories that threaten to change the lens through which we view reality, including not only the world around us, but our view of ourselves.

The primary consequence of such defensiveness is the reluctance of people to learn and their resulting inability to respond properly to feedback and change—even when the personal consequences of not responding are great. These non-rational responses are evident throughout organizations and society. Examples include the tendency of people to overrate themselves systematically in rankings of their peers, the infrequent use of pay-for-performance compensation systems, the common refusal of people to welcome feedback on their errors, and the systematic tendency for corporate managers to overpay for acquisitions and to fail to adapt to changes in the competitive environment in the absence of an organizational crisis.[5] These non-rational responses lie, for example, at the heart of the failure of corporate internal control systems that led to the waste of hundreds of billions of dollars and the failure of a number of crown jewels of corporate America over the last two decades.[6]

While grounded in the flight-or-fight response—a mechanism that has contributed to survival for millions of years—the human responses to emotional or psychic pain appear to be highly counterproductive in our densely populated and complex modern industrial world. Such defensiveness reduces people's capacity to assimilate new information and adapt to an environment in which continuous change is increasingly becoming the rule. People become wedded to their own theories in ways that make them systematically worse off.

An interesting aspect of this non-rational behavior is the tendency for humans to hold views of themselves and their behavior—"espoused theories," in the language of Chris Argyris—that are false. They are false because they are inconsistent with the theories on which the individuals act—what Argyris calls their "theories in use."[7] Discovering these violations of our own principles and beliefs amounts to discovering our "irrationality," and this is highly threatening to an individual's self esteem. The brain's fear response and the associated anxiety then severely limits our ability to perceive when our espoused theories are false. It is obviously difficult to change incorrect behavior under such circumstances.

Moreover, this common discrepancy between espoused theories and theories in use undermines the premise of Brennan's argument for limiting students' opportunities to learn that people are generally self interested. In his opening words, he suggests that people's espoused theories largely determine their behavior. "Self-image is a major determinant of behaviour. If I think of myself as an

3. To some extent, this non-optimal behavior can be incorporated into REMM by recognizing that individuals' visions of the world and their ability to act or react depend on various factors (such as the intensity of emotions) that have the power to change, if only temporarily, their perception of "goods." Such an expanded model could explain deviant behavior as the result of maximizing actions in situations where an individual's perceptions of the world are systematically different, or more constrained, than normal. For a survey of the effects of stress on the behavior of humans that is consistent with such a view, see Karl E. Weick, "Stress in Accounting Systems," *Accounting Review*, Vol. LVIII, No. 2 (April, 1983).

4. See LeDoux, Joseph, "Emotion, Memory and the Brain," *Scientific American*, V. 270, (June 1994), pp. 50-57, and the references therein, as well as the September 1992 *Scientific American* special issue on the brain.

5. For example, in large sample surveys, almost no one ranks themselves below the 50th percentile of their peers. For discussion of these phenomena see George Baker, Michael Jensen, and Kevin Murphy, "Compensation and Incentives: Practice vs. Theory," *J. Finance*, 43 (1988); Michael Jensen and Kevin Murphy, "Performance, Pay and Top Management Incentives," *J. Political Economy* (April, 1990); G. W. Schwert "Mark-up Pricing in Mergers and Acquisitions," Unpublished manuscript, University of Rochester (1993), and the references therein.

6. See Jensen (1993), cited above.

7. See Chris Argyris, *Knowledge for Action, A Guide to Overcoming Barriers to Organizational Change* (San Francisco, California, Jossey-Bass Inc., 1993); and "Teaching Smart People How To Learn," *Harvard Business Review* (May-June 1991), pp. 99-109.

> **The central proposition of agency theory is that rational self-interested people involved in cooperative endeavors *always* have incentives to reduce or control conflicts of interest so as to reduce the losses resulting from them.**

honest person, I shall behave in an honest way." Evidence to the contrary is all around us.

PAM and the Normative Import of REMM

As stated above, the combination of REMM and PAM leads to a richer positive description of behavior. Even more important, this dualistic model will lead to more effective normative propositions, including programs and methods for helping people reduce the counterproductive, self-debilitating aspects of their own behavior.

Note that these tendencies for individuals to act in ways that are inconsistent with their self-interest are another source of conflicts with employees, employers, partners, mates, colleagues, and so on. In this sense, they are another source of agency costs. Along with the conflicts of interest *among* people discussed by traditional agency theory, such *internal* conflicts[8] must also be addressed in any cooperative effort. And this, in turn, leads us to a structure for thinking about how to use group processes and organizational procedures to limit the unwanted effects of non-rational behavior.

In this expanded view of human behavior, REMM becomes more than a positive description of human behavior—it also becomes a prescriptive model that says this is how humans should behave. Consistent with this view, the solutions suggested by the psychological and psychiatric professions are best interpreted as helping people learn to correct their "mistakes" in order to behave in more REMM-like ways.[9] In short, the problem is not to persuade people to stop acting in their own self-interest, but to help them learn to avoid the systematic mistakes that make themselves, and those around them, worse off.

SOME CLOSING THOUGHTS

Professor Brennan laments that the teaching of agency theory and the use of incentives will somehow "coarsen" humanity and make the world we live in a less hospitable place. Although this issue is worthy of careful research, it does not follow logically from the content of the theory, nor does his conjecture fit with my observations from 20 years of teaching this material.

When I teach agency theory, I do not find my students surprised by the existence of conflicts. They live in the midst of them—and those conflicts which are not experienced personally can be shared in the daily torrent of offerings from the world's media. Because of the universality of conflict, the danger is that we may take it for granted and thus fail to see it at all.

I find that students and business people are excited by the central proposition of agency theory. And the proposition that excites them is *not* that people are self-interested, or that conflicts abound. The central proposition of agency theory is that rational self-interested people involved in cooperative endeavors *always* have incentives to reduce or control conflicts of interest so as to reduce the losses resulting from them. The gains can then be shared by some or all of the parties.

Perhaps Professor Brennan and others object to the fact that agency theory holds out no encouragement that human nature can be improved, and that society, organizations, and even individuals themselves can rid themselves of these costly conflicts of interest. The reality, however, is that even if we could instill more of a spirit of altruism in everyone, agency problems would not be solved. Put simply, altruism, the concern for the well-being of others, does not turn people into perfect agents who do the bidding of others.

I am skeptical of our ability to change human nature. Thousands of years of effort by all great religions of the world have failed to eradicate the reality of self-interest. Instead, I place my bets on the institutional structures, contracts, and informal arrangements that we create to reduce conflict, to govern our relations, and to increase the extent of cooperation and the benefits we reap from it. Such efforts, which arise from self-interest, are privately rewarding and improve the quality of life in our society.

---

8. As Richard Thaler has put it, people face agency problems in the form of conflicts with themselves. See Richard T. Thaler and H. M. Shefrin, "An Economic Theory of Self Control," *Journal of Political Economy*, Volume 89, Number 2 (April, 1981): 392-406. I am embarrassed to admit that Richard was a colleague at Rochester at the time he did this original work, and although I always found it interesting, I failed for more than a decade to see the generality and the importance of this self-control issue.

9. See Argyris (1991, 1993) and M. Scott Peck, *The Road Less Traveled* (Simon & Schuster, 1978), pp. 11-77. Consistent with this, there is some evidence that those behaving according to the REMM model live more successful lives. See, for example, R. P. Larrick, R. E. Nisbett and J. N. Morgan, "Who Uses the Cost-benefit Rules of Choice? Implications for the Normative Status of Microeconomic Theory," *Organizational Behavior and Human Decision Processes* (December, 1993, pp. 331-347.)

BAYLOR UNIVERSITY ROUNDTABLE ON

INTEGRITY IN FINANCIAL REPORTING

November 1, 2002   *Waco, Texas*

BILL THOMAS: Good afternoon, and welcome to this discussion of corporate financial reporting. I'm Bill Thomas, the J. E. Bush Professor of Accounting here at Baylor's Hankamer School of Business, and I will serve as a co-moderator. The other co-moderator will be my colleague John Martin, who joined the Baylor faculty a little over four years ago as the Carr P. Collins Professor of Finance. Before coming here, John spent 18 years on the finance faculty of the University of Texas at Austin.

The idea of putting on such a roundtable came to us about a year ago, in the fall of 2001, just after the news of the collapse of Enron and the impending fall of Arthur Andersen. The fall of Enron has hit us very hard, and the fall of Andersen even harder, because those were two of the major recruiters on our campus. Our students are now having a much harder time finding jobs than they did just a year and a half ago. And at least part of the problem they're

now facing had its genesis, we think, in some business practices that became especially prevalent in the 1990s, when things were going very well and the prospects for corporate growth and profitability seemed almost limitless. But, as recent events have made clear, those practices contained considerable potential for abuse.

So we felt we had an obligation to provide our students with some insight into the nature of the problem they are now facing—and by "insight" I mean the kind of knowledge and expertise that is not generally found in popular magazines and the business sections of our newspapers. And that's why we decided to hold this conference: to bring to our campus a group of people with demonstrated knowledge and accomplishments in the area of corporate governance who could shed some light on these issues.

First let me tell you a little about the participants in this discussion, and I will proceed in alphabetical order:

ROBERT ALSPAUGH was recently elected Chief Executive Officer of KPMG International, which is one of the largest public accounting and professional services firms in the world. Bob started working for KPMG in 1970, the year after he graduated from this university—and his degree, according to our records, was awarded summa cum laude. Throughout his 33-year career with KPMG, Bob has served as the lead partner for a diverse array of clients across a range of industries, including energy, manufacturing, and financial services.

STUART GILLAN is Assistant Professor of Finance at the University of Delaware's College of Business and Economics, as well as Director of Research at the college's recently established Center for Corporate Governance. Before going to Delaware, Stu was a Senior Research Fellow with the TIAA-CREF Institute in New York City, where he conducted research on corporate governance issues and worked closely with the staff of TIAA-CREF's Corporate Governance Assessment Program, providing input on policy developments and analysis of corporate governance issues. Prior to joining TIAA-CREF, Stu was Associate Chief Economist at the SEC.

WILLIAM KINNEY holds the Charles & Elizabeth Prothro Regents Chair in Business at the University of Texas at Austin. Bill has done considerable research in the areas of auditing standards, auditor independence, and the use of accounting in decision-making, with particular focus on issues of the economics of auditing and internal control. He has also consulted extensively on accounting issues with Big Five auditors, the American Institute of Certified Public Accountants, and the government.

CHARLES NIEMEIER is Chief Accountant for the enforcement division of the U.S. Securities and Exchange Commission in Washington, D.C. But I should also tell you that Charlie has just been appointed to the new Public Company Accounting Oversight Board that was mandated by the recently passed Sarbanes-Oxley Act. *[Ed. Note: On January 8, 2003, Niemeier was named acting chairman of the new board.]* That board, which will operate under the auspices of and report to the SEC, has been given the job of steering the course for reform of the accounting industry and also aspects of corporate governance. Charlie holds a law degree from Georgetown, but before earning his JD he did his undergraduate work in accounting here at Baylor.

WILLIAM POLLARD was, until a few months ago, Chairman of the Board of The ServiceMaster Company, a Chicago-based provider of residential and commercial services with $3.6 billion in revenues and over 70,000 employees. After a distinguished career as a corporate lawyer, Bill joined the company in 1977 and later served not once but twice as its CEO—first from 1983 through 1993 and then again from October 1999 through February 2001. Under Bill's leadership, ServiceMaster was recognized by *Fortune* magazine as the #1 service company among the *Fortune* 500 and was included in *Fortune*'s list of most admired companies. During Bill's tenure, the company also achieved market leadership in each of its business units and provided an average compounded annual total return for its shareholders of 20%. Bill continues to serve the company as Chairman of the Board's Executive Committee. In addition to his corporate accomplishments, he is also the author of a bestselling business book called *The Soul of the Firm*.

BENNETT STEWART is Senior Managing Partner of Stern Stewart & Co., the company that is best known for refining and popularizing a measure of corporate performance called EVA. I should warn you that Bennett is carrying around with him a copy of what he calls his "radical manifesto," which aims at nothing less than a complete overhaul of Generally Accepted Accounting Principles—and I'm sure we'll hear more about this soon.

Now that I've introduced the panelists, I'm going to turn the floor over to my colleague John Martin.

Does Financial Reporting Matter?

JOHN MARTIN: Thanks, Bill. Our plan is to have a conversation for the next hour or so about the current state of financial reporting: Is it in need of reform and, if so, how can that be done? There will be no formal presentations. Instead I'm going to start by posing a question or two for our panelists, and we'll see where that takes us. I think you're in for a very interesting afternoon.

If you've been reading the paper or watching television at all, you're aware that this topic is receiving a good deal of attention. According to the popular media, our reporting system is at the center of a serious crisis in corporate governance. Of course, this is not the first financial crisis we've ever had. As Keynes put it over 50 years ago, "The amount of time between crises is the time it takes us to forget the last one." But even if the term "crisis" seems a bit overused, there is no denying that the investment community is now scrutinizing corporate financial statements with an intensity that seems unprecedented. People everywhere seem to be asking the question: Can we believe the numbers that are being reported to us in financial statements? And what are the numbers really telling us?

But before we try to answer those questions, we have to start with an even more basic question: Does financial reporting really matter and, if so, why? As Bill Thomas told you, I'm a professor of finance, and in our finance courses we teach our students a theory that is known as "efficient markets." According to this theory, all relevant information about a company's current earnings prospects should be reflected in its current stock price. Now, to the extent that this theory is an accurate description of the world, a company's financial state-

ments should not provide all that much new information. Accounting earnings, after all, are for the most part a backward-looking measure of performance; and because of all the non-cash charges and the mixing of stocks and flows that Bennett Stewart likes to complain about, reported earnings often do a poor job of reflecting what investors are supposed to care about—a company's ability to generate cash flow on a recurring or sustainable basis. For this reason, our theory suggests that the most sophisticated investors in our capital markets, the "lead steers" who are supposed to set prices at the margin, rely on more forward-looking indicators of corporate performance.

But the events of the past two years have caused many of us to question these assumptions—in particular, the market's ability to see through accounting earnings to underlying and sustainable cash flow. In a number of high-profile cases like Enron and WorldCom, the market seemed to be completely fooled by the accounting numbers. And even if these cases turn out to be aberrations, and investors in general can be counted on to penetrate accounting fictions, it's also clear that reported financial statements now serve many other uses in our economic system than helping investors value securities. The business press, following the practice of most sell-side analysts, dutifully reports the latest EPS figures as the most relevant gauge of corporate performance. And, perhaps not surprisingly, many companies tend to evaluate their own performance and to compensate their top executives according to these measures—something we continue to warn our students against in the classroom.

So, my message here is this: Whether we like it or not, financial reporting seems to have become a key element

in the overall process of U.S. corporate governance. It is an important part of the process by which management communicates with all its key stakeholders, including of course its shareholders. If the quality of those communications becomes suspect and investors feel they can no longer trust the numbers, then the general level of confidence falls and the value of all companies tends to drop. And that creates a problem for everyone in this room. Although many of you are too young to even think about your retirement programs, at some point the issues we're wrestling with today are going to affect your life. I've started referring to my 401(k) as my "201(k)." But if we are successful in addressing this and some of the associated governance problems, it may become a 401(k) again. I certainly hope so.

And it's not just the shareholders of public companies who have an interest in restoring the confidence of the investment community. Thanks in significant part to the plunge in the stock market, budget surpluses at all levels of government have turned into large deficits. And to the extent that the lower stock prices can themselves *cause* lower corporate growth by making outside capital more expensive, a crisis of confidence can end up hurting all corporate stakeholders—not just the IRS, but suppliers and employees and the local communities that benefit from corporate employment and activities. So it seems to me that we all have a common interest in ensuring the integrity of financial reporting.

Let me begin the discussion, then, by asking about the magnitude or scope of the problem that we face today. Our newspapers, as I mentioned earlier, are saying that we've got a serious problem of public confidence. President Bush, on the other hand, has tended to downplay the

IN A NUMBER OF HIGH-PROFILE CASES LIKE ENRON AND WORLDCOM, THE MARKET SEEMED TO BE COMPLETELY FOOLED BY THE ACCOUNTING NUMBERS. AND EVEN IF THESE CASES TURN OUT TO BE ABERRATIONS, AND INVESTORS IN GENERAL CAN BE COUNTED ON TO PENETRATE ACCOUNTING fictions, it's also clear that reported financial statements now serve many other uses in our economic system than helping investors value securities. For example, many companies evaluate their own performance and compensate their top executives according to these accounting measures—something we continue to warn our students against in the classroom.

—JOHN MARTIN

problem, stating in a nationally televised speech back in July that the problem is the result of "a few bad apples." But is our current corporate governance problem more serious than that? Does it run deeper than just a few companies that have pushed the edge of the envelope?

And I'm going to ask Bill Pollard to start us off. As a former lawyer and then as the Chairman and CEO of a large public corporation, Bill is probably in the best position of any of us here to see the nature of the crisis we face today. He is one of those exceptional corporate leaders whose companies have not only performed well for shareholders, but have appeared year after year on *Fortune*'s most admired list. Bill, what do you think about the current problem with financial reporting? Are we facing a crisis of confidence—and, if so, what will it take to pull us through?

Crisis in Corporate Governance?

WILLIAM POLLARD: Thanks, John, for the kind words. As you say, this is clearly not the first time we've seen evidence of greed at work in the marketplace, nor is it the first time we've seen a general lack of confidence from the investment community. A number of people have described the recent scandals as comparable to those that gave rise to the Depression-era legislation, including the Securities Acts of 1933 and 1934 that created our present-day SEC. And there was clearly a crisis of confidence at that time.

Today's situation is somewhat different, though there are some common elements. There is clearly a popular perception today that the leadership of corporate America can no longer be trusted. And it's not hard to see why. As *The Financial Times* reported recently, the CEOs of the 25 largest companies that went bankrupt in the last 18 months sold over $3.3 billion of stock in the year or so leading up to their bankruptcy filings. And the continuing media focus on such examples has clearly cast a pall over all of corporate America.

But, when evaluating these statistics, it's important to keep in mind that there are well over 10,000 publicly traded companies in this country—and I continue to believe that these 25 CEOs represent only a very small segment of corporate America. They are the exception rather the rule. But the exception is significant and has created very real problems for the rest of us. And I don't want to minimize the importance of the lack of confidence that has resulted from the actions of a fairly small number of people.

The actions of these people have exposed and caused us to pay more attention to weaknesses in our overall reporting and governance system. And we are now in the midst of a process of correcting those weaknesses. I think the recent steps taken by our President and the Congress have been on the whole very positive. For example, there are aspects of board independence addressed in the recent Sarbanes-Oxley Act, such as the strengthening of the board's role in hiring and firing outside experts, that should prove quite valuable. But, at the same time, I don't believe legislation can dictate integrity. Legislation cannot replace the effectiveness of a board composed of honest, ethical people who are involved with and understand the business. If you don't have people on the governing body with these traits, they can be "independent" by any legal definition you choose but they will not be good directors.

Besides focusing on board independence, we're also now working through a process that I hope will end up strengthening our financial reporting. But this is a major challenge.

THE NEED FOR A BETTER DEFINITION OF EARNINGS HAS A LOT TO DO WITH OUR CURRENT CORPORATE GOVERNANCE PROBLEMS, AND WE ARE NOW IN THE PROCESS OF DEVELOPING NEW GROUND RULES FOR HOW WE MEASURE AND REPORT EARNINGS. THERE IS GREAT UNCERTAINTY today about the usefulness of reported earnings—about what those numbers really mean in the process of establishing the market value of a company. And my feeling is that, until we get agreement on and understanding of some of the changes in the accounting ground rules that will support a closer link of reported earnings to corporate value, the market is going to continue to distrust reported EPS.

—BILL POLLARD

We are in the process of developing new ground rules for how we measure and report earnings. Market valuations of companies are typically expressed in terms of price/earnings ratios, or P/E multiples. But there is great uncertainty today about the usefulness of reported earnings—about what those numbers really mean in the process of establishing the market value of a company. And my feeling is that, until we get agreement on and understanding of some of the changes in the accounting ground rules that will support a closer link of reported earnings to corporate value, the market is going to continue to distrust reported EPS. So, again, the need for a better definition of earnings has a lot to do with our current corporate governance problems, and I hope we make some progress toward this result very soon.

BENNETT STEWART: I agree completely with Bill's statement that our accounting system is a major source of uncertainty and confusion—and it is true, as Bill Thomas said earlier, that I'm carrying around a paper that proposes a complete rethinking of GAAP accounting. But before we get into these accounting issues, I want to point to another factor that may have played

an even larger role in our current so-called "governance crisis."

I think that the fundamental reason we are all talking about corporate governance today is that our stock market turned out to be grossly overvalued. But I hasten to add that it's only with the benefit of hindsight that we can now say that the market was wrong. For a time, our economy was running an experiment called the New Economy. Advocates of the New Economy proposed that, thanks to the Internet and advances in telecommunications technologies, companies like Amazon and eBay were carving out very profitable niches. But it now seems clear—though it was far from clear at the time—that we were wrong. We now know that the technologies that looked so promising are going to take time to implement, and that many of the Old Economy companies are more likely to capitalize on those values than the startup dot-coms.

And while I agree with Bill Pollard that accounting may have played some role in this overvaluation, to blame our current problems on accounting is akin to blaming the thermometer for the cold weather. The current economic and investment climate in the U.S.—which is certainly no worse than what people are experiencing

abroad—is first and foremost the result of some very real changes in our economy, particularly a pronounced change in demand and massive overinvestment in our telecom and high-tech sectors. Now, it's true that inflated stock prices played some role in this overinvestment, and that the fraudulent behavior of some corporate executives contributed to those inflated prices. But my feeling is that the sins of a handful of executives are now being used as a pretext to justify excessive re-regulation of our markets. And though I share Bill's skepticism about accounting earnings, my biggest concern is that the net effect of all the new regulations will be less competitive U.S. financial markets and a less productive economy.

THOMAS: Charlie, as a representative of the SEC, what's your take on this?

CHARLES NIEMEIER: Contrary to the popular belief that Enron and WorldCom are anomalies, we at the SEC have found that the number of financial reporting failures—that is, cases where earnings had to be restated—has increased in every year from the mid-'90s on. But more significant than the increase in the number of these failures is the jump in the size of the companies involved. So, our greatest fear—the failure of the

SARBANES-OXLEY TOOK A MAJOR STEP FORWARD FOR THE ACCOUNTING PROFESSION BY ESTABLISHING THE NEW PUBLIC COMPANY ACCOUNTING OVERSIGHT BOARD. THIS BOARD REPRESENTS THE FIRST TIME THAT THE ACCOUNTING PROFESSION HAS BEEN REGULATED. THERE is now a crisis of confidence in our financial reporting system, and the audit opinion is the basis on which that system is founded. Now, part of this crisis may well be more perception than reality. But because of the role that investor confidence plays in our financial markets, perception is an important element of the reality. The goal of this new accounting board is to restore investor confidence in corporate audit committees and in accounting results generally.

—Charles Niemeier

largest companies in our system—has in fact materialized, and almost completely without warning.

We like to make our case with a corny little story. If you take a frog and put it in boiling water, it will jump out. But if you take that same frog and put it in cool water and slowly heat it to a boil, it will cook to death. That is the way financial fraud works in financial markets, and that's what has happened in our system. Somewhere along the way we stopped looking at the largest companies, and those companies didn't believe they would ever get caught. Investors never thought the companies would resort to improper accounting, and their auditors never thought that anyone would look over their shoulders. But improper accounting has happened, it now appears to have the makings of a trend, and it's not something that we can ignore.

STEWART: My problem with your story, Charlie, is that Cisco and Nortel and Lucent all experienced multibillion dollar declines in value without the kind of financial fraud that appears to have taken place in these other instances.

NIEMEIER: Bennett, while I'm not at liberty to comment on ongoing SEC investigations, some of the cases you just mentioned may not end up sup-

porting your argument. I certainly agree that fraud is not a complete explanation for our current problems. And I also agree with Bill Pollard's suggestion that most companies try to do a good job in reporting their financial results. But let's face it: it takes the failure of only a few companies—especially if they're very large and well known—to create a crisis in confidence. We want our least sophisticated and most vulnerable investors to feel confident that their life savings are protected. But we have now reached the point where many of these investors feel they just can't trust stock prices because they're not sure whether companies are telling the truth.

THOMAS: Bob Alspaugh, from your vantage point as CEO of KPMG International, do you think that we are now facing a crisis in financial reporting?

ROBERT ALSPAUGH: I'm not very comfortable applying the word "crisis" in this case. We have just lived through a period that looks a lot like a stock market bubble. And although we can debate whether the prices reached levels that were completely irrational, what is clear is that when the bubble burst, a lot of people lost a lot of money. A lot of 401(k)s, as John said, became 201(k)s. And it's

also true, of course, that some corporate executives cashed out their holdings near the top while issuing financial reports—in some cases in compliance with GAAP, in other cases not—that misrepresented the true condition of their companies. But based on my 33 years of experience with KPMG, I feel pretty confident in saying that these people represent a tiny fraction of the population—less than 1%, if I had to give you a number.

Now, I do agree with Charlie that when some of the companies under the radar screen are large, heavily followed ones—the kinds of companies that are watched by millions of investors as market bellwethers—it does raise a genuine concern. But, in reflecting on what went wrong here, I keep coming back to my belief that 99% of the people know what's right and are trying to do what's right in their disclosures and in the way they record transactions. And, as I said earlier, there is also a very, very small percentage of people who will always do the wrong thing given sufficient temptation and the opportunity. Given Charlie's policing role, he clearly sees more of these types than others of us at this table do.

Now, to me, the real question we should be asking ourselves is this:

IN THIS COUNTRY, WE HAVE RULES FOR USING ACCOUNTING METHODS THAT RUN TO HUNDREDS OF PAGES. I WILL TELL YOU FRANKLY THAT OUR KIND OF RULES-BASED SYSTEM CREATES WHAT I CALL *SUBOPTIMAL* ACCOUNTING. AND I BELIEVE THAT WE IN THE U.S. SHOULD FIND SOME common ground with our brethren in other parts of the world who look at these accounting issues on a principles basis. We should ask ourselves, "What is the right answer? What would a reasonable and prudent person in the same or similar circumstances think the answer should be?" Efforts are underway to harmonize U.S. and international accounting standards, but much more needs to be done to promote these changes.

—ROBERT ALSPAUGH

What should we do about that very small percentage of companies that look at opportunities to mislead investors and say, "What's the risk-reward ratio? Will I get caught for doing something that I perhaps shouldn't do?" And I think that's the question that's on the table now. What's the role of the accounting firms, the regulators, the analysts, the investment bankers, and the lawyers in deterring that 1% of our companies from crossing over the line?

But, again, I don't think we're really experiencing a crisis of confidence. Instead, we're attempting to apply some fixes—important fixes, to be sure—to what has otherwise proved to be a very productive financial and economic system. Americans are pretty resilient, and what I hear people in the investment community saying is something like this: "We think we understand what's happened here. Part of it resulted from an inflated market. But there are also flaws in our reporting and governance system, and some reform is necessary. We'll take steps to improve those things that clearly need improving, and our economy will bring back most of the good things we've had in the past."

MARTIN: Let me turn to my colleague Stuart Gillan. Stu, based on your re-

search and recent experience with TIAA-CREF, what do you think about the nature and scope of the current governance problem? Are we in the midst of a crisis?

STUART GILLAN: I agree that we are focusing on the tail end of the distribution, on a small number of very large firms that have attracted a huge amount of attention. And while I continue to believe that the U.S. corporate governance system is by far the strongest in the world, I also think that these few cases have revealed some significant flaws in our system. The real issue here, it seems to me, is that despite all the different checks and balances that were in place—the external auditors, the internal compliance systems, the Wall Street analysts, the regulators—the entire system seems to have failed in this handful of cases. And I think that should give us all pause. The issue is not only how we catch those folks at the extreme end of the distribution, but what mechanisms need to change.

Ever since Berle and Means published their famous book in the early 1930s, business and finance scholars have pointed to the separation of ownership from control, and proposed ways of reducing the conflict between managers and shareholders.

And, as recent events have shown, that conflict is still very much with us. In some ways the accounting issues are symptoms of a bigger governance problem, and it strikes me that the role of the board of directors is critical here. The board has the power and the duty to hire, fire, and compensate managers. From this perspective, the board must set the right "culture" or "tone at the top" by hiring the right managers and then holding them accountable for their actions. But to do so the board must be active, informed, and capable of asking the management team probing questions.

Nowhere has this been more true than in the case of Enron. The evidence suggests that Enron's board and audit committee were aware of numerous red flags, including concerns about Enron's accounting policies; yet they approved the adoption of the firm's financials year after year. But an accounting system that drives a wedge between economic reality and what we see in financial statements does not help matters, as Bill Pollard has already suggested. Too much accounting flexibility may have aided some managers in taking the first steps on the slippery slope to financial fraud.

Changes in Accounting

THOMAS: Let's take a closer look at this issue of accounting. Bob, given the breakup of Arthur Andersen, are you and your competitors approaching audits differently? What, if anything, has changed in the public accounting profession as a result of Andersen's fate?

ALSPAUGH: I can only tell you about KPMG's experience, but I suspect that what I'm going to say is true of all the big public accounting firms. What we're all facing today is reputational risk. We all need to make sure that we understand who it is we're doing business with. A critical part of that process is just a matter of having sound intuition and exercising good judgment about the character of our clients. Another part of the process has to do with strengthening the auditing procedures themselves; as just one example, we're now considering incorporating a more forensic piece into what we already do. And a third important element in managing reputational risk is ensuring that we have the right system of checks and balances within our own firm. Have we effectively separated the function of risk assessment of our clients from the revenue-producing side of the

business? You've got the partners out there in the field doing the audit engagements. How do you make sure that there is sufficient oversight of those partners within the organization?

At KPMG, we have always separated those two functions. But we've recently taken the additional step of having our risk assessment people report directly to the relevant CEO. For example, the people who evaluate and monitor the risks of our global clients report to me; and the people who assess the risks of our domestic U.S. clients report to our Vice Chair of Risk and Regulatory Matters—a position that reports directly to the Chairman and sits on our U.S. Management Committee.

POLLARD: As the former CEO of a public company and a board member of three public companies, I have already seen some significant changes in auditing procedures. One thing I've seen very clearly in the past year is that the partners assigned to our account do not have the discretion they once had. The power to sign off on major decisions about accounting treatment has been transferred to more technical people who are sitting at world headquarters, or at any rate are somewhere removed from the client. But while tightening up the auditor's

internal controls, this separation of functions has created problems of communication. It has made the task of gaining clarification on the application of accounting rules very clumsy, especially in the case of quarter-by-quarter reviews.

WILLIAM KINNEY: I think we will end up viewing that clumsiness as one of the costs of making what is otherwise a very beneficial change. It was the failure to separate these two functions—risk assessment and revenue production—that brought down Arthur Andersen. And I agree with Bob that auditing firms should be transferring more of their decisions on accounting policy back to the executive offices—to partners who spend their entire workday thinking about accounting principles. These partners by definition have less involvement with the client company than does the engagement partner, and to me that's the essence of independence—someone who has expertise and who is looking out for the firm's reputation and the audit firm's reputation overall, but who has no direct relationship with or dependence on a particular firm as a client. To protect investors, it's this separation of expertise and interests that our accounting firms really need to ensure.

—BILL KINNEY

Now, Bill, you said that you find this whole process cumbersome and slow, especially for quarterly reviews. Does that mean you think we're going down the wrong path, or do you think this is a one-time continuity problem that will eventually sort itself out?

POLLARD: I'm not sure whether it's the right way or the wrong way to do it. All I can tell you is that the people in the back room, the technical people who think all day about the technical rules, do not necessarily understand how a business runs or operates. And this can create real problems in communication, both internally and in reporting to investors. I have already run into situations where, by adhering to the literal interpretation of the rule, we have been forced to report accounting results that just don't follow the business. I remember one case where I said to the auditor, "If we follow this rule as you suggest, doesn't this mean that even if the business starts going south we will still show higher profits for at least three years?" And his answer was "Yes, but that's what the rule says." Now, to me there's something very wrong with that result.

KINNEY: So, it sounds like the problem here is the auditor's need to adhere to a "bright line" standard, which is unfortunately limiting the engagement partner's ability to use his or her judgment about what is really going on in the business. But I think that's a somewhat different issue, though it's one that we certainly have to resolve.

POLLARD: All I can say is that this use of technical people to make all the accounting decisions is a work-in-progress. It is not working smoothly yet, but that may come with time.

The Case for Accounting Reform

STEWART: Bill, in your opening comments, you mentioned the need for a better definition of earnings. But I think there is a more fundamental question here: namely, what is it that accounting earnings are supposed to measure? What we've ended up with is a Pachinko game of rules that have been formed through the tugs and pulls of various factions, and so what drops out at the bottom has very little meaning as a measure of corporate performance. And because accounting has little economic relevance, it has also lost much of its moral authority.

Some executives—the fewer than 1% that Bob Alspaugh was telling us about—have clearly chosen to inflate their companies' profits by ignoring the letter as well as the spirit of GAAP. But, in a great many other cases, otherwise decent and respectable corporate leaders have responded to the arbitrary nature of GAAP—to its failure to reflect economic value—by using the flexibility built into GAAP to put the best possible face on their performance. My sense is that if accounting were reformed in such a way that reported earnings were closer to an economist's definition of profit, this would provide an ethical guidepost that could have two beneficial effects. First, it would help restore investors' faith in financial statements. But perhaps even more important, it would give corporate managers the sense that reported earnings actually reflect their contribution to value. And this would in turn increase the probability that most managers would use their financial statements not to mislead the market, but rather as a valuable opportunity to communicate relevant, forward-looking information to the investment community.

To illustrate what's wrong with GAAP accounting, let me offer you a simple example. Here we are at Baylor University, which has a very fine MBA program. Now, if you take a class in the corporate finance department, you

IN A GREAT MANY CASES, OTHERWISE DECENT AND RESPECTED CORPORATE LEADERS HAVE RESPONDED TO THE ARBITRARY NATURE OF GAAP—TO ITS FAILURE TO REFLECT ECONOMIC VALUE—BY USING THE FLEXIBILITY BUILT INTO GAAP TO PUT THE BEST POSSIBLE FACE ON THEIR performance. If accounting were reformed so that reported earnings were closer to an economist's definition of profit, this could have two beneficial effects. It would help restore investors' faith in financial statements. And perhaps even more important, by giving corporate managers the sense that reported earnings actually reflect their contribution to value, it would increase the probability that most managers would use their financial statements not to mislead the market, but rather as a valuable opportunity to communicate relevant, forward-looking information to the investment community.

—BENNETT STEWART

will learn how to make decisions that maximize the value of the company. You will be introduced to a principle called "the net present value rule," which says that you should invest capital in all projects that will produce a cash flow rate of return in excess of the cost of capital.

But when you take the accounting courses, you will be taught something very different. You will discover that the way companies are required to measure earnings can be completely unrelated to the way companies make decisions aimed at maximizing shareholder value. For example, although companies are permitted to capitalize and then amortize investments in plant and equipment, they must immediately expense almost all outlays for research and development, advertising and promotion, and other investments with a longer-term payoff. Many companies also use LIFO inventory costing, report deferred taxes they never expect to pay, and take depreciation charges that are far higher than the annual expected cost of replacing assets—all of which, in the name of accounting conservatism, cause financial statements to understate companies' economic profit. At the same time, the requirement that interest on debt be expensed while the cost of

equity capital (and stock options) is effectively assumed to be zero has the effect of mixing operating and financing decisions; it involves a flagrant contradiction of the basic capital budgeting principle that corporate investment decisions should not be affected by how the investment is financed.

Faced with these conflicts between finance and accounting, senior executives are forced to live uncomfortably in two worlds. They might use value-based management techniques for *internal* purposes, such as making strategic investments, measuring divisional results, and establishing bonuses for their people. But at the same time, they are forced to use GAAP accounting to meet the demands of external financial reporting. With the principles of value-based management often running counter to GAAP, many corporate leaders have chosen to report their results using alternative measures like EBITDA or "operating" earnings or economic profit. I view this migration to "black market metrics" as a kind of managerial protest against GAAP earnings. And as I said earlier, this managerial vote of no confidence has caused accounting to lose much of its moral authority.

So, the failure of accounting to count what counts and provide a

meaningful measure of value is a central issue in our current corporate governance debate. Given their feeling that accounting numbers are meaningless, many business leaders appear to have ended up with the view that the main aim of corporate accounting is to prettify the reports to meet the quarterly earnings expectations of Wall Street. (At the same time, a handful of companies like Gillette and Coca-Cola have even declared their intent to stop making earnings forecasts altogether.) And until our accounting authorities develop rules that will do a better job of measuring economic profit, I fear that manipulation of accounting rules will be a recurring problem for our economy.

THOMAS: But, Bennett, once you start giving companies more discretion in capitalizing R&D and other expenditures, don't you open the door to even more litigation? We all know that the U.S. is the most litigious society on earth. And it would seem to me that, as you add more and more subjectivity to the process, we're going to have even more lawsuits—and I think most of us would agree that our public accounting firms are already swamped with frivolous suits.

STEWART: That's a possible outcome, of course. But part of my proposal is

ONCE YOU START GIVING COMPANIES MORE DISCRETION IN CAPITALIZING R&D AND OTHER EXPENDITURES, DON'T YOU OPEN THE DOOR TO EVEN MORE LITIGATION? WE ALL KNOW THAT THE U.S. IS THE MOST LITIGIOUS SOCIETY ON EARTH. AND IT WOULD SEEM TO ME THAT, AS YOU add more and more subjectivity to the process, we're going to have even more lawsuits—and I think most of us would agree that our public accounting firms are already swamped with frivolous suits.

—BILL THOMAS

to fundamentally change the accountants' mission and, in so doing, to narrow the scope of their liability. Accountants should not be held liable, as they effectively are today, for measuring the value of the assets that appear on corporate balance sheets. Their sole mission should be to measure and report economic profit. As I wrote in my "manifesto," the only real asset a company has is its ability to generate profit. The balance sheet is always and everywhere a record of liabilities; it simply represents the monies invested that give rise to an expectation of a return by investors, otherwise known as the cost of capital. The balance sheet is a record only of what companies have spent, not what they expect to get out of the business. And until we recognize this reality, and narrow the accountants' scope accordingly, the accountants will continue to be sued for things they should not be sued for, and they will always adopt an excessively conservative perspective when measuring earnings. And this in turn will continue to make managers distrust those earnings and look for ways around them. That's basically at the root of our problem with financial reporting.

ALSPAUGH: I agree with much of Bennett's argument. And in fact it

really raises the whole question of the rules-based accounting model that is used in this country, as contrasted with the principles-based model used in Europe and Japan. In this country, as you all know, we have rules for using accounting methods that run to hundreds of pages. And so when your client asks you the question, "How do you account for something?," you end up saying, "Well, let me go to the cookbook and show you."

I will tell you frankly—and we've been saying this for some time—that our kind of rules-based system creates what I call *suboptimal* accounting. And I believe that we in the U.S. should find some common ground with our brethren in other parts of the world who look at these accounting issues on a principles basis and collectively ask ourselves, "What is the right answer? What would a reasonable and prudent person in the same or similar circumstances think the answer should be?" Efforts are underway to harmonize U.S. and international accounting standards, but much more needs to be done to promote these changes.

There is one very good explanation for the system that we have developed. As Bill Thomas commented earlier, one thing we worry a lot about

in our profession is lawsuits. And when you have specific rules, it's much easier to defend yourself in a litigious society by saying, "Look, we did what this rulebook said." In environments like Japan and Europe, which are not nearly as litigious, you can make your decisions on the basis of principles with much less fear of being second-guessed by plaintiff lawyers.

More on Accounting

POLLARD: I'd like to come back to Bennett's comments. In my judgment, there's real merit in what he said about the problems with GAAP accounting. ServiceMaster uses the concept of economic value added, or EVA, to guide our investment and operating decisions, to evaluate our own performance, and to some extent as a basis for rewarding our operating managers. And I'm on the board of another company, Herman Miller, that uses EVA very effectively. When the managements of these companies present their annual operational reviews to their boards, they often start out by saying, "Here are our accounting results. This is what we reported to the public." But then they go on to say, "Now, here are the economic value added figures; these numbers show how much value we added to the enterprise during the past year."

So, what management in effect is telling the board is that accounting is not economic reality. And so, Bennett, though I have clearly not thought as long and hard about these issues as you have, it has become very apparent to me that GAAP accounting often fails to provide a useful guide to managerial decision-making.

Take the issue of accounting for goodwill. In running a service company that has grown in large part through acquisitions, I have been frustrated for years by the fact that we have had to write off the goodwill from these transactions. Goodwill is essentially the difference between the book value of the assets and the price we paid for them. And because we paid those prices with the expectation of earning an adequate return on investment, it makes no sense at all to include an arbitrary non-cash charge like goodwill in our measure of earnings. Under the EVA system, we add back the annual amortization of goodwill to get a measure of economic profit. Now, I realize that recent changes in the accounting rules have somewhat resolved this issue—all acquisitions are now treated on a purchase accounting basis and amortization of goodwill is no longer required. But this change was a long time in coming, and we continue to have other problems with GAAP.

The assets in our company walk out the door every day—and the same is true of IT companies. While some changes have been made, GAAP has a long way to go to reflect this reality. And, as Bennett just suggested, the only place we can really account for the value of intangible assets is on the income statement. Maybe it's just the complexity of business and how fast things are changing, but I feel strongly that the accounting profession should be devoting much more thought and effort to making financial reporting of transactions consistent with economic value and with how a business operates and creates value.

STEWART: Let me point to another example. Right now, pension fund accounting permits companies to take any surplus of the value of pension fund assets over the pension liability, and essentially smooth that over 15 years and bring it into earnings. You can also change the rate of return you expect to earn on your pension fund assets and, by increasing that return, report lower pension costs. In fact, many companies over the past four or five years have actually been reporting pension *income*.

And as I argue in my paper, pension fund accounting has seduced many executives into investing much of their pension assets in the equity markets, in large part because the accounting smoothes out the risks and permits them to manage earnings. General Motors, for example, has followed this strategy. And thanks to swings in the stock market, their pension fund has swung from a big surplus to a big deficit. The net result is that most of GM's net discretionary cash flow for the next ten years will be used to shore up its pension fund.

So I think that the GAAP rules themselves are so far removed from reality that they have become a major part of the problem. And one of the main reasons GAAP is so flawed, as Bill Thomas said, is that the tort lawyers won't let accountants do things that make sense. So, ultimately, of course, any effort to improve our public accounting system will have to be accompanied by major tort reform. As Shakespeare put it, we will have to "kill all the lawyers."

NIEMEIER: Bennett, you've got a lawyer sitting right next to you...But I agree that there are some problems with our current accounting model that need to be addressed. To go back to my earlier point, though, the real origin of the fall of WorldCom and Enron was not problems with GAAP. There were some far more basic problems of personal integrity at work in both of these cases. The solution comes down to observing a pretty simple rule: Don't lie to your investors about how you're doing. When you know you're not doing well, you need to say that. The issue is not that complicated.

POLLARD: Charlie, I agree with you. But I also think that investors will try to protect themselves against such behavior by placing greater emphasis on cash flow instead of earnings. The cash that is coming in the front door and going out the back door is real and easy to verify. It's reporting a fact, not a judgment. Now, it's also true that there are all kinds of reasons why the amount of cash coming in or going out in a particular reporting period may not be representative of a company's earnings power. But if anybody had really focused on the cash flow of companies like Enron and WorldCom, I think they would have discovered the problem much sooner.

Toward a Solution

MARTIN: Okay, let's take stock for a moment. I've heard basically three main responses to my question about the causes of our current reporting and corporate governance problems. One is that the so-called New Economy didn't work out as well as we thought it would, and we now are in the midst of an economic downturn resulting from what was in some sense a failed business model. A second issue is that accounting rules are in need of a major fix because they give executives incentives to smooth and inflate earnings in ways that don't make economic or business sense. And the third major point is that a certain number of CEOs have turned out to be fundamentally dishonest people—they committed fraud.

Charlie, where do you see us going from here? What are the main things that need fixing from the SEC's vantage point?

NIEMEIER: I believe that we've already taken the most important step to restoring confidence by admitting that we have a problem. A year ago, when I went out to visit people and talk about potential problems, I would generally get blank stares, as if to say, "What are you talking about? We don't have a problem with our system."

Today we don't talk about whether or not there's a problem. We talk about what we are going to do about it. And the problem here is not just accounting. Yes, there are problems with accounting and problems with lawyers; but there are also problems with corporate boards and managers, with the investment bankers who work for them, and with the securities analysts who are supposed to be looking out for the investment community.

If I had to choose a single "fix," it would be to instill in people a stronger morality, a greater sense of fairness and ethics. But, at the same time, I recognize that we'll always need a well-crafted set of laws, together with vigorous enforcement of those laws, as a deterrent to fraud. Basically what we are asking our companies to do is to provide better disclosure—to report their results fairly, to tell their investors, using words as well as numbers, what happened in a way that can be easily understood. Years ago I remember being taught in my finance class that the market imposes a discount for uncertainty. And for that reason alone, it seems to me that it is in a company's own economic interest to increase the quality if not the quantity of its disclosure, and to promote more of a dialogue with investors.

STEWART: Charlie, I agree completely with your point about the value of better disclosure. But to simply exhort people to do the right thing sounds like utopianism. James Madison said that if men were angels, no government would be necessary. But men, as I think we all agree, are not angels—and the jury is still out on women. It seems to me that there are only three main ways to really influence behavior. One is by exhortation or inspiration. Two is by regulation and other forms of coercion. Number three is through institutions and incentives. Unfortunately, we cannot rely just on inspiration and exhortation. We have to rely on laws and regulation, as you suggest. And in order to keep regulations and their enforcement from becoming too burdensome, we have to design our institutions and incentives to encourage the kind of behavior that we want. My basic point here is that present-day GAAP accounting does not encourage the kind of value-maximizing behavior that we expect from our corporate leaders.

NIEMEIER: One step I would like to see is to break the chain that now forces corporate leaders to meet the quarter-by-quarter expectations of sell-side analysts—and to report good news *all* the time. That pressure often gets transmitted to auditors, who may be asked to come up with "creative" accounting solutions to help management meet the analysts' expectations. These pressures were clearly at work in cases like Enron and WorldCom, and I feel pretty certain they are creating problems in lots of other companies, in some cases pushing managements to make unwise business decisions to pump up EPS.

STEWART: I agree. But the big challenge here will be persuading corporate managements to ignore GAAP when it tells them to do something foolish to boost reported earnings

that will end up reducing value. As long as they continue to hear sell-side analysts clamoring for ever more earnings, and as long as our financial media continue to take reported earnings at pretty much face value—unless, of course, there is evidence of fraud—then U.S. managers will be slow to follow Gillette's and Coca-Cola's example and will remain slaves to GAAP.

GILLAN: This is where the role of the board is critical. The board should hold management's feet to the fire and maintain a focus on long-term shareholder value—not quarterly earnings targets. But at the same time, the board must give management the leeway to say no to Wall Street.

The Challenge of Complexity

THOMAS: Bill Pollard mentioned the increased complexity of the business environment as a possible contributor to our current governance problems. In the case of Enron, to cite just one example, the complexities of the derivatives and their use in managing earnings were well beyond the comprehension of people without considerable quantitative training and skills. What does that tell us about how we need to respond? Integrity alone may not be enough. We may have to surround ourselves with people capable of detecting the schemes that are being perpetrated. Given this problem, how should educators like us be preparing our students to operate as auditors in the future?

ALSPAUGH: In the public accounting profession, the first principle is to make sure you have the right kind of people serving an account. They must have industry expertise and specialized knowledge of the kinds of transactions that go on in that industry. To put the case as simply as possible, it's not effective to have an oil and gas expert audit a bank. And to audit a company like Enron, you would have to have people who understand derivatives and structured finance deals in the context of energy-related transactions. So, having the necessary training and expertise for a given assignment is clearly an essential part of dealing with a very complex world.

The same is true of the people who serve on the audit committees of corporate boards. Do they have the financial expertise and relevant industry knowledge to ask probing questions and carry on an intelligent dialogue with the auditors?

KINNEY: The question about education is a difficult one—and you're right to identify complexity as a big part of our problem. First of all, there are not many accounting professors who know enough about derivatives—and the problem is compounded by the fact that available derivatives are changing all the time. Yet the auditor is required to audit these derivatives with some fairly difficult-to-apply disclosure criteria.

But that's just one part of the new educational requirements for being an auditor. Another part has to do with complaints about public accountants not knowing enough about detecting fraud. Some people think that accounting classes like those at Baylor should teach future accountants how to catch employees stealing nickels and dimes from the company. But this is nonsense, in my view. Detection of minor misappropriation fraud can't be done economically by the independent auditor. That's got be the job of the internal auditor and the internal controls that the company has in place to protect itself.

The new Sarbanes-Oxley Act has a requirement that the auditing firm pass judgment on the company's internal controls, which I think is a potentially wonderful idea. Under the new provision, the company's management must state whether or not

they think they have a "good" system of internal controls, and the auditor is required to say whether they agree with management's statement. We don't yet know how this will play out in practice. For example, it isn't clear whether the auditor will express a positive opinion that controls comply with, say, COSO as the measurement criterion, or will instead express "negative assurance" that no material weakness or reportable condition was found. This is one of the things that Charlie's board will have to decide in the next year or so. But it's a great step forward because investors will now be able to tell whether the company's statements came directly from their internal systems and were then audited by the auditor—or whether the records first had to be reprocessed to get ready for an audit. Investors should care about internal controls because a company that has good controls every day of the year is much less likely to fail in the marketplace than a company with lousy controls, and is much more likely to anticipate and detect risks that might blow them out of the water.

But let me come back to this question of educating future accountants. Students must learn about GAAP—and they should know something about detecting material misappropriation fraud by employees and misrepresentation fraud by management. And they need to learn enough about finance and derivatives to stay ahead of the financial engineers. This brings me to a piece of Sarbanes-Oxley that I think will turn out to be a mistake—namely, barring public accounting firms from even a single dollar of fees for some kinds of consulting activities. Our government seems bent upon limiting the use of all the knowledge students gain about accounting and business here at Baylor. For example, if an auditor finds a serious problem in a client's internal control or risk

management systems, and the client says, "Okay, how can I fix it?," the auditor has to say, "I can't tell you. I'm allowed only to look out the back window to see where your car has been. I can't tell you how your car could run better or how you might avoid bumps on the road ahead."

Students who go to work for an auditing firm as auditors can't use their full set of skills, and clients are denied a potentially low-cost means of improving operations. Independence is critically important, but it isn't clear that banning all services is the only or best way to achieve it. But that's the direction we're moving in, even though it's under the guise of protecting the independence of the auditor. Again, I believe it's the wrong solution. The independence of the auditor comes from Bob and his counterparts *monitoring their own partners,* so that the auditing firm is not swayed by an overly aggressive engagement partner or client.

My point, then, is that taking away the consulting relationship will certainly raise costs, yet not address the independence problem. There are sometimes strong incentives to look the other way even without consulting revenue. Audit firms must have controls in place in order to resist the incentives to acquiesce with an aggressive client—incentives that will exist in any auditing relationship, regardless of whether there is some opportunity for consulting. I hope Charlie's board addresses this issue soon—that is, the procedures that KPMG and Deloitte & Touche and Ernst & Young and Pricewaterhouse-Coopers and smaller firms should have in place to ensure that they are monitoring their own people. Because that's the only way they can really protect investors.

GILLAN: I want to go back to Bob's earlier point about the importance of having a knowledgeable and well-informed board of directors. At a fundamental level, the board of directors is the entity that is appointed on behalf of the shareholders to oversee management. In the case of Enron, it's absolutely clear that very complex derivative transactions were being used. But at the same time, the board had apparently been informed by Arthur Andersen that Enron's accounting techniques and procedures were pushing the limits. The Enron board also approved the waiver of the code of ethics that allowed the CFO to be the lead partner in an entity that would undertake transactions with Enron.

So, part of the challenge of serving on corporate boards is to wrestle with complex issues. But another part involves just adhering to some basic rules that all board members should know. For example, Sarbanes-Oxley mandates that audit committee members not receive compensation other than what they are paid for being a board member—so no consulting arrangements for audit committee members. Of course, it doesn't take a rocket scientist to see the potential conflicts of interest here, so the mere fact that it has to be legislated suggests that some board members have really fallen down on the job. Another requirement is a ban on loans to executives. Although this may help address extreme cases like those we saw at Enron and WorldCom, these extremes are indicative of board failure rather than a problem with loans per se.

Interestingly, other than the audit committee, S-O is silent on board independence. In fact, the NYSE has taken the lead here by proposing that a majority of all board members of NYSE-listed firms be independent within the next two years.

STEWART: Most of the suggestions for improving corporate governance have focused on the responses of our legislators and regulators. But I think the market itself is also beginning to

respond to the problem with some promising innovations. Standard & Poor's and Moody's, for example, are now in the process of developing their own corporate governance rating systems. In the case of S&P, that process started because a handful of well-run Russian companies found that they were all being tarred with the same brush. And I think it was Lukoil that went to S&P and said, "Can you come in and audit our governance procedures? And if you like what you see, we will be able to show the world S&P's seal of approval, which in turn will give investors the confidence to invest in us." I've also heard that Moody's recently hired one of Stu Gillan's former colleagues from TIAA-CREF with the idea of incorporating more governance issues into their bond-rating process. In another interesting development, Institutional Shareholder Services, which is a corporate watchdog funded by large institutional investors, has developed what's known as the corporate governance "quotient," which can be used to guide large investors when voting proxies.

Another innovation we may soon see is a new independent agent called a chief governance officer, or governance auditor—someone who can be retained by the board to ensure that the company's governance structure and procedures are adequate. And I think that as long as government regulation does not become too onerous, the market will find many clever ways to address this issue over the next few years—ways that are likely to be more cost-effective than what comes out of the various government authorities.

GILLAN: Bennett, I have to tell you that I'm more than a little skeptical about the usefulness of these new corporate governance ratings. The fact that the rating itself can be expressed as a single number—just like

an audited earnings number—says to me that we're going to have to exercise a lot of caution and judgment in using the ratings. We now have at least three bond rating services— Moody's, S&P, and Fitch—all doing bond ratings on the same companies. But that doesn't seem to work all that well in the sense that the market tends to anticipate changes in credit ratings. That is, rating changes generally end up being lagging instead of leading indicators. Why should the rating agencies work any better in the context of governance? My point is that as with bond ratings, these governance rating systems are going to come up with a single number. And if you add to that the reality that these numbers are going to be *relative* as opposed to absolute measures of governance, I'm just not convinced that they will be the silver bullet for corporate governance problems.

STEWART: I see your point, but there are some important differences here. First, if every company were audited by three accounting firms instead of one, we would have a more competitive auditing market and more reliable numbers. And I think that's what is emerging on the governance side. And while you're right that bond prices and yields do in fact tend to change before the ratings change, that simply raises the question: What is the real function of the rating agencies? The answer, according to finance scholars at least, is that the agencies play an important certification role in the capital-raising process. The mere fact that the issuer has gone through this drill and shared inside information with the agency enables the company to sell its bonds at higher prices. I think our bond rating system works pretty well on the whole, and it's not clear to me how we could come up with a better system. And I would expect these governance ratings to function in much the same way.

The Promise of Sarbanes-Oxley

THOMAS: A number of our panelists have mentioned certain aspects of the Sarbanes-Oxley Act, which of course represents the legislative and regulatory solution to our current problems. I would like to wrap up the discussion by asking our panelists for their individual views of what's right and what's wrong with this new piece of legislation. Did it go far enough? Or did it go too far, and will it perhaps have some unintended and unwanted consequences?

GILLAN: My answer is "yes" to all of the above. There are a couple of things that came out of Sarbanes-Oxley that I like a lot. One is clearly the development of the new Public Company Accounting Oversight Board. The previous oversight board that was given this role was viewed—and I think correctly—as having been pretty much ineffective. The new board will be independently funded, and so it will be insulated from threats to funding that have plagued accounting standard setters in the past. There is also a sense that the new board, with strong regulatory backing and oversight by the SEC, will be given the power to conduct investigations, impose sanctions, and review the quality of audit procedures—a big change from before.

The other major contribution of Sarbanes-Oxley, one that has received a lot of good press, is its strengthening of the authority of the audit committee to appoint the external auditors. This step should help auditors maintain a greater degree of independence from management, and make them better able to withstand pressure to bend the rules to meet earnings targets.

My principal concern about Sarbanes-Oxley is, as Bill suggested, the possibility of major unintended consequences. Will the new requirements of this act end up imposing material costs on companies? One possible outcome is that many corporate leaders become so caught up with ensuring compliance with all these new rules and regulations that they can no longer focus on running the business. For example, the rules also apply to mutual funds. And this means, for example, that Fidelity's CEO will now have to sign off on statements for over 5,000 entities—and on a quarterly basis going forward. So what does this imply for the amount of time spent on compliance versus key corporate issues?

Another concern is that reforms may encourage a checklist mentality on the part of corporate board members. Take the audit committee. The word on the street is that some governance advisors have developed a set of 37 questions that the audit committee needs to ask the external auditor. While this gives the audit committee a guide as to what's important, the disadvantage is that they may simply check off the boxes rather than asking probing, substantive questions.

STEWART: My feeling is that there will almost surely be unintended consequences from this legislation. One of the most likely is that companies that might have gone public will now choose not to—and companies that are now public may tend to go private. That is, a lot of firms may choose to opt out of, or never to enter, a financial system where the regulatory costs outweigh the benefits of access to capital. I know my friends in the private equity business are just delighted by Sarbanes-Oxley because it's herding the sheep right into their fold.

Now, I'm not opposed to regulation per se, and there are pieces of Sarbanes-Oxley that I think will help. But excessive regulation is a silent killer. And my concern is that we won't really see the damage that is done until it's too late.

ALSPAUGH: I totally agree with Stu Gillan's two observations—first about the value of the new Accounting Oversight Board, and second about the requirement that the corporate board of directors, and not management, be responsible for hiring the auditor. I think both of these provisions are very positive developments. But I will also tell you that, as someone who travels a good deal in Europe and Asia, the extraterritorial piece of this legislation is not being viewed at all positively around the rest of the world. Having said that, I doubt that many foreign companies that are now registered in U.S. markets will decide to delist. But a lot of other companies that might have considered coming to our markets may now choose not to. We have the deepest, most liquid capital markets in the world. But my concern is that we may have put our markets at a competitive disadvantage with that piece of the legislation.

KINNEY: I too have some reservations about Sarbanes-Oxley. Like both Stu and Bob, I think having the auditor report to the audit committee of the board is a good idea in principle—though I'm not sure how this will work out in practice. But the best feature of the legislation, as I said earlier, is its requirement that the auditor evaluate and sign off on the company's internal controls, with management's assertion and the auditor's report then made available to investors.

One of the worst features, as I also mentioned before, is banning even one dollar of some types of consulting services by auditors. Many people assume that it was Enron's $27 million in fees for consulting services that must have turned Andersen's head, and they say nothing about the $25 million fee for auditing services. But independence cannot be guaranteed even by banning all non-audit service fees. The real solution to cases like

Andersen and Enron is, as Bob said earlier, to ensure the separation of risk assessment and reporting decisions from the revenue side of the business. Andersen's downfall was more likely a quality control matter of the executive office partner not being allowed to override Enron's engagement partner whose main livelihood was derived from a single client. But that problem is not directly addressed by the legislation.

And there is one last thing that troubles me about Sarbanes-Oxley: its failure to do anything about the politicization of accounting standards that, for example, has obstructed better accounting for stock options. The actions of Congress, under pressure from corporate executives, to prevent changes in stock options accounting have served only to legitimize and provide incentives for managements' efforts to manage earnings, to take the flexibility that's properly in GAAP and exploit it to pump up the stock price for short-term personal gain. And members on both sides of the aisle, Democrats as well as Republicans, are responsible for our lack of progress on these accounting policy issues.

Somehow we've got to convince Congress to depoliticize the process of setting accounting standards, and to resist the temptation to intervene with short-term and partial fixes under pressure. Financial reporting, GAAP, GAAS, ethics, and quality controls must be trusted, must have integrity, and must provide relevant information. It is dangerous for society to decide the basic structure of financial reporting after only a few weeks of occasional work by our elected officials.

MARTIN: Charlie, you are on the new Public Company Accounting Oversight Board. Can you tell us what you intend to do and how you think the board is going to help?

NIEMEIER: Let me start by saying that Sarbanes-Oxley took a major step forward for the accounting profession by establishing this board. But it's a complete startup. This board represents the first time that the accounting profession has been regulated. It's a very serious issue and a very important one.

Let me also say that there is now a crisis of confidence in our financial reporting system, and that the audit opinion is the basis on which that system is founded. Now, part of this crisis may well be more perception than reality. But because of the role that investor confidence plays in our financial markets, perception is an important element of the reality. And the goal of this new accounting board is to restore investor confidence in corporate audit committees and in accounting results generally.

This is not something that's going to happen overnight. This is a marathon. We can't look for quick fixes. We've got to make sure we do it right. And I agree that we have to be concerned about the effects of possible overregulation. When the pendulum swings, it usually swings too far. But if we don't let it swing so far this time, and if we give ourselves enough time, I think we can get closer to the point of having just the right amount and kind of regulation.

So I'm honored by the opportunity to serve on this board. I think there's a lot that we can accomplish, although it's going to take a lot of discussion and require a lot of input from various constituencies.

STEWART: Charlie, let's say that five years from now we could come back and evaluate whether you have made the kind of contribution that you hoped for. What indicators or criteria would you choose to be judged by?

NIEMEIER: My hope is that, five years from now, our economy will be booming, and the stock market will have recovered most if not all of the ground it has lost. And my expectation is that the public at large will look upon this board as having made an important contribution to the restoration of confidence in our financial markets.

ALSPAUGH: From the perspective of our profession, I would like to think that, in five years' time, financial reporting has ceased to make headlines and be at the center of all the media coverage it's getting today. And inside the companies themselves, my hope is that the quality of financial reporting will receive a healthy and proper degree of focus. I foresee that top managers will be telling their boards and perhaps the investment community, "Look, we've got a financial reporting process in place that works. We have the right kind of oversight, including strong internal controls. Our auditing firm is completely independent and has the right kind of quality controls. We're doing all we can to ensure that the role of the audit committee is clear and that investors can have confidence in our audit opinion."

Of course, there will always be exceptions—those who think they can play fast and loose with the rules. But with new systems in place, the right kind of people on the board, and a healthy regulatory approach—including a positive relationship between the oversight board and the accounting profession—today's problems will disappear from the newspapers.

CHAPTER 2

INTERNAL GOVERNANCE

147

CHAPTER 2: SECTION 2.1
Boards of Directors

Corporate boards of directors can be viewed as the lynchpin of internal corporate governance. As the representatives of shareholders, boards are charged with hiring, firing, and compensating the senior management team. But, in ***The Director's New Clothes (Or, The Myth of Corporate Accountability)***, Robert Monks and Nell Minow, long time participants in the corporate governance arena, suggest that since the board is *"selected by management, paid by management and—perhaps most important—informed by management, it is easy for directors to become captive to management's perspective."* The authors contend that the idea of boards being accountable to shareholders is a myth—the reality is that boards are beholden to management. Moreover, a theme throughout the article is that management control of the director nominations process implies current board structures are self-perpetuating. Consequently, shareholders' ability to seek genuine board representation is severely restricted. This observation is quite pertinent in today's environment with reports that Securities and Exchange Commission is exploring whether or not the director nominations process should be more accessible to shareholders.

In the ***Continental Bank Roundtable on the Role of Corporate Boards in the 1990s***, a number of corporate CEOs and directors discuss the state of U.S. corporate governance with two general partners of LBO investment firms and an academic well known for his critical view of corporate boards. To the extent anything like a consensus emerges, it is that many if not most corporate managements are dedicated to increasing shareholder value, and that many corporate boards conscientiously perform their oversight function. But even the most vigorous defenders of the status quo suggest that boards are clearly failing in something like 20% of all U.S. public companies. And, given the absence of takeovers, no one professed to have a solution to the problem of management entrenchment at persistently underperforming companies.

Nonetheless, one hint of a possible solution was contained in the discussion's clear suggestion of profound differences in the governance systems of public companies and those taken private in LBOs. As James Birle of the Blackstone Group commented, the two necessary conditions for effective board oversight are "adequate information and accountability, neither of which is likely to hold for many public companies." In sharp contrast to the boards of public companies, LBO boards are comprised principally of the company's largest stockholders. And, as Birle suggests, the oversight of a financially interested board makes for significantly tighter financial controls and more demanding performance standards than those typically imposed in public companies. Besides greater accountability, the directors of LBO companies also have far greater knowledge about the companies as a result of participating in the intensive due diligence performed when they first invested in the company.

In the third and final article in this section, Paul MacAvoy and Ira Millstein focus on ***The Active Board of Directors and Its Effect on the Performance of the Large Publicly Traded Corporation***. During the '90s, argue MacAvoy and Millstein, boards of directors have become more active and independent of management in pursuing shareholder interests. But there has been little empirical evidence that active boards help companies produce higher rates of return for their shareholders. In this article, after describing the new board activism, the authors argue that past failures to document an association between independent boards and superior corporate performance can be explained by two features of the research: its concentration on periods prior to the 1990s (when most boards were largely irrelevant) and its use of unreliable proxies (such as a minimum percentage of outside directors) for a well-functioning board. The authors hypothesize that an independent and resourceful board takes steps that require management to increase earnings available to investors. To test their hypothesis, the performance of a sample of large U.S. corporations was examined over the period 1991-1995 using two proxies for the "professionalism" of each company's board: (1) the letter grades (A+ – F) assigned by CalPERS for corporate governance; and (2) a "presence" or "absence" grade based on the evaluation of three key indicators of professional board behavior. Both of these governance metrics were associated in statistically significant ways with superior corporate performance as measured by earnings in excess of cost of capital and net of the industry average.

THE DIRECTOR'S NEW CLOTHES

(OR, THE MYTH OF CORPORATE ACCOUNTABILITY)

by Robert Monks,
Institutional Shareholder Partners, Inc.,
and
Nell Minow,
Institutional Shareholder Services, Inc.*

A scene in *Barbarians at the Gate* frames the question of accountability of corporate management perfectly. Ross Johnson, the man who somewhat impetuously initiated the leveraged buyout of RJR-Nabisco, met with Henry Kravis and George Roberts of Kohlberg, Kravis, Roberts to discuss it. There was a brief discussion of the business before Johnson's central questions came up. "Now Henry, if you guys get this, you're not going to get into chickenshit stuff about planes and golf courses, are you?" (Johnson's perquisites included corporate jets and membership fees at 24 country clubs.[1]) Kravis was eager to gloss over this question, but Roberts was more candid. "Well, we don't want you to live a spartan life. But we like to have things justified. We don't mind people using private airplanes to get places, if there's no ordinary way. It is important that a CEO set the tone in any deal we do."

Johnson stated his concern more directly. "I guess the deal we're looking for is a bit unusual." Johnson, as it turned out, wanted to keep significant control of the company. Roberts responded even more directly: "We're not going to do any deal where management controls it. We'll work with you. But we have no interest in losing control." Johnson asked why.

"We've got the money," Roberts said. "We've got the investors, that's why we have to control the deal." From the look in Johnson's eyes, Roberts could tell it wasn't the message he wanted to hear. "Well, that's interesting," Johnson said. "But frankly, I've got more freedom doing what I do right now."[2]

There's something wrong with this picture, because it took debt to make management accountable. It should have been accountable to shareholders, to the people who have "got the money."

---

*This article is an excerpt from Chapter 3 of *Power and Accountability* (HarperBusiness, 1990). Reprinted here with permission of the publisher.

1. Bryan Burrough and John Helyar, *Barbarians at the Gate* (Harper & Row, 1990), p. 93. The book also notes that "Johnson's two maids were on the company payroll."
2. Ibid., p. 255.

What's wrong with this picture is the discrepancy between the expectations of the law and reality. The law generally assumes that "All corporation power shall be exercised by or under the authority of, and the business and affairs of the corporation managed under the direction of, its board of directors, subject to any limitation set forth in the articles of incorporation."[3] According to Melvin Eisenberg, "All serious students of corporate affairs recognize that notwithstanding the statutory injunction, in the typical large publicly held corporation the board does not 'manage' the corporation's business in the ordinary meaning of that term. Rather, that function is vested in the executives."[4] This reality is reflected in the erosion of the standard of performance for directors. *Barbarians at the Gate* documents in devastating fashion the way that Ross Johnson handled his boards, with a combination of lavish perquisites and meager information. While he was dazzling his hand-picked directors, who could expect them to complain about his jets and country clubs?

The corporate structure was designed to maximize profits through competition in the marketplace, but it has proven to be more successful at making profits, whether maximum or not, by imposing costs on others. Every single mechanism that has been set up as some kind of check to prevent this externalizing of costs has been neutralized, short-circuited, or co-opted. Shareholders, directors, state and federal legislatures—even the marketplace itself—all are part of the myth of corporate accountability, and all are part of the reality of corpocracy. In this article, we look at the convenient myth behind the mechanisms established to make sure that corporate activity was consistent with the public interest, and the more convenient reality of the failure of these mechanisms to do so.

THE MYTH OF THE DIRECTOR'S DUTY

In a corporation, management acts as agent for the owner, but it does not always have the same interests and incentives. What can we do to require—or at least encourage—people to treat other people's property with as much care as if it were their own?

The law has tried to answer this question of agency costs by developing its highest standard of behavior, the fiduciary standard, and applying it to those who hold and manage property for others. This standard applies to several different players in the process for establishing corporate behavior, including directors. At least in theory, they are fiduciaries for the shareholders. And the law books are filled with attempts, some almost poetic, to define that duty. Their actions must be "held to something stricter than the morals of the marketplace," with a "punctilio of an honor the most sensitive."[5]

That there is a fiduciary standard is perhaps the most powerful myth underlying the corporate system. Why is it so important to make clear that directors must take extraordinary measures to make sure that they are protecting the rights of shareholders? The reason is our belief that those who exercise power should be accountable to those who are affected by it. We delegate authority to the directors of private companies because they are accountable to the shareholders, just as we delegate authority to government officials because they are accountable to the electorate. Accountability is what makes delegated authority legitimate; without accountability, there is nothing to prevent abuse.

This was the conundrum that almost stopped corporations before they began. Karl Marx and Adam Smith did not agree on much, but they both thought that the corporate form of organization was unworkable, and for remarkably similar reasons. They questioned whether it is possible to create a structure that will operate efficiently and fairly, despite the fact that there is a separation between ownership and control. Put another way, is there any system to make a manager care as much about the company's performance as a shareholder does? Harvard Law School's Dean Robert Clark describes this issue when he says that the major problem addressed by corporate law is how to keep managers accountable to their fiduciary duties of care and loyalty while allowing them great discretionary power over the conduct of the business.[6]

This is a key question, for both economic and public policy reasons. The separation of ownership and control leads to externalities, imposition of costs

---

3. See Committee on Corporate Laws of the Section of Corporation, Banking and Business Law, American Bar Association, *Model Business Corporation Act,* Prentice-Hall Law and Business, 1990, p. 781. "Thirty-two jurisdictions follow the language of the Model Act. . . the remaining 20 jurisdictions provide the corporation's affairs should be managed by a board of directors," p. 788.

4. Melvin Aron Eisenberg, *The Structure of the Corporation: A Legal Analysis,* Little, Brown, Boston, 1976, p. 140.
5. Benjamin N. Cardozo, *Meinhard v. Salmon,* 249 N.Y. 458, 464 (1928).
6. Robert Clark, *Corporate Law,* Little, Brown, Boston, 1986, pp. 33-34.

Karl Marx and Adam Smith did not agree on much, but they both thought that the corporate form of organization was unworkable, and for remarkably similar reasons. They questioned whether it is possible to create a structure that will operate efficiently and fairly, despite the fact that there is a separation between ownership and control.

on others—including shareholders, taxpayers, and the community. For example, a company that discharges untreated effluent into a river is making the community pay some of the costs of production, through government services for clean-up or increased health care costs. A company that uses political pull at the state level to thwart a worthwhile takeover attempt is making the shareholders foot the bill, not just for the lobbying efforts, but for the lost premium, and possibly for a less competitive company. And, of course, it was the shareholders who were paying for Ross Johnson's 24 country club memberships and (at least by one account) for his dog's trip on a jet from the corporate fleet, to say nothing of the devastatingly expensive mistake of the "smokeless cigarette."

The answer to this problem was supposed to be the board of directors, elected by shareholders and acting as fiduciaries on their behalf. The board is responsible for setting overall goals and making sure they are met, for hiring the CEO and monitoring his performance, and for watching corporate management on behalf of the shareholders, to make sure that the corporation is run in their interest. That's the theory—and the myth. The reality is that directors are "merely the parsley on the fish"[7] or the "ornaments on a corporate Christmas Tree."[8] As Peter Drucker put it many years ago, "Whenever an institution malfunctions as consistently as boards of directors have in nearly every major fiasco of the last forty or fifty years, it is futile to blame men. It is the institution that malfunctions."[9]

The Convenient Myth—and the More Convenient Reality

How can we justify a system in which investors purchase shares in a company that is far too big and complex to permit any meaningful shareholder involvement in governance? In theory, the accountability in our system is the enforceable allegiance that corporate directors and managers owe to shareholders. And that allegiance is enforceable in two ways. Dissatisfied shareholders can sue for violation of fiduciary duty, or, through the electoral process

(proxy voting), they can throw the bums out and vote in directors who will do better.

Although difficult to believe in today's world, it is from the premise that shareholders can respond effectively to inadequate boards that much of corporate decision-making gets its legitimacy. It is directors, after all, who appoint the officers and determine their level of compensation, and who set the long-term goals and make sure that management takes appropriate steps to carry them out. The fiduciary standard is supposed to ensure that they take all of these actions on behalf of the shareholders. But this is little more than a vestigial notion in modern times. As the creation of instruments to finance takeovers of any company, of virtually any size, has presented directors with unprecedented challenges, they have found, as have the shareholders, that the traditional notion of a director's duty—and authority—is more myth than reality.

Dance with the One Who Brought You—or Else

Barbarians at the Gate detailed Ross Johnson's techniques for the care and feeding of his directors—everything from arranging for them to rub shoulders with celebrities to endowing chairs at their alma maters. Perquisites such as the use of corporate planes and apartments made it hard for directors to push him on tough questions. The same is true at most corporations. Directors are picked because the CEO knows them and knows that they are likely to be on his side. Many of them—even those termed "outside" directors by the New York Stock Exchange's definition—have some business or personal relationship with the CEO.[10] We were once informed by an investor of a prominent electronics company that the head of the board of directors' compensation committee was the chancellor of a college. The president of the company, in turn, was the chairman of the college's board of trustees, and the company has been a big contributor to the school—a nice, cozy arrangement.

Directors are not picked for their ability to challenge management. On the contrary, they are

7. Arthur Fleischer, Jr., Geoffrey C. Hazard, Jr., and Miriam Z. Klipper, *Board Games*, Little, Brown, Boston, 1988, p. 3.

8. Jay W. Lorsch with Elizabeth MacIver, *Pawns or Potentates: The Reality of America's Corporate Boards*, Harvard Business School Press, Boston, 1989, p. 4.

9. Peter Drucker, "The Bored Board," in *Toward the Next Economics and Other Essays*, Harper & Row, New York, 1981, p. 10.

10. According to preliminary figures in the ISS Database, 843 out of 5,848 director positions in the ISS Director Database were "affiliated" outsiders, with some business connection to the company.

more often chosen for their business or personal ties, or for their ability to add symbolic luster. Compensation expert Graef Crystal describes boards as "ten friends of management, a woman and a black."

A vice president of one of the nation's largest conglomerates told us that during one period his company's board included a much-loved TV personality. "He always made a hit at annual meetings, where shareholders greeted him with long applause," said the vice president. "After the meeting, the directors would have cocktails and lunch, and the star would regale them with anecdotes and jokes. Then, when the Chairman banged the gavel, the star would put his head down on the table and sleep until the meeting was over. Someone sitting next to him would cast his vote, when required, claiming he or she had checked the star's position." On another board, a Nobel Prize-winning scientist was selected by management. An observer told us that "he always made a point to ask questions during board meetings, the kind of questions that an intelligent but uninformed layman might ask, but his material contributions were nil."

Since they are selected by management, paid by management, and—perhaps most important—informed by management, it is easy for directors to become captive to management's perspective. Information is the key, and it is often frustrating to directors to have such limited access. Former Supreme Court Justice Arthur Goldberg, a member of the board of TWA, suggested that the board form a committee to make periodic reports on the company's operations and that it have its own staff of experts, including a scientist, an economist, a public relations expert, an auditor, and perhaps, a financial expert. The proposal was turned down, and Goldberg resigned from the board.[11]

Other directors who have tried to question management have fared even worse. Those directors who cannot be shmoozed, ignored, or avoided can be silenced. Ross Perot was brought to the General Motors board just to bring the skills and experience that had made his company, EDS, so successful. When he tried to give the board the benefit of that skill and experience, CEO Roger Smith paid Perot $742.8 million—$33 a share for stock that closed at $26 7/8 on the day of the trade, plus another $346.8 million for contingent notes and tax compensation—in order to get him off the board.[12] GM even established a $7.5 million penalty to be levied if either Perot or GM criticized each other, and they set up a three-man arbitration panel to evaluate possible violations.[13] So there was no opportunity for the shareholders to find out Perot's concerns about the company. There was also no opportunity for them to get that price; GM refused to buy back other shareholders' stock for the price they paid Perot.

An outside director of a company that went private in an MBO told us that his every attempt to question management was thwarted. The special committee convened to oversee the deal was made up of directors selected for their history of going along with whatever management proposed. The projections for segments of the company previously expected to do well suddenly became dismal, as all of the assumptions changed to justify a low price. Even if a company is operating as a public company, it has every incentive to present its most optimistic forecasts to directors and shareholders. But a buyer and a seller have two different ways of valuing assets, and in an MBO, management switches sides. The "independent" investment banking firms hired to provide "fair" evaluations of the value of the assets owe their allegiance to management. Who owes allegiance to shareholders? In theory, it is the board of directors, who, as fiduciaries, are supposed to be better to shareholders than they would be to themselves. But the theory of fiduciary duty has given way to the reality of a duty so threadbare that it covers as little as the fabled emperor's new clothes.

THE EMPIRE STRIKES BACK: THE BUSINESS ROUNDTABLE

With the birth of the Roundtable, big business in the United States may at last be said to have come of political age.[14]

The Business Roundtable is an association of approximately 200 of the country's largest publicly held corporations, who have joined together to examine public issues that affect the economy and

11. Lorsch, cited in note 8, pp. 57-58.
12. Maryann Keller, *Rude Awakening: The Rise, Fall, and Struggle for Recovery of General Motors*, William Morrow, New York, 1989, p. 188.
13. Doron P. Levin, *Irreconcilable Differences: Ross Perot versus General Motors*, Little, Brown, Boston, 1989, p. 324.

14. Kim McQuaid, *Big Business and Presidential Power: From FDR to Reagan*, William Morrow, New York, 1982, p. 308.

Since they are selected by management, paid by management, and—perhaps most important—informed by management, it is easy for directors to become captive to management's perspective. Information is the key, and it is often frustrating to directors to have such limited access.

to develop positions that reflect "sound economic and social principles. The objectives of the Roundtable include fostering economic policies conducive to the wellbeing of the nation and its people."[15]

The Roundtable came about, indirectly, because its predecessor, the Business Council, was part of the Department of Commerce—a fact Kennedy's first commerce secretary, Luther Hodges, did not appreciate. Hodges felt the council, a group that advised him as commerce secretary yet would not allow him to select its members or determine their meeting agendas, should not have a "special channel to government thinking."[16] Hodges and the council remained at loggerheads until the council went to Kennedy and told him that they would operate as a private group. Business was then represented by different umbrella organizations over the next decade, including a revived private Business Council, the U.S. Chamber of Commerce, the National Association of Manufacturers, and the National Federation of Independent Business. From the point of view of the business community, the inadequacy of its governmental relations was never more painful than during the Nixon and Ford administrations, when wage and price controls were installed, with almost no input from the business sector. According to one scholar, it was John Connally, long an ally of big business, who made it clear to prominent business leaders that "businessmen had to improve in political sophistication and techniques in Washington or else face political impotence."[17]

In March 1972, Frederick Borch of General Electric and John D. Harper of Alcoa convened about a dozen corporate CEOs as "the March Group" to involve themselves directly in lobbying and influencing. The result was the Business Roundtable, a disciplined, sophisticated, and effective political fighting machine. Its success is attributable to the prestige and effort of the leaders: Harper, Irving Shapiro of Dupont, Reg Jones of GE, GM's Thomas Murphy, Exxon's Clifton Garvin, and, more recently, GM's Roger Smith and Union Pacific's Drew Lewis.

The Roundtable's direction comes from its executive and policy committees. The organization has three unique characteristics. First, the CEOs are personally involved. Second, membership is limited to CEOs of large companies; there are no small or medium-sized businesses whose interests and priorities might be different—or inconvenient. Third, the organization carefully avoids involving itself with a single company or a single-interest pressure group. The Roundtable speaks for "big business," and it does so through its task forces. Typically, a subject for special attention will be selected and then a "lead company" designated. Usually its CEO directs the task force, supplying the critical personnel from his or her own corporation or using people made available by other corporations. The Roundtable itself stays relatively small and discrete.

"Unable to persuade Congress to pass legislation curbing hostile takeovers,"[18] the Roundtable has devised an ambitious strategy to protect its members, including the devotion of substantial attention and energy to questions of internal corporate governance as a way of allowing what is, in essence, a hostile takeover from the inside. Although a great deal of the Roundtable's energy has been devoted to opposition to federal authority over corporate governance and support for state antitakeover legislation, one of its initiatives is noteworthy here: the recent drastic revisions of the Roundtable's own well-researched and thoughtful 1978 Statement on Corporate Governance.

THE ROUNDTABLE ON GOVERNANCE, 1978 AND 1990

There is no clearer indication of the Roundtable's views on corporate governance than in its own reports on the subject. In its brief existence, the Roundtable has profoundly changed its views, as revealed by a comparison of its papers issued in 1978 and 1990.

In January 1978, the Business Roundtable issued a statement entitled *The Role and Composition of the Board of Directors of the Large Publicly Owned Corporation*. The paper was the culmination of a project responding to a pattern of corporate criminal behavior involving illegal campaign contributions, bribery, and illicit involvement in the elections of other countries. The CEO members of the Roundtable evaluated how corporate boards of directors are selected, constituted, and function, in order to understand and to avoid further criminal behavior.

---

15. Brief of petitioner The Business Roundtable, Case #99-1651, Court of Appeals, D.C. Circuit (August 22, 1989), p. ii.
16. McQuaid, cited in note 14.

17. Ibid., p. 284.
18. Tim Smart, "Knights of the Roundtable: Tracking Big Business' Agenda in Washington," *Business Week*, October 21, 1988, p. 39.

A distinguished scholars group was chaired by Dean David S. Ruder of Northwestern University School of Law (who later became chairman of the SEC during the last part of the Reagan administration). He reported to the Roundtable's Committee on Corporate Organization Policy, chaired by J. Paul Austin (CEO of the Coca-Cola Company).

Their report was the state-of-the-art explanation in 1978 for the legitimacy of private power. It relies heavily on accountability as the safeguard from criminal and other activity that is contrary to the interests of society. The report describes the constraints on corporate action that are traditionally used to support its legitimacy. All of the limits listed in the report, however, were more myth than reality, and more often breached by corporate management than observed. The most noteworthy constraint cited by the Roundtable was its accountability to boards and shareholders—noteworthy precisely because, as that myth began to become reality with the takeovers of the 1980s, the Roundtable reversed its position. The 1990 version had the pomp of the earlier version, without the circumstance—no blue-ribbon panel of academics was brought in this time.

The 1978 report specified the accountability imposed by economic constraints—inadequate response to competition, both domestic and foreign—and raised the prospect of lower share prices, higher cost of capital, vulnerability to takeover, and diminished personal job security. It also cited accountability imposed by the formidable array of legal and regulatory requirements to which corporate management is subject: "Moreover, we have witnessed in recent years an increasing rigor on the part of state courts in applying fiduciary standards to evaluate behavior of corporate management. Contrary to some misconceptions, actions for management misconduct are in fact imposed and constitute an impressive system of deterrence."[19]

The Roundtable in 1978 was acutely conscious of the necessity of an independent board of directors. In order to have meaningful independence, the report recognized that it might be necessary to give shareholders an explicit right to nominate directors.

The following statement from the 1978 report may be the best definition of the ideal role of a board of directors: "The board of directors, then, is located at two critical corporate interfaces—the interface between the owners of the enterprise and its management, and the interface between the corporation and the larger society. The directors are stewards—stewards of the owners' interest in the enterprise and stewards also of the owners' legal and ethical obligations to other groups affected by corporate activity."[20] If only the Roundtable had stuck with it.

THE ROUNDTABLE RETREATS: CORPORATE GOVERNANCE IN 1990

The transformation of the issues of corporate governance in the 1980s is reflected in the revisionist approach taken 12 years later in the Roundtable's 1990 report, *Corporate Governance and American Competitiveness*. Its basic conclusion is that American business is doing just fine and does not need interference from anyone, especially shareholders. The Roundtable responded to the threat of government involvement in 1978 by emphasizing private accountability; it responded in 1990 to the threat of private accountability by stressing CEO supremacy.

Whereas the 1978 report contemplated a board of directors directly accountable to shareholders and constructively capable of independent evaluation and monitoring of management, the 1990 statement's version is closer to a structure of vertical authority, with the CEO on top and the board of directors one among several operating departments. The report contemplates the selection of directors who are acceptable to the CEO,[21] who attend meetings presided over by the CEO, and who discuss agenda items selected by the CEO.[22]

As a practical matter, the board contemplated by the report is self-perpetuating; there is no more suggestion of shareholder involvement in nominations, even informally. And the essence of the report is that owners cannot be trusted and therefore should not be permitted to make the fundamental decisions concerning the corporation's operations.

19. The Business Roundtable, *The Role and Composition of the Board of Directors of the Large Publicly Owned Corporation* (available from the Business Roundtable, 200 Park Ave., New York, NY 10166), 1978, p. 3.

20. Ibid. p. 8.

21. The Business Roundtable, *Corporate Governance and American Competitiveness* (available from the Business Roundtable, 200 Park Ave., New York, NY 10166), 1990, p. 13 ("...while the CEO must be involved...").

22. Ibid., p. 14 ("To ensure continuing effective board operations, the CEO can periodically ask the directors for their evaluation of the general agenda for board meetings and any suggestions they may have for improvement.")

"Shareholder voting on such things as acquisitions and divestitures can put immediate shareholder financial return ahead of sound longer-term growth which may have the potential of being even more rewarding to the corporation, its shareholders and its other stakeholders."[23]

This begs the question. No one is in favor of an overly short-term outlook, but *long term* may be a euphemism for something that never happens. The real question is whose perspective is riskier. Why aren't shareholders—as those whose interest is at risk—just as knowledgeable and even more entitled than directors to set the overall direction of the company? Whose perspective is likely to be longer-term—the index fund[24] pledged to hold the stock indefinitely or the CEO, who could lose his job in a change of control?

The critical question is on what basis directors and managers will make their choices. To the extent that directors have authority to allocate corporate resources on any basis other than long-term value enhancement, they are undermining the basis for the grant of power to private entities in a free society.

The 1990 Roundtable report, in all its essentials, is a wiring diagram for CEO monarchy. First, it cautions against direct shareholder involvement: "Excessive corporate governance by referendum in the proxy statement can also chill innovation and risk-taking."[25] Second, it diminishes the authority and independence of the board by depicting it as a necessarily self-perpetuating body ("Because effective corporate boards function as a cohesive whole, the directors are in the best position to recommend the slate of nominees for board membership which is presented to the shareholders for election at the annual meeting"[26]) and by implying that the chairman and presiding officer of the board must be the CEO ("To ensure continuing effective board opera-

tions, the CEO can periodically ask the directors for their evaluation of the general agenda items for board meetings and any suggestions they may have for improvement"[27]).

In the fall of 1990, the Business Roundtable further demonstrated its view of the role of shareholders by telling all of its members to refuse to respond to a survey of directors submitted by the California Public Employees' Retirement System. The Roundtable responded as if merely asking questions of directors to determine their personal views was not appropriate:

Some of the questions do not lend themselves to broad generalizations because the answers depend on particular facts and circumstances, others require a more complex response than the questionnaire's format allows, and still others suggest that directors' responses will be used to create 'good' and 'bad' rankings for director nominees in spite of the disavowal of any such intent...[28]

The letter itself provides the most telling evidence of the Roundtable's vision of the role of shareholders, directors and management: it assumes that when shareholders seek information about the directors they are asked to elect, managers have not only the right but the obligation to interfere.[29]

This is quite a departure from the earlier commitment to acting as stewards for owners. Indeed, other than a vague acknowledgment of the obligation to maximize value, shareholders are only mentioned in the context of either being incapable of providing direction or having their rights considered along with those of other "stakeholders." This diminished role for shareholders is a startling retreat for the Roundtable. It also parallels the diminished role for the shareholders' representatives, the board.

23. Ibid., p. 16.
24. An index fund is a type of "passive portfolio" that tracks an index. An example is the Standard & Poor's Index. Investment managers do not make buy/sell decisions based on analysis of individual companies but hold the stock as long as it is in the index.
25. The Business Roundtable, *Corporate Governance and American Competitiveness*, p. 16.
26. Ibid., p. 9.
27. Ibid., p. 14.
28. Letter from Bruce Atwater, chairman, Corporate Governance Task Force of the Business Roundtable, November 7, 1990.
29. "We suggest you advise your directors not to respond. . ." (Ibid.).

BENNETT STEWART: Yesterday, we heard Michael Jensen talk about the role of the board of directors in creating shareholder value (though after listening to Michael, I suppose we should really think of it as the board of "accommodators"). Professor Jensen identified four main roles our boards *ought* to play in public companies, but in many cases do not. Stated as briefly as possible, they are the hiring, firing, counseling, and compensating of top management. In today's discussion, we will further explore the role of the board with a distinguished panel of senior executives and directors brought together by the Continental Bank.

Current compensation practices are clearly one area where boards seem to be failing—and we will likely talk a little about that today. But there are also more fundamental issues about the relationship between professional management and corporate boards, such as:

- Who really should nominate the board of directors?
- Is it appropriate for management to sit on the board?
- Should the CEO of the company also fulfill the role of the chairman of the company?
- How can we improve the dialogue and decision-making that takes place as a result of the board process?

It would also be interesting to hear the panel's assessment of the import of some current trends. For example, there are a number of public companies that are beginning to feel more pressure from institutional investors to reform the role and function of the board. It can't have escaped anyone's attention that various shareholder interest groups have risen up in recent years to express their dissatisfaction with managements and boards.

Robert Monks, for example, has formed a firm called Institutional Shareholder Partners whose aim is to act with major shareholders to help—

or, in some cases, prod—companies into creating shareholder value. You may recall that Monks waged a well-publicized proxy contest with Sears a while back that was designed to serve as a catalyst for change. The United Shareholders Association (USA), a group started by Boone Pickens and now run by Ralph Whitworth, has achieved some modest successes in influencing the corporate governance

February 29, 1992 ■ *Beaver Creek, Colorado*

CONTINENTAL BANK ROUNDTABLE ON

THE ROLE OF CORPORATE BOARDS IN THE 1990s

process. For instance, after a vigorous campaign, USA managed to change the compensation plan of the chairman of ITT; and there are intimations that perhaps more dramatic changes in the overall structure of the company may be forthcoming. So it would be interesting to speculate here about the expected impact of the increasing activism of institutional investors on corporate managements and boards.

To discuss these issues this morning, the Continental Bank has assembled a really first-rate panel. Let me now introduce the panel (and I will do so in alphabetical order).

JAMES BIRLE is a General Partner with The Blackstone Group, the well-known New York investment firm. One of his principal responsibilities at Blackstone is to serve as the co-chairman and CEO of Collins & Aikman Group, Inc., formerly the Wickes Companies, an organization I would describe as a $3 billion conglomerate. Jim also serves on a variety of boards, including that of Transtar, a railroad business acquired by Blackstone in a leveraged buyout from USX. Given that Jim also spent 30 years with General Electric, I expect him to give us some insights as to how internal corporate governance mechanisms differ between public companies and private companies run by so-called financial investors like Blackstone.

WADE CABLE is CEO and a director of The Presley Companies, a prominent California homebuilder. The company went through an initial public offering of stock this past October, largely because of the difficulty most real estate developers have today in convincing their banks to lend to them. So Wade is living proof of the credit crunch.

MICHAEL JENSEN, whose name I've already mentioned several times, is the Edsel Bryant Professor of Business Administration at the Harvard Business School, and among the most vocal and controversial critics of corporate governance in the U.S.

trial installation. Like John's former employer, Johns Manville, the Fibreboard Corporation faces a massive potential liability from asbestos litigation—which, I'm sure, has made John's current job most challenging.

WILLIAM ROPER is Senior Vice President and CFO of Science Applications International Corporation, which claims to be the largest em-

and governance structure—one that may have valuable lessons for our public companies.

JOHN TEETS is Chairman, President, and CEO of The Dial Corp. John presided over a radical restructuring of the company in the 1980s—one which included the sale of the Armour meat-packing business in 1983, the sale of the Greyhound bus lines in 1987, and the recently

ROGER LEE is Senior Vice President-Finance and Administration, as well as a director, of Caesars World, a company which fought off a hostile suitor by undergoing a leveraged recap about five years ago. Roger will thus provide the perspective of—and presumably defend—the management and directors of our public companies.

JOHN ROACH is the Chairman, President, and CEO of Fibreboard Corporation, also a publicly traded company. The company has approximately $300 million in sales and focuses on wood products and indus-

ployee-owned company in America. The company certainly represents an interesting paradigm for us to consider this morning. The firm has approximately $1.2 billion in revenues, and is involved primarily in systems development work.

FRED SIMMONS is a General Partner of Freeman Spogli, an investment company that has been very successful in executing LBOs of 15 companies in a variety of industries, including seven supermarket chains. As I suggested earlier in introducing Jim Birle of Blackstone, Fred also represents an alternative ownership

announced spin-off of Greyhound Financial Corporation, or GFC, to its stockholders. It should be interesting to hear from John about this process, and about the role of the board in overseeing this restructuring.

I am BENNETT STEWART, Senior Partner of Stern Stewart & Co., a corporate finance advisory firm that specializes in valuation, restructuring, and management incentive compensation. I'm not a director of any major company, which is probably the surest sign of the failure of our corporate governance system.

The Case of Dial Corp

STEWART: Let me begin this discussion with John Teets. John, as I just mentioned, last October your company announced its decision to spin off Greyhound Financial Corporation to its shareholders, which caused the firm's stock price to increase from $35 to about $41 a share. And your share price now trades in the vicinity of $50, if I'm not mistaken. The company must be doing something right.

Would you share with us the dynamics of that decision to spin off GFC? And what role did the board play in that process?

TEETS: Well, the decision to sell Greyhound Financial was really made several years ago. At that time we decided The Dial Corp would pursue a strategy focused on consumer products and services. So we knew then that GFC was not part of our long-range plan.

But it turned out to be very difficult to get out of the finance business. We let Salomon Brothers try to sell it for over a year. Then we gave the job to Merrill Lynch, which also had it for over a year without success. GFC has a good record, five years of 15-20% growth in earnings, and a $2 billion portfolio with only 3% non-earning assets. But no one was interested in paying 100 cents on the dollar for a $2-billion portfolio.

Some time later, we realized when we wanted to divest Verex, our mort-gage insurance business, we were not going to be able to sell that operation either. In this case, we also faced a tax problem. The business was carrying a $100 million investment tax credit going forward that would have been triggered by a sale of the business. Our solution, which we devised with the help of Gleacher and Company, was to package GFC together with Verex and spin them off to our shareholders. In fact, the new securities will begin to trade on March 4 this year.

What was the board's role in this decision? For the past nine years, we have apprised our board that we want to keep moving into the consumer products and services area. That is our long-term strategy, and our board has been kept informed throughout the process. In the course of this nine year program, we have sold close to 20 businesses for about $3.2 billion, and have bought others worth about $1.4 billion.

So we have been moving slowly in the direction we want to go. It's been like moving a giant, but we're finally reaching a point where it's starting to pay off.

STEWART: Well, John, your stock has gone up quite dramatically. Is that something that the board is pleased about? Or do they just not care?

TEETS: Our stock has gone from $13 when I took over to almost $50 today. Our board does not sit around looking at the stock on a daily basis, if that's

your point. But they have played, and continued to play, an important role in the company's success in adding value for stockholders.

Let me also add here that I think statements like Professor Jensen's that boards are incapable of bringing about necessary change are greatly exaggerated. For one thing, boards often exercise their power to fire CEOs. And most boards understand their responsibility to monitor management and represent stockholders' interest. Now, there are clearly some cases where the board doesn't function and the system doesn't work. We all know the companies that are not performing. But that is probably true in no more than, say, 20% of American companies today. So, the system *is* working.

In my own case, *all* my board members are outsiders and they are all CEOs of other companies. And they are very thorough in their examination of proposals. For example, when we proposed the spin-off of GFC and Verex to our board last August, what was scheduled to be a one-hour meeting turned into a four-hour meeting. And the proposal was not approved at that meeting, but only after further research and discussion.

So, in our case, the governance process works quite well. And the board has been pleased with what we've succeeded in accomplishing for our stockholders. Some of our board members have also participated directly them-

In the past few years, I have seen a pronounced change in the way institutional investors are exerting their influence over corporate management. We now appear to have a solid base of fairly long-term institutional investors. They spend the time to come out and talk with us at length about the long-term strategy of the company. Our institutional investors are proving to be a very constructive force.

—Roger Lee

selves in our shareholder gains. We give our board members the option to take their fees in stock or cash. And one of our directors recently reminded me that he has now accumulated a million-dollar's worth of our stock through this program. So he is, I think, quite aware of the fact our stock price is significantly higher today than it was six months ago.

STEWART: John, you mentioned a one-hour meeting that turned into a four-hour meeting. I'm just interested in the kinds of questions and concerns that surfaced during that dialogue.

TEETS: Professor Jensen yesterday objected that the code of politeness that prevails in board meetings prevents serious disagreements from being aired. But that's misleading. It's true that directors don't go to meetings with the idea of antagonizing the CEO, but nor are they the rubber stamp that Jensen suggests. They ask tough questions. They debate important issues.

As I mentioned, our plan to spin off some of our businesses clearly raised questions and concerns among the board. In fact, our original proposal called for combining our bus manufacturing operation along with the finance companies. One important issue the board was especially concerned about was the funding of the spun-off company: They asked questions such as: How could this new entity be financed so as to satisfy the banks and stand up to the scrutiny of S&P and Moody's. How could the banks and

rating agencies be made to accept what amounts to a mini-conglomerate? Wouldn't it be too complicated to understand? (You can't be too careful, I'm told, in explaining these matters to bankers.)

So, it was only after a lot of thought and a long debate that we ultimately decided to spin off GFC and Verex together, and then either sell or spin off the bus manufacturing company as a stand-alone operation. And our board members played an important role in helping us reach this decision.

The Case of Caesars World

STEWART: John mentioned that all of his company's board members are outsiders except himself. Now let me turn to Roger Lee. Roger, you are the Senior Vice President and CFO of Caesars World, as well as a director. Is the composition of your board like that of John's company?

LEE: No. We have a nine-person board that consists of four insiders and five outsiders. We are probably tilting too much to the inside. I personally think there should probably be at least two outsiders for every insider on the board, maybe more. Other companies I've served on have had at most two insiders on the board.

STEWART: Do you think that difference affects the quality of the dialogue that takes place between the board and top management?

LEE: I think it can reduce the amount of dialogue and may tend to create some passivity on the part of the board members. It makes the outsiders more reluctant to take on such a solid nucleus of people in one room at one time.

STEWART: Roger, Caesars World went through a defensive, and fairly dramatic, leveraged restructuring a number of years ago. Can you tell us a little about how what happened, why the company recapitalized itself the way it did, and what the role of the board was during this difficult process?

LEE: We were the target of a hostile takeover bid. The board responded by introducing an in-depth review of values and alternative courses of action, using both management input and several consultants. Based on the specifics of our situation, it was determined that the bid price was considerably lower than the company's value. Further it was believed that an alternate approach—a corporate restructuring using additional leverage to fund a large one-time cash dividend—could deliver more value to shareholders while preserving their proportional ownership in the company.

We aggressively pursued this alternative, eventually gaining shareholder approval and forcing withdrawal of the opposing bid. But one of the casino control commissions that regulate our industry unexpectedly refused to permit the restructuring. The board then investigated alternative courses of action, and decided to use substantially less leverage and repurchase approximately one-third of the outstanding common shares in a Dutch auction—the kind of auction that calls for each shareholder to name his own price within a range of values specified by the company.

Throughout this entire sequence of events, the board was the focal point for initiating, evaluating, and taking actions. It was a difficult task accomplished under enormous pressure.

**The Case of the
Presley Companies**

STEWART: Wade, your company has recently gone public. Could you give us a little background on your company, and tell us how it got to be where it is now? And do you think the corporate governance process and the role of the board will change much as a result of your transition from a private to a public company?
CABLE: Our company was in fact a public company from 1971 through 1984. In 1984 it was acquired by what was then Pacific Lighting. They have since changed their name to Pacific Enterprises. So I've seen a public board of directors at work in a very large, diverse company.

Michael Jensen would probably have some fun looking at how the board of Pacific Lighting performed. As as example, consider the decision the board made in voting to sell the Presley Companies, along with its other real estate companies. At about the same time, Pacific Lighting decided to buy Thrifty Drug Stores for something in the neighborhood of $870 million. To give you a rough sense of how these two transactions affected the shareholder value of Pacific Lighting, Thrifty Drug Stores made approximately $35 million the first year they owned it. The Presley Companies would have made approximately $100 million in the first year we owned it, had it still been owned by Pacific Lighting. Recently, Pacific Enterprises completely elimi-

nated its dividend to shareholders and announced very large losses as a result of its decision to divest their retail businesses. This is a board that, at least in this instance, did not do well by its shareholders.

When we completed our LBO of the Presley Companies from Pacific Lighting in 1987, the deal was reported to be leveraged with a debt-to-equity ratio of 57 to 1. Actually, the entire deal was leveraged, with the equity piece being subordinated debt. We were able to pay down the debt very quickly; and in just two years following the close of the deal, we had a company with a debt-to-equity ratio of less than 4 to 1. We thought this was terrific, feeling that we had hit the home run of all times.

The problem we ran into was that the world changed and suddenly FIRREA-regulated commercial banks changed their view of what constituted an acceptable amount of leverage for a real estate developer. As a consequence, we chose to take our company public in October 1991 in an effort to access other capital markets.
STEWART: What was the role of the board in this decision to go public?
CABLE: Extensive. As a private company, we had a board that was composed entirely of insiders and manager-owners who were very active in the decision to take the company public. On the subject of the role of the board, I was never once asked by potential investors, "Who's on your board?" I don't think institutions that invested in this company really gave a damn. I think they looked at the management and said, "What can you do and what can't you do?" Their decision to buy stock was based on the company's track record and the perceived ability of the management to perform.

Now consider our current board, which is made up of a broad spectrum of people that includes insider owner-managers, our largest shareholder, a university president, other business executives, and an investment banker. I am

confident this board would have taken equally as active a role as our former board in vital decisions such as going public. Our current board is a very astute group of people with a wide variety of backgrounds and expertise; and I am confident that we, as a company, will benefit from their involvement. For example, we currently have an investment banker on our board. This is significant because in our industry the major problem today is capital and how to access sources that we have traditionally not had relationships with.

STEWART: Are you assuming that unless you have an investment banker on your board, you would not be able to get access to capital?
CABLE: No, but we've been forced to educate ourselves very quickly about raising capital from sources that we have had no experience in dealing with. Two years ago, financing in the residential real estate business was pretty simple. We simply asked ourselves, "To which commercial banker were we going to give the honor of making us this loan?" They were lined up outside the door. The only question was, "Who was going to provide the most credit at the lowest rate?" There was little negotiation required, and frankly, our biggest problem was that we could not satisfy all the lenders we had three years ago.

But credit availability has now changed drastically. In the past, profits from our business accrued almost totally to the developer. Now the capital providers are demanding a much larger share.

So, in answer to your question, we could obviously hire an investment banker. But because we had so little experience in this area, we felt it would be advantageous to have someone on our board who could provide us with the benefit of his experience and ideas. Our strategy was not simply go public, pay the banks down, and go on with business as usual. Instead, we viewed going public as a major first step in a long-range

> *We were able to pay down the debt very quickly; and in just two years following the close of the deal, we had a company with a debt-to-equity ratio of less than 4 to 1. We thought this was terrific, feeling that we had hit the home run of all times. The problem we ran into was that the world changed and suddenly FIRREA-regulated commercial banks changed their view of what constituted an acceptable amount of leverage for a real estate developer.*
>
> *—Wade Cable*

strategy to make our balance sheet match the future capital requirements of our business. To do that effectively, we thought it would be helpful to have an investment banker on the board.
STEWART: But don't you think this investment banker might have an agenda with you as far as maximizing his bank's wealth, possibly at your expense. Doesn't that give you cause for concern, Wade?
CABLE: No. On the contrary, I always like to have somebody whom I know is motivated by profit. This way his motivation is the same as our company's. And if we do another offering, which is something we undoubtedly will explore in the future, his company may or may not be part of that offering.
FRED SIMMONS: So, Bennett, you're suggesting that perhaps Wade should hire a firm like Stern Stewart as his financial adviser, one that couldn't

take him public—so this way there couldn't be any conflict of interest?
STEWART: Well, I must confess the thought did flit through my mind, but only for an instant.
CABLE: Gee, Bennett, I didn't realize that's what you were driving at. I think I'll stick with my investment banker.

The Case of Fibreboard

STEWART: Well, let's change the subject. Let me turn now to John Roach, CEO of Fibreboard. What makes John's company especially interesting, as I mentioned earlier, is that the company is dealing with a major asbestos litigation problem. The stock price, as a consequence, is down to $3 a share. There are four million shares outstanding, so the company has a total market equity capitalization of $12 million.

John, I'm just wondering how the board of your company responds to an obviously very challenging situation—one where you have what appears to be a viable operating business on the one side of the balance sheet, with this terrific liability on the other. All of this would seem to increase the threat of legal liability for the board.
ROACH: At Fibreboard the majority of the board has turned over in less than a year. Four out of seven of our current directors are brand-new, including myself. I am the only insider,

and I believe very strongly that all board members should be outsiders unless there are special circumstances—say, heavy ownership by an individual in the company or by a family. Another likely exception is when a company makes a major acquisition. It then may want to have the CEO of the acquired company on the board. But, aside from these special circumstances, I find it difficult to believe that insiders who spend every day dealing with management and management issues could have an independent perspective on things like executive compensation and the hiring or firing of the CEO.

But, in the case of Fibreboard, as I said, four board members are new. The reason I'm there now is that the prior board finally pulled the plug on the prior CEO. That was an action brought about rather dramatically by some angry shareholders. They were able to put one person on the board. And I have put two new representatives on the board, both CEOs of other firms. Like John Teets, I think the value of having other CEOs on the board is enormous. They understand the issues, they're rarely shy individuals, and they understand the pressures the company is facing. And in this case we needed that kind of experience.
STEWART: John, you mentioned that there was a group of shareholders who were instrumental in tossing your predecessor out of the company. How did that happen?
ROACH: Most of them were from New York, like you, and were very vocal.
STEWART: That's shocking—and how unlike my fellow New Yorkers!
ROACH: So, it wasn't really through the normal process of governance, it was just by being vocal.
STEWART: How much stock did the group own? Was it a formal group of shareholders?
ROACH: It wasn't a formal group. At least they didn't file anything formal. But their combined holdings were on the order of about 30 percent. They had

a sizable ownership stake, and they forcefully expressed their view that there was a need for change at the top. So they triggered the change. And when they brought me on, I then had to rebuild the board.

A somewhat similar experience occurred at Manville Corp., a company that also had an asbestos exposure problem. When Manville finally came out of its Chapter 11 proceedings in November of 1988, 11 out of the 13 board members were replaced during the next two-year period. In both these situations, there were unusual opportunities to transform boards into effective agents for necessary change.

But, in both of these cases, it was a crisis, the great sense of urgency, that allowed the changes to take place. Short of a crisis, however, it seems to me very difficult to get boards to assume the role of initiators of dramatic change. But, in these two cases, the new boards were not constrained by the old rules, by the old ways of doing things. It was clear the board was there to enact change. In these two cases, both the board and management had a strong common interest in getting out of a difficult situation and doing what was best for the company.

Now, there are cases where what may be best for the shareholders—or, at least certain shareholders—may not be what's best for the long-term value of the company. I firmly believe that the job of management and the board is to increase the total value of the firm, or the value of the enterprise. There is, however, a secondary issue of how you get that value into the hands of the shareholders; and this is one area where conflict can arise between even conscientious managements and shareholders, and between long-term owners and short-term speculators. This conflict I have in mind really comes down to a matter of financing. Whereas shareholders might prefer a large increase in the firm's debt-equity ratio, perhaps

combined with a major share repurchase program, management may want to capitalize the firm more conservatively—perhaps to protect the value of the firm's human and organizational "capital" from the costs of financial trouble. So, the issue of value maximization gets more complicated when you consider the corporate obligations to creditors, employees, and other constituencies.

But, with that qualification, I do believe the boards of public companies can and should be integrally involved in increasing that shareholder value. This is not to say that the board should initiate or implement policy; they should not attempt to manage the company. But they should have a voice in questions of long-term strategy, in matters like major divestitures, acquisitions, and capital expenditure programs.

At the same time, I think top managements, particularly the CEOs and the CFOs, could do a far better job in educating and informing their boards. I wrote an article a couple of years ago arguing that the CFO, the comptroller, and the financing staff should not view themselves as simply bean counters and opportunistic fund-raisers, but rather as strategic architects who help the CEO do his job better. That same process is an opportunity to provide the board with the kind of information that would enable the board to help evaluate strategic direction

and major decisions to allocate corporate resources. In many companies, top management simply does not provide enough information to the board to allow the board to do its job.

STEWART: As we discussed earlier, John Teets's company spun off Greyhound Financial. John, you have a destination resort that doesn't seem to fit in your kind of company. Now, if you were to consider divesting or spinning off this resort, would you expect the board to *initiate* a discussion about such an opportunity to restructure the company? Or is the board's role simply one of responding to management's proposals?

> *At* least once a year management ought to share with the board its long-term view of the company's strategic plan. And there ought to be periodic updates detailing the company's progress in executing the plan. Such meetings should serve to define the corporate goals and performance parameters that Mike Jensen was insisting on yesterday.
>
> *—John Roach*

ROACH: First of all, let me say that we currently have no intention of divesting or spinning off any of our businesses. Our objective is to enhance the strategic value of each of our businesses and, in so doing, maximize the value of the company.

In response to your question, I think the board should feel free to initiate any idea that management is not smart enough to initiate on their own. It's the management's responsibility, but if management's dragging its feet and doesn't bring that idea forward, any board member should feel completely free to do so.

STEWART: Is that what typically goes on, in your experience? Let me give you an example. Suppose management brings to the board's attention a major capital project for approval. At that point, it's almost too late, it seems to me, for the board to understand all of the factors that could affect the economics of that project. So, given the process, the board is almost put in a position of rubber-stamping a decision that management has initiated. So I'm just wondering whether the board *can* really play an effective role.

ROACH: If that's the way the board is run, they don't have an opportunity to add value. But there is another way—one that I recommended when I was a strategy consultant, and one that we now use at Fibreboard. And that is to have the

company review once a year with its full board the long-term strategy of the company and its individual businesses.

Now, that doesn't have to be more than a quick update if it's been done in great depth before. But, at least once a year management ought to share with the board its long-term view of the company's strategic plan. And there ought to be periodic updates detailing the company's progress in executing the plan. Such updates should tell the board what management expects to accomplish during the year, given the state of the economy and the current competitive environment. Such meetings should shape the board's expectations, it should serve to define the corporate goals and performance parameters that Mike Jensen was insisting on yesterday.

And all this has got to be done within a broad strategic context. So, for example, if management is contemplating a major acquisition in consumer products, the acquisition should not come as a surprise to the board. The same holds if management decides it wants to sell a major line of business. The board should be prepared for such decisions, and should be prepared to understand them as part of a larger strategic plan.

Managements often make the mistake of presenting their boards with acquisitions and then asking them for approval—all during the same meeting. I believe very strongly in putting major projects in front of the board well before a decision is required. Boards ought to be given the opportunity to be educated about such decisions. They should be given the chance to consider and discuss such issues without the pressure that comes from an impending vote.

Governing Private Companies

STEWART: Let me turn now to Fred Simmons. Fred, as a general partner of an LBO firm like Freeman Spogli, you have a very strong ownership interest in the companies on whose boards you serve. To a far greater extent than in the case of public companies, you and your fellow partners have the power to shape the board and to make it what you want it to be. So, given this power, do the boards of your companies end up working differently from what you've heard John Teets and John Roach describe?

SIMMONS: It was very interesting for me to listen to Mike Jensen's comments yesterday about corporate governance by LBO firms—I believe "LBO associations" was the term he used for firms like KKR, Forstmann Little, and our own—because the model of governance Jensen sets forth really does a nice job of describing how Freeman Spogli functions as a firm.

I was struck especially by his discussion of the intensity of the due diligence process that takes place when we first consider investing in companies. As Jensen suggests, the process generates a tremendous amount of research and information about questions that corporate managers are supposed to be asking themselves all the time: Are assets being used correctly? Is management focused in the right problem areas in the business? Is the company spending too much or too little on capital expenditures? Are we financing our assets in the best way possible? Are we in the right businesses? Are we dealing with the competition successfully? Such issues are all looked at in great detail initially upon doing the transaction.

Once our investment is made, the role of the board then becomes one of continually monitoring the company's progress. You continually revisit all those kinds of issues to make sure that the original design is being carried out as was originally planned. And you also re-examine the original plan: Is it still the proper course, or do you need to modify the plan in light of new information?

In putting together our LBO deals, we follow the industry standard of projecting cash flows five or six years into the future. Those estimates determine both the price we are willing to pay and the capital structure we will use in funding our investment in the company.

Another critical determinant of the price we pay for companies—indeed, of our willingness to invest at all—is the extent of the management team's willingness to invest in the deal (and you have to keep in mind that, because of the amount of leverage involved, management's investment is very highly charged equity). If management doesn't want to invest, we get very worried. But if they do want to invest we get very excited. That is a real bellwether for us, an important signal of management's confidence in its ability to achieve projected levels of performance.

STEWART: Fred, do you often see sharp conflicts between the board and the management? Or is it better described as a collaborative interface?

SIMMONS: We try, and generally succeed, in keeping things as collaborative as possible. Of course, there are always issues where there's a natural conflict of interest between management and the board—for example, when it comes to management's compensation. But our philosophy as a firm is that when management invests side by side with us in the equity of the company, then those conflicts are minimized; the goals and interests of the investors and managers are pretty well aligned.

STEWART: How do you combine management ownership with the issue of setting goals and rewarding performance in the company? And what role does the board play in the goal-setting process?

SIMMONS: As majority owners, we clearly call the shots and set the goals in our companies. But before describing our governance process, let me try to explain our investment philosophy. First of all, we try to buy premium companies, well-run companies. We're not in the business of breaking up conglomerates that have problems coordinating all their businesses, nor are we in the business of engineering turnarounds. Our aim is to buy premium companies and then put a lot of capital into them and make them even better.

In the process of investing, we initiate a dialogue with management in which we attempt to come up with a mutually agreeable five-year plan. And, as I mentioned, in our average deal, management typically is asked to buy 5 to 10 percent of the equity of the company up front. They typically buy half of it for cash and half on a full recourse loan. And the company lends them the money at the prime rate of interest, payable quarterly.

So the management has highly charged equity. If the company is leveraged, say, 3 to 1, and management borrows to fund half its equity purchase, then management has highly leveraged equity. And this equity is also supplemented by performance options that vest over a five-year period. So we feel that management is in there with us with both feet. They're committed to making good on their projections.

STEWART: But because the projected payoffs are highly illiquid—the payoff on their options is at least five years down the road—it also forces management to take a somewhat longer view of the firm's performance. It's forces them to consider longer-run investment as well as near-term efficiency.

SIMMONS: That's right. If the company were sold in less than five years at a premium, the performance options might well vest in part or in full.

STEWART: And this effect is actually quite different from that of the standard stock options given to the managements of most public companies. In most of our public companies, management has an incentive to exercise their options and sell the stock as soon as the options have significant trading value. And this, needless to say, only reinforces whatever pressures management may feel to increase short-run value at the expense of the long term.

Fred, do you ever consider having just regular options as part of your compensation program?

SIMMONS: No, I don't see any purpose to having straight options. The way they're often granted by public companies causes them to be much less efficient than options tied to performance. Let's face it, management can increase earnings, and thus the value of vested options, on a short-term basis. But this may well be to the detriment of medium- or longer-term shareholder value.

ROACH: As long as we're on the subject, let me say a word on behalf of stock options. We have just adopted an unusal option program for senior management. As I mentioned earlier, our longer-term mission at Fibreboard is to deal effectively with our asbestos litigation problem. But if we can find a solution to the problem, and increase the profitability of our basic operations at the same time, then there's a tremendous potential upside. Our stock price, as mentioned before, is down to $3.

In order to avoid diluting shareholder value, and yet provide manage-

ment strong incentives at the same time, we have decided to set up our option plan so that the prices at which the options can be exercised are considerably higher than today's price of $3. Specifically, one third of management's options will be exercisable if the price hits $10, a second third if the price hits $15, and the final third if the price hits $20. So, our option program will not really pay off unless until our shareholders experience a significant—for example, a five-fold—increase in their wealth. I think that's a good plan, given our current situation. Although I agree that stock options may be abused by some public companies, this is a good use of stock options.

SIMMONS: I agree, John. Although we have not used escalating option prices, that arrangement would seem to create much the same effect as options tied to medium-term or longer-term performance.

The Case of the Blackstone Group

STEWART: Let me ask Jim Birle, who comes from a similar organization, The Blackstone Group, to comment on his views of the governance process. Jim, as both a general partner of The Blackstone Group and co-chairman and CEO of the Collins & Aikman Group of Companies (or what used to be called the Wickes Companies), what do you view as the principal function of the board of directors?

BIRLE: I'm a great believer in the principle that accountability is what makes delegated authority legitimate. In the case of LBO boards, the board delegates to the management of the company the responsibility for managing the enterprise. The board's job is to set the goals for the company and then keep track of whether those goals are being met. If they are not, then it is the board's responsibility to intervene and get things right.

One of the differences between our LBO boards and those of public companies is that if one of our companies fails to meet goals, the consequences to the board members are very significant. We are in the business of investing money on behalf of insurance companies and pension funds. The contractual duration of our fund is 10 years, which means there is a specified time frame within which we have to provide our investors with a competitive return on their invested capital. If we fail to provide adequate returns within the time frame, then we are going to have a hard time raising capital to fund our next set of investments.

And the fact that time is really working against us in terms of providing returns creates a tension between management and the board. The pressure to ensure that the goals are being met is just far greater than that which exists in most public companies. At the same time, this sense of urgency does not prevent us from setting and pursuing long-range goals and encouraging long-term thinking. We spend considerable time and effort analyzing how to strategically reposition some of the Collins & Aikman businesses and we undertake major reinvestment programs— programs that, in some cases, will not pay off for several years. Our goal is maximizing shareholder value, and you can't command a high price for a business if all you've been doing is liquidating its assets and failing to invest in its future earning power.

But to return to my original point, if the management of one of our companies fails to meet its goals, there's a degree of tension at our board meetings that I think is very healthy—and quite different from some of my prior experiences with public companies. Unlike LBO groups, public companies have the staying power that may permit them to accommodate a standard of performance that is significantly below what would be considered satisfactory by The Blackstone Group or other similar merchant bankers.

STEWART: Jim, can you tell us a little about your role as CEO of the Collins & Aikman Companies, and what you have done to turn things around there?

BIRLE: In the case of Wickes, I am in the unique position of being co-chairman of a board in which the partners are a combination of Blackstone General Partners and Wasserstein Perella General Partners, all of which are major stockholders and thus directly affected by the performance of the company. I'm CEO of the Holdings Company to which the individual operating units report.

When we acquired Wickes in December of 1988, it was an overleveraged and underperforming conglomerate comprised of a diverse group of retail, distribution, and manufacturing components. We immediately set up a holding company structure and reassigned to operating managers the functions necessary for them to operate these businesses as self-standing enterprises. Through the divestiture of 25 units, we paid down $1.5 billion in debt during the first two years of ownership. At the same time we also brought in stronger operating executives who put in place new investment and growth strategies for the strongest units. Having a knowledgeable and involved board made it possible to effect tremendous changes in a troubled company in a short period of time.

STEWART: What kind of periodic performance measures do you use in evaluating operating management's performance?

BIRLE: We have much a tighter performance measurement system, by necessity, than most public companies I'm familiar with. In collaboration with management, the board sets both

> *O*ne critical determinant of the price we pay for companies— indeed, of our willingness to invest at all—is the extent of the management team's willingness to invest in the deal. If management doesn't want to invest, we get very worried. But if they do want to invest we get very excited. That is a real bellwether for us, an important signal of management's confidence in its ability to achieve projected levels of performance.
>
> *—Fred Simmons*

yearly targets as well as longer-term growth goals.

STEWART: What is the nature of the goals?

BIRLE: There are basically two: growth in operating income and return on capital employed. Both of these measures are formulated in terms of cash flow rather than earnings and both are used in evaluating long-term as well as short-term performance. Since management are major equity holders in the company, we are confident that they are constantly attempting to balance short-term versus long-term goals in creating value.

STEWART: Does the board set the goals, or does it instead just ratify goals that have been set by the management in a negotiation throughout the company?

BIRLE: I would say it's more of a negotiation. But, unlike the boards of many public companies, our board members come to the table already knowing a great deal about the operations and the expected behavior of the businesses in various economic and competitive situations. This knowledge comes from the extensive due diligence process we have conducted just prior to the acquisition. So we are able to determine when management has really gotten off the track far more quickly and confidently than most public company directors.

Although we do allow the CEOs to present their own budgets to be ratified by us, there has already been a vigorous dialogue between the CEO and the board when the CEO's plan is presented for ratification. We try and work together with operating management in framing the boundary conditions for performance. For example, what should we expect if the economy turns down? And if the CEO and his management team exceed their targeted goal, they're handsomely rewarded.

STEWART: Is there a cap on the bonus?

BIRLE: For the top guys, yes, there's generally a cap on annual awards. It's roughly twice their base salary. But if they miss on the downside, then their bonus will be zero. So it's very much a pay-for-performance system. Our system is designed such that the people who really perform can make themselves a lot of money in the short term. And the ones who don't perform are really made to feel the pain of failure. To supplement these short-term programs, we put in place long-term capital

accumulation programs where clearly superior performance really translates into significant wealth accumulation.

Employee Ownership and the Case of SAIC

STEWART: Let me just finish my tour of duty here by asking Bill Roper to describe what is probably the unique ownership structure of his company. It may even have considerable value as a model for the future.

ROPER: I am the CFO of a company called Science Applications International Corporation, or SAIC for short. The company was founded in 1969 by four scientists who wanted to do some interesting work with the government. One of their aims was to generate enough revenues to be able to pay themselves a reasonable salary and live in La Jolla, California.

We just completed a year in which our revenues were about $1.3 billion. We

have about 14,000 employees. We've grown at an average compound rate in the high teens; and although the rate of growth is slowing a little bit, it still is in double digits. The company has had revenue and earnings increases in every year of its existence. We are primarily a government contractor; we do almost two thirds of our work for the government.

The company was founded as an employee-owned company, and it has

> **W**e are in the business of investing money on behalf of insurance companies and pension funds. The contractual duration of our fund is 10 years, which means there is a specified time frame within which we have to provide our investors with a competitive return on their invested capital. And the fact that time is really working against us creates a tension between management and the board. The pressure to ensure that the goals are being met is just far greater than that which exists in most public companies.
>
> —James Birle

remained that way since 1969. Some 10,000 of the 14,000 employees directly own stock in the company. By that, I mean they have either written a check or have had money withheld from their paychecks to purchase stock or exercise options. Virtually all full-time employees own stock through our retirement programs as well.

STEWART: What price do the employees pay for the stock? As a private company, SAIC doesn't have a stock price. So is the purchase price based on some kind of periodic appraisal?

ROPER: The shares are sold for a price based on a formula. There's a quarterly setting of value of the company that is determined by a formula that relates to earnings, book value, and market comparables.

I think an important component of our company has been from the beginning that most employees, and every member of the management team from middle management on up, make a significant financial commitment to own stock in the company. Our stock programs—which, again, consist of options, direct purchases, and voluntary contributions to retirement programs—encourage key managers and employees toward greater ownership as they rise through the organization. The higher paid you are, and the faster that you move through the orga-

nization, the more the system forces you to forgo current cash for future earnings from your ownership.

STEWART: Are you saying that as people move up through the company they're *obligated* to buy stock?

ROPER: Not obligated technically, but the system drives you to do that. For example, we have a bonus system that covers about 40% of all employees. Bonuses are typically paid out half in stock and half in cash. The stock is vested immediately, so it's taxable. So if you get 50 percent of your bonus in cash and 50 percent of it in stock, you don't have a lot of cash left over after you pay the tax liability.

But it's a great wealth accumulator. I wish I had brought a chart showing the rise of our stock value; it's the most beautiful parabolic curve you've ever seen. Our stock has probably grown about 20 percent a year compounded over 20 years.

STEWART: So the higher you go in the organization, the more stock you're *allowed* to buy?

ROPER: That's right. It's not an obligation, it's a privilege. But it would be very unusual to have any senior management members who didn't have a substantial ownership stake in our firm.

STEWART: But isn't this somewhat of a Ponzi scheme—something that works as long as it works?

ROPER: We joke a little bit about that around the shop. The system recycles a lot of money. When people leave the company and the company repurchases their stock, it recycles a lot of money. So, if there is a sharp downturn, then there will have been a transfer of value from the people still in the system to those who have left. But, as long as the company remains profitable and growing, it pays for people to forgo current cash for future earnings, and the system works. It's all driven on the fact that the company is profitable and growing.

STEWART: To what extent do you think the company's success is due to employee ownership—or is the combination of ownership structure and success just a coincidence?

ROPER: It's very easy to see that widespread employee ownership and significant senior management ownership of the company drive an awful lot of things that we do. It is clearly responsible for a good amount of the success of the company.

STEWART: Can you give us an example where people inside the company sit down and have an informal, "mini-shareholder" meeting to make an important decision? By the way, is that an accurate description of the process?

ROPER: That's essentially correct. The management philosophy is very decentralized; it is slightly to the right of anarchy. Many meetings are very contentious. People at all levels feel free to tell you what they think about how you are spending *their money!* Perhaps the most forceful objection to a proposed management

decision is the statement, "Well, as a major shareholder, I disagree with your proposal to spend my money this way."

So it's an interesting environment. There's an awful lot of challenge and an awful lot of accountability. It ranges from issues as trivial as how much you spend on your office furniture to major expenditures and acquisitions.

MICHAEL JENSEN: Bill, let me ask a question about your plan. Take a middle manager who's been in the company for, say, 10 years. What kind of money would he or she have invested in the stock, and what would the value of that stock be worth today?

ROPER: Well, let me change your question a little, and let's take the case of a hypothetical senior scientist in our company—because scientists, along with engineers and computer programmers, are really the guts of our company. We don't have a lot of management types.

Let's say a typical scientist has been with the company for 15 years, and is making a base salary of $80,000 along with a cash bonus of $10,000. Over the years, that person has likely put into the company in one form or another—exercising options, payroll deductions, or just direct cash purchases, as well as some retirement contributions—that person is probably out of pocket about $100,000. And the stock purchased by that cash is today probably worth half a million. That seems to me to be a representative case at our firm.

STEWART: Are there any openings at your company?

Well, Bill, your company seems to function as a largely self-regulating, self-governing company. In your case, the role of the board of directors has got to be much less important—because the internal control mechanism is literally woven into the share ownership of the key people throughout the company. Would you agree with that statement, especially in view of the other public companies you've been associated with?

> *T*he management philosophy [of SAIC] is very decentralized; it is slightly to the right of anarchy. Many meetings are very contentious. People at all levels feel free to tell you what they think about how you are spending their money! *Perhaps the most forceful objection to a proposed management decision is the statement, "Well, as a major shareholder, I disagree with your proposal to spend my money this way."*
>
> —*William Roper*

ROPER: That's clearly the case. I think that's a very wise observation. In thinking about the subject of this panel, and especially Mike Jensen's comments yesterday, it became clear to me that our board does not really fit the model Jensen was holding out for public companies. We have a large board. It's composed of 23 members, six of whom are insiders. They meet quarterly for a few hours. I think it's virtually impossible on a quarterly basis to communicate a lot of detailed information about a very complex company. Now, there are other forums where the board members learn about the company. There's a lot of informal contact with them. But our board clearly does not exercise the kind of oversight that, say, the principals of LBOs or venture capital firms do. And yet we have a company that for 23 years running has been phenomenally successful.

So there seem to be two possible answers here: Either we were just lucky for 23 years in a row, or you guys are all full of hot air and we need to have more unwieldy boards packed with insiders. More seriously, I think we are successful largely because of the internal mechanisms and the management ownership structure that the company has maintained throughout its existence. This makes the board's job fairly easy.

STEWART: Bill, I was struck by the similarity of your company to one that I have some familiarity with, Arthur Andersen. I would also describe that company as a self-governing, self-regulating organization. There are 2500 key partners who own the company. The company is extremely successful; it has been quite profitable even in the face of a shrinking market for public accounting services. It's also extremely entrepreneurial. For example, they built the immensely successful Andersen Consulting from nothing. And they're now a competitor of yours.

ROPER: Yes, and I wish they weren't.

STEWART: And that company too is controlled chaos. In the early 1980s, we made a presentation to a group of top partners in the company; and they were extremely enthusiastic about the possibility of adopting our corporate finance program throughout the organization. So I said to one of the top partners, "We have to find a way to get others in Arthur Andersen to hear this message; so why don't you just send out an edict throughout the organization?"

And the partner said to me, "Bennett, you don't understand the way it works around here. We have offices throughout the world, and they are each run by the partners in charge of those offices. There's nothing that comes from the top down. It's kind of a neural network in which proposals within the organization are transmitted from the outlying areas to the center. And when they reach the center, there are ad hoc committees and structures put in place to evaluate them."

What's also interesting about Arthur Andersen—and most of the other accounting firms, too—is that without the pressure of external capital markets, the public accounting industry has gone through a major restructuring and rationalization over the past 10 years. It is no longer the Big 8, it's now the Big 6. And maybe it will be the big five at some point. So this partnership model can work in mature, no-growth industries as well as growth industries like Bill's.

So, Bill, perhaps we can view SAIC as pointing the way towards a new kind of organization—one that reduces the importance of the board in the monitoring process and replaces it with widespread ownership.

JENSEN: Well, Bennett, I'm not sure how far you can extend the application of this model. Both of these companies, Arthur Andersen and SAIC, seem to me classic examples of companies that can't be run any other way than by diffusing ownership throughout the company. In the case of the typical law firm or professional consulting organization, you can't have a complicated control mechanism in which decision initiatives are bucked up a hierarchy—because by the time they get there, the chance to exploit the opportunity has already passed. The specific knowledge that is required for many impor-

tant corporate decisions often lies deep in the organization in small teams. The decisions often have to be made there, and they have to be made quickly.

So, if you tried to take either of these companies and turn them into public companies, it just wouldn't work. You could try and substitute the complicated control mechanisms used by public companies, but they wouldn't work very well in that kind of situation. The substitute for those complicated mechanisms is, as Bennett suggested, to push the equity ownership or partnership shares down and throughout the organization. (Besides the two companies you've mentioned, Gore Associates is another good example of this employee ownership model; and it's an industrial company rather than a consulting operation.)

And let me explain why I asked Bill how much money the typical manager has at stake. If people have a significant investment in the firm, you can be much more comfortable turning them loose to make their own decisions because they are going to be motivated not only by their own financial interests, but by their colleagues' financial interests as well. And it's not just money. It's the fact that they've got the right orientation; they have got the interest of the organization at heart. This is really the only way you can run people-intensive as opposed to capital-intensive organizations.

STEWART: Bill, do you think the kind of employee ownership structure that you've put in place would work for, say, a diversified consumer products company?
ROPER: It's really hard to say. Our main asset is our people. While we do make some products, our principal business is technological consulting, systems development and integration, and other things like that. For this reason, our main asset is the brains and experience of our people. Our company is organized around, and driven by, the need to find and retain good people—getting them on board, motivating them, and rewarding them.
JENSEN: I don't know your company, but I would also predict that this kind of employee ownership works best when you have a technology that's not very capital intensive.
ROPER: That's correct. Over the years, we have had lots of debates about going into capital-intensive businesses. But there's only so much capital that you can aggregate among the body of people that work for you. And so it does work better for those businesses that don't require a lot of capital.
JENSEN: I'm not talking about just your ability to raise large amounts of capital. I'm thinking more about what happens to management incentives after you succeed in raising the capital. If you have a lot of capital assets lying around, partnerships and organizations like yours

with lots of owners run into big problems. Companies with highly decentralized ownership structures will likely start to have major internal conflicts when making decisions about what to do with large capital assets. When do you sell such assets, if ever, and distribute their value to partners? Even owning buildings causes partnerships big problems over issues like this. Having lots of owners with different time horizons makes the decision-making a lot harder.

For this reason, partnerships and 100% employee ownership are well suited for companies that don't invest in major capital assets, but that have a sort of constant flow of capital in and out of the business.

Shareholder Activism and Corporate Accountability

STEWART: Let me ask our representatives of public companies whether they are feeling more pressure to be accountable to their shareholders as a result of some of the increasing shareholder activism that is taking place? John, what about The Dial Corp?
TEETS: The only instance of shareholder pressure I can think of has come from Boone Pickens's group—I think they call themselves the United Shareholders Association. My sense is that Boone got burned pretty badly by the Unocal decision; and after he ran with his tail between his legs, he decided to

start this shareholder voting project. So, because Boone has decided he doesn't like poison pills, we now have a vote every year on whether or not to rescind our poison pill. And that's okay. Members of Boone's group own a small amount of our stock, and they are entitled to propose measures like this and to vote on them. That's the way the system works.

But we have not had any pressure from any of the major funds that own our stock. We have excellent relationships with all of them, and we invite them every year to meet our management team. They are allowed to voice their concerns, and we attempt to respond to them as best we can.

STEWART: But my sense is that the role of most institutional investors is really to try to figure out how much the company is worth and not to make recommendations for change. We have this peculiar state of affairs in this country where institutional investors are looked upon as short-term investors on the one hand, and yet are expected to behave like owners. Or, at least, when they behave more like speculators than owners, people profess to be disappointed by their "short termism."

So my question is the following: How do we turn investors—people who are inclined to short the stock if the company does poorly—into owners interested in participating in the effort to maximize long-run value? It seems to me that our current system does not allow, much less encourage, institutional investors to become owners in that classical sense. For one thing, they don't have board representation.

So, John, would you encourage institutional investors to nominate and elect a minority of independent directors to your board? This way they might be more inclined to become long-term holders.

TEETS: Any shareholder has the right to nominate a director and vote for him or her. So it's not whether I agree or disagree, that's the way the system is set up.

Would I want to have an institutional investor on my board? Our board is picked by consensus, and I doubt very much that any of the ten outside board members would even consider having someone who is in the business of managing funds sit on our board and tell us how we are supposed to run the business to increase shareholder wealth. But, then again, I can't really speak for my board on this. We've never had the issue on the agenda and we've never discussed it.

STEWART: John, you took a proactive role in restructuring your company several years ago. Do you feel that boards are going to become much more active in the future in terms of initiating restructurings to increase shareholder value? For example, do you think they'll be more aggressive in recommending the increased use of leverage for underleveraged companies? I personally think that boards today are much less likely to view a triple-A rating as an unambiguous sign of corporate success. What are your views in terms of the initiatives that corporate boards will most likely be taking in the future?

TEETS: I can't speak for other boards. But our board often challenges our direction. We go into great detail on both the targeted and the realized return on assets of each of our subsidiaries. Our board members also participate in regular on-site visits in which they meet and question the managers that run those businesses.

In fact, I am skeptical about the idea that boards are becoming *more* challenging today. I think they have always been challenging. The average tenure of a CEO is about six years in the United States. CEOs are fired by their boards all the time. It's not like being a tenured professor in a university—a system that guarantees a job for life. (Let me also say that I think the colleges and universities in the United States are among the most poorly run group of organizations in the country, particularly in how they nominate their board and how they function. It's almost impossible to function within their own system.)

I think some boards are becoming more proactive today. There are clearly companies that have not performed well, and where boards have failed to act. And we all know which

companies they are; they are in the newspaper every day. At the same time, of course, we never read about the vast majority of companies in which the boards do a good job.

STEWART: John, what is it that makes a board function well and what makes a board function poorly? What are the key ingredients for success in creating a board that will add value?

TEETS: Well, I think it's important for the CEO to make the best use of the board. He should regularly seek the counsel of the board and listen to their suggestions. Board members have exceptional talent and experience, and the CEO ought to make the best possible use of them. They really do bring different kinds of expertise to the table. They see things I don't see, and I think it's important to have advisers like that.

So I think it's up to the CEO to draw out the expertise of the board. At the same time, though, the board members are the bosses. They have the power to hire and fire top management. If the board does not exercise this power when the company is doing poorly, then there can be a problem. As our professor friend suggested yesterday, this is a very complex issue because each company and board operates differently. Let me also say I just don't think consultants and college professors—that is,

But there are a couple of things running through my mind that maybe you can help me understand. I'm sure there are many CEOs who behave exactly the way you say they do; they make a conscientious effort to use their boards properly and to do the right thing by their shareholders. But even in these cases, there's a potential problem. CEOs get older, they may tend to get set in their ways, but meanwhile the world moves on. We

problem we face in these organizations is how to put in place a control mechanism that creates a healthy tension between management and the board—one that ensures that when management does begin to go off-course, the correction happens sooner rather than later.

Let me tell you about a conversation I had when returning from a board meeting with a fellow member on an airplane. There had been some frank discussion during the meeting, some disagreements with the CEO. This board member is also a very senior executive on the board of his own company, and he was one of those who voiced sharp disagreement with the CEO during our meeting. And this board member explained to me that such frank discussion and disagreements would never happen on his own board. His own CEO would simply take the person aside who asked the hard questions, and then make it very clear that either he was going to get on the same track, or one of them was going to leave. And it was also clear which one of them was going to leave.

We've all seen boards operate this way, John. So what can be done about it?

TEETS: Let me remind you that, although the board can fire the CEO, the CEO cannot fire a board member—or not at least without the approval of the other board members.

JENSEN: But how will you make this organization work so that the CEO will get a message he doesn't want to hear? Because that's when it counts. It's not when the CEO understands that the world is changing and that the corporation has to change with it. It's the opposite situation; the one when the company is off on the wrong track, and the CEO wants to persist with the old strategy. That is precisely when the unpleasantness has to occur, and that is where our current system breaks down. Under the current governance system,

> *With the threat of raiders largely gone, many companies now seem to be looking seriously for new models of corporate governance. In many cases, they are looking for ways of bringing about voluntarily some of the productive changes that were forced upon them during the '80s. One solution is to make the managers and the employees in the company into significant owners. By adopting this self-governing, self-regulating model of governance, we wouldn't have to rely on the capital markets or on the board to bring about change.*
> *—Bennett Stewart*

people who are not active in running businesses themselves—are likely to make good board members. They are not fighting in the war, and they thus have a tendency to be less proactive in many cases than people who are out there facing the competition every day.

JENSEN: John, can I push you a little on that?

TEETS: You're *asking* me?

JENSEN: It's only rhetorical.

STEWART: He's gonna get back at you, John.

JENSEN: By the way, John, I completely agree with your comments about the governance of universities and the way they function—and also about the value of the university tenure system. In fact, I should tell you that I have resigned my tenure at both of the institutions that have granted it to me by submitting unconditional letters of resignation.

all see the world through our own eyes, and it's a very natural and understandable human tendency for people to fail to see the need for radical change.

Now, the problem that troubles me arises when the CEO or the management team begins to get off track—and organizations do this all the time. If the burden is on the CEO and top management to seek out the flagellation from others that will force them to face up to the truth, then we have a serious problem with our system. That is just not going to happen—or not until the deterioration has gotten so bad that it's almost too late to save the organization. (This, incidentally, is my feeling about what has happened recently at General Motors—and maybe even IBM, too, although the organizational changes they just made give me hope for them.) The

the company has to confront a crisis before the board will intervene. GM had to lose several billion dollars in a single year before management was forced to recognize the need for radical change. And Digital Equipment had to lose about 80% of its market value before its CEO was finally removed by the board.

TEETS: I've sat on a number of boards. And although some disagreements are brought up at board meetings, I generally think it's better practice to take up major issues privately with the CEO first. Then, if they come out at the board meeting later, some of the defensiveness of the CEO will have been removed.

But let me say that I don't have the answer to the problem you're talking about. This issue of the board and the CEO is very complex. Obviously, some boards work and some don't. You can see well-publicized cases in the *Wall Street Journal* where boards are not working. On the other hand, you see many cases where they're working very well. I would also insist that there are a lot more CEOs who are canned than we know about because they generally resign. It looks better that way.

JENSEN: But the research on total CEO turnover suggests that, even when companies perform poorly, the likelihood of a CEO being fired is less than one in ten. And these numbers attempt to include all those cases where the CEO seems to resign. In fact, a couple of years ago former SEC Commissioner Joseph Grundfest used to say that it was more likely for a Congressman to be indicted for cheating than for a CEO to be fired by a board. But, with the recent cases at GM and DEC, things seem to be changing somewhat.

Information and Accountability

BIRLE: Michael, my opinion is that the current governance system of public companies is based on two important premises—adequate information and accountability—neither of which is likely to hold for the boards of many public companies. If the board is not properly informed, they are really operating in the dark. If they don't understand there is a problem in the first place, then they are not going to be able to take the appropriate action with the CEO.

One of the advantages that Fred Simmons and I have, as controlling owners of private companies, is that we do the due diligence on the companies we buy. We understand the quality of management, the corporate strategy, the operational plan, the competitive environment, the balance sheet issues—we have a good working knowledge of all those factors that differentiate between success and failure. And then after we make our investment, performance factors are very closely monitored by the board as we go forward.

In public companies, by contrast, board members are brought in with little, if any, knowledge of the company. It's really a ceremonial invitation. And, as I said, if that board member does not really understand what is going on inside the company, his ability to add value is limited. So I think it's up to the CEO to make sure that he gives the board members opportunities to add value at both the committee and full board levels.

As John Roach suggested earlier, issues should be presented to the committees as possible steps under consideration, not as final decisions to be ratified. And as the board becomes more informed about what's going on at the committee level, the discussion at the general board meetings becomes much more constructive and proactive. Armed with greater knowledge, board members will not be as reluctant to ask penetrating questions. Asking such questions may in turn stimulate a lot of dialogue in the full board meeting. And, as a consequence, even more information comes to light, and the board can then begin to do its job of holding management to something like accountability. As a party to the decisions, the board members are also likely to feel a greater sense of responsibility to shareholders about the outcome of corporate decisions.

So, again, in my way of looking at it, it's just really a combination of information and accountability. I think you have to build that accountability within your board. It's not something that happens automatically.

STEWART: Besides information and accountability, couldn't financial incentives also serve as an important contributor to board effectiveness? Incentives are likely to make the board work harder to get the necessary information from management; and, once having the information, then to act on it.

Bob Kidder, the CEO of Duracell, said something very similar to your point, Jim. He said that just the process of going through the LBO gave him and his management team a great deal of new insight into their business; it completely changed how they ran the company after the LBO. There were also tighter financial controls put on management; but he also stressed the importance of financial incentives, the carrot as well as the stick, in motivating improvements in performance.

When I was later working with a very large, extremely diversified company, I suggested that they go through a kind of "practice" LBO in order to discover where the value was coming from in their own businesses, and how things might be improved. I even suggested that management put together a mock prospectus saying that a tender offer had been made for the company, and that each one of the units of the company would be challenged to come up with its own plan to maximize value under the new corporate structure.

Initially, top management was extremely enthusiastic about the whole idea. But then the general counsel of the company stepped in and killed the idea. This was several years ago, before the deal market fell apart; and uncovering break-up values was likely getting too close to reality.

There has, however, been one important benefit from the eclipse of the junk bond and takeover markets. With the threat of raiders largely gone, many companies now seem to be looking seriously for new models of corporate governance. In many cases, they are looking for ways of bringing about voluntarily some of the productive changes that were forced upon them during the '80s.

ROACH: Bennett, I'm not so sure the issue is governance. I think there are two structural problems that don't have ready-made solutions. I think the majority of companies are run by CEOs who are genuinely interested in their shareholders and clearly want the board to play the role of active counselors. They solicit board members who are very talented and directed individuals.

But what if you have a company where the CEO is neglecting shareholders and doesn't really want counsel from his board? He's perfectly happy flying around in his Gulfstream, and the directors are perfectly happy collecting their directors' fees, and not getting involved in conflicts. The issue then becomes: Who is going to intervene on behalf of the shareholders to correct such a situation?

The other problem I don't have a solution for has to do with the time horizon of shareholders. Many managements are skeptical about the ability or willingness of shareholders to give them credit for their long-term investment strategies. Now, if management were confident they had a set of classical owners interested in maximizing the long-term value of the firm, then they might be much more enthusiastic about entering into a more collaborative relationship with institutional investors. But what happens if most of your shareholders are speculators? Do you man-

age the company to maximimize the next quarter's EPS, or do look to strengthen the company's competitive position for the long haul? I don't see any obvious way out of this dilemma.

STEWART: Well, one solution, John, is to make the managers and the employees in the company into significant owners. By adopting such a self-governing, self-regulating model of governance, we wouldn't have to rely on the capital markets or on the board as forces for bringing about change.

For example, in the case of CSX, some 160 of the company's top managers came together as a group to purchase a large number of shares. The typical person invested $35,000 to buy stock leveraged 20 to 1. This meant that a typical CSX manager virtually overnight became the owner of $700,000 worth of stock. To avoid diluting the public stockholders, moreover, the exercise price was indexed to the company's borrowing rate. Since this plan was put in place in 1990, the stock's gone up 50 percent. The other perceptible consequence is that you have to look both ways before you cross the railroad tracks because they only run express trains now.

The Search for
More Permanent Owners

JENSEN: I would like to go back to John Roach's comment about the effect of speculators' stock holdings on management's investment decision-making. If John had raised this issue ten years ago, I would have said, "You don't understand financial economics. Short-term prices reflect long-term values." But I think that some financial economists are now coming to understand that the point you're making may be an important one.

Michael Porter, for example, is now arguing in his Council on Competitiveness project that there's a good chance that we have gotten the wrong corpo-

rate ownership and governance system in the United States. Another Harvard colleague of mine, Amar Bhide, has partly convinced me that we as a nation have put too much emphasis as a matter of public policy on having highly liquid securities market with lots of disclosure and constraints on insider trading. This emphasis on liquidity and disclosure requirements has combined with a whole set of laws enacted since the Great Depression to make it very costly for either individuals or institutions to both hold large amounts of stock in single companies and to become involved in the strategic direction of the firm.

Such legislation and public policy have led to a progressive widening of the rift between ownership and control over the past 50 years—a period, incidentally, in which CEOs' percentage ownership of their companies' stock fell by a factor of 10. This separation of ownership from control has in turn created enormous information and agency costs for investors, who have basically been shut out of the governance process. With imperfect information, and little ability to intervene and change the corporate direction if things go wrong, our institutional investors have been forced to keep management on a short tether, selling shares when earnings turn down.

And this of course creates a problem for management: How can management really make long-term value-maximizing decisions when all they've got is a bunch of transitory shareholders that the law prevents them from communicating effectively with?

By contrast, the Japanese and the Germans have legal and regulatory structure systems that encourage strong relationships and information-sharing among management, the company's major banks (which often hold large equity stakes in the companies they lend to), and other major shareholders. It's difficult for management to build trust and informal agreements with a constantly churning group of outside investors who really don't know (or care) very much about what's going on inside the company.

At the same time, there are institutions that have said to me, "Look, we know we're making long-term investments, but we have no way to talk to management or to enter into a contract, and we're certainly not getting an adequate return for placing long-term money." So this is a real problem. It lies at the heart of the problems that show up with large organizations like General Motors where our governance system seems to be failing us.

As I have also argued, the LBO association model that firms like KKR and Forstmann Little have borrowed from the venture capital industry—one in which a principal equity investor controls the board and represents the interests of the major debtholders as well—is at bottom an attempt to deal with these information and agency problems that now bedevil our public companies. As another example, institutional investors delegate to the Blackstone Group, to people like Jim Birle, the job of being their representative, their active investor. Warren Buffett does something quite similar through the vehicle of Berkshire Hathaway (of which he is the 45% owner). And so does Lazard Freres' Corporate Partners.

So, given the demonstrated effectiveness of these kinds of investors, it may be time for major changes in our legal system and in the structure of regulations of our capital markets. Let me also say, however, that the proposed changes to the current system being put forward by Porter and others are not ones that most CEOs are likely to welcome. They call for larger stakes and greater involvement by investors in return for less emphasis on diversification and liquidity.

LEE: Mike, I think our system may already be evolving somewhat in this direction, even under the current legal and regulatory structure. In the past few years, I have seen a pronounced change in the way institutional investors are exerting their influence over corporate management. Caesars World is a publicly held company. Management does not have a major stake collectively; it's only a 4% position in the company. We also have about 75% institutional ownership.

Five years ago, when financial engineering and leveraged restructuring was reaching its peak of activity, we found out that the time horizons of our institutional owners were very, very short. In one 10-day period, we discovered that our stock had moved almost entirely into the hands of the arbitrage community, whose time horizon was between 15 and 20 seconds. That was a real learning experience for us. As I mentioned earlier, we managed to exit from that predicament only by restructuring the company and making a healthy offer to let the arbitrageurs sell their shares. All this happened 21 days before the market crash. And, although our shareholders ended up very happy with the consequences, we took on considerable leverage in order to deliver that value to shareholders.

We now are back up to 75% institutional ownership, but we have noticed a profound change in their behavior. We now appear to have a solid base of fairly long-term institutional investors. They spend the time to come out and talk with us at length about the long-term strategy of the company. And a number of them seem to understand it fairly well and to have done a lot of homework. We were pleasantly surprised at the amount of time they spend studying us. They often have contrary ideas on what we should be doing in order to maximize value; so we have nice, lively discussions. These institutions, I should also point out, are not for

the most part the ones you read about in the newspapers, the ones who have the strong vocal positions on the top 25 corporations in the country.

So our institutional investors are proving to be a very constructive force. My only objection is that, despite their lip service to saying management should have larger shareholdings, several of them have refused to vote for authorization for issuing more stock. So it's not clear to me the how theory and practice of maximizing shareholder value are going to come together—at least on this issue. But I do really detect a much deeper involvement and sense of purpose among institutional shareholders than I did five and ten years ago. It's been a major change.

TEETS: We have had a very similar experience with our institutional investors. For example, representatives of the Delaware Fund, which own almost 10% of our stock, come out to visit us regularly. They've held the stock now for eight years. They've been long-term holders. Fidelity is another. In fact, I could list ten institutional shareholders who have held our stock for a long time, who regularly come out to confer with us, and whom we also visit on a regular basis.

We are very much open to having such investors. They can talk to whomever they want in the company, we open our books to them. They spend time with us, and we have an excellent relationship with all of our institutional shareholders. They have made a lot of money from investing in our stock, and we have made believers out of them. So, by demonstrating good performance and an openness to your institutional investors, I think it's possible—and indeed quite valuable—to build strong relationships between management and investors.

STEWART: Well, let me end our discussion on that positive note, and add my own wish that such a trend continues. Thank you all for participating.

THE ACTIVE BOARD OF DIRECTORS AND ITS EFFECT ON THE PERFORMANCE OF THE LARGE PUBLICLY TRADED CORPORATION

by Paul W. MacAvoy, Yale University, and Ira M. Millstein, Weil, Gotshal & Manges*

P ursuant to state law, the board of directors is charged with managing the affairs of the corporation[1] in the best interests of the shareholder. In practice, boards have for decades delegated to managers the daily running of the business, giving them the authority to make most investment and operating decisions, while regularly monitoring management's performance. Further, by the mid-20th century, when the separation of corporate ownership from managerial control was virtually complete, professional managers of leadership and experience were able to dominate their boards of directors by controlling strategic decision-making in addition to daily operations. In practice, board members were chosen by management from among its own ranks of large-company executives and from among its professional associates in law and finance; the chosen ratified decisions that management deemed to be "good for the company."

Board service was largely viewed as honorific and responsive to management concerns. The arm's-length relationship implied in the board's monitoring role over management was replaced by a collegial relationship—one closer to that implied by membership in a Yale secret society than that required for effective oversight. As recently as 1986, Peter Drucker described the board of directors as "an impotent, ceremonial, and legal fiction."[2] But, in the last decade, and especially in the past five years, boards of directors of large publicly traded corporations have begun to shed their passivity and dependence.

* A longer, more technical version of this article appeared in *Columbia Law Review*, Vol. 98 (June 1998), pp. 1283-1322. This research has been funded by the John M. Olin Foundation program in government-business relations at the Yale School of Management and by Weil, Gotshal & Manges LLP. Olin Senior Fellows Karen Lamb and Gary Davison, assisted by SOM students Michael Asato and Mangesh Mulgaonkar, contributed materially to implementation of the research design. The authors wish to express their gratitude to the following scholars and experts in the field for their valuable input and insights: William J. Baumol, Holly J. Gregory, Jim Hawley, Thomas R. Horton, Tim Koller, Richard H. Koppes, Paula Lowitt, Chris McCusker, Richard A. Miller, Robert A.G. Monks, Alan J. Patricof, James Phills, Ned Regan, Martin Shubik, John G. Smale, Michael I. Sovern, Robert B. Stobaugh, Kenneth West, and Andy Williams. We would like to extend special thanks to Kayla Gillan, General Counsel of CalPERS; Richard H. Koppes, former General Counsel of CalPERS; and Kenneth West, Senior Consultant to TIAA-CREF, for providing us with access to governance data considered for analysis in this paper.

1. See Delaware General Corporation Law, Del. Code Ann. tit. 8, § 141(a) (1991) ("The business and affairs of every corporation organized under this chapter shall be managed by or under the direction of a board of directors...").

2. As quoted by Charles A. Anderson & Robert N. Anthony in *The New Corporate Directors: Insights for Board Members and Executives* (1986), p. 1. The passive culture of the traditional board, and the practices that have supported that culture, are also described in Jay W. Lorsch & Elizabeth MacIver, *Pawns or Potentates* (1989); and in Robert A.G. Monks & Nell Minow, *Power & Accountability* (1991).

The evolution of boards from managerial rubber-stamps to active and independent monitors has been in large part the result of efforts to address or avoid serious problems with corporate performance associated with managerial entrenchment. By the early 1990s, many of the largest corporations were faltering. For example, IBM, General Motors, and Sears—which, in 1972, ranked first, fourth, and sixth, respectively, in the total market value of their outstanding common shares—were no longer in the top 20 by the end of 1992. And these three companies, which together lost more than $30 billion of market value in 1992 alone,[3] represented only the tip of the iceberg. Throughout the 1970s and 1980s, management-dominated corporations pursued growth and diversification strategies that expanded corporate size for its own sake, but provided limited returns to investors.

The resulting low returns to investors in turn prompted a new activism. Board members had to respond to increasing pressures from (1) institutional shareholders, primarily large public pension funds; (2) active investors, particularly takeover firms; and (3) the courts, whose decisions called for directors to take more responsibility for investors.[4] Further-

more, attacks by the media ultimately raised directors' concerns for their responsibilities and, indeed, their own reputations.[5] Essentially, the response has consisted of the exercise of board authority already there to actively monitor management.

Many boards of large companies now operate in a different mode than they did a few short years ago. Director interviews and surveys conducted in the last few years show that, for most large, publicly traded corporations, a majority of directors are not members of management.[6] For the trend-setting corporations, new independent directors are selected in consultation with management by a wholly independent board committee such as the "nominating" or "governance" committee.[7] Most important, there is more board participation in agenda-setting and in determining information flow.[8] And executive sessions of independent directors that *exclude* management, rather than being considered high treason, have become customary for evaluating management.[9] Relatively few boards, however, have gone so far as to embrace the separation of the roles of board chairman and CEO.[10] Instead, some corporations have created a leader of the independent directors (a "lead director") or some

3. This calculation appears in Carol J. Loomis, "Dinosaurs?," *Fortune*, May 3, 1993, which attributes corporate failures partly to a dominant managerial system acting without true accountability.

4. A series of Delaware court decisions in the 1980s concerning the contours of the business judgment rule in the context of board response to a change of control situation emphasized the role of informed independent directors. See generally Dennis J. Block et al., *The Business Judgment Rule: Fiduciary Duties of Corporate Directors*, pp. 340-48 (4th ed. 1993 & Supp. 1995), which discusses the impact of recent Delaware court decisions; and Robert A. Ragazzo, "Unifying the Law of Hostile Takeovers: The Impact of QVC and Its Progeny," 32 *Hous. L. Rev.* (1995), pp. 945, 976, which traces evolution of judicial definition of board duties.

5. See Memorandum from William T. Allen, Chancellor, Delaware Court of Chancery, to the 1993 Tulane Corporate Law Institute 11 (undated) (on file with the *Columbia Law Review*), which discusses the role of "'soft' concepts like reputation, pride, fellowship and self-respect" in motivating directors to become more active. See also Ira M. Millstein, "The Evolution of the Certifying Board," 48 *Bus. Law.*, pp. 1485, 1488 (1993).

6. The Korn/Ferry 24th Board Study noted that, by 1996, insiders occupied just 18% of board seats, with an average of two insiders sitting on an 11 member board; in 1992, corporate insiders occupied 25% of the seats, which in turn was a decrease from 38% 25 years earlier. (See Korn/Ferry Int'l, Board Meeting in Session: 24th Annual Board of Directors Study (1997), p. 19.) See also Krista J. Berk & Stephen R. Tobey, Investor Responsibility Research Center, *Board Practices 1996: The Structure and Compensation of Board of Directors at S&P 500 Companies* (1996) [hereinafter IRRC Board Practices 1996], which reports that, on average, 65.8% of directors at the 435 S&P 500 companies having annual meetings between January and September 1996 were independent; and that about four out of five company boards had a majority of independent directors (pp. 3-6).

7. See, for example, IRRC Board Practices 1996, cited above, which notes a greater proportion of companies with completely independent nominating committees (40.2%) and an increase in corporate governance committees that often oversee director nomination functions and are typically composed of non-employee directors (p. 9). The study also observes that "Most governance committees have been formed within the last three years, spurred by the widely publicized corporate governance initiatives of Campbell Soup and General Motors." (p. 12)

8. See, for example, The Conference Board, "The Corporate Board: A Growing Role in Strategic Assessment," (1996), which notes that 51% of respondents reported that their boards had a "'greater role' in strategy" than three years earlier, and nearly 49% reported that their board is "'actively engaged in the choice of strategic options'." (p.12, quoting respondents to a 1995 Conference Board survey).

9. The Korn/Ferry 24th Board Study notes that 62% of its respondents reported that in 1996 their outside directors met in executive sessions other than for compensation matters (p. 21); and that 69% reported that their boards have instituted a formal process for evaluating CEO performance (p. 23). See also Towers Perrin, "Perspectives on Best Practices in Corporate Governance," (1996), which reports increased board independence in the form of more rigorous CEO evaluation (p.2).

10. Over half of the institutional investors surveyed (51%) in Russell Reynolds 1997 Survey of Institutional Investors stated their preference that the CEO and chairman positions be separated, and three in ten (32%) strongly support separation. Nevertheless, in 1996 only 6% of respondents to the Korn/Ferry 24th Board Study reported having a separate chairman who was neither a current nor a former employee (p. 21). See also The Conference Board, "Corporate Directors' Compensation," (1996) [hereinafter Conference Board 1996 Compensation Study], which reported that the CEO was chairman in 68% of companies reporting, another employee served as chairman in 9% of companies reporting, and the chairman was a non-employee at 18% of companies reporting (p. 7). IRRC Board Practices 1996 reported finding that only 7 of 435 S&P 500 companies had an independent board chairman and 72 such companies (16.6%) split the position between the CEO and an outside director (p. 1).

The debate over separation of the CEO and chairman roles is likely to continue, with pressure to adopt such separation arising from the public pension funds and opposition originating, not surprisingly, from management groups. For example, CalPERS recently issued governance principles recommending that "[w]hen selecting a new chief executive officer, boards should reexamine the traditional combination of the 'chief executive' and 'chairman' positions." CalPERS, Corporate Governance Core Principles and Guidelines, Governance Guideline A3 (April 13, 1998).

other non-management board leadership position,[11] or have designated a "special-purpose" director for specific leadership in negotiation with management (for example, on a management buyout proposal). Moreover, many boards have become sufficiently concerned about their *own* performance to evaluate themselves as organizations in efforts to increase their effectiveness in making corporate performance more accountable to shareholders.[12]

This evolution in the relationship of management and the board has been the focus of a number of "best practices" publications. The Business Roundtable, the American Law Institute, the National Association of Corporate Directors (NACD), the Conference Board, and the Business Law Section of the American Bar Association have all published white papers on improving practices and procedures in corporate governance that, to varying degrees, provide the basis for strengthening a board's ability and motivation to monitor managerial performance.[13] They describe how to position a board to "incentivize" management to focus on returns to shareholders and to monitor management's performance.[14]

Such doctrine on governance practices had a role in creating an environment in which change could take place, but it was change itself in the governance of a select few of the largest corporations that set the pace. The General Motors board, in discharging the company's CEO in October 1992, reconstituted itself as an "active organization" in the true sense of that term. Shortly thereafter, in January of 1993, both the Westinghouse and IBM boards asserted themselves by discharging their respective companies' CEOs, not because of disastrous performance, but because "no improvement" did not constitute acceptable corporate performance.

In the spring of 1994, the GM board issued guidelines setting forth procedures it had designed to ensure that it or any other currently independent board would actively monitor management. Key provisions included the following: (1) the board has independent leadership in the form of either a separate chairman or a lead director; (2) the independent directors meet without management present at least two or three times a year to discuss management performance and to evaluate the CEO; (3) the CEO's evaluation is based on how the business measures up against its strategic objectives; (4) the board formally evaluates itself annually; (5) the independent directors determine how the board structures its governance processes; (6) the independent board leadership (the separate chairman or the lead director) establishes the board agenda together with the CEO, employing additional input from board members (and concise information on agenda items circulates in advance, with board meetings reserved for discussion); and (7) the independent directors, through a committee, select candidates for board membership, with input from the board leadership and the CEO, and invitations to join the board are extended by the board itself, together with the board leadership and the CEO.[15]

The General Motors board guidelines were widely circulated. Indeed, CalPERS wrote to the board chairs of the 300 largest public companies and requested that their boards consider the GM guidelines and compare them to their own board practices. In May 1995, CalPERS published "grades" ranging from "A" to "F" based on these companies' responses—specifically, whether and to what degree the response indicated board involvement in

---

11. Twenty-four percent of the respondents in Korn/Ferry's 24th Board Study (1997) reported that their board had a lead director in 1996, up from 22% in 1994, but down from the high of 27% in 1995 (p. 21, tbl. 5). For those companies without a lead director, 4% were considering implementing it and 49% said they "believe the concept is a good idea."

12. Twenty-five percent of respondents of the respondents in Korn/Ferry's 24th Board Study (1997) reported that the board's performance is formally evaluated on a regular basis. While this is a decline from the 36% reported in 1995, the decline is attributable to the large number of smaller companies (under $3 billion) that responded in 1996. At the largest companies ($20 billion and over), 41% of respondents reported that the board performed regular self-evaluation (p. 24). Moreover, from the cottage industry developing it appears that an increasing number of directors are attending training programs and seminars. See National Ass'n of Corp. Directors (NACD), Report of the NACD Blue Ribbon Commission on Director Professionalism 15-19 (1996) [hereinafter NACD Report on Director Professionalism].

13. See, especially, The Business Roundtable, Statement on Corporate Governance (1997) [hereinafter BRT 1997 Statement on Corporate Governance] (suggesting, for example, that the board meet periodically outside the presence of the CEO and other inside directors); Committee on Corporate Laws; American Bar

Association, Corporate Director's Guidebook (2d ed. 1994) (discussing various proposals to increase the role of independent directors); NACD Report on Director Professionalism (1996), as cited earlier (suggesting ways to increase the professionalism of boards); ALI Recommendations on Corporate Practice supra note 2, §§ 1.01-6.02 (a comprehensive analysis of all aspects of corporate governance); and "The Working Group on Corporate Governance, A New Compact for Owners and Directors," *Harv. Bus. Rev.*, July-Aug. 1991, [hereinafter Working Group Compact on Governance] (suggesting guidelines for both directors and shareholders to follow to reduce tensions between them).

14. The various "best practices" documents agree about the importance of director independence and, specifically, the need for non-management directors to control the audit, compensation, and nominating functions and the evaluation and compensation of the CEO.

15. See General Motors Board of Directors, Corporate Governance Guidelines on Significant Corporate Governance Issues, (Jan. 1994 & revised Aug. 1995, June 1997) [hereinafter GM Corporate Governance Guidelines]. These guidelines are consistent with the principles of board governance advocated by The Working Group on Corporate Governance, a coalition of lawyers for large public companies and leading institutional investors.

The evolution of boards from managerial rubber-stamps to active and independent monitors has been in large part the result of efforts to address or avoid serious problems with corporate performance associated with managerial entrenchment.

developing an independent monitoring relationship, and whether the relationship was formally established.[16]

The CalPERS focus on formal board procedures underscores the evolutionary shift from domination *by* management to independent director monitoring *of* management in carrying out its responsibility to the shareholders. But with what result? Notwithstanding boards' increased activism and independence, there is still the question as to the extent to which an active, independent board actually has an impact on corporate performance.

BOARD IMPACT ON CORPORATE PERFORMANCE

The determinants of corporate performance—strategic, managerial, and environmental—are complex and interrelated, and in the last decade some or all of them may have offset the positive effect of board activism. Additionally, from outside the corporation looking in, it is difficult to determine whether active boards have actually had to make decisions that could improve managerial performance. Given these complications, it is understandable that numerous attempts to determine whether board activism improves performance have not resulted in consensus.

Even so, who would assert that corporations would be equally or better situated if management is not governed? An active and independent board of directors working for shareholders clearly benefits the corporation by reducing the "agency problem" that arises from the separation of ownership from control in the modern corporation. It does so by acting as agent for owners in controlling a management whose principal motive is *not* to maximize value but rather to enhance its own

position. Any resulting change in management's behavior, no matter how limited, should increase returns to the owners as residual claimants.

In the modern corporation, owners provide investment capital in return for stock, and professional managers carry on the business based on their decisions about how best to employ the capital. This separation of the roles of owner and management has proven successful in aggregating capital to be put at the disposal of talented managers. Nonetheless, as Adam Smith pointed out over 200 years ago, human nature being what it is, managers as agents for shareholders will tend to be less vigilant in pursuing owners' interests than if they themselves were the owners.[17] As explained by Berle and Means (and later by their successors Jensen and Meckling), managers pursue their own interests, at least sometimes, at the expense of the shareholder.[18] When management compensation systems reward growth in corporate sales, then management's plans more likely than not call for larger, more diversified organizations that are not as profitable. The board of directors provides a functional response by downgrading performance based on strategic decisions to expand unless such expansion proves to be in the best interests of the shareholders.

But, to serve as effective monitors, directors must be independent of the management they monitor.[19] Directors who are members of management, or are otherwise closely linked to management, have the same interest as management in perpetuating corporate performance measured in terms of growth for its own sake.[20] A board composed of a majority of independent directors and with leadership independent of management is less likely to accept managerial strategies that extend the size of the corporation at the same or lower rate of return on investment.

16. See CalPERS, Press Release, CalPERS Announces Results of Governance Survey, May 31, 1995 (on file with the *Columbia Law Review*) [hereinafter CalPERS 1995 Press Release].

17. As Smith wrote in *Wealth of Nations*, "[t]he directors of such [joint stock] companies,... being the managers rather of other people's money than of their own, it cannot well be expected, that they should watch over it with the same anxious vigilance with which the partners in a private copartnery frequently watch over their own.... Negligence and profusion, therefore, must always prevail, more or less, in the management of the affairs of such a company. (*An Inquiry Into The Nature and Causes of The Wealth of Nations*, Vol. 2, pp. 264-65 (Edwin Canaan ed., University of Chicago Press 1976) (1776).

18. For the seminal discussion of the separation of ownership from control in the U.S., see Adolph Berle & Gardiner Means, *The Modern Corporation and Private Property* (1932). For the systematic formulation and incorporation into finance theory of Berle and Means's argument, see Michael C. Jensen & William H. Meckling, "Theory of the Firm: Managerial Behavior, Agency Costs and Ownership Structure," *J. Fin. Econ.* (1976).

19. See, e.g., NACD Report on Director Professionalism, cited earlier) (suggesting steps for ensuring director independence and providing various definitions of director independence); Ira Millstein, "The Evolution of the Certifying Board," 48 *Bus. Law.*, pp. 1488, 1490-91 (1993) (discussing the relationship between director independence or responsibility and the deference paid to directors by courts); Ira Millstein, "The Professional Board," 50 *Bus. Law.* 1427, 1430-31 (1995) [hereinafter Millstein, The Professional Board] (recommending processes for increasing director independence); and Working Group Compact on Governance, cited above (outlining the role of outside directors as part of "new compact for owners and directors").

20. Definitions of director independence (or, conversely, "affiliation" with management) generally center on the likelihood of a relationship between a director and senior management that might make the independent exercise of judgment less likely. See, for example, ALI Recommendations on Corporate Governance, § 3A.01(a) (boards should be composed of a majority of directors "who are free of any significant relationship" with senior management). A "significant relationship" includes current employment or employment within the past two years, and certain personal or business relationships with the company. See id. at § 1.34.

Our observation is that even in large-scale, highly bureaucratic corporations, Darwin's logic applies: That is, if one organism has even a tiny advantage over the others, that advantage can be "a grain in the balance" that determines which organism survives over time.[21] We accept the notion that, at the least, an independent board of directors can be such a "grain in the balance."

But notwithstanding Darwin's logic—and the increasingly important role of the board and, specifically, independent directors—there remains a reluctance to conclude that the activist board is in fact the solution to the agency problem. Our hesitancy follows in part from not being able to conclude from the historical studies that there is a significant relationship between good performance and good governance. This failure to detect a relationship may be largely the result, however, of looking at performance and governance through a rear-view mirror. Throughout much of the past half century, the board of directors as an institution has in fact been passive to the point of irrelevance to corporate performance. There has been a significant disparity between board duties as formally described and as actually practiced.[22] A search for proof that active governance leads to better performance using data prior to the last decade encounters almost exclusively the behavior of rubber-stamp boards. Studies based on data from the 1970s and 1980s thus do not lead to the conclusion that boards cannot be relied upon to motivate management to improve corporate performance.

In our view, that boards were passive by itself led to the adoption of various other remedies for the agency problem. These remedies, however, in turn failed to completely resolve the problem. The remedies included using shareholder pressure, media scandal, and litigation against directors as mechanisms for making management work more in the interests of the shareholders. While they have had an important role in reducing management fraud and self-dealing, it is less clear that they have succeeded in focusing management strategies on increasing corporate earnings and shareholder returns.[23] Shareholder pressure and media attention have been insufficient motivators for management to undertake just those investments that are expected to achieve the highest possible returns to investors over the long term rather than the highest rate of corporate growth. Nor has the threat of litigation been sufficient, given that the court system is slow, often makes counterproductive decisions, and the associated costs are likely to outweigh the benefits. As recognized by the courts, and expressed in their business judgment rule, ex post facto second-guessing of business decisions in litigation is not the road to corporate accountability to investors.

For another reason, attempts to link board governance to corporate performance have produced inconclusive results.[24] Most research studies have been based on methodology that links elements of board structure to financial measures of corporate performance or to a single corporate event. For example, early studies focused on whether the percentage of non-management directors on a board correlated with frequency of CEO replacement,[25] response to takeover bids,[26] or variations in

---

21. "More individuals are born than can possibly survive. A grain in the balance will determine which individual shall live and which shall die—which variety or species shall increase in number, and which shall decrease, or finally become extinct." Charles Darwin, *On the Origin of Species by Means of Natural Selection* 467 (1859), quoted in Daniel C. Dennett, *Darwin's Dangerous Idea* 41 (1995).

22. As Myles Mace found in his classic work on boards, *Directors: Myth & Reality* (1971), the literature that describes the traditional functions of boards typically includes three roles: "(1) establishing basic objectives, corporate strategies, and broad policies; (2) asking discerning questions; and (3) selecting the president" (p. 184). However, Mace found that it was senior managers—and not directors—who establish corporate strategy, and, except in severe situations of malfeasance or underperformance, managers and not directors chose the successor president. As for asking "discerning" questions, Mace found that directors either lacked sufficient information or felt that such questioning was simply inappropriate within the collegial boardroom culture. See id., pp. 186-88.

23. See, for example, Bernard S. Black, "The Value of Institutional Investor Monitoring: The Empirical Evidence," 39 *UCLA L. Rev.* (1992), which finds only "modest support" for the proposition that oversight by large shareholders can add value.

24. For an overview of the research literature, see generally Laura Lin, The Effectiveness of Outside Directors as a Corporate Governance Mechanism: Theories and Evidence, 90 *Nw. U.L. Rev.* 898 (1996); and Roberta Romano, Corporate Law and Corporate Governance, *Indus. & Corp. Change* (1996), who describes the board as a "general purpose technology" that is less effective than

"special purpose technologies" such as protective covenants or grievance arbitration for safeguarding investments. As Romano also points out, empirical research indicates that "independent directors are most effective... during financial distress and takeovers [and] the ultimate controls of performance where ownership is diffuse... are the markets in which these firms operate..." (p. 331).

25. See, generally, Michael S. Weisbach, "Outside Directors and CEO Turnover," 20 *J. Fin. Econ.* (1988) (CEO turnover was more sensitive to firm performance in firms with a higher proportion of outside directors; boards with at least 60% independent directors were more likely than other boards to fire a poorly performing CEO; but CEO termination rate for firms ranked in the bottom decile for one measure of stock price performance was only 1.3% higher for firms with 60% independent boards than for firms with 40% or fewer independent directors).

26. See, for example, John W. Byrd & Kent A. Hickman, "Do Outside Directors Monitor Managers?: Evidence from Tender Offer Bids," 32 *J. Fin. Econ.* (1992) (tender offer bidders with majority-independent boards offer lower takeover premia and earn roughly zero returns on average; bidders without such boards suffer losses during takeovers of 1.8% on average); James F. Cotter et al., "Do Independent Directors Enhance Target Shareholder Wealth During Tender Offers?," 43 *J. Fin. Econ.* (1997) (tender offer targets having majority-independent boards realized roughly 20% higher stock price returns between 1989-1992 than targets without majority-independent boards; the initial tender offer premium, the bid premium revision, and the target shareholder gains over the tender offer period were higher; it appears that such independent boards were more likely to use resistance strategies to enhance shareholder wealth).

> The professional board is an active monitoring (but not meddling) organization that participates with management in formulating corporate strategy, develops appropriate incentives for management and other employees, and judges the performance of management against the strategic plan.

stock price.[27] Their results disagreed about the statistical significance—and, in some cases, even about the positive or negative character—of the relationship. But, as these results suggest, it is naive to think that any single structural characteristic of a board, without further analysis of its implications for board activism, can correlate with better corporate performance.

There is another research route to be followed—one based on the alternative methodology that led Darwin to his conclusion. We have observed that certain changes in board structure and conduct have brought activism to the boardrooms of numerous large corporations, and that those activist boards monitor management to deliver strategies to enhance returns to shareholders. Our hypothesis, then, is that independent and active boards are now working to enhance corporate performance. We then take two steps: (1) identify those boards that embrace a culture of professionalism in recognition of their unique function distinct from management and that assert control over processes to maintain independence; and (2) correlate the presence (or absence) of such boards with higher (or lower) earnings performance of the company.

Our experience is that boardroom behavior is what is critical, and that the professional board is an active monitoring (but not meddling) organization that participates with management in formulating corporate strategy in the interest of the shareholders, develops appropriate incentives for management and other employees to harness their interests to achieve the agreed-upon strategic plan, and judges the performance of management against the strategic plan. Given this position, one cannot identify whether a board is performing effectively by examining generic structural characteristics such as the number of outside directors and the number of board meetings per year. The only certain way to know whether a board is performing is to be present in the boardroom, and we of course cannot be present— the doors of some 300 corporate boardrooms are not open to us. But, as we now discuss, there are elements of board process that can serve as reliable indicators of the presence of an independent and effectively monitoring board of directors.

METRICS FOR INDEPENDENCE AND PERFORMANCE

Metrics for Board Independence

We have not been able to observe and record that boards have been participating in strategic planning, incentivizing and monitoring management performance, and disciplining failing managers in a timely fashion. Based on our experience with numerous boards as members or advisors, however, we believe that the following are acceptable surrogates for direct observation of effective behavior by professional boards:

■ Independent board leadership, whether through a non-executive chair or a lead director, so that directors are able to act without relying solely on initiatives from a management chairman;

■ Periodic meetings, without management, of the independent directors to provide the opportunity for the directors to evaluate management against the strategic plan for corporate performance; and

■ Formal rules or guidelines establishing an independent relationship between the board and management.

Each of these surrogates departs from the traditional system that allows the board to be dominated by management, and the presence of any one of them suggests to us that traditional board culture has been displaced in favor of an independent and professional approach in board decisions. Thus, for purposes of this study, we assume that when one or more of these indicators is present, the board is independent and hence can serve as the "grain in the balance" that tips the scales in favor of better corporate performance.

Boards do not disclose detailed information about how they operate, and therefore even documentation about the indicators set forth above is limited.[28] However, the responses that CalPERS

---

27. See, e.g., Benjamin E. Hermalin & Michael S. Weisbach, The Effects of Board Composition and Direct Incentives on Firm Performance, 20 *Fin. Mgmt.* (finding no strong relationship between percentage of outside directors and firm performance); David Yermack, Higher Market Valuation of Companies with a Small Board of Directors, 40 *J. Fin. Econ.* (1996) (finding negative correlation between board size and Tobin's Q, and between board size and several accounting measures of profitability); Sanjai Bhagat & Bernard Black, "Board Composition and Firm Performance: The Uneasy Case for Majority-Independent Boards," (paper presented at "Does Good Corporate Governance Pay?," American Bar Ass'n, Section of Bus. Law, Comm. on Corp. Governance, Feb. 21, 1997) (finding "no convincing empirical evidence" that the proportion of independent directors impacts future firm performance as measured by a variety of stock price and accounting measures).

28. See Constance E. Bagley & Richard H. Koppes, Leader of the Pack: A Proposal for Disclosure of Board Leadership Structure, 34 *San Diego L. Rev.* (1997) (recommending that the New York Stock Exchange and the National Association of Securities Dealers amend their listing policies to require listed companies to disclose in proxy statements whether the company has a separate independent chairman and, if not, whether the board has designated an independent director to function as a leader of the board's independent directors).

generated by asking companies to review the General Motors guidelines contain information about the extent to which companies satisfy these three criteria for a well-functioning board.

In a May 12, 1994 letter to the chairpersons of the boards of the 200 largest companies (a list that was later expanded to include the next largest 100 companies), CalPERS noted that the board of directors of General Motors had completed a self-imposed process of reviewing various corporate governance models. As a result of that review, the GM board had published 28 specific governance guidelines. CalPERS challenged other large companies to follow that lead and undergo the same type of self-analysis. CalPERS's request to the 300 largest companies was aimed at engaging boards as to their own decision processes; it was not concerned with the substance of board decisions, and expressly was not seeking wholesale adoption of the GM guidelines by the boards. Each response was evaluated against specific criteria and "graded" from "A+" to "F." The grading criteria were as follows: "A+" ("submitted a comprehensive list of guidelines" and "the board of directors was clearly involved in the process"); "A" (provided a list of its guidelines but not clear as to "involvement by the Board in the process"); "B" ("responded with a minimal list of guidelines" but "still currently active in the self-evaluation process"); "C" ("acknowledged corporate governance as an issue for Board involvement" and left the impression that action in the future by the board was possible); "D" ("satisfied with 'own' corporate governance guidelines," "saw no benefit in formalizing such practices," and "usually no board involvement"); "F+" ("sent a letter that essentially "saw no need to formalize corporate governance guidelines"); and "F" ("chose not to respond").[29] Thus, the grading criteria were based on whether the company had guidelines similar to those of GM, or was in the process of reviewing its governance structure.

Although the responses were not standardized, indicators of professionalism can be inferred from these letters from the 300 companies to CalPERS.[30]

In these letters, many of the respondents described their board practices in detail. Most provided some indication as to whether the board had independent leadership through a non-executive chairman or lead director or by scheduling regular meetings of the outside directors. Moreover, where such specific information was not included, if a company represented that it followed "substantially all" of the GM guidelines, we concluded that professional board governance could be associated with that company. But we emphasize that this evaluation was based on how each company *chose* to report to CalPERS.[31] We did not conduct interviews, nor did we attempt to substitute any knowledge that we may independently have possessed about the company or the professionalism of its board.

Having once identified professional boards by company, we hypothesized that such companies exhibit better economic performance, on average, than other companies. To test this hypothesis, we used two metrics. The first was the grade assigned to companies by CalPERS during its survey of 300 large companies undertaken in 1994-1995. Using CalPERS grades A+ through F, we assigned all corporations to one of six groups ranging from "well" to "poorly" governed. (As discussed below, the initial sample of 300 was reduced to 154 companies; and the CalPERS grade distribution of those firms was as follows: A+ (63); A (27); B (20); C (23); D (12); F+ (9).)[32]

A second metric was also developed from the information in the CalPERS letter responses. We asked a law firm associate not involved in this testing process to identify, using our criteria, the presence or absence of a professional board based on reading each CalPERS response letter. That person was unaware of any company's performance record. This analysis distinguished between well- and poorly-governed firms simply by assigning a value of "one" to the former and "zero" to the latter. Using this binary criterion, a company was deemed to have the value of "one," indicating board independence, if at least one of the following was

29. CalPERS, Final Report: Company Responses to Request for Board Governance Self-Evaluation, at iii (1995). A listing of firms included in the database is on file with P. W. MacAvoy.

30. The CalPERS year-long survey did not consist of any formal, specific questions, but rather encompassed a request addressed to the chairman of the board that the directors "pursue the task of defining the structure by which the board will operate, and the criteria or disciplines the board will follow, in fulfilling those duties and responsibilities." Letter from Dale M. Hanson to Companies (May 12, 1994) (on file with *Columbia Law Review*) 1.

31. The first 200 companies were graded in the fall of 1994, and the grades received considerable publicity. The first set of companies all had the opportunity to improve their grades by supplementing their responses prior to the final report—and many did. The companies in the second set of 100 had reason to understand the consequences of their response, and therefore had the opportunity and knowledge to do whatever was necessary for a "good" grade if so inclined.

32. In this study, we did not use the 76 companies assigned "F" grades (for failure to respond), and we relabeled the nine companies with "F+" grades as "F."

> **For the purpose of matching board governance with corporate financial performance, EVA has a major advantage over a stock-price measure of performance: It measures what the company actually accomplishes rather than what investors predict it will do in the future.**

present: (1) a non-executive chairman or lead director; (2) scheduled meetings of outside/independent directors without management present; or (3) substantial adherence to the GM guidelines. (For the final sample of 154 firms, this grading process yielded the following distribution: "present" (44); "absent" (102); inadequate data (8).) This grading system seems much more severe than CalPERS' letter grade system because of the former's reduced emphasis on board involvement in the process establishing guidelines and greater emphasis on board conduct under the formal guidelines.

Having devised these two measures of governance, the next step was to determine the extent, if any, to which higher governance measures have been associated with better corporate performance. In order to examine this association, we first had to come up with an appropriate measure of corporate performance.

Metrics for Corporate Performance

Analysts of performance use a variety of measures to evaluate corporations based on criteria that range across "production and allocative efficiency, progress, full employment, [and] equity."[33] Measures that are central to fulfilling goals for investors, and thus for ensuring company access to capital, include revenues, earnings, and returns to investors. Measures of shareholder returns include earnings per share, earnings growth, and discounted future earnings, as well as a relatively new measure, "Economic Value Added," or "EVA." While each of these measures yields valuable information, we chose EVA as our measure of corporate performance because it provides a metric that is widely accepted as representing a company's ability to generate *economic*

profits, and thereby create wealth for shareholders.[34] EVA is "residual income"—what remains after a charge for the cost of *all* capital employed in the business has been subtracted from after-tax operating (i.e., pre-interest) earnings. As an indicator of corporate performance, the principal advantage of EVA over conventional accounting measures is that it holds management accountable for the cost of *equity* capital—a cost that does not appear on the income statement.[35]

Even so, this measure of corporate performance is subject to limitations. Because it is a retrospective measure of performance (that is, based on *historical* operating revenues and operating costs), year-to-year changes in EVA are not likely to serve as an accurate measure of current shareholder returns. In any given year, shareholder returns, measured as dividends plus share-price appreciation, are likely to reflect not only the performance of the company in that period, but also changes in the market's *expectations* about future operating and share-price performance. This tendency of stock prices to reflect macro variables and expected performance means that *no* single-year operating performance measure—whether it be EVA or any other—is likely to have a strong correlation with same-year stock returns.[36]

So, why not use stock returns to evaluate performance? The problem with using stock prices for this study is precisely their tendency to reflect not actual performance, but expected future performance. For this reason, even if management produces extraordinary performance over a given period, if the market has already anticipated such performance (or more), the stock return over that period will be merely "normal" (or worse). Stock returns in any given year are thus likely to be a

33. See F.M. Scherer & David Ross, *Industrial Market Structure and Economic Performance* (3d ed. 1990), pp. 4-5.

34. For a discussion of the inadequacy of earnings per share, return on investment, and return on equity as performance measures, see Alfred Rappaport, *Creating Shareholder Value: The New Standard For Business Performance* 19-49 (1986). For a discussion of the advantages of EVA over conventional measures, see the comments of Joel Stern and Bennett Stewart in "Stern Stewart EVA Roundtable," *J. Applied Corp. Fin.*, Summer 1994, [hereinafter Stern Stewart Roundtable].

35. Another advantage of EVA over conventional measures is that it can be used to correct distortions of performance that are built into GAAP accounting. As Bennett Stewart states, "In defining and refining its EVA measure, Stern Stewart has identified a total of 164 performance measurement issues [that arise from] shortcomings in conventional GAAP accounting... For most of these accounting issues, we have... devised a variety of practical methods to modify reported accounting results in order to improve the accuracy with which EVA measures real economic income.... in practice Stern Stewart addresses 20 to 25 necessary key issues for an individual company in detail and recommends 5 to 10 adjustments." ("EVA: Fact and Fantasy," *J. Applied Corp. Fin.*, Summer 1994, pp. 76-77)

Although Stern Stewart & Co. recommends that individual companies adopt "highly customized" EVA definitions, our implementation of the EVA metric in this study relies solely on raw GAAP data, given that we cannot make such adjustments. We cannot evaluate the differences this creates in estimates, but rather rely on the methodology and the known quality of GAAP published data.

36. At a more practical level, it is well-known that EVA and other annual performance measures explain considerably less than half of the variance in share value from company to company; the rest is random, or dependent on shareholder assessments of future prospects. See Rawley Thomas, The Boston Consulting Group, "Economic Value Added (EVA) Versus Cash Value Added (CAV): Stern Stewart Versus BCG/HOLT: Empirical Comparisons" (1993) (on file with the *Columbia Law Review*), which reports finding that the percentage of stock price variation explained by variation in EVA (the R^2) never exceeded 0.33 in any year from 1982 to 1991. But, as reported by P. Easton et al. in "Aggregate Earnings Can Explain Most Security Returns," *Journal of Accounting and Economics* 15 (June/ Sept. 1992), no accounting-based performance measure explains more than 10% of the variation in stock prices.

highly "noisy" indicator of management's delivered performance.[37]

For the purpose of matching board governance with corporate financial performance, then, EVA has a major advantage over a stock-price measure of performance: It measures what the company (and its board of directors) actually accomplishes rather than what investors predict the company (and board) will do in the future. In so doing, it also provides a measure that is less subject than stock returns to macro-economic factors beyond the company's control, such as changes in interest rates and inflation.

The Calculation. EVA is estimated by subtracting a company's cost of capital from its pre-interest, but after-tax earnings. For example, if Company A has after-tax operating earnings of $150 million on total (debt and equity) capital of $1 billion, and has a weighted average cost of (debt and equity) capital equal to 10%, its EVA would be $50 million. As this simple example illustrates, EVA is a *dollar* measure of shareholder value added. But, for the purpose of comparing company performance, dollar measures are not meaningful for companies of different sizes. The larger company would be identified as the better performer even though its ability to generate large amounts of EVA may be a function of size alone rather than superior managerial acumen.

To control for differences in size when evaluating corporate performance, we use a variant of EVA that we term "excess return," or ER, which is the difference, or "spread," between a company's rate of return on total capital employed and its cost of capital. The rate of return on total invested capital (ROIC) is estimated by dividing net after-tax operating earnings (NOPAT)[38] by the value of total capital.[39] The weighted average cost of capital[40] (WACC) equals the cost of the company's debt, preferred, and equity financing, as "weighted" by the relative proportion that each represents in the company's capital structure.

THE RELATIONSHIP BETWEEN GOVERNANCE AND CORPORATE PERFORMANCE

Of the 300 firms in the CalPERS sample, two firms that were undergoing restructuring and 76 firms that failed to respond to CalPERS were eliminated.[41] For the remaining 222 firms, the COMPUSTAT®[42] database was used to retrieve data to generate WACC and ROIC for the period 1991-1995. An additional 68 firms were eliminated because of lack of data necessary to compute WACC or ROIC, leaving a final sample of 154 firms.[43] This time period, consisting of the three years prior to the CalPERS study and the year afterwards, should be sufficient to calculate long-run values for ROIC and WACC while accounting for year-to-year changes in industry and general economic conditions.

Given that board independence is not the sole determinant of economic performance, we attempted through regression analysis to identify the effect of other determinants and to control for them. Two important candidates are the economic performance of a firm's industry and the life-cycle position of the firm within that industry. Industry performance matters because some firms are in industries that were experiencing substantial demand growth,

---

37. See Jeffrey M. Bacidore et al., "The Search for the Best Financial Performance Measure," *Fin. Analysts J.*, May-June 1997, p. 11. Using stock price change and dividends as a measure of Market Value Added for the sample described below, the 1991-1995 industry-adjusted return for CalPERS (A+) firm was –3.05%.

38. NOPAT is Net Operating Profit After Taxes, as estimated using Generally Accepted Accounting Practices. NOPAT = EBIT – Taxes on EBIT – Change in Deferred Taxes. EBIT represents the pretax "bottom line" of operations, and is computed as follows: Net Sales – Cost of Goods Sold – Selling, General, and Administrative Expenses – Depreciation + Other Operating Expense/Income + Adjustment for Operating Leases + Adjustment for Retirement-Related Liabilities.

39. The denominator of the ROIC calculation—Operating Invested Capital—is defined as follows: Operating Working Capital + Net Plant, Property & Equipment + Other Assets + Other Liabilities + Value of Operating Leases. Goodwill is excluded from capital stock. Operating Working Capital, in turn, is defined as follows: Operating Cash + Excess Marketable Securities + Accounts Receivable + Inventories + Other Current Assets (Less Excess Marketable Securities) – Accounts Payable – Other Current Liabilities.

40. For a discussion of WACC, see T. Copeland et al., *Valuation: Measuring and Managing the Value of Companies* (2d ed. 1995), pp. 239-73. In our calculations, we used the equation on page 240. To calculate the denominator of WACC, we used figures from COMPUSTAT for the total amount of debt, preferred shares, and common stock. To determine the numerator of WACC, we calculated (1) the cost of debt, which equals interest expense (less the tax shield effect of

interest deductibility); (2) the cost of preferred stock, which equals dividends paid to preferred shareholders; and (3) the cost of common stock, which equals the opportunity cost to investors of holding the stock—i.e., the "minimum rate that the firm must earn to entice an investor to invest in [its] equity." The cost of a company's equity, which is estimated from stock market data using the Capital Asset Pricing Model.

41. Our decision to exclude companies that did not respond to CalPERS leaves us open to the charge of "selection bias"—namely, that because companies deserving low grades are probably under-represented in our sample, the behavior of our sample is probably not representative of the population of all corporations. However, we are not seeking to provide a depiction of the economy-wide impact of improvements in corporate governance. Rather we are seeking to determine whether corporations with governance improvements have significantly better performance than those without such improvements. That test is not affected by the relative numbers in the sample. If it is mainly the worst-governed companies that did not respond to CalPERS, and these firms also tend to have the worst economic performance, then our findings are likely to *underestimate* the actual economic benefit of a well-functioning board.

42. COMPUSTAT® is a registered trademark of the McGraw-Hill Companies.

43. The initial sample consisted of the 300 largest domestic equity holdings in the CalPERS portfolio, exclusive of General Motors (which was the promulgator of the standards). A full description of how the final sample of 154 firms was derived can be found in Appendix A of the original *Columbia Law Review* article, and a complete listing of the firms is on file with the *Columbia Law Review*.

The set of 63 companies that received an "A+" grade from CalPERS was the only group to demonstrate a positive *mean* differential spread over the five-year period. Firms that received lesser grades produced ERs that were at least 4.07%—and as much as 7.20%—lower than the highest rated companies.

while others are in industries that were stagnant, in the first half of the 1990s. For example, a company in the aluminum industry, which supplies a mature, commoditized product, is likely to have lower EVA than a similarly sized company in the pharmaceutical industry, with significant new product development and annual increases in demand.

A second factor in corporate performance is the company's current position in its life cycle given the industry's growth profile. Many of the most successful companies in the CalPERS sample such as Intel, Home Depot, and Wal-Mart are early in the lifetimes of new product development, and have high ERs for that reason alone. In many cases their founders have remained in charge and own significant shares, so that these companies do not encounter agency problems, and have had less pressure on the board to protect the interests of shareholders. In addition, there is a selection bias involved in including these firms in the sample: any newly large company that emerges from the hundreds of thousands of new enterprises will have superior management and thus is likely to experience greater growth after it has emerged as a leading corporation. Thus, irrespective of board practices, newer companies in the sample of the largest in the economy are likely to realize better economic performance than that of older companies.

Data Aggregation and Analysis

For each of our remaining 154 companies, we calculated ERs by subtracting WACC from ROIC for each of the five years 1991-1995. The resulting five one-year values were then indexed by calculating the geometric mean.[44] This geometric mean of the ER spread was used to represent the corporate performance of management over the period. Once the five-year series for all companies was generated, each of the 154 firms was assigned to one of 19 industrial groups.[45] For each industry, geometric mean values were generated for each year's ROIC, WACC, and ER. For each firm, we then created a set

of "industry-adjusted" ERs that are equal to the difference between that firm's performance and the industry average.

The last step in the analysis was to adjust for differences in size among the firms in our sample. For the set of companies with the same CalPERS grade, we calculated a weighted average ER in which the weight for each firm's ER was the firm's total assets as a percentage of the total assets of all firms in that set. This weighting process serves as a proxy for firm age, since asset-weighting gives more importance to older, larger firms.

Results

The industry-adjusted ERs by CalPERS grade for 1991-1995 are presented in Table 1. The set of 63 companies that received an "A+" grade from CalPERS was the only group to demonstrate a positive *mean* differential spread over the five-year period. Firms that received lesser grades produced ERs that were at least 4.07%—and as much as 7.20%—lower than the highest rated companies. The "presence" of a professional board also demonstrated impressive explanatory power. The "present" set of 44 companies experienced a weighted average ER that was 3.89% higher than that of its industry peers over 1991-1995. By contrast, the industry-adjusted ER of the "absent" group (102 companies) was a negative 1.05%, for a total difference of almost 500 basis points per year between the ERs of the two groups. This difference was present in each of the five years of the study, ranging between 1.27% in 1993 and 8.23% in 1995.

To test for the statistical significance of observed differences, we also developed a regression analysis of ERs using all year-to-year data for firms in the sample. The aim of this analysis was to filter out the effects on corporate profitability of not only differences in industry, but also of the 1991-1995 business cycle. We defined ER spread as the dependent variable and regressed it on binary (0,1) independent variables representing the year, the

---

44. For the initial cross-sectional data analysis, we used the geometric mean, which de-emphasizes the effect of year-to-year variation upon the rate of return, instead of the arithmetic mean. The geometric mean of the spread results from calculating the spread for each year for each company, then generating a geometric mean based on each year's spread calculation, as opposed to generating a geometric mean for ROIC and WACC and subtracting. Calculating spreads on a year-by-year basis before generating the geometric mean allows us to view the spread statistic as an annual one, which is preferred when confronting data that may have missing entries due to bad data or merger activity.

45. We chose to eliminate regulated electrical and telecommunications utilities from the sample. While virtually all industries encounter regulation, the effects on profitability are particularly noticeable in electric power and telecommunications, where companies must cope with regulatory regimes that limit the rate of return (ROIC) to the cost of capital. Under such regimes, management has reduced incentive to generate surplus value, since any such gains are as likely to be allocated to consumers in reduced prices as to investors in increased returns.

	Percentage Annual Rate of Return					
Grade	1991	1992	1993	1994	1995	Geometric Mean, 1991-1995
CalPERS						
A+	2.97	3.27	1.05	4.64	6.08	3.59
A	−1.38	−2.64	−1.02	2.51	0.20	−0.48
B	−3.12	−3.94	0.51	−3.67	−1.60	−2.38
C	−1.53	−2.32	0.15	−5.54	−8.55	−3.61
D	−0.55	1.83	−0.67	−3.97	−3.95	−1.49
F	−5.45	−3.24	−3.22	−2.46	−0.11	−2.91
GRADE AGGREGATE						
A+, A, B	1.18	0.82	0.42	2.93	3.50	1.76
C, D, F	−2.06	−1.32	−0.62	−4.52	−5.72	−2.87
PRESENCE/ABSENCE						
Presence	2.96	4.35	1.12	4.60	6.50	3.89
Absence	−0.82	−1.19	−0.25	−1.24	−1.73	−1.05
No Data	−1.72	−2.33	−1.02	−2.09	−3.36	−2.11

TABLE 1
CORPORATE VALUE-ADDED PERFORMANCE* GIVEN THE PRESENCE OR ABSENCE OF A PROFESSIONAL BOARD (1991-1995, WEIGHTED IN ASSETS)

*Measured by Differential Spread.
Source: As described in the text, differential spread equals company excess earnings rate of return, weighted by company assets, subtracted from industry average excess earnings.

industry, and the CalPERS grade.[46] We also regressed ER on the same determining variables except that the presence/absence binary variable was substituted for the CalPERS grade.

As summarized in Table 2, the regression results reinforce our findings that professional boards have been associated with (statistically) significantly greater excess returns in the first half of the 1990s. Our regression results suggest, for example, that to have been a "C" rather than an "A+" company was to have settled for ERs that were 7.4% less per year on average. Similarly, the presence vs. absence of an "activist" board produced ER spreads of 4.4% per year. Moreover, this difference was found to persist in more recent years. For 1997, the last year for which data are complete, the ER for A+ firms is 4.52% and for all other firms is −2.33%.

CONCLUSION

In the 1990s, boards of directors have become active and more independent of management in pursuing shareholder interests. We believe that increased board activism in monitoring management against the company's competitive strategy—especially when combined with well-designed management incentive compensation plans—has become an important internal force pushing management to produce higher levels of corporate performance over this period. Nevertheless, there is still intense debate over the extent to which active and independent boards have made a difference in corporate performance. Attempts to confirm empirically a relationship between independent boards and superior corporate performance have produced mixed results. We believe these results have followed from concentrating on earlier periods (when boards *were* largely irrelevant) and from using unreliable proxies (such as a minimum percentage of outside directors) for a well-functioning board. To improve on these results, we posit that active, independent monitoring is the only kind of board behavior that can be expected to generate increases in corporate earnings.

To test this proposition, we examined 154 large U.S. corporations using two proxies for the activism of a company's board: first, the grade assigned by

46. The regression equation took the following form: Company Excess Earnings = Constant + Σ Coefficient$_i$ * Year + Σ Coefficient$_i$ * Industry$_i$ + Σ Coefficient$_i$ * Grade$_i$. It should be noted that in specifying the regression equation, it is not possible to include dummy variables for all years, industries, and grades. For example, including the variables for 1995, when variables for 1991-1994 are already included, adds no information to the regression equation. In selecting which dummy variables to eliminate from the equation, the intent was to choose a variable near the mean to reduce the mean squared error in the regression and make it easier to reject the null hypothesis that the regressors are zero. In the regressions we used 1992, the metals industry, the "A+" CalPERS grade, and the "presence" grade (where appropriate) as the baseline, and thus eliminated them from the equation.

Our regression results suggest, for example, that to have been a "C" rather than an "A+" company was to have settled for ERs that were 7.4% less per year on average.

TABLE 2 ■ REGRESSION RESULTS FOR SINGLE COMPANY: ANNUAL SPREAD VS. CALPERS GRADES AND BOARD ACTIVITY

	Regression Equation Number					Regression Equation Number			
	(1)	(2)	(3)	(4)		(1)	(2)	(3)	(4)
Constant	4.280	3.299	1.293	3.302	Miscellaneous	−1.829	0.034	−0.368	0.022
	4.862	4.836	4.761	4.830		4.804	4.819	4.774	4.786
1991	−18.598**	−18.568**	−18.574**	−18.568**	Oil/Gas	30.672**	31.471**	31.701**	31.471**
	1.795	1.805	1.802	1.804		5.004	4.988	4.981	4.985
1993	4.968**	4.974**	4.959**	4.974**	Retail	−6.199	−5.234	−3.216	−5.237
	1.755	1.765	1.762	1.764		9.425	9.452	9.402	9.444
1994	13.050**	13.061**	13.041**	13.061**	Telecom Equip.	0.722	1.784	1.299	1.777
	1.740	1.749	1.747	1.748		5.291	5.301	5.269	5.287
1995	−11.512**	−11.478**	−11.501**	−11.478**	Transportation	−2.198	−0.485	−0.229	−0.485
	1.714	1.724	1.721	1.723		5.447	5.399	5.391	5.396
Aerospace	16.098**	16.735**	17.403**	16.735**	CalPERS A Grade	−4.945**			
	5.621	5.478	5.470	5.474		1.790			
Automotive	10.476**	8.272	10.298**	8.273	CalPERS B Grade	−3.716			
	5.175	4.894	4.959	4.890		2.204			
Chemicals	9.569	10.511**	10.511**	10.511**	CalPERS C Grade	−7.418**			
	5.351	5.277	5.266	5.273		1.903			
Computers	1.014	2.388	3.218	2.379	CalPERS D Grade	−7.373**			
	5.111	5.072	5.041	5.054		2.731			
Consumer Goods	5.469	3.862	5.795	3.864	CalPERS F Grade	−4.811			
	5.171	4.953	5.032	4.948		2.724			
Electrical Equip.	13.761**	13.555**	14.205**	13.554**	Active Bd. Absent		−4.437**		
	5.565	5.570	5.577	5.566			1.429		
Foods	23.257**	24.573**	24.611**	24.575**	Active Bd.—No Data		−4.487		
	5.184	5.168	5.157	5.163			2.434		
Health Care	23.083**	25.702**	24.425**	25.703**	CalPERS Grade CDF			−4.637**	
	5.383	5.310	5.290	5.306				1.370	
Machinery	6.470	6.232	6.638	6.231	Active Bd.— Fail/No Data				−4.443**
	5.080	5.106	5.098	5.103					1.402
					R^2 (adj.)(%)	51.48	51.09	50.93	50.99

Notes: Sample size = 154. All figures are percentages. Top number is the coefficent for the data; standard error is listed underneath. Statistically significant data at 5% level are denoted by **.

CalPERS for governance; second, a "presence" or "absence" grade we assigned based on our evaluation of three key indicators of professional board behavior. For the period 1991-1995, both of these governance metrics were statistically significant determinants of superior corporate performance as measured by a company's earnings in excess of the cost of its capital net of the industry average. In general, over that five-year period, the 63 companies receiving the highest CalPERS grade ("A+") achieved average annual, industry-adjusted returns on capital that were more than 700 basis points higher than the returns of the 44 firms rated "C."

Although we recognize that correlation does not *prove* causation, we believe that the superior economic performance in this period is in no small part a result of activist corporate governance. Skeptics may argue that causality runs the other way, and that only superior managers, confident of their ability to generate higher returns, are willing to assume the risks associated with working under a professional board. But it seems highly implausible to us that good corporate governance is simply a luxury of firms that are performing extraordinarily well. We believe that the corporate governance revolution in the '90s has had significant positive effects on the earnings and value increases achieved by many large U.S. corporations. In the year 2000 and after, it may well prove the "grain in the balance" that causes many companies to prevail while others disappear.

CHAPTER 2: SECTION 2.2
Compensation

Executive compensation is another key element of internal corporate governance. An effective compensation plan rewards, retains, and motivates employees while aligning employee interests with those of shareholders. However, the level and form of compensation—for employee and executives alike—is the subject of much controversy.

Most of the emphasis in the business press is on the *level* of pay. But in the first article in this section, which was published in 1990, Michael Jensen and Kevin Murphy argue that the relentless focus on how much CEOs are paid diverts public attention from the real problem—how CEOs are paid. Based on their analysis of the salaries and bonuses of 2,505 CEOs in 1,400 publicly held U.S. companies from 1974 through 1988, the authors conclude that the total compensation of top executives of most public companies is virtually independent of performance. "Is it any wonder then," the authors ask, "that so many CEOs act like bureaucrats rather than the value-maximizing entrepreneurs companies need to enhance their standing in world markets?"

In the decade following publication of Jensen and Murphy's classic paper, the use of equity-based compensation exploded, particularly in the form of stock options. One clear reason for the popularity of stock options has been their unrealistic accounting treatment. In *The Case for Expensing Stock Options Against Earnings*, the late Merton Miller and compensation consultant Graef Crystal provide a succinct and compelling argument as to why stock options are an expense, and expose the logical inconsistencies behind the widespread opposition to expensing.

In *Has Pay for Performance Gone Awry? Views from a Corporate Governance Forum*, Stuart Gillan discusses the issues raised by participants at a Corporate Governance Forum on Executive Compensation, Stock Options, and the Role of the Board of Directors that was hosted by the TIAA-CREF Institute on April 2001. The Forum brought together a diverse set of participants, including corporate officers and directors, academic and other researchers, compensation consultants, corporate human resources personnel, institutional investors, regulators, and other practitioners. In so doing, it provided an opportunity for an open exchange of views on current trends in compensation practice, accounting

for stock-based compensation, the appropriate use of stock options, and alternatives to standard at-the-money options. Also discussed were the role of shareholders in approving compensation plans and the importance of the board of directors and board compensation committee in determining compensation policy.

In *Golf Tournaments and CEO Pay—Unraveling the Mysteries of Executive Compensation*, John Martin reveals trends in executive pay during the 1990s and then suggests that the economic theory of "tournaments" may provide a rationale for the pattern, if not the level, of executive pay. Specifically, it finds that the total compensation of the five highest-paid executives in a cross-section of new and old-economy firms is very similar to the pattern of payouts to players in a golf tournament. The author also reports that recent studies show a significant increase in the pay-for-performance correlation throughout the 1990s. But whether that correlation is as high as it should be, and whether current levels of CEO pay are socially "optimal," are questions that remain unanswered.

In *Option-Based Compensation: Panacea Or Pandora's Box?*, Stuart Gillan begins by noting that during the past decade, investors have become increasingly concerned about the proliferation and size of stock option plans. Shareholder concerns center on four main issues. First, the cost of option-based compensation may exceed the associated benefits, resulting in excessive transfers of wealth from shareholders to optionholders. Second, the current accounting for and disclosure of option-based compensation may not be adequate for valuation purposes. Third, although many companies submit option plans to a shareholder vote, it appears that some companies may use exchange and market rules to avoid the shareholder approval process. Given the potential for stock option plans to transfer large amounts of wealth from shareholders to optionholders, the ability of shareholders to vote on option plans is seen as a critical corporate governance issue. Fourth and finally, with recent stock-price declines, many employees now hold out-of-the-money or underwater options. In order to retain and motivate employees, some corporations have responded by repricing or replacing underwater options with new grants. This replenishment has raided shareholder concern that the practice effectively rewards employees for failed performance, and that repricing undermines the rationale for using options as incentive compensation in the first place.

Our next three papers discuss the overall design of compensation programs. In *Twelve Ways to Strengthen Your Incentive Plan*, David Glassman argues that incentive compensation plans are ineffective for a variety of reasons, including the following: too many performance measures and too much complexity; arbitrary targets that are subject to intense lobbying by executives; caps and floors that narrow the payout range and stifle incentives; performance measured at a level too high to be meaningful for most managers, or too low to encourage teamwork; and a failure to integrate the incentive plan into the overall compensation philosophy. After examining these problems, the author offers 12 suggestions for implementing plans that support management's aspirations to create value for shareholders, with an emphasis on EVA.

In *Evidence on EVA*, Gary Biddle, Robert Bowen, and James Wallace summarize the authors' research on the performance of companies adopting EVA (or "residual income") compensation plans. They begin by reviewing the theory that links the underlying concept of residual income to shareholder value. Second, they discuss how Stern Stewart modifies residual income to produce its proprietary EVA metric and show how median EVA compares with residual income, net income, and operating cash flows over the period 1988-97. Third, they examine the claim that EVA is more closely associated with stock returns and firm value than is net income. Their evidence indicates that EVA does not dominate net income in associations with stock returns and firm values. Fourth, they examine a second claim that compensation plans based on residual income motivate managers to take actions consistent with increasing shareholder value. Here the evidence (from a study by Wallace) suggests that managers do respond to residual income-based incentives by, for example, increasing asset sales, cutting capital expenditures, repurchasing stock, and producing higher levels of residual income. The authors conclude by arguing that a metric such as EVA can be effective for internal incentive purposes even if it conveys little news to market participants regarding the firm's valuation.

In the final paper in this section, *Six Challenges in Designing Equity-Based Pay*, Brian Hall notes that the past two decades have seen a dramatic

increase in the equity-based pay of U.S. corporate executives, an increase that has been driven almost entirely by the explosion of stock option grants. When properly designed, equity-based pay can raise corporate productivity and shareholder value by helping companies attract, motivate, and retain talented managers. But there are good reasons to question whether the current forms of U.S. equity pay are optimal. In many cases, substantial stock and option payoffs to top executives—particularly those who cashed out much of their holdings near the top of the market—appear to have come at the expense of their shareholders, generating considerable skepticism about not just executive pay practices, but overall quality of U.S. corporate governance. At the same time, many companies that have experienced sharp stock price declines are now struggling with the problem of retaining employees holding lots of deep-underwater options.

This article discusses the design of equity-based pay plans that aim to motivate sustainable, or long-run, value creation. As a first step, the author recommends the use of longer vesting periods and other requirements on executive stock and option holdings, both to limit managers' ability to "time" the market and to reduce their incentives to take short-sighted actions that increase near-term earnings at the expense of longer-term cash flow. Besides requiring "more permanent" holdings, the author also proposes a change in how stock options are issued. In place of popular "fixed value" plans that adjust the number of options awarded each year to reflect changes in the share price (and that effectively reward management for poor performance by granting more options when the price falls, and fewer when it rises), the author recommends the use of "fixed number" plans that avoid this unintended distortion of incentives. As the author also notes, there is considerable confusion about the real economic cost of options relative to stock. Part of the confusion stems, of course, from current GAAP accounting, which allows companies to report the issuance of at-the-money options as costless and so creates a bias against stock and other forms of compensation. But coming on top of the "opportunity cost" of executive stock options to the company's shareholders, there is another, potentially significant cost of options (and, to a lesser extent, stock) that arises from the propensity of executives and employees to place a lower value on company stock and options than well-diversified outside investors. The author's conclusion is that grants of (slow-vesting) stock are likely to have at least three significant advantages over employee stock options: they are more highly valued by executives and employees (per dollar of cost to shareholders); they continue to provide reasonably strong ownership incentives and retention power, regardless of whether the stock price rises or falls, because they don't go underwater; and the value of such grants is much more transparent to stockholders, employees, and the press.

CEO INCENTIVES—IT'S NOT HOW MUCH YOU PAY, BUT HOW*

by Michael C. Jensen,
Harvard Business School, and
Kevin J. Murphy,
University of Rochester

The arrival of spring means yet another round in the national debate over executive compensation. Soon the business press will trumpet answers to the questions it asks every year: Who were the highest paid CEOs? How many executives made more than a million dollars? Who received the biggest raises? Political figures, union leaders, and consumer activists will issue now-familiar denunciations of executive salaries and urge that directors curb top-level pay in the interests of social equity and statesmanship.

The critics have it wrong. There are serious problems with CEO compensation, but "excessive" pay is not the biggest issue. The relentless focus on *how much* CEOs are paid diverts public attention from the real problem—*how* CEOs are paid. In most publicly held companies, the compensation of top executives is virtually independent of performance. On average, corporate America pays its most important leaders like bureaucrats. Is it any wonder then that so many CEOs act like bureaucrats rather than the value-maximizing entrepreneurs companies need to enhance their standing in world markets?

We recently completed an in-depth statistical analysis of executive compensation. Our study incorporated data on thousands of CEOs spanning five decades. The base sample consists of information on salaries and bonuses for 2,505 CEOs in 1,400 publicly-held companies from 1974 through 1988. We also collected data on stock options and stock ownership for CEOs of the 430 largest publicly-held companies in 1988. In addition, we drew on compensation data for executives at more than 700 public companies for the period 1934 through 1938.

All told, for the median executive in the subsample, a $1,000 change in corporate performance translates into a $2.59 change in CEO wealth.

Our analysis leads us to conclusions that are at odds with the prevailing wisdom on CEO compensation.

Despite the headlines, top executives are not receiving record salaries and bonuses. Salaries and bonuses have increased over the last 15 years, but CEO pay levels are just now catching up to where they were 50 years ago. During the period 1934 through 1938, for example, the average salary and bonus for CEOs of leading companies on the New York Stock Exchange was $882,000 (in 1988 dollars). For the period 1982 through 1988, the average salary and bonus for CEOs of comparable companies was $843,000.

Annual changes in executive compensation do not reflect changes in corporate performance. Our statistical analysis posed a simple but important question: For every $1,000 change in the market value of a company, how much does the wealth of that company's CEO change? The answer varied widely across our 1,400-company sample. But for the median CEO in the 250 largest companies, a $1,000 change in corporate value corresponds to a change of just 6.7 cents in salary and bonus over two years. Accounting for all monetary sources of CEO incentives—salary and bonus, stock options, shares owned, and the changing likelihood of dismissal—a $1,000 change in corporate value corresponds to a change in CEO compensation of just $2.59.

Compensation for CEOs is no more variable than compensation for hourly and salaried employees. On average, CEOs receive about 50% of their base pay in the form of bonuses. Yet these "bonuses" don't generate big fluctuations in CEO compensation. A comparison of annual inflation-adjusted pay changes for CEOs from 1975 through 1988 and pay changes for 20,000 randomly selected hourly and salaried workers shows remarkably similar distributions. Moreover, a much lower percentage of CEOs took real pay cuts over this period than did production workers.

With respect to pay for performance, CEO compensation is getting worse rather than better. The most powerful link between shareholder wealth and executive wealth is direct stock ownership by the CEO. Yet the percentage of stock ownership by CEOs in large public companies was *ten times* greater in the 1930s than in the 1980s. Even over the last 15 years, CEO holdings as a percentage of corporate value have declined.

Compensation policy is one of the most important factors in an organization's success. Not only does it shape how top executives behave but it also helps determine what kind of executives an organization attracts. This is what makes the vocal protests over CEO pay so damaging. By aiming their protests at compensation *levels*, uninvited but influential guests at the managerial bargaining table (the business press, labor unions, political figures) intimidate board members and constrain the types of contracts that are written between managers and shareholders. As a result of public pressure, directors become reluctant to reward CEOs with substantial (and therefore highly visible) financial gains for superior performance. Naturally, they also become reluctant to impose meaningful financial penalties for poor performance. The long-term effect of this risk-averse orientation is to erode the relation between pay and performance and entrench bureaucratic compensation systems.

Are we arguing that CEOs are underpaid? If by this we mean "Would average levels of CEO pay be higher if the relation between pay and performance were stronger?" the answer is yes. More aggressive pay-for-performance systems (and a higher probability of dismissal for poor performance) would produce sharply lower compensation for less talented managers. Over time, these managers would be replaced by more able and more highly motivated executives who would, on average, perform better and earn higher levels of pay. Existing managers would have greater incentives to find creative ways to enhance corporate performance, and their pay would rise as well.

These increases in compensation—driven by improved business performance—would not represent a transfer of wealth from shareholders to executives. Rather, they would reward managers for the increased success fostered by greater risk-taking, effort, and ability. Paying CEOs "better" would eventually mean paying the average CEO more. Because the stakes are so high, the potential increases in corporate performance and the potential gains to shareholders are great.

HOW COMPENSATION MEASURES UP

Shareholders rely on CEOs to adopt policies that maximize the value of their shares. Like other human beings, however, CEOs tend to engage in activities that increase their own well-being. One of

What really matters is *the percentage of the company's outstanding shares the CEO owns*... By controlling a meaningful percentage of total corporate equity, senior managers experience a direct and powerful "feedback effect" from changes in market value.

THE WEAK STATE OF PAY FOR PERFORMANCE	A $1,000 Change in Shareholder Wealth Corresponds to . . .	Median	Middle 50%		
	Change in this year's and next year's salary and bonus	$0.067	$0.01	to	$0.18
	Present value of the two-year change in salary and bonus	0.44	0.05	to	1.19
Estimates for CEOs in the 250 Largest Companies	Change in the value of stock options	0.58	0.16	to	1.19
	Wealth effect for change in likelihood of dismissal	0.05	0.02	to	0.14
	Total change in all pay-related wealth	$1.29	$0.43	to	$2.66
	Change in value of direct stockholdings	0.66	0.25	to	1.98
	Total change in CEO wealth	$2.59	$0.99	to	$5.87

Note: The median individual components do not add to the median total change in CEO wealth since sums of medians do not in general equal the median of sums.

the most critical roles of the board of directors is to create incentives that make it in the CEO's best interest to do what's in the shareholder's best interest. Conceptually this is not a difficult challenge. Some combination of three basic policies will create the right monetary incentives for CEOs to maximize the value of their companies:

1. Boards can require that CEOs become substantial owners of company stock.

2. Salaries, bonuses, and stock options can be designed to provide big rewards for superior performance and big penalties for poor performance.

3. The threat of dismissal for poor performance can be made real.

Unfortunately, as our study documents, the realities of executive compensation are at odds with these principles. Our statistical analysis departs from most studies of executive compensation. Unlike the annual surveys in the business press, for example, we do not focus on this year's levels of cash compensation or cash compensation plus stock options exercised. Instead, we apply regression analysis to 15 years' worth of data and estimate how changes in corporate performance affect CEO compensation and wealth over all relevant dimensions.

We ask the following questions: How does a change in performance affect current cash compensation, defined as changes in salary and bonus over two years? What is the "wealth effect" (the present value) of those changes in salary and bonus? How does a change in corporate performance affect the likelihood of the CEO being dismissed, and what is the financial impact of this new dismissal probability? Finally, how does a change in corporate performance affect the value of CEO stock options and shares, whether or not the CEO exercised the options or sold the shares?

The table "The Weak State of Pay for Performance" provides a detailed review of our main findings for a subsample of CEOs in the 250 largest publicly-held companies. Together, these CEOs run enterprises that generate revenues in excess of $2.2 trillion and employ more than 14 million people. The results are both striking and troubling. A $1,000 change in corporate market value (defined as share price appreciation plus dividends) corresponds to a two-year change in CEO salary and bonus of less than a dime; the long-term effects of that change add less than 45 cents to the CEO's wealth. A $1,000 change in corporate value translates into an estimated median change of a nickel in CEO wealth by affecting dismissal prospects. At the median, stock options add another 58 cents worth of incentives. Finally, the value of shares owned by the median CEO changes by 66 cents for every $1,000 increase in corporate value. All told, for the median executive in the subsample, a $1,000 change in corporate performance translates into a $2.59 change in CEO wealth. The table also reports estimates for CEOs at the lower and upper bounds of the middle two quartiles of the sample. (For an extensive review and comparison of the pay-for-performance relation for individual CEOs, see "A New Survey of Executive Compensation" that follows this article.)

This degree of pay-for-performance sensitivity for cash compensation does not create adequate incentives for executives to maximize corporate value. Consider a corporate leader whose creative strategic plan increases a company's market value by $100 million. Based on our study, the median CEO can expect a two-year increase in salary and bonus of $6,700—hardly a meaningful reward for such outstanding performance. His lifetime wealth would increase by $260,000—less than 4% of the

From 1970 through 1988, the average annual compound stock return on the 25 companies with the best CEO incentives was 14.5%, more than one-third higher than the average return on the 25 companies with the worst CEO incentives.

present value of the median CEO's shareholdings and remaining lifetime salary and bonus payments.[1]

Or consider instead a CEO who makes a wasteful investment—new aircraft for the executive fleet, say, or a spanking addition to the headquarters building—that benefits him but diminishes the market value of the company by $10 million. The total wealth of the CEO, if he is representative of our sample, will decline by only $29,900 as a result of this misguided investment—not much of a disincentive for someone who earns $20,000 per week.

One way to explore the realities of CEO compensation is to compare current practices with the three principles that we outlined earlier. Let's address them one at a time.

CEOs should own substantial amounts of company stock. The most powerful link between shareholder wealth and executive wealth is direct ownership of shares by the CEO. Most commentators look at CEO stock ownership from one of two perspectives—the dollar value of the CEO's holdings or the value of his shares as a percentage of his annual cash compensation. But when trying to understand the incentive consequences of stock ownership, neither of these measures counts for much. What really matters is *the percentage of the company's outstanding shares the CEO owns*. By controlling a meaningful percentage of total corporate equity, senior managers experience a direct and powerful "feedback effect" from changes in market value.

Think again about the CEO adding jets to the corporate fleet. The stock-related "feedback effect" of this value-destroying investment—about $6,600— is small because this executive is typical of our sample, in which the median CEO controls only .066% of the company's outstanding shares. Moreover, this wealth loss (about two days' pay for the average CEO in a top-250 company) is the same whether the stock holdings represent a big or small fraction of the CEO's total wealth.

But what if this CEO held shares in the company comparable to, say, Warren Buffet's stake in the Berkshire Hathaway conglomerate? Buffet controls, directly and indirectly, about 45% of Berkshire Hathaway's equity. Under these circumstances, the stock-related feedback effect of a $10 million

decline in market value is nearly $4.5 million—a much more powerful incentive to resist wasteful spending.

Moreover, these differences in CEO compensation are associated with substantial differences in corporate performance. From 1970 through 1988, the average annual compound stock return on the 25 companies with the best CEO incentives (out of the largest 250 companies examined in our survey) was 14.5%, more than one-third higher than the average return on the 25 companies with the worst CEO incentives. A $100 investment in the top 25 companies in 1970 would have grown to $1,310 by 1988, as compared with $702 for a similar investment in the bottom 25 companies.

As a percentage of total corporate value, CEO share ownership has never been very high. The median CEO of one of the nation's 250 largest public companies owns shares worth just over $2.4 million—again, less than 0.07% of the company's market value. Also, 9 out of 10 CEOs own less than 1% of their company's stock, while fewer than 1 in 20 owns more than 5% of the company's outstanding shares.

It is unreasonable to expect all public-company CEOs to own as large a percentage of their company's equity as Warren Buffet's share of Berkshire Hathaway. Still, the basic lesson holds. The larger the share of company stock controlled by the CEO and senior management, the more substantial the linkage between shareholder wealth and executive wealth. A few companies have taken steps to increase the share of corporate equity owned by senior management. Employees of Morgan Stanley now own 55% of the firm's outstanding equity. Companies such as FMC and Holiday have used leveraged recapitalizations to reduce the amount of outstanding equity by repurchasing public shares, and thus allow their managers to control a bigger percentage of the company. After FMC adopted its recapitalization plan, for example, employee ownership increased from 12% to 40% of outstanding equity. These recapitalizations let managers own a bigger share of their company's equity without necessarily increasing their dollar investment.

Truly giant companies like IBM, General Motors, or General Electric will never be able to grant

---

1. The median CEO in our sample holds stock worth $2.4 million. The average 1988 salary and bonus for the CEOs in our sample was roughly $1 million. At a real interest rate of 3%, the present value of the salary and bonus for the next five years to retirement (the average for the sample) is $4.6 million. Thus total lifetime wealth from the company is $7 million.

their senior executives a meaningful share of outstanding equity. These and other companies should understand that this limitation on executive incentives is a real cost associated with bigness.

Cash compensation should be structured to provide big rewards for outstanding performance and meaningful penalties for poor performance. A two-year cash reward of less than 7 cents for each $1,000 increase in corporate value (or, conversely, a two-year penalty of less than 7 cents for each $1,000 decline in corporate value) does not create effective managerial incentives to maximize value. In most large companies, cash compensation for CEOs is treated like an entitlement program.

There are some notable exceptions to this entitlement pattern. The cash compensation of Walt Disney CEO Michael Eisner, whose pay has generated such attention in recent years, is more than ten times more sensitive to corporate performance than the median CEO in our sample. Yet the small number of CEOs for whom cash compensation changes in any meaningful way in response to corporate performance shows how far corporate America must travel if pay is to become an effective incentive.

Creating better incentives for CEOs almost necessarily means increasing the financial risk CEOs face. In this respect, cash compensation has certain advantages over stock and stock options. Stock-based incentives subject CEOs to vagaries of the stock market that are clearly beyond their control. Compensation contracts based on company performance relative to comparable companies could provide sound incentives while insulating the CEO from factors such as the October 1987 crash. Although there is some evidence that directors make implicit adjustments for market trends when they set CEO pay, we are surprised that compensation plans based explicitly on relative performance are so rare.[2]

The generally weak link between cash compensation and corporate performance would be less troubling if CEOs owned a large percentage of corporate equity. In fact, it would make sense for CEOs with big chunks of equity to have their cash compensation less sensitive to performance than CEOs with small stockholdings. (For example, Warren Buffet's two-year cash compensation changes

only a penny for every $1,000 increase in market value.) In some cases, it might even make sense for pay to go up in bad years to serve as a financial "shock absorber" for losses the CEO is taking in the stock market. Yet our statistical analysis found no correlation between CEO stock ownership and pay-for-performance sensitivity in cash compensation. In other words, boards of directors ignore CEO stock ownership when structuring incentive plans. We find this result surprising—and symptomatic of the ills afflicting compensation policy.

Make real the threat of dismissal. The prospect of being fired as a result of poor performance can provide powerful monetary and nonmonetary incentives for CEOs to maximize company value. Because much of an executive's "human capital" (and thus his or her value in the job market) is specific to the company, CEOs who are fired from their jobs are unlikely to find new jobs that pay as well. In addition, the public humiliation associated with a high-visibility dismissal should cause managers to weigh carefully the consequences of taking actions that increase the probability of being dismissed.

Here too, however, the evidence is not clear: the CEO position is not a very risky job. Sports fans are accustomed to baseball managers being fired after one losing season. Few CEOs experience a similar fate after years of underperformance. There are many reasons why we would expect CEOs to be treated differently from baseball managers. CEOs have greater organization-specific capital; it is harder for an outsider to come in and run a giant company than it is for a new manager to take over a ball club. There are differences in the lag between input and output. The measure of a baseball manager's success is the team's won-lost record this year; the measure of a corporate manager is the company's long-term competitiveness and value. For these and other reasons, it is not surprising that turnover rates are lower for CEOs than for baseball managers. It is surprising, however, that the magnitude of the discrepancy is so large.

On average, CEOs in our base sample (2,505 executives) hold their jobs for more than ten years before stepping down, and most give up their title (but not their seat on the board) only after reaching

---

2. See Robert Gibbons and Kevin Murphy, "Relative Performance Evaluation for Chief Executive Officers," *Industrial and Labor Relations Review*, February 1990, p. 30-S.

CEOs of companies that rank in the bottom 10%...are roughly twice as likely to leave their jobs as CEOs whose companies rank in the top 10%. Yet the differences—a 3% chance of getting fired for top performers versus a 6% chance of getting fired for laggards—are unlikely to have meaningful motivational consequences for CEOs.

normal retirement age. Two recent studies, spanning 20 years and more than 500 management changes, found only 20 cases where CEOs left their jobs because of poor performance.[3] To be sure, directors have little to gain from publicly announcing that a CEO is leaving because of failure—many underperforming CEOs leave amidst face-saving explanations and even public congratulations. But this culture of politeness does not explain why so few underperforming CEOs leave in the first place. University of Rochester's Michael Weisbach found that CEOs of companies that rank in the bottom 10% of the performance distribution (measured by stock returns) are roughly twice as likely to leave their jobs as CEOs whose companies rank in the top 10% of the performance distribution. Yet the differences that Weisbach quantifies—a 3% chance of getting fired for top performers versus a 6% chance of getting fired for laggards—are unlikely to have meaningful motivational consequences for CEOs.

Our own research confirms these and other findings. CEOs of large public companies are only slightly more likely to step down after very poor performance (which we define as company earnings 50% below market averages for two consecutive years) than after average performance. For the entire 1,400-company sample, our analysis estimates that the poor-performing CEOs are roughly 6% more likely to leave their jobs than CEOs of companies with average returns. Even assuming that a dismissed CEO never works again, the personal wealth consequences of this increased likelihood of dismissal amount to just 5 cents for every $1,000 loss of shareholder value.

With respect to pay for performance, there's no denying that the results of our study tell a bleak story. Then again, perhaps corporate directors are providing CEOs with substantial rewards and penalties based on performance, but are measuring performance with metrics other than long-run stock market value. We tested this possibility and reached the same conclusion as in our original analysis. Whatever the metric, CEO compensation is independent of business performance.

For example, we tested whether companies rewarded CEOs on the basis of sales growth or accounting profits rather than on direct changes in shareholder wealth. We found that while more of the variation in CEO pay could be explained by changes in accounting profits than stock market value, the pay-for-performance sensitivity was economically just as insignificant as in our original model. Sales growth had little explanatory power once we controlled for accounting profits.[4]

Of course, incentives based on other measures will be captured by our methodology only to the extent that they ultimately correlate with changes in shareholder wealth. But if they don't—that is, if directors are rewarding CEOs based on variables other than those that affect corporate market value—why use such measures in the first place?

Moreover, if directors varied CEO compensation substantially from year to year based on performance measures not observable to us, this policy would show up as high raw variability in CEO compensation. But over the past 15 years, compensation for CEOs has been about as variable as cash compensation for a random sample of hourly and salaried workers—dramatic evidence of compensation's modest role in generating executive incentives.[5] The exhibit "Common Variability: CEO and Worker Wages" (see next page) compares the distribution of annual raises and pay cuts of our CEO sample with national data on hourly and salaried workers from 1975 through 1986. A larger percentage of workers took real pay cuts at some time over this period than did CEOs. Overall, the standard deviation of annual changes in CEO pay was only slightly greater than for hourly and salaried employees (32.7% versus 29.7%).

LOOKING BACKWARD: PAY FOR PERFORMANCE IN THE 1930s

CEO compensation policies look especially unsatisfactory when compared with the situation 50 years ago. All told, CEO compensation in the 1980s was lower, less variable, and less sensitive to corporate performance than in the 1930s. To compare the current situation with the past, we collected a longitudinal sample of executives from the 1930s using data collected by the Works Projects Admin-

3. See Jerold B. Warner, Ross L. Watts, and Karen H. Wruck, "Stock Prices and Top Management Changes," *Journal of Financial Economics*, January-March 1988, p. 461; and Michael S. Weisbach, "Outside Director and CEO Turnover," *Journal of Financial Economics*, January-March 1988, p. 431.

4. For more detail on these tests, see our article, "Performance Pay and Top-Management Incentives," *Journal of Political Economy*, April 1990.

5. Data on hourly and salaried workers come form the Michigan Panel Study on Income Dynamics. The sample includes 21,895 workers aged 21 to 65 reporting wages in consecutive periods. See Kenneth J. McLaughlin, "Rigid Wages?" University of Rochester Working Paper, 1989.

For the entire 1,400-company sample, our analysis estimates that the poor-performing CEOs are roughly 6% more likely to leave their jobs than CEOs of companies with average returns.

COMMON VARIABILITY:
CEO AND WORKER WAGES

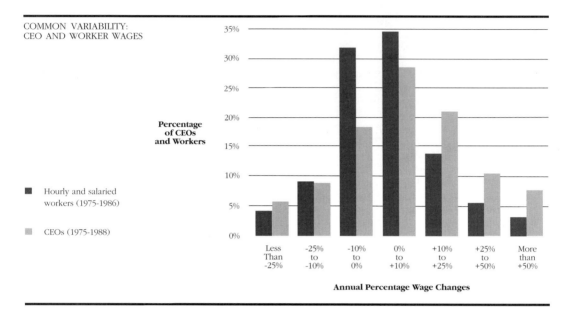

Percentage
of CEOs
and Workers

■ Hourly and salaried
workers (1975-1986)

▨ CEOs (1975-1988)

Annual Percentage Wage Changes

istration. The WPA data, covering fiscal years 1934 through 1938, include salary and bonus for the highest paid executive (whom we designate as the CEO) in 748 large U.S. corporations in a wide range of industries. Nearly 400 of the WPA sample companies were listed on the New York Stock Exchange, and market values from these companies are available on the CRSP Monthly Stock Returns Tape. In order to compare similar companies over the two time periods, we restricted our analysis to companies in the top 25% of the NYSE, ranked by market value. WPA compensation data are available for 60% of this top quartile group (averaging 112 companies per year), while data for more recent times are available for 90% of the top quartile companies (averaging 345 companies per year).

The results are striking. Measured in 1988 constant dollars, CEOs in top quartile public companies earned an average salary and bonus of $882,000 in the 1930s—more than the 1982 through 1988 average of $843,000 and significantly more than the 1974 through 1981 average of $642,000. Over this same time period, there has been a tripling (after inflation) of the market value of top quartile companies—from $1.7 billion in the 1930s to $5.9 billion in 1982 through 1988. Coupled with the decline in salaries, the ratio of CEO pay to total company value has fallen significantly—from 0.11% in the 1930s to

0.03% in the 1980s. Compensation was more variable in the 1930s as well. The average standard deviation of the annual pay changes—the best statistical measure of the year-to-year variability of compensation—was $504,000 in the 1930s compared with $263,500 in the 1980s.

The incentives generated by CEO stock ownership have also declined substantially over the past 50 years. To test this trend, we reviewed stock ownership data for CEOs in the 120 largest companies (ranked by market value). In 1938, CEOs (and family members) held .3% of outstanding stock, in 1974 .047%, and in 1988 .037%, a decline by roughly a factor of ten over the fifty-year period. The trend is unmistakable: as a percentage of total market value, CEO stock ownership has dropped substantially in the last half-century and is continuing to fall.

THE COSTS OF DISCLOSURE

Why don't boards of directors link pay more closely to performance? Commentators offer many explanations, but nearly every analysis we've seen overlooks one powerful ingredient—the costs imposed by making executive salaries public. Government disclosure rules ensure that executive pay remains a visible and controversial topic. The benefits of disclosure are obvious; it provides safe-

Over the past 15 years, compensation for CEOs has been about as variable as cash
compensation for a random sample of hourly and salaried workers—dramatic
evidence of compensation's modest role in generating executive incentives.

guards against "looting" by managers in collusion with "captive" directors. The costs of disclosure are less well appreciated but may well exceed the benefits.

Managerial labor contracts are not a private matter between employers and employees. Third parties play an important role in the contracting process, and strong political forces operate inside and outside companies to shape executive pay. Moreover, authority over compensation decisions rests not with the shareholders but with compensation committees generally composed of outside directors. These committees are elected by shareholders but are not perfect agents for them. Public disclosure of "what the boss makes" gives ammunition to outside constituencies with their own special-interest agendas. Compensation committees typically react to the agitation over pay levels by capping—explicitly or implicitly—the amount of money the CEO earns.

How often do shareholder activists or union leaders denounce a corporate board for *under*paying the CEO? Not very often—and that's precisely the problem. Most critics of executive pay want it both ways. They want companies to link pay to performance, yet they also want to limit compensation to arbitrary amounts or some fuzzy sense of "what's fair." That won't work. Imposing a ceiling on salaries for outstanding performers inevitably means creating a floor for poor performers. Over time, by cutting off the upper and lower tails of the distribution, the entire pay-for-performance relation erodes. When mediocre outfielders earn a million dollars a year, and New York law partners earn about the same, influential critics who begrudge comparable salaries to the men and women running billion-dollar enterprises help guarantee that these companies will attract mediocre leaders who turn in mediocre performances.

Admittedly, it is difficult to document the effect of public disclosure on executive pay. Yet there have been a few prominent examples. Bear, Stearns, the successful investment bank, went public in 1985 and had to submit to disclosure requirements for the first time. CEO Alan Greenburg's $2.9 million salary and bonus was the nation's fourth highest that year, and his ranking drew attention to the firm's compensation system. Under private ownership, compensation of the firm's managing

directors was set at a modest $150,000 base plus a bonus pool tied to earnings—a tight link between pay and performance. Because the firm was so profitable in 1986, the bonus pool swelled to $80 million, an average of $842,000 for each of the firm's managing directors. A public outcry ensued. Six months after going public, Bear, Stearns announced it was lowering the bonus pool from 40% to 25% of the firm's adjusted pre-tax earnings in excess of $200 million. According to one account, the firm's business success had "yielded an embarrassment of riches for top executives."[6]

More recently, we interviewed the president of a subsidiary of a thriving publicly traded conglomerate. This president is compensated with a straight fraction of his subsidiary's earnings above a minimum threshold, with no upper bound. Today he makes roughly five times what he made before his operation was acquired by the conglomerate, and corporate headquarters recognizes him as one of the company's outstanding executives. Why doesn't he want to be an officer of the conglomerate? For one, because his salary would have to be made public—a disclosure both he and the CEO consider needless invitation to internal and external criticism.

We are not arguing for the elimination of salary disclosure. (Indeed, without disclosure we could not have conducted this study.) But it's time compensation committees stood up to outside criticism and stopped adopting policies that make their companies' incentive problems worse. The costs of negative publicity and political criticism are less severe than the costs to shareholder wealth created by misguided compensation systems.

CORPORATE BRAIN DRAIN

The level of pay has very little to do with whether or not CEOs have incentives to run companies in the shareholders' interests—incentives are a function of how pay, whatever the level, changes in response to corporate performance. But the level of pay does affect the quality of managers an organization can attract. Companies that are willing to pay more will, in general, attract more highly talented individuals.

So if the critics insist on focusing on levels of executive pay, they should at least ask the right question: Are current levels of CEO compensation

---

6. *Wall Street Journal*, March 21, 1986.

high enough to attract the best and brightest individuals to careers in corporate management? The answer is, probably not.

Who can disagree with these propositions?

■ It is good when our most talented men and women are attracted to the organizations that produce the goods and deliver the services at the heart of the economy.

■ People evaluate alternative careers at least in part on the basis of lifetime monetary rewards.

■ If some organizations pay more on average and offer stronger pay-for-performance systems than other organizations, talent will migrate to the higher paying organizations.

These simple propositions are at the heart of a phenomenon that has inspired much handwringing and despair over the last decade: the stream of talented, energetic, articulate young professionals into business law, investment banking, and consulting. Data on the career choices of Harvard Business School graduates document the trend that troubles so many pundits. Ten years ago, nearly 55% of newly graduated HBS students chose careers in the corporate sector, while less than 30% chose investment banking or consulting. By 1987, more than half of all HBS students entered investment banking or consulting, while under 30% chose careers in the corporate sector. Last year, just over one-third of all graduating HBS students chose corporate careers, while nearly 40% chose careers in investment banking or consulting. And Harvard Business School is not alone; we gathered data on other highly-rated MBA programs and found similar trends.

We don't understand why commentators find this trend so mysterious. A highly sensitive pay-for-performance system will cause high-quality people to self-select into a company. Creative risk takers who perceive they will be in the upper tail of the performance and pay distribution are more likely to join companies who pay for performance. Low-ability and risk-averse candidates will be attracted to companies with bureaucratic compensation systems that ignore performance.

Compensation systems in professions like investment banking and consulting are heavily weighted toward the contributions made by individuals and the performance of their work groups and companies. Compensation systems in the corporate world are often independent of individual, group, or overall corporate performance. Moreover, average levels of top-executive compensation on Wall Street

or in corporate law are considerably higher than in corporate America. Financially speaking, if you are a bright, eager 26-year-old with enough confidence to want to be paid based on your contribution, why would you choose a career at General Motors or Proctor & Gamble over Morgan Stanley or McKinsey & Company?

Most careers, including corporate management, require lifetime investments. Individuals must choose their occupation long before their ultimate success or failure becomes a reality. For potential CEOs, this means that individuals seeking careers in corporate management must join their companies at an early age in entry-level jobs. The CEOs in our sample spent an average of 16 years in their companies before assuming the top job. Of course, many people who reach the highest ranks of the corporate hierarchy could also expect to be successful in professional partnerships such as law or investment banking, as proprietors of their own businesses, or as CEOs of privately-held companies. It is instructive, therefore, to compare levels of CEO compensation with the compensation of similarly skilled individuals who have reached leadership positions in other occupations.

The compensation of top-level partners in law firms is one relevant comparison. These numbers are closely guarded secrets, but some idea of the rewards to top partners can be gleaned from data on average partner income reported each year in a widely-read industry survey. The table "Salaries for Top Lawyers Are High..." reports 1988 estimated average incomes earned by partners in the highest paying corporate law firms. These five firms paid their 438 partners average incomes ranging from $1.35 million to nearly $1.6 million. Partners at the very top of these firms earned substantially more. When comparing these results with corporate compensation, the appropriate question to ask is "How many public companies paid their top 67 or 177 executives average salaries of $1.6 million or $1.2 million in 1989?" The answer is, few or none. How surprising is it, then, that law school classes are bulging with some of the country's brightest students?

Compensation for the most successful corporate managers is also modest in comparison with compensation for the most successful Wall Street players. Here too it is difficult to get definitive numbers for a large sample of top executives. But the most recent annual survey, as reported in the

When mediocre outfielders earn a million dollars a year, and New York law partners earn about the same, influential critics who begrudge comparable salaries to the men and women running billion-dollar enterprises help guarantee that these companies will attract mediocre leaders.

SALARIES FOR TOP LAWYERS ARE HIGH...

Rank	Firm	Average Income per Partner	Number of Partners
1	Cravath, Swaine, & Moore	$1,595,000	67
2	Cahill Gordon & Reindel	$1,420,000	57
3	Sullivan & Cromwell	$1,375,000	91
4	Wachtell, Lipton, Rosen & Katz	$1,350,000	46
5	Skadden, Arps, Slate, Meagher & Flom	$1,155,000	177

Source: *The American Lawyer*, July-August 1989, p.34.

...SO ARE SALARIES ON WALL STREET

Firm	Number of Partners Earning More Than $3 Million in 1988	Average Earnings for Partners Earning More Than $3 Million in 1988
Drexel Burnham Lambert	20	$18,000,000
Goldman, Sachs	18	$ 9,100,000
Morgan Stanley	11	$ 4,300,000
Sterling Group	6	$36,700,000
Kohlberg Kravis Roberts	5	$59,000,000
Lazard Freres	5	$17,200,000
Salomon Brothers	5	$ 4,700,000
Neuberger & Berman	5	$ 4,700,000

Source: *Financial World*, July 11, 1989. Average earnings are based on *FW*'s lower bound earnings estimate, p.32.

table "...So Are Salaries on Wall Street," documents the kinds of rewards available to top investment bankers. At Goldman, Sachs, for example, 18 partners earned more than $3 million in 1988, and the average income for those partners was more than $9 million. Only nine public-company CEOs had incomes in excess of $9 million in 1988 (mostly through exercising stock options), and no public company paid its top 18 executives more than $3 million each. The Wall Street surveys for 1989 are not yet available, but consistent with high pay-for-performance systems, they will likely show sharp declines in bonuses reflecting lower 1989 industry performance.

The compensation figures for law and investment banking look high because they reflect only the most highly paid individuals in each occupation. Average levels of compensation for lawyers or investment bankers may not be any higher than average pay levels for executives. But that's not the relevant comparison. The very best lawyers or investment bankers can earn substantially more than the very best corporate executives. Highly talented people who would succeed in any field are likely to shun the corporate sector, where pay and performance are weakly related, in favor of organizations where pay is more strongly related to

performance—and the prospect of big financial rewards more favorable.

MONEY ISN'T EVERYTHING

Some may object to our focus on monetary incentives as the central motivator of CEO behavior. Are there not important nonmonetary rewards associated with running a large organization? Benefits such as power, prestige, and public visibility certainly do affect the level of monetary compensation necessary to attract highly qualified people to the corporate sector. But unless nonmonetary rewards vary positively with company value, they are no more effective than cash compensation in motivating CEOs to act in the shareholders' interests. Moreover, because nonmonetary benefits tend to be a function of position or rank, it is difficult to vary them from period to period based on performance.

Indeed, nonmonetary rewards typically motivate top managers to take actions that reduce productivity and harm shareholders. Executives are invariably tempted to acquire other companies and expand the diversity of the empire, even though acquisitions often reduce shareholder wealth. As prominent members of their community, CEOs face pressures to keep open uneconomic factories, to

Are current levels of CEO compensation high enough to attract the best and brightest individuals to careers in corporate management? The answer is, probably not.

keep the peace with labor unions despite the impact on competitiveness, and to satisfy intense special-interest pressures.

Monetary compensation and stock ownership remain the most effective tools for aligning executive and shareholder interests. Until directors recognize the importance of incentives—and adopt compensation systems that truly link pay and performance—large companies and their shareholders will continue to suffer from poor performance.

■ APPENDIX: A NEW SURVEY OF EXECUTIVE COMPENSATION

Routinely misused and abused, surveys contribute to the common ills of corporate compensation policy. Surveys that report average compensation across industries help inflate salaries, as everyone tries to be above average (but not in front of the pack). Surveys that relate pay to company sales encourage systems that tie compensation to size and growth, not performance and value. Surveys that

rank the country's highest paid executives stir public outrage, raise legislative eyebrows, and provide emotional justification for increased demands in labor negotiations.

The basic problem with existing compensation surveys is that they focus exclusively on *how much* CEOs are paid instead of *how* they are paid. Our focus on incentives rather than levels leads naturally to a new and different kind of survey. Instead of reporting who's paid the most, our survey reports who's paid the best—that is, whose incentives are most closely aligned with the interests of their shareholders.

Our survey considers incentives from a variety of sources—including salary and bonus, stock options, stock ownership, and the threat of getting fired for poor performance. It includes only companies listed in the *Forbes* executive compensation surveys for at least eight years from 1975 through 1989, since we require at least seven years of pay change to estimate the relation between pay and performance.

THE 25 CEOs OF LARGE COMPANIES WITH THE BEST INCENTIVES

			Total Effects (over Two Years) on CEO Wealth Corresponding to Each $1,000 Change in Shareholder Wealth		
Rank	Company	CEO	Change in All Pay-Related Wealth	Change in the Value of Stock Owned	Change in Total CEO Wealth
1	Castle & Cooke	David H. Murdock	$7.29	$224.24	$231.53
2	Amerada Hess	Leon Hess*	$0.02	$152.71	$152 73
3	Wang Laboratories	An Wang*	$0 84	$137.83	$138.68
4	Aon Corp.	Patrick G. Ryan	$0.76	$137 46	$138.22
5	Loews	Laurence A. Tisch	$0.00	$126.40	$126.40
6	Ethyl	Floyd D. Gottwald, Jr.	-$0.25	$90.73	$90.48
7	Marriott	J. Willard Marriott, Jr.*	$1.55	$72.58	$74.14
8	MCA	Lew R. Wasserman	$0.05	$70.10	$70.15
9	Paine Webber Group	Donald B. Marron	$55.59	$11.44	$67.03
10	Paccar	Charles M. Pigott	$2.25	$50.86	$53.12
11	Times Mirror	Robert F. Erburu	$3.29	$45.39	$48.67
12	Coastal Corp	Oscar S. Wyatt, Jr.*	$0.43	$44.33	$44.75
13	Archer-Daniels-Midland	Dwayne O. Andreas	-$0.15	$41.23	$41.07
14	Carter Hawley Hale	Philip M. Hawley*	$23.36	$16.25	$39.60
15	McDonnell Douglas	John F. McDonnell*	$0.09	$33.79	$33.88
16	CBS	Laurence A. Tisch	$1.79	$31.58	$33.37
17	Humana	David A. Jones*	$1.34	$25.88	$27.22
18	Winn-Dixie Stores	A. Dano Davis	$2.72	$23.22	$25.95
19	Masco	Richard A. Manoogian	$8.78	$14.08	$22.86
20	American Int'l Group	Maurice R. Greenberg	$0.50	$21.72	$22.22
21	Digital Equipment	Kenneth H. Olsen*	$1.00	$19.06	$20.07
22	MCI Communications	William G. McGowan*	$1.77	$17.95	$19.73
23	Cummins Engine	Henry B. Schacht	$18.46	$0.87	$19.33
24	Walt Disney	Michael D. Eisner	$15.62	$2.88	$18.50
25	FMC	Robert H. Malott	$8.43	$7.04	$15.47

Note: Sample consists of CEOs in the 250 largest companies ranked by 1988 sales. *Denotes founder or founding-family CEO.

Highly talented people who would succeed in any field are likely to shun the corporate sector, where pay and performance are weakly related, in favor of organizations where pay is more strongly related to performance—and the prospect of big financial rewards more favorable.

Compensation surveys in the business press, such as those published by *Fortune* and *Business Week*, are really about levels of pay not about pay for performance. Yet they often include an analysis or ranking of the appropriateness of a particular CEO's pay by relating it to company performance in some fashion. The methods adopted by *Fortune* and *Business Week* share a common flaw. CEOs earning low fixed salaries while delivering mediocre performance look like stars; on the flip side, CEOs with genuinely strong pay-for-performance packages rank poorly. For example, *Business Week*'s 1989 survey calculates the ratio of the change in shareholder wealth to the CEO's total compensation, both measured over three years. Executives with the highest ratios are labeled the "CEOs Who Gave the Most for Their Pay." Low-ratio CEOs purportedly gave shareholders the least. *Fortune*'s 1989 compensation issue uses a regression model to estimate how compensation varies with factors such as the CEO's age and tenure, company size, location, industry, and performance. Although the author cautions against taking the results too literally, CEOs earning more than predicted are implicitly designated as "overpaid," while those earning less than predicted are "underpaid."

Consider the case of Disney's Michael Eisner. By all accounts, Mr. Eisner's pay is wedded to company performance—in addition to loads of stock options, he gets 2% of all profits above an annually increasing threshold. Shareholders have prospered under Eisner, and few have complained that his compensation is unreasonable in light of the $7 billion in shareholder wealth he has helped create since joining the company in 1984. But *Business Week* ranks Eisner second on the list of CEOs who gave their shareholders the least (right behind option-laden Lee Iacocca, who over the past decade helped create $6 billion in wealth for Chrysler shareholders), while *Fortune* flags Eisner as the third most overpaid CEO. Surveys measuring Eisner and Iacocca low are clearly not measuring incentives. In contrast, our survey ranks Eisner and Iacocca as the nation's fourth and ninth respectively

THE 25 CEOs OF LARGE COMPANIES WITH THE WORST INCENTIVES			Total Effects (over Two Years) on CEO Wealth Corresponding to Each $1,000 Change in Shareholder Wealth		
Rank	Company	CEO	Change in All Pay-Related Wealth	Change in the Value of Stock Owned	Change in Total CEO Wealth
226	Central & South West	Merle L. Borchelt	$0.14	$0.32	$0.46
227	Campbell Soup	R. Gordon McGovern	$0.07	$0.38	$0.44
228	3M	Allen F. Jacobson	$0.28	$0.11	$0.39
229	Sears Roebuck	Edward A. Brennan	$0.17	$0.20	$0.37
230	AMP	Walter F. Raab	-$0.03	$0.39	$0.36
231	Consolidated Edison	Arthur Hauspurg	$0.22	$0.12	$0.34
232	Detroit Edison	Walter J. McCarthy, Jr.	$0.24	$0.07	$0.31
233	Commonwealth Edison	James J. O'Connor	$0.24	$0.06	$0.30
234	Texas Utilities	Jerry S. Farrington	$0.23	$0.07	$0.29
235	Exxon	Lawrence G. Rawl	$0.19	$0.11	$0.25
236	AT&T	Robert E. Allen	$0.19	$0.04	$0.24
237	ARCO	Lodwrick M. Cook	-$0.10	$0.33	$0.23
238	IBM	John F. Akers	$0.13	$0.06	$0.19
239	Borden	Romeo J. Ventres	-$0.20	$0.38	$0.18
240	Eastman Kodak	Colby H. Chandler	$0.09	$0.08	$0.17
241	R.R. Donnelley & Sons	John R. Walter	-$0.18	$0.34	$0.16
242	Johnson & Johnson	Ralph S. Larsen	$0.11	$0.15	$0.15
243	Chevron Corp.	Kenneth T. Derr	$0.04	$0.15	$0.11
244	GTE	James L. Johnson	$0.04	$0.07	$0.11
245	Pacific Gas & Electric	Richard A. Clarke	$0.06	$0.04	$0.10
246	Philadelphia Electric	Joseph F. Pasquette	$0.07	$0.01	$0.08
247	PacifiCorp	Al M. Gleason	-$0.04	$0.08	$0.04
248	Honeywell	James J. Renier	-$0.51	$0.40	-$0.10
249	Carolina Power & Light	Sherwood H. Smith, Jr.	-$0.61	$0.45	-$0.16
250	Navistar International	James C. Cotting	-$1.61	$0.20	-$1.41

Note: Sample consists of CEOs in the 250 largest companies, ranked by 1988 sales.

"best paid" CEOs measured on the basis of pay-related wealth alone.

We estimated the pay-for-performance relation for each of the 430 companies for which we have sufficient data. The results are summarized in the four nearby tables. Three of the tables include results for the 250 largest companies ranked by 1988 sales. The 25 CEOs with the best and worst overall incentives, as reflected by the relation between their total compensation (composed of all pay-related wealth changes and the change in the value of stock owned), are summarized in the first two tables. Castle & Cooke, whose current CEO is David Murdock, ranks first with a total change in CEO wealth of $231.53 for every $1,000 change in shareholder wealth. His stockholdings contribute $224.24 of this amount, while the change in all pay-related wealth adds another $7.29.

With a few exceptions, it is clear that the best incentives are determined primarily by large CEO stockholdings. Donald Marron of Paine Webber is such an exception, with more than $55 of his total of $67 coming from changes in pay-related wealth.

So too are Philip Hawley of Carter Hawley Hale, Henry Schacht of Cummins Engine, and Disney's Eisner.

The 25 companies providing their CEOs with the worst total incentives are led by Navistar International whose CEO James Cotting on average receives a $1.41 increase in wealth for every $1,000 decrease in shareholder value. Carolina Power & Light's Sherwood Smith, Jr. receives a 16-cent increase for every $1,000 decrease in shareholder wealth. Other well-known corporations whose CEOs appear on the worst-incentive list include Chevron, Johnson & Johnson, Eastman Kodak, and IBM.

Although one has to recognize that there is statistical uncertainty surrounding our estimates of pay-related wealth sensitivity, no CEO with substantial equity holdings (measured as a fraction of the total outstanding equity) makes our list of low-incentive CEOs. As we point out in the accompanying article, an important disadvantage of corporate size is that it is extremely difficult for the CEO to hold a substantial fraction of corporate equity.

THE BEST OF THE REST: CEO INCENTIVES IN SMALLER COMPANIES			Total Effects (over Two Years) on CEO Wealth Corresponding to Each $1,000 Change in Shareholder Wealth		
Rank	Company	CEO	Change in All Pay-Related Wealth	Change in the Value of Stock Owned	Change in Total CEO Wealth
1	Berkshire Hathaway	Warren E. Buffett	$0.06	$446.77	$446.83
2	Williamette Industries	William Swindells, Jr.	$0.64	$427.10	$427.75
3	Riggs National	Joe L. Allbritton	$1.22	$358.19	$359.40
4	Hilton Hotels	Barron Hilton*	$0.85	$245.90	$246.75
5	Timken	William R. Timken, Jr.*	$5.20	$142.46	$147.66
6	United Missouri Bancshares	R. Crosby Kemper	$1.08	$118.65	$119.73
7	Zions Bancorporation	Roy W. Simmons	$2.76	$89.17	$91.93
8	First Empire State	Robert G. Wilmers	$18.72	$71.63	$90.36
9	Florida National Banks	John D. Uible	$1.85	$87.66	$89.51
10	Equimark	Alan S. Fellheimer	$15.53	$72.28	$87.81
11	W.W. Grainger	David W. Grainger*	$0.21	$79.13	$79.34
12	Fin'l Corp. of Santa Barbara	Philip R. Brinkerhoff	$54.68	$21.41	$76.09
13	Golden West Financial	Herbert M. Sandler*	$4.48	$67.36	$71.83
14	Merchants National	Otto N. Frenzel III	$9.59	$60.19	$69.79
15	First City Bancorp of Texas	A. Robert Abboud	-$0.21	$58.75	$58.54
16	First Security	Spencer F. Eccles	$2.63	$44.84	$47.47
17	Central Bancshares of the South	Harry B. Brock, Jr.*	$4.89	$38.25	$43.15
18	Fruehauf	T. Neal Combs	$16.20	$21.14	$37.34
19	Holiday	Michael D. Rose	$14.01	$20.94	$34.94
20	Cullen/Frost Bankers	Thomas C. Frost*	$8.90	$25.95	$34.85
21	Beneficial Corp.	Finn M.W. Caspersen	$3.37	$29.87	$33.23
22	Yellow Freight System	George E. Powell, Jr.	$0.86	$30.90	$31.76
23	Data General	Edson D. deCastro*	$1.89	$29.79	$31.68
24	Equitable Bancorporation	H. Grant Hathaway	$11.01	$17.23	$28.24
25	Imperial Corp. of America	Kenneth J. Thygerson	$24.98	$2.52	$27.51

Note: Sample consists of CEOs in companies ranked 251 to 430 by 1988 sales. *Denotes founder or founding-family CEO.

The inverse relation between size and stockholdings (and therefore the negative effect of size on incentives) is readily visible in the much higher sensitivities shown for the top 25 CEOs in smaller companies, those ranking from 251 to 430 in 1988 sales. (See the table "The Best of the Rest: CEO Incentives in Smaller Companies.") Warren Buffett of Berkshire Hathaway leads this list with $446 per $1,000, followed by William Swindells, Jr. of Williamette Industries, Joe Allbritton of Riggs National, and Barron Hilton of Hilton Hotels. Again, the importance of large stockholdings is clear.

Indeed, one problem with current compensation practices is that boards often reward CEOs with substantial equity through stock options but then stand by to watch CEOs undo the incentives by unloading their stockholdings. Boards seldom provide contractual constraints or moral suasion that discourage the CEO from selling such shares to invest in a diversified portfolio of assets. One of the

ironies of the situation is that the corporation itself often funds executive financial counseling by consultants whose common mantra is "sell and diversify, sell and diversify." While this can be personally advantageous to executives, it is not optimal for shareholders or society because it significantly reduces CEOs' incentives to run their companies efficiently.

Pay-related incentives are under the direct control of the compensation committee and the board. The table "Best Paid CEOs of Large Companies" lists the 25 companies that reward their CEOs in a way that provides the best incentives from pay-related wealth alone—changes in salary and bonus, long-term incentive plans, dismissal likelihood, and stock options. Each of these estimates is given in the table, along with the sum of the effects in the last column. The table makes clear that the major contributors to pay-related incentives are stock options and the present value of the change in salary and bonus.

BEST PAID CEOs OF LARGE COMPANIES			Change in Pay-Related Wealth Corresponding to Each $1,000 Change in Shareholder Wealth				
Rank	Company	CEO	Change in Salary + Bonus over Two Years	Present Value of Pay Change	Change in Wealth due to Dismissal Likelihood	Change in Value of Stock Options	Change in All Pay-Related Wealth
1	Paine Webber Group	Donald B. Marron	$4.11	$46.91	$1.18	$7.51	$55.59
2	Carter Hawley Hale	Philip M. Hawley*	$0.03	$0.54	$0.98	$21.83	$23.36
3	Cummins Engine	Henry B. Schacht	$1.11	$18.29	$0.03	$0.14	$18.46
4	Walt Disney	Michael D. Eisner	$0.72	$11.35	$0.00	$4.27	$15.62
5	George A. Hormel	Richard L. Knowlton	$0.76	$7.47	$0.19	$4.70	$12.36
6	UAL	Stephen M. Wolf	$0.01	$0.45	$0.02	$11.57	$12.05
7	Fleet/Norstar	J. Terrence Murray	$0.72	$10.93	$0.03	$1.02	$11.98
8	Continental Bank	Thomas C. Theobald	$0.26	$2.01	$0.04	$9.40	$11.46
9	Chrysler Corp.	Lee A. Iacocca	$0.43	$5.38	$0.02	$4.74	$10.14
10	Zenith Electronics	Jerry K. Pearlman	$0.77	$7.44	$0.05	$2.27	$9.76
11	NCNB	Hugh L. McColl, Jr.	$0.76	$8.43	$0.01	$0.63	$9.07
12	Masco	Richard A. Manoogian	$0.01	$2.38	$0.16	$6.24	$8.78
13	FMC	Robert H. Malott	$0.01	$0.13	$0.47	$7.82	$8.43
14	Turner	Alfred T. McNeill	$2.01	$4.27	$0.27	$3.52	$8.06
15	B.F. Goodrich	John D. Ong	$0.51	$4.73	$0.14	$2.85	$7.72
16	Alco Standard	Ray B. Mundt	$0.88	$5.46	$0.88	$1.28	$7.61
17	Black & Decker	Nolan D. Archibald	$0.25	$3.89	$0.34	$3.30	$7.53
18	Castle & Cooke	David H. Murdock	$0.77	$3.70	$0.04	$3.54	$7.29
19	Brunswick Corp.	Jack F. Reichert	$0.40	$6.59	$0.26	$0.00	$6.85
20	Mellon Bank	Frank V. Cahouet	$0.42	$3.69	$0.65	$2.38	$6.72
21	Enron	Kenneth L. Lay	$0.46	$3.99	$0.05	$2.58	$6.62
22	Pan Am	Thomas G. Plaskett	$0.25	$0.77	$0.13	$5.55	$6.46
23	Toys "R" Us	Charles Lazarus*	-$0.13	$1.06	$0.11	$5.27	$6.45
24	Norwest	Lloyd P. Johnson	$0.22	$1.30	$0.10	$4.98	$6.37
25	First Union	Edward E. Crutchfield, Jr.	$0.48	$5.59	$0.03	$0.08	$5.71

Note: Sample consists of CEOs in the 250 largest companies, ranked by 1988 sales. *Denotes founder or founding-family CEO.

THE CASE FOR EXPENSING STOCK OPTIONS AGAINST EARNINGS

by Merton H. Miller,
University of Chicago, and
Graef S. Crystal,
University of California at Berkeley

I n normal times, placidity reigns at the Norwalk, Connecticut, offices of the Financial Accounting Standards Board (FASB), the rule-making body for American accounting. But these are not normal times. FASB is under siege for proposing that companies charge reported earnings for the cost of stock options they grant.

Corporate tempers have flared over FASB's plan to such a degree that the Senate and the Administration have been forced to take sides. The Senators favoring the FASB proposal are led by Carl Levin (D-Mich.). Those opposed are led by Joseph Lieberman (D-Conn.), who along with Dianne Feinstein (D-Calif.), Barbara Boxer (D-Calif.) and Connie Mack (R-Fla.), has sponsored a bill ordering the U.S. Securities and Exchange Commission (SEC), which oversees FASB, to kill the plan to charge earnings. Bill Bradley (D-NJ) sponsored a less extreme "sense of the Senate" resolution urging FASB to reconsider. Treasury Secretary Lloyd Bentsen and Commerce Secretary Ronald Brown have joined the Senate critics in offering objections. For his part, President Clinton has expressed sympathy for both sides.

Just what has FASB done to generate such contention? To see, consider a typical company granting its CEO an option on 100,000 shares of company stock, trading that day at $50 per share. The option gives the CEO the right, but not the obligation, to purchase the shares for $50 any time after the first four years of the option's ten-year life. The CEO thus stands to make $100,000 for each $1 per share the stock price rises during the term of the grant. Programs offered by Wall Street firms allow CEOs to realize these option gains in cash, immediately on exercise, without putting up any money of their own, and, thanks to the forbearance of the SEC, without triggering the insider trading restrictions. If the stock price falls below $50 per share and never recovers, the CEO simply elects not to exercise the option.

A "heads I win, tails I don't lose" proposition like that is worth about $1.8 million to the CEO. Under FASB's rules, that sum, minus what the company could obtain through corporate tax deductions, must be charged pro rata against the company's income during the four years following the grant.

So if that's how FASB is proposing to charge earnings for options granted, what's being done now? The answer, believe it or not, is nothing! Stock options of this kind currently are not charged to earnings either when granted or when exercised. This curious treatment, which is accorded no other form of expense—whether compensation or not—dates from the 1950s, when options first came into widespread use. The accountants grappling with the issue then couldn't figure out how to price a stock option, so they turned to a number of academics for guidance. Faced with widely-varying opinions from these outside experts, the accountants chose to do nothing—even though no serious academic, then or now, has ever concluded that an option had no worth or was not properly included as a compensation expense on the income statement. FASB, at long last, proposes to correct this cop-out.

Until it does, however, companies' decisions as to forms of compensation for attracting, retaining, and motivating their employees will continue to be distorted. If the company pays an executive a $100,000 cash bonus, that bonus is charged to earnings, thereby decreasing pre-tax profits by $100,000. But if the same executive earns $100,000 through the exercise of a stock option, reported earnings are the same as if the company never granted the executive a stock option. (Needless to say, however, both the cash bonus and the gain on option exercise are fully deductible for corporate income tax purposes. Not even FASB's harshest critics object to that!)

The arbitrary difference between the accounting for stock options and for alternative forms of compensation produces other bizarre results. At General Mills, for example, executives can forgo bonuses and even part of their base salaries in return for larger-than-normal stock options. General Mills defends its plan as a way of improving the relation between pay and performance, which may well be true. But one thing is certain: By substituting stock options for cash bonuses or salaries, General Mills will be reporting higher profits even if performance stays the same.

This type of pay-shifting may soon get a boost from the new law limiting pay deductions of public corporations to no more than $1 million per year for each of its five most highly-compensated executive officers. But the law also offers ways around that limit, notably by allowing the company, with shareholder approval, to grant any number of stock option shares to its top officers and to exempt from the $1 million deduction cap any compensation they receive by exercising those options.

Many companies will also be induced to use conventional stock options in preference to other plans more directly linked to performance. Our CEO, for example, would earn $5 million by exercising the 100,000 share option if the stock price rises from $50 to $100. But what if the overall stock market had also doubled in the same period? The CEO gets $5 million for simply staying even with the market. Free-riding of that kind could be remedied, of course, by adjusting the fixed $50 exercise price of the option by the gain or loss in a broad market index (or perhaps by an index predicated on competitor stocks). But options like that don't qualify under the current no-charge rules FASB is trying to change. A company will thus be rewarded for its devotion to tying pay to real performance by being forced to charge earnings and hence report lower profits to its shareholders.

Or consider a company with a number of autonomous divisions operating in a variety of industries. To grant the General Manager of Division A an option on the parent corporation's stock may be totally inappropriate because that General Manager has so little influence on the results of the overall corporation. But to grant a synthetic stock option on the long-term results of his or her own division, though far more motivational, will force the company to take charges to its earnings.

Despite these distortions under the current arrangements, virtually every company in the land is fighting FASB's proposal, along with some strange allies, like the Council of Institutional Investors, a prestigious group of major pension funds. They have raised a number of objections.

One is that granting stock options is not compensation to a corporate employee but an equity transaction between shareholders and the executive. This curious theory, however, flies in the face of centuries of legal, accounting, and tax precedents that the corporation is an entity separate from the shareholders. Worse, the notion that shareholders are somehow dealing directly with executives, if carried to its logical conclusion, would result in no charge to earnings, not merely for stock options, but for any executive compensation transaction involving the company's stock, like the grant two years ago to Roberto C. Goizueta, the CEO of Coca-Cola of totally-free shares worth $56 million. What value would company income statements have for stockholders and investors if they omitted such transactions?

The most frequently-heard objection to FASB's proposal centers on the difficulty of determining with precision what an option is worth when it is granted. Back in 1950, when options were first used, that may well have been the case; hence, the disagreement among the academics previously noted. But in 1973, two pioneering economists, Fischer Black and Myron Scholes, developed a valid method for putting a price tag on a stock option—even, as it turns out, an executive stock option. Their so-called Black-Scholes model (and its many descendants) is widely used today all over Wall Street.

To be sure, pricing an option by the Black-Scholes formula does require an estimate of the stock's future price volatility as well as the stock's likely future dividends. And estimates can be wrong. But company income statements are full of estimates. You must depreciate a new computer over its useful life. But how do you know now what that useful life will be? Or you must estimate the present value of future pension costs. But how do you know now what interest rates, inflation rates, and labor costs will really be in the year 2030? As Warren Buffett puts it: "I have far more confidence in our company's ability to determine an appropriate price to pay for an option than I have in our ability to determine the proper depreciation rate for our corporate jet."

Consider also that many of the firms proclaiming that options cannot be valued need only turn to the financial pages of any newspaper to see publicly-traded options on their very own stock. Those options do have much shorter terms than the usual ten-year executive stock option, which must also typically be forfeited on leaving the company. But many Wall Street firms would be happy to help the company hedge the grant by selling comparable ten-year options to the company which would, by the same token, remove any uncertainty to the company about the value of the option at the time of granting. As for the possibility of forfeiture, the original charge to earnings would be reversed if the executive left the company without exercising the option. Note as well that, for companies with no listed stock or past history of stock prices, the FASB proposal permits a number of highly conservative alternatives to the Black-Scholes model.

Another objection is that FASB's action will hurt the "little people," the employees below the top management. Faced with a charge to earnings, the argument goes, companies heretofore open-handed with their stock option grants will cut off anyone but the most senior executives. This argument has particular currency in Silicon Valley, because not a few companies there do, in fact, offer option grants to almost all employees. But if granting options to such employees really does pay off in increased motivation, then these companies, which are already bearing the true economic costs of option grants, would be foolish to abandon them simply because they now must recognize that reality on their income statements.

A final complaint—also frequently heard in Silicon Valley—is that if companies must charge their earnings for stock option grants, their stock prices will plummet, and they will find it too costly to raise the further investment capital they need to grow. Clearly, charging earnings for stock option grants will lower reported earnings. But stock prices are not some simple multiple of current or past earnings per share. Stock prices are based on the market's estimate of future earnings. The analysts and brokers following a company's stock already know how many option shares the company has granted and have factored the potential future dilution into their calculations. And to the extent they have not, and the stock price adjusts, the adjustment, up or down, is *correcting* an error in valuation, not *causing* one.

A number of possible compromise approaches have been suggested to FASB, such as that by the Shadow SEC (a group of five academics including one of the authors, Merton Miller), under which companies would report their earnings before the cost of all performance-based plans (not merely stock options) was charged to earnings; the companies would also report their earnings after the costs of such plans were charged to earnings, exactly as they now report earnings per share on both a primary and a fully-diluted basis when they have convertible securities outstanding.

The Shadow SEC's proposal underscores another point, namely, that nothing prevents any company from giving its shareholders more information than the minimum required by accounting rules. Those rules already let a firm distinguish between its net *operating* income and its ultimate net *income*, taking into account extraordinary charges. So if a Silicon Valley company is about to see its net income move from a profit to a loss because of the new charges it must take for stock option grants, that company can provide extra lines in its income statement to help shareholders understand that the decrease in profits is not simply cash frittered away but rather a reflection of the company's significant commitment to employee motivation.

In sum, stock options are valuable forms of compensation and, as such, are surely a cost to shareholders. America deserves accounting policies based on those realities, not on fallacious arguments backed by political pressure.

HAS PAY FOR PERFORMANCE GONE AWRY? VIEWS FROM A CORPORATE GOVERNANCE FORUM

by Stuart L. Gillan,
*TIAA-CREF Institute**

An important way in which many large institutional investors, including TIAA-CREF, attempt to serve the interests of their constituents is by promoting good corporate governance practices in the public corporations in which they invest. While there are several ways in which TIAA-CREF and other entities pursue this goal, an important first step in evaluating the appropriateness of any governance practice is thoughtful research and open discussion of the issues.

Some of the most controversial governance-related issues that have arisen in recent years involve executive and employee compensation. Investors, the press, and the public have expressed concern over (1) escalating executive pay packages and (2) the growing use of stock options. These two trends raise several complex governance issues that have significant implications for all investors.

Indeed, compensation issues have become an increasingly important component of corporate governance for a number of reasons. First, well-designed compensation programs should serve to align the interests of executives and employees with those of shareholders. It is also clear that an effective compensation policy is critical in attracting, motivating, and retaining employees. However, the costs and benefits of large pay packages and option grants—to executives in particular—are not always obvious. Second, in many companies, particularly knowledge-based companies, the role of workers or "human capital" has become critical in generating returns to shareholders. Many employees recognize

this, and justifiably desire a "piece of the action," that is, to be compensated with equity for their contributions to value creation. Third, an explosion in the use of option-based compensation during the past decade has led to concerns about how much this is costing shareholders. Finally, there is a concern that misuse of stock-based compensation, particularly in the context of a booming economy and rising stock market, has led to a fundamental disconnect in the relationship between pay and performance.

Motivated by these concerns and others, on April 5, 2001, the TIAA-CREF Institute, in cooperation with the TIAA-CREF corporate governance staff, sponsored a Corporate Governance Forum, *Executive Compensation, Stock Options, and the Role of the Board of Directors*, at which the issues of executive compensation and the use of stock options were examined and discussed in detail. By bringing together a diverse audience, including corporate officers and directors, academic and other researchers, compensation consultants, corporate human resources personnel, institutional investors, regulators, and other practitioners, the Forum provided an opportunity for an open exchange of views among groups that do not often meet together. Participants discussed current trends in compensation practice, the accounting for stock-based compensation, the appropriate use of stock options and alternatives to standard at-the-money options. They also reviewed and debated the role of shareholders in approving compensation plans, and the importance of the board of directors and board compensation committee in determining compensation policy.

* Reprinted with permission from TIAA-CREF © 2001 TIAA-CREF Institute. This article was reprinted from the No. 68 July 2001 issue of the TIAA-CREF Institute *Research Dialogue*. I thank John Ameriks, Ken Bertsch, Dolph Bridgewater, Elizabeth Fender, Mark Warshawsky, and Ken West for helpful comments and

discussions. The opinions expressed in this article are those of the author and not necessarily those of TIAA-CREF or its employees. Additional conference-related materials are available at http://www.tiaa-crefinstitute.org (select "Corporate Governance" then "Programs").

This article discusses the important issues raised by conference participants and attempts to provide an overview of the comments and observations of both panel members and the audience. The article first provides a primer on stock options and related compensation issues, then generally follows the order of the conference sessions: (1) Executive Compensation and Executive Stock Options, (2) the General Use of Stock Options and Dilution Issues, and (3) the Role of the Board of Directors and the Compensation Committee. Necessarily, there is some overlap within each of the three broad topics. This article is not a transcript of the Forum, a comprehensive background on compensation programs, or a statement of best practices as it relates to compensation policies. Rather, the goal is simply to share some of the insights and information presented at the conference with a broader audience.

A PRIMER ON STOCK OPTIONS

A basic understanding of what options are and how they work is a prerequisite for thinking about the governance issues related to their use; thus, a brief outline of stock options is presented here. When a stock option is granted to an employee, a company gives the employee the right to purchase a share of her company's stock at a future date, at a prespecified price—the so-called exercise price. (Typically, the exercise price is set at the market price of the stock as of the date of grant.) Although the difference between the exercise price and the market price on the grant date is zero, the possibility that the stock price will increase gives the option an economic value. After the grant date, if the price of the underlying stock increases above the exercise price of the option, the value of the employee's option increases—so she can effectively buy the stock at a discount.

Thus, owning an option gives an employee the incentive to act in such a way as to increase the company's stock price, and hence the value of her stock options. Shareholders also benefit from any increases in the stock price. While this seems to be a remarkable win-win situation for shareholders and employees alike, there is an important secondary effect of rising stock option values: As the value of the options held by employees rises, the obligation of the company to honor these options also increases. Thus, it is vital to recognize that the use of

stock options benefits shareholders only so long as the gains from compensating employees with options exceed the costs of doing so.

By the early 1990s, stock options were viewed by many investors as an effective means of aligning the interests of executives and shareholders. Consequently, options have been increasingly used to compensate senior executives. For example, in 1992 the median value of options granted to CEOs at S&P 1,500 firms was approximately 16% of their total compensation. By 1998, this had increased to 35% of total compensation.[1] Similarly, the use of options to compensate employees beyond the executive suite also expanded rapidly during the nineties. In her presentation at the Forum, Ms. Pearl Meyer noted that "option overhang" (defined as shares reserved for outstanding option grants, plus shares available for future grant, divided by the weighted average shares outstanding) for the top 200 industrial and service companies increased from 6.5% in 1989 to approximately 15% by 2000. Moreover, average annual grants increased from just over 1% to approximately 2.3% of shares outstanding during the same time period. At 100 "dot-com" companies surveyed in 2000, grants averaged 10.7% of shares outstanding, and option overhang averaged approximately 37% of shares outstanding.

AN OUTLINE OF COMPENSATION ISSUES

Increased use of stock options has led to greater scrutiny of option-based compensation. A key concern, sparked by large gains for executives and employees in the face of a bull market, is that the cost of stock options to shareholders may exceed the benefits from their use. This reflects, in part, the idea that stock prices may be poor measures of employee performance, because stock price changes are beyond the control of most employees. A clear question is whether option-based compensation rewards employees for their own performance, for their company's performance, or for the performance of the economy (or stock market) as a whole. Put another way, the issue is whether option plans reward employees for superior individual performance—or for luck.

Two other issues have led to questions about the appropriateness of using options to compensate employees. First, academic research suggests that employees place a lower value on stock options than

---

1. See Table 2 in Perry and Zenner (2000).

Under SFAS 123, Accounting for Stock-based Compensation, companies are required to estimate the fair value of options at the grant date and typically do so using an option-pricing model, usually Black-Scholes. Companies must then either take a charge to income or else (as almost all do) include a note to the financial statements that shows net income and earnings per share as if that cost had been charged to income. The estimated cost of each year's grant is allocated equally over the vesting period.

Under SFAS 128, Earnings per Share, diluted earnings per share (EPS) is reported for both continuing operations and the "bottom line" corporate earnings number. In each case, shares underlying in-the-money options are considered to be shares outstanding, and are added to current shares outstanding in the denominator of the earnings per share calculation. However, that denominator is reduced by the number of shares that could be purchased in the open market with option exercise proceeds. Options "at-the-money" or "out-of-the-money" do not result in EPS dilution. Researchers argue that existing shareholders experience dilution from all options, not just those in-the-money. Any increase in firm value as a result of an increase in future earnings accrues in part to all optionholders, and this takes place at the expense of current shareholders.

the potential cost of those options to shareholders.[2] If true, then the rationale for using a form of compensation that costs shareholders more than its perceived value to employees is unclear. Second, it has been argued that option-based compensation may not be appropriate for employees at lower levels in the corporation because of the risk involved.

Another important aspect of the current compensation environment is the way in which companies account for option-based compensation. Granting employees stock options "at-the-money" (with an exercise price equal to the market price of the company's stock as of the date of grant) generally does not result in a compensation expense in corporate financial statements—in contrast to other types of options and forms of compensation. (See box.) Thus, the reported income of many companies (i.e., their profits or losses) does not reflect the full cost of their option-based compensation programs. Similarly, measures of diluted earnings per share, calculated in accordance with current accounting rules, do not reflect the economic cost or full dilution resulting from option grants. These accounting practices raise at least two issues for consideration. First, do financial statements reflect the economic reality of the cost of stock options? Many would argue that they do not. Second, and perhaps more important, does the current accounting treatment encourage the use of at-the-money options in preference to potentially superior alternatives, simply because at-the-money options receive favorable accounting treatment?

Another significant issue deserves mention as part of a general introduction. Recently, option repricing has served to focus attention on many of the issues pertaining to option-based compensation. Stock market declines have left many employees holding "out-of-the-money" or "underwater" options (i.e., options that give the employee the right to purchase shares at a price above the current market price of the stock). Although these options continue to have value, because stock prices may rise again in the future, they could not be profitably exercised at the current share price. As of January 2001, option grants made during 1999 were underwater for approximately 40% of S&P 1,500 companies.[3] To address this issue, many companies have moved to restore all or part of the option value by means of a "repricing." A repricing often takes the form of granting employees new options with a new exercise price equal to the current market price, effectively reducing the price that employees must pay to exercise their options.

Investors are concerned that repricing rewards employees for poor stock price performance and undermines the rationale for using options as incentive compensation. This asymmetry, where employees are rewarded in a rising market and made whole in the face of a market decline, has been viewed as a "heads I win, tails you lose" arrangement. Moreover, repricing stock options is perceived as providing employees with a benefit that is not available to shareholders, who have also suffered a decline in the value of their investment but cannot recover their losses.

---

2. Hall and Murphy (2000).

3. Gillan (2001).

High-powered executives may end up negotiating for pay with part-time directors
who have difficulty valuing the job of the CEO, which can create a dynamic favoring
CEOs, if not creating a systematic bias toward management.

In contrast, many companies argue that in a tight labor market, failure to reprice options may result in poorly motivated employees and/or undesirable employee turnover. For example, employees can effectively "reprice" their underwater options by leaving their current jobs and getting new options from a new employer. Thus, failure to reprice may result in additional costs to the company and shareholders in the long run. Finally, the current regulatory environment allows companies to adopt some stock option plans without shareholder approval. Thus, a central governance concern relates to the right of shareholders to approve stock option plans that have the potential to dilute their voting power and their wealth.[4]

EXECUTIVE COMPENSATION AND STOCK OPTIONS

The first session of the day addressed *Executive Compensation and Executive Stock Options*. In focusing on executive compensation, the discussion related not only to the use of options per se, but also to the overall levels of compensation and the mechanisms that govern the pay-setting process at corporations. This session focused primarily on the state of CEO pay in general and features of the compensation environment that may tend to undermine the potential incentive effects of option-based compensation.

Presenting a view of compensation practices and trends from the perspective of an experienced compensation consultant, Mr. Frederic W. Cook highlighted several factors considered influential in driving CEO pay to high levels. Among these is the public company board model. The public company board places an emphasis on independent outside directors, with no affiliations to the company other than stock ownership. Mr. Cook argued that this is a useful governance model that ensures general accountability to shareholders, but it can result in an imbalance in the pay-setting process. High-powered executives may end up negotiating for pay with part-time directors who have difficulty valuing the job of the CEO, which can create a dynamic favoring CEOs, if not creating a systematic bias toward management.

Mr. Cook contended that a reliance on surveys in setting pay may also lead to higher compensation. Surveys lead to asymmetry in compensation practices, emphasizing pay for performance when companies are performing well, and offering peer group pay norms when companies are not performing well. Moreover, Mr. Cook suggested that companies relying more heavily on surveys tend to be poor performers. This leads to performance-related differences in compensation practices: strong-performing companies tend to link pay to performance, while weaker performing companies rely on surveys. The result is that the pay-to-performance link is weakened, and pay levels ratchet ever upward.

Mr. Cook suggested there has been a cultural shift toward pay aggressiveness, and that "the cult of the CEO as a star" impacts compensation practices. He observed that in the past, CEOs were embarrassed to have their pay packages publicized, but now some CEOs enjoy being mentioned in the listings of top-paid executives, such as the annual review by *Business Week*. The "total pay model" also seems to influence the level of compensation and the link between pay and performance. The idea of the total pay model is that companies grant stock options annually based on competitive guidelines irrespective of recent corporate performance. The value of option grants has come to dominate changes in annual pay. This, in turn, may result in total pay rising in the face of poor performance and an apparent disconnect between pay and performance.

Professor David Yermack's comments focused on the growing evidence of a disconnect between pay and performance. As noted earlier, it seems clear that the aim of incentive-based compensation is to align the interests of executives and shareholders. That is, shareholders should want to see the executive's personal fortunes tied to the stock price of the company that he or she manages. However, the aspects of executive behavior that Professor Yermack highlighted suggest that option-based compensation may not be achieving this objective. For example, one of the often-stated reasons companies award stock options is to encourage ownership by management. There is evidence, however, that executives rarely continue to hold the stock acquired from exercising options. Indeed, by encouraging cashless exercise of stock options, companies may even encourage executives not to hold stock acquired from option exercise. Professor Yermack also noted that option recipients tend to sell stock when they receive new grants of stock options. Although taxes and/or incentives for

---

4. Gillan (2001).

executives to diversify their personal holdings may partly explain this behavior, he noted that the selling of company stock does not appear to be in the interests of their firms. Moreover, it contradicts one of the stated reasons why equity compensation plans exist.

In contrast, Professor Brian Hall highlighted evidence on managerial stock holdings, suggesting that executive stock ownership has grown by a factor of 10 during the last two decades. During the flat stock market of 1994, 25% of executives "lost money," given pay and the net change in the value of their equity. This demonstrates that changes in executives' wealth constitute "pay for performance."

Professor Yermack raised a related point regarding the "shadowy hedging market." Basically, this market enables executives to trade out of their personal equity positions using strategies such as equity swaps, put options, "collars," and secured borrowing using the stock as collateral. These practices provide executives with an opportunity to undo the incentives that firms impose on them when stock options are awarded. To the extent that executives can undo the incentive structures, the rationale of using incentive-based compensation is undermined.

The appropriateness of "reload options," a variation on standard options, was also discussed. An executive with reload options triggers the "reload" feature by exercising the option and paying the exercise price with shares of company stock he already owns. For every share surrendered, the executive receives one new option with an exercise price equal to the current market price of the stock. Professor Yermack argued, essentially, that by exercising and reloading, executives can insure themselves against stock price declines. Furthermore, the use of an incentive contract that makes executives better off in the face of falling stock prices than they otherwise would have been does not appear to be in shareholders' interests.[5]

Another compensation puzzle discussed by Professor Yermack is evidence suggesting that executives tend to exercise standard stock options earlier than might be expected under financial theory. When executives exercise options early, they receive the difference between the current stock price and the option exercise price, while essentially donating back to their employers the further upside potential of the option.

Professor Hall offered several explanations for observed early exercise. First, risk-averse executives rationally seek to diversify their personal portfolios, so they have an incentive to exercise early. Second, in part because of a desire for diversification, risk-averse executives may place a lower value on stock options than the potential cost to shareholders. Finally, because of executive incentives to diversify, short vesting periods (as opposed to longer vesting periods) may contribute to early exercise.

Professor Yermack also noted that some research shows stock option awards tend to occur at times favorable to the executives involved. For example, evidence suggests a close association between option award dates and the release of news, such as earnings announcements, that push company stock prices higher. Other research reports similar patterns of "fortuitous timing" for option repricing: Options tend to be repriced when the stock price hits a low point relative to the recent past. This pattern has striking similarities to what would otherwise be considered illegal insider trading, and raises a question as to why such practices are not curtailed through better corporate governance, improved disclosure, or enforcement actions by the SEC.

THE GENERAL USE OF STOCK OPTIONS, DILUTION, AND RELATED ISSUES

The second session of the Forum emphasized the use of stock options beyond the executive suite. Moreover, other general issues related to stock option use were also discussed, including measuring the cost of stock options, option repricing, shareholder concerns, and shareholder voting.[6]

In many industries, stock options have become standard compensation practice. Thus, given competitive labor markets, the use of options to attract talent, particularly in the context of high-tech or knowledge-worker reliant companies, has become something of a necessity. Furthermore, there is a strong perception that options are a source of competitive advantage in the U.S., and are linked to value-building performance. Indeed, Mr. Larry G. Stambaugh argued that the boom in U.S. productivity and innovation has been enhanced by the use of stock options.

---

5. Although reload options were not debated at the Forum, Mr. Cook has subsequently argued that, while reload options allow executives to "dampen" their losses relative to standard optionholders who did not exercise, the reload mechanism does encourage stock ownership.

6. Although the discussion at the Forum regarding share repurchases actually took place during the morning session, it is incorporated here for ease of exposition.

To the extent that the costs of option-based compensation exceed the perceived benefits, it implies the destruction of shareholder value as opposed to the creation of shareholder value.

However, the appropriateness of using options at all levels of the organization has been subject to question. For example, Mr. Michael Mauboussin argued that, at best, most employees can have only a small impact on overall corporate performance. In addition, even if individual employees can directly contribute to corporate performance, there is a question as to what extent their contributions are reflected in the stock price. There is also a potential "free-rider" problem, in that an employee incurs all the costs of working hard to increase the stock price, but any consequent increase in corporate value will be divided among all stockholders and all optionholders. Thus, option-based compensation may provide weak incentives for employees to increase stock price.

Mr. Eric D. Roiter highlighted this issue by questioning whether option-based compensation serves to reward performance or, rather, encourages a "lottery ticket" mentality on the part of employees. He also noted shareholders' concerns about the potential reallocation of ownership rights as a result of option-based compensation and the associated value transfers from shareholders to employees. To the extent that the costs of option-based compensation exceed the perceived benefits, it implies the destruction of shareholder value as opposed to the creation of shareholder value.

Ultimately, the panel concluded that companies with perceived high levels of dilution and poor compensation practices will face financial constraints as they return to the capital markets for additional funding.

Mr. Stuart L. Gillan's presentation focused on the implications of option repricing. Given recent stock market declines, option repricing has become a highly contentious compensation issue. Even when the option exercise price is above the current market price (options are underwater), the options still have economic value (share prices may rise again in the future). However, underwater options are typically considered to be "worthless" by employees. When employees hold underwater options, companies have a number of concerns, such as how to deal with demoralized employees and how to approach a repricing given shareholder apprehension over dilution in general and repricing in particular.

As highlighted by Mr. Cook earlier in the day, there are numerous approaches companies can use to deal with underwater options. These alternatives range from doing nothing to making employees entirely whole for the value decline they have experienced by means of a repricing.

Recent FASB rulings, however, require that companies repricing options must adopt "mark-to-market accounting" for the repriced options and have those adjustments flow through the income statement. In other words, the cost of the repricing would have to be reflected in reported income. A key element of the FASB's ruling is that any stock option issuance within six months of a cancellation constitutes a repricing for accounting purposes. To avoid this definition, and the associated charge to earnings, some companies have adopted a "synthetic repricing" strategy in which they leave six months *and one day* between option cancellation and reissuance.[7]

Another approach to dealing with underwater options is "on-top" grants. On-top grants simply award employees additional options at a lower exercise price, while allowing them to keep their underwater options. Mr. Gillan noted that although this may alleviate the employee morale issue, underwater options do have value and, in fact, they represent a significant potential value transfer from shareholders to optionholders. Most option grants have a 7-to-10-year life; and if stock prices increase dramatically, it could prove very costly to shareholders at these companies to double-up option grants.

On a related issue, an audience member made the observation that repricing relates to the extent to which employee compensation is at risk, and one could argue that lower-level workers should not have a significant element of pay at risk.[8] High-level employees, on the other hand, should have risk—but real risk, both upside and downside. These arguments have a great deal of merit; indeed, it would seem that they provide the rationale for the current wave of repricing, as many companies apparently face pressure to readjust employees' "at-risk" compensation now that the "risk" has been realized. This need for companies to reprice options provides evidence that the standard practice of granting at-the-money options to a broad range of employees does not always work well.

---

7. See "Options Overdose," *Wall Street Journal*, page C1, June 3, 2001.

8. It could also be argued that individuals receiving option-based compensation have chosen to accept a risky compensation package.

The gaming of the accounting rules to effectively reprice options and avoid an accounting charge raises questions as to whether a focus on earnings numbers results in the choice of compensation strategies that may be inferior relative to alternatives. For example, Mr. Mauboussin proposed the use of indexed options, which would adjust the option exercise price to reflect changes in some benchmark, say the return on the S&P 500. As the return on the index increases, the exercise price would also rise. Similarly, if the market declines, the exercise price is adjusted downward by the change in the index. Only when a company's stock return outperforms the index (in either up or down markets) do employees get a payoff. That is, indexed options reward superior performance in all markets, whether the market trend is up or down. However, current accounting requires that a cost for indexed options be charged to earnings, again highlighting the notion that disparate accounting treatments may disadvantage some compensation plans relative to others.

Given shareholder concerns about compensation practices in general and the use of options in particular, shareholders want the ability to approve option plans. Many companies actively seek shareholder approval for all stock option plans, and still others have adopted plan restrictions prohibiting future repricing without shareholder approval. However, past repricing activity can serve as a trigger for institutions to vote against new option plans. Similarly, high dilution levels have surpassed "vote no" thresholds for many institutional investors. Indeed, increased dilution levels have heightened shareholder concerns relating to the potential costs of option-based compensation. Evidence of shareholder concern is apparent when one focuses on shareholder voting on stock option plans. Average shareholder votes cast against proposed stock option plans have reached more than 20%—which is very high relative to other management issues put to a shareholder vote.[9]

Mr. Gillan noted that by assuming all grants will be exercised, standard dilution measures effectively provide an upper estimate of the potential cost of option grants to shareholders. When one considers other factors, the expected cost of the grant as a proportion of market value may be markedly lower than standard dilution measures would suggest. For example, when employees exercise their options, companies are generally able to deduct the difference between the market price and the exercise price from taxable income. This can represent a significant reduction in the estimated economic cost of the options to shareholders. Similarly, to the extent that companies have large numbers of stock options outstanding, the cost of future grants will be shared by both current shareholders and current option holders. Finally, (1) adjusting the estimated cost for possible cancellations as employees leave prior to exercising their options and (2) using option-valuation approaches based on financial theory, will lead to lower estimates of the cost of stock options relative to the company's market value.

The conference discussion earlier in the day also focused on the use of share repurchases to offset dilution from stock options. Many companies explicitly state that they repurchase shares to accomplish one of two goals: (1) limit the dilution of existing shareholders and (2) influence the accounting measure of earnings per share.

As noted by an audience member, boards who repurchase think they can give more options because they believe they are countering dilution effects.

Conference participants were generally dismissive of the notion that repurchases offset dilution in a value sense. It is true that repurchases offset the dilution of current shareholders' voting power. It is also true that repurchases can be used to maintain the number of shares outstanding, and thus prevent lowering earnings per share. However, repurchases cannot "undo" the value transfer from shareholders to employees that occurs from granting options to employees. Thus, limiting dilution and preserving earnings per share do not seem relevant in a financial sense.

Although repurchases may have potential benefits—for example, investing in the company's undervalued stock, curbing wasteful investment programs, achieving tax savings relative to dividend payments, or maintaining a target capital structure—it is not clear how these benefits interact with the presence of stock options, if at all. As noted by Professor Yermack, repurchasing stock creates value only if the company acquires shares below their true worth. In general, if a stock trades at $50 per share and the firm pays the $50 market price to repurchase it, no one is any better or worse off. Likewise, "dilution" from option grants does not harm

---

9. Bethel and Gillan (2001).

Despite the friction between corporate America and investors over stock option use, there remains a commonality of interests between investors and employees. In the evolving economy, both financial capital (from shareholders) and human capital (from employees) have the opportunity to benefit from each other.

existing shareholders if the services contributed by employees equal the value of the option compensation awarded. Simply managing earnings per share numbers cannot increase the value of the firm. It was further suggested by Mr. Samuel C. Scott that the decision to use options and the decision to repurchase shares are fundamentally separate issues. One (the use of options) is a compensation issue, whereas the other (share repurchases) is an issue of capital budgeting and corporate capital structure.

THE ROLE OF THE BOARD OF DIRECTORS AND THE COMPENSATION COMMITTEE

The capstone session of the day addressed the role of the board of directors, the compensation committee, and its chairperson. As with the earlier sessions, several common themes arose in relation to the corporate governance environment and the role of corporate boards. Many conference speakers and participants viewed compensation policy, particularly executive compensation policy, as a window through which the effectiveness of the board may be viewed.

Professor Joseph L. Bower presented evidence suggesting that, despite substantial destruction of shareholder value at some U.S. corporations, CEOs at those companies have received very large salary and bonus increases. This appears inconsistent with the concepts of pay for performance and aligning management incentives with those of shareholders—which in turn suggests that pay for performance is something of a myth. Other aspects of current compensation policy are also troubling, particularly "megagrants" (very large option grants) and retirement awards, where the relationship to shareholder interests is obscure.

As the last speaker in the conference session on dilution, Mr. Peter N. Larson stressed that despite the friction between corporate America and investors over stock option use, there remains a commonality of interests between investors and employees. In the evolving economy, both financial capital (from shareholders) and human capital (from employees) have the opportunity to benefit from each other. Nevertheless, the board of directors and its compensation committee play crucial roles in addressing the governance of compensation.

Both Mr. Sanford R. Robertson and Mr. Clayton Yeutter echoed these sentiments. Mr. Robertson noted that many questions about the use of stock options center on high-tech companies that use stock options broadly and deeply down the corporate hierarchy. The nature of the company, as interpreted by the board, may significantly impact compensation policies in these types of companies. Thus, the board of directors is critical in not only determining the company's strategic direction, but also the compensation policies to achieve that direction. Mr. Yeutter stressed that corporate boards need flexibility to assess the nature of compensation for a particular company, in a particular set of economic and company-specific circumstances. There is not a "one-size-fits-all" compensation policy, particularly for companies heavily reliant on knowledge workers for innovation, growth, and returns to shareholders.

Professor Bower also highlighted aspects of compensation policy that boards need to address including: the underlying philosophy of compensating employees, retaining employees, designing severance packages, and ensuring that compensation packages are equitable internally and relative to the external labor market. This encompasses not only the use of equity-based compensation, but also aligning expectations as to employee performance and sharing in the firm's success.

While the inclusion of performance-based measures in compensation programs may be desirable, Mr. Yeutter suggested that care must be taken to avoid unintended consequences. For example, if a performance award pays off only in a period where earnings reach a certain level, there may be an incentive for employees to game the system, for example, by managing earnings numbers to achieve the goal.

Several speakers throughout the day, including Professor Bower, considered the role of the compensation committee chair to be critical. The chair must lead the compensation committee, work with the CEO to oversee management development and performance appraisal, and approve and oversee compensation policy. The task of the compensation committee also extends beyond that of just compensation to evaluating the CEO and succession planning.

Input is also needed from consultants, including good, detailed information on true comparables. However, as was discussed throughout the day, care must be taken to avoid the so-called "Lake Woebegone" effect, in which many firms attempt to have an "above average" compensation policy.[10] Other inputs may also be of use to compensation committees. For example, there was an overall sense that industry guidelines on appropriate levels of dilution would provide a signal to management and boards as to the appropriate levels of option use without foreclosing the possibility of exceeding a guideline when the board judges it to be appropriate and can explain why.

In his observations regarding the development of prescriptive compensation policies, Mr. Yeutter suggested that care must be taken to ensure that boards are not hamstrung by excessive oversight. He also suggested, however, that concerned shareholders can seek to address compensation practices. Shareholders can discuss compensation practice and philosophy with boards, critiquing performance (including the performance of the compensation committee) and the pay-to-performance relationship, and communicating with directors and managers. Moreover, shareholders can withhold votes for directors where circumstances warrant a strong signal.

SUMMARY AND CONCLUDING REMARKS

The Forum provided the opportunity for an exchange of views on compensation-related issues. Clearly, stock- and option-based compensation can be powerful motivators. However, at least two features of the compensation environment lead one to question the overall efficacy of option-based compensation. First, the Forum discussion highlighted an apparent disconnect between pay and performance, a disconnect that is exacerbated in the context of option repricing. Second, there is evidence suggesting that employees undervalue options relative to the potential cost to shareholders. This is not a condemnation of all option-based compensation. Rather, it is a prelude to the idea that a judicious and informed approach is needed in the design and implementation of compensation programs.

Two observations suggest that financial accounting considerations may unduly influence compensation policy: first, the continued use of standard at-the-money options relative to potentially superior alternatives such as performance-based options; and second, the gaming of the accounting system, particularly in the case of synthetic six-month-plus-one-day repricings. The proclivity of companies to adopt compensation policies to avoid a charge to earnings is somewhat disturbing. Indeed, it leads one to question whether a myopic focus on measured earnings and earnings per share distorts economic decisions and results in the adoption of suboptimal compensation programs.

A related concern is that if standard options are viewed as "free" from an accounting perspective, it may well lead to their overuse. Moreover, if firms compete for talent on the basis of "free" stock options, it may inflate the potential costs to shareholders. An understanding of the costs, benefits, advantages, and disadvantages of standard at-the-money options relative to alternatives is essential. In addition, an understanding of the incentive effects of option-based compensation and the actions that employees can take to undo or limit those incentive effects is critical. It is particularly important that boards of directors and compensation committees understand these issues. This is especially true in the context of governing the pay setting process for senior executives.

The Forum itself produced a general consensus that there is an ongoing need to address compensation issues. Several important themes emerged throughout the course of the day, and comments at the Forum appeared to reflect the beginnings of a broad, if somewhat general, consensus on a number of issues:

1) Legitimate shareholder concerns exist regarding the potential costs of option-based compensation; option plans should be submitted to shareholders for approval.

2) In an increasingly knowledge-based economy, employees will continue to demand a "piece of the action."

3) Conventional measures of dilution may not be the best way to determine the "cost" of stock options; however, such measures may be useful in identifying companies at which compensation practices may be worthy of increased scrutiny.

4) The repricing of employee stock options has focused attention on some of the more controversial aspects of option-based compensation.

5) Common guidelines and general education regarding the use and operation of stock options would serve the interests of all parties involved.

---

10. A number of observers noted that a significant proportion of companies target pay levels above the 50th percentile, and few target below that level. The effect over time is to cause pay levels to "ratchet" upward. See Bizjak, Lemmon, and Naveen (2001).

6) The development of "best practices" from accounting, board, investor, and company perspectives is essential.

7) Compensation policies are not a matter of "one size fits all," but there are common problems with many current compensation practices.

8) Board and committee governance is critical.

9) Leveling the accounting "playing field" so that alternate forms of performance-based compensation are not disadvantaged relative to standard at-the-money options is desirable.

10) There may be a role for a task force of qualified representatives to focus on the elements of compensation policy and the pay-setting process.

While certainly not the last word on the issues discussed, these observations, and the insights of the Forum participants may provide a basis for progress toward the development and implementation of compensation practices that can benefit employees and shareholders alike.

BIBLIOGRAPHY

Jennifer E. Bethel and Stuart L. Gillan (2001) "The Impact of Broker Votes on Shareholder Voting and Proposal Passage," working paper, TIAA-CREF Institute.

John M. Bizjak, Michael L. Lemmon, and Lalitha Naveen (2001) "Has the Use of Peer Groups Contributed to Higher Levels of Executive Compensation?" working paper, Portland State University.

Stuart L. Gillan (2001) "Option-based Compensation: Panacea or Pandora's Box?" working paper, TIAA-CREF Institute.

Brian J. Hall and Kevin J. Murphy (2000) "Stock Options for Undiversified Executives," working paper, Harvard Business School.

Tod Perry and Marc Zenner (2000) "CEO Compensation in the 1990s: Shareholder Alignment or Shareholder Expropriation?" *Wake Forest Law Review*, Spring 2000, 31, 1:123-152.

GOLF TOURNAMENTS AND CEO PAY—UNRAVELING THE MYSTERIES OF EXECUTIVE COMPENSATION

*by John D. Martin, Baylor University**

C EO pay reached astronomical levels at the close of the 1990s, and public concern has risen commensurately. *BusinessWeek*'s prize for top CEO compensation for 1999 went to Charles Wang, CEO and founder of Computer Associates International, who was reported to have received more than $650 million. According to financial economist and compensation expert Kevin Murphy, concern over executive pay stems from at least three basic factors: (1) the undisputed escalation in compensation—S&P 500 CEO median cash compensation has doubled since 1970 in constant 1996 dollars and total compensation (including realized gains from options) has quadrupled; (2) the populist attack on the excesses of the '80s, coupled with the perception that high CEO compensation is tied to layoffs, plant closing, and corporate downsizing; and (3) the bull market of the '90s, which has created windfalls for CEOs whose pay has been increasingly tied to stock performance.[1]

Public concern focuses on both the level of CEO pay and the growing gap between CEO compensation and that of the average worker. For example, the average CEO compensation package in 1999 was valued at about $13 million, which was more than 400 times the pay received by the average worker on the factory floor. Even the most ardent supporters of CEO pay find it increasingly difficult to rationalize the facts of CEO compensation.

There are two opposing views on the matter. On the positive side are those who think that the labor market for CEOs works well and that these individuals are paid their just reward. They argue that the job of CEO requires very specialized talents and that the CEO can be compared to the winner of a long and arduous tournament. The size of the compensation received by the CEO simply reflects the cost of enticing the most capable managers into a tournament that only one of them can win. On the other end of the spectrum are those who think that CEOs are simply looting the corporate coffers by using their power to influence their own pay. They argue that the system of corporate governance in many U.S. firms works for the managers, not the stockholders.

*The author would like to acknowledge the helpful comments of Spencer Case, Robert Darden, Stuart Gillan, Brian Hall, Steve Rich, Laura Starks, and Mike Stegemoller.

1. See Kevin Murphy, "Executive Compensation," *Handbook of Labor Economics*, Vol. 3, North Holland, Orley Ashenfelter and David Card, eds., 1999.

HOW MUCH DO CEOs REALLY GET PAID?

Senior executives typically receive three forms of compensation: salary, bonus, and long-term compensation. Salary for the year is set before the beginning of the year and is paid out to the executive regardless of how the firm performs. The bonus component is generally linked to firm performance and is paid out in a lump sum at the end of the year. Long-term compensation is generally paid out over multiple years and is contingent on firm performance and/or CEO longevity. Long-term compensation consists of stock options, restricted stock awards, or other payments designed to reflect the returns earned by the firm's stockholders.

Since long-term compensation is frequently the largest element of a CEO's pay, let's investigate its component parts in detail. Stock options awarded to executives are technically call options and they now constitute the largest component of CEO compensation.[2] Executive stock options confer rights to the executive to buy the stock of the granting firm at a pre-specified price known as the exercise price (usually the current market price at the time the option is granted)[3] during a specific period of time (usually 10 years). Although the options are valuable, the executive does not actually receive any cash at the time of the option grant and generally is restricted from selling the options for some specified period of time.[4] Ultimately, the amount of compensation received is equal to the difference between the market price of the stock and the exercise price paid for the shares.

Restricted stock awards are shares of the firm's common stock that are either given to the executive or sold to him or her for less than the current market price. These awards are frequently restricted. For instance, the shares cannot be sold until a specified revenue growth target is met or until the executive has been in the employ of the firm for a specified number of years.

Companies can also compensate their executives based on stock price performance without actually giving them stock. In a phantom stock plan, units that correspond to common stock but carry no ownership claim are awarded to the executive. The executive then receives the share price appreciation and dividends that are earned by the firm's common stock. Similarly, stock appreciation rights (SAR) are sometimes used whereby the executive receives an amount equal to the share price appreciation on a specified block of shares over time.

Reporting Executive Compensation in the Financial Press

Both *BusinessWeek* and *Forbes* publish annual surveys of CEO pay for a sample of the largest U.S. companies. The *BusinessWeek* 2000 survey, which reflects year-end 1999 compensation for 362 companies, reported that CEO pay increased 17% from 1998 to 1999, and valued the average CEO compensation package at $12.8 million.[5] In addition, average CEO compensation in 1999 was six times the compensation level in 1990, and CEO pay in 1980 was roughly

---

2. A recent study by Brian Hall and Jeffrey Liebman ("Are CEOs Really Paid Like Bureaucrats?," *Quarterly Journal of Economics* 113, 3, 1998, 653-691) reports that in fiscal 1998 the value of stock option grants accounted for 40% of total pay for S&P 500 CEOs, which was up from 25% in 1992. They further note that stock options are becoming increasingly important for rank-and-file workers as well with 45% of U.S. companies awarding options to their exempt salaried employees in 1998, while 12% and 10% awarded options to their non-exempt and hourly employees, respectively. Furthermore, a recent study by Brian Hall and Kevin Murphy ("Stock Options for Undiversified Executives," Harvard Business School, unpublished working paper, June 2000) observes that in 1998, 97% of S&P 500 companies granted options to their top executives compared to 82% in 1992.

3. Hall and Liebman (1998), cited in footnote 2, report that 94% of the option grants to S&P 500 CEOs in 1998 were at-the-money grants as opposed to discount options offering exercise prices below the grant date stock price, premium options carrying exercise prices above the current stock price, or indexed options whose exercise price is contingent on an industry or market index. Alfred Rappaport (in "New Thinking on How to Link Executive Pay with Performance," *Harvard Business Review*, March/April 1999, 91-101) argues for the use of indexed options on the basis that setting the exercise price equal to or below the current market price will reward below market performance during bull markets. However, few companies (Broomfield, Colorado-based Level 3 Communications, Inc. is an exception) use indexed options in spite of some very high profile proponents including Warren Buffett and Alan Greenspan, among others. A sticky problem appears to be the accounting treatment accorded to executive stock options. When an option is granted at or above the current market price, the firm doesn't have

to record any charge to firm earnings. However, when an indexed option is used with its variable strike price, the difference between the grant price and the exercise price must be recognized as a compensation expense. Although the charge is noncash, it does impact reported earnings and some executives evidently feel that investors cannot or will not see through the charge.

4. That is, unlike calls options purchased in the public market, executive stock options are not transferable immediately. Hall and Murphy (2000), cited in footnote 2, point out that this non-transferability feature reduces their value to the executives who receive them, yet the rights they confer are the same from the perspective of the granting firm. This drives a wedge between the value of the options received and the cost of the options to the granting institution, and makes options an expensive way to compensate employees. Very simply, the value received by the executive is less than the value granted (thus its cost) by the firm. Furthermore, even when the options are exercised and the executive buys the shares, she may be restricted to holding the shares for some prescribed period of time before she can sell them and receive cash.

5. Estimates of average CEO compensation vary depending upon the sample used. For example, executive pay expert Graef Crystal, who writes a compensation column for Bloomberg, estimated average CEO compensation for 1999 to be $10.4 million based on the 439 CEOs in his database; the New York consulting firm of Pearl Meyer and Partners estimated average compensation at $11.9 million; a compilation quoted by the AFL-CIO puts the figure at $12.4 million; and a survey of the top paid 200 CEOs made for *USA Today* found average pay at $17.6 million. No matter what estimate you choose to believe, the numbers are huge.

TABLE 1
BUSINESS WEEK'S TOP 10 CEOS RANKED IN TERMS OF THEIR COMPENSATION RECEIVED IN 1999 (THOUSANDS OF DOLLARS)

Rank	CEO and Company	Salary and Bonus	Long-term Compensation	Total Reported Pay Received
1	Charles Wang, Computer Associates	$4,600	$650,824	$655,424
2	L. Dennis Kozlowski, Tyco Intl.	4,550	165,446	169,996
3	David Pottruck, Charles Schwab	9,000	118,900	127,900
4	John Chambers, Cisco Systems	943	120,757	121,700
5	Stephen Case, America Online	1,575	115,510	117,085
6	Louis Gerstner, IBM	9,266	92,983	102,249
7	Jack Welch, General Electric	13,325	79,813	93,138
8	Sanford Weill, Citigroup	10,181	80,049	90,230
9	Peter Karmanos, Jr., Compuware	2,200	85,321	87,521
10	Reuben Mark, Colgate-Palmolive	4,200	81,117	85,318

Legend:
Salary—Salary for the year is set before the beginning of the year and paid out to the executive regardless of how the firm performs.
Bonus—The bonus component is generally linked to firm performance and paid out in a lump sum at the end of the year.
Long-term Compensation—Long-term compensation is generally paid out over multiple years and is contingent on firm performance and/or CEO longevity. Furthermore, long-term compensation can be composed of stock options, restricted stock awards, and other payments designed to mimic the returns earned by the firm's stockholders.

40 times the compensation paid to the average factory worker. The gap widened to 208 times in 1996 and reached a whopping 419 times in 1999.[6] Compensation expert Graef Crystal extrapolated this trend out to 2015 and estimated that the ratio of the average chief executive's pay to that of the average worker will approach levels that existed in 1789, when Louis XVI was king of France.[7] (And we know what happened to him.)

Table 1 contains *Business Week*'s top ten CEOs ranked in terms of compensation for 1999. Note that the size of the payouts is driven by the long-term compensation component of CEO pay (not salary and bonus). Furthermore, the importance of salary and bonus has decreased dramatically in recent years. In 1994 salary plus bonus constituted 54% of CEO pay, but by 1999 the percentage had fallen to 23%.[8] A change in the tax code in 1994 disallowed the tax deductibility of executive pay in excess of $1 million unless it was tied to performance, and this change is credited with stimulating the increased use of stock and options and the diminished use of salary as components of executive compensation.

The key to understanding CEO pay, then, is coming to grips with the long-term compensation component. However, the long-term compensation data reported in the financial press by *Business Week*

and others is very different from the compensation reported to the SEC and to stockholders in the firm's annual proxy statement. Specifically, the financial press reports long-term compensation as the sum of the value of restricted stock grants that *become vested* in the year, plus stock gains realized from the *exercise* of options. Since the exercise of stock options is the primary determinant of CEO compensation and the CEO determines when they exercise the options received from grants they received in prior years, CEO compensation reported in the financial press are largely determined by the CEOs themselves.

Table 2 provides an indication of the size of the caches of unexercised stock options that have been awarded, but whose income effects have not been reported in the financial press. When CEOs do exercise their options, the value at exercise may bear little or no relationship to the firm's current period performance or the compensation awarded to them for the period.

Reporting Executive Compensation to the Securities and Exchange Commission

The Securities Act of 1933 and Securities Exchange Act of 1934 mandated that information regarding executive compensation be made avail-

---

6. See "Share and Share Unalike," *Economist* (August 7, 1999).
7. See Kathleen Day, 2000, "Soldiers for the Shareholder," *The Washington Post* (August 27), H01.

8. See "I'll Take Stock," *Forbes*, May 15, 2000.

TABLE 2 ■ CEOS WITH HUGE AMOUNTS OF UNEXERCISED STOCK OPTIONS

Executive and Company	Value of non-exercised stock options ($K)	Executive and Company	Value of non-exercised stock options ($K)
Timothy Koogle, Yahoo	$2,251,451	Henry Silverman, Cendant	$684,683
Stephen Case, America Online	1,263,767	John Chambers, Cisco Systems	482,453
Barry Diller, USA Networks	1,033,984	Louis Gerstner, IBM	481,350
Glen Meakem, Freemarkets	751,140	Joseph Nacchio, Qwest Communications	467,546
Millard Drexler, GAP	685,003	William Esrey, Sprint Fon Group	452,837

Source: *Business Week*, April 17, 2000.

TABLE 3 ■ ANNUAL CEO COMPENSATION PAID BY THE HALLIBURTON CORPORATION TO MR. RICHARD CHENEY: 1998-1999

Year	Salary	Bonus	Restricted Stock Award Value	Securities (#)	Options Award Value[a]	Other Compensation	Total Compensation
1999	$1,283,000	$—	$—	300,000	$7,452,401	$640,914	$9,376,315
1998	1,183,257	1,154,704	1,525,000	100,000	1,768,766	564,771	6,196,498

Source: Halliburton Proxy Statements for 1999-2000.
a. This estimate of the value of options granted in the period represents the potential realizable value based on an assumed annual rate of stock price appreciation over the 10-year term of the option equal to 5% per year.

able for publicly held corporations. However, in 1992 the rules governing the disclosure of executive compensation were revised to require companies to report the value of the compensation awards to their five highest-paid executives in their annual proxy statements. In the SEC filing, the value of restricted stock and option grants is reported in the year of the award. This contrasts with the reporting of compensation in the financial press, where income is recorded only when restricted stock vests and options are exercised. The SEC has taken the position that these stock and option grants have value to the CEO at the time of the award, and that an estimate of their value should be reported to stockholders. To illustrate, consider the compensation awarded by the Halliburton Corporation to then-CEO Richard Cheney (found in Table 3). The 1999 Halliburton proxy reported that Mr. Cheney received total compensation valued at $ 9,376,315. Salary and bonus represented only $1,283,000 of that total, while options accounted for the bulk of the remainder.[9] Interestingly, Mr. Cheney's total compensation reported in the *Forbes*

annual survey was only $3,601,000, which meant that the value of his option award for 1999 exceeded the value of any options he exercised during the year.

Table 4 contrasts the compensation awarded for the year (and reported to the firm's shareholders via the annual proxy statement) and the compensation realized and reported in the financial press for the highest-paid CEOs in the *Forbes* annual survey of executive compensation for 1996-1999. We see that the annual compensation reported to stockholders in the proxy statement sometimes bears little resemblance to the compensation reported in the financial press. For example, *Forbes* reported that in 1998 Michael Eisner, CEO of Disney, received total compensation just over $589 million (Panel B of Table 4). However, the value of his compensation reported in the firm's proxy statement for the year was just under $6 million. The difference in these figures represents the value of options that Eisner exercised in 1998 on 22 million shares of stock that he had received over a period of nine years.[10] But, as in the case of Dick Cheney cited above, the compensation of Lawrence

9. Mr. Cheney also received *other* compensation composed of $6,400 in 401 (k) matching contributions, ERISA limitation accruals of $113,874, supplemental retirement plan contributions of $500,000 (the minimum set in his employment contract), and above market earnings on amounts deferred under elective deferral plans of $15,564 (Halliburton Proxy Statement for 2000).

10. Jennifer Reingold ("Special Report: Executive Pay," *BusinessWeek*, April 17, 2000, 100-112) reports that if Eisner's stock options had been indexed to the S&P 500 index, they would have been worth only $257.5 million since Disney's shares outperformed the S&P by a relatively narrow margin of 22% compared to 18%.

The SEC has taken the position that these stock and option grants have value to the CEO at the time of the award and an estimate of their value should be reported to the stockholders.

TABLE 4 ■ REPORTED COMPENSATION VERSUS THE ANNUAL COMPENSATION AWARD—TOP CEO PAY FOR 1996-1999

PANEL A. COMPENSATION REPORTED TO SHAREHOLDERS AND THE SEC IN THE ANNUAL PROXY STATEMENT

Year	CEO and Company	Salary	Bonus	Value of restricted stock granted in the year	Value of options granted in the year	Other Comp.	Total Comp.
1999	Charles Wang, Computer Associates	$1,000,000	$3,600,000	$650,812,050	$—	$35,948	$655,447,998
1998	Michael Eisner, Disney	764,423	5,000,000	—	—	3,820	5,768,243
1997	Sanford I. Weill, Travelers Group/Citigroup	1,025,000	6,168,034	3,109,288	39,307,207	261,673	49,871,202
1996	Lawrence Coss, Green Tree Financial	433,608	102,015,158	—	38,834,243	—	141,283,009

PANEL B. *FORBES* REPORTED TOTAL COMPENSATION

Year	CEO and Company	Total Comp.
1999	Charles Wang, Computer Associates	$650,048,000
1998	Michael Eisner, Disney	589,101,000
1997	Sanford I. Weill, Travelers Group/Citigroup	227,618,000
1996	Lawrence Coss, Green Tree Financial	102,449,000

Coss, CEO of Green Tree Financial, illustrates that the amount reported in the financial press is not always more than the amount reported for the year to the SEC. In 1996 Coss received options whose reported value in the firm's proxy statement exceeded the value of options exercised and reported in the *Forbes* survey. Although both these compensation totals are informative, the SEC filing seems more relevant when trying to understand how much a firm decides to pay an executive in a particular year.

Where's the Cash?

To this point we have not made a clear distinction between cash and non-cash compensation. The fact is that the great majority of CEO compensation in any given year (and reported to the SEC) is not paid in cash, and the actual amount the CEO will ultimately receive can be highly uncertain. To illustrate, consider the case of Computer Associate's Charles Wang, whose reported compensation for 1999 was more than $650 million (see Table 4). Almost all of this came in the form of a grant of

restricted stock that he could neither sell nor borrow against for a period of seven years. Furthermore, he had to pay taxes on the income immediately.[11] This example illustrates the fact that the form of payment used for CEOs is often designed to tie them to the company (i.e., golden handcuffs). This evidently was what Computer Associate's board had in mind. When asked about the size of the grant, a spokesman for the board of directors alluded to the board's concern that Wang might someday leave the firm and start a new company.

Not only is reported CEO pay not immediately convertible into cash, but the final payout can be highly uncertain. Consider the case of Webvan CEO George Shaheen, who owned options and shares valued at $815 million on the first day of Webvan's initial public offering in November 1999. Six months later, the stock had fallen to $7, reducing the value of the options dramatically, and his shares dropped in value to only $8.8 million.[12] The message here is simple: the total dollar value of options and restricted shares is uncertain and may not be what they appear to be in the firm's annual proxy statement.

---

11. See Anthony Bianco, "The Package that Launched a Dozen Lawsuits," *BusinessWeek* (April 17, 2000), p. 108.

12. The fact that the options were "out of the money" at a $7 price does not mean that they are worthless (unless the term of the option has expired). However,

they are certainly worth "less." In addition, a common practice among firms whose share prices have dropped dramatically is the repricing of their executive's stock options by dropping the exercise price down to the current market price of the shares.

TABLE 5 ■ GOLF TOURNAMENT PRIZES FOR THE PARTICIPANTS IN THE 2000 U.S. AND BRITISH OPEN

Rank	U.S. Open	Prize	Multiples[a]	British Open	Prize	Multiples[a]
1	Tiger Woods	$800,000	1.00	Tiger Woods	$759,150	1.00
2	Ernie Els	$390,150	2.05	Thomas Bjorn	$371,983	2.04
3	Miguel Jimenez	$390,150	2.05	Ernie Els	$371,983	2.04
4	John Juston	$212,779	3.76	Tom Lehman	$197,379	3.85
5	Padraig Harrington	$169,526	4.72	David Toms	$197,379	3.85
:	:	:	:	:	:	:
Last	Robert Damron	$10,862	73.65	Peter Senior	$10,628	71.43

a. The multiple represents the prize winnings of the winner of the tournament (Tiger Woods) divided by the prize received by each player. We only include the prizes earned in each tournament although the value of endorsements and other associated benefits of winning the tournament can be several times the actual prize money. For example, Tiger Woods' original Nike endorsement provided him with $40 million and the contract being negotiated in 2000 is valued at $100 million.

WHY ARE CEOs PAID SO MUCH?

Two opposing theories have been offered for the high levels of CEO pay, and both rely on the fact that ownership (stockholders) and control (managers) are separated in large public corporations.[13] The first theory suggests that CEOs should be provided with powerful monetary incentives to maximize shareholder value. According to this view, when it comes to determining CEO pay, boards of directors are by and large *doing the right thing*. This view is founded on the belief that the boards exercise control over the firm's management and not the other way around.

The second theory of CEO compensation argues that the board often *does the wrong thing* when they set CEO pay. You can arrive at this conclusion in either of two ways. First, management may exercise enough control over the board of directors and its compensation committee that they effectively set their own compensation and, in so doing, "skim" value from the shareholders and transfer it to themselves. Second, setting CEO pay so as to align CEO and stockholder interests is not an easy thing to do and boards have simply not been up to the task.

It's The RIGHT Thing to Do

For those who believe that CEOs are being properly rewarded for the job they are doing, theoretical justification is derived from the principal-agent model of the firm. This model views managers as agents of the firm's stockholders, who are the owners and principals. In the absence of perfect oversight, or compensation plans that provide them with incentives to do otherwise, executives can act in their own interests rather than those of the firm's stockholders. So, as the argument goes, boards of directors design compensation plans that provide management with incentives that will make it in their interest to maximize shareholder value.

But however plausible this theory seems, there are two features of CEO pay that are particularly difficult to rationalize. The first is the sheer size of the payments in absolute terms. The second is the difference between the compensation of the CEO and lower ranking executives (i.e., the pay gap).

Tournaments and CEO Pay. One theory that has been used to shed some light on both these issues is the economic theory of tournaments. A tournament is simply a contest in which the participants are ranked based on their relative performance. The size of the prize then reflects the order of finish in the tournament.

To see why tournaments might provide a useful analogy to the competition for top corporate jobs, consider the prizes awarded to the contestants in the 2000 British and U.S. Open golf tournaments that are shown in Table 5. Tiger Woods won both tournaments and his prize money for each was approximately twice that of the runner-up and more than 70 times that of the last person in the tournament.

---

13. Adolph Berle and Gardner Means (*The Modern Corporation and Private Property*, New York, 1932) first warned of the potential dangers of separating ownership and control in the modern corporation. More recently Michael Jensen and William Meckling ("Theory of the Firm: Managerial Behavior, Agency Costs, and Ownership Structure," *Journal of Financial Economics* 3, no. 4 (October 1976)) laid the foundations for understanding the implications of the relationship between stockholders and managers as a principal-agent relationship.

Forbes reported that in 1998 Michael Eisner, CEO of Disney, received total compensation just over $589 million. However, the value of his compensation reported in the firm's proxy statement for the year was just under $6 million.

Presumably the size of the total purse reflects the cost of attracting the most talented players to the tournament.[14] But why are the differences in the prizes awarded to the contestants so large?

The economic theory of tournaments suggests that effort and performance in tournaments are sensitive to the size and distribution of the prizes. For example, a 1990 study by Ronald Ehrenberg and Michael Bognanno showed that larger prizes were associated with lower scores in men's professional golf tournaments. They found that raising the total prize money by $100,000 lowered each player's score an average of 1.1 strokes over a 72-hole tournament. Since the monetary gain to finishing first rather than second is much greater than the gain to finishing second rather than third and so forth, there is a greater marginal gain to the player who lowers his final round score by a stroke when he is among the leaders after the first three rounds than when he is at the back of the pack. Supporting this contention, the researchers found that, in the final round of play, the tournament leaders improved their score more than did the laggards.

These results suggest that it may make sense to think of the contenders for the CEO position as contestants engaged in a very long and arduous tournament that extends over many years. Since only one of them can become CEO, companies may want the labor market for corporate CEOs to be designed to elicit the same type of effort as in a golf tournament. This logic suggests that the CEO's compensation should be considerably higher than the next tier of managers and should be sufficiently large so as to draw the best candidates into the competition.

But does the reward structure of corporate executives who are potential candidates for the CEO position look similar to the prize structure in a tournament? Earlier we noted that in 1999 the average CEO compensation was 419 times that of the average factory worker. This is a much wider than the 70-plus multiple we saw in the 2000 British and US open golf tournaments. However, this is not a fair comparison for we only considered the winnings of the subset of golfers who qualified for the two major tournaments. A more reasonable comparison might

be between the average CEO earnings and the average earnings of CEO contenders. For example, in 1995 the average pay for a manager of a $100 million division or subsidiary in the U.S. was $190,000 (salary plus bonus). Comparing this figure (and it would be higher in 1999 and higher yet if the value of stock options were included) to average CEO compensation in 1999 of approximately $13 million, the resulting multiple of CEO to manager compensation drops to 68 times. This multiple is very nearly the same as we saw in the comparison of first- and last-place contestants in the two open golf tournaments.

A quick (and admittedly unscientific) survey of five new-economy and five old-economy firms provides further anecdotal evidence that is consistent with a tournament theory of executive compensation. Table 6 contains the 1999 compensation reported in company proxy statements by each firm.[15] The value of options granted during the year is calculated using an assumed growth rate in share price of 5% per year (as reported to the SEC and the firm's stockholders). We compare the total compensation of the highest-paid executive to the lower-paid company executives using the ratio of the dollar values of their total compensation packages.

As can be seen in panel C of Table 6, the range of pay for the top five executives exhibits roughly the same dispersion as we saw in the top five finishers in the two golf tournaments reported in Table 5 (that is, the highest-paid received about four times that of the lowest-paid). However, the difference in compensation for the top two executives is not quite as great as the difference in the top two prizes in the two open golf tournaments. This may reflect the fact that executives, unlike golfers, must rely on cooperation to succeed and paying too large a differential between the two top officers may encourage destructive competition.

It's The WRONG Thing to Do

But not everyone believes that CEO pay reflects proper payment for services rendered. Some argue that the CEOs exercise substantial control over their own compensation while others suggest that well-meaning

---

14. We recognize that the prize winnings to the top finishers are actually a relatively small portion of their "winnings" since they each make substantial sums from product endorsements. For example, Tiger Woods signed an agreement with Nike in 1996 valued at $40 million and following his very successful 2000 tour is rumored to be negotiating a new agreement worth $100 million.

15. The compensation paid to Mr. Gates and the Microsoft executives may be surprising but no option grants were made to these employees during 1999. Don't be too concerned about Mr. Gates being able to support his lifestyle on a mere $623,373. He still owns 15% of Microsoft's 787,055,600 shares making him one of the richest men in the world. In fact, the executive officers and directors of Microsoft as a group own 25.7% of the firm's shares (Microsoft 1999 Annual Proxy Statement).

TABLE 6 ■ RELATIVE COMPENSATION FOR TOP FIVE EXECUTIVES OF NEW AND OLD ECONOMY FIRMS—1999

Name	Title	Salary	Bonus	Restricted Stock Grants	Other LT Comp.	Option Grants[a]	Total LT Comp.	Total Comp.	Relative Comp.
PANEL A. NEW ECONOMY FIRMS									
ORACLE									
Gary Bloom	EVP	$888,864	$2,352,919	—	—	$18,167,219	$18,167,219	$21,409,002	1.00
Lawrence Ellison	CEO	1,000,000	2,752,000	—	—	15,761,640	15,761,640	19,513,640	1.10
Raymond Lane	COO	1,000,000	2,250,000	—	—	11,821,230	11,821,230	15,071,230	1.42
Jay Nussbaum	EVP	525,000	1,151,730	—	—	11,496,980	11,496,980	13,173,710	1.63
Jeffrey Henley	CFO	727,500	1,334,609	—	—	6,304,656	6,304,656	8,366,765	2.56
YAHOO									
Timothy Koogle	CEO	295,000	—	—	660	38,438,436	38,439,096	38,734,096	1.00
Jeffrey Mallett	COO	260,000	—	—	300	28,883,558	28,883,858	29,143,858	1.33
Anil Singh	CMO	202,375	75,000	—	2,905	13,056,049	13,058,954	13,336,329	2.90
Farzad Nazem	CTO	212,500	—	—	2,905	13,056,049	13,058,954	13,271,454	2.92
Gary Valenzuela	CFO	205,000	—	—	2,800	10,853,149	10,855,949	11,060,949	3.50
MICROSOFT									
Robert Herbold	COO	562,465	363,693	—	50,997	—	50,997	977,155	1 00
Steven Ballmer	PRES	388,392	272,181	—	4,800	—	4,800	665,373	1.47
William Gates	CEO	400,213	223,160	—	—	—	—	623,373	1.57
Paul Maritz	GVP	331,213	246,647	—	4,940	—	4,940	582,800	1.68
Michel Lacombe	SVP	356,983	222,796	—	—	—	—	579,779	1.69
SUN MICROSYSTEMS									
William Joy	Founder	398,519	471,393	1,199,750	6,496	20,283,992	21,490,238	22,360,150	1.00
Edward Zander	COO	750,000	1,630,125	—	7,553	19,223,073	19,230,626	21,610,751	1.03
Scott McNealy	CEO	116,154	3,622,500	—	5,583	3,844,615	3,850,198	7,588,852	2.95
Michael Lehman	CFO	600,000	869,400	—	6,400	3,844,615	3,851,015	5,320,415	4.20
William Raduchel	CSO	400,000	581,149	—	6,400	2,883,461	2,889,861	3,871,010	5.78
E-TRADE									
Christos Cotsakos	CEO	522,789	1,140,999	—	17,428	26,219,000	26,236,428	27,900,216	1.00
Kathy Levinson	COO	357,404	562,934	—	6,829	13,911,000	13,917,829	14,838,167	1.88
Debra Chrapaty	CMediaO	260,288	260,098	—	15,066	5,524,000	5,539,066	6,059,452	4.60
Jerry Gramaglia	CMktO	267,635	229,121	—	64,577	4,546,000	4,610,577	5,107,333	5.46
Judy Balint	CIO	260,288	266,774	—	9,644	4,018,000	4,027,644	4,554,706	6.13

(CONTINUED ON FOLLOWING PAGE)

boards are not up to the task of tying compensation to performance. Either way, CEO pay cannot be defended on the grounds that it aligns the CEO's interests with those of the stockholders.

Who sets CEO pay? Technically, CEOs do not set their own pay. The majority of large U.S. corporations have a compensation committee made up of at least two outside board members.[16] However, even though the presence of outside board members on the compensation committee may guarantee the appearance of independence of the committee's actions, it doesn't mean that the CEO is without

---

16. Regulators, stock exchanges and institutional shareholders generally define an outside board member as someone who is neither a current or past employee, and who has no significant business ties to the corporation (e.g., consultants). The IRS includes in its definition of insiders former employees who were compensated in the past year. However the Council of Institutional Investors is even more stringent by including relatives of employees, and other shareholder groups even include recipients of the firm's charitable giving as insiders. Furthermore, companies need a compensation committee with at least two outside members to qualify for exemption under IRS § 162(m), which places a $1 million limit on the deductibility of CEO compensation and other executives named in the company proxy statement.

It may make sense to think of the contenders for the CEO position as contestants engaged in a very long and arduous tournament that extends over many years.

TABLE 6 (CONTINUED)

Name	Title	Salary	Bonus	Restricted Stock Grants	Other LT Comp.	Option Grants[a]	Total LT Comp.	Total Comp.	Relative Comp.
PANEL B. OLD ECONOMY FIRMS									
FORD									
Alex Trotman	CEO	2,500,000	10,000,000	—	2,369,280	3,951,624	6,320,904	18,820,904	1.00
Jacques Nasser	COO	1,050,000	5,000,000	—	64,142	8,933,812	8,997,954	15,047,954	1.25
Edw. Hagenlocker	V Chrman	840,000	3,100,000	—	608,895	1,646,510	2,255,405	6,195,405	3.04
Wayne Booker	V Chrman	714,166	3,100,000	—	459,201	987,906	1,447,107	5,261,273	3.58
Kenneth Whipple	CFO	710,000	3,100,000	—	365,654	987,906	1,353,560	5,163,560	3.64
SEARS									
Arthur Martinez	CEO	1,200,000	2,198,550	—	725,686	3,840,002	4,565,688	7,964,238	1.00
Julian Day	COO	415,479	517,625	1,093,750	—	3,419,118	4,512,868	5,445,972	1.46
Anastasia Kelly	EVP	386,849	581,854	1,028,250	84,375	1,943,700	3,056,325	4,025,028	1.98
Mark Cohen	CMktO	500,068	623,009	1,125,000	262,616	1,085,000	2,472,616	3,595,693	2.21
Alan Lacy	PresSvcs	566,712	827,256	1,125,000	185,060	620,000	1,930,060	3,324,028	2.40
WAL-MART									
Lee Scott	CEO	800,000	1,215,385	—	90,685	4,867,073	4,957,758	6,973,143	1.00
David Glass	Chrmn	1,406,154	2,540,000	—	566,719	2,060,392	2,627,111	6,573,265	1.06
Thomas Coughlin	EVP	700,000	1,008,000	—	137,493	2,433,548	2,571,041	4,279,041	1.63
John Menzer	EVP	567,308	805,385	—	58,846	1,676,104	1,734,950	3,107,643	2.24
Donald Soderquist	VChrmn	1,046,389	1,500,000	—	122,663	—	122,663	2,669,052	2.61
U.S. STEEL									
T.J. Usher	CEO	1,241,667	1,400,000	—	132,768	5,903,058	6,035,826	8,677,493	1.00
R.M. Hernandez	CFO	573,750	600,000	—	62,970	2,186,317	2,249,287	3,423,037	2.54
P.J. Wilhelm	VChrmn	604,167	600,000	—	56,825	2,147,054	2,203,879	3,408,046	2.55
D.D. Sandman	SVP	425,000	425,000	—	52,103	1,093,159	1,145,262	1,995,262	4.35
V.G. Beghini	VChrmn	687,500	1,000,000	—	108,088	—	108,088	1,795,588	4.83
EXXON-MOBIL									
L.R. Raymond	CEO	2,110,147	13,900,000	8,356,250	222,571	22,334,603	30,913,424	46,923,571	1.00
L.A. Noto	VChrmn	1,048,334	8,598,300	2,089,063	2,111,007	26,292,438	30,492,508	40,139,142	1.17
E.A. Renna	SVP	828,750	2,880,500	835,625	1,172,501	16,563,305	18,571,431	22,280,681	2.11
H.J. Longwell	SVP	953,333	2,640,000	835,625	5,485	10,510,401	11,351,511	14,944,844	3.14
R. Dahan	SVP	953,333	2,640,000	835,625	5,485	10,510,401	11,351,511	14,944,844	3.14

PANEL C. STATISTICS ON COMPENSATION RELATIVE TO HIGHEST PAID EXECUTIVE FOR NEW AND OLD ECONOMY FIRMS

Rank[b]	Averages		Maximums		Minimums		Medians	
	New	Old	New	Old	New	Old	New	Old
1	1.00	1.00	1.00	1.00	1.00	1.00	1.00	1.00
2	1.36	1.50	1.88	2.54	1.03	1.06	1.33	1.25
3	2.69	2.26	4.60	3.04	1.42	1.63	2.90	2.11
4	3.18	3.10	5.46	4.35	1.63	2.21	2.92	3.14
5	3.88	3.50	6.13	5.06	1.60	2.70	3.50	3.43

a. Value as reported in the company proxy statement.
b. Rank reflects the total compensation award and although the top rank usually corresponds to the CEO, it does not always.

influence. In fact, the firm's management (through its human resources department) generally prepares recommendations for the compensation committee that are sent to the firm's top executives for their blessing before being forwarded on to the board's compensation committee. The compensation committee then either accepts the recommendation or sends it back for revision before forwarding it to the board of directors for final approval.[17]

If CEOs have the power to influence board decisions regarding executive compensation, what, if anything, constrains their greed? The fact is that corporate CEOs find themselves under growing pressure to improve their record of pay for performance. An important source of pressure comes from institutional investors that have become actively involved in the governance of their portfolio companies. One such institutional investor is TIAA-CREF, the largest U.S. pension fund, which has recently published its suggested guidelines for corporate governance including explicit guidelines for executive compensation.[18] The policy guidelines speak directly to potential sources of abuse in the use of stock option and grant programs. The types of abuse they are concerned about are reflected in the following list of decision rules designed to guide TIAA-CREF's voting on proxies related to compensation issues:

1. excessive dilution from stock-based plans;
2. the use of reload options that automatically lock in the gains from increased stock price that occur over the duration of the option;
3. options that have no termination date (i.e., evergreen options);
4. option mega-grants that are excessive in relation to other forms of pay or in relation to other executives in the corporation;
5. the use of an unspecified exercise price or exercise price less than 85% of the fair market value of the stock on the date of the grant;
6. plans that are limited to a small number of senior executives;
7. option repricing to lower the exercise price of options already awarded where the market price of

the stock has declined below the original exercise price (i.e., underwater options); and
8. bundling of votes on executive compensation with one or more unrelated items.

Moreover, it's not just the large institutional investors that are watching over the compensation policies of corporate boards. The Internet has made it possible for large numbers of very small investors to coordinate their concerns about what they feel are aberrant management practices. For example, the Internet site eRaider.com provides an opportunity for individual investors to share their concerns and coordinate activities when it comes time to vote their shares at the annual shareholder meeting.[19]

Are there cases where CEOs exercise what may be undue influence over their board of directors? Nell Minow, outspoken shareholder rights activist and founder of the activist LENS fund, clearly thinks so. For example, she notes that "when it appeared that shareholders were about to defeat an exceptionally lucrative stock option proposal at Citrix Systems, the company closed the polls on all other items but left it open on the stock options for an additional ten days, so they could solicit support." They did not inform their shareholders about what they were doing, and the plan was eventually passed. In another example, she describes what Conseco's board did when it paid incoming chairman Gary Wendt a $45 million signing bonus and simultaneously paid the outgoing CEO $50 million as a goodbye package. In her words, the board of Conseco had effectively declared, "Let the shareholders eat dividends."

Certainly not all firms engage in the type of abuse alleged here. However, the actions of corporate boards are now visible to investors via reported compensation required in the firm's annual proxy statement and the large institutional investors are watching. When they find evidence of abuse they can and will move to influence board policies.[20]

The compensation of 52-year-old retiring Coca-Cola Co. CEO Douglas Ivester provides an example of the fuel that feeds the fires of public concern over

---

17. If you saw Michael Douglas' speech at the shareholders meeting of the fictitious Teldar Paper company in the movie "Wall Street," you probably got the impression that stockholders exercise very little control over corporate management. And there are many firms in corporate America whose shareholders have very limited representation on the board of directors even though the board is ostensibly there to direct management in the interests of the shareholders. Consider the composition of the board of directors of the John Deere Corporation in 1989, which was comprised of thirteen members, of which eight were current or retired employees of John Deere. Clearly the fox was in charge of the hen house. Following

a lengthy period of poor firm performance, the board of directors was restructured such that by 1996 it consisted of eleven members and included only two insiders (the firm's current and immediate past CEO).
18. See http://www.tiaa-cref.org/libra/governance/index.html.
19. See Kathleen Day, "Soldiers for the Shareholder," *The Washington Post* (August 27, 2000), H01.
20. As one sign of a growing movement, on July 13 and 14, 2000, a total of 339 institutional shareholders from around the world representing $10 trillion in invested capital, met in New York to talk about issues of corporate governance.

Corporate CEOs find themselves under growing pressure to improve their record of pay for performance. An important source of pressure comes from institutional investors that have become actively involved in the governance of their portfolio companies.

CEO compensation. When Ivester announced his retirement, Graef Crystal, Bloomberg's executive compensation columnist and frequent critic of CEO pay, made the following observation: "Here is a man who is resigning after a two-year tenure as CEO that produced a return for shareholders of a negative 7.3 percent. For that, he is walking away with stock, options and other goodies worth at least $120 million."[21] In addition to his retirement plan benefits, Ivester negotiated a separation agreement that includes (among other things) annual payments of $1.5 million, additional monthly payments of $66,300, medical benefits for himself and his wife, office space and secretarial services, maintenance of his home security system and club dues for his existing club memberships, as well as title to his company car, cell phones, and computer.[22]

However, there are some notable instances of CEO pay "heroes." For example, Apple Computer's Steve Jobs, Masco Corporation's Richard Manoogian, and Pepsico's Roger Enrico all work for a base salary of $1.00 per year. At the same time, they own significant interests in their respective firms and are working for themselves as owners. Enrico's story is particularly interesting. He asked his board to cut his salary to $1.00 and donate the difference to scholarships for the children of Pepsico's front-line employees. The board complied and donated $1 million.

Paying for performance is not easy and some boards do it badly. An alternative to the manager-controlled board story is the inept board story. In this scenario, the board of directors tries to do the right thing but simply does it badly because it's hard to do. Let's consider what the ideal CEO compensation program is trying to accomplish: First, the total package must have sufficient total value to attract and retain the caliber of talent the firm must have to compete effectively in its product or service markets. In practice this means that the firm must meet a market test for the level of talent it requires.

The second objective of the CEO compensation program is to provide incentives that will elicit effort as well as the optimal amount of risk-taking by the CEO. Encouraging the CEO to succeed at his job is typically accomplished by using various forms of incentive pay that kick in only when performance targets are met. However, inducing the CEO to take risks poses a particularly difficult challenge. Taking risks opens the CEO to the possibility of failure and possible job loss. Thus, to encourage the CEO to undertake risky strategies, companies usually include features in the CEO's employment contract that take the sting out of failure. Specifically, CEO compensation packages almost always include a fixed salary component combined with a generous severance package should the firm falter so badly that the CEO would be replaced. The combined effect of these two elements of the compensation package serves to provide at least partial insulation for the CEO from the personal costs he or she might suffer from undertaking a failed strategy.[23] Unfortunately, neither of these measures distinguishes between good decisions that just did not pan out and bad decisions that made little economic sense from the start.

Finally, the CEO compensation program must be structured to align shareholder and manager interests so that the CEO will "think like an owner." The most obvious way to do this is to make him an owner by giving him stock and options, right? Not necessarily. If the CEO's personal well being becomes too dependent on the fortunes of the firm, then he may refuse to undertake risks that shareholders, who own diversified portfolios, would like the company to undertake.[24] In fact, some CEOs are finding that shareholdings in their own firm are so out of balance that they are engaging in external market transactions known as equity swaps to limit their personal exposure to the vagaries of the stock market. But this just undoes the intended effects of the stock options.[25]

---

21. The Crystal Report.
22. Company Proxy Statement filed with the SEC on March 3, 2000.
23. For example, Rebecca Mark vied with Jeff Skilling for the CEO post at Enron by promoting a strategy reliant on owning huge amounts of productive assets. Mr. Skilling promoted a different strategy for Enron and eventually won out. You can either look at this as a personal tragedy for Ms. Marks or a very successful tournament for the CEO position that elicited two very different strategies from two hard-working contenders (*Wall Street Journal*, August 27, 2000, A1).
24. Brian Hall and Kevin Murphy ("Stock Options for Undiversified Executives," Harvard Business School unpublished working paper, June 2000) point out the lengthy set of problems that arise where undiversified, risk-averse executives are paid using non-tradable stock options.
25. A study by Lisa Meulbroek ("Does Risk Matter? Corporate Insider Transactions in Internet-based Firms," Harvard Business School working paper

#00-062, 2000) documents the propensity for Internet executives to sell their stock and rationalizes the practice as a means of reducing the executive's excessive exposure to the fortunes of their employer firm. She also finds that on average investors don't seem to mind that the executives are selling as the stock price of the firm tends to increase upon the announcement of insider sales. This contrasts with previous research in which insider investors have interpreted sales by executives of more traditional firms as a signal that the firm's shares are overvalued. Similarly Eli Ofek and David Yermack ("Taking Stock: Equity-based Compensation and the Evolution of Managerial Ownership," *Journal of Finance* 55, 2000, 1367-1384) study more than 18,000 executives who received an annual average of 57,250 new options on shares of their firms' stock in the mid-1990s and found that their average annual change in stock ownership actually declined by −6,340 shares. They document that executives sell virtually all they acquire through the exercise of option grants (with the exception of lower-ownership managers).

DO CEOs EARN THEIR PAY?

This is where the rubber meets the road. The number of studies that have tried to resolve this issue has grown exponentially over the last decade,[26] but the connection between CEO pay and firm performance has proven a difficult one to test. As we just seen, CEOs get paid for just showing up (salary), for having a good year (bonus), and to encourage them to work hard for the company's future (options and grants of shares—long-term compensation). So, what period should we use when evaluating pay for performance? Just measuring recent past performance is not sufficient since some part of a CEO's pay is designed to encourage him or her to undertake strategies that pay off in the future.

What has been carefully tested is the relationship between a CEO's pay and the stock price performance of the firm he or she manages. Specifically, much of this research has tried to estimate just how much a CEO's compensation changes in response to a $1,000 change in shareholder value for the firm they lead. In his 1999 report cited earlier, Kevin Murphy offers four basic findings that have come from these studies: First, the pay-performance relationship for CEOs is driven primarily by stock options and stock ownership (as opposed to salary and bonus). For example, 95% of the pay-performance sensitivity for CEOs in manufacturing companies is a result of the CEO's holdings of stock options and stock. Furthermore, as reported in a 1998 study by Brian Hall and Jeffrey Liebman, the effect of stock and options on the pay-performance relationship is 53 times larger than the effect of salary and bonus. Second, pay-performance sensitivities vary considerably across industries. For example, in 1996, according to Murphy, CEOs in mining and manufacturing firms received $5.90 per $1,000 of shareholder value created, compared to $1.22 for a utility CEO. Third, the pay-performance sensitivity has increased dramatically over the decade of the 1990s, again driven primarily by the use of stock options and restricted stock. Murphy notes that in 1992 a CEO in

Mining and Manufacturing realized $3.72 for each $1,000 of wealth created, but by 1996 this had risen to $5.90.[27] Fourth and finally, the increase in pay-performance sensitivity has been almost exclusively due to stock option grants.

Let's accept, for the moment, that higher CEO pay is linked to higher corporate performance, as the principal-agent theory would suggest. Even so, several nagging questions remain. First, is the performance that the CEOs get paid for producing a direct result of the exercise of their managerial talents or sheer luck? A recent study examined the effects of "luck" in the form of windfall changes in oil prices for firms in the oil industry and found that the luck-skill split is about 50-50.[28] Furthermore, the study found that companies with better governance structures (as evidenced by the presence of large shareholders, a smaller board of directors, and a larger fraction of the board made up of insiders) tend to pay less for luck than those that are not so well governed.

Second, is the pay-performance sensitivity optimal? That is, should the CEO of a mining or manufacturing firm receive more or less than $5.90 per $1,000 of shareholder wealth created? We simply don't know the answer to this question. As Hall and Liebman conclude in their 1998 study, "We do not claim the current relationship between CEO pay and firm performance is sufficiently strong or that current contracts are efficient. Indeed, our findings point to some potentially serious deficiencies in current CEO compensation packages."[29] Finally, the evidence supporting a strong link between CEO pay and performance relies almost exclusively on what Kevin Murphy refers to as the "explicit linkage" provided by CEO holdings of stock and options as opposed to the "implicit linkage" provided by salary changes and bonuses (typically based on year-to-year measures of firm performance). What is the proper mix of implicit pay (based on backward-looking accounting profitability) and explicit pay (based on forward-looking stock prices)? These and related questions will provide the fuel for many volumes of future research.

26. Kevin Murphy ("Executive Compensation," *Handbook of Labor Economics*, Vol. 3, North Holland, Orley Ashenfelter and David Card, eds., 1999) reports that the one to two studies per year of CEO pay prior to 1985 jumped to sixty by 1995.

27. Brian Hall ("What You Need to Know about Stock Options," *Harvard Business Review* (March-April 2000), 121-129) documents a steady rise in the sensitivity of CEO pay to corporate performance (measured by annual stock returns) over the period 1980-2000. For example, in 1980 a one-percentage point

increase in firm value resulted in a $43,000 increase in CEO compensation, and by 1994 a similar increase in firm value increased CEO pay by $124,000. Similar increases were documented for three other measures of pay-performance sensitivity.

28. See Marianne Bertrand and Sendhil Mullainathan, "Do CEOs Set their Own Pay? The Ones without Principals Do," NBER Working Paper No. 7604 (March 2000).

29. Hall and Liebman (1998), cited in footnote 2, p. 686.

The pay-performance sensitivity for U.S. CEOs has increased dramatically over the decade of the 1990s, driven primarily by the use of stock options and restricted stock.

SUMMARY REMARKS

Many people, including a number of prominent financial economists, think that CEO compensation is out of control and that something needs to be done about it. Even among those economists and practitioners who feel the CEO labor market is working well, there is a clear sense that the media, stockholders, and other corporate constituencies (particularly, rank-and-file workers) need to be educated about the workings of this market.

The controversy over CEO pay has brought together some strange bedfellows as shareholders and labor unions find themselves on the same side of the issue. Consider the AFL-CIO's four-part plan to reform the way that CEO pay is awarded.[30] First, it calls for the use of independent directors on the compensation committee. In support of the need for such a change, it points out that, in 1998, the Investor Responsibility Research Center identified nearly 150 directors serving on the compensation committees of S&P 500 companies who had affiliations with the firm that compromised their independence. Second, they make the case for more uniform disclosure of the value of option grants in an effort to make CEO pay more transparent to stockholders and the general public. Third, they argue that CEO pay should be linked to clear performance standards and that, at a minimum, CEO pay should reflect the company's economic health, including its stock price. Finally, they call for fairness in the compensation practices for all employees throughout the firm. Here they suggest linking CEO pay proportionally to average pay to employees in the firm. With the possible exception of item four, you might assume this proposal came from a shareholder group.

Studies have shown that the CEO receives higher pay when the firm realizes higher performance, and that such pay for performance is largely due to the effects of stock and stock option ownership by the CEO. So when we read stories of very large CEO compensation awards, isn't this simply evidence that stockholders are "sharing the value pie" created by the CEO? In part the answer to this question must be affirmative for studies have shown that changes in CEO pay are driven almost exclusively by changes in the stock price of their firm's shares. Even so, there remain some troubling questions: First, did the CEO bring about the changes that increased shareholder returns or simply enjoy a "free ride"? In one study it was found that about half of oil company CEO compensation could be attributed to changes in oil prices, a variable over which they have no control. Second, was it really necessary to give the CEO so much of the value pie? Did a wise and knowing board of directors reward the CEO appropriately, or did the CEO exercise influence over the board's compensation decision? Rewarding executives is an inexact science and it is certainly understandable that corporate boards can and will make mistakes. In other cases the CEO may well be exerting undue influence over the board's compensation process, thereby extracting excessive compensation for him or herself.

Perhaps our problem with understanding CEO compensation comes from the fact that financial economists have not thought deeply enough about the pay-for-performance issue. A notable exception is Michael Jensen, long an outspoken critic of corporate pay practices (though not of *levels* of pay) and other managerial practices that do not give priority to shareholder interests. In the article that precedes this one, Jensen argues that the proper goal of the firm should be *enlightened value maximization*. He points out that the long-standing goal of value maximization, accepted by virtually all financial economists, provides a way to measure success or failure, but says nothing about how to create a superior vision or strategy to achieve the goal of value creation. To a greater extent than its predecessor, *enlightened* value maximization places special emphasis on the importance of building and maintaining good relations with customers, employees, suppliers, local communities, and other corporate "stakeholders." One possible corollary of Jensen's argument is that we may have gone too far in our quest to "incentivize" the CEO to maximize shareholder value.

---

30. See http://www.aflcio.org/paywatch/2cl_bd.htm.

OPTION-BASED COMPENSATION: PANACEA OR PANDORA'S BOX?

by Stuart L. Gillan,
TIAA-CREF Institute*

D uring the past decade, investors have become increasingly concerned about the proliferation and size of stock option plans. Shareholder concerns center on four main issues. First, the cost of option-based compensation may exceed the associated benefits, resulting in excessive transfers of wealth from shareholders to optionholders. Second, the current accounting for and disclosure of option-based compensation may not be adequate for valuation purposes. Third, although many companies submit option plans to a shareholder vote, it appears that some companies may use exchange and market rules to avoid the shareholder approval process. Given the potential for stock option plans to transfer large amounts of wealth from shareholders to optionholders, the ability of shareholders to vote on option plans is seen as a critical corporate governance issue.

Fourth and finally, with recent stock-price declines, many employees now hold out-of-the-money or underwater options. In order to retain and motivate employees, some corporations have responded by repricing or replacing underwater options with new grants. This replenishment has raised shareholder concern that the practice effectively rewards employees for failed performance, and that repricing undermines the rationale for using options as incentive compensation in the first place.

Along with increased shareholder concern has been an increase in the perceived importance of human capital—employees—in determining corporate profitability and shareholder returns at many companies. Proponents of option-based compensation argue that it aligns employee and shareholder interests. Moreover, it has been suggested that options are critical not only in motivating and retaining employees, but also in fueling economic growth. It is difficult, however, to measure the benefits of compensating employees with stock options.

Similarly, assessing the cost of stock options can be complex. Although an economic transfer from shareholders to employees takes place at the time an option is granted, the option exercise occurs some time in the future. This raises the issue of how to measure the potential wealth transfer from shareholders to optionholders resulting from option grants. One approach is to develop an estimate of the expected value transfer at the time of the grant—using dilution measures or option pricing tools. Alternatively, given sufficient disclosure in corporate financial statements, one could focus on actual option exercises and measure the realized value transfers.

Although recognizing that there are potential benefits of option-based compensation, the primary focus of the paper is on (1) measuring the "cost" of option-based compensation, (2) management actions to deal with underwater options, and (3) shareholder concerns about the use of stock options. Shareholder concerns suggest that the use of option-based compensation will continue to be a hot-button corporate governance issue.

*An earlier version was presented at the TIAA-CREF Institute Corporate Governance Forum 2001: Executive Compensation, Stock Options, and the Role of the Board of Directors. I would like to thank John Ameriks, Ken Bertsch, Jennifer Bethel, Jay Hartzell, Jacob Rugh, Lelia Stroud, and Mark Warshawsky for helpful comments and discussions. The opinions expressed in this article are those of the author and not necessarily those of TIAA-CREF or its employees.

DILUTION

One of investors' primary concerns about stock option plans is the extent to which shareholder value may be diluted—that is, transferred to optionholders. This section examines several dilution measures that can be used to benchmark the potential value transfers. While commonly used, dilution measures implicitly assume that each option granted will be exercised when it is deep in-the-money. That is, the dilution measures assume that the exercise price will be paid in exchange for a share of stock with a much higher market value. The actual value transfer from shareholders to optionholders will depend on the difference between the option exercise price and the market price of the share at exercise. This section illustrates how dilution measures provide an upper bound on the potential cost. Alternate approaches to dilution are discussed later in the paper.

The term dilution is used in a number of different ways in different contexts. *Basic Dilution* provides an overall measure of dilution from stock options by dividing options granted during a year by the number of shares outstanding at year-end. *Full Dilution* estimates the portion of the current shareholders' value transferred to employees if employees exercise their options. Full Dilution recognizes that on exercise there are additional shares outstanding. *Potential Dilution,* often referred to as the option *overhang,* which can be measured either in Basic or Full terms, incorporates the number of options the company has *available* for grant into the numerator of the dilution calculation.

EXAMPLE 1: MEASURES OF DILUTION

Suppose a company has 100 shares outstanding and a current price of $30. Some time ago the company granted employees 16 options, and the company has an additional 16 shares available to grant as options.

BASIC DILUTION
= (options granted / current shares outstanding)
= (16/100)
= 16%.

POTENTIAL BASIC DILUTION
= ([options granted + options available for grant]/ current shares outstanding)
= (32/100)
= 32%.

Once the options are exercised the company will have 116 shares outstanding. Each share has an equal claim on the company's assets.

THE FULL DILUTION IS:
= (options granted/[current shares outstanding + options granted + options outstanding])
= (16/(100+16+0))
= 13.8%

The original shareholders owned 100% of company prior to exercise, but only 86.2% after exercise (100 shares out of 116).

POTENTIAL FULL DILUTION
= ([options granted + options available for grant] / [current shares outstanding + options granted + options available for grant])
= (32/132)
= 24.2%.

Note that Potential Dilution can be measured using Basic and Full approaches by adding shares *available* for grant to the options granted in each calculation.

Suppose that the company issues an additional 10 options. The company has 100 shares outstanding, 16 options from the original grant, and 10 newly granted options. The potential wealth transfer resulting from the new grant is borne by current shareholders *and* current optionholders.

Following the Potential Dilution example, current shareholders own 100 shares, so 100 / [100 + 16 + 10] represents the proportion of the potential transfer from shareholders to new grant recipients. Similarly, with 16 current optionholders, 16 / [100 + 16 + 10] represents the magnitude of the potential transfer from current optionholders to new grant recipients.

To provide a perspective on how the examples work in practice, Table 1 reports on option granting activity at Microsoft during 1999. The Full Dilution resulting from the new options granted is 1.32%. Put another way, the 1.32% Full Dilution represents the portion of the company that new optionholders may

TABLE 1 ■ DILUTION AT MICROSOFT

The table reports measures of Basic and Full Dilution for Microsoft during Fiscal 1999. Shares outstanding is reported as of fiscal year-end. Option activity is as reported in Microsoft's 1999 10-K. Note that options outstanding of 766 million include the current year grant of 78 million options.

	Options (millions)	Basic Dilution	Full Dilution
Granted	78	(78/5,141) = 1.52%	78/(5,141 + 766) = 1.32%
Outstanding	766	(766/5,141) = 14.90%	766/(5,141 + 766) = 13.14%
Available	980	(980/5,141) = 19.06%	980/(5,141 + 766 + 980) = 14.23%
Potential Dilution	1,746	(1,746/5,141) = 33.96%	1,746/(5,141 + 766 + 980) = 25.35%
Shares Outstanding	5,141		

TABLE 2 ■ BASIC DILUTION IN A LARGE SAMPLE

The table reports summary statistics on Basic Dilution for a broad set of U.S. companies tracked by the IRRC. The sample comprises the S&P 1,500 and approximately 500 other companies with broad institutional ownership. Basic Dilution is measured in percentage terms as 100 × (Options/Shares outstanding as at year-end.) Statistics for potential dilution are reported only for companies where shares available for grant at year-end can be determined.

	Grants 1997	Grants 1998	Grants 1999	Options Outstanding 1999	Available for Grant at year-end 1999	Potential Dilution 1999
Average	2.70	2.98	2.85	9.00	4.79	13.93
Median	1.67	1.78	1.94	7.65	3.42	11.83
95th Percentile	8.87	10.03	8.61	21.06	9.62	31.41
Number of Companies	1,517	1,589	1,655	1,680	1,340	1,340

Source: Author's calculations based on IRRC data.

ultimately receive. However, as noted in the hypothetical example, the dilution falls on shareholders *and* optionholders.[1] The optionholders prior to the new grant face a potential value transfer in the proportion of: [688/(766 + 5,141)] = 11.7%. Shareholders prior to the new grant face a potential value transfer in the proportion of: [5,141/(766 + 5,141)] = 87%. For this reason, current shareholders have not really given away a full 1.32% of their wealth in the company. Rather current shareholders face a potential wealth transfer of around 1.17% of the value of the company—their 87% "share" of the 1.32% Full Dilution.

Dilution in a Broad Sample of Companies

To examine the issue of dilution further, the following table reports measures of dilution and potential dilution using Basic Dilution (options as a percentage of shares outstanding) for a large sample of U.S. companies. The sample is based on a set of companies tracked by the Investor Responsibility Research Center (IRRC) that includes the S&P 1,500

and approximately 500 other companies with broad institutional ownership. Complete 1999 data for this analysis was disclosed by 1,680 companies. Table 2 reports summary statistics on Basic Dilution for the 1,680 companies, including option grants in each year 1997-1999, options outstanding at the end of 1999, options available for grant, and potential dilution.

The "Run-rate" (sometimes referred to as the option "burn-rate") is annual option grants as a percentage of shares outstanding. A constant or declining run-rate may indicate a stable compensation policy, whereas an increasing run-rate is likely to indicate increasingly aggressive granting of options.

As shown in Table 2, in 1999 companies on average granted options equal to 2.85% of shares outstanding, an increase from 2.7% in 1997. Median grants exhibit an increasing trend from 1.67% in 1997 to 1.94% by 1999. Median grant levels are somewhat lower than the average, suggesting that companies with a higher level of option use raise the average. Some companies were particularly aggressive in their option granting practices, with those at the 95th percentile making annual grants in the 8.6-10%

---

1. Jennifer Carpenter and David Yermack (2001) "Dilution from stock-based compensation," working paper, New York University.

range. At the end of 1999, the average level of options outstanding as a proportion of shares outstanding was 9% (median 7.65%.) At the upper end of the distribution, the company at the 95th percentile had options outstanding equal to over 21% of current shares outstanding.[2]

The last two columns of Table 2 report on shares available for option grants and potential dilution (the total of shares available for grant and options outstanding) for the three-quarters of the sample for which the required information is available. Each measure is reported as a percentage of year-end shares outstanding. Comparing shares available for grant to past grants indicates that companies had between one and two years' worth of option grants on hand. This could provide an indication as to whether or not the company is running out of shares for option grants, and at what point the company may need to adopt additional option plans.

Table 3 provides perspective on how grant practices vary across industries by reporting industry-level Basic Dilution. Industry groups are based on 2-digit SIC codes. Table 3 reports option activity for three industries with a low use of option grants, and three industries with a high use of option grants. There is considerable variation in grant practices across industries, with *Electric, gas and sanitary services* at the low end of the scale and *Engineering and management* at the high end. The median level of dilution from prior grants (options outstanding) ranges from 2.35% to 13.78%. Median grants during 1999 ranged from 0.88% to 5.03%, and dilution from options outstanding at the 95th percentile ranges from 9.8% to 26.91%.

There is also substantial variation in grant practices among companies in the same industry. For example, the median company in the *Food stores* industry had dilution from 1999 grants of 1.28% and options outstanding of 4.25%. In contrast, the company at the 95th percentile in *Food stores* had 1999 grant dilution at 4.42% and options outstanding equal to 15.63%.

Estimated Value Transfers of Option Grants

Whereas dilution measures provide a basis for benchmarking option use, the issue quickly turns to one of the "cost" to shareholders. Although the dilution measures discussed above provide estimates of the upper bound of potential wealth transfers from shareholders to optionholders (as a proportion of the equity that optionholders may ultimately receive), option pricing tools are typically used to estimate the dollar value of grants, which may then be benchmarked against market values. Typically, the deeper in-the-money the options are, the closer they are economically to a share of stock. This implies that if the majority of options are deep in-the-money, the potential value transfer can be approximated by Full Dilution. To the extent that options are not deep in-the-money, value estimates as a proportion of current market value will be lower than the Full Dilution.

To illustrate, during 1999 Microsoft reported grants of 78 million options to employees. The estimated value transfer at the time of grant (explained later in this section) amounted to about $967 million, representing approximately 0.2% of Microsoft's 1999 year-end market value. This is an estimate of the *expected* value transfer at the time of grant, based on assumed inputs and the Black-Scholes option pricing model. Consequently, the estimates are subject to criticisms of the model and the inputs used. For example, option pricing models are designed to value exchange-traded options, not employee stock options. Employee stock options typically have a much longer maturity than exchange-traded options, vesting restrictions, non-transferability features, and other characteristics that may imply different valuations relative to exchange-traded options. Moreover, there is evidence that employees tend to exercise options early, sacrificing a significant portion of the value. On the other hand, many employee stock options in practice have value-enhancing features not captured by standard option pricing models. For example, employee stock options are American options (which permit exercise before the expiration date), whereas the standard Black-Scholes model is designed to value European options (which can be exercised only on the expiration date). Some employee stock options also have reload features or may ultimately be repriced, which enhances their value relative to estimates using standard option pricing models. Similarly, at least for some employees, informational advantages may add substantial value by permitting "fortuitous" timing of option grants and exercises.[3] Moreover, it has been suggested that, although option pricing approaches may provide an estimate of the potential cost to

---

2. By way of comparison, John Core and Wayne Guay (2001) "Stock option plans for non-executive employees," forthcoming *Journal of Financial Economics*, report average options outstanding during the 1994-1997 period of 6.6% (median 5.2%) for a large sample of firms.

3. David Yermack (1997) "Good timing: CEO stock option awards and company news announcements," *Journal of Finance* 52, 449-476.

Whereas dilution measures provide a basis for benchmarking option use, the issue quickly turns to one of the "cost" to shareholders.

TABLE 3 ■ INDUSTRY-LEVEL BASIC DILUTION

The table reports summary statistics on Basic Dilution for selected industries. Industry groups are based on 2-Digit SIC codes. Basic Dilution is measured in percentage terms as 100 × (Options / Shares outstanding as at year-end.) Panel A reports on three industries with low levels of options outstanding relative to other industry groups. Panel B reports on three industries with high levels of options outstanding relative to other industry groups.

	Grants 1997	Grants 1998	Grants 1999	Options Outstanding 1999	Available for Grant 1999	Potential Dilution 1999
PANEL A: LOW OPTION-USE INDUSTRY GROUPS						
DEPOSITORY INSTITUTIONS						
Mean	1.51	1.56	1.57	5.77	4.24	10.24
Median	1.16	1.20	1.22	4.39	2.72	8.59
95th Percentile	3.74	5.63	4.74	13.01	14.98	23.90
Number of companies	85	92	91	94	72	72
ELECTRIC, GAS, AND SANITARY SERVICES						
Mean	1.08	1.18	1.47	3.84	3.58	8.23
Median	0.51	0.57	0.88	2.35	3.12	6.45
95th Percentile	4.03	2.96	4.15	9.80	11.83	18.96
Number of companies	59	69	80	84	53	53
FOOD STORES						
Mean	1.55	1.45	1.53	5.14	1.82	6.94
Median	0.85	1.02	1.28	4.25	1.74	6.19
95th Percentile	4.01	5.96	4.42	15.63	3.42	17.60
Number of companies	8	9	9	9	8	8
PANEL B: HIGH OPTION-USE INDUSTRY GROUPS						
SECURITY, COMMODITY BROKERS, AND SERVICES						
Mean	2.69	2.85	3.09	10.38	8.23	18.1
Median	2.2	2.14	2.43	9.35	4.93	14.26
95th Percentile	10.37	6.97	9.1	19.7	40.87	49.86
Number of companies	19	21	23	23	18	18
BUSINESS SERVICES						
Mean	5.64	6.03	5.40	13.96	6.42	20.40
Median	3.98	4.53	4.28	12.51	4.62	19.14
95th Percentile	18.04	14.99	13.04	25.56	20.62	41.49
Number of companies	144	154	165	165	136	136
ENGINEERING AND MANAGEMENT SERVICES						
Mean	4.29	4.61	5.61	14.03	5.45	19.83
Median	3.33	3.80	5.03	13.78	6.19	18.72
95th Percentile	9.82	15.04	13.24	26.91	13.24	38.88
Number of companies	20	20	19	19	15	15

shareholders, risk-averse employees typically assign a much lower value to the option grant.[4] There are also other potential, if even more difficult to quantify, costs. For example, options may provide senior managers with incentives to increase risk or reduce dividend payments, which may not be in the interest of shareholders.

Despite such criticisms, the use of option pricing tools provides a useful alternative approach in benchmarking the level of expected value transfers from shareholders to optionholders. To illustrate the application of option pricing techniques, the remainder of this section follows the approach of Michael Mauboussin to value option grants at Microsoft.[5]

---

4. Brian Hall and Kevin Murphy (2000) "Stock options for undiversified executives," NBER working paper 8052.

5. Michael Mauboussin (1998) "A piece of the action: employee stock options in the new economy," *Frontiers of Finance*, Credit Suisse First Boston.

Using the Black-Scholes option pricing formula, and the company's assumptions for volatility, risk-free rate, average exercise price ($54.62), and weighted-average option life (6.2 years), the base estimate of the value transfer from options grants on 78 million shares during 1999 is $1.78 billion. Note, however, that as employees leave the company and their options expire, options are cancelled. Cancellations at Microsoft have averaged around 3.3% of options outstanding per year. Using 3.3% as an estimate of the rate of future cancellations, the value transfer estimate declines to $1.71 billion.[6]

As noted in the earlier examples, if a company has significant stock options outstanding, the value transfer resulting from new grants is from shareholders *and* current option holders. With 5.14 billion shares outstanding and 688 million options granted in prior years, Microsoft notionally has 5.83 billion shares with a potential claim on earnings.[7] After the new grant of 78 million options, Microsoft notionally has 5.91 billion shares with a potential claim on earnings. Thus, future cash flows will flow to current shareholders in the proportion of (5.14/5.91= 87%) and to current optionholders in the proportion of (0.69/5.91=12%).[8] By implication, when new options are granted, both current shareholders and current option holders are diluted. The value transfer from current shareholders is 87% of $1.71 billion, or approximately $1.49 billion.

Finally, for tax purposes, Section 422 of the United States Internal Revenue Code allows companies to expense the difference between the market price and the exercise price when employees exercise their options.[9] Assuming that the tax benefit is the tax rate of 35% multiplied by the estimated value transfer, the estimated after-tax value transfer from incumbent shareholders is $967 million, which is approximately 0.2% of Microsoft's year-end market value. Recall from the earlier analysis that the Full Dilution approach resulted in an estimated value transfer of 1.17% of market value. The option pricing approach captures the fact that new grants are not deep in-the-money and provides a lower estimate of the expected value transfer.

There is considerable debate about how to measure the value transfers resulting from option grants. This debate spans a number of issues, including the legitimacy of using standard option pricing models and the appropriate time to estimate or measure value transfers (whether at grant date, vesting date, or exercise date). There is also vigorous debate as to whether or not any estimates should be treated as an expense in the income statement. The next section focuses on an alternative to using option pricing models at grant date by examining realized value transfers on option exercise.

Realized Value Transfers

The value transfer approach based on an option pricing model is, by its nature, a forward-looking exercise. Moreover, the focus is on grant-date *estimates* of the *potential value transfer*. An alternate approach is to use information at the time of exercise to measure *realized value transfers*. This section first presents examples of measuring realized value transfers, and then examines realized value transfers in a large sample.

Illustrating Realized Value Transfers

EXAMPLE 2: VALUE TRANSFER

Suppose that a company has 100 shares outstanding and assets of $3,000. Some time ago the company granted employees 16 options with an exercise price of $10. On exercising their 16 options, employees pay the company the $10 exercise price per share for a total of $160. The $160 cash payment increases the company's assets to $3,160, and shares outstanding increases to 116 as employees receive 16 shares. Each share has an equal value of ($3,160/116) = $27.24.

CASE 1: LARGE MARKET VALUE INCREASE SINCE GRANT DATE
The employees' net gain:
= (value of shares acquired – total exercise price paid)
= ([16 shares @ $27.24] – $160) = $276.

---

6. Ideally we would like to estimate cancellations as a proportion of annual grants.
7. All numbers have been rounded for ease of exposition.
8. This provides an upper bound as not all options outstanding are "in-the-money."

9. Under IRS regulations, some options do not qualify for tax deductions. To the extent that such options are granted by companies, calculations using the reported tax benefit will understate the potential value transfer.

The value transfer from the original share-holders:

Value before exercise – Value after exercise

= $3,000 – (100 shares @ $27.24)

= $3,000 – $2,724 = $276

= ($276/$3,160), or 8.7% of the market value of the firm.

CASE 2: ENORMOUS MARKET VALUE INCREASE SINCE GRANT DATE

If the value of the firm prior to exercise were to increase to say, $1,000,000, then on exercise each outstanding share would be worth ($1,000,160/116) = $8,622.07.

The employees' net gain:

= (value of shares acquired – total exercise price paid)

= ([16 shares @ $8,622.07] – $160) = $137,793.

The value transfer from the original shareholders:

Value before exercise – Value after exercise

= $1,000,000 – (100 shares @ $8,621.69)

= $1,000,000-$862,169 = $137,793.

= ($137,793/$1,000,000), or 13.8% of the market value of the firm.

As in the earlier dilution examples, any subsequent option issuance transfers value from current shareholders and current optionholders to new grant recipients.

The realized value transfer of $276 in Case 1 of Example 2 equates to 8.7% of the market value of the company on the exercise date (which includes the $160 employees pay to exercise their options). In Case 2, where the market value of the company increased dramatically, the wealth transfer was 13.8%. The potential value transfer is capped at the level of Full Dilution, in this case 13.8% of the market value on the exercise date.

As noted earlier, for tax purposes companies are permitted to expense the difference between the market price at exercise and the option exercise price. As a result, companies may report the associated tax savings in their financial statements. For example, Microsoft reported in its 1999 10-K a tax saving associated with option exercises of $3.1 billion. The tax saving is equal to the tax Microsoft did *not* pay—that is, the tax rate multiplied by the difference between the market price and the exercise price (0.35 × (Market price – exercise price) = $3.1 billion). This implies that the pre-tax amount was ($3.1 billion/0.35) = $8.86 billion, or $5.76 billion after tax. This $5.76 billion after-tax figure amounts to a realized value transfer equal to 1.25% of Microsoft's year-end market value.

Realized Value Transfers in the S&P 500

Table 4 reports realized value transfers for S&P 500 firms during the period 1997-1999. Note that the tax benefit from stock option exercise was readily available for less than one-third of all S&P 500 firms each year.[10] Panel A of Table 4 focuses on after-tax value transfers as a percentage of year-end market value. Assuming a tax rate of 35%, the median estimated after-tax value transfer each year from option exercises ranges from 0.38% to 0.44% of market value, with an increasing trend during the period. Average values are somewhat higher, in the range of 0.58%-0.62% range. In Panel B the emphasis is on measuring the aggregate value transfers at the sample companies. These aggregates, which would contribute to any economy-wide measure of labor costs, range from $11.9 to $28.4 billion while averaging $19.7 billion a year during the three-year period. These value transfers reflect exercises of past option grants. It would seem reasonable to "allocate" a portion of the realized value transfer to prior years rather than view this as the "cost" of stock options in a particular year. Nevertheless, measuring realized value transfers over time is analogous to measuring option run-rates; it provides an indication of annual realized value transfers, and may suggest a trend.

To evaluate the potential value transfers in the time between grant and exercises, one could take the following approach: At grant dates, use an option pricing model to estimate the value transfer and the sensitivity of options granted (and outstanding) to the price of the underlying stock. As the stock price changes, estimate the change in the value of the options, and the resulting increase or decrease in the expected value transfer. Upon exercise there could then be a reconciliation between the current estimate and the realized value transfer.

---

10. It has been suggested that the tax disclosures are "hard to come by" and are not plainly visible in the income statement, see Jack Ciesielski (2000) "1999 S&P 500 stock compensation: The fluff grows," *The Analyst's Accounting Observer.*

**Stock-based compensation is viewed by many as being a critical component of
compensation programs with many potential benefits.**

TABLE 4 ■ REALIZED VALUE TRANSFERS AT S&P 500 COMPANIES
The table reports on estimated realized value transfers at approximately 162 S&P companies for which information on tax benefits from option exercise was available. Panel A reports on the after-tax value transfer as a proportion of current stock market value. Panel B reports on the aggregate dollar amount of the after-tax value transfers.

PANEL A: AFTER-TAX VALUE TRANSFERS AS A PERCENTAGE OF MARKET VALUE				
	1997	**1998**	**1999**	**3-year Average**
	%	%	%	%
Mean	0.58	0.62	0.54	0.58
Median	0.38	0.40	0.44	0.41
Number of companies for which tax benefit information is available	155	161	162	

PANEL B: AGGREGATE AFTER-TAX VALUE TRANSFERS $ BILLION				
	1997	**1998**	**1999**	**3-year Average**
Tax benefit	6.4	10.1	15.3	10.6
Implied cost	18.4	28.9	43.7	30.4
Implied after-tax cost	11.9	18.8	28.4	19.7
Number of companies for which tax benefit information is available	155	161	162	

Source: Author's calculations based on data from FACTSET and *The Analyst's Accounting Observer.*

Although we can estimate value transfers, such estimates are imprecise by virtue of both the information available and the limitations of the models used. Many companies disclose information on option grants only in 10-K reports, which typically are available after fiscal year-ends and announcements of fourth quarter earnings. Inevitably, the question then arises as to whether option related disclosures are timely and relevant for investment decision making.

GENERAL DISCLOSURE ISSUES

Under Generally Accepted Accounting Principles (GAAP) and Securities and Exchange Commission (SEC) requirements, two main types of option-based compensation disclosure are required in corporate financial statements.[11] The first set of disclosures requires an estimate of compensation costs at grant date. The second set requires a three-year summary of option granting activity.[12]

The primary accounting rule governing accounting for stock options is SFAS 123. Under SFAS 123 companies must either take a charge to income or, as almost all do, provide additional footnote disclosures reporting net income and earnings per share *as if* the costs had been charged to income. (The *as-if* estimates are referred to as "pro-forma" disclosures.) Companies are granted considerable latitude in making assumptions about inputs into option pricing models, including the expected life of the option, stock price volatility, dividend yield, and the risk-free rate. Although such assumptions must be fully disclosed, different assumptions can lead to quite different estimates of the cost of stock options. Companies can then allocate estimated costs over the expected life of option grants; that is, only a portion of the current year's option grant is treated as an expense in the current fiscal year's *as-if* estimates of net income and earnings per share. The portions of the estimated costs from prior grants allocated to the current fiscal year are also included in the *as-if* estimates of net income and earnings per share.

The value of prior-year grants is not updated to reflect changes in the market price of the stock, which suggests that, everything else being equal, the footnote values may over- or under-estimate the

11. This discussion relates to company-wide option disclosures, and not specifically those required for senior executives under the proxy rules.

12. In addition, under SFAS 128, Earnings per Share, in-the-money options are considered to be shares outstanding when calculating the number of shares to determine *diluted* earnings per share. Options "at-the-money" or "out-of-the-money" do not result in EPS dilution.

"costs" conditional on the change in the stock price since the grant date. Recent research suggests, however, that perhaps "everything else" is not equal when it comes to the accounting estimates of option grants. For example, a 1998 study by David Yermack reports that companies choose methods that tend to minimize the reported value of option grants.[13]

The three-year summary of option activity includes a statement of options: (1) outstanding at the beginning of the year, (2) outstanding at the end of the year, (3) exercisable at the end of the year, (4) granted, (5) exercised, (6) forfeited, or (7) expired during the year. Specifically, for each item companies are required to disclose the number of options, a "meaningful" range of exercise prices, and a weighted-average exercise price for each range. Additional information is required for options outstanding and options currently exercisable (items (2) and (3) above.) This additional disclosure entails a breakdown into finer price ranges, with the number of options, weighted-average exercise price, and weighted-average remaining contractual life reported for each price range. Finally, the number of shares represented by in-the-money options must be added to the number of shares outstanding when reporting fully diluted earnings per share.[14]

SEC rules also require disclosure of the material features of a compensation plan in the proxy statement when it is submitted to shareholders for approval. However, the disclosures need only relate to the plan being voted on, not all plans at the company. Thus, shares available for grant under all company plans may be difficult to ascertain. The SEC currently has a release out for public comment on this issue. Proposed changes include the disclosure of shares available for grant under all stock option plans and an indication as to whether or not each plan was approved by shareholders.[15]

In the section on Realized Value Transfers earlier in the paper, disclosures of the tax benefit associated with option exercises were used to estimate realized value transfers. However, not all companies have this information readily available. In the earlier analysis, tax information was readily available for only one-third of the S&P 500 companies studied. Similarly, in a sample of 15 of the largest companies in the NASDAQ 100 index, Bear Stearns' analysts found explicit disclosures on the tax benefit from option exercise for only six of the 15. For another five companies the analysts were able to estimate a tax benefit from other disclosures. Two companies had insufficient information available to ascertain the tax benefit.[16] It is apparent that companies have some leeway in determining if, and how, they disclose the tax benefit information. And, in July 2000, the FASB's Emerging Issues Task Force (EITF) reached a consensus in support of improved disclosure of the tax benefit in the statement of cash flows.

SHAREHOLDERS AND CORPORATE GOVERNANCE CONCERNS: PANDORA'S BOX

As noted earlier, this paper focuses on the "costs" of stock options. But this focus is not meant to imply that options have no benefits. Rather it is an acknowledgement that the benefits of option based compensation are difficult to measure. Stock-based compensation is viewed by many as being a critical component of compensation programs with many potential benefits. Such benefits may include:

Incentive effects: Stock options may align employee interests with those of shareholders. If an employee holds stock options, then the value of those options increases as the stock price rises. Employees with significant amounts of options have a strong incentive to work to increase company value; that is, employee and shareholder incentives are aligned.

Employee retention: Stock options may help companies retain employees, particularly in a competitive labor market. Fresh option grants over time create incentives for employees to stay, especially when options are in-the-money and close to vesting or when employees must forfeit options when leaving the company.

Financing: To the extent that options are substituted for other forms of compensation, they may reduce other labor costs, conserve cash, and provide a form of contingent financing for the company.[17]

---

13. David Yermack (1998) "Companies' modest claims about the value of CEO stock option awards," *Review of Quantitative Finance and Accounting,* 10, 207-226

14. Under the "Treasury Stock" method, the number of shares subject to option included in fully-diluted shares outstanding can be reduced by the number of shares that could be purchased with the exercise proceeds. See John Core, Wayne Guay and S.P Kothari (2001) "The economic dilution of employee stock options: diluted EPS for valuation and financial reporting," working paper, Wharton School, University of Pennsylvania.

15. SEC Release No. 34-43892, Jan. 26, 2001, Disclosure of Equity Compensation Plan Information Reference: File No.: S7-04-01.

16. See Pat McConnell, Janet Pegg, and David Zion (2000) "Accounting issues: Employee stock options," *Bear Stearns Equity research, Accounting and Taxation.*

17. Edward Lazear (1999), "Output-based pay: incentives or sorting?" NBER working paper 7419.

FIGURE 1
AVERAGE VOTES CAST
AGAINST STOCK OPTION
PLANS 1988-1999

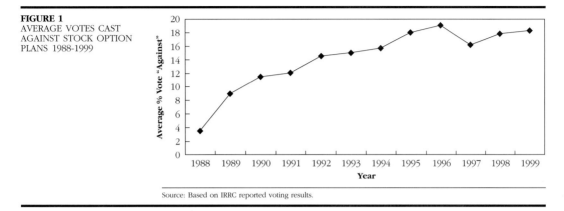

Source: Based on IRRC reported voting results.

Ultimately option-based compensation should be used only so long as it increases the market value of the firm. That is, the economic benefits of option-based compensation should exceed the economic costs. It is also important to consider what types of companies are likely to benefit from option-based compensation, the types of employees that should receive option-based compensation, and the extent to which companies should use option-based compensation. These questions in turn raise issues as to the role of shareholders in approving option plans, the basis for their decisions, and any shareholders' concerns about the use of option-based compensation.

Shareholder Voting

Depending on a stock option plan's characteristics, companies may need to seek shareholder approval. In doing so, however, some companies appear to "game the system" by taking advantage of exchange rules to garner votes. Specifically, if beneficial owners fail to vote their shares or to provide voting instructions on some management proposals, the NYSE and Amex permit member brokers to vote the shares. The NYSE and Amex permit brokers to vote on management proposals seeking the authorization or issuance of stock or stock options to directors, officers, or employees in amounts that are less than 5% of outstanding common shares as routine. Although the NASD does not currently have a parallel rule governing broker voting, many NASD brokers, who are also members of the NYSE or Amex, vote uninstructed shares of NASDAQ-listed firms for beneficial owners. As a result, some companies will seek authorization for option plans by requesting a number of shares less than or equal to 5% of current shares outstanding.

There is compelling evidence that brokers vote in favor of management proposals, and, further, that the level of broker votes can be significant—often 10-15% of shares outstanding.[18] Thus, for some companies, "shareholder approval" of an option plan may hinge on votes cast by brokers in favor of the management proposal. The use of broker votes to pass stock option plans has been characterized by some as "ballot stuffing," and is of concern to shareholders given high potential dilution at some companies.[19] One indication of general shareholder concern about stock option plans is illustrated in Figure 1, which shows the rising average percentage of votes cast *against* stock option plans during the period 1988-1999.[20]

In general, the higher the potential dilution resulting from options outstanding and options sought, the greater the opposition from shareholders.

---

18. Jennifer Bethel and Stuart Gillan (2001) "The impact of broker votes on shareholder voting and proposal passage," working paper, TIAA-CREF Institute.
19. Council of Institutional Investors http://www.cii.org/brokervoting.htm.

20. Based on S&P 1,500 companies as tracked by the IRRC – see Drew Hambly (2000) "Management proposals on executive compensation plans," Investor Responsibility Research Center, Corporate Governance Service Background Report A.

Ultimately option-based compensation should be used only so long as it increases the market value of the firm.

This concern about dilution persists despite the earlier analysis suggesting that economic approaches to benchmarking option use result in lower estimates of the cost of stock options relative to the company's market value (as compared with standard dilution measures). It is perhaps surprising that corporations do not encourage an economic option pricing approach to measuring dilution, as opposed to the standard dilution approach (although one would expect a high correlation between the two measures). It is not clear, however, to what extent institutional voting thresholds would change using an economic approach as opposed to a dilution approach.

The trend toward more votes against options plans, with some plans even failing on rare occasions, indicates that shareholders are apprehensive about levels of potential dilution at some companies. Past repricing of options at a company are especially likely to trigger "no" votes by many shareholders.

Concerns About Repricing

The rationale for voting against stock option plans at companies that have repriced is twofold. First, it is perceived as rewarding employees for failed performance, thus undermining the rationale for using options as incentive compensation. Second, the repricing of employee stock options is often criticized as providing employees a benefit that is not available to shareholders who have suffered a decline in the value of their investment.

The counter argument is that, in a tight labor market, failure to reprice may result in poorly motivated employees and undesirable employee turnover (as employees effectively reprice their underwater options by getting new options from a new employer). Thus, a failure to reprice may cost the company and shareholders more in the long run.

To assess the degree to which companies have underwater options, Figures 2 and 3 report the cumulative distribution of option "in-the-moneyness." Figure 2 reports on the degree to which options granted during 1999 were in-the-money at the end of January 2001. In-the-moneyness is measured in percentage terms as 100 × ([January 2001 closing price – Weighted average price for 1999 grants]/ Weighted average price for 1999 grants).

Negative in-the-moneyness indicates that options were, on average, underwater. Specifically, a negative 50% on the horizontal axis in Figure 2 indicates that the January 2001 market price was 50% below the weighted average exercise price of options granted during 1999. Figure 3 is similar but reports in-the-moneyness for options *outstanding* at year-end. In-the-moneyness is measured as 100 × ([January 2001 closing price – Weighted average price of options outstanding at fiscal year-end 1999] /[Weighted average price of options outstanding at fiscal year-end 1999]).

Two features of Figures 2 and 3 are worth highlighting. First, in many cases options issued during 1999 and outstanding as of year-end were deep in-the-money, thus highlighting potentially large wealth transfers from shareholders to optionholders. However, as one would expect, options were underwater by a large amount at many other companies. Figure 2 shows that grants made during 1999 were underwater for approximately 40% of companies. Similarly, based on the weighted average price of options outstanding, Figure 3 suggests that approximately 35% of companies had 1999 or prior option grants that were underwater. Some 10% of companies had either 1999 grants or options outstanding at year-end that were underwater by more than 50%.

Table 5 expands the analysis by reporting on selected industry groups where there is substantial variation in the degree of in-the-moneyness. Specifically, Table 5 reports a set of industry groups in which some companies had outstanding options deep in-the-money, whereas other companies had options outstanding underwater by at least 30%. Take, for example, the *Business services* group, which includes a large number of hi-tech companies. *Business services* had 59 companies with underwater options, and 107 with options in-the-money. Companies where options are underwater had options outstanding with an exercise price that was on average 46.4% above the stock market price at the end of January 2001. Options were in-the-money for the other 107 firms by an average of 220.5%. Similar patterns can be seen for other industry groups.

Such markedly different levels of in-the-moneyness suggest considerable variation in individual company performance, or in sub-sector performance. Companies with options deep underwater face pressure to reprice to address employee incentive and retention concerns. Such pressures may be heightened given that there are other firms in similar industries performing well.

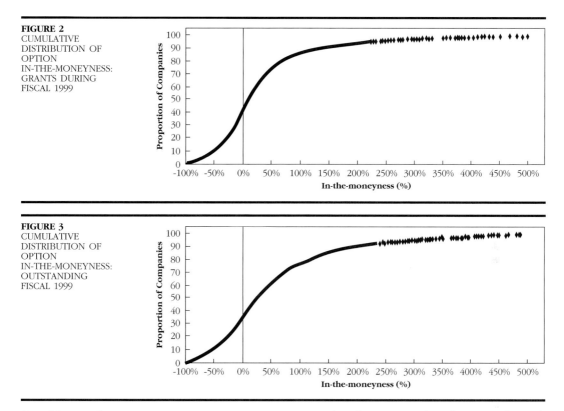

FIGURE 2
CUMULATIVE
DISTRIBUTION OF
OPTION
IN-THE-MONEYNESS:
GRANTS DURING
FISCAL 1999

FIGURE 3
CUMULATIVE
DISTRIBUTION OF
OPTION
IN-THE-MONEYNESS:
OUTSTANDING
FISCAL 1999

Breathing Underwater

When employees hold underwater options, companies typically worry about employee retention and morale. Some companies consider repricing options, but doing so risks angering shareholders who are apprehensive about dilution in general and repricing in particular. Companies can undertake a pure repricing by lowering the exercise price of prior grants. This is usually implemented by canceling underwater options and simultaneously granting replacement options at the current market price. In some cases, companies will make a grant equal in present value (using an option pricing model) to the initial award rather than replace underwater options on a one-for one basis. Recent clarifications by FASB

require that if a company alters the terms of a stock option plan—in effect undertaking a repricing—the plan must be treated as "variable" for accounting purposes.[21] The FASB pronouncement, which is retroactive to December of 1998, requires that an estimate of the cost of the options at grant date be made, charged as an expense to earnings, and then marked to market on a quarterly basis. Although some companies such as Amazon.com have recently repriced stock options, it is likely that repricing will be used less frequently given the reluctance of many companies to take a charge to earnings.[22]

A key element of the FASB ruling is that any issuance within six months of a cancellation constitutes a repricing for accounting purposes. This clarification has led some companies, Sprint being

---

21. Broadly speaking, stock option plans are classified as variable compensation if the full terms of the plan (e.g., number of underlying shares and / or exercise price) are unknown at the time of grant, or a pre-specified performance hurdle must be met. Such plans result in an expense recorded on the income statement.

22. For an analysis of companies that have repriced in the past see Mary Ellen Carter and Luann Lynch (2001) "The effect of accounting on economic behavior: Evidence from stock option repricing," working paper, Columbia University Graduate School of Business

**....underwater options do have value and represent a potential value transfer from
share-holders to optionholders.**

TABLE 5 ■ UNDERWATER AND IN-THE-MONEY OPTIONS OUTSTANDING BY INDUSTRY GROUP
The table reports the extent to which options outstanding as of fiscal year-end 1999 are in- or out-of-the-money. In- and out-of-the-moneyness are calculated as 100 × ([January 2001 closing price – Weighted average price of options outstanding at fiscal year-end 1999]/ Weighted average price of options outstanding at fiscal year-end 1999].) The table reports on two sets of companies within each industry group: First, companies where outstanding options are underwater (Panel A), and second, companies in the same industry where outstanding options were in-the-money (Panel B). Specifically, Panel A reports the average out-of-the-moneyness for those industry groups where average out-of-the-moneyness was 30% or more. Panel B reports the average level of in-the-moneyness for companies within the each industry where options were in-the-money.

Industry Group (2-digit SIC code Classifications)	Panel A ■ Outstanding options underwater (out-of-the-money)		Panel B ■ Outstanding options in-the-money	
	Number of Companies	Average amount underwater (% relative to Jan. 01 stock price)	Number of Companies	Average amount in-the-money (% relative to Jan. 01 stock price)
Business services	59	-46.4%	107	220.5%
Communications	14	-58.2%	48	186.4%
Eating and drinking places	6	-41.6%	18	85.0%
Electrical and electronic equipment	28	-35.2%	92	303.7%
Engineering and management services	11	-50.7%	9	187.6%
Food and kindred products	9	-38.2%	31	53.2%
Furniture, home furnishings and equipment stores	2	-41.7%	7	91.5%
General merchandise stores	9	-43.8%	12	163.9%
Health services	5	-38.1%	14	140.1%
Heavy construction contractors	1	-70.0%	5	101.2%
Industrial machinery and equipment	35	-32.7%	63	159.7%
Instruments and related products	13	-35.2%	43	139.6%
Insurance agents, brokers, and service	2	-42.7%	8	177.0%
Insurance carriers	20	-36.4%	46	64.7%
Metal mining	5	-60.2%	1	123.7%
Miscellaneous retail	16	-54.5%	17	92.7%
Motion pictures	2	-91.7%	2	138.0%
Motor freight transportation and warehousing	1	-76.6%	11	110.6%
Nondepository credit institutions	6	-60.3%	13	108.2%
Primary metal industries	25	-46.8%	10	114.9%
Security, commodity brokers, and services	2	-62.8%	21	137.7%
Transportation equipment	21	-39.1%	23	66.2%
Wholesale trade—durable goods	20	-40.1%	20	58.7%

among the first, to adopt a "synthetic" repricing strategy. Sprint announced that it would give employees a choice to hold onto their current grants or hand them back to the company with the promise that a replacement grant would be made in six-months and one-day at the then market price—thus circumventing the definition of a "repricing."

Alternatively, companies with sufficient options available for grant, such as Lucent and Microsoft, have simply issued employees replacement options while leaving prior underwater grants outstanding.

While this may help maintain employee morale, the fact remains that underwater options do have value and represent a potential value transfer from shareholders to optionholders. In the event that there is a dramatic increase in the stock price at such companies, this doubling of grants could prove very costly to shareholders.

In the face of insufficient shares available for grant, some companies may take advantage of exchange and market rules permitting the adoption of plans without shareholder approval.[23] In the

23. NYSE Listed Company Sections 312.01, 312.03 and 312.04 exemption of shareholder approval for "broad-based" stock option plans which and NASD Marketplace Rules Section 4310. The rules suggest that non-approved plans of up to 20% of current shares outstanding may be possible.

absence of any change to current rules, one would expect the adoption of more plans without shareholder approval, particularly at those companies facing shareholder opposition to new option plans. Moreover, given current disclosure requirements, it is difficult to determine the extent to which companies are using non-shareholder-approved plans. IRRC reported that, as of July 2000, 52 out of 1,157 (approximately 4.5%) S&P 1,500 companies reported having plans in place that had not been approved by shareholders.[24] This 4.5% estimate is likely to understate number of non-approved plans because it includes only those companies where plan disclosures were readily available. More recently, the compensation consulting firm iQuantic reported that during 1999 more than 70 out of 200 technology companies surveyed (35%) adopted option plans without shareholder approval.[25]

In contrast, many companies seek shareholder approval for all stock option plans. Others have adopted plan restrictions prohibiting future repricing without shareholder approval. Indeed, some companies have sought and received shareholder approval to reprice stock options. Repricing, however, remains a focal point of shareholder concern, a concern exacerbated by what are perceived to be high levels of potential dilution.

CONCLUSION

Determining the "cost" of option-based compensation is a complex task, for shareholders and employees alike. More importantly, to the extent that there is a difference between the value placed on options by employees and the economic cost of options to shareholders, it raises questions about the economic efficacy of this form of compensation. Put another way, are employees being paid in a currency (stock options) that is significantly less valuable to them than to shareholders?

Another valuation issue is that standard at-the-money options are "free" from an accounting perspective; that is, they generally do not result in a compensation expense. This raises questions regarding the extent to which accounting considerations may influence compensation policy. For example, do the current accounting rules result in a preference for standard options over potentially superior alternatives (such as indexed- or performance-based options) simply because they do not result in an expense? Similarly, does the absence of an expense lead to the overuse of standard options?

Despite the difficulties in valuing options, shareholders monitor option use and have actively voted against management-proposed stock option plans they believe to be excessive. However, exchange and market rules allow companies to adopt some stock option plans without shareholder approval. In the absence of any change to current rules, one would expect more companies to avoid shareholder approval, particularly when facing shareholder opposition to new option plans. A central governance question, then, is whether exchange and market rules permitting companies to avoid shareholder approval of stock option plans disenfranchise shareholders.

Focusing solely on dilution, repricing, and the cost of stock options begs the question on a number of issues, notably: what types of companies may benefit from option-based compensation, what types of employees should receive option-based compensation, and whether or not the benefits of option-based compensation outweigh the costs. Nevertheless, shareholder concerns suggest that option-based compensation will continue to be a focal point for controversy. Pandora's box is open.

---

24. Annick Siegl (2001) "Potential dilution 2000: Potential dilution from stock plans at S&P 1,500 companies," Investor Responsibility Research Center.

25. Ted Buyniski and Daniel Silver (2000) "Trends in equity compensation: An executive summary of iQuantic's high-tech equity practices survey 1996–2000," iQuantic report.

TWELVE WAYS TO STRENGTHEN YOUR INCENTIVE PLAN

by David Glassman,
Stern Stewart & Co.

F ew areas of corporate governance generate as much divisiveness and distrust as incentive compensation. From determining the key measures, to setting the targets, to establishing the payout range, companies seem continuously to undermine their own plans, processes, and credibility.

With great fanfare new incentive schemes are rolled out that few understand. Worse, new plans from the outset are viewed as the "flavor of the month," likely to be changed again next year. Lack of credibility diminishes the buy-in of managers and, along with it, the enthusiasm, motivation, and drive the plans are intended to generate. For investors, this makes the incentive plan a low rate-of-return initiative.

Our experience at Stern Stewart suggests that the problems besetting incentive plans are surprisingly similar across companies and even across apparently dissimilar industries. Most plans are ineffective because of:
- Too many performance measures;
- Measures that motivate the wrong behavior;
- Too much complexity;
- Arbitrary targets that are subject to intense lobbying by executives;
- Too much managerial discretion;
- Performance measured at a level too high to be meaningful, or too low to encourage teamwork;
- Caps and floors that narrow the payout range and stifle incentives;
- A failure to integrate the incentive plan into the overall compensation philosophy; and
- Ineffective or non-existent communication.

Obviously, companies do not set out to develop convoluted programs. So why does it happen? Why are incentive plans so poorly constructed when CEOs recognize their importance for corporate governance? And why are plans so complicated when simplicity is so clearly a priority?

This paper identifies why incentive plans are unproductive, and offers 12 suggestions for implementing plans that support management's aspirations to create value for shareholders. The remedies described below are not difficult to execute and, judging from the evidence, are remarkably effective. But they require the strong commitment and attention of senior management. Left solely to the human resources staff, capable as they may be, institutional resistance will be overwhelming.

1. IMPROVE FOCUS AND GET THE MEASURE RIGHT

Most companies ask too much of their incentive plans. Obviously, they aim to motivate improvements in financial performance, but how is this defined? Growth is a key goal, so a target for Sales gains plays a role. Profit (or EPS), of course, is highlighted in the incentive plan. And Finance often proposes a balance sheet measure, such as inventory turns or Return on Investment. With these three measures, the Compensation Committee believes that all financial bases are covered. In fact, the problems are just beginning.

One problem is that any particular initiative is likely to push different financial measures in conflicting directions. Sales may rise but the gain may be too costly, leaving profits unchanged, or even below where they started. Or an SKU reduction initiative may reduce sales and profit but increase inventory turns and ROI. Instead of guiding decisions, the measures create confusion. And, to add to the confusion, management also inserts non-financial considerations into the incentive plan. These may include customer and employee satisfaction, safety and environmental compliance, investment for the long term, leadership, and so forth.

Also, the many measures influencing bonuses diffuse, rather than concentrate, the focus of executives. Worse, they can even encourage counterproductive behavior. At one company that used Sales and Profit measures for its incentive plan, a particularly candid manager admitted that in a recent year his business was unlikely to achieve the Profit component. When asked how this influenced decision-making, he said, "We made sure we hit the Sales target." How? By discounting product in the fourth quarter. Margins suffered, profits were down, but at least part of the bonus was salvaged.

Management can improve the focus of incentive systems by using just one financial measure, Economic Value Added (EVA). EVA, measured as the profit after deducting a charge for all capital, internalizes the tradeoff between income statement reductions and improvements in capital productivity. As Peter Drucker said recently in *Fortune*:

"there is no profit unless you earn the cost of capital. Alfred Marshall said that in 1896, Peter Drucker said that in 1954 and in 1973, and now EVA (economic value added) has systematized this idea, thank God."[1]

EVA contains in one measure the benefits of Sales and Margin gains offset by increases in Capital that may be required. An internal study performed by Stern Stewart, and summarized in the same *Fortune* article, indicates that companies adopting EVA for incentive compensation outperform peer companies in the stock market. The 67-company sample of EVA firms provided an average annual return of 21.8% vs. 13.0% for industry peers.

Some companies add EVA to the menu of compensation measures, but without eliminating measures like sales and EPS growth. This both adds to the confusion and double counts gains or losses in sales and earnings. Sales, obviously, is a key driver of EVA, but it can be improved without necessarily benefiting EVA. The same is true of EPS. Stern Stewart performed a study of the largest 1,000 companies in the U.S. to determine the extent to which EPS and EVA move together. The results indicate that, when EVA increases, EPS increases in 82% of the cases. But when EVA decreases, EPS still grows 57% of the time.[2] In other words, set your sights on EVA growth and favorable EPS results will follow. But the reverse is uncertain.

EVA focuses incentive plans on the right motivations—growing the business profitably while taking into account all costs of doing business. But this focus is undermined when EVA is forced to share the stage with other financial measures. Eliminate them.

2. ABANDON ATTEMPTS TO MEASURE WHAT EXECUTIVES "CONTROL"

Conversations about development of incentive plans almost always begin with instructions to "Keep it Simple." At the same time, however, CEOs and human resource directors want to pay managers only for what they control. This is a combination sure to cause frustration. Unanticipated events during the year convert up-front simplicity into back-end complexity. Complexity results from the failure to

---

1. September 28, 1998, Q&A with Peter Drucker.

2. Annual data from the *Stern Stewart 1,000*, 1988-97. The reason why EPS does not increase in even more cases can be attributed to accounting restructuring charges, and increases in R&D. While they diminish EPS, these items are capitalized for EVA purposes.

In a study of the largest 1,000 companies in the U.S., Stern Stewart found that when EVA increases, EPS increases in 82% of the cases. But when EVA decreases, EPS still grows 57% of the time.

consider, and incorporate into bonus programs, the tendency for events to overtake plans.

Despite evidence to the contrary, managers enter the year believing they can estimate within a relatively tight range the performance that can be expected. Yet, time and again, "surprises" early in the year make a mockery of expectations. Surprises result from changing trends in economic and industry growth, interest rate and commodity price volatility (either for inputs or outputs), regulatory changes, competitor initiatives, unusual weather patterns, legal actions, and the like. Because these are viewed as "out of the control" of managers an after-the-fact adjustment to the bonus plan is proposed.

This is where it gets complicated. While out of management's control, aren't investors exposed to such events? How is a change to be explained to the Board? And what will be the harm to management's political capital with Directors? Of greatest importance, shouldn't managers be required to respond swiftly to changes in their markets? While outside of management's control they are the reality. And managers must internalize an urgency to anticipate such possibilities, build contingency plans, and execute them swiftly to limit losses and capitalize on the opportunities offered by change. Insulating executives from the impact of market fluctuations denies reality and gets in the way of the necessary responses.

It is easier and simpler to forbid incentive plan adjustments during the year. In place of such adjustments, establish realistic multi-year EVA improvement targets (discussed in a later section) driven by shareholders' requirements for earning an adequate return on investment. Missing the target in the current year, for whatever reason, is penalized with a reduction from the target bonus. But, if the shortfall is judged by top management to have been caused by factors beyond management's control, the improvement target could then be lowered, using as a new base the current (disappointing) level of profitability. By making such an adjustment, executives are given the opportunity to earn an attractive award in the following year by recovering lost ground.

The principle underlying this plan is that managers should share with investors the value they create. And, using EVA as the key performance measure ensures that each dollar of improvement drives additional value for shareholders as well as more bonus compensation for participants. Accord-ingly, the bonus plan motivates managers to think, and act, like owners.

But owners also face risk. They can lose some or all of their money. Accordingly, an EVA Bonus Plan sets aside a portion of outstanding awards in a Bonus Reserve (or Bonus "Bank"). The set-aside is paid to executives if performance is sustained; but if EVA subsequently declines below a defined threshold, the deferred amount can be lost. In other words, a "negative bonus" is a key feature of the EVA Plan. This ensures that, among other things, decision-makers are properly focused on the long-term consequences of today's actions.

What executives control is difficult to determine, and in the end does not much matter. Results matter. And results are more likely to be achieved if executives face the downside risk associated with unanticipated events. Economists call this "moral hazard." If managers know they will be given relief for what they cannot control, their incentive to plan for such events is reduced, making the consequences more severe.

3. USE INVESTORS', NOT MANAGEMENT'S, EXPECTATIONS TO SET TARGETS

Typically, companies rely on the budget process to determine incentive targets. This is a mistake, one that corrupts both planning and incentives. And, because each is a critical element of corporate governance, they should be separated. The reason is that managers tend to water down their plan for next year in the hope of achieving a soft performance target.

Knowing that managers have the incentive to hide opportunities, headquarters stretches the performance targets. The result is a cycle of managers submitting plans, headquarters rejecting them, managers recycling them, and so on. For almost all companies, negotiating budgets is a time-consuming process that makes adversaries of line and staff. Instead, they should be collaborating to find solutions to the problems they face and to identify opportunities to grow.

To make the planning process more effective, bonus targets should be set in advance for a multiyear period without referencing the budget or business plan. Breaking the link enables managers to craft a Budget that beats the target, instead of developing a Budget to negotiate a target. And, because the target is known in advance, management can plan for an EVA improvement that will earn them and their team a satisfactory award.

But this still leaves the original question: How much EVA improvement is necessary to pay a target bonus award? Managers should be awarded a target bonus when they provide investors with a competitive stock market return. This takes into consideration the demands of investors now owning or buying the stock, and recognizes that performance must improve to deliver a competitive return. This required return is the company's cost of capital.

When shareholders each day determine the price at which they are willing to buy or sell the company's stock, they signal their perception of the company's management, its strategies, prospects, and risks. Investors today are making a statement: a stock price and market value that represents a premium over and above the capital currently used in the business is a vote of confidence in management's ability to produce positive EVA in the future. In fact, the amount of the premium provides an indication of the amount of EVA *growth* expected by investors.

Thus, we can use the current stock price and market value premium (a measure we call the "Market Value Added," or MVA) to "back into" the necessary growth in EVA to justify today's price and earn competitive returns for our current shareholders. Further, we can establish the growth targets for a multi-year period. This eliminates the counterproductive and frustrating annual negotiation, and frees managers to craft a budget to beat the already defined targets.

Outperforming the growth targets will then drive outstanding returns to investors and superior bonuses for executives. Similarly, failing to achieve the targets will disappoint shareholders and generate a less than target bonus for managers.

An important feature of the EVA plan is that it establishes at the outset the growth track that will drive a target award. To illustrate, let's suppose that the result of the analysis indicates that the company must improve EVA by, say, $10 million per year for each of the next three years. If EVA then improves by $20 million in the first year, a substantial bonus would be awarded. (Not all of the award would be paid; a portion would be set aside in the Bonus Reserve.) But in the next year, an improvement of another $10 million would be required to earn a target award. The Plan is demanding; it pays for growing value but always asks for more improvement in the next year.

Eli Lilly implemented such an EVA plan in 1995. Randall Tobias, then the company's CEO, says:

We saw as a shortcoming of our incentive system that executive pay was linked to sales and net income. There just wasn't a very good correlation at all with shareholder value... Basically, Lilly's bonus plan now requires managers to achieve continuous year-to-year improvements in EVA. Each year we have to beat that target—and each year the bar is raised. It's a small percentage increase, but it keeps pounding at you. Whatever you did yesterday, you need to do better tomorrow to keep raising shareholder value.[3]

Of course, it is always possible that EVA improvement will be below the target. Let's say it grows by just $3 million in the first year, $7 million short of the target. In this case a less-than-target award is paid, and $10 million is established as next year's growth target. Some may suggest requiring associates to make up the shortfall in the second year; that is, why not add $7 million in EVA growth to the goal to make the target $17 million in improvement?

This would be unfair to managers. They have already been penalized for the performance shortfall. Raising the target in the next year imposes a second penalty. For example, if the company were to achieve the $17 million, managers will have earned a target bonus in Year 2, but would still have less than the targeted bonus for the two years *combined.*

To see this, note that the annual EVA improvement target of $10 million means that EVA must grow by $20 million for two years. If the company grows EVA by $3 million in the first year and $17 million in the second, it would achieve the target on a cumulative basis. But, by requiring the company to recoup the first year shortfall in Year 2, the plan would allow managers to earn only a target in the second year. And, combined with a less-than-target award in Year 1, managers would earn below-target bonuses for the two years together.

This is important for companies implementing EVA after several years in which EVA has declined.

---

3. *Fortune,* September 9, 1996.

The goal is to achieve a substantial "bounceback," but management should resist incorporating this into the incentive targets. We should recognize that the company was not focused on increasing EVA in the past. As in the case of Lilly before it adopted EVA, management was focused on other measures. Holding managers accountable now for something that was not then the goal seems inappropriate.

4. SET STRETCH GOALS

This does not suggest that the CEO should abandon setting stretch goals. Quite the contrary. The company's leaders should emphasize that merely achieving the incentive target is not the goal. Instead, we are aiming higher: to achieve not just acceptable returns for our investors, but consistently outstanding performance. Further, to accomplish this, we must outperform the EVA incentive goal. And if we can do it, then the bonuses for associates will also be outstanding.

What then is the role of the Budget? If the Company achieves the stretch goals incorporated in the Budget, it will earn a greater-than-target award. And this is not unusual. In most cases the Budget is not the most likely outcome; nor should it be. The Budget is a positive statement of management's *objectives*, not the highest-probability result. We should recognize that achieving the Budget requires a strong and sustained focus, some difficult decisions, and a change in mindset to consider the cost of capital involved both in major and minor initiatives.

John Blystone, formerly of General Electric, became Chairman and CEO of SPX Corporation in 1996. Blystone brought to the $1 billion auto parts company a philosophy of stretch targets that he has combined with an EVA program. The EVA target for incentive purposes was established at a $4.2 million improvement in the first year. This was calculated to be the amount necessary to provide investors with a competitive capital market return. At the same time, Blystone set a stretch target of $25 million improvement—and, if this was achieved the bonus plan would pay over five times the target bonus. Blystone says, "we're not going to shoot a manager for doing all the right things and still not getting a stretch goal. What we're going to shoot you for is if you set too low a target and easily blow by it."[4]

His experience is that the combination of stretch goals and EVA works well because "EVA strikes the proper balance between the income statement and the balance sheet... This makes it safer to push for stretch EVA goals than it is to drive for a single income statement or balance sheet improvement. We found that you can push very, very hard from an EVA standpoint without breaking anything."[5]

The Company actually increased EVA in 1996 by $26.6 million. The stock price jumped from $15.38 to $40.38; and the following year, 1997, the stock closed at $69. Says an analyst at Bear Stearns: "Of anything automotive—the Big Three, parts companies, you name it—SPX is the single most focused company on shareholders, bar none."[6]

5. REDUCE SUBJECTIVITY

Bonus awards should be predictable. Executives at the end of the year—and even during the year—should be able to estimate their own bonus based on the performance of the company. This desirable objective is undermined when companies incorporate an element of subjectivity into the bonus determination. The reasons for subjectivity are understandable and generally relate to providing competitive compensation to managers even during years of company underperformance. The fear is retention risk—that is, the possibility that the company may lose able managers to competitors. In addition, efforts made by management in poor years are cancelled by the financial results, but nevertheless deserve recognition, or so the reasoning goes.

But there is a downside both to the logic and to the practical consequences of this approach. First, let's examine the logic. Shareholders receive their return from the financial results of the company. Poor results, poor return. Why do managers acting as the steward of the shareholders' investment, and presumably being paid a competitive salary, deserve a bonus? Instead, they should be provided only a realistic chance next year to recover the bonus lost by improving performance from the disappointing level suffered in the current year.

---

4. *EVA: The Real Key to Creating Wealth*, by Al Ehrbar, John Wiley and Sons, Inc., 1998. Page 188.

5. From the proceedings of the *EVA Institute*, March 19-21, 1998; published in the *EVAngelist*, Volume 2, No. 2.

6. "Another GE Veteran Rides to the Rescue," *Fortune*, December 29, 1997.

On the practical side, subjectivity often results in arbitrary goals and evaluations. The goals may include difficult-to-measure judgements about leadership, employee satisfaction, or other MBOs that are rarely judged negatively. Over time they become an entitlement, just another way of ensuring a payout even in bad times.

6. DON'T ENCOURAGE PAROCHIAL BEHAVIOR

One of the most difficult incentive issues involves drawing the balance between awarding bonuses based on a business unit's performance, or the accomplishments of a functional area, versus that of the total company. A manager obviously has the greatest influence on his or her business unit, and therefore should be compensated on this area's performance. This works well when the business units are separate and there is little value to collaboration.

But this describes very few companies today. The era of conglomerates has long past. Virtually all companies are comprised of at least somewhat related businesses that profit by working in concert. And each individual business unit is comprised of inter-related processes—research and product development, procurement and manufacturing, information technology, marketing and sales, and so forth. In cases where such interactions are significant, incentives that focus managers only on their individual businesses and functions could turn out to be counterproductive. They create silos where teamwork is required. They impede communication and lead to the hoarding of resources and information instead of the sharing of best practices.

Consider an example of a retail company organized along two dimensions: Store Operations and Merchandise categories. EVA can be calculated for each, but the EVA of the Company is best served by having the two areas collaborate. Merchandise managers oversee the mix (styles, colors, sizes, etc.) but can take other actions that will benefit Stores. For example, they can negotiate the shipping of merchandise that is "floor-ready," or . . . require vendors to apply ink tags to the goods. The vendors will charge a higher cost for the merchandise, but in each case the initiative eliminates the need for handling once merchandise reaches the Store. "Merchandise" EVA declines, but the Stores benefit. If their line of sight is their own EVA, Merchandise managers will fail to take the appropriate actions that could benefit the Company.

One way to solve this problem is to use total company performance to determine the bonus. All managers will be rewarded or penalized together, as a team. It removes the (explicit monetary) incentive for parochial behavior. But using total company performance dilutes all incentives. One manager's contribution is obscured by the results of the other businesses. This creates what economists call the "free rider" problem: all managers have the incentive to shirk and hope that others perform well—and the total business suffers.

So what is the right balance? In principle, the goal should be to focus on individual activities. However, the greater the interrelationships among different areas, the more that can be gained from collaboration. Accordingly, *joint* incentives—based on the aggregate performance of the relevant areas—produce the best balance.

Operationally, it is difficult to apply a general template to the specific circumstances that will influence the decision for a particular company. But we can offer some general guidelines.

Some of the issues that affect how, and how fast, EVA incentives are introduced include the level of business literacy, sophistication of information systems, and the degree to which the performance of business units is independent and separable. Generally, a top-down approach to phasing in EVA incentives is the most prudent. First, integrate EVA into the management system—measurement, reporting, planning, capital budgeting, and communications. At the same time, involve the businesses in training managers about the levers they have available to influence the company's EVA. And incorporate EVA into the incentive plan of the primary business units where the lines distinguishing their activities are clear, where interrelated activities are few, and where asset and other allocation problems can be most easily resolved.

In subsequent years, related EVA measures for key functions and processes—manufacturing, logistics, real estate, product development, sales, marketing, and so on—can be developed using more sophisticated transfer-pricing techniques that reliably measure the EVA contribution made by these areas. But first the new measures must be given time to be tested and accepted by the managers that will be judged on this basis.

> **The Genzyme structure provides focus both for executives and for investors and sharpens accountability for creating value within the key divisions. At the same time, it enables the small units to take advantage of the larger company's infrastructure.**

This approach argues against evaluating functional managers using measures related solely to their processes—for example, using cost per unit, productivity, defect rates, yields, and cycle times to establish bonus targets for manufacturing managers. All such measures are drivers of success, but each can be managed separately to produce a favorable result while at the same time damaging other parts of the business. Instead, incentive compensation for these managers should be more heavily weighted to the performance of the business units they serve. Extensive training and communication can then be provided to make managers aware of the critical role they play in the success of the business, and the tradeoffs that must be balanced between the critical measures bearing on their activities and the overall company objective of growing EVA and value.

7. TRACKING STOCK: ANOTHER WAY TO MEASURE AND MOTIVATE

The equity markets provide an alternative approach to governance and incentive compensation for EVA Centers. An interesting example of this is Genzyme Corporation, which is based in Cambridge, Massachusetts. Genzyme provides products and services for the pharmaceutical and health care market. The company is organized in three divisions, each of which has common stock traded in the public markets. Accordingly, investors can take positions in Genzyme General—the core of the company's activities—Genzyme Tissue Repair, Genzyme Molecular Oncology, or Genzyme Transgenics. Stock in the first three units represent separate classes of Genzyme Corporation stock, similar to the way General Motors organized its EDS and Hughes subsidiaries. This means that the value of these shares is linked to the performance of the subsidiary, but that the shares do not represent ownership in the divisions. Instead, investors own shares in a special class of stock in Genzyme Corporation. Genzyme Transgenics, on the other hand, is owned 41% by Genzyme General, with the balance held by outside investors.

While the separate classes of stock add to the complexity of the structure, it simplifies incentives. First, the share price reflects a direct assessment by the market of the company's success. Managers owning the shares receive ongoing feedback that directly impacts their personal wealth.

The separate tracking stocks also provide other benefits. As Genzyme indicates in its literature, the structure:

- Provides investors an opportunity to invest selectively in the businesses of interest;
- Enables each business to raise capital directly;
- Creates a separate focus for each business; and
- Captures the efficiencies of shared resources in capital formation, research and development, clinical and regulatory affairs, and manufacturing.

The Genzyme structure thus has multiple benefits. It provides focus both for executives and for investors and sharpens accountability for creating value within the key divisions. At the same time, it also enables the small units to take advantage of the larger company's infrastructure. In addition, taxes are filed on a consolidated basis so that the losses incurred in one division can offset the taxable profit of another division.

Of course, the complexity of the structure increases governance costs, particularly where transfers of costs and assets are at issue. General and administrative costs are allocated to the divisions based on usage estimates. Also, the Genzyme Board can reassign assets, products, and development programs from one division to another. However, compensation based on market value must be paid (in cash or in equivalent value) to the unit surrendering the program. And, in the case of Genzyme Tissue Repair and Genzyme Molecular Oncology, a vote of the holders of the class of stock is necessary for carrying out the transfer of a program.

This makes governance clumsy for management, but more transparent for shareholders. That key interdivisional resource allocation decisions require shareholder approval makes cross subsidies difficult to sustain. Instead, each division must raise capital on its own merits, and therefore faces the urgency to maintain an attractive stock price. The discipline imposed by the market aligns the interests of management with those of investors.

It is not just high-technology companies that use tracking stock. Georgia-Pacific has also created this structure to isolate the value of its stable, cash-generating timber products business from the cyclical capital intensive pulp and paper operations. As the company's 1997 Annual Report points out, "Integrated companies compound the problem by using cash flows from timberlands to finance manufacturing investments that do not earn their cost of capital. This will no longer be an option at Georgia-Pacific." Use of two classes of tracking stock means that "Excess cash from timberlands will be paid out to investors. The other operations of the company will have to compete for capital on the merits." As the company also notes, this step is "a natural outgrowth of EVA" because "separating assets makes each group's use of capital easier to evaluate."

The tracking stock also provides for investors a pure play opportunity in a focused business with managers, through stock options, being rewarded for the value they add to the business they oversee.

8. DON'T FORGET TOP MANAGEMENT'S ROLE

Ultimately, even the suggestions offered above may not be sufficient to diminish local management's inclination toward parochial behavior. Any individual manager will wish to stand out from his peers by demonstrating superior performance in his business. Such achievements attract rewards over and above those held out by any bonus plan—in the form of promotions, special attention from superiors, and so forth.

The solution, therefore, must also come from outside the bonus plan. Controlling the tendency for parochial behavior is a challenge for *management*, not just the incentive program. Creating a culture, through example and leadership, that emphasizes individual performance while valuing teamwork is what senior executives are supposed to do. Asking the incentive system to do this without additional reinforcement from top management passes the buck. It puts too great a burden on the plan.

9. ELIMINATE CAPS AND FLOORS

In all incentive systems there is a tension among competing objectives, some of which have already been noted and discussed (such as preserving simplicity vs. rewarding for what managers control, and promoting teamwork vs. creating a local line of sight). One of the most critical (and generally mismanaged) tradeoffs involves the management of cost and retention risk vs. the objective of providing true incentives.

Traditional compensation philosophy aims to provide an executive with pay that is competitive in the labor markets. To manage the risk of losing good managers in bad times some minimum compensation is required. And to avoid excessive costs to shareholders a maximum is established. In the process however, motivation is lost.

The narrowing of the difference between pay for good and poor performance stifles in-

centives. In good years the incentive is to ensure that performance does not exceed the point at which the maximum bonus is achieved. Executives will book business for delivery next year, and discretionary expenses that would otherwise be scheduled for next year will be accelerated to the current year's fourth quarter. If SPX had used bonus caps, you can bet that EVA would not have improved by $26.6 million when the target was $4.2 million. Nor would the stock have appreciated by 163%. (What's more, Blystone views the EVA plan as also helping to attract extraordinary talent to the company.)

There is a similarly perverse incentive on the downside. At one company, an executive said that "in the 16 years, I have been with the company, whenever we have missed the threshold for a payout, we never *just* missed a payout." He described how bad years were made worse by the incentive to defer revenues, accelerate expenses, and take write-offs because the bonus could not be any worse. In other words, the traditional incentive system breaks down when times are particularly good or bad, as if companies believe that incentives don't matter during such periods. Worse, companies implicitly are directing managers to take actions that diminish current year's results.

This problem is fixed by removing the cap and floor on potential pay. Like SPX, allow bonuses to grow, as EVA grows, without limit. Preserve the marginal incentive to reach for the next dollar. The company need not pay everything in the short term. In fact, as noted earlier, EVA companies use a Bonus Reserve, an account to which all awards are credited. If the balance is sufficient, the Reserve each year pays out a target bonus plus some proportion of the excess that remains (say one-third or one-half). The remainder is carried forward in the Reserve, but is at risk for future performance. If the company has an unusually poor year—a substantial decline in EVA—a negative bonus can reduce the Bonus Reserve.

In this way managers are encouraged to stretch, even in good years, and are discouraged from making a difficult year even worse. It also guards against short-term "windfalls" that are not sustainable over time. It does not ensure competitive pay in any single year, but the system is calibrated to provide competitive pay over a multi-year cycle. This is discussed at greater length in the next two sections.

10. FIT THE INCENTIVE PLAN INTO THE TOTAL COMPENSATION ARCHITECTURE

Any incentive plan, even a well-designed EVA plan, is not a stand-alone management tool. It must be designed to fit the company's general compensation architecture, one that rewards managers in a variety of ways—base salary, cash incentive plans, equity programs, pension benefits, perquisites, promotions, and so on. Changing the incentive plan alters the overall risk-reward dynamics of the compensation structure.

For example, the EVA plan typically introduces more variability into total compensation, because the removal of caps and floors generally makes it riskier than the plan it replaces. Absent any adjustment for the higher risk, introduction of the EVA plan is a net loss to participants. Several clients prior to adopting EVA had an "incentive" program with a minimum payout of 50% of the target bonus. The reason, they said, is that base salaries were low relative to their competition. In such cases, it would be naïve to simply mix in the more aggressive principles of an EVA plan and expect the outcome not to create unrest.

But rather than modify the EVA plan, these companies increased either the base salaries or the target bonus amounts. They recognized that, under the old plan, deferred salary was essentially masquerading as incentive pay. This looked good in the proxy but misrepresented the process.

Management and the Board of Directors are responsible for articulating a compensation philosophy, what they hope to achieve from the combination of base salary, short-and long-term incentive plans, and non-monetary programs. As discussed earlier, they must determine the balance between the strength of the incentive on one hand, and the impact this will have on the cost to shareholders in good times and the retention risk borne during bad times. To minimize turnover, some companies design stable compensation programs with little variability. Others prefer more volatility, offer more upside opportunity, and recognize that they will not attract risk-averse managers.

In many cases, however, management does not fully understand the fundamental risk-reward characteristics of the compensation structure. They have not modeled in a sophisticated way how total compensation can be expected to behave over a multi-year period. Companies generally rely on static compensation surveys describing the practices of peer companies. They tell us the base salary and bonus opportunity of comparable positions, but fail to provide insight into risk—how compensation fluctuates with the performance of the company. The next section describes an analysis that provides insight into the dynamics of compensation, a much more important element of the design structure.

11. STRESS TEST THE COMPENSATION ARCHITECTURE

Like a piece of machinery, the compensation system must be tested to determine how it performs under stress. This means modeling the interplay between various realistic business scenarios, financial results, and total compensation. To the degree that traditional approaches address these dynamics at all, they do so in an incomplete way; they look only at how changes in financial results create volatility in the annual bonus. Typically overlooked is how a manager's personal *wealth* is affected by changes in company performance and value. For our purposes, a manager's wealth is defined as the current value of stock and options owned, plus the present value of expected future compensation, including salary, bonus, option (or stock) grants, and pension benefits.

To arrive at an overall compensation strategy, one key issue is how sensitive should managers' wealth be to a change in shareholder wealth? We call this "wealth leverage." Leverage of 100% indicates that a 10% increase in company value increases an executive's wealth by 10%. This would be true of the entrepreneur that receives compensation only in the form of company stock. Bill Gates and Warren Buffett each have wealth leverage that is close to 100%.

Alternatively, an executive whose compensation consists entirely of base salary and guaranteed pension benefits would have wealth leverage of zero; his wealth is independent of the company's stock price performance. This compensation mix is analogous not to that of a stockholder, but rather to that of a lender. The lender receives his return even if the stock price performs poorly; he has a fixed claim on the company's profit.

The calculations of a manager's wealth, and the changes in wealth for given performance scenarios, are somewhat complex, but computer spreadsheets enable us to perform these analyses quickly. To fully appreciate the dynamics of the incentive system, we simulate (using Monte Carlo analysis) changes in shareholder wealth and managers' wealth for as many as 100 different performance scenarios over a five-year period. For each scenario, we measure the ratio of the change in managers' wealth to the change in shareholder wealth.

My former colleague, Steve O'Byrne, describes one insight provided by this analysis as follows:[7] Consider an executive whose total compensation is delivered through a mix of 30% salary, 20% target bonus, and 50% stock options. A traditional compensation approach would suggest that 70% of this executive's compensation is "at risk." But our calculation indicates that, over a five-year period, this executive's wealth leverage is only 40%. The reason is that, under traditional stock options programs, options are granted each year at the prevailing stock price. This means that, if the price falls, more options are granted at the lower price. If the stock rises, fewer options are granted at a higher price. The mix re-balances to make compensation less leveraged. Executives each year are granted options that provide a competitive compensation package. Failing to account for how the pay mix fluctuates with performance misleads executives as to the true nature of the compensation plan.

Management can increase the leverage but at the cost of more retention risk. If stock option grants are front loaded, or are unaffected by share price fluctuations (i.e., the number of options granted is fixed each year), leverage increases to approximate the position of a shareholder having 70% of his wealth invested in company stock. The executive truly has 70% of his compensation at risk. But this means that in bad times there will be a large gap between actual pay and what would be considered "competitive." The risk of losing key executives is high when performance is poor. And when performance is strong, the cost to shareholders is high.

These are the key tradeoffs in structuring compensation, issues that are often overlooked in the heat of preparing for a compensation committee presentation about the proposed bonus plan. The cost of an incomplete analysis is the future need to modify the incentive plans because of events not anticipated at the outset.

12. COMMUNICATE

Once the changes are made communication is vital. A variety of audiences should be targeted, including the Board of Directors, who must approve the plan, key investors, who must approve of the plan, and participants, who must understand it. Incentive plans often fail to achieve credibility because they are not explained adequately. Uncertainty creates doubt, and doubt undermines success.

Analysts and investors often ask us how to differentiate between companies embracing EVA as a fad and those that are using it to create positive and sustained change. The answer can be found in the incentive plan. If the focus is on the same old EPS growth objectives, the company has not adopted EVA. Integrating EVA into the incentive plan, among other important benefits, provides a powerful signal of the company's commitment to increasing shareholder wealth. Companies must disclose the plan in the Proxy statement. Many are taking communication a step further and describing the plan in their Annual Reports.

For example, Herman Miller after describing the EVA concept in its 1998 Annual Report goes on to say:

We took EVA a step further by linking our incentive-based compensation to it. All of our executive incentive compensation plans as well as all of our employee gain-sharing programs at each of the business units have been linked to this measure. Using EVA-based plans shifts the focus from budget performance to long-term continuous improvements in shareholder value. The EVA target is raised each year by an improvement factor, so that increasingly higher EVA targets must be attained in order to earn the same level of incentive pay. Our Board of Directors has set the EVA improvement factor for a period of three years.

Herman Miller then presents its EVA calculation to investors for 1996-98. It shows an increase from $10.3 million in 1996, to $40.9 million in 1997, to $78.4 million in 1998.

Best Buy, a Minneapolis retailer, announced its intention to adopt EVA in a public press release dated

---

7. Steve writes about the wealth leverage framework in an article, "Total Compensation Strategy," published in the *Journal of Applied Corporate Finance,* Summer 1995, Volume 8 Number 2.

Analysts and investors often ask us how to differentiate between companies embracing EVA as a fad and those that are using it to create positive and sustained change. The answer can be found in the incentive plan.

November 18, 1998. The headline was "Best Buy Teams with Stern Stewart to Adopt Economic Value Added (EVA) Framework." Best Buy's founder and CEO, Richard Schultze, stated that

The implementation of the EVA framework is a key element of our continuing efforts to evolve as a world class organization and deliver sustainable value to our shareholders, customers and employees. EVA will foster our entrepreneurial culture and focus management to think like shareholders.

Best Buy's stock price increased from $46 to about $50 per share by the close of trading.

Of course, communicating the plan to internal constituents is important too. Further, communication should not end with the initial workshops and written materials associated with the rollout. Updates indicating how the company is performing against the incentive target should be a regular part of monthly (or, at a minimum, quarterly) communications. This way participants have the information they need to assess their position, and understand what they must do to improve their bonus during the balance of the year. The bonus announced by headquarters at the end of the year should therefore contain no surprises. It merely verifies the calculation made by the individuals themselves.

SUMMARY

Designing and implementing an effective incentive compensation plan is not just the responsibility of the human resources team. Human resources organizes and facilitates the overall process, but eliminating the cynicism and distrust surrounding the effort is a job for everyone.

First, the CEO and the Board must provide direction, balancing the tradeoffs between the strength of the incentive, the cost to shareholders, and the level of retention risk that is tolerable. Financial executives must support EVA as the critical financial measure used to judge performance. They also have to be prepared to report EVA results on a regular basis, and assist in the analytical effort necessary to establish performance targets.

Of greatest importance is obtaining the buy-in of operating managers early in the process. This provides them the opportunity to help craft the application of EVA to their businesses and managers. When the plan is then rolled out to participants, the operating executives will be better prepared to explain and champion the plan to their organizations.

The executive responsible for investor relations will be asked to assist in the public communication of the company's policy. Internal training and communications resources help in organizing and sponsoring workshops at which customized case studies are reviewed to help managers understand the levers they have available to influence EVA.

A poor implementation process can be worse than no process at all. Without collaboration with other areas of the company, participants have no ownership in the plan. It is "their" plan, not ours. Worse, the plan can get in the way of the right decision and strategy because it is not well understood, it may focus on too many different and (conflicting) measures, involve adversarial negotiations of performance targets, encourage short-term gaming that may be costly in the long term, and reward a parochial focus at a local level that may be counterproductive for the total company.

The challenge presented by these problems is less intellectual and more one of commitment. Management must have the will to persevere in making changes, and not just to the incentive system. It requires first a commitment to shareholder value, one that permeates all key process of the company. The EVA companies that have succeeded in outperforming peers use EVA as the focus of performance measurement and reporting, planning and budgeting, and capital allocation and communication. Making EVA the key to incentive compensation then fuels the company's fire to produce continuous growth in shareholder wealth.

EVIDENCE ON EVA

*by Gary C. Biddle,
Hong Kong University of Science &
Technology and University of Washington,
Robert M. Bowen,
University of Washington, and
James S. Wallace,
University of California at Irvine**

E VA, an acronym for economic value added, is the registered tradename of Stern Stewart & Company for their version of a long-known and compelling concept called residual income. Hailed by *Fortune* as the "New Key to Creating Wealth" and "Today's Hottest Financial Product," EVA has recently attracted considerable attention as a valuation and incentive tool. With a host of consultants now marketing related metrics, numerous claims have been made—most based on anecdotal evidence or in-house studies. However, little independent evidence has existed until recently regarding EVA's alleged advantages. This article helps fill this void by presenting results from recent academic research.

We first review briefly the theory that links residual income to shareholder value. We then discuss how Stern Stewart modifies residual income to produce its proprietary EVA and show how it compares with residual income, earnings, and operating cash flows over the period 1988-1997. Next we examine evidence regarding the claim that EVA has a stronger association with stock prices and firm values than traditional accounting measures. We then examine a second claim that compensation plans based on residual income motivate managers to take actions consistent with increasing shareholder value. Finally, we discuss and integrate recent findings on the usefulness of residual income metrics in valuation and incentive compensation.

*The comments of Robert Higgins, Jane Kennedy, Jennifer Koski, Suil Pae, Terry Shevlin, and seminar participants at Hong Kong University of Science & Technology are greatly appreciated.

THE THEORY

EVA is the leading example of a new class of metrics that attempt to measure an underlying concept called residual income. Recognized by economists since the 1770s, residual income is based on the premise that, in order for a firm to create wealth for its owners, it must earn more on its total invested capital than the cost of that capital.[1] Whereas traditional accounting net income measures "profits" net of interest expense on debt capital, residual income measures "profits" net of the full cost of both debt and equity capital.

To compute residual income, begin with net operating profits after tax (NOPAT) and subtract the total cost of capital measured as the weighted-average cost of capital (WACC) times the total invested capital (CAPITAL).[2] Notationally, residual income (RI) for period t is:

$$\text{Residual Income}_t \ (RI_t) = NOPAT_t - [WACC_t \times CAPITAL_{t-1}] \quad (1a)$$

Since NOPAT can be expressed alternatively as a rate of return on invested capital (i.e., return on assets, ROA) times capital, residual income can be restated as in (1b). Expression (1b) is intuitively appealing because it separates total return on capital from the total cost of capital.

$$RI_t = [ROA_t \times CAPITAL_{t-1}] - [WACC_t \times CAPITAL_{t-1}] \quad (1b)$$

Regrouping the right hand side terms of (1b), we also can observe in (1c) that firms producing positive residual income earn a positive "spread" between the percent return on invested capital and the percent cost of capital:

$$RI_t = [ROA_t - WACC_t] \times CAPITAL_{t-1} \quad (1c)$$

Put still another way, residual income can be seen in (1d) to equal traditional accounting net income (NI) minus a charge for the cost of *equity* capital, where the cost of equity capital can be expressed as the beginning-of-period book value of equity (BV) times the cost of equity capital (k). That is,

$$RI_t = NI_t - [k_t \times BV_{t-1}] \quad (1d)$$

A look at the right hand sides of expressions (1a) to (1d) suggests that there are three main opportunities to increase residual income and owners' wealth. Other things equal, managers will increase residual income to the extent they increase NOPAT and ROA, decrease WACC (though this is inherently more difficult), or reallocate capital away from negative-"spread" toward positive-"spread" investments. These opportunities become incentives when managers are evaluated or compensated based on residual income (or EVA). Later in this article, we review evidence on the effects of these incentives on managers' actions.

To see more clearly how residual income relates to shareholder wealth, consider the familiar discounted dividends model of equity valuation, where the market value of equity, V_t, is expressed as the net present value of future dividends:

$$V_t = \Sigma_{\tau=1}^{\tau=\infty} D_{t+\tau}/(1+k)^{\tau} \quad (2)$$

This expression can be restated using the so-called "clean surplus substitution," where clean surplus is the accounting convention that the accounting book value of equity (also called surplus) is changed only by earnings and dividends:[3]

$$BV_t = BV_{t-1} + NI_t - D_t, \quad (3)$$

1. See R. Hamilton, *An Introduction to Merchandize*, Edinburgh (1777), and A. Marshall, *Principles of Economics*, MacMillan Press Ltd., London, New York (1890). Coined residual income by General Electric in the 1950s, this concept also has been labeled "excess earnings" by J. Canning, *The Economics of Accountancy*, Ronald Press, New York (1929) and G. Preinreich, "The Law of Goodwill," *Accounting Review*, Vol. 12 (1936), 317-329, G. Preinreich, "Goodwill in Accountancy," *Journal of Accountancy* (July, 1937), 28-50, G. Preinreich, "Annual Survey of Economic Theory: The Theory of Depreciation," *Econometrica* (January 1938), 219-231; "super-profits" by H. Edey, "Business Valuation, Goodwill and the Superprofit Method," *Accountancy*, (January/February, 1957); excess realizable profit by E. Edwards and P. Bell, *The Theory and Measurement of Business Income*, University of California Press, Berkeley (1961); "excess income" by J. Kay, "Accountants, Too, Could Be Happy in a Golden Age: The Accountant's Rate of Profit and the Internal Rate of Return," *Oxford Economic Papers*, Vol. 28 (1976), 447-460; and "abnormal earnings" by K. Peasnell, "On Capital Budgeting and Income Measurement" *Abacus*, Vol. 17 (1981), 52-67, K. Peasnell, "Some Formal Connection Between Economic Values and Yields and Accounting Numbers,"

Journal of Business Finance and Accounting, Vol. 9 (1982), 361-381 and G. Feltham and J. Ohlson, "Valuation and Clean Surplus Accounting for Operating and Financing Activities," *Contemporary Accounting Research*, Vol. 11 (1995), 689-731.

2. Capital is generally defined to be assets (net of accumulated depreciation and amortization) invested in going-concern operating activities or, equivalently, contributed and retained debt and equity capital at the beginning of the period (net of non-operating capital). Non-interest bearing debt capital (e.g., accounts payable) is sometimes subtracted from total capital under the argument that it does not require a return.

3. See, for example, Peasnell (1982), cited above; Ohlson (1995), cited above; Feltham and Ohlson (1995), cited above; and J. O'Hanlon and K. Peasnell, "Wall Street's Contribution to Management Accounting: The Stern Stewart EVA Financial Management System," *Management Accounting Research*, Vol. 9, No. 4 (1998), 421-444. Clean surplus generally holds under U.S. accounting principles, with limited exceptions such as foreign currency translation gains and losses. Additional exceptions arise in the accounting principles of other countries.

Which measure conveys more information about future residual income: current
residual income or current earnings? It could be that other metrics better reveal this
future than do past and current observations of residual income (or EVA).

where D_t is the net "dividends" paid to owners for period t (i.e., cash dividends plus share repurchases net of capital contributions). Solving equation (1d) for NI_t, equation (3) for D_t, and substituting into the discounted dividends model (2), we can express equity value in terms of discounted residual income and equity book values (4a):

$$V_t = \Sigma_{\tau=1}^{\tau=\infty}[RI_{t+\tau} + (1 + k)BV_{t+\tau-1} - BV_{t+\tau}]/(1 + k)^\tau \ (4a)$$

If we further assume that $BV_{t+\tau} / (1+k)^\tau$ approaches 0 as τ approaches ∞, equity value can be expressed solely in terms of beginning book equity and discounted residual income:[4]

$$V_t = BV_t + \Sigma_{\tau=1}^{\tau=\infty}RI_{t+\tau}/(1 + k)^\tau \qquad (4b)$$

Because this relationship with equity value described in (4b) holds for residual income but not for accounting earnings (because accounting earnings does not include a charge for equity capital), one might expect that residual income should therefore be superior to accounting earnings in explaining firm values and stock returns. As we shall see, however, a key problem with this inference is that stock market participants have only past and current data to use as a basis for estimating the model's future residual income.

Thus, the empirical question becomes: Which measure conveys more information about future residual income: current residual income (or EVA) or current earnings? It could be that other metrics do a better job of revealing future residual income than do past and current observations of residual income (or EVA).[5] Before presenting evidence on this issue, however, we first describe Stern Stewart's version of residual income called EVA.

EVA

First introduced in the late 1980s, Stern Stewart's EVA has generated considerable publicity and over 300 client adoptions to date, including major international corporations such as Coca-Cola, Eli Lilly, and Siemens.[6] EVA also has attracted competitors who offer related or competing metrics. The resulting intense competition has been referred to as "metric wars" in the financial press.[7]

Figure 1 summarizes the steps that transform underlying cash flows from operations (CFO) into Stern Stewart's economic value added (EVA). Adjusting CFO for accounting accruals (such as depreciation and interest expense) yields bottom line accounting earnings (NI). Adding back after-tax interest expense to NI yields net operating profits after tax (NOPAT). Subtracting the current cost of both debt and equity capital from NOPAT yields residual income (RI). To compute economic value added (EVA), Stern Stewart adjusts the NOPAT and capital components of residual income for what are termed "accounting anomalies" or "distortions."[8] Some of their more common adjustments are shown in Table 1. Some of these adjustments undo traditional accounting accruals (such as eliminating deferred tax accounting in favor of actual cash taxes paid). Other adjustments switch accrual methods (e.g. from LIFO to FIFO). Still others introduce new accruals not used in traditional GAAP-based accounting (e.g., capitalization and amortization of marketing and R&D expenditures).

Stern Stewart argues that these EVA adjustments produce a better measure of residual income that enhances comparability and also reduces distortions of managerial incentives introduced by standard GAAP accounting.[9] For example, certain adjustments remove or reduce managers' discretion in computing EVA (e.g., the opportunity to influence bad debt

---

4. EVA (discussed below) can be substituted for residual income without loss of equivalence. When applying (4b), analysts truncate the infinite series and attempt to capture residual income beyond the forecast horizon in a "terminal value" term.

5. Similar reasoning explains why earnings have been found to better explain stock returns and firm values than cash flows, even though firm values can alternatively be modeled in discounted (free) cash flows (see, e.g., Gary C. Biddle, Gim S. Seow and Andrew F. Siegel, "Relative versus Incremental Information Content," *Contemporary Accounting Research* (Fall 1995), 1-23).

6. Stern Stewart also advocates a second performance metric based on (4b). Subtracting BV_t from both sides yields "market value added" (MVA), a measure of the equity value created by management beyond contributed equity capital, expressed in terms of discounted expected residual income: $MVA_t = V_t - BV_t = \Sigma_{\tau=1}^{\tau=\infty}RI_{t+\tau}/(1 + k)^\tau$. A "Performance 1000" ranking based on MVA has appeared annually in *Fortune* since 1993.

7. R. Myers, "Metric Wars," *CFO*, Vol. 12 (October 1996), 41-50. Performance measures marketed by competing firms include cash-flow return on investment (CFROI) by HOLT Value Associates, total business return (TBR) by Boston Consulting Group, shareholder value added (SVA) by LEK/Alcar, discounted economic profits (EP) by Marakon Associates, and economic value management (EVM) by KPMG. For further discussion, see also Christopher D. Ittner and David F. Larcker, "Innovations in Performance Measurement: Trends and Research Implications," *Journal of Management Accounting Research*, Vol. 10 (1998), 205-238.

8. Stern Stewart has reportedly developed over 160 proprietary adjustments to NOPAT and CAPITAL (although generally only a few are employed in each client application).

9. They also undoubtedly increase marketing effectiveness by creating a proprietary measure available only from Stern Stewart.

FIGURE 1
RECONCILING OPERATING
CASH FLOWS, NET
INCOME, OPERATING
PROFITS, RESIDUAL
INCOME AND ECONOMIC
VALUE ADDED*

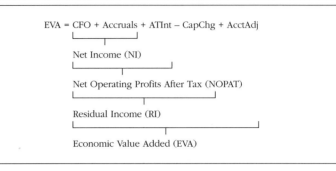

*This figure shows the relation between cash from operations, accounting earnings, residual income, and economic value added. Definitions of each component are below:
- CFO = cash flow from operations
- Accruals = accruals introduced by the financial accounting process
- NI = net income before extraordinary items
- ATInt = after-tax interest (added back to produce an operating performance number that is before the cost of financing)
- NOPAT = net operating profits after tax (not to be confused with Stern Stewart's NOPAT that includes adjustments to accounting earnings and capital)
- CapChg = charge for the estimated current cost of debt and equity capital
- AcctAdj = Stern Stewart's adjustments to NOPAT and Capital for alleged accounting distortions
- EVA = economic value added (registered tradename of Stern Stewart & Company)

TABLE 1
EXAMPLES OF TYPICAL
STERN STEWART
ADJUSTMENTS FOR
ALLEGED ACCOUNTING
DISTORTIONS

Common Areas where GAAP-based Accounting is Adjusted*	GAAP Treatment	Nature of Adjustments**
Marketing and R&D costs	Expense	Record as asset and amortize
Deferred taxes	Record as asset and/or liability	Reverse recording of asset and/or liability to reflect cash basis reporting
Purchased goodwill	Record as asset; amortize over up to 40 years	Reverse amortization to reflect original asset amount
Operating leases	Expense	Record asset and amortize; record liability and related interest
Bad debts and warranty costs	Estimate accrual	Reverse accruals to reflect cash basis reporting
LIFO inventory costing	LIFO permitted	Convert to FIFO
Construction in progress	Record as asset	Remove from assets
Discontinued operations	Include in assets and earnings	Remove from assets and earnings

*Common examples of Stern Stewart's adjustments. For example, the effect of capitalizing R&D is to add to CAPITAL (assets) past R&D expenses, less accumulated amortization. The effect on NOPAT (earnings) is to add back current R&D expenses and subtract the period's amortization of capitalized R&D. For a firm experiencing growth (decline) in R&D, the adjustment increases (reduces) contemporaneous NOPAT. The effect on EVA depends on the amount of capitalized R&D. For a firm in steady state, the adjustment has little net effect on NOPAT, but increases CAPITAL, thereby reducing EVA.
**Stern Stewart's rationales for these adjustments include: a) to better represent the underlying economics of the transactions; b) to reduce incentives for dysfunctional or suboptimal decision making; and c) to improve comparability externally (across firms) and internally (e.g., across divisions) by putting the accounting on a similar basis. Not all rationales apply to each adjustment.

The difference between EVA and RI is relatively small, suggesting that the net effect of Stern Stewart's accounting adjustments is not large on average.

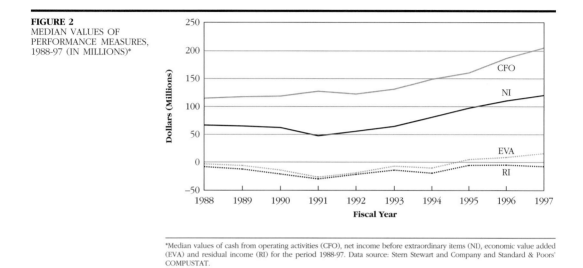

FIGURE 2
MEDIAN VALUES OF
PERFORMANCE MEASURES,
1988-97 (IN MILLIONS)*

*Median values of cash from operating activities (CFO), net income before extraordinary items (NI), economic value added (EVA) and residual income (RI) for the period 1988-97. Data source: Stern Stewart and Company and Standard & Poors' COMPUSTAT.

accruals). Other adjustments reduce incentives to make operating, investing, and financing choices that boost earnings and EVA in the short term, but reduce shareholder wealth. Examples of such myopic decision-making include cutbacks in positive-NPV capital investments, marketing, and R&D expenditures. These adjustments are particularly relevant when executive pay is closely linked to EVA—a situation that can produce incentives for short-term "gaming." Other mechanisms used in conjunction with EVA to help control "short-termism" include bonus banks and EVA-based stock option plans.[10]

Figure 2 plots median values of four alternative performance measures—net income (NI), residual income (RI), EVA, and Cash Flow from Operations (CFO)—over the period 1988-1997.[11] Since accounting accruals generally reduce net income (e.g., due to depreciation and amortization expense), it is not surprising that median NI plots well below median CFO in each year. EVA and RI both lie well below NI because of the incremental charge for equity capital. However, the difference between EVA and RI is relatively small, suggesting that the net effect of Stern

Stewart's accounting adjustments is not large on average.[12] Interestingly, although the sample is drawn from among the largest firms in the U.S. economy, median EVA is negative until 1995, and median RI is negative in every year. Near zero EVA and RI is consistent with a competitive economy in which even the typical large firm has difficulty earning more than its cost of capital. Low values of EVA and RI also are also consistent with a potential upward bias in Stern Stewart's cost of capital estimates (which are used here for computing RI).

CLAIM #1 — EVA BETTER EXPLAINS STOCK RETURNS AND FIRM VALUES

Proponents of EVA and other residual income measures have made two primary claims about EVA and/or residual income: (1) they better explain stock returns and firm values than traditional accounting earnings; and (2) they better motivate managers to create shareholder wealth. In this section and the next, we examine recent independent evidence that bears on each claim.

10. See, for example, Stephen F. O'Byrne, "Does Value Based Management Discourage Investment in Intangibles?" working paper, Shareholder Value Advisors Inc. (1999), which discusses adverse incentives associated with acquisitions and investments, and illustrates that the typical practice of using straight-line depreciation in EVA creates incentives to forgo positive net present value investments.

11. The data are from Stern Stewart's publicly available database and the Standard & Poors COMPUSTAT database. The Stern Stewart data are summarized in *Fortune*'s annual Performance 1000 issue.

12. For example, in any period, current R&D costs can be approximately equal to the amortization of past capitalized costs. And even if, say, capitalized R&D costs are large and growing, any expense reduction due to capitalization will be offset by higher cost of capital charges due to capitalized R&D in the capital base.

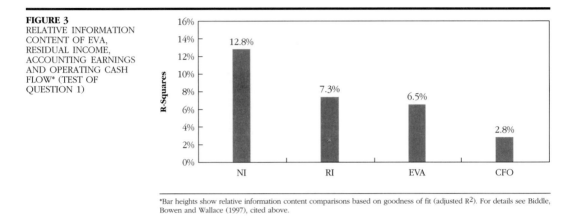

FIGURE 3
RELATIVE INFORMATION CONTENT OF EVA, RESIDUAL INCOME, ACCOUNTING EARNINGS AND OPERATING CASH FLOW* (TEST OF QUESTION 1)

*Bar heights show relative information content comparisons based on goodness of fit (adjusted R^2). For details see Biddle, Bowen and Wallace (1997), cited above.

Evidence on Associations with Stock Returns and Firm Values

In our recently published article, entitled "Does EVA Beat Earnings? Evidence on Associations with Stock Returns and Firm Values,"[13] we provide evidence on the first claim by examining whether EVA and residual income (RI) are more closely associated with stock returns and firm values than two currently mandated performance metrics: net income (measured as earnings before extraordinary items) and cash flow from operations.[14] Specifically, we examine three related questions, the first of which is:

Q1: Do EVA and/or RI dominate earnings (NI) and operating cash flow (CFO) in explaining contemporaneous stock returns?

We examine a sample of 6,174 firm-years over the period 1984-1993. As a test of association (or "goodness of fit"), we use adjusted R-squared (Adj. R^2) from a regression of stock returns on each performance metric.[15] Our results, as summarized in Figure 3, indicate that current period accounting earnings (NI) is significantly more highly associated with market-adjusted annual stock returns (Adj. R^2 = 13%) than are RI (Adj. R^2 = 7%) and EVA (Adj. R^2 = 6%), and that all three dominate cash flows from operations, CFO (Adj. R^2 = 3%).[16] This finding is

supported across a number of alternative specifications. These results do *not* support the claim that EVA dominates earnings in its association with stock returns. On the contrary, NI appears to outperform EVA on average.

A second and related question that we examine is whether EVA and/or RI *complement* currently mandated performance measures by conveying information beyond that contained in contemporaneous NI and CFO:

Q2: Do components unique to EVA or RI help explain contemporaneous stock returns beyond that explained by CFO and NI?

To address this question, we decompose EVA into its component parts as shown in Figure 1 (e.g., cash from operations, operating accruals, capital charge, and net accounting "adjustments") and evaluate the contribution of each component toward explaining contemporaneous stock returns. We find that EVA components add little to the explanatory power of the regressions. Further, tests across alternative specifications indicate that, while traditional earnings components such as operating cash flow and accruals are consistently significant, components unique to EVA—that is, the capital charge and accounting adjustments—are often not significant in explaining contemporaneous returns. These results

13. Gary C. Biddle, Robert M. Bowen and James S. Wallace, "Does EVA Beat Earnings? Evidence on Associations with Stock Returns and Firm Values," *Journal of Accounting and Economics*, Vol. 24, No. 3 (December 1997), 301-336.

14. For examples of such claims, see G. Bennett Stewart, *The Quest for Value* (Harper Business, New York (1991), 2 and 66; *Harvard Business Review* (November-December, 1995), 20; and G. Bennett Stewart, "EVA: Fact or Fantasy," *Journal of Applied Corporate Finance* Vol. 7, No. 2 (Summer 1994), 75.

15. See equation (6), Figure 3 and related text in Biddle, Bowen and Wallace (1997), cited above, for an elaboration on this regression and related statistical tests.

16. The strength of the relation between stock returns and contemporaneous performance is a function of the length of the time frame or 'window' over which returns and performance are measured. For example, Adj. R^2 for regressions over 5-year windows were NI (31%), CFO (19%), EVA (14%) and RI (11%). Again, we find no evidence of EVA or RI 'beating' earnings over five-year intervals.

Our evidence suggests that realized earnings are a better predictor of future EVA than realized EVA itself.

FIGURE 4
ASSOCIATIONS BETWEEN
CONTEMPORANEOUS
STOCK RETURNS AND EVA,
RESIDUAL INCOME,
ACCOUNTING EARNINGS
AND OPERATING CASH
FLOW* (TESTS OF
QUESTIONS 1 AND 2)

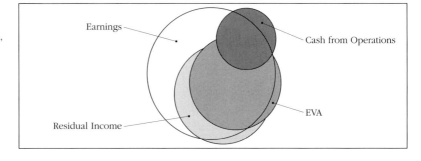

*This figure combines *relative* information content comparisons (Adjusted R^2s) for question 1, shown as circle *sizes*, and *incremental* information content comparisons (F-statistics) for question 2, shown as relative positioning or lack of *overlap* (with *less* overlap indicating more incremental information content). For details see Biddle, Bowen and Wallace (1997), cited above.

suggest that EVA components contribute only marginally to the information already available to market participants in NI.

Figure 4 summarizes our overall findings on the value-relevance of EVA versus the other performance measures. It combines comparisons of *relative* information content (Adj. R^2s) from question 1 (which are shown as circle *sizes* in the figure), and comparisions of *incremental* information content (F-statistics) from question 2, shown as relative positioning or lack of *overlap* (with *less* overlap indicating more incremental information content). Overall, neither EVA nor RI appears to dominate NI in its association with stock market returns. NI has the largest relative information content (as indicated by the largest circle) and the overlap between circles is large, suggesting that there is little incremental information content in EVA, RI, and CFO beyond that contained in NI.

We also examine a related claim that EVA is more highly associated with firm values (versus stock returns considered above):

Q3: Does EVA dominate earnings in explaining firm values?

To address this question, we replicate and extend a study authored by former Stern Stewart vice-president Stephen O'Byrne that appeared in the Spring 1996 issue of this journal.[17] O'Byrne first compares Adj. R^2s from regressing firm value on EVA and on earnings measured as NOPAT. He reports an Adj. R^2 of 31% for the EVA regression and 33% for the NOPAT regression. Next, he adjusts the EVA regression by: (1) allowing separate coefficients for positive and negative values of EVA; (2) including the natural log of capital in an attempt to capture differences in the way the market values firms of different sizes; and (3) including 57 industry dummy variables in order to capture potential industry effects. When all of these adjustments are included, O'Byrne obtains a larger Adj. R^2 for the enhanced EVA regression (56%) than for NOPAT (33%).

Notice, however, that O'Byrne makes such adjustments only to the EVA regression. When we "level the playing field" by applying the same adjustments to the NOPAT regression and also examine NI, EVA's superiority disappears. The NI regression has a significantly higher association with firm value (Adj. R^2 = 53%) than the EVA regression (Adj. R^2 = 50%) and the NOPAT regression (Adj. R^2 = 49%). The latter two are statistically indistinguishable. Thus, as with our stock returns tests, these results do not support the contention that EVA outperforms earnings in explaining firm values. On the contrary, our evidence suggests that earnings more often dominates EVA in value-relevance to market participants.[18]

17. Stephen F. O'Byrne, "EVA and Market Value," *Journal of Applied Corporate Finance*, Vol. 9, No. 1, 116-125.

18. Other independent studies report similar findings. See S. Chen and J. Dodd, "Economic Valued Added EVA: An Empirical Examination of a New Corporate Performance Measure," *Journal of Managerial Issues* (Fall 1997), 318-333; S. Chen and J. Dodd, "Usefulness of Accounting Earnings, Residual Income, and EVA: A Value-relevance Perspective," working paper, Clarion University (1997); Pamela P. Peterson and David R. Peterson, "Company Performance and Measures of Value Added," *The Research Foundation of the Institute of Chartered Financial Analysts* (1996), Chapter 4; and R. Bernstein, *Quantitative Viewpoint, An Analysis of EVA —Part II*, Merrill Lynch & Co. Global Securities & Economics Group, Quantitative & Equity Derivative Research Department, (February 1998).

Why Don't Residual Income and EVA "Beat" Earnings?

There are several potential explanations as to why RI and EVA do not dominate earnings in associations with stock returns and firm values. First, recall that the valuation model in equation (4b) is specified in terms of discounted future RI (or EVA)—not on past and current realizations. In this light, our evidence suggests that realized earnings are a better predictor of future EVA than realized EVA itself.[19] Also recall that the key difference between NI and RI is the cost of equity capital, and that the key difference between RI and EVA are Stern Stewart's accounting adjustments (such as the capitalization of R&D). Earnings could dominate RI if market participants use cost of capital estimates that are different than those provided by Stern Stewart. Earnings could dominate EVA if Stern Stewart's accounting adjustments have the effect of "undoing" discretionary accruals that market participants use to infer firms' future prospects. Alternatively, the market may make a set of accounting adjustments that are different from those applied by Stern Stewart. Even if the market adjustments are similar to Stern Stewart's, they may contain little news. If earnings already conveys essential economic news (e.g., unexpected revenues and costs)—and the market provides its own cost of capital estimate—there may be little left to glean from RI and EVA. It also is possible that, for the time period we studied, the market had yet to recognize valuable incremental information contained in EVA and RI numbers.

CLAIM #2 — EVA BETTER MOTIVATES MANAGERS TO INCREASE SHAREHOLDER WEALTH

A second principal claim is that residual income-based incentive schemes are better than earnings-based plans in motivating managers to create shareholder wealth. For example, Stern Stewart advertisements often include testimonials and charts showing rising EVA and share prices. They suggest that EVA adoption is responsible for increased shareholder wealth by better aligning internal management incentives with owners' interests.[20] Because it can be shown that discounted future RI is equivalent to discounted future cash flows in a capital budgeting decision,[21] RI-based incentives are claimed to better motivate managers to select positive net-present-value investments than traditional accounting metrics. As we noted earlier, both RI- and EVA-based compensation should reward managers for increasing operating profits (NOPAT) and return on capital (ROA), reducing the weighted average cost of capital (WACC), and reallocating capital from negative spread (ROA minus WACC) activities toward positive spread activities. We next present evidence on whether managers actually respond to these incentives at firms that adopt residual income-based metrics.[22]

Evidence on Incentives and Performance

In a recently published paper entitled "Adopting Residual Income-Based Performance Plans: Do You Get What You Pay For?,"[23] Wallace provides independent evidence on this second set of claims. Specifically, he examines what amounts to a precondition for the possibility that managers of firms adopting RI-based plans (including EVA) create wealth for their shareholders: namely, that the managers change their operating, investing and financing decisions in response to RI incentives. Evidence consistent with this precondition does not prove that RI (or EVA) creates shareholder wealth, but it provides a necessary first step by demonstrating that RI-based incentive compensation plans are effective in altering management decisions.

---

19. Realized earnings are similarly more predictive of future free cash flows than are cash flow themselves. This is not surprising since earnings smooth irregular cash flow realizations and accruals allow managers to convey to market participants inferences regarding their firms' future prospects.

20. Of course, some EVA adopters have prospered (e.g., Coca-Cola and Eli Lilly), others have not fared well (e.g., Quaker Oats) and others have dropped or de-emphasized EVA (e.g., AT&T, Monsanto). For further elaboration of such claims, see G. Bennett Stewart (1991), cited above.

21. For example, see Robert M. Bowen and James S. Wallace, "Interior Systems" case, *Issues in Accounting Education* (1999), forthcoming.

22. Another Stern Stewart claim is that EVA is applicable to virtually any type of firm. Although residual income type measures like EVA are indeed widely applicable, they are, like earnings, inherently backward looking. As a result,

earnings-based metrics (including EVA) can be more difficult to implement as a management incentive tool in settings where the benefits of management actions are delayed. Consider the Boeing Company, where the effects of management actions to land a large order for new aircraft may not appear in sales, earnings or EVA for as long as five or ten years. For this reason, Boeing employs one of a class of forward-looking metrics based on projected cash flows. Other industries where the effects of current actions can be seriously delayed include biotechnology, internet, software development, and wireless communications. Stern Stewart has proposed a solution to this problem in an article called "EVA for the Oil and Gas Industry," *Journal of Applied Corporate Finance*, Vol. 11, No. 3. (Fall 1998).

23. James S. Wallace, "Adopting Residual-Income-Based Compensation Plans: Do You Get What You Pay For?," *Journal of Accounting & Economics*, Vol. 24, No. 3 (December 1997), 275-300.

Asset dispositions increased 100% and new investment decreased 21% after adoption for the residual income firms relative to the control firms.

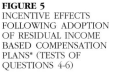

FIGURE 5
INCENTIVE EFFECTS
FOLLOWING ADOPTION
OF RESIDUAL INCOME
BASED COMPENSATION
PLANS* (TESTS OF
QUESTIONS 4-6)

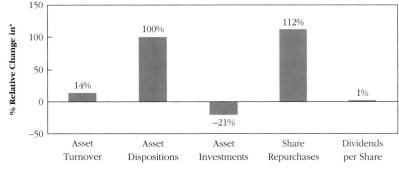

*Percentage changes in selected actions of firms that adopt residual income based compensation plans (relative to a control group of non-adopters). For example, asset turnover increased 14% relative to a control group when compared to the pre-adoption period. More specifically, the percentage change in 'asset turns' equals the average asset turnover for the treatment (adopter) group (= 1.24) less the average asset turnover for the control (non-adopter) group (= 1.08), with this difference scaled by the average asset turnover for both groups in the period before adopting RI based compensation plans (= 1.125). In numbers, (1.24 - 1.08) / 1.125 = .14 or a 14% relative increase in asset turnover subsequent to adoption of residual income based plans. For more details on these results, see Wallace (1997), cited above.

For each of the four research questions listed below, 40 firms that adopted residual income-based compensation plans were compared with 40 matched-pair control firms that continued to use traditional compensation schemes. The results are summarized in Figure 5, where "% relative change" indicates average percentage changes in selected actions of firms that adopt residual income-based incentives relative to the non-adopters.

Operating decisions that use invested capital more efficiently will boost NOPAT and ROA and, other things equal, increase RI. For this reason, we would expect actions consistent with residual income incentives to increase asset turnover measured by sales over total assets:[24]

Q4: Does asset turnover increase for firms adopting residual income-based compensation plans (relative to non-adopters)?

As shown in Figure 5, total asset turnover increased by an average of 14% for firms adopting residual income plans relative to control firms in the period after adoption. This increase is statistically significant at conventional levels.

Investing decisions also boost RI to the extent they re-allocate capital away from activities that earn less than their capital costs and toward activities that

earn more. If the adoption of a RI-based compensation plan simultaneously introduces greater awareness of the higher hurdle rate for investments (now explicit in the full weighted average cost of capital, WACC), other things equal, we should observe increased asset divestitures and decreased new investments:

Q5: Do asset dispositions increase and asset acquisitions decrease for firms adopting residual income-based compensation plans (relative to non-adopters)?

As depicted in Figure 5, asset dispositions increased 100% and new investment decreased 21% after adoption (compared to pre-adoption levels) for the residual-income firms relative to the control firms. It is important to note that each of these results is driven by actions in the post-adoption period. In fact, the firms adopting residual income actually were investing more relative to the control firms in the pre-adoption period. Each of these changes is significant at conventional levels. However, it is difficult to interpret whether an observed reduction in net investment is a value-increasing action since it is possible that managers are reducing positive NPV projects—not just projects earning below their cost of capital. Critics of RI-based compensation plans claim that they provide incentives for manag-

---

24. For example, after adopting EVA, a large west coast manufacturing firm realized that, while its purchasing group had incentives to cut costs (and thus the input price of component parts), they had little incentive to control the level of parts inventory. Senior management quickly decided that it was more effective to cut inventory (and thus capital) than to minimize price. As a consequence, they moved

a large amount of their purchases to wholesalers instead of buying directly from manufacturers who imposed higher order minimums and inflexible delivery schedules. Allegedly, this firm was willing to pay up to 15% more than past prices to achieve lower target inventory levels.

ers to underinvest in positive-NPV projects. Proponents and users of RI-based incentives claim otherwise and, in fact, argue that RI encourages investments that increase shareholder wealth.[25]

Financing decisions also should be influenced by the adoption of RI-based incentives. Given that holding capital that earns less than the WACC reduces RI, we expect to observe increased payouts to shareholders. If these payouts reflect discrete, one-time responses to new RI-based compensation incentives and tax incentives, we are more likely to see an increase in share repurchases than in regular cash dividends:[26]

Q6: Do share repurchases and dividend payouts increase for firms adopting residual income-based compensation plans (relative to non-adopters)?

As shown in Figure 5, both repurchases per share and dividends per share increase in the post-adoption period relative to the pre-adoption period. Relative to the matched-pair control firms, residual income adopters dramatically increased repurchases per share—by $1.09 (or 112%) on average, but only slightly increased dividends per share—by $0.13 (1%). Only repurchases per share are significant at conventional levels. These findings suggest that managers faced with higher investment hurdle rates under RI return excess capital to shareholders in a tax-favored manner that does not signal a permanent change in dividend payout.

Finally, if managers take actions consistent with RI incentives, firms that adopt RI incentives should produce increased residual income:

Q7: Does residual income increase for firms adopting residual income-based compensation plans (relative to non-adopters)?

Here the evidence reveals that following adoption of RI-based incentive plans, the RI firms relative to the control firms increased residual income by a statistically significant average of nearly $190 million annually (almost 1300%). This result is consistent with the adage that you get what you measure and reward.

Although these results suggest that the adoption of residual income-based incentives alter management decisions in ways that should contribute to shareholder wealth, several caveats are in order. First, firms that adopt new incentive plans may simultaneously change other aspects of their operations that also could influence management decisions (e.g., management realignments, strategic repositionings, restructurings, etc.). Thus, observed changes in management behavior could be due at least in part to these other effects. Second, our sample is not random since firms choose voluntarily to adopt residual income-based plans. It could be, for example, that managers opt for RI-based compensation when they forecast success unrelated to the incentives in the plan.[27] Finally, one should be careful not to interpret these results strictly as confirming shareholder value creation. While they suggest changes in management behavior that are consistent with RI incentives, it remains for future research to confirm that resulting benefits have been realized by shareholders.

DISCUSSION AND SUMMARY

The introduction of EVA and competing performance metrics can rightly be regarded as one of the most significant management innovations of the past decade. As key components of the shareholder value movement, they have stimulated both management interest and academic research. A variant of the long-appreciated concept of residual income (RI), EVA is well understood to provide desirable management incentives under appropriate conditions. Less self-evident are two key claims that have been made about EVA as part of a heated competition that has emerged among metrics providers. These are that EVA (RI) better explains stock returns and firm values than traditional accounting earnings and that EVA better motivates managers to increase shareholder wealth. This article provides evidence from recent independent research regarding these claims.

Regarding the first claim that EVA is more closely associated with stock returns and firm value than is net income, independent research suggests that EVA (RI) does not dominate traditional ac-

---

25. If their pay or prospects are tied to periodic accounting performance, managers may avoid positive-NPV projects that are slow to pay off. It has been argued that RI, because it tends to apply a higher investment hurdle rate of return, will exacerbate this tendency. Perhaps one of the most vocal critics is the consulting firm Boston Consulting Group. See, for example, Eric Olsen in the October 1996 Boston Consulting Group publication, *Perspectives.* For a rebuttal, see John Shiely, COO of Briggs and Stratton, an EVA firm. Mr. Shiely's response was published in the February 1997 Stern Stewart publication, *EVANGELIST™.*

26. Share repurchases are tax favored over dividends in two respects: they are taxed at a lower rate for many taxpayers and taxpayers can choose whether to receive and thus be taxed on them.

27. See, for example, Chris Hogan and Craig Lewis, "The Long-Run Performance of Firms Adopting Compensation Plans Based on Economic Profits," working paper, Vanderbilt University (1999), who argue that managers adopt RI-based plans opportunistically in anticipation of increased profitability and that adopting firms do not significantly outperform peer companies in creating shareholder wealth.

counting earnings in associations with stock returns and firm values. On the contrary, the evidence suggests that earnings generally beats EVA in value relevance to market participants. One possible explanation is that Stern Stewart's proprietary adjustments to GAAP earnings "undo" informative accounting accruals contained in earnings (e.g., bad debts and deferred taxes). Another possibility is that EVA and residual income contain little news beyond that already contained in earnings. For example, if net income measures convey news about unexpected revenues and costs, and if the market provides its own cost of capital estimate, there may be little left to glean from EVA and residual income. Alternatively, market participants may apply a different set of adjustments than those provided by Stern Stewart e.g., different amortization periods for capitalized marketing and R&D costs). It also is possible that, in the time periods studied, market participants had yet to recognize the information contained in EVA and residual income.

Regarding the second claim that EVA and residual income better motivate managers to increase shareholder wealth, independent evidence suggests that firms that adopt residual income-based incentives tend to (1) improve operating efficiency by increasing asset turnover, (2) dispose of selected assets and reduce new investment (which adds value provided these assets were failing to earn adequate returns when compared to the firm's overall cost of capital), and (3) repurchase more shares (consistent with distributing underperforming capital to shareholders). Firms that adopt RI incentive plans also exhibit increased residual income, confirming the adage that you get what you measure and reward. These findings support a pre-condition for shareholder wealth creation by confirming that managers respond to RI-based incentives.

At this point a reader might ask how these results can be reconciled. Is it possible that residual income-based incentives can motivate managers to take actions consistent with shareholder wealth creation when earnings beats EVA and residual income in associations with stock returns and firm values? We believe so. As argued by Jerold Zimmerman in a previous edition of this journal, these issues are separable. As Zimmerman puts it,

the success of a given performance measure in tracking near-term changes in a company's stock price is unlikely to be the most important consideration in choosing a measure as a basis for managerial rewards.... The best performance measure is the one that without imposing excessive costs gives managers the strongest incentives to take actions that increase firm value.[28]

Thus, it is possible for a metric to be quite useful for internal incentive purposes even though it conveys little if any news to market participants regarding the firm's future prospects. Similarly, a measure that is useful to capital market participants for determining share prices is not necessary useful as a management incentive tool. Therefore, EVA and residual income could prove effective in motivating shareholder wealth creation without conveying new information to investors, and claims linking the two should be interpreted with care. Ultimately, if an internal metric or compensation plan is more effective in motivating shareholder wealth creation, shareholders should benefit *regardless* of its correlation with stock returns and firm values. Whether implementations of EVA and residual income-based incentives have been truly effective in this regard remains an open question for further research.

---

28. Jerold L. Zimmerman, "EVA and Divisional Performance Measurement: Capturing Synergies and Other Issues," *Journal of Applied Corporate Finance*, Vol. 10, No. 2 (1997), 98-109.

SIX CHALLENGES IN DESIGNING EQUITY-BASED PAY

by Brian J. Hall,
Harvard Business School*

T here has been a dramatic change in both the level and composition of executive pay in the U.S. during the last two decades. Executive compensation has increased sharply, driven almost entirely by an explosion in stock option grants. What's more, the trend toward equity-based pay appears to be spreading to the rest of the developed world.

But what has equity-based pay really accomplished, and what can we expect in the future? Let's start with what can go right. Besides attracting and retaining a high-quality management team, well-designed stock and stock option packages can increase corporate productivity and value by better aligning top managers' interests with those of the shareholders. And despite all of the recent controversy, research shows that the increased use of stock options has greatly strengthened the link between executive pay and corporate performance during the last decade or two. In their much-cited 1990 study of U.S. companies in the 1970s and early 1980s, Michael Jensen and Kevin Murphy reported that for every $1,000 change in a company's market value in a given year, the average CEO's total compensation for that year changed by *only* about three dollars. In a study almost a decade later, Jeff Liebman and I found that by the end of the 1990s, the pay-to-performance link for U.S. CEOs had jumped almost tenfold since 1980—due almost entirely to the proliferation of stock options during the 1990s.[1]

Yet this change in no way suggests that the stock option revolution has been all to the good. Indeed, recent events suggest that the current method of rewarding executives has significant flaws. The top executives of many companies cashed out significant portions of their options during the end of the bull market of the 1990s, a period when stock prices proved unsustainably high. And whether achieved by accident or design, the resulting transfer of wealth to selling managers from existing (and particularly buying) shareholders generated considerable skepticism about corporate governance in general and executive compensation in particular. At the same time, companies whose stock prices

*This article was prepared with the assistance of research associate Aaron M. G. Zimmerman. It draws heavily on material in *Incentive Strategy II: Executive Compensation and Ownership Structure* (HBS No. 902-134).

1. See Michael C. Jensen and Kevin J. Murphy, "Performance Pay and Top Management Incentives," *Journal of Political Economy*, April 1990, pp. 225-265; Brian J. Hall and Jeffrey B. Liebman, "Are CEOs Really Paid Like Bureaucrats?," *Quarterly Journal of Economics*, August 1998, pp. 653-691; and Brian J. Hall, "What You Need to Know About Stock Options," *Harvard Business Review*, March-April 2000, pp. 121-129.

have plummeted are now struggling with the dual problem of retaining employees with deeply underwater options and placating shareholders strongly opposed to repricing those options.

What has also become clear is that designing an effective equity-based compensation plan—one that motivates *long-term* value-maximizing behavior—is not a simple task. There are difficulties associated with time horizons, opportunistic selling, the gaming of accounting numbers and stock prices, risk-taking, fairness, and what I call option "fragility." Moreover, as this article will make clear, most stock options are worth considerably less to the executives they are meant to motivate than to the shareholders of the companies that grant them. This "wedge" in value represents a significant cost to the firm's shareholders—one that could tilt the balance toward the use of restricted stock or cash-based compensation instead. Until recently, corporate decisions to grant options rather than restricted stock have clearly been influenced by a quirk of accounting—the fact that companies need not expense option grants on their income statements, whereas the cost of restricted stock, indexed options, and virtually all other executive compensation must flow through the P&L. But a growing sensitivity to the drawbacks of options (which will only be reinforced if the accounting treatment is changed) is likely to cause many companies to consider restricted stock and cash-based compensation as more cost-effective alternatives to options.

In this article, I discuss the major challenges in designing equity-based pay plans that effectively link executive compensation to long-run shareholder value. Besides encouraging executives to balance long-term performance goals against the pressures to meet near-term earnings targets, corporate pay plans must also perform another difficult balancing act—maintaining a strong pay-for-performance link (including reduced rewards when stock prices fall) while at the same time retaining capable executives. There are dramatic differences in equity-based pay plans, and the way companies set up these plans can have powerful effects on both incentives and retention. But incentives can be a double-edged sword and must be carefully managed to prevent the loss of shareholder confidence and value.

EXECUTIVE COMPENSATION: RECENT HISTORY AND TRENDS

As late as 1984, fewer than half of the CEOs of publicly traded U.S. companies were granted any stock or stock options in a given year. With hindsight, it now seems clear that the resulting misalignment of incentives between managers and owners was a major contributor to the wave of U.S. corporate restructurings in the 1980s. Private equity firms like Kohlberg Kravis Roberts & Co. (KKR) and Clayton Dubilier & Rice bought up underperforming companies—or, in many cases, subsidiaries of large conglomerates—and achieved remarkable performance improvements by forcing managers to focus on profitability and shareholder value. The change in managers' motivation came from three main sources: meaningful equity ownership, high debt payments that provided a new discipline by leaving managers with little free cash flow, and more active monitoring by a board made up entirely of major equity investors.[2]

George Roberts, one of the founders of KKR, summed up the prevailing view of the importance of ownership incentives as follows:

Just as you are likely to take better care of a home you own than one you rent, managers and boards with a financial commitment to their business are virtually always more effective in creating both short- and long-term value...Companies perform better when all important parties—management, employees, and directors—have the incentive of ownership in the business.[3]

In virtually all of these transactions, the top managers became co-owners by purchasing stock with their own or borrowed money and through compensation in the form of stock and options. And the fact that the early buyout firms referred to their transactions as "*management* buyouts" (rather than "leveraged buyouts," as they later became known) reflected the conviction that in terms of motivating executives to increase profitability and firm value, ownership structure and incentives were more important than the way the transactions were financed.

2. See Steven Kaplan, "The Evolution of U.S. Corporate Governance: We Are All Henry Kravis Now," *Journal of Private Equity*, 1997, pp. 7-14; Bengt Holmstrom and Steven Kaplan, "Corporate Governance and Takeovers in the U.S.: Making Sense of the '80s and '90s," *Journal of Economic Perspectives*, Spring 2001, pp. 121-144; and Bengt Holmstrom and Steven Kaplan, "The State of U.S. Corporate Governance: What's Right and What's Wrong?," *Journal of Applied Corporate Finance*, in this issue.

3. George R. Roberts, "Corporate Governance and the Power of Ownership," *The Corporate Board*, September/October 1998.

There are dramatic differences in equity-based pay plans, and the way companies set up these plans can have powerful effects on both incentives and retention. But incentives can be a double-edged sword...

FIGURE 1
THE LEVEL AND
COMPOSITION OF MEDIAN
CEO PAY IN THE U.S.
FROM 1980 TO 2001 (IN
2001 DOLLARS)

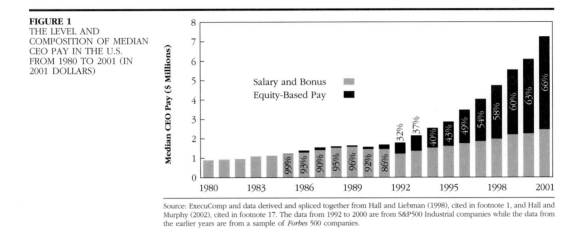

Source: ExecuComp and data derived and spliced together from Hall and Liebman (1998), cited in footnote 1, and Hall and Murphy (2002), cited in footnote 17. The data from 1992 to 2000 are from S&P500 Industrial companies while the data from the earlier years are from a sample of *Forbes* 500 companies.

The success of the management buyouts in raising productivity and shareholder value did not go unnoticed by the shareholders of public companies.[4] In the early 1990s, after the leveraged restructuring movement had been shut down by a combination of market and regulatory forces, institutional investors began to use their power as owners to push managers to increase returns to shareholders. This development, along with the sharp rise of venture-backed companies, led to an enormous increase in the proportion of stock and (especially) stock options in top management compensation packages.

Figure 1 shows the level and composition of top executive pay over the period 1980-2001. By 2001, equity based pay constituted about two thirds of the median annual total pay of U.S. top executives, up from zero as late as 1984. What's more, by the end of the 1990s, annual changes in the value of executives' portfolios of company stock and options were swamping annual changes in cash pay. In fact, studies estimated that, in a year of "normal" stock price volatility, changes in the value of executive stock and options were as much as 50 times the annual change in cash pay.[5]

Perhaps even more striking is the sharp increase in the *level* of top executive pay during the period.

The median CEO pay package rose from about $1 million in 1980 to over $7 million in 2001 (measured in 2001 dollars). Thus, while the pay of the average rank-and-file worker increased (in inflation-adjusted terms) by about 15% over the past 20 years, CEO pay increased by nearly 600%. The only major groups with commensurate or larger percentage pay increases during this period were "superstar" actors and professional athletes.[6]

And U.S. trends in executive pay appear to be spreading internationally. Table 1 shows changes in the composition of pay between 1996 and 2001 in 23 of the wealthiest countries (averaged by continent). In each of the groups, the share of equity-based pay (as a percentage of total pay) increased by 12 percentage points or more, and such increases were all within range of the 19-percentage-point increase in the U.S. (The main difference, of course, is that the proportion of equity-based pay in the U.S. in 1996 was already much higher than in other countries.) And the same pattern emerges in the share of total "at-risk" pay—that is, cash bonus plus equity-based pay. The percentage-point increase in U.S. at-risk pay is comparable to that in the other countries, although the U.S. share again begins and ends at a much higher level.

4. For evidence that LBOs raised productivity and shareholder value, see, for example, Steven Kaplan, "The Effects of Management Buyouts on Operations and Value," *Journal of Financial Economics*, Vol. 25 (1989), pp. 217-254; and Krishna G. Palepu, "Consequences of Leveraged Buyouts," *Journal of Financial Economics*, Vol. 27 (1990), pp. 247-262.

5. See Hall and Liebman (1998), cited earlier; and surveys by Kevin J. Murphy, "Executive Compensation," in *Handbook of Labor Economics*, Vol. 3 (1999), edited by O. Ashenfelter and D. Card; Robert M. Bushman and Abbie J. Smith, "Financial

Accounting Information and Corporate Governance," Working Paper, University of North Carolina, April 2001; and John E. Core, Wayne Guay, and David F. Larcker, "Executive Equity Compensation and Incentives: A Survey," Working Paper, University of Pennsylvania, January 2002.

6. Brian J. Hall and Jeffrey B. Liebman, "The Taxation of Executive Compensation," in *Tax Policy and the Economy*, NBER volume edited by J. Poterba, MIT Press, Vol. 14 (2000).

TABLE 1
CHANGES IN EXECUTIVE
PAY COMPOSITION:
INTERNATIONAL
COMPARISONS

	Share of Equity-Based Pay			Share of At-Risk Pay		
	1996	2001	Change	1996	2001	Change
Europe (9)	6%	18%	12%	24%	37%	13%
Asia (6)	6%	24%	18%	23%	39%	16%
Latin America (4)	0%	21%	21%	26%	45%	19%
Commonwealth (3)	8%	20%	12%	27%	46%	19%
U.S. (1)	32%	51%	19%	51%	68%	17%
Average (of 23 countries)	6%	22%	16%	26%	42%	16%

Source: Author's calculations using data supplied by Towers Perrin. The data are for industrial companies with at least $500 million in sales. The commonwealth countries are Australia, New Zealand, and Canada. The share of equity-based pay includes the present value of "long-term incentives," which primarily consist of stock, options, and other equity-like pay. The number in parentheses indicates the number of countries included.

Equity-based pay has also increasingly become part of the compensation package for lower-level managers and workers. Indeed, a 1999 study by William M. Mercer found that about 40% of all large U.S. companies granted stock options to at least half of their employees, more than doubling from the early 1990s. And this trend is particularly prevalent in the high-tech sector. For example, at Akamai, an e-business infrastructure services provider, the heavy use of stock options is said to reflect management's and the board's belief that "all employees should be owners and have equity."[7] In the words of Akamai president Paul Sagan, "Equity was a way of doing something that was psychological as well as financial—it was motivational to people and made them part-owners. The sense was that we were working to build a new endeavor. It was a big idea, but not without some risk—so there ought to be some big upside reward that comes with that risk."[8]

It is hard to estimate precisely the degree to which equity-based pay motivates managers and employees to increase shareholder value since cause and effect are difficult to disentangle. Nevertheless, there is now a considerable body of empirical evidence that suggests that equity holdings motivate executives to raise profitability and increase shareholder value. For example, several recent studies have found that increases in stock-based pay are followed by improvements in both accounting and stock price performance.[9]

CHALLENGES IN EQUITY-BASED PAY DESIGN

Incentives, however, can cut both ways. If not designed with care, equity-based pay plans can end up motivating behavior that *destroys* value. There are six fundamental challenges in designing equity-based pay plans that correctly align managerial (and employee) incentives with the pursuit of shareholder value:

1. mismatched time horizons;
2. gaming;
3. the value-cost "wedge";
4. the leverage-fragility tradeoff;
5. aligning risk-taking incentives; and
6. avoiding excessive compensation.

Understanding these six challenges provides important insight into the design of equity-based pay.

Challenge 1: Mismatched Time Horizons

Well-designed equity plans motivate *sustainable*, or long-run, value creation. One advantage of stock-based pay in this regard is that while accounting profits measure the past, stock prices reflect expectations about the future; they represent the market's best forecast of how current actions will affect future profitability. And investors, who can lose a lot of money by being wrong, have strong incentives to scrutinize executive decisions closely.

7. Brian J. Hall, Houston Lane, and Jonathan P. Lim, "Akamai's Underwater Options (A)," HBS Case No. 902-069, p. 5.

8. Ibid.

9. See John E. Core and David F. Larcker, "Performance Consequences of Mandatory Increases in Executive Stock Ownership," *Journal of Financial Economics*, Vol. 63 (2002), pp. 315-40. For similar evidence, see also Hamid Mehran, "Executive Compensation Structure, Ownership, and Firm Performance," *Journal of Financial Economics*, Vol. 38 (1995), pp. 163-184; John J. McConnell and Henri

Servaes, "Additional Evidence on Equity Ownership and Corporate Value," *Journal of Financial Economics*, Vol. 27 (1990), pp. 595-618; and Melissa Frye, "Equity-Based Compensation for Employees: Firm Performance and Determinants," Working Paper, University of Central Florida, 2001. Other studies describe and analyze the reasons why such evidence is hard to interpret; see, for example, Murphy (1999), Bushman and Smith (2001), and Core, Guay, and Larcker (2002), all cited in footnote 5.

**Equity-based pay is often criticized as encouraging executives to manage short-term
earnings to appease Wall Street instead of managing for long-run value creation.
Solving, or at least limiting, the problem of short-termism requires lengthening
vesting periods and strengthening executive "ownership requirements."**

Viewed in this light, equity incentives are the best protection against short-term thinking.

But even so, equity-based pay is often criticized as encouraging executives to manage short-term earnings to appease Wall Street instead of managing for long-run value creation. And given the market's occasional bouts of excessive optimism, executives may be tempted to fool the market by figuring out ways to temporarily prop up their stock prices and then cash out their equity holdings. Under pressure to boost the stock price, for example, managers may cut R&D or take other actions that increase short-term earnings at the expense of (appropriately discounted) long-run cash flow. Such "short-termism" is likely to be especially tempting for managers nearing retirement or whose jobs are on the line because of weak performance.

Solving, or at least limiting, the problem of short-termism requires lengthening vesting periods and strengthening executive "ownership requirements." While many stock and option plans have vesting periods of four or five years, others have considerably shorter vesting periods. Al Dunlap of Sunbeam had stock and options that vested over his first two years as CEO, and when Sunbeam's stock price surged, the contract was renegotiated to *reduce* the vesting period.[10] Virtually all executive contracts trigger "accelerated" vesting when an executive retires, which is likely to limit the value-creation horizons of executives approaching retirement.

Why are vesting periods so short? Executives prefer short vesting because it makes their compensation less risky, and they are often able to get their boards to go along. But boards should ask why an executive is "demanding" a short vesting period. What does that say about the executive's future plans and motivations? Or about the executive's confidence that he or she can successfully lead the company over the long haul?

Although vesting periods of five years or longer—and that extend beyond an executive's tenure with the firm—represent a significant step in the right direction, longer vesting alone is not a perfect solution to the horizon problem. Requiring executives to build up and hold company stock over a period of time—by purchasing the stock or by holding on to some portion of the stock after an option exercise—is also important for ensuring that executives have long horizons. Indeed, nearly half of large companies have formal "ownership guidelines" that require their top executives to acquire (over some number of years) company stock holdings with a value equal to some multiple (four to seven is the typical range) of annual salary.[11] Long vesting of current equity compensation, combined with requirements that executives continue to amass and hold significant equity stakes, can go a long way toward lengthening managerial value-creation horizons.

Challenge 2: Gaming

A close cousin of the horizon problem is the "gaming" problem. Equity-based pay, combined with the intense pressure to meet Wall Street's expectations, can push some executives to use accounting tricks or outright falsification of information to artificially boost the stock price.[12] Unfortunately, high-powered equity-based pay—particularly when combined with very short or no vesting restrictions—can encourage actions that are unethical and wasteful at best, and massively value-destroying and fraudulent at worst.[13] The incentives to "game the system" and engage in questionable or illegal behavior are especially strong for managers in "overpriced" companies, where the pressure to meet the unrealistic expectations of Wall Street can be very great.[14]

More generally, the temptation to game the system increases with the potential rewards (or lack of punishments) associated with gaming. Thus, managing the gaming problem requires boards and

10. See Brian J. Hall, Rakesh Khurana, and Carleen Madigan, "Al Dunlap at Sunbeam," HBS Case No. 899-218, 1999.

11. Approximately 45%; see Frederic W. Cook & Co.'s study of the 250 largest U.S. companies according to market capitalization, "2002 Top 250."

12. Some of the recent corporate scandals appear to have been associated with sharp increases in equity-based pay without a strengthening of checks and balances. In the case of Enron, for example, these internal controls and boundary systems seem to have been quite weak. See Malcolm Salter, "Innovation Corrupted: The Rise and Fall of Enron," HBS Case No. 903-032, 2003.

13. According to one study, option grants are followed by abnormal company returns, suggesting that executives are using their inside information about company performance to affect the timing of option grants (see David Yermack,

"Good Timing: CEO Stock Option Awards and Company News Announcements," *Journal of Finance*, June 1997, pp. 449-476). But another study (Jennifer N. Carpenter and Barbara Remmers, "Executive Stock Option Exercises and Inside Information," *Journal of Business*, Vol. 74 (2001), pp. 513-534) found no evidence that abnormal negative stock price performance follows executive stock sales, implying either that this type of gaming is not widespread or that executives trying to time sales are simply not very good at it. Neither study rules out the possibility that some executives have successfully gamed the system by timing the sales of their company stock.

14. Joseph Fuller and Michael C. Jensen, "Just Say No to Wall Street: Putting a Stop to the Earnings Game," *Journal of Applied Corporate Finance*, Winter 2002, pp. 41-46.

companies to pay close attention to these temptations and, especially, to strengthen internal controls. This means devoting resources to building and reinforcing corporate systems designed to monitor risky behavior and to detect and deter gaming. It may also call for improvements in the way the company communicates to its employees (through corporate codes of ethics, for example) the kinds of actions and behaviors that are clearly off-limits.[15]

One way to interpret the recent corporate scandals is that the massive increase in equity-based pay during the previous decade or two created a corresponding increase in the temptations to game without the appropriate increase in internal controls and other checks against cheating. In some respects, boards became less focused on measuring and evaluating executive performance since so much of executive compensation was tied to stock price performance and so little to other measures of executive performance. Put another way, boards had "outsourced" performance evaluation to the stock market. But while the market is a powerful and useful measure of executive performance, the heavy reliance on equity-based pay calls for perhaps more, not less, rigorous evaluation of CEO actions and performance.

Challenge 3: The Value-Cost "Wedge"

Mismatched time horizons and gaming are two fairly well-known problems that arise with equity-based pay. But an even more fundamental issue is the potentially significant disparity between the real cost of an equity grant and the value of that grant to the executive or employee. For the company, the market value of an equity grant represents the economic or "opportunity" cost of the equity—the amount the company could receive if the equity were sold to an outside investor rather than given to an executive or employee.[16] But because executives and employees are risk-averse and tend to hold personal asset portfolios that are "undiversified,"

they generally value equity-based pay at less than its market value (as estimated using standard models such as Black-Scholes). That is, because executives are forced (by vesting requirements, insider sales restrictions, or board pressure) to hold more company equity—and usually much more—than is desirable from a portfolio-diversification standpoint, they discount the value of their company equity holdings.[17]

As a general rule, then, the value to the executive of equity pay is generally lower than its cost to the company's shareholders. The value-to-cost (V/C) ratio depends on a number of factors,[18] including:

1. the degree of diversification in the executive's holdings (greater diversification increases V/C);

2. the risk aversion of the executive (greater risk aversion lowers V/C);

3. the volatility of the stock (higher volatility lowers V/C);

4. the vesting period of the equity (longer vesting lowers V/C); and,

5. in the case of stock options, the extent to which the options are in the money (the further in the money, the higher is the V/C).

In the case of stock grants, the V/C discount is fairly modest, generally on the order of 15% (or a 0.85 ratio) for an average-volatility stock. But for standard at-the-money stock option grants, there is often a significant gap between value and cost, with V/C ratios ranging in most cases from 0.8 to as low as 0.4. This suggests that option grants must be discounted (relative to their Black-Scholes value and assuming the options are not forfeited) by 20% to 60%—with 30% to 40% being "typical"—in order to determine the *executive value* of an option. And that 30% to 40% represents a "deadweight loss" to the company's shareholders—a discount that, along with the market value of the option grant itself, must be justified by performance improvements stemming from the options-linked strengthening of retention and ownership incentives.

In sum, the V/C wedge is a significant part of the price that companies must pay in order to generate

---

15. See Robert Simons, *Performance Measurement and Control Systems for Implementing Strategy* (Upper Saddle River, NJ: Prentice Hall, 2002) for a more detailed analysis of internal controls and boundary systems.

16. But if the company's cost of equity pay is thus reasonably approximated by its market value, that value must be adjusted for early exercise and expected forfeiture, both of which lower the cost on average. Furthermore, the cost to shareholders is independent of whether companies pay for the options by dilution (issuing new shares to pay option holders) or through share repurchases (which creates a cash cost). See Brian J. Hall, "Exercise on Employee Stock Option Dilution," HBS Case No. 902-162, 2002.

17. See Brian J. Hall and Kevin J. Murphy, "Optimal Exercise Prices for Executive Stock Options," *American Economic Review*, May 2000, pp. 209-215, and "Stock Options for Undiversified Executives," *Journal of Accounting and Economics*, Vol. 33 (2002); for a more detailed analysis, see also Richard A. Lambert, David F. Larcker, and Robert E. Verrecchia, "Portfolio Considerations in Valuing Executive Compensation, *Journal of Accounting Research*, Vol. 29 (1991), pp. 129-150, and Lisa K. Meulbroek, "The Efficiency of Equity-Linked Compensation: Understanding the Full Cost of Awarding Executive Stock Options," *Financial Management*, Vol. 30 (2001), pp. 5-45.

18. See Hall and Murphy (2002), cited earlier.

An even more fundamental issue is the potentially significant disparity between the real cost of an equity grant and the value of that grant to the executive or employee.

TABLE 2		Market Value		Executive (Employee) Value		Normalized Executive Value	
COMPARING THE UPSIDE POTENTIAL AND DOWNSIDE RISK OF STOCK AND OPTIONS	Stock Price	Stock	Options	Stock	Options	Stock	Options
	$0	$0	$0	$0	$0	0.00	0.00
	25	25	8	21	1	0.25	0.02
	50	50	31	43	12	0.50	0.14
	75	75	63	64	35	0.75	0.54
	100	100	100	85	65	1.00	1.00
	125	125	140	105	98	1.24	1.50
	150	150	183	126	140	1.48	2.15

Source: Executive value calculations are risk-adjusted measures (certainty equivalents), taken from Hall and Knox (2002), cited in fn. 19, and Hall and Murphy (2002), cited in fn. 17. The right-hand columns show normalizations—equal to 1.00 when the options are at-the-money to highlight percent changes in option values as they move into or out of the money. Market value calculations are based on Black-Scholes assuming 50% volatility, five-year maturity, no dividend, and a 6% risk-free interest rate.

the benefits of equity-based pay. And, as I discuss later in more detail, this inefficiency could cause many companies to shift from option awards to restricted stock, or perhaps to shift some compensation away from equity and toward cash.

Challenge 4: The Leverage-Fragility Tradeoff

Partly offsetting the value-cost inefficiency of options is the fact that they are a "leveraged" incentive device. That is, companies can grant employees more stock options than shares for the same cost to the company, since each option has a lower per-share cost than a share of stock. As a result, for a given increase in the stock price, the upside gain from a given (market) value of options is generally higher than that of stock.

Table 2 shows how the value of stock or options changes with the stock price. The entries in the table assume that one employee receives a share of stock worth $100 and another receives two at-the-money options, also worth $100. The entries in the left half of the table show how the *market value* of the stock and options (based on Black-Scholes) changes when the stock price changes. Increases in the stock price lead to exactly proportionate increases in the value of the stock award but proportionately greater increases in the value of the options package. For example, a 50% increase in the stock price (from $100 to $150) results in a 50% increase in the value of the stock award but an 83% increase in the options package.

This analysis, however, fails to take into account the value-cost wedge—which, again, stems from the tendency of risk-averse and undiversified employ-

ees and executives to value options (and stock) at less than their market values. The risk-adjusted *executive values* of stock and options are shown in the middle column of Table 2, and their "normalized" values are shown in the right-hand columns to show percentage changes in values.

Accounting for risk aversion increases the difference between option and stock values. While the value of risk-adjusted stock still moves roughly in proportion with the stock price, the value of stock options increases even more sharply (in percentage terms) when the stock price increases. Option values rise sharply in percentage terms as options move into the money. Options have great upside potential, and this leverage effect increases when the value-to-cost (V/C) ratio is taken into account.

Option Fragility. But the leverage of options operates in both directions. As shown in the table, the value of options also *falls* sharply in response to stock price *decreases*. For example, a 50% fall in the stock price (from $100 to $50) lowers the value of the options by 69% (from $100 to $31)—and by 82% (from $65 to $12) when executive risk aversion is taken into account. This helps explain why risk-averse individuals perceive far-underwater options as being almost worthless. While perhaps an attractive feature in terms of "punishing" executives (and employees) for decreases in the stock price, it also makes option incentives *fragile*. That is, as options move farther out of the money, they tend to lose their power both to motivate and to retain executives.

Moreover, the probability of options falling underwater is significant. Even at the height of the bull market in 1999, about one-third of all options held by U.S. executives in publicly traded companies were underwater.[19] In 2001, this number averaged over 50%. Although options are more fragile in bear markets, they are also fragile incentive instruments in bull markets.[20]

Managing Leverage and Fragility. Designing option packages that properly balance the tradeoff between leverage and fragility is a difficult task. There are three basic types of option plans, each of which varies in terms of leverage and fragility.[21] Large, upfront grants (also known as "megagrants"), which fix the exercise price and number of options at the beginning, are highly leveraged and have the desirable feature (especially from the perspective of the recipient) of producing a very high payoff when the stock price increases. Megagrants thus provide powerful incentives initially, but these incentives will erode if the stock price falls substantially. And if the drop in stock price is due mainly to factors beyond management's control, the result may well be the loss of good managers.

Fixed-value plans, which pay a certain predetermined Black-Scholes value each year, have the opposite problem. They are not as highly leveraged on the upside; in fact, if the stock price increases in a given year, the recipient receives fewer options and at higher exercise prices at the beginning of the next. But such plans are much more robust in the event of stock price declines. If the stock price drops in a given year, the executive actually receives a larger number of options (at the now lower exercise price) in order to hold constant the value of the annual grant.

But if fixed-value plans can help retain executives who might be demoralized by a drop in the company's stock price, the fact that such a policy can end up rewarding poor performance (by granting *more* stock options after down years) means that it can also work to undermine incentives. A partial solution to this incentive problem is provided by multi-year plans that pay a fixed *number* of at-the-money options each year. Such fixed-number plans represent a compromise between megagrants and fixed-value plans. They provide smaller rewards for exceptional performance than megagrants but stronger incentives (and hence retention power) in the event of stock price declines. At the same time, they avoid the distortion of incentives in fixed-value plans by increasing the value of option grants following good years and decreasing their value after down years.

In designing equity-based pay packages, then, companies must carefully weigh the incentive benefits of leverage against the retention costs of fragility.[22] The challenge in designing multi-year option plans is to create sufficient upside potential for incentive alignment purposes while at the same time preserving the company's ability to retain and motivate executives if the stock price falls sharply. After large price declines, many companies, in practice, grant "extra" options the following year—a form of back-door repricing.[23] But if this response makes sense when price declines are caused by factors that are clearly beyond the executives' control, it is likely to provoke unrest among stockholders when poor management and not poor market conditions is to blame.

The Case for Indexed Options. Many academics, and some in the press, argue that indexed options—where the exercise price is tied to some market or industry index—create the possibility of a tighter link between pay and performance without jeopardizing executive retention. With indexed options, executives are rewarded (or punished) according to their success in outperforming their competitors or the broad market. Yet despite what appear to be significant advantages to indexed options, they are virtually nonexistent. A survey of one thousand companies found that only one company had an indexed option plan.[24] Of course, indexed options are somewhat complex and can introduce difficult design problems. For example, what index should be used? Should the index be "beta" adjusted? Do we always want to remove industry or market changes?[25] Will executives and employees understand them?

---

19. Brian J. Hall and Thomas A. Knox, "Managing Option Fragility," NBER Working Paper No. w9059, July 2002.

20. Ibid.

21. Hall (2000), cited earlier, and Brian J. Hall, "The Design of Multi-year Stock Option Plans," *Journal of Applied Corporate Finance*, Vol. 12, No. 2 (Summer 1999), pp. 97-106.

22. For more detailed analysis of the relative merits of each of these types of plans, see Hall (2000), cited earlier.

23. See Hall and Knox (2002), cited earlier.

24. Note that the fact that indexed options are rarely used even by companies with large owners, who have strong incentives to design equity-pay instruments well, is a challenge to the view that any type of indexed options are a good idea.

25. For evidence and analysis regarding indexed options, see Lisa K. Meulbroek, "Restoring the Link Between Pay and Performance: Evaluating the Costs of Relative-Performance-Based (Indexed) Options," HBS Working Paper 02-021, 2001, and "Designing an Option Plan that Rewards Relative Performance: Indexed Options Revisited," HBS Working Paper 02-022, September 2001; see also Shane A. Johnson and Yisong S. Tian, "Indexed Executive Stock Options," *Journal of Financial Economics*, Vol. 57 (2000).

The challenge in designing multi-year option plans is to create sufficient upside
potential for incentive alignment purposes while at the same time preserving the
company's ability to retain and motivate executives if the stock price falls sharply.

TABLE 3 INCENTIVES TO TAKE RISKS: HOW OPTION VALUE CHANGES AS VOLATILITY CHANGES	At the Money	In the Money	Out of the Money
OPTION VALUE			
▪ At 50% volatility	$65.83	$180.67	$20.52
▪ At 55% volatility	$69.86	$184.78	$23.32
INCREASE IN OPTION VALUE	6%	2%	14%
RISK-TAKING ELASTICITY	0.6	0.2	1.4

Notes: All options have a five-year duration; dividends are assumed to be zero and the risk-free rate is 6.3%. For at-the-money options, the stock price is $129 and the exercise price is $129. For in-the-money options, the stock price is $260 and the exercise price is $129. For out-of-the money options, the stock price is $65 and the exercise price is $129. Risk-taking elasticity is the percentage increase in option value divided by the percentage increase in volatility.

But the main obstacle to indexed options is probably their unfavorable accounting treatment—the cost of such options must be expensed on corporate income statements. If the same treatment is eventually extended to standard at-the-money options, we are likely to see more interest in the design of indexed equity pay.[26]

Challenge 5: Aligning Risk-Taking Incentives

One of the most commonly alleged benefits of options is that they help overcome managers' natural aversion to risk. Although it is hard to know the optimal level of risk-taking for a given company, there are good reasons to believe that, without the risk-taking incentives provided by equity-based pay, executives would be overly conservative with the corporate assets they manage. There are two main reasons for this. First, it is not irrational for executives to want to avoid risky bets that may jeopardize their positions. Since they are much more likely to be fired for poor company performance, they may be wary of taking bets—even bets with high expected payoffs—that have a significant chance of failure. Second, risk-averse executives with a disproportionate amount of financial and human capital invested in one firm will rationally tend to take fewer risks (harking back to the value-cost wedge). Options promote more risk-taking because increases in the volatility of a company's stock price actually increase

the value of its options (while leaving stock prices unaffected). Options can thus add value by encouraging managers to move the firm closer to its optimal level of risk.[27]

But *standard* options do not necessarily induce more risk-taking because there are two opposing forces at work. Managers with lots of at-the-money (or in-the-money) options can become *overly* cautious, unwilling to jeopardize a large anticipated payoff that will accrue even if the stock price increases at just the T-bill rate. On the other hand, options increase in expected value in response to higher volatility and risk. Thus, although the risk aversion of executives makes them want to reduce risk following the option grant, the higher expected payoff encourages more risk-taking—and the net effect of these two factors is uncertain.

Although the effect of executive risk aversion is hard to measure, the relationship between greater risk-taking and higher payoffs can be quantified. Table 3 shows how the value of at-the-money options (where both the strike price and the stock price are equal to $129) changes when volatility increases by 10% (or five percentage points), from 50% to 55%. The option value increases by about 6%, from $65.83 to $69.86. This represents a "risk-taking elasticity" of 0.6—that is, a 10% increase in volatility causes a 6% increase in option value.

Note that the risk-taking elasticity is much smaller when the options are substantially in the

26. WebScale in "Sara's Options" (Brian J. Hall, Peter Tufano, and Joshua Musher, HBS Case No. 201-005, 2001) is a rare example.

27. Options can also encourage overly risky behavior, either because they more than offset natural biases against risk-taking or because these biases are inconsequential, especially if the options are way out of the money. Perhaps the most direct evidence we have on this issue relates to the behavior of S&L managers and owners. When the S&Ls became insolvent, or nearly so, in the 1980s, the owners/managers of these institutions were confronted with option-like payoffs (and federal deposit insurance enabled them to "borrow" from depositors without

paying for their risk-taking behavior). They would become very wealthy if the risky loans paid off, and would lose little or nothing if the bets did not pay off. The result was the S&L crisis, which necessitated a taxpayer-financed bailout on the order of hundreds of millions of dollars. For details about risk-taking incentives and behavior in banking, see Benjamin C. Esty, "Organizational Form and Risk Taking in the Savings and Loan Industry," *Journal of Financial Economics*, April 1997, pp. 25-56, and "The Impact of Contingent Liability on Commercial Bank Risk Taking," *Journal of Financial Economics*, February 1998, pp. 189-218.

money. For example, if the stock price is twice the strike price, the elasticity is only 0.2. In-the-money options thus create risk-taking incentives that are not too dissimilar from ordinary stock. Conversely, options that are substantially out of the money—in the example in the table, the stock price is half the strike price—have a risk elasticity of 1.4, or more than twice the risk elasticity of the at-the-money options.

Out-of-the-money options, then, are quite responsive to changes in volatility. And it is not hard to see why: as options fall farther out of the money, the only way to produce a positive payoff is to pursue riskier investments that widen the tails of the distribution of possible outcomes. Risk-taking incentives are thus strongest for out-of-the-money options and weakest for in-the-money options (and weaker still for stock).[28] In fact, standard (at-the-money) options—especially options that have moved significantly into the money—may actually cause executives to take *fewer* risks.[29]

Challenge 6: Avoiding Excess

Equity-based pay, especially option-based pay, generally consists of complex financial instruments, which can make valuation difficult. This presents two problems. First, to the extent that boards, managers, and employees fail to understand the value of options, and how option values change with stock price fluctuations, the usefulness of options as a compensation and incentive device is undermined. Second, the complexity of equity-based pay may lead to abuses and misallocations of value, since boards do not always understand how much value they are transferring to executives when they make option grants. And even if they do understand, boards that are overly friendly with top executives may use the complexity—and lack of transparency—of equity packages to make overly generous grants to their friends.

Apple CEO Steve Jobs was given an option grant with a Black-Scholes value in excess of $500 million.[30] Likewise, Tyco's CEO Dennis Kozlowski was granted nearly six million options—5.1 million new options in Tyco, plus 800,000 options in the Tycom subsidiary—with a Black-Scholes value of $81 million.[31] It is hard to imagine that the size of these packages was necessary for either motivation or retention purposes. Did the board fully understand the value of the transfer they were making? Would such grants have been possible if the value of the (expected) transfer from shareholders to executives was less complex? Determining the optimal level of equity-based pay is a major challenge for boards.

THE CASE FOR STOCK vs. OPTIONS

Much of the preceding discussion of the challenges in equity-pay design has focused on options, since options have been the predominant form of equity-based pay for U.S. executives during the previous two decades. Yet if the key goal of equity-based pay is to create owners out of managers, why not use stock? After all, owners are stockholders, not option holders. Using the principles discussed so far, I now outline some of the significant advantages of restricted stock—stock that vests slowly over time—relative to options.

First, the incentives provided by stock ownership to improve performance and add value—and, in fact, to stay in the current job—are not so dramatically affected by changes in the stock price. As we saw earlier, the incentives created by options are fragile in the sense that both the incentive and retention effects of options diminish as the stock price falls. This fragility of option incentives is the reason why many companies have faced an underwater options crisis. Stock has the important advantage of not being able to fall underwater. Akamai, for example, addressed its underwater options problem

---

28. Note that the risk-taking incentives for options also increase as the option package (especially an underwater package) moves close to the maturity date. That is, the "end game" for underwater options can be particularly destructive.

29. For evidence that options increase risk-taking relative to stock, see Peter Tufano, "Who Manages Risk? An Empirical Examination of Risk Management Practices in the Gold Mining Industry," *Journal of Finance*, Vol. 51 (1996). He finds evidence regarding risk management in the gold mining industry: Managers who hold options manage less gold price risk while managers who hold common stock manage more gold price risk. See also Richard A. Lambert, David F. Larcker, and Robert E. Verrecchia (1991), cited earlier, who fail to find evidence that options increase risk-taking behavior. Indeed, their evidence suggests (weakly) the opposite.

30. This is based on the author's Black-Scholes calculation. See also Geoffrey Colvin, "The Great CEO Pay Heist," *Fortune*, June 25, 2001.

31. Also, he received 800,000 shares of restricted stock on January 22, 2002, in a "retention agreement" detailed in the Tyco September 30, 2001 10-K filing. Unlike the millions of shares Kozlowski was granted in the past, 100,000 shares of this grant vest annually regardless of Tyco's performance. With the stock price closing at $47.55 a share on the day they were granted, the 800,000 shares of restricted stock were worth $38 million. Mark Maremont, "Tyco CEO's Stock Options Yield $99.9 Million Gain," *Wall Street Journal*, January 30, 2001.

Managers with lots of at-the-money (or in-the-money) options can become overly cautious, unwilling to jeopardize a large anticipated payoff...

by allowing its executives and employees to exchange their options for shares of *stock* (albeit fewer shares). That is, the company's management decided that the key advantage of options—its upside potential—was more than offset by its countervailing disadvantage—its fundamental fragility. Although less leveraged than options, restricted stock continues to provide reasonably strong ownership and retention incentives whether the stock price rises or falls.

Second, the value/cost ratio is generally higher for stock. As stated earlier, the value of equity-based pay to recipients is generally less than its true cost. Although the value/cost differential between stock and options varies with factors such as the diversification and risk aversion of the executive and the volatility of the stock, estimates suggest that the value-to-cost discount for stock is two to three times less than that of options under the most plausible assumptions. That is, while an executive holding a grant of restricted stock might value it at 80% to 90% of its cash value, he or she might value an (at-the-money) options grant at only 50% to 75% of its cash value, all other things constant.[32] And critically important, because stock is more highly valued by executives and employees (per dollar of expected cost to shareholders), it can generate stronger and more cost-effective ownership incentives than options in a wide variety of cases.[33] The relative merits of stock are particularly high when executives are fairly risk-averse and undiversified.

Finally, stock grants are much less complex to value and much more transparent—to stockholders, employees, and the press—than option grants. Deriving the value of an at-the-money option package is far trickier and involves use of a complex (and poorly understood) valuation model that produces what many practitioners call a "theoretical value." When *Fortune* magazine put Steve Jobs on the cover of a June 2001 issue and claimed that his options package was the largest-ever compensation package at $872 million, Jobs countered that his option package was worth zero since the options were underwater. An argument in which the two sides differ by nearly a billion dollars suggests a fair degree of complexity. The package had a Black-Scholes value of about $170 million at the time the article was written. But the fact that the package could be said

to be worth zero creates confusion about the issue, and confusion can lead to abuse.

It is noteworthy that most of the seemingly outrageous executive pay packages have involved options rather than stock, in part because boards better understand what they are giving away when they grant stock. To the extent that the complexity of option valuation contributes to excesses in pay, a change from option-based to stock-based pay should help curb such excesses.

BUT IS EXECUTIVE PAY REALLY "EXCESSIVE"?

With the surge in equity pay, newspapers and media reports have become saturated with stories about "executive greed" and "out-of-control pay." But despite the large increases in executive pay over the past two decades, and fairly convincing evidence of excesses in particular cases, it is hard to determine whether the overall level of executive pay is too high by looking at pay *outcomes* alone. The chief difficulty is that there is no obvious benchmark. What is "excessive"? Should executive pay be compared to employee pay? To the pay of investment bankers? The pay of European executives? What percentage of the upside (or downside) of shareholder value *should* executives receive?

Although it is hard to make strong statements about executive pay levels by looking at pay outcomes, it is possible to shed some light on this issue by looking at the pay-setting *process.* That is, it is hard to determine whether a pick-up baseball game was played fairly by looking only at the final score. But a close examination of the circumstances would allow such a determination—for example, did both teams have the same number of players, the same number of outs, and so forth.

One measure of "appropriate executive pay" is the level of compensation determined in *competitive labor markets* with a *sound process* overseen by an *independent board.* Let's analyze U.S. executive pay with regard to each of these three criteria.

Although there is clearly some degree of competition in executive labor markets, it varies widely by specific circumstances. Some executives compete with a large number of fairly similar candidates, while other executives—particularly at the CEO level—vie for positions among a pool with only a

---

32. See Hall and Murphy (2002), cited earlier.
33. Ibid.

few candidates. In such situations, the CEO has great bargaining power and the executive labor market is not highly competitive.

A second clear contributor to the rise in CEO pay is an upward bias that is built into the executive pay-setting process. The compensation committees of boards make heavy use of "pay surveys" compiled by compensation consultants on executive pay at companies that are comparable (in terms of size, industry, and so on). But since most boards feel that their executives are "above average," they elect to pay in the upper half of the distribution—for example, at the 60th or 75th percentile. Although hard to prove conclusively, the proposition that the increased use of compensation surveys has contributed to the rise in executive pay is consistent with both the views of practitioners—including executives and compensation consultants themselves—and the findings of empirical studies.[34]

In a related vein, the use of surveys was encouraged by rule changes in 1993 that required companies to detail more fully the pay of their top executives in company proxy statements. One of the hopes of the new rules was that greater disclosure would slow the increase in executive pay, with the publicity about high pay working to curb abuses. But once executives began to see more clearly how much their peers were making, they wanted more—and boards granted more. Thus, although disclosure generally curbs excesses, in this case it may have had the opposite effect.

A third potential contributor to pay excesses is the lack of board independence. While some companies have strong and independent boards, other boards are filled with close associates of the CEO who are reluctant to rein in the CEO's pay, corrupting the pay process.[35] Consistent with this, academic research suggests that companies with weaker governance structures award greater pay to top executives than do firms with stronger governance.[36] Stronger boards can play an important role both in checking the power and influence of CEOs and in curbing excessive compensation.

In sum, there are good reasons to believe that the executive pay *process* leads, at least in some cases, to excessive pay. The upward pressures on pay are particularly strong when the dominant form of executive pay is a complex and hard-to-value equity instrument like options.

ACCOUNTING FOR OPTIONS

Standard at-the-money option grants do not create an expense to the P&L, either at the time of grant or at the time of exercise. By comparison, a restricted stock grant creates an immediate expense (as does the use of nonstandard options). Options are approximately 15 times more common than stock grants in the U.S. While there are many possible explanations for the dominance of options over stock, managers and other practitioners often claim that the accounting treatment of options is among the most important. Despite the fact that companies must disclose option compensation in mandatory footnotes, a surprisingly high percentage of managers believe that investors will punish the stock price if options are expensed, forcing their companies to cut back on their use.

The accounting treatment of options is currently at the center of a heated debate. Proponents of expensing options argue that options are a genuine cost to shareholders. As Warren Buffett has observed, "If options are not compensation, what are they? If compensation is not an expense, what is it? If expenses don't go on the P&L, where do they go?"[37] Opponents of expensing options argue that options are hard to value, do not represent a cash expense, and—perhaps most important, especially in the high-tech sector—would cause companies to scale back option-based pay. According to venture capitalists John Doerr and Frederick Smith, "Counting options as an expense would actually distort and confuse the picture considerably. It could also prevent millions of workers from sharing in the success of their firms through employee ownership."[38]

34. See John M. Bizjak, Michael L. Lemmon, and Lalitha Naveen, "Does the Use of Peer Groups Contribute to Higher Levels of Executive Compensation?," Working Paper, Portland State University, December 2000, and Jay W. Lorsch, "Compensating CEOs: A Process View," Working Paper 99-013, Harvard, 1998, for evidence and analysis.

35. See Lucian A. Bebchuk, Jesse M. Fried, and David I. Walker, "Managerial Power and Rent Extraction in the Design of Executive Compensation," *University of Chicago Law Review*, Vol. 69 (3), pp. 751-846, for evidence and analysis that CEOs have too much power in the pay-setting process.

36. John E. Core, Robert W. Holthausen, and David F. Larcker, "Corporate Governance, CEO Compensation, and Firm Performance," *Journal of Financial Economics*, Vol. 51 (1999), pp. 371-406.

37. B. Quinn, "Letters to the Editor: Stock Options: Heads We Win, Tails You Lose," *The Wall Street Journal*, April 19, 2002.

38. John D. Doerr and Frederick W. Smith, "Leave Options Alone," *New York Times*, April 5, 2002.

> **Because stock is more highly valued by executives and employees (per dollar of expected cost to shareholders), it can generate stronger and more cost-effective ownership incentives than options in a wide variety of cases.**

But none of this alters the reality that options represent a real cost to shareholders, and that treating one type of costly compensation instrument as "free" while expensing others creates an uneven playing field that distorts executive (and employee) pay practices. The current accounting controversy raises the possibility that options are also being overused for rank-and-file employees. U.S. companies have increasingly pushed their option plans lower into the organization. As mentioned earlier, a recent study by William M. Mercer found that about 40% of all large companies have granted options to at least half of their employees, a more than doubling from the early 1990s. Moreover, a high percentage of options—about two-thirds according to one study[39]—are held by non-executive employees.

Although options clearly help firms attract and retain employees (option fragility notwithstanding), the evidence that broad-based plans are effective in increasing firm performance is at best mixed.[40] While a broad-based option plan has the advantage of reminding employees that the firm has owners, and perhaps contributes to an "ownership culture," such plans are a fairly blunt incentive instrument. From the perspective of any one worker in a very large company, the connection between effort and value is fairly small and likely to be swamped by other factors. The fact that broad-based option plans are not a very targeted incentive device, combined with the low value/cost efficiency of options, suggests that options are being used too heavily in broad-based compensation plans, and that companies should consider making greater use of restricted stock and cash-based compensation.

CONCLUSION

There has been a dramatic rise in equity-based pay during the past two decades. When structured properly, equity pay can add value by aligning the incentives of managers and shareholders while attracting and retaining qualified executives. But it is not at all clear that equity pay has been well structured, especially given its uneven accounting treatment, which may well have created a value-destroying bias in favor of options and against cash, stock, and other forms of compensation.[41] Without rules that level the accounting playing field between options and other forms of pay, it is difficult to know the extent of this bias or how much corporate value, if any, is being destroyed.

In the coming years, new rules and regulations, and perhaps changes in corporate governance, may slow or even reverse the growth in equity-based pay for executives. But while the form of equity pay may change, the large and growing influence of institutional investors is likely to ensure that equity-based pay remains a significant component of executive compensation in the U.S. during the next decade. For good reasons, owners want managers to hold equity. Thus, although some of the methods have been called into question, the goal of creating ownership incentives is unlikely to disappear. The challenge that remains is curbing pay excesses while experimenting with new (and old) ways of linking executive rewards and long-run value creation.

39. John E. Core and Wayne R. Guay, "Stock Option Plans for Non-Executive Employees," *Journal of Financial Economics*, Vol. 61 (2001), pp. 253-287.

40. See Core and Guay (2001), cited above; Richard A. Lambert, David F. Larcker, and Christopher D. Ittner, "The Structure and Performance Consequences of Equity Grants to Employees of New Economy Firms," Working Paper, University of Pennsylvania, January 2001; and Simi Kedia and Abon Mozumdar, "Performance Impact of Employee Stock Options," Working Paper, Harvard, August 2002, for evidence.

41. Brian J. Hall and Kevin J. Murphy, "Expense Options to Level the Playing Field," *Boston Globe*, October 6, 2002.

CHAPTER 2: SECTION 2.3
Incentives and Organizational Structure

The first two sections of this chapter focus on the Board and incentive compensation. But these internal governance mechanisms do not arise in a vacuum. Rather, the leadership provided by CEOs, the business environment, the structure of the organization (be it centralized or decentralized decision-making), and the firm's financing polices all interact to influence other elements of a firm's governance structure.

In *The CEO: A Visible Hand in Wealth Creation?*, C.K. Prahalad and Yves L. Doz suggest that the role of the CEO in the corporate value creation process has increased significantly in recent years. In defining the CEO's role, the article begins by noting that there are three distinct elements of sustained wealth creation in large corporations with multiple lines of business. The first and most basic is portfolio selection, the choice of the lines of business in which to operate. The second is formulation of the value creation model, which must explain how this particular set of businesses expected to add value over and above the sum of the individual parts. The third element is the internal governance system, which establishes the corporate structure and the performance measurement and incentive system, and, perhaps even more important, defines and communicates the corporate values that are expected to inform the strategic and operational priorities of all managers and employees.

Prahalad and Doz argue that "the essence of the work of the CEO" is to develop and maintain a balanced relationship among these three elements of wealth creation. In working to achieve this balance, CEOs are inevitably faced with "dilemmas" that must be managed—in particular, the need to balance continuity and change and to maintain the integrity of short-term performance disciplines while encouraging not only investment in growth opportunities (which can hurt near-term performance), but also experimentation and collaboration among business units (which are difficult to measure and reward with most performance measurement and incentive schemes).

Our next two articles illustrate aspects of incentives and organization structure at particular companies. In *Decentralization, Incentives, and Value Creation: The Case of JLG Industries*, Heidi Treml and Ken Lehn provide a case study of JLG Industries,

a manufacturer of aerial work platforms, over the period 1993-1998. During that period, the company achieved dramatic improvements in operating efficiency and created substantial value for shareholders. Most of the value created by JLG was traced to three factors: a highly successful product development program that generated substantial revenue, large cost savings resulting from improvements in operations, and a dramatic reduction in inventories. The authors attribute JLG's success to a strategic initiative that focused attention on key value drivers, decentralized decision-making, and strengthened incentives for employees throughout the organization. In the early 1980s JLG adopted several knowledge-based management techniques, including TQM and just-in-time inventory, but at that time the company's decision-making was more centralized and employee incentives did not correspond to strategic goals. After the departure of its founder in 1993, JLG decentralized decision-making, strengthened employees' incentives, and achieved enormous success. Evidence from the JLG case supports the argument that the benefits of TQM and related management techniques are most likely to be achieved when companies have organizational structures and incentives that encourage the most effective use of those techniques.

In *Adding Value for Shareholders in South Africa: An Analysis of the Rembrandt Restructuring*, Brian Kantor focuses on restructuring by "unbundling," which involves the selling or otherwise splitting off of unrelated businesses. The focus of this paper is on the South African corporate landscape, which has recently changed from a system dominated by family-controlled groups of companies. Holding companies like Anglo-American, the largest and best known of all the family groups, have become more focused and more international (in those lines of business they have chosen to retain). At the same time, they have relinquished a good deal of control to outside shareholders.

But if unbundling has succeeded in adding value in some cases, it is by no means a panacea for shareholders. Value is likely to be added for shareholders only when such restructurings are expected to increase the efficiency of existing operations, discontinue value-destroying investments, or encourage new investment only in projects that are expected to return more than their cost of capital. For this reason, a restructuring like the one recently completed by the Rembrandt group—one that simply divided the company into two major parts while retaining the old managerial control structure—does not hold out much promise for shareholders.

The final two articles in the section focus on highly leveraged transactions and the effect of corporate financing decisions on managerial decision making and performance.

In *Leveraged Recaps and the Curbing of Corporate Overinvestment*, David and Diane Denis conclude from their study of 29 large leveraged recapitalizations that the companies were overinvesting prior to undertaking these highly leveraged transactions. As Michael Jensen has suggested, the massive substitution of debt for equity in such recaps, typically undertaken in response to hostile takeover pressure, forced managements to pay out "free cash flow" rather than continue seeking corporate growth at the expense of their shareholders. To cite a representative example, in the case of Goodyear Tire, the company's leveraged payout of $2.2 billion to shareholders brought about a reversal of the company's disastrous diversification strategy (into oil, natural gas, and aerospace), forcing it to return its focus on the tire industry, where it now appears to be prospering.

In *Performance, Leverage, and Ownership Structure in Reverse LBOs*, Robert Holthausen and David Larcker analyze the performance of LBO companies that return to public ownership through an IPO. The aim of the study was to track the performance of reverse LBOs and to reveal any association between operating performance and changes in leverage and ownership structure. Among the principal findings of the study were the following: Despite a substantial decline in leverage ratios and equity ownership by insiders at the time of the IPO, the equity ownership of reverse LBOs remained more concentrated and the leverage remained higher than that of public companies in the same industries. The operating performance of reverse LBOs was significantly better than that of the median firm in their industries both in the year prior to and the year of the IPO. Although there is some evidence of deterioration in the performance of the reverse LBO firms, they continue to outperform their industry competitors for four fiscal years after the IPO. Moreover, larger reductions in the percentage of equity owned by managers and other insiders at the time of the IPO were associated with larger declines in operating performance. The stock price performance of reverse LBOs after going public also appears more "rational" than that of other IPOs; that is, there was less initial underpricing and no sign of the negative longer term returns associated with IPOs in general.

THE CEO: A VISIBLE HAND IN WEALTH CREATION?

by C. K. Prahalad, University of Michigan, and
Yves L. Doz, INSEAD*

D uring the past decade, many CEOs of large companies have become highly visible public figures. Lee Iaccoca of Chrysler, in particular, can be credited with launching a new style of corporate leadership—one that includes a public persona for the CEO. Consider, for example, the visibility of Jack Welch, Bill Gates, Anita Roddick of the Bodyshop, Jeff Bezos of Amazon.com, and, most recently, Carly Fiorina of Hewlett-Packard. The actions of these CEOs are chronicled by business journalists and their strategies held up to public scrutiny. The performance of companies, good or bad, is often attributed—not only by the press, but by the directors and shareholders of the companies—to the CEO's personal business savvy and leadership.

But if greater visibility has certainly focused attention on CEOs as individuals, does a more visible corporate leadership reflect a new reality in the internal governance of large corporations? Do CEOs now matter more than they did before? In exploring these issues, we will focus on a more fundamental set of questions: How does the CEO help create wealth in a large firm? What is the value added of the CEO and the top management team in the new competitive environment? And does the emergence of the CEO as a public figure necessarily represent a clear gain for the firm, or does it create a new set of problems that must be addressed?

THE GROWING IMPORTANCE OF THE CEO AND TOP MANAGEMENT

The past decade has brought unprecedented change for many companies and their CEOs. A wide variety of factors—deregulation, global competition, emerging markets, knowledge-driven competition, technological discontinuities, hostile takeovers, excess capacity, growing customer expectations, and the rise of nontraditional competitors—have forced a fundamental reexamination of the wealth-creation process in large corporations.[1] Industry and corporate transformation is occurring everywhere, from utilities to financial services. The job of the CEO is to help navigate the firm through this complex and continuously evolving competitive terrain.

In the face of such change, top managers cannot take a "hands off" approach or content themselves with effective stewardship of the assets they inherit at the beginning of their tenure. Shareholders demand value creation and, in many cases, this requires strategic action by the CEO. Active investors have also shown themselves increasingly willing to force the issue. In North America, institutional investors played a major role in ousting the CEOs of General Motors, Westinghouse, American Express, and Sears—and the CEOs of Suez and Alcatel in Europe experienced a similar fate. Bigger risks beget bigger rewards, and over the past decade CEO compensation has risen spectacularly, as well as becoming

---

*An earlier draft of this paper was presented at the Twentieth Anniversary Conference of Euroforum, El Escorial, Spain, in September 1995. Support from Euroforum in preparing this paper is gratefully acknowledged.

1. See G. Hamel and C.K. Prahalad, "Competing for the Future," *Harvard Business Review*, Vol. 72, No. 4 (July-August, 1994), pp 122-130.

FIGURE 1
THE CEO: A VISIBLE HAND IN STRATEGIC ARCHITECTURE

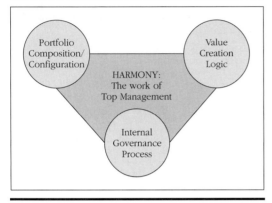

more closely tied to the firm's performance. At the same time, stock prices have become more responsive to who is appointed to the top position; investors clearly believe the CEO matters.

The role of top management is no longer just control and coordination; it is anticipating, leading, and managing change—and articulating the rationale for such change to employees as well as to securities analysts. Change involves re-examining the firm's portfolio of businesses, rethinking how that portfolio creates value for shareholders, and reworking the internal processes of governance—in short, it involves reinventing the company. Top managers must simultaneously manage the process of "forgetting old ways" and "learning new ones" both *for themselves* and for their organizations. At the same time, CEOs must recognize the existing strengths of their organizations and strike a balance between necessary change and the continuity that is essential to the self-confidence and commitment of managers and employees. The task is intellectually demanding, politically sensitive, and administratively complex.

In the pages that follow we examine the role of the CEO and wealth creation in three parts. First, we outline a framework for thinking about wealth creation in a diversified firm. This involves careful management of the interactions between the business units that make up the firm's portfolio of assets, the CEO's logic for value creation, and the firm's internal governance process. Second, we identify some of the key dilemmas CEOs face in the process—for example, how to resolve tensions that arise

in decentralized governance structures between the discipline of meeting near-term financial targets and a company's ability to pursue longer-range growth opportunities (particularly those requiring cooperation among business units). Finally, we discuss the implications of the emergence of the CEO as a public persona for the effectiveness of wealth creation.

THE WEALTH CREATION PROCESS

Our understanding of the process of sustained wealth creation in the context of rapidly changing competition can be thought of as the interaction of the three interlinked elements shown in Figure 1. Sustained wealth creation begins with a company's portfolio of businesses. In a changing environment, managers must periodically reevaluate this portfolio in the context of the assets and resources that they want to own (or at least have access to). For this reason, portfolio reconfiguration tends to be high on the list of new CEOs, who are typically less constrained than incumbents by past commitments.

A business portfolio carries with it, whether explicitly or not, a value creation logic (or "business model," as many people call it) that answers the question: How is this particular portfolio of assets expected to create value over and above the sum of the values of each business or asset category standing alone? A portfolio of businesses is expected to add value in a particular way, which in turn affects the choice of assets to be added to or eliminated from the portfolio. Thoughtful CEOs work on both portfolio configuration and the business model at the same time because the two must be consistent with and reinforce each other.

The portfolio composition and the business model then drive the design of the firm's internal governance system. Governance starts with a decision about corporate structure—that is, where to establish the boundaries between the basic organizational building blocks (or business units) that constitute the diversified firm. The governance system also includes the processes and values that govern the performance disciplines and strategic and operational priorities of the different business units, and the relationships and dialogue between them. Defined in this way, internal governance has a significant influence on how the portfolio of businesses is managed. It is the value creation logic in action, and can profoundly affect the capacity of the firm to create wealth.

As we emphasize throughout this paper, wealth creation demands a constructive and harmonious relationship among these three key elements: the business portfolio, the approach to value creation, and the internal governance system. Developing and maintaining such a relationship—and ensuring that it evolves in the face of changing circumstances—is the essence of the work of top management. We examine each of the three aspects of wealth creation below, while stressing the importance of their interdependencies.

Assets and Resources: The Portfolio Configuration

Portfolio reconfiguration is perhaps the most visible manifestation of CEO action in most large corporations today. Many companies undertook extensive diversification programs in the 1970s and early 1980s only to refocus their portfolios in the late 1980s and early 1990s. What was the rationale for all this activity?

In almost all cases, portfolio reconfiguration is based on a fresh assessment of the meaning, basis, and value of relatedness among businesses in the portfolio, often resulting from a new value creation logic. Relatedness is hardly a new concept in strategic management, but the emphasis has shifted from viewing it as an objective, economic *given* to seeing it as the partly subjective result of managerial thought and imagination—of management choices about the kind of value creation logic they wish to pursue. Richard Rumelt's 1974 study of corporate diversification has served as the foundation for a large body of research on diversification and performance that has grown up in the last 25 years.[2] Rumelt came up with four classifications of multi-business companies— "related," "related linked," "related constrained," and "unrelated or conglomerate"—based on three variables: (1) specialization ratio (percentage of business attributable to the firm's largest single business), (2) vertical ratio (percentage of revenues attributable to the largest group of vertically integrated businesses within the firm), and (3) related ratio (percentage of revenues attributable to the largest group of related businesses within the firm). While sales data were used to sort the diversification patterns into one of the four diversification strategies, the underlying logic for classification was based on similarities among product markets and technology. The tests of relatedness in this schema are objective in the sense that an outsider studying the portfolio should arrive at the same conclusion as insiders.

In an extension of Rumelt's work, a 1994 study[3] concluded that many firms are "coherent" diversifiers, in the sense that their pattern of diversification is consistent with their learning and skill base. This pattern of diversification is "idiosyncratic" or "path-dependent"—that is, not likely to be produced by a different management team with a different set of skills or experience or even by the same management team at a different starting point. What might appear to be unrelated diversification in the earlier Rumelt schema may appear to be "coherent" here.

If relatedness can be defined along various dimensions, then here are some different ways to think about it:

1. Business selection: One of the cornerstones of General Electric's strategy has been to choose only businesses in leading positions, or with the potential to achieve such positions. This value creation logic was clearly articulated by CEO Jack Welch. It is based on dominating an industry—being #1 or #2, or out. Less clearly stated, but well understood, are other assumptions behind the logic, including relentless cost reduction and avoiding businesses subject to intense foreign competition. When Jack Welch became CEO, many of GE's businesses, such as lighting, appliances, and medical systems, were already dominant players with world-scale (if not worldwide) operations. Extensive cost cutting prepared them for effective global competition. These underlying strengths allowed the creation of considerable shareholder value from selective divestitures and acquisitions.

Business selection can also be premised on industry consolidation. Highly fragmented industries, because of the large number of small firms, are often characterized by a low average level of general management skills, underinvestment in technologies, and an inability to capture the value of scale that may be *invisible to the incumbents*. In such circumstances, an effective management team with access to capital can achieve scale economies and perhaps create barriers to entry by assembling a large portfolio of industry assets (typically through acquisi-

2. R. Rumelt, *Strategy, Structure and Economic Performance* (Boston, Harvard University Press, 1974).

3. G. Dosi, D. Teece, and S. Winter, "Understanding Corporate Coherence," *Journal of Economic Behavior & Organization*, Vol. 23, (1994), pp. 1-30.

Over the past decade CEO compensation has risen spectacularly, as well as becoming more closely tied to the firm's performance. At the same time, stock prices have become more responsive to who is appointed to the top position; investors clearly believe the CEO matters.

tions) with the aim of rationalizing the industry. This approach was used repeatedly in the U.S. and U.K. during the 1960s and '70s to consolidate industries such as cement, elevators, and retailing. Today it can be seen operating in industries like financial services, entertainment, telecom, and the airlines. ABB's strategy of consolidating the electrical power business is a good example of this approach. Corning's highly successful entry into medical diagnostics labs is another.

2. Parenting similarities: Creating value from a diverse corporate portfolio is easier when the businesses share common strategic and managerial characteristics. For example, Hanson Trust until recently could be characterized as an "unrelated diversifier," with businesses as varied as brick making, coal, jacuzzis, and chemicals. Nevertheless, Hanson's managers believed that their businesses had common characteristics and required similar management skills. Hanson's criteria for fit into their portfolio were as follows: basic businesses providing essential products (as opposed to high-tech, people-intensive businesses); good management at the operating level; reasonable asset backing; stable rate of change; and strong and predictable cash flow.[4] This view is based on what Goold and Campbell have called the "parenting advantage"[5]—the capacity of corporate management to add value to the business units based on a common set of corporate capabilities. Interestingly, though, Lord Hanson was not convinced that Hanson's advantage was sufficiently corporate (rather than individual) that the firm's prosperity would survive the death of his partner and his own imminent retirement. In early 1996, he announced the split of Hanson Trust into four separate companies in different sectors.

3. Core Competencies: Considering relatedness from the standpoint of core competencies yields a different view from that of parenting advantage.[6] A highly diversified portfolio like Cargill's (consisting of commodity trading, meat processing, salt, fertilizer, mini steel mills, financial services, orange juice, animal feeds, and seeds) would clearly be classified by outsiders as "unrelated." But the firm's top managers think and act otherwise, as reported by Cargill's CEO Whitney MacMillan:

Experience in the handling of bulk commodities, knowledge of trading, processing expertise, international understanding, risk management; these are the attributes of Cargill that underpin all our businesses. These core competencies represent the collective learning and judgment of our 125 years of experience in all our businesses. They have been built over the years as the result of an unending process of refinement and improvement. They help hold us together and give us a sense of unity of purpose that would otherwise be difficult to define. They drive our development of new business opportunities and shape our ability to respond to future challenges.

The concept of relatedness at Cargill is based not on product-market configuration or technology similarities, but on shared competencies and knowledge. Different businesses within Cargill demand different skills from the parent (in contrast to Hanson's approach), but all share a common set of core competencies. Cargill is not alone in taking this approach. Many other seemingly diversified firms—3M, Canon, NEC, Sony, P&G, and ABB are examples that come to mind—would consider their diversification strategy as "related" in the same way.

4. Interbusiness linkages: In some portfolios, managing the interlinkages provides value. For example, the distribution efficiencies and clout with retailers of a Procter &Gamble are greater than if each of its stand-alone businesses independently negotiated terms with major distributors such as Wal-Mart. Similarly, ABB involves many of its different businesses in major contracts in emerging economies such as China and India, and GE adds the strength of its financial service operations to support such deals. Thus, P&G, ABB, and GE have to manage their businesses differently from Hanson, which deliberately sacrificed any benefits from coordination in order to emphasize accountability for performance. Hanson made no pretense of encouraging synergies between its acquisitions, as illustrated by the operation of two of Hanson subsidiaries, Imperial Tobacco Limited and Elizabeth Shaw (a chocolate firm). Although both were based in Bristol, England, and delivered goods to newsagents and corner shops throughout the U.K., Hanson

4. P. Haspeslagh and C. Taubmann, *Hanson Plc.*, INSEAD case study (1992).
5. M. Goold and A. Campbell, "How Corporate Parents Add Value to the Stand-Alone Performance of their Business," *Business Strategy Review*, Vol. 5,

No. 4 (Winter 1994), pp. 33-56.
6. C. K. Prahalad and G. Hamel, "The Core Competence of the Corpora-

opposed any sharing of distribution resources on the ground that any economies of scale would likely be outweighed by "the general sloppiness that would result if each company thought that distribution was the other's problem."[7]

5. Complex Strategic Integration: Core competencies that transcend individual businesses in the portfolio not only create the basis for value creation by enabling the discovery of valuable new interlinkages, they also help identify new business opportunities that draw on competencies from multiple units and reconfigure them in creative ways.[8] The goal here is to create a portfolio that is capable of generating new businesses *internally*, thereby building a capacity for self-revitalization. Hewlett-Packard, with its clear focus on creating businesses at the intersection of Measurement, Computing, and Communications (its so-called "MC2" strategy), represents one such portfolio. In 1994, more than 60% of HP's sales came from businesses that did not exist in 1990, and nearly all the growth came from products and businesses that were developed internally. Value creation in such cases is as much about growth and reinventing the business portfolio based on core competencies as about rationalizing existing assets or defending existing businesses.

In sum, identifying the appropriate configuration of the portfolio is a top management task—one that often involves pursuing more than just conventional notions of "relatedness." In approaching this task, CEOs must attempt to answer the following questions:

1. Is the value of the bundle of assets and businesses combined within a single company greater than the sum of the values of these businesses as independent units? The portfolio must benefit the business units, and the business units must add value to the portfolio. The relatedness, or potential for "synergies," among the businesses in the portfolio may not be obvious, and thus the most valuable dimensions of relatedness often need to be discovered.

2. What is the underlying value creation logic for the chosen portfolio? While some CEOs such as Lord Hanson focus on maximizing efficiency at the business unit level, CEOs like Percy Barnevik at ABB attempt to develop a composite value creation strategy that takes advantage of synergies among

businesses. How good is the match between a company's portfolio of assets and its value creation model? The attempt to define the portfolio's logic raises two questions: What kinds of assets do we want and what connections between them do we need? The answers to these questions are clearly interdependent. The logic of the portfolio is the result of two things: the history of the company (the cards that one is dealt) and the creative interpretation of opportunities by top management of the firm (what one does with the hand). By developing a process for this creative interpretation of opportunities, the CEO plays an important role in determining the composition of the portfolio.

The Value Creation Logic: The CEO's Theory of Relatedness

Implicit in the choice of portfolio configuration, if not explicitly articulated by the CEO, are assumptions about how the firm will compete and create value over and above what its separate businesses could achieve. Value creation logic is about understanding the business model, resource intensity, risks, and the critical competencies needed for success as a diversified corporation. To clarify the point, let us consider some explicit statements of the value creation logic.

Each one of Hanson Trust's businesses is strategically defensible and differentiated. Each commands significant market share. These businesses are unlikely to attract new competitors or be subject to radical technological change. Under these circumstances, good general management disciplines—budgeting, controls, incentives, autonomy, and low overheads—can provide opportunities for extraordinary value creation. From the perspective of a business, the advantage of belonging to the Hanson portfolio is derived from the general management disciplines provided (or imposed) by the parent. From the perspective of the group, it is having strategically defensible businesses that enjoy monopoly types of advantage. Further, high quality managerial skills might not be available to the businesses as stand-alone entities in some mature industries. In sum, Hanson is able to attract and retain better managers than "member" companies could on their own and to give them better management tools.

---

tion," *Harvard Business Review* (May-June 1990), pp. 79-91.

7. Haspeslagh and Taubmann (1992), cited earlier.
8. R. Burgelman and Y.L. Doz, "Complex Strategic Integration in the Lean

To an extent General Electric follows a similar logic, but on a global scale. As stated earlier, the original portfolio logic was to assemble "good businesses." GE sold businesses such as consumer electronics where the #1 or #2 criteria could not be met and built up its activities where it could—for example, in medical imaging. The portfolio restructuring at GE during Jack Welch's regime was accomplished by divesting more than $7 billion worth of businesses and acquiring more than $17 billion. More than 52% of GE today is in financial services. As in the Hanson business model, the GE management process imposed discipline on the various businesses and improved their performance. But, at the same time—and in contrast to the value creation logic of Hanson and other conglomerates—GE has also been successful in selectively managing *interbusiness* linkages—for instance, using its finance arm to lease large systems such as jet engines, power plants, or medical systems. On the other hand, GE has not succeeded in creating new opportunities in emerging businesses such as "factory with a future," where being #1 or #2 had no meaning. When GE invested in it, the factory automation industry was just emerging, boundaries of businesses were unclear, and the firm faced nontraditional competitors. In this business as in others, GE went for scale. After a series of acquisitions and some experimentation, GE quit the business. The GE approach to portfolio selection applies only to existing businesses with reasonably clear boundaries. Being #1 in the multimedia industry, at its current stage of development, means very little, as it did in factory automation ten years ago.

While the value creation logic at GE is clear (and blindly adopted by many CEOs as a model for their own company) and its success widely acknowledged, it is important to recognize that Welch started with a distinctive set of endowments—one available to few other firms or their CEOs. Take the case of Motorola, which did not begin with a stable of large, dominant businesses that could be sheltered from Japanese and European competition. Motorola's value creation strategy had to be different. It is based on uncompromising pursuit of quality ("6 sigma"), continuous and radical improvements ("10 X"), and positioning the firm at the beginning of the wave of growth in emerging businesses such as semiconduc-

tors and mobile and cellular communication and in emerging markets such as China, the ASEAN, and India. Another key element in Motorola's strategy is the integration of new technologies and markets into mutually supportive patterns. Implicit in the company's value creation logic is the capacity to bet on new products, scale up, grow rapidly, price aggressively, be global, and cannibalize old products with new.

Dynamic Evolution. In developing their portfolio configuration and value creation logic, managers must develop a view of likely patterns of industry development as well as a strategy for influencing that development. Intellectual leadership of an industry is a critical ingredient in developing new businesses.[9] There are many examples of inventing new value creation models for single businesses, even in well-established industries. Here are a few:

■ Swatch took leadership in the wristwatch business by bringing high fashion, European design, excellence and low cost in manufacturing and technology, and continuous product development to an industry where the Swiss had lost leadership. It is the marriage of high fashion with high technology and efficiency that represents a new model of value creation. Seiko and Citizen also improved efficiency, but failed to recognize the demand for fashion à la Swatch.
■ Nike brought advertisement intensity, design, advanced technology, market segmentation, and global logistics to an old, traditional industry.
■ Levi is experimenting with mass customization—uniquely fitted jeans "just for you"—based on new information technology and new manufacturing as well as logistics capability.

Benetton, Charles Schwab, Wal-Mart, CNN, Southwest Airlines, and British Airways are other examples of companies that have invented a new model of value creation for a business.

Discovery of a new value creation model starts with developing industry foresight through a thoughtful and imaginative assessment of underlying market drivers, trends, and critical discontinuities. Top managers must ensure that the industry foresight is based on a deep understanding of the forces of change. This calls for a process of discovery inside the firm—one that involves a large enough number of people at all levels in the organization to ensure that a wide variety of inputs are gathered and

Multibusiness Corporation," INSEAD Working Paper, 97/03/SM (1997).

processed.[10] The goal of this process is not to accumulate more analytical insights, but to create a new "synthesis," if you will—one that draws on perspectives from all the different disciplines within the firm to identify new opportunities that are often "invisible" to industry incumbents.[11] Having used this process to develop a working hypothesis, managers then need to validate it through a process of market-based experiments at low cost.

Moving from individual businesses to companies consisting of related, but diverse competencies and markets adds a level of complexity. Part of the difficulty stems from how well the portfolio and the value creation logic hold together. An innovative business model and the discovery of new opportunities are bound to influence the approach to portfolio configuration. By the same token, a decision on the portfolio suggests an implicit value creation logic. For example, Hanson and Hewlett-Packard differ sharply in their portfolio, in their opportunity horizon, and therefore in their value creation logic. Few CEOs deal with this relationship explicitly. While the portfolio is frequently reconfigured, the underlying value creation model is not explicitly reexamined. Identifying a set of business opportunities based on *existing* core competencies and identifying a set of core competencies that will be needed to manage a desired portfolio of businesses *in the future* are both critical tasks—and both call for creative thinking. Forward-looking managers will use such competency assessments to discover new patterns of relationships in their current portfolio of businesses as well as new businesses that could profitably expand the portfolio.[12]

The value creation logic then becomes the intellectual link between the actual business portfolio and the governance of the firm. Together with the tangible assets necessary to execute it, the basic business models for individual businesses and for their integration determine the competencies that have to be developed and maintained. For example, in a portfolio where value is created by continuous development of new products and businesses drawing on competencies and expertise that cut across existing business unit boundaries, it is important to manage relationships between the business units. Also critical is a company's ability to shift resources across boundaries to address emerging opportunities.[13] In this sense, stability of business unit charters is not necessarily a virtue—and is likely to become a handicap.[14]

Articulating the Reason for the Portfolio. Articulating the linkage between portfolio configuration and the value creation logic is not easy for most CEOs. First of all, the two often remain separate in their minds. While CEOs are willing to discuss the logic for the portfolio configuration very explicitly, they do not often articulate a model of value creation. The failure to do so often leads managers to evaluate major acquisitions and other investment opportunities largely on their own merits—a practice that results in systematic underestimation of the value of interbusiness linkages and limited potential for more valuable portfolio configurations.

Second, highly popular business models—again, like GE's—are often uncritically adopted by managers, who are thereby prevented from taking a more strategic look at their portfolio configuration. Restructuring and reengineering are among the most popular "non-strategic" value creation approaches; both are fundamentally cost-reduction models. Cycle time reduction is another. While attention to cost, productivity, and cycle times is crucial, the focus is only on efficiencies. Wealth creation is also about growth and new business development. Once a top management team accepts the idea that sustained wealth creation must include the achievement of profitable growth, cost-reduction models become less important. While the continuous push for efficiencies remains critical, the quest for growth assumes an even larger role in the value creation logic and portfolio decisions. The vogue of reengineering, and the very real productivity gains that have been achieved from it, have blinded many CEOs to the need to be strategic in how they think about value creation in their firms.

Third, the portfolios of firms are not always amenable to a coherent value creation logic. Take the case of Kodak. In the early 1990s, then-CEO Kay Whitmore struggled to identify and validate a port-

---

9. See Hamel and Prahalad (1994), cited earlier.
10. See G. Hamel, "Strategy as Revolution," *Harvard Business Review*, Vol. 74, No 4 (July-August, 1996) pp. 69-83.
11. See G. Szulanski and Y. L. Doz, "Strategy Formulation as Disciplined Imagination," INSEAD Working Paper, 95/56/SM (1995).

12. See Burgelman and Doz (1997), cited earlier.
13. See C. Galunic and S. Rodan, "Resource Combinations in the Firm: Knowledge Structures and the Potential for Schumpeterian Innovation," INSEAD Working Paper, 97/75/OB (1997).
14. See C. Galunic and K. M. Eisenhardt, "The Evolution of Intracorporate Domains: Divisional Charter Losses in High-Technology, Multidivisional Corpora-

> While the continuous push for efficiencies remains critical, the quest for growth assumes an even larger role in the value creation logic and portfolio decisions. The vogue of reengineering, and the very real productivity gains that have been achieved from it, have blinded many CEOs to the need to be strategic in how they think about value creation.

folio logic; and some of his assumptions, such as the advantage of being active in both chemicals and pharmaceuticals, were questioned from the start. In 1993 Kodak's portfolio consisted of chemical imaging (film and paper), copiers, printers, medical reagents, over-the-counter and proprietary drugs, bulk chemicals, and cleaners. Under the next CEO, George Fisher, the portfolio was pruned and redefined as Imaging Businesses (chemical and electronic) designed to capitalize on linkages and new opportunities. Other businesses were divested, including Eastman Chemicals, Sterling Drugs, and Lysol Cleaners.

Fourth, because the process of developing a value creation model and integrating it with the business is a creative and time-dependent process, mistakes can and often do happen. For example, Daimler-Benz diversified all through the 1980s due to the conviction of Edzard Reuter and his team that they would become a "one-stop shop" for all the travel and communication needs of society—with major investments in businesses ranging from motor, air, and rail transportation to telecommunications. (Similar visions of one-stop shopping supplied the rationale for large numbers of acquisitions in the financial services and multimedia products industries.) However, developments since then suggest that consumers do not place a high enough value on one-stop shopping to justify the costs associated with building a network of unrelated businesses. Recognizing this, Reuter's successor, Jürgen Shrempp, quickly started shedding businesses such as Fokker and Dornier in commuter planes, and most of AEG's businesses in electronics. Other businesses were put into joint ventures with partners for which they are more strategic—for example, rail transportation joined with ABB, and missiles and satellites with Matra—perhaps as a prelude to divestment. In contrast to Daimler-Benz under Reuter, other companies may suffer when the CEOs' value creation logic is too limiting, putting too much emphasis on business autonomy and so neglecting opportunities for valuable interunit linkages. AT&T's conspicuous failure to penetrate emerging markets and its ultimate split-up into three companies may be examples of underachievement stemming from a flawed design. Al-

though the company's portfolio of businesses suggested a value creation model premised on synergies and integration of business units, the governance structure emphasized business autonomy.

Fifth, the value creation logic can become obsolete, but CEOs do not always recognize it. Intel had become much more successful at microprocessors than at memories before its CEO noticed.[15] In the airline industry, British Airways, among all European airlines, noted the importance of information technology and adopted yield management innovations much earlier than its competitors, who remained wedded to a technical (e.g., Lufthansa) or political (e.g., Air France) model of value creation.[16]

Internal Governance: Value Creation in Action

Portfolio choices and formulation of the value creation logic are almost never independent exercises performed by the CEO alone. They are determined at least in part by the internal strategy process and the interplay of business unit with corporate interests and perspectives. In that sense tomorrow's value creation logic results from yesterday's internal governance process—not necessarily an ideal situation! In many companies, vested interests and concerns about centralization and corporate vs. business unit roles cloud the debate and prevent the incumbent CEO from discovering or implementing a new value creation model. In such cases the CEO is hostage to the existing governance system.

Internal governance provides the structure for the relationships of the parts to the whole in a diversified firm. How are the parts defined? How do they relate to corporate management as well as to each other? Is the governance structure consistent with the portfolio and value creation logic? These are some of the critical questions that CEOs face. An internal governance process that is inconsistent with the value creation model will prevent the firm from realizing the potential of the portfolio.

We believe that a systematic approach to understanding the logic of the internal governance system is a necessity. Such a logic is based on three building blocks:

tions," *Organization Science*, Vol. 7, No. 3 (1996), pp. 255-282.

15. See R. Burgelman, "Fading Memories: A Process Theory of Strategic Business Exit in Dynamic Environments," *Administrative Science Quarterly*, Vol. 39, No. 1 (March 1994), pp. 24-56; and R. Burgelman and A. Grove, "Strategic Dissonance," *California Management Review*,

Vol. 38, No. 2 (Winter 1996) pp. 8-28.

16. See M. Lehrer, "Comparative Institutional Advantage in Corporate Governance and Managerial Hierarchies: The Case of European Airlines," Unpub-

1. Structural clarity that is based on a determination of the basic administrative units into which the firm is divided;

2. Administrative processes that allow for dialogue between units, measurement of performance, and a system of accountability and rewards;

3. Basic premises or key assumptions about the kind and quality of interactions between the building blocks of the company, as well as well as other *values and behaviors* that all employees are expected to understand and uphold.

We examine each of these below:

Structural Clarity. Regardless of the portfolio configuration of the firm, a large company has to disaggregate itself into smaller administrative units to be managed effectively. Companies can be organized by product and business areas, functional expertise, and/or by geographic location. In many situations, individual programs or projects can also be units of disaggregation. But at least in all large firms, there is a need for *business, geography, and functional* building blocks.

In most firms, the debate is not about the need for three dimensions, but about the relative roles of the three dimensions. Which of the three ways of organizing—by product, function, or geography—provides the most sensible basis for structuring units, and for managing interactions between them?[17] Having answered this question, the key issues then become: How large should a business unit (or SBU) be? Should each SBU have the complete set of resources it needs? And, finally, how self-contained should its mission be?

Some companies have broken themselves up into many units to set up an internally "competitive" environment, either among existing activities (which was part of Barnevik's motive in choosing ABB's decentralized organization) or among new growth initiatives proposed by individual managers (as in the cases of Johnson & Johnson, 3M, and Matsushita). While a firm is going through a process of rationalization, disaggregating the firm into small, self-contained units can make sense; it provides a focus and clear accountability for cost reduction. But the case for such radical decentralization grows weaker as cross-unit linkages and core competencies be-

come more important. ABB, for instance, has backed away from its extreme decentralization in order to capture potential synergies among its business units. Moreover, in companies that face few, but very large, investment decisions, such decisions are almost never left to the managers of the business units. Take the case of aerospace groups. Although some are relatively diversified, most have only a dozen or so key product programs; and the major decisions to invest in such programs cannot be decentralized in the same way as decisions at 3M, with its 60,000 products.

Yet it is important to recognize that no resource allocation process can enable top managers to cope with choices in any substantive depth if the number of business units becomes too large—30 to 40 is widely considered to be pushing the limit. Some of the problems associated with having lots of small business units can be limited by having sector or "group" heads allocate resources to units within their sectors in a multi-stage, multi-level allocation process. And intermediate-level managers can encourage business units to collaborate with others for growth by identifying opportunities that, although transcending the scope of their individual business units, promise benefits to each. But even with these compensating features, a governance structure made up of lots of very small business units is still likely to produce underinvestment in critical technologies and in emerging markets. Thus, while firms such as ABB may continue to describe their approach to decentralization as "managing a large number of entrepreneurial units," the demands of internal growth and the increasing pressure for resource shifts across major businesses and geographies in most firms will require top managers to deal with fewer and larger aggregations. It will also require paying greater attention to the role of intermediate-level managers in encouraging cooperation among business units.

In a decentralized and diversified company, managers responsible for an administrative unit (be it an SBU or a territory) will argue for a self-contained mission and a full complement of resources. This makes them operate as if they were independent units, selectively drawing on corpo-

---

lished Ph.D. dissertation, INSEAD (1997).

17. The problems that tend to arise in matrix organizations—the tensions over relative influence of the three dimensions in strategy and operational direction, and the destructive consequences of unresolved conflicts between

them—are sufficiently well documented not to deserve special attention here. See, for example, S. Ghoshal and C.A. Bartlett, "Matrix Management, Not a Structure, A Frame of Mind," *Harvard Business Review*, (July-August, 1990), pp. 138-145; and C. K. Prahalad and Y. L. Doz, *The Multinational Mission:*

While a firm is going through a process of rationalization, disaggregating the firm into small, self-contained units can make sense; it provides a focus and clear accountability for cost reduction. But the case for such radical decentralization grows weaker as cross-unit linkages and core competencies become more important.

rate services only as they deem fit. This approach to governance may be fine for Hanson (given its portfolio and value creation logic) but it will not work at HP or Kodak. At such companies there are too many opportunities that cut across any given configuration of administrative unit lines (say, a large project that cuts across several SBUs, or global account management that crosses several countries)—opportunities that are likely to "fall between the cracks" created by SBU boundaries.

To ensure that all promising opportunities are identified and pursued, the organization is likely to need "semi-permeable membranes" rather than brick walls separating the administrative units. But then what is the meaning of a unit—a temporary project, a focal point for concentrating efforts and allocating resources? While R&D organizations have long operated in this way, can this approach be extended to an entire corporation?

Administrative Processes. The *nature of the dialogue* between administrative units and corporate management must be consistent with the value creation logic adopted by the CEO. The administrative and technical infrastructure provides a formal basis and framework for dialogue within the firm in the form of business plans for the year, quarterly budgets and performance expectations, and common design disciplines (based on common CAD tools). The design of the infrastructures supporting these processes and the way they are used can have a major effect on the kind of dialogue that takes place between staff and line managers. The dialogue can be arms' length, as in the case of Hanson. In this approach, the dialogue is primarily through the administrative systems; hence the need for strong budgeting controls and a strong management team at the business units. A key assumption of this approach, however, is "few surprises"—one that is tenable only in slow-moving, mature businesses.

But now consider the case of Canon, which operates in high-growth, rapidly changing markets. There the dialogue between business units has been described as "heart-to-heart, mind-to-mind" communication. Consensus decision making and thorough knowledge of the businesses and markets by people at all levels have been critical to the company's success. The administrative control process can act as the backbone of, but is by no means a substitute for, frequent and intense personal communications across levels of management.

Basic Premises, Values, and Behaviors. While structural clarity and administrative processes provide the anatomy and the physiology of the company, the psychology of the company—how it acts within the broad framework of its structure—is determined by its basic premises and by its values, beliefs, and behaviors. By "basic premises" we mean the key expectations of managers and employees imposed by the CEO and top managers. For example, a basic premise in companies like HP and 3M is the expectation of continuous business renewal (as measured by the percentage of sales from new businesses). This imposes an expectation of not just growth, but *internal* growth. At Motorola, the premise of "6 sigma" suggests that the company will strive for perfection in all it does and in all its relationships, including those with their suppliers.

One important goal of a CEO in setting and communicating basic premises in an organization should be to make clear the expected kind and quality of interactions among business units and other structural building blocks—an expectation that is difficult to convey in an administrative process like the firm's measurement and control system. For example, in the case of GE, after the initial decentralization Jack Welch established the basic premise of "boundaryless" behavior to encourage the sharing of information and best practices across all boundaries—across hierarchical levels, countries, and businesses within the company. In this case, the assumption that a large firm represents a laboratory of good practices and that there is value in sharing these across boundaries takes precedence over the autonomy built into the structural and administrative processes.

While such processes provide the basic framework for organizing and monitoring the resources of the company, communicating best practices and instilling the right values and behavior are essential to create a favorable learning environment for managers and employees. Basic premises and values must be accepted companywide to overcome the fragmenting effect of a decentralized administrative structure, and CEOs often sponsor initiatives to communicate such premises and values to managers and employees throughout the organization.

Clearly understood and shared values and behaviors are important for two main reasons. First, in a volatile industry environment, no structure can anticipate all the adjustments that sometimes need to be made by managers and employees. Managers must go beyond predefined roles and respond in ways that increase the value of the entire organization, not just their own business units. Second is the demand for profitable growth. In many if not most businesses, there is growing pressure to discover new opportunities that enable companies to leverage their competencies. Constant reconfiguration of competencies to address new opportunities will force frequent changes in structure, and business unit boundaries may have to be redrawn. Maintaining continuity in values and principles generally allows room for substantive changes in the business portfolio as well as changes in the internal governance system. Given today's emphasis on flexibility and profitable growth, values and norms of behavior are likely to become as important as the formal structure as the source of organizational clarity and stability in an era of constant change in competitors, products, prices, and customers.

The Search for Harmony

At bottom, getting the right internal governance system is about achieving harmony between the three elements of the governance system: structure, administrative process, and basic premises and values. It is the job of the CEO and top management to bring about this harmony and to manage apparent contradictions, such as demanding control and accountability of performance of unit managers while at the same time giving them sufficient leeway to experiment and create new "white space" opportunities for growth that lie outside the existing structure.

The key to internal governance, then, is understanding the implications of the portfolio composition and value creation logic and using the three elements of governance to harmonize the complex and conflicting demands. Such harmonization can take a number of different forms. At Hanson Trust, there is what we would describe as a harmonious but essentially *static* relationship between the portfolio composition decision, the value creation logic, and the internal governance process selected by Lord Hanson. At Hewlett-Packard and Canon, by contrast, this relationship can be seen operating beneath continuously changing configurations. In such cases, the harmony is *dynamic*, continuously evolving and embedded

within the change processes. Where Hanson puts emphasis on formal structures and processes, Canon and HP stress the continuity of their basic premises and principles and behavioral norms. The value creation logic of HP and Canon emphasizes distributed entrepreneurship and evolving business portfolios, all built upon core competencies. Although the relationships among portfolio composition, value creation, and governance may appear to shift continuously, the underlying rationale is to maximize the firm's *capacity to adapt* to changes in the business environment.

Maintaining strategic harmony is a challenge for most CEOs, who typically approach internal governance in one of two ways. In one approach, the management style of the CEO drives the process. The CEO's preferred style, whether explicitly control-driven or nominally hands-off and decentralized ("you're okay as long as you meet the budget"), takes precedence over, and often conflicts with, the value creation model.

In the other popular approach, tools are sometimes expected to take the place of personal leadership, as an increasingly formal approach to internal governance is fueled by the groundswell of enthusiasm for decentralization and performance measures like economic value added. What is not often recognized is that decisions by top management to measure the contribution of a business unit by its EVA tend to require considerable decentralization of decision-making, including at least partial decentralization of investment decisions. But is the disaggregation of the firm into stand-alone business units necessarily appropriate in all cases? We believe not. Governance approaches such as division of the firm into EVA centers (or other forms of SBUs), matrix organizations, teams, and decentralization must all be evaluated carefully in the context of a company's portfolio and business model.

CEO DILEMMAS AND INTERVENTION CAPABILITIES

Most corporate governance systems at least profess allegiance to a democratic "rule of law" as opposed to a "rule of men." But, even in the most rules-bound corporations, there is some room for "intervention" by the CEO, for setting aside the administrative processes when they get in the way of the desired outcome or behavior. For example, in a

> Given today's emphasis on flexibility and profitable growth, values and norms of behavior are likely to become as important as the formal structure as the source of organizational clarity and stability in an era of constant change in competitors, products, prices, and customers.

firm where division managers' incentive pay is based solely on hitting divisional performance targets, the CEO may reserve the right to override the corporate bonus system by rewarding a manager for exceptional teamwork even when his division fails to meet its target. Especially in diversified companies, there are bound to be circumstances in which all governance approaches are likely to impose a dominant logic that acts as a straitjacket on some businesses.[18] But with a variety of different intervention models to choose from, CEOs can adjust their governance systems to accommodate the needs of the portfolio and the value creation logic.

In determining when and how to intervene, CEOs need to consider a number of important questions:

1. What in the internal governance process is *nonnegotiable and mandatory?* First are legal and regulatory matters, as well as compliance with accounting procedures. Many firms also require conformity with the technical architecture, which is often a critical precondition for sharing competencies and components across business units. Achievement of performance standards is also often mandatory; in many firms, meeting budgets is necessary to receive bonus awards, and failure to do so over a longer period of time could lead to dismissal. Adherence to corporate values is frequently nonnegotiable. Mistreatment of customers or failure to uphold a standard of quality may not be tolerated even when accompanied by outstanding financial performance.

2. Can some aspects of the internal governance system be allowed to deviate from corporate-wide policy and be *tailor-made* for a specific business unit, function, or geographic setting? For example, an unusual compensation scheme designed to attract the right talent for a specific business can be made a local prerogative.

3. What is the role of *perceived fairness in the system?* It is very important that employees at all levels of the firm see the system as inherently fair. Building employee commitment, loyalty, and excitement requires a deep commitment to fairness. But fairness is as much perception as reality. In practicing selective intervention, a CEO must worry about its being interpreted as unfair practice. More-

over, fairness is not the same as uniformity of systems and procedures. Uniformity can easily be seen as lack of fairness and courage—for instance, when all units, no matter how successful, are required to cut investment.

4. *How can mixed signals in the organization be avoided?* Attempts to fine tune the system can easily create multiple interpretations of the expectations imposed on the organization by top managers. For example, a demand for growth coupled with pressure for profit improvement can be seen as a mixed (up!) signal if it is not properly explained to the organization. Mixed signals can paralyze an organization. However, creating the right level of tension and anticipation cannot be achieved without complex signals. Achieving balance is the key to high performance.

5. What is the balance between the investment in the *continuity and stability* of the enterprise and the investment in *change and flexibility?* Governance mechanisms such as reengineering, downsizing, and multiple restructurings have the potential not only to demoralize managers and employees, but to limit the company's ability to accumulate and exploit knowledge. Continuity of the team and processes within the firm dramatically reduces the costs of transactions as individuals start to work with each other, establish patterns of interactions, develop trust, and accumulate intellectual assets.[19] On the other hand, too much emphasis on stability in the context of dramatic changes in the external environment will create paralysis. Change and flexibility, which alter the pattern of interactions, work flow, and skill mix in the organization, are critical for survival. The degree of harmony between the firm's business model and its governance system is measured not just by how well they knit together at a given point in time, but by the firm's ability to encourage the next round of capability development.

In thinking about their role in achieving this harmony, CEOs must recognize the inherent difficulties. In addition to the challenges listed above, CEOs have to deal with other major issues. For example, a significant part of the wealth creation opportunity is centered around stretching the imagination of the organization and focusing it on aspirations that are beyond the range of the current resources of the

---

Balancing Local Demands and Global Vision (New York: The Free Press, 1987).

18. C.K. Prahalad and R.A. Bettis, "The Dominant Logic: A New Linkage Between Diversity and Performance," *Strategic Management Journal*, Vol. 7:36

(November-December 1996), pp. 485-501.

19. See Y.L. Doz and B. Chakravarthy, "Managing Core Competence Dynamically," working paper presented to the Strategic Management Society International Conference, Mexico City 1995.

company. "Stretch goals" are highly motivating when employees voluntarily commit to them because of their understanding of the rationale for it. In such cases the organizational goal of stretch is transformed into the personal imperative to "reach." But if imposed administratively (as often happens with budgets), it can lead to fear, anxiety, and dishonesty; managers stop being candid and start hiding slippage and sandbagging numbers. Reach is about commitment and not compliance—about managers and employees volunteering their discretionary time, effort, and imagination.

Similarly, a CEO in a large organization must strive to provide clarity to the tasks, values, performance expectations, and standards. This is the function of "keeping the machine well oiled and reducing the frictional losses" in the system. But too much emphasis on clarity can kill enthusiasm for experimentation. Experiments that are likely to change the way the system is currently managed and challenge the dominant logic are a critical source of longer-term vitality in a large firm. CEOs must demonstrate commitment to the current system while planting the seeds that will challenge it.

CEO EFFECTIVENESS AND PUBLIC IMAGE

The challenge for the CEO, then, is to manage the interactions between portfolio configuration, value creation, and governance in a way that ensures harmony. But harmony depends not just on analytical skills but also on the capacity to motivate and provide an emotional dimension to the company. Analytics and passion, clarity and experimentation, efficiency and innovation must all coexist; the CEO's job is to strike an ideal balance between them.

Unless they are very careful, CEOs are likely to become too distant from the reality of the businesses that they are managing. A check on the calendar of a CEO can provide very useful hints of the existence of such a problem. Outside commitments, routine corporate reviews and the corporate calendar, and personal style and preferences can leave very little time for in-depth understanding of the emerging opportunities, be they in the laboratories, in manufacturing, or in the changing mix of customers. Although distance is a natural outcome of the job, staying informed about the key issues is a result of active management of one's time and of installing ad

hoc processes that bypass and transcend the formal ones. CEOs don't have to be gluttons for detail, but they must have enough understanding of the emerging detail to extract the essence. For example, a CEO today must know what is happening with information technology to recognize its likely effects on distribution and retailing, customer interface, focused marketing, logistics, distance collaboration, the nature of dialogue between individuals, teams, and administrative units, and the cost structure of businesses. The goal is not to become an expert on the details of "virtual reality" or large database construction techniques, but to recognize their implications for the firm's business model and internal governance processes. The goal is for CEOs to listen to the arguments, suspend judgment, and recognize that they cannot and need not have a solution to all the problems that the organization faces. Many of the solutions evolve and CEOs must unburden themselves from the self-imposed (and sometimes culturally imposed) burden of "knowing the answer" to all questions.

The reality, of course, is that CEOs, like all of us, have their limitations, including those stemming from their background and management style. While many CEOs recognize the potentially negative impact of their style on the internal governance processes, few understand how to limit or counteract this effect. The difficulty is in modifying behavior patterns and questioning managerial assumptions that one has grown up with. The search for an outside CEO is often triggered by an intuitive sense, on the part of directors, of the need for a new value creation strategy and business portfolio. Boards come to the conclusion, often painfully, that nobody from the inside can break away from the ingrained managerial mindset and style fast enough. Employing an outsider becomes a way of dealing with the limitations of the incumbent CEO and his team. The changes in top management at companies like Alcatel, IBM, Kodak, Sears, K Mart, and American Express during the early '90s are all examples of this process.

Public image is the source of another, somewhat subtle, limitation on the effectiveness of a CEO. The public image of CEOs can either expand or limit their capacity for managing the interactions among the different business units and, more generally, between the business model and the governance system. The public image can be built through a conscious effort by the CEO to use it to influence the

Even in the most rules-bound corporations, there is some room for "intervention" by the CEO, for setting aside the administrative processes when they get in the way of the desired behavior.

organization—say, to cut through layers of bureaucracy and reach the rank and file directly—or it can be left largely to the press, with little or no cooperation by the CEO. But like politicians running for office, CEOs cannot ignore their public images; nor can they fail to recognize that such images are subject to change and require continual "maintenance."

The public image of the CEO is reflected in the organization. All employees have access to that image and interpret it. For example, the popular image of Jack Welch as "Neutron Jack" has doubtless help persuade GE's managers that maintaining profitability and a dominant industry position are "musts." Also associated with Welch's image are other, related messages: outsourcing is acceptable; lack of internal growth may be tolerated (given profitability); divestment of businesses is part of corporate strategy and the company is not committed to any single business; and the "new social contract" is about ensuring employability, not employment.

The public image of Bill Gates is somewhat different from Welch's. At Microsoft, the emphasis is on growth, market dominance, establishing products as the industry standard, "take no prisoners, winner take all," a wide scope of businesses, enormous technical and market foresight and imagination, brashness and irreverence. Microsoft employees recognize that individual contributions are greatly valued; that their firm is constantly increasing the scope of what they do and challenging incumbents in major industries such as banking and education by attempting to change the dynamics of those industries. Of course, CEOs can also acquire a negative public image—a reputation for indecision, unwillingness to change, and lack of connection with the realities of new competition. Given a CEO with such an image, are employees likely to be willing to commit to change?

A strong public image has a number of important benefits:

■ It can build stockholder confidence. Jack Welch and the late Roberto Goizueta (of Coca Cola) built impressive reputations as allies of stockholders and builders of market value. Or think about what happens when a company simply announces that Warren Buffett is taking an equity stake; the consequences of bringing in a highly regarded CEO are often the same.

■ It can scare competitors. Being #1 or #2, or Bill Gates's approach to launching "Windows 95," can give second thoughts to competitors.

■ It can inspire confidence in the company, as in the cases of Bob Galvin during the 1980s at Motorola, George Fisher at Motorola and later at Kodak, and Percy Barnevik at ABB.

On the other hand, there are also highly visible companies with strong reputations, such as 3M, Marriott, Rubbermaid, and the present-day Motorola, whose CEOs do not have well-defined public images. Why is this? Visibility and a public image are often thrust upon (if not sought by) CEOs involved in major restructuring and reengineering efforts. Such events provide for the kind of drama relished by the media. Companies like Motorola or 3M that have not made big and dramatic takeover bids, whose strategic change has been based on a longer-term view of the industry's evolution, are less likely to draw media attention. For these companies, the reinventing of the company is an ongoing, intense, but "low decibel" effort. Their change efforts tend to be "middle-out" initiatives that rely heavily on the efforts of mid-level as well as top managers, a much less visible process than the traditional strategizing at the top followed by asset and organizational restructuring. There are benefits to having a low-visibility CEO, in particular the greater freedom to communicate and manage the balance among the three key value creation elements within the firm. The disadvantage, however, is that it forgoes the ability of the the highly visible CEO to use the public image to amplify his or her message.

In short, public image for the CEO is a mixed blessing. Once a strong public persona is created, it is not easy for the CEO to provide a credible message to the organization that conflicts with the image. In this sense the CEO becomes hostage to the image. How long do public images last? Should we be thinking about public image as a "brand franchise," with all its attendant benefits and limitations?

Today's CEO has to ask the following questions: Can I afford to ignore the public image that may be emerging, and its effect on the firm and my ability to manage? How do I ensure that my values, concerns, and goals are consistent with those implied by the emerging public persona? How can I effectively change my message, perhaps even more than once? (This can become a problem, especially when the CEO has ten or more years in the job—although GE, with its shift in focus toward soft issues since 1991, is proof that such a change can be made without loss of credibility.) And, finally, what is the impact of a "barrage" of publicity on the CEO as a person?

CONCLUSION

The CEO has become critical in the wealth creation process. Managers and employees at all levels have become significant contributors to the competitiveness of the firm, and quality leadership can encourage this by creating a favorable environment for employee participation. We believe that the process of creating this environment begins by developing a harmonious relationship between the portfolio of businesses, the value creation logic, and the internal governance system. In most large companies today, particularly those in growth businesses, developing and maintaining such a harmony is an evolving, dynamic process. Moreover, CEOs will inevitably be faced with dilemmas in managing this delicate process—in particular, the need to maintain the integrity of near-term performance disciplines while encouraging experimentation, investment in growth opportunities (that can hurt near-term performance), and collaboration among business units (which is difficult to incorporate into performance measurement and incentive schemes). Managing such dilemmas demands a good sense of timing and sequencing, as well as considerable social and intercultural sensitivity. Management styles must be recognized and, in cases where they interfere with effective management, set aside. Finally, CEOs must ask themselves if they should (or even can) avoid creating a public image—and, if the answer is no, how they can use that image to strengthen the commitment of their employees and investors.

DECENTRALIZATION, INCENTIVES, AND VALUE CREATION: THE CASE OF JLG INDUSTRIES

*by Heidi E. Treml,
Marconi PLC, and
Kenneth Lehn,
University of Pittsburgh*

T his paper examines the strategic and organizational changes that led to the creation of substantial value at JLG Industries, a 30-year-old manufacturer of aerial work platforms. One dollar invested in JLG stock at the end of 1992 would have been worth $15.82 at the end of 1998, whereas one dollar invested in a portfolio of industry peers would have grown to only $1.48 over the same period. Almost all of the increase in JLG's value can be traced to three factors: substantial revenue growth, large cost savings, and a dramatic reduction in inventories.

We show that the creation of value at JLG occurred simultaneously with dramatic changes in the company's organizational structure and compensation plans for executives and other employees. Prior to 1993, JLG had been managed in a highly centralized manner by its founder, John Grove. After Mr. Grove was removed as chairman in April 1993, the company changed to a much more decentralized governance structure that sought greater employee involvement in both product and process design.

As it decentralized decision-making, JLG revised the compensation plans of top executives and other employees throughout the organization to encourage value creation. The compensation of top executives became much more tied to JLG's stock price performance. For example, the percentage of their total compensation derived from stock option grants increased from 7% during 1990-1992 to 43% during 1993-1998. JLG strengthened the incentives of other employees by increasing gain-sharing bonuses and rewarding employees in non-pecuniary ways, such as regular employee breakfasts and large celebrations on the achievement of corporate goals.

After the changes in JLG's governance structure and compensation plans, JLG's operating performance improved dramatically and it created substantial value for investors. The strategic initiatives that contributed to JLG's stellar performance after 1993 actually originated in 1983, when JLG introduced a "Seven-Part Strategy to Resume Growth." The initiative included an increased focus on accelerating new product development, improving manufacturing processes, and reducing costs. Although JLG performed reasonably well in the 1980s, the strategic initiative did not result in substantial value gains until it changed its organizational structure and compensation plans in 1993.

The increase in JLG's value over 1993-1998 can be traced to changes in key value drivers associated with the strategic initiative. JLG's revenue grew at an average rate of more than 30% per year during 1993-1998, due in large part to a proliferation of new products. The ratio of its cost of goods sold to sales declined by two percentage points over this period, reflecting improvements in JLG's manufacturing processes. The ratio of JLG's selling, general, and administrative expense to sales fell in half over this period (from 0.20 to 0.10), reflecting both the economies of scale associated with overhead and better control of overhead expenses. Perhaps most notably, JLG slashed its inventories-to-sales ratio dramatically over this period, from 0.234 in 1992 to 0.090 in 1998. We estimate that this accomplishment alone, which resulted from its successful implementation of just-in-time production (JIT) and continuous flow manufacturing (CFM), accounts for roughly $500 million of additional value.

The JLG experience is consistent with arguments made by scholars in the organizational economics literature. For example, in two articles published in this journal in 1997—one by Karen Wruck and Michael Jensen and the other by Jim Brickley, Cliff Smith, and Jerry Zimmerman[1]—the authors emphasize the importance of coordinating organizational change with the adoption of management techniques such as total quality management (TQM), just-in-time production (JIT), and continuous flow manufacturing (CFM). Both of these papers adopt the perspective that the choice between centralized versus decentralized decision-making involves a tradeoff: The major disadvantage of centralization is that decision makers are likely to lack information that front-line employees have about market conditions, technology, costs, and so forth. This, of course, argues for transferring decision rights to front-line employees with better information. However, the major disadvantage of decentralized decision-making is that front-line employees are less likely to use decision rights to maximize firm value, since their interests are more parochial than those of senior managers, who are responsible for the performance of the entire organization. Hence, as decision rights are decentralized it becomes important to consider changes in the structure of employee compensation plans to align their incentives with the creation of value.

Both Wruck and Jensen (1997) and Brickley, Smith, and Zimmerman (1997) argue that implementing science-based management techniques such as TQM, JIT, and CFM requires the use of information that is scattered across functional areas and various levels of a business organization. Consequently, the relative costs of centralized decision-making are high for companies using these techniques, since the likelihood of making ill-informed decisions is especially high. Therefore, the successful execution of these management techniques may require organizations to adapt towards more decentralized governance structures.[2] As described above, when decision-making becomes less centralized, compensation plans should change to provide stronger incentives for employees to use their decision rights in ways that create value.

The JLG case illustrates the importance of linking the adoption of management techniques such as TQM, JIT, and CFM with decentralization of decision-making and changes in incentives for employees. JLG had adopted these management techniques several years before its performance improved so dramatically during 1993-1998. In 1993, however, following the departure of the company's founder as chairman, JLG adopted the strategic initiative that emphasized greater decentralization, more employee involvement in decision-making, greater use of teams, and more reliance on incentive compensation. Following this shift in hierarchy, JLG achieved enormous success in implementing these techniques and creating value.[3]

JLG BEFORE 1993

John L. Grove, who developed the first self-propelled boom lift, founded JLG Industries in 1969. This product revolutionized the construction industry by allowing work to be completed more quickly and safely than with ladders and scaffolding. During the late 1970s the company expanded its product line from its trademark boom lifts to include scissor lifts, helping to round out its product line. Rental companies, JLG's major customers, needed both types of lift equipment to meet the demands of its customers. JLG also needed to ward off competitors' entry into its domain and its key distribution channels.

Like other manufacturers of capital goods, JLG's fortunes are closely tied to conditions in the overall economy and, in particular, to the highly cyclical construction industry. After growing the company to $60.4 million dollars in revenues by 1980, JLG weathered the 1982-1984 economic recession with sales declining to $50 million, $32.8 million, and $38.7 million. By 1985 sales were once again on the upswing, and by 1988 they reached $81.5 million. During 1988 and 1989, JLG was recognized by such publications as *Fortune* magazine as one of the top three (out of 33) industrial and farm equipment manufacturers based on ROA, ROI, and return-on-sales.

---

1. Karen Hopper Wruck and Michael C. Jensen, "Science, Specific Knowledge, and Total Quality Management," *Journal of Applied Corporate Finance* (Summer 1997), 8-23; and James Brickley, Clifford W. Smith, Jr., and Jerold L. Zimmerman, "Management Fads and Organizational Architecture," *Journal of Applied Corporate Finance* (Summer 1997), 24-39.

2. Wruck and Jensen (1997) argue that this is not necessarily the case for all firms: "While the writings of quality experts appear to encourage massive decentralization, the optimal policy is far more subtle....Successful TQM firms must establish a system for assigning decision rights that curbs managers' tendency to overcentralize, but at the same time provides a structure to guard against excessive decentralization (p. 12).."

3. The evidence from JLG's experience also is consistent with recent data compiled by *Industry Week*. Data gathered in the Second Annual *Industry Week* Census of Manufacturers revealed that plants that embraced "employee empowerment" demonstrated consistently superior improvement in performance compared with plants that were not focused on this effort. See Jim Cauhorn, "Empowered Employees Are Key to Success," www.industryweek.com, April 12, 1999.

As the economy and construction industry turned down in the early 1990s, JLG experienced hard times. Its sales dropped from $149 million in 1990 to $94 million in 1991 and $110 million in 1992. JLG reported operating losses of $4.2 million in 1991 and $4.4 million in 1992. Net income per share dropped from $2.42 in 1990 to losses of $0.91 in 1991 and $0.85 in 1992, and the company's stock price fell from $16 at the beginning of 1990 to roughly $10 in the fall of 1991. In late 1991, JLG omitted its quarterly dividend.

As JLG's performance declined during the 1991-1992 recession, it became embroiled in two corporate control battles. On October 9, 1991, the company received an unsolicited letter from Lawrence F. Orbe, a lawyer representing an unidentified investor group, outlining a conditional offer to buy 1.8 million shares (50.4% of outstanding shares) for $16 a share. JLG's board questioned the substance of the offer, since the investor group was unidentified and the offer was conditional. Furthermore, JLG's founder and chairman, John L. Grove, controlled 19.4% of the shares and indicated no interest in selling his shares. Nonetheless, Lawrence Orbe continued to nip at JLG's heels through the summer of 1992, at one point even threatening to challenge the incumbent slate of directors in a proxy fight.

Meanwhile, the company was sustaining an internal dispute between Grove and the senior management team at JLG. In 1990, JLG had selected L. David Black as president, chief operating officer, and heir apparent to Grove as chief executive officer of JLG. Before joining JLG, Black had been president and chief executive officer of ARO Corp., a manufacturer of pumps, pneumatic tools, and other types of industrial equipment. As planned, in July 1991 Black was named as chief executive officer and Grove retained his position as chairman. Disharmony prevailed at the firm, however, as Grove continued to be involved in day-to-day management and disagreed with senior managers on important issues, including whether or not the company should be sold. On July 17, 1992, JLG announced that a special committee of outside directors had reviewed the performance of JLG's senior management and concluded that they should continue in their positions. Furthermore, the special committee stated that "it was now appropriate for the chairman of the board, John L. Grove, to concentrate on board activities and withdraw from day-to-day operational responsibilities" (JLG Press Release, July 17, 1992). Grove

continued to have strong disagreements with JLG's senior management and openly expressed his concerns within the firm. The leadership conflict at JLG culminated in the removal of Grove as chairman in April 1993. In September 1993, JLG agreed to buy Grove's equity stake for $17 per share.

The Seven-Point Program

In 1983 JLG developed the first iteration of "A Seven-Part Strategy to Resume Growth"; however, the strategy was not actively used until the late 1980s. Moreover, it was not until early 1993 that JLG's management team tied incentives to the seven points by bringing in a facilitator with a wealth of experience and knowledge to help develop a cohesive management group committed to the same goals, with the same focus. This management group included more than two dozen people whom JLG's executives felt would be the key individuals responsible for realizing these goals. The result of several iterations was the strategic plan known as the "Seven Point Program for Long-Term Growth" to strengthen the company, reduce its dependence on the U.S. economy, and make it less vulnerable to recessions like the one experienced during 1991-1992.

Black did not want the initial plan to focus exclusively on financial measures of performance. He emphasized developing initiatives that focused on being the market leader through "delighting their customers." After the operating plan was completed, they looked at the financial impact of the various projects. If they found the financials displeasing they would return to the operating plan for improvement. Through this approach, the company embarked on what it called its "Journey to Excellence." Under this plan, everyone in the company would work toward continuous improvement rather than toward a specific financial goal (and "settling" when it was reached). The initiative was overseen by the executive committee and monitored by the board of directors. In accordance with the strategy, the executives made known their intentions by decentralizing decision-making and allowing employees to move rapidly forward in the stated areas. Employees were empowered to improve processes in their functional areas and work as a corporate team to achieve their mission of delighting their customers.

The seven points consisted of the following initiatives: improve processes and reduce costs; accelerate new product development; expand glo-

The JLG case illustrates the importance of linking the adoption of management techniques such as TQM, JIT, and CFM with decentralization and stronger incentives for employees. Although the company performed reasonably well in the 1980s, the strategic initiatives launched in the '80s did not result in substantial value gains until it changed its organizational structure and compensation plans in 1993.

FIGURE 1
TOTAL NUMBER AND
AVERAGE NUMBER OF
STOCK OPTIONS GRANTED
TO FIVE HIGHEST PAID
EXECUTIVES, 1990-1998*

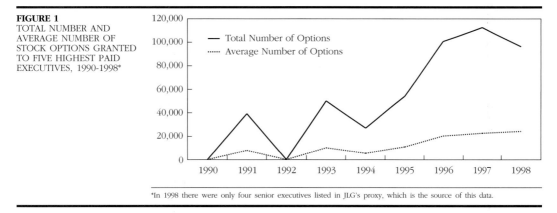

*In 1998 there were only four senior executives listed in JLG's proxy, which is the source of this data.

bal distribution; enhance customer support services; grow JLG Equipment Services; strengthen employee involvement; and pursue strategic acquisitions. Of these strategies, process improvement and cost reduction, new product development, and strengthened employee involvement were the key factors in generating the growth spurt that JLG experienced from 1993 to 1998. The key—strengthened employee involvement—enabled the full implementation of the other strategies. According to the Second Annual *IndustryWeek* Census, employee dedication cannot be bought with wages or other monetary rewards. Employees like to feel that they are part of the company, and provide important contributions to the company's success.[4] JLG embraced this theory, making it the key to its continuous improvement.

1993 AND BEYOND

Beginning in fiscal year 1993 (JLG's fiscal year ends on July 31), JLG had a senior management team that had just received the endorsement of the board in its conflict over corporate strategy with founder Grove. The team consisted of Black; Charles H. Diller, executive vice president and chief financial officer; Rao G. Bollimpalli, senior vice president–engineering; Michael Swartz, senior vice president–marketing; and Raymond F. Treml, senior vice president–operations. Although the team had been in place for several years, 1993 was the first fiscal year in which they had the board's blessing to operate the firm on a day-to-day basis, free of Grove's control.

This marked the beginning of decentralized decision-making and employee incentives tied directly to the strategic plan.

The Key to JLG's Success: Stronger Incentives and Greater Employee Involvement

Executive compensation. In 1993, the structure of executive compensation changed markedly at JLG, with much greater emphasis on stock-based forms of compensation. Before 1993 stock option grants accounted for only a small percentage of executive compensation at JLG. For example, from 1990 to 1992, stock option grants accounted for only 7% of the total compensation for both the CEO and the five highest-paid executives of JLG.[5] Beginning in 1993, JLG dramatically increased its reliance on stock option grants as a component of executive pay. In 1993, 36% of the CEO's and 44% of the five highest-paid executives' compensation consisted of stock option grants. From 1993 to 1998, 35% of the CEO's and 43% of the five highest-paid executives' total pay consisted of stock option grants.

Figure 1 shows the total and average number of stock options granted to the five highest paid executives at JLG during the period 1990 to 1998. The figure shows a steady increase in the number of stock options granted to JLG executives over this period. No stock options were granted in 1990, 39,100 were granted to the five executives in 1991, and none were granted in 1992. With the organizational changes in 1993, the number of stock options granted to JLG

---

4. See Jim Cauhorn, www.industryweek.com, "Empowered Employees are Key to Success," April 12, 1999

5. We used the Black-Scholes model with continuously paid dividends to value the executive stock options.

executives increased substantially, to 50,000. After declining in 1994, this number increased steadily to 112,600 in 1997. The figure shows a decline in the total number of options granted JLG executives in 1998, but this is because JLG only reported compensation data for the four highest paid executives in its 1998 proxy. In fact, the average number of stock options granted executives listed in JLG's proxy increased from 22,520 in 1997 to 24, 075 in 1998.

Non-executive compensation and incentives. As part of the decentralization initiative, JLG's goal after 1993 was to gain input from all employees on all plant changes. Along with process improvements, decentralization endeavors led to an improvement in revenue dollars per employment from $80,000 in 1992 to $190,000 in 1997.[6]

JLG sought input from all employees by posting all planned changes, including blueprints and floor plans, and allowing all employees to offer suggestions for improving the plan. This input was integrated into the redesign and final design of the proposed changes. As the company restructured its material flow, employees saw their suggestions being implemented in the new processes. JLG also developed teams who were responsible for completing various projects, which contributed to the corporate goals. These teams were aware of the link between their project and the corporate goal, affording the members the understanding of how their initiative would relate to corporate success. Teams were developed to reduce material handling, improve processes, and reduce process and setup time, along with many other initiatives.

JLG offered employees improved financial rewards by increasing the bonuses they were eligible to receive. Due to the lull in the economy and its poor performance, JLG did not award bonuses from 1990 to 1992. During this time, the company also instituted a wage freeze, providing only one across-the-board raise of three percent for all employees (in 1991). In 1993, the Company instituted the Profitability and Productivity Improvement Award (PPI) program. Employees could receive a maximum of 4% of their salary in 1993, based on corporate financial performance. The company achieved the financial measures, and all employees received the 4% raise in 1993. In a series of increases during the period 1993 to 1998, JLG gradually increased the bonus percent

from 4% to 10%, reflecting its growing effort to reward employees based on performance.

The PPI provided a cash award or bonus for each employee based on the company's net income, which was closely tied to the Seven Point program. The fulfillment of JLG's strategic initiatives would relate to an increase in revenues and a decrease in costs, thus directly affecting the net income. JLG set three levels for bonuses: a threshold, a target, and a distinguished bonus. In each year from 1993 to 1998, employees received the highest possible percentage bonus because the performance measures always reached the "distinguished" target.

In addition to financial measures, JLG increased the number of social activities to help increase employee interaction and reduce barriers between functional departments and management levels. These activities included company sponsored lunches, picnics, amusement park visitations, and, the most favored by many employees, "JLG Days" at local ballparks, race tracks, and resorts. When JLG's boom-lift facility reached a long anticipated goal of reducing cycle time to 10 days, they hired a marching band and disc jockeys to provide entertainment for a plant-wide celebratory barbecue. To emphasize the "speed" theme, they had nationally famous racecar drivers on hand to sign autographs. JLG also holds focus group breakfasts with officers and randomly selected employees, where employees provide input through direct communication with the executives on problems in their area and contribute suggestions for improvement.

Employee surveys indicate a generally positive work environment, which is also reflected by a low employee turnover rate. The company is currently drawing employees from a 70-mile radius. The company's preparation and continuing adherence to ISO 9000 certification has also forced cross-training and led to skill-based pay, which rewards employees for the additional skills they acquire through various corporate training initiatives.

JLG's Performance, 1993-1998

Table 1 shows the dramatic improvement in JLG's performance using two sets of performance measures: accounting profits and economic profits. Panel A, which contains data on accounting profits,

6. "Journey to Excellence," Raymond F. Treml and Thomas A. Horejs, JLG Industries, Inc.

Process improvement and cost reduction, new product development, and strengthened employee involvement were the key factors in generating the growth spurt that JLG experienced from 1993 to 1998. But it was the greater employee involvement that enabled the full implementation of the other strategies.

TABLE 1
PERFORMANCE DATA FOR JLG, 1990-1998*

PANEL A: ACCOUNTING PROFIT MEASURES

Year	Operating Income	Net Income	Return on Assets	Return on Equity
1990	$14.9m	$8.5m		
1991	–4.2m	–3.2m	–5.6%	–8.4%
1992	–4.4m	–3.0m	–6.0	–8.2
1993	4.9m	3.2m	6.8	8.3
1994	15.0m	9.5m	16.4	20.9
1995	32.7m	20.8m	27.3	30.3
1996	64.7m	42.1m	35.4	37.2
1997	71.9m	46.1m	28.8	28.5
1998	71.1m	46.5m	23.1	22.4

PANEL B: ECONOMIC PROFIT MEASURES

Year	Market Value	Capital	Market Value Added	Return on Invested Capital	Cost of Capital	Economic Profits
1990						
1991	$61.8m	$50.4m	$11.4m			
1992	56.1m	47.0m	9.1m	–12.5%	9.9%	$–11.2m
1993	68.1m	41.5m	26.7m	4.7	9.8	–2.2m
1994	142.4m	49.5m	92.9m	15.5	12.4	1.2m
1995	272.7m	66.2m	206.5m	37.9	10.2	11.9m
1996	817.4m	106.1m	711.2m	63.6	12.6	28.5m
1997	500.1m	141.0m	359.2m	48.7	11.6	29.6m
1998	701.3m	188.8m	512.5m	28.8	10.9	21.6m

*This table includes various performance measures for JLG Industries annually during the period of 1990 through 1998. The measures include operating income, net income, return on assets (defined as the ratio of operating income to the book value of assets), return on equity (defined as the ratio of net income to the book value of equity), market value added (defined as the difference between the market value of JLG's assets and its capital), and economic profits (defined as the product of invested capital and the difference between return on invested capital and the cost of capital). Sources of data include JLG's annual reports for operating income, net income, book value of assets, book value of equity and capital. The market value of assets is computed with data from JLG's annual reports and Standard & Poor's *Daily stock price record*. Return on invested capital is computed as the ratio of net operating profit less adjusted taxes (NOPLAT) to capital. The cost of capital is computed as the weighted average cost of capital. See Thomas Copeland, Tim Koller, and Jack Murrin, *Valuation,* John Wiley & Sons, 1994 for details on the computation of cost of capital, return on capital, cost of capital, and economic profits.

reveals that JLG's operating income increased steadily and substantially over the period, from $4.9 million in 1993 to $71.1 million in 1998. Net income followed a similar pattern, increasing from $3.2 million in 1993 to $46.5 million in 1998. Return on assets (ROA), defined as operating income divided by the book value of assets, increased from 6.8% in 1993 to 23.1% in 1998, reaching a peak of 35.4% in 1996. Return on equity (ROE), defined as net income divided by the book value of equity, showed a similar pattern and also peaked in 1996.

Panel B contains estimates of economic profits (often referred to as EVA, the trademark name for economic profits used by Stern Stewart, a management consulting firm) and market value added

(MVA). Economic profits measures value creation by subtracting a capital charge from earnings, on the grounds that investors could have earned the capital charge if they had invested capital in other assets with comparable risk. Since managers create value only if they generate earnings in excess of the capital charge, many argue that economic profits serves as a better measure of performance than accounting profits. Market value added (MVA) is the difference between the market value of a firm and its invested capital. This measure reflects the market's expectations about a firm's future economic profits.

The data reveal that both JLG's economic profits and MVA increased substantially over the period. JLG's economic profits (computed as return on

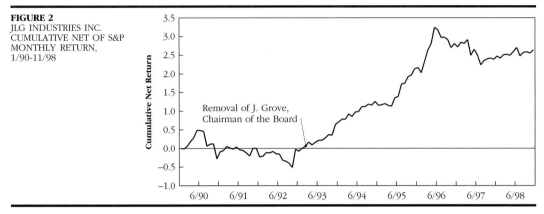

FIGURE 2
JLG INDUSTRIES INC.
CUMULATIVE NET OF S&P
MONTHLY RETURN,
1/90-11/98

invested capital less the cost of capital, times invested capital) increased from a negative $2.2 million in 1993 to $21.6 million in 1998, peaking at $29.6 million in 1997. The company's MVA increased in a similar fashion, from $26.7 million in 1993 to $512.5 million in 1998. From 1993 to 1998, JLG's invested capital increased by only $147 million (from $41.5 million to $188.8 million), while its market value increased by $633 million (from $68.1 million to $701.3 million). The large difference between the change in JLG's invested capital and the change in its market value reflects the market's assessment that JLG was likely to generate returns far in excess of its cost of capital on the newly invested capital.

Finally, Figure 2 shows the cumulative net of market returns on JLG's stock during 1990-1998. The graph shows that, from 1990 until the summer of 1993, the company's cumulative net of market return hovered around zero (i.e., its stock return was roughly the same as the return on the overall market). Almost immediately after the management change in the summer of 1993, JLG's market-adjusted stock price began its meteoric rise. By the end of 1998, its cumulative net of market stock return was 230 percentage points higher than the returns on the overall market.

To determine whether JLG's stock returns were driven by industry-wide factors, we computed buy-and-hold stock returns for JLG and six industry peers (Case, Caterpillar, Deere, Dover, Omniquip, and Terex) during the period 1993-1998.[7] JLG's buy-and-hold return over this period was $15.82, indicating that one dollar invested in JLG stock at the end of 1992 was worth $15.82 by the end of 1998. The corresponding buy-and-hold return for the equally-weighted portfolio of six industry peers was only $1.48, revealing that JLG's stock price performance over the period handily outpaced that of other firms in the industry. Among the six industry peers, the highest buy-and-hold return was only $2.71 (Caterpillar), far short of JLG's return over the period.

The evidence on buy-and-hold returns suggests that the value created by JLG over the period is due to factors unique to JLG, and not due simply to favorable industry conditions. As the data below suggest, the bulk of the value created by JLG over this period can be attributed to the successful cost reduction, inventory reduction, and revenue enhancement that resulted from the seven-point program.

Improved Processes and Reduced Costs

From 1993-1998, JLG completed a series of continuous process improvement measures designed to reduce manufacturing time and costs. First, it completely reengineered the material flow through the McConnellsburg plant and increased the size of the paint shop. JLG added a new finishing system in 1997 and a new final prep building in 1998, which increased the total plant size from 500,000 to 750,000 square feet, thereby relieving the bottleneck associ-

---

7. The industry portfolio was identified from a list of firms in the same 4-digit SIC codes as JLG by Charles Diller, executive vice president and chief financial officer of JLG.

Employees could receive a maximum of 4% of their salary in 1993, based on
corporate financial performance. In a series of increases during the period 1993 to
1998, JLG gradually increased the bonus percent from 4% to 10%, reflecting its
growing effort to reward employees based on performance.

TABLE 2 COST OF SALES AND SELLING, GENERAL AND ADMINISTRATIVE EXPENSES AS PERCENTAGES OF SALES, JLG, 1990-1998*	Year	Cost of Sales to Sales Ratio	Selling, General and Administrative Expenses to Sales Ratio
	1990	0.747	0.146
	1991	0.787	0.228
	1992	0.796	0.199
	1993	0.771	0.190
	1994	0.761	0.154
	1995	0.755	0.124
	1996	0.737	0.107
	1997	0.753	0.107
	1998	0.759	0.105

*The ratio of cost of sales to sales and selling, general, and administrative expenses to sales for JLG Industries, 1990-1998. All data for these computations are taken from JLG's annual reports.

Cost of Sales. Table 2 reveals that the ratio of JLG's costs of sales to sales fell by roughly two percentage points, from 0.77 in the early 1990s to 0.75 during 1996-1998. To quantify the impact of this reduction on JLG's value, we estimated a discounted cash flow (DCF) model of JLG's value as of the end of 1998. In short, the model enables one to quantify how different assumptions about variables such as the costs to sales ratio affect a company's free cash flows and hence its value. In this case, we estimated the incremental change in JLG's value if its costs-to-sales ratio had remained at 0.77 in 1998, its level at the beginning of the decade. The model assumes that all other variables affecting free cash flow are unaffected by this assumption, which allows us to estimate the independent effect of costs on value. This exercise reveals that if JLG had not reduced its cost-to-sales ratio from 0.77 to 0.75, its value at the end of 1998 would have been approximately $150 million lower than it actually was.

To examine whether the reduction in JLG's costs-to-sales ratio differed from the industry trend, we estimated this ratio for its industry peers as the ratio of the sum of their costs to the sum of their sales in each year during 1990-1997. These data show that the costs-to-sales ratio for the industry follows a remarkably similar pattern as that for JLG, declining through most of the 1990s and then turning up in 1997 and 1998. We can think of three possible inferences to draw from this figure. First, it may be that other firms in the industry adopted process improvements to lower costs in the early to mid-1990s. Second, the reduction in costs-to-sales for both JLG and its industry counterparts may reflect economies of scale in this industry, since units of production increased substantially over the period. Third, the pattern may reflect changes in input prices that had similar effects on both JLG and its competitors.

Selling, general, and administrative expense. Table 2 also contains data on the ratio of JLG's selling, general, and administrative (SG&A) expense to its sales in each year 1990-1998. As the data reveal, this ratio fell dramatically, especially after 1993. During 1990-1992, SG&A amounted to 18.5% of sales. By 1998, SG&A had fallen to 10.5% of sales.

To determine whether the decline in JLG's SG&A-to-sales ratio differs from the industry trend, we examined this ratio for both JLG and the six industry peers. The data show a substantially larger decline for JLG during the 1990s. Whereas the industry ratio hovers between 0.12 and 0.16 over this period, JLG's ratio varies much more widely. At the beginning of the decade, the company's SG&A-to-sales ratio was roughly eight percentage points higher than the industry average. In 1995, it fell below the industry average, where it has since remained.

Inventory Management

JLG eliminated its warehouse and moved to point-of-use and in-transit inventory. The receiving area was changed to the "Transit Area" to indicate that all material must be quickly transported to the point-of-use. With point-of-use inventory, parts are delivered directly to the work cell or line where they will be used, and are replenished throughout the day based on the production schedule. Work in process is moved through the plant on rolling skids and

	Year	Total inventories	Finished goods	Work in process	Raw materials
TABLE 3 INVENTORIES DATA FOR JLG, 1990-1998*					
	PANEL A: DOLLAR VALUE OF INVENTORIES				
	1990	$41.9m			
	1991	37.6m	$12.6m	$15.4m	$9.7m
	1992	25.8m	8.8m	9.4m	7.6m
	1993	19.5m	4.2m	8.5m	6.8m
	1994	23.2m	5.0m	9.2m	9.0m
	1995	33.2m	7.6m	13.4m	12.5m
	1996	39.4m	12.9m	14.0m	12.5m
	1997	53.7m	30.4m	12.1m	9.3m
	1998	47.6m	27.8m	9.3m	15.1m
	PANEL B: INVENTORIES AS PERCENT OF SALES				
	1990	28%			
	1991	40	13%	16%	10%
	1992	23	8	9	7
	1993	16	3	7	6
	1994	13	3	5	5
	1995	12	3	5	5
	1996	10	3	3	3
	1997	10	6	2	2
	1998	9	6	2	3

*Various data on inventories for JLG Industries, 1990-1998. All data are taken from JLG's annual reports over this period.

production scheduling ensures that fabricated parts arrive at the appropriate work area precisely when they are needed.

The result of these changes includes the reduction of average cumulative manufacturing lead-times (for boom-lifts) from 76.1 days in fiscal year 1992 to 9.8 in 1998. Additionally, annual inventory turns, excluding finished goods, improved from four in 1992 to 12 in 1998.[8]

As Table 3 reveals, the value of JLG's inventories changed relatively little as the 1990s progressed, despite large increases in its sales. For example, in 1990, JLG had inventories of $41.9 million; by 1998, inventories had increased to only $47.6 million. Over the same period, JLG's sales increased from $149 million to $531 million. The ratio of JLG's inventories to sales fell steadily, from roughly 0.3 in the early 1990s to less than 0.1 during 1996-1998.

As described previously, the improvements that JLG made to its manufacturing processes are likely to have especially large effects on two components of inventories—work in process and raw materials. Table 3 shows that indeed this was the case. JLG's work-in-process inventories actually peaked at $15.4 million in 1991. By 1998, it had fallen to only $9.3 million, despite the large increase in JLG's sales. As a percentage of sales, JLG's work in process inventories fell from 16% in 1991 to less than 2% in 1998. A similar, albeit less dramatic pattern exists for both raw materials and finished goods. Raw materials inventories as a percentage of sales fell from 10% in 1991 to only 3% in 1998. The corresponding percentage for finished goods inventories fell from 13% in 1991 to 6% in 1998.

The dramatic improvement in JLG's inventory management over this period has had a huge effect on its value. To demonstrate this, we again use the DCF model discussed above. In computing free cash flow, one subtracts the cash outflows associated with gross investment from the gross cash flow from operations. A major component of gross investment is the investment that a firm makes in its operating

---

8. "Journey to Excellence," Raymond F. Treml and Thomas A Horejs, JLG Industries

JLG's EVA and MVA increased substantially over the period. EVA increased from a negative $2.2 million in 1993 to $21.6 million in 1998, peaking at $29.6 million in 1997. The company's MVA increased in a similar fashion, from $26.7 million in 1993 to $512.5 million in 1998.

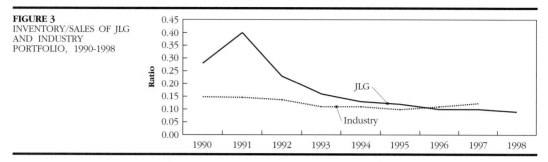

FIGURE 3
INVENTORY/SALES OF JLG AND INDUSTRY PORTFOLIO, 1990-1998

working capital. In turn, a large component of investment in operating working capital is investment in inventories, computed as the change in inventories from one year to the next.

When JLG's inventory-to-sales ratio was 0.25, as it was in the early 1990s, its investment in operating working capital represented 6.5% of sales. As it lowered its inventory-to-sales ratio to 0.10, JLG's investment in operating working capital fell to only 2.5% of sales. We estimate that this reduction in operating working capital has increased the value of JLG by more than $400 million.

To compare the change in JLG's inventory management with that of its competitors, we plot the annual inventory-to-sales ratio for JLG and the seven industry cohorts in Figure 3. The graph shows that JLG accomplished a much greater reduction in this ratio than the industry as a whole. The inventory-to-sales ratio oscillated between 0.10 and 0.15 for the industry over the period, while it fell from 0.30 to 0.10 for JLG.

Accelerated New Product Development

From 1995 to 1998 JLG increased research and design spending by 73%, confirming their commitment to accelerate new product development. JLG introduced 40 new products from 1994 through 1998 while the nearest competitors introduced 10 booms and 14 scissors in the same timeframe. The expansion of new products included both innovative products and replacements of complete families of machines.

According to Rao Bollimpalli, senior vice president of engineering, the two key contributors to the growth in new product development were the integrated product development teams (IPD) and the technological tools. The IPD teams allowed the development to be proactive and enabled a shorter development cycle while lowering expenses. New technology including the CAD system also allowed JLG to reduce time to market and costs. Technology helped the company to move closer to three NPD goals of (1) first-pass design, (2) solid modeling on the CAD system, and (3) production of prototypes on the assembly line. These strategies have improved the accuracy of first design from 60% with hard prototypes to 85% with the use of technology.

As shown in Table 4, JLG's sales grew almost fivefold over the 1993-1998 period, from $110.5 million in 1992 to $530.9 million in 1998. They grew especially fast in 1995, 1996, and 1997, with annual increases of $93 million (53% growth), $144 million (54% growth), and $113 million (27% growth), respectively. The table also shows that a high percentage of JLG's sales in each of these years was accounted for by new (i.e., developed within the past two years) or redesigned products. Of the $257 million increase in sales from 1995 to 1997, only $80 million, or 30%, came from existing products; the remaining 70% came from new or redesigned products, indicating that JLG's product development efforts accounts for a large proportion of its sales growth during 1993-1998.

Table 4 also reveals that JLG increased its international sales markedly over the period. In 1992, global sales amounted to $19 million, or 17% of total sales. By 1998, global sales had increased ninefold, to $170 million, or 32% of sales. This evidence indicates that JLG accomplished its goal of expanding global distribution by a sizable amount.

Figure 4 plots JLG's annual sales growth rate from 1990-1998 and the corresponding aggregate sales growth rate for the seven industry cohorts listed previously. The figure shows that JLG's sales growth rate exceeded that of the industry by a sizeable margin over 1993-1998. While the industry sales growth rate hovered between 5% to 15%, JLG achieved growth rates of 43% in 1994, 53% in 1995,

	Year	Sales	Sales Growth Rate	% of Sales from New or Redesigned Products	International Sales as % of Total Sales
TABLE 4 SALES AND NEW PRODUCT DATA FOR JLG, 1990-1998*	1990	$149.3m			
	1991	94.4m	−37%		
	1992	110.5m	17	18%	17%
	1993	123.0m	11	18	18
	1994	176.4m	43	25	25
	1995	269.2m	53	24	18
	1996	413.4m	54	27	24
	1997	526.3m	27	46	30
	1998	530.9m	1	32	32

*Various data on JLG's sales, 1990-1998. Source: JLG's annual reports, 1993-1998.

FIGURE 4
JLG INDUSTRIES INC. SALES GROWTH RATE VS. INDUSTRY PORTFOLIO, 1990-1998

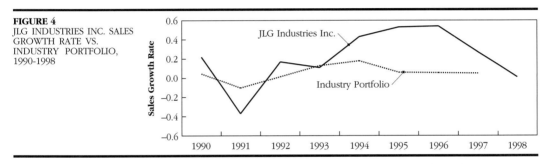

54% in 1996, and 27% in 1997.

Concluding comments

A major challenge facing corporate managers, consultants, and business scholars is understanding why corporations often fail to achieve the goals embodied in strategic plans. Recent studies suggest that an important but often ignored factor is the coordination of organizational changes with the adoption of management techniques, such as TQM and JIT, that require the use of knowledge that is diffused throughout the organization. In particular, successful implementation of these programs is likely to require more involvement of front-line employees in decision-

making and a strengthening of employee incentives to align their incentives with value creation.

The case of JLG Industries illustrates the importance of combining knowledge-based management techniques with decentralized decision-making and strong employee incentives. JLG adopted several of these techniques, but did not achieve the expected results until it shifted from a centralized governance structure to one that encouraged the involvement of front-line employees with important information that proved useful in redesigning both products and processes. The combination of these management techniques, decentralization, and heightened incentives resulted in the proliferation of dozens of new products, spectacular improvements in operating efficiency, and the creation of immense value.

ADDING VALUE FOR SHAREHOLDERS IN SOUTH AFRICA: AN ANALYSIS OF THE REMBRANDT RESTRUCTURING

by Brian Kantor,
University of Cape Town*

S outh African companies, long inhibited by exchange control and international opprobrium, are responding energetically to the opportunities and threats, to the risks and rewards, provided by increasingly global capital markets, of which the Johannesburg Stock Exchange (JSE) is now so much more an accepted part. It has taken the new democratic dispensation in South Africa, the removal of sanctions, and the relief of exchange control to encourage this process of change. The tightly controlled JSE-listed companies have in response become both more specialized and much more international in their operations, and they now appear to attach much less importance to the need to maintain their control structures.

The South African corporate landscape has in fact changed quite materially from the system dominated by family-controlled groups of companies that I described in this journal six years ago.[1] The Anglo-American Corporation (Anglo), by far the largest of these groups listed on the JSE, has been in the vanguard of such responses. Anglo has also listed on the London Stock Exchange and moved its head office to the U.K. in 1999. More important, the cross holdings between Anglo and the De Beers Corporation, which effectively secured the Oppenheimer family control over Anglo and De Beers, were eliminated in June 2001. De Beers itself was delisted and converted into a private diamond mining and distribution company, in which the Oppenheimer family company and

*I should like to thank Investec Securities for permission to apply some of their tables and analysis and in particular Kalinka Anjelopolj and Anthony Geard of Investec Securities for their most helpful assistance. I must also thank my colleague Graham Barr for his advice and assistance with the model building exercises. The responsibility for any errors and inadequate analysis is of course mine alone.

1. Graham Barr, Jos Gerson and Brian Kantor, "Shareholders as Agents and Principals: The Case for South Africa's Corporate Governance System," *Journal of Applied Corporate Finance*, Vol. 8 No. 1 (Spring 1995).

Anglo each holds 45% of the shares (and which the family effectively controls). The other 10% of the new De Beers is held by the Botswana government. In this way, Anglo has become a management-controlled company with a highly diffuse group of shareholders, none of which holds more than a minor stake in the company.[2]

South African Breweries (SAB), the largest industrial company listed on the JSE, also moved its primary listing to London. It did so after unbundling and selling much of its non-brewing portfolio to focus on its international brewing business. The holding company Bevcon, which held a 30% stake in SAB and through which Anglo, with others, exercised shareholder control over SAB, distributed its SAB shares to its shareholders in an unbundling operation.

The two major mutual life assurance companies that controlled two other important groups of companies on the JSE, Sanlam and the Old Mutual, have given up their mutual status and become stock exchange-listed companies themselves. And the Old Mutual has also become a U.K.-domiciled company with its primary listing on the LSE.

The Rembrandt group, the other major family-controlled group of companies listed on the JSE, has undergone a major restructuring designed to simplify its conglomerate nature and split the company into two more specialized parts. The founding families, however, continue to maintain control over the two new JSE-listed components of the group. And the Rembrandt restructuring is one of the main subjects of this paper.

In the pages that follow, I begin by analyzing the general forces that determine the value of a holding company whose most important assets are shares held in a variety of listed subsidiary or associate companies. I explain why unbundling, while reducing the discount to what is described as Net Asset Value, does not necessarily add value for shareholders. And, as I go on to suggest, adding value for shareholders requires changes that are much more fundamental than those that are likely to be accomplished by the recent restructuring of the Rembrandt group.

WHY NAV IS THE WRONG INDICATOR OF SHAREHOLDER VALUE ADDED

Given the opportunities provided the SA groups to restructure and unbundle, the spotlight has been cast ever more brightly upon what is widely assumed to be the counterproductive for shareholders—namely, the conglomerate nature of many of the South African groups.[3] In attempting to arrive at an assessment of what is popularly called "the conglomerate discount," financial analysts and asset managers pay particular attention to the relationship between the market value and the net asset value (NAV) of the South African Holding companies. On the basis of such calculations, almost all of the listed holding companies have a market value that is less than their NAV—that is to say, they trade at a discount to their NAV. And from this finding alone, analysts often infer that the company would be worth more to its shareholders if its assets were liquidated. That is, either the constituent parts should be sold off and the cash distributed to shareholders; or the shares they own in other companies (which account for most of the NAV) should be distributed to their shareholders. This kind of "unbundling," it is widely argued, would eliminate the discount to NAV and thereby add value for shareholders generally.

Some Leading Questions

To show why this argument is misleading if not wrong, we need to explore the following questions:

1. When will the value of a holding company stand at a discount to its NAV?

2. Why does the discount go up or down?

3. When will unbundling reduce or eliminate the discount to NAV?

4. How can unbundling hope to add value for shareholders?

The simple answer to question 1 is that the market believes the management of the holding company will destroy shareholder value by making future investment decisions that cost shareholders more than they prove to be worth—and,

---

2. Full details of these transactions are to be found on the Anglo American plc web site, www.angloamerican.co.uk

3. Such controversies are by no means unique to South Africa but occur wherever the system of listed holding and subsidiary companies is applied, as for example in continental Europe. By way of illustration there is at this time of writing a dispute between Investment Banks UBS Warburg and Lazards concerning three French holding companies run by Lazards in which UBS holds stakes, Eurafrance

SA, Azeo SA and Societe Immobiliere Marsellaise SA. To quote *The Asian Wall Street Journal* (Ruling Escalates Tension between Lazard, Warburg) November 24-26, 2000 p. 13, "Warburg believes that the companies, which trade below the value of their assets, should be broken up to release their latent value for shareholders ...." See also (Truce Agreed in Battle at Lazard) *Financial Times* November 28, 2000 p. 17.

> The fact that the shares of Berkshire Hathaway are worth more than the sum of the values of its publicly traded subsidiaries (and at least the book value of its untraded assets) reflects the expectation that Warren Buffett will continue to make investments with above-normal returns.

more generally, by the pursuit of corporate empire building rather than value maximization. The upfront discount has the effect of compensating new shareholders for these disadvantages by converting expected below-normal *operating* rates of return on investment into expected, normal *share market* returns.

The opposite is true of the rare holding company that stands at a premium to its NAV. Take, for example, Warren Buffett's Berkshire Hathaway. In that case, the fact that its shares are worth more than the sum of the values of its publicly traded subsidiaries (and at least the book value of its untraded assets) reflects the expectation that management will continue to make above-normal returns. As the history of Berkshire Hathaway suggests, shareholders are willing to pay a premium for the privilege of sharing in those returns. In other words, investors have to pay to enter the premium club and are offered a discount to join the low-life types at the back of the bus.

A little bit of algebra can make this point very clearly and help us address some of the further implications indicated above.

$$\%\text{Discount} = 100*(\text{MVAdjNAV} - \text{MV})/\text{MVAdjNAV}\% \quad (1),$$

where MV represents the market value of the holding company and MVAdjNAV represents its NAV (or rather, as discussed below, its market value adjusted NAV). If MVAdjNAV>MV, as is almost invariably the case, the holding company will trade at a positive discount. But in cases where MVAdjNAV<MV, the discount will be a negative number and called a "premium."

The Different Definitions of NAV

First let us be perfectly clear what we mean about the NAV of a holding company when we refer to a discount to its NAV. Most important is to recognize that this NAV is *not* what is usually meant by the NAV of a company, which is simply the *book value* of its assets less its debts. In what has become a common practice not only in South Africa, but in equity analysis throughout the world, the NAV of a holding company is calculated by continuously converting the value of the holding company's assets

from book to market value. It is therefore best described as a market value adjusted net asset value, or MVAdjNAV.

Following the practice of the South African Mining Houses,[4] this MVAdjNAV can in turn be defined as follows

$$\text{MVAdjNAV} = \text{ML} + \text{BU} + \text{Cash} - \text{Debts} \quad (2),$$

where ML represents the market value of the listed assets of the holding company and BU represents either the book value of the unlisted assets of the company or the director's estimate of that value (which in most cases would exceed the original book value).

Alternatively, an analyst might substitute for BU an estimate of the market value of its unlisted assets, in which case:

$$\text{MVAdjNAV} = \text{ML} + \text{MU} + \text{Cash} - \text{Debts} \quad (3)$$

Using some of the same terms, we can define the market value of the holding company as follows:

$$\text{MV} = \text{ML} + \text{MU} + \text{MH} + \text{MP} \quad (4)$$

That is, market value can be expressed as the sum of the market value of its listed assets (ML) and the market value of its unlisted assets (MU), plus two other variables: MH and MP. MH can be thought of as the market value of the holding company's head office operations that provide services (and charge fees) to the subsidiary companies—both listed and unlisted. MH will usually, though not always, have a positive value, especially if the subsidiary companies receiving these financial and technical services are paying above market-related fees for the services provided. (Thus, another way of viewing MH is as the net present value of the wealth transfers from the subsidiaries to the parent.)

This brings us to MP, which is really the critical variable in the valuation of a holding company, as well as the most important determinant of how a holding company trades in relation to its NAV. MP reflects the net present value of all the projects the management of the holding company is expected to undertake in the future, as well as the likelihood that management will either

---

4. The mining houses, which reported such numbers in their annual reports, must have thought it advantageous to point to the fact that their NAV was greater than their market values. They did so presumably because it improved their credit worthiness.

discontinue current value-reducing investments, or convert them into value-increasing investments. Net present value is the difference between the present value of the operating surpluses the investment is expected to realize and the cost of undertaking these investments. This may be their acquisition costs or the value of a series of disbursements that might have to be made over time to bring a green-field project to completion. MP represents the market's estimate of the value of the gleam in the management's eye. If these projects are expected to add value for shareholders over and above the value of the cash that will be paid out to undertake the projects, then MP will have a positive value. If not, MP will take on a negative value.

Reformulating the Calculation of the Discount

If we now substitute for MVAdjNAV from equation 3 and for MV from equation 4 into equation 1 we get the following expression for the discount from NAV:

$$\% \text{ Discount} = [ML + MU + Cash - Debt - (ML + MU + MH + MP)] / (ML + MU + Cash - Debt)$$

The MLs and MUs cancel out in the numerator, reducing the expression to the following:

$$\% \text{ Discount} = [(Cash - Debts) - MH - MP] / [ML + MU + (Cash - Debt)] \quad (5)$$

If we instead use the mining house definition from equation 2, the equation would take the form

$$\% \text{ Discount} = [BU + (Cash - Debt) - MU - MH - MP] / [ML + MU + (Cash - Debt)] \quad (6)$$

A number of points become clear when we examine the right hand side of equation 5.

First of all, the larger the absolute value of the numerator, the larger will be the discount. At the same time, the larger is the absolute value of the denominator, the smaller the discount will be. Thus, for any increase in the market value of the listed or unlisted assets of the holding company, which are represented in the denominator of equation 5, the discount will be smaller.

What is important to recognize, then, is that the discount will change in response to market-wide changes in the value of assets, changes over which management has little if any control. If underlying market conditions improve, the value of a holding company's investments will rise and the discount will narrow; but the discount will widen if general market conditions deteriorate. In such cases, to repeat, the movement in the discount mostly will have nothing to do with the actions of the managers of the holding company who exercise control over the managers of their listed and unlisted subsidiaries.

A True Value Proposition

But in cases where the value of the assets under holding company control moves independently of the broad market, it may make sense to praise or blame the management of the holding company for the lower or higher discount to MVAdjNAV. The value added or lost might then be properly attributed to the exercise of effective or ineffective corporate governance by the controlling shareholders over the managers of their subsidiaries. The opportunity for the holding company to exercise shareholder control over the management of a listed or unlisted subsidiary may add value to it and, in so doing, reduce the size of the discount. This essentially is the justification for a closely controlled (if not owned) holding company—namely, that it provides the means for superior managers to exercise shareholder rather than management control over companies at all levels of the group structure.[5]

Let us now turn to the numerator of equation 5. There it can be seen that the greater the expected market value of new projects (MP), the smaller the absolute value of the numerator and so the lower the discount. It thus becomes clear from equation 5 that a persistently large discount reflects in large part investors' pessimism about the value of the future investment program of the holding company (as well as the extent of management's commitment to maximizing the

---

5. See, again, my article with Graham Barr and Jos Person, cited in footnote 1.

MP, which is the really critical variable, reflects the net present value of all the projects the management of the holding company is expected to undertake in the future, as well as the likelihood that management will either discontinue current value-reducing investments, or convert them into value-increasing ones.

value of existing operations). That is, the appearance of a persistently large discount will reveal that a large negative value has been attached to MP. This would be especially true in cases where the market value of listed and unlisted assets, represented in the denominator, is large and therefore will tend to reduce the discount. The more valuable are these assets, the larger is the market value of ML and MU, the larger the absolute size of the denominator, and so the smaller the discount—for any given value of the numerator. MH is unlikely to have a material effect on the value of the numerator, given that the present value of head office fees over the cost of providing service is unlikely to be material one way or another for most large companies.

Thus, in order for the management of a large holding company to reduce the discount, it would have to increase MP, the net present value of their investment program. (Alternatively, it would have to convince the market that it was committed to either ending or improving the efficiency of existing value-destroying operations.) Naturally words alone cannot hope to overcome a high degree of market skepticism as reflected in a large discount. It would require the convincing adoption of a clearly more disciplined process for undertaking investments—one in which the firm demonstrated its commitment to pursue only those investment projects that promised to provide returns exceeding the opportunity cost of the capital invested.

UNBUNDLING BY ITSELF IS NOT THE SOLUTION

Unbundling is the distribution of listed assets held by the holding company to its shareholders. This action by itself cannot add value for shareholders—and for essentially the same reason that 4 minus 2 is equal to 2 and not 3. What is gained by shareholders in the form of shares previously held on their behalf by the holding company must by the same token mean a less valuable holding company. In fact, simply distributing some listed assets to shareholders, all other things (especially MP) remaining the same, will actually increase rather than reduce the discount. A reduction in the ML of equation 5 means a smaller denominator and so a

larger ratio or discount, provided MP, the negative value attached to the company's investment program, is unaffected.

If all the listed assets were distributed to shareholders, the company would cease to be a holding company for which a market value adjusted NAV could be calculated. But if a separate market value was attached to some of its important unlisted assets, especially if they were less than wholly owned, then a discount to MVAdjNAV would still be possible. And if book values or directors' valuations were instead used to estimate MVAdjNAV as per equation 2, then the discount (applying the original mining house convention) would decline after distribution or sale of an asset, provided the book or directors' valuation exceeded the market value of the listed or unlisted asset being disposed of or unbundled to shareholders. But if book values fell short of the implicit market value of the unlisted subsidiaries, then the opposite would happen—the discount would widen.[6]

For this reason, then, an unbundling exercise with no significant change in managerial control or decision-making is unlikely to add value for shareholders even if the discount increases or decreases. In other words, the critical issue is the relevance of any unbundling exercise for the value of MP of equation 5. Will unbundling lead to better investments or, perhaps better yet, be associated with the complete abandonment of clearly failing investment programs? Or, to propose the unthinkable, would the managements of some holding companies even choose to liquidate their entire firms? In cases where MP has a sufficiently large negative value, such acts of managerial self-abnegation would surely add value for shareholders.

Is Balance Sheet Strength Good or Bad?

To expect the managers or owner-managers of a holding company—especially one with a successful track record of adding value for shareholders—to give up simply because the market is skeptical about their investment program is usually to expect too much of managers. They will be well aware that the judgment of the market is subject to change. And given a degree of insensitivity to market valuations by controlling managers or shareholders, the fact that the holding company has a significant portfolio

---

6. The numerator and denominator would both decline by the same amount causing the ratio to decline that is provided BU>ML.

of cash and other liquid listed assets will be highly relevant for the estimation of MP and the market value of a holding company. When the holding company has valuable assets in the form of cash and shares in listed companies, it has the power to pursue projects relatively unhindered by the need to raise additional finance from the capital markets. Listed assets are almost as good as cash for the purpose of financing investment decisions. This is especially true if the sales of shares in the listed subsidiaries or divisions can be affected without reducing the holding company's control of the subsidiary. This will be the case when the holding company holds significantly more than the 50% of the voting rights in the subsidiary or tracked division, or when control can be maintained in other ways even when the controller's share falls below 50%.

But financial strength is not always a source of value. In cases where a company's future investments are not regarded as promising by the market, but are expected to be undertaken anyway because of the financial strength of the holding company, then more balance sheet strength is a disadvantage rather than an advantage to shareholders. In short, the value of MP becomes even more negative for companies that can afford to ignore financial markets. And in the case of holding companies with listed assets, it is not only the waste of cash that may be of concern to shareholders, but also the waste of the listed assets that can easily be converted into cash.

Signals From Management

Thus the greater the firepower of a holding company in the form of cash and shares held in listed companies, the more vulnerable are shareholders to the danger of poor investments that are expected to have little or even negative value for investors. Such dangers will be reflected in a lower market value for the holding company and a large discount to MVAdjNAV.

In such cases, unbundling of listed assets may add value simply by signalling to the market that management is about to take a more disciplined approach to investment. The willingness of a holding company to reduce the strength of its balance sheet and dispose of its highly liquid listed assets could be a sign to shareholders that management will be less likely to proceed with unprofitable projects in the future. A similarly positive signal would be provided by the holding company's announcement of its plan to buy back its shares with surplus cash or with cash generated through disposals of assets.

Value can only be added for shareholders if projects are undertaken that are expected to return more than their cost of capital. This criterion applies equally to stand-alone, single-business companies and to diversified holding companies. Holding companies can add value to their listed subsidiaries by ensuring that the managers of the listed subsidiaries they control undertake only those projects that promise to add value for all their shareholders.

In effect the market is judging the value of a holding company as it judges a successful stand-alone company—primarily on the basis of its future performance not its past record of achievement (which can be inferred from a large positive market-to-book ratio). Converting book NAV into market adjusted NAV is consistent with such a forward-looking approach. But when used for purposes of internal performance evaluation, there is a problem with this approach. Requiring the managers of holding companies to achieve market values in excess of their market-adjusted NAVs effectively sets the bar too high. By converting book values into current market values, stock analysts are asking already successful companies to continually exceed the expectations created by their past successes.

In many cases, then, the market is clearly skeptical about the ability of managers of holding companies to add additional value in the future. In such cases, an unbundling strategy that promises major improvements in operating and investment strategy could succeed in adding significant value— and perhaps even in eliminating (at least for a time) the discount to NAV. But for those holding companies with a highly successful track record of delivering value to shareholders, selling at a discount to a market value adjusted NAV is not a sufficient reason to unbundle. Indeed, the only way that a consistently successful value-adding holding company can continue to add value is by continuously exceeding the market's expectations—that is, by continually surprising the market with new and even more profitable investments. But since markets are forward looking, once the company fails to match the expectations built into its listed assets, any premium of its market value to its MVNAV will quickly turn into a discount.

Requiring the managers of holding companies to achieve market values in excess of their market-adjusted NAVs effectively sets the bar too high. By converting book values into current market values, stock analysts are asking already successful companies to continually exceed the expectations created by their past successes.

FIGURE 1
REMBRANDT AND THE
MARKET (A ONE YEAR
PERSPECTIVE)

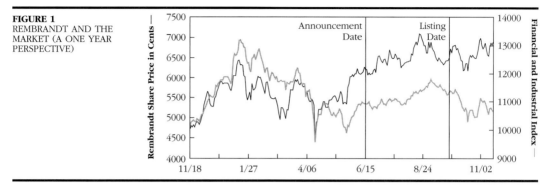

A MEASURE OF WEALTH CREATION: THE CASE OF THE REMBRANDT UNBUNDLING

A case study of the effects of unbundling is provided by the restructuring and unbundling exercise conducted by the Rembrandt Group of companies in the year 2000. The holding company, Rembrandt Group Limited, was converted into two listed entities Venfin, which now holds the group's technology interests, and Remgro, which houses the more traditional industrial interests of Rembrandt. The restructuring was also accompanied by the removal of the four listed pyramid holding companies through which family control of Rembrandt had been secured. The controlling stake in Rembrandt was held through a tier of JSE listed holding companies,[7] conferring the equivalent of a 6.7% ownership stake, which was swapped for B shares in the new companies. These unlisted B shares came with with highly differential voting rights that maintained family control. In this way the structure of assets was changed, but without any change in the control structure.

As I argued earlier, unbundling in and of itself will not add value for shareholders unless the unbundling exercise is regarded as a reliable signal of improved investment decisions and greater operating efficiency. Unfortunately, there is no obvious reason to believe that the Rembrandt unbundling provides such a signal. The fact that the two new companies are closely

controlled by the same group of shareholders and managers that controlled the old Rembrandt was not likely to encourage the market to believe that the investment process has changed materially.

Has this transaction added value for shareholders? The proof of the pudding is in the eating—that is, how has the market responded to the announcement of the Rembrant unbundling on June 15, 2000, and how have the shares of Remgro and Venfin performed since the restructuring exercise concluded on September 26, 2000?

Conducting an Event Study

The most challenging part of any such calculation of value creation following some important event of this kind is to factor out the impact of the market itself on shareholder returns. This therefore presumes a significant statistical relationship between the value of the shares and the market itself.[8] In Figure 1, we show the relationship between the market and the value of Rembrandt between November 1999 and November 2000, some two months after the unbundling was concluded. (As can be seen from the figure, the relationship between the market and Rembrandt appears to be a very close one.) In the period immediately before the announcement of the intention to unbundle on June 14, Rembrandt shares do seem to gain relative to the market. This

7. The pyramid structure that secured family control of Rembrandt Group Limited consisted of a tier of holding companies, four of which were listed on the JSE. At the apex of the structure was a private company Rembrandt Trust that held 44.5% of the shares in a listed company TIB. TIB in turn held 60.4% of the listed company Tegkor. Tegkor in turn held 40.6% of RBB, another listed subsidiary. The only asset of RBB was a 51.1% controlling stake in the parent company, Rembrandt Group Limited. The ownership stake of the unlisted family controlled Rembrandt Trust in the Rembrandt Group Limited that secured control of the major holding company was thus approximately 5.6%. (44.5*60.4*40.6*51.1) Some additional

direct holdings took the effective ownership stake of the families to the 6.7% ownership share represented by the B shares.

8. Any statements one could make about unbundling in general, as opposed to the value created or lost in a particular unbundling exercise, would require a relatively large sample of similar unbundling exercises in order to reduce the influence of possibly idiosyncratic forces acting in a particular case. A large sample of South African case studies is however not available. And so we procede with an analysis of the Rembrandt unbundling seen in isolation.

TABLE 1
REGRESSION RESULTS: DAILY CHANGES IN REMBRANDT EXPLAINED BY DAILY CHANGES IN THE FINANCIAL AND INDUSTRIAL INDEX

Dependent Variable:	DREM (daily changes in Rembrandt)		
Method:	Least Squares		
Sample(adjusted):	11/19/1999 6/14/2000		
Included observations:	149 after adjusting endpoints		

Variable	Coefficient	Std. Error	t-Statistic	Prob.
C	0.130028	0.164309	0.791363	0.4300
DFI	1.163293	0.105037	11.07507	0.0000

R-squared	0.454	Mean dependent var	0.188
Adjusted R-squared	0.451	S.D. dependent var	2.705
S.E. of regression	2.00	Akaike info criterion	4.242
Sum squared resid	590.71	Schwarz criterion	4.28
Log likelihood	−314.0375	F-statistic	122.65
Durbin-Watson stat	1.85	Prob(F-statistic)	0.000000

FIGURE 2
FORECAST AND ACTUAL VALUE OF REMBRANDT (SINCE THE UNBUNDLING ANNOUNCEMENT AND FOR A LIMITED PERIOD AFTER THE LISTING)

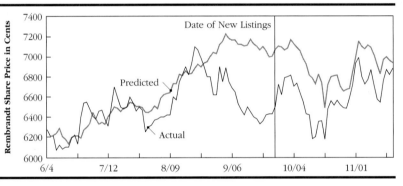

relative advantage then seems to have been maintained up until and after the listing of the separate unbundled parts on September 26.

A significant statistical relationship between changes in the daily value of Rembrandt and the market, as represented by the Financial and Industrial Index of the JSE, was found for the months leading up to announcement of its intent to restructure, which was made on the June 15, 2000. Having established this statistical relationship, which is reported in Table 1,[9] it was then possible to use this equation to predict, taking into account the actual behavior of the market after June 15, what the value of a combined holding in Venfin and Remgro might have been in the absence of the unbundling exercise. The difference between the predicted by the model value and the actual value may then be attributed, within appropriate confidence limits, to the event—in this case the unbundling and restructuring of Rembrandt.[10]

In Figure 2 we show a comparison of the value of Rembrandt, as predicted by the market model, with its actual value from June 15, when the announcment was made, until November 17, 2000 when the statistical analysis was concluded . After the unbundling on September 26, "Rembrandt" is represented by the sum of the share prices of the newly listed Venfin and Remgro.[11] The results of this exercise are ambigous. As

---

9. As can be seen in Table 1, daily movements in the Index explain about 45% on average of the daily movement in Rembrandt. The Rembrandt beta is 1.16.

10. The model as may be seen is estimated in daily change form. These daily changes and their values, as forecast by this model, given the actual fluctuations in the market, have been converted into a series of actual share prices for easier reference.

11. We regard a period of two months after the unbundling as sufficient time for the benefits of the unbundling to reveal itself. Furthermore the model, based upon the relationship between the combined Rembrandt and the market in the period leading up to the announcment, could not be expected to apply indefinitely to the separately listed Venfin and Remgro. The two new companies with a different character will establish their own different market betas over time.

Unbundling in and of itself will not add value for shareholders unless it is regarded as a reliable signal of improved investment decisions and greater operating efficiency. Given that the two new companies are closely controlled by the same group of shareholders and managers who controlled the old Rembrandt, there is no obvious reason to believe that the Rembrandt unbundling provides such a signal.

indicated, the actual and expected values of Rembrandt shares move closely together after the announcement on June 15. Then, immediately prior to the listing, Rembrandt shares appear to fall back relative to their estimated values. After the unbundling, the combined value of the new Venfin and Remgro seem to closely conform to the values expected of them, given the behavior of the market generally.

Thus, as we might have predicted, Rembrandt's unbundling appears to have had no material benefits for its shareholders.

CONCLUSION—COSMETIC CHANGES VERSUS VALUE-ADDED RESTRUCTURING

Value can be added for shareholders only if restructurings are expected to (1) increase the efficiency of existing operations; (2) discontinue value-destroying investments; or (3) encourage investment only in projects that are expected to return more than their cost of capital. This criterion applies equally to stand-alone companies and to holding companies. Holding companies can add value to their listed subsidiaries and to themselves if they ensure that the managers of the listed subsidiaries they control only undertake projects that return more than their cost of capital.

Clearly, in many cases, the market is skeptical about the ability of managers of holding companies, even those with a good track record, to add additional value in the future. In the case of a holding company, this skepticism reveals itself in a discount to market value-adjusted NAV. For managers of holding companies that are subject to a discount to market-adjusted NAV, it is important to realize that if they succeed in their mission of identifying investments that return more than their cost of capital, they may take the market by surprise and be rewarded with a higher share price. But their shares are still unlikely to trade at a premium to MVNAV. A premium is only awarded to those few holding companies that are expected to find *new* cost of capital-beating investments, not merely to those with a history of them.

LEVERAGED RECAPS AND THE CURBING OF CORPORATE OVERINVESTMENT

*by David J. Denis and
Diane K. Denis,
Virginia Tech*

D uring the 1980s the number and size of leveraged buyouts and leveraged recapitalizations increased dramatically. Proponents of such highly leveraged transactions (HLTs) argued that the combination of high leverage and increased management stock ownership would strengthen management incentives to increase operating efficiency and resist the temptation to "overinvest," thereby increasing share values and corporate competitiveness.[1] Critics of HLTs claimed that the heavy debt loads would force cutbacks in productive investment and impose a short-term orientation, thus reducing competitiveness.

In this article, we offer further insights into the economic consequences of HLTs by presenting the findings of our recently published study of 29 leveraged recapitalizations completed between 1984 and 1988.[2] Unlike LBOs, companies undergoing leveraged recaps remain publicly traded after the transaction, thus affording us greater opportunity to observe changes in internal operating and investment decisions *after* the transactions. Our study was designed to answer two questions: Did HLTs in fact reduce the amount of internally-generated funds available for investment—and thus the actual level of investment? And if so, did these constraints on investment serve to increase or decrease shareholder value?

By way of a brief preview, we reached the following conclusions about companies undergoing leveraged recaps:

- their stock prices outperformed the market by 26%, on average, in the period surrounding the recap;
- in the first year after the recap, their ratio of operating (pre-interest) income to assets increased by over 20%;
- even with such an increase in operating cash flow, a 250% increase in interest payments led to a 30% reduction in their undistributed cash flow, and a 35% reduction in capital expenditures;
- over the five-year period *prior* to the recap, the stock market reaction to their announcements of major corporate investments (including acquisitions) was systematically negative;
- after the recap, the market reaction to their (much less frequent) announcements of investments was statistically indistinguishable from zero.

In short, our study provides striking evidence that HLTs added value by forcing management to pay out excess capital rather than diversify through acquisitions or continue to make unprofitable investments in mature businesses.

---

1. Major substitutions of debt for equity—as argued notably by Michael Jensen—would compel managements accustomed to reinvesting in low-return projects to pay out their "free cash flow" to investors. See Michael C. Jensen, "Agency Costs of Free Cash Flow, Corporate Finance, and Takeovers," *American Economic Review* (May 1986), pp. 323-329 and Rene M. Stulz, "Managerial Discretion and Optimal Financing Policies," *Journal of Financial Economics* (July 1990), pp. 3-28.
2. See David J. Denis and Diane K. Denis, "Managerial Discretion, Organizational Structure, and Corporate Performance: A Study of Leveraged Recapitalizations," *Journal of Accounting and Economics* (January, 1993).

TABLE 1
MEAN AND MEDIAN*
CHANGES IN OWNERSHIP
AND CAPITAL STRUCTURE

Variable	Pre-Recap	Post-Recap	P-Value[a]
Beneficial Ownership of Officers and Directors[b]	5.2%	7.7%	0.003
	(1.7%)	(3.6%)	0.001
Ownership of Officers, Directors and Employees	9.4%	18.6%	0.000
	(5.9%)	(14.7%)	0.000
Total Debt/Total Assets[c]	41.3%	102.9%	0.000
	(44.6%)	(86.1%)	0.000
Long-term Debt/Total Assets	18.1%	69.2%	0.000
	(15.1%)	(49.9%)	0.000

*Medians in parentheses.
a. P-values measure the statistical significance of pairwise changes in the variables and are computed using a standard t-test for differences in means and the Wilcoxon signed-ranks test for differences in medians.
b. Beneficial ownership of officers, directors, and employees is obtained primarily from corporate proxy statements. Where proxy statements are unavailable, ownership information is obtained from *Value Line* and *Spectrum 6*. Changes in ownership structure are measured from the last reported ownership prior to the recapitalization to the first report of ownership following the recapitalization.
c. The change in total and long-term debt to total assets is computed from Compustat data and is measured from the last fiscal year prior to the recapitalization to the first full year following the recapitalization.

WHAT ARE LEVERAGED RECAPS?

Leveraged recapitalizations, also sometimes referred to as "leveraged cash-outs," typically involve significant payouts to common shareholders financed by new borrowings. Although most recaps are set up as large one-time dividend payments, they can also be structured as share repurchases or exchange offers in which some combination of cash, debt securities, and new common shares is exchanged for existing shares. In many recaps, share-owning managers and directors choose not to participate in the cash portion of the distribution, thereby increasing their proportional share ownership. Thus, as in the case of LBOs, leveraged recaps result in significant increases not only in leverage, but also in management's percentage share ownership.

Take the case of Kroger Co. In 1988, responding to takeover pressure from the Haft family and then a formal bid by KKR, Kroger gave its shareholders, in exchange for each share of stock, a $40 dividend, a junior subordinated debenture valued at $8.69, and a new "stub" share of common stock (that initially traded at $8.875). Two months before the

Haft family came into the picture, Kroger's stock had been trading at just below $40. The total value of the recap package, estimated at roughly $57.50 per share, thus represented an over 40% gain for Kroger's shareholders (although it was still more than 10% lower than KKR's bid, valued at $64 per share).

Because Kroger's senior management and directors chose to forgo the cash and debt part of the distribution for a portion of their shares, their percentage equity stake more than doubled, from 1.4% to 3.0%. In this respect, the Kroger deal was fairly representative of our entire sample of 29 recaps; as shown in Table 1, the median percentage stock ownership of management and directors increased from 1.7 to 3.6%.[3]

The financing for Kroger's recap, which consisted of almost $3 billion in net new bank borrowings, $1 billion of increasing rate notes, and $704 million of subordinated debt held by selling shareholders, raised the company's debt-to-total capital ratio from just under 30% to over 90%. As shown in Table 1, the median debt-to-capital ratio for the 29 recaps in our sample increased from 45% to 86%.

---

3. For the changes in managerial ownership following large management buyouts in the 1980s, see Steven N. Kaplan and Jeremy C. Stein, "The Evolution of Buyout Pricing and Financial Structure in the 1980s," in *Journal of Applied Corporate Finance*, Vol. 6 No. 1, Spring 1993. For a sample of 124 large management buyouts between 1980 and 1989, they find that managers own 5.0% of the firm's equity prior to the buyout and 22.3% after the buyout.

THE DATA

We began our study by defining leveraged recaps as any payout to common shareholders financed by new borrowings. In searching the *Dow Jones News Retrieval Service* over the period 1984-1988, we found 39 cases in which companies *proposed* such transactions. The 39 companies consisted mainly of fairly large, well-established firms. At the time of the transactions, the companies had median total assets of over $2.2 billion and had been incorporated a median of 66 years.

Of these 39 companies, 35 had experienced some takeover threat (either explicit or rumored) before making the recap proposal. In 24 of these cases, management received a formal offer for the company. Thus, although leveraged recaps are technically "voluntary" actions taken by management, they were seldom made without outside pressure. This may explain why managers would propose a transaction that would severely limit their discretion over corporate operating and investment policies.

The proposed recapitalizations were completed in 29 of the 39 cases. The remaining ten proposals were not completed; in fact, nine of these companies were acquired. Our study focused on the 29 completed recaps. (For a listing of such companies, see the Appendix.)

The Stock Market Response

We attempted to measure the stock market's reaction to our sample of leveraged recaps by calculating cumulative daily stock price changes—adjusted for broad market movements and differences in risk—for each company over the period surrounding the recap and any associated takeover activity. In the 25 cases of recaps preceded by a takeover threat, we measured the stock price movements over a period extending from 40 trading days prior to the first public mention of outside takeover interest until the day we determined all uncertainty about whether the recap would go through was resolved. In the four cases where there was no indication of a takeover threat, we started our

calculation of daily stock price movements 40 days before the initial announcement of the recap.[4]

The process of summing these daily market-adjusted stock price changes across the recapitalized companies produced a measure of corporate stock market performance known as a "cumulative abnormal return," or CAR. For example, in the case of Colt Industries, on July 21, 1986, management proposed a recapitalization that gave shareholders $85 cash and one new share for each share currently owned. Adding the daily market-adjusted stock price changes from May 22, 1986 through this date, we calculated a CAR of +38%.

For the entire sample of 29 recaps, we found that the shareholders of companies that proposed leveraged recaps experienced substantial increases in value—increases very similar in size and consistency to those observed in LBOs. The median CAR for our sample of completed recaps was +26.2%, and almost 90% of the completed recaps had positive CARs.

THE EFFECT OF LEVERAGED RECAPS ON INVESTMENT POLICY

As stated earlier, one of the two principal aims of our study was to determine the extent to which leveraged recaps limited management's ability to reinvest corporate cash flow. To answer this question, we examined percentage changes in selected operating variables for the 29 completed recaps extending from the last fiscal year prior to the recap (year −1) to the first two full years after the recapitalization was completed (years +1 and +2).

We started by analyzing changes in operating income and undistributed cash flow, each scaled by the corresponding level of total assets. Operating income was measured before depreciation and thus provided an estimate of the cash generated from current operations. Undistributed cash flow was defined as operating income minus the sum of taxes paid, interest payments, and preferred and common stock dividends.[5] (Following leveraged recaps, common dividends and, to a lesser extent, preferred dividends are sharply reduced if not eliminated altogether.) By measuring after-tax cash flows not

---

4. It is possible that recapitalized companies are viewed by the market as still "in play," even after completion of the transaction. If so, the positive CARs would reflect the expected value of a forthcoming bid for the company rather than the value added by the recap itself. But the fact that only one of the 29 firms completing recaps was acquired over the subsequent three-year period would seem to contradict this argument.

5. For the use of this variable as a measure of free cash flow, see Kenneth Lehn and Annette Poulsen, "Free Cash Flow and Stockholder Gains in Going Private Transactions," *Journal of Finance*, (July 1989), pp. 771-788.

Although leveraged recaps are technically "voluntary" actions taken by management, they were seldom made without outside pressure. This may explain why managers would propose a transaction that would severely limit their discretion over their companies' operating and investment policies.

distributed to security holders, we aimed to produce a direct estimate of the extent to which discretionary (or "reinvestable") cash flows were reduced in the post-recapitalization period.

We also reported percentage changes in the above variables relative to a sample of 29 comparable control firms to account for possible industry- or economy-wide factors. In constructing the control group, each of the 29 recap companies was matched with the company in the same industry that was closest in size. For each of the 29 recaps, we then calculated the "control-adjusted" change in each of the operating variables—that is, the percentage change in the operating variable for the recapitalized company minus the percentage change for the comparable control firm over the same period.

Changes in Operating Variables

Increases in Operating Efficiency. As summarized in Table 2, our sample companies achieved substantial improvements in operating performance after the recap.[6] For example, the median increase in the ratio of operating income to total assets from year −1 to year +1 was 21.5%. The control-adjusted change was 21.8% over the same time period, suggesting that the operating performance of the control companies remained essentially unchanged over the same time period. In almost 80% of the cases, moreover, the ratio of operating income to total assets increased for the sample company relative to its control firm.

Reductions in Discretionary Cash Flow. Despite the significant increases in operating cash flow accompanying recaps, the large-scale substitution of debt for equity in these transactions led to significant reductions in the ratio of undistributed cash flow to assets, at least in the first year after the transaction. Relative to the control firms, however, the reductions in these ratios were considerably smaller (and statistically insignificant).

Reductions in Investment. Although the above measure suggests that undistributed cash flow was reduced following the recaps, it did not address the possibility that cash could have been generated by selling assets of the firm, thereby increasing cash available to management for investment. We accord-

ingly addressed the question of whether recaps limited new investment more directly by examining changes in capital expenditures.

For the sample firms, the median percentage reduction in the level of capital expenditures was 35.5% over the −1 to +1 period, and 41.5% over the −1 to +2 period (although only the second measure was statistically significant). These results were even more suggestive when we compared these changes in capital expenditures for the recapitalized companies to those of the control firms. The median control-adjusted reduction in capital expenditures was 46% over the −1 to +1 period and 65% over the −1 to +2 period. These findings show that the recap companies sharply reduced new investment relative to their industry peers following the transactions.

Reductions in Size. Changes in total assets provide a measure of the firm's *net* investment. The reductions in total assets reported in Table 2 indicate the sample companies actually disinvested on net— that is, they paid out to security holders more than their (pre-interest) operating earnings—in the years following the recaps. The median percentage reduction in total assets over the −1 to +1 period was 6.1%, and the median reduction in the level of total assets was just under $70 million. Much more strikingly, relative to their industry counterparts the recapitalized firms reduced their total assets by 42% through the first year, and by 57% through the second.

More Tests of Effects on Investment

In order to conclude that leveraged recaps reduced managerial discretion over cash flow, we felt we had to establish a more direct link between the reductions in internally generated cash flow and the reductions in capital expenditures. For example, if the reduced year +1 cash flow would still cover the year +1 capital expenditures expected in the absence of the recap, then the link was weak at best.

Accordingly, we calculated the ratio of year +1 undistributed cash flow to three alternative estimates of what year +1 capital expenditures *would have been* if the recaps had not occurred. The first measure assumed that year +1 capital expenditures would have been the same as year −1 capital

---

6. These findings are consistent with research demonstrating significant operating improvements by companies undergoing LBOs. See, for example, Steven N. Kaplan, "The Effects of Management Buyouts on Operating Performance and Value," *Journal of Financial Economics* (October 1989), pp. 217-254, Chris J. Muscarella and Michael R. Vetsuypens, "Efficiency and Organizational Structure:

A Study of Reverse LBOs," *Journal of Finance* (December 1990), pp.1389-1413, and Abbie Smith, "Corporate Ownership Structure and Performance: The Case of Management Buyouts," *Journal of Financial Economics* (October 1990), pp. 143-164 for LBO results.

TABLE 2

CHANGES IN OPERATING
INCOME, UNDISTRIBUTED
CASH FLOW, CAPITAL
EXPENDITURES, AND
TOTAL ASSETS[a]

Operating Variable[b]	Year −1 Level	Change Between Years	
		−1 and +1 (N = 29)	−1 and +2 (N = 17)
Percentage Change			
■ Operating Income/ Total Assets	0.152	21.5%** (62.1)	14.9% (58.8)
■ Undistributed Cash Flow/ Total Assets	0.076	−31.1%** (37.9)	−14.5% (37.5)
■ Capital Expenditures	$153.1m	−35.5% (27.6)	−41.5%** (23.5)
■ Total Assets	$2,234.8m	−6.1%** (31.0)	−5.7% (41.2)
Control-Firm-Adjusted Percentage Change[c]			
■ Operating Income/ Total Assets		21.8%*** (79.3)	17.7%* (64.7)
■ Undistributed Cash Flow/ Total Assets		−17.6% (41.3)	−8.4% (47.1)
■ Capital Expenditures		−45.6%** (32.1)	−65.3%*** (18.8)
■ Total Assets		−42.3%*** (24.1)	−56.6%*** (17.6)

a. Medians are listed with percentage positive changes listed in parentheses below.
b. Operating income is measured before depreciation and is scaled by the book value of total assets. Undistributed cash flow is defined as operating income minus the sum of interest expenses, tax expense, preferred stock dividends, and common stock dividends and is also scaled by total assets.
c. Control-firm-adjusted change is defined as the percentage change of the sample firm minus the percentage change of the control firm over the same interval. A control firm is defined as that firm with the same 4-digit SIC code that is nearest in market value of equity to the sample firm.
***, **, and * denote significance at the 0.01, 0.05, and 0.10 levels, respectively.

expenditures. The second assumed that a firm's capital expenditure growth rate between years −1 and +1 would have been the same as the rate over the previous two-year period. The third assumed that the sample firms' capital expenditures would have grown at the same rate as the control firms' between year −1 and +1.

The results of this exercise, as shown in panel A of Table 3, clearly indicated that management's ability to invest was sharply curbed by the recaps. Assuming the same level of investment in year +1 as year −1, undistributed cash flow would have covered only 63% of capital spending. Assuming growth rates in investment equal to those of the past and to the control firms', undistributed cash flow would have covered only 46% and 34%, respectively.

As shown in Panel B, moreover, the reductions in discretionary cash flow described above were almost entirely attributable to the sharp increases (257% in the median case) in interest payments. The increased debt-servicing costs far outweighed the positive effects on distributable cash flow of increases in operating income, tax savings from interest shields, and the reductions in dividends on common and preferred stock.

Overall, then, the changes in operating variables documented by our study suggest that the increased debt served to increase operating efficiency, reduce managerial discretion over cash flow, and reduce excess investment.

The Case of Holiday Corp. To illustrate our general findings in a specific context, consider the

Over the five-year period *prior* to the recap, the stock market reaction to announcements of major corporate investments (including acquisitions) by recapitalized companies was systematically negative.

TABLE 3
MEDIAN RATIOS OF YEAR +1 UNDISTRIBUTED CASH FLOWS TO THREE ALTERNATIVE MEASURES OF PREDICTED YEAR +1 CAPITAL EXPENDITURES

A. Undistributed Cash Flow / Predicted Capital Expenditure

		Capital Expenditure Measure	
	Year –1[b]	Two-Year Growth-Adjusted[c]	Control Firm Growth-Adjusted[d]
Median Ratio	.634	.464	.343
Percentage < 1.0	75.9	75.9	72.4
Percentage < 0.8	72.4	69.0	69.0

MEDIAN PERCENTAGE CHANGES IN THE INDIVIDUAL COMPONENTS OF THE FIRMS' UNDISTRIBUTED CASH FLOW RATIOS BETWEEN YEAR –1 AND YEAR +1[a]

B. Percentage Changes in Individual Components of Undistributed Cash Flow

Variable	Median Percentage Change Year –1 to Year +1
Operating Income	12.7
Tax	–73.4***
Interest	256.6***
Dividends on Preferred	–57.8
Dividends on Common	–75.2***

a. Year 0 is defined as the fiscal year during which the recap is completed.
b. Predicted year +1 capital expenditure equals year –1 capital expenditure.
c. Predicted year +1 capital expenditure equals year –1 capital expenditure times one plus the sample firm's percentage growth in capital expenditure between year –3 and year –1.
d. Predicted year +1 capital expenditure equals year –1 capital expenditure times one plus the control firm's percentage growth in capital expenditure between year –1 and year +1.
***, **, and * denote significance at the 0.01, 0.05, and 0.10 levels, respectively.

recapitalization of Holiday Corp. in 1986. Following its $2.8 billion payout to shareholders in the form of a special dividend of $65 per share, Holiday's operating income increased from 18.6% of total assets to 24.7%, a gain of nearly 33%, representing an increase of $105 million in operating cash flow. Because of the increased debt payments accompanying the recap, the firm's cash flow available for investment was still approximately $50 million less than the level of capital expenditures ($245 million) in the year prior to the recap. And, indeed, Holiday's management actually reduced capital expenditures by over $70 million (to $173 million) in the first year after the transaction.

IS REDUCED INVESTMENT REALLY GOOD FOR SHAREHOLDERS?

As stated earlier, reductions in managerial discretion over a company's investment policy will increase its value only if the company is "overinvesting"—that is, investing in negative-NPV projects to pursue goals like growth or market share. The alternative possibility, however, is that the debt load

from recaps compels management to forgo valuable investments with longer-run payoffs. The second major aim of our study was to attempt to distinguish between these two hypotheses.

The Stock Price Response to Investment Decisions

We do not know what future investments would have been made by the recapitalized firms in the absence of the recap. We simply assumed that companies that had systematically made value-increasing or -reducing investments in the past would, unless acted upon by an outside force, continue to do so.

We identified 79 announcements of acquisitions and 88 announcements of other major investments by our 29 sample firms over the five years preceding their completed recaps. The number of announcements made by each company ranged from 0 (in five cases) to 29, with a median of 5. We also examined announcements of 63 acquisitions and 44 other investments reported by the control firms over the same five-year period.

TABLE 4
THE STOCK MARKET
RESPONSE TO
ANNOUNCEMENTS OF
INVESTMENT DECISIONS

A. Abnormal Returns[a]

	Sample Firms		Control Firms	
Type of Investment	[–1, 1]	[–5, 1]	[–1, 1]	[–5, 1]
All Investments	–0.90%	–0.88%	–0.17%	–0.46%
	(–4.09)***	(–2.84)***	(–0.63)	(–1.21)
	[n = 167]	[n = 167]	[n = 107]	[n=107]
Acquisitions	–0.89%	–0.82%	–0.41%	–0.81%
	(–2.62)***	(–1.71)*	(–1.11)	(–1.53)
	[n = 79]	[n = 79]	[n = 63]	[n = 63]
Non-Acquisitions	–0.91%	–0.92%	0.17%	0.02%
	(–3.14)***	(–2.24)**	(0.38)	(0.03)
	[n = 88]	[n = 88]	[n = 44]	[n = 44]

B. Pairwise Differences in Average Abnormal Returns[b]

	Sample	Control	Difference
Mean	–0.56%	0.05%	–0.61%
t-stat	–2.95***	0.16	–1.64*
Fraction Negative	0.71**	0.56	0.64*
Number of Firms	28	28	28

a. In panel A, mean CARs are reported with t-statistics in parentheses and sample size in brackets below for all announced investment decisions and for acquisition and non-acquisition subsamples.
b. In panel B, average abnormal returns for each firm are defined as the average of the three-day [–1,1] CARs associated with the firm's announced investment decisions.
***, **, * denote significance at the 0.01, 0.05, and 0.10 levels respectively.

As shown in Panel A of table 4, the average stock price reaction to announcements of these investment decisions by recapitalized companies was negative (about 1%), and significantly different from zero (at the 99% confidence level). This is evidence that the recap companies were systematically making value-reducing investments in the years preceding their recaps.

As also shown in the top of Table 4, the market reacted uniformly negatively to announcements of normal capital investment plans as well as to announcements of acquisitions. The negative, non-acquisition CARs are especially notable in light of previous evidence showing that announcements of increased capital spending and increased R & D programs are generally greeted positively by the stock market (with average stock price increases of about 1%).[7] These results support the hypothesis that the correction of value-reducing investment strategies was both a motive for the attempted takeovers of the sample firms and a benefit of reducing managerial discretion over investment decisions.[8]

The Case of Goodyear. A clear example of this pattern of past overinvestment leading to hostile

7. See John J. McConnell and Chris J. Muscarella, "Corporate Capital Expenditure Decisions and the Market Value of the Firm," *Journal of Financial Economics* (September 1985), pp. 399-422 and John J. McConnell and Timothy J. Nantell, "Corporate Combinations and Common Stock Returns: The Case of Joint Ventures," *Journal of Finance* (June 1985), pp. 519-536.
8. Studies of past corporate investment behavior have come to similar conclusions in examining LBO companies for which there is publicly available information. LBOs are associated with significant reductions in capital expenditures and are characterized by poor investment decisions in the years prior to the buyout. See Steven Kaplan, Chris Muscarella and Michael Vetsuypens, and Abbie Smith cited in note 7. For the wealth effects of pre-LBO investment decisions, see David J. Denis, "Corporate Investment Decisions and Corporate Control: Evidence from Going Private Transactions," *Financial Management*, (Autumn 1992).

> Goodyear's leveraged recapitalization limited its ability to continue making value-destroying, diversifying investments. In so doing, it effectively redirected the company's focus back upon the tire business, where it now appears to be having considerable success.

TABLE 5
THE SHAREHOLDER
WEALTH EFFECTS OF PRE-
AND POST-RECAP
INVESTMENT DECISIONS

A. Abnormal Returns[a]

	Pre-Recap	Post-Recap	Difference
Mean	–0.90%	–0.26%	–0.64%
t-stat	–4.09***	–0.47	–1.16
Frac. Neg.	0.66***	0.56	
Number	167	36	

B. Pairwise Differences in Average Announcement Effects Per Firm[b]

	Pre-Recap	Post-Recap	Difference
Mean	–0.56%	–0.28%	–0.28%
t-stat	–2.95***	–0.70	–0.82
Frac. Neg.	0.71*	0.53	0.57

a. Abnormal returns are three-day [–1,1] CARs associated with announced investment decisions.
b. Panel B presents a pairwise comparison of the average pre- and post-recap average announcement effects for each firm.
***, **, * denote significance at the 0.01, 0.05, and 0.10 levels respectively.

pressure and a defensive recapitalization is contained in the recent history of Goodyear Tire and Rubber Co. When Goodyear announced its diversifying acquisition of Celeron Oil for $800 million in 1983, the stock value fell by over 10%, representing a shareholder loss of almost $250 million.[9] In response to hostile threats from Sir James Goldsmith, whose announced intent was to reverse the company's disastrous diversification, Goodyear paid out $2.2 billion to buy back all of Goldsmith's holdings and an additional 36.5% of the outstanding stock. Following its leveraged repurchase of shares, Goodyear reduced investment from $1.7 billion to under $670 million. Between the period 40 days prior to Goldsmith's first threat through the execution of the share repurchase, shareholders experienced a market-adjusted return of 22.5%, representing an increase of nearly $760 million. As suggested, this is a clear case of a leveraged recapitalization that limited Goodyear's ability to continue making value-destroying, diversifying investments. In so doing, it effectively redirected the company's focus back upon the tire business, where it now appears to be having considerable success.

Interestingly, our sample of control firms did not exhibit the same tendency to "overinvest" as the recapitalized companies. Stock price reactions to control firm announcements of investments, whether acquisitions or otherwise, were not significantly different from zero.

Better Investment Decisions?

We also examined the stock market reaction to announcements of major investment decisions *after* the recaps. The 29 sample firms announced only 36 such investments in the three years following their recaps. This, needless to say, was a dramatic reduction relative to the number of investments made in the years prior to the recap, from a median of 1.2 investments per firm per year to 0.3 investments.

As shown in Panel A of table 5, there was some difference between the market reactions to announcements of major pre- and post-recap investment decisions. Post-recap investment decisions were associated with an average CAR of –0.28%—statistically indistinguishable from zero. Moreover, only 56% of the post-recap announcements were associated with negative CARs. (Nevertheless, the difference in average announcement effects between the pre-recap and post-recap samples was not statistically distinguishable from zero, as is

9. See Mark Mitchell and Ken Lehn, "Do Bad Bidders Become Good Targets?" *Journal of Applied Corporate Finance* (Summer 1990), pp. 60-69.

confirmed by the pairwise comparisons presented in panel B.)

This last finding led us to conclude that high leverage is beneficial primarily because it constrains investment; there is little evidence of improvements in those investments that companies do make following the recapitalizations.

The Case of Unocal. That curbs on investment can reverse the shareholder losses of recapitalized firms is well illustrated by the case of Unocal. In the five years leading up to its leveraged recapitalization, the company announced five major investments that collectively reduced shareholder value by $640 million. In the three years following its recap, Unocal did not announce any major new investments.

The experience of Unocal appears to have been fairly typical. We computed a measure of the aggregate dollar change in shareholder wealth associated with announced investment decisions in the pre-recap years, and then computed the same measure for the post-recap years. Specifically, we multiplied the percentage two-day stock price reaction for each investment decision by the market value of the firm at the time of the investment, and then summed these wealth effects across all investments. As a group, the sample firms' investment decisions reduced aggregate shareholder wealth by $477.3 million *annually* over the five years prior to their recaps. In contrast, after the recaps, the same companies' investment decisions reduced aggregate shareholder wealth by only $16.0 million annually.

Do Operating Changes Explain Recap Increases in Shareholder Value?

To the extent that curbing overinvestment was the principal source of expected value added in leveraged recaps, we might expect to find a significant positive correlation between the stock market reactions to individual recaps and the extent of the investment reductions that later actually took place. And, indeed, using a statistical measure called Spearman rank correlation, we found that reductions in the levels of capital expenditures and total assets were positively correlated with the size of the initial stock market reaction.

When these investment reductions were measured relative to control firm capital expenditures, however, the correlations were still evident, but statistically insignificant. We found no significant correlations between the size of the market reaction and the changes in operating income or in undistributed cash flow.

CONCLUSIONS AND POLICY IMPORT

The findings of our recent study of 29 leveraged recapitalizations are broadly consistent with the argument that increased debt plays a valuable role in restricting management's discretion over "free cash flow" in companies with limited growth opportunities. Leveraged recaps sharply reduced the amount of corporate reinvestment by the recapitalized companies, and the curbs on investment appear to have significantly increased the market value of such companies. The size of the initial shareholder gains, moreover, were directly correlated with the percentage reductions in investment we observed after the recap. Also telling, our study suggests that the recapitalized companies systematically misallocated resources through poor investment decisions in the years leading up to the recaps.

These results have important implications for the public policy debate surrounding highly leveraged transactions. Failures in the financial sector and by certain well-publicized HLTs created a political climate that led to increased regulation of such transactions, leading to a dramatic reduction in both their size and numbers.[10] Moreover, strengthened state antitakeover laws and more sophisticated takeover defenses have reduced the possibility of a successful hostile takeover. This in turn has greatly reduced the pressure on managers to engage in HLTs to preserve their independence.

To this day, the popular view of HLTs is that they forced cutbacks in productive investment, thereby damaging the long-run competitiveness of the levered firms. Our evidence, however, suggests that the primary consequence of HLTs was to prevent managements in low-growth industries from either "overinvesting" in their core businesses or diversifying away from them. By forcing management to return excess capital to investors and focus on increasing operating efficiency, they appear to have achieved significant increases in competitiveness as well as shareholder value.

---

10. See Michael C. Jensen, "Corporate Control and the Politics of Finance," *Journal of Applied Corporate Finance* (Summer 1991), pp. 13-33.

This appendix contains a brief description of the 29 completed recapitalizations in the sample. Each description contains a synopsis of the relevant events surrounding the recapitalization transaction, and, when available, the dates of the relevant events. We also include the cumulative abnormal return (CAR) and the abnormal dollar change in the market value of the firm's equity (Value) associated with each recapitalization.

■ **CBS Inc.**   CAR = 24.7%, Value = $531.5 million

CBS offered to repurchase 21% of its common stock (7/5/85). The move was in response to a takeover bid by Ted Turner. The contest began with a proposed proxy contest by a politically conservative group (2/8/85) and ended with management retaining control after executing the repurchase (8/2/85).

■ **Caesars World Inc.**   CAR = 26.8%, Value = $153.1 million

Caesars World announced plans to pay a $26.25 special dividend and add $1 billion of new debt (4/6/87). The move was designed to defeat a hostile takeover bid. Caesars World later dropped its recapitalization plan and instead launched a plan to repurchase 31% of its shares (9/8/87). The contest began with a hostile bid by Martin Sosnoff (3/9/87) and ended with Sosnoff dropping its bid (6/16/87) and managers retaining control.

■ **Carter Hawley Hale**   CAR = 28.0%, Value = $156.8 million

Carter Hawley Hale announced plans to spin off a division to shareholders and make a special payout of $325 million (12/9/86). The contest began with a hostile bid from Limited (11/26/86) and ended with the announced restructuring.

■ **Colt Industries Inc.**   CAR = 37.8%, Value = $457.1 million

Colt proposed a recapitalization that would give shareholders a special dividend of $85 and 1 new share in exchange for each share (7/21/86). The move was financed through $1 billion in bank borrowing and $500 million in new debentures.

■ **FMC**   CAR = 25.7%, Value = $432.1 million

FMC announced plans for a recapitalization that would give shareholders a special dividend of $80 per share and 1 share in the recapitalized firm in exchange for each share (2/24/86). The plan would increase insider ownership from 19% to 41%. The board acknowledged concern about the possible emergence of an unfriendly suitor.

■ **GenCorp**   CAR = 34.9%, Value = $577.4 million

GenCorp announced plans to buy back 54% of its stock for $1.6 billion (4/7/87). The move was designed to fight a hostile takeover bid by a partnership consisting of AFG Industries and Wagner & Brown. The contest began with the hostile bid (3/18/87) and ended when W&B dropped its bid in the face of the repurchase tender offer (4/8/87).

■ **Gillette Co.**   CAR = 18.9%, Value = $405.8 million

Gillette blocked a takeover attempt by Revlon by agreeing to buy Revlon's 13.9% interest. The firm also announced plans to buy as many as seven million of its shares in the open market or through private transactions (11/25/86). The contest began with a hostile bid by Revlon (11/14/86) and ended with the targeted repurchase and announcement of the open market repurchases.

■ **Goodyear Tire and Rubber Co.**   CAR = 22.5%, Value = $759.0 million

Goodyear announced a plan to repurchase as many as 20 million of its shares and sell as many as three major units (11/7/86). The contest began with the disclosure of a large stake held by Sir James Goldsmith (10/29/86) and ended with the firm buying back Goldsmith's stake and announcing a tender offer for a further 36.5% of the firm's shares (11/21/86).

■ **HBO & Co.**   CAR = 135%, Value = $0.2 million

HBO proposed a recapitalization, citing the need to maintain shareholder value and defend against a possible hostile takeover (5/29/86). The firm later withdrew the recapitalization plan and proposed to purchase as much as 26% of its shares in the open market (8/7/87).

■ **Harcourt Brace Jovanovich**   CAR = 63.1%, Value = $674.5 million

Harcourt announced plans to recapitalize by increasing debt and paying a large special dividend (5/27/87). The move was designed to defeat a hostile bid by British Printing & Communications. The contest began with the hostile bid (5/19/87) and ended with the implementation of the recapitalization plan (7/27/87).

■ **Holiday Corp.**   CAR = 30.8%, Value = $471.6 million

Holiday proposed a special dividend of $65 per share (11/13/86). The contest began with a rumored hostile takeover by Donald Trump (9/29/86) and ended with the approval of the recapitalization plan (3/2/87).

■ **Inco Ltd.**   CAR = –6.3%, Value = $–145.7 million

Inco announced plans to distribute more than $1 billion to shareholders in a special dividend intended to thwart any takeover attempts (10/4/88).

■ **Interco**   CAR = 40.8%, Value = $475.9 million

Interco's board approved a $2.8 billion restructuring program consisting of a special dividend of $14 cash and $11 in senior subordinated debentures per share (9/21/88). The move was aimed at thwarting a hostile takeover bid from a group led by the Rales brothers (7/29/88). The firm retained control after amending its recapitalization plan to consist of cash and securities valued at $71 a share (11/23/88).

■ **Kroger**   CAR = 50.4%, Value = $979.9 million

Kroger announced a restructuring proposal which would possibly include a special dividend (9/14/88). The move was in response to the Haft family's receipt of federal clearance to accumulate an unspecified stake in Kroger (9/13/88). Kohlberg, Kravis, Roberts and Co. (KKR) made a subsequent unsolicited bid. The contest ended when KKR ended its bid and left Kroger to pursue its special dividend and restructuring plan (10/12/88).

■ **Multimedia**   No stock returns data available

Multimedia's board approved a cash-and-debt recapitalization plan which included an option to take a reduced amount of cash and retain some equity interest (4/9/88). The contest began with an LBO proposal by a management-led group of investors (2/4/85) and became a recapitalization proposal when the option to retain equity was added. The contest ended when shareholders approved the recapitalization (9/27/85) after purchasing the 10% stake of a competing bidder.

■ **Newmont Mining Corp.**   CAR = –9.9%, Value = $–185.7 million

---

Newmont announced plans for a major restructuring that included a $33 per share dividend (9/22/87). The move was designed to defeat a bid from Ivanhoe Partners. The restructuring would grant minority owner Consolidated Gold Fields a bigger stake in the firm. The contest began with the disclosure of a 9.1% stake held by Ivanhoe (8/14/87) and ended with Ivanhoe withdrawing its bid (11/19/87).

■ **Optical Coating Laboratories**   CAR = 11.4%, Value = $9.8 million

---

Optical Coating's board approved a recapitalization plan which involved a $13 per share cash payout (1/6/88).

■ **Owens Corning**   CAR = 40.7%, Value = $454.8 million

Owens Corning announced a recap plan, which would give shareholders $52 plus $35 face amount of new junior debt in exchange for each share (8/29/86). The contest began with a hostile bid from Wickes (8/6/86) that was later dropped (9/2/86).

■ **Phillips Petroleum Co.**   CAR = 10.3%, Value = $545.1 million

---

Phillips announced plans to recapitalize the company by more than doubling the firm's debt while reducing public ownership of the firm (12/24/84). The contest began with a takeover bid from T. Boone Pickens (11/8/84) and ended with Pickens dropping his bid and accepting the recapitalization (12/24/84).

■ **Phillips-Van Heusen**   CAR = 10.8%, Value = $26.5 million

---

Phillips-Van Heusen announced an acquisition program and a stock buy-back of 5.2 million shares at $28 each (7/31/87). The move may have been designed to make the company less attractive as a takeover target. The contest began with a hostile bid by Rosewood Financial (7/13/87) and ended with Rosewood dropping its bid in light of the repurchase tender offer (8/4/87).

■ **Quantum Chemical**   CAR = 0.4%, Value = $9.1 million

Quantum announced a recapitalization plan involving a $50 per share special dividend (12/29/88).

■ **Santa Fe Southern Pacific**   CAR = 96.6%, Value = $4,491 million

---

Santa Fe announced that it would pay shareholders at least $4 billion in a restructuring of the firm (12/14/87). The contest began with the announcement that Henley Group held a 5.03% stake in Santa Fe (3/31/87) and ended with the announced restructuring.

Appendix (Cont.)

■ **Shoney's**	CAR = 0.7%, Value = $5.4 million

Shoney's board approved a recapitalization plan involving a cash-and-debt special dividend (3/8/88).

■ **Standard Brands Paint Co.**	CAR = −12.5%, Value = $−29.3 million

Standard Brands offered to buy as much as 53% of its common stock in a recapitalization plan (11/11/87). The contest began with a hostile offer from Entregrowth (7/22/87) and ended with the successful repurchase tender offer (1/5/88).

■ **Swank Inc.**	CAR = 19.2%, Value = $11.2 million

Swank announced a recapitalization plan that included a share repurchase in which most shareholders received $17 in cash and a share of new common stock (9/30/87). The firm also declared a distribution of a preferred stock purchase right. The measures were designed to fend off a hostile takeover.

■ **UAL Corp. (Allegis)**	CAR = 63.9%, Value = $1,675.7 million

Allegis announced a plan to pay a dividend of $60 per share that would be financed primarily through additional borrowing (5/29/87). The action came after the disclosure that Coniston Partners held a large stake in the firm. The contest began with an offer from the pilots union to buy Allegis (4/6/87) and ended with the resignation of the chairman (6/11/87) and a repurchase tender offer for 63% of its shares (2/1/88).

■ **USG Corp.**	CAR = 81.3%, Value = $1,609.7 million

USG announced a recapitalization and restructuring plan that offered holders $37 a share in cash, debt and stock (5/3/88). The contest began with the acquisition of a 9.8% stake by Desert Partners (10/6/87) and ended with shareholders approving the recapitalization plan (7/11/88).

■ **Union Carbide Corp.**	CAR = 56.6%, Value = $1,464.3 million

Union Carbide announced an offer to exchange cash and debt securities for 35% of its shares (12/16/85). The firm was seeking to fend off a hostile takeover attempt by GAF Corp. The contest began with rumors of a GAF bid (8/30/85) and ended with GAF abandoning its bid in the face of the buyback offer (1/9/86).

■ **Unocal Corp.**	CAR = 3.3%, Value = $209.4 million

Unocal announced a plan to repurchase 49% of its shares using $6.28 billion face value of notes (4/17/85). The $72 per share offer would be made only if a T. Boone Pickens group succeeded in acquiring a majority of Unocal shares in its $54-per-share bid. The contest began when the Pickens group acquired a 7.9% stake (2/15/85) and ended with management retaining control by defeating a Pickens-led proxy bid and completing the repurchase (5/30/85).

PERFORMANCE, LEVERAGE, AND OWNERSHIP STRUCTURE IN REVERSE LBOs

by Robert W. Holthausen and David F. Larcker, University of Pennsylvania*

T he performance of leveraged buyouts has received considerable attention in the finance literature. Michael Jensen has argued that LBOs and LBO-like organizations add value by reducing incentive problems faced by more traditional corporate organizations, especially in slow-growth sectors of the economy. He postulates that high leverage, concentrated equity ownership by managers, and monitoring by an LBO sponsor firm work together to create an organizational form with an incentive structure that leads to value maximization. In particular, increasing the proportion of equity owned by managers can provide stronger incentives for managers to create shareholder wealth. In addition, substantial debt service obligations can force managers to avoid investing in negative net present value (NPV) projects, which is particularly useful in mature industries generating substantial "free cash flows" (that is, cash in excess of that required to fund all profitable investment opportunities). Finally, nonmanagement insiders (such as an LBO sponsor firm) typically own a significant proportion of the outstanding equity and exercise considerable control over managers through the board of directors, thus improving monitoring within the organization. Given the potentially superior incentive structure that comes with these changes, Jensen goes so far as to suggest that LBOs, or public corporations that imitate the incentive structures of LBOs, could supplant the more typical public corporation in mature industries.[1] At the very least, Jensen argues, many public companies could benefit substantially by adopting aspects of the LBO form such as higher leverage, larger equity stakes for managers, and perhaps the participation of large blockholders.

---

*This article draws heavily on "The Financial Performance of Reverse Leveraged Buyouts," by Robert W. Holthausen and David F. Larcker, *Journal of Financial Economics* 42, 1996, pp. 293-332.

1. See Michael C. Jensen, "The Eclipse of the Public Corporation," *Harvard Business Review* 67 (1989), pp. 61-74. Although supported by G. Bennett Stewart (see "Remaking the Public Corporation from Within," *Harvard Business Review* 68 (1990), pp. 126-137), Jensen's view of LBO's is controversial. For example, Alfred Rappaport argues that LBO-like organizations are inherently transitory in nature and that they are not likely to supplant the public corporation. In particular, Rappaport argues that concentrated equity ownership and high leverage make it difficult for the organization to be flexible enough to respond to changing economic conditions and competitive pressures, and that demand for capital, liquidity desires, and risk-sharing incentives will eventually force the public sale of the LBO organization (see Alfred Rappaport, "The Staying Power of the Public Corporation," *Harvard Business Review* 68 (1990), pp. 96-104).

A number of previous empirical studies have provided convincing evidence of improvements in the performance of firms that undergo LBOs.[2] To our knowledge, however, no studies have directly examined the association between the *extent of the change in organizational incentives* at the time of the LBO and the subsequent change in performance. Nor have researchers documented the performance of reverse LBOs—those LBO firms that choose to go public again in an IPO—after they return to public ownership to see whether such performance improvements are sustained under a different organizational structure.

In a study published in 1996, we examined the performance of reverse LBOs in order to provide additional evidence about the extent to which leverage and concentration of ownership provide desirable incentives within organizations. The premise of our study was that if the high leverage and concentrated equity ownership of LBOs motivate these firms to operate more efficiently while they are private, we would expect the decline in leverage and the dispersion of equity ownership to lead to a decline in performance after they go public. At the same time, though, we might also expect to find lingering effects from the LBO; that is, to the extent that reverse LBOs continue to have higher leverage and more concentrated ownership than their industry competitors, the reverse LBOs might continue to outperform their industries.

Notwithstanding the incentive arguments presented by Jensen, other financial economists have offered competing predictions about the effects of changes in leverage and managerial equity ownership. For example, while increased managerial ownership of the firm's common equity could improve financial performance because the key officers have a greater stake in any value-increasing actions that are taken, it is also possible that increased managerial ownership could hurt performance because of managers' risk aversion and the potential underdiversification of their wealth. For example, managers with large equity stakes in highly leveraged firms may reject some higher-risk but more profitable (higher NPV)

projects, and accept lower-risk but less profitable (lower NPV) projects. Indeed, it seems plausible that managers in LBOs, faced with the pressure of servicing a substantial amount of debt, would not even consider all available projects, concentrating instead on only those where the payoffs are relatively assured and immediate.

In our study, we conducted a detailed examination of the performance and change in organizational structure (leverage and equity ownership) of a sample of 90 LBOs that went public between January 1983 and June 1988. At the time of the IPO, there was a substantial decline in the mean leverage ratio and the average equity ownership by insiders (all officers, directors, and employees). Even so, equity ownership by managers and other insiders remained more concentrated and leverage remained higher than that of typical public corporations. Thus, when these LBOs returned to public ownership, they became "hybrid" organizations that retained some of the important features of the LBO organization.

The key findings of our study are summarized below:

- The operating performance of reverse LBOs, as measured by operating income/assets and operating cash flow/assets, is significantly *better* than that of the median firm in their industries in the year prior to and in the year of the IPO. Moreover, the reverse-LBO firms continue to outperform their industry competitors for at least the first four fiscal years after the IPO (though the evidence in the third year is less strong). Nevertheless, there is some evidence of a deterioration in the performance of the reverse-LBO firms after the IPO.
- Reverse-LBO firms spend less on capital expenditures than the median firms in their industries prior to the IPO. After the IPO, their capital expenditures return to the median level of their industry counterparts.
- Reverse-LBO firms have significantly smaller amounts of working capital than their industry counterparts both before and after the reverse LBO. There is evidence, however, of an increase in the amount of working capital held by reverse-LBO firms after they go public.

2. See Steven Kaplan, "The Effect of Management Buyouts on Operating Performance and Value," *Journal of Financial Economics* 24 (1989), pp. 217-254, Chris Muscarella and Michael Vetsuypens, "Efficiency and Organizational Structure: A Study of Reverse LBOs," *Journal of Finance* 45 (1990), pp. 1389-1413, and Abbie Smith, "Corporate Ownership Structure and Performance: The Case of Management Buyouts," *Journal of Financial Economics* 27 (1990), pp. 143-164.

For a case study illustrating improvements in both organizational incentives and monitoring, see also George Baker and Karen Wruck, "Organizational Changes and Value Creation in Leveraged Buyouts: The Case of the O.M. Scott & Sons Company," *Journal of Financial Economics* 25 (1989), pp. 163-190. A shorter, less technical version of this study appears in Vol. 4 No. 1 of this journal.

- Changes in operating performance (measured from one year before to up to four years after the reverse LBO) are unrelated to the change in leverage at the time of the reverse LBO. At the same time, we find that greater declines in the percentage equity owned by operating management and other insiders at the time of the reverse LBO are associated with larger declines in operating performance.
- Changes in working capital and capital expenditures are negatively related to the percentage equity owned by nonmanagement insiders. In particular, as nonmanagement insider ownership falls, working capital and capital expenditures increase.

Although these findings are generally consistent with the argument that organizational incentives affect performance, there is another possible explanation: LBO managers and other owners may believe either that firm performance has "peaked" or that the IPO market is willing to pay more than the firm's earnings prospects would justify. According to this explanation, reverse LBOs could thus reflect manager-owners' attempts to take advantage of a temporary market mispricing.

To test this possibility, we examined the stock market performance of reverse LBOs. If managers were able to issue shares at temporarily inflated values, we would anticipate *negative* stock market performance for reverse LBOs. Our evidence, however, shows that the stock market returns of LBOs outperform (or at worst equal) those of the broad market after the IPO.

CHANGES IN LEVERAGE AND OWNERSHIP STRUCTURE

Our sample of 90 reverse LBOs comes from an October 1988 report by Kidder, Peabody & Co. entitled "Analysis of Initial Public Offerings of Leveraged Buyouts." The data represent all IPOs of LBOs identified by IDD Information Services, Inc. that occurred between January 1, 1983 and June 30, 1988 and raised at least $10 million in the common stock offering. Our sample of LBOs was concentrated in the 1985 to 1986 period, and the associated IPOs were concentrated in 1986 and 1987.

Financial information, such as changes in leverage and ownership structure at the time of the IPO, was obtained from the prospectuses for the public offering. Stock return data were taken from the files of the Center for Research in Security Prices (CRSP). Accounting data were collected from prospectuses and the *Compustat* annual industrial, research, and full coverage files. We obtained information about the ownership structure and board structure three years after the IPO from proxy statements.

Using these sources of information, we examined changes in the financial and organizational structure (leverage, ownership, and board of directors) of reverse-LBO firms around the time of the IPO. The mean leverage ratio (based on book values) fell from 83% prior to the IPO to 56% after the IPO, where leverage is defined as the sum of long-term debt, short-term debt, capitalized leases, and redeemable preferred stock divided by the sum of all of the above plus the book value of common equity.[3] Debt reduction was the primary use of the proceeds, with 57% of the firms using 100% of the proceeds to reduce debt, 28% of the firms using 50% to 99% of the proceeds to reduce debt, and only 5% of the firms using none of the proceeds to reduce debt. Other commonly cited purposes for the proceeds cited in the prospectuses were working capital, general corporate purposes, capital expenditures, retirement of preferred stock, and acquisitions.

There were also substantial shifts in the concentration of ownership at the time of the IPOs. The average ownership of insiders declined from 75% before the IPO to 49% after the IPO. Insiders include all officers, directors, employees and their relatives, and all holdings voted by these people. The equity ownership of a firm that organizes and/or invests in LBOs, such as Kohlberg, Kravis and Roberts, would be included in insiders' holdings because of its representation on the board of directors.

The average equity ownership of operating management fell from 37% of the outstanding equity prior to the IPO to 24% after the IPO. (Operating management is defined as operating management and other employees (if disclosed) and excludes directors who have no operating responsibilities.) On average, managers sold 8% of their stake. Nevertheless, in over half (59%) of the transactions, managers sold none of their equity—and in some cases their proportional ownership actually

---

3. Pre-IPO levels refer to the data just prior to the IPO and post-IPO levels refer to pro forma data for the period immediately after the IPO as described in the prospectus.

increased. At the same time, the average equity ownership by nonmanagement insiders (all officers and directors who are not considered part of operating management) fell from 38% before the IPO to 25% after the IPO.

In the process of going public, 34% of the outstanding equity of the average firm was transferred to public hands (that is, it was no longer owned by insiders or other pre-IPO equity holders, such as private investors, debtholders, or funds without board representation). Moreover, following the IPOs, there was a broad range of public ownership in the sample, with the percentage of equity publicly held by outsiders varying from 4% to 88% of the outstanding equity.

While the leverage and concentration of equity ownership decreased substantially when these firms went public, the leverage and ownership of equity by managers and other insiders was still large relative to the leverage and insider equity ownership of the typical public corporation. For example, median insider ownership after the IPO was 51.3%, whereas insider ownership was approximately 5.0% for 1,000 nonfinancial companies followed by *Value Line* in 1986. Further, the leverage of the reverse-LBO firms after the IPO was approximately 44% higher, on average, than for firms in their industry.

Even though the average declines in the ownership stake for management and nonmanagement insiders were approximately the same (−13%), the changes in ownership for operating management and nonmanagement insiders were inversely correlated (correlation of −0.404). This suggests that even though both management and nonmanagement ownership generally declines, larger declines in ownership by one group tend to be associated with more modest declines in ownership by the other. Further, despite the declines in both leverage and equity ownership by insiders, the correlation between the leverage changes and ownership changes is very small and insignificant.

We also examined the composition of the board of directors for our sample. There were an average of seven directors for our sample firms at the time of the IPO. On average, 34% of the board of directors were operating managers, while 33% of the board were nonmanagement capital providers (such as representatives of leveraged buyout firms, debtholders, or other investors owning 5% or more of the equity who are not operating managers). External board members constituted 27% of the

board, on average, and 6% of the seats were vacant. (Nonmanagement board members were classified as external if they owned less than 5% of the shares or if they represent an organization that owned less than 5% of the shares. If the board member or affiliated organization owns 5% or more, the board member was classified as a nonmanagement capital provider.)

While there are no well-defined criteria for judging whether these boards of directors are unusual, the size of the boards of reverse-LBO firms is clearly smaller than the board sizes typically reported in studies of board structure. Moreover, there is far more representation by nonmanagement capital providers (active investors) who have a significant ownership stake in the organization.

There is not much evidence of a significant change in either management or the board of directors at the time of the IPO. Of all board members currently serving, only 12.5% (or about one in eight), on average, were appointed within six months of the IPO, and these new board members did not necessarily replace former board members. More likely, the board size was increased and these were new appointments. Because the prospectuses rarely disclose changes in the size of the board, it was difficult to obtain information on changes in board structure. In only one case was a dramatic change in the board disclosed (in this case, 80% of the board was replaced). Moreover, only three out of 90 CEOs changed within six months prior to the IPO date.

Interestingly, the period of public trading in the reverse-LBO firms was quite short for many of them. Through the end of 1993, 36 of the 90 companies had been acquired by another corporation and eight had completed another LBO. For these 44 acquired firms, the average time to acquisition was 30 months. Eight companies had a significant event of default (violating a covenant, missing an interest or principal payment, or filing for bankruptcy) and 37 were still public as of December 31, 1993.

THE OPERATING PERFORMANCE AND INVESTMENT DECISIONS OF REVERSE LBOs

To assess the relative operating performance of reverse LBOs, we measured operating performance using two different (although related) accounting ratios that are widely used as measures of performance: operating income and operating cash flows. We did not use common stock returns to measure relative operating performance since any expected decline in the performance of the company attributable to its reversion to a public corporation should be impounded in the offering price; and, to the extent this is so, changes in organizational structure observed at the IPO would be uncorrelated with subsequent returns.

To avoid the mechanical effect of leverage on the results, both variables measured flows on a before-tax and before-interest basis. In addition, we used several different benchmarks for assessing expected performance, including "unadjusted" and "industry-adjusted" benchmarks. Only firms that were private for the full fiscal year prior to the fiscal year of the IPO were used in subsequent tests, a condition that caused us to eliminate eight of the 90 firms from consideration.

The first operating performance measure we examined was the ratio of operating earnings *before depreciation, interest, and taxes* as a percentage of total assets (denoted "OPINC/assets"). The second measure was the ratio of operating cash flow before interest and taxes as a percentage of total assets ("OCF/assets"). The primary difference between the OCF measure and the OPINC measure is that the OCF measure eliminates many accounting accruals. And, since the accounting accrual process tends to smooth reported earnings relative to cash flows, the OCF measure exhibits more variability than the OPINC measure. OPINC, however, is more highly correlated with stock returns than OCF. Nevertheless, one advantage of the OCF measure is that by eliminating many accruals (which are at least partially at the discretion of management), the measure is less susceptible to manipulation. Another advantage of the OCF measure is that it is directly affected by changes in working capital management.

As mentioned, we assessed the performance of our sample firms using two different benchmarks. First, we examined a "raw" or unadjusted measure. Second, we calculated an industry-adjusted performance measure, one that controls for time period and industry effects by examining the performance of the reverse-LBO firm after subtracting the contemporaneous *median* performance of the firms with the same two-digit SIC code as each reverse-LBO firm.

The Operating Performance of Reverse LBOs

Panel A of Table 1 presents median operating performance measures from one year before the IPO (year –1) to four years after the IPO. Year 0 is defined as the fiscal year that *includes* the IPO.[4] Thus, when we refer to performance two years after the IPO, we do not literally mean the performance over the two years after the company goes public, but rather the performance over the two *fiscal years* since the fiscal year in which the company went public.

Given that a large number of reverse-LBO firms are later acquired or go bankrupt and that our tests require the use of accounting data that are not generally available for those firms, the number of observations available varies across years. As can be seen from Panel A of Table 1, the performance of the reverse LBOs dominates that of their industries in the year prior to the IPO. In year –1, the median OCF/assets and OPINC/assets for the reverse-LBO firms were 19.3% and 19.5%, respectively, as compared to approximately 10% and 12% for the median firm in the industry. Reflecting these differences between our sample firms' and their competitors' performance, the median industry-adjusted OCF/assets was 9.2% and the median industry-adjusted OPINC/assets was 7.7%.[5]

Results for the years after the IPO suggest that these firms continue to outperform their industries for the four years following the IPO, as the median industry-adjusted performance for OPINC/assets and OCF/assets is positive (and significantly different from zero, though the evidence in year +3 is weaker than in years +1, +2, or +4). But even though the median reverse-LBO firm continues to outperform its industry, as we discuss below, the margin of superiority appears to shrink over time.

In Panel B of Table 1, we examine *changes* in operating performance for the reverse LBOs. This analysis is conducted to test the possibility that the level of a firm's performance could be significantly better than its industry throughout the period in question (years –1, 0, +1, +2, +3, and +4), while the firm also experiences a significant change (decline or improvement) in its performance relative to its own prior performance or that of its industry. The fiscal year prior to

---

4. While year 0 is the fiscal year of the IPO, we have no control over when in the fiscal year the IPO occurs. Hence, for some firms, year 0 may be based largely on the operating results of the firm when it is private and for others the results may be based largely on a period when the firm is public.

5. These results should not be interpreted as evidence that LBO firms in general outperform their industries, because of the potential selection bias associated with the subset of LBO firms that have a subsequent public offering.

Median insider ownership after the IPO was 51.3%, whereas insider ownership was approximately 5.0% for 1,000 nonfinancial companies followed by *Value Line* in 1986. Further, the leverage of the reverse-LBO firms after the IPO was approximately 44% higher, on average, than for firms in their industry.

TABLE 1
OPERATING
PERFORMANCE OF
REVERSE LBOS[a]

PANEL A: RESULTS ON THE LEVELS OF OPERATING PERFORMANCE

	Year −1	Year 0	Year +1	Year +2	Year +3	Year +4	Avg Years +1 to +4
Median level of OCF/assets (%)							
Firm	19.3%***	14.6%***	11.9%***	14.3%***	13.5%***	15.4%***	15.0%***
Industry–adjusted	9.2%***	4.7%***	1.4%	4.0%***	2.3%	2.9%**	4.1%***
# observations	54	58	55	45	44	39	37
Median level of OPINC/assets (%)							
Firm	19.5%***	19.8%***	17.5%***	17.1%***	14.7%***	15.3%***	16.7%***
Industry–adjusted	7.7%***	7.9%***	5.2%***	5.4%***	2.9%*	4.3%***	4.7%***
# observations	62	66	56	47	44	39	38

PANEL B: RESULTS ON THE CHANGES IN OPERATING PERFORMANCE

	Year −1 to Year 0	Year −1 to Year +1	Year −1 to Year +2	Year −1 to Year +3	Year −1 to Year +4	Year −1 to Avg Years +1 to +4
Median change in OCF/assets (%)						
Firm	−4.7%***	−6.2%***	−4.4%*	−4.5%*	−2.1%	−2.6%
Industry-adjusted	−4.3%**	−6.5%***	−4.5%*	−5.2%**	−3.1%	−3.2%
# observations	51	51	42	40	36	35
Median change in OPINC/assets (%)						
Firm	0.4%	−1.3%	−2.2%	−4.1%***	−3.4%**	−2.0%
Industry-adjusted	0.2%	−1.6%	−1.9%	−3.6%**	−2.0%*	−1.5%
# observations	62	55	46	43	38	37

a. Year −1 is the fiscal year ending prior to the IPO completion year of Year 0.
*,**,*** — Significantly different from 0 at the 10%, 5% and 1% levels, respectively (two-tailed test).

the fiscal year of the IPO (year −1) was used as the benchmark in assessing the extent of such changes.

Results using the change in unadjusted firm performance provide evidence of a significant decline in OCF/assets from the year prior to the IPO to years 0, +1, +2, and +3, but not to year +4 (although one should keep in mind that the sample size has declined to 36 observations by year +4). Using the OPINC/assets performance measure, we find no evidence of a statistically significant decline from year −1 to years 0, +1, or +2, but there are significant declines in years +3 and +4. At the same time, however, when using either measure of operating performance we found no significant differences between the performance in year −1 and the average

performance from year +1 to +4. The results using industry-adjusted performance measures parallel those using the unadjusted measures in terms of the years in which declines are significant for both performance measures.

In general, then, the evidence in Table 1 suggests that the operating performance of firms that complete a reverse LBO exceeds the performance of their industries at the time of the IPO. Moreover, the evidence is reasonably consistent with the conclusion that this superior performance lasts for at least four fiscal years after the fiscal year of the IPO. But there is also some evidence of a decline in performance after the IPO, although this result is sensitive to the performance measure and benchmark used.[6]

6. The choice of benchmarks is obviously important for interpreting our results. In our original paper published in the *Journal of Financial Economics*, we also used a performance-matched benchmark that takes the perfomance of the reverse-LBO firm and subtracts the contemporaneous median performance of all firms in the same two-digit SIC code whose operating performance was similar to that of the reverse-LBO firm in the year prior to the IPO. Since firms that are performing very well or very poorly tend to achieve subsequent performance that is closer to the norm for their industry, the performance-matched benchmark

allows us to assess whether the performance observed for the reverse-LBO sample (which undergoes changes in organizational structure) is different from the performance observed for a sample of firms in the same industry that are chosen *solely* on the basis of having performance similar to that of the reverse-LBO firm in the reverse-LBO firm's year −1. In general, we find that reverse-LBO firms perform similarly to the firms in the performance-matched benchmark from years −1 to year +4. For more detail on this comparison, please refer to the article published in the *Journal of Financial Economics* (cited on the first page of this article).

TABLE 2
CAPITAL EXPENDITURES
AND WORKING CAPITAL
OF REVERSE LBOS[a]

PANEL A: RESULTS ON THE LEVEL OF CAPITAL EXPENDITURES AND WORKING CAPITAL

	Year –1	Year 0	Year +1	Year +2	Year +3	Year +4	+1 to +4
Median level of capital expenditures/assets (%)							
Firm	4.3%***	4.8%***	5.3%***	4.7%***	5.4%***	4.4%***	5.6%***
Industry-adjusted	–1.3%**	–0.5%	0.0%	–0.5%	0.0%	–0.4%	0.4%
# observations	61	66	55	47	43	37	36
Median level of working capital/assets (%)							
Firm	14.4%***	14.5%***	15.0%***	13.8%***	13.1%***	14.5%***	13.4%***
Industry–adjusted	–14.0%***	–13.6%***	–10.1%***	–10.7%***	–12.1%***	–10.6%***	–11.5%***
# observations	54	53	55	45	43	38	37

PANEL B: RESULTS ON THE CHANGES IN CAPITAL EXPENDITURES AND WORKING CAPITAL

	Year –1 to Year 0	Year –1 to Year +1	Year –1 to Year +2	Year –1 to Year +3	Year –1 to Year +4	Year –1 to Avg Years +1 to +4
Median change in capital expenditures/assets (%)						
Firm	0.8%**	0.6%	–0.0%	0.7%	–0.2%	0.7%
Industry-adjusted	1.2%***	1.2%*	0.6%	1.4%	1.1%	1.5%
# observations	61	53	45	41	35	34
Median change in working capital/assets (%)						
Firm	0.0%	1.5%	0.8%	0.5%	1.3%	0.8%
Industry-adjusted	1.1%	3.4%**	3.8%**	3.6%**	5.1%**	4.3%**
# observations	49	53	43	41	36	35

a. Year –1 is the fiscal year ending prior to the IPO completion year of Year 0.
*,**,*** — Significantly different from 0 at the 10%, 5% and 1% levels, respectively (two–tailed test).

Capital Expenditures and Working Capital of Reverse LBOs

In addition to investigating operating performance, we examined working capital management and capital expenditures. In particular, we were interested in determining whether capital expenditure patterns and working capital management of reverse-LBO firms were significantly different from those of their industry counterparts, and whether those patterns changed over time. The previously cited studies on LBOs found that firms reduce some of their expenditures on discretionary items and manage working capital more efficiently after going private in an LBO. Thus, another potential manifestation of poor performance would be that newly public firms begin to overinvest in capital expenditures and manage working capital less efficiently.

Panel A of Table 2 provides an analysis of the unadjusted and industry-adjusted level of capital expenditures and working capital, both as a percentage of total assets. Reverse-LBO firms spent signifi-

cantly less than the industry norm on capital expenditures in the year prior to the IPO, but in later years there was no difference in capital expenditures between the reverse-LBO firms and their industry medians. The industry-adjusted ratio of working capital to assets was significantly negative in every year, indicating that the reverse-LBO firms carried significantly less working capital than other firms in their industry. Indeed, the reverse-LBO firms carry approximately half of the working capital carried by the typical firm in their industry.

Panel B of Table 2 provides an analysis of *changes* in capital expenditures and working capital. Unadjusted changes in capital expenditures showed a significant increase from year –1 to year 0, but none of the other differences was significant. Industry-adjusted changes in capital expenditures increased significantly between years –1 and 0 and year –1 and +1; but although subsequent years generally saw increases relative to year –1, no other observed changes were statistically significant. Changes in the level of capital expenditures in years 0 and +1 are

*The operating performance of reverse LBOs is significantly **better** than that of the
median firm in their industries in the year prior to and in the year of the IPO.
Moreover, the reverse-LBO firms continue to outperform their industry competitors
for at least the first four fiscal years after the IPO.*

probably expected, given the infusion of cash into these firms from the public offering. Further, although there is no evidence of an increase in the level of unadjusted working capital for these firms, industry-adjusted working capital for these firms increased.

LINKING CHANGES IN PERFORMANCE TO CHANGES IN OWNERSHIP AND LEVERAGE

Up to this point, we have examined the median levels and changes in performance, capital expenditures, and working capital. While interesting, these results do not provide evidence on whether the changes in performance are systematically related to changes in organizational structure. In order to provide evidence of a systematic linkage between incentives and performance, we designed a series of regressions intended to reveal the relationship between changes in performance and changes in leverage and ownership structure.

For purposes of these regressions, our primary measures of the change in performance were the changes in OPINC/assets and OCF/assets (measured in percent) between year −1 and year +1, and the changes of the same two ratios between year −1 and the average of years +1 to +4. We also used as performance measures the changes in working capital and the changes in capital expenditures over the same two periods. The variables measuring change in organizational structure were the change in leverage and the changes in the percentage of equity owned by operating management and non-management insiders.

Moreover, the changes in the organizational structure variables were measured at the time of the IPO, regardless of whether we examine the change in accounting performance between years −1 and +1 or between years −1 and the average of years +1 to +4. Thus, we effectively assumed that the change in incentives that occurred in year 0 was related to subsequent changes in performance. Since we do not know how quickly a change in performance arising from a change in incentive structures would be reflected in the financial statements, we examined the two alternative intervals.

If reducing leverage and the concentration of ownership reduces managers' incentives to achieve superior performance, we should expect to find positive coefficients on the leverage and ownership variables when OCF/assets and OPINC/assets are the dependent variables. If, however, very high leverage and concentrations of ownership constitute a relatively poor incentive structure, reducing leverage and ownership concentration should improve performance and the coefficients on leverage and the ownership variables should be negative. Moreover, if reducing leverage and the concentration of ownership reduces managerial incentives to perform, and if increases in working capital and capital expenditures imply poorer performance because managers are paying less attention to working capital management and are relaxing constraints on capital expenditures, then the signs on leverage and ownership should be negative.

As presented in Table 3, the results of the first four regressions[7] provide no evidence that changes in leverage are associated with changes in accounting performance. By contrast, the changes in the percentage ownership by operating management and nonmanagement insiders are generally significant and positively associated with changes in accounting performance.[8] The positive coefficients on the percentage of equity owned by operating management and other insiders indicate that the greater the decline in the percentage of outstanding equity owned by these groups, the greater the decline in subsequent accounting performance.[9]

To get a sense of the economic importance (as opposed to the statistical significance) of the ownership coefficients, consider the regression of OCF/assets in Panel A from year −1 to the average of year +1 to +4, where the estimated coefficients on the change in the two equity positions are 0.44 for operating management and 0.35 for nonmanagement insiders. Recall also that the median OCF/assets in year -1 for this sample was 19.3%. On average, the firms that enter this regression experienced a 13% drop in both the percentage of equity owned by operating management (that is, their average ownership fell from 37% to 24%) and in the percentage

---

7. The results reported in Table 3 use the "raw" or "unadjusted" firm performance measures. In results not reported here, we have also included controls for industry performance. The coefficients and significance levels are almost identical to those reported.

8. The F-statistics of the regressions are generally significant and the adjusted-R^2's of the equations range from 6.4% to 33.5%.

9. Note also that the coefficients on the effect of ownership changes are generally unaffected by the time period used to measure the change, but are approximately twice as large for the OCF/assets equations than for the OPINC/assets equations. But, since there is a much smaller change in the OPINC/assets than in the OCF/assets numbers (see Table 1), this is perhaps not surprising.

TABLE 3 ■ THE ASSOCIATION BETWEEN OPERATING PERFORMANCE, LEVERAGE, AND OWNERSHIP[*, a]

Dependent Variable	Intercept	Independent variables			Adj R²	F- Stat	No. Obs.
		Change in Debt/Capital	Change in Mgmt. % Equity	Change in Non- Mgmt. Insider % Equity			
Change in firm OPINC/assets from year −1 to +1	2.76 (0.220)	0.89 (0.853)	0.13 (0.042)	0.17 (0.029)	7.3%	2.39 (0.088)	54
Change in firm OPINC/assets from year −1 to the average of years +1 to +4	4.26 (0.136)	−1.87 (0.776)	0.22 (0.025)	0.21 (0.050)	11.9%	2.57 (0.071)	36
Change in firm OCF/assets from year −1 to +1	1.73 (0.636)	−7.61 (0.317)	0.38 (0.001)	0.40 (0.002)	22.9%	5.95 (0.002)	51
Change in firm OCF/assets from year −1 to the average of years +1 to +4	6.25 (0.065)	−3.55 (0.641)	0.44 (0.000)	0.35 (0.006)	33.5%	6.71 (0.001)	35
Change in firm working capital/ assets from year −1 to +1	−2.96 (0.297)	3.26 (0.586)	−0.23 (0.007)	−0.24 (0.017)	12.3%	3.37 (0.026)	52
Change in firm working capital/ assets from year −1 to the average of years +1 to +4	−1.34 (0.611)	4.16 (0.505)	−0.07 (0.448)	−0.28 (0.008)	14.2%	2.77 (0.060)	33
Change in firm capital expenditures/ assets from year −1 to +1	−1.29 (0.292)	−4.40 (0.084)	0.00 (0.940)	−0.08 (0.054)	10.0%	2.88 (0.045)	52
Change in firm capital expenditures/ assets from year −1 to the average of years +1 to +4	−0.95 (0.454)	−1.78 (0.541)	0.01 (0.739)	−0.08 (0.095)	6.4%	1.73 (0.183)	33

[*] Cross-Sectional Regression Analysis of changes in percentage firm performance after the initial public offering as a function of changes in leverage, change in the percentage of equity owned by operating management, and change in the percentage of equity owned by non-operating management insiders for 90 reverse-LBO firms.
a. Year +1 is the fiscal year ending after the IPO completion year of Year 0. The significance levels for each estimated regression coefficient are reported in parentheses below the estimate. All reported significance levels are two-tailed.

of equity owned by nonmanagement insiders (which dropped from 38% to 25%). According to our regression results, a firm experiencing this average (13%) decline in the percentage equity owned by management sees its OCF/assets ratio decline by 5.7% (that is, from 19.3% to 13.6%) relative to a firm whose managers' percentage equity owned does not decline, other things equal. And a firm experiencing the average decline in the percentage equity owned by nonmanagement insiders (also 13%) loses an additional 4.55% in OCF/assets, relative to a firm whose nonmanagement insiders' percentage equity owned does not decline, other things equal. Given the median OCF/assets in year −1 of 19.3%, these losses *each* represent about 25% of the ratio's value in year −1.

The last four regressions in Panel A use working capital and capital expenditures as the dependent variables. Again, there is no evidence that changes in leverage are associated with changes in working capital, and only very weak evidence of a negative association between changes in leverage and changes in capital expenditures. Further, there is only very weak evidence of a negative association between changes in managerial ownership and changes in working capital, and no evidence of an association between changes in managerial ownership and capital expenditures.

However, there is strong evidence of a negative association between changes in nonmanagement insider ownership and both working capital and capital expenditures. That is, as nonmanagement

There is strong evidence of a negative association between changes in nonmanagement insider ownership and both working capital and capital expenditures. That is, as nonmanagement insiders' equity decreases, working capital and capital expenditures increase.

insiders' equity decreases, working capital and capital expenditures increase. The coefficients on nonmanagement insider ownership in the working capital regressions (which range from –0.24 to –0.28) suggest that a firm experiencing the average decline in the percentage equity owned by nonmanagement insiders (13%) sees its working capital/assets ratio increase by about three percentage points relative to a firm whose nonmanagers' percentage equity did not decline. Given the median working capital/assets in year –1 of 14.4%, this represents more than a 20% increase in working capital relative to the value in year –1. A similar calculation using the nonmanagement insider ownership coefficient from the capital expenditure regressions of –0.08 implies an increase in capital expenditures/assets of 1.04%, which approximates a 25% increase in the level of capital expenditures relative to year –1.[10]

THE STOCK MARKET PERFORMANCE OF REVERSE LBOs

Overall, Table 3 provides evidence that changes in accounting performance observed after the reverse LBO are related to changes in the concentration of ownership by operating management and nonmanagement insiders. One interpretation of the evidence is that reductions in the concentration of ownership lead to an inferior incentive structure and therefore performance deteriorates. An alternative interpretation, however, is that managers optimally choose the timing of the IPO transaction to take advantage of an information "asymmetry"—that is, a significant disparity between their private information and the information known to the market that might cause public investors to overpay in an IPO. According to this interpretation, managers reduce their ownership stake more as their expectation of performance falls. (Of course, examining the relation between changes in equity ownership and

operating performance is only tangentially related to this timing explanation because it does not directly relate to changes in shareholder wealth.) In this section, we examine the stock market performance of reverse LBOs to determine if there is any evidence that managers act opportunistically.

If managers take advantage of their private information to sell their shares at an inflated offering price, we would anticipate significantly negative shareholder returns following the IPO. Previous studies have documented that the stock price performance of IPOs in the 1975-1984 period (not reverse LBOs) underperforms the value-weighted New York and American Stock Exchange Index by approximately 25% over the first three years of listing (excluding the day of listing). A similar finding in the reverse-LBO data would be consistent with managers' taking advantage of an informational asymmetry.

The mean opening-day raw return for the 89 reverse-LBO firms for which opening-day closing price data was available on the CRSP tapes was 2.03%. Of these, 43 had a positive return, 24 had a negative return, and 22 had a zero return. Previous studies on IPOs (excluding reverse LBOs) generally document mean first-day returns above 10%. Thus, the initial day's return is much smaller for the sample of reverse LBOs than for IPOs in general.

To examine this issue further, we investigated longer holding periods beginning with the closing price on the opening-day. In assessing the longer-term stock market performance of reverse LBOs, we used three different metrics: buy-and-hold returns; buy-and-hold returns in excess of the buy-and-hold returns for the value-weighted New York and American Stock Exchange Index (market-adjusted returns); and Jensen alphas.[11] The three different measures were calculated for 12-, 24-, 36-, and 48-month holding periods beginning with the closing price on the date of the IPO.

10. One difficulty associated with interpreting the working capital and capital expenditure regressions is that many firms explicitly indicate that they are going public in order to raise funds for the purposes of increasing working capital and capital expenditures. Of interest to us is the effect of the incentive structure on capital expenditures and working capital. We are not interested in the effects of an infusion of cash on working capital and capital expenditures if that was the purpose of the equity offering, *assuming that the effects of that infusion do not represent incentive problems.* As the ownership stakes of the managers and nonmanager insiders fall, more capital is likely to be raised by the firm, and thus the negative association between ownership and both working capital and capital expenditures may be due to the cash infusion. To see whether our results on leverage and ownership are sensitive to controlling for the capital infusion into the firm, we reran all of the working capital and capital expenditure regressions with an additional control variable for the net proceeds of the offering less the amount

used to retire debt (deflated by assets). The regression results were not sensitive to the inclusion of this variable. Therefore, the associations between ownership and working capital and capital expenditure do not appear to be mechanically induced by the IPO.

11. Jensen alphas assume that the Capital Asset Pricing Model is correctly specified. The Jensen alpha for each firm is the intercept from estimating a firm-specific time series regression of monthly firm excess returns (the firm's returns in excess of one-month U.S. Treasury Bill returns) on the value-weighted NYSE/AMEX excess returns (the value-weighted NYSE/AMEX return in excess of one-month U.S. Treasury Bill returns). Regressions use the maximum number of observations available up to the number of months in the reported holding period. (The mean and median betas for the reverse LBOs vary between 1.3 and 1.5 depending on the time period examined.)

Our examination of longer-term performance yielded no evidence of negative returns subsequent to the reverse LBO. In particular, mean and median returns, market-adjusted returns, and Jensen alphas at 12 months were all insignificantly different from zero. At 24, 36, and 48 months, mean and median raw returns were positive and significantly different from zero. Mean and median market-adjusted returns were positive at 24, 36, and 48 months, but only the 24-month return was significant at conventional levels. For the Jensen alphas, the means at 24, 36, and 48 months were all positive and also significant at the 10% or better level at 24 and 36 months, while the medians were always negative but never significantly different from zero at conventional levels.

Overall, then, the market performance of the reverse LBOs after their public offerings was either positive or insignificantly different from zero, depending on the time period and performance metric chosen. Since there was no evidence of statistically negative excess returns, there is no support at the overall sample level for the hypothesis that managers were able to take advantage of an information asymmetry to enrich themselves. Moreover, the pricing of reverse LBOs seems quite rational relative to the pricing of other IPOs, for reverse LBOs experience neither a large increase in value on the offering date nor a large decline in value over the subsequent three years.

We also examined the extent to which cross-sectional variation in excess returns can be explained by the change in leverage and ownership structure. If the initial public offering market is efficient, we would *not* anticipate that the change in organizational structure variables would explain any of the cross-sectional variation in subsequent market performance, since those variables are known at the time of the offering. While the amount that insiders sell in the offering or by which they reduce their percentage ownership of the firm would likely affect the offering price, it should not affect subsequent market performance in an efficient market. If subsequent market performance is found to be uncorrelated with the organizational structure variables—in particular, with the change in the percentage equity owned by operating management and nonmanage-

ment insiders—that would be additional evidence that is inconsistent with the information asymmetry explanation for the observed association between operating performance measures and ownership.

In a series of tests whose findings are not reported here, we found no association between stock market performance and either changes in leverage or changes in the percentage equity owned by managers and other insiders. Thus, there is no evidence that operating management and other insiders were able to use an information asymmetry to increase their wealth. The offering price appears to have reflected any change in performance arising from the change in the leverage and ownership structure.

INTERPRETATION AND SUBSEQUENT CHANGES IN ORGANIZATIONAL STRUCTURE

Our major findings, then, are that reverse-LBO firms outperform their industries for the four years following the IPO. At the same time, however, there is some evidence of a decline in performance in that period. Further, reverse LBOs both increase capital expenditures and levels of working capital after the public offering. *Most important*, cross-sectional tests indicate that firm performance decreases with declines in the concentration of equity ownership by operating management and other insiders, but is unrelated to changes in leverage. Finally, both capital expenditures and working capital appear to increase with declines in the concentration of equity ownership by nonmanagement insiders.

One interpretation of our findings is that there are positive incentive effects associated with more concentrated ownership by managers and active investors who monitor management, and that these organizational changes contribute to superior performance. At the same time, we find no evidence of positive incentive effects associated with greater leverage in the sense that post-IPO performance is unrelated to changes in leverage at the time of the IPO.[12]

These results leave us with a bit of a puzzle, however. If LBOs are value-increasing events when undertaken, can reverse LBOs also be value-increas-

---

12. If the reverse LBOs are generally constrained in their ability to make investments, this sample of firms is unlikely to exhibit the positive incentive effects associated with debt, since those effects are typically discussed in the context of firms with free cash flow generating ability and no profitable investment opportunities. Moreover, evidence from our sample indicates that capital expenditures increase after the reverse LBO which is consistent with these firms being cash constrained prior to the reverse LBO.

> The pricing of reverse LBOs seems quite rational relative to the pricing of other IPOs, for reverse LBOs experience neither a large increase in value on the offering date nor a large decline in value over the subsequent three years.

ing? If reverse LBOs are not value-increasing, why are they undertaken? One possibility is that, as the value of the firm increases with improved performance, the owners of the LBO firm begin to place a higher value on having more marketable claims and more diversified holdings. And, so, even if their decision to sell is expected to cause performance to decline somewhat after going public, the managers still prefer to hold claims that are marketable.

Another potential answer to the puzzle, however, is that the change in organizational structure occurs because of some major change in the external business environment that affects, say, the firm's investment opportunities. For example, suppose that profitable investments become available to the firm on a larger scale than had been available previously, but that the firm's current owners are reluctant to provide more funding because of their lack of diversification. Moreover, financing the new investment with debt is precluded by the already high leverage levels. In this case, the shift to a public firm could be optimal, and the fundamental cause of such a shift would be the underlying change in the firm's investment opportunities. It is in this sense that the organizational structure of the reverse-LBO firm may well have been optimal both when the firm was private, and when it returned to public ownership.[13]

Since our tests provide at least some evidence that changes in performance subsequent to the reverse LBO are related to the change in the ownership structure, it is interesting to examine changes in organizational structure after the reverse LBO. If the change in organizational structure that occurs at the time of the reverse LBO is *less efficient* than the LBO structure, we would expect firms to switch back towards their LBO-like structure.

To see whether the board and ownership structure of the reverse-LBO firms changes after the reverse LBO, we obtained proxy statements for the 44 firms in our sample that were still publicly listed three years after the reverse LBO. Our analysis indicates that these firms were still hybrid organizations—that is, they retained some of the own-

ership and board structure characteristics of the leverage buyout. At the same time, they also appeared to be continuing to evolve *toward* the board and ownership structure of a more typical U.S. corporation, as opposed to moving back toward an LBO-like structure.

In particular, we found that for the firms that were still public three years after the reverse LBO, the mean and median percentages of equity owned by operating managers were 22.4% and 12.6%, respectively. For nonmanagement insiders, the mean and median ownership percentages were 16.4% and 5.3%, respectively. Thus, although ownership by operating managers and nonmanagement insiders was still more concentrated than for the typical corporation, the ownership positions of these organizations had become much less concentrated than they were immediately after the IPO. (The median declines in ownership for management and nonmanagement insiders were −14.9% and −24.1%, respectively.)

We also found that the board structure of these companies was evolving toward a more standard corporate structure. In particular, three years after the IPO, approximately 46% of the board members were external members with no significant equity stakes (less than 5% of the equity), 35% of the board members were internal board members, and the remaining 19% of the board members were significant investors (representatives of LBO buyout firms, debtholders, and other significant investors). Of the external members with no significant equity stakes, approximately 7% were significant investors immediately after the IPO but were no longer significant investors.

Thus, the major shift that occurred in the board structure in the three years after the IPO was away from nonmanagement capital providers to external directors with limited equity stakes. Though the median board size did not increase (and average board size increases by less than one person), approximately one-third of the board members were new since the reverse LBO.

---

13. One possibility that we cannot rule out is that the association between ownership and performance detected by our tests is not caused by the incentive effects associated with increased ownership, but rather that the shifts in the firm's investment opportunities are driving both the changes in ownership and the positive correlation between ownership and performance. In many cases, low profitability and the presence of few promising investment opportunities might have been responsible for the initial decision to lever up and concentrate ownership through an LBO. However, after capturing the gains from the LBO, these firms may may have faced expanded investment opportunities with positive-NPVs, but with lower operating performance ratios than those taken while the firm was private. High leverage and concentrated ownership are likely to have constrained the firm from making such investments. To the extent this is so, it would be the company's new investment opportunities (with positive NPVs, but lower rates of return) that are effectively driving management's decision to return to less concentrated public ownership and cause the reduction in operating performance. Thus, it would be these new investment opportunities, as opposed to the changes in incentives, that are driving the association we document between ownership and performance.

Overall, the results in this paper add some intriguing evidence on the link between performance and organizational incentives. In particular, there is strong evidence of a positive association between performance and managerial ownership and ownership by active investors (monitors). Moreover, the results provide further insights on the transition from the LBO form.

CHAPTER 3
EXTERNAL GOVERNANCE

CHAPTER 3: SECTION 3.1
Ownership and Control

We begin our foray into external governance mechanisms by focusing on the role of outside shareholders. Ownership structures, and thus the strength of incentives for shareholders to monitor corporate management, vary dramatically across companies and across countries. Our readings in this chapter focus on the potential for external shareholder monitoring in France, Germany, and the U.K., as well as in the U.S.

In *The Growth of Institutional Stock Ownership: A Promise Unfulfilled*, Frank Edwards and Glenn Hubbard argue that despite the substantial growth of institutional ownership of U.S. corporations in the past 20 years, there is little evidence that institutional investors have acquired the kind of concentrated ownership positions required to be able to play a dominant role in the corporate governance process. Institutional ownership remains widely dispersed among firms and institutions, in large part because of significant legal obstacles that discourage institutional investors both from taking large block positions and from exercising large ownership positions to control corporate managers. Thus, although much of the growth of institutional ownership since 1980 has been accounted for by the growth of mutual funds and private pension funds, there continue to be strong deterrents to the accumulation and use of large ownership positions to influence corporate managers.

Another potentially important factor discouraging concentrated investments are incentive schemes that effectively reward money managers for producing returns that track the S&P 500 (or whatever sector the manager is supposed to be representing). Using a very different incentive scheme that offers managers a share of the excess returns (as well as penalties for failure to meet benchmarks), a relatively new class of "hedge funds" has emerged that provides both more concentrated ownership positions and higher risk-adjusted rates of return.

To encourage mutual funds to take a more activist corporate governance role and to behave more like hedge funds, the authors recommend that current legal restrictions on mutual funds be relaxed so that mutual funds have a greater incentive to hold large ownership positions in companies and to use those positions to more effectively monitor corporate managers. In particular, the "five and ten"

portfolio rules applicable to mutual funds could be repealed and replaced with a standard of prudence and diligence more in keeping with portfolio theory; mutual funds could be given greater freedom to adopt redemption policies that would be more conducive to holding larger ownership positions; and institutional investors could be permitted to employ a variety of incentive fee structures to encourage fund managers to pursue more pro-active investment strategies. The prospect of actively involving institutional fund managers in the corporate governance process in a constructive way may be our best hope for improving corporate governance in the U.S.

In *Corporate Ownership and Control in the U.K., Germany, and France*, Julian Franks and Colin Mayer argue that, like its U.S. counterpart, the U.K. corporate ownership and governance system can be characterized as an outsider system with a large number of public corporations, widely dispersed ownership (though with growing concentrations of institutional shareholdings), and well-developed takeover markets. By contrast, the much smaller number and proportion of publicly traded German and French corporations are governed by insider systems—those in which the founding families, banks, or other companies have controlling interests and in which outside shareholders are not able to exert much control.

The different patterns of ownership in the U.K. and in France and Germany give rise to different incentives and corporate control mechanisms. Concentrated ownership would seem to encourage longer-term relationships between the company and its investors. But while perhaps better suited to some corporate activities with longer-term payoffs, concentrated ownership could also lead to costly delays in undertaking necessary corrective action, particularly if the owners receive "private" benefits from owning and running a business. And although widely dispersed ownership may increase the likelihood that corrective action will be sought prematurely (as outsiders rush to sell their shares in response to a temporary downturn), the presence of well-diversified public owners may also be more appropriate for riskier ventures requiring large amounts of new capital investment. Thus, concentrated ownership, while having the potential to reduce information costs and to strengthen incentives to maximize value, can also impose costs in two ways: (1) by forcing managers and other insiders to bear excessive company-specific risks that could be transferred to well-diversified outsiders; and (2) by allowing insiders to capture private benefits at the expense of outsiders.

In *Large Bank Stockholders in Germany: Saviors or Substitutes?*, William Carney argues that differences between Germany and the U.S. in the importance of trading markets and the role of banks as monitors can be explained in large part by actions of German banks that blocked the development of German capital markets and provided big banks with informational advantages over other traders. Markets are likely to be more effective monitors than large banks because of the banks' conflicts of interest as both creditors and underwriters and market-makers for German firms.

Nevertheless, as Carney also argues, there is more diversity in the ownership structure of U.S. corporations than the current governance debate would suggest. In the U.S. there are many publicly owned companies that are either closely held or have reverted to private ownership through LBOs. This in turn suggests that U.S. capital markets have devised means for bringing about concentrated stock ownership in those cases where large stockholder monitoring is likely to be more efficient. Thus, to the question what is likely to happen to U.S. corporate ownership structure if remaining legal constraints on stock ownership by U.S. banks are relaxed, the answer this article offers is "not much." Indeed, if one considers increasing U.S. institutional ownership together with recent SEC attempts to liberalize shareholder communications, there appears to be a striking trend toward a new concentration of voting power—one that may ultimately rival that of the German banks.

THE GROWTH OF INSTITUTIONAL STOCK OWNERSHIP: A PROMISE UNFULFILLED

by Franklin R. Edwards and R. Glenn Hubbard, Columbia University*

A cademics have pointed to the dramatic growth of institutional stock ownership in the United States during the past 20 years as our best hope for reversing the shift in power from corporate owners to corporate managers that began in the 1930s.[1] In their 1932 classic, *The Modern Corporation and Private Property*, Berle and Means recognized what was to become the dominant corporate paradigm of 20th-century American capitalism: the transfer of effective control from stockholders, the owners, to professional corporate managers. In their words, "[T]he central mass of the twentieth century American revolution [is a] massive collectivization of property devoted to production, with [an] accompanying decline of individual decision-making and control, [and] a massive dissociation of wealth from active management." The "[s]tockholder [vote] is of diminishing importance as the number of shareholders in each corporation increases—diminishing in fact to negligible importance as the corporations become giants. As the number of stockholders increases, the capacity of each to express opinions is extremely limited."[2] Berle and Means correctly foresaw that shareholders would become "passive" investors, leaving corporate managers in full control of their corporations. For many, the growth of institutional stock ownership that has occurred during the last two decades—institutions now hold nearly 56% of outstanding stock in the U.S.—is a hopeful development that promises to change the face of American

capitalism in the next century.[3] As large shareholders, institutions have a greater incentive to be active shareholders and to monitor corporate managers than do small shareholders. In particular, institutions are better able to overcome the agency costs and information asymmetries associated with diffuse stock ownership.[4] In principle, therefore, institutional stock ownership should result in improved corporate governance generally and an accompanying increase in corporate efficiency and shareholder wealth.

This promise of better corporate governance through more active institutional shareholders has been reinforced by a recent empirical study of institutional ownership by Paul Gompers and Andrew Metrick, who find that in the U.S. "...the concentration of institutional ownership... has risen sharply since 1980."[5] Based on this growth in institutional ownership, they conclude that "...the importance of large [institutional] shareholders for corporate governance in the United States will increase" in the future.[6]

Such optimism about the prospects of a corporate governance revolution led by a growth in "institutional-investor capitalism" may be premature. First, while institutional stock ownership concentration has indeed increased since 1980, it is generally still quite low. Second, there are good reasons to believe that, unless significant changes are made in the legal and cultural environment of institutional funds management, ownership concentration

---

*The authors wish to thank Eric Engstrom for invaluable research assistance.

1. See, for example, Bernard Black, "Next Steps in Proxy Reform," *Journal of Corporation Law* 18 (1992); and Mark J. Roe, *Strong Managers, Weak Owners: The Political Roots of American Corporate Finance.* Princeton, N.J.: Princeton University Press, 1994.

2. See Roe, 1994, p. 6, cited above.

3. See, for example, Financial Economists Roundtable, "Statement on Institutional Investors and Corporate Governance." *Journal of Financial Services Research* 15 (February 1999): pp. 77-79.

4. See Andrei Shleifer and Robert Vishny, "A Survey of Corporate Governance," *Journal of Finance* 52 (1997): pp. 737-784.

5. Paul A. Gompers and Andrew Metrick, "How Are Large Institutions Different from Other Investors? Why Do These Differences Matter?" Working Paper, Harvard Business School, March 1998, pp. 22 and 30.

6. *Ibid*, p. 32.

in the U.S. is unlikely to reach the level at which institutional investors will have a powerful voice in corporate boardrooms. Third, institutional fund managers face significant legal and institutional constraints that deter them from both accumulating large ownership positions and attempting to use those positions to control corporate managers.[7] Finally, notwithstanding journalistic accounts of the rise of institutional shareholder activism, empirical studies suggest that such activism has had at best a modest effect on the performance of targeted firms.[8]

Our primary message in this paper is that, despite the increase in institutional stock ownership that has occurred since 1980, institutional investors are unlikely to alter significantly the way U.S. corporations are governed in the future unless changes are made in the laws and the institutional structure that govern the behavior of institutional fund managers. Indeed, to date institutional investors have done little to change the structure of corporate governance in the U.S. Apart from the episodic activities of a few large public pension funds, institutional investors on the whole have not taken an active role in corporate governance.[9]

The rest of this paper is organized in the following four sections. In the first, we examine the data on institutional ownership and draw somewhat different conclusions from prior studies about the growth of institutional ownership and in particular about the growth of ownership concentration. The second section explores the determinants of institutional ownership and again reaches some conclusions that differ from those of prior studies. The third section describes the legal and institutional obstacles faced by fund managers in both taking large ownership positions and in using those positions to influence corporate managers. The fourth section discusses changes in the legal and institutional structure that we believe would encourage a more active involvement of institutional investors in corporate governance. Some of these recommendations derive from the legal and organizational structure currently used by hedge funds.

INSTITUTIONAL OWNERSHIP REVISITED

We first examine the growth of institutional ownership and ownership concentration. In particular, based on the quarterly 13F reports submitted to the SEC on all common-stock positions greater than 10,000 shares or $200,000, CDA/Spectrum has compiled a data base on institutional ownership. We use those data for the years 1980, 1985, 1990, and 1995 through 1997. In organizing these data Spectrum assigns one of the following manager types to each reporting institution: (1) bank; (2) insurance company; (3) investment company (mutual fund); (4) independent advisor (usually a large brokerage firm or securities firm); or (5) other (public pension funds and university and charitable foundation endowments).[10]

This classification is not always precise. In particular, if a fund manager reports that more than 50% (say, 55%) of the total assets that it has under management fall into category (4), all of the assets managed by that manager are then classified as being in category (4), even though the other 45% of the assets managed by the manager may be in mutual funds. In this case category (4) assets will be overstated and category (3) assets understated. Alternatively, the reverse could be true. This reporting problem is likely to be greater for categories (3) and (4) than for other institutional categories because the same fund managers are active as both mutual fund managers and private pension fund managers. While in principle this reporting problem could result in either overreporting or underreporting of the assets in either category (3) or (4), our findings indicate that in practice it results in the overstating of category (4) assets and the understating of category (3), or mutual fund assets. This underreporting of mutual fund assets is exacerbated by the fact that mutual fund assets managed by banks and insurance companies also are reported as being in categories (1) and (2) rather than in category (3).

To obtain a better estimate of category (3) assets, we supplemented the CDA/Spectrum classification system with separate data on all mutual funds with

7. See Robert C. Pozen, "Institutional Investors: The Reluctant Activists." *Harvard Business Review* (January/February 1994).

8. See, *e.g.*, Bernard Black, "Shareholder Activism and Corporate Governance," in Peter Newman, ed., *The New Palgrave Dictionary of Economics and Law*, London: MacMillan Reference Limited, (1998), pp. 459-464; Stuart L. Gillan and Laura Starks, "A Survey of Shareholder Activism: Motivation and Empirical Evidence," *Contemporary Finance Digest* 31 (Autumn 1998); and Jonathan M. Karpoff, "Does Shareholder Activism Work?: A Survey of Empirical Findings." Mimeograph, April 1998.

9. See, for example, the review of studies of the role of institutional investors and the interviews of institutional investors reported by Gile R. Downes, Jr., Ehud Houminer, and R. Glenn Hubbard, *Institutional Investors and Corporate Behavior*, American Enterprise Institute, 1999.

10. Analysis of flow-of-funds data on private, defined-benefit, pension funds suggests that category (4) closely parallels the growth of defined-benefit pension funds. However, category (4) managers also include private equity funds, hedge funds, venture capital funds, etc.

TABLE 1		1980	1985	1990	1995	1996	1997
INSTITUTIONAL EQUITY HOLDINGS BY TYPE OF INSTITUTION, BILLIONS OF DOLLARS	**ALL INSTITUTIONS**						
	Total	504.27	986.29	1522.97	3785.51	4845.76	6390.74
	Average Size	0.91	1.26	1.59	2.99	3.66	4.38
	Pct. of U.S.	36%	45%	51%	56%	59%	60%
	Top 5/Class	10%	10%	12%	18%	19%	19%
	BANKS						
	Total	222.91	342.91	407.24	781.94	948.09	1236.58
	Average Size	0.99	1.43	1.88	3.80	5.10	6.87
	Pct. of 13F	44%	35%	27%	21%	20%	19%
	Pct. of U.S.	16%	16%	14%	12%	12%	12%
	Top 5/Class	20%	26%	31%	41%	42%	44%
	INSURANCE COMPANIES						
	Total	59.07	80.10	111.34	350.91	423.89	577.77
	Average Size	0.84	1.13	1.61	4.50	5.81	7.31
	Pct. of 13F	12%	8%	7%	9%	9%	9%
	Pct. of U.S.	4%	4%	4%	5%	5%	5%
	Top 5/Class	45%	50%	54%	66%	68%	68%
	INDEPENDENT ADVISORS						
	Total	110.35	338.02	611.68	1301.25	1690.75	2140.00
	Average Size	0.84	0.99	1.20	1.59	1.86	2.09
	Pct. of 13F	22%	34%	40%	34%	35%	33%
	Pct. of U.S.	8%	15%	21%	19%	21%	20%
	Top 5/Class	26%	16%	21%	18%	20%	23%
	PUBLIC AND NON-PROFIT						
	Total	60.86	112.58	182.26	316.43	346.65	453.35
	Average Size	0.79	1.31	2.00	4.06	4.50	5.46
	Pct. of 13F	12%	11%	12%	8%	7%	7%
	Pct. of U.S.	4%	5%	6%	5%	4%	4%
	Top 5/Class	31%	31%	39%	42%	44%	44%
	MUTUAL FUNDS						
	Total	51.07	112.68	210.44	1034.98	1436.38	1983.05
	Average Size	0.30	0.47	0.72	1.87	2.49	3.35
	Pct. of 13F	10%	11%	14%	27%	30%	31%
	Pct. of U.S.	4%	5%	7%	15%	17%	19%
	Top 5/Class	26%	26%	34%	34%	35%	37%

more than $100 million under management. The drawback of this procedure is that it does nothing to correct problems in measuring category (4) assets, and may result in some double-counting, which may in turn cause total institutional ownership to be overstated. Despite this drawback, we prefer this procedure because it enables us to obtain a more accurate picture of mutual fund assets, the fastest-growing type of institutional investor.

Using our data sources, we find that mutual funds accounted for 10% of all reported 13F assets in 1980 and 31% in 1997. Correspondingly, assuming that the persistent underreporting of mutual fund assets that we find occurred largely because of an over-reporting of category (4) assets, we estimate that category (4) assets (independent advisors) would have represented 33% of 13F equity in 1997 (see Table 1).

OWNERSHIP CONCENTRATION

We measure institutional ownership (IO) as the proportion of a company's outstanding stock owned by all types of institutional investors, and ownership concentration (C5) by the proportion of a company's outstanding stock owned by the five largest institutional owners. (We also examine alternative measures of concentration, such as C1, C10, and a block ownership measure, and find a high degree of correlation among these measures.) Our figures on institutional ownership and on ownership concentration are based on the firms reported in the CDA database. We make no assumption about the institutional ownership of firms not included in the CDA database.[11] We find that, in the median CDA firm, the five-investor concentration ratio (C5) increased from 9% in 1980 to 17% in 1997, an increase of eight percentage points; and that, in the 75th percentile firm, C5 increased from 16% in 1980 to 26% in 1997, an increase of 10 percentage points (see Table 2).

The question, of course, is of what importance is the growth in ownership concentration. Does, for example, a figure of 17% for C5 for the median CDA firm suggest that institutional investors are now in position to influence or control most corporate managers? To begin with, C5 is probably not a very good measure of ownership power. A 15% figure for C5 could mean that five different institutions each owned three percent of the firm, or that one institution owned 11% and four owned one percent each. Clearly, the incentive to exercise control over managers would be much stronger for an institution owning 11% of the firm than for an institution owning only three percent. Thus, the distribution of stock ownership among the large owners can make a significant difference in both the incentive and ability of an owner to exercise control. The more equal it is, the less the incentive for any one institution to exercise ownership power, and probably the higher the costs of coordinating joint ownership activities.

To capture differences in the distribution of ownership shares among institutional owners we use a version of the Herfindahl Index (H).[12] An increase in H can occur if the ownership shares increase or if ownership shares become more unequal. The higher the value of H the more unequal are ownership shares, and the more likely it is that some institutional investors will have an incentive to influence corporate managers. We find that increases in H since 1980 have not been particularly significant: H increased from 6% in 1980 to about 10% in 1997 for the median firm, and increased from 10% to 15% for the 75th percentile firm (see Table 2). Further, in absolute terms, a Herfindahl index of 10 to 15% is typically not considered to be a high level of concentration (by, for example, antitrust standards, where the ability to undertake coordinated activities is of paramount importance).

Another way of viewing ownership concentration is in terms of large block ownership. Arguably, unless an institution owns a sizeable block of a company's stock, it has little incentive to expose itself to the costs and risks associated with activities directed at controlling or influencing corporate managers. It might simply opt to sell its shares in an under-performing company. We define a "block owner" as an owner who owns at least five percent of a company's shares (BO), and we measure ownership concentration as the percentage of a company's shares owned by all block owners (BOC). For the median firm, BOC increased from zero in 1980 to 6% in 1997; and for the 75th percentile firm BOC increased from 7% in 1980 to 17% in 1997. Thus, for most firms, there is no more than one block owner even today, and for the 75th percentile firm all block owners control only 17% of outstanding shares (see Table 2).

Examining the pattern of institutional ownership concentration also reveals why concentration has not increased as fast as has total institutional ownership in CDA firms. Since 1980, total institutional ownership in the median CDA firm went from 12 to 29%, and from 29 to 57% in the 75th percentile CDA firm. In contrast, ownership concentration (C5) has risen only from 9 to 17% in the median CDA firm, and from 16 to 26% in the 75th percentile CDA firm (see Table 2). Ownership concentration has not risen as fast as total institutional ownership because institutional investors have increasingly diversified

---

11. In contrast, Gompers and Metrick use a sample consisting of all companies reported by CRSP and assume that any CRSP company not included in the CDA data has zero institutional ownership. *Ibid.* We found many instances of large firms with institutional ownership that were inexplicably omitted from the CDA data, especially in the earlier years.

12. *H* is the root sum of squared ownership shares of all institutional owners of a stock.

TABLE 2		1980	1985	1990	1995	1996	1997
INSTITUTIONAL OWNERSHIP CONCENTRATION, CDA FIRMS*	**TOTAL OWNERSHIP**						
	Mean	18%	24%	27%	31%	33%	35%
	Median	12%	18%	20%	25%	26%	29%
	25%-ile	3%	6%	5%	8%	9%	9%
	75%-ile	29%	38%	43%	51%	53%	57%
	CONCENTRATION 1						
	Mean	6%	6%	6%	7%	7%	7%
	Median	4%	5%	5%	6%	6%	6%
	25%-ile	2%	2%	2%	3%	3%	3%
	75%-ile	7%	8%	8%	9%	9%	9%
	CONCENTRATION 5						
	Mean	11%	14%	15%	17%	18%	18%
	Median	9%	12%	13%	15%	16%	17%
	25%-ile	3%	5%	5%	7%	7%	8%
	75%-ile	16%	20%	22%	25%	26%	26%
	CONCENTRATION 10						
	Mean	14%	18%	19%	22%	23%	24%
	Median	11%	16%	16%	20%	21%	22%
	25%-ile	3%	5%	5%	8%	9%	9%
	75%-ile	21%	26%	29%	34%	35%	36%
	HERFINDAHL INDEX						
	Mean	7%	8%	9%	10%	10%	11%
	Median	6%	7%	7%	9%	9%	10%
	25%-ile	2%	3%	3%	4%	4%	5%
	75%-ile	10%	11%	12%	14%	14%	15%
	TOTAL OWNERSHIP OF BLOCK OWNERS[a]						
	Mean	5%	7%	8%	9%	10%	11%
	Median	0%	0%	0%	6%	6%	6%
	25%-ile	0%	0%	0%	0%	0%	0%
	75%-ile	7%	11%	13%	15%	16%	17%

*Concentration X is defined as the total shares held by the top X institutions divided by a company's outstanding shares. The Herfindahl Index is the root sum of squared institutional holdings of a firm's stock.
a. Block ownership is defined for a firm as the sum of ownership positions that individually comprise at least 5% of shares outstanding.

their holdings to more (and smaller) firms as the size of their portfolios has increased. In particular, the percentage of institutional investors' equity portfolios accounted for by either their largest stock position or their largest ten stock positions has declined significantly since 1980: the percent accounted for by the largest ten positions, for example, has fallen from 43 to 34% (see Table 3).

THE DETERMINANTS OF INSTITUTIONAL OWNERSHIP

Institutional investors also prefer to invest in companies that can be characterized as "prudent" investments: large companies that pay dividends, have highly liquid stocks that have performed well in the recent past, and can be viewed as "value"

If acquiring control were an important objective, we would expect to see institutions taking large ownership positions in smaller companies where they could obtain a much larger voice in the corporate governance process. Further, since such investments would presumably be more long term, stock liquidity should be much less of a consideration.

TABLE 3		1980	1985	1990	1995	1996	1997
PERCENTAGE OF INSTITUTIONAL INVESTORS' EQUITY PORTFOLIOS ACCOUNTED FOR BY LARGEST EQUITY POSITIONS, CDA FIRMS	**LARGEST POSITION**						
	Mean	14%	12%	10%	9%	9%	9%
	Median	8%	8%	6%	5%	5%	5%
	75%-ile	14%	13%	10%	9%	9%	9%
	90%-ile	28%	23%	19%	16%	17%	17%
	LARGEST TEN POSITIONS						
	Mean	47%	45%	43%	38%	38%	38%
	Median	43%	42%	39%	34%	34%	34%
	75%-ile	55%	54%	52%	47%	47%	48%
	90%-ile	75%	71%	70%	66%	66%	66%

TABLE 4	Pooled OLS		Industry (SIC4) Effects		Firm-Fixed Effects	
DETERMINANTS OF INSTITUTIONAL OWNERSHIP	Coefficient	t-stat	Coefficient	t-stat	Coefficient	t-stat
Log Size	0.092	49.12	0.091	59.03	0.027	13.35
Log Size Squared	−0.005	−32.43	−0.005	−39.25	0.002	11.44
Log Momentum	−0.606	−4.53	−0.053	−0.85	0.304	8.07
Log Price	0.038	28.17	0.064	55.88	0.023	14.63
Log Volatility	−0.456	−9.01	−0.358	−11.60	−0.027	−1.43
Log Dividend Yield	−2.943	−22.89	−1.710	−11.95	0.482	4.49
Log Book-to-Market	0.007	6.99	0.079	59.74	0.037	20.18
Log Turnover	0.044	73.77	0.043	83.56	0.004	9.29
S&P 500 Dummy	0.069	26.19	0.056	20.97	−0.002	−0.47
Constant	−0.437	−65.59	−0.571	−95.35	−0.030	−4.01
Obs.		66197		66197		66197
R-Squared		0.47		0.41		0.33
			pval - ind.eff.	0.00	pval - firm.eff.	0.00

Note: Time dummies are included in all specifications, but are not reported. The sample period is 1995:1 to 1997:4. The sample includes all CDA firms for which both COMPUSTAT and CRSP data are available.
Variable Definitions are as follows. **Ownership Measures**: *IO*: Total shares owned by institutional investors divided by a firm's total outstanding shares. *C1,C5,C10* :Total shares owned by the 1, 5, or 10 largest institutional investors for a firm divided by the firm's total shares outstanding. *Block IO*: Total shares owned by institutions that hold at least five percent of a firm's total outstanding shares divided by the firm's total outstanding shares. *Herfindahl Index*: The root sum of squared institutional holdings of a firm's stock. **Firm Characteristics**: *Size*: Total shares outstanding for a firm multiplied by price per share at end of quarter. *Momentum*: Total per share return calculated over the last twelve months excluding the most recent three months. *Price*: Price per share of a firm's stock calculated at end of quarter. *Volatility*: Standard deviation of daily returns calculated over the current quarter. *Dividend Yield*: Dividends per share divided by price per share for the current quarter. *Book-to-Market*: Book value of a firms total assets divided by its market capitalization (size). *Turnover*: Average daily volume of shares traded divided by total shares outstanding for a firm. *S&P 500 Dummy*: Bivariate dummy variable set to 1 if the firm was included in the S&P500 Index for at least two months of the current quarter and 0 otherwise.

stocks.[13] In other words, institutions take large ownership positions in companies that fund managers can easily defend as "prudent" investments and that can be sold quickly if they perform poorly.

Table 4 reports our estimates of the determinants of institutional ownership. This table shows the results for three estimated equations: a pooled OLS equation for all CDA firms over the 12 quarters from 1995:1 through 1997:4, including time dummies for each quarter; the same equation with dummy variables added for all four-digit-SIC industries; and a firm-fixed-effects specification that removes firm-

13. See Diane Del Guercio, "The Distorting Effect of the Prudent-Man Laws on Institutional Equity Investments." *Journal of Financial Economics* 40 (1996), pp. 31-62; S.G. Badrinath, G.D. Gay, and J.R. Kale, "Patterns of Institutional Investment and the Managerial 'Safety-net' Hypothesis," *Journal of Risk and Insurance* 56 (1989), pp. 605-629; and Gompers and Metrick, cited above.

TABLE 5		C1			C5		
DETERMINANTS OF OWNERSHIP CONCENTRATION (C1,C5), FIRM-FIXED-EFFECTS ESTIMATION		Coefficient	t-stat		Coefficient	t-stat	
	Log Size	0.008	8.08		0.025	16.72	
	Log Size Squared	−0.001	−9.23		−0.002	−15.43	
	Log Momentum	0.036	1.90		0.094	3.37	
	Log Price	0.004	5.48		0.013	11.05	
	Log Volatility	0.013	1.37		−0.009	−0.61	
	Log Dividend Yield	0.061	1.15		0.094	1.18	
	Log Book-to-Market	0.005	5.92		0.018	13.49	
	Log Turnover	−0.002	−10.11		−0.003	−9.12	
	S&P 500 Dummy	−0.001	−0.48		−0.006	−1.80	
	Constant	0.047	12.62		0.063	11.29	
	Obs.		66197			66197	
	R-Squared		0.01			0.07	
	pval - ind.eff.					0.00	

Note: Time dummies are included but are not reported. The sample period is 1995:1 to 1997:4. The sample includes all CDA firms for which both COMPUSTAT and CRSP data are available.

specific means of the variables.[14] Although the third model is the most informative, we report results for all three equations.

The results for the pooled OLS equation indicate that total institutional ownership is higher in larger companies and in companies with higher stock prices (expressed as dollars per share), greater stock turnover (or more liquid stocks), higher book-to-market ratios (or are "value" companies), and for those included in the S&P 500 Index. Institutional ownership is lower in companies that have more volatile stock returns and, surprisingly, in firms that pay relatively high dividends and whose stock prices have increased significantly in the last year (momentum stocks). Estimates from our second model, which includes industry dummy variables, yield similar conclusions, except that the momentum variable becomes insignificant.

When we estimate the firm-fixed-effects model, however, important differences emerge. First, the sign on the dividend yield is reversed, suggesting that institutions do in fact prefer companies that pay higher dividends. This result is more consistent both with conventional wisdom and most academic work. Second, the coefficient estimate for the momentum variable is now posi-

tive and significant, suggesting that institutional investors are indeed momentum investors, which again is more consistent with academic studies.[15] Third, neither stock volatility nor membership in the S&P 500 index is now significant. Last, the sign of the variable "size squared" is reversed, indicating that institutional ownership rises at an increasing rate as firms become larger.

Thus the view that fund managers take stock positions out of a desire to gain an advantage either by obtaining "inside" information about a firm's prospects or by improving corporate efficiency by better monitoring of corporate managers is not consistent with the types of firms in which they hold stock. If acquiring control were an important objective, we would expect to see institutions taking large ownership positions in smaller companies where they could obtain a much larger voice in the corporate governance process. Further, since such investments would presumably be more long term, stock liquidity (such as turnover) should be much less of a consideration, as would whether a company pays a dividend. Indeed, this is exactly what we find when we examine the determinants of large ownership positions represented by C5: neither the turnover nor the dividends variable has a significantly positive coefficient (see Table 5).

14. The sample includes all CDA firms for which both COMPUSTAT and CRSP data are available.

15. See, for example, Mark Grinblatt and Sheridan Titman, "Momentum Investment Strategies, Portfolio Performance, and Herding: A Study of Mutual Fund Behavior," *American Economic Review* 85 (December 1995), pp. 1088-1103.

> Both corporate culture and law combine to discourage private pension funds from owning sizeable blocks of stock, or from adopting an active corporate governance policy. On the cultural side, corporate managers effectively control their own pension funds, and few of them may want to meddle in the affairs of other companies.

To summarize, although both total institutional ownership and ownership concentration have increased significantly during the last fifteen years, this growth has not translated into institutions taking controlling positions in major U.S. companies. It seems premature, therefore, to conclude that the growth of institutional ownership heralds an end to managerial capitalism and the beginning of a new age of more active stockholders. In the next section we discuss reasons why institutional investors have not attempted to hold controlling positions in companies and why they are unlikely to do so in the future as well.

DETERRENTS TO ACTIVE INSTITUTIONAL OWNERSHIP

Most of the increase in institutional ownership that has occurred since 1980 is due to the rapid growth of two types of fund managers: mutual funds and independent advisors, which together account for all of the 17 percentage point increase in total institutional ownership since 1980. Ownership concentration (C5) is also much higher for these two types of fund managers than all other institutional investors. If the growth of institutional investors offers the promise of better corporate governance in the future it will have to come largely from the actions of mutual fund managers and independent advisors (private, defined-benefit pension plans now make-up most of this category). Thus we focus on legal and institutional constraints that prevent mutual funds and private pension fund managers from playing a more active role in the governance of corporations.

Mutual Funds

A number of regulations combine to restrict or at least discourage mutual funds from taking significant ownership positions. First, the "five and ten" rule contained in the Investment Company Act of 1940 is a clear attempt to limit mutual fund ownership. These provisions require that at least 50% of the value of a fund's total assets must satisfy the following two criteria: the value of an equity position can not exceed five percent of the value of the fund's total assets, and the fund cannot hold more than ten percent of the outstanding securities of any company.[16] The ten-percent rule is obviously directed at limiting the ability of mutual funds to take controlling positions in companies, and to ensure that mutual funds do not play a significant role in corporate boardrooms. The effect of the five-percent rule on ownership concentration is subtler. This rule is ostensibly a "diversification" rule, and is usually viewed as an attempt to ensure that mutual funds remain sufficiently diversified to meet unanticipated redemptions without appreciable changes in the net asset value of the fund. However, as a diversification requirement, this rule is not terribly effective, and its intent can be easily circumvented. For example, it does not require a mutual fund to diversify across industries—all of a fund's portfolio can legally be invested in companies in the same businesses or sectors of the economy, with highly correlated returns. Indirectly, the five-percent rule also is an important ownership constraint. It prevents all but the very largest mutual funds from taking sizeable ownership positions in a company's stock, since such positions could violate the rule. The data examined in the prior section support this conclusion.

Section 16(b) of the Securities and Exchange Act of 1934 is another obstacle to mutual funds taking large equity positions. This law requires that a shareholder who owns ten percent or more of a company's stock, or *any* director of a company, must return *any* "short-swing" profits to the company (profits on the sale of stock held for less than six months). Because mutual funds typically trade frequently, if only to meet redemptions, this law effectively makes holding large blocks of stock impractical for mutual funds. Further, the law discourages mutual funds from placing a director on a portfolio company's board of directors, or from even being identified too closely with any director of the company for fear of becoming liable.[17]

---

16. Investment Company Act of 1940, sec. 4(b)(3); I.R.C. sec. 852(b)(4). If a mutual fund violates these provisions it risks losing its pass-through tax status for federal income tax purposes on its entire portfolio, since the tax law allows only "diversified" funds to pass income through to shareholders. The result would be triple taxation of the fund's earnings, which would destroy the economic viability of the fund. It is not clear whether the "five and ten" rule applies to a mutual fund "family" (such as Fidelity Management) or to each of the fund's portfolios separately. Mutual funds have generally not challenged the SEC on this issue.

17. Bernard Black, "Next Steps in Proxy Reform," *Journal of Corporation Law* 18 (1992), also cites a number of other laws that discourage active institutional involvement, such as Schedule 13D of the Securities and Exchange Act of 1934, the pre-merger notification rules of the Hart-Scott-Rodino Act, state corporate law, corporate antitakover provisions, and the "change of control" provisions commonly contained in corporate contracts, such as employment contracts.

Private Pension Funds

Both corporate culture and law combine to discourage private pension funds from owning sizeable blocks of stock, or from adopting an active corporate governance policy. On the cultural side, corporate managers effectively control their own pension funds, and few of them may want to meddle in the affairs of other companies for fear of provoking a similar reaction on the part of the pension funds controlled by those companies.[18] On the legal side, ERISA (the Employee Retirement Income Security Act) poses significant legal risks to pension fund managers who acquire large blocks of stock or are active in corporate governance. Roe argues that the primary effect of ERISA is to encourage pension fund managers to imitate prevailing practice in order avoid legal liability for imprudent behavior. In particular, ERISA requires a standard of diligence that uses as a benchmark the "conduct of an enterprise of a like character and with like aims."[19] Thus, because the prevailing practice in pension fund management is to hold a diversified portfolio consisting mostly of small ownership positions, a manager who deviates from this practice runs a serious risk of liability in the event that the fund loses a substantial amount of money in any position. Further, to the extent that a pension fund would benefit from taking more concentrated positions in firms, such benefit accrues largely to the fund's beneficiaries and not to the fund managers. There is, therefore, little incentive for fund managers to take concentrated positions in firms; they assume all the risks and the beneficiaries get most of the benefits.

In addition, standard trustee law, which is not part of ERISA, discourages managers from taking block positions because trust law "antinetting" rules typically prevent trustees (or fund managers) from defending against a loss on a block position by pointing to other large gains in the portfolio, or to the general overall sound performance of the portfolio. Under the law, each block position must be evaluated separately as a distinct investment in order the show that the manager did not act irresponsibly. Thus, by employing a portfolio strategy of great diversification and avoiding sizeable block holdings,

fund managers can avoid liability for "big" mistakes. Finally, the incentive of pension funds to acquire large blocks of stock in order to obtain a seat on a corporate board is largely negated by ERISA's "prudent expert" standard, which may expose pension fiduciaries (or their agents) to even greater liability than the typical corporate director.[20]

Thus our empirical findings that, since 1980, institutional ownership concentration has increased much less than has total institutional ownership is not surprising given the ownership constraints faced by mutual fund and private defined-benefit pension plans. These institutions account for most of the growth in institutional ownership since 1980, and the U.S. legal structure strongly discourages them from holding sizeable positions in companies. Further, because future growth in institutional ownership is most likely to occur through mutual funds and pension funds, there is unlikely to be a substantial change in the present pattern of corporate governance in the U.S. without significant changes in the legal and institutional structure governing mutual funds and pension funds.

IMPLICATIONS FOR PUBLIC POLICY

If institutional investors are to play a greater role in corporate governance, we will have to increase the incentives of mutual fund and pension fund managers to take larger ownership positions and to be more active in monitoring the performance of corporate managers, and will have to remove or at least moderate the current legal and institutional obstacles that discourage them from pursuing this strategy. Fund managers must also believe that a more pro-active investment strategy will pay off; that is, they must believe that portfolio performance will be enhanced by working with companies over a longer horizon to improve company performance, rather than their following the "Wall Street rule" of simply ridding their portfolios of poorly performing stocks.

There is reason to believe that, if fund managers were able to hold larger ownership positions in companies, a pro-active investment strategy would enhance their performance. In particular, the exist-

---

18. The Employee Retirement Income Security Act (ERISA) permits the firm's own "officer, employee, agent, or other representative" to run the fund (ERISA, sec. 408(c), 29). Over half of private pensions are managed in-house (see Roe, 1994, cited above, p. 133).

19. See Employee Retirement Income Security Act (ERISA) of 1974, sec. 404(a), 29 U.S.C. sec 1104(a) (1988).

20. Non-fiduciary corporate directors can use the "business judgment" rule to defend themselves against a lawsuit, whereas fiduciaries are likely to be held to the tighter ERISA prudent expert rule (see Roe, 1994, cited above, pp. 142-3).

The recent growth of money flowing into venture capital firms and hedge funds taking long stock positions provides some evidence of the potential profitability of a more pro-active investment strategy. These funds typically hold relatively large equity positions in companies (albeit usually in smaller companies) and take a more hands-on approach to managing their investments than do mutual funds.

ence of asymmetric information (wherein corporate managers know more about the company than do stockholders) together with the separation of ownership from control stemming from the dispersed ownership structure common to U.S. corporations typically causes a principal-agent problem that is costly for stockholders to overcome. Under this structure it is reasonable to believe that there is some slack in corporate performance that could be eliminated if stockholders had a greater incentive to become informed about company performance and to provide greater monitoring of corporate managers. One low-cost way to capture these inefficiencies is to permit mutual fund and pension fund managers to hold larger ownership positions, which would both enhance their incentive to be active corporate monitors and reduce the free-rider problem inherent in a dispersed ownership structure. Further, by capturing the gains from reducing corporate inefficiencies, fund managers will be able to enhance their portfolio performance, which will benefit themselves and their clients, as well as improving the performance of the overall economy.

The recent growth of money flowing into venture capital firms and hedge funds devoted to holding long stock positions provides some evidence of the potential profitability of a more pro-active investment strategy. These funds typically hold relatively large equity positions in companies (albeit usually in smaller companies) and take a more hands-on approach to managing their investments than do mutual funds. Another indication of the potential profitability of this strategy is the recent proliferation of "select" or "focus" mutual funds. These funds typically hold 25 or fewer stocks, and may invest more than ten percent of the fund's assets in a single stock.[21] They may also impose a stiff (two percent) redemption fee to encourage investors to take a longer-term view of performance.

One policy reform, therefore, could be to reduce the legal and institutional obstacles to holding larger equity positions in companies. Mutual fund managers currently face several such obstacles, such as the "five and ten rule." Although this rule is often confused with limiting a fund's riskiness by requiring portfolio diversification, its primary effect, as we have already pointed out, is to restrict large

ownership. Thus, a first step should be to eliminate "the five and ten rule." The legal standards of diligence and prudence applicable to mutual funds should instead be based solely on a fund's disclosure documents. Mutual funds are already required to describe their investment philosophies and strategies in their prospectuses and disclosure documents, and these documents would also include an explicit statement about a fund's strategy with respect to its portfolio concentration. The appropriate legal standard should be whether mutual funds adhere to the investment policies and strategies set forth in their disclosure documents.

Managers of open-end mutual funds also may fear holding large equity positions because of liquidity concerns. Open-end mutual funds are required to redeem their shares on a daily basis, and cannot postpone the payment of redemption proceeds for more than seven days after the tender of the shares offered for redemption. Large portfolio positions may be difficult to unload in a hurry without affecting stock prices adversely. Further, open-end mutual funds are required to maintain at least 85% of their portfolios in assets that can be sold in seven days at approximately the prices used in determining net asset value of the fund's shares. Large equity positions may be more difficult to value because of the difficulty of estimating the liquidity effect. These legal requirements, therefore, discourage fund managers from holding large ownership positions in companies.

We believe that this "illiquidity" obstacle to holding large equity positions can be substantially mitigated by permitting open-end mutual funds to redeem their shares on an interval basis of their choosing. At present all open-end mutual funds are required under section 22(e) of the Investment Company Act of 1940 (the "Act") to redeem their shares on a daily basis. An alternative approach would be to allow mutual funds to adopt any redemption policy they wish so long as this policy is fully disclosed to investors. As long as the funds are required to disclose their redemption policies to investors, and are held legally accountable for the valuations that they put on the assets they redeem, investors will be adequately protected. Greater freedom to limit redemption privileges would enable

---

21. See "Sharp Focus: How 'Select' Mutual Funds Do It," *The Wall Street Journal*, March 5, 1999, p. C1, col. 3; and "Montgomery Gets 'Focused' With Funds," *The Wall Street Journal*, April 11, 2000, p. C27, col. 1.

mutual funds to hold less liquid (*i.e.*, larger) owner-ship positions in companies, and to pursue less liquid portfolio strategies generally. In particular, fund managers could hold larger blocks of stock without fear of having to liquidate those positions to meet unanticipated redemptions, and they could plan to hold these blocks for longer time periods. Thus freed from the threat of having to redeem their shares on a moment's notice, some mutual funds could be expected to take a longer-term perspective on corporate performance in the hopes of achieving superior portfolio performance through a more pro-active strategy.

The legal mechanism (or loophole) for permitting greater freedom in funds' redemption policies already exists, and the SEC could expand this. In October 1998, under section 6(c) of the Act, the SEC granted Emerging Markets Growth Fund, Inc. ("EMGF") an exemption from section 22(e) and rule 22c-1 of the Act.[22] Section 22(e) requires an open-end fund to permit its shareholders to redeem shares on a daily basis and to make payments on redemption requests within seven days following tender to the fund. Rule 22c-1 effectively requires an open-end fund to calculate its Net Asset Values (NAV) each day and to price its shares for sale or redemption on a daily basis. EMGF was a closed-end mutual fund that held primarily equity securities of issuers located in developing countries, which were generally not very liquid. It proposed to convert to a registered open-end mutual fund and to redeem its shares on a monthly rather than daily basis.

EMGF's application had several features that are important for interpreting the scope of the SEC's approval of its application. First, EMGF proposed to limit all new investors to "qualified purchasers" within the meaning of section 2(a)(51) of the Act and the rules and SEC interpretive positions under the Act. Section 2(a)(51) generally defines qualified purchasers as persons who own $5 million of investments and institutions that own or manage on a discretionary basis $25 million of investments. Second, EMGF proposed that at least 85% of its assets must either mature by the next Redemption

Payment Date or be capable of being sold between the Redemption Request Deadline and the Redemption Payment Date at approximately the price used in computing its NAV. Third, EMGF proposed that its redemption policy be stated on the cover of its prospectus and in any marketing materials and that it would not hold itself as a "mutual fund," but would instead hold itself out to be an open-end "interval" fund.

Thus the SEC's approval of EMGF's application is conditioned on a mutual fund adhering to a "qualified purchaser" standard and on its not being able to market itself as an open-end mutual fund. This obviously severely restricts the scope of the SEC permitted exemption from the daily redemption requirement under section 22(e) to the same small segment of the investor population that is able to avail themselves of hedge funds. Nonetheless, the EMGF order clearly carves out a legal precedent for the SEC under section 6(c) of the Act to exempt open-end mutual funds from having to redeem daily. The SEC could consider expanding the scope of this exemption to a broader segment of the investor population, and permit so-called interval funds to hold themselves out as open-end mutual funds, so long as a fund's redemption policies are clearly stated in a fund's prospectus and marketing materials.

Even if the legal impediments to mutual funds taking large ownership positions are reduced, there is still the problem of fund manager incentives. Under the current "flat fee" structure used by most mutual funds (and by many other institutional fund management companies), fund managers do not have a great incentive to take unusual risks, such as those associated with holding a less diversified portfolio or making big bets on a particular company by holding a large ownership position in that company.[23] The compensation of most mutual fund managers depends largely on the amount of assets under management, and there is no guarantee that investment flows into the fund will increase substantially if a fund manager outperforms her peers. Although there is some evidence that investment

---

22. Securities and Exchange Commission, Release No. 23481, October 7, 1998. Section 6(c) permits the SEC to exempt any person or transaction from any provision of the Act, if such exemption is necessary or appropriate in the public interest and consistent with the protection of investors and the purposes fairly intended by the policies of the Act.

23. The Investment Advisors Act of 1940 does not permit the use of asymmetrical "incentive fee" contracts—where money managers (or advisors)

receive a base fee plus a bonus for surpassing some benchmark return, but do not receive less if performance falls short of that benchmark. However, an amendment to the 1940 Act does permit performance-based fees if management compensation is computed symmetrically around some chosen benchmark return, where the fees decrease when managers underperform in the same way that they increase when managers outperform. Few mutual funds, however, have adopted this type of "fulcrum" fee structure.

Even if the legal impediments to mutual funds taking large ownership positions are reduced, there is still the problem of fund manager incentives. Under the current "flat fee" structure used by most mutual funds, fund managers do not have a great incentive to take unusual risks, such as those associated with making big bets on a particular company by holding a large ownership position.

flows do respond positively to superior mutual fund performance, it seems unlikely that fund managers would nevertheless be willing to take large risks on the chance of this happening, since underperforming could mean the loss of their jobs.[24]

More specifically, a fund manager cannot expect to outperform by a wide margin without making some big bets, and big bets cannot be expected to pay off every year. At best they pay off on the average and, when they do lose, they typically lose a lot. Fund managers are unlikely to want to take such risks in today's financial environment, in which investors and financial consultants have become increasingly intolerant of returns below a specified industry benchmark. Beating the benchmark by only a small amount is acceptable, while falling behind by a large amount is a death sentence—investment flows may turn negative and fund managers may lose their jobs. Thus, the compensation structure in the mutual fund industry encourages fund managers to stay with the "herd" and to eschew taking big portfolio risks or deviating very much from what other fund managers are doing.

Not surprisingly, mutual fund managers wishing to pursue more risky strategies are increasingly moving to hedge funds, where the incentive compensation structure provides a greater payoff for superior managers.[25] Hedge funds, which have grown significantly over the past ten years, are to a large extent a regulatory creation developed to take advantage of the gaps in the fund management marketplace created by legal restraints on mutual funds. Unlike mutual funds, hedge funds can adopt whatever redemption policies they wish (most permit only periodic redemptions, such as quarterly or even once each year or less frequently), and are not encumbered by diversification, liquidity, ownership, and disclosure requirements. Hedge funds also typically employ asymmetrical incentive fee structures, which reward managers handsomely for superior performance (usually 20% of profits above a specified hurdle rate).

Mutual funds could be given greater freedom to experiment with the use of incentive fees to encourage fund managers to take large ownership positions and to be willing to hold these positions for a longer period of time. In particular, incentive fees could be structured in a way that rewards fund managers for successfully identifying undervalued companies and working with corporate managers to improve corporate performance over a longer time period than is now fashionable in the fund management industry. The evidence from hedge funds is consistent with this view. In a recent study, one of the authors of this paper examined the relationship between hedge fund performance and the incentive fee structure used by a hedge fund, using a sample of approximately 1,000 hedge funds over a period of ten years. Hedge fund performance (risk-adjusted) was found to be markedly better when fund managers were paid a higher incentive fee.[26]

Finally, the accepted rationale for restricting what open-end mutual funds can do is "investor protection." Hedge fund investors are limited to "qualified purchasers": individual investors with at least $5 million of investments and institutions that own or manage on a discretionary basis at least $25 million of investments. These investors are presumably sophisticated and well informed. In contrast, many mutual funds investors have relatively little wealth and are arguably less sophisticated, and therefore may need to be protected by regulations restricting the amount of risk that mutual funds can take. While for some investors there may be truth to this argument, the effect of current mutual fund regulations is to exclude virtually all mutual fund investors from participating in pro-active investment strategies that may yield superior returns. If government protection of small and unsophisticated mutual fund investors were deemed necessary, there is still substantial scope to relax the current restrictions on mutual funds. For example, investors with a net worth of $1 million arguably do not need to be protected from the risks associated with a fund taking, say, large ownership positions in ten companies (such individuals would generally be permitted to invest in illiquid private equity investments, for example). Indeed, it may be sufficient simply to

---

24. See, for example, Erik R. Sirri and Peter Tufano, "Costly Search and Mutual Fund Flows," Working Paper, Harvard Business School, 1999; Ajay Khorana, "Top Management Turnover: An Empirical Investigation of Mutual Fund Managers." *Journal of Financial Economics* 40 (1996), pp. 403-427; and Judith Chevalier and Glenn Ellison, "Career Concerns of Mutual Fund Managers," Working Paper No. 6394, National Bureau of Economic Research, February 1998.

25. "Hedge Funds' Heat Generates Allure for Mutual-Fund Firms," *The Wall Street Journal*, August 7, 2000, p. R1, col 1.

26. See Franklin R. Edwards, and Mustafa O. Caglayan. "An Analysis of Hedge Fund Performance: Excess Returns, Common Risk Factors, and Manager Skill," Working Paper, Columbia Business School, August 2000. See also Sanjiv Ranjan Das and Rangarajan K. Sundaram, "Fee Speech: Signaling and the Regulation of Mutual Fund Fees," Working Paper No. CLB-98-020, Center of Law and Business, New York University, April 1999.

require all mutual funds to clearly disclose to investors their holdings, strategies, past performance, redemption policy, fees, and governance and management structure. Thus there is ample scope for the SEC to free open-end mutual funds from the legal restrictions that currently discourage them from taking larger ownership positions in companies and from pursuing more pro-active investment strategies.

CONCLUSION

Despite the very substantial growth of institutional ownership of U.S. corporations in the past 20 years, there is little evidence that institutional investors have acquired the kind of concentrated ownership positions required to be able to play a dominant role in the corporate governance process. Institutional ownership remains widely dispersed among firms and institutions. The key reason for this is that there exist significant legal obstacles that discourage institutional investors both from taking large block positions and from exercising large ownership positions to control corporate managers. In particular, much of the growth of institutional ownership since 1980 has been accounted for by the growth of mutual funds and private pension funds, but there continue to be strong deterrents to these institutions using large ownership positions to influence corporate managers.

To encourage mutual funds to take a more activist corporate governance role, we recommend that current legal restrictions on mutual funds be relaxed so that mutual funds have a greater incentive to hold large ownership positions in companies and to use those positions to more effectively monitor corporate managers. In particular, the "five and ten" portfolio rules applicable to mutual funds could be repealed and replaced with a standard of prudence and diligence more in keeping with portfolio theory; mutual funds could be given greater freedom to adopt redemption policies that would be more conducive to them holding larger ownership positions; and institutional investors could be permitted to employ a variety of incentive fee structures to encourage fund managers to pursue more pro-active investment strategies. The prospect of actively involving institutional fund managers in the corporate governance process in a constructive way is probably our best hope for improving corporate governance in the U.S.

CORPORATE OWNERSHIP AND CONTROL IN THE U.K., GERMANY, AND FRANCE

by Julian Franks,
London Business School, and
Colin Mayer,
Oxford University*

Differences among national financial systems have been a subject of continuing debate for well over a century. The primary distinction drawn by economists has been that between "bank-based" and "market-based" systems.[1] In the stylized description of bank-based systems, companies raise most of their external finance from banks that have close, long-term relationships with their corporate customers. By contrast, the market-based systems of the U.K. and the U.S. are characterized by arm's-length relationships between corporations and investors, who are said to be concerned primarily about short-term returns.

While these distinctions cannot be dismissed, they have proved to be difficult to formulate with much precision. Empirical evidence does not provide grounds for the sharp distinction that would have been expected if there were fundamental differences in the structure and operation of national economies. Nevertheless, there is one area in which there are clear differences in the structure and conduct of economies that are deep-rooted and open to quite precise quantification. These differences concern the ownership and control of corporations.

In their 1932 classic, *The Modern Corporation and Private Property*, Adolph Berle and Gardiner Means warned that the growing dispersion of ownership of U.S. stocks was giving rise to a potentially value-reducing separation of ownership and control.[2] In 1976, the general argument of Berle and Means was given a more rigorous formulation by Michael Jensen and William Meckling in their theory of "agency costs."[3] Agency costs, loosely speaking, are reductions in value resulting from the separation of ownership from control in public corporations. Pointing to a roughly tenfold decline in the percentage of managerial stock ownership of large U.S. public companies between the 1930s and the 1980s, Jensen argued that dispersed ownership was leading to major inefficiencies in U.S. companies, particularly in the form of widespread conglomeration. In this view, the rise of hostile takeovers and LBOs in the 1980s was a value-increasing response by U.S. capital markets—one that reduced agency costs by removing inefficient managers and, especially in the case of LBOs, concentrating corporate ownership.[4]

More recently, however, a study by Harold Demsetz and Kenneth Lehn has argued that concentrated ownership is likely to have had significant costs as well as benefits.[5] That is, besides providing stronger incentives to maximize value, concentrated ownership can impose costs in two ways: (1) by forcing managers and other inside shareholders to bear excessive company-specific risks—risks that could be borne at lower cost by well-diversified outside stockholders; and (2) by allowing inside owners to capture private benefits at the expense of minority or outside owners. In the view of Demsetz and Lehn, ownership patterns should reflect a trade-off between the incentive benefits of concentrated

*This paper is a revised version of a paper entitled "Ownership and Control" that was written for the International Workshop at the Kiel Institute on "Trends in Business Organization: Increasing Competitiveness by Participation and Cooperation," June 13 and 14, 1994. It is based on an inaugural lecture that was given by Colin Mayer at the University of Warwick on February 1, 1993. It is part of a project funded by the ESRC (no. W102251003) on "Capital Markets, Corporate Governance and the Market for Corporate Control." We are grateful to participants at the workshop for helpful comments and in particular to our discussant, Martin Hellwig. We are also grateful to Marc Goergen and Luis Correia da Silva for research assistance on the project.

1. For recent interesting examples of this, see F. Allen and D. Gale, "A Welfare Comparison of the German and US Financial Systems," CEPR-Fundacion BBV

Conference, April 1994; and J. Edwards and K. Fischer, *Banks, Finance and Investment in Germany* (Cambridge: Cambridge University Press, 1994).

2. A. Berle and G. Means, *The Modern Corporation and Private Property* (New York: MacMillan, 1932).

3. For the original formulation of agency theory, see M. Jensen and W. Meckling, "Theory of the Firm: Managerial Behavior, Agency Costs and Ownership Structure," *Journal of Financial Economics*, No. 3 (1976).

4. See M. Jensen, "The Agency Costs of Free Cash Flow: Corporate Finance and Takeovers," *American Economic Review* 76 (May, 1986); and M. Jensen, "The Eclipse of the Public Corporation," *Harvard Business Review* (1989).

5. H. Demsetz and K. Lehn, "The Structure of Corporate Ownership: Causes and Consequences," *Journal of Political Economy*, 93 (1985), 1155-77.

ownership and the expected costs arising from excessive concentration of risk and the potential for expropriating minority holders.

In this paper, after a brief summary of existing theories of corporate ownership and control, we describe patterns of ownership in France, Germany, and the U.K. We also review the evidence (much of it our own) on the operation of the market for corporate control in the U.K. and Germany. As we conclude, none of the existing theories offers a completely satisfying explanation of the differences between the *insider* ownership systems of Germany and France, on the one hand, and the *outsider* systems of the U.S. and the U.K. on the other. Nevertheless, given the durability of the two systems, both appear to have devised effective ways of disciplining poor managers and otherwise promoting efficiency.

THEORIES OF OWNERSHIP AND CONTROL

There are two strands of literature that are relevant to this discussion. The first concerns the determinants of corporate ownership, and the second focuses on the operation of the market for corporate control.

With regard to ownership there are three classes of models. The first is the industrial economics literature on vertical relationships—for example, those between manufacturers and their suppliers. This class of models seeks to explain the tendency of upstream and downstream firms to own each other (or to remain independent companies) in terms of the "externalities" that may exist between the parties.[6] For example, upstream firms will not always take full account of the interests of downstream firms in the prices that they charge and the way in which they treat their purchasers. In such a case, joint ownership may be required to "internalize this externality" in the absence of suitable contractual alternatives.

A second, related, class of literature on ownership argues that transaction costs may make transactions through markets more costly than internal activities within the firm.[7] It may be difficult or costly to write the contracts necessary to undertake transactions between firms through the marketplace. Discouraging "opportunistic" breaches of implicit contracts may be accomplished more effectively inside the firm than through the marketplace.

A third literature on ownership is concerned with the effect of incomplete contracts on the incentives that firms have to make long-term, highly specialized investments—the kind of investments that would have little value if transferred beyond the context of the particular firm.[8] Joint or vertical ownership is viewed as a means of encouraging such "firm-specific" investments by guaranteeing that important parties will honor their implicit commitments to projects involving joint effort (for example, those involving suppliers and manufacturers).

According to this theory, one would expect to see joint ownership where (1) it is difficult to use contracts to avoid expropriation of subsequent returns; (2) there is a high degree of "complementarity" between the assets of the two firms; and (3) one of the assets or one of the owners of the assets is particularly important to the other party and should therefore become the owner of both the assets. These theories suggest that we would expect patterns of ownership to reflect complementarities in production.

The second major strand of literature is concerned with corporate control. Separation of ownership and control in outsider systems like the U.S. and the U.K. has prompted the rise and refinement of a number of mechanisms designed to limit the agency problems with dispersed ownership.[9] Such mechanisms include monitoring and control by non-executive (or "outside") directors, pay-for-performance management incentive systems, and a market for corporate control.

---

6. See, for example, A. Dixit, "Vertical Integration in a Monopolistically Competitive Industry," *International Journal of Industrial Organization*, 1 (1983), 63-78; M. Salinger, "Vertical Merger and Market Foreclosure," *Quarterly Journal of Economics*, 103 (1988), 345-56; and W. Waterson, "Vertical Integration, Variable Proportions and Oligopoly," *Economic Journal*, 92 (1982), 129-44.

7. See, for example, R. Coase, "The Nature of the Firm," *Economica*, 4 (1937), 386-405; O. Williamson, *Markets and Hierarchies: Analysis and Anti-Trust Implications* (New York: Free Press, 1975); O. Williamson, *The Economic Institutions of Capitalism* (New York: Free Press, 1985); and M. Aoki, B. Gustafsson, and O. Williamson, *The Firm as a Nexus of Treaties* (London: European Sage, 1988).

8. See, for example, B. Klein, R. Crawford, and A. Alchian, "Vertical Integration, Appropriable Rents and the Competitive Contracting Process," *Journal of Law and Economics*, 21 (1978), 297-326; S. Grossman and O. Hart, "The Cost and Benefits of Ownership: A Theory of Vertical and Lateral Integration," *Journal of Political Economy*, 94 (1986), 691-719.; O. Hart and J. Moore, "Property Rights and the Nature of the Firm," *Journal of Political Economy*, 98 (1990), 1119-58.

9. See H. Manne, "Mergers and the Market for Corporate Control," *Journal of Political Economy* (1965), 110-20; and A. Alchian and H. Demsetz, "Production, Information Costs and Economic Organization," *American Economic Review*, 62 (1972), 777-95; and E. Fama and M. Jensen, "Separation of Ownership and Control," *Journal of Law and Economics*, No. 26 (1983).

Most financial economists' attention to date has focused on the operation of the corporate control market or, in popular parlance, the takeover market. In the standard conception of this market, corporate raiders identify companies that are not being managed so as to maximize shareholder value. Raiders launch bids for controlling ownership that, if successful, give them the right to bring about value-increasing changes in strategy and, in many cases, top management.

PATTERNS OF OWNERSHIP IN FRANCE, GERMANY, AND THE U.K.

The stereotypical description of the structure of corporate sectors runs as follows: There are a large number of small companies that are privately owned by individuals, families, and partners; and there are a much smaller number of large companies that are quoted (or "publicly traded") on the stock market and owned by a large number of individual shareholders. Complicating this pattern somewhat, a significant fraction of the shares of quoted companies are owned by institutional investors—in particular, pension funds, life insurance firms, and mutual funds.

Corporate Ownership in the U.K.

The above description fits the U.K. reasonably well. There are over 2,000 U.K. companies quoted on the stock market out of a total population of around 500,000 firms. Almost 80% of the largest 700 companies are quoted on the stock market, and the value of companies quoted on the stock market is around 81% of the GDP. Approximately two-thirds of the equity of quoted U.K. companies is held by institutions.

But this pattern of ownership is by no means universal; on the contrary, it appears to be the exception rather than the rule. Although the U.S. has more quoted companies than the U.K., in most other countries the number of quoted companies is far lower. In Germany, for example, there are fewer than 700 quoted companies and in France less than 500 (see Figure 1). In both countries, the value of quoted companies amounts to only 25% of GDP (Figure 2). In short, quoted companies in Germany

and France account for a much smaller fraction of total national corporate activity than those in the U.K. and the U.S.

In the U.K. and the U.S., moreover, ownership is widely dispersed among a large number of institutions or individuals. Most of the equity of quoted U.K. companies is held by institutions, but no one institution owns very much of any one company. In the U.S., the largest category of shareholders is individuals.

In most of continental Europe, however, ownership is much more concentrated. Consider the ownership pattern revealed in Figure 3, which shows the percentage of (approximately) the largest 170 quoted companies in France, Germany, and the U.K with a single large (at least 25%) shareholder. In only 16% of the U.K. companies did a single shareholder own more than 25% of the shares. By contrast, in nearly 85% of the German firms there was at least one shareholder owning more than 25%; and almost 80% of the French companies had at least one shareholder with more than 25% ownership. In short, concentration of ownership is much greater in corporations based outside the U.K. and the U.S.[10]

Corporate Ownership in Germany and France

In France and Germany, by far the single largest group of shareholders is the corporate sector itself. Figure 4 breaks down large share stakes in 171 large quoted German companies by different groups of investors—banks, investment institutions, companies, government, and so forth. It reveals that a majority of the large share stakes are held by companies. The next largest group is families, followed by trusts, institutional investors, and foreign companies.

Although there is a commonly held view that banks control corporate Germany, banks actually come far down the list of large stakeholders. Nevertheless, the control exerted by banks is significantly greater than their direct equity holdings would suggest. As holders of the bearer shares owned by their customers, they are able to exercise proxy votes on behalf of dispersed shareholders. (And, since all the companies studied here are quoted, at least a portion of the shares are widely held.)

---

10. For a comparison of ownership in Japan and the U.S. that makes a similar observation, see S. Prowse, "The Structure of Corporate Ownership in Japan," *Journal of Finance*, 47 (1992), 1121-40. In the case of Japan, the largest group of shareholders is financial institutions.

Almost 80% of the largest 700 U.K. companies are quoted on the stock market, and the value of companies quoted on the stock market is around 81% of the GDP. Approximately two-thirds of the equity of quoted U.K. companies is held by institutions.

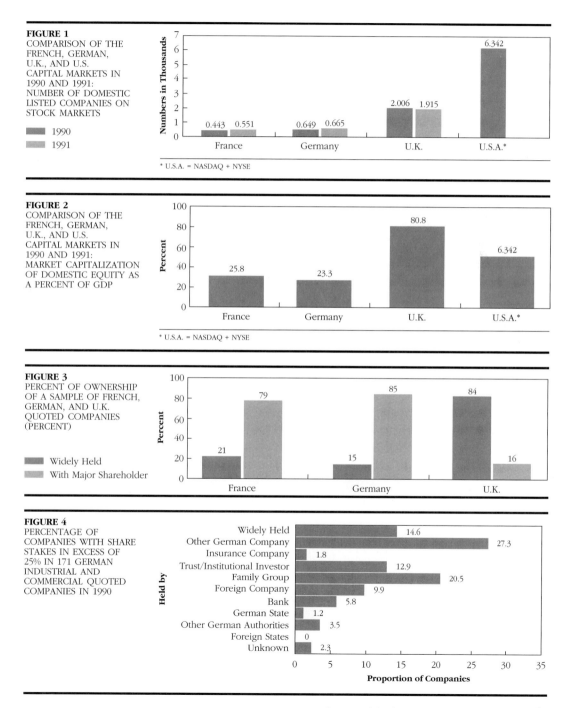

FIGURE 1
COMPARISON OF THE FRENCH, GERMAN, U.K., AND U.S. CAPITAL MARKETS IN 1990 AND 1991: NUMBER OF DOMESTIC LISTED COMPANIES ON STOCK MARKETS

◼ 1990
◼ 1991

Numbers in Thousands

France 0.443 0.551
Germany 0.649 0.665
U.K. 2.006 1.915
U.S.A.* 6.342

* U.S.A. = NASDAQ + NYSE

FIGURE 2
COMPARISON OF THE FRENCH, GERMAN, U.K., AND U.S. CAPITAL MARKETS IN 1990 AND 1991: MARKET CAPITALIZATION OF DOMESTIC EQUITY AS A PERCENT OF GDP

Percent

France 25.8
Germany 23.3
U.K. 80.8
U.S.A.* 6.342

* U.S.A. = NASDAQ + NYSE

FIGURE 3
PERCENT OF OWNERSHIP OF A SAMPLE OF FRENCH, GERMAN, AND U.K. QUOTED COMPANIES (PERCENT)

◼ Widely Held
◼ With Major Shareholder

Percent

France 21 79
Germany 15 85
U.K. 84 16

FIGURE 4
PERCENTAGE OF COMPANIES WITH SHARE STAKES IN EXCESS OF 25% IN 171 GERMAN INDUSTRIAL AND COMMERCIAL QUOTED COMPANIES IN 1990

Held by

Widely Held 14.6
Other German Company 27.3
Insurance Company 1.8
Trust/Institutional Investor 12.9
Family Group 20.5
Foreign Company 9.9
Bank 5.8
German State 1.2
Other German Authorities 3.5
Foreign States 0
Unknown 2.3

Proportion of Companies

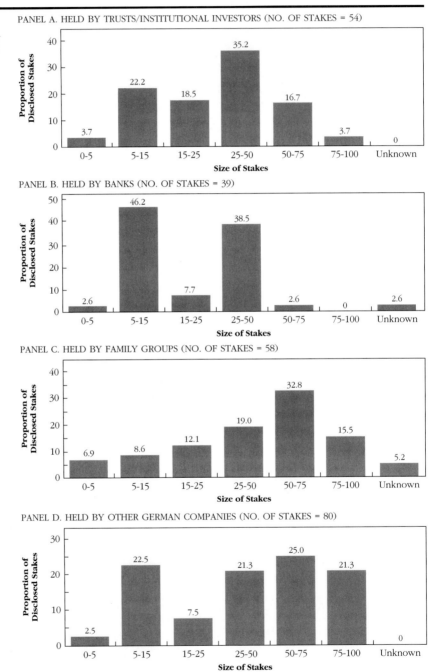

FIGURE 5
PROPORTION OF
DISCLOSED STAKES BY
SIZE OF STAKES IN 171
GERMAN INDUSTRIAL
AND COMMERCIAL
QUOTED COMPANIES
IN 1990

PANEL A. HELD BY TRUSTS/INSTITUTIONAL INVESTORS (NO. OF STAKES = 54)

PANEL B. HELD BY BANKS (NO. OF STAKES = 39)

PANEL C. HELD BY FAMILY GROUPS (NO. OF STAKES = 58)

PANEL D. HELD BY OTHER GERMAN COMPANIES (NO. OF STAKES = 80)

In nearly 85% of the German firms there was at least one shareholder owning more than 25%; and almost 80% of the French companies had at least one shareholder with more than 25% ownership.

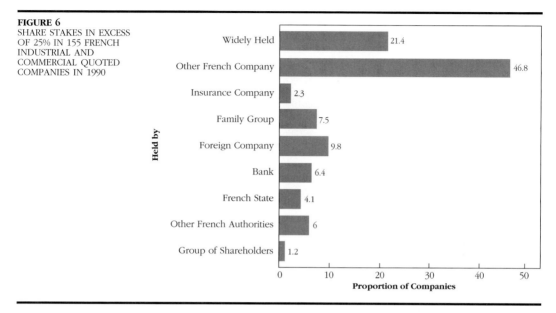

FIGURE 6
SHARE STAKES IN EXCESS OF 25% IN 155 FRENCH INDUSTRIAL AND COMMERCIAL QUOTED COMPANIES IN 1990

Figure 5 provides more detail on the ownership of the 171 large German companies analyzed in Figure 4. As shown in Figure 5A, trusts and institutional investors are sometimes large shareholders in German companies. However, their share stakes are rarely majority holdings. The same holds for banks (Figure 5B): there are some large share stakes but rarely majority holdings. This contrasts with the pattern of family ownership. In almost one-third of the cases, families appear to be majority holders of German companies (Figure 5C).

In examining these figures, one should keep in mind that they refer to the *largest* German companies. Thus, in contrast to our earlier description of the U.K. ownership structure, large-block family ownership is a highly representative feature of the largest enterprises in Germany. This raises the interesting question (to which we return later) of how and why German (and French) families play a much more significant role in corporate ownership than, say, their U.K. counterparts.

The other group that emerges as having majority shareholdings in Germany is the German corporate sector (Figure 5D). Not only do German companies have many and large stakeholdings in other German firms, but also these intercorporate shareholdings are often majority ones. What makes such corporate equity stakes in other firms especially

noteworthy is that these are all quoted companies, not just subsidiaries of other companies.

In sum, then, while German banks do have quite large share stakes, they are rarely majority shareholders. The pattern for insurance companies, trust, and institutional investors is very similar—some large but rarely majority shareholdings. The two dominant investor groups in German companies are families and other German firms.

A remarkably similar pattern emerges for France. First, as noted above, the proportion of large stakeholdings in total is about the same as in Germany. Figure 6 summarizes the ownership distribution for 155 large quoted French companies. As in the case of Germany, a majority of these stakes are held by other companies. Other large stakeholders in French firms are foreign companies, families, and banks.

Further detail on the ownership of these 155 French companies is provided in Figure 7. As we saw in the case of Germany, there are some large stakes held by insurance companies but these are rarely majority holdings (Figure 7A). Banks have some large minority shareholdings, often in excess of 25% (Figure 7B). But, as in Germany, it is French families (Figure 7C) and other French companies that have the largest proportion of majority shareholdings (Figures 7C and 7D).

FIGURE 7
STAKES HELD IN 155
FRENCH INDUSTRIAL
AND COMMERCIAL
QUOTED COMPANIES IN
1990

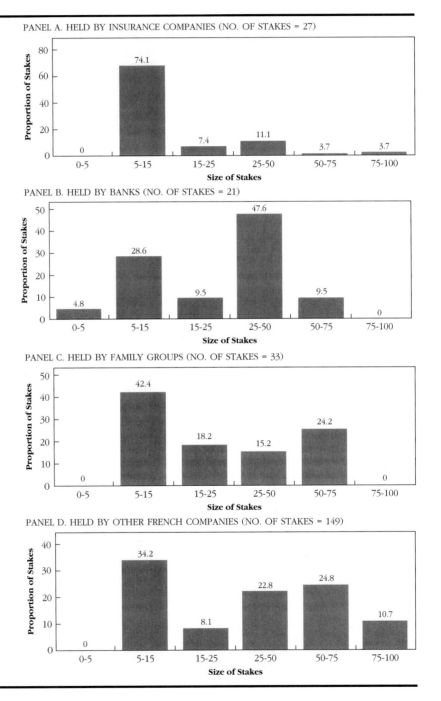

PANEL A. HELD BY INSURANCE COMPANIES (NO. OF STAKES = 27)

PANEL B. HELD BY BANKS (NO. OF STAKES = 21)

PANEL C. HELD BY FAMILY GROUPS (NO. OF STAKES = 33)

PANEL D. HELD BY OTHER FRENCH COMPANIES (NO. OF STAKES = 149)

Although there is a commonly held view that banks control corporate Germany,
banks actually come far down the list of large stakeholders. Nevertheless, the control
exerted by banks is significantly greater than their direct equity holdings
would suggest.

FIGURE 8
PROPORTION OF
DISCLOSED STAKES
HELD BY THE STATE IN
GERMANY[1] AND
FRANCE[2]

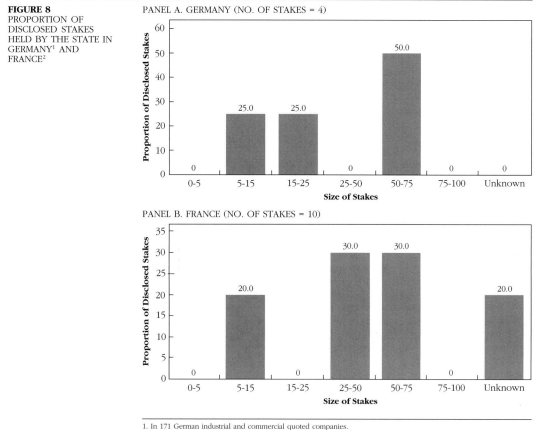

PANEL A. GERMANY (NO. OF STAKES = 4)

PANEL B. FRANCE (NO. OF STAKES = 10)

1. In 171 German industrial and commercial quoted companies.
2. In 155 French industrial and commercial quoted companies.

There is, however, one notable difference between France and Germany, and that is the comparative importance of state ownership of large companies. As shown in Figure 8, share stakes by the state are more prevalent and tend to be larger in France than in Germany.

Four Cases of German and French Corporate Structure

The ownership patterns of individual firms reveal a number of characteristics that are hidden in the aggregate data. Figures 9, 10, and 11 show the ownership structures of three prominent and representative German companies—Renk AG, Kromschroder AG, and Metallgesellschaft AG. Fig-

ure 12 describes the ownership of the French water company, Degremont.

What can we learn from these exhibits?
■ First, they show the extent of equity holdings of corporations in each other's shares. These investments are frequently in quoted companies and are often by firms in a related or the same industry. Figure 9, for example, shows a large holding by MAN AG, a large German engineering company that produces buses, lorries, and machines, in Renk AG, another mechanical engineering company. Ruhrgas (shown in Figure 10) is a gas company that owns Elster, another gas company.
■ Second, the other corporate owners are frequently *not* trading partners. For example, the gas company

FIGURE 9

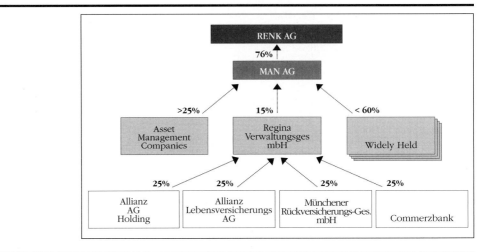

FIGURE 10

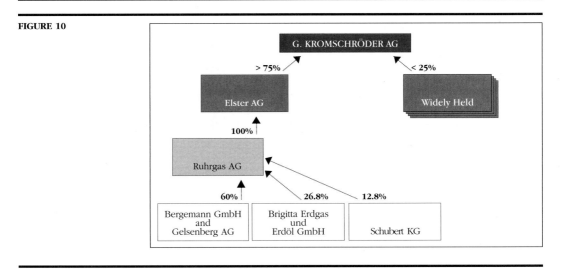

Elster holds Kromschroder, a precision mechanics and optics company.

- Third, banks and insurance companies often emerge higher up in the ownership tree. For example, partnerships between Allianz, which is a German insurance company, and German banks show up in a number of large corporations. Allianz and Deutsche Bank between them have a controlling interest in the holding company of Metallgesellschaft (Figure 11). Allianz, Allianz's life insurance company, and Commerzbank have

a controlling interest in a holding company that has a large stake in MAN. And, as shown in Figure 12, Compagnie Financiere de Suez, Credit Lyonnaise, and UAP all have significant holdings in Société Lyonnaise des Eaux-Dumex, which in turn owns Degremont.

Thus, institutional owners play a prominent role in all three countries. But, whereas institutional ownership is highly dispersed in the U.K., it is highly concentrated in France and Germany. And, as the above illustrations further suggest, the

The German and French corporate governance systems are perhaps best described as *insider* systems—those in which the corporate sector has controlling interests in itself and in which outside investors, while participating in equity returns through the stock market, are not able to exert much control.

FIGURE 11

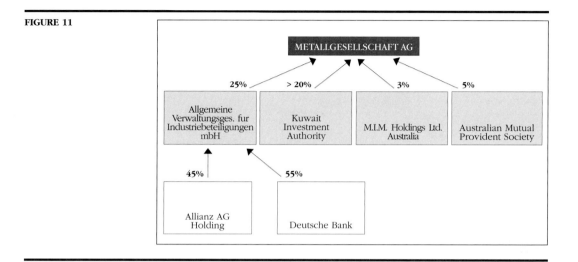

FIGURE 12

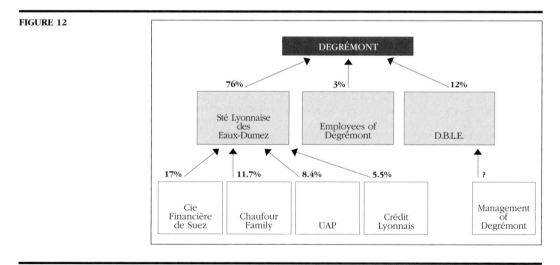

corporate governance role of outside shareholders in France and Germany is even less significant than the small number of quoted companies in these countries would suggest. For, even in those cases in which companies are quoted on the stock market, controlling shareholdings often reside with other companies.

Therefore, as we noted earlier, the German and French corporate governance systems are perhaps best described as *insider* systems (see Figure 13). Insider systems are those in which the corporate sector has controlling interests in itself and in which outside investors, while participating in equity returns through the stock market, are not able to exert much control. By contrast, the U.K. and the U.S. are *outsider* systems of corporate control, in which there are few controlling shareholdings (what controlling blocks do exist are rarely associated with the corporate sector itself). And, as we discuss below, these differences in ownership systems give rise to very different forms of corporate control.

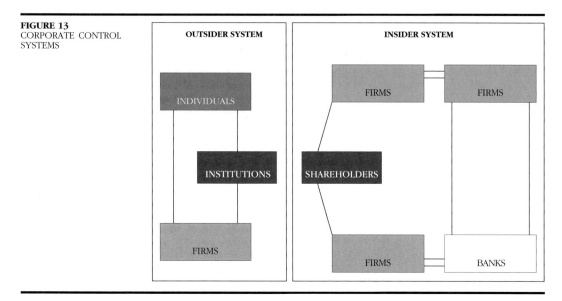

FIGURE 13
CORPORATE CONTROL
SYSTEMS

OUTSIDER SYSTEM

INDIVIDUALS

INSTITUTIONS

FIRMS

INSIDER SYSTEM

FIRMS

FIRMS

SHAREHOLDERS

FIRMS

BANKS

THE MARKET FOR CORPORATE CONTROL IN THE U.K.

The takeover market is active in the U.K. During the merger waves at the beginning of the 1970s and the end of the 1980s, as much as 4% of the total U.K. capital stock was acquired by takeover (or merger) in one year.[11] Furthermore, it has been estimated that about 25% of takeovers in the 1980s were "hostile" in the sense of being rejected initially by the incumbent management.[12] Of those bids that were hostile in nature, approximately one-half were successfully completed.

There are two empirical studies of takeovers that have attempted to distinguish takeovers designed to correct past managerial failure from those that were not. In a 1991 study of the U.S. market, Kenneth Martin and John McConnell investigated the disciplinary role of corporate takeovers in the U.S. over the period 1958 to 1984, using a sample of 253 successful tender offers. They classified a takeover as "disciplinary" if there was any change in the CEO of the target firm. Their study, somewhat surprisingly, reported no difference in bid premiums associated with disciplinary and non-disciplinary takeovers and only moderate evidence of differences in the share price performance of targets of disciplinary and non-disciplinary bids prior to takeover.

In a study published in 1995, we reported similar results for a sample of 80 contested bids in the U.K. in 1985 and 1986.[13] We found that for a range of financial variables, including share price returns, dividends, and cash flow rates of return, the performance of targets of hostile bids in the six years prior to a bid was not statistically distinguishable from that of samples of either accepted bids or non-merging firms. In fact, the dividend performance of targets of both friendly and hostile bids was *appreciably better than* that of firms in the lowest deciles of share performance. Whereas poorly performing firms frequently reduced their dividends, targets of hostile and friendly bids rarely reduced their dividends in the two years prior to a bid.[14]

We also repeated our analysis of U.K. firms using Martin and McConnell's definition of managerial failure as replacement of top management. But, again, we found found little evidence that managerial control changes in takeovers were a response to

11. See our article, "Corporate Ownership and Corporate Control: A Study of France, Germany and the UK," *Economic Policy* (1990).
12. T. Jenkinson and C. Mayer, *Hostile Takeovers* (London: MacMillan, 1994).
13. J. Franks and C. Mayer, "Hostile Takeovers and the Correction of Managerial Failure," *Journal of Financial Economics* 40, (1996), 162-81.

14. Although it appears inconsistent with standard explanations of the control market, such a finding is consistent with Jensen's free cash flow theory of takeovers, in which companies with excess capital tend to overinvest. See Jensen (1986), cited earlier.

There have been just four recorded cases of hostile takeovers in Germany since World War II, and three of those four have occurred within the last six years.

poor financial performance. The past performance of acquired firms where managers were replaced was not significantly worse than the performance of those targets in which top managers were retained.

All these results question the common association of markets for corporate control with the correction of managerial failure. Nevertheless, even in the absence of poor pre-merger performance, we did find evidence of considerable restructuring after takeovers. More precisely, we found that levels of asset disposals and restructurings were significantly higher in cases where bids were either hostile or followed by managerial control changes. Furthermore, we found that managerial dismissals were much higher in hostile than in friendly bids. Indeed, nearly 80% of executive directors either resigned or were dismissed within two years of a successful hostile bid.

In sum, then, while the market for corporate control does not appear to be associated with the correction of managerial failure as measured by past corporate performance (which we henceforth refer to as *ex post failure*), it does give rise to substantial corporate restructurings in the form of asset disposals and executive dismissals (*ex ante failure*). One possible interpretation of these results is that hostile bids can occur, even in the absence of any evidence of poor past performance, in the expectation that the acquiring firm will implement a new and more valuable policy in the future (an explanation that would fall under the classfication of *ex ante failure*). In support of this argument, we found in the previously mentioned study of takeovers that hostile bidders paid much larger premiums over market than friendly acquirers, which is consistent with higher expected benefits from the planned restructurings of targets of hostile bids.[15]

THE MARKET FOR CORPORATE CONTROL IN GERMANY

In a recently published study, we found that during the 1980s the total number of mergers in Germany was only about one-half of those in the U.K.[16] More significantly, in contrast to the active market in corporate control in the U.K., there have been just four recorded cases of hostile takeovers in Germany since World War II, and three of those four have occurred within the last six years.

Several explanations have been suggested for the low level of hostile takeovers in Germany. The first focuses on the dominant position of banks resulting from owning corporate equity and sitting on the supervisory boards of many quoted German companies. As noted earlier, German banks' holdings of equity are a quite modest proportion of the total, but they exercise considerable control by virtue of their ability to vote in proxy contests the bearer shares they hold in custody for customers.

The second explanation is that voting right limitations prevent predators from acquiring controlling interests in firms. German companies frequently pass resolutions at shareholders' meetings limiting the voting right of any one shareholder to a maximum of 5%, 10%, or 15% of total votes, irrespective of the size of the shareholding. The justification for such voting restrictions is that, in the absence of a U.K.-style takeover code, they protect minority shareholders from predators who, after acquiring a controlling interest, attempt to dilute the value of the minority's investments.

The third explanation is that it may prove difficult to remove members of the supervisory board and thereby gain control of a company, even when a majority of the shares are tendered. The supervisory board comprises representatives of employees as well as shareholders. For an AG (public limited company), 50% of the board is composed of employee representatives, who by tradition vote with the incumbent management.

Case studies of hostile takeovers in Germany provide evidence of the effectiveness of these institutional features as barriers to takeover.[17] The unwelcome bid by Pirelli for Continental, Germany's largest tire manufacturer, was launched in September 1990. During the course of the bid, substantial share stakes were acquired by allies of the two parties: Italmobiliare, Mediobanca, and Sopaf in the Pirelli camp; BMW, Daimler-Benz, and Volkswagen in the Continental camp. These share stakes were in large part acquired from individual investors and investment institutions.

At the time of the Pirelli bid, there was a 5% limitation on the voting rights that could be exercised by any one shareholder. Prior to launching the bid, Pirelli attempted to have the 5% limitation removed so as not to dilute the voting rights of its own (and its partners') holdings. A motion for removal of the

---

15. J. Franks and C. Mayer, "Corporate Control: A Synthesis of the International Evidence," mimeo.

16. J. Franks and C. Mayer, see [13].
17. Ibid.

restriction was passed at a shareholders' meeting in March 1991, thereby paving the way for Pirelli to launch a tender bid for Continental. Nevertheless, the removal was delayed (and never implemented) due to a court action by shareholders objecting to rule violations of minority interests.

The Continental case illustrates that voting right restrictions can introduce a two-stage procedure into German takeovers. In the first stage, predators solicit the support of small shareholders to have voting right limitations removed. In the second stage, a normal tender can be launched. The Continental case suggests that the first stage can represent a significant, though not necessarily insurmountable, barrier to takeover.

Although the management board of Continental was resolutely opposed to the merger, the supervisory board showed itself more willing to explore merger possibilities with Pirelli. This difference in approach resulted in the dismissal of the chairman of the management board in May 1991. He was replaced by a chairman who was more sympathetic to merger discussions.

The Continental case suggests that neither proxy votes nor voting right restrictions are absolute defences against hostile takeovers, though the latter certainly slows down the process. Furthermore, the supervisory board may remove members of the management board, though this is less easy to achieve than in the U.K.

The main impediment, however, to an Anglo-American market for corporate control is the ownership structure of German companies. In the Continental case, there was no major shareholder who owned a stake of 25% or more, thus allowing Pirelli and its partners to build large holdings. Two other hostile takeovers in Germany—that of Feldmühle Nobel and the bid by Krupp for Hoesch—were also for firms in the small set of German companies with dispersed shareholdings. In the latter case, Krupp was able to amass a stake of 24.9% without the knowledge of Hoesch or the investment banking community. The purchase of this stake took more than five months to complete, involved purchases on the German, London, and Swiss stock exchanges, and was a crucial tactic in gaining control. Without such a stake, a merger would have proved unlikely or impossible, since all previous attempts at friendly mergers in the industry had failed.

Where ownership is concentrated, direct control is effectively exercised by boards. This is reflected in a close association between ownership and representation on supervisory boards, in particular in the all-important position of chairman. In the small proportion of companies where ownership is dispersed, bank representation on supervisory boards is more in evidence. This suggests that, in widely held companies, proxy votes and voting restrictions together permit banks to exercise effective control through board representation.

A DISCUSSION OF THE EVIDENCE

The evidence presented above on national differences between corporate ownership and control can be summarized by the following observations:

1. There are marked differences in the ownership structures of similar companies in different countries.

2. Intercorporate holdings of companies are very significant in some countries but not others.

3. Large shareholdings by families are of much greater importance in some countries than others.

4. Markets for corporate control are little in evidence in countries with concentrated ownership.

5. Even where companies are widely held, markets for corporate control are seriously restricted in some countries.

6. Bank control is associated primarily with widely held companies where the market for corporate control is restricted.

7. There is little association of the market for corporate control with poor past performance (or *ex post failure*).

8. Corporate control transactions such as takeovers lead to substantial restructuring and management changes (which can be interpreted as evidence of *ex ante failure*).

How well do the theories of ownership and the market for corporate control square with these observations? The answer is not well at all; they leave a large number of unresolved issues.

First, it would not be expected that the broadly similar production technologies that are employed in different countries would give rise to the marked variations in ownership patterns recorded in this paper. Moreover, it is difficult to imagine that there are sufficient differences in production complementarities across countries to explain much larger intercorporate holdings in some countries than in others.

Second, the large family holdings in France and Germany suggest that families in those countries either (1) possess greater managerial skills or (2) derive larger "private" benefits from control (larger at least in relation to the value they could realize by selling their controlling interest) than their English and American counterparts. It is possible that regulation may create greater private benefits in some countries, for example, by being more permissive towards insider trading or providing less protection of minority interests.[18] In this respect, regulation may have important consequences for the structure of corporate organization.

Third, if markets for corporate control improve corporate efficiency, why are they largely absent in some countries? For example, it is very difficult to understand why markets for corporate control in Germany are restricted by bank intermediation *even* in cases of widely held companies where there are weak incentives for shareholders to exert control directly themselves.

On the other hand, if the market for corporate control really does work to correct managerial failure, the puzzle posed by the U.K. is why there is so little evidence of poor pre-bid performance. And, in the absence of poor pre-bid performance, why is there so much restructuring after the takeover?

In this sense, then, current theories of ownership and control fail to provide adequate explanations for the ownership structure and operation of either U.K. or Continental European capital markets. For example, there is clearly more to the determination of ownership in the U.K., Germany, and France than complementarity in production. Moreover, the market for corporate control does not appear to perform its assumed function of correcting managerial failure—or not at least the kind of failure that manifests itself in substandard operating and shareholder returns.

One might suggest that dispersed public ownership, because of its efficiencies in risk-bearing and the liquidity of public markets, is better suited to providing capital for large-scale corporate expansions. But this ignores the reality that even companies with concentrated share ownership can raise external equity while retaining control through either the issuance of dual class shares or the "pyramiding" of intercorporate holdings (as illustrated earlier in the case of several German and French companies).[19] It also ignores the

fact that active secondary markets can be (and are) organized in shares other than those that are part of the controlling block.[20]

Concentrated ownership, as suggested by Demsetz and Lehn, is likely to occur for one or both of the following reasons: (1) the greater potential for owners to exercise control over managers increases the value of the enterprise (relative to the value it would command under dispersed ownership), or (2) there are "private" benefits to owners of exercising control—that is, benefits that do not accrue to (and may even come at the expense of) minority stockholders. Both of these factors are likely to explain the extent of family ownership in Germany and France. Concentrated ownership allows investors to exert *direct* control, which is presumably much less costly than the indirect control exerted by takeover markets (especially given restrictions on takeovers in Continental markets). And the private, perhaps even non-monetary, benefits of owning a large enterprise (which may include greater powers to keep minority shareholders at bay) may well be larger in France and Germany than in the U.S. or the U.K.

Nevertheless, the differences in the extent of family ownership of public corporations among these nations remain a puzzle. Unless the relative costs of direct and indirect control can be shown to vary greatly among countries, or unless families in different countries attach very different values to private benefits, the diverse forms of ownership cannot be readily explained.

The hypothesis we offer is that the different patterns of ownership across countries are associated with different forms of corporate control that allow for different kinds of correction. Large share stakes and concentrated ownership are likely to be more effective in responding to *ex post* managerial failures (poor past performance), in large part (as we will argue below) because of the "information and agency costs" that confront dispersed shareholders. And there is at least one piece of supporting evidence for this argument: In a recent study (with a colleague), we found that those companies in the bottom decile of corporate performance were far

18. And differences in estate taxes may lead to differences in ownership; for example, many large family interests in U.S. companies are reportedly sold to pay estate taxes.

19. For a defense of the economic efficiency of the pyramid ownership structure, see Brian Kantor, "Shareholders as Agents and Principals: The Case for South Africa's Corporate Governance System," *Journal of Applied Corporate Finance*, Vol. 8, No. 1 (Spring 1995).

20. For a paper arguing that this may be an important source of information for structuring incentives for management, see B. Holmstrom and J. Tirole, "Market Liquidity and Performance Monitoring," *Journal of Political Economy*, 101 (1993), 678-709.

more likely to replace their managers than those with dispersed ownership.[21] By contrast, dispersed ownership seems to be more effective in correcting *ex ante failure*—that is, in bringing about valuable restructuring and management changes in cases where financial performance has been adequate, but managers have failed to maximize value.

At first sight, this argument would appear to suggest that national systems with dispersed ownership will tend to achieve more efficient resource allocations than those with concentrated ownership. Nevertheless, there is a problem presented by dispersed ownership—namely, the inability of a large number of small shareholders to make "commitments" to other key corporate stakeholders such as employees and suppliers.

A simple example illustrates the point. Consider a company with 100,000 shareholders each owning one share in a firm. An alternative prospect, for example, a proposed acquisition emerges. A sale of a majority of shares results in a change in corporate policy to the detriment of existing stakeholders (suppliers, purchasers, and employees). Individually, shareholders base their decision to sell purely on the price which they are offered since the action of any one shareholder has no effect on policy. In addition, the loss sustained by stakeholders in the event of a change in policy cannot be attributed to the actions of any one shareholder. In contrast, large shareholders know that if they sell their shares, they will affect corporate policy to the detriment of stakeholders. Their decisions will be affected by the loss of their reputation as well as the price for their shares

According to this description, the key distinction between corporate systems concerns the degree of anonymity of shareholders. To a much greater extent than in the U.S. or the U.K., the Continental system allows a large number of small investors to buy and sell shares without having any effect on control. At the same time, large investors such as families or other companies—those who are likely to have the best information about the firm's long-run prospects—effectively guarantee the ability of the firm to make good on strategic commitments.

On the other hand, the advantage of dispersed ownership is that outside shareholders who are not bound by prior commitments are more likely to seek the highest value control group *at any point in time*. Thus, dispersed share ownership achieves value maximization, at least over the short run, although possibly at the expense of valuable long-term relationships with other stakeholders.[22]

It is in this sense, then, that the U.K. and the U.S. financial markets may be considered "short-term." Dispersed shareholders cannot commit to the same extent as concentrated owners and cannot therefore sustain the same set of prior relations. This kind of short termism thus does not represent a mispricing of securities or excessive trading of shares, but is rather a direct result of the structure of ownership. And if the short-term orientation of dispersed shareholders limits their ability to commit to key corporate stakeholders, it also provides a potentially valuable flexibility (an ability to reduce operating leverage, if you will, by converting fixed into variable costs). For this reason, in cases where little investment is required of other stakeholders, or relationships can be sustained through explicit contracting, dispersed share ownership may well lead to more efficient allocation of resources than a concentrated ownership burdened by commitments.[23]

Moreover, while it is possible to provide a rationale for high levels of concentration of ownership, majority (or large minority) intercorporate ownership remains very hard to explain. Indeed, the main puzzle presented by the Continental ownership structure is this: Where control is retained within the corporate sector through large corporate shareholdings and corporate representatives who serve on supervisory boards, management is likely to enjoy a high degree of protection from external influences. Managerial failure will not be corrected, either directly by large outside shareholders such as families or indirectly by takeovers, as in economies with dispersed shareownership. Thus, one plausible view of the insider system holds that the complex web of intercorporate holdings in France and Germany is designed, not to promote efficiency, but to perpetuate control within the corporate sector itself.

---

21. J. Franks, C. Mayer, and C. Renneboog, "The Ownership and Control of Poorly Performing Companies in the U.K.," working paper (1995).

22. This provides the basis for the Shleifer and Summers assertion that shareholders are unable to make commitments to other stakeholders and employ managers to do this on their behalf. The observation here is that through concentrated ownership some financial systems permit investors to make commitments. (See A. Shleifer and L. Summers, "Breaches of Trust in Hostile Takeovers," in *Corporate Takeovers: Causes and Consequences*, ed. Alan Auerbach (University of Chicago Press for National Bureau of Economic Research, 1988).)

23. Franks and Mayer (1996), cited above, emphasize another distinguishing feature of insider and outsider systems and that is the importance of committees. Control in insider systems is exercised by committees that can reflect the interests of parties who, for credit constraint reasons, are underrepresented in ownership stakes. In Germany, stakeholder representation on boards is in part dictated by legal considerations.

> **Besides providing stronger incentives to maximize value, concentrated ownership can impose costs in two ways: (1) by forcing managers to bear excessive company-specific risks that could be borne by well-diversified outside stockholders; and (2) by allowing inside owners to capture private benefits at the expense of outside owners.**

CONCLUSIONS

There are pronounced differences in the ownership patterns of corporate sectors across countries. The U.K. and the U.S. have large quoted sectors with share ownership dispersed across a large number of investors. (In the U.K. the dominant shareholding group is institutional investors; in the U.S. it is individual investors.)

In contrast, France and Germany have small quoted sectors. Perhaps more significant, even the largest quoted companies in France and Germany typically have at least one shareholder owning more than 25% of the equity and, in many cases, even a majority shareholding. Such large shareholdings tend to be held either by the founding family or by other corporations. In this sense, both France and Germany can be seen as having "insider systems" of corporate ownership, as contrasted with the "outsider systems" of the U.K. and the U.S.

The different ownership systems are associated with very different forms of corporate control. There is an active market for corporate control in the U.K. and the U.S., but very little in the way of a market for corporate control in France and Germany. In the case of Germany, even in the comparatively small widely held component of the quoted sector, the market for corporate control is impeded by proxy votes and voting right restrictions that effectively confer more power on banks than on the concentrated ownership segment.

Some economists have suggested that complementarities in production can make vertical relationships (including intercorporate block holdings) a cost-effective way of reducing transaction costs or "completing" incomplete contracts. Nevertheless, the patterns of intercorporate ownership we observe in France and Germany do not appear to be particularly closely associated with trading relationships. And, in further contradiction of this theory, similar companies have quite different ownership structures in the U.K., on the one hand, and France and Germany on the other.

In theory, the market for corporate control should be closely associated with the correction of managerial failure. In practice, however, there is very little evidence of a relation between the incidence of hostile takeovers and poor corporate performance. The performance of targets of hostile takeovers in the U.K. is close to that of the average quoted company. At the same time, however, hostile takeovers do result in considerable restructuring and managerial turnover. This can be construed as evidence that targets, while performing up to averages, were failing to *maximize* shareholder value.

The different patterns of ownership in the U.K. and in France and Germany create different incentives and corporate control mechanisms. Concentrated ownership would seem to encourage longer-term relationships between the company and its investors. But, while perhaps better suited to some corporate activities with longer-term payoffs, concentrated ownership could also lead to costly delays in undertaking necessary corrective action, particularly if the owners receive non-monetary benefits from owning and running a business. And although widely dispersed ownership may increase the likelihood that corrective action will be sought prematurely (that is, in cases where the firm is suffering a temporary downturn and outsiders rush to sell their shares), the presence of well-diversified public owners may also be more appropriate for riskier ventures requiring large amounts of new capital investment.

In short, different forms of ownership would appear to be suited to promoting different types of activity. Concentrated ownership may be necessary where investment by other stakeholders is important and cannot be promoted contractually, but dispersed ownership will be advantageous where little investment is required by non-investor stakeholders or where adequate contracts can be written that protect their interests. What is finally very hard to explain, however, is the high level of intercorporate holdings in the French and particularly the German systems. Such holdings, while possibly achieving some coordination benefits, are also likely to create insider systems that are largely immune to necessary corrective intervention by outside investors.

LARGE BANK STOCKHOLDERS IN GERMANY: SAVIORS OR SUBSTITUTES?

*by William J. Carney,
Emory University Law School**

M ark Roe's book is a singular achievement, largely because of the breadth of
his scholarship and his ability to bring
several disciplines—law, American history, economics, and political science—to bear on
the subject of U.S. corporate governance. The book
carefully documents the role that laws, interest
groups, ideology, and perhaps historical accident
played in keeping U.S. financial institutions from
playing a significant role as stockholders in American corporations. In so doing, it provides an important "counter-story" to the received view of the Berle
& Means corporation, with its widely dispersed
shareholdings and professional (non-owner) managers, as the logical culmination of industrial development. While I am not yet persuaded by parts of
his story, that in no way detracts from its importance.

The main lessons of the book are two-fold: first,
that the domination of the Berle & Means style of
firm in the United States may not be as inevitable as
most of us have thought; and second, that the
predominance of the Berle & Means firm in the U.S.
may be a function of the pervasive bias of U.S.
politics, laws, and regulations against control of
corporations by large financial institutions.

In this paper, I will limit my remarks to the first
lesson—the inevitability of the Berle & Means form
in advanced industrial societies. Although Roe is
surely right in identifying barriers to concentrated
holdings by financial intermediaries as a cause of
dispersed share ownership in the U.S., his book—

in my view at least—pays too little attention to
important developments in American markets designed to achieve some, if not most, of the benefits
of concentrated holdings.

In making my case, moreover, I find it useful
and instructive to compare the evolution of the U.S.
governance system with developments in Germany
over the same period. Such a comparison leads me
to the following two propositions:

■ First, the differences between the U.S. and German corporate governance systems may have more
to do with the success of German banks in blocking
the growth of strong financial markets in Germany
than with political constraints on large banks in the
U.S. American financial markets are more developed and efficient than those found in Germany;
and, to the extent U.S. markets provide more cost-
effective monitoring of managers than large bank
shareholders, bank monitoring should be viewed
as a second-best solution—one that can be expected to prevail only where monitoring by strong
markets is not possible.

■ Second, American corporate laws give shareholders of U.S. companies a more effective voice in corporate governance than company laws in Germany.
By so doing, they may facilitate shareholder monitoring and accountability in ways that reduce the need
for concentrated bank ownership. Put another way,
concentrated ownership may be necessary in Germany in order to offset the disadvantages that German laws have imposed on German investors.

*This paper is based on a presentation delivered at a conference on Mark Roe's
book, *Strong Managers, Weak Owners: The Political Roots of American Corporate* *Finance*, at the Law & Economics Center of George Mason University School of Law
on May 4, 1996.

376 ■ CHAPTER 3: EXTERNAL GOVERNANCE

In short, my view of Roe's evidence might be titled "Strong Managers, Strong Markets." Although Roe may be right to suggest there may *still* be an important role for financial institutions in U.S. corporate governance, the potential for concentrated ownership by financial institutions to add value to American companies can be as large as Roe suggests *only* if you view U.S. markets as suffering from some serious "failures"—and, as I argue in the following pages, there is not much evidence to support that view. Stock prices are sensitive indicators of expected performance; and, insofar as they reflect investors' collective assessment of managers' efficiency in using resources, they impose real constraints on companies seeking capital for new projects. Even for those firms not presently seeking outside financing, stock prices send signals about management's performance to prospective bidders for control as well as to large shareholders who might launch proxy fights. Moreover, for those managers whose compensation is tied to the firm's performance through stock-based incentive programs, these same price signals provide powerful incentives for efficiency.

THE DEVELOPMENT OF U.S. SECURITIES MARKETS

Securities markets in America developed to a remarkable degree during the 19th century. While the origins of the New York Stock Exchange go back to 1792, it was not until after the Civil War that the market grew significantly, with railroads constituting a significant portion of the early listings. By 1880 trading volume reached sufficient levels that a continuous auction market system was instituted, and securities of the growing industrial sector began to be listed.[1]

Although Berle and Means are remembered largely for their description of dispersed ownership of American corporations, they really provided much more. As early as 1932, they described U.S. stock markets in terms that today's finance scholars would recognize as the "semi-strong form" of market efficiency.[2] New York Stock Exchange rules required annual financial reports, and encouraged quarterly reports as well, all before adoption of the securities

laws.[3] Offering disclosures for new issues were roughly similar to the current S-1, S-2, and S-3 registration statement standards, although they lacked the overlay of trivial detail that the SEC has since mandated. Even at this early date the NYSE was competing on a "quality margin," as evidenced by the fact that its best practices in the prospectus area were used as the basis for the mandatory regulation that followed. So, even if these markets had been left unregulated, we would have expected competition on quality margins to have continued, and these standards would have embraced the thousands of new issuers who sought public capital over the decades.

The accounting standards that we employ today have been left largely in the hands of the private sector, with only minimal interference from the SEC.[4] With the onset of regulation, these essentially private standards were mandated and refined through SEC regulation to provide the most detailed disclosure and financial reporting requirements in the world. If they are to be faulted, it is because too much, rather than too little, information is required to be disclosed.

U.S. capital markets raise in excess of $1 trillion per year, which has been estimated to be more than the combined total of all other capital markets.[5] In 1980 the market capitalization of the New York Stock Exchange exceeded the combined capitalization of the exchanges in Tokyo, London, Montreal, Frankfurt, Toronto and Paris.[6] While American markets are less dominant today, this comparison demonstrates the lead that the U.S. had in the development of efficient capital markets for many decades.

While Roe's book focuses on the role of U.S. laws in restricting bank ownership and control of equity capital, there are developments in the markets for debt securities that suggest that mature markets may use fewer intermediaries to perform monitoring functions. In the past two decades, our debt markets have moved dramatically in the direction of market-based borrowing rather than lender-based borrowing. Disintermediation has been one of the most dramatic developments in U.S. markets during that period. First, the development of junk bond markets shifted unsecured borrowing from banks to capital

1. J. Edward Meeker, *The Work of the New York Stock Exchange* (rev. ed. 1930), pp. 67-72.
2. A. A. Berle and Gardiner C. Means, *The Modern Corporation and Private Property*, 294 (1932).
3. Meeker, cited above, 581.

4. George J. Benston, The Effectiveness and Effects of the SEC's Accounting Disclosure Requirements, in *Economic Policy and the Regulation of Corporate Securities* (H. Manne, ed. 1969) 23, 27-30.
5. Richard C. Breeden, "Foreign Companies and U.S. Securities Markets in a Time of Economic Transformation," 17 *Fordham Int'l L. J.* S77, S81 (1994).
6. Joseph Blum, "The Regulation of Insider Trading in Germany: Who's Afraid of Self-Restraint?," 7 *J. Int'l L. Bus.* 507, n. 4 (1986).

markets. Second, securitization of a wide variety of liquid assets has replaced secured lending.

Moreover, this movement of debt markets away from intermediaries has happened without the kind of political interference Roe describes with respect to equity markets. Indeed, the junk bond market developed in the face of political opposition. Thus, the U.S. experience with debt markets that were not hampered by the kinds of regulations Roe describes seems to suggest that highly liquid capital markets are the final stage of development of corporate finance.

In short, we have lived with relatively efficient capital markets for most of this century. Liquidity in these markets is relatively high, even for smaller companies, compared to liquidity throughout much of the world. It is this liquidity and transparency that have attracted foreign investors to our markets for decades.

DEVELOPMENT OF THE GERMAN MARKET

German capital markets may provide an even more dramatic story of political interference than the U.S. story, except in this case the story might well be how the big German banks succeeded in blocking the development of efficient securities markets. German markets appear to have imposed higher transactions costs on trading, set up higher barriers to entry by upstart firms, and furnished investors with lower-quality disclosures and less liquidity than U.S. markets. While I have not investigated all of the reasons for these differences, they all furnish an opportunity for big banks to provide substitute markets, and to play a monitoring role that might otherwise be played by the markets themselves.

Let me begin with transaction costs. In an article that preceded his book, Mark Roe pointed out that stock transfer taxes in Bismarck's Germany, besides retarding the development of securities markets, gave banks control over corporate proxy machinery.[7] Because shareholders wished to avoid transfer taxes, they delivered their shares to the banks, which held them in the banks' names. Thereafter when a shareholder wished to sell, he preferred to sell to another customer of the same bank because such intra-bank transactions—thanks in part to the banks' successful lobbying—were not treated as taxable transfers. Obviously customers preferred dealing with large banks because of their greater ability to match customers' sales and purchases.[8]

It would be fascinating, from an interest-group perspective, to know the sponsors of this legislation, as well as that which followed it. Transaction costs remain high today for individual shareholders who might wish to hold or transfer their own certificates, because an extra charge is imposed under these circumstances.[9] This has allowed German banks to function as combination stock exchanges and nominee corporations, in the process excluding real owners from control of their shares. While banks must seek instructions from depositing shareholders about how to vote their shares, in practice few shareholders exercise this power, and the banks are free to vote virtually all deposited shares. With big banks in control of proxies for most voting shares, one wonders what role they played in seeing that corporations imposed such certificate charges.

Barriers to entry to capital markets were first created in 1884 when German law restricted corporations' access to the stock exchanges. This was accomplished by increasing the minimum size of a public offering and the length of time a company had to be in existence before it could list its shares on an exchange.[10] Such restrictions on listing, by forcing smaller companies to deal with the banks, ensured that debt would become the dominant form of financing in Germany—and not equity, as in the United States.

At the same time, the big banks, which are both the relevant markets as well as underwriters, appear to use their market power over secondary trading activity to dominate the primary markets for new issues and the underwriting process in most instances. The banks are said both to underprice new issues to assure their "success," and to charge relatively high underwriting fees.[11] And their combined positions as major stockholders, creditors, and underwriters provided the big banks with an opportunity for insider trading, which was not legally prohibited until 1994.

While American securities markets appear to compete vigorously with each other on quality

---

7. Mark J. Roe, "Some Differences in Corporate Structure in Germany, Japan and the United States," 102 *Yale L. J.* 1927, 1971 (1993).

8. Ibid. at 1971.

9. Theodor Baums, "Corporate Governance in Germany: The Role of the Banks," 40 *Am. J. Comp. L.* 503, 506 (1992).

10. William L. Horton, Jr., "The Perils of Universal Banking in Central and Eastern Europe," 35 *Va. J. Int'l L.* 683 694, text at n. 51 (1995).

11. Herman H. Kallfass, "Forum: The American Corporation and the Institutional Investor: Are There Lessons from Abroad? - The German Experience," 1988 *Colum. Bus. L.Rev.* 775, 779-80.

margins, the same does not appear to be true in Germany. Only part of the German market has been regulated (in the sense of self-regulation by stock exchanges), until recent laws passed in response to European Community directives. There has been "unofficial" and unregulated trading in some corporate stocks at the German stock exchanges. Primary offerings were often made in the unofficial markets without any prospectus whatever.

I mentioned that disclosure standards in Germany are not up to U.S. standards. Let me take the particular example of accounting standards as a final explanation for why German stock markets are less appealing to investors, thus necessitating the development of financial intermediaries as substitutes. The American accounting profession has provided relatively uniform standards for a long time, thus allowing outsiders to perform reasonably accurate comparisons of firms and their securities. After 1934, of course, these requirements became legally enforceable, and over time the financial statement requirements for large reporting companies went beyond GAAP, and became more detailed. Markets are able to use this information with a relatively high degree of confidence. It has facilitated monitoring by market participants, and by the market for corporate control.

German accounting systems appear to provide far less reliable information than the U.S. system. A wide variety of accounting methods are available to German firms that make comparisons difficult if not impossible. German corporations can freely create reserves that can be used to mask earnings dips in bad years. It is hard to believe that accounting standards that permit huge reserves to be declared as current profits at management's discretion can provide the same transparency as GAAP reporting.

To be sure, there is some evidence that suggests that German financial statements provide the same quality disclosures as the U.S.,[12] but I am skeptical of these studies. The studies deal only with the *transactional* efficiency of the German market; that is, they examine only whether market prices react quickly to new accounting information. They do not test the *allocative* efficiency of the German market

compared to that of the U.S. market, and the only way I know to test that is to examine price reactions when companies restate their results under another accounting system. Until recently, even the largest German corporations have been reluctant to list their securities for trading in the U.S., largely because of their reluctance to submit to SEC accounting requirements. That could be explained either because compliance with GAAP was not thought to provide value for firms and their investors, or because managers were reluctant to be held more accountable under these standards.

The Daimler Benz experience is the only example of a company reconciling its statements with U.S. standards. At one point Daimler Benz had reserves equal to about 40% of its balance sheet assets, thus giving it the ability to cover up its losses with these reserves. When Daimler Benz brought its financial statements into conformity with U.S. GAAP, a reported profit of DM200 million was turned into a loss of DM1 billion. Remarkably, even with the revelation of such losses, the company's announcement that it was going to reconcile its financial statements with U.S. GAAP was interpreted as good news, with its stock price rising over 5% against the German average.[13] If German financial statements are as obscure as this suggests, accurate monitoring of German firms by market participants must be all but impossible. Only the big banks seem likely to have access to accurate information about the performance of most firms. Because of the informational advantages possessed by the big banks, there was little incentive for other analysts to engage in costly research and analysis of publicly-available information.

German stock markets remain relatively small and illiquid compared to American markets. Only about 2,800 German corporations are stock corporations (AGs), while the vast majority, approximately 220,000, are limited liability companies without tradeable shares (GmbHs).[14] Only a small number of firms, approximately 650, have shares traded on the exchanges.[15] Even many of those companies are not actively traded, and they have floats that are less than one-half of their outstanding shares.[16] Only 100 firms are widely held.[17]

---

12. William J. Baumol & Burton G. Malkiel, "Redundant Regulation of Foreign Security Trading and U.S. Competitiveness," in *Modernizing U.S. Securities Regulation: Economic and Legal Perspectives* (Kenneth Lehn and Robert Kamphuis, eds., 1992) 35, 42-43; James L. Cochrane, "Are U.S. Regulatory Requirements for Foreign Firms Appropriate?," 17 *Fordham Int'l L. J.* S58, S62 (1994).

13. Breeden, cited above at S91-S92.

14. Baums, cited above at 504.

15. Gerhard Wegen, "Congratulations from Your Continental Cousins, 10b-5: Securities Fraud Regulation from the European Perspective," 61 *Ford. L. Rev.* S57, S61 (1993).

16. As of 1990, only 6% of the firms listed on the Frankfurt Exchange had more than half their stock publicly traded. Horton, supra note at 696, n. 74. Approximately thirty stocks account for 68% of total value of all shares traded on all German stock exchanges. Kallfass, cited above at 786.

17. Baums, cited above at 504.

As a result of big bank dominance and weak capital markets, the frequency with which German companies resort to public capital markets is much lower than in the U.S.[18] German corporations are forced to borrow from banks to a far greater extent than their American counterparts, with two obvious consequences: First, debt-equity ratios in Germany are much higher than in the United States.[19] Second, it has been suggested that banks have charged German corporations excessive rates for borrowing, thus restricting the growth of German industry.[20] These characteristics hardly describe a mature and developed capital market by U.S. standards. Finally, no market for corporate control exists in Germany to cure even the most extreme monitoring problems.[21]

One would expect investor skepticism and higher capital costs in such markets. Individual participation in the German stock market has been very low when compared to that in the United States. As a result, the big banks have had a monitoring role to play in Germany that may not be required in the United States.

U.S. MARKETS: EFFECTIVE MONITORS?

While I hope this evidence is at least suggestive of why German banks dominate share ownership and voting in Germany, it is not a complete challenge to Roe's suggestion that such ownership may provide better monitoring than that furnished by U.S. markets. To complete the picture, I want to suggest first that large block ownership isn't nonexistent in the United States—just that it isn't necessary for all firms. Second, I want to take a moment or two to challenge Roe's view of some of the weaknesses of U.S. markets that might provide a useful role for monitoring by financial institutions.

Given the sharp growth of U.S. institutional ownership and activism in recent years, Roe's use of the Berle & Means label for the modern American corporation probably overstates the current degree of management control. Ownership concentration patterns are hardly uniform across all corporations, and in that sense the Berle & Means model is merely a stereotype, and perhaps a misleading one. In their day, Berle & Means found significant control blocks in many corporations, and the "management control" that resulted from dispersed ownership was just one of the forms they observed. Indeed, they characterized only 44% of the 200 largest industrial corporations as management controlled. At least some of the variance in ownership patterns seems attributable to the incidence of agency costs in various types of firms. One study, for example, has shown that those companies more prone to conflicts of interest between managers and outside shareholders—those characterized by high nonsystematic risk and the large potential for personal consumption of firm resources—also tend to be firms with relatively concentrated ownership.[22]

There have also been a number of other modern studies that show concentrated ownership in some significant number of U.S. corporations. For example, three different studies of companies adopting two-tier voting systems in the 1980s reported the median percentages of shares held in large blocks to be 30%, 46%, and 62%.[23] While this was not a sample of all large firms, but only of a self-selected set where powerful owners would presumably benefit from a recapitalization, it represented a significant number of companies in the 1980s.

Consistent with this evidence of concentrated holdings, a 1972 House subcommittee study found that the percentage ownership held by the 30 largest shareholders of 25 major U.S. corporations then ranged between 11.9% and 49% of the voting shares.[24] A 1978 Congressional study went so far as to describe excessive concentration of ownership of large corporations as a "problem."[25] (This statement alone shows how much lawyers' and economists' views of concentrated ownership have changed over the past 20 years—in part, I suspect, because of Mark Roe's writings.) That study found that the House of Morgan remained the largest shareholder in a substantial number of corporations, as it had been much earlier in the century.

18. Kallfass, cited above at 775, reports that in 1986-87 roughly 50 times as many companies were admitted to stock exchange trading in the U.S. as in Germany, and that the relationship of market value of traded companies to GDP is much lower in Germany (14%) than in the United States (49%) or Japan (55%).

19. Blum, cited above, at 507-8.

20. Horton, cited above, at 694, n. 45.

21. Baums, cited above, at 505.

22. Harold Demsetz and Kenneth Lehn, "The Structure of Corporate Ownership: Causes and Consequences," 93 *J. Pol. Econ.* 1155 (1985).

23. Jeffrey Gordon, "Ties that Bond: Dual Class Common Stock and the Problem of Shareholder Choice," 76 *Calif. L. Rev.* 3, 36-37 (1988).

24. Subcommittee on Intergovernmental Relations and Budgeting Management, and Expenditures, of the Senate Committee on Government Operations, 93rd Cong., 1st Sess., Disclosure of Corporate Ownership 6, 17 (Comm. Print 1973).

25. "Voting Rights in Major Corporations: A Staff Study," prepared by the Subcommittee on Reports, Accounting and Management of the Committee on Governmental Affairs, U.S. Senate, 252-258 (95th Cong. 1st Sess. 1978).

German corporations can freely create reserves that can be used to mask earnings dips in bad years. It is hard to believe that accounting standards that permit huge reserves to be declared as current profits at management's discretion can provide the same transparency as GAAP reporting.

In the past two decades, institutional ownership of corporate stock has increased dramatically, with institutions owning 53% of all public equity by 1990.[26] (In contrast, German banks and insurance companies owned only 21% of equity of publicly held German corporations in 1988.[27]) And so, if one considers increasing U.S. institutional ownership together with recent SEC attempts to liberalize shareholder communications, there appears to be a striking trend toward a new concentration of voting power—one that may ultimately rival that of the German banks.[28] But even if this movement continues, German banks are still likely to have greater clout than U.S. institutions because of their ability to vote nominee shares on a discretionary basis, which U.S. nominees cannot do because of rules of self-regulatory organizations.[29]

Roe argues that monitoring by large bank shareholders could cure possible market failures that he suggests may exist in the U.S. The first of these involves product market "imperfections" that may, in his words, "allow managers considerable slack, because monopoly rents can be earned from sunk capital for a considerable period of time." This is an old—and I would have thought discredited—argument that was made in support of greater regulation of corporations during the course of the ALI debates in the 1980s. The difficulty I have with this argument is that Roe mentions as examples companies that have been hammered by vigorous competitors, and that have been forced to make dramatic adjustments—companies like Sears, General Motors, American Express, Westinghouse, Kodak and IBM. All of these companies, with the possible exception of Sears, experienced turnover in their CEOs during their difficulties. Furthermore, recent stories about European companies operating in U.S. product markets report that their managers have

been surprised by the degree of competitiveness they have encountered here.[30] So, when our product markets are characterized as lacking competitiveness, one might fairly ask, "compared to what?"

Roe's second illustration involves the alleged failure of financial markets to evaluate properly "soft" or private information about such things as the quality of management and the expected value of long-term research. According to this story, short-termism creeps into management's decision-making processes as a result. This is a well-worn story of corporate critics from the 1980s, when the prevailing view was that U.S. competitors were being outperformed by their more "farsighted" Japanese and German competitors—and I think it's a story that contains far less than meets the eye. While I don't want to deny that markets may have some difficulties with this kind of information, there is also evidence that markets do indeed value long-term research projects.[31] This evidence also shows that R&D activity is positively correlated with institutional ownership, suggesting that managers can communicate the expected values of such projects to investors, even when they lack the close relations that exist between banks and corporations in Germany and Japan.[32]

In short, there is little reason to believe that there is a pervasive and serious information problem that exists because of the current patterns of dispersed stock ownership in the U.S. I don't want to suggest that all information is perfectly evaluated by financial markets, but I do feel more comfortable with the consensus valuation of participants in these markets than I would with the evaluation of representatives of a single big bank that is both a lender and a stockholder, and may suffer from a conservative creditor's bias.[33]

26. Bernard Black, "Agents Watching Agents: The Promise of Institutional Investor Voice," 39 *UCLA L. Rev.* 811, 827 (1992).

27. John C. Coffee, Jr., "Liquidity Versus Control: The Institutional Investor as Corporate Monitor," 91 *Colum. L. Rev.* 1277, 1303, n. 98 (1991), citing a 1989 study by Coopers & Lybrand.

28. See Securities Exchange Act Rule 14a-2(b)(1), exempting certain shareholder communications not soliciting proxies.

29. Voting by U.S. nominees is governed by a combination of SEC rules providing an obligation to deliver proxy materials to beneficial owners (Securities Exchange Act Rule 14b-1) and rules of exchanges and the NASD, which generally only permit nominees to vote if beneficial owners do not return proxies. See, e.g., N.Y.S.E. Rule 451, N.Y.S.E. Guide (CCH) ¶2451; Rules 574-579, Am. Stock Exch. Guide (CCH) ¶¶9526-31; NASD, Rules of Fair Practice, art. III, §1 NASD Manual (CCH) ¶2151. Under NYSE rules, for example, a broker-dealer cannot vote shares on contested matters in the absence of instruction (N.Y.S.E. Rule 452). In contrast, German nominees can vote shares when beneficial owners do not provide instructions. Wegen, cited above at 104.

30. Bernard Wysocki, Jr., "Rhone-Poulenc Prepares to Concentrate on Margins, Not Acquisitions in U.S.," *Wall St. J.*, Apr. 12, 1996, A7A.

31. Office of Chief Economist, SEC, "Institutional Ownership, Tender Offers, and Long-Term Investments" (1985). See also Su Han Chan, John Martin and John Kensinger, "Corporate Research and Development Expenditures and Share Value," 26 *J. Fin. Econ.* 255 (1990); but see John Doukas and Lorne Switzer, "The Stock Market's Valuation of R&D Spending and Market Concentration," 44 *J. Econ. & Bus.* 95 (1992), which reports finding insignificant stock price effects.

32. For one recent study that shows that markets can evaluate the impact of R&D on profits, see Anant K. Sunaram, Teresa A. John and Kose John, "An Empirical Analysis of Strategic Competition and Firm Values: the Case of R&D Competition," 40 *J. Fin. Econ.* 459 (1996) (finding that stock prices rise only for announcing firms in industries where competitors will not emulate their R&D strategy).

33. See Jonathan Macey and Geoffrey Miller, "Corporate Governance and Commercial Banking: A Comparative Examination of Germany, Japan, and the United States, *Stanford Law Review* Vol. 48 No.1 (Nov. 1995), pp. 73-112.

> If one considers increasing U.S. institutional ownership together with recent SEC attempts to liberalize shareholder communications, there appears to be a striking trend toward a new concentration of voting power—one that may ultimately rival that of the German banks.

While my comments on Roe's description of the U.S. market can fairly be described as quibbles, I make them because they are the beginning of my attempt to provide a different balance in the description of the benefits and costs of the two systems that Roe has offered. My real point is that it seems likely that concentrated bank ownership is not a superior form of monitoring for companies with particularly difficult agency or informational problems, but rather that bank ownership is a substitute for the market-based monitoring that has been foreclosed by German institutions. If I am correct, then the absence of bank ownership in the U.S. might be explained just as well by the superiority of market-based forms of monitoring as by the U.S. laws and regulations that precluded bank monitoring. If this is so, the answer to the question of what would happen if U.S. regulatory barriers to stock ownership and control by financial institutions were repealed is likely to be "not much."

IS BANK CONTROL A SUBSTITUTE FOR REAL CORPORATE DEMOCRACY?

Another part of the story of why banks play such a different role in Germany may have to do with the role that corporate laws play in allowing shareholder monitoring and voice. In this story, concentrated ownership is a substitute for more vigorous corporate democracy.

German stock corporations generally issue *bearer shares* that conceal the identity of the holder, so that reporting directly to shareholders, and communications among shareholders are impossible. Corporations cannot communicate directly with their shareholders when they do not know who they are. The substitute form of communication is publication of disclosures in a national journal. Nevertheless, mandatory disclosures by firms in Germany, as we have seen, are different in kind and quality from those found in the U.S., and are limited almost entirely to financial information. Proxies cannot be solicited directly, and any communications with shareholders are unregulated. There are no requirements that qualitative or evaluative information be provided to shareholders.[34]

While a shareholder is entitled to information about the company at the annual meeting, this right is useless in soliciting proxies, and is circumscribed by exceptions. As a result, there are no quorum requirements for shareholders meetings in Germany or most European nations. Insurgents, unable to learn the identity of their fellow shareholders from corporate records, are hardly in a position to solicit proxies to contest management's tenure or its proposals. Under such a system, the low levels of attendance by German shareholders at meetings should come as no surprise.

While some American commentators have complained about shareholder apathy in the United States, the level of public shareholder participation in Germany is far lower than in the U.S. There is no proxy solicitation system comparable to the U.S. system. Few individual owners of shares bother to attend shareholders' annual meetings in Germany, even by proxy, except where [when] their shares are deposited with big banks.[35] As a result, these banks cast over 90% of the votes at meetings of widely held corporations, and in most cases hold a majority of the shares present and voting.[36] Because these banks generally hold over three-quarters of all shares present and voting, they have the power to amend articles of incorporation and bylaws.[37] It should hardly be surprising that most corporations have bylaw provisions preventing any one shareholder from voting more than 5% of the company's stock, with an exception for shares voted by banks in their capacity as custodians.[38]

CONCLUSION

Roe's book has provided a rich history of the development of regulation of financial institutions in the United States, and the limits imposed on them as influential stockholders. A similar history of Germany might provide an equal and opposite story—of how financial markets were suppressed for the benefit of big banks. Ultimately, if these banks are viewed as caretaker voters of deposited shares, one has to wonder if their interests as creditors have sometimes outweighed their interest as shareholders. Their monitoring may be effective, but for whose benefit?

---

34. The European Community Directives now require disclosures equivalent to "Management's Discussion and Analysis" in the context of mergers, but these requirements are recent and do not reflect past practices in Europe. Third Council Directive as of 9 October, 1978, 78/855/EEC, Art. 10, reprinted in Commission of the European Communities, Harmonization of Company Law in the European Community: Measures Adopted and Proposed: Situation as at 1 March 1992, (1992).

35. Kallfass, cited above, at 782.
36. Id. Baums, cited above, at 507, puts the number at 82%.
37. Id.
38. Baums, cited above, at 507-08.

CHAPTER 3: SECTION 3.2
Markets

Many different market forces may influence corporate governance to different degrees. For example, the market for corporate control (mergers and acquisitions) is viewed by economists as a mechanism for transferring corporate assets to their highest value use. Put another way, if the current management team is not using corporate assets efficiently, other management teams compete to replace the incumbents and put the assets to better use. The readings in this section focus on aspects of the market for corporate control, with the last two articles emphasizing how the legal environment and financial markets may influence external mechanisms, including the market for corporate control.

In *Takeovers, Management Replacement, and Post-Acquisition Operating Performance: Some Evidence from the 1980s*, James Parrino and Robert Harris report that the most important determinant of superior post-merger operating performance for a sample of 197 U.S. takeovers from the 1980s was whether the target company's management was replaced or retained. When the target CEO was replaced, the post-merger firm's annual cash flow returns outpaced industry standards by 2 to 3%. In contrast, when target top management stayed in place, operating returns did not exceed industry averages. Moreover, the effect of management replacement was even more pronounced in those cases where the industry was consolidating. By contrast, for those takeovers that were followed by significant corporate investment (and thus presumably in growth industries), management replacement did not make a significant difference in post-acquisition performance.

In *The Corporate Restructuring of the 1980s— and Its Import for the 1990s*, Gordon Donaldson argues that the primary accomplishment of restructuring in the '80s was to expose business units once protected by the conglomerate structure and "financial slack" to direct product market competition, thereby forcing increases in focus and efficiency. In the '90s, however (and this article was published in 1994), Donaldson predicted that the shareholder momentum behind such changes was likely to yield to demands by corporate managers and other stakeholders for more diversification and unprofitable growth, and less debt financing.

In *Recent Developments in German Capital Markets and Corporate Governance*, Eric Nowak begins by noting that financial economists continue to point to Germany as a relatively successful model of a bank-centered as opposed to a market-based economy. But few seem to realize that leading up to World War I, German equity markets were among the most highly developed in the world. Although there are now only about 750 companies listed on German stock exchanges, in 1914 there were almost 1200 (compared to only about 600 on the NYSE). Since German reunification in 1990, there have been signs of a possible restoration of the country's equity markets to something like their former prominence. The last 10 years have seen important legal and institutional developments that can be seen as preparing the way for larger and more active German equity markets together with a more shareholder friendly corporate governance system. In particular the 1994 Securities Act, the Corporation Control and Transparency Act passed in 1998, and Fourth Financial Market Promotion Act all contain legal reforms that are essential for well functioning equity markets. Such legal and regulatory changes have helped lay the groundwork for more visible and dramatic milestones, such as the Duestche Telecom IPO in 1996, the opening of the Neuer Market in 1997, and, perhaps most important, the acquisition in 2000 of Mannesmann by Vodafone, the first successful takeover of a German company.

In *Corporate Governance in an Emerging Market: The Case of Israel*, Asher Blass, Yishay Yafeh, and Oved Yosha argue that, despite significant capital-market reforms in the mid-1980s, the Israeli government and banks continue to play an unusually dominant role in Israeli financial markets. Israeli banks operate as merchant banks and, through pyramid structures of ownership, control large segments of manufacturing, construction, insurance, and services. In addition, the banks dominate all facets of the capital market, including underwriting, brokerage, investment advice, and the management of mutual and provident funds. Because of this dominance by the banks, several important mechanisms of corporate governance are missing: there is no effective market for corporate control; institutional investors have little incentive to monitor corporate managers; and those managers in turn have little incentive to improve firm performance and increase shareholder value. To be sure, there has been an impressive wave of IPOs on the Tel Aviv Stock Exchange (TASE) in the 1990s. But those firms' stocks have substantially underperformed the market since going public, and many "higher-quality" Israeli firms have chosen in recent years to list their securities on the NASDAQ and not at home. The main reason the most promising Israeli firms go public in the U.S. is because that is where U.S. and other foreign investors want to buy them; such investors want the assurances that come with the U.S. corporate governance system.

TAKEOVERS, MANAGEMENT REPLACEMENT, AND POST-ACQUISITION OPERATING PERFORMANCE: SOME EVIDENCE FROM THE 1980s

by James D. Parrino, Babson College, and Robert S. Harris, University of Virginia

A cquisition continues to be management's favorite growth strategy, and understanding which acquisition strategies have the highest success rates is useful for managers, corporate advisers, and investors. But how do we know if an acquisition has been successful? And are some acquisition strategies more successful than others?

We know a great deal about how the market values acquisitions upon their announcement. However, the evidence that would allow us to determine whether post-acquisition operating performance gains are actually achieved is inconclusive. We know even less about how various acquisition strategies are linked to post-acquisition operating performance. Although acquisitions come in many different sizes and shapes, most of the research on post-acquisition performance treats acquisitions as homogenous events.

We recently completed a study of almost 200 U.S. acquisitions in the 1980s that attempts to answer two fundamental questions: First, do acquisitions produce the "real business" gains that appear to be anticipated by the stock market at the time of the transaction? The answer is "yes" on average, though not without some disagreement about the appropriate benchmark for evaluating "operating improvement." Second, are the prospects of realizing post-acquisition operating gains better for certain acquisition strategies than for others? In other words, are acquisition gains the result of operating synergies, financial synergies, better management, or some other factors? One popular acquisition theory is that some firms are more valuable under the direction of a new management team. Our study provides support for this theory by showing that when the target management is replaced, acquisitions had significantly better post-acquisition operating performance than when management was retained. Other popular acquisition strategies showed no evidence of significant improvement in post-acquisition operating performance.

EVIDENCE FROM PRIOR STUDIES

Before analyzing the impact of acquisition strategies on post-acquisition performance, let's briefly review what we know from previous research. Evidence on the effects of acquisitions yields mixed signals. On the positive side of the ledger, many studies have documented significant share price gains (on average) at the time of acquisition announcements—with the lion's share, if not indeed *all*, of the wealth gains going to target firm shareholders.[1] These wealth gains are often cited as evidence of the financial market's anticipation of post-acquisition improvements. But despite the notable announcement wealth gains to shareholders, the evidence to support the realization of post-acquisition benefits is less conclusive. Practitioners note the difficulties of managing post-acquisition integration and cite frequent disappointments in their ability to achieve planned synergies.

There are two general approaches for examining post-acquisition performance: share-price analysis and analysis of operating performance. Share-price studies measure the long-term impacts of acquisitions by comparing the combined firms' post-acquisition share price returns to some benchmark return based on beta risk and/or broad market indices. If the future benefits from the acquisition are correctly assessed by the market upon the acquisition announcement, then post-acquisition share price performance should equal (on average) the benchmark return. Empirical research on share prices shows that post-acquisition share price performance is often substandard, suggesting that the anticipated acquisition gains are not accomplished. However, there is little evidence on whether any operational gains materialize and, in cases where they do, how such gains are linked to particular acquisition strategies.[2]

Post-acquisition operating performance is measured from reported financial and accounting data

on the acquiring firm. The advantage of this approach is a performance measure and benchmark that are not directly dependent upon the current market price and therefore reduces the impact of the market's continual re-evaluation of the future—which is likely to include the effect of non-acquisition related events. Given that announcement returns are positive on average, one would expect post-acquisition operating performance to be positive to reflect the upward adjustment in the stock prices of the target and acquiring firms.

While some evidence supports this conjecture, other studies show poor post-acquisition operating performance.[3] Using cash flow operating returns, Healy, Palepu, and Ruback (1992) find that median post-acquisition operating performance is positive (although one-fourth of their sample firms had negative post-acquisition performance).

ANALYZING ACQUISITION STRATEGY

Recognizing that acquisition strategies are not mutually exclusive, we use the term "acquisition class" to encompass acquisitions with similar and identifiable characteristics. Many theories purport to explain the underlying resources available to generate economic value through acquisitions. Most of these theories are based on efficiencies in management, operations, or finance.[4] The strategy literature tends to focus on operational efficiencies, highlighting possible synergistic gains. Much of the finance literature, however, focuses on acquisitions as a disciplinary device for managers in the market for corporate control.

We explore three common acquisition classifications: Management Replacement, Industry Consolidation, and Growth Resource Imbalance.

Management Replacement refers to transactions in which the top manager (CEO) of the target firm changes. In one sense, by definition, an acquisition changes the overall management structure, but

---

1. The empirical evidence on shareholder wealth effects is voluminous. For evidence through the late 1980s see Michael C. Jensen, "The Takeover Controversy: Analysis and Evidence", *Midland Corporate Finance Journal*, (Summer 1996) and the references therein. For more recent findings, see Lance Nail, William Megginson, and Carlos Maquieira, "How Stock-Swap Mergers Affect Shareholder (and Bondholder) Value: More Evidence of the Value of Corporate Focus," *Journal of Applied Corporate Finance*, Vol. 11 No. 2 (Summer 1998).

2. For evidence on post-acquisition share price performance see Franks, Harris and Titman (1991) and Agrawal, Jaffe and Mandelker (1992). In general, existing post-acquisition stock price studies provide no strong evidence to relate acquisition strategies to performance.

3. For studies that provide evidence on post-acquisition operating performance, see Ravenscraft and Scherer (1987), Kaplan & Weisbach (1992), and Healy, Palepu, and Ruback (1992). Possible reasons for the conflicting results include use of different time periods and different post-acquisition performance benchmarks.

4. The strategy literature tends to focus on operational efficiencies (see Walter Goldberg, *Mergers: Motives, Modes and Methods*, Nichols, NY (1983); and Michael Porter, "From Corporate Advantage to Corporate Strategy," *Harvard Business Review*, May-June (1987)). Much of the finance literature focuses on acquisitions as a disciplinary device for managers in the market for corporate control (see Jensen (1986) and Andrei Shleifer and Robert Vishny, "Value Maximization and the Acquisition Process," *Journal of Economic Prospectives*, Vol. 2 No. 1 (Winter 1998)). For a summary of commonly cited acquisition motivations, see Fred Weston, Kwang Chung, and Susan Hoag, *Acquisitions, Restructuring and Corporate Control*, Prentice Hall (1990).

it does not necessarily mean that the target managers themselves will be replaced. If acquisition gains are synergistic, their realization may not require changing a manager. Moreover, in some cases the acquiring firm may have every intention of retaining target management; indeed, the strength of incumbent target management may have been a key factor in motivating the acquisition.

In contrast, the corporate control literature often depicts takeovers as a means of replacing a management team that is not working in shareholder interests.[5] This could result because managers are simply inept, or because they may not have strong enough incentives to work in shareholder interests. As evidence for the latter possibility, some point to the large operating gains that take place in management buyouts where only the incentives change, but not the management team itself.

Our proxy for management replacement is based upon management turnover after the transaction. This measure does not rely on public statements that may often be difficult to interpret in terms of voluntary versus forced management change. As described in the Appendix, our procedures classify a transaction as Management Replacement if the pre-acquisition target CEO is not employed by the post-acquisition firm one year after the acquisition and is under 60 years old at the time of the acquisition. The age cut-off is used as an approximate control for voluntary retirement. While one can observe management turnover, it is often difficult to be sure of the reasons for the change. Managers of target firms may be ready to retire even without an acquisition. At times, managers reap large financial gains and want to move on to other pursuits. In contrast, some target managers are replaced because the acquiring firm decides that new leadership is needed. Since our proxy makes a correction only for retirement (and then only crudely), our management replacement class likely overestimates the number of cases in which target managers left against their own wishes.

The Industry Consolidation class includes transactions where the number of firms in the target industry is shrinking in the years surrounding the acquisition. Typically, these are transactions in industries where scale economies in production are important determinants of success. The scale economies may be driven by lower-cost technology, more efficient industry distribution channels, or other changes in market conditions. It is important to note that operating synergies are not necessarily dependent upon the merged firms being in the same industry. Technological changes, or market structure changes, can create operational efficiencies that are not subject to standard industry classifications.

The common characteristic of these acquisitions is that they typically result in a consolidation of the target industry as assets are redeployed. A typical example in recent times is the consolidation in the retail drug-store industry. HMOs have become a powerful force in the distribution of pharmaceutical drugs through their reimbursement polices. As a result, margins have been squeezed at smaller retail drugstore companies with little negotiating power. The result has been a wave of acquisition activity that has reduced the number of small chain stores.[6]

An example of an industry that was consolidating in the 1980s is the operation of nursing homes. Purchasing economies of scale and centralized administration for the increasingly complex regulatory environment in health care spurred industry consolidation. From 1980 to 1985, the number of companies in this industry (SIC code 8051) declined by more than 10%.[7]

The Growth Resource Imbalance class includes transactions in which the post-acquisition firm's rate of capital expenditures (as a percent of revenues) is higher than that of the combined target and acquirer in the years before the acquisition. This proxy is designed to capture a type of synergy that some have argued may result from combining firms. As the argument goes, acquirers may purchase a company with good growth prospects, but limited financial or managerial capacity to capitalize on potential growth. From the target firm's perspective, the acquisition may provide benefits (such as financial strength or managerial capacity) that are not as readily or efficiently attainable in other ways. The acquiring firm may view the transaction as a way to enter a new business or to invest in underutilized capacity.

As suggested, the common characteristic of these acquisitions is an increased rate of investment after the transaction.[8] A recent example is Walt

---

5. For a review of general issues in corporate governance across a number of countries, see Schleifer and Vishny (1998).

6. For example, in 1997, there was a 5% drop of 190 stores from 3,720 to 3,530. According to Chain Drug Review, April 27, 1998.

7. Based on information obtained from the Compustat Industrial Data Base.

8. Smith and Kim (1994) focus on announcement returns of acquisitions between high cash flow firms and slack-poor, high-growth firms and use a classification scheme similar to our treatment of growth resource imbalance. Their research focuses on how acquisitions can be used to mitigate the underinvestment and free cash flow problems.

Disney Company's acquisition of Infoseek Corporation, an internet service provider and search engine. Disney is expected to continue to invest in internet technology to broaden the distribution channel for its products. For Infoseek, the acquisition brings a parent company with the financial capacity to fund research and development for the forseeable future.

An illustration of a Growth Resource Imbalance transaction from our sample is the 1987 acquisition of Conrac Corporation by Mark IV Industries. Conrac was essentially a single product firm, producing Code-a-phone answering machines. Mark IV, a diversified manufacturer of plastic products and electronic parts, was able to enter and grow the answering machine business through continued investment after the acquisition.

While these three classifications do not describe all acquisition activity, they encompass a large percentage of frequently discussed acquisition theories and motivations. Notice that we do not attempt to make the popular distinction between conglomerate and non-conglomerate acquisitions—a distinction that focuses on the relatedness of the buyer and seller industries as opposed to the motivation for the acquisition. Our classification scheme attempts to capture the *motivation* for the acquisition. For completeness, however, we do measure business overlaps between the merging firms using Standard Industrial Codes (SICs). In so doing, we find that relatedness is not linked to post-acquisition operating performance.[9]

MEASURING OPERATING PERFORMANCE

After an acquisition, there is no longer independent data on two separate firms. Our procedures measure the performance of the entire post-acquisition firm and thus capture operating improvements whether they occur in the original businesses of the target or derive from synergies across businesses.

Developing a post-acquisition performance benchmark from accounting data is difficult because of the many biases that can lead to distortions. As detailed in the Appendix, we measure operating performance using cash flow returns defined as operating cash flow divided by the market value of

assets. These cash flow returns are converted to industry-adjusted cash flow returns (IACFR) by subtracting the median industry performance. IACFR becomes our primary measure of post-acquisition performance. A positive IACFR suggests that the firm is outperforming most of its industry peers.

Our measure of return addresses a number of difficulties that surface in creating a post-acquisition performance benchmark using accounting data. Since operating cash flow is derived before depreciation, amortization, interest, and taxes, it is less subject to distortions introduced by accounting methods. Moreover, using market values of assets avoids changes to equity that result purely from the accounting treatment of the acquisition transaction as opposed to economic performance. For instance, the choice of an acquisition accounting method (purchase or pooling) can produce substantial differences in the accounting treatment of tangible and intangible asset values, and their subsequent write-offs through depreciation and amortization charges.[10]

THE STUDY

We examined 197 transactions in which U.S. public companies merged during the period 1982-1987. The median asset size (book value of debt plus the market value of equity in the year prior to acquisition) of the acquiring companies was $1.0 billion, as compared to $145 million for the target companies. The median ratio of target asset size to acquiring company size was 25% (mean of 47%), which suggests that the transactions were typically a significant economic event for the acquiring company. (See the Appendix for more detail on our sample selection procedures, data sources, and construction of variables.)

Consistent with prior work, the stock market reactions to the acquisition announcements in our sample show investors capitalizing expected acquisition benefits, with essentially all of the gains accruing to target shareholders. For the total sample, target shareholders averaged large announcement gains (21.1%), acquiring firm shareholders earn essentially zero returns, and the combined an-

---

9. For a recent study that finds that relatedness has a positive effect on the combined firms securities upon the acquisition announcement, see Lance Nail, William Megginson, and Carlos Maquieira, "How Stock-Swap Mergers Affect Shareholder (and Bondholder) Value: More Evidence of the Value of Corporate Focus," *Journal of Applied Corporate Finance*, Vol. ll No. 2 (Summer 1998).

10. Comparing cash flow returns to an industry median provides a useful benchmark, but admittedly does not address the specific risk-adjusted return that may be anticipated by the market for each firm. For an alternative measure that may provide a valuable extension to our work, see Sirower and O'Byrne (1998).

TABLE 1	Classification	Percent[a] of Sample
MERGER CLASSIFICATIONS FOR SAMPLE	Management Replacement(MR)	62%
	Industry Consolidation(IC)	15%
	Growth Resource(GR)	40%
	Other	22%

Composition of Management Replacement Observations	Percent of MR observations
Management Replacement only	42%
MR and IC (without GR)	12%
MR and GR (without IC)	41%
MR and IC and GR	5%
Total	100%

Management Replacement(MR)—CEO of target company is no longer employed by the acquiring firm one fiscal year after the merger. If the CEO of the target firm is over 60 years old and the second ranking officer remains with the acquiring firm the observation is not classified as management turnover. In only one case both of the top two officers were over 60 and both were no longer employed one year after the merger. This instance was not classified as MR in the data reported above.
Industry Consolidation(IC)—Number of firms in the target firm's 4-digit SIC drops by more than five percent (exclusive of the target firm acquisition itself), measured from two years before the merger to two years thereafter.
Growth Resource(GR)—The postmerger acquiring firm's ratio of capital expenditures to sales is higher than the ratio for the combined premerger firms, measured using two year average ratios immediately after and before the merger year.
Other—Not classified in one or more of the three categories above.
a. Percentages do not add to 100 due to category overlaps.

nouncement return is 4.9%, which is significantly different from zero.[11]

As shown in Table 1, our acquisition classes encompass the vast majority of the sample; only 22% of the transactions do not fall into at least one of our three acquisition categories. The figures also show that there is overlap among classes with some transactions being placed into more than one category. The largest single grouping is Management Replacement. In 123 of the 197 transactions, representing 62% of our sample, the target CEOs were replaced after the acquisition.[12] The relatively large number of Growth Resource transactions (79, or 40%, of the sample transactions) indicates that, in many cases, the rate of capital expenditures increases after the acquisition. Industry consolidations are less frequent in our data (only 15% of the sample) but still comprise 30 transactions.

The second set of data in Table 1 shows the overlap of management replacement (MR) with the other acquisition classes. As indicated, management was replaced in 70% of the industry consolidation transactions and in 71% of the growth imbalance deals. Thus, the frequency of the other two classes among MR observations mirrors the overall sample proportions. Only a small number of observations qualify for all three classes.

Post-Acquisition Operating Performance

Table 2 shows that post-acquisition operating performance exceeds industry standards for our sample. The sample average post-acquisition industry-adjusted cash flow return (IACFR) was 2.1% (and significantly different from zero).[13] Our results thus suggest that, on average, merged companies show post-acquisition improvement in operating performance.

When we segment the results by acquisition class, we find that the transactions where manage-

11. In an analysis of 41 empirical studies Datta, Pinches and Narayanan (1992) find that the average announcement return for target companies is 22% and gains to bidders are less than one-half percent.

12. This rate is much higher than normal CEO turnover in U.S. firms. In random samples of both acquired and non-acquired firms, top management turnover (including retirement) is between 35 and 40% over a five-year period. The 62% figure in our sample is comparable to the rate of turnover others have found after proxy contests. See W.H. Mikkelson and M.M. Partch, "The Decline of Takeovers and Disciplinary Managerial Turnover," *Journal of Finance*, 46 (1997); J.A. Krug

and W.H. Hagerty, "Postacquisition Turnover among U.S. Top Management Teams: An Analysis of the Effects of Foreign vs. Domestic Acquisitions of U.S. Targets," *Strategic Management Journal*, 46 (1997); and J.H. Mulherin and A.B. Poulsen, "Proxy Contests and Corporate Change: Implications for Shareholder Wealth," *Journal of Financial Economics*, 47 (1998).

13. These results are consistent with Healy *et al.* (1992), who find that post-acquisition cash flow returns exceed the industry by 2.4% for a small sample of 50 observations.

When we compared transactions based on whether target management was replaced or not, the average IACFR for the MR transactions was 2.8% higher than the comparable figure in the cases where target management remains in place.

TABLE 2 POST-MERGER INDUSTRY ADJUSTED CASH FLOW RETURNS (IACFR): AVERAGE ANNUAL RETURNS OVER THE FIVE YEARS AFTER MERGER	Entire Sample	Management Replaced	Industry Consolidation	Growth Resource	Other
Number	197	123	30	79	44
IACFR Mean	2.1%	3.1%	1.7%	1.0%	1.1%
IACFR t-value	3.50***	3.88***	1.06	1.00	1.00

***, **, and * denote significance at the .01, .05, and .10 levels, respectively, based on a two-tailed test.

ment is replaced have positive and statistically significant post-acquisition operating performance. These transactions have an average IACFR of 3.1%. In contrast, transactions in the other acquisition classifications do not have significant positive post-acquisition operating performance. Moreover, when we compared transactions based on whether target management was replaced or not, the average IACFR for the (123) MR transactions was 2.8% higher than the comparable figure in the (74) cases where target management remains in place.[14]

The bottom line from this analysis is that superior post-acquisition operating performance appears to occur when there is a change in the top managers of the acquired firm. When the incumbent manager remains, post-acquisition cash flow returns meet but do not exceed industry standards. The other two acquisition classes do not appear significantly linked to post-acquisition operating returns.

Regression Analysis

Regression analysis provides additional insight into the links between post-acquisition performance and acquisition classes. First, since some observations fall into more than one class, regression analysis allows us to control for multiple effects at the same time. Second, we can control for pre-acquisition operating results to shed light on whether post-acquisition operating results are simply a continued trend of pre-acquisition performance.

We estimated the following cross-sectional regression (following the general methods of Healy, Palepu and Ruback (1992)):

(1) $IACFR = a + b*PIACFR + c*MR + d*IC + e*GR$

IACFR is the annual (five-year average) industry-adjusted cash flow return for a company from the post-acquisition years. PIACFR is the comparable pre-acquisition mean (five-year) formed as a weighted average of returns for the target and acquiring firm that merged. Each of the zero-one dummy variables MR, IC, and GR takes on a value of one (1) if an acquisition falls into that acquisition class. As a result, the slope coefficient (b) captures any correlation in cash flow returns between the pre- and post-acquisition period. The coefficients on the dummy variables (c, d and e) capture differences in post-acquisition performance related to an acquisition class, having controlled for pre-acquisition performance.

Table 3 presents key results. The third regression includes all of our variables. The slope coefficient on pre-acquisition returns is .33 and statistically significant, indicating that pre-acquisition industry-adjusted returns tend to persist over time. The .33 figure suggests, however, that only about a third of any pre-acquisition advantage over the industry is maintained across our sample.[15] Apparently, competitive markets make it likely that firms move toward the industry average over time.

Even controlling for pre-acquisition performance, the regression signals a significant positive association between management replacement and post-acquisition cash flow returns. The coefficient on MR is 2.8% and is significantly different from zero. Coefficients on IC and GR are both negative (though significantly so only in the latter case). Thus, the data in Table 3 support the contention that acquisitions lead to superior post-acquisition operating performance, but only in the case of management replacement transactions. If anything, the other acquisition categories are linked to subpar performance.

---

14. This difference is significantly different from zero (a t-value of 2.47). We did similar comparisons based on the IC classification and on the GR classification. While observations in each of these groupings had lower average IACFR values (compared to the grouping's complement), the differences were not statistically significant.

15. Our sample consists of merged firms only so we do not test the rate of performance erosion for non-merging firms.

TABLE 3

REGRESSION ANALYSIS OF POST-MERGER INDUSTRY ADJUSTED CASH FLOW RETURNS

Regression	Intercept	Pre-merger Return	MR	IC	GR	R-squared
1	0.00%	0.331***	2.40%**			0.08
2	0.90%	0.334***	2.90%**	−1.50%	−2.50%**	0.10

***, **, and * denote significance at the .01, .05, and .10 levels, respectively.

The dependent variable is a firm's average annual industry adjusted cash flow return over the five years after the merger (IACFR). The coefficient entries for MR,IC and GR show the effects of being classified in one of the merger categories. The coefficient on the pre-merger return (five year annual average) indicates that independent of the merger category effects about .33 of a firm's pre-merger industry adjusted performance typically persists after the merger.

Other researchers have analyzed whether or not the degree of relatedness of the buyer and seller industries is linked to post-acquisition performance. Using SIC codes as a proxy for relatedness, we test whether our variable for management replacement remains significant if we control for the relatedness of the two firms as measured by SIC codes. Regression four in Table 4 includes the dummy variable RELATE, which takes on the value of one (1) if the primary businesses of the buyer and seller are in the same two digit SIC code.[16] The results suggest that, for our sample, relatedness, as measured by SIC overlaps, was not a factor in post-acquisition performance. Additionally, when controlling for business overlaps, the impact of replacing the target management remains significant.[17]

Further Analysis of Management Replacement Transactions

We further explored the effects of management replacement to address two issues. First, does management replacement follow substandard pre-acquisition operating results? For our sample the answer is "no." We examined the pre-acquisition industry adjusted cash flow performance of the combining firms, as well as the target and acquirer separately. For the combined pre-acquisition firm, PIACFR is positive for MR transactions and not significantly different from the comparable value when management is not replaced. There are also no significant differences in PIACFR for targets or buyers when MR transactions are compared to the

rest of the sample.[18] In some respects, our evidence contrasts with some findings that management is replaced in response to poor performance. We note, however, that poor past operating performance is not necessarily a precondition for a disciplinary takeover. For instance, incumbent managers may be reluctant to pay out cash flow that is the very result of good economic times for the firm. Replacement might be needed to avoid plowing funds into value-destroying internal investments. Moreover, even if an acquisition is truly synergistic, management change may be necessary to accomplish the new policies to make operating improvements.

Second, do the effects of management replacement differ across our two other acquisition classes? The answer is "yes." Table 4 partitions the management replacement acquisitions based on the other acquisition categories. Comparison of the first and second rows shows that the effect of management replacement is slightly more pronounced when the industry is consolidating than in the sample overall; the IACFR for that group is 3.5%, as compared to 3.1% for all MRs. In contrast, for Growth Resource transactions management replacement does not make a significant difference in post-acquisition performance.[19] The lower IACFR in GR transactions is similar to the negative coefficient in earlier regressions. The final row of Table 4 shows that for the 52 observations that were classified as MR but fell into no other class, IACFR is a significant 4.2%.

In sum, Table 4 shows that management replacement seems to matter both by itself and in

---

16. Using a four-digit SIC code did not materially change the results presented.

17. In a separate paper, we test alternative measures of relatedness. We find that SIC codes may not accurately define whether or not the two firms have common business lines and/or related technologies. We define relatedness based on a review of the publicly available information at the time of the transaction. With this methodology we fine that relatedness is linked to significantly positive post-acquisition performance. The management replacement transactions remain significant and the results and conclusions stated in this paper are unaffected.

18. While our data do not allow strong statistical conclusions, there is weak evidence that buyers in MR transactions may have better pre-acquisition operating results, perhaps suggesting an ability to transfer management expertise.

19. We also estimated regressions allowing for interactions of acquisition classes. For instance, we created a dummy variable that took on the value of one only if the acquisition fell into both the MR and IC classes but not in the GR class. Results of these regressions are consistent with the results presented in the text.

The effect of management replacement is even more pronounced when the industry is consolidating than in the sample overall; the IACFR for that group is 3.5%, as compared to 3.1% for all MRs. In contrast, for Growth Resource transactions management replacement does not make a significant difference in post-acquisition performance.

TABLE 4
POST-MERGER INDUSTRY ADJUSTED CASH FLOW RETURNS (IACFR), SEGMENTED BY MANAGEMENT REPLACEMENT AND OTHER MERGER CLASSES: AVERAGE ANNUAL RETURNS OVER THE FIVE YEARS AFTER MERGER

Observations		Replaced	Management Not Replaced	Management Difference
Full Sample	Mean	3.1%	0.3%	2.8%
	t-value	3.88***	0.38	2.47***
	N	123	74	
Industry Consolidation	Mean	3.5%	-2.60%	6.1%
	t-value	1.94***	-0.81	1.66**
	N	21	9	
Growth Resource	Mean	1.4%	-0.1%	1.5%
	t-value	1.08	-0.10	0.91
	N	56	23	
Management Replacement Only	Mean	4.2%	n a	n a
	t-value	3.21***		
	N	52		

***, **, and * denote significance at the .01, .05, and .10 levels, respectively.

combination with industry consolidation, but it is less important in GR transactions. One interpretation of these results is that GR transactions afford less opportunity for acquisition gains and that replacing managers does not change that picture. In other transactions in which gains are available, realization of such gains is, at least on average, dependent on replacing incumbent target managers. Another possibility is that GR transactions represent high R&D investments with longer-term payoffs that are not captured by our method of measuring operating improvements.

CONCLUSION

Any acquisition classification scheme is subject to flaws, given the complexity of the data, and our classification scheme is not an exception. However, our results clearly show that acquisitions in the 1980s in which the target management was replaced had greater post-acquisition operating success than other acquisitions. Replacing target management appears linked to higher cash flow returns than the industry average.

We also looked at situations in which the target firm is in a consolidating industry. Such instances might present opportunities for synergistic gains but also may involve particularly hard decisions for incumbent managers if they are to choose policies that serve shareholder (versus employee or management) interests. In such consolidating industry situations, target CEO replacement is accompanied by above-average operating performance but management retention is not. Management replacement seems to play less of a role when firms are increasing their rate of capital expenditures. In these cases there is no evidence of superior operating results even when management is replaced.

The results have several interesting implications for acquisition planning in today's environment. For one thing, our findings support the contention of most financial economists that acquisitions play a key role in the overall corporate governance system of monitoring managerial performance and thereby improving corporate efficiency. Moreover, our results also help explain why some acquisition strategies common in the 1980s have if anything accelerated in the '90s. In particular, industry consolidation through merger has continued to proceed in utilities, telecommunications, banking, and several other industries involved in roll-up strategies. Growth resource imbalance transactions, as illustrated by the "strategic" (as opposed to "financial") deals of the 1990s, have been particularly well-represented in the current market for Internet-based technology companies. Our findings also suggest that, particularly in consolidating transactions (where downsizing is likely to be necessary), acquiring management should be wary of its ability to achieve operating gains if it plans to leave incumbent target management in place. While takeover gains depend on many factors, our results suggest that replacing target management is typically necessary to achieve above-average operating performance.

The sample includes 197 transactions during the 1982-1987 period in which both the bidder and target firm were New York or American Stock Exchange listed companies. We eliminated transactions in heavily regulated industries (SIC groups 4000-4999, 6000-6999, and 9000-9999) because of the potentially non-competitive nature of those transactions. We also eliminated observations in which the acquiring firm was private or a non-U.S. company and hence data are unavailable. Our final screen required the availability of financial statement data from the Compustat Research and Industrial files.

Using data from the CRSP daily files, we compute daily abnormal stock returns defined as the return on the stock minus the value weighted return for all firms on the New York and American Stock Exchanges. To estimate an announcement effect for a target firm, these daily abnormal returns are cumulated from 20 days before the first bid by any bidder until 5 days after the final bid. For an acquiring firm, the window used is 20 days before the acquiring firm's first bid until 5 days after the last bid. The combined announcement effect (target plus bidder) is a value-weighted average using equity market values from 20 days before the first bid.

We measure operating performance using cash flow returns defined as operating cash flow divided by the market value of assets.[1] Operating cash flow is defined as: Sales - Cost of Goods Sold - Selling, General and Administrative Expenses + Depreciation and Amortization. Cash flow is calculated for each of ten years including the five years prior to (years -5 to -1) and the five years after the acquisition year (years 1 to 5). The year of the acquisition (year 0) is excluded to eliminate any potential bias from one-time accounting charges such as consulting fees and restructuring charges. To measure pre-acquisition performance, the cash flow returns of the target and acquiring firms are aggregated to create a pro-forma measure of the combined entity, weighted by beginning year asset values. Post-acquisition performance is measured using the cash flow return of the post-acquisition company.

The market value of assets is measured at the beginning of each year and defined as the book value of debt and preferred stock plus the market value of equity. Following Healy, Palepu, and Ruback (1992), the announcement impact on the equity values of both companies is excluded from the asset base in post-acquisition years. Without this adjustment, computed cash flow returns may not reflect operational improvements if the market has already incorporated these into its initial assessment of the acquisition. Dollar-based announcement impacts are estimated by multiplying the percentage combined announcement effect (discussed earlier) by the market value of equity at the beginning of the announcement window.

We then compute for each acquirer an *industry-adjusted* cash flow return (IACFR), which is the operating cash flow return minus the industry cash flow return. The industry return is the median cash flow return for all firms listed in the Compustat Industrial and Research tapes for a four-digit SIC code. Before the acquisition, industry returns are developed by weighting the target and acquiring firms' industry returns by the relative asset values of the two firms at the beginning of each year. In the post-acquisition years, the industry returns are weighted by the average asset values for the two years preceding the acquisition. Our industry adjustment generally follows the work of Healy, Palepu, and Ruback (1992) except that we employ the more commonly used Compustat SIC codes to define industries. Healy *et al.* use broader Value Line industry definitions.

An alternative, broader benchmark is also employed to test the sensitivity of results. A market-adjusted cash flow return is calculated as the raw cash flow return minus a market cash flow return. The market return is the median cash flow return for all firms listed in the Compustat Industrial and Research tapes for all SIC codes represented in the sample.

Each transaction is examined one fiscal year after the acquisition to determine the status of the target management. The names of the top two officers of the target company are retrieved from Section

---

1. Our procedures generally follow Healy, Palepu, and Ruback (1992); see also Anna and Singh (1997). Barber and Lyon (1996) provide a discussion of a range of measures used in past studies of operating performance.

Ten, Part III of the last 10k filing of the target company. The Standard & Poor's Register of Corporations, Directors, and Executives is used to determine if the management of the target company is retained in the year following the acquisition. If the top officer of the target company is no longer employed by the acquiring company, and is less than 60 years old at the time of acquisition, the transaction is classified in the Management Replacement class. In 31 observations, the top officer was no longer employed at the company but was over 60 years old. In these cases, the status of the second ranking officer of the target company is examined. If the second ranking officer is no longer with the new firm and is less than 60 years of age, the transaction is placed in the Management Replacement category.

Industry Consolidation transactions are based on the change in the number of companies Compustat lists in the target firm's four-digit SIC industry. If the number of firms two years before the acquisition is five percent or more larger than the "adjusted" number two years after the acquisition, the transac-tion is classified as Industry Consolidation. The "adjusted" post-acquisition number is simply the number of firms plus one (1) to eliminate the direct consequence of the acquisition itself. Sensitivities were examined using a cutoff threshold of 10% with no material change in the results.

A Growth Resource Imbalance transaction is characterized by an increased investment by the combined firm after the acquisition. We use Compustat data to proxy the rate of investment as the ratio of capital expenditures to revenues. We compare the ratio for the post-acquisition firm (average for the two years after the acquisition) to the combined ratio for the target and acquiring firms (average for the two years preceding the acquisition). The reported results classify any acquisition that has a post-acquisition ratio greater than the pro-forma combined ratio as a Growth Resource Imbalance. We also used a more stringent screen that required the post-acquisition ratio to be at least 1.05 time the pre-acquisition ratio and this led to no material changes in the results.

THE CORPORATE RESTRUCTURING OF THE 1980s—AND ITS IMPORT FOR THE 1990s*

*by Gordon Donaldson,
Harvard Business School*

T he 1980s will be remembered in the annals of corporate America as the decade of confrontation. Managers whose claim to leadership was based on a lifetime of corporate service were under attack from external critics who asserted a widening gap between investor expectations and corporate performance. Charges of incompetence, inefficiency, indifference, wastefulness, and self-dealing were used to arouse a traditionally passive shareholder electorate to vote for new leadership. In the political vernacular of the 1990s—it was time for a change.

To those who had grown up in an era when the professionalization of business management in America had been hailed as a home-grown national treasure and a unique competitive advantage for the second half of the twentieth century, this came as a shock. The drama of a rising tide of corporate takeovers caught the public attention: corporate gladiators fighting to the death before an audience eager for the promised riches of escalating equity values. The business press seized on the excitement of the struggle for personal power and potential wealth to bring corporate affairs into the range of vision of the average citizen far beyond what had ever occurred. Hitherto unfamiliar corporate names and anonymous corporate leaders, obscure individuals suddenly appearing as sinister "raiders," and Wall Street money managers all became part of the weekly news parade of personalities involved in companies under siege.

Unfortunately, media accounts of the restructurings of the '80s have emphasized primarily the human drama of the power struggle—the personalities and the personal wealth won or lost. Even the more thoughtful academic writings, which have focused on the "market for corporate control," have tended to limit their attention to the near-term consequences for shareholder wealth. Largely missing from these analyses has been the corporate perspective: the forces driving the evolution of corporate priorities, the management process, and the operation of the traditional governance system, which continues to run the vast majority of business enterprises.

One thing is very clear. The events of the 1980s were precipitated in large measure by the common perception among investors that many of the business strategies of the 1960s and 1970s had tipped the balance of corporate priorities in favor of career employees, including professional management. As a result, the wealth of the owners was being dissipated, or so it was increasingly alleged. The phrase "management entrenchment" became popular in academic research, even in schools of business administration—a startling reminder of how far we had come from the days when the excellence of American professional management was widely proclaimed as a unique competitive advantage.

An aroused investment community sensed that there could be a payoff in the challenge initiated by a new generation of activists, outside the corporate establishment, and supported by allies on Wall Street and lending institutions looking for exceptional returns at limited risk. An increasing number of traditionally passive fund managers were no longer willing to express discontent simply by selling the stock; they began to speak out. We have seen the results.

*Excerpted and reprinted by permission of Harvard Business School Press from Chapters 1, 2, 9, 10, and 11 of the forthcoming book, *Corporate Restructuring: Managing the Change Process Within* by Gordon Donaldson. Copyright © 1994 by the President and Fellows of Harvard College; all rights reserved. To obtain copies of *Corporate Restructuring*, call 1-800-545-7685, or outside the continental U.S., 617-495-6192.

THE STRUCTURE OF THE 1970s: THE ORIGINS OF INVESTOR DISCONTENT

Why were strategies that appeared to serve these corporations so well in the 1960s and 1970s, and that were generally accepted and even applauded by investors, analysts, and the business press of the time, suddenly so radically wrong for the 1980s? Some observers believe that the answer lies in gross mismanagement by an all-powerful and self-serving group of professional managers acting with the tacit approval of a negligent board of directors.

Certainly self-interest is a part of the motivation of most, if not all, managers, as it is in other walks of life. However, the strategy and actions of large publicly owned corporations cannot be sustained merely to serve the will of incumbent chief executives. They must also serve the self-interest of some or all of the major constituencies that voluntarily cooperate to produce a profitable product or service: employees, unions, suppliers, customers, shareholders, and host communities. Thus, to understand the restructuring of the 1980s we must understand the economic rationale behind the structure of the 1960s and 1970s, which explains the motivations of managements and the interests served and why they prevailed so broadly and so long.

In the late 1960s and most of the '70s, the typical mind-set of top management can be described as follows: an introverted, corporate-centered view of the business mission focused on growth, diversification, and opportunity for the "corporate family." In the corporate rhetoric of that period, reference to the stockholder interest was strangely absent, and there was often even a renunciation of "purely economic" goals. It was a period when the social and legal climate encouraged management to adopt a pluralistic view of their responsibility to the various corporate constituencies. As career employees themselves, it was natural for management to identify with all constituents who were long-term investors in the enterprise and to view shareholders in the same light. "Loyalty" was the key word—commitment to the success of an enterprise within which each constituent found economic and social fulfillment.

But shareholders were increasingly looking beyond the individual corporate entity to find greater investment potential with the help of a new generation of fund managers who were investing in the securities of the market as a whole. New investment opportunity meant that shareholders no longer identified with individual entities but with a broad corporate portfolio. To corporate leadership, stockholders—or those who represented them—were increasingly diversified and mobile—and therefore, by definition, "disloyal"—just at the time when other constituents—notably career jobholders—were increasingly undiversified and immobile. This was significantly affected by, among other things, the two-income family anchored to a single geographic location.

Conflict over Growth, Diversification, and Financial Self-Sufficiency

Financial economists often wonder why *growth* is so central to management thinking. For the career jobholder the answer is obvious. First, growth and market share are central to most product-market strategies, keeping pace at least with the growth rate of primary demand in the industry and demonstrating competitive superiority by gaining share on one's closest rivals. Growth is also the environment that best promotes employment opportunity, improved compensation, and upward mobility. It is a more exciting environment in which to work. Finally, a growth environment is an easier setting in which to manage: more resources, more room to negotiate, easier to mask or excuse mistakes.

For the highly mobile and diversified portfolio manager, by contrast, it is the growth rate of the economy as a whole, or sectors of the economy, that is important, not that of any one company. It is the *quality* of the earnings of the individual company that matters, not quantity. If smaller means a better return on investment, then small is beautiful. If loyalty means holding resources captive to inferior rates of return, then loyalty is a bad word. There is little concern for the growth or even the survival of the individual firm. It is not surprising that the individual chief executive found this to be heresy.

There is a similar divergence of views between management and investors regarding *diversification*. At certain stages of industry and company history, diversification is essential to the preservation of management careers and to corporate survival. When product markets mature and rates of return begin to erode, it is inevitable that the corporation will search for new sources of revenue and growth potential. "Growth" and "stability" are the two words most commonly used to justify diversification. In the late 1960s, James McFarland, chief executive of

In the late 1960s and most of the '70s, the typical mind-set of top management can be described as follows: an introverted, corporate-centered view of the business mission focused on growth, diversification, and opportunity for the "corporate family." In the corporate rhetoric of that period, reference to the stockholder interest was strangely absent...

General Mills, launched an era of aggressive diversification and coined the phrase "The All-Weather Growth Company," a term designed to capture the unqualified commitment of both jobholders and stockholders.

For the jobholder it was an easier sell. One more leg on the corporate stool, as it was sometimes described, made job potential, particularly at upper levels, more secure and exciting. If the corporation was viewed as a portfolio, then growing markets could pick up the slack from mature markets in performance and resource utilization. When one market was down another would, it was hoped, be up. Thus a new base of earnings would ensure the long-term survival of the corporate entity. In keeping with the corporate portfolio concept, many corporate names were changed to a more universal image: Corn Products to CPC International, Household Finance to Household International, Armco Steel to Armco Inc., Sun Oil to the Sun Company.

At a more personal level, a motive for diversification in a company struggling to cope with the problems of corporate old age is weariness and boredom on the part of management. In private conversations, top managers admit to becoming worn down by another round with the same intractable problems. Diversification offers the prospect of new and exciting frontiers. One can only speculate as to how far personal considerations rather than corporate priorities influenced these decisions.

A third central management concern of the time, *financial self-sufficiency*, also pitted jobholder against stockholder. The men leading corporate enterprises in the 1960s and 1970s were the children of the Great Depression who, through their own experience or that of their parents, had learned to be wary of dependence on fickle capital markets and unreliable institutional relationships—to be independent, self-reliant, and self-sufficient both in personal and in corporate life. Post-war managers were thus unwilling to trust the availability of resources critical to the future of the enterprise to an unpredictable place in the queue at the capital-market window, where timing was all-important. Career jobholders particularly benefit from an internal capital market with reserves on which to draw in time of emergency, and are unaware of and unaffected by any financial sacrifice this places on equity investors.

Financial investors, on the other hand—particularly diversified ones—would prefer that the firm be dependent on explicit and regular capital-market approval for major new investment decisions. The risk that a key strategic action might be delayed or aborted by the capital-market process, which looms large to the individual CEO and the individual company, is inconsequential to the diversified portfolio holder.

Thus the central precepts that governed the corporate financial structure of the 1960s and 1970s had a clear, if unconscious, bias in favor of the investors of human capital. In defense of the managements of the time, it is not at all clear that they saw the trade-offs, so convinced were they that the corporate self-interest, and therefore the presumed self-interest of all constituencies, was being served. And, as we shall see later, the signals from the capital market regarding the strategies of the 1970s were, on the whole, supportive of management.

The Social Environment

The political, fiscal, and regulatory environment of the 1960s and 1970s represented a powerful social endorsement of the corporate strategies of the period. Most of the companies included in this study were not only large but were also market leaders. It is an axiom of competition that, as share of market increases, it becomes increasingly difficult to make further inroads on competitors' entrenched positions. Thus the rate of growth of the mature market leader tends to drift down toward the rate of growth of the industry as a whole.

In the U.S., a major factor accelerating this trend after World War II era was the active intervention of the federal government through regulation and antitrust action. It was apparent that, for these companies, further penetration into competitors' market share, particularly by acquisition, could invoke legal action that at best would involve costly delays and at worst abort the intended expansion. As a result, leading companies, particularly in mature industries, turned to unrelated diversification at home and to expansion abroad as the means of maintaining a vigorous and "hassle-free" growth environment within the company.

The pattern of funding for growth and diversification was also strongly influenced by the intended and unintended regulatory and fiscal policies of the federal government. I have already noted management's preference for financial self-sufficiency. In particular this meant the virtual exclusion of the unreliable equity markets as a source of ongoing cash requirements. This was motivated for two primary reasons. The key index of equity performance at the time was earnings per share (EPS); an increase in the number of shares, in advance of the profitable investment of the funds provided, was a sure way to slow the growth of EPS. In contrast, shares issued for the purchase of a newly acquired subsidiary or industry partner brought an immediate and usually fully offsetting increase in earnings.

The second reason to avoid new equity issues for cash was the active involvement of the government through the Securities and Exchange Commission oversight process. Designed to protect unwary investors from abuse by incompetent or unscrupulous corporate managers, it focused an uncomfortable public spotlight on a firm's investment program at a time when it might prefer anonymity. More important, the process imposed a lengthy review process of uncertain duration when timing of an issue was absolutely critical. In contrast, corporate requirements demanded access to the external equity market when the funds were needed and at a price that justified the investment. If the needed equity funds could be obtained internally, even at some delay, the planning process could be more reliable.

Happily for management, the internal equity capital market—that is, retained earnings—was encouraged and justified in shareholders' eyes by the tax policies of the federal government. The fact that most shareholders are in upper-income brackets and that tax rates favor capital gains over dividends leads to a preference for earnings retention and reinvestment over dividend distribution. One can, of course, imagine circumstances where, even with the tax differential, it might be better for shareholders to invest dividends elsewhere than to recommit earnings to perpetuate inferior returns in a weak or declining industry. Management, however, with its accustomed optimism about the latest strategic plan to rejuvenate earnings, would make no such assumption.

Overall, then, society appeared to endorse the investment and funding policies of the 1970s that were also in the corporate self-interest.

The Voice of the Capital Markets

If, as suggested previously, a management preoccupation with growth for growth's sake, unre-lated diversification, and independence from the direct discipline of the capital markets was harming investor interests during the 1970s, why was there no outcry? There were several reasons.

One was the traditional passivity of the public shareholder who, with access to a well-organized capital market, minimized the cost of real or perceived mismanagement by the quick and certain process of selling the stock rather than by the long and highly uncertain process of attempting to change management behavior. Proxy votes and the archaic ritual of the shareholders' meeting had no real power. Similarly, the growing number of potentially influential portfolio managers who were judged by year-to-year performance found selling the stock the only practical way to maximize return or to minimize the cost of investment error. There were no natural champions of the stockholder interest who would or could take on corporate leadership. The financial backing and incentive structure were not yet in place.

In the early days of these companies, there was usually a concentrated block of equity in the hands of the founders or their heirs. So a distinctive and influential equity constituency was represented. As these concentrations dispersed, management began to listen with some care to the professional security analyst and, to a lesser extent, the business press. This was particularly true of industry analysts who had built a reputation for astute interpretation of industry and company trends. Of course, management's natural tendency is to welcome favorable reports and screen out unfavorable ones, but it is hard to ignore persistent criticism from acknowledged industry experts.

But, from the viewpoint of an objective market discipline, there was a potentially fatal flaw inherent in the job analysts were assigned to do. Like individual corporate managers, they had a major long-term investment in intimate knowledge of particular industries and particular companies. A solid relationship with management was an important avenue of information. Their recommendations to buy, sell, or hold related to particular stocks of particular companies, not to portfolios. Their standard of comparison was, like management's, primarily the company's own past performance and its principal industry competitors.

In these respects, most of the companies in this study did well in the 1970s. They showed regular improvement and at least held their own in their

> The basic problem of the '70s was a gradual and, at the time, imperceptible drift in the focus of the management of resources that was eroding equity returns. It was what economists would call the opportunity cost of underutilized resources— mismatched product lines lacking real synergy and critical mass, and organizational and operational slack from which constituencies other than shareholders benefited.

industry. After all, if the number of shares was not growing and total earnings were, however slowly, earnings per share would show a positive upward trend. In a generally buoyant economy, this was to be expected: a rising tide raises all boats. As a result, the firms received their fair share of positive recommendations from industry analysts. A study of analysts' reports and the business press of that time fails to reveal widespread or persistent criticism of general corporate strategy, and certainly no consensus.

The basic problem of the period was one common to most firms: a gradual and, at the time, imperceptible drift in the focus of the management of resources that was eroding equity returns. It was what economists would call the opportunity cost of underutilized resources—mismatched product lines lacking real synergy and critical mass, and organizational and operational slack from which constituencies other than shareholders largely benefited. With hindsight, the trends were strikingly clear; looking forward from the early 1970s, they were not.

THE CORPORATE RESTRUCTURING OF THE 1980s

The 1980s yielded many examples of financial restructuring under the pressure of a direct challenge to the authority of incumbent management. Under threat of a hostile bid for control, the imperative for change is obvious: do what has to be done to retain the confidence of the constituency represented by the challenger. Some of these responses were in the first instance purely defensive; but even if successful in fending off the attackers, they were usually followed by genuine restructuring designed to address lingering problems of concern to one or more constituencies whose support was essential to the long-term viability of the enterprise.

There were three distinct, but related consequences of the changes in strategy and structure widely adopted by corporate America during the 1980s. The first was the rejection of the concept of unrelated product-market diversification, the extreme form of which was the unrestrained conglomerate enterprise. In its place, the new concept was a return to the core competence of the enterprise and the shedding of all corporate activity which did not draw heavily on that core competence. In capital-market jargon, it was a return to "pure plays."

The second consequence of the 1980s was the abandonment of the concept of financial self-sufficiency—of the firm as its own internal capital market,

largely independent of the external (public) debt and equity markets for the funding of new investment. Financial self-sufficiency was a goal pursued not only through product-market diversification but also with conservative debt policy and heavy reliance on retained earnings and accumulated reserves.

The third consequence, not unique to the 1980s, was progress (or lack of it) on the persistent need for renewal of the primary source of long-term earning capacity of the enterprise. Some of the businesses discussed in this study have been locked into mature products, markets, and technologies that have persistently frustrated management's search for a secure basis for long-term growth and profitability. If the core of the enterprise has these characteristics, a return to the core has an ominous ring to it. Long-term and even short-term survival hang on the success of a renewal process, and one is struck by the sharp contrast between the restructuring of those companies in which the core remained healthy (food processing, in the case of General Mills) and those in which it was seriously impaired (steel, in the case of Armco).

As explained earlier, the corporate drive for diversification was widely and uncritically accepted in the late '60s and early '70s. Indeed, it became a central theme of the then current theory of best management practice. For example, the Boston Consulting Group's concept of the corporate product "portfolio"—as represented graphically by a two-by-two matrix of cash generation and use—called for infant market positions to be fed by mature market positions ("cash cows"). But all this was changed in the 1980s. The concept of self-sustaining growth continues to be an essential concept for small privately financed enterprise, but is now out of date for the public corporation.

What changed was the rejection of the idea that the public corporation should be insulated from the discipline of the capital markets that is imposed when the company is required to come to the equity and debt markets on a regular basis for new infusions of long-term investment capital. This discipline is reimposed when the internal capital market is broken up, peripheral business entities are sold or spun off, and the company returns to its traditional or redefined core business. We saw this when General Mills sold off its toy and fashion businesses, among others, and went back to concentrating on its historic strength in consumer foods. We also saw it when Burlington Northern split off its resources business from the railroad and when CPC divested its European corn wet-milling business.

In the process, inefficient market positions were no longer sustained indefinitely by their more successful corporate siblings but were released, either to survive independently in the marketplace or be absorbed by larger, more efficient companies in the same industry. General Mills' Kenner Parker toys division survived quite successfully for a time as an independent company, but was eventually absorbed by Tonka. An important side effect of this disaggregation process for investors was that financial information was also disaggregated and the market got a better insight into the unique financial condition of each company.

During the period when many companies were pursuing their particular conglomerate strategy, the core business was going through a transformation, surrounded and obscured by the cocoon of diversified business segments. Many of these conglomerates looked back on the 1960s and 1970s and concluded that they had "lost their way"—that is, their unique product-market identity. In this sense, the 1980s were a time for rediscovery of that identity, and to the general benefit of the economy.

In addition to the benefit from a more narrowly defined and reenergized product-market mission, the release of excess funds from overcapitalized balance sheets benefited the economy by allowing such funds to seek their most profitable use. The repurchase of stock and increased dividends were the means by which this was accomplished. While the motive in some cases may have been self-preservation—that is, by removing one of the motives for hostile takeovers—the results were nevertheless beneficial in forcing a more aggressive cash management of remaining resources.

The impact of restructuring on the mix of corporate funding between debt and equity was of more questionable benefit. One of the effects of the post-Great Depression swing to deep financial conservatism by many companies, as evidenced by triple-A bond ratings and negligible debt-equity ratios, was to reduce the influence of long-term lenders on the strategic direction of enterprise. Those of us who served on corporate boards (and I have served on several over the past 30 years) when bankers were more frequent fellow board members recall the persistent concerns of a representative of the long-term investor. With the disappearance of a dominant equity investor in the person of the founder or his heirs—as noted in several of the companies in this study—and their replacement by anonymous, transient investment institutions, these boards lost the single-minded investor viewpoint and, perhaps, their defense against unfocused investment.

On the other hand, going from one extreme to the other is hardly the solution. The dramatic run-up of the debt-equity ratio resulting from the substitution of debt for equity as a defensive redistribution of invested capital, which we saw in cases like Martin Marietta, Safeway, and CPC, imposed an unsustainable debt-servicing burden that could be met only in the short term by asset liquidation (or, as in the case of Martin Marietta, in combination with the subsequent issuance of new preferred and common equity). The first order of business was to get the debt burden back down to levels that could be supported by continuing operations. The defensive maneuver of highly leveraged transactions can produce a level of financial risk that no management would tolerate under normal circumstances. In following that path, management is betting on the probability of a subsequent period of sustained cash flow for however many months or years it takes to return debt to normal levels. Meanwhile, myopic or dysfunctional cash management may neglect everything but the most urgent short-term expenditures. As a result, a window of strategic advantage may open to competitors if they choose to act at a moment of weakness.

Overall, however, these consequences of the restructuring of the 1980s were healthy for the economy. In recent years, much has been made of the breakdown of U.S. competitiveness in global markets, attributed, partially at least, to a preoccupation with quarter-to-quarter performance and lack of commitment to long-term investment. This study suggests an alternative explanation to that of simple investment myopia. It posits that by following a strategy of diversification and financial self-sufficiency, the corporate enterprise insulated itself from the discipline of both the product and capital markets and as a result became less sensitive to the competitive demands for long-term survival in any of its individual product-market positions. Competitive weakness in an individual product market, which would not have been tolerated in a stand-alone enterprise dependent on public capital, was often tolerated and sustained by infusions of capital from other, more successful product-market affiliates.

The primary thrust of restructuring in the 1980s was to expose individual product positions to the competitive forces of their own product and capital markets. Inefficient market positions were no longer sustained indefinitely by their more successful corporate siblings but were released, either to survive independently or be absorbed by larger, more efficient companies in the same industry.

On a stand-alone basis the unit would have found a way to succeed, have failed, or been merged with a more successful enterprise.

The primary thrust of restructuring in the 1980s was therefore to expose individual product-market positions to the competitive forces of their own product and capital markets—domestic and foreign—and in the process the fittest would survive and prosper. Viewed as a whole, the restructuring of the 1980s was a necessary adjustment to correct a fundamental divergence between corporate strategy and structure and the environment of the late twentieth-century product and capital markets. The economic pain inflicted arose primarily from the sudden imposition of long-overdue change and the shattered expectations of those who had come to rely on the strategy in place. And, as always happens, some excesses and mistakes occurred in the process.

ISSUES FOR THE 1990S

The actions of 1980s' equity investors in curtailing the scope of corporate investment, shrinking the discretionary reserves, and forcing the return of surplus funds to the direct control of the owners can be read as a vote of "no confidence" in the control exercised by professional management in the past. It is unlikely, however, that this mood of mistrust will survive a return to a healthy economy, or that the strategy and structure which the restructuring of the 1980s has produced will remain intact. After all, professional investors must in the long run place their investable funds in the custody of professional managers—they have no other choice.

In particular, the forces that have constrained investment in the 1980s with respect to diversification and growth will in the longer run be confronted with inherent organizational counterforces that cannot be suppressed indefinitely. I have pointed out that one of the primary errors committed in the 1960s and 1970s was the trend to unrelated diversification of product markets, resulting in excessive fragmentation and in the perpetuation of uneconomic entry-level product-market operations. But we clearly have not seen the end of corporate diversification, or even of completely unrelated diversification.

It is inherent in every self-perpetuating organization that it seeks to maintain a base of earnings capable of sustaining the enterprise in the long term. It is particularly true of businesses that find themselves on the downward slope of a mature

industry in which it is increasingly difficult to maintain an adequate return on investment that they will begin to probe the boundaries of investment and seek new investment opportunities with greater earnings potential.

It is difficult, however, if not impossible, to make a sudden and complete transfer of investment from one earnings base to another. Thus the typical response is to initiate diversification into a new or related product market while continuing with the old. We have seen many such examples in the case histories presented in this book. Like a person crossing a stream on stepping-stones, balance is sustained by maintaining a footing on the last stone before a confident footing is reached on the next. The trouble was that many companies, having successfully diversified into a new and more promising earnings base, never lifted their foot off the last stone. Or, having unsuccessfully probed a new product-market position, proceeded to a third and a fourth stone without conceding mistakes and abandoning the unstable footing.

There is a school of thought which says companies that find themselves in a mature and declining product-market position ought to face up to reality and go out of existence. Uneconomic enterprise ought not to be perpetuated. Liquidation or bankruptcy is the Darwinian solution for economic weakness. It is not surprising, however, that corporations (which by law have unlimited existence) and their career managers continue to explore diversification as an escape into a new and more promising environment. Efforts at diversification will continue, though it is hoped with a more focused and disciplined approach to the range of options that can be successfully exploited.

Related to the instinct for long-term survival is the organizational need for growth. It is interesting how quickly many of the businesses whose initial response to restructuring was a sharp curtailment of expansion soon followed up with a renewed growth strategy. The drive to grow is the most elemental expression of the priorities of the investors of human capital, in contrast to the desire of investors of financial capital for conservation and maximum return on investment. Surges of new investment, particularly for long-term development, inevitably undermine the ROI in the near term. This tension between the priorities of different constituent interests can be expected to persist in the large-scale publicly funded enterprise.

The Propensity to Overcapitalize

One of the consequences of the 1980s restructuring for many companies was a swing from the overcapitalization of the 1970s to undercapitalization: to a deficiency of equity funding and a just-in-time funding policy. As noted, a legitimate complaint of the earlier postwar decades was the tendency of corporations to develop a high degree of financial self-sufficiency, which meant low debt levels and substantial redundancy in asset holdings. Since funding policy is a process of anticipating uncertain future needs, and the determination of appropriate risk levels is a matter of judgment and personal risk preference, there is no scientific answer to the question of the "right" amount of redundancy to build into a financial system.

As a consequence, the tendency is for funding practice to swing, over time, from one extreme to another: from overfunding to underfunding, and back again. In all aspects of financial policy, there is a predisposition to bury one's corporate financial identity in the averages—not to appear at an extreme and thus to attract attention—to conform to the norm. Hence, there is a pendulum-like secular movement in aggregate behavior. The 1980s was a time to move in the direction of undercapitalization, lean asset structure, and excessive debt. The debt was often produced by a defensive disgorgement of excess cash, with debt-equity ratios suddenly multiplied by substituting debt for equity.

We have noted the universal tendency of companies caught in this process to then give priority to cash conservation and accelerated debt reduction. Sensing unusual vulnerability, companies moved quickly to restore normal debt levels. The extended period of recession that marked the end of the 1980s and the beginning of the 1990s has underlined the wisdom of that response for those which had time to recover their solvency. The recession, which has also served as a crash course in survival tactics for a new generation of senior managers, has undoubtedly conditioned investment and funding strategy in this decade.

Therefore, the decade of the 1990s is likely to be marked by a renewed dedication to the minimization of financial risk, the restoration of financial reserves, and perhaps a renewed interest in financial self-sufficiency. The recession of the early 1990s cannot be compared to the Great Depression of the 1930s in its impact on the management psyche, but

chief executives who have been buffeted by a strained banking system and rebellious shareholders are likely to seek the comfort of deeper corporate pockets when the opportunity recurs.

The Competition for Corporate Value-Added

I have recorded how the ultimate purpose of the restructuring of the 1980s was to improve the quality of investment performance and to increase the ROE, both by reducing investment and by increasing the bottom-line return to equity holders. The cases in this book illustrate the substantial gains that were achieved in this respect. I have also noted that for there to be substantial winners—most obviously, shareholders—there had to be substantial losers—some professional managers and employees—as the corporate value-added was transferred from one constituent group to another. This trend has been reinforced by the subsequent recession.

It is impossible to predict whether the circumstances that caused power to flow into the hands of the shareholders—and in particular, into the hands of equity-oriented activists operating in the market for corporate control—will recur in the near future. The public reaction to the era of junk bonds and the tarnished reputation of Wall Street middlemen suggest that time must elapse for memories to fade before there will again be free access to the more extreme forms of financial brinksmanship. The financial institutions that provided a ready market for low-grade bonds and the bridge financing associated with takeovers have undergone a severe reexamination of their loan portfolios and are unlikely to repeat that experience anytime soon. The decade of the 1990s is likely to be an era of relative financial conservatism and caution by both borrowers and lenders.

This lessening of raw financial power in the hands of would-be corporate interventionists must be balanced against the evidence of a new and persistent mood of active oversight by some institutional equity holders which, if it continues, will keep attention focused on the stockholder interest. How successful it will be in sustaining attention to current priorities remains to be seen. Experienced managers have noted, however, that it is difficult in a large organization to maintain a high level of financial discipline continuously over long periods of time, particularly when there is a return to prosperity, profitability, and full employment. Every organizational

The forces that have constrained investment in the 1980s with respect to diversification and growth will in the longer run be confronted with inherent organizational counterforces that cannot be suppressed indefinitely. Efforts at diversification will continue, though it is hoped with a more focused and disciplined approach to the range of options that can be successfully exploited.

system works "better," from a management perspective, when there is a degree of slack in the system.

As Peter Magowan, CEO of Safeway, has said, it is difficult to wring concessions from union negotiators when you are reporting record profits. This is a reminder that prosperity and full employment strengthen the bargaining position of the investors of human capital. A return to full employment is likely to restore some or all of the give-up that occurred when equity holders had the upper hand. Thus, financial efficiency, from an equity holder perspective, is likely to be eroded at some time in the future, though perhaps not to the full extent of the 1960s and 1970s.

In summary, the several elements of financial restructuring in the 1980s were directed at the reordering of corporate priorities, which ebb and flow with the balance of power within the business organization. The interests that produced the priorities of the 1960s and 1970s are still present and will be heard from again.

The Future of Restructuring—Voluntary or Involuntary?

The principal focus of this study has been on the capacity of the modern large-scale, professionally managed business enterprise *voluntarily* to effect major structural change in a timely and efficient manner. The case studies have provided illustrations in which this complex and difficult task has been executed repeatedly and with exceptional skill. Of course, the words "timely" and "efficient" are relative terms and, with the benefit of hindsight, even management itself will conclude it could have been done better. There are also illustrations in which the system broke down and the end result was hostile external intervention. On the whole, however, were this sample assumed to be representative of the whole system, the study demonstrates a powerful instinct in modern enterprises for survival, self-renewal, and independence.

The fundamental question currently under debate concerns the extent to which professional investment managers who now dominate equity ownership should assert more direct control over the formation of strategy and structure in the companies that comprise their portfolios. Were the process of voluntary restructuring as I have defined it to continue, professional investors would refrain from intervention in direct control except as they influence the functioning of the board.

In considering possible changes in the corporate governance process, it is essential that we be informed by the experiences of the past. The observations of this study contribute important insights into the working of the system and how it is likely to perform in the future. One of these concerns the fundamental difference between the capital markets and the product markets on the dimension of efficiency and speed of response. Investors in financial assets, particularly in the United States, have become accustomed to instantaneous and frictionless reinvestment and restructuring of portfolios in response to new information or changed priorities. In contrast, investors in real assets operate in a relatively inefficient product market where a critical resource is the time necessary to effect a change in resource allocation and revenue distribution. As a result, professional investors typically lack the experience, expertise, and particularly the patience needed to manage a major corporate restructuring.

It is obvious that the resource of time is placed in the hands of one chief executive whose unique vision of the future will dominate corporate strategy as long as he or she remains in that position. Past experience suggests that the normal term of office of a new chief executive, barring ill health, obvious mismanagement, or abuse of office, is a minimum of five to ten years, during which the CEO must be allowed wide discretion—the freedom to succeed and the freedom to fail. This reality of the cycles of power in a corporation places severe constraints on the "efficiency" with which adjustment to change occurs, particularly when viewed through the eyes of the capital markets.

If used wisely, the resource of time will serve to confirm the nature of the needed change, to gain the commitment of the top management team, to carefully explore options, and, particularly, to choose the timing of change for maximum benefit or minimum loss. We have noted the time-consuming process of renegoting constituency contracts, a matter uniquely suited to career professional managers capable of delivering on those contracts. In a number of cases this entire process has taken the greater part of a decade to bring to completion, even by leaders totally dedicated to the restructuring mission.

We have observed that it is unusual for a major change in strategy and structure to be initiated and executed by the same administration responsible for the prior strategy. It is more commonly executed by a successor, with or without the intervention of the board. Hence another reason why the voluntary process takes time—the time necessary for incumbent management to recognize the need for change and step aside, or to reach normal retirement. This is the element of the process in which the voluntary system is most vulnerable since, in the absence of a vigilant and assertive board, extended delay may occur.

The advantages we have seen when the voluntary restructuring process works well are highlighted by the experience of companies in which the voluntary system has broken down and hostile external intervention has occurred. The collapse of the time frame for restructuring, which inevitably accompanies hostile intervention, necessarily restricts options, seriously weakens bargaining position, forces action regardless of the conditions of the capital and product markets, exposes the business to competitive vulnerability and excessive financial risk. By definition, restructuring, whether voluntary or involuntary, involves an element of catch-up in a deteriorating condition. However, the convulsive response to sudden external intervention imposes severe penalties that an orderly voluntary process can avoid or minimize.

Critics of voluntary restructuring under the internal governance system as practiced over recent decades will focus primarily on the "excessive" delays in response—some, but not all of which, I have described as inherent in the management of a product-market investment process. One further element of the voluntary process which we have recognized will also be a subject of debate. It is that, on the whole, restructuring voluntarily implemented by incumbent management is more "humane" than restructuring imposed by a new ownership group intent on maximizing equity values as quickly as possible. It is more humane to the extent that a deliberate objective of the restructuring process is to cushion the shock of the necessary changes on career employees, particularly those who are innocent victims of a changing corporate environment. The longer the lead time on change, the greater the opportunity.

Economists will argue that "humanity" has nothing to do with "efficiency" and that the pain inflicted by a sudden realignment of corporate goals is an inevitable consequence of an efficient market system operating in an uncertain environment. The humane treatment of employees is, however, an important element of efficiency in practice, as an essential ingredient of trust between management and long-term contractors of human capital. "Loyalty"—two-way loyalty—is a key building block of management authority.

In summary, it is my view that the evidence of this study clearly supports the desirability of a process of voluntary restructuring as the primary means by which the private enterprise system adapts to change. However, there is a recognized cost to dependence on voluntary response, which is made most apparent when the internal governance system breaks down. Thus the potential for external intervention by capital-market agents is needed as a last resort, the threat of which helps keep management focused on action necessary to preserve its cherished independence.

PROPOSALS FOR IMPROVING BOARD OVERSIGHT

Among the companies included in this study, a significant number showed that the board of directors can play a significant role in precipitating and influencing a necessary restructuring process. This evidence is contrary to a popular impression created by critics of the current corporate governance process that boards of public companies have generally failed to exercise effective oversight on behalf of the interests of the shareholders they are elected to represent. On the other hand, there were also cases in which boards appeared to be entirely passive in the face of mounting evidence of deteriorating performance. Clearly, voluntary restructuring, particularly the board oversight function, does not work perfectly.

Looking to the 1990s, these shortfalls in the governance process cannot be ignored. The future of the internal governance process as we have known it, and of voluntary restructuring, will depend largely on our success in increasing the effectiveness of the board of directors in performing its oversight function.

Of course, no governance system that depends primarily on voluntary response to a perceived need for fundamental restructuring performs to everyone's satisfaction—or even, on some occasions, to anyone's satisfaction. Nevertheless, some individual governance processes have clearly been more responsive,

> In pursuit of a defined corporate mission, the CEO must necessarily gain and maintain the full commitment of *all* constituencies to the common objective, and in the process strike a balance among the competing interests and rewards to each constituency.

timely, and efficient than others. Thus, drawing attention to the unique characteristics of these processes provides an opportunity to make the self-governance system more efficient and less dependent on the threat of external intervention. Alertness to the opportunity for improvement is the responsibility of everyone directly or indirectly involved in the current corporate governance process.

The characteristics of a responsive system are presented as follows:

The Allocation of Accountability

Because of the common practice of vesting in one person the dual responsibilities of chief executive and chairman of the board, the important differences in responsibility and accountability of the two offices become blurred. The chief executive is, by definition, the leader of a coalition of constituencies, the most important of which are the long-term investors of human and financial capital—the primary risk takers. In pursuit of a defined corporate mission, the CEO must necessarily gain and maintain the full commitment of *all* constituencies to the common objective, and in the process strike a balance among the competing interests and rewards to each constituency.

In this regard the CEO, his or her own rhetoric to the contrary notwithstanding, cannot place the interests of one constituency always ahead of the others, particularly the interests of the shareholders. The history of corporate restructuring described in this study documents that this is, in fact, the case. The ebb and flow of priorities between investors of human capital and investors of financial capital is the primary characteristic of change from decade to decade. To use the phraseology of economic theory, the chief executive cannot be expected to place the maximization of shareholders' wealth as the number one priority at all times.

At the same time, the shareholders can be expected to press for that objective and to demand that their elected representatives, the board, do likewise. The events of the 1980s have produced a renewed sensitivity to the shareholder interest. The goal of sustained improvement in the return to investors of financial capital, which the study has documented in demonstrated results, benefits not only shareholders but, to the extent that increased profitability is retained and wisely reinvested, the long-term investors of human capital as well.

Nevertheless, there is an implicit and real tension between the tests of accountability appropriate to the board and to the chief executive.

Recent efforts of some state legislatures to broaden the constituency base of boards of directors to include the interests of "investors" other than the shareholders (by means of "stakeholder statutes") may have the tendency to confuse the essential distinction between the executive and the oversight responsibility. On the one hand, it is prudent to give boards the latitude to accommodate the broader mandate of the chief executive. On the other, the primary responsibility of boards to their unique constituency remains. As Delaware Court Chancellor W.T. Allen has stated,

In most contexts, the director's responsibility runs in the first instance to the corporation as a wealth producing organization. Promotion of the long-term, wealth producing capacity of the enterprise inures ultimately to the benefit of the shareholders as the residual risk bearers of the firm, but it also benefits creditors, employees as a class, and the community generally.

When one draws the distinction between the responsibilities and accountability of the board and the chief executive, the merit of separating the office of chairman and of chief executive becomes more apparent. The call for separation, which has been receiving increasing support as a means of strengthening the oversight capacity of the board, is meeting some response in corporate practice. However, there will be strong resistance from chief executives who see the potential for mischief in divided authority. Nevertheless, the justification for a separation of accountability is clear.

An effective alternative to the preferred separation of office has been the appointment or election of a governance committee chaired by a board member other than the chief executive. Such a committee deals with the key issues of governance as they arise, and its chairman acts as board liaison with the chief executive and therefore as a shadow chairman.

Board Composition

Observation of those boards which have been most effective in influencing the course and timing of restructuring, particularly at the moment of succession to the office of CEO, suggests the need for a rethinking of the sources from which board membership is drawn. As has been noted, timely intervention, when it occurs, is never initiated by the board as a collective body, but rather by an individual board member with a unique voice of authority and the motivation and determination to act. In the individual case, this has been a former CEO, a senior lender, a founder or his descendant, or a respected senior board member.

One of the reasons for the apparent decline in board oversight and justifiable intervention is the homogenization of board membership and the disappearance of recognized "voices of authority" on the board besides the chairman. Inevitably, founding families fade away, senior lenders have been discouraged from participation on the boards of companies to which they lend—on the whole, an unfortunate development—and, for obvious reasons, former CEOs are an uncomfortable presence.

It is a common practice today for boards to be composed of a minority of inside directors and a majority of outside members, the latter drawn from the ranks of senior or chief executives of other companies, from "experts," including academics, and from political constituencies. On such boards the independent voice of authority is likely to be another chief executive who speaks from a base of experience comparable to that of the incumbent CEO—and chairman. However, as a potential voice of dissent on behalf of the stockholder interest, the outside CEO-board member has one fatal flaw. His (or her) primary allegiance is to *his* stockholder group, not to that of the company in question. He therefore has little appetite or incentive to invest precious time and attention in what will likely be an open-ended commitment, not just to start a debate on leadership but to bring it to a meaningful conclusion. There is no payoff equal to the cost.

It is no surprise, therefore, to see that it was a *retired* CEO who took on the huge personal cost and risk of confronting the incumbent chief executive of General Motors. It would be highly beneficial to the boardrooms of corporate America if greater use was made of retired CEOs as board members who would bring their experience, maturity, objectivity, *and discretionary time* to the oversight process. With careful choice, this need not create an adversarial environment and should not be threatening to a self-confident and successful chief executive.

The Function of a Strategic Audit Committee

It is common practice for boards to set aside a day or two each year for a strategic and long-range planning review. It provides an opportunity to react to the strategic plan in place and, especially, to evaluate the input from individual members of the senior management team who are potential successors to the current CEO. As is appropriate, however, the entire agenda is firmly in the control of the chief executive, who is responsible for the success of the plan. Inevitably all the focus—the specific goals and the means and time frame by which they will be achieved—is on the future.

While this exercise is always interesting and even exciting, it involves the board at the wrong end of the strategic review. To put the matter in somewhat oversimplified terms, the future is the prerogative of the incumbent chief executive, the past the unique prerogative of the board. In short, the board must make its judgments primarily on the basis of past performance, not future promise. The only real way for the board to influence the future materially is to replace the chief executive.

To draw an analogy from one of the industries included in this study—railroads—the role of the CEO in the customary strategic planning meeting is like the engineer of a train who invites the board for a brief visit to the cab of the lead engine to view with him the prospect of the elevated landscape that lies ahead. The board has no way of knowing whether the scene is reality or mirage. By definition, future plans always promise improved performance. In terms of strategic review, the proper place for the board is at the rear of the train in the caboose, in the role of brakeman, observing the slope of the terrain already traveled and whether in the longer term it has represented incline or decline. That evidence defines a credible baseline from which to judge the probability of future promise.

As a practical solution, I suggest the formation of a strategic audit committee of the board composed primarily of and chaired by outside board members. This committee would direct the gathering and presentation of the information needed to map past performance upon which informed judgments can be made. Once established, it could convene on, say, a regular three-year cycle or for a specific purpose such as the impending retirement of the CEO.

Such a committee would need modest staff support. In this respect it is important that the process

The future is the prerogative of the incumbent chief executive, the past the unique prerogative of the board. In terms of strategic review, the proper place for the board is at the rear of the train in the caboose, in the role of brakeman, observing the slope of the terrain already traveled and whether in the longer term it has represented incline or decline.

of data gathering be initiated in a period when the data are not seen as threatening to anyone. It should not be necessary, therefore, for the board to have its own analyst, but it could draw on corporate staff for this function. The role of strategic analyst is, however, a sensitive one that could at some time place the individual in the line of crossfire between management and the board.

Board Empowerment: Information

The power of a board to exercise the oversight function so as to influence the course of corporate affairs lies not in legal or organizational authority, but in access to the information that compels attention and demonstrates the need for change. If there is any one agenda item that this study lends to the governance debate more than any other, it is that:

- in cases of major restructuring, voluntary or involuntary, the evidence of serious and persistent erosion of financial performance and structural integrity was clear and unambiguous for anyone with access to the data; and that
- consistent tracking and regular monitoring of this information by the board is essential to potential board intervention in the strategic process, normally at times of management succession.

The case histories presented here illustrate both the nature and content of such information, which offers evidence that the corporation is substantially and persistently underperforming its competition in major respects. It is information that is clear, unambiguous, in the public domain, and therefore accessible to public investors and professional analysts. It appears in a form that uses the common language of management reporting.

As illustrated in the case histories of General Mills, Burlington Resources, and CPC presented in earlier chapters, a consistent and consecutive set of data should provide information on the record of investment and return on investment with respect to *all* of the following over the past decade or so:

(1) the company's own past performance, particularly, the long-term trends in ROE, and the market-to-book and price-earnings ratios;

(2) the performance of the company's principal competitors in the same product market and for the industry as a whole;

(3) the performance of the company's principal competitors for funds in the capital market that lie in a comparable investment-risk category; and

(4) the response of investors to this performance—particularly, shareholder returns relative to industry-average as well as S&P 500 returns—over an extended period of time.

These are the types of data and the extended time frames that should come under regular board surveillance. These are the data that no board, in company with the chief executive, could persistently ignore. For a board of directors, information is at the center of its potential power.

It may seem surprising to those unfamiliar with the internal governance process that this information is not commonly available to board members. The fact is, however, that it is unusual for consistent information to be regularly provided by management because of either benign or deliberate neglect—as much the former as the latter. "Movers and shakers" are typically singularly uninterested in the past; for them, only the future moves and shakes.

But it is also true, of course, that when the past—particularly when viewed in a comparative and competitive context—is an embarrassment, management has little interest in bringing it to anyone's attention, especially that of the board of directors. Instead, management normally prefers to emphasize plans for the future and make presentations regarding goals and implementation of strategies to achieve goals. Such forward planning, after all, is what management is all about. Goals are by definition an optimistic assertion of the upside potential designed to overcome any shortfall of the past.

It is accomplishment, then, not promise, that should be the metric of board oversight. Board time and attention to monitoring executive performance should be focused primarily on the past. Usually it is not, because adequate information is not consistently provided. *The board should insist on, and be directly involved in, determining the content of such information.*

It is curious, moreover, that in all the talk about greater involvement by professional analysts and portfolio managers, no one seems to talk about the weapon of information. If the facts of poor performance are so abundantly clear to these professionals with a stake in ownership, why do they not target individual members of the boards of offending companies and regularly confront them with the information they may be denied on the inside?

The Capacity for Intervention

Board oversight is a meaningless concept unless it includes a willingness to engage a management team in a serious dialogue on strategic direction and, if necessary, to confront an unresponsive CEO and intervene to initiate change. On the other hand, previous chapters have illustrated the fact that if product-market enterprise is to succeed, it needs extended periods of stability and continuity during which the collective investment, broadly defined, can be focused on specific economic objectives. The threat of frequent or random interruption or intervention to countermand established directives erodes morale and weakens commitment and trust. Even new CEOs, who have an implicit mandate for change, usually move cautiously in their early incumbency unless an obvious crisis is evident.

Thus the consideration of fundamental restructuring should be, and normally is, approached with proper care and caution. The essential ingredients for voluntary restructuring are convincing proof of the need for change, opportunities for near-term improvement, consensus among the board members and top management, and a visible mandate for change. Corporate activists in the field of restructuring are understandably impatient with the necessity for these conditions and despair of the time frame involved. Those accustomed to the instantaneous and continuous execution and feedback of the capital-market investment process find the product-market investment environment frustrating. This accounts for much of the persistent tension between corporate management and corporate ownership.

The issue of timing in the success of voluntary restructuring is of key importance and relates to the need for a visible mandate for change. The two most common mandates are the retirement and replacement of a chief executive and a sudden and significant deterioration in performance, particularly following a negative trend. Both pose a threat to the continuity of established initiatives and are widely apparent throughout an organization, putting it on notice of possible change. The window of opportunity is likely to open suddenly and perhaps briefly; unless the initiative is seized, the opportunity may pass. There are always those who have a strong vested interest in the status quo and actively seek to frustrate change. A second opportunity may be long in coming, as when a retiring CEO promotes a successor in his own image.

As we have seen, however, the easy cases are those in which the need for change is suddenly and dramatically apparent. The more difficult—and more common—cases are those in which there is gradual or erratic erosion over extended periods of time and no one increment of decline is an obvious mandate for board intervention into what is normally the prerogative of the chief executive and the management team.

It is therefore necessary to elevate and legitimate a periodic dialogue between the board and the chief executive on long-term strategy and structure, not about the future promise of current plans and action, but about the present and past reality of demonstrated accomplishment. The strategic audit committee can provide a mandated cycle of review that, based on consistent and objective historical evidence, invites a genuine dialogue in which, it is hoped, consensus rather than confrontation can be the outcome.

Self-Renewal and the Need for Governance Reform

Undoubtedly these suggestions for a more responsive internal governance process capable of timely and effective structural evolution will encounter the crossfire of both critics and practitioners of the established system. Critics will be skeptical of the capacity of a "failed system" to engage in a process of self-renewal. Practitioners, specifically chief executives, will be wary of changes that encourage a proactive strategic oversight process led by outside board members and a more independent boardroom relationship.

The prospect for voluntary reform of the governance process depends on the extent to which the experience of the 1980s has had a significant and lasting impact on the corporate board's sense of vulnerability to external intervention in cases of serious structural imbalance. Enough turmoil has been created to make it credible that the traditional independence of governance of the private enterprise could be lost or substantially modified by political, legal, or institutional intervention. If so, managements as well as boards may be ready for self-imposed reform that will preserve the essential managerial discretion. The price of independence is active self-discipline.

At the moment the threat of external intervention has receded. Despite its absence, the restructuring

In cases of major restructuring, the evidence of serious and persistent erosion of financial performance and structural integrity was clear and unambiguous for anyone with access to the data. Consistent tracking and regular monitoring of this information by the board is essential to potential board intervention in the strategic process.

process continues to surface in wave after wave of downsizing as corporations reach for solid footing on which to base the next recovery. Public attention is preoccupied with the more fundamental issues of national deficits, unemployment, and foreign competition. Corporate governance reform is not just on a back burner—it is off the stove. Under the circumstances, the temptation to slip back into old and familiar patterns of governance and oversight will be strong.

Yet if history is any guide, the next period of renewed economic growth will spawn new corporate strategies and structures responsive to the new environment. In time they, too, will outlive their relevance and the old issues of restructuring will reappear, undoubtedly accompanied by a renewed debate over corporate governance. When this happens, it is to be hoped that the real lessons of the 1980s will be remembered.

This experience has provided a vivid reminder that the real discipline on those who wield corporate power, management and its governing boards, derives not from formal legal or organizational structures, but from the forces of the markets in which the business enterprise exists. A firm survives only if it is able to meet the competitive demands of all its principal markets: for its products or services, for capital, and for human resources. The lesson of the 1980s was that in seeking to insulate the firm from the discipline of the capital markets, through financial self-sufficiency, and from the product markets, through diversification, management's sensitivity to the needs of those two critical constituencies had been weakened or temporarily lost. In many cases, the restructuring of the 1980s was a dramatic reversal of that trend.

Reform of the governance process will function best if it does not presume to be a substitute for market discipline. By enhancing the means by which both management and the board are fully informed on the evolving market environment, the corporate governance process will offer the best assurance that enlightened and informed self-interest will produce the appropriate response.

RECENT DEVELOPMENTS IN GERMAN CAPITAL MARKETS AND CORPORATE GOVERNANCE

by Eric Nowak,
Goethe University*

F inancial economists have acquired the habit of classifying all national economies into one of two groups: (1) those with "market-based" corporate finance and governance systems, as exemplified by the U.S. and the U.K.; and (2) those with "bank-centered," or "relationship-based," systems, as represented notably by Japan and Germany. Ten years ago, there was a vigorous debate about the relative merits of the two systems, with many scholars emphasizing the farsightedness of relationship-based systems in contrast to the "myopia" of capital markets. But with the plunge of the Japanese economy in the 1990s, the pendulum began to swing back toward focus on the benefits of capital markets in disciplining corporate managers. More recently, a number of financial economists have proposed that there is a natural course of economic development—one that leads *from* bank-dominated systems, which tend to be effective in earlier stages of industrial development, *to* market-based systems.[1] But the debate continues on, with no resolution in sight.

And none of these proposals (or theoretical "models") offers anything like a perfect fit with the development of German corporate finance and governance. Although economists continue to point to Germany as a relatively successful model of a bank-centered economy, few have mentioned (or showed any awareness of) an intriguing historical reality: In the years leading up to World War I, German equity capital markets were among the most highly developed in the world. Although there are now only about 750 companies listed on German stock exchanges, in 1914 there were almost 1,200 (as compared to only about 600 stocks listed on the New York Stock Exchange).[2] Equally remarkable, between 1905 and 1914, over 300 German companies were taken public in initial public offerings. In short, the prosperous pre-War German economy was supported by vigorous capital market activity and a vibrant "equity culture."

But after World War II, the role of the equity markets in funding corporate growth was largely taken over by the German "universal banks." As one indication, a 1994 study reported that German companies borrow more than $4 (as contrasted with just 85 cents for U.S. companies) for every $1 they raise in capital markets.[3] Nevertheless, in the decade that has passed since German reunification in 1990, there have been some important signs of a possible restoration of the country's equity markets to something like their former prominence. For example, thanks in large part to the opening of the Neuer Markt

---

*The author wishes to acknowledge valuable comments from Don Chew (the editor), Andreas Dische, Olaf Ehrhardt, Matthias Heuser, Christoph Kaserer, Max Koch, Harry Schmidt, and Niko Weber-Henschel. He also thanks Franz-Josef Leven (Deutsches Aktieninstitut) for providing data.

1. Raghuram G. Rajan & Luigi Zingales, "Which Capitalism? Lessons from the East Asian Crisis," *Journal of Applied Corporate Finance* 11 (1998), 40-48.

2. Source: Steffen Eube, *Der Aktienmarkt in Deutschland vor dem Ersten Weltkrieg*, Frankfurt am Main: Knapp, 1998. NYSE figure as reported by William N. Goetzmann, Roger G. Ibbotson & Liang Peng, "A New Historical Database for the NYSE 1815 to 1925: Performance and Predictability," *Journal of Financial Markets* 4 (2001), 1-32.

3. J. Mark Ramseyer, "Explicit Reasons for Implicit Contracts: The Legal Logic to the Japanese Main Bank System," in Masahiko Aoki & Hugh T. Patrick (eds.), *The Japanese Main Bank System: Its Relevance for Developing and Transforming Economies.*, Oxford University Press, 1994.

410 ■ CHAPTER 3: EXTERNAL GOVERNANCE

in 1997, the number of publicly traded German companies increased from just over 600 companies in 1989 to 753 in July 2001—and the total market capitalization of the German stock market has more than tripled (from $392 billion to $1.27 trillion) during that period. But even if it is now the fifth largest in the world,[4] the market cap of the German market seems unimpressive when considered in relation to the size of the German economy. At the end of 2000, the total market cap of German stocks amounted to 67.6% of total German GDP, as compared to 184% in the U.K., 153% in the U.S., and an overall European average of 108%.

In sum, the statistics do not suggest that the German corporate finance and governance system is about to be transformed into a U.S.-style market-based system.[5] But, as discussed in this paper, the last decade has seen important legal and institutional developments that can be seen as preparing the way for larger and more active German equity markets, together with a more "shareholder-friendly" corporate governance system. In particular, the 1994 Securities Act, the Corporation Control and Transparency Act passed in 1998, and the just released Fourth Financial Market Promotion Act and Take-over Act all contain legal reforms that are essential conditions for well-functioning equity markets. Such legal and regulatory changes have helped lay the groundwork for more visible and dramatic milestones, such as the Deutsche Telekom IPO in 1996, the opening of the Neuer Market in 1997, and, perhaps most important, the acquisition in 2000 of Mannesmann by Vodafone, the first successful hostile takeover of a German company.

In this paper, I provide a chronicle of these major events in the context of some of the legal reforms that helped make them possible. But before I begin the story, let's briefly consider some broad-based evidence of progress in improving German corporate governance.

SOME EVIDENCE OF CHANGE

In an article published in this journal in 1998, Jonathan Macey proposed three objective indicators for evaluating the relative effectiveness of national corporate governance systems: (1) the voting rights premium (with large premiums indicating lack of protection for minority shareholders); (2) the number of IPOs; and (3) the frequency of management replacements.[6] In the rest of this section, I discuss why these measures are important, and the extent to which they reflect progress in strengthening German corporate governance.

The first measure of the three measures—the size of the control premium that voting shares have over non-voting shares—can be viewed as a proxy for the extent that the majority owner of a company receives "private benefits" from control that often come at the expense of minority shareholders.[7] The basic idea is that, in economies with limited protection for minority holders, concentrated ownership allows wealth transfers from minority shareholders to a controlling stakeholder.[8] A recent study by Tatiana Nenova shows that this control or voting rights premium differs significantly across countries and legal environments.[9] In civil law countries such as Italy and France (where average voting rights premiums range from 23-36%), the value of control is generally higher than in common law countries like the U.S. or the U.K (where the average premium is less than 5%). Germany, although also a civil law country, is reported to have control premiums in the range of 10-15%.[10]

However, Nenova's study covers only the year 1997, in which the voting rights premium in Germany was unusually low. An examination of the average voting rights premium of all German firms that issued dual-class shares from 1989 to1998 yields further insights.[11] First of all, as shown in Figure 1, the voting rights premium has been highly volatile,

4. The four largest markets in the world are, in order of size, the U.S., U.K., Japan, and France. The data were provided by the Deutsches Aktieninstitut (DAI).

5. R. Schmidt, A. Hackethal and M. Tyrell find that during the period 1980-1998 the German financial system continued to be bank-dominated, the British system market-dominated. See "Disintermediation and the Role of Banks in Europe: An International Comparison," *Journal of Financial Intermediation* 8 (1999), 36-67.

6. Jonathan R. Macey, "Measuring the Effectiveness of Different Corporate Governance Systems," *Journal of Applied Corporate Finance* 10 (1998), 16-25.

7. Luigi Zingales, "The Value of the Voting Right: A Study of the Milan Stock Exchange Experience," *Review of Financial Studies* 1 (1994), 125-148.

8. La Porta, Rafael, Florencio Lopez-de-Silanes, Andrei Shleifer, & Robert Vishny (LLSV), "Investor Protection and Corporate Valuation," *Journal of Finance*, forthcoming.

9. Tatiana Nenova, "The Value of Corporate Votes and Control Benefits: A Cross-country Analysis," *Harvard University Economics Working Paper*, Sep 21, 2000.

10. LLSV show that shareholder protection is weaker in civil law countries like Germany as compared to common law countries like the U.S. or the U.K. In a related paper we show that private benefits in Germany have been extremely high in the past, but this has not necessarily been reflected in the control premium. Olaf Ehrhardt & Eric Nowak, "The Effect of Going Public on German Family-Owned Firms: Governance Changes, Ownership Structure, and Performance," *Journal of Small Business Management*, forthcoming.

11. Data were provided by Stefan Daske & Olaf Ehrhardt, "Der Kurs- und Renditeunterschied von Stamm- und Vorzugsaktien—eine Untersuchung am deutschen Kapitalmarkt," *Humboldt University Working Paper*, 2001.

From 1980 to 1989, there were only 147 IPOs of German companies. The following decade, 1990 to 1999, saw 412 German companies go public. Moreover, the lion's share of these IPOs—almost 300 in number—have come since the opening of the Neuer Markt in 1997.

FIGURE 1
VOTING RIGHTS PREMIUM
IN GERMANY, 1989-1998

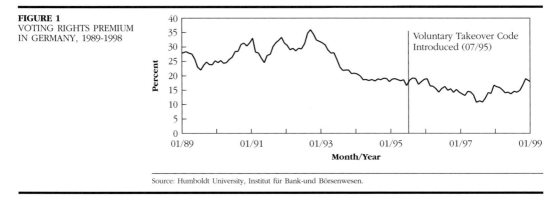

Source: Humboldt University, Institut für Bank-und Börsenwesen.

ranging from a high of 36% in December 1992 to a low of 11% in June 1997. Perhaps most telling, however, is that the voting premium fell dramatically in the second half of the 1990s, and was below 20% at the end of 1998 (the last period for which sufficient data were available to make the calculation). This reduction in the control premium can be attributed to the introduction of the voluntary Takeover Code in July 1995, as well as to other significant changes in corporate governance mechanisms that I discuss later.[12]

The second measure of comparative corporate governance is the "ability and willingness of entrepreneurs to make initial public offerings of stock."[13] Why are IPOs a good indicator of a well-functioning governance system? The short answer is that, in order for companies to go public, minority shareholders must be willing to pay a high enough price (relative to earnings) to induce the controlling shareholders to give up partial ownership. And, to be willing to pay such high price-to-cash flow multiples, minority investors must have a good deal of confidence in both management and the legal system. In the absence of legal protection and a strong governance system, both companies and investors should be reluctant to enter the IPO market—the former because they will not get an appropriate price for the shares, the latter out of a fear of expropriation.[14]

In the past decade, as shown in Figure 2, Germany saw a sharp increase in IPOs, both in terms of number and market capitalization. From

1980 to 1989, there were only 147 IPOs of companies with a combined market value of 50 billion euro. The following decade, 1990 to 1999, saw 412 German companies go public with a market value of 157 billion euro. Moreover, the lion's share of these IPOs—almost 300 in number—have come since the opening of the Neuer Markt in 1997. As in the U.S., the high point of the German IPO wave came in 1999, when 175 German companies went public and raised a total of 35 billion euro in equity capital.

The third measure proposed by Macey is the effectiveness of the corporate governance system in replacing poorly performing managements. There is little empirical evidence on management turnover in Germany prior to 1995, when the Securities Act (discussed below) required listed firms to disclose material news. One exception is a 1994 study of 42 German firms by Steve Kaplan, which reported that poor stock performance and negative earnings increased the likelihood of management turnover.[15] A much more recent study by Julian Franks and Colin Mayer also finds that supervisory and management board turnover are closely related to poor performance, as indicated mainly by accounting earnings losses.[16] But I would argue that, to the extent that German managers have discretionary power to smooth reported earnings, those companies that could not avoid reporting negative earnings were likely to be in *deep* trouble indeed. And given such

---

12. Support for this argument comes from a study by Ulrike Hoffmann-Burchardi, "Corporate Governance Rules and the Value of Control–A Study of German Dual-class Shares," *FMG Discussion Paper* 315 (1999), London School of Economics.

13. Macey (1998), p. 19.

14. Franco Modigliani & Enrico Perotti, "Security versus Bank Finance: The Importance of a Proper Enforcement of Legal Rules," *MIT Working Paper* (2000).

15. Steven N. Kaplan, "Top Executives, Turnover, and Firm Performance in Germany," *Journal of Law, Economics, and Organization,* 10 (1994), 142-159.

16. Julian Franks & Colin Mayer, "Ownership and Control of German Corporations," *Review of Financial Studies* 14 (2001), 943-977.

FIGURE 2
STOCK MARKET
CAPITALIZATION, AND
NUMBERS OF IPOS, IN
GERMANY, 1990-2000

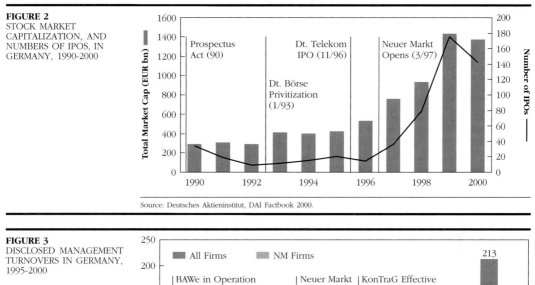

Source: Deutsches Aktieninstitut, DAI Factbook 2000.

FIGURE 3
DISCLOSED MANAGEMENT
TURNOVERS IN GERMANY,
1995-2000

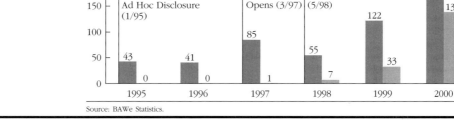

Source: BAWe Statistics.

latitude in accounting methods, the past record of German supervisory boards in replacing managers in response to earnings disappointments may not be evidence of vigilant monitoring.

But this evidence all pertains to the past. How have German boards performed more recently in replacing substandard management? In a very simple procedure, I examined the number of replacements of managing board members disclosed by listed firms since the ad-hoc reporting requirement was enacted in 1995. As can be seen from Figure 3, over the past six years, the number of top management turnovers has almost quintupled from 43 in 1995 to 213 in 2000.

In sum, to the extent we can judge from these three objective measures of effective corporate governance, the German system appears to be improving. Now I consider some of the major legal and institutional developments that have accompanied and helped bring about these changes.

AN OVERVIEW OF DEVELOPMENTS IN THE GERMAN CAPITAL MARKET

Following Columbia law and economics professor John Coffee, I find it useful to discuss changes in corporate governance systems by dividing them into four categories: (1) formal legal and regulatory changes; (2) changes in the structure of share ownership; (3) growth of the stock market; and (4) emergence of a market for corporate control.[17] Although no one would deny that changes in one of these categories could affect the others, there is considerable scholarly disagreement about which of these kinds of changes are more important, or more

17. John C. Coffee, "The Rise of Dispersed Ownership," *Columbia Law School Working Paper* No. 182, 2001.

> In the case of Germany, legal developments have *combined* with changes in stock ownership in ways that are likely to alter the relationship between management and shareholders in many German companies.

WHY LAW MATTERS

When corporate governance mechanisms fail, it may be because the legal system does not provide investors with sufficient protection for capital markets to work properly. In a series of published studies (see footnotes 8 and 18), Rafael La Porta, Florencio Lopez-de-Silanes, Andrei Shleifer, and Robert Vishny (LLSV) have shown that differences among countries in legal codes and enforcement may account for much of the differences in the size and development of their financial markets. According to LLSV, the single most important "law-related" determinant of the strength of a nation's capital markets appears to be whether its legal system originates in a common law tradition (where changes in law are effectively accomplished by judges' rulings) or in the civil law tradition (where changes are made by parliament) that prevails in most of Continental Europe, including Italy, France, Germany, and Scandinavia. Countries with a common law framework also tend to exhibit other signs of an investor-friendly legal system—such as provisions for disciplining negligent directors, adherence to a one-share-one-vote principle, and creditor rights—most of which are generally lacking in civil law countries. LLSV and others (again, see footnote 18) have shown that such indicators of investor protection are associated with dispersed ownership structures, higher dividend payout policies, lower private benefits of control, and less of a tendency to "manage" earnings.

Germany is a civil law country where, until quite recently, shareholder protection has been quite limited. Consistent with LLSV's argument, German capital markets have been relatively undeveloped. On the other hand, the legal protection of creditors has traditionally been strong, leading to the evolution of a relationship-oriented banking system. Thus, in order to develop its capital markets, the German legal system has had to reform itself in ways that afford greater protection for shareholders.

"fundamental," in the sense of *causing* other changes. For example, one school of thought holds that law "matters a lot,"[18] while another argues that law and regulation are likely to be an outgrowth or result of the economic system.[19] What seems clear enough from the case of Germany, however, is that legal developments have *combined* with changes in stock ownership in ways that are likely to alter the relationship between management and shareholders in many German companies. Accordingly, in the pages that follow, I describe in roughly chronological order both major legal changes and the most important capital market and corporate governance developments since the dismantling of the Berlin Wall in 1989.

1989-1992: Reunification, Takeover Attempts, and the Invention of Capital Market Law

As noted earlier, until the Vodaphone acquisition of Mannesmann last year, a German company had never been acquired in a hostile take-over.[20] Nevertheless, there were three widely publicized takeover contests for German firms in the period surrounding German Reunification in 1990. One was the merger bid by Pirelli Spa for Continental AG in 1990; another was the bid first by the Flick brothers and then by Veba AG for the former family-owned Feldmühle Nobel AG in 1988 and 1989; and a third was the somewhat "friendly" takeover of Hoesch AG by Fried. Krupp AG in 1991. To be sure, none of these three attempts was a hostile takeover in the U.S.-U.K. sense since none involved a tender offer made directly to shareholders. But, in retrospect, they appear to signal the beginnings of what economists refer to as the "market for corporate control." In each occasion, there was an unsolicited and unwelcome expression of interest by one management team in a company run by another. What was lacking in each of these cases, however, was support by the target firm's shareholders and a set of legal guidelines for takeovers (not to

---

18. See Mark Roe, "The Political Roots of American Corporate Finance," *Journal of Applied Corporate Finance* 9 (1997), No. 4. For an empirical demonstration of how law affects economic systems, see La Porta, Rafael, Florencio Lopez-de-Silanes, Andrei Shleifer, & Robert Vishny, "Legal Determinants of External Finance," *Journal of Finance* 52 (1997), 1131-1150; LLSV, "Law and Finance," *Journal of Political Economy* 106 (1998), 1113-1155. LLSV, "Investor Protection and Corporate Governance," *Journal of Financial Economics* 58 (2000), 3-28. On the role of the accounting system, see Christian Leuz, Dhananjay Nanda & Peter D. Wysocki, "Investor Protection and Earnings Management," *Wharton School Working Paper,* 2001.

19. See Frank Easterbrook, "International Corporate Differences: Markets or Law?," *Journal of Applied Corporate Finance* 9 (1997), No. 4.

20. But the accumulation of hostile stakes probably acted as a partial substitute for takeovers. See Tim Jenkinson and Alexander Ljungqvist, "The Role of Hostile Stakes in German Corporate Governance," *Journal of Corporate Finance* (2001), forthcoming.

mention acceptance by the German public). But, as I discuss below, the initial main concern of German legislators in reforming German capital markets was not to make things easier for raiders, but to provide guidance for issuers of securities and protection for investors by reforming the laws governing capital markets.

In fact, there was no unified capital market law in Germany until 1990. Prior to that time, rules and regulations governing the issuance and trading of securities were found in various parts of the law—particularly in stock corporation law, securities exchange law, and banking law. The Prospectus Act ("*Verkaufsprospektgesetz*"), which was released in 1990, was the first legal act to have as its primary goal the protection of investors in German capital markets.[21] The act governs the prospectus requirements for all securities that are offered to the public for the first time and have not previously been registered to trade on a German stock exchange. And although the requirements were not as detailed and far-reaching as those imposed by the U.S. SEC, the combination of the requirements with enforceable liability standards was clearly a necessary first step toward increased securities issuance.

The second major legal innovation in 1990 was the First Financial Market Promotion Act ("*Erstes Finanzmarktförderungsgesetz*," or FFG I). FFG I is an aggregation of drafts of several capital market-related laws. In particular, the following changes were important: (1) drafting of investment guidelines; (2) removal of some anachronistic taxes, such as the capital transfer tax and the stock exchange turnover tax; and (3) legal expansion of business opportunities and investment possibilities for trust companies and mutual funds. Like the new disclosure requirements, these three changes were only small steps towards a modern securities market law, but they were steps in the right direction. (And in fairness to German legislators, much of their attention was focused in those days on Reunification and the political and economic restructuring of the East.)

1993-1995: Securities Markets Think Global— Securities Laws Act Local

The following years saw major changes driven by international developments. Competitive pressure from European financial integration and growing demand for equity investments accelerated the modernization and internationalization of the Frankfurt Stock Exchange (which was founded before 1585).[22] On January 1993, the former mutual Frankfurt Stock Exchange was privatized by its members and became part of the newly founded Deutsche Börse AG (DBAG). DBAG, which now operates the largest German stock exchange and markets a cutting-edge electronic trading system (Xetra), later formed the highly successful joint cross-border derivates market Eurex (along with the Swiss Exchange), which have both proved successful in attracting capital from overseas investors.[23]

At the same time the German stock exchange began to modernize, German issuers also went "global" by raising equity in stock markets abroad. The listing of Daimler-Benz AG on the New York Stock Exchange on October 5, 1993, was part of a comprehensive financing strategy designed to end the company's reliance on domestic providers of capital.[24] It made Daimler the first German company to reconcile its financial statements with U.S. GAAP, resulting in a troublesome 1.8-billion-deutschmark adjustment of the company's reported earnings.[25] Despite such obstacles, however, it was clear that Daimler would not be the last German company seeking to list on the NYSE. And so German legislators had to make the capital market more attractive for both issuers and investors by strengthening its legal foundation. This is what the next major piece of German capital market legislation set about to accomplish.

The Second Financial Market Promotion Act ("*Zweites Finanzmarktförderungsgesetz*," or FFG II) can be regarded as the watershed event in the legal development of the German securities market. FFG II overhauled German financial law completely

---

21. Siegfrid Kümpel, in Assmann & Schneider (eds.), *Wertpapierhandelsgesetz*, 1999, § 15 supra note 15.

22. Bernd Baehring, *Börsen-Zeiten. Frankfurt in vier Jahrhunderten zwischen Antwerpen, Wien, New York und Berlin*, Vorstand der Frankfurter Wertpapierbörse (eds.), Frankfurt, 1985.

23. Interestingly, due to political struggles and provincial egoism, the other regional stock exchanges in Germany have not taken comparable steps, the most important of which would be to merge their redundant operating activities.

24. Lee Radebaugh, Günther Gebhardt & Sidney Gray, "Foreign Stock Exchange Listings: A Case Study of Daimler-Benz," *Journal of International Financial Management and Accounting*, Vol 6, No. 2, Autumn 1995.

25. Trevor S. Harris, "Understanding German Financial Statements—Lessons From Daimler-Benz's Listing," *Salomon Brothers United States Equity Research*, 1993.

The listing of Daimler-Benz AG on the New York Stock Exchange on October 5, 1993, was part of a comprehensive financing strategy designed to end the company's reliance on domestic providers of capital. It made Daimler the first German company to reconcile its financial statements with U.S. GAAP.

and established a regulatory apparatus comparable to that in the U.S. Released in July 1994, the act expresses the German Government's commitment to establishing international standards in its own securities laws and to ensuring the enforcement of those standards—all with the ultimate aim of promoting the growth of German financial markets.[26]

The core element of FFG II is the Securities Trading Act ("*Wertpapierhandelsgesetz*," or WpHG), which, among its other innovations, established a Federal Securities Supervisory Office, issued the first formal German prohibition of insider trading, and greatly expanded reporting requirements for German companies. The Securities Trading Act is a "law in action," in the sense that its formulators understood that it would be subjected to interpretation by both the financial and legal communities and continuously updated to reflect new market realities.

The Federal Securities Supervisory Office ("*Bundesaufsichtsamt für den Wertpapierhandel,*" or BAWe), the German equivalent of the SEC, opened in Frankfurt am Main on January 1, 1995.[27] The BAWe is an independent superior federal authority under the German Ministry of Finance whose mission is to ensure the proper functioning of the securities and derivatives markets by pursuing the underlying principles of investor protection, market transparency, and market integrity. Most of the staff of the BAWe have a legal or public administration background, and thus it is not surprising that the agency continues to be criticized as a sluggish, bureaucratic institution. (And Americans, of course, often say the same about the SEC.)

One of the key features of the WpHG, as mentioned above, is its prohibition of insider trading.[28] Prior to release of the act in 1994, there was only a *voluntary* insider code, which was governed by a self-organizing insider commission under private law. Although most stock companies accepted and attempted to adhere to the code, it was never-

theless just a "gentleman's agreement" that did not seem to impose a credible threat upon insiders and clearly failed to measure up to international standards.[29] Under the Securities Trading Act, the BAWe now has the power to investigate all suspected cases of insider trading.[30]

Another major breakthrough for investor protection and capital market transparency was the introduction of "ad-hoc disclosure" ("*Ad-hoc-Publizität*") requirements. Since January 1, 1995, the issuers of securities trading on a German stock exchange have been required to disclose immediately any "private" information that is likely to have a material effect on the profitability, value, or financial condition of the issuer. If irregularities are discovered, proceedings are instituted by the BAWe, which has the power to impose fines of up to deutschmark 3 million.

But this innovation has not been entirely successful. Even though six years have passed since the introduction of the ad-hoc disclosure rules, there is still considerable uncertainty among German companies as to how to meet the legal requirements. Determining which *kinds* of information are likely to be deemed material by the law has proven especially difficult. Given this uncertainty, ad-hoc disclosures have frequently been misused by some issuers as a public relations tool, while many other issuers have not disclosed a single statement.

Nevertheless, ad-hoc corporate disclosures have increased sharply, rising from 991 notifications in 1995 to 5,693 disclosures in 2000. And it seems indisputable that these two aspects of the Securities Act—the ad-hoc disclosure requirements and the insider trading prohibition—have been critically important legal milestones in providing a level of investor protection comparable to that of the U.S. market. Indeed, I would argue that a significant part of the German stock market boom in the second half of the 1990s can be attributed to these two changes alone.

26. Klaus Hopt, *Company Law in the European Union: Harmonization or Subsidiarity*, 1998.

27. Most of the following information as well as the legal text is directly provided by the BAWe through its website www.bawe.de.

28. According to Section 13 of the WpHG, *insiders* are "persons who, due to their function or by any other way, have learned of non-public and price-sensitive information."

29. Joseph Blum, "The Regulation of Insider Trading in Germany: Who's Afraid of Self-Restraint?," *Northwestern Journal of International Law & Business* 7 (1986), No. 3.

30. Issuers of insider securities must, upon request, disclose to the BAWe all documents and details about events and developments on a given inside information. If an insider deal is suspected, the BAWe has to pass the case on to a public prosecutor, who may (or may not) conduct further investigations and criminal prosecution. The BAWe's lack of authority to file criminal actions on its own is often cited as the main cause of the low number of successfully prosecuted insider cases. For example, from 1999 to 2000, the BAWe started 90 investigations, and passed on 35 cases to public prosecutors. The prosecutors, during the same period, turned down 83 cases, settled 14 with a down payment, and convicted only one insider in a case brought to court.

1996-1998: New Markets, New Mergers, New Corporate Governance Rules

The privatization of the former state monopolist Deutsche Telekom in November 1996 set off an unprecedented IPO boom in Germany. The Telekom IPO, which was the largest ever flotation of equity securities in Europe, was offered globally with a dual listing on the NYSE. Because of its symbolic impact and its success with first-time shareholders, many believe the IPO was *the* crucial step in popularizing equity investments in the Germany.[31]

But if there is some truth to this view, the key role of the Deutsche Börse in generating an unforeseen boost in equity investments should not be underestimated. Challenged by pan-European competitors like London Stock Exchange (LSE) and Euronext—the later merger of the Paris, Amsterdam, and Brussels exchanges—the DBAG had to respond with innovative action.

The most remarkable step was its opening of the Neuer Markt Exchange in March 1997. Much like the U.S. NASDAQ, Neuer Markt (NM) is designed to attract listings by technologically innovative, high-growth companies. Because it is organized under private law, DBAG was able to impose stricter admission and disclosure requirements for NM than for the Official Market (*Amtlicher Handel*). And today, what started as a simple replica of the NASDAQ has become Europe's biggest exchange for securities of growth companies, having attained in 2000 a market share of well over 50% in both issuance volume and market capitalization. Although a number of other European growth markets have emerged—for example, the Nouveau Marché (Paris), the Nuovo Mercato (Milan), the SWX New Market (Zürich), the Alternative Investment Market (AIM) in London, and NASDAQ Europe in Brussels (EASDAQ)—they have been significantly less popular with European issuers than the Neuer Markt. As of January 2001, 338 companies were listed on NM with a combined market value of 121 billion euro.

Much of the success of the NM can be attributed to the "Rules and Regulations—Neuer Markt" (RRNM), which are designed to achieve the greatest possible "transparency." The RRNM require the following:

(1) adherence to detailed specifications of the content of the IPO prospectus; (2) publication of annual and quarterly reports in accordance with internationally accepted accounting standards (IAS or U.S. GAAP); (3) issuance of ordinary shares with voting rights only (no dual-class issues); (4) issuance of a minimum of five million euro and placement of at least 20% of shareholders' equity; (5) a mandatory six-month "lock-up" provision for former shareholders and management; and (6) two designated sponsors guaranteeing bid and offer quotes that ensure sufficient liquidity for trading the shares at all time (without affecting the market price). In theory, the legal framework of the RRNM is comparable to and, in some respects, even stricter than the admission requirements and post-listing duties under the SEC regime in the U.S.[32] In practice, however, as I discuss later, the system has been hampered by inconsistent enforcement.

On April 1, 1998, the Third Financial Market Promotion Act ("*Drittes Finanzmarktförderungsgesetz*," or FFG III) went into effect, bringing about further changes in German corporate and securities trading law. Most of these changes were amendments to prior capital market reforms such as the Securities Trading Act and the Prospectus Act. The legal innovations in FFG III were designed primarily (1) to expand the access to capital of small- and medium-sized enterprises by reducing transaction costs incurred in raising equity on the stock market; (2) to broaden the range of futures exchange products for investment companies; (3) to approve pension plan investment funds, which were now allowed to offer new products particularly designed for private pension schemes; and (4) to expand the supply of financing for non-listed companies. These changes made private equity investments much more attractive and helped prepare the way for a massive increase in German venture capital funding in the 90's.[33] (As discussed in the box on the next page, however, a large portion of this capital went to fund MBOs, LBOs, and other forms of private equity rather than high-tech start-ups.)

But if Germany had succeeded in creating the legal and institutional framework for high-tech IPOs, venture capital investments, and private pension plans, was it ready for hostile takeovers? The answer is almost but not quite. The nearest approach

---

31. Rüdiger von Rosen, "Is There an Equity Culture in Germany?" Lecture given at Brandeis University, Waldham, April 26, 1999.

32. Sherman & Sterling, "Does German Capital Markets Law Meet International Standards?," in Deutsche Börse (ed.), *Neuer Markt Report: Gateway to European Capital Markets – Key to Growth*, Frankfurt, 2001, 53-89.

33. Stefan Feindegen, Ulrich Hommel & Mike Wright, "Zum Stand der Beteiligungskapitalfinanzierung in Deutschland," *Finanz Betrieb* 10 (2001).

Much like the U.S. NASDAQ, Neuer Markt (NM) is designed to attract listings by technologically innovative, high-growth companies. What started as a simple replica of the NASDAQ has become Europe's biggest exchange for securities of growth companies, having attained in 2000 a market share of well over 50% in both issuance volume and market capitalization.

THE RISE OF THE GERMAN PRIVATE EQUITY MARKET: THE CASE OF GROHE AG

"To go or not to go public" is a major decision in the corporate lifecycle and, until today, most firms that make up the German middle market (*Mittelstand*) have decided to obtain corporate financing from sources other than the stock market, particularly through long-term loans from their *Hausbank*. But of those that have chosen to go public, an increasing number have decided to go private again. In the late 1990s, many small and medium-sized firms—particularly those operating in mature industries like automotive, textile, or construction—began to feel neglected by stock analysts and the investment funds. At the same time, there were massive inflows into German private equity funds, making going private an attractive alternative to public ownership. As a consequence, a number of German companies have bought back their companies from the minority shareholders or sold their companies (or divisions of them) to private equity firms.

The most prominent example of this going private trend is the recent LBO of Grohe AG, which, with a purchase price equal to $1 billion, is the largest LBO in German history. The fate of Grohe is not only a milestone in the development of going-private transactions, it also illustrates possible disadvantages of being a listed stock from the point of view of small and medium-sized family-owned firms.

Friedrich Grohe AG & Co. KG, which was founded in 1911, manufactures "sanitation" products that range from single faucets to electronic water management systems. In 1991, the company went public both to gain access to funds for growth and to enable the family owners to cash in some of their stakes at attractive terms, given the favorable market situation. At the offering, Friedrich Grohe AG floated 1.3 million non-voting shares to the public, with the Grohe family holding all of the remaining 1.7 million ordinary shares. Members of the Grohe family also took all seats in the supervisory board.

But in the late 1990s, with the stock trading at disappointing levels, the Grohe family decided to delist and go private again. The reasons given were as follows: (1) to eliminate ongoing listing costs; (2) to prevent a possible hostile takeover by a competitor; (3) to achieve greater flexibility from operating as a different legal corporate entity; and (4) the family's unwillingness to raise seasoned equity at the low prices commanded by its stock. As the company's major shareholder, the Grohe family felt their firm belonged to an industry that investors considered "boring and unattractive." As a result, the company found itself in the undesirable position of being unable to attract further capital through seasoned offerings, while at the same time constrained by the "inflexible legal duties" of a listed stock corporation.

The Grohe family together with an advisory bank decided to take the company private by means of a private placement of their share blocks. In April 1999, negotiations started with the pan-European private equity firm BC Partners, who offered to buy 75% of the ordinary shares in a private block trade. In a second stage, the general meeting voted to switch to no-par shares, a stock split, and empowered management to buy back shares. The closing of the deal in July 1999 in turn initiated the buyback of the shares owned by the general public. BC Partners made the minority shareholders an offer to buy back all non-voting stock at 300 euro per share—representing a premium of 30% above the average price over the prior six-month period—provided at least 95% of the shares were tendered. Upon reaching this threshold, BC Partners finished the transaction and Grohe became a private company once more—but with a new investor with (presumably) considerable control. According to the new and old shareholders of Grohe, the LBO was very successful and had the following advantages: (1) flexible legal form; (2) access to financing for future acquisitions; (3) close ties between management and shareholders; (4) flexible tax shields; and (5) a clean exit of the founding family.

---

to a successful hostile acquisition in Germany was the Thyssen-Krupp merger that finally took place in 1998. In March of 1997, Hoesch-Krupp (Krupp) made a bid for Thyssen AG in the form of a tender offer to all Thyssen's shareholders at a 25% premium over the prevailing market price. Not surprisingly, the bid provoked an outbreak of public opposition from politicians, union representatives, the media, and employees, as well as the management of the target company.[34] The leader of the IG Metall union,

---

34. Theodor Baums, "Corporate Governance in Germany—System and Current Developments," *University of Osnabrück, Institut fuer Handels und Wirtschaftsrecht*, Working Paper No. 70 (1998).

FIGURE 4 ■ VENTURE CAPITAL IN GERMANY, 1990-2000

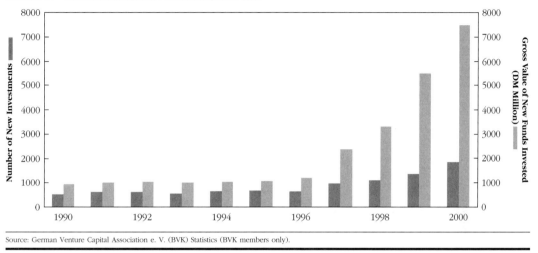

Source: German Venture Capital Association e. V. (BVK) Statistics (BVK members only).

Klaus Zwickel, accused the Krupp management of using "wild west" methods. And Chancellor Helmut Kohl urged both parties to find a "prudent solution" based on careful consideration of their "social responsibility."

After several weeks of public opposition, Krupp finally withdrew its formal takeover bid and then began talks about a friendly merger with Thyssen in September 1997. In January 1998, the supervisory boards of both companies approved the merger plan. And in December 1998, the merger was approved in special stockholders' meetings of both companies. Owing to a quirk in U.S. GAAP rules, the merger had to be accounted for as if Thyssen had acquired Krupp. But the reality was that Krupp's management was finally successful in achieving control of the combined company, as reflected in their dominant positions on the executive board.

Another supposedly friendly merger in 1998 was no less remarkable. The cross-border merger between Daimler Benz and Chrysler Corporation created what can be called the first *truly global* company. Many Americans objected to the fact that the resulting business entity was incorporated in Germany and viewed the merger as "a disaster from day one."[35] But the merger had profound implica-

tions for *German* capital markets simply by virtue of the fact that it "injected a substantial element of U.S.-style shareholder activism into the governance of a major German corporation."[36] In effect, the Daimler-Chrysler merger established a new model of cross-border corporate governance, prompting a new series of legal changes intended to support the globalization of German firms.

One such change was the Raising of Equity Relief Act ("*Kapitalaufnahmeerleichterungsgesetz,*" or KapAEG) which, starting in February 1998, allowed German stock companies to use internationally accepted accounting standards. More precisely, it allows listed group parents to prepare consolidated financial statements that are made in accordance with either IAS or U.S. GAAP. The most obvious beneficiaries of the KapAEG were those German companies like Daimler or Deutsche Telekom with securities listed on U.S. stock exchanges that were *required* to prepare U.S. GAAP financial statements. But other companies benefited, too, including NM companies (which, as noted earlier, are required to use IAS or US GAAP for consolidated financial reporting) and the increasing number of foreign companies now listed on German stock exchanges (and whose financial statements conform

---

35. Robyn Meredith, "The Anti-Iacocca," *Forbes Magazine*, August 20, 2001.

36. Jeffrey N. Gordon, "Pathways to Corporate Convergence? Two Steps on the Road to Shareholder Capitalism in Germany: Deutsche Telekom and DaimlerChrysler," *Columbia Journal of European Law*, Vol. 5, No. 219, Spring 1999.

> The cross-border merger between Daimler Benz and Chrysler Corporation had profound implications for *German* capital markets simply by virtue of the fact that it "injected a substantial element of U.S.-style shareholder activism into the governance of a major German corporation."

to U.S. GAAP). In this sense, the KapAEG further encouraged the internationalization of German equity markets.

Another legal milestone in 1998 was the Corporation Control and Transparency Act (*KonTraG*). A number of cases of supervisory board and audit failure in the effective monitoring of German companies gave rise to calls for legal reform of the corporate governance system.[37] The KonTraG, which became effective in May 1998, provided some gradual but very important changes in German corporate governance law as well as new regulations affecting almost every corporate legal institution. Its primary goals were to improve the monitoring effectiveness of German supervisory boards and corporate disclosure to the investment community.

The KonTraG imposes stronger duties on the management board, which is now required to implement adequate risk management and internal revision systems. Legal liability of the management board in case of dishonest or fraudulent behavior was also tightened. And to provide the management with proper performance-based incentives, the KonTraG simplifies the use of stock option programs through share buybacks and capital increases. To strengthen the role of the supervisory board of quoted stock companies, the law limits the maximum number of supervisory board seats an individual may hold and requires quarterly meetings. To counteract the problem of interlocking shareholdings, the use of voting rights in the election of supervisory board members of affiliated companies is forbidden.

The KonTraG also introduced some amendments to the Stock Corporation Act intended to limit the role of banks in board representation and proxy voting. The law prohibits deviations from the one share-one vote principle by abolishing multiple voting stock and caps on voting rights for listed stock. Further rules were introduced in the KonTraG designed to ensure the independence and quality of the financial audit by excluding auditors with close ties to their clients and by increasing auditor liability from 500,000 to 8 million deutschmark for quoted companies. Also, the auditor must be chosen by the supervisory board, attend the board meetings, and deliver his audit report to every board member in advance.

The KonTraG also laid the groundwork for accounting reform by requiring mandatory segmentation and cash flow statements and for the establishment, in March of 1998, of a privately organized standard-setting body called the German Accounting Standards Committee (GASC). The GASC develops proposals for application of the basic principles of group accounting and represents Germany in meetings of international standard-setting bodies such as the International Accounting Standards Committee (IASC).[38]

In sum, by the end of 1998, the legal and institutional framework for the rapidly developing German capital market was closing in on the goal of meeting international standards for investor protection and corporate governance. However, there were more accomplishments and some setbacks to come.

1999-2001 Monetary Union, Hostile Takeovers at the Gate, and Bursting Bubbles

Whether European Monetary Union is doomed to fail or succeed, the decision to make Frankfurt the location of the European Central Bank ECB constituted another advantage for the German financial marketplace. Contrary to many U.S. economists, I am convinced that the introduction in 1999 of the euro as the single currency for 300 million EU citizens will provide many benefits with respect to investment and finance. By eliminating exchange rate risk and transaction costs, adoption of the euro will also lead to increased cross-border competition by stock exchanges for company listings. And greater integration of the capital market infrastructure in Europe will in turn have a strong impact on financial development in Europe.

What evidence do we have that the promised financial integration is really taking place? Perhaps most convincing is the emergence of a cross-border market for corporate control in Europe. As stated earlier, the recent acquisition of Mannesmann AG, a German telecom company, by Vodafone Airtouch, a U.K. competitor of roughly the same size, was the first successful hostile takeover accomplished by public tender offer in Germany. Vodafone's initial bid for Mannesmann came in November 1999. As in the Krupp-Thyssen

---

37. Prominent cases are Metallgesellschaft, Klöckner-Humboldt-Deutz, Schneider, Balsam-Procedo, Bremer Vulkan. Some of them are described by Ekkehard Wenger & Christoph Kaserer, "The German System of Corporate Governance—A Model Which Should Not Be Imitated," in Black and Moersch (eds.), *Competition and Convergence in Financial Markets*, North-Holland, 1998.

38. Charter of the GASC on www.dasc.de.

case, public opinion in Germany was strongly against the takeover. Chancellor Gerhard Schröder expressed concern about "certain methods that foreign firms undertake to buy German companies" and argued that "hostile takeovers destroy the corporate culture." But this time, in spite of major opposition, the German capital markets—and in particular the shareholders of Mannesmann—were determined to see the deal get done. In February 2000, the supervisory board of Mannesmann agreed to the terms of an agreement whereby the German company would become a part of the Vodafone group. And the agreement received clearance by the European Commission in April 2000.

Besides representing the largest cross-country merger ever, this 200 billion euro transaction marked a giant leap forward in establishing the legitimacy of corporate control contests in Germany. And, in fact, the second successful German hostile takeover has just been announced. On October 15, 2001, the management board of FAG Kugelfischer Georg Schäfer AG said it had reached an agreement regarding a public tender offer from competitor INA-Holding Schaeffler KG. After initial opposition to the bid, FAG finally recommended that shareholders

The recent acquisition of Mannesmann AG, a German telecom company, by Vodafone Airtouch, a U.K. competitor of roughly the same size, was the first successful hostile takeover accomplished by public tender offer in Germany. It appears that hostile takeovers have finally achieved acceptance as a means of improving corporate governance.

accept the offer. Perhaps even more important, in this case the takeover was not accompanied by a public outburst by politicians and the media. Thus it appears that hostile takeovers have finally achieved acceptance as a means of improving corporate governance.

Besides the advent of hostile takeovers, the new Millennium also witnessed the bursting of the high-tech bubble. Since its peak in March 2000, the NEMAX index of all shares on the Neuer Markt has lost more than 80% of its value. As has often happened in the U.S., the collapse of stock prices has led many small shareholders to seek legal remedies for foolish investments; and several German law firms have begun to specialize in U.S.-style securities litigation.[39] A number of scandals involving misleading disclosure practices, insider trading, and, in some cases, outright fraud have put NM companies under pressure from investors, investigators, and the media. In the year 2000 alone, 102 companies were officially criticized for inadequate quarterly reporting. Although DBAG introduced contractual penalties as a sanctioning mechanism, some companies still refuse to publish quarterly reports.[40] As of August 31, 2001, four companies had been delisted because of bankruptcy and seven more due to takeovers, while a growing number of issuers decided to move into less regulated market segments.

What's more, on September 24, 2001, a German court decided for the first time ever in favor of shareholders in a case of fraudulent disclosure. As a consequence, the NM software firm Infomatec is required to repay losses resulting from investor stock purchases following management's misleading statements about future sales. In response to the scandals and related public criticism, the DBAG has announced its intent to tighten disclosure rules. Starting in March 2001, new rules were introduced regulating the disclosure of directors' stock sales and purchases as well as the extension and standardization of quarterly reporting. And in July of 2001, the DBAG announced a delisting rule for NM companies that is comparable to standards set by NASDAQ.

THE FUTURE: GREATER SHAREHOLDER PROTECTION AND MORE M&A

Not surprisingly, the combination of the stock market crash with the aforementioned scandals has shaken investor sentiment in Germany. And the complexity of the Securities Trading Act (as well as its weak enforcement by the BAWe) has also come under harsh criticism. Partly in response to such problems, the German Ministry of Finance released on September 4, 2001 its long-awaited draft proposal for the Fourth Financial Market Promotion Act ("*Viertes Finanzmarktförderungsgesetz*," or FFG IV). This act represents another major initiative toward greater investor protection, transparency, and market integrity.

FFG IV introduces far-reaching amendments to both the Stock Exchange Act and the Securities Trading Act. Market and price manipulation will be punishable as a criminal act, provided the company can be shown to have made intentionally false statements deemed to have a *material* effect on the valuation of its securities.[41] The BAWe will now monitor all investigations of manipulative cases as the central federal institution. (Prior to this, stock exchange monitoring commissions in all German states had legal jurisdiction on market manipulation.)

In response to recent cases of very large share sales by founding shareholders and management members of NM firms, the act also intends to limit the possibility of "cashing out" shortly after IPOs through the enforcement of lock-up provisions. An amendment to the Stock Exchange Act will require complete disclosure of lock-up agreements in the offering prospectuses for all IPOs. Furthermore, the stock exchanges themselves will be able to "lock" the shares on specified accounts, thus making illegal sales impossible. The draft proposal also contains an amendment to the Securities Trading Act requiring Internet disclosure of all stock sales and purchases by both management and supervisory board members (as well as their relatives).

Ad-hoc disclosure requirements will also be clarified. And in response to their frequent abuse as

---

39. Stefan Rützel, " Der Anlegeranwalt—ein Neues Bankenrisiko?," *Die Bank* 9 (2001), 666-669.

40. For example, issuers Porsche AG and Spar AG were even excluded from the MDAX for that reason.

41. The proof of significance or materiality of the price change is now the critical criterion for conviction of a criminal act. And I expect this small amendment to lead to the frequent use of *event studies* in German courtrooms. See Mark L. Mitchell & Jeffrey M. Netter, "The Role of Financial Economics in Securities Fraud Cases: Applications at the Securities and Exchange Commission," *The Business Lawyer*, 1994, 545-590.

a public relations tool, disclosures deemed to be misleading will be punished with fines of up to 1.5 million euros. Of perhaps greatest importance for shareholders, private securities litigation will now be possible for the first time, thus allowing shareholders to sue issuers for untimely, false, or misleading ad-hoc statements as well as for failure to disclose material information. Though it remains to be seen how such shareholder litigation cases will be handled in practice, this development represents a major step in moving the German civil law system toward Anglo-American case law.

In addition to stronger shareholder protection measures, a significant change in German corporate tax law will also stimulate capital market activity. Beginning in 2002, capital gains from the sale of cross-corporate shareholdings will generally be exempted from tax. This change is expected to have a major positive effect on the sale of stakes and hence on the volume of mergers and acquisitions.[42] Mainly in response to this tax change, banks and other financial institutions have already announced their intent to sell off many of their large equity stakes in industrial companies, leading to what has been called the "unbundling of Germany AG."

CONCLUSION

During the last decade, there have been major changes in German capital markets and corporate governance. As a consequence of legal reforms over this period, including the recent Fourth Financial Market Promotion Act, German corporate and capital market law has been elevated to international standards. Indeed, German law now provides investors with assurances that, at least in theory, are comparable to those afforded by the U.S. Securities and Exchange Commission. The remaining challenge for the German regulatory system is thus achieving credible *enforcement* of a now modern and investor-oriented capital market law.

But if recent legal and institutional developments bode well for the emergence of a new German equity culture and a shareholder-friendly governance system, there are obstacles. Perhaps the most formidable are the after-effects of the plunge in Neuer Markt prices (even more devastating than that of the NASDAQ) and the current threat of global recession. Only the future will tell if German companies and investors are committed to pursuing what in the late 1990s appeared to be the beginnings of a revolutionary change in corporate finance and governance.

---

42. Deborah Orr, "Germany Faces the Future," *Forbes Global*, July 23, 2001.

CORPORATE GOVERNANCE IN AN EMERGING MARKET: THE CASE OF ISRAEL

by Asher Blass, Bank of Israel, Yishay Yafeh, Hebrew University, and Oved Yosha, Tel Aviv University

C onsiderable research has been devoted in recent years to the role of corporate governance and the ways in which corporate managers are monitored by their stockholders. Most of this research has focused on countries with the most highly developed economies, notably the U.S., the U.K., Japan, and Germany.[1] But it is also important to develop a better understanding of corporate governance in emerging markets, if only because of their growing share in world markets. In recent years, U.S. and other investors have earmarked increasing amounts of funds for portfolio investment in emerging markets. In 1996, such investment exceeded $90 billion, 15 times what it was in 1990. During this same period, the foreign stock component of U.S. investors' portfolios doubled from 3% to 6%.[2]

The large increase in foreign portfolio investment in emerging markets, among them Israel, has been attributed to several factors. First, returns have been relatively high and are expected by many to remain high, on average. Moreover, portfolio investors can reduce risk by diversifying into emerging markets since their returns are poorly correlated with those of developed markets.[3] Second, there has been a move toward less stringent capital controls in many emerging market countries, thereby facilitating foreign inflows. Third, as a result of stock offerings and new listings, stock exchanges in emerging market countries have grown considerably. Fourth, privatization of large state-owned enterprises (SOEs), often through equity issues, has further increased the supply of shares of well-known companies available to foreign investors on the local exchanges.

In recent years, the Israeli stock market has produced high returns and diversification for foreign investors. Yet, although many capital controls have been lifted, most foreign investment on the Tel Aviv Stock Exchange (TASE) continues to take the form of controlling rather than passive interests.[4] Passive portfolio investments have been relatively small, totaling just $335 million in 1996 and $720 million in 1997.[5] And, whereas foreign portfolio investors in most emerging markets have purchased locally traded shares, foreign portolio investors in Israeli companies have tended to limit their purchases to companies listed *not on the TASE, but on the NASDAQ*—and, to a lesser extent, on the New York Stock Exchange and the British AIM. From 1990 through 1996, over 50 Israeli firms went public on the NASDAQ. As a result, the number of Israeli firms listed on that exchange (in most cases, in the form of non-ADR shares that are not dually listed in New York and in Tel Aviv) is greater than that of any foreign country other than Canada.

---

1. A notable exception is the survey of corporate governance in several dozen countries, classified according to their legal traditions, by Rafael LaPorta, Florencio Lopez-de-Silanes, Andrei Shleifer, and Robert Vishny, "Legal Determinants of External Finance," *Journal of Finance*, Vol. 52 No. 3 (1997), pp. 1131-1150.

2. J. Cochrane, J. Shapiro, and J. Tobin, "Foreign Equities and U.S. Investors," *Stanford Journal of Law, Business, and Finance*, Vol. 2, No. 2 (1996), pp. 241-261; and The World Bank, Global Development Finance, 1997.

3. International Finance Corporation, Emerging Stock Markets Factbook, 1997.

4. In addition, considerable investments have been made in non-listed companies, also usually in the form of controlling interests.

5. Annual Reports of the Supervision of Foreign Currency, Bank of Israel.

To illustrate the dominant corporate governance mechanisms in Israel, we first provide an overview of the evolution of Israeli capital markets in recent years. The government initiated many reforms in the mid-1980s that, by reducing the extent of its intervention in credit and financial markets, allowed companies to raise funds. Nevertheless, the government and the banks continue to dominate financial markets, with banks playing an even greater role than that of their counterparts in bank-dominated European countries.

Second, we identify the largest institutional investors—mutual funds, pension funds, and retirement provident funds—and show that such investors operate in an environment that discourages them from providing adequate monitoring of firm managers.

Third, we analyze ownership patterns of publicly traded firms on the TASE. Our main findings are that ownership concentration in these firms is extremely high, and that banks and affiliated institutional investors hold a substantial portion of the publicly traded shares not held by insiders, while the stakes of the public at large (the "free float") are even lower than those in continental Europe. As a consequence—and notwithstanding a regulatory environment (including disclosure regulations and legal treatment of minority shareholders) similar to that in the U.S.—the takeover market in Israel is very thin.

Fourth and last, we describe the IPO wave of Israeli companies in the U.S., and compare those IPOs (most of them traded on the NASDAQ) to recent IPOs on the TASE. In the TASE IPOs, Israeli banks operate as lenders, underwriters, brokers, investment advisors, and subscribers. And such bank involvement underscores a key theme of this paper—namely, that despite some very important reforms, banks still play an unusually dominant role in Israeli financial markets. Some corporate finance and governance scholars have argued that there are economic efficiencies associated with a bank-based financial system, including the potential for better corporate monitoring (by insiders familiar with the business) and more reliable funding during periods of financial distress. But the Israeli experience mostly suggests that such benefits are outweighed by the disadvantages, including the lack of a takeover market and major conflicts of interest—and that governance problems stemming from such conflicts have only been exacerbated by the extensive market and political power of the Israeli banks.

We argue that the decisions by many Israeli firms to list their securities on the NASDAQ and not at home may be driven, in large part, by their desire to raise funds and establish a liquid market for their shares outside of the realm of influence of the Israeli banks. Listing abroad is likely to serve as a signal of "quality" to foreign investors and customers. Furthermore, it seems plausible that U.S. and other foreign portfolio investors have shied away from the Israeli stock market and chosen Israeli companies listed on the NASDAQ in order to avoid corporate governance problems associated with the TASE.

REFORMS AND NON-REFORMS

Several welcome capital market developments have occurred over the past 12 years. In the past, the government issued special subsidized and illiquid bonds to pension funds and retirement provident funds. (The latter are funds that, much like 401(k) and 403(b) plans in the U.S., are based on employee and employer contributions and enjoy generous tax benefits.) The government decided to stop selling these securities to the provident funds in the mid-1980s as part of a fiscal package aimed at cutting structural budget deficits. The banks were also formerly required to hand over to the government most of the funds they received from depositors—and much of those funds were channeled by the government into subsidized loans to certain favored industries. The banks are no longer required to deposit these funds with the Treasury and are now permitted to extend loans directly to the business sector with little government intervention. In addition, corporations have been allowed to issue bonds without explicit Treasury approval on an issue-by-issue basis (as in the past), many foreign currency restrictions have been removed, and access to capital markets abroad has been eased. In particular, companies are now allowed to raise equity capital on overseas stock exchanges and to borrow from foreign banks.

In the wake of such reforms, the Tel Aviv Stock Exchange has grown significantly (though from a very small initial base), and many Israeli firms, mainly specializing in high-tech, have issued equity in the United States. But if these accomplishments have contributed to a more developed and competitive financial system, the dominant role of banks and government in the economy continues to block the further development of capital markets in Israel. A

Despite some very important reforms, banks still play an unusually dominant role in Israeli financial markets. The dominant role of banks and government in the economy continues to block the further development of capital markets in Israel.

small number of commercial banks—the largest of which are partially owned by the government[6]—still provide virtually all bank credit. The assets of the two largest banks in Israel constitute almost three quarters of the country's total bank assets! And the reforms that reduced the government's role as a financial intermediary ended up actually expanding the banks' role in allocating credit and, hence, the extent of their influence.

Moreover, the banks' role is not limited to commercial operations. They also operate as merchant banks and, through pyramidal structures of ownership, control large segments of manufacturing, construction, insurance, and services. In addition, the banks dominate all facets of the capital market, including underwriting, brokerage, investment advice, and the management of mutual and provident funds. There has been virtually no new entry into commercial banking, whether by foreign banks or other entities.

Israeli capital market assets—primarily government bonds—totaled approximately $110 billion at the end of 1996.[7] Two thirds of these assets are held by institutional investors such as bank-managed provident and mutual funds, pension funds, and life insurance programs. Direct household holdings are minimal. The huge role of government in Israeli capital markets is reflected in the fact that government bonds account for two thirds of all capital market assets (and 96% of all bonds). The large share of government debt in the market is the result of past deficits generated by excessive government spending. Had spending been lower, private savings would have been channeled into corporate bonds and stocks instead of government bonds.

The government's role in the market is further enlarged by its significant ownership stakes in large commercial banks as well as in many other large companies. Among such enterprises are public utilities, defense, infrastructure, and transportation companies, as well as ports, airports, construction authorities, and hospitals. In recent years, the Israeli government has sold at least partial ownership stakes in some state-owned enterprises (SOEs) to the public via the TASE, with the proceeds generally being used to retire government debt. Such sales of

SOEs have two potential effects on the corporate governance system: one fairly immediate and direct, the other longer-range though potentially even more important. SOE sales have immediate governance benefits in the sense that many if not most of the sold enterprises are inherently inefficient. Often, managers owe their position to patronage, not competence, while employment policies result in over-staffing. Some enterprises are never forced to meet financial and budgetary constraints; when faced with losses, they lobby for subsidies or help in keeping competition out.

The longer-range benefits of SOE sales on the Israeli corporate governance system could come from their potential to generate more liquidity on the TASE. To the extent they succeed in attracting broader participation by both local and foreign investors, such sales could end up creating a larger constituency for reform of Israeli corporate governance. But, since the pace of privatization has until very recently been quite slow, this prospect is as yet largely unrealized.

In order to reduce the banks' involvement in capital markets, a number of mild reforms have been proposed by several recent government-appointed blue ribbon committees, although few of their recommendations have been implemented. One reform proposes reductions in bank holdings of large equity blocks in non-financial firms. On the one hand, as mentioned earlier, concentrated bank holdings could have the advantages of better monitoring of performance by insiders, a higher probability of distressed firms receiving financial assistance, and perhaps more informed underwriting.[8] But such large bank holdings, in combination with the banks' range of activities and political and market power, create conflicts of interest that could lead to expropriation of minority stockholders and widespread failure to maximize value.

For example, a bank's fund-management subsidiary might purchase shares of a company, part of whose equity is owned by the parent bank, even if it were not in the best interest of the funds that it manages. This is especially likely to happen in a public offering of stock if purchases made by the investment funds are likely to increase the price of

---

6. The government became the owner of most of the banking system following the 1983 stock market crash. For the most part, it has not interfered with bank operations (except for the appointment of senior managers and directors and in some debt restructuring plans), and is now in the process of privatizing the banks. See A. Blass and R. Grossman, "Financial Fraud and Banking Stability? The Israel

Crisis of 1983 and Trial of 1990," *International Review of Law and Economics*, Vol. 16, No. 4 (1996), pp. 461-472.
7. The figure does not include foreign debt and government-owned shares.
8. For evidence of this, see H. Ber, "Money Markets and Corporate Governance," Ph.D. thesis, Hebrew University, 1997.

the public offering. The bank in question will have an incentive to use investors' money to support a higher offering price for the shares that it owns, even if shares of other corporations represent better investments. Banks can also use their fund subsidiaries to strengthen their effective control of industrial companies by having them buy additional shares in the secondary market, even though such purchases may not be in the best interests of the funds' investors.[9]

Banks' credit operations can also, in principle, lead to conflicts of interest with their underwriting, fund-management, and investment-advisory roles. For example, a bank concerned that a company to which it loaned funds was about to default might persuade the company to issue stock through its underwriting subsidiary. Moreover, the bank would know that its fund-management subsidiary would purchase shares on behalf of the funds that it manages. The bank would thereby effectively transfer the credit risk associated with a bad loan away from its commercial banking department to investors in its fund-management subsidiaries. Nevertheless, a recent study concludes that banks in Israel underwrite companies with above average post-IPO accounting performance, thus suggesting that there is an informational advantage associated with bank-affiliated underwriting.[10] The study also finds, however, that the benefits from these issues do not accrue to investors, but to the banks who tend to overprice these issues, causing subscribers to realize relatively large capital losses.

Another distortion related to credit operations is the tendency for banks to extend credit on preferred terms to customers who accept its investment advice and purchase shares of bank-affiliated mutual funds or bank-underwritten IPOs, thereby generating additional fees for its affiliates.[11] The temptation to make such biased lending decisions is enlarged by the fact that Israeli banks also act as brokers and investment advisers to most households and firms.

Finally, and further embedding such conflicts of interest within the system, the Israeli combination of universal banking, extensive ownership of firms, and market concentration gives bank managers and directors substantial political influence—influence that the bankers have not been reluctant to use to block competitive reforms.

THE INSTITUTIONAL INVESTORS: PROVIDENT, MUTUAL, AND PENSION FUNDS

The provident funds are by far the largest institutional group, and investments through the funds have in the past accounted for approximately 30% to 40% of overall household savings. These funds are long-term saving instruments, favored with considerable tax benefits, that can be redeemed after a period of 15 years. Most (about 95%) of the funds are managed by bank-owned subsidiaries, with the three largest banks controlling about 75% of this market.[12] Commission income from provident funds constituted about 4% of total bank revenue in 1995, and profits from fund management represent a large share of overall profits.

Provident funds are organized as defined contribution (as opposed to defined benefit) plans so that the proceeds received upon retirement depend on fund performance. The funds hold few corporate bonds, stocks, and foreign securities, and invest mostly in illiquid deposits and government bonds (Figure 1).

In recent years, however, the share of government bonds in provident funds holdings has declined. As mentioned earlier, in the past most fund holdings consisted of illiquid special-issue government bonds bearing above-market rates of interest. The government stopped issuing those bonds to the provident funds in the mid-1980s, and subsequently changed the investment guidelines so that fund managers could invest greater portions of their holdings in non-governmental financial assets. As a result, new inflows, as well as the proceeds from maturing bonds, were invested in negotiable (though still mostly government) bonds and stocks, as well as in bank deposits. This shift in provident fund holdings provided much of the impetus for the wave of Israeli IPOs in the 1990s.

9. While investment funds in Israel are prohibited from investing in the shares of the parent bank in Israel, the potential for other distortions related to purchasers of subsidiaries and controlled affiliates is generally unfettered. Empirical evidence can be found in A. Blass, "Performance and Market Structure of Provident Funds: 1987-1994," *The Economic Quarterly*, Vol. 43, No 2 (1996), pp. 260-279; and in H. Ber, Y. Yafeh, and O. Yosha, "Conflict of Interest in Universal Banking: Evidence from the Post-issue Performance of IPO Firms," Tel Aviv University Discussion Paper No. 97-18 (1997).

10. Ber, Yafeh, and Yosha (1997), cited above.

11. Instances of such abuse are well-documented. For example, according to a report issued by the Bank of Israel (see Supervisor of Banks Reports, Bank of Israel), many of the largest commercial banks provided high-percentage margin loans to clients in the early l990s on condition that they invest the proceeds in bank-managed mutual funds.

12. Blass (1996), cited above.

Israeli banks operate as merchant banks and, through pyramid structures of ownership, control large segments of manufacturing, construction, insurance, and services. In addition, the banks dominate all facets of the capital market, including underwriting, brokerage, investment advice, and the management of mutual and provident funds.

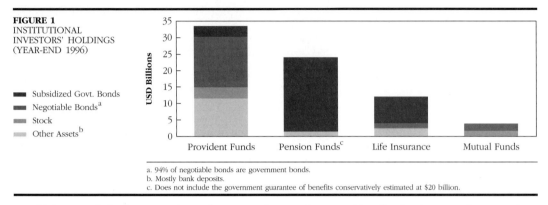

FIGURE 1
INSTITUTIONAL
INVESTORS' HOLDINGS
(YEAR-END 1996)

■ Subsidized Govt. Bonds
■ Negotiable Bonds[a]
■ Stock
■ Other Assets[b]

a. 94% of negotiable bonds are government bonds.
b. Mostly bank deposits.
c. Does not include the government guarantee of benefits conservatively estimated at $20 billion.

Unfortunately for investors, the performance of the provident funds since the govermnent stopped issuing the special bonds has been poor. Not only were fund returns low, but volatility has been relatively high. The average returns for all of the provident funds from 1987 through 1994 were lower than the returns on *any* of the main asset classes in which they invest. And not only were the averages low, *virtually all* of the funds underperformed.[13]

This underperformance can be explained in large part by both poor selections of individual securities and a poor allocation of investments between bonds, stocks, and deposits. As suggested above, part of the explanation has to do with the incentives for bank fund managers to make investment decisions aimed not to produce the highest returns for the fund's holders, but rather to strengthen the bank's network of affiliations and increase overall bank profits. Another, related contributor to such low returns has been high management fees and high commission costs from excessive trading by fund managers seeking to generate fees for their brokerage affiliates.

The poor performance results raise the question of why there has been little entry of new provident fund firms producing better results than the bank-managed funds. A number of barriers have prevented entry. New entrants are required to pay discriminatory bank commissions when investors transfer funds, whereas bank-affiliated provident funds are not required to pay fees. The tax code also makes fund-to-fund transfers unduly burdensome. A corporate entity with an ongoing relationship with a commercial bank might not find it in its interest to transfer a provident fund retirement plan away from a bank-controlled fund. In fact, there is a strong tendency for corporations controlled by bank affiliates to invest in provident funds run by the same bank, suggesting that commercial banking relationships indeed influence the choice of provident fund.

Similar arguments apply to the smaller mutual funds, which typically invest a larger proportion of their assets in equities. More than 75% of mutual fund assets are managed by the three largest banks, and an additional 12% are managed by four other banks. The concentration in mutual funds is, therefore, also very high. Like the bank-run provident funds, the bank-affiliated mutual funds have also generally underperformed.

Recent legislation has attempted to address the problem of poor mutual-fund performance—and to make mutual funds a more effective source of corporate monitoring as well—by requiring mutual fund representatives to attend and vote at shareholders meetings. But such a measure seems cosmetic at best. As in the case of the provident funds, the mutual funds' affiliation with commercial banks constitutes a continuing source of conflicts of interest—conflicts that seem likely to perpetuate ineffective monitoring and low returns for fundholders.

In light of these conflicts, some economists have suggested that the banks should be required to spin off their fund management operations and be further prohibited from running provident funds in the future. Not surprisingly, the banks and some regulators have objected to this proposal. Their main contention is that, by forcing banks to spin off their

13. Ibid.

fund operations and depriving them of a major profit center that provides both high returns and diversification, the stability of the banking system could be impaired. Although such concerns are greatly overstated,[14] political resistance to such a reform is likely to prove effective, at least for the foreseeable future.

But if the bank-dominated provident and mutual funds are unlikely to play a major governance role in the near future, what about the pension funds? Pension fund assets represent more than one-fifth of all capital market assets in Israel. Virtually all of the funds are run by the Histadrut Trade Union, and 95% of pension assets are invested in the subsidized bonds that the government continues to issue to the pension funds. In addition to the subsidies and tax benefits (which exceed those in most other countries), the government has agreed to cover the substantial actuarial deficits accrued over time. The cumulative effect of the benefits and guarantees is that the government has effectively promised real double-digit rates of return to Union-affiliated pension fund holders, thus distorting the relation between risk and return.[15] In addition, the pension funds cannot serve as useful intermediaries between household savers and business because their investments are channeled almost entirely into government bonds.

In short, Israeli pension funds—like the provident and mutual funds—are not well-suited to play a significant role in corporate governance.

CORPORATE GOVERNANCE—OWNERSHIP CONCENTRATION AND THE EQUITY MARKET

The picture that emerges is that the Israeli capital market is still dominated by the government and the banks, corporate debt and equity holdings remain relatively small, and institutional investors do not adequately monitor corporate performance. Moreover, while the banks that often hold significant equity blocks could theoretically monitor firm managers, there is little evidence of such monitoring. Still, it would be worthwhile to establish whether the equity market, perhaps via other mechanisms, serves as a vehicle through which managers can be monitored.

According to some measures, corporate governance in the Israel stock market would appear to be satisfactory. Volume and turnover ratios are reasonable, while the underlying legislation and the powers of the regulatory bodies are modeled on those of the U.S. SEC. Almost all listed companies have moved to one class of shares. Disclosure and accounting rules are also strict.

Share ownership patterns, however, point in another direction. The ownership distribution of the $50 billion Israeli market is different from that of most countries. The government's stake is high—over 18%; and the ownership stakes of other publicly-traded corporations and the banks are also significant (22% and 5%, respectively), while the share of the investing public-at-large is relatively limited (Figure 2).

Of the ten largest Israeli companies, which account for 40% of the total market capitalization of the TASE, eight are controlled either by the government or by the IDB group. Of the largest 25 companies, which account for approximately 60% of market value, ownership is truly dispersed in only one—"Teva" (the largest of the 25). The rest are controlled by nine different groups—the government, four banks, and four conglomerates. The largest 100 companies, which represent more than 80% of market value, are overwhelmingly controlled by eight key groups (see Table 1), which in turn are mostly government- or bank-related. Moreover, in 99 of the 100 (and 243 of the top 250), strategic investors control at least 25% of outstanding stock, while in 88 they control at least 50%. These figures are extreme even in comparison to "insider markets" such as Germany and France.[16]

For a typical listed industrial firm, 80% of its shares are held by large shareholders.[17] Again, this seems to be far higher than in most developed economies, including Germany and France. Individuals, often belonging to the founding family, reportedly hold directly about 40% of the equity, non-financial corporations hold another 25%, while banks own (directly and through mutual and provident funds) at least 15%.[18]

---

14. Yosha (1995) focuses on the effect of such a structural change on the degree of competition in the banking sector. The main conclusion of this analysis is that the gains from increased competition are likely to outweigh the potential economies of scale and scope that would be lost if the funds were spun off. (See O. Yosha, "Privatizing Multi-Product Banks," *Economic Journal*, Vol. 105, No. 433 (1995), pp. 1435-53.)

15. A. Blass "The Cost of Pension Arrangements in Israel," mimeo, Bank of Israel (Hebrew) (1997).

16. See J. Franks and C. Mayer, "Corporate Ownership and Control in the UK, Germany, and France," *Journal of Applied Corporate Finance*, Vol. 9, No. 4 (1997), pp. 30-45.

17. Ber, Yafeh, and Yosha (1997), cited above.

18. Ber (1997), cited above.

Large bank holdings, in combination with the banks' range of activities and political and market power, create conflicts of interest that lead to expropriation of minority stockholders and widespread failure to maximize value.

FIGURE 2
DISTRIBUTION OF
OWNERSHIP ON THE TASE
(YEAR-END 1995)

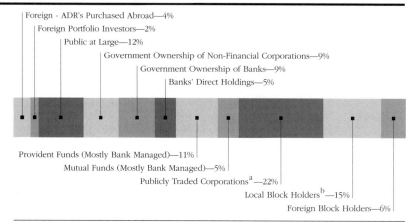

Foreign - ADR's Purchased Abroad—4%
Foreign Portfolio Investors—2%
Public at Large—12%
Government Ownership of Non-Financial Corporations—9%
Government Ownership of Banks—9%
Banks' Direct Holdings—5%

Provident Funds (Mostly Bank Managed)—11%
Mutual Funds (Mostly Bank Managed)—5%
Publicly Traded Corporations[a]—22%
Local Block Holders[b]—15%
Foreign Block Holders—6%

a. Other than banks and government susidiaries.
b. Other than the government, banks, publicly traded corporations, and financial institutions.

TABLE 1
CONTROL PATTERNS OF
100 LARGEST COMPANIES
TRADED ON TASE*

	Number of Companies Controlled by Group	% of Market Value that These Companies Constitute
IDB Group[a]	29	26.0%
Bank Hapoalim[b]/Koor	14	20.2%
Eisenberg Group	8	9.4%
Bank Leumi[b]	4	9.3%
Teva[c]	1	8.8%
Other Government Co's	2	7.5%
Zelkind	6	3.7%
Saffra	3	3.2%
Others	33	12.0%

Source: Tel Aviv Stock Exchange Publications and calculations of the Research Department, Bank of Israel —end of year 1995 figures.
*Representing 81.5% of total market value.
a. IDB is controlled by the Recanati family and holds a 13% stake in the third largest bank.
b. Controlled by the government.
c. The only company among the largest 100 with dispersed ownership.

Institutional shareholders other than bank-managed funds play a relatively small role in the ownership of Israeli manufacturing firms, in part because, as noted above, pension funds as well as life insurance programs are almost fully invested in subsidized government bonds. This situation is not conducive to the operation of an active market for takeovers, which until now has been virtually nonexistent. And the privatization process, instead of attempting to remedy this situation by creating a more dispersed stock ownership, has often exacerbated the problem by placing blocks of SOE shares in the hands of "strategic investors," most of whom already control other large corporations.

As suggested earlier, although a highly concentrated ownership structure can create incentives for large shareholders to monitor firms, it can also lead to conflicts of interest that end up reducing value, at least for minority stockholders. Extensive anecdotal support for this argument now exists in the form of newspaper accounts of losses suffered by minority shareholders at the hands of banks and other controlling shareholders. But broad-based statistical evidence of shareholder losses from concentrated ownership is hard to come by.[19]

What is abundantly clear, however, is that managerial compensation and incentive schemes are not used in Israel to motivate efficient management as intensively as in the U.S. For example, one recent study demonstrated that levels of executive pay have no significant correlation with various widely accepted measures of firm performance.[20] Instead, managerial compensation seems to be more strongly influenced by firm size and the strength of the manager's family ties with the controlling shareholder.

ISRAELI IPOs AT HOME AND IN THE U.S.

The recent IPO wave on the TASE was impressive by OECD standards. From 1990 through 1996, more than 160 Israeli manufacturing and software corporations and 300 firms in real estate and services issued stock through IPOs. During the same period, moreover, most previously listed firms sold additional shares. As a result of the secondary stock offerings and new listings, Israel has been one of the fastest growing equity markets in the world over the last decade. The number of listed companies is now approximately 700, and market capitalization has grown to over $50 billion today from $7 billion in 1989. The amount of funds raised through stock offerings was also substantial, financing a third of all equipment purchases in Israel, an exceedingly high ratio compared to other countries such as the U.S., the U.K., or Germany.[21]

Most firms sold no more than 20% of their equity in the IPO, thus keeping post-IPO ownership extremely concentrated. Moreover, the bank-controlled provident and mutual funds purchased most of these shares. In almost a third of the IPOs, a single bank-controlled provident or mutual fund affiliate acquired at least 5% of the company's equity.[22]

As in many countries, the IPOs (as well as the seasoned offerings) were facilitated by a rising stock market. From 1991 through 1993, Israeli stock market prices rose at a real annual average rate of 43%. The large-scale immigration from the former Soviet Union that began in 1989 and the prospects of a "peace dividend" following the 1991 Madrid Conference and the 1993 Oslo Accords led many to believe that the economy might grow rapidly for several years. Previous work has shown, however, that growth rates required to support the run-up were much higher than those predicted by most observers and probably were not plausibly attainable.[23] The subsequent stock market decline from 1994 through 1996 suggests, in retrospect, that greater emphasis should have been placed on economic fundamentals.

Despite the large number of IPOs on the TASE in recent years and the growth of its market value, most foreign portfolio investors have stayed away from the TASE, purchasing instead Israeli shares listed on the U.S. exchanges (usually non-ADR shares on the NASDAQ). Indeed, there are more Israeli firms listed on the NASDAQ than firms from any other foreign country except Canada.

With few exceptions, moreover, Israeli firms in New York are quite different from Israeli IPOs in Tel Aviv. As shown in Table 2, the Israeli IPOs in New York are relatively young, with an average life of nine years, as compared to 21 years for the TASE-listed IPOs. Virtually all of the New York IPOs are high-tech firms (primarily in electronics or software), as compared to only one-third of the TASE's industrial IPOs. Although the New York-listed companies pre-IPO operating margins are lower than the pre-IPO margins of the TASE firms, the revenue of the New York IPOs doubles, on average, every two years. The Israeli firms that list in the U.S. also spend relatively large amounts of money on R&D and marketing, and more than three quarters of their revenue is derived from exports. By contrast, Tel Aviv IPO's derive only a quarter of their income from exports. Indeed, half of the TASE IPOs in the electronics and software industries have no export income at all!

19. One study, for example (Ber, Yafeh, and Yosha (1997), cited above), shows that reported accounting profits decline following IPOs in Israel, which could indicate that monitoring becomes less effective after firms go public. On the other hand, the same study also detects a positive correlation between the change in accounting profits for these firms and the level of ownership concentration, which suggests that concentration induces better monitoring. It is not clear, however, whether ownership concentration improves performance due to mitigation of managerial moral hazard problems, or if instead. original owners tend to keep higher stakes in "good" firms. There is also some doubt whether shifts in accounting profits accurately reflect corresponding shifts in economic profits.

20. S. Bar Yossef and E. Talmor, "Performance and Corporate Control: What Motivates CEOs and Other Top Executives in Israel," The Economic Quarterly, Vol. 44, No. 2 (1997), pp. 171-192 (Hebrew).

21. See C. Mayer, "Financial Systems, Corporate Finance and Economic Development," in G. Hubbard, ed., Asymmetric Information, Corporate Finance and Investment (Univ. of Chicago Press, 1990).

22. Ber, Yafeh and Yosha (1997), cited above.

23. See A. Blass, "Are Israeli Stock Prices Too High?", Bank of Israel Review, forthcoming.

The superior performance of U.S. IPOs suggests that, in general, higher-quality Israeli firms issue shares in the United States while lower-quality firms issue shares on the TASE. Underwritings in the U.S. under the auspices of reputable U.S. investment banks may signal that the firm is of high quality, and that it expects to grow rapidly and provide investors with substantial returns over time.

TABLE 2
ISRAELI INDUSTRIAL IPOS IN TEL AVIV AND IN NEW YORK 1990-1996

	Tel Aviv IPOs	Tel Aviv IPOs in Electronics and Software	New York IPOs
Pre-issue Balance Sheet Total (Mil $):			
Mean	14.3	6.3	25.3
Median	6.2	3.7	5.4
Age (Years)	21	16	9
Ownership Concentration[a]	4,900	4,950	2,900
Exports as a % of Revenue:			
Mean	24%	27%	77%
Median	2%	2%	90%
% of IPO Proceeds Designated for R&D	1%	3%	15%
% of IPO Proceeds Designated for Marketing	1%	1%	16%
Operating Margin (median)[b]	17%	19%	10%
Annual Revenue Growth (%)[b]	18%	23%	38%
% Employees in R&D:			
Mean	12%	30%	45%
Median	3%	24%	47%
Number of Employees (median)	93	69	86
Number of Observations	163	56	52

Source: Blass and Yafeh (1997).
a. Herfindahl Index.
b. Pre-IPO.

Another difference between Israeli IPOs in New York and those in Tel Aviv is that the ownership structure of U.S. IPOs is typically more diverse before they go public—and even more so afterwards, since U.S. underwriters usually offer relatively large amounts of new stock, thereby further diluting the stakes of strategic investors. Indeed, portfolio investors on average own 35% of U.S. issuers after they go public. By contrast, in only one TASE industrial offering did portfolio investors collectively attain a 35% stake.

As for post-IPO stock performance, a recent study by two of the present authors finds a substantial difference between the TASE and U.S. IPOs.[24] U.S. issues are substantially underpriced, generating first-day returns of almost 20%. They also exhibit relatively high (albeit statistically insignificant) market returns for another 18 months after the IPO (Figure 3).[25] By contrast, local IPOs do not exhibit positive first-day returns and, over time, they have

significantly underperformed the market. Moreover, this overpricing and substandard longer-run performance seems to be especially pronounced in cases involving bank underwriters and, hence, suggests there are conflicts of interest in Israeli universal banking. Indeed, one study of TASE IPOs shows that performance was worst (i.e., the overpricing greatest) when the same bank performed the following three roles: major lender to the issuing firm; lead underwriter of the IPO; and significant purchaser (through its provident or mutual funds) of the offered equity.[26] In other words, the poor performance of provident funds discussed earlier is at least in part due to the fact that they purchased overvalued offerings from affiliated underwriters.

The superior performance of U.S. IPOs suggests that, in general, higher-quality Israeli firms issue shares in the United States, while lower-quality firms issue shares on the TASE. Although the shares of U.S.

24. A. Blass and Y. Yafeh, "Vagabond Shoes Longing to Stray—Why Israeli Firms List in New York—Causes and Consequences," mimeo, Bank of Israel Discussion Paper No. 98-02 (1998).

25. These results are different from the study by Jay Ritter (1991), which shows that investors purchasing IPO shares at the closing market price on the first day of

trading realize significantly low returns over time. (J. Ritter, "The Long-Run Performance of Initial Public Offerings," *The Journal of Finance*, Vol. 46, No. 1 (1991), pp. 3-27.

26. Ber, Yafeh, and Yosha (1997), cited above.

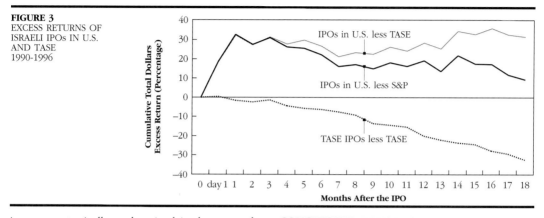

FIGURE 3
EXCESS RETURNS OF
ISRAELI IPOs IN U.S.
AND TASE
1990-1996

issuers are typically underpriced in the sense that one-day returns are abnormally high, the offering prices may still have been higher than those that could have been attained had the shares instead been issued in Israel. That could be so because issuing stock in the U.S. might enhance firm value. The benefits for Israeli firms from listing in the U.S. are likely to include not only monitoring by a more effective corporate governance system (i.e., that provided by U.S. institutional investors) but also greater investor recognition, thereby gaining continued access to a large financial market. U.S. listing could also give Israeli firms greater visibility and name recognition among potential clients, many of whom are in the U.S. More generally, listing and underwriting in the U.S. under the auspices of reputable U.S. investment banks may signal that the firm is of high quality, and that it expects to grow rapidly and provide investors with substantial returns over time.[27] In sum, the main reason the most promising Israeli firms go public in the U.S. is because that is where U.S. and other foreign investors want to buy them; and such investors want to buy them on U.S. exchanges because they want the assurances that come with the U.S. corporate governance system.

Israeli portfolio investors might continue to invest locally (especially in TASE IPOs), in part because of the conflicts of interest noted earlier. In addition, foreign currency regulations and tax distortions have limited the ability of provident funds and other institutional investors to invest abroad.

CONCLUDING REMARKS

The financial system in Israel is dominated by banks and bank-affiliated institutions, and the government also continues to play an important role. Ownership of publicly traded companies tends to be extremely concentrated. As a result, several important mechanisms of corporate governance are missing. Most important, there is no market for corporate control; institutional investors have little incentive to monitor corporate managers; and those managers in turn have little incentive to improve firm performance and increase shareholder value. There is no clear evidence for the existence of effective bank monitoring of corporate managers.

To improve corporate governance in Israel, further reduction of the government's involvement in capital markets is essential. If, for example, government debt is reduced, corporate securities markets will become more liquid, thus giving minority investors stronger incentives and greater ability to monitor managers more effectively. Government debt can be ultimately reduced, however, only if fiscal discipline is maintained. Privatization through sales of stock to the public at large could also add to the depth and liquidity of the equity market, and further improve market discipline. Reforms that would induce pension funds to invest in equity rather than rely on non-tradable government bonds are also likely to contribute to the development of governance mechanisms.

---

27. For a paper that models listing abroad as a means of signaling quality, see S. Cheung and J. Lee, "Disclosure Environment and Listing on Foreign Stock Exchanges," *Journal of Banking and Finance*, Vol. 19, No. 2, (1995), pp. 347-362. In this model, however, the signal is broadcast by additional disclosure costs associated with listing in the U.S.

> The main reason the most promising Israeli firms go public in the U.S. is because
> that is where U.S. and other foreign investors want to buy them; and such investors
> want to buy them on U.S. exchanges because they want the assurances that come
> with the U.S. corporate governance system.

Other measures for improving corporate governance should address the structure of the financial system. For example, if provident and mutual funds were made independent of bank control (either through legislation or if the government, as a majority shareholder in some banks, forced the banks to spin off the funds), both the banks and the funds would have clearer incentives to monitor the firms to which they lend or whose equity they hold. If such changes take place, they are likely to affect patterns of foreign investment in Israel in the following sense: Rather than purchasing controlling interests, or buying shares of Israeli firms issued in New York as they do now, investors are likely to include in their portfolios small stakes of Israeli firms traded in Tel Aviv.

CHAPTER 3: SECTION 3.3
Financial Reporting

As a number of articles throughout this book suggest, part of the present U.S. corporate governance problem can be traced to U.S. accounting rules and the tendency of top executives to pursue continuous increases in reported earnings per share as their primary corporate goal. Besides misleading investors, corporate efforts to "manage" earnings often involve the sacrifice of long-term value through shortsighted cutbacks in R&D and other forms of corporate investment that must be immediately expensed under U.S. GAAP. The readings in our final section focus on financial reporting and U.S. accounting.

The effect of corporate disclosure on the cost of equity capital is a matter of considerable interest and importance to both corporations and the investment community. But, as Christine Botosan begins by observing in *Evidence That Greater Disclosure Lowers the Cost of Equity Capital*, the relationship between level of disclosure and cost of capital is not well established and has proved difficult or researchers to quantify. After examining the annual reports of 122 manufacturing companies, the author concludes that companies providing more extensive disclosure had a lower (forward-looking) cost of equity capital (measured using *Value Line* forecasts with an EBO valuation formula derived from the dividend discount model). For companies with extensive analyst coverage, differences in disclosure do not appear to affect cost of capital. But for companies with limited analyst coverage, differences in disclosure do appear to matter. Among this group of companies, the firms judged to have the highest level of disclosure had a cost of equity capital that was *nine percentage points lower* than otherwise similar firms with a minimal level of disclosure. Moreover, analysis of some specific disclosure practices also suggests that, for small firms with limited analyst coverage, there are benefits to providing more forward-looking information, such as forecasts of sales, profits, and capital expenditures, and enhanced disclosure of key non-financial statistics, such as order backlogs, market share, and growth in units sold.

In *R&D and Capital Markets*, Baruch Lev argues that the substantial growth of R&D expenditures, together with the continuous substitution of knowledge (intangible) capital for physical (tangible) capital in corporate production functions, has elevated the importance of R&D in the performance of business enterprises. At the same time, however, the evaluation of corporate R&D activities by investors has been seriously hampered by antiquated accounting rules and insufficient disclosure by corporations. Despite the fact that the expected benefits of R&D stretch over extended periods of time, corporate investments in R&D are immediately written off in financial reports, leaving no trace of R&D capital on balance sheets and causing material distortions of reported profitability.

After a brief review of statistics documenting the growth and economic importance of corporate R&D in the U.S., the article presents a comparison of R&D disclosure regulations among industrialized nations that shows U.S. rules to be the least flexible in allowing management discretion in how they measure and report R&D. Next the author surveys the large and growing body of empirical research on R&D, which provides strong testimony to the substantial contribution of R&D to corporate productivity and shareholder value. Moreover, despite widespread allegations of stock market "short termism" throughout the 1980s and early '90s, the research indicates "unequivocally" that capital markets consider investments in R&D as a significant value-increasing activity.

But if investors clearly demonstrate a willingness to take the long view of R&D, there is also evidence of undervaluation of some R&D-intensive companies—particularly those with low profitability—as well as other potential costs to corporations and investors stemming from inadequate public information about R&D. To help correct the reporting biases and distortions of R&D, the author offers some suggestions for investors and analysts that follow R&D-intensive companies. In particular, he proposes (1) adjustment of reported data to reflect the capitalization and amortization of (instead of expensing) corporate R&D and (2) the use of various quantitative measures for gauging research capabilities and output including citations of the firm's patents and measures indicating the share of current revenues coming from products developed within recent years.

In *Goodwill Accounting: Everything Has Changed and Nothing Has Changed*, Martin Ellis begins by noting that in issuing Statements No. 141 and No. 142, the FASB has attempted to make accounting statements better reflect the economics of the exchange of value that takes place in business combinations. At the very least, requiring a single method of accounting reduces the costs of accounting, puts all acquirers on an equal accounting footing, and removes the incentive to incur significant costs to be able to report on a pooling-of-interests basis. But if the FASB rules have changed significantly, investors' expectations for acquiring companies have not. Therefore, accounting rules should have no impact on acquisition pricing or structuring unless they affect cash flows. Recorded goodwill and return on capital are the artificial result of accounting rules, and largely without economic content.

However, understanding the growth value implicit in the price paid is key to helping ensure that acquisitions create value. Boards of directors and executives must understand the minimum annual performance targets they have set for themselves by paying a premium to acquire a company. The ideal measure of goodwill, which has not been contemplated by the FASB, would capture the premium of the current acquisition price over the value of the target firm's current operating value—that is, the discounted NPV of its current operating cash flows. Using such an economist's definition of goodwill, financial analysts could then come up with the variable that is of greatest interest to investors—namely, the expected improvements in operating performance that are necessary to justify the acquirer's investment in the target company. The economic framework and future growth value analysis based on EVA can be used to answer this question, regardless of the accounting rules *du jour*.

In *How to Fix Accounting—Measure and Report Economic Profit*, Bennett Stewart proposes to remedy this problem with a complete overhaul of GAAP that aims to measure and report *economic* profit. Stated in brief, Stewart's concept of economic profit begins with an older, now seldom used, definition of accounting income known as "residual income" and then proposes a series of additional adjustments to GAAP that are designed to produce a reliable measure of a company's sustainable annual *cash*-generating capacity.

In *Accounting Doesn't Need Much Fixing (Just Reinterpreting)*, George Benston responds to Stewart with a classic defense of traditional accounting practices and standards. Like the recent efforts of the FASB to achieve greater balance-sheet realism through "fair value accounting," Stewart's call to make economic profit the centerpiece of GAAP is said to stem from the mistaken premise that audited financial statements are

intended *primarily* to guide equity investors in setting stock prices. But if he rejects Stewart's proposal, Benston nevertheless agrees with his claim that GAAP accounting is of limited use for investors in valuing companies and that the single-minded pursuit of higher GAAP earnings by corporate managers can lead to value reducing investment and operating decisions. Accordingly, he endorses many of Stewart's proposed modifications of GAAP both for *internal* purposes, such as performance evaluation and incentive compensation, and for *voluntary supplemental* reporting to the investment community.

We conclude this chapter, and the book, where we began—with insights from Michael Jensen, this time with Joseph Fuller. In *Just Say No to Wall Street: Putting a Stop to the Earnings Game*, Fuller and Jensen argue that CEOs are in a bind with Wall Street. Managers up and down the hierarchy work hard at putting together plans and budgets for the next year only to discover that the bottom line falls far short of Wall Street's expectations. CEOs and CFOs are therefore left in a difficult situation; they can stretch to try to meet Wall Street's projections or prepare to suffer the consequences if they fail. All too often, top managers react by suggesting or even mandating that middle-and lower-level managers redo their forecasts and budgets to get them in line with external expectations. In some cases, managers simply acquiesce to increasingly unrealistic analyst forecasts and adopt them as the basis for setting organizational goals and developing internal budgets. But either approach sets up the firm and its managers for failure if external expectations are impossible to meet.

Using the recent experiences of Enron and Nortel, the authors illustrate the dangers of conforming to market pressures for unrealistic growth targets. They emphasize that an overvalued stock, by encouraging overpriced acquisitions and other value-destroying forms of overinvestment, can be as damaging to the long-run health of a company as an undervalued stock. Ending the "expectations game" requires that CEOs reclaim the initiative in setting expectations and forecasts so that stocks can trade at close to their intrinsic value. Managers must make their organizations more transparent to investors; they must promise only those results they have a legitimate prospect of delivering and be willing to inform the market when they believe their stock to be overvalued.

EVIDENCE THAT GREATER DISCLOSURE LOWERS THE COST OF EQUITY CAPITAL

by Christine A. Botosan,
The University of Utah

Providing information to the capital markets is not a costless undertaking. Among the costs of disclosure are the costs of creating and distributing the information, costs imposed on the firm by competitors who exploit the information to the detriment of the disclosing firm, and litigation costs that arise when a firm is sued in connection with a disclosure.

While much attention is paid to the costs of disclosure, it is important not to overlook the benefits. The ultimate benefit of providing more information to the capital markets is a lower cost of equity capital and thus a higher stock price (for a given level of earnings). But, of course, if the costs of providing more information include a proliferation of shareholder lawsuits or a weakening of the firm's competitive position, then future earnings—and hence the stock price—will be lower as a consequence. Thus, like most corporate decisions, the decision to disclose more or different kinds of information to the capital markets should be based on a cost-benefit analysis that shows the benefits outweigh the costs.

Although this concept is easy to state, it is difficult to apply in practice. Both the costs and the benefits of disclosure are difficult to observe and quantify. Yet the costs of disclosure, perhaps because they seem more concrete and direct, are widely accepted as real and significant. The benefits of disclosure, on the other hand, are much less accepted, whether in terms of their size or their existence. In this environment of uncertainty, cautious managers might be inclined to place too much weight on the costs of disclosure and too little on the benefits, thus leading to too little disclosure.

For many years, academic research on the benefits of disclosure was mainly theoretical and empirically untested. But, during the past five years, a number of empirical studies have attempted to detect and quantify the benefits of providing improved disclosure to the capital markets. In 1997 I published a study of 122 industrial companies that provides direct evidence of a negative association between cost of equity capital and the level of voluntary disclosure. But this association holds only for smaller companies with little or no analyst following; for larger firms with extensive analyst coverage, there is no detectable relationship. The findings of my study also suggest that, in the case of smaller, less-followed companies, the firm providing the highest level of disclosure has a cost of capital that is *nine percentage points lower* than that of the least forthcoming firm, even after controlling for differences in market beta and firm size.

The purpose of this paper is twofold: (1) to review some of this evidence with the aim of increasing awareness of the benefits of providing enhanced disclosure to the capital markets; and (2) to offer some guidance as to where firms should concentrate their efforts to receive the maximum benefit from enhancing their disclosures.

FIGURE 1
DISCLOSURE BENEFITS
FRAMEWORK

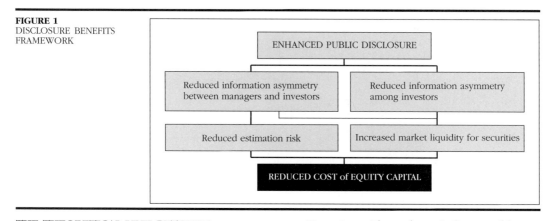

THE THEORETICAL LINK BETWEEN
DISCLOSURE AND THE COST OF CAPITAL

Finance theory suggests that corporate managers have the potential to increase the value of their company's shares by reducing investor uncertainty about future corporate performance. Of course, risk and uncertainty are inherent in business activity, and thus there is much uncertainty that can never be eliminated. What can be largely eliminated, however, are disparities in information between market participants—or, to use the academic term, "information asymmetries."

Information asymmetries arise when market participants are privy to different levels of information. For example, managers often have better information about the firm's prospects than investors. Information asymmetries can also exist among investors, such as when certain investors gain access to private information. By increasing disclosure to the capital markets, and so making some private information public, corporate managers can reduce both kinds of information asymmetries. And to the extent investors are reassured that they are at less of an informational disadvantage, the theory suggests they will require a lower required rate of return, or "cost of capital," for holding the firm's shares.

Figure 1 provides a schematic diagram of the two main ways that enhanced corporate public disclosure can lead to a lower cost of equity. One path to a lower cost of equity capital involves reducing the so-called *estimation risk* that confronts all investors.[1] In setting stock prices, investors use all available information to estimate variables such as the extent to which the returns on the firm's future investments are likely to exceed the cost of capital. Such estimates are formed based on the firm's return history and other information available about the firm. When less information is forthcoming, investors are more uncertain about their estimates, which injects an additional element of risk into their assessments of the value of the firm. Investors require compensation for this element of risk—in the form of a higher cost of capital—if it cannot be diversified away.

A second path to a lower cost of equity capital is through greater liquidity in the market for the firm's securities.[2] Greater liquidity leads to lower transaction costs. Faced with lower transaction costs, investors are willing to pay more for the firm's securities resulting in a lower cost of equity capital. Greater liquidity can also increase the demand for a firm's securities, which raises the price of the firm's stock, leading to a lower cost of equity capital.

1. Klein, R., and V. Bawa, 1976, The Effect of Estimation Risk on Optimal Portfolio Choice, *Journal of Financial Economics*, 3, 215-231, were perhaps the first to consider estimation risk. More recent work includes Barry, C., and S. Brown, 1985, Differential Information and Security Market Equilibrium, *Journal of Financial and Quantitative Analysis*, December, 407-422. Coles, J., and U. Loewenstein, 1988, Equilibrium Pricing and Portfolio Composition in the Presence of Uncertain Parameters, *Journal of Financial Economics*, 279-303. Handa, P., and S. Linn, 1993, Arbitrage Pricing with Estimation Risk, *Journal of Financial Economics*, March, 81-100. Coles, J., U. Loewenstein, and J. Suay, 1995, On

Equilibrium Pricing Under Parameter Uncertainty, *Journal of Financial and Quantitative Analysis*, September, 347-364. Clarkson, P., J. Guedes, and R. Thompson, 1996, On the Diversification, Observability, and Measurement of Estimation Risk, *Journal of Financial and Quantitative Analysis*, March, 69-84.

2. See for example Amihud, Y., and M. Mendelson, 1986, Asset Pricing and the Bid-ask Spread *Journal of Financial Economics* 17, 223-249. Also, Diamond D., and R. Verrecchia, 1991, Disclosure, Liquidity and the Cost of Equity Capital, *The Journal of Finance*, September, 1325-1360.

THE EMPIRICAL LINK BETWEEN DISCLOSURE AND THE COST OF CAPITAL

Although the theory suggests that better disclosure can reduce the cost of capital, is there any empirical support for this conclusion? A number of studies have provided what amounts to indirect evidence by showing that more extensive disclosure is associated with more accurate analyst forecasts, (somewhat) lower levels of disagreement among analysts, and higher levels of stock liquidity (as indicated by increased institutional ownership and reduced bid-ask spreads).[3] But while the findings of this research are consistent with a negative association between disclosure level and cost of equity capital, they do not provide definitive evidence of this relationship because they do not examine the impact of disclosure on the cost of equity capital itself.

Estimating Cost of Equity Capital

The main reason for the dearth of studies on how disclosure affects the cost of capital is that the cost of equity capital is difficult to estimate. Traditional approaches either estimate cost of equity capital using a model that provides no role for information, or they yield estimates with so much "noise" that any effect on cost of capital would be obscured. For example, the traditional Capital Asset Pricing Model defines expected return as the sum of the expected risk free rate and the product of a firm's estimated market beta and the expected market risk premium. Thus, the CAPM assumes that variations in market beta alone explains differences in cost of equity capital among companies. In short, the model provides no role for differences among companies in disclosure policy. Estimating cost of equity capital based on average realized returns is not a viable alternative approach because average realized returns provide an extremely noisy measure of cost of equity capital.

In a study published in the *Accounting Review* in 1997,[4] I circumvented these problems by devising a test of the association between the level of disclosure of 122 industrial companies and their forward-looking, or *expected,* cost of equity. The companies in my sample represented three SEC industry groups: primary metals, fabricated metal products, and industrial and commercial machinery. My forward-looking estimates were based on a single point in time: June 30, 1991.

For each of the 122 companies, I estimated the expected cost of equity capital by "backing it out" of an accounting-based valuation formula known as the EBO (short for Edwards-Bell-Ohlson)[5] formula. The EBO formula is derived directly from the well-known dividend discount model, and it yields the same answer, provided all gains and losses that affect forecasted book value flow through forecasted earnings (a condition known as "clean surplus accounting").

The EBO formula[6] estimates the current stock price as the sum of three components:

(1) current book value;

(2) the present value of future earnings in excess of a normal return on book value; and

(3) the present value of the terminal value in excess of book value.

In applying the formula, I used 1990 year-end book values and stock prices on June 30, 1991, together with *Value Line* forecasts of earnings, book values, and future stock prices (which were used as terminal values). With all the other variables so defined, I was then able to solve for the single remaining unknown, the cost of equity capital. Reduced to its essentials, my estimate of cost of capital can be thought of as the discount rate that reconciles the firm's current stock price with the expected future cash flows implied in current book values and

---

3. See Mark Lang and Russell Lundholm, "Corporate Disclosure Policy and Analyst Behavior, October 1996; and Paul Healy, Amy Hutton, and Krishna Palepu, "Stock Performance and Intermediation Changes Surrounding Sustained Increases in Disclosure," *Contemporary Accounting Research,* forthcoming.

4. Christine Botosan, 1997, Disclosure Level and the Cost of Equity Capital, *The Accounting Review,* July, 323-349.

5. The EBO formula has been developed by accounting researchers over the past 40 years. The original conception was provided by E. Edwards and P. Bell, 1961, The Theory of and Measurement of Business Income, University of California Press. This original concept was revised and extended in two fairly recent articles: James Ohlson, 1995, Earnings, Book Values, and Dividends in Security Valuation, *Contemporary Accounting Research,* Spring, 661-687; and Gerald Feltham and James Ohlson, 1995, Valuation and Clean Surplus Accounting for Operating and Financial Activities, *Contemporary Accounting Research,* Spring, 689-731.

6. The EBO valuation formula is:

$$P_t = b_t + [\Sigma_{\tau=1}^{T}(1 + r)]^{-\tau} E_t[x_{t+\tau} - rb_{t+\tau-1}] + (1 + r)^{-T} E_t(P_T - b_T)$$

Where: r = cost of equity capital; P_t = price at date t; $E_t(\circ)$ = the expectations operator; b_t = book value at time t; and x_t = earnings for year t.

Setting the forecast horizon t to four years, I used *Mathematica* software to solve the equation for r (the cost of equity capital). This procedure yields four unique formulas for r. Each formula defines r as a different combination of the following set of variables: current price, forecasted price four years into the future, current book value, forecasted book value and forecasted earnings 1, 2, 3, and 4 years out. I solved each of the four equations for each firm. In all cases, two of the four solutions are undefined and one is unrealistic (a negative number typically in the neighborhood of –2). The remaining solution is my estimate of the firm's cost of equity capital.

For many years, academic research on the benefits of disclosure was mainly theoretical and empirically untested. But, in the past five years, a number of empirical studies have attempted to detect and quantify the benefits of providing improved disclosure to the capital markets.

TABLE 1

	Sign	Coefficient	Variable	t-statistic
Cost of Equity Capital =		0.2050	Intercept	(0.0001)
	Plus	0.0661	Beta	(0.0037)
	Plus	−0.0155	Market Value of Equity	(0.0007)
		13.7%	Adjusted R²	

Value Line's forecasts of future earnings, book values, and stock prices.

The average cost of equity capital computed in this manner for the entire 122 companies was 20.1%.[7] Then I divided the sample into two groups—those companies with a large analyst following and those with a small following—based on whether the firm was followed by more or less than the median number of analysts. The average cost of equity capital for the companies with a large analyst following was 18%, well below the 22% for the firms followed by few analysts.

The next step was to perform a regression analysis to help determine whether the EBO valuation formula was producing estimates of the cost of capital that varied across companies in a sensible way. Specifically, I regressed the cost of equity capital on both the firm's market beta and on its size (as measured by market equity capitalization), and obtained the results shown in Table 1. As the CAPM would lead us to expect, the cost of equity estimates produced using the EBO formula were found to be an increasing function of beta; and the coefficient on beta was 0.066, which is consistent with a market risk premium of 6.6%. But, also consistent with the well-documented small-firm effect—the tendency of small firms to produce higher returns than those predicted by the CAPM—the cost of capital fell with increases in firm size. In short, the results of this regression analysis suggest that the EBO valuation formula does a reasonably good job of capturing variations in the cost of capital among different firms.

Measuring Disclosure Level

For each of the 122 companies, I then produced a quantitative measure of their disclosure level using a disclosure "index" that reflects both the amount and kind (though not necessarily the "quality") of information provided in their 1990 annual reports to shareholders. This was done by reading each annual report and awarding points if certain items of information were disclosed. The items included in the disclosure index were drawn from five categories of voluntary information identified by investors and financial analysts as useful in investment decision making: (1) background information; (2) summary of historical results; (3) key non-financial statistics; (4) forward-looking information; and (5) management discussion and analysis. (A brief description of each category is provided in the box on the next page.)

While recognizing that most companies have means of communicating with market participants other than the annual report, I used the disclosure score for the firm's annual report as my indicator of the effectiveness of its overall disclosure policies. Although perhaps an unreliable assumption for large companies, it seems reasonable for small and mid-sized companies. Because such companies tend to receive little coverage by analysts, their ability to communicate through channels other than the annual report is fairly limited, thus making the report a more significant part of the disclosure process. This was my primary reason for dividing my sample into companies with a large analyst following and those followed by few if any analysts. The firms in the small-analyst group, which had median following of five analysts, tended to be small in size as well, with median market value of equity of $90.7 million. By contrast, the median firm in the large analyst group was covered by 15 analysts and had an equity market cap of $592 million.

Association Between Disclosure Level and Expected Cost of Equity Capital

The next step was to examine the association between disclosure level and cost of equity capital

---

7. In assessing the reasonableness of this figure, I drew on the research of M. Ehrhardt, *The Search for Value: Measuring the Company's Cost of Capital* (Boston: Harvard Business School Press, 1994). Ehrhardt's work produces estimates of the risk free rate that range between 6.0% and 9.25%, with associated risk premiums of 8.2% and 7.8%. Using the midpoint of Ehrhardt's estimates and the sample average beta of 1.146, my CAPM estimate of the cost of equity capital was 17.4%. This crude approximation suggests that, on average, information (i.e., estimation risk) might add as much as 2.7% to the cost of equity capital.

Background information: Includes statements regarding management's objectives and business strategy, the firm's competitive environment, the principal products it produces, and its principal markets. Firms were awarded one point for each background item that they disclosed and one additional point per item if they provided information of a quantitative nature not recoverable from the basic financial statements.

Summary of historical results: The information included in these summaries varies ranging from a complete balance sheet and income statement to the minimum required for the 10-K. I awarded the sample firms points based on the information required to compute the following basic profitability ratios: return-on-assets, net profit margin, asset turnover and return-on-equity. Firms generally presented either five or ten years of annual data, but because users typically prefer ten years I awarded firms twice as many points if they provided a summary of ten or more years than if they provided a summary of shorter duration.

Key non-financial statistics: Includes items such as market share, units sold, number of employees, order backlog, and average compensation per employee. A firm was awarded two points for each non-financial statistic disclosed in its annual report.

Forward looking information: Includes discussion of management's future plans and the possible impact on sales and/or profits of existing or anticipated opportunities, industry trends and risks. Also includes forecasted sales, operating earnings, capital expenditures and market share. I awarded two points for a directional prediction (i.e. qualitative forecast) and three points if the forecast includes a point estimate (i.e. quantitative forecast).

Management discussion and analysis: Includes discussion of year-to-year changes in items such as sales, operating income, various expense categories, inventory, accounts receivable, market share, etc. The scoring procedure assigned one point for each item discussed provided a detailed explanation, not recoverable from the basic financial statements or footnotes, was given for the change. One additional point per item was given if the explanation included quantitative data also not recoverable from the basic financial statements or footnotes.

for each of the two subsamples by estimating a regression of expected cost of equity capital on disclosure level, market beta, and market value of common equity. The results of this analysis are summarized in Table 2.[8] (Except for the p-value on the intercept, all p-values are for one-tailed tests of significance.)

The results suggest that, for firms with a large analyst following, cost of equity capital increases with market beta, but is unrelated to disclosure level and firm size. However, the proper interpretation of the insignificant coefficient on disclosure level is not clear. It is consistent with the possibility that greater annual report disclosure does not provide much benefit to large firms with a heavy analyst following. But it may also reflect the possibility, as suggested above, that large firms have effective disclosure alternatives.

In contrast, for firms with a low analyst following, the cost of equity is also an increasing function of market beta, but it decreases with increases in both firm size and disclosure level. The size of the coefficient on disclosure level suggests that, among the firms with a small analyst following, the *most* forthcoming firm enjoys about a 9% reduction in its cost of equity capital relative to the *least* forthcoming firm. So, for example, if the worst disclosing firm has a cost of equity of, say, 25%, the cost of equity for the best discloser, holding all else equal, would be about 16%.

SOME EVIDENCE ON TYPES OF DISCLOSURE

In the final part of my 1997 study, I attempted to gain some insight into the kinds of disclosure that are likely to be most effective in reducing the cost of capital. Because companies bundle together a variety of different kinds of information in their disclosure packages—and, in some cases, have multiple channels for disseminating the same type of information—it is difficult to design a test that can isolate a

---

8. Table 9 in Botosan (1997) reports the results corresponding to those presented above. However, the model estimated and reported on in that study uses the full sample and allows the association between disclosure level and cost of equity capital to vary for high and low analyst following sub-samples by including an indicator variable in the model. Estimating the model for the high and low analyst following sub-samples separately produces the results reported here. Primary conclusions regarding the impact of disclosure level on cost of equity capital are insensitive to these alternative specifications.

The findings of my study suggest that, in the case of smaller, less-followed companies, the firm providing the highest level of disclosure has a cost of capital that is *nine percentage points lower* than that of the least forthcoming firm, even after controlling for differences in market beta and firm size.

TABLE 2

Expected cost of equity capital =	High Analyst Following				Low Analyst Following			
	Sign	Coefficient	Variable	t-statistic	Sign	Coefficient	Variable	t-statistic
		0.094	Intercept	(0.2719)		0.250	Intercept	(0.0019)
	Plus	0.097	Beta	(0.0031)	Plus	0.068	Beta	(0.0512)
	Plus	0.034	Disclosure Level	(0.8462)	Plus	−0.090	Disclosure Level	(0.0256)
	Plus	−0.008	Mkt. Value Equity	(0.1836)	Plus	−0.018	Mkt. Value Equity	(0.0711)
		16.2%	Adjusted R²			11.4%	Adjusted R²	

single aspect of disclosure, particularly with a sample that contains only 122 firms.

But, as a tentative first step in this direction, I examined the effect of each of the five categories of disclosure on the cost of equity capital by estimating the above regression model using my five categories of disclosure in place of the overall disclosure score. My principal finding was that, for companies with a small analyst following, cost of equity capital decreased with increases in the level of two categories: (1) forward looking information, such as forecasts of sales, profits, and capital expenditures; and (2) key non-financial statistics, such as order backlogs, market share, and growth in units sold. I also found that, in the case of companies with large analyst followings, although the cost of capital is not affected by increases in *overall* disclosure level, it tends to fall with increases in one particular category of disclosure: the historical summary.

These findings are consistent with results of a 1987 survey of investors conducted by SRI International (formerly the Stanford Research Institute).[9] According to the survey, individual investors value financial projections in the annual report to a greater extent than analysts or portfolio managers ("professional investors") while the opposite relation holds with respect to historical summary information. The suggestion from both the survey and my regression analysis is that forecast information may be particularly valuable to investors when a firm is not followed by a large number of analysts; that is, individual investors are forced to rely on management forecasts when analysts' forecasts are not readily available. But, for companies with heavy analyst coverage, the provision of more extensive historical information appears to be valued by financial analysts.

MORE EVIDENCE ON CORPORATE DISCLOSURE PRACTICES

Although not part of my published 1997 study, I have also performed some additional analysis of disclosure practices in corporate annual reports using a sample of 247 industrial companies (a group that includes the 122 firms discussed above).[10] The main finding of this analysis—which is based, once again, on an examination of the companies' 1990 annual reports—is that smaller companies followed by few analysts tend to provide less information in all categories of disclosure than companies with more analyst coverage.

In this study, I started by dividing the entire sample of companies into *three* groups according to the size of their analyst following. Of the 247 companies, 80 fell into the "low analyst" group (firms followed by at most one analyst); 104 companies were considered to have "moderate" followings (those with from two to nine analysts); and the remaining 63 "high" analyst firms were followed by ten or more analysts. As in the study discussed earlier, analyst following varies directly with size. For example, the low analyst firms had a median market value of equity of only $10.8 million. In contrast, the median market value of the firms with moderate analyst followings was almost $50 million; and the high analyst sample consisted of much larger companies, with a median market value of close to $600 million.

For each of the three groups of companies, I calculated an average disclosure score for each of the five disclosure categories as well as an average score for overall disclosure. These average disclosure scores were also relative scores in the sense that they

9. SRI International, 1987, *Investor Information Needs and the Annual Report*, Morristown, New Jersey, Financial Executives Research Foundation. The survey indicates that 61.5% of individuals favor including forecast information in the annual report as compared to 54.5% of professionals. In contrast, only 46.2% of individual investors view the historical summary as important, compared to 69.6% of professional investors.

10. See also my Ph.D. doctoral dissertation, "The Effect of Disclosure Level on the Cost of Equity Capital and Stock Market Liquidity," University of Michigan, 1995.

TABLE 3		High Analyst Following	Moderate Analyst Following	Low Analyst Following
DISCLOSURE SCORE BY CATEGORY DIVIDED BY MAXIMUM SCORE	Overall disclosure	0.656	0.508	0.412
	Background information	0.723	0.563	0.436
	Summary of historical results	0.692	0.592	0.448
	Key non-financial statistics	0.458	0.273	0.227
	Management discussion and analysis	0.544	0.489	0.429
	Forward looking information	0.279	0.212	0.175

TABLE 4	Attribute	Percentage of High Analyst Following Firms	Percentage of Moderate Analyst Following Firms	Percentage of Low Analyst Following Firms
DESCRIPTIVE STATISTICS CONCERNING FUTURE ORIENTED DISCUSSION	Trends	19.0%	5.8%	1.3%
	Opportunities	11.1%	9.6%	3.8%
	Risks	1.6%	1.9%	0.0%

were computed for each firm by dividing the firm's "raw," or absolute, score by the highest disclosure score earned by any sample firm in a given category.

As shown in Table 3, the average firm in the high analyst group achieved an overall disclosure score of 0.656, as compared to the 0.508 and 0.412 for the moderate and low analyst subsamples. (The differences were statistically significantly at a 1% level.) Moreover, the disclosure pattern across categories is similar for all three groups of firms. That is, in each of the three cases, the average firm posts its best performance in the background and historical summary information categories closely followed by their scores in the management discussion and analysis category. At the same time, the average sample firm in each of the three groups achieves its worst performance in the forward-looking information and key non-financial statistics categories.

Although the pattern of disclosure across the categories is similar, the firms in the high analyst group outperformed the firms in the moderate and low analyst subsamples by providing significantly more disclosure in each of the five categories. The moderately followed firms also outperformed the low analyst firms in all categories except two: (1) forward-looking information and (2) key non-financial statistics. In this respect, my analysis makes the disclosure policies of small firms appear more sensible; for, as reported earlier, it is improvement in precisely these two categories that appear to hold out the largest cost-of-capital reductions for such firms.

Several conclusions can be drawn from this evidence. First, relative to the benchmark of the most forthcoming firm, there appears to be room for im-

provement in the disclosure practices of firms in all three groups, particularly with respect to forecast information and key non-financial statistics. But such results are not completely surprising, given the potential costs associated with such disclosures (including the possibility of lawsuits and revelation of proprietary information). Also not surprising, disclosure levels are highest in all subsamples for those categories where disclosure costs are likely lowest: background and historical summary information.

Additional Analysis of Disclosure of Forward Looking Information

To examine further the possibility that companies are neglecting an opportunity to lower their cost of capital by providing more forward-looking information, I looked more closely at the forecasting behavior of the sample firms. As suggested above, forward-looking information in the annual report may be particularly important to parties that invest in companies with low to moderate analyst followings.

Table 4 shows the percentage of companies in each of the three groups whose annual report mentioned the expected impact on future sales or profits of existing or anticipated industry trends, opportunities, or risks. The data indicate that few firms provide this type of discussion in their annual report. However, the firms with higher analyst following do so significantly more often than firms with lower analyst following. The percentage of firms discussing the potential impact of industry trends ranged from 1.3% (low analyst following) to 19.0% (high analyst following); while the proportion

My principal finding was that, for companies with a small analyst following, the cost
of equity capital decreased with increases in the level of two categories:
(1) forward looking information, such as forecasts of sales, profits, and capital
expenditures; and (2) key non-financial statistics, such as order backlogs,
market share, and growth in units sold.

	Forecast Attribute	Qualitative	Quantitative	Mixed	% of Firms
TABLE 5 DESCRIPTIVE STATISTICS CONCERNING TYPE OF FORECAST	**PANEL A: HIGH ANALYST FOLLOWING**				
	Operating income	84.4%	12.5%	3.1%	50.8%
	Sales	81.5%	14.8%	3.7%	42.9%
	Capital expenditures	12.8%	87.2%	0.0%	61.9%
	Market share	100.0%	0.0%	0.0%	14.3%
	PANEL B: MODERATE ANALYST FOLLOWING				
	Operating income	90.7%	7.0%	2.3%	41.3%
	Sales	84.2%	2.6%	13.2%	36.5%
	Capital expenditures	14.3%	85.7%	0.0%	47.1%
	Market share	87.5%	12.5%	0.0%	7.7%
	PANEL C: LOW ANALYST FOLLOWING				
	Operating income	94.3%	2.9%	2.9%	43.8%
	Sales	82.1%	10.7%	7.1%	35.0%
	Capital expenditures	33.3%	66.7%	0.0%	45.0%
	Market share	100.0%	0.0%	0.0%	5.0%

of firms discussing the potential impact of opportunities ranges from 3.8% (low analyst growth) to 11.1% (high analyst group) (Both differences are statistically significant at a 1% level of significance.) At the same time, the percentage of firms discussing the future impact of risks is uniformly low, not exceeding 2% for any group.

The percentage of companies providing forecasts of operating income, sales, capital expenditures, or market share is shown in the last column of Table 5. This table also provides, for each of the three groups of companies, a breakdown of forecasts between qualitative and quantitative forecasts (quantitative forecasts are defined as those that provide point estimates or stated minimums, maximums, or ranges). The "mixed" category refers to firms that provide a mixture of quantitative and qualitative forecasts for various business segments.

As can be seen in Table 5, the pattern across the various forecast attributes is similar for all three groups of firms. Capital expenditure forecasts are the most common, with 61.9%, 47.1% and 45.0% of the high, moderate, and low analyst following firms providing them. Operating income and sales forecasts are provided somewhat less often, while market share forecasts are relatively rare.[11] Moreover, the vast majority of firms that offer forecasts of sales,

operating income, or market share provide directional predictions only. In contrast, capital expenditure forecasts tend to take the form of estimated amounts. The frequency with which forecasts are provided is statistically similar across the three groups of firms with one exception: companies in the high analyst group are more likely to provide a capital expenditure forecast than firms in the other two subsamples.

Table 6 summarizes evidence on forecast *direction*. All forecasts were classified as either "good" (if the forecasted attribute was expected to increase), "bad" (if it was expected to decrease), or "neutral" (if no change was expected). A forecast was classified as "mixed" if the forecast direction varied for different divisions of the same organization.

As can be readily seen from the table, regardless of what variable they were forecasting—whether operating income, sales, or market share—the companies in my sample were much more likely to provide a good news forecast than any other type. Across the three groups of firms, at least 65% of the forecasts of operating income, 50% of the sales forecasts, and 75% of the market share forecasts anticipated increases in the coming year. (Differences among the three subsamples were not statistically significant.)

---

11. The results presented in the table with respect to sales and operating income forecasts are similar to those presented in Peter M. Clarkson, Jennifer L. Kao and Gordon D. Richardson, 1994, The Voluntary Inclusion of Forecasts in the MD&A Section of Annual Report, *Contemporary Accounting Research*, Fall, 423-450 who find that approximately 36% of their sample firms provide directional forecasts of net income, cash flow or sales in their annual reports.

Forecast Attribute	Good	Bad	Neutral	Mixed
PANEL A: HIGH ANALYST FOLLOWING				
Operating income	68.8%	15.6%	0.0%	15.6%
Sales	66.7%	18.5%	3.7%	11.1%
Market share	100.0%	0.0%	0.0%	0.0%
PANEL B: MODERATE ANALYST FOLLOWING				
Operating income	65.1%	16.3%	7.0%	11.6%
Sales	50.0%	18.4%	5.3%	26.3%
Market share	87.5%	0.0%	12.5%	0.0%
PANEL C: LOW ANALYST FOLLOWING				
Operating income	68.6%	17.1%	5.7%	8.6%
Sales	60.7%	17.9%	7.1%	14.3%
Market share	75.0%	0.0%	25.0%	0.0%

TABLE 6
DESCRIPTIVE STATISTICS CONCERNING DIRECTION OF FORECAST

These results suggest that, in most respects, the forecasting behavior of companies with a moderate to low analyst following is similar to those of firms with a high analyst following. Specifically, forecast frequency, type (qualitative vs. quantitative) and direction (good, bad, or neutral) is similar across all three groups for forecasts of income, sales and market share. These results suggest that managers behave as if they are aware of the potential benefits of providing forward looking information. Nevertheless, there are two areas where managers of companies followed by fewer analysts appear to have an opportunity to make improvements: (1) disclosure of capital expenditure forecasts and (2) discussion of the expected impact of industry trends on future sales and profits.

SOME NEW EVIDENCE ON FREQUENCY OF DISCLOSURE

In a very recent, and as yet unpublished, study, Mark Lang and Russell Lundholm[12] (LL) examined the disclosure practices and associated stock market responses of 41 small companies around the time of seasoned equity offerings. The first question that LL address is: Can managers positively affect their stock price by managing the tone and frequency of their disclosures prior to a stock offering? They find that, during the half-year period leading up to 6 months

prior to the equity offering announcement, the disclosure activity of the issuing firms was indistinguishable from that of a matched sample of non-issuing firms.[13] However, during the six months prior to the announcement of the offering, the issuing firms made an average of 4.86 more disclosure statements than their non-offering counterparts.[14] Moreover, the authors also find that this increase in disclosure activity was associated with a run-up in the stock prices of the offering firms (relative to those of the non-offering firms) prior to the announcement of the offering. Specifically, each additional positive disclosure statement was associated with a 1.6% higher pre-announcement return.

The second question the study addresses is: Are the increases in stock price sustainable after the intent to go public is announced? If the market on the announcement of the stock issue views the pre-announcement disclosure activity as simply a means of hyping the stock without economic basis, the announcement should result in a stock price correction. LL examine this issue by regressing the difference in the announcement period returns (measured over days −2 to +2 around the announcement) both on the level of and the change in disclosure frequency. (All variables are measured as the difference between the value of the variable for an offering firm relative to that of its non-offering matched firm.)

12. Mark Lang and Russell Lundholm, 1999, Voluntary Disclosure During Equity Offerings: Reducing Information Asymmetry or Hyping the Stock, University of North Carolina and University of Michigan Working Paper.

13. For the most part, firms are matched on firm size, industry, exchange listing and fiscal year end.
14. More precisely what is being compared is the increase from one six month period to the next by the issuers relative to the increase by non-issuers.

> **A higher level of disclosure in the pre-announcement period is associated with a less negative stock price reaction to the announcement of a seasoned equity offering. Nevertheless, the price drop is larger if the firm achieved its disclosure level by increasing its disclosure activity in the period leading up to the announcement.**

LL find a significant positive coefficient on the level of disclosure frequency and a significant *negative* coefficient on the *extent of change* in disclosure frequency. Since announcement period returns are negative on average, this suggests that a higher level of disclosure in the pre-announcement period is associated with a less negative stock price reaction to the announcement of a seasoned equity offering. Nevertheless, after controlling for the level of the disclosure, the price drop associated with the announcement is larger if the firm achieved its disclosure level by increasing its disclosure activity in the period leading up to the announcement. (These firms are referred to as "stock price hypers.")

Their regression indicates that a company that makes one more disclosure statement than an otherwise identical firm can expect to have a return that is 0.4% less negative. But if this same firm added this extra disclosure statement during the pre-announcement period, the beneficial effect of greater disclosure is offset by a 0.5% lower stock return attributable to the increased frequency of the disclosure.

The final question addressed by LL is whether the stock price correction upon the announcement of the issue is "complete." If the stock price correction is complete, there should be no association between disclosure patterns in the pre-announcement period and post-announcement returns. LL examine this issue by regressing the post-announcement return (measured over days +3 to +390 after the announcement) on the level and change in disclosure frequency in the pre-announcement period.

Once again, LL find a significant positive coefficient on the level of disclosure frequency and a significant negative coefficient on the change. This suggests that a higher level of disclosure in the pre-announcement period is associated with a less negative stock price reaction during the post-announcement period. However, after controlling for the level of the disclosure, firms that increased disclosure just prior to the announcement suffer a larger price drop during the post-announcement period than a matched non-issuing firm. Stated in quantitative terms, LL's analysis suggests that a company with one more disclosure statement in the pre-announcement period has a 2.8% higher stock return during the post-announcement period. But if the firm added this extra disclosure statement during the pre-announcement period, then the positive influence on the stock return is offset by a 2.1% lower stock return due to the increased frequency of disclosure. This implies that the price reaction at the announcement date is not complete for firms that increase their disclosure activity during the six months preceding a stock offering announcement.

Overall, then, the story that emerges from LL's study is the following: On average, a higher level of disclosure during the period leading up to a stock offering announcement is associated with higher stock returns. On the announcement date, however, the market penalizes firms that achieved higher levels of disclosure by changing their previous disclosure patterns. However, the full penalty is not imposed on the "stock price hypers" on the announcement date. Instead, the stock prices of these companies continue to decline long after the equity offering is announced. Thus, all else equal, the cost of equity capital is lower for companies that provide greater disclosure prior to a stock issuance. However, the benefit is greatest for firms that provide consistently high disclosure, as opposed to those that increase their disclosures in anticipation of a stock offering.

CONCLUSION

The effect of disclosure on cost of equity capital is a matter of considerable importance. While there is room for additional research into this issue, the research completed to date tells a consistent and compelling story. Greater levels of disclosure are associated with a lower expected cost of equity capital in general and with higher stock prices around the time of seasoned equity offerings.

There is also some evidence to suggest that type of disclosure matters. Companies with moderate to low analyst followings appear to benefit most from providing greater forward-looking information and key non-financial statistics. As a result, these are the areas managers should focus on when considering enhancing their disclosures to the capital markets.

R&D AND CAPITAL MARKETS

*by Baruch Lev,
New York University**

E conomic growth and the consequent welfare improvement of nations and individuals are driven mainly by *technological change*, as manifested by the introduction of new products and services, the development of more efficient systems of production, and improvements in the organization and management of commerce and industry. Research and development is the major driver of technological change—hence the central role of R&D in economic growth and welfare improvement. The impact of R&D and technological change on economic growth has long been recognized by proponents of free market economies such as Adam Smith, Marshall, Keynes, and Solow. Even two of the most ardent critics of capitalist societies, Marx and Engels, argued in the *Communist Manifesto* that capitalism depends for its very existence on the constant introduction of new products and processes.

This sequence of effects—from R&D to technological change to increases in productivity and growth—holds not only for nations, but for individual companies and business units as well. A large and growing number of empirical studies have confirmed a significantly positive association between national, industry, and corporate R&D expenditures, on the one hand, and economic growth, productivity gains, and increases in corporate earnings and market values.[1]

The growth of R&D expenditures over the last two or three decades, together with the continuous substitution of knowledge (intangible) capital for physical (tangible) capital in firms' production functions, has elevated the importance of R&D in the performance of business enterprises. The ability to evaluate the risk and eventual payoffs from corporate R&D is therefore of considerable importance to capital market practitioners and researchers. The evaluation of R&D activities is seriously impeded,

however, by antiquated accounting rules and insufficient disclosure by corporations. Despite the obvious benefits of R&D, which generally stretch over extended periods of time, this investment is immediately expensed (written off) in corporate financial reports, leaving no trace of R&D capital on firms' balance sheets and causing material distortions of reported profitability.[2] Immediate expensing is practiced not only for internally generated R&D, but also in the growing number of acquisitions involving large amounts of "R&D-in-process," further distorting reported performance.[3]

The fact that only scant information on R&D and other innovative activities is publicly disclosed by firms compounds the information problems of investors when evaluating high-tech companies. Investors are generally told little about the nature of firms' research activities, such as the share of total R&D devoted to basic research, new product development, or efforts to increase the efficiency of production processes (known as "process R&D"). Nor is information typically furnished about the expected benefits and duration of products under development. Even the total R&D expense reported in corporate income statements often misrepresents the extent of activities aimed at producing innovations, particularly for small companies that do not formally classify such activities as R&D.

Given the importance of corporate research activities to capital market practitioners and researchers, and the inadequacy of public information on R&D, I provide in this essay:
- salient statistics about recent trends in corporate R&D;
- a brief summary of international disclosure regulations;
- a survey of the major empirical findings concerning R&D and its benefits, particularly as reflected in capital markets; and
- some guidelines for investors and analysts engaged in the valuation of R&D-intensive enterprises.

*I am grateful to Mark Hirschey, Frank Lichtenberg, Min Wu and Anne Wyatt for their assistance and suggestions.

1. See, for example, Griliches 1995, Hall 1993a, Lev and Sougiannis 1996, Coe and Helpman 1995. Full citations for all studies cited in the text and notes of this paper appear in the References section at the end of the article.

2. The most obvious effect of this accounting practice is to reduce current earnings for companies with high R&D growth. But, as discussed later in this paper, a more subtle distortion is the tendency to *inflate* popular return-on-investment measures like ROE and ROA.

3. Deng and Lev (1998).

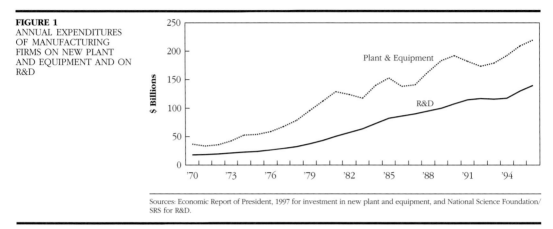

FIGURE 1
ANNUAL EXPENDITURES
OF MANUFACTURING
FIRMS ON NEW PLANT
AND EQUIPMENT AND ON
R&D

Sources: Economic Report of President, 1997 for investment in new plant and equipment, and National Science Foundation/SRS for R&D.

RECENT TRENDS IN R&D

Total annual R&D expenditures in the U.S. increased from $26 billion in 1970 to $206 billion in 1997, representing an average yearly growth rate of 8.0%, while investment in plant and equipment over the corresponding period increased annually by 6.8%, on average.[4] By comparison, the aggregate growth rate of R&D in the European Union countries during 1991-1996 was about half the U.S. rate. Of the $206 billion devoted to R&D in the the U.S. in 1997, $151 billion (or 73.3% of the total) was industry R&D, while the rest was sponsored by the federal government ($16.5 billion, or 8.0%), universities ($27 billion, 13.1%), and other institutions (5.6%).

Some perspective on the relative magnitude of industry R&D is provided by Figure 1, which portrays the relationship over the last 25 years between total annual expenditures of U.S. manufacturing firms on new plant and equipment (tangible investment) and their expenditures on R&D. While investment in plant and equipment has been very volatile, exhibiting sensitivity to economic conditions (particularly the recessions of the early 1980s and 1990s, which led to *decreases* in plant & equipment investment), expenditures on R&D have increased smoothly due to the constantly expanding opportunities in emerging technologies, such as biotech, computers, and telecommunications.

Besides increasing steadily in absolute terms, corporate investment in R&D has also increased relative to the scale of firms' operations. Figure 2 presents the annual average "R&D intensity" (that is, R&D as a percentage of revenues) of Compustat companies that report R&D (upper curve) and of all Compustat companies (lower curve). As shown in the upper line of Figure 2, for the former group, R&D expenditures as a percentage of revenues more than doubled from 1.9%, on average, in 1978 to 4.0% percent in 1997.[5] And the R&D intensities of high-tech, science-based companies have been substantially higher than the overall averages shown in Figure 2. For example, in 1996 the average R&D intensities of electronics, drugs, software, and biotech companies were, respectively, 6.1%, 12.0%, 17.8%, and 41.0%.[6]

Structural changes that occurred in the U.S. economy during the 1980s and early 1990s helped to increase the relative role of R&D in publicly traded companies. The increased focus of manufacturing firms on core operations accomplished by restructurings and spinoffs had the economy-wide effect of moving capital out of low-R&D sectors, such as chemicals, metals, and machinery, and into the high-tech sectors of pharmaceuticals, biotech, software and electronics.[7] The R&D intensity of the public-company sector increased further because the firms that went private through LBOs or were

---

4. The statistical data in this section are derived from the Economic Report of the President, 1997; the National Science Foundation/SRS; and the OEDC publication : Main Science and Technology Indicators, 1998.

5. The increase of R&D intensity is not due to increases in R&D input prices, rather to enhanced R&D activities of corporations (see Scherer, 1992, p. 1428)
6. Computed from Compustat, for SIC codes: 3600-3699, 2834, 2836, and 7372.
7. Hall (1993a).

R&D expenditures as a percentage of revenues more than doubled from 1.9%, on average, in 1978 to 4.0% percent in 1997. And the R&D intensities of high-tech, science-based companies have been substantially higher than the overall averages.

FIGURE 2
AVERAGE R&D INTENSITY (R&D OVER REVENUES) OF FIRMS HAVING R&D AND ALL FIRMS

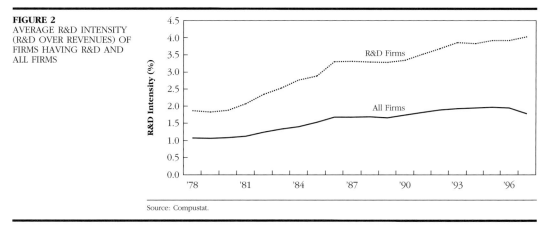

Source: Compustat.

acquired by foreign companies during the 1980s tended to be low in R&D (such as food companies and retailers). At the same time, the majority of the new entrants to capital markets in the 1980s and 1990s were high-tech firms traded on the NASDAQ.

Disclosure Regulations

Disclosure requirements in corporate financial reports for *internally generated* R&D vary across countries.[8] The main differences concern the income statement and balance sheet treatment of R&D. Public companies in the U.S. are required to expense all R&D outlays as incurred.[9] German companies also generally expense all R&D outlays, to conform to tax regulations. But most other developed countries allow—and, under certain circumstances, require—the capitalization (i.e., recognition as an asset) and subsequent amortization of certain R&D outlays, particularly identifiable product costs. For example, in the U.K., Canada, France, Australia, the Netherlands, Israel, and Sweden, public companies may capitalize the costs of development (but generally not basic research) when the projects under development are clearly defined and the expenditures separately identifiable. Japanese companies may capitalize R&D, but have to amortize it within five years. The amortization of the R&D capital is determined by the expected useful life of the projects.

Most countries require disclosure in the financial reports of the amounts of R&D expensed or capitalized, typically in footnotes. Moreover, in September 1998, the International Accounting Standards Committee (IASC) issued Standard No.38 on Intangible Assets, which calls for the capitalization of R&D costs for projects that meet certain criteria. Most important are that the projects (1) be clearly identified (i.e., costs and expected revenues are clearly separable from general corporate R&D), (2) have passed a technological feasibility test, and (3) be shown capable of recovering the capitalized costs.

In recent years, an increasing number of firms have been *purchasing* "R&D-in-process" (i.e., still incomplete projects and processes), generally through a corporate acquisition. Here, too, U.S. reporting standards are less flexible than those of most other countries. In the U.S., the purchasing companies are required to write off immediately the entire value of the acquired R&D-in-process. In contrast, the U.K., Canada, Australia, and New Zealand, as well as countries that have adopted the international standard, allow the capitalization of acquired R&D, which then must be amortized over its expected useful life.

As should be evident from this brief international survey, the required public disclosure of R&D activities by U.S. companies—essentially a single line item in the income statement—is wholly inad-

---

8. Information on international R&D disclosure regulations was obtained from Coopers & Lybrand (1993).

9. The only major exception in the U.S. to the immediate expensing of R&D are software development costs (FASB Statement No. 86) which have to be capitalized when a product passes successfully a technological feasibility test. Pre-feasibility development costs are expensed as incurred.

equate for the purpose of financial and security analysis. Reported profitability is seriously distorted; sometimes understated, often overstated. And the absence of R&D capital from financial reports denies investors the ability to assess the firm's return on innovative activities.

THE EMPIRICAL RECORD

Systematic economic research on the relationship between R&D and the attributes of firms and the markets in which they operate was initially motivated by Joseph Schumpeter's (1942) hypothesis that large and monopolistic companies have significant advantages in conducting research and developing products, mainly due to their sustained profitability and access to relatively inexpensive capital. Extensive empirical research, however, failed to substantiate a reliable association between either input or output measures of R&D and individual company or market attributes, such as size or the extent of competition in the product market.[10] In fact, the success of many small software, electronics, biotech, and pharmaceutical companies in conducting R&D and marketing products within highly competitive environments clearly runs counter to Schumpeter's hypothesis.

Research on R&D and Productivity

From examining industrial organization and market structure issues, mainstream economic analysis of R&D largely shifted in the 1970s to investigating the social and private returns to investment in R&D. This empirical work, which started with extensive historical case studies and proceeded to large-sample cross-sectional analyses of the impact of R&D on productivity and growth, was aimed mainly at assessing the consequences of R&D investment and addressing public concerns such as the role of R&D in the protracted productivity slowdown in the U.S. in the 1970s and early 1980s.[11]

This research effort yielded several important findings:[12]

■ R&D expenditures contribute significantly to the productivity (value added) and output of firms, and the estimated rates of return on R&D investment are quite high—as much as 20-30% annually—although varying widely across industries and over time.[13] Indeed, the estimated returns to R&D are more than double the returns to tangible capital, reflecting the higher productivity as well as riskiness of R&D capital relative to physical assets.

■ The contribution of *basic* research—research aimed at developing new science and technology—to corporate productivity and growth is substantially larger than the contribution of other types of R&D, such as product development and process R&D. In fact, the estimated contribution differential is about 3-to-1 in favor of basic research[14]—a finding that is particularly intriguing, given the widespread belief that firms have been recently curtailing expenditures on basic research and the skepticism expressed by many financial analysts and institutional investors about basic research.[15] Basic research is, of course, more risky than applied R&D, but it is inconceivable that risk differentials account for a 3-to-1 productivity superiority of basic research.

■ The contribution of privately financed corporate R&D to productivity growth is larger than that of corporate R&D that is financed by the government (granted primarily to government contractors). The fact that most contracts with the government are based on "cost plus" terms may partly explain this finding. Nevertheless, the contribution to the technological infrastructure of industry of government-funded research conducted by government agencies and in federal laboratories (such as, for example, the National Institute of Health) as well as university research is very significant.[16]

---

10. For surveys of this research, see Cohen and Levine (1989) and Scherer (1992).

11. See, for example, Lichtenberg and Siegel (1991).

12. For a discussion of these findings and the methodological issues involved in analyzing the cost-benefit relationship of R&D, see Griliches (1995).

13. See Hall (1993a); and for estimates of returns on tangible capital, see Poterba (1997). Documenting a positive contribution of R&D to productivity and growth is hardly surprising; why else would managers invest so heavily in R&D? Yet, this finding stands in stark contrast to a major assertion underlying the Financial Accounting Standards Board's (FASB) requirement for the immediate expensing of R&D in financial reports: "A direct relationship between research and development costs and specific future revenue generally has not been demonstrated, even with the benefit of hindsight." (FASB, 1974, p. 14).

14. See Griliches (1995). Related findings concern the importance of university research to industrial innovation (e.g., Mansfield 1991, Acs et al. 1994).

15. First-hand evidence of adverse analyst attitudes towards basic research can be found in an article by Richard Mahoney, former chairman and CEO of the Monsanto Company, describing how Monsanto developed over an extended period its biotechnology capacity, while analysts "naysayers offered a constant drumbeat of advice: reduce R&D, sell off any asset that wasn't nailed down and use the cash proceeds to buy back shares." (*The New York Times*, May 31, 1998).

16. See Mansfield (1991). Striking examples of major contributions of government R&D to industry are the Internet, funded originally by the Department of Defense as a bomb-resistant communicvations network, and later developed by the National Science Foundation, and the Human Genome Project, initiated by the National Institute of Health, now leading to revolutionary advances in biomedicine.

> Despite widespread allegations of stock market "short termism" throughout the 1980s and early '90s, the research indicates persuasively that capital markets consider investments in R&D as a significant value-increasing activity.

■ The gap between the private and social benefits of R&D is wide. R&D "spillovers"—that is, benefits to one firm (industry or nation) from another firm's (industry or nation's) R&D or pool of knowledge—are substantial. Consequently, the "social" rate of return on R&D is considerably higher than the return to individual firms.[17] This finding generated extensive analysis of the adequacy of corporate incentives to conduct R&D, and the optimal design of arrangements for appropriating R&D benefits (e.g., patents, trademarks).

Because of the scarcity and other shortcomings of information *published* by individual companies, the research findings outlined above were based primarily on survey data and industry aggregates. In fact, none of the examined variables and attributes—return on R&D capital, basic vs. applied research, company vs. government sponsored R&D, and private vs. social benefits of R&D—can be directly estimated for individual companies from information publicly disclosed to investors. Thus, one of the most promising uses of the above findings is to suggest the kinds of information and data that investors should seek from R&D-intensive companies and that companies should consider disclosing to investors.

Research on R&D and Capital Markets

The research effort surveyed above related R&D inputs (intensity, capital) to firms' productivity, sales, or profit growth in an attempt to estimate the return on corporate investments in innovation-producing activities. But this approach encounters various problems. Perhaps most obvious, the time lag between the investment in R&D and the realization of benefits is generally unknown and often long (particularly for basic research), increasing the uncertainty about the estimated regression parameters. Furthermore, biases and distortions in reported profits (such as those arising from "opportunistic" decisions by managers to cut back or expand

R&D to "smooth" reported income) may cloud the intrinsic relationship between the cost of R&D and its benefits.

Such measurement difficulties have prompted a search for alternative and more reliable indicators of R&D *output* than conventional profitability measures. Two measures have received considerable attention—patents and capital market values—and they are discussed in the following review of the growing number of studies examining the relation between R&D and market values.[18]

Investors' Recognition of R&D Value. Despite widespread allegations of stock market "short termism" throughout the 1980s and early '90s, the research indicates persuasively that capital markets consider investments in R&D as a significant value-increasing activity. Thus, for example, a number of "event studies" register a significantly positive investor reaction to corporate announcements of new R&D initiatives, particularly of firms belonging to high-tech sectors and operating on the cutting edge of technology.[19] Moreover, when information is available, investors distinguish among different stages of the R&D process, such as program initiation and commercialization, rewarding in particular mature R&D projects that are close to commercialization.[20] Furthermore, econometric studies that relate corporate market values or market-to-book ratios to R&D intensities consistently yield positive and statistically significant association estimates.[21] Further probing into such associations suggests that firm size affects the valuation of R&D in the sense that investors value a dollar R&D spent by large firms more highly than R&D of small firms, perhaps due to better information available on large firms.[22] The evidence thus indicates unequivocally that the stock market views R&D expenditures as enhancing the value of firms, on average, and that investors also demonstrate some ability to differentiate the value of R&D across industries, firm sizes, and stage of R&D maturity.[23,24]

Estimating R&D Capital (Cost Basis). While R&D capital is the major asset of most high-tech and

---

17. (Griliches 1995)

18. The research using patent counts and citations as R&D output measures is voluminous, and is summarized in Griliches (1989) and Hall et al. (1998).

19. See, for example, Chan et al. 1992. It was widely believed in the 1980s and early 1990s that, prodded by investors' "obsession" with quarterly earnings, U.S. managers routinely sacrificed the long-term profitable growth of their firms by curtailing investments, such as R&D, with long payoffs but immediate hits to earnings. The evidence of investors' positive reaction to R&D increases, despite the negative effect of such increases on near-term earnings (due to the immediate expensing of R&D), largely dispels the allegation of investor myopia, at least with respect to R&D.

20. (Pinches et al. 1996)

21. (Ben-Zion 1978, Hirschey and Weygandt 1985, Bublitz and Ettredge 1989).

22. (Chauvin and Hirschey 1993)

23. Hall (1993a, 1993b) reports an intriguing finding that investors' valuation of R&D decreased substantially during the mid-to-late 1980s. This decrease, however, was found to be most evident in the electronics sector and has been largely reversed in the 1990s.

24. While investors as a group reward R&D expenditures, a recent study (Bushee 1998) found that institutions engaged in momentum trading (i.e., short-term oriented investors) tend to have large holdings in firms that "manage" earnings by cutting R&D to reverse earnings declines.

science-based companies, its value is nowhere to be found in financial reports. Obviously, the absence of a major asset from the book value (equity) or total assets of firms reduces the reliability and usefulness of conventional return-on-investment measures like ROE and ROA for performance evaluation. The assessment of companies' effectiveness in using investor capital requires that estimates of their investment in R&D be considered.

Economists often estimate the value of firms' R&D capital by assuming a uniform 10-15% annual amortization rate, which implies an amortization period, or average economic life, for R&D investment that ranges from roughly six to ten years. The assumed amortization rate is then used to "build up" a firm's R&D capital in cost terms. For example, based on a straight-line 15% annual amortization assumption, a firm's R&D capital at the end of a given year would be equal to 85% of its R&D expenditure in that year, plus 70% of R&D in the prior year, plus 55% of R&D expenditure in the year before that, and so on until a fully amortized R&D layer is reached.[25]

Since the pattern of R&D benefits varies across firms and industries, an industry- or firm-specific amortization rate is likely to do a better job of reflecting economic reality than a universal 10-15% rate. In a study published in 1996, Theodore Sougiannis and I estimated industry-specific R&D amortization rates using a (simultaneous equations) model that relates companies' operating profits to their tangible assets, advertising expenditures (proxying for brands), and the time series of their annual R&D expenditures extending back ten years.[26] The derived R&D lag structure allowed us to estimate the contribution to current profits of R&D expenditures made ten years ago, nine years ago, and so forth, ending with the contribution of current year's R&D to current profits. For example, in applying our model to pharmaceutical companies, our findings suggest that a dollar spent on R&D today increases future profits by $2.63, on average, and that the average life of R&D projects is 9 to 10 years.

The pattern of lagged contributions to future profits by R&D spending in turn allowed us to estimate firm-specific R&D capital for about 1,500 companies spanning a large variety of industries. In the case of Merck, for example, we found that an appropriate R&D-adjusted balance sheet would contain R&D capital with a value of some $3 billion at the end of 1991. This would represent a 60% addition to Merck's equity capital base.[27]

To examine the potential relevance of our estimates of R&D capital for investors, we used the estimates to calculate *capitalization-adjusted* earnings and book values and then ran a series of regressions to estimate the strength of the correlation of such *capitalization-adjusted* measures with stock prices and returns. Our regression analysis confirmed that the adjustments of both reported earnings and book values for the immediate expensing of R&D yield performance measures that are more strongly associated with market values than reported earnings and book values.

Firm-specific estimates of R&D capital, based either on a uniform (15%) amortization schedule or on industry-specific rates, could prove useful in the kind of corporate performance evaluation that relies heavily on financial ratio analysis.

Estimating R&D Capital (Market Values). Given the magnitude of corporate expenditures on R&D (over $150 billion in 1997) and ever-increasing demand for technology, one would expect *markets* for R&D to develop. Of course, markets for patent rights and the licensing of R&D have long been in operation. But recent years have witnessed a relatively new development—a large number of corporate acquisitions in the software, pharmaceutical, biotech, and electronics industries in which *R&D-in-process* was by far the major asset acquired. This became evident due to an accounting requirement ("purchase accounting" for acquisitions) that acquiring companies estimate separately the fair market value of the acquired assets, including R&D-in-process. In a recent study of such acquisitions, Zhen Deng and I found that the fair market values of acquired R&D (yet-to-be-completed R&D projects) amounted, on average, to 75% of the acquisition price.[28] Such acquisitions, numbering in the hundreds per year, are primarily trades in R&D and technology.

---

25. Sometimes a geometrically decaying R&D capital is assumed.

26. Lev and Sougiannis (1996). The rationale for estimating industry- rather than firm-specific amortization rates in our study was similar to that underlying the use of industry- rather than firm-specific beta values in cost of capital estimation. That is, the loss of specificity involved in an industry estimate is likely to be compensated for by reduction of noise in the industry data.

27. For a detailed example of the computation of firm-specific R&D capital for Merck & Co., see the appendix of the Lev and Sougiannis paper.

28. Deng and Lev (1998)

> **In applying our model to pharmaceutical companies, our findings suggest that a dollar spent on R&D today increases future profits by $2.63, on average, and that the average life of R&D projects is 9-10 years.**

The fair market values assigned by management to acquired R&D-in-process are generally based on the present value of estimated cash flows from projects under development.[29] Our study finds that those fair values are closely associated with stock prices of acquiring firms, which in turn lends some credibility to management estimates. Moreover, a recent study of Australian companies reported that revaluations of intangibles (a procedure allowed in Australia but not in the U.S.) are significantly associated with stock prices, suggesting once more that investors pay attention to managers' assessments of market values of R&D.[30]

In addition to acquisitions where R&D is the prime asset acquired, another manifestation of developing markets for R&D are the "targeted stocks" issued in recent years by high-tech companies such as Alza and Genzyme. In those still small number of cases, the value of the security is derived from a specific R&D program or pool of patents transferred by the patent company to the new entity, thus representing a further step in the progressive securitization of intangibles.[31] In time, the prices observed in such markets will provide "comparables" or multiples for the purpose of intangibles' and enterprise valuations.

Nonfinancial Indicators of R&D Value. In search of reliable measures of R&D *output*, economists have experimented with various nonfinancial indicators, such as the number of patents registered by a company (patent counts), patent renewal and fee data, number of innovations, and citations of patents.[32] Patent counts and the number of innovations emerging from a company's R&D program have been found to be associated with both the level of corporate investment in R&D and with firms' market values. It is clear, however, that those R&D output measures are rather noisy due to the "skewness" of their value distributions—that is, the tendency of a few patents or innovations to generate substantial returns, while most turn out to be virtually worthless.[33] Citations (references) of a firm's patents included in subsequent patent applications ("for-ward citations") offer a more reliable measure of R&D value than the absolute number of patents, since such citations are an objective indicator of the impact of a firm's research activities on the subsequent development of science and technology.[34]

Various studies have shown that patent citations capture important aspects of R&D value. For example, Trajtenberg (1990) reports a positive association between citation counts and consumer welfare measures for CAT scanners; Shane (1993), in examining 11 semiconductor companies, finds that patent counts weighted by citations contribute to the explanation of cross-sectional differences in Tobin's q measures (market value over replacement cost of assets); and Hall et al. (1998) report that citation-weighted patent counts are associated with firms' market values (after controlling for the firms' R&D capital).[35]

In a direct test of the usefulness of patent citations to investors, Deng et al. (1999) and Hirschey et al. (1998) examine the ability of various measures derived from patent citations to *predict* subsequent stock returns and market-to-book (M/B) values in various R&D-intensive industries. The following three measures were all found to be significantly associated with future market-to-book values and stock returns of up to three years: (1) the number of patents granted to the firm in a given year; (2) the intensity of citations of a firm's patents in subsequent patents; and (3) a "science linkage" measure that reflects the number of citations in a firm's patents ("backward citations") of scientific papers and conferences (in contrast with citations of previous patents). The science linkage indicator is of special interest since it reflects the extent to which the firm engages in science-related or basic research as opposed to product development or process improvement. Furthermore, the predictive power of the science linkage measure with respect to stock performance is consistent with previously mentioned research that finds the contribution of basic research to firm productivity substantially larger than that of applied research aimed at product development.

---

29. See, for example, IBM's description in its 1995 annual report of the way it estimated Lotus' value of R&D-in-process ($1.84 billion).

30. Barth and Clinch (1998)

31. See Solt (1993) on R&D targeted securities and Beatty et al. (1995) on other R&D financing arrangements.

32. For a survey of this research, see Griliches (1989).

33. See, for example, Patel and Pavitt (1995).

34. The compilation of citations of previous patents or scientific studies in patent applications is of considerable importance and is checked carefully by patent examiners since patent citations assist in delineating the "claims," or property right boundaries, of the invention. Indeed, patent citations are used as evidence in patent infringement lawsuits. See Lanjouw and Schankerman (1997).

35. In two other studies, Austin (1993) reports that patents identifiable with end products tend to be more valued by investors than the average patent, and Megna and Klock (1993) find that patents of rival firms have a negative effect on a company's q-ratio.

As noted earlier, information about the nature of a company's R&D activities is generally not available in its financial statements. But, as the research just summarized suggests, non-financial indicators of R&D output such as number of patents, innovations, and trademarks—and in particular measures based on patent citations—offer a promising set of measures for firm valuation and security analysis.[36]

Firms' Capitalization of R&D. Software development costs are the major exception in the U.S. to the uniform expensing of R&D. FASB Statement No. 86 (enacted in 1985) requires companies to capitalize software development costs incurred after a project under development has reached technological feasibility (as generally evidenced by a working model or pilot).[37] The cumulative capitalized development cost (net of amortization) is presented as an asset on the balance sheet, while the periodic capitalized amount is subtracted from quarterly or annual development costs, which are then expensed in the income statement.

The amount of subjective judgment involved in the determination of technological feasibility of projects and the amortization of the capitalized asset led certain analysts and investment advisors to view software capitalization skeptically as detrimental to the quality of financial information. For example, the Association for Investment Management Research states: "We are not enamored of recording self-developed intangible assets unless their values are readily apparent; it usually is next to impossible to determine in any sensible or codifiable manner exactly which costs provide future benefit and which do not."[38]

But some recent empirical research suggests that the capitalization of intangibles may in fact provide useful information to investors. When David Aboody and I examined capitalization data disclosed during 1986-1995 by 168 software companies, we found that:

■ annually capitalized software development costs (i.e., the part of the total development cost that is not expensed) are positively and significantly associated with stock returns;

■ the value of the software asset that is reported on the balance sheet is reliably associated with stock prices; and

■ software capitalization data improve the prediction of future earnings.[39]

Particularly intriguing, moreover, was our finding that software companies that consistently expensed all their development costs (about a third of the examined sample) experienced positive abnormal return *drifts* that persisted for at least three years after the cost expensing, while firms that capitalized development costs did not. This evidence is consistent with some undervaluation of the shares of fully expensing firms, attributable perhaps to the lack of timely information about the progress and success of their software development programs (information that could be partly disclosed by the capitalization process).[40]

The evidence thus suggests that despite the subjectivity involved in the capitalization of software development costs, this procedure provides useful information to investors. The extent to which this conclusion can be generalized to other types of R&D (e.g., drug development) awaits further research. Nevertheless, it is worth noting that a recent simulation study clearly demonstrates the superiority of intangibles' capitalization over expensing in providing meaningful earnings data to investors. The simulation model measures the performance of pharmaceutical companies under immediate expensing of R&D and alternatively under capitalization, and compares the performance measures with economic returns and values (based on future cash flows). The results show that capitalization-based performance measures explain twice the variation in value as expensing-based measures.[41]

R&D and the Deteriorating Usefulness of Financial Information. It is widely acknowledged that the accounting measurement and reporting system has failed to keep up with recent sweeping changes

---

36. Stephan (1998) reports that the number of scientific publications of scientists associated with biotech startups is positively correlated with the IPO prices of these companies.

37. FASB Statement No. 86 applies to software developed for *sale*. In March 1998, the Accounting Standards Executive Committee of the AICPA (AcSEC) issued a statement of position (SOP 98-1) which applies the main criteria of FASB Statement No. 86 to software developed for *internal use*.

38. (AIMR 1993, p.50)

39. Aboody and Lev (1998). This predictive ability of capitalized values is consistent with the FASB's capitalization criterion—the establishment of technological feasibility. Projects achieving technological feasibility are more likely to

generate higher earnings in the near future than earlier-stage projects, hence the association between the amounts capitalized and subsequent earnings.

40. The subsequent return drifts associated with full expensing software companies is consistent with a similar finding in Lev and Sougiannis (1996, section 6), indicating that the shares of firms intensive in R&D (which is fully expensed in the U.S.) are associated with subsequent positive returns, after controlling for various risk factors. Relatedly, Chan et al. (1998) report that poorly performing firms that continue to invest substantially in R&D are also characterized by subsequent positive abnormal returns, which is consistent with undervaluation.

41. Healy et al. (1998)

The extent of the association between earnings and stock returns has continuously decreased over the past 20 years.

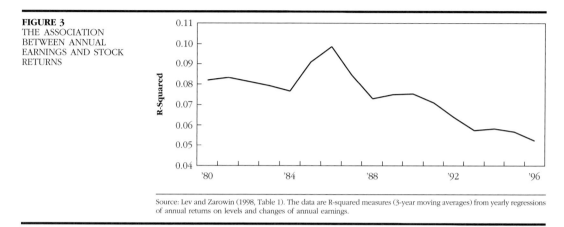

FIGURE 3
THE ASSOCIATION
BETWEEN ANNUAL
EARNINGS AND STOCK
RETURNS

Source: Lev and Zarowin (1998, Table 1). The data are R-squared measures (3-year moving averages) from yearly regressions of annual returns on levels and changes of annual earnings.

in the economy. Such changes have been driven by the continuous restructuring of firms' operations and the extensive deregulation of important economic sectors (such as telecommunications), as well as by the innovation-producing activities of companies that are the focus of this paper. Various public committees that have examined the usefulness of financial information to investors report widespread concerns of financial statement users with both the timeliness and relevance of information conveyed by corporate reports.[42] The popularity of business performance measures like EVA, which makes potentially large adjustments to reported earnings, also attests to the dissatisfaction of users, both internal and external to the firm, with the product of the accounting measurement system.

In a recent study, Paul Zarowin and I examined changes in the usefulness of financial information by analyzing the association over the last 20 years between stock prices and returns, on the one hand, and key financial variables such as earnings, cash flows, and book values.[43] This research comes to the following conclusions:

- the extent of the association between stock returns (prices) and financial variables has continuously decreased over the examined period, as portrayed in Figure 3 for earnings and stock returns;

- the major culprit responsible for the deteriorating usefulness of financial information is *business change*, since the costs and benefits associated with change are mismatched in the computation of earnings;[44] and

- R&D, a major driver of change, is directly associated with the decreasing usefulness of earnings.

More specifically, our study finds that firms that increased their R&D intensity over the 1977-1997 period experienced an above-average *decrease* in the association between earnings and stock returns, while firms whose R&D intensity declined experienced an *increase* in the strength of their returns-earnings association.[45]

The capital market consequences of informationally deficient financial reports have yet to be fully established, but some recent studies suggest they could be significant. For example, Boone and Raman (1998) report that unexpected changes in R&D are associated with a widening of the bid-ask spreads of stocks (an expected market-maker reaction to an increase in information asymmetry), leading to increased investors' transaction costs and decreased stock liquidity. Barth et al. (1998) document an increased level of analysts' efforts and possible mispricing of securities associated with high levels of R&D intensity. Aboody and Lev (1998) find

---

42. See, for example, AICPA (1993).

43. Lev and Zarowin (1998).

44. The costs associated with change (e.g., restructuring charges, R&D expenditures) are recognized immediately in the financial reports, while the benefits are reflected in future periods. Such a mismatching of costs and benefits adversely affects the informativeness of earnings and book values.

45. A mini-research industry has recently developed around the examination of temporal changes in the usefulness of financial information. Essentially all studies document a decrease in the returns-earnings association. On the other hand, Collins et al. (1997) report that the decrease in the returns-earnings association was compensated for by an increase in the stock price-book value association. Chang (1997) corroborates the Lev and Zarowin (1998) findings of a temporal decrease in the informativeness of both earnings and book values.

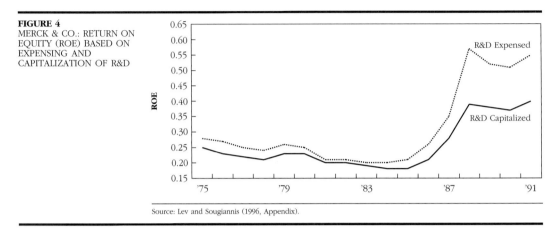

FIGURE 4
MERCK & CO.: RETURN ON
EQUITY (ROE) BASED ON
EXPENSING AND
CAPITALIZATION OF R&D

Source: Lev and Sougiannis (1996, Appendix).

that officers of R&D-intensive firms gain from insider trading significantly more than their counterparts in firms not engaged in R&D. And Lev and Sougiannis (1996), Aboody and Lev (1998), Chan et al. (1998), and Lev et al. (1999) all report evidence consistent with mispricing (generally undervaluation) of the shares of R&D-intensive companies. Finally, there is also evidence that some firms "manage" their reported earnings—say, by cutting R&D in response to shortfalls in operating earnings—which further compounds the information problems confronting investors in high-tech companies.[46]

In sum, the preliminary evidence suggests that the information and reporting deficiencies related to R&D activities have various adverse capital market consequences, which in turn may reduce firms' value by increasing monitoring costs and the cost of capital.[47]

OPERATING INSTRUCTIONS

What inferences can capital market practitioners draw from the empirical research on corporate R&D? I will classify such inferences, or "operating instructions," into two themes: (1) those that can be applied to the on-going performance evaluation of firms and (2) those useful for special purpose assignments, such as valuations for IPO pricing and corporate control transactions such as acquisitions and divestitures.

Performance Evaluation

Financial statements of R&D-intensive companies fail to provide adequate information for the assessment of profitability, growth, and enterprise risk. Contrary to widespread beliefs, the immediate expensing of intangible investments—including expenditures on brand maintenance and human resources as well as R&D—is not even necessarily a conservative practice. In fact, for firms with relatively low growth rates of intangibles—that is, the typical mature company—the immediate expensing of intangibles leads to a substantial *overstatement* of reported profitability.[48] In such cases, the effect of excluding intangible capital from the denominator of profitability ratios like ROE and ROA far outweighs the increased earnings under capitalization.[49] For example, as shown in Figure 4, the reported ROE (with immediate expensing of R&D) of Merck & Co.

---

46. See, for example, Baber et al. (1991).

47. In a similar vein, Bronwyn Hall (1993a p.290) comments: "asymmetric information between firms and investors implies that, to fund [R&D] projects about which they do not have full information, investors will demand a 'lemons' premium in the form of a higher rate of return." Obviously, in assessing the desirability of increased disclosure about firms' R&D activities, the competitive harm to firms from such disclosure and its effect on incentives to engage in R&D should be considered.

48. The exact relationship between ROE (ROA) under expensing and capitalization of intangibles is as follows: When the firm's growth rate of intangible investment is higher than its return on equity (which is typical of young firms and

industries), ROE (ROA) under expensing will be lower than under capitalization. But ROE and ROA under expensing will be higher for firms whose growth rate of intangibles is lower than their return on equity. For details, see Lev et al. (1999).

49. Under intangibles' expensing, earnings are charged with the periodic R&D expenditure, while under capitalization the amortization of the R&D capital (asset) is subtracted from earnings. For firms with a low growth rate of R&D, the difference between R&D expenditure and amortization will be relatively small, leaving the numerator of ROE (ROA) little changed, while the denominator is highly understated due to the absence of the intangible capital.

in the late '80s and early '90s was around 50-55%; but if Merck had instead capitalized and amortized its R&D, its ROE in that period would have ranged from 35-40%.[50]

Moreover, in a recent study, Bharat Sarath, Theodore Sougiannis, and I analyzed the impact of R&D expensing on reported earnings *growth*, which is the primary focus of many investors.[51] Our study demonstrated that firms whose growth rate of R&D falls below their growth in earnings will report higher earnings momentum when R&D is fully expensed than when R&D is capitalized and amortized. Thus, in this case as well—typical of mature companies— the expensing of R&D is far from conservative.

These biases in the reported performance of R&D-intensive companies are aggravated by the fact that U.S. firms expense not only *internally generated* R&D, but also *acquired* R&D. As noted earlier, acquired R&D amounts to 75%, on average, of the total acquisition price in those deals in which it is involved.[52] Obviously, the immediate expensing of the lion's share of the acquisition price substantially inflates the reported profitability of acquiring firms in the years after the acquisition. Post-acquisition earnings from the acquired entity are unencumbered by the previously expensed R&D, and the reported total assets or equity of the acquiring company reflects only a small portion of the total investment in the acquired entity. Thus, the full-expensing of R&D, internal as well as acquired, tends to inflate the reported profitability of R&D-intensive enterprises as well as the rate of growth of their reported earnings.

Financial analysts can partly correct for the reporting biases and distortions discussed above by a systematic reversal of R&D expensing—that is, by capitalizing and amortizing both internal and acquired R&D.[53] This adjustment involves adding back to earnings the expensed R&D and subtracting from earnings the amortization of the capitalized R&D. On the balance sheet, the R&D capital (net of amortization) should be added to total assets and equity (book value).[54]

To perform such a capitalization adjustment, the value of acquired R&D, which is provided in financial statement footnotes, should first be added to assets and equity. In contrast, the capitalized value of internal R&D has to be estimated. The key to the capitalization and amortization of internal R&D is the assumed *amortization rate*, or *average expected life*, of R&D projects, which is not reported by firms. As mentioned earlier, in estimating firms' R&D capital economists often use uniform annual amortization rates that range between 10% and 15%. But it is obviously preferable, whenever possible, to use industry- or firm-specific rates that reflect differences in technology and the appropriability of R&D benefits (relatively high in chemicals and drugs, where R&D is effectively protected by patents, and low in software and instruments) across industries and companies. Using the industry-specific amortization rates estimated by Lev and Sougiannis (1996) and other sources,[55] the following annual amortization rates seem suitable for R&D capitalization in the process of financial analysis:

- 8-10% (or amortization periods of 10-12 years) for pharmaceutical companies;
- 12-15% (6-8 years) for chemicals;
- 17-20% (5-6 years) for computer hardware, electronic equipment, and transportation vehicles; and
- 25% (4 years) for scientific instruments and software.

Despite the coarseness of the proposed capitalization and amortization estimates, it is inconceivable that investment analysis based on the uniform 100% amortization of R&D that now underlies reported earnings and book values could not be improved by the adjustment procedure outlined above.[56] Furthermore, the proposed capitalization procedure overcomes a disturbing inconsistency in accounting practices related to internally developed vs. acquired R&D products (e.g., scientific instruments). When a company acquires such a product it is recorded as an asset, whereas when the product is internally developed, all or most of the development costs are

---

50. Among the reasons for the increasing divergence between Merck's ROE (expensing) and ROE (capitalization) in the late 1980s (see Figure 4) is the considerable slowdown in its R&D growth. While Merck's average annual growth rate of R&D between 1977 and 1987 was close to 30%, its average annual R&D growth from 1987 to 1991 decreased to 18.6%. Ceteris paribus, the lower the growth rate of R&D, the larger the overstatement of reported profitability relative to profitability based on the capitalization of intangibles.

51. (Lev et al.1999).

52. (Deng and Lev 1998); sample period ended in 1997.

53. Note that the EVA performance evaluation system also reverses the immediate expensing of intangibles.

54. For firms whose R&D expenditures are stationary (zero growth), capitalization will not affect earnings (in a steady state), but will affect book value and total assets. For all other firms, the proposed capitalization will affect both earnings and book values. For details of the capitalization procedure, see Lev and Sougiannis (1996, Appendix).

55. See, for example, Deloitte & Touche 1996 annual survey of the software industry.

56. This conclusion is also supported by (Chambers et al. 1997), which shows that the explanatory power of earnings and book values with respect to stock prices increases when the financial variables are adjusted to reflect the capitalization of R&D.

expensed. The comparability of financial information between purchasing and developing companies can be restored by capitalizing the development costs of the latter companies.

Finally, it should be noted that the capitalization procedure outlined above is no substitute for the procedure for capitalizing intangibles that is currently required for software companies. Because such capitalization begins only after projects under development pass a technological feasibility test, the capitalization data provide investors with important information about the progress and probable success of firms' development programs. Furthermore, the writeoff of capitalized assets that are no longer commercially viable provides additional important information to investors. Such information, needless to say, is not reflected in the mechanical capitalization procedure proposed above.

In-Depth Assessment of Innovative Capabilities

The valuation and due diligence of R&D-intensive enterprises performed for corporate control transactions or IPOs require a thorough understanding and assessment of the innovative capabilities of the examined enterprise and its capacity to produce and market the developed products. Such assessment should begin with an analysis of the enterprise's R&D *strategy*—an analysis that determines the extent to which the firm primarily *develops* products and services, *shares* development with others through alliances, or *acquires* R&D. The strategy analysis should then attempt to ascertain the proportions of resources devoted to basic research vs. product development and cost reduction ("process R&D"), and to an assessment of the firm's capability to *use* rather than to *perform* R&D—that is, its record of learning from other companies' (and universities') innovations and adapting quickly to external technological changes. Learning from others requires an adequate scientific and engineering capacity as well as flexibility of organizational design. An examination of an enterprise's research strategy and capabilities will also shed light on the riskiness of investment in R&D. Obviously, the heavier the investment in basic vs. applied research, and the larger the proportion of in-house R&D vs. that developed in alliance with other firms, the riskier are the firm's R&D activities.

Research capability should be assessed primarily by *output* measures, such as the number of new products that have emerged from the development process, as well as the number of patents, patent citations, and trademarks registered (as discussed earlier, each of these measures of R&D output have been demonstrated to have a strong positive correlation with stock-price performance). Most important, efforts should be made to quantify the contribution of R&D activities to sales, cost savings, and earnings. Various quantitative measures can be used to gauge research output, such as citations to the firm's patents and measures indicating the share of current revenues coming from products developed within the last three or five years. The latter measure indicates the firm's ability to quickly "bring products to the market," a capacity which often differs from the ability to develop products.

R&D strategy should be evaluated in the context of the firm's overall strategic position. Is the firm an industry leader, reaping the advantages of a "first mover"; or is it a "follower" in introducing new products and innovations? What is the firm's record in appropriating the benefits of its innovative activities, such as successfully defending its patents from infringement and maximizing licensing revenues? Answers to these and similar questions will shed light on the firm's innovative capabilities.

Finally, the firm's product *pipeline* has to be considered. Even when accompanied by an impressive historical record of developing and marketing products, an impoverished pipeline of projects does not bode well for the future. This calls for a thorough examination of products under development, such as drugs in FDA approval process, as well as patents and trademarks pending registration. Also to be examined are current and expected revenues from licensing agreements and the activity level of research and development performed within alliances and joint ventures. When *valuation* of R&D-in-process is required (as in the case of corporate acquisitions), the future cash flows from pipeline projects should be estimated, accounting among other things for synergies with the acquiring entity's R&D. Such cash flow-based valuations of R&D-in-process are now common, given the large volume of technology company acquisitions.

An assessment of firms' product development and marketing capacity should also take into consideration managers' incentives to "manage" reported performance. As mentioned earlier, research indicates that under certain circumstances managers will change periodic R&D expenditures to

Efforts should be made to quantify the contribution of R&D activities to sales cost savings, and earnings. Various quantitative measures can be used to gauge research output, such as citations of the firm's patents and measures indicating the share of current revenues coming from products developed within the last three or five years.

achieve earnings targets or conform with investors' expectations.[57] Such "management" of R&D and the resulting effect on reported earnings should be adjusted for in the evaluation of R&D capabilities and consequences.[58]

SUMMARY

Although R&D is the major productive factor and the principal asset of high-tech and science-based companies, public information about firms' R&D activities and their benefits is wholly inadequate for investment research and analysis. This paper begins with a brief review of statistics that show the growth of U.S. corporate R&D expenditures outstripping the growth of corporate investment in tangible assets. Next, in comparing R&D disclosure regulations among industrialized nations, I show that U.S. rules are the least flexible in allowing management

discretion in the measurement and reporting of R&D (e.g., capitalization vs. expensing). Then I survey the large and growing body of empirical research on R&D, which demonstrates unequivocally that (1) the contribution of R&D to productivity and shareholder value is substantial and (2) that capital markets reflect such contributions in stock prices. But if investors clearly demonstrate a willingness to take the "long view" of R&D in many cases, there is also some evidence of undervaluation of R&D-intensive companies as well as other potential costs to some corporations and investors stemming from inadequate public information about R&D. In the final section, I offer some operating guidelines for investors and analysts that follow R&D-intensive companies, suggesting a number of adjustments of financial data (in particular, capitalizing instead of expensing some forms of R&D) designed to better reflect corporate performance and value.

---

57. See, for example, Perry and Grinaker (994), Baber et al. (1991), Bushee (1998).

58. Incentive compensation plans, such as EVA, that capitalize R&D expenditures reduce but do not eliminate incentives to manage earnings via R&D.

REFERENCES

■ **Aboody, D. and B. Lev**, 1998, "Information Asymmetry and Insider Gains: The Case of R&D-Intensive Companies," NYU working paper.

■ **Aboody, D. and B. Lev**, 1998, "The Value-Relevance of Intangibles: The Case of Software Capitalization," *Journal of Accounting Research*, forthcoming.

■ **Acs, Z., D. Audretsch and M. Feldman**, 1994, "R&D Spillovers and Recipient Firm Size," *Review of Economics and Statistics*, 76, 336-340.

■ **American Institute of Certified Public Accountants**, 1993, The AICPA Special Committee on Financial Reporting, "The Information Needs of Investors and Creditors," New York: AICPA.

■ **Association for Investment Management and Research (AIMR)**, 1993, *Financial Reporting in the 1990s and Beyond.*

■ **Austin, D.**, 1993, "An Event-Study Approach to Measuring Innovative Output: The Case of Biotechnology," *The American Economic Review*, 83, 253-258.

■ **Baber, W., P. Fairfield and J. Haggard**, 1991, "The Effect of Concern about Reported Income on Discretionary Spending Decisions: The Case of Research and Development," *The Accounting Review*, 66, 818-829.

■ **Barth, M. and G. Clinch**, 1998, "Revalued Financial, Tangible, and Intangible Assets: Associations with Share Prices and Non-Market-Based Value Estimates," Stanford University, working paper.

■ **Barth, M., R. Kasznik and M. McNichols**, 1998, "Analyst Coverage and Intangible Assets," Stanford University, working paper.

■ **Beatty, A., P. Berger and J. Magliolo**, 1995, "Motives for Forming Research & Development Financing Organizations," *Journal of Accounting and Economics*, 19, 411-442.

■ **Beaver, W. and S. Ryan**, 1996, "Biased Recognition (Conservatism) and Delayed Recognition in Accounting and Their Effects on the Ability of the Book-to-Market Ratio to Predict Book Return on Equity," NYU working paper.

■ **Ben Zion, U.**, 1978, "The Investment Aspect of Nonproduction Expenditures: An Empirical Test," *Journal of Economics and Business*, 30, 224-229.

■ **Boone, J. and K. Raman**, 1998, "Unrecognized R&D Assets and the Market Microstructure," University of North Texas working paper.

■ **Brown, S., K. Lo, and T. Lys**, 1998, "Use of R2 in Accounting Research: Measuring Changes in Value-Relevance over the Last Four Decades," Northwestern University, School of Business.

■ **Bublitz, B. and M. Ettredge**, 1989, The Information in Discretionary Outlays: Advertising, and Research and Development, *The Accounting Review*, LXIV, 108-124.

■ **Bushee, B.**, 1998, "The Influence of Institutional Investors on Myopic R&D Investment Behavior," *The Accounting Review*, 73, 305-333.

■ **Chambers, D., R. Jennings and R. Thompson**, 1997, "Evidence on the Usefulness of Capitalizing and Amortizing Research and Development Costs," working paper, University of Texas at Austin.

■ **Chan, L., J. Lakonishok and T. Sougiannis**, 1998, "The Stock Market Valuation of Research and Development Expenditures," working paper, University of Illinois.

■ **Chan, S., J. Kensinger and J. Martin**, 1992, "The Market Rewards Promising R&D—and Punishes the Rest," *Journal of Applied Corporate Finance*, Vol. 5 No. 2 (Summer), 59-66.

■ **Chang, J.**, 1998, "The Decline in Value Relevance of Earnings and Book Values," Harvard University, working paper.

■ **Chauvin, K. and M.Hirschey**, 1933, "Advertising, R&D Expenditures and the Market Value of the Firm," *Financial Management*, 128-140.

■ **Coe, D. and E. Helpman**, 1995, "International R&D Spillovers," *European Economic Review*, 39, 859-887.

■ **Cohen, W. and R. Levine**, 1989, "Empirical Studies of Innovation and Market Structure," R. Schmalensee and R. Willig, eds., *Handbook of Industrial Organization Vol. II*, Elsevier Science, Amsterdam.

■ **Collins, D., E. Maydew and I. Weiss**, 1997, "Changes in the Value-Relevance of Earnings and Book Values over the Past Forty Years," *Journal of Accounting and Economics*, forthcoming.

■ **Coopers & Lybrand**, 1993, *International Accounting Summaries*, New York, John Wiley & Sons.

■ **Deloitte & Touche LLP**, 1996, "Research and Development Survey of Software Companies," New York.

■ **Deng, Z., B. Lev and F. Narin**, 1999, "Science & Technology as Predictors of Stock Performance," *Financial Analysts Journal*, forthcoming.

■ **Deng, Z. and B. Lev**, 1998, "The Valuation of Acquired R&D," NYU working paper.

■ **Financial Accounting Standards Board (FASB)**, 1985, SFAS No. 86, "Accounting for the Costs of Computer Software to be Sold, Leased, or Otherwise Marketed."

■ **Financial Accounting Standards Board**, 1974, "Accounting for Research and Development Costs," *Statement of Financial Accounting Standards No. 2.*

■ **Francis, J. and K. Schipper**, 1997, "Have Financial Statements Lost Their Relevance?" University of Chicago, working paper.

REFERENCES (Continued)

■ **Freeman, C.,** 1996, "Innovation and Growth," *Handbook of Industrial Innovation,* Dodgson and Rothwell, eds., Brookfield, US: Edward Elgar, 78-93.

■ **Griliches, Z.,** 1990, "Patent Statistics as Economic Indicators," *Journal of Economic Literature,* 92, 630-653.

■ **Griliches, Z.,** 1989, "Patents: Recent Trends and Puzzles," Brookings Papers on Economic Activity: Microeconomics, 291-319.

■ **Griliches, Z.,** 1991, "Market Value, R&D, and Patents," *Economic Letters,* 7, 183-187.

■ **Griliches, Z.,** 1995, "R&D and Productivity: Econometric Results and Measurement Issues," *Handbook of Economics of Innovation and Technological Change,* P. Stoneman, ed., Oxford: Blackwell.

■ **Hall, B., A. Jaffe and M Trajtenberg,** 1998, "Market Value and Patent Citations: A First Look," UC Berkeley and NBER.

■ **Hall, B.,** 1993a, "Industrial Research during the 1980s: Did the Rate of Return Fall?" Brookings Papers on Economic Activity: Microeconomics 2, 289-393.

■ **Hall, B.,** 1993b, "The Stock Market Valuation of R&D Investment during the 1980s," *American Economic Review,* 83, 259-264.

■ **Healy, P., S. Myers, and S. Howe,** 1998, "R&D Accounting and the Relevance-Objectivity Tradeoff: A Simulation Using Data from the Pharmaceutical Industry," Working Paper, Harvard Business School and MIT Sloan School of Management.

■ **Hirschey, M. and J. Weygandt,** 1985, "Amortization Policy for Advertising and Research and Development expenditures," *Journal of Accounting Research,* 23, 326-335.

■ **International Accounting Standards Committee,** 1998, "Intangible Assets," *International Accounting Standard No.38,* London.

■ **Lanjouw, J. and M. Schankerman,** 1997, "Stylized Facts on Patent Litigation: Value, Scope and Ownership," National Bureau of Economic Research, working paper No. 6297.

■ **Lev, B., B. Sarath and T. Sougiannis,** 1999, "Reporting Biases Due to Intangibles' Expensing," Working Paper, NYU.

■ **Lev, B. and P. Zarowin,** 1998, "The Boundaries of Financial Reporting and How to Extend Them," NYU working paper.

■ **Lev, B. and T. Sougiannis,** 1996, "The Capitalization, Amortization, and Value-Relevance of R&D," *Journal of Accounting and Economics,* 21, 107-138.

■ **Lev, B. and T. Sougiannis,** 1998, "Penetrating the Book-to-Market Black Box: The R&D Effect," *Journal of Business, Finance and Accounting,* forthcoming.

■ **Lichtenberg, F. and D. Siegel,** 1991, "The Impact of R&D Investment on Productivity—New Evidence Using Linked R&D-LRD Data," *Economic Inquiry,* 29, 203-228.

■ **Mansfield, E.,** 1991, "Academic Research and Industrial Innovation," *Research Policy,* 20, 1-12.

■ **Marx, K. and F. Engels,** 1848, "The Communist Manifesto," English translation, *Karl Marx Selected Works, Vol.1,* Marx-Engels-Lenin Institute, Moscow, 1935.

■ **Megna, P. and M. Klock,** 1993, "The Impact of Intangible Capital on Tobin's q in the Semiconductor Industry," *The American Economic Review,* 83, 265-269.

■ **OECD Directorate for Science, Technology and Industry - Industry Committee Report,** 1998, "Industrial Performance and Competitiveness in an Era of Globalization and Technological Change," DSTI/IND(97) 23/FINAL

■ **Patel, P. and K. Pavitt,** 1995, "Patterns of Technological Activity: Their Measurement and Interpretation," *Handbook of the Economics of Innovation and Technological Change,* Paul Stoneman, editor, Great Britain, Blackwell Publishers Ltd., 14-51.

■ **Perry, S. and R. Grinaker,** 1994, "Earnings Expectations and Discretionary Research and Development Spending," *Accounting Horizons,* 8, 43-51.

■ **Pinches, G., V. Narayanan and K. Kelm,** 1996, "How the Market Values the Different Stages of Corporate R&D — Initiation, Progress, and Commercialization," *Journal of Applied Corporate Finance,* Vol. 9 No.1 (Spring), 60-69.

■ **Poterba, J.,** 1997, "The Rate of Return to Corporate Capital and Factor Shares: New Estimates Using Revised National Income Accounts and Capital Stock Data," National Bureau of Economic Research, working paper no. 6263.

■ **Scherer, F.,** 1992, "Schumpeter and Plausible Capitalism, *Journal of Economic Literature,* XXX, September, 1416-1433.

■ **Schumpeter, J.,** 1942, *Capitalism, Socialism, and Democracy,* New York: Harper.

■ **Shane, H.,** 1993, "Patent Citations as an Indication of the Value of Intangible Assets in the Semiconductor Industry," Philadelphia, PA: The Wharton School, University of Pennsylvania.

■ **Shevlin, T.,** 1991, The Valuation of R&D Firms with R&D Limited Partnerships, *The Accounting Review,* 66, 1-21.

■ **Solt, M.,** 1993, "SWORD Financing of Innovation in the Biotechnology Industry," *Financial Management,* 173-187.

■ **Stephan, P.,** 1998, "Capitalizing the Human Capital of University Professors: The Case in Biotechnology," Georgia State University, School of Policy Studies.

■ **Trajtenberg, M.,** 1990, "A Penny for Your Quotes: Patent citations and The Value of Innovations, "*Rand Journal of Economics,* 21, 172-187.

GOODWILL ACCOUNTING: EVERYTHING HAS CHANGED AND NOTHING HAS CHANGED

by Martin Ellis,
Stern Stewart & Co.

ill the Financial Accounting Standards Board's new reporting procedures for business combinations cause a slowdown in M&A activity? Acquisitions initiated after June 30, 2001 must now be recorded using the purchase method, with any premium over book value reported as goodwill on the balance sheet of the acquirer (FASB Statement No. 141). Goodwill is no longer amortized against earnings, although it must be periodically reviewed for "impairment," and occasional write-downs may be necessary (FASB Statement No. 142). Pooling-of-interests accounting—with the balance sheets of the acquirer and target merely added together, or "pooled"—is no longer permitted. But while these changes are significant, do the new FASB rules really alter the merger and acquisition landscape to the extent that advisors and executives should be concerned about the impact on acquisition activity?

Practitioners differ in their assessment of the effects of the FASB rules changes. A recent article in *The Daily Deal* written by a "valuation specialist" from a leading investment bank stated that companies in industries such as energy and financial services will see their stock prices rise because the end of goodwill amortization will increase their earnings. He went on to suggest that M&A deal volume will increase because "companies that were previously unattractive acquisition candidates, because of size and high price-to-book ratios, will become attractive," and "U.S. companies will be more competitive in their bids against foreign buyers because the new rules put them on a similar accounting footing."[1] In stark contrast, another M&A analyst wrote, "Mergers done with stock can no longer avoid the gremlin of goodwill...and many companies will opt out of the acquisition game rather than face goodwill write-downs that could 'hammer' earnings."[2] Echoing this, a partner at Pricewaterhouse-Coopers commented: "It [recording goodwill] will take certain companies out of the picture and have a depressing effect on asset prices."[3]

In the hype and debate over the impact of the FASB rules changes, however, little attention has been paid to the underlying value and economic impact of business combinations. Despite the changes to GAAP for acquisitions, investors' expectations have not changed. Accounting goodwill is merely the premium over historical book value; what investors care about is the premium over the current operating value of the target firm and whether the acquiring firm can achieve the value creation implicit in that premium. The concern over EPS and the accounting impact of business combinations ignores the fundamental economics of acquisitions, which relate to the exchange of value, not to accounting rules. The key question is still whether an acquisition benefits the acquiring firm's stockholders—and the economic value added (EVA) framework, which links value, goodwill, and investor expectations, can help to answer that question.

---

1. Lorre F. Jay, "Acquiring Goodwill," *The Daily Deal*, July 18, 2001
2. David Carey, "A World Without Goodwill," *The Daily Deal*, May 31, 2000.
3. Ibid.

IMPACT ON M&A ACTIVITY

There is ample record of the fear—whether justified or not—that the end of pooling-of-interests accounting, and other changes to the accounting rules for business combinations, will affect M&A activity. The technology industry in particular—which frequently used pooling-of-interests accounting—has expressed concern that having to record goodwill would make growth through acquisition unprofitable and unviable. John Chambers, CEO of Cisco Systems, voiced this concern in a 1999 quarterly earnings release regarding the proposed changes to the rules for accounting for goodwill and suggested that Cisco would likely change its acquisition strategy and/or its valuation methodology.

It appears that in the heated discussion about accounting rules, however, we have forgotten about the stockholders—and after all, they are the constituency that we should really be concerned about. Target company stockholders typically make out all right, with premiums of 30%, 40%, and higher. But the real question is whether an acquisition increases the wealth of the acquiring firm's stockholders—whether it adds to the market value of their ownership—and whether accounting goodwill has any bearing on their wealth or value expectations. The relationship between investor expectations and the acquisition price determines the wealth impact of an acquisition. Simply put, if the acquisition price is greater than the present value of the target's expected cash flows—including synergies—then the market value of the acquirer will fall.

Many acquisitions have been structured to increase reported earnings per share in the belief that an increase in reported earnings will create value for the acquirer's shareholders. However, acquiring firms frequently discover only fool's gold when they structure deals to be EPS accretive, since earnings accretion does not necessarily equal value accretion—and if it does, it is only by coincidence. In fact, transactions can be structured to be EPS accretive even if they *destroy* value for the acquirer. The market sees through the accounting fog, however, and penalizes acquirers that pursue value-destroying deals, including deals that boost EPS.

In chasing EPS, many companies have been willing to pay significant premiums in order to be able to account for a transaction on a pooling-of-interests basis, notwithstanding the abundant empirical evidence that pooling-of-interests accounting does not benefit shareholders. A 1996 study of the purchase versus pooling controversy found that the average premium over book value was nearly three times greater in poolings than in purchase transactions.[4] As a result, companies that pooled were more likely to overpay, and subsequently to underperform, than those using purchase accounting. One interpretation is that because acquirers believed that using their stock as an acquisition currency is free, they were seduced into paying higher premiums for the cosmetic benefits of pooling. Moreover, poolings lulled management into a false sense of security about the higher premiums since the return on capital is typically higher than for companies using purchase accounting—operating profits are unchanged but capital is lower than with purchase accounting by the amount of goodwill. But return on capital can be as misleading as any other measure of performance in analyzing an acquisition. For instance, are investors better off when an acquisition—using purchase accounting—results in no goodwill being recorded because the price paid is less than book value, and thus return on capital increases (because capital is lower)? If managers believe that by not recording goodwill they remove the requirement to meet the implicit value expectations of investors—since there is no goodwill to amortize and thus return on capital is higher—or that they will be rewarded by investors for higher earnings, they are mistaken in both instances.

A study of AT&T's controversial 1991 merger with NCR concluded that AT&T overpaid for NCR by anywhere from $60 to $101 per share on a final $111-a-share offer.[5] Moreover, AT&T was willing to incur at least $50 million in additional out-of-pocket expenses for lawyers and accountants to meet pooling-of-interests criteria. When allowed by the Securities and Exchange Commission to use pooling, AT&T paid an additional $5 to $7 per share to get NCR to unwind certain past transactions—NCR's special dividend and share repurchases—that would have frustrated pooling, thereby increasing the $7.5

---

4. Michael L. Davis, "The Purchase vs. Pooling Controversy: How the Stock Market Responds to Goodwill," *Journal of Applied Corporate Finance*, Vol. 9, No. 1 (Spring 1996).

5. Thomas Lys and Linda Vincent, "An Analysis of Value Destruction in AT&T's Acquisition of NCR," *Journal of Financial Economics* 39 (1995).

In the hype and debate over the impact of the FASB rules changes, little attention has been paid to the underlying value and economic impact of business combinations. The key question is still whether an acquisition benefits the acquiring firm's stockholders—and the EVA framework, which links value, goodwill, and investor expectations, can help to answer that question.

billion all-stock purchase price by as much as $500 million. The acquisition of NCR decreased the wealth of AT&T stockholders by between $3.9 billion and $6.5 billion and resulted in negative synergies of as much as $3.0 billion—even though the deal boosted EPS by 17%. The final word on the value creation of the merger, however, came six years later when, after investing a further $2.8 billion in NCR, AT&T spun the computer company off to shareholders in a transaction worth only $3.4 billion.

Given many acquirers' proclivity to avoid purchase accounting, it would appear that the devil is in the details of goodwill. But does purchase accounting really change anything? Although the evidence confirms that companies earn higher stock returns when they account for acquisitions as a purchase rather than as a pooling-of-interests, this does not imply that the new FASB rules will necessarily result in acquirers earning higher returns. The objective of the acquirer should be to maximize the wealth of its stockholders, and thus it is the exchange of value—not accounting rules—that should be the focus. The only way to truly evaluate the exchange of value and the relationship between the price paid, current performance, and goodwill is to use the economic value added (EVA®) valuation framework, which explicitly links value, goodwill, and investor expectations. The EVA valuation framework can thus provide unique insights into structuring and pricing acquisitions.

ECONOMICS OF ACQUISITIONS

In principle, mergers and acquisitions are undertaken to create value for shareholders. Certainly acquisitions are good for the national economy since they ensure the free flow of capital to its most productive uses. Moreover, the evidence shows that acquisitions do create wealth for shareholders.[6] But while acquisitions create value for all shareholders as a group, numerous studies confirm that all too frequently, much of the value created goes to the shareholders of the *target* company. In fact, approximately two-thirds of all deals *destroy* value for the acquiring firm's shareholders.[7]

The stock price reaction to an acquisition announcement speaks volumes about the exchange of value and what investors expect from a business combination. Clearly, if the stock price of the acquirer drops on announcement, investors' "unbiased" estimate of the additional value created by combining the two companies is less than the premium paid by the acquirer, irrespective of whether the deal is earnings accretive or accounted for on a purchase or pooling-of-interests basis. Mergers are all about the exchange of value, and the evidence indicates that the shareholders of the acquirer are often on the short end of that exchange.[8] The FASB's requirement to record goodwill documents the exchange of book value and total market value, but does it truly address the exchange of economic value—the price paid versus the value based on current and future operating performance? The FASB has, at least in its own mind, tried to address these issues with its Statement No. 141 and Statement No. 142.

What Is Goodwill?

The definition of goodwill is quite clear. Goodwill is the excess of the cost of an acquired entity over the net of the amounts assigned to assets acquired and liabilities assumed. Simply put, it is the premium paid for the net book assets of a business. The FASB's new Statement No. 141 requires that any applicable goodwill be recorded for all mergers and acquisitions, meaning that all transactions are accounted for using the purchase method. The rationale for the change in the accounting rules is that the new rules more appropriately capture the economics of merger and acquisition transactions since they will result in financial statements that:[9]

■ *Better reflect the investment made in an acquired entity as it reflects the exchange of value and provide information about total purchase price paid which allows a meaningful evaluation of subsequent performance.*

■ *Improve the comparability of reported financial information.*

6. Michael Bradley, Anand Desai, and E. Han Kim found that the combined value of the target and the acquirer, as measured by market capitalization, increased by an average of 7.4% over the five-day period prior to the first bid for the target through the five days after the announcement of the ultimately successful bid; see "Synergistic Gains from Corporate Acquisitions and Their Division Between the Stockholders of Target and Acquiring Firms," *Journal of Financial Economics* 21 (1988).

7. Mark L. Sirower, *The Synergy Trap* (New York: The Free Press, 1997).

8. Tim Loughran and Anan Vijh studied the post-acquisition returns of 947 companies from 1970-1989 and found that all acquirers—irrespective of how the acquisition was financed—earned 6.5% less than matching non-acquirers over the five years after the acquisition, and the returns were 24.2% less than matching companies when stock was used; see "Do Long-term Shareholders Benefit from Corporate Acquisitions?," *Journal of Finance*, Vol. 52, No. 5 (1997).

9. Statement of Financial Accounting Standards Board No. 141.

■ *Provide more complete information through expanded disclosure requirements.*

At a minimum, the new FASB requirements will remove the incentive for companies to incur significant costs to be able to report on a pooling-of-interests basis—like AT&T in its acquisition of NCR—and will thus benefit the acquirer's shareholders whose shareholder value will no longer be destroyed just to meet accounting rules. Requiring that a single method of accounting be used to account for business combinations also reduces the costs of accounting. But while the definition of goodwill is clear, its relationship to the required operating performance of acquired companies is less obvious.

Economics of Goodwill

Goodwill is not just about intangibles—it is directly related to current and future operating performance, or EVA. Companies that are well managed and earn a return on capital that exceeds their cost of capital tend to be valued at a premium over the capital invested in them—the ratio of market value to book value is greater than one. Investors will pay a premium over the dollar amount of invested capital to own the shares of these companies where, they believe, management will continue to be successful in adding value to their investment. One measure of the premium shareholders are willing to pay for successful companies is market value added (MVA). Mathematically, MVA is the absolute dollar spread between a company's total market value and the book capital—both debt and equity capital—invested in it. Capital can also be thought of as the net (of non-interest-bearing current liabilities) book assets of a company.

$$MVA = Total\ Market\ Value - (debt + equity\ capital)$$

Every year *Fortune* magazine publishes a ranking of the 1,000 largest companies according to the absolute dollar amount of wealth, or MVA, that these companies have created for their stockholders. In the latest ranking General Electric is rated number one, having created some $426 billion in wealth for its investors.[10] MVA, while a measure of wealth, is also the "goodwill" that companies have generated

for their investors. In fact, if no premium is paid to acquire a company, then accounting goodwill—assumed to include any allocation of premium over net assets to other intangibles—is quite simply equal to MVA, or total market value less net book assets.[11] Any premium over the pre-acquisition stock price of a target company simply increases pre-acquisition MVA by the premium. Since goodwill is equal to the total purchase price less net book assets,

$$Goodwill = MVA.$$

Inasmuch as investors are forward looking, MVA and goodwill must be directly related to investors' expectations of the future operating performance of a company. Merton Miller and Franco Modigliani demonstrated 40 years ago that the total market value of the firm is equal to the present value of its future free cash flows (FCFs) discounted at an appropriate weighted average cost of capital.[12] While FCF is an excellent measure of value, it is a poor measure of period performance since it subtracts the full cost of a capital investment in the period in which it occurs. This results in volatile FCF from one year to the next. As a result, it is very difficult to define required annual FCF targets that meet investors' expectations, since FCF could be positive or negative in any one year depending on a company's growth opportunities and investment schedule.

While discounted FCF may be the basis for determining value and the price to be paid in an acquisition, it is of little help in guiding management as to the level of operating performance that their investors expect of them based on their willingness to pay a premium over the capital invested in a target. Accounting goodwill measures the exchange of total value and book value, but there is no explicit link between goodwill and required operating performance. Goodwill is akin to knowing the total miles you have to travel but with no insight into the speed at which you need to travel to reach your destination on time, or how that speed varies depending on the route followed.

The EVA valuation framework, on the other hand, avoids the shortcomings of FCF and provides unique insights into acquisitions, goodwill, and current and implied future operating performance.

---

10. *Fortune*, Investor Guide, 2001, forthcoming.
11. Assumes that the recorded book value of the assets remained unchanged, i.e., no write-up or write-down of the book value.

12. Merton Miller and Franco Modigliani, "Dividend Policy, Growth and the Valuation of Shares," *Journal of Business*, Vol. 34 (October 1961).

Transactions can be structured to be EPS accretive even if they destroy value for the acquirer. The market sees through the accounting fog, however, and penalizes acquirers that pursue value-destroying deals, including deals that boost EPS.

Unlike FCF, EVA capitalizes investments, rather than expensing them, and imputes a capital charge at the cost of capital on the investment. EVA is defined as net operating profits after tax (NOPAT) minus a capital charge equal to total capital multiplied by the cost of capital (C). Equivalently, it is the return on capital (R)—defined as NOPAT divided by capital—minus the cost of capital, multiplied by total capital.

$$EVA = NOPAT - (C \times Capital), \text{ or}$$
$$EVA = (R - C) \times Capital$$

Assume that a target company has NOPAT of $60 million, total capital of $500 million, and a 10% cost of capital. The calculation of EVA is simple: NOPAT of $60 million less 10% of $500 million, which results in EVA of $10 million. In other words, the target is generating real profits of $10 million—not merely accounting profits—by earning sufficient NOPAT to more than cover the 10% cost of its capital.

The present value of FCF is exactly equal to the present value of EVA plus invested capital, since the sum of the present value of depreciation and the capital charge is equal to the initial investment for FCF purposes. As a result,

$$Total\ Market\ Value = Capital + Present\ Value\ of\ EVA$$

We have already seen that total market value is equivalent to invested capital plus MVA. But since goodwill is equal to MVA, goodwill is then also equal to the present value of future EVA. As a result, the EVA valuation methodology provides managers of acquiring firms with a framework—directly related to period performance—for determining the operating profitability necessary to justify the price paid for a target.

Return on Capital Is Misleading

One of the FASB's objectives with its new rules is to improve the comparability of reported information. While it will be easier to make comparisons among acquiring firms, goodwill makes return on capital comparisons between acquiring and non-acquiring companies meaningless. Acquisitive companies will systematically have lower returns on capital, except in special circumstances.

The return on capital is key to the calculation of EVA, since EVA is equal to the return on capital minus the cost of capital, multiplied by the total capital invested in a business. In order to create value, the return on capital—over time—must exceed the cost of capital so that the net present value of the investment is positive. Notwithstanding the trend over the past decade toward value-based metrics and a focus on the return on capital, the return on capital can be particularly misleading when corporate acquisition criteria require that the pro forma return on capital exceed some hurdle rate, and if not immediately, then within a short period of time. Take for instance an industry that is undergoing consolidation, such as the electronics distribution industry, where an Arrow or an Avnet continue to make one or more large acquisitions every year. In such industries, consolidation may be necessary for survival as well as value creation. Acquirers are able to eliminate the duplicate fixed costs of their competitors—such as corporate overhead and excess distribution facilities—as well as realize synergies by picking up additional product lines and increasing sales volumes through existing distribution facilities, thus increasing the return on capital, or EVA, of those facilities. However, as new acquisitions are made—and the target's capital is marked-to-market—the acquirer's goodwill balance continually expands, and it is unlikely that return on capital will exceed the cost of capital until many years after the company ceases making acquisitions. Yet each one of these deals may create value even though the return on capital for the acquirer may not exceed the cost of capital for some time.

Return on capital is an even bigger problem in high-growth companies such as technology and biotechnology companies. These companies typically have a low capital base and very high returns on capital; it is not unusual for technology companies to have returns on capital that exceed 50%. When capital investments are small relative to total market value, MVA and hence goodwill will dwarf the current capital base. For example, a biotechnology company with invested capital of $50 million and NOPAT of $30 million will have a return on capital of 60%. If the company trades at a PE of 25, the current value of the company will be $750 million, and MVA is $700 million. If this company were acquired for a 33% premium, the acquisition price would be $1,000 million and the acquirer would record $950 million in goodwill. Pro forma return on capital would plummet from 60% to 3% because NOPAT is still $30 million but capital is now $1,000 million.

FIGURE 1 ■ INDUSTRY FUTURE GROWTH VALUES

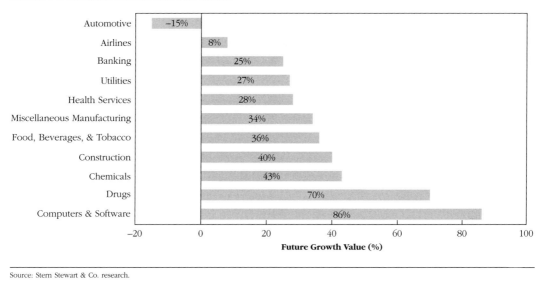

Source: Stern Stewart & Co. research.

As a result, positive EVA—where the return on capital exceeds the cost of capital—is highly unlikely in the short term and possibly for many years. This analysis of pro forma accounting for acquisitions of technology companies reveals why the new FASB requirements on recording goodwill give many CEOs heartburn. But recording goodwill and measuring the return on capital are merely the result of the accounting rules for business combinations. Rather than being concerned with the accounting implications, the directors and executives of acquiring firms should ask what the implicit expectations are for the future operating performance of the target, in order to justify the price paid.

Future Growth Is Key

The Miller and Modigliani valuation formula also laid the groundwork for one of the EVA valuation methodology's biggest benefits, which is its ability to disaggregate a company's total market value into two components: the value of current operations and a growth component equal to the future growth value. A company's future growth value is that part of its total value which is based on investors' collective expectations that management will improve operating performance,

or EVA, in the future. It is simply the present value of improvements in EVA over and above the current level of EVA. There is a growth component implicit in all stock prices, but it is typically larger for technology companies than, say, for steel companies. Figure 1 gives an indication of how growth values vary across industries.

The value of current operations, by contrast, assumes no growth in the current levels of EVA—that is, the company sustains its current level of operating performance into perpetuity. If investors expected no improvement in a company's EVA, its total market value would be equal to the value of its current operations. Incorporating the current operating value and the future growth value into the EVA valuation formula results in:

$$\text{Total Market Value} = \text{Capital} + \text{EVA}/c + ((1+c)/c) \times \sum_{t=0}^{\infty} \Delta \text{EVA}_i/(1+c)^i$$

Establishing a company's future growth value raises one of the most important questions about analyzing an acquisition: Can management achieve the growth implicit in a target's stock price? Future growth value has considerable importance in M&A, where the acquiring firm's management must deliver on both the growth value embedded in the pre-

A 1996 study of the purchase versus pooling controversy found that the average premium over book value was nearly three times greater in poolings than in purchase transactions. As a result, companies that pooled were more likely to overpay, and subsequently to underperform, than those using purchase accounting.

FIGURE 2

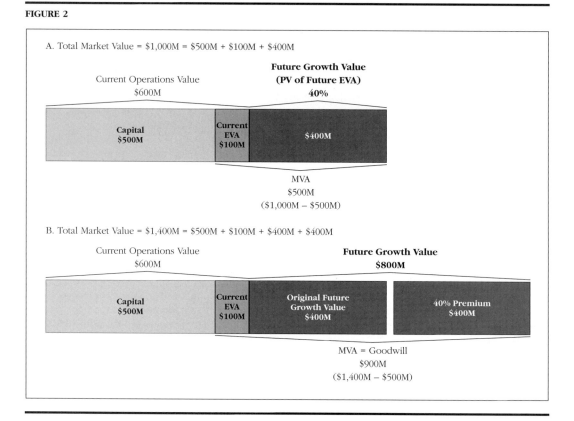

acquisition value of the target plus the increase in that growth value implicit in the premium paid to acquire the target. To evaluate how much future growth is implicit in the price paid, the acquirer's due diligence first must confirm the target's current operations value. Next, the acquirer must analyze the additional improvements in performance required to justify the premium over the current operations value at which the target trades to determine whether they are realistic and achievable. Finally, the acquirer must figure out how much further the target EVA will have to improve to justify the premium paid over the current market value.

EVA EXPLAINS ACCOUNTING GOODWILL

EVA clarifies whether the exchange of value is fair. The acquirer, knowing the purchase price, can determine exactly what level of future operating performance must be achieved with its new acquisition in order to receive fair value in return. Let's assume that a target acquisition company has a total market value of $1 billion and total book or invested capital of $500 million—see Figure 2(A). The difference of $500 million is the wealth, or MVA, that has been created for shareholders, but it is also the present value of an expected future stream of EVA. Assume that current annual EVA of $10 million is sustainable forever and is worth $100 million at a 10% cost of capital. Adding this $100 million to the $500 million of capital establishes the company's current operations value of $600 million. Since the company has a total market value of $1 billion, the remaining $400 million, or 40% of the total market value, is the future growth value.

When an acquirer pays a premium to acquire this target company, the acquirer commits not only to deliver the required earnings growth implicit in the $400 million future growth value, but also to deliver the necessary improvements to earn back any premium paid—see Figure 2(B). If the premium over market value is 40%, or $400 million, so that the acquisition price is $1,400 million, then the acquiring firm's management has doubled the target firm's future growth value to $800 million from $400 million, and has thus doubled the required level of annual improvements in EVA. With invested capital of $500 million, goodwill of $900 million will be recorded ($1,400 million – $500 million). Unfortunately, free cash flow and other performance measures do not provide any insight into what the post-acquisition required performance should be to justify $900 million in goodwill. However, the EVA valuation formula fully accounts for all the goodwill—$100 million is accounted for by the current operating performance of the target and $800 million is accounted for by future growth or improvements in EVA. Thus, an EVA analysis allows the acquiring firm to determine the required EVA improvement for the target firm based on its pre-acquisition market value as well as the additional required improvement in EVA necessary to justify the $400 million premium over market value. As a result, EVA accounts for every dollar of accounting goodwill.

Future Growth Value Is Acquisition Goodwill

The future growth value has far greater implications for acquirers than merely helping to tote up accounting goodwill. The future growth value is the true economic or acquisition goodwill, or the purchase price less the value of the existing business, since it represents the premium over the current operations value. The future growth value, or acquisition goodwill, is the premium that management must recover in order to make its stockholders whole; accounting goodwill is not relevant. It is quite possible for a target company to have positive MVA—and thus goodwill will be recorded—but have zero or negative future growth value, or alternatively to record no accounting goodwill but have significant acquisition goodwill, or future growth value. As a result, the debate and concern over the impact on M&A activity of the FASB's new rules has focused on the wrong issue. The real issue is acquisition goodwill rather than accounting goodwill.

For example, Philip Morris and Intel have both created prodigious wealth for their shareholders and thus have positive MVA, whereas AT&T has de-

stroyed significant value and was in fact ranked number 1,000 in *Fortune* magazine's December 2000 ranking of "America's Best and Worst Wealth Creators," having destroyed $34.4 billion in shareholder value. Acquiring Philip Morris or Intel, excluding a premium for the sake of simplicity, would result in significant goodwill being recorded—$55.7 billion in an acquisition of Philip Morris and $281.8 billion in an acquisition of Intel. However, acquiring AT&T would result in no goodwill being recorded, since its book value exceeds its total market value. With zero goodwill recorded, is an acquisition of AT&T a better deal for the acquiring firm's stockholders than an acquisition of Philip Morris or Intel? One hopes that the acquiring firm would not make that case on the economically bankrupt argument of not having to record goodwill.

Table 1 provides even further insights into goodwill. Table 1 presents three companies as hypothetical acquisition targets. Company PM has been structured to look like Philip Morris, AT to look like AT&T, and IN to look like Intel. PM, AT, and IN each have a total market value of $1 billion. However, PM has MVA $250 million, AT has MVA of –$500 million, and IN has MVA of $800 million. Based on their current total market values and operating performance, PM has a future growth value of –$250 million, whereas AT's future growth value is $500 million and IN's future growth value is $700 million. If a 30% premium is offered to acquire control—assuming that all three companies are financed with 40% debt on a market value basis—then a premium of $180 million will be paid (equal to 30% of $600 million in equity). Acquiring either PM or IN will result in goodwill being recorded, whereas the acquisition of AT results in no goodwill being recorded. Notwithstanding the FASB's stated desire to reflect the economics of acquisitions, the recording of accounting goodwill does not provide adequate insight into the economics of an acquisition, and thus accounting goodwill is irrelevant.

The only way to evaluate the required performance implicit in the goodwill, or lack thereof, is to analyze the future growth value. PM's future growth value of –$250 million implies that investors expect current performance to be unsustainable—current EVA capitalized is greater than MVA, so future performance is expected to deteriorate. In other words, accounting goodwill of $430 million—even including the $180 million (30%) premium—is more than accounted for by the current level of operating

While acquisitions create value for all shareholders as a group, numerous studies confirm that all too frequently, much of the value created goes to the shareholders of the *target* company. In fact, approximately two-thirds of all deals *destroy* value for the acquiring firm's shareholders

TABLE 1

	Philip Morris	AT&T	Intel
MVA ($ Billions)	$55.7	($34.4)	$281.8
EVA ($ Billions)	$6.6	($6.4)	$4.7
Future Growth Value	(25.2%)	55.8%	79.4%

	PM	AT	IN
Invested Capital	$750	$1,500	$200
Total Market Value	1,000	1,000	1,000
MVA	250	(500)	800
NOPAT	125	50	30
Cost of Capital	10%	10%	10%
Return on Capital	16.7%	3.3%	15.0%
Current EVA	50	(100)	10
Current EVA Capitalized	500	(1,000)	100
Current Operations Value	1,250	500	300
Future Growth Value	(250)	500	700
Future Growth Value (%)	(25%)	50%	70%
30% Premium	180	180	180
Goodwill (Including 30% Premium)	430	0	980
Total Deal Value (Including 30% Premium)	1,180	1,180	1,180
Pro Forma Return on Capital	10.6%	4.2%	2.5%

Source for Philip Morris, AT&T, and Intel results: *Fortune* Ranking 12/18/00.

performance. In the case of a Philip Morris, this may be quite realistic given increasing public resistance to tobacco products and the possibility of further significant class action lawsuits. Focusing on the fact that investors expect future performance to deteriorate is of far greater importance for the acquirer than worrying about book values, PE ratios, and goodwill and its potential impact on reported earnings and return on capital.

In the case of AT, no goodwill is recorded, even at a 30% premium. However, investors have significant expectations for improvement in EVA with a future growth value of $500 million. If investors expected AT to realize its growth value over a ten-year horizon, EVA would have to increase by $7.4 million every year for ten years (based on the equation for future growth value presented earlier).

Knowing how much performance must improve annually is of far greater relevance than celebrating not having to record goodwill, writing down assets, and increasing the return on capital from 3.3% to 4.2%. If the present value of synergies is less than the premium of $180 million, then the acquirer has destroyed shareholder value even though it has managed to increase the return on capital by 90 basis points.

Like PM, IN has positive MVA, but like AT it has created significant expectations for improvements in performance with a future growth value of $700 million. As with PM, significant goodwill will be recorded in an acquisition of IN—$980 million, including the 30% premium. However, current EVA accounts for little more than one-tenth of goodwill. With a future growth value of $700 million plus a premium of $180 million, investors have significant expectations for growth, or improvements in EVA, and thus goodwill includes a substantial growth component. Recording goodwill does not change these expectations; even if IN were acquired using the old pooling-of-interests accounting, the future growth value would remain unchanged, as would investors' expectations. In addition, the earlier comments about growth values and return on capital for technology companies are relevant for IN, our version of Intel. Pro forma return on capital falls from 15% to 2.5%. Even if all synergies are realized immediately—assume after-tax cost savings of $18 million a year—making the acquisition value neutral, the pro forma return on capital is still only 4.1%.

In summary, acquisitions of high-growth companies—such as technology companies—will result in significant levels of accounting goodwill being recorded and a significant growth component to this goodwill, and return on capital will fall dramatically. An acquisition of either PM (Philip Morris) or IN (Intel) would result in substantial balances of goodwill being recorded, but implicit in this accounting goodwill are widely different expectations for growth and improvements in profitability, with the market forecasting weakening performance for PM and significant improvements for IN. Nor does return on capital provide any real insight. Without a rigorous analysis of future growth value, or acquisition goodwill, an acquirer cannot make an informed decision about the required level of performance implicit in the premium paid, thus increasing the likelihood that the acquisition is ultimately value destroying.

Understanding future growth value is key to helping ensure that acquisitions create value. Far too many acquirers spend too much of their effort and resources on the wrong issues, such as figuring out ways to make deals EPS accretive and focusing their due diligence on existing operations rather than on the future growth value, which is the component of value that is most uncertain.

CONCLUSION

In issuing Statements No. 141 and No. 142, the FASB has attempted to better reflect the economics of the exchange of value that takes place in business combinations. At the very least, requiring a single method of accounting for business combinations reduces the costs of accounting, puts all acquirers on an equal accounting footing, and removes the incentive for companies to incur significant costs to be able to report on a pooling-of-interests basis. Yet while the FASB rules for accounting for business combinations have changed significantly, investor expectations of acquirers have not. Unfortunately, the new rules do not provide any real insight into what investors expect of acquirers.

Accounting rules should have no impact on acquisition pricing or structuring, unless they affect cash flows. Nonetheless, there is a continued obsession with pooling-of-interests and EPS accretion, rather than price paid, value received, and the economic implications of future growth. It has even been reported that the demise of pooling will limit how much corporations can afford to bid for assets and will make financial buyers more competitive, since LBO firms can acquire significant ownership stakes through leveraged recapitalizations and not record goodwill. There is already anecdotal evidence that companies are structuring deals with LBO partners where economic stakes are split 50:50 but voting control is greater than 80% for the LBO partner so that goodwill does not have to be recorded.

To ensure that acquisitions are fair to the acquirer's stockholders, boards of directors and executives must understand the minimum annual performance targets they have set for themselves by paying a premium to acquire a company. They must also have an integration and operating plan to achieve those performance targets. Accounting goodwill does not hold anyone accountable for the price paid, and can be very misleading when the current operations value of a target is significantly different from book value and thus accounting goodwill deviates significantly from acquisition or economic goodwill.

Ideally, corporate incentive plans would reward wealth creation rather than accounting measures of performance. If they did, the obsession with goodwill would disappear. All too often, incentive plans get in the way of ensuring that acquisitions are value creating by rewarding managers for EPS or income growth rather than wealth creation. Even using other value-based metrics in measuring post-acquisition performance, such as return on capital, can provide the wrong incentives and lead to value-destroying behavior.

Achieving the expected improvements in EVA implicit in the future growth value, or economic goodwill, is what investors expect of acquirers to make them whole. Without holding themselves accountable for investors' expectations, executives will continue to pursue acquisitions that boost EPS. As a sage once said, any fool can grow profits; the real test is whether profits can be grown profitably. The EVA valuation framework helps to meet that test. The economic framework and future growth value analysis of EVA always remain applicable, whatever the accounting rules *du jour.*

HOW TO FIX ACCOUNTING— MEASURE AND REPORT ECONOMIC PROFIT

*by G. Bennett Stewart III,
Stern Stewart & Co.*

An upheaval in corporate accounting is underway. Declaring an end to the era of low standards and false profits, President Bush has created a new oversight board to regulate accounting standards. Hoping to get ahead of the curve, companies are lining up to deduct the cost of granting employee options. Finance officers everywhere are scrambling to disclose more data.

Welcome as these changes are, they chiefly attack symptoms instead of providing a cure. The real issue is not that a handful of companies like Enron and WorldCom broke rules to inflate their earnings—deplorable as that is—but that almost every company has been bending accounting rules to smooth earnings and meet analyst expectations. Finance chiefs have routinely changed key assumptions, plundered reserves, and timed the recognition of gains and losses if that's what was necessary to keep reported profits on track.

Even more disturbing, most business leaders appear to see no harm in taking advantage of accounting flexibility. "Lots of companies managed their earnings, and I think that's okay within reason," cable entrepreneur Craig McCaw opined in a recent *Fortune* magazine interview.[1] GE's Jeff Immelt has also publicly defended the active management of corporate earnings.

When decent men like McCaw and Immelt condone deceptive behavior, something has gone wrong. Bending accounting rules is not substantively different from breaking them. But fudging financial results has become so ingrained in corporate culture that even ethical business leaders have succumbed to the temptation to mislead the public while meeting analysts' demand for smoothly rising earnings.

A sudden outbreak of greed is not to blame for this. The real source of our present maladies is that accounting has become unhinged from value; it is no longer counting what counts. It has been set adrift by a thousand tugs and pulls of competing factions, each vying to mold accounting pronouncements to their own purposes. Those in charge have not been wise or strong enough to resist their ploys and to make the auditor's definition of earnings a reliable measure of value. As accounting has lost its anchor to value, it has forfeited its stature and authority. It has degenerated into a game whose main aim is prettifying earnings reports. When there is no standard or overarching mission, and the corporate accountant's charge is simply to "beat the Street," Enron and WorldCom are but a step removed.

---

1. "The Man Who Would Save Satellites," *Fortune*, June 24, 2002.

Corporate executives have known for some time that accounting no longer measures what matters. They understand full well that many of their wisest decisions diminish their reported profit, at least initially—things like stepping up promising research spending, developing new brands, or investing heavily in a six-sigma quality initiative. They also realize that many dumb strategies are available to give their earnings a boost. Postponing a restructuring or pouring more funds into low-return business units are classic examples of bad decisions that accounting makes good. Smart managers have responded by opting out of the accounting system. They have been moving toward substitute measures, including pro forma income, core earnings, EBITDA, and, in some cases, EVA[2] or the Balanced Scorecard.[3] Corporate managers' disenchantment with reported earnings has been shared by the business press and the investment community. As a *BusinessWeek* article concluded, the reason for calculating "a second set of earnings" is simple:

...the numbers reached by applying generally accepted accounting principles (GAAP) are woefully inadequate when it comes to giving investors a good sense of a company's prospects. Many institutional investors, most Wall Street analysts, and even many accountants say GAAP is irrelevant. "I don't know anyone who uses GAAP net income anymore for anything," says Lehman Brothers Inc. accounting expert Robert Willens.[4]

The proliferation of alternative metrics is a clear sign that something is systematically wrong with accounting, and that a systematic response is called for. Stopgap rule changes of the kind now being proposed will only backfire; for if they do not bring accounting into accord with economic value, they will only set the stage for the next round of scandals. A deep reformation in accounting principles is required. What the public demands, and what in fact is needed, is a measure of earnings that offers a reliable guide to intrinsic value.

But not everyone agrees. In fact, some of the most sophisticated observers of stock market behavior—the so-called "efficient" market theorists—point out that astute, price-setting investors look beyond reported earnings and take into account all publicly available information relevant to the valuation of shares. They think the aim of reform should simply be fuller information disclosure, and regard as folly the idea that a single "true" earnings measure can be defined. A recent *Wall Street Journal* editorial by regular columnist Holman Jenkins is representative of this school of thought:

Studies galore show that stock prices already behave as if investors understand what options cost them in terms of potential dilution of their ownership stakes. The issue has been fully aired and the proposed rule, if adopted, would have no impact on share prices.[5]

Jenkins and other like-minded souls are correct as far as the professional investor is concerned. But they are mistaken if they think that the auditor's definition of earnings has no important consequences. Consider, for example, the following statement that appeared the same day in another *Wall Street Journal* article:

As companies begin expensing options, they are almost certain to get stingier about handing them out because it will hurt their bottom line. That will have major implications for how a wide array of employees negotiate their compensation packages.[6]

The media, government agencies, board members, employees, and top managers all tend to take reported earnings seriously—and at face value. The press judges business leaders by the amount of earnings they book. Union leaders base their wage demands on disclosed corporate profit. Accountants are sued when their profit reports are alleged to be misleading.

Most damaging of all, bonuses for corporate top brass are almost universally tied to reported

---

2. EVA® stands for economic value added. It is a special method to measure economic profit and can be used in making business decisions and in motivating managers and employees to think and act like owners by paying them like owners.

3. The Balanced Scorecard was developed by Robert Kaplan (Harvard Business School) and David Norton (Balanced Scorecard Collaborative). The Balanced Scorecard suggests that management develop metrics, collect data, and analyze results in each of these four perspectives: (1) learning and growth; (2) business processes; (3) customer; and (4) financial. The scorecard approach

explicitly rejects the usefulness of reported financial results in managing and measuring the value of a business.

4. "Confused About Earnings?," *BusinessWeek*, Nov. 26, 2001.

5. Holman W. Jenkins, Jr., "Much Ado About Stock Options—Act Two," *The Wall Street Journal*, August 7, 2002.

6. "What the New Option Rules Mean for Your Pay," *The Wall Street Journal*, August 7, 2002.

As accounting has lost its anchor to value, it has forfeited its stature and authority. It has degenerated into a game whose main aim is prettifying earnings reports.

net income measures, and that can distort almost every major decision they make, including how they manage risk. Consider the following testimony by law professor Frank Partnoy before the U.S. Senate:

Enron's risk manual stated the following: 'Reported earnings follow the rules and principles of accounting. The results do not always create measures consistent with underlying economics. However, corporate management's performance is generally measured by accounting income, not underlying economics. Risk management strategies are therefore directed at accounting rather than economic performance.' This alarming statement is representative of the accounting-driven focus of U.S. managers generally, who all too frequently have little interest in maintaining controls to monitor their firm's economic realities.[7]

Professor Partnoy has pointed to the cause of the accounting scandals: the failure of accounting to measure economic value. Reported earnings are indeed of considerable practical importance, and a far better definition is needed.

But the proposed reforms now making the rounds are much too limited for the task at hand. Yes, employee stock options should be expensed, and pension fund gains should be eliminated from income. But such proposals have more to do with appearances—forcing companies to report lower earnings—than the real issue of getting a more relevant measure of earnings.

The substantive changes necessary to make earnings a meaningful indicator of value would challenge some of the most basic assumptions on which our accounting framework now rests. As accounting scholars will tell you, our present system was *originally* designed to provide information about corporate assets that was intended mainly for use by creditors; it was basically an auditing function aimed at verifying the existence (as opposed to the value) of corporate assets and at deterring theft and fraud.[8] What this article proposes is a fundamental

change in the accountant's mission—one in which the primary aim becomes the measurement and reporting of *economic* profit (or, alternatively, economic value added, or "EVA").

Stated in brief, my concept of economic profit or EVA begins with an older, but now seldom used definition known as "residual income" (basically standard net income minus a charge for the cost of equity capital), and then proposes a series of additional adjustments to GAAP accounting that are designed to produce a reliable measure of a company's annual, sustainable *cash*-generating capacity. In contrast to the definition of income as the change in the stock measure of wealth from period to period, as originally proposed by the economist John Hicks, my definition of economic profit aims to provide a purely "flow" measure of income. The basic intent in so doing is to provide a measure of income that, when capitalized at a multiple that reflects a company's cost of capital, accounts for the premium at which a company's market value stands in relation to the book value of its net assets.[9]

Narrowing the accountant's responsibility to that of measuring and reporting the economic profit their clients have earned would remove any legal liability associated with the valuation of corporate assets, which is properly the role of security analysts and one for which accountants are not particularly well suited. Nonetheless, accountants are increasingly being asked to play this role. The recently enacted FAS 144, for example, directs auditors to write down long-term assets such as acquisition goodwill that they determine to have shrunk in value. But this is a ticking time bomb of legal exposure and negative publicity. The next time a major acquisition disintegrates in a cloud of layoffs, the firm's auditors will be skewered for not anticipating the loss with a goodwill write-down. Lawsuits and an erosion of investor confidence will surely follow. But even so, we are now hearing calls to expand the auditor's valuation responsibilities to include providing estimates of the market value of such

---

7. Hearings before U.S. Senate Committee on Government Affairs, Jan. 24, 2002.

8. See, for example, George Benston, "Accounting Doesn't Need Fixing (Just Some Reinterpreting)," *Journal of Applied Corporate Finance*, Vol. 15, No. 3 (Spring 2003).

9. Economic theory and substantial empirical evidence suggest that a company's market value is determined by its book capital plus the present value of its recurring flow of economic profit. Expressed as an equation, Market Value

= Book Value of Capital + Present Value of Economic Profit. For more on the connection between economic profit (EVA) and value, refer to G. Bennett Stewart III, *The Quest For Value* (New York: HarperBusiness, 1991), pp. 250-350, and also to Ronald E. Shrives and John M. Wachowicz, Jr., "Free Cash Flow (FCF), Economic Value Added (EVA®) and Net Present Value (NPV): A Reconciliation of Variations of Discounted-Cash-Flow (DCF) Valuation," *The Engineering Economist*, Vol. 46 (2001), No. 1, pp. 36-52.

difficult-to-value and firm-specific corporate assets as research and brand names. Yet broadening the accountant's mandate in this way will lead only to more punitive lawsuits and force even greater concentration among accounting firms.

The solution is to accept that valuation is the market's job and to limit the accountant's responsibility to providing information about economic profit. Accountants must surrender the illusion that balance sheets can and should measure "value"—a forward-looking measure of the resources that investors can expect eventually to take out of a business—and accept that balance sheets can only measure "capital," a necessarily backward-looking measure of the resources that have been put into a business. At present, accounting rules have made the balance sheet an arbitrary combination of assets, value, and capital. In so doing, they have diminished the usefulness of income statement information, they have left the accountant's mission and the definition of earnings ambiguous, and they have needlessly exposed audit firms to liabilities they should not bear.

The most significant change needed to make the income statement more useful is to recognize that *all* capital—equity as well as debt—is costly. The failure to recognize that shareholders as well as lenders expect and deserve to earn a fair return on their investment is by far the grossest and most pervasive source of earnings overstatement. Including the cost of equity as a cost of doing business ought to be at the top of everyone's list of reforms. But this is only a first step down the path to converting accounting profit into economic profit. Other reforms on a "top-ten" list are:
- insulating profit from the impact of transitory financing decisions;
- hauling off-balance-sheet financing into the light of day;
- bringing pension assets and liabilities onto corporate balance sheets, and eliminating speculative pension fund gains and losses from operating income;
- measuring the recurring cash flows from operations as opposed to the liquidation value of assets, thereby addressing the concerns of risk-taking shareholders more than those of conservative bankers;
- closing the lid on cookie-jar reserves;
- recording investments in intangibles as balance-sheet capital and making similar allowances for other strategic investments that take time to bear fruit;
- shifting from successful efforts to full-cost, cash accounting;
- measuring depreciation so that it leads to a steady measure of economic profit rather than book profit; and
- expensing stock option grants.

Besides shoring up the audit profession, changing the way accountants are supposed to keep score can also improve the quality of corporate governance and restore the public's confidence about investing in equities. But let us not expect too much from this alone. Shady managers and shoddy auditors can undermine any system of accounting rules and overstate profit. Stiff jail sentences, financial penalties, and peer pressure must be vigorously applied to those who defraud the public or neglect professional responsibilities. The rules must be followed if they are to be of value.

Accounting fails to measure economic profit in many ways. In the sections that follow, several notable shortcomings are examined in more detail. A number of rule changes are also proposed that, if enacted, would result in a comprehensive new statement of economic profit and loss to replace the accountant's current flawed definition of earnings.

EQUITY CAPITAL IS COSTLY

The most egregious error accountants are now making is to treat equity capital as a free resource. Although they subtract the interest expense associated with debt financing, they do not place any value on the funds that shareholders have put or left in a business. This means that companies often report accounting profits when they are in fact destroying shareholder value.

Economic profit eliminates this distortion. It more accurately measures corporate performance by subtracting the cost of all resources used to generate revenues, including the cost of equity capital. In its most basic form (which accounting scholars refer to as "residual income"),

Economic Profit = Accounting Profit – The Cost of Equity

Unlike interest or wages, the cost of equity is not a cash cost, but rather an opportunity cost. It is the return that a firm's shareholders could expect to earn by purchasing a portfolio of stocks in other companies of comparable risk. If a firm cannot give its

Smart managers have responded by opting out of the accounting system. They have been moving toward substitute measures, including pro forma income, core earnings, EBITDA, and, in some cases, EVA or the Balanced Scorecard. The proliferation of alternative metrics is a clear sign that something is systematically wrong with accounting.

shareholders at least the return that they could earn by investing on their own, it will lose value. Thus, in an economist's view, a company does not begin to earn a profit until it can cover the opportunity cost of its equity capital.

The return that investors expect from investing in equity portfolios has been the subject of intense theoretical and empirical research by finance scholars. The finding that has stood the test of time is that investors want to be compensated for bearing risk—and, over time, they are. When establishing the price they will pay for a company's shares, shareholders discount a firm's future prospects in such a way that they are likely to earn a return well above the yield available from relatively risk-free government bonds. Of course, it doesn't work out for each stock in every year. But over time, a portfolio of common stocks tends to provide investors with a 2% to 7% return premium over the risk-free rate, which compensates them for risk. With government bonds currently yielding about 5%, shareholders are now demanding long-run returns from their equity investments that range from 7% to 12% per annum, depending on the risk of the investment. Companies must earn that return as a cost of doing business.

Although abstract in nature, the cost of equity is as real as any cost in terms of its implications for a company and its shareholders. If a firm cannot earn a return on equity above its cost, its shareholders will abandon their support for the stock and set its price at a discount to book value. But if a return above the cost of equity can be achieved, the company will sell for a premium over its book value, and it will have created wealth for its shareholders. The cost of equity is the cutoff rate necessary to create value with investor capital, an invisible but profound dividing line between superior and inferior corporate performance.

The difference between accounting profit and economic profit is often considerable. A company with reported net income of $80 million may seem healthy enough. But if it ties up $1 billion in shareholder capital on its balance sheet, and if its cost of equity is 10%, the firm is actually producing a $20 million economic loss compared to the alternative investment uses of that capital:

Economic Profit = Accounting Profit – Cost of Equity

−$20 million = $80 million − (10% × $1 billion)

The likely consequence is that the firm will trade for a market value significantly less than its $1 billion book capital, the difference reflecting the shareholder wealth that has been lost through misallocation or mismanagement of capital. Many of the past decade's high flyers like WorldCom and Enron would surely have been more deliberate in their growth had they been forced to recognize the cost of all the equity capital they were pouring into their businesses.

How substantial is the accountant's neglect of the cost of equity? The 1,000 largest U.S. firms ended 2001 with book equity of about $2.9 trillion. At a 10% rate, the annual cost of that capital is on the order of $290 billion. To put that in perspective, the equity capital charge is more than three times as large as the $96 billion in aggregate net income those firms reported that year. Ignoring the cost of equity capital is not only a major oversight, it is perhaps the single most significant governance issue in the accounting system.

Accounting for the Cost of Equity

The accounting change needed to fix this flaw is elementary: debit earnings for the cost of equity, and add back the same charge with a credit to book equity. The entry does not change the balance sheet or cash flow, but it does begin to bring net income in line with economic profit.

The cost of equity cannot be measured precisely. But since the accounting framework assumes it is zero, any systematic measurement technique that conforms to modern finance theory will be a significant improvement and provide profit figures that are generally more relevant and more accurate. A 10% charge levied on the book value of equity would be better than continuing with the current assumption that equity is costless, though greater precision is certainly possible. In fact, most companies are already making an assumption about the cost of equity when they estimate the returns they expect to earn on equity investments in their pension fund (as discussed later, accountants use that expected return in determining the annual pension cost). General Motors, for example, is currently assuming it will earn a 10% return on its pension fund assets. So why not turn around and charge GM's net income at the same rate? How can GM executives expect to earn a 10% return from their pension assets if they do not demand it of themselves?

DON'T MIX OPERATING AND FINANCING DECISIONS

A second fallacy built into our accounting framework is its misleading association of financing sources with investment uses. The root of the problem is that traditional accounting measures look very different depending on whether debt or equity finances a new investment. When funding an investment entirely with debt, all management has to do is cover interest—which might cost only about 3% to 4% after taxes these days—and the investment will increase the company's reported earnings and returns. A new common stock issue sets a far higher hurdle because it expands equity capital and the number of shares outstanding. Thus, a project that is financed with stock will generally have to produce a lot more profit to keep a firm's EPS and ROE on a roll. Simply put, debt exaggerates the apparent payoffs that a company earns from its investments, whereas equity financing tends to understate them.

Because of that disparity, managers face temptations to misallocate capital. They may take on weak projects that they can dress up with attractive debt financing, and pull back from worthwhile projects if they no longer can tap debt sources and must raise expensive new equity. What's worse, managers can become so enamored of the financial attractions of debt that they leverage up to the brink of financial ruin.

Enron is a classic example of the hazards of mixing operating and financing decisions. Management announced in its 2001 annual report that "we are laser-focused on earnings-per-share," and so they were. Enron executives were so preoccupied with giving their EPS and ROE a ride that they began to use debt very aggressively to fund such questionable projects as overseas water utilities and broadband telecom networks. Even as leverage climbed to dizzying heights, the firm's top brass could not bring themselves to tap the equity markets to relieve the financial stress.

Once a company runs down the path of leveraging its growth, it is difficult to reverse course. Confronted with a higher cost of equity (or fearing the consequences of diluting EPS or ROE), managers become reluctant to raise equity to finance even sound projects. Instead, they keep borrowing from the future and hoping for the best today.

Corporate finance theory has an answer to this problem. According to a well-known principle called the "net present value rule," management should evaluate potential investment projects on their own merits rather than penalizing or subsidizing them according to how each is financed. To apply this rule, the costs associated with all of a company's major sources of capital are combined into one overall blended cost known as the weighted average cost of capital; and that WACC, as it is known in financial circles, is used as the hurdle rate for judging all projects (of average corporate risk), regardless of how the individual projects are actually financed. The rule thus implies that the actual debt or equity a company employs in funding any given project is misleading and irrelevant. What matters is whether a project would look good assuming it was financed with a prudent and sustainable blend of debt and equity.

Most companies today do use an overall WACC to measure the value of investment projects and as a key input in deciding which ones to accept or reject. The problem, however, is that an investment's return on capital relative to its WACC is not the *only* criterion managers use in making decisions. Many top executives also feel they must keep an eye on how new investments will affect their overall ROE and EPS results, measures that unfortunately fail to separate operating and financing decisions. By their failure to align accounting principles with economic value, accountants are forcing managers to live uncomfortably in two worlds—the "internal" world in which resources are allocated according to the net present value rule, and the "external" world of public accounting in which the choice of debt or equity financing affects reported results.

Regulators and other accounting authorities have a responsibility to relieve management of this tension, and to make GAAP accounting conform to the established principles and practices of value-based management. What's needed is a new accounting standard that makes financial reporting consistent with the capital budgeting techniques most companies now use for internal resource allocation decisions.

The recommended accounting treatment is straightforward: Put all of the operating results on one side of the economic profit calculation and then subtract all financing costs on the other side. The first step in this separation process is to measure profit before subtracting any financing charges. The result

**The most egregious error accountants are now making is to treat equity capital as a
free resource. This means that companies often report accounting profits when they
are in fact destroying shareholder value.**

is known as net operating profit after taxes, or
"NOPAT" for short.[10] Unlike book net income,
NOPAT is a measure of pure operating results that is
not affected by temporary shifts in capital structure
or interest rates. Dividing NOPAT by the sum total of
a firm's debt and equity capital provides a rate of
return that measures how productively management
has managed corporate assets, regardless of how it
has financed them. Because it removes the effects of
financing differences, NOPAT/Total Capital is far
more reliable than ROE as a basis for comparing a
company's performance from one year to the next or
across a group of companies within the same year.

Having measured operating results, the second
step is to subtract all financing costs as represented
by the weighted average cost of capital. The result
is a popular measure of economic profit called
economic value added, or EVA:[11]

$$EVA = NOPAT - (WACC\% \times \$Total\ Capital)$$

WACC is computed by weighting the after-tax cost
of each capital component by its proportionate
representation in an ideal capital structure mix.
Finance staffs carefully select their target capital
structures by balancing the benefit of cheap debt
financing against their need to preserve financing
flexibility with an equity cushion. The target capital
structure is also one that management should be
committed to maintaining on average and over time.

Under our current accounting system, if the
firm's capital structure deviates temporarily from its
long-run target, the accounting measures will shift
because such measures effectively mix financing
costs with operating results. But the economic
measures will not be affected; they remove the
effects of temporary financing fluctuations and remain rock-solid performance indicators. The firm's
WACC stays the same because it is assumed that

management remains steadfastly committed to its
target capital structure. Provided they understand
and believe that the policy will be maintained,
investors will view current deviations from the target
as temporary and expect them to be reversed in due
course.[12]

To be consistent with the net present value rule,
then, the EVA reporting scheme requires that the
actual interest expense and other financial charges
a firm incurs not be deducted on its statement of
economic profit and loss. Such charges could, however, be presented in a footnote section containing
a wealth of information pertinent to measuring the
firm's cost of capital. So long as the information is
disclosed there, creditors and others interested in
debt capacity and creditworthiness can make assessments of coverage ratios and the like without
disrupting the main objective of reporting the firm's
economic profit to the shareowners.

In sum, divorcing financing decisions from
investment uses will encourage managers to deploy
capital in the long-run interests of shareholders. And
it will let managers happily live in one world instead
of two, the world of legitimate value creation as
opposed to that of financial manipulation.

PENSION PLAN ACCOUNTING: A SPECIAL CASE OF MIXING OPERATING COSTS AND FINANCIAL RETURNS

The accounting rules for defined-benefit pension plans are almost totally misleading. The gap
between appearance and economic substance is
probably as great in this area as any other. Accountants intertwine the pension cost with how it is
funded; they systematically understate the expense
of paying for a retirement plan; and they ignore risk
by smoothing results. The overall effect is that
accounting rules have seduced usually staid finance

---

10. The term NOPAT was coined by Joel Stern in the late 1960s following the
seminal articles on corporate valuation theory by Nobel laureates Merton Miller and
Franco Modigliani. Because NOPAT is a measure of after-tax operating profitability,
the tax bill should also be grossed up for the additional taxes that would have been
paid had interest expense not sheltered the operating profit from being fully taxed.
The benefit that a company realizes from deducting interest and not paying those
taxes already appears elsewhere in the EVA calculation. It is in the cost of capital,
for the after-tax cost of borrowing money is used to compute it.

11. In a comprehensive EVA accounting system, all financing costs should be
backed out of NOPAT and impounded into the cost of capital in order to clearly
and totally separate operating and financing decisions. For instance, off-balance-
sheet lease commitments should be discounted to a present value and included
as part of debt capital for the purpose of measuring the overall cost of capital, and
the implied after-tax interest component of the annual rents should be added back
to NOPAT. As already required under current accounting rules, the debt and

interest associated with special purpose entities in which the company holds more
than a 50% economic interest should continue to be included in calculations of the
firm's capital, and be made part of its calculations of its cost of capital and NOPAT
as well.

12. One practical consideration is how auditors should verify a firm's target
capital structure. The best solution would be for the SEC to mandate disclosure by
managers of their target capital structure policy. The targets should be based on
book value proportions rather than market value weights because managers do
not control the firm's market value in the short term. The disclosed targets are apt
to be credible in the main because investors, analysts, and the media will hold
managers' feet to the fire if they do not achieve their declared objectives over time.
Alternatively, auditors could use a company's trailing three-year average debt/
equity mix as the implied target. The trailing average is simple and auditable, and
will certainly be more accurate than taking any one year's leverage ratio at face
value.

managers into being far too adventuresome with their pension fund assets.

Almost all companies today are running far too great a risk of joining GM in having to hand over more cash to their pension plan just after the market has taken a nosedive and they are least prepared to make the extra payments. As reported in a recent *Wall Street Journal* article,

Despite favorable performance, GM Chief Financial Officer John Devine said most of the $3.5 billion in cash the company generated in its auto business in the latest quarter went to fund contributions for retiree costs. Depending on how the markets perform, he said, GM might have to contribute $6 to $9 billion to its pension plan over the next five years to meet regulatory requirements... GM's shares, which have fallen sharply in the past few weeks amid concerns about the pension-fund issue, fell 4.3% to $45.84 on the New York Stock Exchange.[13]

The crux of the problem is that accountants do not treat pension accounts as true corporate liabilities and assets when in fact they are. For starters, ERISA regulations require a company to maintain minimum funding of its future pension liabilities—hence the urgency of GM's move to bump up its pension contributions. If a company is caught short and goes belly-up without a fully funded plan, the shortfall is covered by a government insurance fund, the Pension Benefit Guarantee Corporation. Employees do not need to lose sleep in a bankruptcy filing, but the firm's lenders do. The PBGC is empowered to recover its advance by filing a claim against the company's assets that has the status of a tax lien.

Whether paid out of cash flow or in bankruptcy, a company's pension liability is senior even to the claims of its most senior lenders. It is not a vague contingent claim that deserves to be relegated to a footnote, but in fact quite the opposite—a liability so binding that it should be boldly printed on a company's balance sheet at the very top of its list of debts. And this means that pension *assets,* although in the control of a trustee and legally segregated for servicing employee retirement benefits, are effectively *corporate* assets because they directly offset the firm's pension liability. They too should appear on the corporate balance sheet.

Accountants also err in the way they record pension expense on corporate income statements. The true pension cost is the present value of the extra retirement payments that employees have earned through their service to the company over the time period in question. Put another way, the true pension cost is represented by the amount of cash that would have to be set aside and invested in a bond fund that would compound in value to meet the additional retiree payments.[14] This "service cost," as it is known, directly increases the firm's pension liability and decreases its market value. It is the amount that should be subtracted as the periodic pension expense in the measurement of a firm's NOPAT and EVA—but under present accounting rules it is not.

Accountants and actuaries have devised a complicated formula to measure a company's pension expense:

Pension Cost = Service Cost − (Fund Return − Liability Interest)

The accountants start off on the right track by setting the pension cost equal to the service cost, but then subtract the spread between the return earned on the pension assets and the interest cost of the pension liability. This formula suggests that earning a higher return on pension fund assets reduces a company's pension cost, but this is not at all correct. The pension expense is the period-to-period increase in the pension liability—that is, in the present value of the promised retirement payments. That increase has nothing to do with the returns actually earned from the pension plan assets. By failing to separate the liability from investment returns, accountants have lured many unsuspecting CFOs into gambling their shareholders' equity on speculative investments.

Given the priority the law accords pension beneficiaries, pension commitments ought to be discounted to a present value at a very low interest rate, a rate even lower than what a company would pay on its most senior debt. We recommend using the yield offered by a portfolio of bonds that is one credit rating "notch" higher than the credit rating of

---

13. "GM Profit Grows, But Pension Costs Worry Investors," *The Wall Street Journal,* July 17, 2002, p. A3.

14. Pension fund consultants often argue that the liability should include the increases in benefits that would be due to future inflationary increases, but that is incorrect. Almost all corporate operating costs, whether for materials or services or labor, will increase due to inflation, and yet such increases are not recorded as current liabilities. In the economic model, the pension liability due to inflation will be recorded only as the inflation occurs and not in advance.

Accounting rules have seduced usually staid finance managers into being far too adventuresome with their pension fund assets… The crux of the problem is that accountants do not treat pension accounts as true corporate liabilities and assets when in fact they are.

the firm itself. For example, a "AAA"-rated credit like GE should discount its pension liability at the U.S. government bond rate of interest, and a "BBB"-rated credit should use the "A" interest rate—always one notch higher because the pension liability is senior to a firm's most senior lenders. While accountants correctly acknowledge that pension liabilities should be discounted, they uniformly discount pension liabilities using a "AA" discount rate. Because a "AA" rate is really only appropriate for "A"-rated credits, this practice understates the liability for big credit-worthy firms and overstates it for smaller, more credit-constrained companies.

The only way a company can be sure it will meet its pension commitments on schedule is to invest its pension fund assets in a diversified bond portfolio that matches the risk profile of its pension liability. Suppose a company with an "A" rating has a $1 billion pension liability—the result of discounting its retiree commitments to a present value at the prevailing "AA" bond yield of 7%. To neutralize the risk to its shareholders, and align portfolio returns with pension commitments, the firm must invest its pension fund assets in a $1 billion, "AA"-rated bond fund that would yield an identical 7% return. By the accountant's reckoning, the interest cost on the pension liability and the return from the mirror-image pension fund asset precisely cancel, leaving the firm's pension cost equal to its service cost.

But from an economist's viewpoint, a company's pension cost must *always* be equal to its service cost, regardless of the investments that are being used to finance the plan. Economists recognize that because investors demand to be compensated for risk, pension plan costs can be measured accurately only when the risk borne by a firm's shareholders is not changed by the introduction of the pension plan. Any deviation from that risk-neutral policy represents a decision by management to enter a separate, "non-operating" line of business—namely, speculative investment. The *expected* NPV of a company's pension plan investments, as discussed in more detail below, is by definition zero. And the *actual* returns on speculative investment should not be commingled with pension liability costs, since that again would be a decision to mix operating and financing decisions. Speculative returns should instead be broken out on NOPAT and EVA statements so investors can judge them as a separate matter.

With considerable encouragement from the accounting system, then, most corporate finance

managers have succumbed to the temptation to speculate. They invest pension assets in securities with risk profiles vastly higher than their pension liabilities. They hope to boost returns, earn a positive spread, reduce their reported pension cost, and perhaps win a bigger bonus. But even if they succeed, they have accomplished nothing of value for their shareholders. Corporate managers can earn a higher return on their pension assets only by taking on more risk—a risk that is passed on to the firm's shareholders. The shareholders will respond by discounting the firm's riskier earnings at a steeper rate (or, what amounts to the same thing, cutting its P/E multiple), and the stock price will not budge. This way, the shareholders will simply earn a higher return commensurate with the additional risk they are forced to take.

Another way accountants overstate the appeal of investing in equities is that overfunded pension plans trigger underreporting of pension costs. Suppose that a firm with a $1 billion pension liability shifted 50% of its pension fund assets into equities during the bull market run of the 1990s, and that the market value of its portfolio has grown to $1.5 billion. Assuming it earns a 7% (risk-free) return, this $500 million overfunding results in a $35 million per year understatement of the true service cost.

Accountants compound this error by assuming that a diversified stock and bond portfolio will earn a higher return than an investment in safe bonds. Suppose management projects that, with the fund partly invested in equities, it can average a 10% return from its pension assets. The financial speculation spread now drives the reported pension cost a full $80 million a year below the true service cost:

$$\text{Pension Cost} = \text{Service Cost} - [(10\% \times \$1.5 \text{ billion}) - (7\% \times \$1 \text{ billion})]$$

In fact, if the investment returns are high enough, a company can even report *negative* pension costs—that is, it can actually book income from its pension plan. This astonishing outcome is the result of mixing the returns from speculative financial investments with the operating cost of providing retirement compensation.

Such results have been made possible by accountants' decision to ignore risk when they measure a firm's pension cost. While it is true that equities are expected to outperform bonds over a long time frame, economists do not expect them to provide a higher *risk-adjusted* return than bonds. An investment of $1,000 in stocks or $1,000 in bonds has the same $1,000 present value even though the stocks are eventually expected to be worth more than the bonds. The mistake that accountants make is assuming that the extra return that common stocks offer over time represents a gain for the firm's stockholders. In fact, the higher return is necessary for the firm's stock portfolio just to break even (on a risk-adjusted basis) with the surer return offered by bonds. Put another way, a company that shifts its pension assets from bonds into stocks will boost its reported earnings and its return on equity over time. But those gains will be completely offset by the lower multiple the market will attach to its riskier, lower-quality earnings stream.

The accounting gets even worse (or better, if you take book earnings at face value) because the pension fund return that appears in the pension cost formula is not the actual return realized from the fund assets. It is an *assumption* about long-run future returns. As a result, pension plan accounting takes no account of risk. Actual pension fund returns may be gyrating up and down, and yet the recorded pension cost blithely assumes away the short-term fluctuations that are the essence of risk.

What's more, managers are able to change the assumed return on the pension assets (even though, again, the only correct assumption is that it is equal to the return used to discount the pension liability) in a way that ends up smoothing earnings. Seeing good times ahead, management lowers the assumed return, boosts the reported pension cost, and so builds up a store of potential earnings for the future. In lean years, managers draw down on the store by ginning up the assumed return and reducing the reported pension cost.

Accountants reserve their most transfiguring powers for smoothing pension plan surpluses and deficits. If pension fund assets exceed (or fall short of) the pension liability by more than 10%, the difference is amortized into the pension cost formula.[15] Any surplus must be amortized into earnings over the remaining service life of current employees (a period of typically five to 15 years), which further reduces the pension cost.[16] The same expense-smoothing treatment is accorded any pension fund deficit. And since those funding shortfalls show up in earnings only over a protracted amortization period, the accounting once again prevents managers from recognizing the considerable investment risks they may be taking with their pension plans.

In fact, most companies' pension plans today do not differ in kind, only in degree, from Enron's reviled Raptor partnerships. Both are (or were) special-purpose entities using off-balance-sheet debt to finance the acquisition of risky assets that are also kept off the balance sheet. In both cases, the accounting treatment hides losses and disguises the risk of the investments. The rules that accountants have developed to measure pension costs have provided managers with strong incentives to play this corporate version of Russian roulette and hope they win. In today's market, they are losing. But, as the market reaction to GM's announcement suggests, sophisticated investors are able to see through the accounting gimmickry to focus on the true underlying cost and risks.

The correct accounting treatment is to put pension assets and liabilities on corporate balance sheets where they belong, to record the service cost as the true pension cost on the income statement, and, if companies persist in gambling on equities in their pension plans, to segregate the actual (unsmoothed) speculation gains and losses and report them as separate line items on the statement of economic profit and loss.[17] Restoring the integrity of earnings and balance sheet presentations, and reducing (off balance sheet) pension leverage in favor of (on balance sheet) corporate leverage, are among the desirable governance outcomes that will likely follow in the footsteps of these proposed accounting reforms.[18]

---

15. The actual accounting rules are more complex. Actual pension fund returns that are above or below the expected return are aggregated and held in an off-balance-sheet reserve. If that reserve exceeds 10% of the pension liability or asset, whichever is greater, the reserve excess is amortized into the pension cost over the remaining service life of current employees. A reserve surplus reduces pension cost and adds to reported earnings; a reserve deficit increases pension cost and reduces book earnings.

16. Pension contributions are deductible for tax purposes and thus a pension fund surplus or deficit is really only worth the after-tax amount to the shareholders.

17. The pension liability should not be subject to the company's overall cost of capital charge (because its return is expected from the pension fund assets), but the pension fund deficit or surplus (resulting from net losses or gains on assets) should be subject to a separate capital charge that reflects the financial speculation risk.

18. Many corporate managers will want to avoid profit swings by swapping pension assets from equities into bonds. By stabilizing earnings and insulating the pension liability risk, they will increase creditworthiness. Many of them will take advantage of their additional debt capacity by borrowing on their corporate books and using the proceeds to buy back their stock. They will increase their EVA and market value by reducing the cost of capital applicable to their business investments.

*Most companies' pension plans today differ not in kind, but only in degree,
from Enron's reviled Raptor partnerships...In both cases, the accounting treatment
hides losses and disguises the risk of the investments.*

DON'T CONFUSE SHAREHOLDERS WITH LENDERS

Another basic flaw is that accounting rules are wired to measure liquidation value more than going-concern value, and to address the concerns of creditors more than the needs of risk-taking shareholders. Burned by lawsuits (many of them without merit), accountants have adopted the motto, "when in doubt, debit"—debit the earnings, that is. They have developed rules designed in large part to minimize their liability exposure. They knowingly understate reported earnings by burying valuable assets in reserves or writing them off entirely. But, in so doing, they have unwittingly created a problem: the accountant's conservatism has created an incentive for managers to work around the rules and restore earnings to what they think is a more accurate result.

As a matter of national policy, companies should be compelled to report information that will enable smart investors to judge the likely future cash flows from a going concern, and that will motivate managers to make decisions that optimize resources and maximize shareholder wealth. As long as they stick to those rules, the auditors should not be culpable if ex ante performance expectations are not realized after the fact.

Corporate income taxes offer a classic example of excessive conservatism. Most companies are lawfully permitted more deductions to compute their income tax than they legitimately recognize when reporting book profit. Companies can, for instance, depreciate assets at an accelerated pace on their tax records. The intent of Congress is to subsidize the purchase of assets that will raise worker productivity.

The accountants, however, both undermine that policy aim and diminish the relevance of reported results by ignoring the taxes a company actually pays. Instead, they concoct a tax expense figure that is typically much higher than what's been paid. They compute the tax a company would owe on *their* definition of income, and they deduct that hypothetical "income tax provision." For example, if a company's taxable income is $100 and its accounting book income is $150, the tax actually paid at a 40% tax rate is $40, but the accountants will instead subtract $60, or 40% of $150. In so doing, accountants deduct taxes that a company has not paid and probably will never pay; for as long as a firm remains in business, it will most likely continue to generate tax deferrals through the acquisition of new assets.

The difference between the fictitious book tax provision and the firm's actual tax bill is accumulated in a balance sheet account called the "deferred tax liability." That liability tends to increase over time as more and more taxes are deferred. At the end of 2001, for example, GE had a deferred tax reserve of $9.13 billion, up from $8.69 billion at the end of 2000. The $440 million increase is an indication of how much the accountants overstated GE's tax and understated its profit in 2001. The $9 billion ending balance is a measure of the cumulative error in measuring GE's recurring cash flow from operations.

The accountants defend this puzzling practice as conservatism designed to protect the interests of creditors. They worry about a company that fails to prosper, no longer generates tax deferrals, and ends up having to repay its deferred taxes. But in their effort to avoid occasionally being wrong about a handful of deadbeat companies, the accountants have chosen to be wrong about the vast majority of businesses that prosper as going concerns. The fact that almost every company in the stock market trades for a value well in excess of its liquidation value is prima facie evidence that the accountants have made a systematically wrong choice.

Accountants should deduct from profit the taxes a company has paid instead of some hypothetical tax provision.[19] That done, the profit that is now being buried in the deferred income tax reserve will be reflected in the NOPAT income statement and make its way into the firm's equity capital via retained earnings. EVA can then be computed using those revised figures.[20]

---

19. To measure NOPAT, as we saw earlier, the tax bill should also be grossed up for the additional taxes that would have been paid had interest expense not sheltered the operating profit from being fully taxed. The benefit that a company realizes from deducting interest and not paying those taxes already appears elsewhere in the EVA calculation. It is in the cost of capital, for the after-tax cost of borrowing money is used to compute it.

20. The year-to-year amount of taxes deferred can be quite volatile since it is geared to investment spending and other fluctuating factors. Policymakers should consider an alternative approach that smoothes the measurement of EVA. The idea is to recognize the benefit of deferring taxes not as a flow-through on the income statement, but rather as a balance sheet reduction in the stock of capital subject to the capital charge. The approach entails accepting the income tax provision (after backing out the tax benefit of debt) as the charge to NOPAT, but then eliminating the balance sheet deferred tax reserve from capital by presenting it as a contra asset.

The deferred tax liability, if it remains of interest to lenders, can be reported in a footnote.[21] Again, lender-oriented information items should step to the rear.

CLAMP DOWN THE LID ON THE COOKIE JARS

Another example of accountants' conservative bias is the way they anticipate losses from uncollectible loans and receivables. Accountants require companies to set up a bad debt reserve that holds an estimate of the amounts owed a company that will not be paid. If the company has $100 million of receivables and the accountants think based on prior experience that 3% of those credits will dodge payment, the bad debt reserve will be set at $3 million. On the balance sheet, the reserve offsets the receivables and the $100 million "face value" of the receivables is reduced to a "net book value" of $97 million. The reserve is used up as receivables go bad, and it is replenished by a charge to earnings each year known as the bad debt provision.

That is the theory, anyway. The practice is a good deal murkier. In flush years, managers are tempted to bump up the bad debt provision to squirrel away earnings in the reserve so that in lean times they can underestimate future losses and import earnings from the balance sheet reserve to the income statement. The reserve provides managers with a ready device for smoothing reported earnings and stabilizing their bonuses. It's the mechanism WorldCom CFO Scott Sullivan used to create an additional $2 billion of income in 1999 and 2000. It's just one of many cookie jars whose lids must be shut tight.

Banks and other financial intermediaries face an even more severe problem. The more new loans or credits they sign up, the more they have to increase the charge to earnings to build up the reserve. If they sign up a lot of new loans at the end of their accounting year, the increase in the provision for bad debts can easily exceed the additional interest income they record from the new loans during that short period of time. Ironically, the more good new loans they sign up, the lower their earnings may go. The antidote to auditors' excessive conservatism is to subtract from NOPAT the actual charge-off of the bad debts as they occur rather than in advance, and to record loans and receivables at face value without

the subtraction of any reserve. This way, not only is the accounting a lot simpler to understand, it strengthens a manager's incentive to recover bad debts and avoid making such loans in the first place. The new accounting rule switches bad debts from the purview of what accountants manage to the realm of what managers should be managing. It elevates economic substance over cosmetic appearance. And it still permits accountants to address creditor concerns by reporting the bad debt reserve and provision in financial statement footnotes.

INNOVATION IS AN INVESTMENT AND NOT AN EXPENSE

Another classic example of the red carpet treatment that accountants accord lenders at the expense of shareholders is the accounting for research and development spending. R&D outlays are unquestionably of vital importance to the economy. Innovation spending helps companies boost their potential for generating sales and earnings through the creation of new products and processes. In theory, such outlays should be capitalized as an asset and written off against earnings over the period that they are likely to contribute to sales and earnings. Yet accountants treat research not as an investment but as an expense. They immediately charge off R&D as it is spent and record nothing on the balance sheet.

Again, the only explanation for this practice is that accounting is clearly designed for bankers, not for shareholders. Bankers write loan covenants against tangible asset values. They want the protection of hard assets that are likely to have a resale or liquidation value in the event a firm goes bankrupt. To accommodate bankers' preference for concreteness, the accountants write off investments in intangible assets like R&D. But in so doing, they take the position that failure is a far more likely outcome than success, and that the company in question is more dead than alive.

Accountants counter that R&D spending has an uncertain payoff and can't be relied upon to create a valuable asset. But by that logic, much spending on hard assets should not be capitalized either. General Motors, for instance, spent a king's ransom on robots in the early '80s with the intent of catching up with Japanese producers, but got nothing in return. The

---

21. It would probably help creditors even more for the auditors to create a supplemental schedule that displays the reversal of deferred taxes that would be expected over the next five years and thereafter, assuming that no additional assets are purchased or pertinent policy changes are made.

In our knowledge-based economy, investments in all intangibles ought to be capitalized like any other asset and depreciated over estimates of their economic lives.

robot investment was a total write-off. Staggering as it was, that debacle pales against the massive losses sustained by telecom firms in recent years in building out big bandwidth networks and paving the way for so-called G3 mobile phones for which the demand has been slow to materialize. The trend toward *hard-asset risk* is if anything accelerating. A strong case can be made that today's economy is particularly geared toward rewarding investments in soft assets, and that the firm's most valuable assets are its people and processes. In fact, the best firms are investing in ideas and software to *limit* their investment in capital and hardware. Is not GE's pervasive "six-sigma" quality capability worth a lot more than the factory assets it uses to make appliances? And yet the investment associated with developing that capability appears nowhere on GE's balance sheet.

In our knowledge-based economy, investments in all intangibles ought to be capitalized like any other asset and depreciated over estimates of their economic lives. Such intangibles would include, among other things, outlays for training and developing people; up-front investments in signing bonuses to lure talented engineers and managers to a firm; advertising and promotion to launch new products, enter new markets, and build brands; the cost of setting up systems to gather information that enhances customer relations, supply chain management, and the sharing of knowledge; and, of course, research and development expenditures.[22] The point is not that each expenditure to create an intangible asset creates value, but that each one is expected to and that, in the aggregate, they do. As a policy choice, the answer is to go with the rule rather than the exception. As for bankers, they are free to rewrite their loan covenants to strike out intangible assets as they have often done in the past with goodwill.

Eminent accounting scholar Baruch Lev agrees that investments in research ought to be capitalized on corporate balance sheets:

The proposed capitalization of intangibles is consistent with recent empirical evidence interpreted within the "residual earnings" valuation framework for analyzing accounting principles issues...This valuation framework equates an enterprise intrinsic value to its current book value plus the present value

of residual earnings (reported earnings minus a charge for equity capital). Accordingly, accounting standards which improve the alignment of reported book value with the firm's intrinsic value (usually proxied by market value) and/or improve the prediction of earnings should be preferred over standards which do not.[23]

USE FULL-COST ACCOUNTING

Some argue that only investment outlays that are clearly successful should be capitalized and put onto a firm's balance sheet and that failures should be expensed. Why treat an expenditure that clearly did not pan out as an asset, they ask? The right answer is to capitalize *all* the outlays because, in any risky business (and what business isn't?), part of the investment required to find winners is investing in losers now and again.

Take drilling for oil as an example. Suppose a company drills wildcat wells in an area that geologists describe as having a "one-in-five" success ratio. The statistic indicates that five wells must be drilled to have a good chance to find one winner. The cost to find one well is thus, by definition, the cost of drilling five wells. Even the four dry holes are valuable because management knows not to drill there again. In the new, intangible economy, knowledge is the capital. The same applies to "drilling" for new products, markets, processes, and capabilities. Failure is a form of learning, and learning is capital.

As a result, accountants should capitalize all the risky outlays, successful or not, and depreciate that total investment over the expected life of the successes—a practice known in audit circles as "full cost" accounting. But this technique is not commonly followed in the oil patch. In another example of their desire to debit earnings as quickly as possible, accountants typically impose "successful efforts" accounting on energy companies. They capitalize only the costs associated with discovering oil and send dry hole costs right down the drain. (Of course, this is not as extreme as the accounting for research and other intangible outlays, which are subject to "unsuccessful efforts" accounting in the sense that *no* outlays are capitalized and *all* must be expensed.)

---

22. Depreciation schedules for intangible assets should not be left up to corporate controllers or individual auditors. Accounting authorities should establish appropriate schedules for various classes of intangibles.

23. Baruch Lev and Paul Zarowin, "The Boundaries of Financial Reporting and How to Extend Them," *Journal of Accounting Research*, forthcoming.

To illustrate the consequences of the accounting methods, suppose that each well costs $20 million to drill, so that the total investment in five wells sums to $100 million. Full-cost accounting puts $100 million on the balance sheet, and successful efforts adds only $20 million to the asset base and charges off the $80 million in dry hole expense. Suppose also that the wildcatters' cost of capital is 10%, and that the NOPAT arising from the drilling campaign is $10 million a year. The project breaks even on EVA and so breaks even on value. From a full-cost accounting point of view, the $10 million NOPAT yields a 10% rate of return on the $100 million investment, and EVA is zero each year. Full-cost accounting gets the economic facts correct right from the start.

With successful efforts, however, an initial charge of $80 million penalizes earnings for the dry hole expense in the first year. But in succeeding years, the $10 million NOPAT gives the appearance of yielding a 50% return on the $20 million invested in the one successful well. EVA looks quite positive—$8 million a year—and the firm, if valued at $100 million, appears to sell for a market value that is five times its book value. But that is an illusion. Successful efforts accounting at first understates and then radically overstates all the relevant measures.

The economic reality of drilling for new products and processes, and investing in intangible assets of all kinds, is essentially the same as drilling for oil. It is precisely because those investments are known to be risky that full-cost accounting ought to be used for all of them. But putting such a change into effect will require a shift in terminology. No longer can the balance sheet be considered an aggregation of "assets." In the economic reporting model, the balance sheet measures "capital," but capital is not an asset and it's not value. In the economic model, capital simply measures the value of the resources that have been put *into* a business, not the value that investors can expect to take out of it. Whether such capital investments translate into market value depends on whether management earns a positive EVA.

A company's real assets are thus on its income statement, and its balance sheet is mainly just a record of liabilities. For this reason, any attempt to record the value of intangibles on balance sheets, as some accounting experts have suggested, is both theoretically wrong and impracticable. The values of all of a company's assets are measured simply, directly, and only by their ability to generate economic profit.

USE FULL-COST CASH ACCOUNTING FOR DIVESTITURES AND RESTRUCTURING TRANSACTIONS

Corporate rightsizing decisions often stumble over accounting roadblocks that hamper a swift reallocation of capital to more promising uses. Divestitures of business lines, sales or disposals of assets, and reorganizations often trigger recognition of book losses even when the decisions produce palpable gains in value. Current accounting rules are forcing managers to choose between making the right restructuring moves in the face of adverse accounting consequences, or keeping accounting profit on track by rejecting economically sound decisions.

A new accounting rule is needed to take corporate managers entirely off the horns of this dilemma. It is also needed because a corollary of the principle that failure is a form of learning is that it pays to fail fast. Current accounting rules make it difficult for managers to own up to a mistake, put it behind them, and move on quickly to the next opportunity.

Suppose a nonproductive asset such as an underperforming business line is carried on a company's balance sheet for a book value of $100 million. Also assume that the business unit produces an uninspiring $4 million in annual NOPAT profit. At a 10% cost of capital, that $4 million amounts to an EVA loss of $6 million a year.

The EVA loss indicates, with hindsight, that management made a poor decision to invest in the business line. However, that decision is by now irrelevant. Shareholders' only concern is that management increase their share value by *increasing* the firm's EVA as much as possible. Making a negative EVA less negative is as valid a way to improve performance and increase the stock price as increasing an already positive EVA.

In economics, this principle is encapsulated in the phrase "sunk costs are irrelevant." It means that the carrying value of an asset on the firm's balance sheet, or what is known as its book value, should be completely unimportant in deciding how to increase its market value going forward. The implication is that bookkeeping gains and losses on asset dispositions simply do not matter. What matters is whether a sale, restructuring, or exit can achieve a higher value than continued operation.

To continue with the above example, assume that the business line has no improvement prospects

Through the EVA prism, restructuring losses are not seen as inexplicable and eminently forgettable charges to earnings. They are memorialized as investments intended to streamline operations.

in the current owner's hands. Earning a $4 million per year NOPAT is the best that can be expected. In that case, the business is worth only $40 million to the current owners, which is the result of capitalizing the $4 million a year NOPAT at the 10% cost of capital. Realizing any value for the unit that is greater than $40 million will make shareholders better off. Selling it for $75 million, for example, will make the current owners $35 million richer. Yet by comparing the $75 million sale value with the unit's $100 million book value, the accountants will record a $25 million book loss on the sale, which in turn reduces profits and total assets. If the accounting is taken at face value, the apparent impact on EVA is to make a good decision look bad.

If management has the fortitude to persist in the sale of the unit, the company's stock price will increase even as reported earnings fall—but try explaining that to a board of directors, much less to the average investor. Confronted with such obstacles, many managers have stopped believing that accounting counts what counts, and have turned to alternatives.

As the new economy wave took hold in the 1990s, companies discovered the need to heave off outmoded assets and outdated business practices with restructuring moves that often triggered large bookkeeping charges. Business leaders and professional investors quickly became disenchanted with the auditor's view of the world. They decided to back out the restructuring charges and concentrate on new measures with names like "core earnings" or "pro forma income." But they forgot that legitimate accounting is always a "double-entry" bookkeeping system. An add-back to "pro forma" earnings must be accompanied by an add-back to the "pro forma" balance sheet. In the EVA accounting system, a restructuring charge or divestiture loss is added back to NOPAT, but it is also added back to capital. In our example, this means that the $25 million bookkeeping loss must be added back both places.

With the proposed double add-back accounting, economic profit is correctly measured as a loss of $2.5 million. It is a loss because the company is stuck with $25 million in unrecouped capital on its balance sheet. Investors had put $100 million in

capital into the business line and have now gotten back only $75 million. At a 10% cost of capital, they are out the $2.5 million a year they could have earned on the $25 million difference. The restructuring cannot erase the loss in value from the original decision to enter the business.

The important point here, however, is not that EVA is still negative, but that it has increased by $3.5 million, from a loss of $6 million to a smaller loss of $2.5 million. That is the measure of the wisdom of the current decision to exit the business line. The measure of the market value added by the exit decision is the capitalized value of the $3.5 million EVA gain at the firm's 10% cost of capital which, as expected, is $35 million ($75 million sales price less $40 million present economic value). When EVA is measured in this way, it provides the reliable signals that investors and managers have always needed to judge the value of restructuring maneuvers.

The proposed new accounting should also have a considerable appeal to the many astute investors who have long championed cash accounting as more reliable than book reporting. Consider that when the dust settles with all the adjustments just described, the net effect boils down to the following changes in the corporate balance sheet. First, the company's cash account is increased by the $75 million in sale proceeds; and second, based on the assumption that the cash is (or will soon be) distributed to investors, the company's capital account ends up being reduced by the same $75 million, leaving a residual $25 million in capital on the firm's balance sheet.[24] Both changes involve pure cash, and avoid the recognition of an arbitrary loss or gain compared to book value.[25]

Sweeping capital gains and losses off the income statement makes sense because capital transactions by their nature should swing through the capital account. Accountants have an unfortunate tendency to mix changes in stock values with flows. In the new accounting, recurring cash flows would go through NOPAT, and adjustments to capital stock would be relegated to the balance sheet. One implication of this treatment is that non-cash restructuring charges have no effect on a firm's

---

24. In the measurement of EVA, it is assumed that the $75 million sale proceeds are used to retire the firm's debt and equity in target capital structure proportions, and that the investors earn the cost of capital on those funds through reinvestment in a comparably risky stock and bond portfolio. If the proceeds are retained for some other purpose, management should still think of the funds as having been paid out and then brought back in at the cost of capital, and the new project's EVA

should be evaluated on its own merits as a separate matter. This is another manifestation of the principle of separating operating and financing decisions.

25. The same treatment would apply if a gain were registered on the sale. The gain is ignored on the income statement, but the excess of sale proceeds over book value leads to a net overall reduction in capital that adds to EVA through a negative capital charge.

EVA. Since the charges do not affect cash flow, they cannot affect value, and so they do not affect EVA either. A good example of a completely inconsequential, non-cash restructuring charge is "goodwill impairment."[26] Although such charges can represent major traumas for reported earnings, the charges are non-cash non-events for EVA. The EVA treatment is entirely consistent with the market's reaction to AOL Time Warner's disclosure that it would take a $54 billion impairment charge to its earnings. Upon the announcement of the massive loss, the company's stock price did not budge. The clear implication is that acquisition goodwill that no longer contributes to operating profit (such as from the AOL merger with Time Warner), and that thus registers a loss in economic profit, will be deducted from market value whether or not it is written off from balance sheet capital. In fact, an accounting write-down—or write-up for that matter—of goodwill or indeed of any asset is superfluous and irrelevant so long as the market has information about the firm's prospects for generating economic profit. Such write-downs provide no useful information about recurring flow of economic profit and should therefore not pass through the statement of economic profit and loss. They should instead be recorded only in financial statement footnotes where the information can be tapped by lenders.

The proposed new accounting also casts a brighter light on decisions to restructure a business. Through the EVA prism, restructuring losses are not seen as inexplicable and eminently forgettable charges to earnings. They are memorialized as investments intended to streamline operations. The effect is to give managers and investors a far better way to judge the incremental value of decisions in a dynamic risk-taking environment and to liberate assets now held hostage by outdated accounting conventions.

STRATEGIC INVESTMENTS

Switching from the back door of investing to the front, strategic investments are new projects that will take some time to fully bear their fruit. They produce insufficient earnings to cover the cost of capital in their early years even though they are likely to produce lots of EVA down the road. A start-up biotech company like Amgen went almost ten years after its public offering before profits began to gush in from its early-stage investments. Even a restaurant chain typically finds that it takes three years from the day a new restaurant is opened before word of mouth builds traffic to the level at which profit can cover the cost of capital. Measuring EVA without an adjustment will lead to a dramatic understatement of performance in the initial building years and an overstatement in the later years. The same is true also for accounting earnings and ROE, but EVA improves on those metrics.

The EVA solution to this problem is to hold back a portion of the capital subject to the capital charge and meter it in with interest over the period that the project is expected to ramp up. Suppose, for example, that new restaurants typically earn 70% of the cost of capital in the first year they are opened, 90% in the second year, and thereafter settle in to a long-run return. The accountants should create a "contra" asset—essentially a negative asset account that has the effect of reducing the book value of capital—in the amount of 30% of capital in the first year and 10% in the next year. With those subtractions, if management is on track with its NOPAT plan in those two start-up years, its EVA will be reported as break even; if it is ahead of plan, EVA will be positive. Once the restaurant is fully operational—for the third year and thereafter—management should be required to earn a return that compensates investors for the cost of waiting by adding interest into the capital base.[27]

A variant of this approach that achieves the same objective is to gross up both NOPAT and capital for the EVA shortfall experienced over the ramp-up period. Electric and gas utilities are the rare exception of an industry for which accountants have long employed this method. It has been applied to utilities because they have significant strategic investments—a new generating plant takes five years or longer to build—and because regulators do not want to pass on to consumers the cost of financing a plant that is not yet operational.

---

26. Under recently promulgated rules, accountants must periodically reassess the value of the goodwill premium over book value that companies have paid to acquire other firms. If the current value of the goodwill is found to be less than what was paid, the goodwill must be written down and charged to earnings. But accountants will not write up the book value of goodwill if it is found to have appreciated in value—yet another sign of their conservative bias.

27. In the first year investors gave up a 10% return on 30% of their capital, or 3%, and in the second year they forfeited a 10% return on 10% of their capital, or 1%. Assuming that the 3% and 1% give-ups were invested at the 10% cost of capital for two years and one year, respectively, they would grow to 3.63% and 1.10%, for a sum of 4.73%, by the third year. To compensate investors for the return shortfall in the first two years the firm's accountants should gross up capital subject to the capital charge for year three and beyond by 4.73%.

Companies have been reporting information about stock options in their financial statement footnotes for some time, and investors have digested the news. Expensing options at this time should not cause any significant revaluation of share values, nor should it reduce companies' ability to access capital.

Suppose a power plant requiring a total outlay of $1 billion is completely constructed in just one year (and for simplicity let's assume the money is all spent on December 31 of the previous year), and has no revenue for that year. With a 10% cost of capital charged against that (beginning-year capital of) $1 billion, the EVA in the first year of that project would ordinarily be recorded as a $100 million loss. Rather than flush the EVA loss down the drain and forget about it, and rather than attempt to pass on the financing charge to consumers for a plant that is not yet generating energy, public utility regulators have instructed accountants to remove the up-front EVA losses from earnings and capitalize them into the firm's asset base in the following period. By making this "allowance for funds used during construction," or AFDC as it is called, accountants ensure that when the plant comes on stream the utility and its shareholders are able to earn a return on the full cost of the plant asset—the actual brick-and-mortar construction outlays plus the time value of the money.

Strategic investment treatment can also be important when a company makes a significant acquisition. Not only does it typically take several years for anticipated merger synergies to materialize, but acquired companies frequently have significant growth potential that warrants a lofty market value premium—a premium that cannot be justified by the current returns.

Consider an all-equity company that trades for a total value that is 16 times its current NOPAT earnings of $1 per share, but that with synergies is worth 25 times its NOPAT (or $25 per share) to a strategic buyer. Suppose a deal closes at a price somewhere in between—say, at $20 per share. The selling shareholders will be 25% richer, and the buyer will acquire its target at a 20% discount to its potential value. The transaction has all the hallmarks of a win-win acquisition, one where the buyer's and the seller's stock prices will both increase. The rub, however, is that if the purchase price is 20 times NOPAT, then NOPAT is only one-twentieth—just 5%—of the capital paid. With an overall cost of capital on the order of 10%, the acquisition will immediately dilute the buyer's EVA and flash the wrong signal.

The key to providing a useful accounting treatment in this situation lies in dividing share values into two components: current operating value and expected future growth value. Consider again the target company that transacts for $20 a share, which is 20 times its current $1 per share NOPAT profit. The present value of its $1 NOPAT at a 10% cost of capital is $10, which is the target's current operating value. Therefore, the $10 balance of its $20 share price can be attributed to the present value of expected EVA growth.

In the early years, the only way to assess whether such an acquisition is earning an appropriate return on the purchase price is to hold back the value of the seller's expected strategic growth from its capital base (in this case, $10 per share), and then meter it in over the period that the EVA growth is expected to materialize.[28] Such strategic investment treatment already has a long and successful application in public utilities. There is no reason why with a little thought and attention it cannot be applied everywhere it pertains.

DEPRECIATION DOES NOT FOLLOW A STRAIGHT LINE

The root of the problem in measuring depreciation is a mathematical conundrum: It is arithmetically impossible to measure a company's accounting profit steadily and also its true rate of return and EVA steadily using the same depreciation schedule. The accountants have decided to use depreciation schedules that aim to produce stable operating profits. That choice makes financial statements less useful to the fundamental valuation of any business (although it is most pronounced for companies that invest heavily in long-lived physical assets), and it presents a nettlesome corporate governance dilemma for managers.

Depreciation stems from the orderly liquidation of the investment in an asset as the asset is used up over its productive life. Because no one knows for sure how an asset will depreciate in value, accountants have devised a number of more or less arbitrary schedules to get the job done. The most popular by far is to assume that plant and equipment assets

---

28. To administer the strategic investment treatment, accountants will need to develop a set of tables setting forth the appropriate deferral periods for various categories of investments or acquisitions. An alternative is to use a uniform assumption, something on the order of an across-the-board three- to five-year phase-in or forgiveness period. In either case, each investment qualifying for the strategic accounting treatment must be subject to board approval as such, and be capable of separate measurement in the company's accounts. The accounting authorities should also establish criteria of materiality, strategic significance, and minimum payoff horizon.

depreciate in value in a straight line. A $10 million asset with a ten-year useful life is written off through a steady $1 million annual depreciation charge to earnings. A level charge-off schedule pleases the accounting crew because it tends to stabilize the measurement of reported profit.

The problem is that "straight-line" depreciation invariably distorts a company's rate of return and its EVA. Those measures are understated after a new asset is first added to a company's balance sheet and then progressively overstated as the asset is depreciated in value over time. Confronted with those misleading signals, corporate managers understandably refrain from adding all the assets they should and are motivated to retain old assets beyond the point of realizing a truly attractive economic return. Here again, a seemingly innocuous accounting practice has become a serious impediment to corporate governance that aims to maximize shareholder value.

The discrepancy between accounting and economic depreciation is most pronounced in asset-intensive businesses like real estate, cable TV and telecom, media and entertainment, hotel chains, and transportation. Not surprisingly, CEOs and CFOs in those firms have been among the most vocal advocates for backing out depreciation and substituting EBITDA (earnings before interest, taxes, depreciation, and amortization) for GAAP earnings. Those executives have correctly diagnosed that depreciation presents a problem, but their proposed remedy is simplistic and draconian, and it has only added to the public's perception that accounting doesn't measure what matters.

Simply ignoring depreciation and embracing EBITDA is to throw out the baby with the bath water. Although it is not a cash cost, depreciation is usually a legitimate charge to earnings.[29] Assets wear out or become obsolete and must be replaced for a company to remain in business and sustain its cash flow. The answer is not to abandon profit and embrace cash flow, but to compute profit with *economic* depreciation in place of book depreciation.

Economic depreciation does not generally follow a straight-line pattern. Instead, like the principal amortization on a mortgage loan, it typically grows larger each period as the asset ages and approaches the point at which it will need to be replaced. Straight-line book depreciation thus tends to overstate true depreciation in the early years and to understate it later on. Hence the common desire of managers to defer new asset purchases and retain old assets, and to argue that depreciation should be ignored when measuring earnings.

Consider a factory asset costing $10 million that will generate $1.8 million in cash flow each year over its ten-year life. With a straight-line depreciation charge of $1 million a year, the accountants are able to report a steady $0.8 million in operating profit.[30] The rate of return measured with those figures is not constant, however. In the first year it is 8%, the result of dividing the $0.8 million profit by the original $10 million investment. Looking five years later, the return seemingly soars to 16%— twice as high—because the asset has been written down halfway in value, from $10 million to $5 million; but the operating profit remains the same. At the outset, the factory asset appears to earn less than the company's 10% cost of capital, and later on a lot more.

The basic problem is that straight-line depreciation leads to an asset charge that is front-end loaded, and that thus makes no sense. What corporate executives would agree to sign up for a financial lease that puts a bigger rent at the front end than the back, forcing them to recognize lower earnings just as they are getting started on a new investment? Yet that is essentially what they are forced to do when they acquire an asset and write it off in a straight line.

To fix the distortion is not hard. Just think like a leasing company. Compute the level payment that a leasing company would need to charge to recover its investment and a 10% return over the asset's life. Subtracting that level payment from NOPAT renders a steady EVA each year. The project is now correctly seen to be profitable and value-adding right from the start.

In the final analysis, only one of the three metrics can be reliably measured with any given depreciation schedule. Policymakers must choose among operating profit, rate of return, and economic

---

29. Some assets may not depreciate in value at all. Prime hotel properties like the Waldorf-Astoria Hotel in New York City or unique entertainment franchises like *The Lion King* are examples of assets that actually may appreciate in value over time. Charging off any depreciation in such cases distorts the measurement of value

no matter which measure is chosen. Accountants need to recognize the existence of such assets and permit the investments in them never to be written off.

30. For simplicity, taxes are ignored and so operating profit in this case is the equivalent of NOPAT.

Accounting and corporate governance are in trouble, but not because a handful of companies have ignored the rules. The problem is that the accounting rules are outdated and misguided, and corporate governance is suffering the consequences.

profit. If accounting for value is the goal, the accounting system should be geared to measuring and reporting EVA, and economic depreciation schedules should be widely substituted for straight-line charts.

STOCK OPTIONS ARE AN EXPENSE

It is by now old news that stock options are a form of compensation that should be expensed as exercise rights vest. Warren Buffett is finally getting his way. Companies like The Washington Post Company and Coca-Cola on whose boards he sits have been among the first to adopt a new policy of recognizing the expense and expensing the options. More (maybe all) companies will follow.

Many corporate managers have found it difficult to understand the cost of handing out options because they have collapsed two steps into one. An employee option grant is substantively the same as compensating the employee with cash—which is an obvious operating expense—and then compelling the employee to turn around and use the cash to purchase an option from the company at its fair market value—which is a separate investment decision. Whether the option is eventually exercised for a gain or allowed to lapse has nothing to do with the cost of granting the option in the first place. The true option expense is given by the option's fair market value on the date of grant. Once the option is outstanding, the employee becomes like any other equity holder, and the gains and losses from exercising the option or letting it expire should not be recognized as a corporate expense or income item.

Companies have been reporting information about stock options in their financial statement footnotes for some time, and investors have digested the news.[31] Expensing options at this time should not cause any significant revaluation of share values, nor should it reduce companies' ability to access capital. What it will likely accomplish, however, is to force managers who have mistakenly thought of options as free to reevaluate the effectiveness of options against other incentive plans, including cash bonus plans that attempt to simulate the incentives of ownership by sharing the economic profit that is earned by a company and its business lines.[32]

SUMMARY

Accounting and corporate governance are in big trouble, but not because a handful of companies have ignored the rules. The problem is that the accounting rules are outdated and misguided, and corporate governance is suffering the consequences.

Accounting is not even close to measuring economic reality. Accountants ought to make the measurement and reporting of economic profit their main mission, and relegate other aims to a decidedly subordinate role. Charging profit for the cost of all capital—shareholders' equity included—is the most fundamental and important reform on the list. Setting up an objective, market-derived hurdle rate should help to rein in managers too willing to pursue growth at the expense of profitability and value, and it could also help prevent small bubbles from growing into larger ones the next time around.

Accountants should also erect a Chinese wall between a company's operating decisions and its investment and financing decisions, breaking out NOPAT on the one side and on the other the strategic cost of financing all the capital invested in the business. Accountants must stop tempting managers to borrow in order to boost their earnings per share and ROE with unsustainable debt. Off-balance-sheet debt-equivalents from operating leases and pension liabilities should be brought out of hiding and into the clear light of day. Financial reporting in general needs to become more transparent by being brought into closer alignment with the capital budgeting techniques most companies now employ internally for measuring value and allocating resources.

Pension fund accounting must be changed to bring the economic reality of pension risks and pension costs onto the income statement and balance sheet and out of the bookkeeping notes, where the information is now revealed only in the most opaque manner imaginable. And the lids of the cookie jars that managers reach into when they need a ready source of earnings must be slammed shut.

Investing in intangibles of all kinds, including failures, is an increasing key to business success and a much more common form of capital investment than accountants now acknowledge. Even losses on asset dispositions and restructuring charges should

---

31. The EVAntage™ database, a joint service of Stern Stewart & Co. and Standard & Poor's, adjusts the earnings and market value of 1,300 of the largest public American companies for stock option grants.

32. See "How to Structure Incentive Plans That Work," by G. Bennett Stewart III, for a detailed description of EVA-based incentive contracts (available at www.sternstewart.com).

be subject to double-entry, full-cost cash accounting. Auditors must also develop techniques to defer the expected up-front losses associated with strategic investments until they can reasonably be expected to pay off.

Depreciation is a noticeable distortion for many companies. Straight-line write-offs do not permit the consistent measurement of economic profit. New economic depreciation schedules ought to be developed and implemented so that even managers of capital-intensive businesses can turn their attention back to reported earnings and away from EBITDA.

And yes, stock options should be expensed.

What we have now is not working. It's time for a reform of accounting to lead the charge to a new and superior form of corporate governance.

ACCOUNTING DOESN'T NEED MUCH FIXING (JUST SOME REINTERPRETING)

by George J. Benston,
Emory University

T his has not been a good time for public accounting. Enron's dramatic failure brought charges of malfeasance against its longtime auditor, Arthur Andersen, and aroused widespread skepticism about the way corporations prepare their financial reports and how auditors attest to the reliability of those reports. Andersen was sued by the Department of Justice for destroying evidence and found guilty by a jury, which led eventually to the dissolution of the firm. WorldCom admitted that it misclassified billions of dollars of operating expenses as assets, thereby grossly inflating its profits, and many other well-known corporations—including Xerox and Adelphia—have had to restate their previously reported net incomes. In fact, accounting manipulation now seems so common that many people would likely agree with Bennett Stewart's observation (in the immediately preceding article) that "almost every company has been bending accounting rules to smooth earnings and meet analyst expectations."[1]

In an effort to stem accounting irregularities and restore credibility to the public accounting profession, the Sarbanes-Oxley Act of 2002 established a Public Company Accounting Oversight Board empowered to impose new regulations on independent public accountants who audit publicly traded corporations. But rather than criticizing corporate managers or auditors, Stewart puts most of the blame on the accounting standards themselves. He argues that "the real source of our present maladies is that accounting has become unhinged from value; it is no longer counting what counts." His solution is "a deep reformation of accounting principles...What the public demands, and what in fact is needed, is a measure

of earnings that offers a reliable guide to intrinsic value." In particular, Stewart proposes "a fundamental change in the accountant's mission—one in which the primary aim becomes the measurement and reporting of *economic* profit."

However, the "economic profit" that Stewart would have accountants measure and report is not the economist's definition. As formulated many years ago by U.K. economist Sir John Hicks, a company's economic profit is the difference between the present values of its assets less liabilities at the end and beginning of a period, adjusted for additional investments by and disbursements to its owners during the period. In contrast to this periodic measure of income, Stewart's concept of economic profit is a "sustainable flow" measure—one that begins with accountants' traditional measure of earnings and then makes a series of adjustments designed to reflect a company's long-term *cash-generating capacity* (as opposed to actual cash flow) net of all capital charges, including the opportunity cost of equity. Stewart's economic profit—or "EVA," as he calls it—can also be thought of as the level of recurring cash earnings (again, after capital charges) that provides a reliable guide to the premium (or discount) at which a company trades relative to its book value.

In the course of developing his measure of economic profit, Stewart proposes several useful reforms that I too would urge the Financial Accounting Standards Board (FASB) to include in generally accepted accounting principles (GAAP). Perhaps most important, Stewart proposes that companies separate the gains and losses on funds set aside for pensions from their annual pension expense. I also agree with his recommendation that corporations

---

1. Bennett Stewart, "How to Fix Accounting—Measure and Report Economic Profit," *Journal of Applied Corporate Finance*, Vol. 15 No. 3 (Spring 2003).

show their opportunity cost of employee stock options as an expense. Both of these changes are consistent with GAAP as it has traditionally been applied.

But, however much I agree with some of Stewart's specific suggestions, I fundamentally disagree with his proposal for comprehensive reform of GAAP accounting. His measure of economic profit introduces major problems and ignores other important functions of accounting. At the same time, though, I agree with Stewart's contention that GAAP accounting numbers have major limitations for investors seeking to establish the economic values of companies and for managers attempting to make value-increasing investment and operating decisions. Although I would oppose incorporating most of Stewart's proposed changes into GAAP, I suggest that many corporations would find it valuable to supplement their traditional GAAP financial statements with reports of their economic profit (pretty much) as defined by Stewart. Toward that end, I endorse many of his proposed modifications of GAAP for *voluntary supplemental* reporting, particularly his suggestion that the cost of equity be reported as an expense. (See the Appendix, where I comment on each of his "top ten" changes.)

In addressing Stewart's arguments, I begin by describing the traditional roles of accounting, how they are valuable to investors and others, and why requiring companies to provide—and auditors to sign off on—statements of economic profit would undermine the accounting profession's ability to serve these roles. From my reading of papers by Stewart and others, and from the FASB's and SEC's championing of "fair-value" accounting, I fear that the benefits of the traditional accounting approach are not fully understood or appreciated. This presentation of traditional financial accounting provides the basis for my analysis of Stewart's proposed alternative to GAAP accounting. I next offer some of my own suggestions for improving the content and application of GAAP. Of greatest importance, the FASB and SEC should reverse their relatively recent efforts to achieve greater balance-sheet realism through fair-value accounting—especially the requirement that certain financial assets be marked to estimated values *when reliable market prices are not available*. I then point out another serious threat to our GAAP accounting framework—namely, its evolution into a "rules-based" system. The article closes with a plea for a principles-based approach, whereby companies would be held responsible for complying

not just with the letter but with the substance of accounting principles. And the principles ought to be those of traditional financial accounting, with its primary emphasis on producing trustworthy numbers that auditors can verify and an income statement that matches expenses to realized or realizable revenues.

THE TRADITIONAL ROLES OF FINANCIAL ACCOUNTING

Financial accounting is, and always has been, a somewhat uneasy mix of responses to two primary—and in some ways incompatible—demands by users of financial statements. One is for "stewardship" and the other is for "valuation." Stewardship refers to the role of the accounting system in tracking the acquisition, use, and disposition of resources in an enterprise. The term "stewardship" derives from the reports compiled by stewards (the pre-20th century equivalent of today's professional corporate managers) to account for their actions to the absent owners who employed them. The stewards kept records, usually in monetary terms, of the resources entrusted to them. These records provided the beginning and ending balances in the accounts for which the stewards were responsible (today known as the "balance sheet") as well as an explanation of changes over the period (now called the "income statement" and "statement of changes in equity"). Reputable independent accounting experts (today's independent public accountants, or IPAs) were hired by the owners to attest to the validity of the stewards' reports.

The emphasis was *not* on measuring and reporting the current *market* values of balance sheet accounts or changes in these values over the period. The primary aims of the financial reports and the audits were—and, to a large degree, still are—much more modest:

■ to detect theft or gross misuse of the resources entrusted to the stewards; and
■ to ensure that the earnings generated by the resources were measured and reported "fairly" and consistently over time in accordance with known and generally accepted accounting conventions or principles (today's GAAP), as verified by an examination that follows generally accepted auditing standards (today's GAAS).

Of course, the owners of resources would also like to know what those resources are worth and

Financial accounting is, and always has been, a somewhat uneasy mix of responses to two primary—and in some ways incompatible—demands by users of financial statements. One is for "stewardship" and the other is for "valuation."

whether and to what extent they have become more or less valuable over time. And they would like to know the sources of changes in those values, and what is likely to happen in the future, so that they can better gauge the current value and prospects of their enterprises. But, as discussed below, GAAP balance sheets do not have a high degree of relevance for valuation purposes. And although GAAP income statements provide a useful measure of past changes in the owners' wealth—one that, *when combined with other sources of information*, can be used to estimate economic values—GAAP net income is clearly not a measure of economic profit.

Moreover, the idea that public accounting was ever intended for use primarily by investors in valuing companies is relatively new. Valuation, it's true, has long been regarded as one of accounting's major uses. But the values reported were generally viewed as having greater relevance for creditors, who are interested in the disposal value of assets and in the amount and kind of outstanding liabilities. It was not until the first decades of the 20th century, when the ownership of U.S. companies became progressively more dispersed and effective control was delegated to professional managers, that the demand by *equity* investors for "value-based" accounting information increased sharply. And it was not until the passage of the Securities Acts in 1933 and 1934, when accounting first became subject to government regulation, that such investors were encouraged to believe that accounting reports contained not just necessary but *sufficient* information for making investment decisions.

Shortcomings of Traditional Historical-Cost Financial Accounting—or Getting the Balance Sheet Right

The expectation that audited financial statements alone would provide a sufficient basis for investing reflects a serious misunderstanding of the principles and methods of public accounting. Let's start with the balance sheet. The values of most assets and liabilities recorded on corporate balance sheets are based on historical costs—the amounts paid for individual assets and incurred for liabilities at the time they were acquired or undertaken, less depreciation and amortization. For this reason, balance sheets need not and—with the exception of current items like cash and marketable securities, and accounts and notes receivable and payable—generally do not reveal the values that could be obtained if the assets were sold or the liabilities paid off. In fact, balance sheet numbers are not even adjusted for changes in the purchasing power of the dollar.

Why do accountants continue to use historical costs? Why not instead mark all corporate assets (and liabilities) to market, since such values would surely be more useful to investors attempting to assess the value of the entire company?

The main reason is that coming up with reliable estimates of the market values of most corporate assets is generally difficult and often impossible. The market values of individual assets depend on such variables as the quantities purchased, market conditions when purchased, and the availability of reliable price quotations. Some assets, particularly work-in-process inventories, typically have no market value until they are completed and, in some cases, until they are sold. Even assets in general use, such as land, buildings, and equipment, often have no objectively determinable market value until they are sold or replaced. And special-purpose tangible assets like tools and computer software programs often have not only no determinable market value but no readily measurable cost of replacement. In fact, many assets would be replaced with a different technology—for example, copper cable in telephone lines might be replaced with fiber-optic cable or with satellite transmissions. And the difficulty of valuing tangible assets pales in comparison to the problem of assigning values to intangibles, such as research and development, advertising, personnel training, trademarks, and customer goodwill, which often are not bought and sold separately from the company that developed them.

To be sure, such difficulties have not discouraged *all* attempts by the accounting profession to build greater economic realism into audited financial statements. But the outcome of such efforts is instructive. For example, when the SEC mandated disclosure of fixed-asset replacement costs in 1976, corporations found the exercise so costly (and often futile) that the requirement was rescinded by FAS 33 in 1978, which called instead for price-level-adjusted figures in a supplementary statement. But even that much more modest attempt to make historical cost numbers more "relevant" proved impracticable and was rescinded in 1982. And, as I discuss below, the more recent attempts at market-value accounting, such as the requirement that derivatives positions be marked to market[2] and financial assets restated at fair values, are also likely to be very costly to comply with and of limited use (if not actually misleading) to investors.

Present Value Estimation: Problems in Getting the Income Statement Right

But even if accountants could measure the market values of assets and liabilities, this is not the information investors really want. Simply adding up the current market values of individual assets and subtracting the market values of liabilities would provide investors with, at best, an estimate of the "break-up" or liquidation value of the firm.[3] For companies that are profitable (or expected to become profitable), it is not the net disposal value of the assets and liabilities that matters for investment purposes, but rather the firm's going-concern value—that is, what outside investors, or another firm, would pay for the company's net assets.

Thus, what investors would really like to know is the net present value (NPV) of the corporation's expected future net cash flows (and not on the balance sheet date, but as of the date they are considering buying or selling shares in the corporation). With this estimate of NPV, they could then determine how much value the managers have added (or lost) in operating the business over a given time period by comparing the NPV at the beginning and end of the period (adjusted for additional investments by and distributions to shareholders).

The problem for accountants, however, is that present values require reliable estimates of future cash inflows and outflows. The cash inflows depend on predictions of physical outputs (production and sales), the demand for these outputs, the prices at which the outputs will be sold, and the actual receipts from these sales. These predictions in turn depend not only on the firm's own actions, but on competitors' actions and reactions as well as the performance of the local and national economy. In addition, estimates must be made of related cash *out*flows during the same period, including outlays for production, distribution, financing, and taxes. Finally, the net operating cash flows must be discounted by the opportunity cost of equity capital,

which requires assumptions about risk premiums and the company's capital structure.

From this very brief recitation of the basic requirements for calculating present values, it should be evident that the process is complicated, highly subjective, and open to a substantial amount of error and manipulation. IPAs and investors thus have had good reason to fear that permitting managers to estimate and discount future cash flows (or even just estimate replacement costs) would compromise the important stewardship function of accounting. IPAs can audit historical-cost-based numbers. But it is much more difficult for them to verify managers' assertions that future cash flows of a particular amount were in fact expected, and that such amounts should have been discounted by the rate specified.

THE TRADITIONAL ACCOUNTING APPROACH: EMPHASIS ON THE INCOME STATEMENT WITH THE BALANCE SHEET AS A "HOLDING PLACE" BETWEEN INCOME STATEMENTS

The accounting profession accordingly has confined its role to a more manageable task—that of producing and auditing financial statements designed primarily to report on managers' stewardship, with emphasis on consistency and trustworthiness in measuring and reporting income. Financial accounting accomplishes this more modest (though still very important) goal by defining net income in a special way. In brief, the accounting statement of periodic net income is a report of net revenue minus expenses incurred to produce that revenue (including losses due to investments and decisions that turned out badly). The amounts and timing of revenues and the "matched" expenses are measured using prices derived from (or based on) actual market transactions and the consistent application from period to period of established accounting procedures. The revenue and matched expenses from the ongoing operations of the company are distinguished from those related to other activities, such as investment and financing operations and the occasional sale of major assets and discontinuance of major businesses.

The balance sheet was—and still largely continues to be—a "holding place" for numbers that have

---

2. See my article, "Back to Basics: Accounting for Derivatives," *Journal of Applied Corporate Finance*, Vol. 10 (Fall 1997), pp. 46-58.

3. And assuming (incorrectly) that assets and liabilities can be sold for the same price at which they could be purchased, these values would be correct only as of the date of the balance sheet.

> The accounting profession has confined its role to a more manageable task—
> that of producing and auditing financial statements designed primarily to report on
> managers' stewardship, with emphasis on consistency and trustworthiness in
> measuring and reporting income.

not yet been credited or charged to an income statement or equity account. Thus, financial accounting has placed greater emphasis on achieving economic realism in the income statement than in the balance sheet. But in addition to serving as a bridge between successive income statements, the balance sheet provides a statement of the values of current (short-term) assets and liabilities on a specified date, because such assets and liabilities can often be reliably valued at market prices and because these numbers are useful to banks and other short-term creditors. These assets and liabilities include cash, securities held for trade or resale, and accounts and notes receivable and payable.

Accounting Rules for Recognizing Income and Expense

Rather than attempting to create balance sheets that reflect economic values, accountants have chosen to maintain the reliability and integrity of financial statements by developing rules for recognizing income and expenses that can reasonably and consistently reflect periodic changes in the value of stockholders' claims to their companies' assets. The profession has adopted two related principles, known as the "critical event" and "matching"—as well as a third modifying rule, "conservatism"—for recognizing when income is earned and when expenses are incurred. These rather simple and time-tested concepts allow accountants and their clients to live with the problem that most assets cannot reliably or efficiently be assigned economic values, while fulfilling the basic goals of verifying stewardship and reporting a consistent, meaningful, trustworthy, and hence useful measure of net income.[4]

Revenue Recognition: The Critical Event. The critical event concept specifies that income—an increase in equity value—is recognized when the certainty and amount of that value increase can be verified objectively. For example, sales income is recognized when title to and control over goods has passed to the purchaser and the amount that the purchaser paid or will pay can be determined. If a customer takes goods on consignment, a sale is not recorded. Nor is income recorded when goods are manufactured but not sold, even when the finished goods are clearly worth more than the sum of the

costs of labor, materials, and overhead incurred in producing the goods. Moreover, income is not recorded when goods are physically transferred but collecting the amount owed from the purchasers is so uncertain that collection becomes the critical event. In that situation, income is recognized when cash is collected. In the case of long-term contracts, although income is often recognized before the contract is completed, it is recorded only when the firm has or can establish valid claims to payments for the work; establishing these claims is the critical event.

Expense Recognition: The Matching Concept. Once income has been recognized and recorded, the matching concept comes into play. Expenses that are incurred to generate income are matched to that income and recognized as reductions in equity value. For example, cash might be exchanged or liabilities incurred for labor and materials used to produce inventory for sale. But the costs of the labor and materials are carried as assets ("work in process" and then "finished goods") until the inventory is sold, at which point the costs of the assets are transferred to an expense account ("cost of goods sold"). When income is anticipated but the critical event has not yet occurred (perhaps because there is insufficient objective, market-based evidence of the revenue amount), the associated expense is deferred and included in the balance sheet as an asset (though in an amount not to exceed the anticipated income).

Of course, some costs cannot be traced directly to revenue. These are either charged as expenses on a predetermined schedule over time (to avoid possible opportunism by managers) or recorded as immediate expenses when future benefits cannot be reliably determined. Depreciation of fixed assets is an example of the former, while R&D expenditures are an example of the latter.

Conservatism. Both the critical event and the matching concepts are often modified by the third concept—"conservatism." Even before it became lucrative to sue accounting firms, accountants tended to be conservative because people are generally upset when things turn out worse than predicted but rarely complain when pleasantly surprised. Hence, assets are usually written down to no more than their net realizable values, but are not written up even when there is clear and objective evidence of an

---

4. This is not to say that some companies do not violate the basic accounting rules or that their IPAs never fail to discover these violations or, when they learn about them, refuse to attest that their clients' statements fairly present their financial condition in accordance with GAAP.

increase in value.[5] Increases in the values of nonfinancial assets or decreases in the amounts of liabilities are generally not recorded until these changes are realized in market transactions. Intangible assets such as advertising and R&D are expensed immediately because of uncertainty as to the value they will generate in future periods. This procedure is "conservative" because it shifts income recognition to future periods while showing expenses in earlier periods.

THE CASE FOR ECONOMIC PROFIT

As stated earlier, the measure of earnings that results from the application of these three principles differs in important respects from what an economist (and presumably sophisticated investors) would call income or "value added." And this brings us to Stewart's concept of economic profit, or EVA, which is an attempt to define (and even institutionalize) such a measure.

When I first heard of Stewart's proposal to reform GAAP accounting, I assumed it was yet another call for marking corporate assets to present values. But in much the same spirit (and for some of the same reasons) as traditional GAAP, Stewart begins by conceding the futility of trying to capture economic reality on a balance sheet. Instead of marking assets and liabilities to present values, he proposes that the balance sheet function simply as a historical record of the amount of capital that investors have committed to the firm. For example, under Stewart's proposal and in contrast to GAAP, writedowns of goodwill and other corporate assets do not reduce reported net profits and equity, but are transferred to an asset-side balance sheet account. Stewart also includes as capital any material off-balance-sheet liabilities that are not included under GAAP, such as operating leases. So defined, total capital provides the basis for calculating the capital charge against earnings (including a cost for equity capital) that is an important distinguishing feature of his definition of economic profit.

Besides expensing the cost of equity, Stewart's plan consists of nine other suggested improvements in GAAP (each of which are discussed individually in the Appendix). Almost all of the proposed changes can be grouped into one of three main categories:

(1) changes intended mainly to capture real economic costs that are not currently reflected in GAAP; (2) changes designed to provide a clearer picture of a company's operating cash flow, mainly by adding back non-cash GAAP expenses to income; and (3) changes that attempt to undo the effects of what he considers excessive accounting conservatism, mainly by capitalizing and then amortizing longer-term investment outlays that are immediately expensed under GAAP.

Under the first general category of improvements—those intended to capture costs not reflected in GAAP—I would include Stewart's proposals to (1) expense the cost to the corporation of stock options granted to employees; (2) remove the effects of pension investment returns from the income statement (thereby providing a more relevant, and generally higher, estimate of pension servicing costs); and (3) include as an expense a charge for the cost of equity. I strongly recommend incorporating the first two of these three suggestions into GAAP. But, as discussed in the Appendix, although I agree that the cost of equity is an expense that should be recognized for the purpose of computing net income, I would not include it in the income statement that is attested to by IPAs.

The second category of Stewart's proposed changes—those designed to reflect cash flow—are adjustments that involve recording expenses only when there are actual cash outflows instead of the customary procedure of accruing expenses applicable to revenue reported in a period. In particular, Stewart would eliminate the periodic provision for deferred taxes and would record as an expense only actual charge-offs of loans and accounts receivable during the period. I have two objections to making these proposed changes part of GAAP. First, accruals are required to match expenses with reported revenues. Second, the cash flows that Stewart wants reported are already provided in the Statement of Cash Flow that GAAP requires of all companies.

The third group of Stewart's proposed changes are those intended to move reported income *away* from cash flow and toward the matching concept. For example, he would have companies capitalize (instead of expense) expenditures that create intangible assets, particularly R&D, and then amortize those

---

5. Notable exceptions to this general rule are marketable financial assets held in a trading account or "available for sale," and all financial assets held by investment and development companies.

> **Rather than attempting to create balance sheets that reflect economic values, accountants have chosen to maintain the reliability and integrity of financial statements by developing rules for recognizing income and expenses that can reasonably and consistently reflect periodic changes in the value of stockholders' claims to their companies' assets.**

amounts in a way that reflects the expected payoffs from those investments. On the same principle, he would attempt to match the cost of "strategic" investments with the higher returns they are expected to yield after they have matured. If these capitalizations and allocations to income were not subject to manipulation by opportunistic or overly optimistic managers, they would be a useful extension of the matching concept. However, I believe that the costs of potential and likely misrepresentation substantially exceed the benefit from improved reporting of periodic net income.

As an economist, then, I find many of Stewart's suggested changes to be useful both for corporate managers making investment decisions and for investors attempting to evaluate the effectiveness of those decisions. For that reason, I would recommend that many companies consider making voluntary disclosures of their economic profit. But as an accountant, I feel strongly that the attempt to incorporate Stewart's measures of economic profit into GAAP would be a mistake. The principle of conservatism that informs the GAAP treatment of revenue and expense recognition is designed to reduce managerial manipulation and protect auditors from criticism. As long as accountants can be sued for estimates of value that turn out to be too high—a condition that Stewart, somewhat naively, assumes can be changed—conservatism will continue to be one of financial accounting's primary "principles."

SUGGESTIONS FOR IMPROVING TRADITIONAL FINANCIAL ACCOUNTING

But my insistence on traditional accounting principles does not mean that I think all is right with GAAP. In fact, there are two fairly recent developments in public accounting that need to be re-examined if not completely reversed. One is the attempt to capture "fair values" on corporate balance sheets and the second is the evolution toward "rules-based" accounting.

Problems with "Fair Value"

For most of the history of accounting, trustworthiness has been ensured by accountants' practice of reporting only numbers derived from arm's-length market transactions that can be verified by auditors. The development of new financial and commodity markets in the past few decades has greatly expanded the range of assets and liabilities that accountants can feel comfortable in revaluing on a periodic basis. And starting around the late 1980s, there has been a growing push by the FASB to reflect the market values of such assets and liabilities on corporate balance sheets. But if the principle of using trustworthy but more relevant numbers is sound, the actual steps that have been taken to implement market value accounting have been seriously flawed.

Take the case of FAS 115 (adopted in 1993), which requires companies to revalue all financial assets traded regularly on recognized securities markets to their market values at the end of an accounting period. Although there is much to recommend this idea, the revaluations are not applied consistently. Debt securities designated as "held to maturity" are not revalued, although their market values must be reported in a note. But if designated as "held for sale," the same securities must be revalued for the balance sheet (though changes in the values are not reported as current income; instead they are relegated to a subsidiary statement called "comprehensive income"). These inconsistencies appear to have been driven by political pressure from some companies, particularly commercial banks, that wanted to shield their income statements from changes in market prices, even though these prices could be easily and reliably determined by anyone with a newspaper or computer. This aberration should be eliminated; at a minimum, all identical or closely comparable assets should receive the same accounting treatment, as long as the matching concept is maintained (that is, one side of a hedging transaction should not be revalued if the other side cannot be reliably revalued).[6]

By contrast, inventories—a much more important asset for most companies than securities—are almost never reported at market values (except in notes), even when they can be reliably valued as of the balance sheet date. Instead they are reported in accordance with measurements that distort either balance sheet values (as in the case of LIFO) or income statement values (when FIFO is used). In place of the current accounting treatment, I recommend that inventories be valued at their opportunity costs

---

6. See Benston (1997), cited earlier.

when these amounts are trustworthy. Such is the case for inventory that is regularly replaced, including raw materials and inventory purchased for resale. (In fact, by the time the financial statements are produced, a substantial portion of many inventories is likely to have been replaced, which would allow IPAs to readily verify their values on the balance sheet date.)

Even manufactured inventories could be reported at reliably determined opportunity costs, which would include only the cost of replacing the inventory (but not arbitrary allocations of fixed expenses). Such a change would eliminate one important method by which managements can manipulate reported net income—namely, manufacturing goods for inventory that are unlikely to be sold so that fixed expenses that otherwise would have been reported as current expenses can be capitalized. Although this kind of manipulation cannot be sustained for long, it is particularly costly since it wastes resources as well as misinforming investors.

The failure of the SEC and FASB to address the valuation of inventories can perhaps be attributed to their fixation on financial assets. But far more troubling than these inconsistencies in applying market value accounting is an associated development called "fair value" accounting—one that is likely to do substantial damage to the trustworthiness of financial accounting statements. A critical event in the rise of fair value accounting occurred in 1992, when the SEC publicly allowed Enron (and presumably other energy firms) to report substantial net profits on contracts to supply power over periods as long as ten years. The reported profits were based *on Enron's managers' estimates* of the present value of future cash flows (including their choice of a discount rate for present valuing those flows).[7]

At about the same time, moreover, the FASB initiated its efforts to extend fair value accounting to derivatives (even those used as hedges). After years of debate, FAS 133 was adopted in 1998, requiring companies to assign fair values to all derivatives other than those used to hedge assets or liabilities (that are not themselves stated at fair values).[8] As a consequence, many derivatives not regularly traded on recognized exchanges must now be "marked to model," which allows managers substantial leeway in calculating the derivatives' fair values.

Further complicating matters, an accounting provision that was initially meant to apply only to investment companies has ended up providing opportunistic managers with another way to use fair value accounting to circumvent IPAs' traditional insistence that numbers reported in financial statements be based essentially on market transactions. Going back at least as far as 1987, the AICPA's Investment Companies Audit Guide has required investment, business development, and venture capital companies to mark their financial assets to fair values, *regardless of whether reliable market prices are available*. In recent years, this requirement has allowed managers of *industrial companies* to restate operating assets at their present values and report the increase (because it is almost always an increase) as operating profit. They first transfer substantial operating assets or divisions to subsidiaries or establish such operations in subsidiaries. Then they create a business development subsidiary, to which the stock of the operating subsidiaries is transferred. Since the stock in the operating subsidiaries is not traded, the revaluations must be based on estimated cash flows and assumptions about key variables, particularly discount rates, relevant to the underlying assets. In this fashion, fair valuation has effectively been extended to all kinds of fixed assets, enabling managers to record income in advance of reliable evidence that it has been earned.[9]

The Problem of Rules-Based Accounting

In the name of economic realism, then, the fair value movement is likely to succeed mainly in expanding the opportunities for managers to manipulate financial statements. Ironically enough, accounting authorities have also sought in recent years to limit such opportunities by formulating

---

7. The FASB extended this as a requirement to all companies in 1998 when its Emerging Issues Task Force adopted EITF 98-10, which held "that energy trading contracts should be marked to market [that is, measured at fair value determined as of the balance sheet date] with gains and losses included in earnings and separately disclosed in the financial statements or footnotes thereto."

8. See Benston, op cit. note 2. FAS 137 delayed required application of FAS 133 to fiscal years ending after June 15, 2000.

9. The AICPA has proposed limiting fair valuation of non-traded securities to registered investment companies and legally and actually separate investment companies, no owner of which owns 20% or more of its financial interests. The AICPA-AcSEC's Proposed Statement of Position *Clarification of the Scope of the Audit and Accounting Guide Audits of Investment Companies and Equity Method Investors for Investment in Investment Companies*, December 17, 2002, was cleared by the FASB. If adopted it would become part of GAAP for fiscal years beginning after December 15, 2003. I would not be surprised if opportunistic managers find a way around this limitation.

> As an economist, I find many of Stewart's suggested changes to be useful both for corporate managers making investment decisions and for investors attempting to evaluate the effectiveness of those decisions. But as an accountant, I feel strongly that the attempt to incorporate Stewart's measures of economic profit into GAAP would be a mistake.

GAAP in highly detailed rules that seemingly attempt to determine precisely what should be done under all possible circumstances. But the effect of such a rules-based system has been far from what the authorities intended.

Under the current rules-based (as opposed to a principles-based) approach, managers and their consultants design accounting procedures that are in technical accordance with GAAP, even though these procedures tend to mislead investors and violate the substance or spirit of GAAP. Accountants not only find it difficult to challenge the use of such procedures, but often propose or assist in their design. In this sense, the practice of public accounting has become quite similar to tax practice, with clients demanding and accountants providing expertise on ways to avoid the substantive requirements of GAAP while remaining in technical compliance.

There are several reasons for this rules-based approach. First, auditors believe that they can avoid losing lawsuits if they can show that they did in fact follow the rules. A second is the fear of losing a client by refusing to attest to an accounting procedure that does, after all, technically conform to GAAP. Third, government agencies such as the SEC tend to establish or support rules and then demand strict adherence to them. This protects the agencies from claims of favoritism and arbitrariness, forestalling political interference.

Last but by no means least, GAAP has been criticized because it permits managers some degree of choice, at least under certain circumstances. For example, when initially purchased, assets may be written down at a slower or faster rate by application of straight-line or sum-of-the-years'-digits depreciation, or in somewhat smaller or larger periodic amounts according to estimates of the assets' useful economic lives and salvage values. Inventory may be valued and charged as cost of goods sold with the assumption that the first goods sold were those purchased first or last (FIFO or LIFO).[10] In fact, the FASB was created in 1973 largely in response to concern about excessive accounting flexibility. Its well-funded professional staff and directors have fulfilled their mandate and

have developed a very large set of detailed rules designed to limit alternative means of compliance with GAAP.

However, the rules-based approach is clearly not working. Accounting firms are sued when a company they audited goes bankrupt, or even when the company's share price drops for some reason. Courts have not accepted as a sufficient defense that specific GAAP rules were followed or not explicitly violated. The SEC and FASB have been severely criticized for allowing companies and accounting firms to violate the spirit of GAAP. Of greatest importance, users of financial statements, who have reason to believe that the numbers presented therein are at least not *deliberately* deceptive, have at times been misled.

The principles of accounting are clear enough. Revenue should not be recognized until there is objective and reliable evidence that it has been earned. Expenses should be matched to the associated revenues or to the time periods in which assets are determined to have lost future value. And, most important, the numbers reported in the financial statements should be trustworthy, as verified by independent public accountants who have conducted audits and ascertained that the numbers reported accord with the basic principles embodied in GAAP. Having satisfied these conditions, the traditional income statement would be a fair and consistent record of a company's operations and would therefore fulfill the stewardship function of public accounting.

But as I have also argued, GAAP accounting does not, cannot, and should not attempt to provide the kind of information about corporate profitability and value that is required for investors' decisions. Nor does GAAP provide the kind of information about value added that should guide corporate managers in their decision-making and serve as the basis for their performance reviews and compensation. For that information one would be better served by using a measure of economic profit. Many companies may find it in their interest to disclose calculations of their economic profit not in place of, but as a supplement to, their traditional GAAP statements.

---

10. The choice among alternatives actually is severely limited. Once adopted, depreciation and inventory valuation methods may rarely be changed. And when permissible changes are made, their effect must be disclosed, thus enabling analysts to compare the numbers reported from period to period. Furthermore, opportunities for managerial manipulation under traditional financial reporting are limited by two factors. One is the inherent limit imposed by accrual accounting. Sales that

are overstated in one period result in lower sales reported in future periods, and lower current depreciation results in higher depreciation later. The other is the real economic cost incurred as a result of some kinds of manipulations. For example, delaying or reducing expenditures to maintain assets clearly exposes the firm to larger costs down the road.

1. Expense the Cost of Equity Capital. As an economist, I agree that the investment of a company's stockholders has an opportunity cost that, in a market economy, must be earned before a company is adding value for its shareholders. For this reason, the cost of equity capital clearly belongs on any statement of economic profit, particularly statements intended primarily for internal uses such as evaluating profitability and establishing the criteria for incentive bonus plans. However, I would not include the cost of equity in GAAP income statements because (1) accountants have no comparative advantage in estimating investors' required rates of return and (2) the *amount* of equity capital for which the company is charged, whether using GAAP or Stewart's proposed balance sheet, would be based on book rather than market values; and, in theory at least, management is supposed to earn an adequate return on the current *market* value of its equity.

2. Haul Off-Balance-Sheet Financing into the Light of Day—But Don't Mix Operating and Financing Decisions. Both as an economist and as an accountant, I agree with Stewart's suggestion that all material off-balance-sheet financings should be included on corporate balance sheets. I should also point out, however, that this requirement is already part of GAAP (FAS 5), which requires reporting in a note the amount and details of contingent liabilities, such as loan or other financial guarantees. What remains to be done, as I suggested earlier, is to close technical accounting "loopholes" by making GAAP principles-based rather than rules-based so companies can no longer avoid reporting material obligations on their balance sheets.

As an economist, I'm also favorably disposed toward Stewart's proposal that corporate returns be measured not on equity capital but rather on total capital (debt and equity) because, as he argues, this allows for cross-company comparisons of operating profitability that are not affected by differences in financing. Stewart also proposes that the capital charge against earnings be determined by multiplying total capital (as he defines it) by a fixed weighted average cost of capital (WACC), which is based on a firm's target capital structure. *Actual* interest expense and finance charges, however, would not be deducted as expenses. Although this procedure might be useful for a supplementary statement, it should not be incorporated into GAAP because it would substitute the manager's estimates of capital costs for market-derived numbers.

Auditors, though, could examine and report on these calculations, as he suggests, if they were used in a supplementary statement.

3. Bringing Pension Assets and Liabilities onto Corporate Balance Sheets, and Eliminating Speculative Pension Fund Gains and Losses from Operating Income. Stewart treats pension fund accounting as an especially egregious case of mixing operating income and financing choices, and I agree. FAS 87 (Employers' Accounting for Pensions) should be changed to exclude interest cost (the assumed discount rate times the pension obligation) and gains or losses on the value of pension fund assets (including a smoothed portion). This change would be consistent with financial accounting generally, wherein financing costs and returns are not included as part of the expenditure that gave rise to them (unless they are a part of the cost of constructing an asset).

4. Focus on Recurring Expected Cash Flow (Not Liquidation Values): The Case of Deferred Taxes. One of Stewart's main objections to GAAP is that "accounting rules are wired to measure liquidation value more than going-concern value, the concerns of creditors more than the needs of risk-taking shareholders," and he goes on to complain that GAAP income statements "consciously understate earnings by burying valuable assets in reserves or writing them off entirely." Stewart's solution: "As a matter of national policy, companies should be compelled to report the information that will enable smart investors to judge the likely future cash flows from a going concern."

In illustrating his proposal for accounting based on *sustainable* cash flow, Stewart focuses on the case of deferred taxes, which he mistakenly identifies as "a classic example of excessive conservatism...designed to protect the interests of creditors." In fact, the GAAP treatment of deferred taxes is a proper application of the matching concept. In accordance with FAS 109, GAAP accounting requires that companies report not the actual amount of income taxes paid, but rather the amount they would have paid had their taxable income been the same as their reported pre-tax GAAP income. Material differences can arise, for example, when a company uses accelerated depreciation for tax purposes and straight-line depreciation for financial reporting. In that case, it will pay less income tax in the early years and higher income tax in the later years (assuming unchanged rates), with the differences

Under the current rules-based (as opposed to a principles-based) approach, managers and their consultants design accounting procedures that are in technical accordance with GAAP, even though these procedures tend to mislead investors and violate the substance or spirit of GAAP.

APPENDIX: ANALYSIS OF STEWART'S "TOP TEN CHANGES" (Continued)

summing to zero. In the interim, the difference is reported as a deferred liability (not a "reserve," as Stewart calls it), on the assumption that it will be offset when straight-line is greater than accelerated depreciation.

Stewart (and others) argue that the deferred taxes are never paid as long as a company continues to add more in depreciable assets than it retires because the deferred tax liability also grows—it is not zeroed out. But based on this observation, one could also say that a growing company does not have a liability for bank loans that increase over time. The mistake is in viewing the deferred tax liability account in its entirety rather than as the summation of accounts for individual assets, accounts that do zero out as the assets are retired. The real problem with FAS 109 is that it disregards the present value of future tax liabilities, thereby overstating the increase in reported tax expense when taxable income is lower than reported income.

5. Clamp Down the Lid on Cookie Jars by Eliminating "Reserve Accounting." Stewart's example of a "cookie jar" is the allowance for doubtful accounts (which, again, is not a "reserve"). But what about excessive writedowns of assets in periods when a company must report losses anyway, or when a new CEO comes on board? How about intangibles that are not capitalized? Now, those are cookie jars! Unfortunately, many such writedowns are within the bounds of managerial discretion (for example, when is an asset really impaired?).

Stewart, though, takes aim at a mere cookie crumb. He would record as an expense only the actual amount of receivables charged off and permit no contra-asset account. My problem with this procedure is that a company could report revenue in a given period, without any offsetting bad debts expense, from a sale "paid for" with a receivable that probably won't be fully collected. Then, in the next period, when the receivable is charged off, the company would report a bad debt expense without any revenue. In short, Stewart would do away with the matching concept and accrual accounting, at least with respect to bad debts. What, then, would "net income for a period" mean, even to smart investors?

I suspect, though, that what Stewart is really complaining about is poorly determined allowances for doubtful accounts. That is the only explanation I have for his example of banks that "sign up a lot of new loans at the end of their accounting year [and increase the provision for loan losses (which, in banking, is the expense account), such that it exceeds]...the additional interest income they record from the new loans during that short period of time." An accountant who made such an entry would in fact be violating GAAP, which does not permit recording a future loss as a current expense. In fact, as long as the interest charged on loans is expected to cover expected losses, under GAAP there should be no increase in the allowance for loan losses and provision for loan losses, unless the expected probability of default had actually increased by the end of the accounting period in question.

6. Innovation Is an Investment and Not an Expense. I agree with this statement, and with Stewart's argument that, in measuring and reporting economic profit (on a voluntary supplemental basis), expenditures on R&D and other valuable intangibles should not be immediately and completely expensed (as now required under GAAP), but should instead be capitalized and amortized over a period that reflects their expected payoff. Stewart's proposal thus effectively calls for treating intangibles in essentially the same way as tangible assets like plant and equipment.

But I would not make this accounting a part of GAAP. For purposes of financial accounting, there are important differences between the two kinds of assets. Unlike most tangible assets, there are few if any markets in which intangible assets like R&D projects are traded. In contrast, the value of a tangible asset can be reliably measured, at least at the time the asset is purchased. And while it can be difficult to confirm the extent to which many tangible assets hold their values over time, in most cases accountants have well-established and reasonably reliable estimates of the assets' expected useful lives, which in turn provide a consistent and predetermined basis for depreciating their value that is difficult for managers to manipulate.

Under Stewart's proposal, by contrast, managers would have the latitude to claim that outlays on R&D, advertising, new product development, and customer and employee development are all expected to reap enormous benefits in the future, and should all be classified as assets rather than expenses (with amortization schedules based on the managers' present value estimates). It's not hard to see how opportunistic managers could (and would) exploit this kind of flexibility. And unless the present scope of accountants' liability were greatly limited (say, as Stewart proposes, to establishing the "reasonableness" of the managers' present value estimates of intangible asset values), then adopting such a scheme for GAAP would surely prove to be a feast for plaintiffs' lawyers.

7. Use Full-Cost Accounting. Under GAAP accounting, many oil and gas exploration companies use a method called "successful efforts," whereby outlays on unsuccessful drilling projects (dry holes) are immediately expensed, while other drilling expenditures are capitalized and amortized over their expected production periods. Stewart proposes that all companies instead be required to use "full-cost accounting," which allows them to capitalize outlays on unsuccessful as well as successful drilling projects. The rationale for such treatment is that "in any risky business…part of the investment required to find winners is investing in losers now and then," and that companies learn from their failures. Although Stewart's proposal is likely to be useful for some companies for internal reporting purposes, it should not be made part of GAAP accounting.

The experience of the FASB and SEC in mandating accounting for oil and gas production provides support for my position. In 1977, the FASB adopted FAS 19, which required the use of successful efforts for oil and gas exploration. Larger companies wanted this to be the required method because they did not want to report higher (read "obscene") profits. Smaller companies, however, wanted to use the full-costing procedure advocated by Stewart because they often had periods when they drilled mostly dry holes. When their well-orchestrated protests led to hearings before the SEC, I was asked to testify on the relative merits of the two methods. In my testimony, I argued that neither method was in accord with economic values, and that the proper way to value an oil field is to estimate the present value of the net cash flow expected from pumping and selling the oil that has been discovered. The SEC adopted my suggestion that the present value of discovered oil is the relevant method; and in Release 33-5969 issued in August 1978, it adopted Reserve Recognition Accounting (RRA) on an experimental three-year basis. But, as in the case of replacement cost accounting, the cost of applying this method was very high, the results were very unreliable, and RRA was not extended (although in November 1982, the FASB issued FAS 69, which required disclosure of much of the information required for RRA).

This experience suggests that the best that GAAP can provide investors is an accounting for the amounts expended on oil and gas development and *consistent* reporting of the amounts capitalized, whether using successful efforts or full-cost accounting. Neither of these amounts equals the economic value of discovered and not-yet-recovered oil and gas, which must be determined independently.

Stewart goes on to propose application of a version of full-cost accounting to asset sales, divestitures, and restructurings involving the writedown of asset values. Under this proposal, any loss on an asset that is sold (as measured by the difference between the asset's book and realized market value) would not be recorded as a reduction in stockholders' equity, but instead be added back to GAAP net income and debited to an asset-side balance sheet account. Such accounting is said to have two purposes: (1) managers would no longer have an incentive to retain assets that are worth more to another firm simply in order to avoid having to report the resulting losses (as required under GAAP); and (2) managers would be held accountable for losses in the sense that total capital (from which Stewart computes the cost of capital expense) still includes the loss amount.

Although consistent with Stewart's concept of economic profit, this application of full-cost accounting should not be adopted for GAAP reporting, which requires that these assets be written down to their net realizable values. If Stewart's change were adopted, managers could avoid recognizing losses on underperforming assets and bad investment decisions (except to the extent that their periodic cost of capital is greater by the WACC times the loss amount). To prevent such practices, the Accounting Principles Board in 1973 formally adopted (in APB 30) the "clean surplus" approach, whereby all but really extraordinary charges must go through the income statement (and even these charges must be reported on a statement of changes in equity).

And this brings us to another fundamental difference between GAAP accounting and Stewart's economic profit. By including losses on asset sales and writedowns in the income statement, GAAP concentrates on amounts that are recognized in a particular accounting period. Stewart's economic profit, by contrast, excludes such substantial losses in an attempt to provide a measure of *sustainable* income, while at the

> GAAP accounting does not, cannot, and should not attempt to provide the kind of information about corporate profitability and value that is required for investors and that should guide corporate managers in their decision-making and provide the basis for their performance reviews and compensation.

same time reflecting, through its use of full costing, the *entire* cost of *investor* capital represented by unsuccessful as well as successful investments. This approach to income measurement—particularly its insistence that writeoffs be added back to the capital base—could be useful to investors as a supplement to the GAAP-determined income statement.

8. Defer the Capital Charge on Strategic Investments. Assuming that his proposal to expense the cost of equity capital were adopted for GAAP accounting, Stewart also suggests that the capital charge be adjusted such that some new ventures with long-term expected payoffs are assigned less capital in their early years, with the amounts not charged placed into a deferred capital account and added back to total capital (from which he calculates the cost-of-capital expense) over time. If adopted, however, this change would undermine the insistence of GAAP that the numbers be trustworthy. Opportunistic or overly confident managers are likely to claim that investments that are currently not doing well really will yield extraordinary future gains. How could an auditor determine the validity of such claims?

As an example of such "strategic investment" accounting, Stewart proposes dividing the cost of an acquisition purchased at a very high multiple of current operating cash flow into two components—current operating value and future growth value—and then recording only the first component in the capital account in the early years of the acquisition. This procedure is based on several key assumptions, including which investments are strategic, when they pass from the formative to the mature stage, what is the expected cost of capital, and the extent to which the investment will have future returns that exceed that cost. Although income statements based on these assumptions and the resulting calculations might be useful for managers' internal decision-making and evaluation of performance, such numbers could not be used to calculate publicly reported GAAP net income without severely compromising its meaning and usefulness to investors.

9. Depreciation Does Not Follow a Straight Line. I disagree with Stewart's assertion that GAAP depreciation schedules are designed primarily to "produce stable operating profits." In fact, depreciation methods are designed to record as an expense the original cost less net salvage value of a fixed asset over its useful economic life—and it accomplishes this in *a predetermined manner that does not lend itself to managerial manipulation.* That is, managers can affect reported net profits only by varying within established constraints the estimated useful lives and salvage values of their assets and then choosing among the few allowable depreciation algorithms (essentially straight-line, double-declining balance, and sum-of-the-years'-digits). This clearly defined and limited set of alternatives makes it difficult for managers to use depreciation to "stabilize" operating profits.

Stewart is correct, however, that accounting depreciation is not the same as economic depreciation, which is the reduction in the present value of a fixed asset over a specified time period. He illustrates this point with an example of an asset that generates a constant net cash flow over ten years, which results in an increasing amount of economic depreciation. But what Stewart seems to fail to recognize is that few, if any, limited-life fixed assets generate a constant or increasing net cash flow. Rather, net cash flow tends to decrease over time, for at least two reasons. First, fixed productive assets wear out with use, which results in higher maintenance and operating costs and/or lower output. Second, as competitors (or the company itself) develop substitutes for the output and as more efficient replacement procedures become available, the net cash inflows produced by the fixed assets decrease.

Given that most fixed assets produce declining net cash flows, the increasing economic depreciation schedule advocated by Stewart will distort economic profit. At the same time, the change in present values determined by declining net cash flows are often closely approximated by straight-line or accelerated accounting depreciation. Table 1 illustrates these relationships for three assets, each with an expected useful life of five years, a constant annual rate of return of 10%, zero salvage value, and a \$1,000 initial year-end net cash flow. Thereafter, I assume that the annual net cash flows for each asset decline by 10%, 20%, or 30%. Economic depreciation (Econ.) is the annual decline in present value. The first line at year 0 gives the purchase price (assumed to be equal to the present value of the net cash flows) and, under accounting depreciation (Acctg.), the amount of straight-line depreciation. For each of the years following, accounting depreciation is computed with the sum-of-the-years'-digits method.

TABLE 1

Year	10% annual rate of cash flow decline			20% annual rate of cash flow decline			30% annual rate of cash flow decline		
	Present Value	Depreciation		Present Value	Depreciation		Present Value	Depreciation	
		Econ.	Acctg.		Econ.	Acctg.		Econ.	Acctg.
0	$3,167		$633	$2,655		$531	$2,239		$448
1	2,483	$683	1056	1,921	$734	885	1,463	$776	746
2	1,832	652	844	1,313	608	708	909	554	597
3	1,205	627	633	804	509	531	510	399	448
4	596	609	422	372	432	354	218	292	299
5	0	596	212	0	372	177	0	218	149
Totals		$3,167	$3,167		$2,655	$2,655		$2,239	$2,239

As the first example illustrates, when the annual decline in cash flow is the same as the rate of return (the case shown in the 10% illustration), straight-line accounting depreciation ($633) is similar to the annual economic depreciation. When the cash flow decline is greater (see the second and third illustrations), the accelerated accounting method yields numbers that are closer to economic depreciation. Thus, although accounting depreciation is not exact, it is not a bad reflection of economic reality and, as stated earlier, it has the advantage of being much less susceptible to managerial manipulation.

10. Stock Options Are an Expense. Stewart concludes—and I agree—that "an employee option grant is substantively the same as compensating an employee with cash" (and the same holds for any property or other corporate asset). The expense is the opportunity cost of the forgone asset (such as cash), or the amount that outside investors would have paid for the options. This amount could be determined from an option pricing model, from expert opinions, or from the price obtained from similar options sold to investors (adjusted, if necessary, for restrictions on employee options). Consistent with the matching concept, the cost of the employee stock options should be charged against revenue in the same periods that the revenue, presumably generated by the employee, is reported, which period should not extend beyond the time when the options vest. Similar to amortization generally, the cost to the corporation of the options could be charged as an expense in equal periodic amounts.

JUST SAY NO TO WALL STREET: PUTTING A STOP TO THE EARNINGS GAME

*by Joseph Fuller,
The Monitor Company, and
Michael C. Jensen,
The Monitor Company and
Harvard Business School**

> "WE DO NOT WANT TO MAXIMIZE THE PRICE AT WHICH BERKSHIRE shares trade. We wish instead for them to trade in a narrow range centered at intrinsic business value… [We] are bothered as much by significant overvaluation as significant undervaluation."
>
> —*Warren Buffett, Berkshire Hathaway Annual Report, 1988*

First there were whispers and informal advisories to favored analysts of what to expect in coming earnings announcements. Then the conversations became more elaborate, engendering a twisted kind of logic. No longer were analysts trying to understand and analyze a company so as to predict what it might earn; instead the discussion revolved around the analysts' forecasts themselves. Will expectations be met? What will management do to ensure that? Rather than the forecasts representing a financial byproduct of the firm's strategy, the forecasts came to drive those strategies. While the process was euphemistically referred to as "earnings guidance," it was, in fact, a high-stakes game with management seeking to hit the targets set by analysts—and being punished severely if they missed.

Last year, the Securities and Exchange Commission recognized that private conversations between executives and analysts had become extensive, with analysts gaining access to critical data not otherwise broadly available to shareholders. The new regulations on fair disclosure addressed the mechanics of the conversation, but did little to change its underlying logic. The result has been blizzards of filings and dozens of press releases, and many more company-run conference calls. But such changes in the outward forms of corporate disclosure have done little if anything to deflect the underlying momentum of the earnings guidance game.

Nevertheless, there are some encouraging signs. In the past few months, a few courageous CEOs—notably, USA Networks' Barry Diller and Gillette's Jim Kilts—have attempted to put a halt to the earnings game by simply saying no. In a recent SEC filing, Diller balked at the sophisticated art form known as managing expectations, saying publicly what many have said privately for a long time: "The process has little to do with running a business and the numbers can become distractingly and dangerously detached from fundamentals."[1]

*© Copyright 2002, The Monitor Company and M. C. Jensen. Excerpts of this article were published in the *Wall Street Journal* "Manager's Journal" column under the title "Dare To Keep Your Stock Price Low," December 31, 2001, and in the *Financial Times,* Jan 22, 2002 under the title "End the Myth-Making and Return to True Analysis." We thank Nancy Nichols, Pat Meredith, Jennifer Lacks Kaplan, Hardy Tey, Stephanie Mayer, and Shibanee Verma, who contributed to this effort. This paper can be downloaded without charge from the Social Science Research Network Electronic Library at: http://papers.ssrn.com/abstract=297156

1. USA Networks. 2001. "USA Provides Internal Budget to Investment Community." *SEC Form 425.1*: October 24, 2001.

AN OVERVALUED STOCK DAMAGES A COMPANY

Witness the part that Wall Street's rising expectations played in the demise of once high flyers like Enron, Cisco, and Nortel. With analysts pushing these companies to reach for higher and higher growth targets, the managements of the companies responded with actions that have generated long-term damage. To resolve these problems, managers must abandon the notion that a higher stock price is *always* better and recognize that an overvalued stock can be as dangerous to a company as an undervalued stock. The proper management of investor expectations means being willing to take the necessary actions to eliminate such overvaluation when it occurs.

In his first meeting with analysts after taking over Gillette, James Kilts stood firm against the tide refusing to be forced into making predictions for his company. *The New York Times* reports that, in a June 2001 meeting with analysts, Kilts remained silent when Wall Street analysts repeatedly asked him for a more specific estimate of the company's performance: "Mr. Kilts stood on the stage, crossed his arms and refused to give it."[2] By taking positions that we believe will benefit all the players in this game, Kilts and Diller have seized an important opportunity— even an obligation—to reshape and reframe the conversation for a new era.

Over the last decade companies have struggled more and more desperately to meet analysts' expectations. Caught up by a buoyant economy and the pace of value creation set by the market's best performers, analysts challenged the companies they covered to reach for unprecedented earnings growth. Executives often acquiesced to increasingly unrealistic projections and adopted them as a basis for setting goals for their organizations.

There were several reasons executives chose to play this game. Perhaps the most important was favorable market conditions in many industries, which enabled companies to exceed historical performance levels and, in the process, allowed executives and analysts alike to view unsustainable levels of growth as the norm. Adding to favorable conditions and exceptional corporate performance was a massive, broad-based shift in the philosophy of executive compensation. As stock options became an increasing part of executive compensation, and managers who made great fortunes on options became the stuff of legends, the preservation or enhancement of short-term stock prices became a personal (and damaging) priority for many a CEO and CFO. High share prices and earnings multiples stoked already amply endowed managerial egos, and management teams proved reluctant to undermine their own stature by surrendering hard-won records of quarter-over-quarter earnings growth. Moreover, overvalued equity "currency" encouraged managers to make acquisitions and other investments in the desperate hope of sustaining growth, continuing to meet expectations, and buying real assets at a discount with their overvalued stock.

Parallel developments in the world of the analysts completed a vicious circle. Once analysts were known to a handful of serious investors and coveted a spot on Institutional Investor's annual All-American team. In recent times, analysts became media darlings. An endless parade appeared on an increasing array of business programming. The views of celebrity analysts were accorded the same weight as the opinions of leading executives. Analysts Mary Meeker and Jack Grubman were quoted in the same breath and, more important, credited with the same insight as Cisco's CEO John Chambers and Qwest's Joe Nacchio. With the explosion in the markets came an explosion in analyst compensation, as leading analysts shared in the bonus pools of their investment banking divisions and thus had incentives to issue reports favorable to their banks' deals. Analysts with big followings, a reputation built on a handful of good "calls," and an ability to influence large investment banking deals sold by their firms commanded multi-million dollar salaries. In sum, analysts had strong incentives to demand high growth and steady and predictable earnings performance, both to justify sky-high valuations for the companies they followed and to avoid damage to their own reputations from missed predictions. In too many instances, too many executive teams and too many analysts engaged in the equivalent of liar's poker.[3]

2. Barnes, Julian E. 2001. "Gillette's Chief Is Critical of the Company's Misstep." *New York Times*, June 7, 2001. http://college2.nytimes.com/guests/articles/2001/06/07/852365.xml

3. Evidence of the distortion of information provided to investors by companies, and of the collaboration of some financial intermediaries and analysts in this distortion, has grown considerably. For an excellent compilation and analysis of this evidence, see the paper by Gene D'Avolio, Efi Gildor, and Andrei Shleifer. 2001. "Technology, Information Production, and Market Efficiency." Harvard Institute of Economic Research Discussion Paper Number 1929, September 2001. Cambridge, MA. This paper can be downloaded without charge from the Social Science Research Network eLibrary at: http://papers.ssrn.com/abstract=286597 and at http://post.economics.harvard.edu/hier/2001papers/2001list.html

With analysts pushing companies like Enron and Nortel to reach for higher and higher growth targets, the managements of the companies responded with actions that have generated long-term damage. Managers must abandon the notion that a higher stock price is *always* better and recognize that an overvalued stock can be as dangerous to a company as an undervalued stock.

Many will say, "So what? If overly aggressive analysts drove executives to create more shareholder value faster, what's the harm?" What they fail to recognize is that this vicious cycle can impose real, lasting costs on companies when analyst expectations become unhinged from what is possible for firms to accomplish. As the historic bankruptcy case of Enron suggests, when companies encourage excessive expectations or scramble too hard to meet unrealistic forecasts by analysts, they often take highly risky value-destroying bets. In addition, smoothing financial results to satisfy analysts' demands for quarter-to-quarter predictability frequently requires sacrificing the long-term future of the company. Because the inherent uncertainty in any business cannot be made to disappear, striving to achieve dependable period-to-period growth is a game that CEOs cannot win. Trying to mask the uncertainty inherent in every industry is like pushing on a balloon—smoothing out today's bumps means they will only pop up somewhere else tomorrow, often with catastrophic results.

More important, we have witnessed the consequences of executives' futile attempts to record growth rates that consistently and materially exceed growth in primary demand in their markets. Stated simply, companies participating in markets with 4% underlying growth in demand cannot register 15% growth in earnings quarter over quarter, year over year, indefinitely.

The technology and telecommunications sectors provide good examples of the effects of sustained pressure from analysts. In the last decade, analysts' expectations consistently and vastly exceeded what high-tech and telecom companies were capable of achieving. Managers collaborated in this fiction, either because they themselves had unrealistic expectations for their companies or, worse yet, because they used analysts' expectations to set internal corporate goals. The resulting destructive effects of overvaluation of corporate equity manifested itself in ill-advised actions aimed at fulfilling these unrealistic expectation—notably, value-destroying acquisitions and greenfield investments. When the fiction finally became obvious, the result was massive adjustments in earnings and growth projections and, consequently, in equity valuations.

In many cases, the very survival of the affected companies came into question. Enron is perhaps the most dramatic example.

THE CASE OF ENRON

Enron was in many ways an extraordinary company. It boasted significant global assets, genuine achievements, dramatic innovations, and a promising long-run future. Taking advantage of a rapidly deregulating market and capitalizing on its deep knowledge of the industry, Enron had seized what was probably a once-in-a-corporate-lifetime opportunity to reinvent itself as a market maker in natural gas and energy.

Wall Street responded to this and other innovations by Enron with a series of positive reports and ever-higher valuations, eventually labeling Enron one of the best companies in the economy, even comparing it to Microsoft and GE.[4] However, the aggressive targets that Wall Street set for Enron's shares made the company a captive of its own success. To be sure, it was a game that Enron willingly played—but it's one the company clearly lost, with considerable consequences for not only the company's stockholders, but for its creditors, customers, employees and other major stakeholders.

To begin to see what went wrong, consider that Enron's peak valuation of $68 billion (in August 2001) effectively required the company to grow its free cash flow at 91% annually for the next six years, (and then to grow at the average rate for the economy)—a pace that required it to continuously come up with what were, in effect, one-time-only innovations. As if to confirm these expectations, one analyst blithely predicted that Enron would come to "dominate the wholesale energy market for electricity, natural gas, coal, energy derivatives, bandwidth, and energy services on three continents."[5] And Enron, to its own detriment, took up the challenge. In seeking to meet such expectations, it expanded into areas, including water, broadband, and even weather insurance, in which it had no specific assets, expertise, or experience.

Yet it didn't have to be this way. Had management not met Wall Street's predictions with its own hubris, the result could have been very different. As

4. Fleischer, David N. 2001. "Enron Corp. Gas and Power Convergence." Conference Call Transcript, Goldman Sachs, July 12, 2001. New York.

5. Tirello, Edward J., Jr. 2000. "Enron Corporation: The Industry Standard for Excellence." Analyst Report, Deutsche Banc Alex. Brown., September 15, 2000. New York.

Gillette's Kilts is demonstrating, managers can refuse to collude with analysts' expectations when they don't fit with their strategies and the underlying realities of their markets. They can decline to bow to analysts' demand for highly predictable earnings.

If Enron's management had confronted the analysts with courage and conviction and resisted their relentless focus on outsized earnings growth, the company could have avoided questionable actions taken to please the analysts and markets. The result may well have been a lower-valued company, but a stable and profitable one with a promising future. And, as in other companies, these questionable actions went beyond the decisions to launch unwise investments and acquisitions, and included apparent manipulation of the information it provided to Wall Street. Some of these practices are currently being investigated by the SEC, including aggressive revenue recognition practices, off-balance-sheet financing that reduced Enron's apparent debt, and partnerships that allowed the company to show higher earnings.

When discovered, such practices—coupled with missed earnings expectations—first stirred Wall Street's concern and eventually caused the crisis of confidence that destroyed the company's most valuable asset—its ability to make markets in energy. As a result, by January of 2002, Enron's stock price had fallen by more than 99% from its peak just four months earlier. While the partnerships brought to the forefront issues of credibility for Enron and the integrity of their financial reporting, they also served to highlight the importance of Wall Street analysts and the nature of their relationship with the companies they cover.

THE CASE OF NORTEL NETWORKS

The story of Nortel is similar. Nortel's CEO, John Roth, launched a strategy in 1997 to transform the company from one dependent on its traditional strength in voice transmission into one focused on data networking. Nortel acquired 19 companies between 1997 and early 2001. And as its stock price soared (to reach a total capital value of $277 billion in July 2000), it came under pressure to do deals to satisfy the analysts' growth expectations. Ultimately, it paid over $32 billion—mostly in stock—for these companies. Most of those acquisitions have now been sold off for modest amounts or shut down and written off entirely.

The quest to transform Nortel clearly damaged this former mainstay of the telecommunication sector. With a year-end 2001 valuation of just $24 billion, the company's stock has fallen by more than 90% from its peak in September of 2000. In July 2001 it reported a record $19.4 billion second-quarter loss followed by a $3.6 billion loss in the third quarter. Its CEO resigned effective November 1, 2001 but remains as vice-chairman until the end of 2002. Employment has shrunk from 72,900 people when Roth took over (and from a high of 94,500) to a projected 45,000 by the end of this year. As of the end of 2001, Nortel's (adjusted) stock price was 44% lower than its level of $13.16 on Oct. 1, 1997 when Roth took over as CEO.[6] As these numbers make clear, the decline suffered by Nortel involved far more than the elimination of its overvaluation; it involved a significant destruction of value, mainly, again, through acquisitions and massive overinvestment. It is this kind of damage that can be stopped if managers can just say no to the pressure to fulfill unrealistic market expectations.

A number of factors encouraged Nortel's managers to collaborate in the fiction of a $270 billion valuation. One was the incentive to maintain the value of managerial and employee stock options. Another was the understandable reluctance of top management to admit they were not as good as analysts were projecting. And a third was management's unwillingness to give up the overvalued equity currency that gave them the leeway (and purchasing power) to make unwise, value-destroying investments. In sum, management's reluctance to bear the unpleasantness associated with correcting the market sooner led to far greater pain down the road.

This cycle is not without its costs for the financial community. Of course, many stockholders have incurred huge losses. Analysts, too, have taken their lumps. Their integrity has been called into question in congressional hearings. The press has pilloried many of the most prominent analysts, contrasting their earnings projections with actual results. Many unhappy clients have terminated long-standing relationships. One even went so far as to sue a prominent

---

6. The breakeven share price for Nortel investors as of 12/31/2001 was $21.33 assuming a 12% cost of equity capital net of dividends. This implies the breakeven total value of Nortel at the end of 2001 was $68.5 billion. Thus investors lost a total of $44.5 billion as a result of the failed strategy.

> **Companies should state their strategies clearly, identify associated value drivers, and report auditable metrics on both. They should also address the "unexplained" part of their firm's share price—that part not directly linked to observable cash flows— through a coherent description of the growth opportunities they foresee *and be willing to tell the markets when they see their stock price as overvalued.***

analyst in federal court.[7] And though that action proved unsuccessful, extensive coverage of the suit in the popular press reflects the depth of disillusionment. Where there is smoke from the public having been burned, political fire soon follows. If the SEC were willing to spend years and significant political capital pursuing restrictions on accounting firms providing consulting services to their statutory audit clients, it cannot be long before regulators become interested in the potential conflict of interest between the investment banking and the security analysis sides of investment banks.

RESTARTING THE CONVERSATION

Putting an end to this destructive cycle will require a new approach to disclosure based on a few simple rules of engagement.

■ Managers must confront the capital markets with courage and conviction. They must not collude with analysts' expectations that don't fit with their strategies and the underlying characteristics of their markets. They must not bow to analysts' demands for highly predictable earnings. The art of analysis includes the capacity to understand phenomena like seasonality, cyclicality, and random events. Companies do not grow in a constant fashion with each quarter's results better than the last. In the long run, conforming to pressures to satisfy the market's desire for impossible predictability and unwise growth leads to the destruction of corporate value, shortened careers, humiliation, and damaged companies.

■ Managers must be forthright and promise only those results they have a legitimate prospect of delivering, and they must be clear about the risks and uncertainties involved. They must dispel any air of unreality that settles over their stock and highlight what they cannot do as readily as they trumpet their prospects. While this can cause the stock price to fall, the associated pain is slight compared to colluding in myth-telling. This reflects more than the good conscience of a Boy Scout. It is, in fact, an act of self-preservation.

■ Managers must recognize that an overvalued stock can be damaging to the long-run health of the company, particularly when it serves as a pretext for overpriced acquisitions. As the experience of companies like Nortel and Worldcom demonstrates, buying overpriced companies with overvalued stock not only fails to add value, but can end up demoralizing once successful organizations. While leveling with the markets can cause the stock price to fall to a sustainable level, the associated personal and organizational pain is slight compared to that arising from colluding in myth-telling.

■ Managers must work to make their organizations far more transparent to investors and to the markets. USA Network's Diller, for example, has chosen to provide analysts with actual business budgets broken down by business segments. At the very least, companies should state their strategies clearly, identify associated value drivers and report auditable metrics on both. They should also address the "unexplained" part of their firm's share price—that part not directly linked to observable cash flows— through a coherent description of the growth opportunities they foresee *and be willing to tell the markets when they see their stock price as overvalued.*

■ Similarly, to limit wishful thinking, managers must reconcile their own company's projections to those of the industry and their rivals' projections. Analysts develop models of an industry's growth. If the company's expectations lie outside what is widely viewed as the industry's growth rate, its managers must be able to explain how and why they will be able to outperform their market. Some executives will be concerned or complain that making this all clear to the analysts will reveal valuable information to their competitors. To this we have a simple response: *If your strategy is based on your competitor not knowing what you are doing, as opposed to not being able to do what you can do, you cannot be successful in the long run no matter who knows what.*

Finally, managers would be wise to remember that analysts are not always wrong. In fact, analysts have a vital monitoring role to play in a market economy. While recent history may have obscured that role, managers should not simply presume that analysts are wrong when disagreement occurs. It is worth noting that during the 1970s and 1980s managers regularly complained that analysts were undervaluing their companies. Yet, analysts were generally correct that managers of that era were not

---

7. Regan, Keith. 2001. "Lawsuit Against Noted Internet Analyst Tossed." *www.EcommerceTimes.com*. August 22, 2001, http://www.newsfactor.com/perl/story/13001.html

making effective use of corporate resources. They continued to invest in industries and activities with substantial excess capacity and consequent low returns, refused to downsize and distribute free cash flow to shareholders, and pursued inefficient value-destroying conglomerate mergers. In response to such value destruction, there emerged an active market for corporate control, as reflected in the wave of hostile acquisitions and LBOs, in which competing management teams took over and replaced the managers and directors of underperforming companies and created vast new value.

Contrasting the decades of the 1970s and 1980s with the recent era thus yields an important lesson: managers and analysts must pay close attention to each other's views. Both analysts and managers bring important information and important perspectives to the conversation and both sides benefit when each does their task well. Managers for their part must stop encouraging analysts to reach for ever-higher valuations and return to managing their companies. Analysts must stop making Nostradamus-like predictions and instead return to their true roots—the creation of original research and analysis.

The Securities Industry Association issued an excellent statement entitled "Best Practices for Research" in 2001 that lays the foundations for resolving many of the conflicts of interest on the part of analysts. We look forward to its early and widespread implementation.[8]

Stock prices are not simply abstract numbers that exist apart from the reality of corporate enterprises. Gyrations initiated by Wall Street or managers have real effects on companies and society. The price that Wall Street puts on a company's securities and the trajectory of those prices affect the nature of the strategies firms adopt and, hence, their prospects for success. Stock prices also drive a company's cost of capital, its borrowing capacity, and its ability to make acquisitions. Ultimately, the viability of the companies themselves is at stake.

A dysfunctional conversation between Wall Street and Main Street is not the esoteric stuff of business school classroom discussions. It can rob investors of savings, cost employees their jobs, erode the nest eggs of retirees, and undermine the viability of suppliers and communities. Clearly, it is time to restart the conversation on a new, stable, and enduring footing.

---

8. Securities Industry Association. 2001. "Best Practices for Research." http://www.sia.com/publications/pdf/best.pdf